CROWN COURT INDEX 2023

CROWN COURT INDEX 2023

FORTY-THIRD EDITION

By

HIS HONOUR JUDGE MARK LUCRAFT KC
Recorder of London

HER HONOUR JUDGE REBECCA TROWLER KC
Senior Circuit Judge at the Central Criminal Court

HIS HONOUR JUDGE SIMON MAYO KC
Senior Circuit Judge at the Central Criminal Court

SWEET & MAXWELL THOMSON REUTERS

Published and typeset in 2023 by Thomson Reuters,
trading as Sweet & Maxwell. Thomson Reuters is registered in England & Wales, Company No.1679046. Registered Office and address for service:
5 Canada Square, Canary Wharf, London, E14 5AQ.

For further information on our products and services, visit
www.sweetandmaxwell.co.uk

Computerset by Sweet & Maxwell.
Printed and bound by CPI Group (UK) Ltd, Croydon, CRO 4YY

Only farmed timber was used and replanted.

A CIP catalogue record for this book is available from the British Library

ISBN (print): 978-0-414-10939-1

ISBN (e-book): 978-0-414-10941-4

ISBN (print and e-book): 978-0-414-10940-7

First published 1964
Thirty-First Edition 2011
Thirty-Second Edition 2012
Thirty-Third Edition 2013
Thirty-Fourth Edition 2014
Thirty-Fifth Edition 2015
Thirty-Sixth Edition 2016
Thirty-Seventh Edition 2017
Thirty-Eighth Edition 2018
Thirty-Ninth Edition 2019
Fortieth Edition 2020
Forty-First Edition 2021
Forty-Second Edition 2022
Forty-Third Edition 2023

FOREWORD

The Crown Courts across England and Wales deal with the complete range of criminal cases, from the relatively straightforward to the most complex. Each case presents its own particular issues which need to be resolved, whether it be a murder case, a burglary, a case involving young defendants, or an absent defendant, but every case will benefit from the concise summaries and checklists which the *Crown Court Index* provides.

Through their editorship of the *Crown Court Index*, Mark Lucraft, Rebecca Trowler and Simon Mayo provide invaluable assistance to the busy judge, recorder and practitioner. This latest edition continues the work of earlier editions and takes on board all the additions and amendments to the Criminal Procedure Rules and Criminal Practice Directions, legislative changes introduced in the last twelve months, as well as key decisions in the Court of Appeal and Supreme Court. The provisions of the Sentencing Act 2020, the Police, Crime, Sentencing and Courts Act 2022 and the Judicial Review and Courts Act 2022 are also clearly set out.

The digital case system has revolutionised the working methods of everyone in the Crown Court and we all continue to spend more time than ever looking at a screen or screens—particularly with the added pressures created by a backlog of cases. Nonetheless, I know that many of us still find it invaluable to have a hard copy of the *Index* to hand to help with all the issues which arise.

Nicholas Hilliard
The Hon. Mr Justice Hilliard

PREFACE

THIS EDITION has been amended in the wake of new legislation. It incorporates updates to both the Criminal Procedure Rules and the Criminal Practice Directions. We have also sought to include all relevant authorities from the last 12 months. In this edition we have set out references to the Sentencing Act 2020 as well as to the Police, Crime Sentencing and Courts Act 2022 and the Judicial Review and Courts Act 2022.

Following the Criminal Procedure Rules 2020 coming into force in October 2020, there have been several sets of changes to the Criminal Procedure Rules during the course of 2021 and 2022. The first set, published in January 2021, and coming into force in February and April, included changes to reflect the new provisions in the Sentencing Act 2020, and to remove references to legislation revoked following the withdrawal of the UK from the European Union. The second set of amendments, published in July and in force from 4 October 2021, included changes to the rules concerning expert evidence, access to information held in court records, and applications to vary restraining orders. The Criminal Practice Directions were amended in November 2020.

In the prefaces to the last editions we have made mention of s.28 of the Youth Justice and Criminal Evidence Act 1999 and the pre-recording of cross-examination and re-examination of those witnesses covered by s.19 of the Act and the proposed rollout of the process. The process was halted, then leapt forward in 2021. The roll-out continues as we go into 2023.

2021 and 2022 saw the coronavirus continue to affect all of our lives. Various measures were introduced to ensure that the Crown Court procedure was able to adapt to ways of working. Although the changes when introduced were temporary, many are now the subject of permanent change through the Police, Crime, Sentencing and Courts Act 2022 and we have made reference to those changes.

Nearly every chapter has been updated and, as with editions over the last few years, a number have been substantially revised. We have again tried to restrict the growth of the text, conscious that one of the principal attractions of the work over the years has been that it provides a practical "way in" to common problems of law and procedure. We express our grateful thanks to a number of people who have been kind enough to read through some of the draft chapters for the 2023 edition. Particular thanks go to Charles de Lacy (the Clinical Nurse Specialist at the Central Criminal Court who retired in September 2021) for looking at the chapters dealing with mentally disordered offenders and unfitness to plead/insanity. We are also grateful to all of the permanent and visiting judges at the Central Criminal Court, and members of the probation service team for making helpful comments on previous editions of this text. The law is stated, unless otherwise indicated, as at 1 October 2022.

TABLE OF ABBREVIATIONS

The following abbreviations appear in the text and refer to the respective enactments shown:

Statutes

ABOOA 1956	Magistrates' Courts (Appeals from Binding Over Orders) Act 1956
AJ(MP)A 1933	Administration of Justice (Miscellaneous Provisions) Act 1933
AJA 1960	Administration of Justice Act 1960
AJA 1970	Administration of Justice Act 1970
AJA 1999	Access to Justice Act 1999
ASBA 2014	Anti-social Behaviour, Crime and Policing Act 2014
AVTA 1992	Aggravated Vehicle Taking Act 1992
B(A)A 1993	Bail (Amendment) Act 1993
BA 1976	Bail Act 1976
BBEA 1879	Bankers' Books Evidence Act
C(IC)A 2003	Crime (International Co-Operation) Act 2003
CA 1971	Courts Act 1971
CA 1989	Children Act 1989
CA 2003	Courts Act 2003
CAA 1968	Criminal Appeal Act
CAA 1981	Criminal Attempts Act 1981
CAA 1995	Criminal Appeals Act 1995
CCA 1981	Contempt of Court Act 1981
CCA 2013	Crime and Courts Act 2013
CDA 1971	Criminal Damage Act 1971
CDA 1998	Crime and Disorder Act 1998
CDDA 1986	Company Directors Disqualification Act 1986
CDSA 2006	Criminal Defence Services Act 2006
CE(WA)A 2008	Criminal Evidence (Witness Anonymity) Act 2008
CEA 1995	Civil Evidence Act 1995
CEMA 1979	Customs and Excise Management Act 1979
CJ(IC)A 1990	Criminal Justice (International Co-operation) Act 1990
CJA 1967	Criminal Justice Act 1967
CJA 1972	Criminal Justice Act 1972
CJA 1982	Criminal Justice Act 1982
CJA 1987	Criminal Justice Act 1987
CJA 1988	Criminal Justice Act 1988

CJA 1991	Criminal Justice Act 1991
CJA 1993	Criminal Justice Act 1993
CJA 2003	Criminal Justice Act 2003
CJCA 2014	Criminal Justice and Courts Act 2014
CJCA 2015	Criminal Justice and Courts Act 2015
CJCSA 2000	Criminal Justice and Court Services Act 2000
CJCSA 2003	Criminal Justice and Courts Services Act 2003
CJIA 2008	Criminal Justice and Immigration Act
CJPA 2001	Criminal Justice and Police Act 2001
CJPOA 1994	Criminal Justice and Public Order Act 1994
CLA 1826	Criminal Law Act 1826
CLA 1967	Criminal Law Act 1967
CLA 1977	Criminal Law Act 1977
CLSA 1990	Courts and Legal Services Act 1990
CMCHA 2007	Corporate Manslaughter and Corporate Homicide Act 2007
CorJA 2009	Coroners and Justice Act 2009
CP(AW)A 1965	Criminal Procedure (Attendance of Witnesses) Act 1965
CP(I)A 1964	Criminal Procedure (Insanity) Act 1964
CP(IUP)A 1991	Criminal Procedure (Insanity and Unfitness to Plead) Act 1991
CPA 1865	Criminal Procedure Act 1865
CPIA 1996	Criminal Procedure and Investigations Act 1996
CRCA 2005	Commissioners for Revenue and Customs Act 2005
CSA 1997	Crime (Sentences) Act 1997
CSA 2010	Crime and Security Act 2010
CTA 2008	Counter Terrorism Act 2008
CYPA 1933	Children and Young Persons Act 1933
CYPA 1963	Children and Young Persons Act 1963
CYPA 1969	Children and Young Persons Act 1969
DTA 1994	Drug Trafficking Act 1994
DTOA 1986	Drug Trafficking Offences Act 1986
DVA 2004	Domestic Violence, Crime and Victims Act 2004
EA 2001	Education Act 2001
EA 2003	Extradition Act 2003
ECHR	European Convention on Human Rights
ESA 1883	Explosive Substances Act 1883
F(A)A 1997	Firearms (Amendment) Act 1997

FA 1968	Firearms Act 1968
FDA 2000	Football Disorder Act 2000
FOD 1999	Football (Offences and Disorder) Act 1999
FrA 2006	Fraud Act 2006
FSA 1989	Football Spectators Act 1989
GA 1986	Gaming (Amendment) Act 1986
HRA 1998	Human Rights Act 1998
HSWA 1974	Health and Safety at Work Act 1974
IA 1971	Immigration Act 1971
IA 1978	Interpretation Act 1978
IA 2000	Insolvency Act 2000
IAA 1999	Immigration and Asylum Act 1999
JA 1974	Juries Act 1974
JPA 1968	Justices of the Peace Act 1968
JPA 1997	Justices of the Peace Act 1997
LA 1964	Licensing Act 1964
LA 1988	Licensing Act 1988
LASPOA 2012	Legal Aid, Sentencing and Punishment of Offenders Act 2012
LP(E)A 1980	Licensed Premises (Exclusions of Certain Persons) Act 1980
M(ADP)A 1965	Murder (Abolition of Death Penalty Act) 1965
MCA 1980	Magistrates' Courts Act 1980
MDA 1971	Misuse of Drugs Act 1971
MH(A)A 1982	Mental Health (Amendment) Act 1982
MHA 1959	Mental Health Act 1959
MHA 1983	Mental Health Act 1983
MHA 2007	Mental Health Act 2007
MSA 2015	Modern Slavery Act 2015
OAPA 1861	Offences Against the Person Act 1861
OMA 2007	Offender Manager Act 2007
ORA 2014	Offenders Rehabilitation Act 2014
PACE 1984	Police and Criminal Evidence Act 1984
PCA 1953	Prevention of Crimes Act 1953
PCA 1995	Proceeds of Crime Act 1995
PCC(S)A 2000	Powers of Criminal Courts (Sentencing) Act 2000
PCP(S)A 1993	Prisoners and Criminal Proceedings (Scotland) Act 1993
PCrA 2009	Policing and Crime Act 2009

PCSCA 2022	Police, Crime, Sentencing and Courts Act 2022
PHA 1997	Protection from Harassment Act 1997
PJA 2006	Police and Justice Act 2006
POA 1907	Prohibition of Offenders Act 1907
POA 1985	Prosecution of Offenders Act 1985
POCA 2002	Proceeds of Crime Act 2002
POrA 1986	Public Order Act 1986
PRA 2002	Police Reform Act 2002
PSIA 2001	Private Security Industry Act 2001
RHA 2006	Racial and Religious Hatred Act 2006
RIPA 2000	Regulation of Investigatory Powers Act 2000
ROA 1974	Rehabilitation of Offenders Act 1974
RSA 2006	Road Safety Act 2006
RTA 1988	Road Traffic Act 1988
RTA 1991	Road Traffic Act 1991
RTOA 1988	Road Traffic Offenders Act 1988
RTRA 1984	Road Traffic Regulation Act 1984
SC 2020	Sentencing Code (Act) 2020
SCA 1981	Supreme Court Act 1981
SCA 2007	Serious Crimes Act 2007
SCA 2015	Serious Crime Act 2015
SCB 2014	Serious Crimes Bill 2014
SOA 1956	Sexual Offences Act 1956
SOA 1997	Sex Offenders Act 1997
SOA 2003	Sexual Offences Act 2003
SOCPA 2005	Serious Organised Crime and Police Act 2005
SVGA 2006	Safeguarding Vulnerable Groups Act 2006
TA 1968	Theft Act 1968
TA 1978	Theft Act 1978
TerrA 2000	Terrorism Act 2000
TerrA 2006	Terrorism Act 2006
VCRA 2006	Violent Crime Reduction Act 2006
YJCEA 1999	Youth Justice and Criminal Evidence Act 1999

Subordinate Legislation

COR 2009	CDS (Contribution Orders) Regulations 2009
COR 2013	Criminal Legal Aid (Contribution Orders) Regulations 2013 (SI 2013/483)
CrimPR	Criminal Procedure Rules 2015 (SI 2015/1490)

CPR 1998	Civil Procedure Rules 1998
CVHCCR 2001	Criminal Defence Service (Choice in Very High Costs Cases) Regulations 2001
DCOR 2013	The Criminal Legal Aid (Determinations by a Court and Choice of Representative) Regulations 2013 (SI 2013/614)
DTLR 2011	Criminal Procedure and Investigations Act 1996 (Defence Disclosure Time Limits) Regulations 2011
DTTO 2002	Drugs Testing and Treatment Order 2002
GR 1986	Costs in Criminal Cases (General Regulations) 1986
GR 2001	Criminal Defence Service (General) Regulations 2001
GR 2013	Criminal Legal Aid (General) Regulations 2013 (SI 2013/9)
GR(A)R 1991	Costs in Criminal Cases (General)(Amendment) Regulations 1981
IJR 2009	Criminal Defence Service (Interests of Justice) Regs (SI 2009/2875)
MC(F)R 1981	Magistrates' Courts (Forms) Rules 1981
PCAO 2003	Proceeds of Crime Act 2002 (Appeals under Part 2) Order 2003
RDCOR 2001	Criminal Defence Service (Recovery of Defence Costs) Regulations 2001
ROA 2006	CDS (Representation Orders; Appeals Etc.) Regulations 2006
RO(A)R 2009	Criminal Defence Service (Representation Orders) (Amendment) Regulations 2009 (SI 2009/3331)
ROAR 2001	Criminal Defence Service (Representation Order: Appeals) Regulations 2001
ROCR 2006	CDS (Representation Orders and Consequential Amendments) Regulations 2006
Miscellaneous	
ASBO	Anti-social behaviour order
CACD	Court of Appeal (Criminal Division)
CCP 2004	Code for Crown Prosecutors 2004
CLAM	Criminal Legal Aid Manual (Issued April 2013)
CPD	*Criminal Practice Directions* at [2019] EWCA Crim 1603
CPS	Crown Prosecution Service
CTL Protocol	Custody time limits Protocol agreed between HMCS and CPS December 2012
DBS	Disclosure and Banning Service
DRC	Director of Revenue and Customs

DSFO	Director of the Serious Fraud Office
EPE	Electronic presentation of evidence
Guide	Guide to Commencing Proceedings in CACD 2008
HO 1990	Home Office publication Sentence of the Court (1990)
ISA	Independent Safeguarding Authority
ISO	Individual Support Order
JSB	Judicial Studies Board (Judicial College)
LAA	Legal Aid Agency
Law Com. No. 324	The *Law Commission Report on The High Court's Jurisdiction in relation to Criminal Proceedings 2010*
LSC	Legal Services Commission
PCMH	Plea and case management hearing
PDC	*Practice Direction (Costs in Criminal Cases)* at [2015] EWCA Crim 1568
PTPH	Plea and trial preparation hearing
RCPO	Revenue and Customs Prosecution Office
RT	Road traffic
SAP	Sentencing Advisory Panel
SCEW	Sentencing Council for England and Wales (created by CorJA 2009)
SFO	Serious Fraud Office
SGC (Y)	SGC Guidelines Overarching Principles – Sentencing Youths
SGC 1	Sentencing Guidelines Council, "Reduction in sentence for a guilty plea"
SGC 2	Sentencing Guidelines Council, "Overarching principles—seriousness"
SGC 2010	Definitive Guidelines Corporate Manslaughter and Health and Safety Offences Causing Death 2010
SGC 3	Sentencing Guidelines Council, "New sentences CJA 2003"
SOCA	Serious Organised Crime Agency
SOPO	Sexual Offences Prevention Order
TerrPro 2007	Protocol on Terrorist Cases, issued by the President of the Queen's Bench Division 2007

TABLE OF CASES

[1969] 2 W.L.R. 92; [1969] 1 All E.R. 25; [1968] 12 WLUK 26; (1969) 53 Cr. App. R. 143; (1969) 133 J.P. 127; (1968) 112 S.J. 987; *Times*, December 7, 1968 QBD 32-034, 32-036

Designated Officer for Sunderland Magistrates' Court v Krager [2011] EWHC 3283 (Ch); [2012] 1 W.L.R. 1291; [2011] 12 WLUK 419 Ch D (Newcastle) 17-014

Director General of Fair Trading v Proprietary Association of Great Britain, sub nom. Medicaments and Related Classes of Goods (No.2), Re [2001] 1 W.L.R. 700; [2000] 12 WLUK 687; [2001] U.K.C.L.R. 550; [2001] I.C.R. 564; [2001] H.R.L.R. 17; [2001] U.K.H.R.R. 429; (2001) 3 L.G.L.R. 32; (2001) 98(7) L.S.G. 40; (2001) 151 N.L.J. 17; (2001) 145 S.J.L.B. 29; *Times*, February 2, 2001; *Independent*, January 12, 2001 CA (Civ Div) 42-044

Director of the Serious Fraud Office v A [2007] EWCA Crim 1927; [2007] 8 WLUK 21; [2008] Lloyd's Rep. F.C. 30; (2007) 151 S.J.L.B. 1058 CA (Crim Div) 54-003

Director of the Serious Fraud Office v Airbus SE [2020] 1 WLUK 435 Crown Ct (Southwark) 25-002

Director of the Serious Fraud Office v O'Brien, sub nom. Director of the Serious Fraud Office v B; OB v Director of the Serious Fraud Office; R. v O'Brien [2014] UKSC 23; [2014] A.C. 1246; [2014] 2 W.L.R. 902; [2014] 2 All E.R. 798; [2014] 4 WLUK 109; [2014] Lloyd's Rep. F.C. 401; *Times*, April 11, 2014 SC 54-012

Director of the Serious Fraud Office v O'Brien, sub nom. Director of the Serious Fraud Office v B; OB v Director of the Serious Fraud Office; R. v O'Brien [2014] UKSC 23; [2014] A.C. 1246; [2014] 2 W.L.R. 902; [2014] 2 All E.R. 798; [2014] 4 WLUK 109; [2014] Lloyd's Rep. F.C. 401; *Times*, April 11, 2014 SC 54-001

DLA Piper UK LLP v BDO LLP [2013] EWHC 3970 (Admin); [2014] 1 W.L.R. 4425; [2013] 12 WLUK 457; [2015] L.L.R. 351 QBD (Admin) 7-067

Donahue v DPP [1992] 3 WLUK 18; [1993] R.T.R. 156 DC 32-038

DPP v Alexander [2010] EWHC 2266 (Admin); [2011] 1 W.L.R. 653; [2010] 7 WLUK 774; (2010) 174 J.P. 519; [2011] R.T.R. 8; [2010] A.C.D. 98 DC 2-011

DPP v Anderson (Keith Anthony), sub nom. Anderson (Keith Anthony) v DPP; R. v Anderson (Keith Anthony) [1978] A.C. 964; [1978] 2 All E.R. 512; [1978] 5 WLUK 173; (1978) 67 Cr. App. R. 185; [1978] Crim. L.R. 568; (1978) 122 S.J. 400 HL 16-003, 24-049

DPP v Ara [2001] EWHC Admin 493; [2002] 1 W.L.R. 815; [2001] 4 All E.R. 559; [2001] 6 WLUK 445; [2002] 1 Cr. App. R. 16; [2001] Po. L.R. 235; (2001) 98(32) L.S.G. 36; *Times*, July 16, 2001 DC 2-005

DPP v B (Daniel Paul) [2008] EWHC 201 (Admin); [2008] 1 WLUK 196; [2008] Crim. L.R. 707 DC 2-001

DPP v Barker [1989] 11 WLUK 34; [1990] R.T.R. 1; *Times*, November 22, 1989 DC 32-038

DPP v Beaumont [2008] EWHC 523 (Admin); [2008] 1 W.L.R. 2186; [2008] 3 WLUK 27; [2008] 2 Cr. App. R. (S.) 98; (2008) 172 J.P. 283; [2008] Crim. L.R. 572 DC 34-006, 34-007

DPP v Boardman, sub nom. Boardman v DPP; R. v Boardman (Derrick Rowland) [1975] A.C. 421; [1974] 3 W.L.R. 673; [1974] 3 All E.R. 887; [1974] 11 WLUK 63; (1974) 60 Cr. App. R. 165; [1975] Crim. L.R. 36; (1974) 118 S.J. 809 HL 39-023

DPP v Bristow [1996] 10 WLUK 252; (1997) 161 J.P. 35; [1998] R.T.R. 100; (1997) 161 J.P.N. 110; *Times*, October 28, 1996 DC 32-034, 32-036, 32-037

DPP v Bulmer [2015] EWHC 2323 (Admin); [2015] 1 W.L.R. 5159; [2016] 3 All E.R. 860; [2015] 7 WLUK 991; [2016] 1 Cr. App. R. (S.) 12; (2015) 179 J.P. 519; [2015] Crim. L.R. 986 DC 21-001

DPP v Christou [2015] EWHC 4157 (Admin); [2015] 10 WLUK 480; [2016] 2 Cr. App. R. 16 DC 53-002

DPP v Conroy [2003] EWHC 1674 (Admin); [2003] 6 WLUK 567; [2004] 1 Cr. App. R. (S.) 37; (2003) 167 J.P. 418; (2003) 167 J.P.N. 591 DC 32-039

DPP v Cox [1995] 5 WLUK 307; [1996] R.T.R. 123 DC 32-037

DPP v Edgar [2000] 2 WLUK 781; (2000) 164 J.P. 471; (2000) 164 J.P.N. 665 DC 2-012, 55-001

DPP v Enston [1995] 2 WLUK 136; [1996] R.T.R. 324; *Times*, February 17, 1995 DC 32-037

DPP v Fell [2013] EWHC 562 (Admin); [2013] 1 WLUK 605 DC 2-005

DPP v Heathcote [2011] EWHC 2536 (Admin); [2011] 7 WLUK 52; (2011) 175 J.P. 530 QBD (Admin) 32-037

DPP v Hussain [1994] 5 WLUK 173; (1994) 158 J.P. 602; (1994) 158 J.P.N. 570; *Times*, June 1, 1994 QBD 2-001

DPP v Jowle [1997] 10 WLUK 548; (1999) 163 J.P. 85; *Times*, December 13, 1997 DC 32-036

DPP v Kinnersley [1992] 12 WLUK 166; (1993) 14 Cr. App. R. (S.) 516; [1993] R.T.R. 105; (1993) 137 S.J.L.B. 12; *Times*, December 29, 1992 DC 32-036

DPP v Knight [1988] 12 WLUK 217; [1994] R.T.R. 374 DC 32-037

DPP v O'Connor; joined case(s) DPP v Allen; DPP v Allett; DPP v Chapman; DPP v

TABLE OF STATUTES

TABLE OF STATUTORY INSTRUMENTS

TABLE OF CRIMINAL PROCEDURE RULES

1. ABSENT/UNREPRESENTED ACCUSED

Quick Guide

A. Absent Accused

1. General

Meaning of "absent"

An accused may be said to be "absent" from proceedings in the Crown Court where: **1-001**

(1) he fails to surrender to custody at the time and place fixed for the proceedings, or having surrendered absents himself;
(2) though physically in the custody of the Crown Court:
  (a) through illness, he is unable; or
  (b) of his own free will he declines to participate in the proceedings; or
  (c) by order of the judge he is removed from the proceedings for misbehaviour or disruption.

He is not "absent" from specified proceedings where he is the subject of a live link order (see LIVE LINKS).

2. Non-appearance

Administrative enquiries

The non-appearance of the accused has been a principal cause of "cracked" or ineffective trials over many years. The reasons may be various: the culpability or negligence of the accused, or lack of communication between the accused and his representatives. The fault may lie with the prosecutor or with the Prison Service. **1-002**

Faced with the absence of the accused, the judge will need to make enquiries of the advocates to identify the position, and to call upon them where appropriate to make administrative arrangements for the accused's attendance.

Where no satisfactory information is forthcoming, or no arrangements can be made, a bench warrant may be issued.

As to the approach to medical certificates purporting to justify non-attendance, see BAIL.

Bench warrant

1-003 A bench warrant may be issued for the arrest of a person:

(1) released on bail in criminal proceedings, and thus under a duty to surrender to the custody of the court who:
  (a) fails to surrender at the appointed time and place; or
  (b) having surrendered, absents himself at any time and before the court is ready to begin or resume the hearing of the proceedings, unless he is absent in accordance with leave given by or on behalf of the court; or
(2) where an indictment has been signed but the person charged has not been sent for trial, and a summons is inappropriate.

In an appropriate case a warrant may be backed for bail.

There is no express requirement that a warrant for arrest issued under BA 1976 s.7 following failure to surrender to bail must state on its face the statutory source of its authority. Lords Wilberforce and Diplock in *R. v IRC Ex p. Rossminster Ltd* (1980) 70 Cr. App. R. 157 HL (suggesting that a warrant should state its statutory authority upon its face), were making a statement of what would be good practice in such circumstances (*R. (on the application of Bromley) v Secretary of State for Justice* [2010] EWHC 112 (Admin); [2010] A.C.D. 43 DC).

As to the terms and contents of a warrant, see CrimPR 13.2 and 13.3. As to the information to be included in it, see CrimPR 13.4.

A warrant that contains an error is not invalid, as long as it was issued in respect of a lawful decision by the court, and it contains enough information to identify that decision.

3. Absconding accused

Trial in absence

1-004 An accused has a right, in general, to be present and to be represented at his trial. He may, however, choose not to exercise those rights (*CPD* III Custody and Bail 14E: Trials in Absence 14E.1) by:

(1) waiving them, separately or together:
  (a) wholly, by voluntarily absenting himself, and failing to instruct his legal representatives adequately so that they can represent him; or
  (b) partly, if, being present and represented at the outset, during the course of the trial behaving in such a way as to obstruct the proper course of the proceedings and/or withdrawing his instructions from those representing him; or
(2) absenting himself immediately before the trial, aware that the prosecutor intends to apply to amend the indictment to add a more serious charge, thus waiving his rights to an arraignment (*R. v K* [2007] EWCA Crim 1339; (2007) 104 (26) L.S.G. 32).

CrimPR 25(2)(b) provides that where a court tries a case or the accused pleads guilty, the judge must not proceed if the accused is absent, unless satisfied:

(a) that the accused has waived the right to attend; and
(b) the trial will be fair despite his absence.

If waiver is to be established, then knowledge of where and when his trial is to take place, and knowledge of, or indifference to, the consequences of being tried in absence ought to be proved.

In such circumstances, the judge has a discretion as to whether a trial should take place, or continue in the absence of the accused, or of his legal representatives.

As to the power to make a confiscation order under POCA 2002, in the absence of an absconding accused, see CONFISCATION ORDERS.

The judge must exercise his discretion to proceed in the absence of the accused with the utmost care and caution. The overriding concern must be to ensure that such trial is as fair as circumstances permit, and leads to a just outcome. Due regard should be had to the judgment in *R. v Jones* [2002] UKHL 5; [2002] 2 Cr. App. R. 9 (see 1-005) in which Lord Bingham identifies the circumstances to be taken into account before proceeding (*CPD* III 14E.3).

Circumstances to be taken into account

In *R. v Jones* [2002] UKHL 5; [2002] 2 Cr. App. R. 9 it was said that in assessing the "overall fairness" of a trial, the judge must consider: **1-005**

(1) the nature and circumstances of the accused's behaviour, in particular whether it is deliberate, voluntary and such as plainly waives his right to appear;
(2) whether an adjournment might result in the accused being apprehended, or attending voluntarily and/or agreeing not to disrupt the proceedings; also the likely length of such an adjournment;
(3) whether the accused, though absent, is, or wishes representation at the trial or whether he has, by his conduct, waived his right to it;
(4) whether the representatives of the absent accused are able to receive instructions from him during the trial, and the extent to which they are able to present his defence;
(5) the extent of the disadvantage to the accused in not being able to give his account of events, having regard to the nature of the evidence against him; and
(6) the risk of the jury, where there is one, reaching an improper conclusion about the absence of the accused.

(*CPD* III 14E.3)

The presence of an advocate on behalf of the accused, who can ensure that all points which can be put forward in the absence of the accused's evidence are clearly before the jury, is a clear, additional safeguard to the fairness of the trial (*R. v Jones* [2002] UKHL 5; [2002] 2 Cr. App. R. 9; *R. v O'Hare* [2006] EWCA Crim 471; [2006] Crim. L.R. 950).

There will be inevitably some unfairness to the accused if a trial begins in his absence after he has absconded. His legal representatives are likely to regard their retainer as terminated by his conduct in absconding; there will be no cross-examination of prosecution witnesses, and no speech to the jury on behalf of the accused. The judge and prosecuting counsel, however well-intentioned, cannot know all the points which might be open to the accused. The answer to this contention is, that one who voluntarily chooses not to exercise a right cannot be heard to complain that he has lost the benefits (Lord of Cornhill, cited in *R. v Wells* [2009] EWCA Crim 2043).

At a PTPH the judge should warn an accused that the trial may proceed in their absence. As from 2 October 2017 CrimPR 3.13 makes clear that the accused must be warned of the possibility of trial in absence and also that if a trial takes place in his absence, that the judge may inform the jury of the reason for absence. Although some judges may not give these warnings in custody cases, it may be prudent to do so.

Public interest to be considered

1-006 While fairness to the defence is of prime importance, fairness to the prosecution must also be taken into account.

The judge needs to consider also:

(1) the general public interest;
(2) the particular interests of the victims and witnesses that a trial should take place within a reasonable time of the events to which it relates, bearing in mind the effect of delay on the memories of witnesses; and
(3) where there is more than one accused, and not all are absent, the undesirability of separate trials and the prospects of a fair trial for those who are present.

The seriousness of the offence, though a relevant factor, is not an overriding consideration. The objective is to secure as fair a trial as the circumstances permit; that objective is equally important, whether the offence charged is serious or relatively minor. The judge should not be reluctant to hear a case in the absence of the accused merely because the charge is a very serious one (*R. v O'Hare* [2006] EWCA Crim 471; [2006] Crim. L.R. 950).

4. Unruly behaviour

1-007 Where the accused behaves in such an unruly manner in court as to make it impracticable for the trial to continue in his presence the trial judge may order his removal (*R. v Lee Kun* (1916) 11 Cr. App. R. 293). In such a case, the judge ought to warn the accused of his intention, and, where appropriate, give him the opportunity to return to court later, provided he behaves.

5. Accused in custody refusing to attend

1-008 An accused in custody refusing or failing to attend, even when he is in the course of giving evidence, presents a special problem.

It is important that the judge is satisfied that the accused has deliberately absented himself (*R. v Amrouchi* [2007] EWCA Crim 3019; *R. v H* [2008] EWCA Crim 620) before making a decision. His attendance should not be compelled by threats of the use of force (*R. v O'Boyle* (1991) 92 Cr. App. R. 202). The case may be adjourned and the accused warned that the case will continue in his absence, or he may be dealt with for contempt, if appropriate (see *R. v Baker* [2008] EWCA Crim 334; [2008] All E.R. (D) 191 (Apr)). There has been an increasing trend for a defendant in custody to refuse to leave his cell or the prison to attend an on-going case at court. In such circumstances it may be possible to arrange a video-link to the prison and for counsel or the judge to speak to the defendant to warn them of the consequences of not attending.

Before the judge proceeds to deal with an accused for contempt in his absence (e.g. where he refuses to come into court), *R. v Jones* [2002] UKHL 5; [2002] 2 Cr. App. R. 9, demonstrates the need for the judge to exercise great caution in deciding whether to proceed; the process should be no less rigorous than would occur in the case of an accused who fails to attend his trial. This must be particularly so where the accused is unrepresented, even if he is experienced in criminal proceedings (*R. v McGrath* [2013] EWCA Crim 1261; [2014] Crim. L.R. 144).

6. Illness of accused

The judge's discretion is not limited solely to cases in which the accused has abused his right to be present or has voluntarily agreed to the trial going on in his absence; for in an appropriate case, the judge has a discretion to continue a trial in the absence of an accused through illness, though this is likely to be sparingly used and never if the accused's defence could be prejudiced by his absence (*R. v Howson* (1982) 74 Cr. App. R. 172; [1981] Crim. L.R. 720). The stage the trial has reached may be material: *R. v Kaur* [2013] EWCA Crim 590 (where the accused had given her evidence and had been cross-examined). **1-009**

7. Legal representation

General

It is generally desirable (*R. v Jones* [2002] UKHL 5; [2002] 2 Cr. App. R. 9) that an accused be represented even if he has voluntarily absconded. The presence throughout the trial of legal representatives, in receipt of instructions from the client at some earlier stage, and with no object other than to protect the interests of that client, provides a valuable safeguard against the possibility of error and oversight. **1-010**

It is not within the province of the judge to dismiss an advocate or solicitor from a case, or to order an advocate to remain if the latter is required by the etiquette of the Bar to withdraw. In the latter event, the most that a judge can do is to invite counsel to assist the court in the manner contemplated by the ruling of the then Council of the Bar (*R. v Shaw* (1980) 70 Cr. App. R. 313).

The Bar Standards Board's most recent Handbook sets out the rules and guidance for the profession. It replaces the Code of Conduct with effect from 6 January 2014. (The latest edition (3.3) came into force in May 2018.)

Rules C25 and C26 set out the rules on returning instructions. Rule C26.8 states that

> "you may cease to act on a matter on which you are instructed and return your instructions if there is some other substantial reason for doing so."

This is subject to Rules C27–C29. Rule C27.1 states that

> "you must not cease to act or return instructions without either obtaining your client's consent or clearly explaining to your client or your professional client the reasons for doing so".

A barrister in this situation could withdraw provided they explained to the professional client their "substantial reason" for doing so. However, for the barrister to do so may well not be in accordance with the Core Duties, which take precedence.

Core Duties 1 and 2 provide that "you must observe your duty to the court in the administration of justice" and "you must act in the best interests of each client". These are likely to be particularly relevant to this type of situation. In addition, the barrister would need to consider whether the client had in fact withdrawn instructions, or whether that could be implied by (for example) failure to comply with contractual terms as to payment. Assuming the barrister was being paid (by legal aid, for example) and was able to continue, then there would be no reason for them not to and it may well be in the interests of both justice and the client for them to do so.

It will, of course, be important for the judge to keep an eye on the overall fairness of the proceedings and to exercise his discretion appropriately to prevent any unfair manipulation of the process by an absent accused, to the disadvantage of the co-accused (*R. v Pomfrett* [2009] EWCA Crim 1939; [2010] 2 Cr. App. R. 28).

Position of legal representative

1-011 In regard to the position of the defence advocate, it should be noted that:

(1) in principle, no distinction is to be drawn between instructions received before and instructions received after the date of absconding; if the defence advocate were not permitted to take into account fresh instructions received from the absent accused it would increase unnecessarily the possibility of error or oversight in the trial and could lead to an advocate having to advance a case wholly at odds with the accused's true case;
(2) it could also prevent counsel from being able to deal effectively with new evidence or new issues, even where the absent accused has valid points to make in relation to them;
(3) the advocate is entitled to ask questions of witnesses for the prosecution in as much detail as he wishes based on his instructions, but without indicating what the accused's evidence might have been, and in the knowledge that he is not able to call evidence to contradict the answers given; and
(4) the defence advocate is entitled to conduct cross-examination on this basis in the hope of either showing that his absent client's instructions are accepted by the witnesses or casting doubt upon the coherence or accuracy of their accounts.

(*R. v Kepple* [2007] EWCA Crim 1339; *R. v Pomfrett* [2009] EWCA Crim 1939; [2010] 2 Cr. App. R. 28).

8. CONDUCT OF TRIAL

1-012 Where the judge decides that a trial should take place, or should continue, in the absence of an unrepresented accused:

(1) subject to the amendment to the CrimPR 3.21 with effect from 2 October 2017 (where a defendant will be warned at a PTPH about a jury being told of the reason for their absence at trial) the situation should be explained to the jury as soon as possible in appropriate terms; where absence is voluntary the jury should not be informed of that fact, and they should be warned not to speculate on the reason for the accused's absence;
(2) the judge is under a duty to ensure that the trial is as fair as circumstances permit, and to consider how the fairness of the trial process can be preserved

at each stage (see *R. v Wells* [2009] EWCA Crim 2043) where the accused was arrested while the trial was proceeding in his absence);

(3) the judge:
   (a) must take reasonable steps, both during the giving of the evidence, and, in summing up, to expose any weaknesses in the prosecutor's case and to make such points on behalf of the accused as the evidence permits; and
   (b) ought to warn the jury, if there is one, that absence is not an admission of guilt, and adds nothing to the case for the prosecution.

As to the directions which should be given to the jury where the trial continues in the absence of the accused, see *R. v Rebihi* [2012] EWCA Crim 2481; also *R. v Umerji* [2014] EWCA Crim 421. As to the warning to the jury under CJPOA 1994 s.35, see ACCUSED NOT GIVING EVIDENCE and *R. v Gough* [2001] EWCA Crim 2545; [2002] 2 Cr. App. R. 8.

B. Unrepresented (but present) Accused

1. General

There is no obligation on an accused person to be represented in criminal proceedings in the Crown Court. He may be unrepresented because he chooses to be, or because he does not qualify for public funding (see LEGAL AID; PUBLIC FUNDING) and is not prepared to fund representation himself. **1-013**

When an accused represents himself problems regularly arise. He may lack that knowledge of procedure, evidence and substantive law, that appreciation of relevance, that ability to examine and cross-examine witnesses and present facts in an orderly and disciplined way, and that detachment which should form part of the equipment of the professional lawyer. These deficiencies exist even where an accused attempts to represent himself in all good faith, but the problems are magnified one hundred-fold where the accused is motivated by a desire to obstruct the proceedings or to humiliate, intimidate or abuse any one taking part in it (*R. v Brown* [1998] 2 Cr. App. R. 364).

2. Advice and assistance to accused

The judge, in his duty to ensure that the proceedings are fair, will need to take such steps as are necessary to assist the accused, without prejudicing the interests of the prosecutor, the witnesses, or the public at large. **1-014**

He may need to:

(1) explain the meaning and content of the counts in the indictment;
(2) advise the accused of any special defences and how they may be established;
(3) indicate relevant rules of evidence, the burden of proof and the nature of any evidential traps into which the accused may fall, emphasising that the rules of evidence apply even-handedly to the prosecution and the defence;
(4) explain the accused's right to cross-examine prosecution witnesses and, if necessary, assist in phrasing the questions the accused seeks to put as well as explaining (if appropriate) there are some witnesses the accused will not be able to cross-examine but will need to have an advocate instructed to do so (see 1-015);

(5) explain the rights and nature of conducting the defence, in particular the accused's right to give evidence and the consequences of not doing so (see ACCUSED NOT GIVING EVIDENCE);
(6) explain the accused's right to address the jury, if there is one, but not to introduce evidence in his speech;
(7) if there is a jury, explain the nature of the verdict; and
(8) on sentence, if the accused is still unrepresented, extract from him such mitigation as is available.

In summing up such a case, it will generally be desirable for a judge to direct the jury that it is always open to an accused to represent himself, but where he chooses to do so, they should bear well in mind the difficulty in properly presenting a defence. It will usually be sensible for the judge to explain some or all of these matters to the jury at the outset of the trial, so that they are able, from that stage, to understand the course which the trial follows.

Statutory restrictions apply in relation to the cross-examination of witnesses by an accused in person, as to which see 1-015.

As to the judge's control over an unrepresented accused, particularly in regard to cross-examination of witnesses, see *R. v Brown* [1998] 2 Cr. App. R. 364.

There is a heavy duty on prosecuting counsel, where an accused is unrepresented, to be scrupulously careful in the way in which the case is presented, so that no unfair prejudice against the accused can arise from the manner in which the trial is conducted (*R. v De Oliveira* [1997] Crim. L.R. 600 per Rose LJ).

3. STATUTORY RESTRICTIONS ON CROSS-EXAMINATION

1-015 Where an accused chooses to represent himself, there are certain circumstances in which the law intervenes to protect witnesses:

(1) YJCEA 1999 s.34 prevents the cross-examination by the accused in person of victims in sexual offences cases;
(2) YJCEA 1999 s.35 prohibits such cross-examination of a child (see SPECIAL MEASURES DIRECTIONS).

If such a situation arises, the judge will ask the accused to instruct an advocate to carry out the cross-examination. Applications for legal aid will be subject to means testing (see LEGAL AID; PUBLIC FUNDING).

If the accused:

(a) fails to choose an advocate; or
(b) has his application for legal aid refused in the magistrates' court; or
(c) appears unrepresented in the Crown Court,

the judge will consider whether he ought to appoint a solicitor or advocate.

If he appoints a representative, payment will be made via Central Funds (*CLAM* Annex 13).

In such cases it will generally be desirable that the trial judge should ask such questions as he sees fit, to test the accuracy and reliability and the possibility of collusion between the prosecution witnesses. Without either descending into the arena on behalf of the defence or, generally speaking, putting any sort of positive case on behalf of the defence, this is a difficult tightrope for the trial judge to walk. However, he must do his best according to the circumstances of the particular case (*R. v De Oliveira* [1997] Crim. L.R. 600 per Rose LJ).

4. JUDGE'S OVERALL CONTROL; SEXUAL CASES

General

The trial judge is obliged to have regard not only to the need to ensure a fair trial for the accused but also to the reasonable interests of other parties to the court process, in particular witnesses, and among witnesses particularly those who are obliged to relive, by describing it in the witness box, an ordeal to which they say they have been subject. **1-016**

The following principles may be stated (*R. v Brown* [1998] 2 Cr. App. R. 364):

(1) it is the clear duty of the trial judge to do everything he can, consistently with giving the accused a fair trial, to minimise the trauma suffered by other participants;
(2) a trial is not fair if the accused, by choosing to represent himself, gains the advantage he would not have had if represented of abusing the rules in relation to relevance and repetition which apply when witnesses are questioned; and
(3) the judge is not obliged to give an unrepresented accused his head to ask whatever questions, at whatever length, he wishes.

The exercise of these powers will always call for the exercise of a very careful judgment, since the judge must not only ensure that the accused has a fair trial but also (which is not necessarily the same thing) that the jury feel he has had a fair trial.

2. ABUSE OF PROCESS

Quick Guide

1. General principles

The underlying principle

2-001 "Abuse of process" has been defined as

"something so unfair and wrong that the court should not allow a prosecutor to proceed with what is, in all other respects, a regular proceeding" (*R. v Hui Chi-Ming* (1992) 94 Cr. App. R. 236 PC).

It is well established that the court has the power to stay proceedings in two categories of case, namely:

(1) where it will be impossible to give the accused a fair trial; and
(2) where it offends the court's sense of justice and propriety to be asked to try the accused in the particular circumstances of the case.

In:

(a) the first category of case, if the judge concludes that the accused cannot receive a fair trial, he will stay the proceedings without more; no question of the balancing of competing interests arises;
(b) the second category of case, the focus is on whether the court's sense of justice and propriety is offended or public confidence in the criminal justice system would be undermined by the trial (*Warren v HM Attorney General of the Bailiwick of Jersey* [2011] UKPC 10; [2011] 2 Cr. App. R. 29 per Lord Dyson); that is not about fairness to the accused.

The two categories are distinct and should be considered separately (*R. v Maxwell* [2010] UKSC 48; [2011] 2 Cr. App. R. 31 per Lord Dyson). The courts have not endeavoured to identify every situation which would come within this second category. Lord Dyson referred to "the infinite variety of cases that can arise". The facts of each case must be examined carefully. Note that it is not necessary for an appellant alleging category 2 abuse to prove misconduct which goes beyond that establishing category 1 abuse (*Hamilton v Post Office Ltd* [2021] EWCA Crim 577).

In the first category the judge has jurisdiction to prevent abuse of the court's process, the discretionary power to stay an indictment (or part of an indictment—*R. v Munro* (1993) 97 Cr. App. R. 183) being conferred to ensure that there is a fair trial. The right to a fair trial is guaranteed by ECHR art.6.

In the second category it should be noted that:

(i) a stay should be granted where necessary to protect the integrity of the criminal justice system;
(ii) a balancing of interests should be conducted in deciding whether a stay is required to fulfil this primary purpose;
(iii) the public interest in ensuring that those charged with grave crimes should

be tried will always weigh in the balance (*R. v Latif* [1996] 2 Cr. App. R. 92 per Lord Steyn);

(iv) the "but for" factor (i.e. where it can be shown that the accused would not have stood trial but for executive abuse of power) is merely one of various matters that will influence the decision; and

(v) a stay should not be ordered for the purpose of punishing or disciplining prosecutorial or police misconduct.

An application to stay is, in effect, a plea in bar of trial and should not succeed where there are other methods of achieving a fair hearing of the case (*DPP v Hussain* (1994) 158 J.P.N. 570 DC). Once a decision has been taken to stay proceedings on grounds of abuse, that is the effective final determination of the case; it is inconceivable that the case could subsequently be pursued (*Council for the Regulation of Healthcare Professionals v GMC* [2006] EWHC 2784 (Admin); [2007] 1 W.L.R. 3094).

An indictment should be stayed only in exceptional circumstances (*DPP v B* [2008] EWHC 201 (Admin); [2008] Crim. L.R. 707) and a stay should not be granted in the absence of prejudice to the accused so serious that no fair trial could be held. It is an exceptional remedy and each case turns on its own facts. *R. v Abu Hamza* [2006] EWCA Crim 2918; [2007] 1 Cr. App. R. 27 does not lay down strict minimum requirements (*R. v Gripton* [2010] EWCA Crim 2260).

Where abuse may arise

The cases show that there may be abuse of process where: **2-002**

(1) the prosecution has manipulated or misused the process of the court so as to deprive an accused of a protection afforded by the law, or to take advantage of a technicality (*R. v Liverpool MC Ex p. Slade* [1998] 1 Cr. App. R. 147);

(2) the proceedings before the court have only been made possible by acts of agents of the state which offend the court's conscience as being contrary to the rule of law, or would otherwise bring the administration of justice into disrepute (e.g. *R. v Horseferry Rd MC Ex p. Bennett (No.1)* (1994) 98 Cr. App. R. 114; *R. v Mullen (No.2)* [1999] 2 Cr. App. R. 143; *R. (on the application of Hausschildt) v Highbury Corner MC* [2009] Crim. L.R. 512; cf. *R. v Mote* [2008] Crim. L.R. 793);

(3) illegal conduct by the police or the prosecutor is so grave as to threaten or undermine the rule of law itself (*R. v Grant* [2005] EWCA Crim 1089; [2005] 2 Cr. App. R. 28);

(4) on a balance of probabilities, the accused has been, or will be, prejudiced in the preparation or conduct of his defence by delay on the part of the prosecution which is unjustifiable, being not due, for example, to:
   (a) the complexity of the enquiry and the preparation of the prosecution case;
   (b) the acts of the accused or one or more co-accused;
   (c) genuine difficulties of service (*R. v Derby Crown Court Ex p. Brooks* (1985) 80 Cr. App. R. 164); or

(5) a prosecuting authority ignores or fails to comply with its own declared prosecuting criteria (*R. v Adaway* [2004] EWCA Crim 2831; (2004) 168 J.P. 645).

Judges should be slow to interfere with the exercise of prosecutorial discretion by the DPP or CPS but may do so where it can be shown that a policy is unlawful or where there was a failure to adhere to a policy, or a decision may be said to be perverse.

The considerations in relation to proceedings in which there is no state involvement are significantly different from those applying to a criminal prosecution or to misuse of executive powers by the state's agents; see *Council for the Regulation of Health Care Professionals v GMC* [2006] EWHC 2784 (Admin); [2007] 1 W.L.R. 3094. There is no reason in principle why, by analogy, a private prosecution should not be considered an abuse of process if the crime which is the subject of the prosecution is one that has been encouraged by the private prosecutor, or when in some other way the private prosecutor has essentially created the same mischief as that about which he complains (*R. (on the application of Dacre) v City of Westminster MC* [2008] EWHC 1667 (Admin); [2009] 1 Cr. App. R. 6). In *Asif v Ditta* [2021] EWCA Crim 1091; [2022] 1 W.L.R. 285 the Court of Appeal concluded that the trial judge had been entitled to conclude that the primary motive of the prosecution was so unrelated to properly constituted proceedings that it rendered the prosecution a misuse or abuse of process.

As to guidance issued by the CACD in cases involving the prosecution of victims of trafficking, see *R. v L* [2013] EWCA Crim 991; [2013] 2 Cr. App. R. 23 and *R. v GB* [2020] EWCA Crim 2. See also *R. v AAD* [2022] EWCA Crim 106; [2022] 1 W.L.R. 4042 and *R. v AGM* [2022] EWCA Crim 920; [2022] 7 WLUK 9.

There is no freestanding ground for staying a criminal case as an abuse of process on the basis that a prosecution is a disproportionate interference with rights pursuant to ECHR arts 10 and 11 (*R. v Brown* [2022] EWCA Crim 6; [2022] 1 WLUK 102).

In *Tague v Governor of Full Sutton Prison* [2015] EWHC 3576 (Admin); [2016] 1 Cr. App. R. 15, the CACD left open the question whether the second category of abuse could be founded on post-conviction misconduct.

Potential prejudice to the accused: a "fair trial"

2-003 The crux of the matter is whether, in all the circumstances, the situation created by any apparent abuse is such as to make any trial unfair (e.g. *Tan v Cameron* (1993) 96 Cr. App. R. 172; *Attorney General of Hong Kong v Cheung Wai-Bun* (1994) 98 Cr. App. R. 17).

Where there is no fault on the part of the police or the prosecutor, it will be very rare for a stay to be justified. Even where the judge finds that there has been an abuse of process in the conduct of the proceedings, whatever the category of abuse, in general he:

(1) must consider, as a "further and separate" question, whether there is potential prejudice to the accused;
(2) has a discretion, even where he finds abuse of process, to allow the trial to proceed where he finds no prejudice to the accused (*R. v Gloucester Crown Court Ex p. Jackman* [1993] 12 C.L. 118; [1993] C.O.D. 100), unless the unlawful acts by the police or the prosecutor are so great an affront to the integrity of the justice system, and therefore to the rule of law, that the associated prosecution should not be countenanced by the courts, whether or not prejudice is caused to the accused (*R. v Grant* [2005] EWCA Crim 1089; [2005] 2 Cr. App. R. 28).

When assessing "serious prejudice" the judge needs to bear in mind, however, his control over the admission of evidence and the important fact that the trial process itself will ensure that all factual issues arising will be properly before the jury (*R. v S (Stephen Paul)* [2006] EWCA Crim 756; [2006] 2 Cr. App. R. 23).

Thus:

(a) it is important to distinguish between the sort of case in which the issues at the trial will depend upon the recollection of witnesses about some event, and a case which turns largely upon documents (*R. v Buzalek* [1991] Crim. L.R. 115 at 116); and

(b) the complexities of the case and the difficulties of investigation are a factor to be considered; there may be cases where the case is so complex that, despite the diligent efforts of the prosecutor, delay, for example, is such that a fair trial is impossible (cf. *R. v Telford Justices Ex p. Badham* (1991) 93 Cr. App. R. 171; *Hayter v L* [1998] 1 W.L.R. 854).

Where confiscation proceedings are properly brought within POCA 2002, they should not be stayed as an abuse of process because the judge considers that they may have an oppressive result (*R. v Nelson* [2009] EWCA Crim 1573; [2010] 1 Cr. App. R. (S.) 82).

2. Instances of abuse

(1) Investigative methods

Action by the investigating body, luring persons into committing acts forbidden by law and then seeking to prosecute them for doing so, may amount to an abuse of the process of the court, and a judge has an inherent power and duty to prevent it. **2-004**

The boundary between acceptable and unacceptable behaviour will depend in each case on its own facts, but a useful guide to identifying the limits of the type of conduct which is acceptable is to consider whether, in the particular circumstances, the investigators did no more than present the accused with an unexceptional opportunity to commit a crime (*R. v Loosely; Attorney General's Reference (No.3 of 2000)* [2001] UKHL 53; [2002] 1 Cr. App. R. 29, recently considered in *R. v Syed* [2018] EWCA Crim 2809; [2019] 1 Cr. App. R. 21).

Thus:

(1) if the conduct of the investigators preceding the commission of the offence was no more than might have been expected from others in the circumstances, they are not to be regarded as having instigated or encouraged or assisted in the commission of the crime;

(2) if they did no more than others might be expected to do, they were not creating crime artificially; but the investigatory technique of providing an opportunity to commit crime should not be applied in a random fashion or be used for wholesale virtue testing without good reason (see *R. v Moore* [2013] EWCA Crim 85; 2014 Crim. L.R. 364 where the issues are discussed in depth; see also *R. v Palmer* [2014] EWCA Crim 1681; [2015] Crim. L.R. 153);

(3) a degree of active involvement by an undercover police officer will not necessarily amount to entrapment (*R. v M* [2011] EWCA Crim 648).

The greater the degree of intrusiveness, the closer will be the need for the judge to scrutinise the reason for using it.

Furthermore:

(a) the investigators must act in good faith, and having reasonable suspicion is one way in which such good faith might be established;

(b) reasonable suspicion of a particular individual will not always be necessary.

In deciding what is acceptable, the judge must have regard to the accused's circumstances, including his vulnerability.

(2) Missing exhibits

2-005 The absence of an exhibit does not, of itself, give rise to abuse of process (*R. v Beckford* [1996] 1 Cr. App. R. 94). See also *DPP v Fell* [2013] EWHC 562 (Admin) where the accused's position could be adequately protected in the trial process, even without the missing evidence. "Mere speculation about what missing documentation might show" does not justify a stay for abuse, contrasting other cases where there was reason to think that specific, but at trial absent, contemporaneous documents would have been decisive (*R. v MacKreth* [2009] EWCA Crim 1849; [2010] Crim. L.R. 226; see also *R. v E* [2012] EWCA Crim 791). A distinction also needs to be drawn between the loss of an exhibit and its deliberate destruction (see *R. v Birmingham* [1992] Crim. L.R. 117). See also *Clay v South Cambridgeshire Justices* [2014] EWHC 321 (Admin); [2015] R.T.R. 1 and *DPP v Patel* [2015] EWHC 48 (Admin); [2015] Crim. L.R. 385.

The principles set out in the leading case of *R. (on the application of Ebrahim) v Feltham MC* [2001] EWHC Admin 130; [2001] 2 Cr. App. R. 23 were more recently re-stated in *R. v Lamont* [2010] EWCA Crim 2144 as follows:

(1) Was the prosecution in breach of a duty in failing to obtain evidence? In determining that question regard should be had to the Code of Practice applicable to prosecuting authorities and the Attorney General's guidelines; if there is no breach of duty, then the question of stay will not arise.

(2) If the prosecution is in breach of duty, have they acted in bad faith or otherwise been in serious default of their duty? If so, then the prosecution should be stayed on that ground alone, irrespective of whether a fair trial would be possible; in these very exceptional cases it is not so much that the accused cannot receive a fair trial but that it would be unfair to subject him to a trial at all (see, e.g. *DPP v Ara* [2001] EWCA Admin 493; [2002] 1 Cr. App. R. 16).

(3) Absent bad faith or serious default, there should be a stay if there is such serious prejudice to the accused that a fair trial cannot be guaranteed.

(4) In most cases, the difficulty arising from the lack of evidence can be dealt with by an appropriate direction in the trial process itself. It is only in exceptional circumstances that a stay is likely.

It is important to bear in mind two points which were emphasised by the court in *Ebrahim*, the first of which is of general application in all cases of abuse, namely that the discretionary power to ensure fairness means fairness to both the accused and to the prosecution; it is important that the guilty are convicted as well as the innocent acquitted.

Secondly, and importantly, there will often be holes in the prosecution case which may result from some failing by the prosecution. If, in such a case, there is sufficient credible evidence, apart from the missing evidence, which if believed would justify a safe conviction, then the trial should proceed, leaving the accused to seek to persuade the jury not to convict because evidence which might otherwise have been available was not before the court through no fault of his. Often the absence of relevant evidence is likely to hamper the prosecution as much as the defence.

See, as to missing video recordings, *DPP v S* 67 JCL 87; as to gaps in video evidence, *R. v Brooks* [2004] EWCA Crim 3537; (2004) 148 S.J. 1031; and as to the absence of CCTV evidence, see *Morris v DPP* [2008] EWHC 2788; (2009) 173 J.P. 41.

For cases considering the impact of a missing ABE interview and a missing interview with the defendant, see *R. v SR* [2019] EWCA Crim 887 and *R. v PR* [2019] EWCA Crim 1225; [2019] 2 Cr. App. R. 22.

(3) Defects in disclosure

A stay on the ground that failures of disclosure by the prosecution have led to an abuse of process will be an exceptional case, particularly where the charges are serious, but see *R. v Birmingham* [1992] Crim. L.R. 117 (where video tape was not disclosed and was later lost). **2-006**

Deficiencies in disclosure may be censured, but it does not follow that the trial should not proceed, particularly where there is no allegation of bad faith on the part of the prosecutor.

Such a ruling should not be made unless it is established that the accused could not have a fair trial. See *Prosecution Appeal; R. v O* [2012] L.S. Gazette 5 January 2012 CA (where the failure was late disclosure, rather than non-disclosure, and there was nothing to indicate that that late disclosure could not have been accommodated during the trial (e.g. by adjournment)).

In *R. v Salt* [2015] EWCA Crim 662; [2015] 2 Cr. App. R. 27 the trial judge had stayed the proceedings as an abuse of process, not because a fair trial was impossible but because to allow proceedings to continue would condone extreme prosecution failings in the conduct of disclosure. The CACD set aside the stay, concluding that it was necessary to balance the public interest in ensuring that those charged with grave crimes should be tried and the rights of the complainants against the need to ensure the proper integrity of the criminal justice system and the fairness of any future trial. Whilst the conduct of the CPS and police had been reprehensible, the failures of disclosure were of limited materiality. See also *R. v Boardman* [2015] EWCA Crim 175; [2015] 1 Cr. App. R. 504.

In *R. v R* [2015] EWCA Crim 1941; [2016] 1 Cr. App. R. 20 the CACD provided guidance in cases where the conduct of the disclosure exercise has resulted in delay. They concluded that the judge had placed too great a weight on the question whether the defendants had suffered personal prejudice, rather than considering whether there was serious prejudice that would deprive them of a fair trial. The delay was not sufficient to warrant the conclusion that there could not be a fair trial. In the event of conviction, the delay might be cured by a reduction in sentence. It is important that conduct or results which might be the result of state incompetence or negligence should not necessarily justify the abandonment of a trial of serious allegations—"there is no bright line and a broad brush approach is likely to be necessary" ([72]). There will be cases where prosecutorial failures can bring a prosecution summarily to an end but these can only be decided on a case by case basis.

More recently in *R. v Akle* [2020] 7 WLUK 755; [2021] Lloyd's Rep. F.C. 306 at the Crown Court at Southwark the trial judge ruled that serious failings in disclosure by the SFO relating to potential inappropriate influence of a third party upon the SFO's decision to prosecute did not justify a stay of the prosecution. When the matter came before the Court of Appeal *R. v Akle* [2021] EWCA Crim 1879; [2021] 12 WLUK 150 the Court upheld the trial judges ruling but quashed the convictions on the basis of the disclosure failings.

For a case considering the impact of a conceded failure to examine the contents of a complainant's mobile telephone, see *R. v E* [2018] EWCA Crim 2426; [2019] Crim. L.R. 151. See also *R. v CB* [2020] EWCA Crim 790; [2020] 2 Cr. App. R. 20, in which the CACD provided guidance on issues arising in criminal investigations concerning the retention, inspection, copying, deletion and disclosure of digital records held on mobile telephones and other digital devices.

(4) Delay

The principles

2-007 The leading cases are *Attorney-General's Reference (No.1 of 1990)* [1992] Q.B. 630; (1992) 95 Cr. App. R. 296; *R. v S (Stephen Paul)* [2006] EWCA Crim 756; [2006] 2 Cr. App. R. 23 and *R. v F(S)* [2011] EWCA Crim 726; [2011] 2 Cr. App. R. 13.

In *Attorney General's Reference (No.1 of 1990)* [1992] Q.B. 630; (1992) 95 Cr. App. R. 296 the CACD stated that:

(1) a stay on grounds of delay is to be imposed only in exceptional circumstances even where the delay was unjustifiable, even more rarely in the absence of fault on the part of complainant or prosecution, and never when the delay is due to the complexity of the case or the actions of the accused; and
(2) no stay should be imposed unless the defence establishes that the accused will suffer serious prejudice because of the delay to the extent that no fair trial can be held; the judge should bear in mind his powers and the trial process itself to provide protection from prejudice.

Where delay in the proceedings is put forward as amounting to abuse, the judge will consider the reasons for the delay and the potential unfairness, if any, to the accused. In considering the question of whether there is potential prejudice to the accused, the cases show that relevant factors will be:

(a) the *length* of the delay;
(b) any *reasons* given by the prosecutor for that delay; and
(c) any *efforts* made by the accused to assert his rights.

The longer the delay the more likely it will be that the prosecution is at fault and that the delay has caused prejudice to the accused; the less the prosecution has to offer by way of explanation, the more easily can prejudice be inferred.

For an example of an extreme delay (events occurring between 39 and 63 years earlier) where a fair trial was held to be possible, see *R. v D* [2013] EWCA Crim 1592.

The approach

2-008 The above principles were re-emphasised in *R. v S (Stephen Paul)* [2006] EWCA Crim 756; [2006] 2 Cr. App. R. 23. The CACD stated that the discretionary decision whether or not to grant a stay for abuse of process because of delay was an exercise in judicial assessment dependent on judgment rather than on any conclusion as to facts based on evidence.

It is therefore potentially misleading to apply to the exercise of that discretion the language of burden and standard of proof, which is more apt to an evidence-based fact-finding process.

The CACD repeated the principles stated in *Attorney General's Reference (No.1 of 1990* [1992] Q.B. 630; (1992) 95 Cr. App. R. 296), adding that when assessing possible serious prejudice, the judge should bear in mind:

(1) his power to regulate the admissibility of evidence; and
(2) the fact that the trial process itself should ensure that all relevant factual issues arising from delay will be placed before the jury for its consideration in accordance with appropriate directions from the trial judge.

If, having considered all those factors, a judge's assessment is that a fair trial would be possible, he should not grant a stay.

A five-judge Court of Appeal approved *R. v S (Stephen Paul)* [2006] EWCA Crim 756; [2006] 2 Cr. App. R. 23 in *R. v F(S)* [2011] EWCA Crim 1844; [2011] 2 Cr. App. R. 28. The CACD said that where abuse of process submissions on the ground of delay are advanced, provided the principles articulated in *R. v Galbraith* (1981) 73 Cr. App. R. 124 and *Attorney General's Reference (No.1 of 1990)* [1992] Q.B. 630; (1992) 95 Cr. App. R. 296, were clearly understood, it is not necessary or appropriate for reference to be made to any decisions of the CACD save for *R. v S (Stephen Paul)* and *R. v F(S)*.

No case submission distinguished

An application to stay for abuse of process on the ground of delay and a submission of no case to answer are two distinct matters requiring distinct and separate consideration. **2-009**

Thus:

(1) an application to stay for abuse of process on the ground of delay cannot succeed unless, exceptionally, a fair trial is no longer possible owing to prejudice to the accused occasioned by the delay which cannot fairly be addressed in the normal trial process; whereas
(2) on a submission of no case the question is whether the evidence, viewed overall, is such that the jury can properly convict.

In *R. v F(S)* [2011] EWCA Crim 1844; [2011] 2 Cr. App. R. 28 it was apparent that the argument, and perhaps in consequence the ruling, represented an amalgam of two distinct questions, namely, should:

(a) the prosecution be stayed for abuse of process on the ground that the accused could not receive a fair trial?; or
(b) the case be withdrawn from the jury on the ground that the evidence was such that a conviction would be unsafe?

The authority of *R. v Galbraith* (1981) 73 Cr. App. R. 124, with its emphasis on the responsibilities of the jury as the fact-finding body responsible for delivering the verdicts, is undiminished. The principles have not been modified or extended (e.g. for the purposes of addressing trials which involve historic unreported sexual crimes). Where, in accordance with the second limb of *Galbraith*, the state of the evidence called by the prosecution and taken as a whole is so unsatisfactory, contradictory, or so transparently unreliable that no jury, properly directed, could convict, it is the judge's duty to direct the jury that there is no case to answer and to return a not guilty verdict. In making that judgment, however, the judge has to bear in mind the constitutional primacy of the jury, and not usurp its function.

Judges will find it easier to ensure that submissions of no case are concentrated on the correct principles if expressions such as "safe to convict" or "safely left to the jury" are avoided.

If the jury convicts, and the conviction may be unsafe, that is a matter which must be dealt with by the CACD. The trial judge is not responsible for assessing whether, in advance of a conviction, the conviction would be unsafe.

Historic sex cases

2-010 In most historic sex allegations the reasons for the delayed complaint, and whether and how the delay is explained or justified, bear directly on the credibility of the complainant. They therefore form an essential part of the factual matrix on which the jury has to make its decision. That is the principal, and in the overwhelming majority of cases, the only relevance of the evidence on those issues.

The authorities show that:

(1) in general, submissions as to whether the trial should proceed at all should take place before the evidence is called;
(2) it is only in exceptional cases, where a fair trial is not possible, that a stay is justified on the ground of delay; and
(3) the question whether the complainant's explanation for the delay in reporting the alleged offence is truthful is a matter capable of exploration at the trial; it does not provide any reason on abuse of process grounds for preventing the trial from taking place.

(5) Serial prosecutions

2-011 There is a general rule of criminal procedure that:

(1) the prosecutor should join in one indictment all the charges that he wishes to prefer in respect of one incident; and
(2) he should not be permitted, *save in special or exceptional circumstances*, to bring a second set of proceedings arising out of the same incident as the first, after the first set of proceedings have been concluded.

The judge has a discretion to stay the subsequent proceedings if to proceed would be oppressive or prejudicial and therefore an abuse of the process of the court. The question for determination in a case of this kind is whether the second set of proceedings arises out of the same, or substantially the same, facts as the first.

Consideration of whether or not the accused can have a fair trial, which is material to applications to stay on grounds of delay (see *Attorney General's Reference (No.1 of 1990)* [1992] Q.B. 630; (1992) 95 Cr. App. R. 296) has no place here. Where a stay is sought on the ground of:

(a) delay, the burden is on the defence to show that, on a balance of probabilities, no fair trial can be held;
(b) a second prosecution, the general rule is that there *should* be a stay unless the prosecutor shows that there are special circumstances why there should not be (see *R. v Phipps* [2005] EWCA Crim 33, where the authorities are

reviewed; cf. *DPP v Alexander* [2010] EWHC 2266 (Admin); [2011] 1 W.L.R. 653. See also *R. v Dwyer (Howard James)* [2012] EWCA Crim 10).

The phrase "special circumstances" originates in the speech of Lord Devlin in *Connelly v DPP* (1964) 48 Cr. App. R. 183 (see also *R. v Beedie* [1997] 2 Cr. App. R. 167 and *R. v Dwyer* [2012] EWCA Crim 10). In each of the latter two cases different constitutions of the CACD found that it was for the Crown first to demonstrate special circumstances and then to demonstrate that to proceed would not be an abuse of process. This is different from the conventional approach to applications to stay a case as an abuse of process, where the burden is on the accused. The principle underlying the general rule is that a trial for different offences arising out of the same facts that led to an earlier trial is prima facie oppressive.

The general rule requires the judge to stay the indictment (that is, order that it remain on the file not to be proceeded with) where he is satisfied that the charges in it are founded on the same facts as the charges in a previous indictment on which the accused has been tried, but note that a second trial on the same or similar facts is not always necessarily oppressive. In *Connelly v DPP* Lord Devlin added that

> "there may in a particular case be special circumstances which make it just and convenient in that case. The judge must then, in all the circumstances of the particular case, exercise his discretion as to whether or not he applies the general rule."

In *R. v Antoine* [2014] EWCA Crim 1971; [2015] 1 Cr. App. R. 8 the CACD distinguished *Beedie* and *Dwyer* on the ground that no one with the responsibility for prosecuting the case had correctly applied their mind to the appropriate charges originally brought and how they should be prosecuted. This was not an escalation from minor charges to more serious charges, contrary to the general rule, but a move from misconceived charges to correct charges. The appellant was aware that appropriate charges were to be brought nine days after sentence was imposed and only 19 days after arrest. The court had no hesitation in concluding that the judge was justified in finding that there were special circumstances here which required that the prosecution continue. The court's sense of justice and propriety was not offended nor was public confidence in the criminal justice system undermined. On the contrary, a stay would have brought the criminal justice system into disrepute.

In *R. v Dunn* [2021] EWCA Crim 439; [2021] 3 WLUK 444 the Court of Appeal found that a re-trial for "forensic alternative" rather than a true alternative offence did not constitute an abuse of process.

For a recent authority considering *Dwyer* and *Beedie* and allowing an appeal against a refusal to stay proceedings, see *R. v Wangige* [2020] EWCA Crim 1319; [2021] 1 Cr. App. R. 6.

(6) Retrials

Whether a retrial, particularly a second retrial, is in the interests of justice (which **2-012**
require a fair trial in circumstances which are neither oppressive nor unjust) is ultimately a question for the trial judge (*R. v Bell* [2010] EWCA Crim 3; [2010] 1 Cr. App. R. 27).

In *R. v Henworth* [2001] EWCA Crim 120; [2001] 2 Cr. App. R. 4, it was accepted that there was a recognised public interest in having a jury decide serious criminal allegations, but that there was a possibility that in any given case a time might come when it would be an abuse of process for the prosecution to try again.

There is a convention that if the prosecutor fails to secure a conviction on two occasions he will not seek a further retrial (*R. v Henworth* [2001] EWCA Crim 120; [2001] 2 Cr. App. R. 4; *DPP v Edgar* (2002) 164 J.P. 471; see also *R. v Bell* [2010] EWCA Crim 3; [2010] Cr. App. R. 27).

In *R. v Bell* [2010] EWCA Crim 3; [2010] 1 Cr. App. R. 27 the CACD identified two characteristics which must be satisfied before a second retrial could take place. These are (a) that the alleged offence is one of extreme gravity; and (b) that the evidence against the defendant is very powerful. The application of the *Bell* test was considered in *R. v Burton* [2015] EWCA Crim 1307; [2016] 1 Cr. App. R. 7, in which the CACD held that the *Bell* test will usually be a sufficient test of where the interests of justice lie, but in some cases a wider consideration may be required. There must be an informed, dispassionate and searching examination of why a third trial was justified if there were no irregularities in the first two trials. The number of cases in which a third trial is permitted must be strictly limited in order to maintain public confidence and provide a degree of finality for the defendant. The court must proceed with extreme caution.

(7) Undertaking not to prosecute; agreement as to plea

2-013 There may be abuse of process where the prosecutor seeks to go back on:

(1) an unequivocal promise made to an accused that he will not be prosecuted; or
(2) a carefully prepared and agreed basis for plea approved by the court (*CPS v Mattu* [2009] EWCA Crim 1483; [2010] Crim. L.R. 220.

A prosecution undertaking ought to be relied on and it is not right to allow a prosecutor to proceed in such circumstances unless he can show affirmatively that the original decision was exclusively evidentially based and was clearly wrong (*DPP v Taylor* [2004] EWHC 1554 (Admin)).

Abuse of process is unlikely to arise unless:

(a) there has been an unequivocal representation by those with the conduct of the prosecution that the accused will not be prosecuted; and
(b) the accused has acted to his detriment on that representation.

Even then, proceedings may not be stayed if fresh material facts have come to light since the representation was made (*R. v Abu Hamza* [2006] EWCA Crim 2918; [2007] 1 Cr. App. R. 27).

The authorities show that, in general, the circumstances of the case need to be exceptional. *R. v Townsend* [1997] 2 Cr. App. R. 540 makes it plain that breach of a promise not to prosecute does not necessarily give rise to abuse (cf. *R. v Bloomfield* [1997] 1 Cr. App. R. 135 where an assurance had been given to the judge that no evidence would be offered). See also *R. v Killick* [2011] EWCA Crim 1608; [2012] 1 Cr. App. R. 10; *R. v Dowty* [2011] EWCA Crim 3138; and *R. v LG* [2018] EWCA Crim 736; [2019] Crim. L.R. 706 (where the accused could not be shown to have acted to his detriment).

Where the prosecutor has elected not to proceed against a co-accused, although such proceedings were possible, such a decision does not amount to an abuse of process (*R. v Forsyth* [1997] 2 Cr. App. R. 299). See also *Environment Agency v Stanford* [1999] Env. L.R. 286.

Where an offender admits an offence and, with his agreement, is formally cautioned by the police under CDA 1998 on their assurance that he will not be brought before a criminal court in connection with the matter, it is an abuse of the court's process to permit the victim subsequently to bring a private prosecution in respect of that offence (*Jones v Whalley* [2006] UKHL 41; [2007] 1 Cr. App. R. 2; cf. *R. v Gore* [2009] EWCA Crim 1424; [2009] W.L.R. (D) 240).

(8) Failure to obey court orders

Orders made by judges must be obeyed; the normal consequence of disobeying such an order, made in the interests of a fair trial, is either: **2-014**

(1) the exclusion of the evidence to which the order relates; or
(2) in a case which is entirely dependent on the evidence in question, a stay of proceedings.

See *CPS v LR* [2010] EWCA Crim 924; [2010] 2 Cr. App. R. 9 in relation to charges of making indecent photographs of children, contrary to the Protection of Children Act 1978. The arrangements suggested by the prosecution to enable the accused and his legal advisers to examine the material had been wholly inadequate. The judge had ordered the prosecutor to supply the court and the accused with the copies of the images but the prosecutor refused to comply with the order.

(9) Adverse publicity

There will be cases where it is argued that a stay should be granted owing to the publicity surrounding a case. The issue (as put succinctly in the High Court of Justiciary in the Scots case of *Montgomery v HMA; Coulter v HMA* [2000] 2 W.L.R. 779) is whether the risk of prejudice resulting from the publicity will be so grave that even careful directions by the trial judge cannot reasonably be expected to remove it. **2-015**

In *R. v Abu Hamza* [2006] EWCA Crim 2918; [2007] 1 Cr. App. R. 27 the CACD, per curiam, stated that the fact that adverse publicity may risk prejudicing a fair trial is no reason for not proceeding with the trial if the judge concludes that, with his assistance, it will be possible to have a fair trial. In considering this question it is right for the judge to have regard to his own experience and that of his fellow judges as to the manner in which juries normally perform their duties. For a recent illustration of the application of these principles, see *R. v C (PM)* [2017] EWCA Crim 557.

In *Attorney General v MGN Ltd* [1997] 1 All E.R. 456, Schiemann LJ suggested that a judge would consider, amongst other matters, in making an assessment of:

(1) the likelihood of a publication coming to the attention of a potential juror:
    (a) whether the publication circulates in the area from which the jurors are likely to be drawn; and
    (b) how many copies were circulated;
(2) the likely impact of the publication on an ordinary reader at the time of publication:
    (a) the prominence of the article in the publication; and
    (b) the novelty of the content of the article in the context of likely readers of that publication;
(3) the residual impact of the publication on a notional juror at the time of the trial:
    (a) the length of time between publication and the likely date of trial;

- (b) the focusing effect of listening over a prolonged period to evidence in a case; and
- (c) the likely effect of the judge's directions to a jury.

As this passage indicates, it is the effect of the publication on the mind of the notional juror at the time of the trial that has to be considered.

The risk assessment exercise requires account to be taken of the factors, including the measures available to the trial judge, that may be expected to reduce the residual impact (per Lord Hope of Craighead in *Montgomery v HMA; Coulter v HMA* [2000] 2 W.L.R. 779).

In *R. v Stone* [2001] EWCA Crim 297; [2001] Crim L.R. 465 the CACD considered that the question should be decided on a balance of probabilities. In that case there was a three-year interval between the majority of the media coverage and the expected date of the retrial. Much of the information would have been forgotten by potential jurors. Even if all the information were not forgotten, it would be easier for a jury member to set aside any information they were told to disregard. Since the impact of the offences had been felt most in the local region, any risk of prejudice would be reduced if the retrial took place away from that local region.

3. Procedure on application

Application to stay case for abuse of process

2-016 Procedure is governed by CrimPR 3.28 which provides that an accused wanting the judge to stay the case on the grounds that the proceedings are an abuse of the court or otherwise unfair must:

- (1) apply in writing:
  - (a) as soon as practicable after becoming aware of the grounds for doing so;
  - (b) at a pre-trial hearing, unless the grounds for the application do not arise until trial; and
  - (c) in any event, before the accused pleads guilty or the jury (if there is one) retires to consider its verdict at trial;
- (2) serve the application on the court officer, and on each other party; and
- (3) in the application:
  - (a) explain the grounds on which it is made;
  - (b) include, attach or identify all supporting material;
  - (c) specify relevant events, dates and propositions of law; and
  - (d) identify any witness he wants to call to give evidence in person.

A party who wants to make representations in response to the application must serve the representations on the court officer, and on each other party, not more than 10 business days after service of the application.

CrimPR 3.28 is supplemented by *CPD* I 3C.2 which provides that a co-accused who wishes to make a like application must give a like notice not later than seven days before the relevant date, setting out any additional grounds relied upon.

The following automatic directions apply to such applications (*CPD* I 3C.3):

- (i) The advocate for the applicant(s) must lodge with the court and serve on all other parties a skeleton argument in support of the application, at least five clear working days before the relevant date; if reference is to be made to any document not in the existing trial documents, a paginated and indexed bundle of such documents is to be provided with the skeleton argument.

(ii) The advocate for the prosecution must lodge with the court and serve on all other parties a responsive skeleton argument at least two clear working days before the relevant date, together with a supplementary bundle if appropriate.

All skeleton arguments must specify any propositions of law to be advanced (together with the authorities relied upon in support, with paragraph references to passages relied upon) and, where appropriate, include a chronology of events and a list of dramatis personae. In all instances where reference is made to a document, the reference in the trial documents or supplementary bundle is to be given (*CPD* I 3C.4).

Time limits

2-017 The above time limits are minimum time limits. In appropriate cases, the court will order longer lead times. To this end, in all cases where defence advocates are, at the time of the preliminary hearing or as soon as practicable after the case has been sent, considering the possibility of an abuse of process application, this must be raised with the judge dealing with the matter, who will order a different timetable if appropriate, and may wish, in any event, to give additional directions about the conduct of the application. If the trial judge has not been identified, the matter should be raised with the Resident Judge (*CPD* I 3C.5).

3. ACCUSED NOT GIVING EVIDENCE

Accused's right to give or not to give evidence

3-001 At the trial of any person who has attained the age of 14 years for an offence, unless:

(1) the accused's guilt is not in issue;
(2) it appears to the judge that the physical or mental condition of the accused makes it undesirable for him to give evidence; or
(3) at the conclusion of the evidence for the prosecution, his legal representative informs the judge that the accused will give evidence, or, where the accused is unrepresented, the judge ascertains from him that he will give evidence,

the judge must, at the conclusion of the evidence for the prosecution, satisfy himself, in the presence of the jury, that the accused is aware that:

(a) the stage has been reached at which evidence can be given for the defence;
(b) he can, if he wishes, give evidence; and
(c) if he chooses not to give evidence, or having been sworn, without good cause refuses to answer any question, it will be permissible for the court or jury to draw such inferences as appear proper from his failure to give evidence or his refusal, without good cause, to answer any question.

Where this provision applies, the jury, in determining whether the accused is guilty of the offence charged, may draw such inferences as appear proper from the failure of the accused to give evidence or his refusal, without good cause, to answer any question.

(CJPOA 1994 s.35)

Accused legally represented

3-002 Where the accused's legal representative informs the judge in the presence of the jury, if there is one, that the accused:

(1) *will give evidence*, the case proceeds in the normal way; or
(2) *does not intend to give evidence* (or the judge is not informed that he does), the judge must address the advocate as follows:

> "Have you advised your client that the stage has now been reached at which he may give evidence and, if he chooses not to do so or, having been sworn, without good cause refuses to answer any question, the jury may draw such inferences as appear proper from his failure to do so?"

If the representative replies that the accused has been so advised, the case will proceed in the normal way; if the judge is informed that the accused has not been so advised, then he will direct the representative to advise his client of the consequences and should adjourn briefly for this purpose before proceeding (*CPD* VI 26P.3).

When an accused chooses not to go into the witness box and give evidence in his own defence, his legal advisers should:

(a) record the fact that he has made that decision and the reasons for it; and
(b) make sure that the accused signs such a record (*R. v Bevan* (1994) 98 Cr. App. R. 354).

Such a note will:
(i) be to the benefit of the client, in that it will serve to ensure that he has been given the appropriate advice; and also
(ii) serve to protect the advocate and his instructing solicitors from criticism based on assertions made after the event by a dissatisfied client (*R. v Anderson* [2010] EWCA Crim 2553; [2011] Costs L.R. Online 109).

In the absence of a written record the CACD will consider the respective accounts of the appellant and his former legal advisers and evaluate them in the light of the relevant circumstances (*R. v Chatroodi* [2001] EWCA Crim 585).

While successful appeals based on the incompetence of an advocate are extremely rare, where it is shown that a decision not to call evidence was made without proper discussion and against all the promptings of reason and good sense, it is open to the CACD to set aside the jury's verdict. The court will assess the effect of the advocate's incompetence on the trial and verdict (*R. v Clinton* (1993) 97 Cr. App. R. 320; cf. *R. v Chatroodi* [2001] EWCA Crim 585, where, although the advocate's failure to maintain such a written record was criticised, it could not be concluded that his advice had been incompetent).

Accused not legally represented

If the accused is not represented, the judge must, at the conclusion of the evidence for the prosecution, in the absence of the jury, indicate what he will say to him in the presence of the jury and ask if he understands and whether he would like a brief adjournment to consider his position. When appropriate, and in the presence of the jury, the judge should say to the accused (*CPD* VI 26P.5): **3-003**

"You have heard the evidence against you. Now is the time for you to make your defence. You may give evidence on oath, and be cross-examined like any other witness. If you do not give evidence or, having been sworn, without good cause refuse to answer any question, the jury may draw such inferences as appear proper. That means they may hold it against you. You may also call any witness or witnesses whom you have arranged to attend court or lead any agreed evidence. Afterwards you may also, if you wish, address the jury. But you cannot at that stage give evidence. Do you now intend to give evidence?"

Direction to the jury

In almost every case the judge will consider it necessary to discuss with the advocates, in the absence of the jury, the form of his direction. **3-004**

In *R. v Cowan* (1996) 1 Cr. App. R. 1 (applied in *R. v Hobson* [2013] EWCA Crim 819; [2013] 2 Cr. App. R. 27), the CACD highlighted certain essentials in directing the jury.

The judge:

(1) must tell the jury that the burden of proof remains upon the prosecution throughout, and define the required standard;
(2) must make clear to the jury that the accused is entitled to remain silent; it is his right and his choice;
(3) must tell the jury that an inference from failure to give evidence cannot, on

its own, prove guilt (it is expressly stated in CJPOA 1994 s.38(3)); therefore, they must be satisfied that the prosecutor has established a case to answer before drawing any inferences from silence;

(4) may tell them that if, despite any evidence relied upon to explain his silence, or in the absence of any such evidence, they conclude that silence can only sensibly be attributed to the accused's having no answer, or none that would stand up to cross-examination, they may draw an adverse inference.

A jury should not draw adverse inferences from the silence of an accused against whom the prosecution have not established a case to answer, and the judge's failure to direct the jury on that precondition may give rise to a risk of injustice (see e.g. *R. v JL Alford Transport Ltd* [1997] 2 Cr. App. R. 326; *R. v Birchall* [1999] Crim. L.R. 311, where the trial judge omitted such a direction).

For an example direction, see the Crown Court Compendium (June 2022) Pt 1 17–8.

Careful thought will need to be given to whether it is appropriate to give both a Lucas direction and a s.34 direction, or a single direction incorporating both elements, where the prosecution rely both on lies told in interview and a failure to mention facts in interview (see e.g. *R. v Wainwright* [2021] EWCA Crim 122; [2021] 2 WLUK 61 and more generally Crown Court Compendium (June 2022) Pt 1 16–3).

Jury's discretion

3-005 It is not possible to anticipate all the circumstances in which a judge might think it right to direct or advise a jury against drawing an adverse inference. In *R. v Cowan* (1996) 1 Cr. App. R. 1 the CACD said that

> "the [jury] has then a complete discretion as to whether inferences should be drawn or not. In these circumstances it is a matter for the [jury] in any criminal case (1) to decide whether to draw inferences or not; and (2) if it decides to draw inferences what their nature, extent and degree of adversity, if any, may be. It would be improper and indeed quite unwise for any court to set out the bounds of either steps (1) or (2). Their application will depend on factors peculiar to the individual case."

The CACD accepted that:

(1) apart from the mandatory exceptions in CJPOA 1994 s.35(1), it will be open to a jury to decline to draw an adverse inference from silence at his trial and for a judge to direct or advise them against drawing such inference if the circumstances of the case justify such a course;

(2) there would, however, need either to be some evidential basis for doing so or some exceptional factors in the case, making that a fair course to take; and

(3) the inferences permitted by the section are only such "as appear proper"; the use of that phrase was no doubt intended to leave a broad discretion to the trial judge to decide in all the circumstances whether any proper inference is capable of being drawn by the jury. If not, he should tell them so; otherwise it is for the jury to decide whether, in fact, an inference should properly be drawn.

The possession of a previous criminal record upon which an accused could be cross-examined (if he has attacked prosecution witnesses) is no good reason for directing a jury that they should not hold his silence against him (see *R. v Becouarn* [2005] UKHL 55; [2006] 1 Cr. App. R. 2).

Counsel is not entitled to give evidence dressed up as a submission; he should not give to the jury reasons for his client's silence at trial in the absence of evidence to support such reasons (*R. v Cowan* [1996] 1 Cr. App. R. 1; *R. v Phillips* [2015] EWCA Crim 836).

The judge should not direct the jury to draw adverse inferences against an absconding accused unless he is satisfied, for the purposes of s.35(2), that the accused knew of the potential consequences of his not giving evidence (*R. v Gough* [2002] EWCA Crim 2545; [2002] 2 Cr. App. R. 8). As to the effect of a direction on co-accused who are present at the trial, see *R. v Hamidi* [2010] EWCA Crim 66; [2010] Crim. L.R. 578.

"Physical or mental condition"

If the judge considers that the accused's physical or mental state makes it undesirable for the accused to give evidence s.35(3) does not apply. **3-006**

The question posed by the section is a wide question for the judgment of the judge. Most difficulties that an accused (or indeed any other witness) may have in giving evidence are factors which are properly to be assessed by the jury. The purpose of s.35(1)(b) is clearly to enable the judge to remove the possibility of adverse inference from the jury if it is undesirable for the accused to give evidence.

Note that:

(1) it is plainly not sufficient that the accused suffers from *some* physical or mental condition;
(2) it must be a mental condition which is such as to make it undesirable for him to give evidence; and
(3) the fact that he may have some difficulty in giving evidence is insufficient to justify the conclusion that it is undesirable that he should do so.

See *R. (on the application of DPP) v Kavanagh* [2005] EWHC 820 (Admin); [2006] Crim. L.R. 370, adopted in *R. v Tabbakh* [2009] EWCA Crim 464; [2010] Crim. L.R. 79 and in *R. v JD* [2013] EWCA Crim 465; [2013] 3 All E.R. 242 as representing the correct approach, and emphasising that the authorities do not support the submission that s.35(1)(b) should be confined to cases where an accused will suffer an adverse impact upon his health or condition (as suggested in *R. v Ensor* [2009] EWCA Crim 2519; [2010] 1 Cr. App. R. 18). See also *R. v Mulindwa* [2017] EWCA Crim 416; [2017] 2 Cr. App. R. 10 (appropriate for psychiatrist to be called before defendant, who suffered from paranoid schizophrenia, to explain the effect of the defendant's condition on his likely presentation as a witness) and *R. v Biddle* [2019] EWCA Crim 86; [2019] 2 Cr. App. R. 20 (s.35 direction appropriate where there was no causative link between the absence of an intermediary and the defendant's decision not to give evidence).

Where it is contended that the accused's physical or mental condition makes it undesirable for him to give evidence, that issue must be properly raised (see *R. v Friend* [1997] 2 Cr. App. R. 231; *R. v A* [1997] Crim. L.R. 883) and must be determined by the judge. If the judge decides in favour of the accused the jury must be directed not to draw any adverse inference.

Absconding accused

As to the position where the accused absconds and the trial proceeds in his **3-007**
absence, see *R. v Gough* [2002] EWCA Crim 2545; [2002] 2 Cr. App. R. 8. See also

R. v Hamidi [2010] EWCA Crim 66; [2010] Crim. L.R. 578 and ABSENT/UNREPRESENTED ACCUSED.

4. AGE OF OFFENDER

In the TABLE at 4-002 an "x" indicates where there is a statutory restriction on the imposition of a sentence or order on an offender of a certain age; an "*" indicates that there is no such restriction. Neither mark should be read as signifying that such a sentence or order is appropriate in the circumstances of the case. An entry in *italics* indicates that a sentence or order of that type may be fixed by law, may be mandatory, or its length may be prescribed. **4-001**

A "#" sign indicates that an order is available even where there is no conviction.

The bracketed numbers refer to the short notes appended at 4-003. These are followed at 4-004 and 4-005 by several statements of principle applicable in determining the age of an offender for the purposes of the proceedings.

Note that two orders refer to corporations, and are therefore outside the scope of this section:

1. Publicity orders, available in the case of corporate manslaughter only: Corporate Manslaughter and Corporate Homicide Act 2007 s.10; as to the use of such orders use the SGC Definitive Guidelines on Corporate Manslaughter & Health and Safety Offences Causing Death 2010 paras 30–32.
2. Remedial orders, available both for corporate manslaughter under the 2007 Act s.9, and under the Health and Safety at Work Act 1974 s.42; as to the use of such orders see the SGC Definitive Guidelines paras 33–36.

4-002

Sentence or order	Under 14	14	15	16	17	18	19	20	21 & over
ASBO	*(1)	*(1)	*(1)	*(1)	*(1)	*(1)	*(1)	*(1)	*(1)
Attendance Centre	x	x	x	*(2)	*(2)	*(2)	*(2)	*(2)	*(2)
Bind over	*(3) #	*(3)#	*(3)#	*(3)#	*(3)#	* #	* #	* #	* #
Committal for contempt	x	x	x	x	*(4)	*	*	*	*
Community order	x(5)	x(5)	x(5)	x(5)	x(5)	*	*	*	*
Company officers Disqualification	*	*	*	*	*	*	*	*	*
Compensation	**(6)*	**(6)*	**(6)*	**(6)*	**(6)*	*	*	*	*
Confiscation	*	*	*	*	*	*	*	*	*
Criminal Behaviour orders	*(7)	*(7)	*(7)	*(7)	*(7)	*(7)	*(7)	*(7)	*(7)
Custody for life	x	x	x	x	x	**(8)*	**(8)*	**(8)*	x
Deportation	x	x	x	x	*(9)	*(9)	*(9)	*(9)	*(9)

Sentence or order	Under 14	14	15	16	17	18	19	20	21 & over
Deprivation	*	*	*	*	*	*	*	*	*
Detention HMP	*\(10)*	*\(10)*	*\(10)*	*\(10)*	*\(10)*	x	x	x	x
Detention for life	*\(11)*	*\(11)*	*\(11)*	*\(11)*	*\(11)*	x	x	x	x
Detention s.250	*(12)	*(12)	*(12)	*(12)	*(12)	x	x	x	x
Detention YOI	x	x	x	x	x	*	*	*	x
Detention & training	*\(13)*	*\(13)*	*\(13)*	*\(13)*	*\(13)*	x	x	x	x
Discharge	*(14)	*(14)	*(14)	*(14)	*(14)	*(14)	*(14)	*(14)	*(14)
Driving disqualification	*\(15)*	*\(15)*	*\(15)*	*\(15)*	*\(15)*	*\(15)*	*\(15)*	*\(15)*	*\(15)*
Extended sentence	x	x	x	x	x	*(16)	*(16)	*(16)	*(16)
Financial circumstance order	*(17)	*(17)	*(17)	*(17)	*(17)	*(17)	*(17)	*(17)	*(17)
Fine, costs etc.	*(18)	*(18)	*(18)	*(18)	*(18)	*	*	*	*
Football banning order	*	*	*	*	*	*	*	*	*
Forfeiture	*	*	*	*	*	*	*	*	*
Guardianship MHA	*	*	*	*	*	*	*	*	*
Hospital order, restriction order	*	*	*	*	*	*	*	*	*
Hospital & limitation direction	*	*	*	*	*	*	*	*	*
Imprisonment	x	x	x	x	x	x(19)	x(19)	x(19)	*
ISO	*	*	*	*	*	x	x	x	x
Licensed premises exclusion	*	*	*	*	*	*	*	*	*
Parenting order	*(20)	*(20)	*(20)	*	*	x	x	x	x
Reparation	*	*	*	*	*	x	x	x	x
Restitution	*	*	*	*	*	*	*	*	*

Sentence or order	Under 14	15	16	17	18	19	20	21 & over
Restraining order	*#	*#	*#	*#	*#	*#	*#	*#	*#
Restraint order	*	*	*	*	*	*	*	*
Serious crime prevention order	x	x	x	x	x	*(21)	*(21)	*(21)	*(21)
Sexual harm prevention order	*(22)	*(22)	*(22)	*(22)	*(22)	*(22)	*(22)	*(22)	*(22)
Sexual offences prevention order	*(23)	*(23)	*(23)	*(23)	*(23)	*(23)	*(23)	*(23)	*(23)
Surcharge	*(24)	*(24)	*(24)	*(24)	*(24)	*(24)	*(24)	*(24)	*(24)
Youth rehabilitation	*(25)	*(25)	*(25)	*(25)	*(25)	*(25)	x	x	x

Notes

(1) As from 20 October 2014 ASBOs were replaced by CBOs. See CRIMINAL BEHAVIOUR ORDERS. 4-003

(2) (PCC(S)A 2000 s.60; part repealed CJIA 2008 s.6 but not repealed or restated in the SA 2020.) Restricted to offenders punishable with imprisonment committed before 30 November 2009, or those 17–21 found in contempt of court. As to attendance centre as a requirement of a community order, see COMMUNITY SENTENCES and YOUTH REHABILITATION ORDERS.

(3) Although available in respect of persons under 18, that person must consent, and if he does not, the judge is, in practice, powerless to compel him. An attendance centre order may be appropriate in the case of a juvenile aged 17, but it is more common in the case of offenders under 18 to bind over the subject's parent or guardian (see BIND OVER).

(4) Attendance centre order may be appropriate.

(5) The appropriate order in this age bracket is a youth rehabilitation order (see YOUTH REHABILITATION ORDERS).

(6) A compensation order is available to a court by or before which an offender is convicted of any offence (SA 2020 ss.130–146). Since the means of the offender are an important factor in making compensation or other financial orders, it may be more appropriate in the case of offenders under 18 to order payment by a parent or guardian (see COMPENSATION ORDERS).

(7) (SA 2020 s.230.) Supercedes ASBO. Cannot stand alone only as an ancillary to sentence or conditional discharge, and only on application by

prosecutor. Where offender under 18, prosecutor obliged to consult youth offending team (see general CRIMINAL BEHAVIOUR ORDERS).

(8) (SA 2020 ss.272–274.) Appropriate where persons 18–20 are convicted of offences other than murder, and such a sentence is appropriate (SA 2020 ss.273 and 274); mandatory in the case of dangerous offenders under SA 2020 s.274 and where an adult would be sentenced to life imprisonment for an offence committed on or after 3 December 2012 (see DANGEROUS OFFENDERS; PROTECTIVE SENTENCES).

(9) (UK Borders Act 2007.) Automatic deportation of "foreign criminals" under the Act requires the prosecutor to inform the judge at the sentencing stage that an offender qualifies as such; no recommendation is required unless the conditions in s.33 of the Act are not fulfilled. See also SA 2020 s.386.

(10) (SA 2020 s.259.) Fixed by law in relation to an offender convicted of murder who appears to have been under 18 at the time the offence was committed (notwithstanding anything in SA 2020 or any other Act).

(11) (SA 2020 s.258.) Mandatory where:
- (a) the conviction is for a serious offence and judge is of opinion that there is a significant risk to members of the public of serious harm occasioned by commission of further specified offences; or
- (b) the offender is liable to detention for life under SA 2020 s.250 and the judge considers the seriousness of the offence(s) such as to justify life (see DANGEROUS OFFENDERS; PROTECTIVE SENTENCES).

(12) (SA 2020 ss.249 and 250.) Applies to an offender:
- (a) under 18 convicted of certain specified offences only, namely an offence:
  - (i) punishable in the case of an offender aged 21 or over with 14 years' imprisonment, not being an offence for which the sentence is fixed by law; or
  - (ii) under SOA 2003 s.3 (sexual assault); or
  - (iii) under SOA 2003 s.13 (child sex offences committed by children or young persons); or
  - (iv) under SOA 2003 s.25 (sexual activity with a child family member); or
  - (v) under SOA 2003 s.26 (inciting a child family member to engage in activity);
- (b) aged at least 14 but under 18 convicted of certain specified offences, namely:
  - (i) causing death by dangerous driving under RTA 1988 s.1; or
  - (ii) causing death by careless driving while under the influence of drink or drugs.

The sentence may not exceed the maximum term of imprisonment to which a person aged 21 or over would be liable.

(13) (SA 2020 ss.233–248.) Available in respect of any offender aged over 12 and under 18 convicted of an offence punishable with imprisonment in the case of an offender aged 21 or over, but:
- (a) in respect of offenders aged under 15 at the time of conviction, he must be, in the judge's opinion, a persistent offender; and
- (b) in the case of an offender under the age of 18 but at least 12 at that time, the offence must have been committed after a date specified by

the Secretary of State, and the judge must be of the opinion that only a custodial sentence would be adequate to protect the public from further offending by him. The term of the sentence must be for 4, 6, 8, 10, 12, 18 or 24 months and must not exceed the maximum term of imprisonment the judge could impose for the offence. An order of at least four months is prescribed in the case of an offender aged 16 but under 18 under PCA 1953 s.1A (threatening article with blade or point or offensive weapon in public place or on school premises) or under CJA 1988 s.139AA (threatening with blade or point or offensive weapon) in the circumstances set out in IMPRISONMENT.

(14) Absolute or conditional (SA 2020 ss.79 and 80). Available in the circumstances outlined in DISCHARGE; ABSOLUTE AND CONDITIONAL. As to combining other orders, see 29-004. Order not to exceed three years.

(15) Available in several different circumstances, see DRIVING DISQUALIFICATIONS; an order is obligatory in the case of certain serious RT offences.

(16) The sentence applies under SA 2020 ss.279–282 (those aged 21 and over), ss.266–268 (those over 18 and under 21) and ss.254–257 (those aged under 18) for certain offences to imprisonment (or detention) where the offender is convicted of certain violent or sexual offences for an offence committed on or after 3 December 2012, and the judge considers that there is a significant risk to members of the public of serious harm occasioned by the offender's commission of further specified offences and the conditions in the section are met (see DANGEROUS OFFENDERS; PROTECTIVE SENTENCES).

(17) (SA 2020 s.35.) Limit on length of order: where offender sentenced to life imprisonment of 20 years, otherwise 15.

(18) Since the means of the offender are an important factor in making compensation or other financial orders, it will be more appropriate in the case of offenders under 18 to order payment by a parent or guardian (see also FINES and SURCHARGES, COSTS AND ASSESSMENT, and COMPENSATION ORDERS).

(19) The custodial sentence appropriate in the case of an offender aged 21 or over. As to the threshold for such sentence, and the length of the term, see IMPRISONMENT. A life sentence may be appropriate. As to:
   (a) life sentences, see LIFE SENTENCES;
   (b) as to prescribed terms, see IMPRISONMENT.

(20) SA 2020 ss.365–375, CDA 1998 s.8(1)–(2).

(21) SCA 2007 s.16 limit on length of order—not more than five years.

(22) SA 2020 s.343.

(23) Now repealed and replaced by SHPOs and powers to vary existing orders as with SHPOs.

(24) (SA 2020 ss.42–43.) Where a fine is imposed, a surcharge must also be ordered. For offences committed on or after 1 October 2012, see TABLE under FINES and SURCHARGES.

(25) (SA 2020 ss.173–186 and Sch.6.) A "community sentence"; the equivalent of a community order in the case of an offender aged 18 or over.

Determination of age

4-004 Where an available sentence depends upon the age of the offender:

(1) the starting point is the sentence which the offender would have been likely to receive if he had been sentenced on the date of his conviction of the offence (*R. v Ghafoor* [2002] EWCA Crim 1857; [2003] 1 Cr. App. R. (S.) 84; *R. v Britton* [2007] 1 Cr. App. R. (S.) 121; *R. v M-F* [2012] EWCA Crim 523);
(2) for the purposes of liability to a custodial sentence, or to a community sentence, the relevant age is the age of the offender on the date of his conviction, whether he pleaded guilty or not (*R. v Danga* (1992) 13 Cr. App. R. (S.) 408; *R. v Robson* [2006] EWCA Crim 1414; [2007] 1 Cr. App. R. (S.) 54); *R. v Robinson* (1994) 98 Cr. App. R. 370);
(3) where the offender has crossed the age threshold into adulthood between the date of the commission of the offence and the date of his conviction, the judge is bound to have regard to CJA 2003 s.141(1) (purposes of sentencing) including deterrence (*R. v Bowker* [2007] EWCA Crim 1608; [2008] 1 Cr. App. R. (S.) 72).

Where the offender's age is in doubt or in dispute, the judge should adjourn and obtain proper evidence of age before sentence.

For the purposes of the following orders, i.e.:

(a) imprisonment;
(b) detention in a young offender institution;
(c) detention under SA 2020 s.250; and
(d) a detention and training order,

the age of the offender is deemed to be, after considering any available evidence on the day of conviction, what it appears to the judge to be: SA 2020 s.405.

As to exceptions to these general rules, see 4-006.

In *R. v Robson* [2006] EWCA Crim 1414; [2007] 1 Cr. App. R. (S.) 54, distinguishing *R. v Ghafoor* [2002] EWCA Crim 1857; [2003] 1 Cr. App. R. (S.) 84, the CACD held that as a matter of statutory construction, the age of the offender for the purpose of determining which of the statutory regimes under Ch.5 of Pt 12 of CJA 2003 applied was the offender's age at the date of conviction.

The sentencing regime under which the appellant is to be sentenced must be determined by what was contemplated by the provisions which created the new sentencing regime.

When sentencing those under 18 at the date of conviction a court must, save for when imposing a mandatory life sentence, a statutory minimum custodial sentence, detention for life under the dangerous offender provisions or when making certain orders under the MHA 1983, have regard to the principal aim of the youth justice system (to prevent offending by children and young people), and the welfare of the child or young person. (SC Definitive Guideline on Sentencing Children and Young People).

Committal for sentence; breaches

4-005 There are, as has been said, a number of exceptions to the general rules stated in 4-004, thus:

(1) an offender committed to the Crown Court for sentence under SA 2020

ss.14–24 must be sentenced on the basis of his age *on the day he appears before the Crown Court*;

(2) an offender subject to a community order who appears before the Crown Court for sentence, while the community order is in force, and where the judge revokes the community order and passes a further sentence for the offence, must be sentenced on the basis of his age *when he appears before the Crown Court*;

(3) an offender who is found to be in breach of a community order and in whose case the order is revoked, must be sentenced on the basis of his age *when he appears before the court which revokes the order*;

(4) an offender who is subject to a community order under SA 2020 and in *whose case the community order is revoked* following a breach or subsequent conviction must be sentenced on the basis of his age *when the original order was made*; and

(5) an offender subject to a conditional discharge convicted of a further offence during the operational period of the order, where the conditional discharge is revoked, any sentence imposed for the original offence must be based on the offender's age *when he is so sentenced* (*R. v Keelan* (1975) 61 Cr. App. R. 212).

Other exceptions

In addition to the cases set out in 4-005, note that: **4-006**

(1) an offender convicted *at any age* of a murder committed when he was under 18 must be sentenced to be detained during His Majesty's Pleasure; and

(2) the power to make a road traffic disqualification order depends upon the offender's age *when he committed the offence*.

5. ALLOCATION AND LISTING OF CASES

Quick Guide

5-001 CPD [2022] EWCA Crim 367 is the most recently published amendment to the consolidated practice directions. It was handed down by the Lord Chief Justice on 23 March 2022 and came into effect on 24 March 2022. The consolidated practice direction itself was handed down on 29 September 2015. Part XIII of the consolidated practice direction deals with listing and allocation. Overall it replaced ss.III.21, IV.31, IV.32, IV.33, IV.38 and IV.41.9 and Annex F of the Consolidated Criminal Practice Direction of 8 July 2002 ([2002] 1 W.L.R. 2870; [2002] 2 Cr. App. R. 35), as amended, which are revoked.

Additionally, the *CPD* consolidated "Deployment and Allocation in Criminal Cases in Class 1, 2 and 3: Guidance for all Resident Judges" issued by the Senior Presiding Judge on 26 May 2005, incorporate parts of the guidance issued by the Senior Presiding Judge and by HMCTS on Custody Time Limits in May 2012 and replaced the guidance on Transfer of Cases to other Crown Courts for sentence issued by the Senior Presiding Judge in March 2009.

Reference is made to recommendations from the Magistrates' Courts Disclosure Review May 2014. Annex 1 incorporates the relevant operational parts of the "Protocol to support judicial deployment in the Magistrates' Courts" issued in November 2012. Annex 2 subsumes the "Sexual Offences Protocol in the Youth Court" issued by the Senior Presiding Judge in March 2010.

A. Judicial Responsibility for listing and key principles

Listing as a judicial responsibility and function

5-002 Listing is a judicial responsibility and function. The purpose is to ensure that:

(1) all cases are brought to a hearing or trial in accordance with the interests of justice;
(2) the resources available for criminal justice are deployed as effectively as possible; and
(3) cases are heard by an appropriate judge [or bench] with the minimum of delay.

(*CPD* XIII Listing A: A.1)

The agreement reached between the Lord Chief Justice and the Secretary of State for Constitutional Affairs and Lord Chancellor set out in a statement to the House of Lords on 26 January 2004 ("the Concordat"), states that judges, working with

HMCTS, are responsible for deciding on the assignment of cases to particular courts and the listing of those cases before particular judges.

Therefore:

(a) the *Presiding Judges* of each circuit have the overall responsibility for listing at all courts, Crown [and magistrates'], on their circuit;

(b) subject to the supervision of the Presiding Judges, the *Resident Judge* at each Crown Court has the general responsibility within his or her court centre for the allocation of criminal judicial work, to ensure the just and efficient despatch of the business of the court or group of courts. This includes overseeing the deployment of allocated judges at the court or group, including the distribution of work between all the judges allocated to that court. A Resident Judge must appoint a deputy or deputies to exercise his or her functions when he or she is absent from his or her court centre (see also 5-004);

(c) the *listing officer in the Crown Court* is responsible for carrying out the day-to-day operation of listing practice under the direction of the Resident Judge. The listing officer at each Crown Court centre has one of the most important functions at that Crown Court and makes a vital contribution to the efficient running of that Crown Court and to the efficient operation of the administration of criminal justice; and

(d) in the *magistrates' courts*, the Judicial Business Group, subject to the supervision of the Presiding Judges of the circuit, is responsible for determining the listing practice in that area. The day-to-day operation of that listing practice is the responsibility of the justices' clerk with the assistance of the listing officer.

(*CPD* XIII Listing A.2)

Key principles of listing

When setting the listing practice, the Resident Judge [or the Judicial Business Group] should take into account the following principles: 5-003

(1) Ensure the *timely* trial of cases and resolution of other issues (such as confiscation) so that justice is not delayed; the following factors are relevant:
  - (a) In general, each case should be tried within as short a time of its arrival in the court as is consistent with the interests of justice, the needs of victims and witnesses, and with the proper and timely preparation by the prosecution and defence of their cases in accordance with the directions and timetable set.
  - (b) Priority should be accorded to the trial of young accused, and cases where there are vulnerable or young witnesses. In *R. v B* [2010] EWCA Crim 4, the Lord Chief Justice highlighted "the importance to the trial and investigative process of keeping any delay in a case involving a child complainant to an irreducible minimum".
  - (c) Custody time limits ("CTLs") should be observed, see 5-019.
  - (d) Every effort must be made to avoid delay in cases in which the accused is on bail.

(2) Provide, when possible, for certainty and/or as much advance notice as possible, of the trial date; and take all reasonable steps to ensure that the trial date remains fixed:

(a) ensure that a judge [or bench] with any necessary authorisation and of appropriate experience is available to try each case; and
(b) wherever desirable and practicable, ensure there is judicial continuity, including in relation to post-trial hearings.

(3) Strike an appropriate balance in the use of resources, by taking account of:
(a) the efficient deployment of the judiciary;
(b) the proper use of the courtrooms available at the court;
(c) the provision in long and/or complex cases for adequate reading time for the judiciary;
(d) the facilities in the available courtrooms, including the security needs (such as a secure dock), size and equipment, such as video and live link facilities;
(e) the proper use of those who attend the Crown Court as jurors; and
(f) the need to return those sentenced to custody as soon as possible after the sentence is passed, and to facilitate the efficient operation of the prison escort contract.

(4) Provide where practicable:
(a) the accused and the prosecution with the advocate of their choice where this does not result in any delay to the trial of the case; and
(b) for the efficient deployment of advocates, lawyers and associate prosecutors of the CPS, and other prosecuting authorities, and of the resources available to the independent legal profession, for example by trying to group certain cases together.

(5) Meet the need for special security measures for category A and other high-risk accused.

(6) Ensure that proper time (including judicial reading time) is afforded to hearings in which the court is exercising powers that impact on the rights of individuals, such as applications for investigative orders or warrants (see 5-025).

(7) Consider the significance of *ancillary proceedings*, such as confiscation hearings (see 5-026 and 5-027), and the need to deal with such hearings promptly and, where possible, for such hearings to be conducted by the trial judge.

(8) Provide for government initiatives or projects approved by the Lord Chief Justice.

Although the listing practice at each Crown Court centre [and magistrates' court] will take these principles into account, the listing practice adopted will vary from court to court depending particularly on the number of courtrooms and the facilities available, the location and the workload, its volume and type (*CPD* XIII Listing A: A.3 and A.4).

Discharge of judicial responsibilities

5-004 The *Resident Judge* of each court *is responsible for*:

(1) ensuring that good practice is implemented throughout the court, such that all hearings commence on time;
(2) ensuring that the causes of trials that do not proceed on the date originally fixed are examined to see if there is any systemic issue;
(3) monitoring the general performance of the court and the listing practices;

(4) monitoring the timeliness of cases and reporting any cases of serious concern to the Presiding Judge; and
(5) maintaining and reviewing annually a list of Recorders, qualifying judge advocates and Deputy Circuit Judges authorised to hear appeals from the magistrates' courts unless such a list is maintained by the Presiding Judge.

(*CPD* XIII Listing: A.5)

B. Classification of offences

The classification structure outlined here (*CPD* Listing B: Classification B.1) is solely for the purposes of trial in the Crown Court. The structure has been devised to accommodate practical administrative functions and is not intended to reflect a hierarchy of the offences therein. **5-005**

Offences are classified as follows:

Class 1: A:

i. Murder;
ii. Attempted Murder;
iii. Manslaughter;
iv. Infanticide;
v. Child Destruction (Infant Life (Preservation) Act 1929 s.1(1));
vi. Abortion (OAPA 1861 s.58);
vii. Assisting a suicide;
viii. Cases including DVA 2004 s.5, as amended (if a fatality has resulted);
ix. Soliciting, inciting, encouraging or assisting, attempting or conspiring to commit any of the above offences or assisting an offender having committed such an offence.

Class 1: B:

i. Genocide;
ii. Torture, hostage-taking and offences under the War Crimes Act 1991;
iii. Offences under ss.51 and 52 International Criminal Courts Act 2001;
iv. An offence under s.1 of the Geneva Conventions Act 1957;
v. Terrorism offences (where offence charged is indictable only and took place during an act of terrorism or for the purposes of terrorism as defined in TerrA 2000 s.1);
vi. Piracy, under the Merchant Shipping and Maritime Security Act 1997;
vii. Treason;
viii. An offence under the Official Secrets Acts;
ix. Incitement to disaffection;
x. Soliciting, inciting, encouraging or assisting, attempting or conspiring to commit any of the above offences or assisting an offender having committed such an offence.

Class 1: C:

i. Prison mutiny, under the Prison Security Act 1992;
ii. Riot in the course of serious civil disturbance;
iii. Serious gang related crime resulting in the possession or discharge of firearms, particularly including a campaign of firebombing or extortion, especially when accompanied by allegations of drug trafficking on a commercial scale;

iv. Complex sexual offence cases in which there are many complainants (often under age, in care or otherwise particularly vulnerable) and/or many defendants who are alleged to have systematically groomed and abused them, often over a long period of time;
v. Cases involving people trafficking for sexual, labour or other exploitation and cases of human servitude;
vi. Soliciting, inciting, encouraging or assisting, attempting or conspiring to commit any of the above offences or assisting an offender having committed such an offence.

Class 1: D:

i. Causing death by dangerous driving;
ii. Causing death by careless driving;
iii. Causing death by unlicensed, disqualified or uninsured driving;
iv. Any Health and Safety case resulting in a fatality or permanent serious disability;
v. Any other case resulting in a fatality or permanent serious disability;
vi. Soliciting, inciting, encouraging or assisting, attempting or conspiring to commit any of the above offences or assisting an offender having committed such an offence.

Class 2: A:

i. Arson with intent to endanger life or reckless as to whether life was endangered;
ii. Cases in which explosives, firearms or imitation firearms are used or carried or possessed;
iii. Kidnapping or false imprisonment (without intention to commit a sexual offence but charged on the same indictment as a serious offence of violence such as under OAPA 1861 ss.18 or 20);
iv. Cases in which the accused is a police officer, member of the legal profession or a high profile or public figure;
v. Cases in which the complainant or an important witness is a high profile or public figure;
vi. Riot otherwise than in the course of serious civil disturbance;
vii. Child cruelty;
viii. Cases including DVA 2004 s.5, as amended (if no fatality has resulted);
ix. Soliciting, inciting, encouraging or assisting, attempting or conspiring to commit any of the above offences or assisting an offender having committed such an offence.

Class 2: B:

i. Any sexual offence, with the exception of those included in Class 1C;
ii. Kidnapping or false imprisonment (with intention to commit a sexual offence or charged on the same indictment as a sexual offence);
iii. Soliciting, inciting, encouraging or assisting, attempting or conspiring to commit any of the above offences or assisting an offender having committed such an offence.

Class 2: C:

i. Serious, complex fraud;
ii. Serious and/or complex money laundering;
iii. Serious and/or complex bribery;
iv. Corruption;

v. Complex cases in which the defendant is a corporation (including cases for sentence as well as for trial);
vi. Any case in which the defendant is a corporation with a turnover in excess of £1 billion (including cases for sentence as well as for trial);
vii. Soliciting, inciting, encouraging or assisting, attempting or conspiring to commit any of the above offences or assisting an offender having committed such an offence.

Class 3:

All other offences not listed in the classes above.

Deferred prosecution agreements

Cases coming before the court under s.45 of and Sch.17 to the CCA 2013 must be referred to the President of the Queen's Bench Division who will allocate the matter to a judge from a list of judges approved by the Lord Chief Justice. Only the allocated judge may thereafter hear any matter or make any decision in relation to that case (*CPD* XIII Listing B: Classification B.2). **5-006**

Criminal Cases Review Commission

Where the CCRC refers a case upon conviction from the magistrates' courts to the Crown Court, this shall be dealt with at a Crown Court centre designated by the Senior Presiding Judge (*CPD* XIII Listing B: Classification B.3). **5-007**

C. Referral of cases in the Crown Court to the Resident Judge and to the Presiding Judges

General

This Practice Direction: **5-008**

(1) specifies:
  (a) cases which must be referred to a Presiding Judge for release; and
  (b) cases which must be referred to the Resident Judge before being assigned to a judge, Recorder or qualifying judge advocate to hear.

(2) is applicable to all Crown Courts, but its application may be modified by the Senior Presiding Judge or the Presiding Judges with the approval of the Senior Presiding Judge, through the provision of further specific guidance to Resident Judges in relation to the allocation and management of the work at their court (*CPD* XIII Listing C: Referral of cases in the Crown Court to the Resident Judge and to the Presiding Judges. C.1);

(3) does not prescribe the way in which the Resident Judge gives is to ensure that there is appropriate judicial control over the listing of cases. However, the Resident Judge must arrange with the listing officers a satisfactory means of ensuring that all cases listed at their court are listed before judges, Recorders or qualifying judge advocates of suitable seniority and experience, subject to the requirements of this Practice Direction. The Resident Judge should ensure that listing officers are made aware of the contents and importance of this Practice Direction, and that listing officers develop satisfactory procedures for referral of cases to him or her (*CPD* XIII Listing C: Referral of cases in the Crown Court to the Resident Judge and to the Presiding Judges. C.2).

In order to assist the Resident Judge and the listing officer, all cases sent to the Crown Court should, where possible, include a brief case summary prepared by the prosecution. The prosecutor should ensure that any factors that make the case complex, or would lead it to be referred to the Resident Judge or a Presiding Judge are highlighted. The defence may also send submissions to the court, again highlighting any areas of complexity or any other factors that might assist in the case being allocated to an appropriate judge (*CPD* XIII Listing C: Referral of cases in the Crown Court to the Resident Judge and to the Presiding Judges. C.3).

Cases in the Crown Court to be referred to the Resident Judge

5-009 All cases in Class 1A, 1B, 1C, 1D, 2A and 2C must be referred to the Resident Judge, as must any case which appears to raise particularly complex, sensitive or serious issues (*CPD* XIII Listing C: Referral of cases in the Crown Court to the Resident Judge and to the Presiding Judges. C.4).

Resident Judges should give guidance to the judges and staff of their respective courts as to which Class 2B cases should be referred to them following consultation with the Senior Presiding Judge. This will include any cases that may be referred to the Presiding Judge (see 5-010). Class 2B cases to be referred to the Resident Judge are likely to be identified by the list officer, or by the judge at the first hearing in the Crown Court. Any appeal against conviction and/or sentence from a Youth Court involving a Class 2B case must be brought to the attention of the Resident Judge as soon as practicable. Where not provided with the appeal papers, the list officer must obtain a full summary of the prosecution case so as to allow an informed allocation decision to be made (*CPD* XIII Listing C: Referral of cases in the Crown Court to the Resident Judge and to the Presiding Judges. C.5).

Once a case has been referred to the Resident Judge, the Resident Judge should refer the case to the Presiding Judge, following the guidance at 5-010, or allocate the case to an appropriate category of judge, and if possible, to a named judge (*CPD* XIII Listing C: Referral of cases in the Crown Court to the Resident Judge and the Presiding Judges. C.6).

Cases in the Crown Court to be referred to a Presiding Judge

5-010 All cases in Class 1A, 1B and 1C *must* be referred by the Resident Judge to a Presiding Judge, as must a case in any class which is:

i. an usually grave or complex case or one in which a novel and important point of law is to be raised;
ii. a case where it is alleged that the defendant caused more than one fatality;
iii. a non-fatal case of baby shaking where serious injury resulted;
iv. a case where the defendant is a police officer, or a member of the legal profession or a high-profile figure;
v. a case which for any reason is likely to attract exceptional media attention;
vi. a case where a large organisation or corporation may, if convicted, be ordered to pay a very large fine; and
vii. any case likely to last more than three months.

(*CPD* XIII Listing C: Referral of cases in the Crown Court to the Resident Judge and to the Presiding Judges. C.7)

Resident Judges are encouraged to refer any other case if they think it is appropriate to do so.

Presiding Judges and Resident Judges should agree a system for the referral of cases to the Presiding Judge, ideally by electronic means. The system agreed should include provision for the Resident Judge to provide the Presiding Judge with a brief summary of the case, a clear recommendation by the Resident Judge about the judges available to try the case and any other comments. A written record of the decision and brief reasons for it must be made and retained.

Once a case has been referred to the Presiding Judge, the Presiding Judge may retain the case for trial by a High Court Judge, or release the case back to the Resident Judge, either for trial by a named judge, or for trial by an identified category of judges, to be allocated by the Resident Judge (*CPD* XIII Listing C: Referral of cases in the Crown Court to the Resident Judge and to the Presiding Judges. C.8, 9 and 10).

D. Authorisation of Judges

Requirement of authorisation ("ticketing")

Judges must be authorised by the Lord Chief Justice before they may hear certain types of case. **5-011**

Judges (other than High Court Judges) to hear:

(1) Class 1A cases must be authorised to hear such cases. Any judge previously granted a "Class 1" or "murder" authorisation is authorised to hear Class 1A cases. Judges previously granted an "attempted murder" (including soliciting, incitement or conspiracy thereof) authorisation can only deal with these cases within Class 1A; and

(2) sexual offences cases in Class 1C or any case within Class 2B must be authorised to hear such cases. Any judge previously granted a "Class 2" or "serious sex offences" authorisation is authorised to hear sexual offences cases in Class 1C or 2B.

It is a condition of the authorisation "for serious sex offences" that it does not take effect until the judge has attended the relevant Judicial College course; the Resident Judge should check in the case of newly authorised judges that they have attended the course. Judges who have been previously authorised to try such cases should make every effort to ensure their training is up-to-date and maintained by attending the Serious Sexual Offences Seminar at least once every three years. See Annex 2 of the *CPD* XIII for guidance in dealing with sexual offences in the youth court.

(*CPD* XIII Listing D: Authorisation of Judges. D.1, 2 and 3)

Cases in the magistrates' courts involving the imposition of very large fines

Where an accused appears before a magistrates' court for an either way offence, to which Annex III of the *CPD* XIII applies the case must be dealt with by a DJ (MC) who has been authorised to deal with such cases by the Chief Magistrate. **5-012**

The authorised DJ (MC) must first consider whether such cases should be allocated to the Crown Court or, where the accused pleads guilty, committed for sentence under PCC(S)A 2000 s.3 (see COMMITTALS FOR SENTENCE), and must do so when he considers the offence or combination of offences so serious that the Crown Court should deal with the accused as if he had been convicted on indictment.

If an authorised DJ (MC) decides not to commit such a case the reasons must be recorded in writing to be entered onto the court register.

(*CPD* XIII Listing D: Authorisation of Judges. D.4)

E. ALLOCATION OF BUSINESS WITHIN THE CROWN COURT

Trial of cases

5-013 Cases may be tried as follows:

Class	Rank of judge	Comments	CPD XIII
1A	Only (i) a High Court Judge, or (ii) a Circuit Judge, or Deputy High Court Judge, authorised to try such cases and provided that the Presiding Judge has released the case for trial by such a judge.		E.1
1B	Only (i) a High Court Judge, or (ii) a Circuit Judge, or a Deputy High Court Judge, provided that the Presiding Judge has released the case for trial by such a judge.		E.2
1C	Only (i) a High Court Judge, or (ii) a Circuit Judge, or a Deputy High Court Judge, or Deputy Circuit Judge, authorised to try such cases (if the case requires the judge to be authorised to hear sexual offences cases), provided that the Presiding Judge has released the case for trial by such a judge, or, if the case is a sexual offence, the Presiding Judge has assigned the case to that named judge.	See also *CPD* XIII Listing C.10	E.3
1D, 2A	Only (i) a High Court Judge, or (ii) a Circuit Judge, or Deputy High Court Judge, or Deputy Circuit Judge, or a Recorder or a qualifying judge advocate, provided		E.4

Class	Rank of judge	Comments	CPD XIII
	that either the Presiding Judge has released the case or the Resident Judge has allocated the case for trial by such a judge; with the exception that Class 2A(i) cases may not be tried by a Recorder or qualifying judge advocate.		
2B	Only (i) a High Court Judge, or (ii) a Circuit Judge, or Deputy High Court Judge, or Deputy Circuit Judge, or a Recorder or a qualifying judge advocate, authorised to try such cases and provided that either the Presiding Judge has released the case or the Resident Judge has allocated the case for trial by such a judge.		E.5
2C	By (i) a High Court Judge, or (ii) a Circuit Judge, or Deputy High Court Judge, or Deputy Circuit Judge, or a Recorder or a qualifying judge advocate, with suitable experience (for example, with company accounts or other financial information) and provided that either the Presiding Judge has released the case or the Resident Judge has allocated the case for trial by such a judge.		
1D, 2A, 2C	Will usually be tried by a Circuit Judge.		E.7

Class	Rank of judge	Comments	CPD XIII
3	Cases in Class 3 may be tried by a High Court Judge, or a Circuit Judge, a Deputy Circuit Judge, a Recorder or a qualifying judge advocate.	A case in Class 3 shall not be listed for trial by a High Court Judge except with the consent of a Presiding Judge.	E.8

Preliminary hearings; PCMH, PTPH

5-014 If a case has been allocated to a judge, Recorder or qualifying judge advocate, the preliminary hearing should be conducted by the allocated judge if practicable, and if not, if possible by a judge of at least equivalent standing. PCMHs and PTPHs should only be heard by Recorders or qualifying judge advocates with the approval of the Resident Judge.

For cases in Class 1A, 1B or 1C, or any case that has been referred to the Presiding Judge, the preliminary hearing, PCMH and PTPH must be conducted by a High Court Judge; by a Circuit Judge; or by a judge authorised by the Presiding Judges to conduct such hearings. In the event of a guilty plea before such an authorised judge, the case will be adjourned for sentencing and will immediately be referred to the Presiding Judge who may retain the case for sentence by a High Court Judge, or release the case back to the Resident Judge, either for sentence by a named judge, or for sentence by an identified category of judges, to be allocated by the Resident Judge.

(*CPD* XIII Listing E: Allocation of Business within the Crown Court. E.9 and 10)

Appellate jurisdiction

5-015 Appeals from decisions of magistrates' courts shall be heard by:

(1) a Resident Judge; or
(2) a Circuit Judge, nominated by the Resident Judge, who *regularly sits* at the Crown Court centre; or
(3) a Recorder or qualifying judge advocate or a Deputy Circuit Judge listed by the Presiding Judge to hear such appeals; or, if there is no such list nominated by the Resident Judge to hear such appeals; and, no less than two and no more than four justices of the peace, none of whom took part in the decision under appeal.

Where no Circuit Judge or Recorder or qualifying judge advocate satisfying the requirements above is available, by a Circuit Judge, Recorder, qualifying judge advocate or Deputy Circuit Judge selected by the Resident Judge to hear a specific case or cases listed on a specific day (*CPD* XIII Listing E: Allocation of Business within the Crown Court. E.11).

Breaches; removal of driving disqualification

Allocation or committal for sentence following breach (such as a matter in which a community order has been made, or a suspended sentence passed), should, where possible, be listed before the judge who originally dealt with the matter or, if not, before a judge of the same or higher level (*CPD* XIII Listing E: Allocation of Business within the Crown Court. E.12). **5-016**

Applications for removal of a driving disqualification should be made to the location of the Crown Court where the order of disqualification was made. Where possible, the matter should be listed before the judge who originally dealt with the matter or, if not, before a judge of the same or higher level (*CPD* XIII Listing E: Allocation of Business within the Crown Court. E.13).

As to the listing of hearings other than trials, see 5-023 and following.

F. Listing of trials, custody time limits and transfer of cases

Estimates of trial length

Under the regime set out in the CrimPR, the parties will be expected to provide an accurate estimate of the length of trial at the hearing where the case is to be managed based on a detailed estimate of the time to be taken with each witness to be called, and accurate information about the availability of witnesses. **5-017**

At the hearing the judge will ask the prosecution to clarify any CTL dates. The court clerk must ensure the CTL date is marked clearly on the court file or electronic file. When a case is subject to a CTL all efforts must be made at the first hearing to list the case within the CTL and the judge should seek to ensure this. Further guidance on listing CTL cases can be found at 5-019 (*CPD* XIII Listing of Trials, Custody Time Limits and Transfer of Cases: F.1 and 2).

Cases that should usually have fixed trial dates

The cases where fixtures should be given will be set out in the listing practice applicable at the court, but should usually include the following: **5-018**

(1) Cases in classes 1A, 1B, 1C, 2B and 2C.
(2) Cases involving vulnerable and intimidated witnesses (including domestic violence cases), whether or not special measures have been ordered by the court.
(3) Cases where the witnesses are under 18 or have to come from overseas.
(4) Cases estimated to last more than a certain time—the period chosen will depend on the size of the centre and the available judges.
(5) Cases where a previous fixed hearing has not been effective.
(6) Re-trials.
(7) Cases involving expert witnesses.

(*CPD* XII Listing of Trials, Custody Time Limits and Transfer of Cases: F.3)

As to changes to the dates of fixed cases, see 5-021.

Custody Time Limits

Every effort must be made to list cases for trial within the CTLs set by Parliament. **5-019**

The guiding principles are:

(1) At the first hearing in the Crown Court, prosecution will inform the court when the CTL lapses.
(2) All efforts must be made to list the case within the CTL. The CTL may only be extended in accordance with s.22 Prosecution of Offences Act 1985 and the Prosecution of Offences (Custody Time Limits) Regulations 1987.
(3) If suitable, given priority and listed on a date not less than two weeks before the CTL expires, the case may be placed in a warned list.
(4) The CTL must be kept under continual review by the parties, HMCTS and the Resident Judge.
(5) If the CTL is at risk of being exceeded, an additional hearing should take place and should be listed before the Resident Judge or trial judge or other judge nominated by the Resident Judge.
(6) An application to extend the CTL in any case listed outside the CTL must be considered by the court whether or not it was listed with the express consent of the defence.
(7) Any application to extend the CTL must be considered as a matter of urgency. The reasons for needing the extension must be ascertained and fully explained to the court.
(8) Where courtroom or judge availability is an issue, the court must itself list the case to consider the extension of any CTL. The Delivery Director of the circuit must provide a statement setting out in detail what has been done to try to accommodate the case within the CTL.
(9) Where courtroom or judge availability is not in issue, but all parties and the court agree that the case will not be ready for trial before the expiration of the CTL, a date may be fixed outside the CTL. This may be done without prejudice to any application to extend the CTL or with the express consent of the defence; this must be noted on the papers.

(*CPD* XIII Listing of Trials, Custody Time Limits and Transfer of Cases: F.4)

As legal argument may delay the swearing in of a jury, it is desirable to extend the CTL to a date later than the first day of the trial (*CPD* XIII Listing of Trials, Custody Time Limits and Transfer of Cases: F.5).

On 9 April 2020 the PQBD issued some guidance on CTLs in the light of the impact of Covid-19 on the work of the Crown Court. That was withdrawn on 2 September 2020. The approach in a time of pandemic is assisted by the decisions of the High Court in *R. (on the application of DPP) v Woolwich Crown Court* [2020] EWHC 3243 (Admin); [2021] 1 W.L.R. 938; *R. (on the application of McKenzie) v Leeds Crown Court* [2020] EWHC 1867 (Admin) and of first instance decisions, cases such as Whipple J in *R. v P* unreported 14 September 2020 Crown Court (Woolwich). The impact of action by the CBA on CTLs was considered in *R. (on the application of the DPP) v Crown Court at Bristol* [2022] EWHC 2415 (Admin).

Re-trials ordered by the CACD

5-020 The Crown Court must comply with the directions of the CACD and cannot vary those directions without reference to that court (*CPD* XIII Listing of Trials, Custody Time Limits and Transfer of Cases: F.6). In cases where a retrial is ordered by the CACD the CTL is 112 days starting from the date that the new indictment is preferred, i.e. from the date that the indictment is delivered to the Crown Court.

Court centres should check that their listing systems have calculated the dates correctly and that it has not used 182 days on cases that have previously been "sent" (*CPD* XIII Listing of Trials, Custody Time Limits and Transfer of Cases: F.7).

Changes to the date of fixed cases

Once a trial date or window is fixed, it should not be vacated or moved without good reason. Under the CrimPR, parties are expected to be ready by the trial date. **5-021**

The listing officer may, in circumstances determined by the Resident Judge, agree to the movement of the trial to a date to which the defence and prosecution both consent, provided the timely hearing of the case is not delayed. The prosecution will be expected to have consulted the witnesses before agreeing to any change. In all other circumstances, requests to adjourn or vacate fixtures or trial windows must be referred to the Resident Judge for his or her personal attention; the Resident Judge may delegate the decision to a named deputy (*CPD* XIII Listing of Trials, Custody Time Limits and Transfer of Cases: F.8, 9 and 10).

Transferring cases to another court

Transfer between: **5-022**

(1) courts on the same circuit must be agreed by the Resident Judges of each court, subject to guidance from the Presiding Judges of the circuit;
(2) circuits must be agreed between the Presiding Judges and Delivery Directors of the respective circuits.

Transfers may be agreed either in specific cases or in accordance with general principles agreed between those cited here (*CPD* XIII Listing of Trials, Custody Time Limits and Transfer of Cases: F.11, 12 and 13).

G. Listing of hearings other than trials

Listing of shorter matters

In addition to trials, the court's listing practice will have to provide court time for shorter matters, such as those listed in this section. These hearings are important, often either for setting the necessary case management framework for the proper and efficient preparation of cases for trial, or for determining matters that affect the rights of individuals. They must be afforded the appropriate level of resource that they require to be considered properly, and this may include judicial reading time as well as an appropriate length of hearing. **5-023**

The applicant is responsible for notifying the court, and the other party if appropriate, and ensuring that the papers are served in good time, including a time estimate for judicial reading time and for the hearing. The applicant must endeavour to complete the application within the time estimate provided unless there are exceptional circumstances.

Hearings other than trials include the following:

- Applications for search warrants and Production Orders (sufficient reading time must be provided, see *CPD* G.8).
- Bail applications.
- Applications to vacate or adjourn hearings.
- Applications for dismissal of charges.

- Preliminary hearings.
- Preparatory hearings.
- Pre-Trial and Preparation case Hearing.
- Applications for disclosure of further unused material under s.8 of CPIA 1996.
- Case progression or case management hearings.
- Applications in respect of sentence indications not sought at the PTPH.
- Sentences.
- Civil applications under ASBA 2014.
- Appeals from the magistrates' court: it is essential in all cases where witnesses are likely to be needed on the appeal to check availability before a date is fixed.
- Appeals from the youth court: where the case involves a Class 2B offence, a directions hearing will be required before the re-hearing to consider special measures, ground rules and appropriate adjustments for the hearing of the trial.

(*CPD* XIII Listing of Hearings other than Trials: G.1, 2 and 3)

Short hearings should not generally be listed before a judge such that they may delay the start or continuation of a trial at the Crown Court. It is envisaged that any such short hearing will be completed by 10.30 or start after 16.30.

Each Crown Court equipped with a video link with a prison must have in place arrangements for the conduct of PCMHs, PTPHs, other pre-trial hearings and sentencing hearings by video-link (*CPD* XIII Listing of Hearings other than Trials: G.4 and 5).

Notifying sureties of hearing dates

5-024 Where a surety has entered into a recognisance in the magistrates' court in respect of a case allocated or sent to the Crown Court and where the bail order or recognisance refers to attendance at the first hearing in the Crown Court, the accused should be reminded by the listing officer that the surety should attend the first hearing in the Crown Court in order to provide further recognisance. If attendance is not arranged, the defendant may be remanded in custody pending the recognisance being provided (*CPD* XIII Listing of Hearings other than Trials: G.6).

The court should also notify sureties of the dates of the hearing at the Crown Court at which the defendant is ordered to appear in as far in advance as possible: see the observations of Parker LJ in *R. v Reading Crown Court Ex p. Bello* [1992] 3 All E.R. 353 (*CPD* XIII Listing of Hearings other than Trials: G.7).

Applications for Production Orders and Search Warrants

5-025 The use of production orders and search warrants involve the use of intrusive state powers that affect the rights and liberties of individuals. It is the responsibility of the court to ensure that those powers are not abused.

To do so the court must be presented with a properly completed application, on the appropriate form, which includes:

(1) a summary of the investigation to provide the context for the order;
(2) a clear explanation of how the statutory requirements are fulfilled; and
(3) full and frank disclosure of anything that might undermine the basis for the application.

Further directions on the proper making and consideration of such applications will be provided by Practice Direction. However, the complexity of the application must be taken into account in listing it such that the judge is afforded appropriate reading time and the hearing is given sufficient time for the issues to be considered thoroughly, and a short judgment given (*CPD* XIII Listing of Hearings other than Trials: G.8).

Confiscation and Related Hearings

Applications for *restraint orders* should be determined by the Resident Judge, or a judge nominated by the Resident Judge, at the Crown Court location at which they are lodged (*CPD* XIII Listing of Hearings other than Trials: G.9). **5-026**

In order to prevent possible dissipation of assets of significant value, applications under POCA 2002 should be considered urgent when lists are being fixed. In order to prevent potential prejudice, applications for the variation and discharge of orders, for the appointment of receivers, and applications to punish alleged breaches of orders as a *contempt of court* should similarly be treated as urgent and listed expeditiously (*CPD* XIII Listing of Hearings other than Trials: G.10).

Confiscation Hearings

It is important that confiscation hearings take place in good time after the offender is convicted or sentenced (*CPD* XIII Listing of Hearings other than Trials: G.11). **5-027**

6. ANCILLARY ORDERS

General

6-001 A number of ancillary orders are available, which may be attached, in appropriate circumstances, to the principal sentence. Orders which form part of a community sentence are not included. With the exception of compensation orders, which may stand alone, all other such orders depend upon there being a principal sentence.

A "plea and sentence document" served on the court (see GUILTY PLEAS) should refer to any ancillary order for which the prosecution intends to apply.

Available orders are:

Name of order	Age restrictions	Section in text	Comment
Anti-Social Behaviour Order (ASBO)			No longer available on conviction; see CRIMINAL BEHAVIOUR ORDERS
Bind Over	none	10	Only with consent; as to binding over parent or guardian of offender under 18, see 10-010 and following
Company Officer's Disqualification Order	none	15	
Compensation Order	none	16	Parent or guardian of under 16 must, and of 16–18 may, be ordered to pay
Confiscation Order POCA 2002	none	17	Enforceable as a fine
Costs	none	19	Parent or guardian of under 16 must, and of 16-18 may, be ordered to pay
Criminal Behaviour Order	none	21	
Default Sentence (Financial Penalties)	—	34	
Deportation Recommendation	none	27	
Deprivation Order	none	36	

Name of order	Age restrictions	Section in text	Comment
Disqualification from Driving	none	32	
Drinking (Banning Order)			No longer available on conviction; see CRIMINAL BEHAVIOUR ORDERS
Exclusion Order (licensed premises)	none	45	
Financial Circumstances Order	none	34	
Financial Reporting Order	NO LONGER AVAILABLE		
Football Banning Order	none	35	Certain offences only; prescribed periods
Foreign Travel Order	none	62	Sexual offences; to be distinguished from TRAVEL RESTRICTION ORDERS
Forfeiture Order (MDA 1971)	none	36	
Hospital and Limitation Direction (MHA)	none	49	
Individual Support Order (ISO)			No longer available in view of abolition of Anti-Social Behaviour Order made on conviction
Knife Crime Prevention Orders (KCPO)	12 or over		In force in Met Police Area for period of 14 months from 5 July 2021 (OWA 2019; SI 2021/762)
Offences taken into consideration (TICs)	over 17	24	
Parenting order	under 18		
Publicity order (under CMCHA 2007)	corporations only	6	See SGC 2010, paras 30–32
Reparation Order	Under 18	12	(reparation other than money) re-

Name of order	Age restrictions	Section in text	Comment
			strictions apply in relation to offences committed before 4 April 2005
Remedial order (CMCHA 2007, HSWA 1974)	corporations only	6	See SGC 2010 paras 33–36
Restitution Order	none	54	
Restraining Order	none	55	
Restriction Order (MHA)	none	49	
Return to custody	18 or over	39	
Serious Crime Prevention Order	18 and over	60	
Sexual Harm Prevention Order	none	62	SOA 2003 s.103A; ASBA 2014 Sch.5
Sexual Offences Notification Requirement	none	62	
(Sexual Offences Prevention Order)			No longer available; superseded by SEXUAL HARM PREVENTION ORDER
Serious Violence Reduction Orders (SVRO)	18 or over		Not yet in force. Ch.1A Pt 11 SA 2020
Sheriff's Award; Commendation	none	63	Should always be considered in appropriate circumstances
Slavery and Trafficking Reparation Order			MSA 2015 s.8
Surcharge	none	66	Applies to offences committed on or after 1 October 2012

Name of order	Age restrictions	Section in text	Comment
Travel Restriction Order	none	68	Drugs; applies to offender convicted of drug trafficking offence on or after 1 April 2002. To be distinguished from FOREIGN TRAVEL ORDER (SOA 2003)

Machinery

In general, unless the statute otherwise permits, all aspects of the sentence (i.e. the principal penalty and any ancillary order) ought to be imposed on the same occasion. **6-002**

However, note that where confiscation proceedings are postponed beyond sentence, consideration of costs, compensation and forfeiture should also be postponed.

In the case of RT disqualifications:

(1) there is nothing to prevent the judge from dealing with the substantive part of the sentence on the day of conviction and postponing ancillary questions of endorsement and disqualification until the licence is produced, and any other relevant information is to hand (*R. v Annesley* (1976) 62 Cr. App. R. 113);
(2) a judge who:
  (a) defers sentence in respect of an offence carrying obligatory or discretionary disqualification; or
  (b) adjourns after convicting an offender of such an offence, before dealing with him,

may order him to be disqualified until he has been dealt with for the offence.

In order to avoid any disconnection between the order made by the judge and that recorded in the Crown Court office:

(i) the judge should insist that ancillary orders sought are put before the court in draft;
(ii) the judge may then either make the order in the form which is tendered, or, if appropriate, amend it;
(iii) the document bearing either his approving initial or the amended terms of the order plus such initial, should then be placed with the papers by the clerk,

and in that way the order will be translated in proper form in the office afterwards.

It will also be sensible if, particularly with orders of this kind, when they are provided to the offender he is asked to sign for receipt, although that is not a formal requirement (per Hughes LJ in *R. v Pelletier* [2012] EWCA Crim 1060).

Sheriff's awards under CLA 1826 ss.28 and 29 and commendation(s) should be considered in appropriate cases (see SHERIFFS' AWARDS; COMMENDATIONS).

7. APPEALS FROM THE CROWN COURT

QUICK GUIDE

The principal avenue of appeal from the Crown Court is to the CACD. Decisions of the Crown Court may also be challenged, in appropriate circumstances, by stating a case for the opinion of the Administrative Division of the High Court, or by seeking judicial review by that court. The Attorney General may refer matters to the CACD under CJA 1988 s.36.

This section covers the principal avenues of appeal from convictions, sentences and other orders made by the Crown Court. Some less common appeals in respect of ancillary orders are dealt with in other chapters.

A. Introduction

Decisions of the Crown Court may be challenged in relation to: **7-001**

(1) conviction and sentence, etc. on indictment, by appeal to the CACD under CAA 1968 ss.1 and 9 by the accused;
(2) interlocutory matters arising during the trial, by the accused or the prosecutor, relating, e.g. to certain rulings;
(3) matters not directly relating to its jurisdiction on indictment, by applying to the Administrative Division of the High Court for judicial review;
(4) its appellate jurisdiction, by way of case stated or judicial review to the Administrative Division of the High Court; and
(5) its jurisdiction in committal for sentence under CAA 1968 s.10 and by judicial review to the Administrative Division of the High Court.

Furthermore, the:

(i) Attorney General may refer a point of law or a lenient sentence to the CACD under CJA 1988 s.36;
(ii) Prosecutor may challenge certain matters under POCA 2002 by appeal to the CACD; and
(iii) CCRC may refer a conviction or sentence to the CACD under CAA 1995; its powers and functions were reviewed in *R. v Criminal Cases Review Commission Ex p. Pearson* [2000] 1 Cr. App. R. 141.

B. Against conviction and sentence

1. General

Rights of appeal

All the usual consequences following from a conviction, etc. on indictment, are susceptible to appeal to the CACD: **7-002**

(1) by a person convicted on indictment—against his conviction and/or sentence (not being a sentence fixed by law);
(2) by a person convicted in the magistrates' court and sentenced on committal to the Crown Court—against that sentence;
(3) by a person in whose case a verdict of not guilty by reason of insanity has been returned—against that verdict;
(4) where there has been a determination under CP(I)A 1964 s.4 of the question of a person's fitness to be tried, and findings that he was under a disability and did the act or made the omission charged against him have been returned—against those findings;
(5) by a person in whose case a hospital order or an interim hospital order is made by virtue of CP(I)A 1964 ss.5 or 5A, or a supervision order is made under s.5—against that order; and

(6) where, upon conviction, judgment is respited and the offender is bound over to come up for judgment when called upon to do so—against any sentence subsequently imposed (*R. v Smith* (1925) 89 J.P. 79).

An appeal also lies to the CACD:

(a) at the instance of an offender, from any order or decision of the Crown Court in the exercise of its jurisdiction to punish for contempt (AJA 1960 s.13) (see 7-040), including an appeal against a refusal of bail made in the course of contempt proceedings (*R. v Serumaga* [2005] EWCA Crim 370; [2005] Cr. App. R. 12);
(b) by an offender upon whom a mandatory life sentence was imposed before 18 December 2003 and whose minimum term set or reviewed by a judge of the High Court (CJA 2003 Sch.22 para.14) (see 7-010). See also SI 2005/2798.

As to the right of appeal to the CACD *after* the determination of an Attorney General's reference of an unduly lenient sentence, see *R. v Hughes* [2009] EWCA Crim 841; [2010] 1 Cr. App. R. (S.) 25.

Appeals by the prosecutor are available only where expressly permitted by statute; see, e.g. 7-030.

Appeal to the CACD (save in respect of a contempt matter brought under AJA 1960 s.13, where appeal lies of right) lies only:

(i) with the leave of the CACD; or
(ii) in an exceptional case, if the judge of the trial court gives a certificate that the case is fit for appeal (see 7-026).

Special rules under CJA 2003 s.84 govern the retrial of an accused person on an indictment preferred by the CACD (see RETRIALS). A failure to strictly comply with directions of the CACD (pursuant to s.8 of the Criminal Appeals Act 1968) in respect of the time within which arraignment should occur following an order for a retrial may invalidate the trial, see *R. v Llewelyn* [2022] EWCA Crim 154; [2022] 2 WLUK 533.

Unsafe conviction; pleas of guilty; mentally disordered offenders

7-003 The single ground for allowing an appeal against conviction is where the CACD finds the conviction is unsafe (see *R. v Graham* [1997] 1 Cr. App. R. 302). This does not preclude an appeal by an accused who pleads guilty at the trial (see *R. v Chalkley* [1998] 2 Cr. App. R. 79, also *R. v Togher* [2001] 1 Cr. App. R. 33 (accused pleading guilty following judge's ruling)).

Note that where, on appeal against conviction, the CACD is of the opinion (CAA 1968 s.6) that:

(1) the proper verdict would have been one of not guilty by reason of insanity; or
(2) the case is not one where there should have been an acquittal, but there should have been a finding that the accused was under a disability and that he did the act or made the omission charged against him,

the court may make a hospital order (with or without a restriction order) a supervision order or an order for his absolute discharge.

In *R. v Tredget* [2022] EWCA Crim 108; [2022] 4 W.L.R. 62 the CACD comprehensively reviewed the authorities on the availability of an appeal following a guilty plea and confirmed that there are three categories of cases in which the CACD has jurisdiction to hear an appeal against conviction following a guilty plea:

(1) where the guilty plea was vitiated (e.g. an equivocal or unintended plea; or where compelled by an adverse and wrong ruling of law by the judge);
(2) in cases of abuse of process where it would be unfair to try the defendant (e.g. entrapment); and
(3) in a small category of cases where it was established that the defendant had not committed the offence and the plea was false.

Absconding appellants; deceased appellants; change in law

Applications for leave to appeal on behalf of *absconding appellants* will be put before the CACD in the ordinary way (*R. v Okedare* [2014] EWCA Crim 228; [2015] 1 Cr. App. R. 9; see also *R. v Charles* [2001] EWCA Crim 129; [2001] 2 Cr. App. R. 15). Applications from absconders will not be treated as ineffective per se. If there are grounds for believing that the absconder has given authority to appeal, or the case is one where the court might wish to intervene in the interests of justice, the CACD will proceed as normal. The single judge may adjourn the application for more information and grant or refuse leave or refer to the application to the full court as usual. If the single judge is satisfied that there is no authority to pursue an application for leave, and the application is not one the court would wish to entertain, he has the power to treat the application as ineffective and time will continue to run. However, this should be the exception rather than the norm. **7-004**

Special rules apply in the case of *persons since deceased*; see CAA 1968 s.44A and *R. v Whelan* [1997] Crim. L.R. 659. Approval for an appeal to be brought will be given only to certain specified persons, and an application for approval must be made within one year of the death. See also *R. v Bentley* [2001] 1 Cr. App. R. 21 and *R. v Hanratty (deceased)* [2002] EWCA Crim 1141; [2002] Cr. App. R. 30.

An extension of time will not be granted routinely in a case simply because there has been a *change in the law*, but only if substantial injustice would otherwise be done to the accused. The mere fact of change of law does not ordinarily create such injustice. Nor is the case where an extension will be refused limited to one where, if the law had been correctly understood at the time of the proceedings in the Crown Court, a different charge or different procedure might well have left the accused in a similar position to that in which he now finds himself: see *R. v Cottrell* [2007] EWCA Crim 2016; [2008] 1 Cr. App. R. 7, applied in (e.g.) *R. v McGuffog* [2015] EWCA Crim 1116; see also the remarks of the Supreme Court in *R. v Jogee* [2016] UKSC 8; [2016] 1 Cr. App. R. 31. Even though a change in the law would provide a defence, there was held to be no substantial injustice where the defendant had been released from prison, his licence had expired and the conviction was spent: see *R. v Ordu* [2017] EWCA Crim 4; [2017] 1 Cr. App. R. 21.

2. Mentally disordered offenders

CAA 1968 gives a right of appeal to an accused against: **7-005**

(1) a verdict of not guilty by reason of insanity (s.12); and
(2) a finding that:
    (a) he was under a disability; or
    (b) he did the act or made the omission charged against him, or both (s.15).

Procedure is, in both (1) and (2), as in the case of appeals against conviction, under CrimPR 39, commenced by service on the Crown Court of an appeal notice within 28 days from the date of the finding.

It should be noted, in considering whether to appeal, that although the CACD is bound to allow the appeal if the conviction is considered unsafe, the court has powers where:

(a) an appeal under s.12 would fall to be allowed and none of the grounds for allowing it relates to the question of the insanity of the accused, to dismiss the appeal if of opinion that, but for the insanity of the accused, the proper verdict would have been that he was guilty of an offence other than that charged (s.13(3));

(b) an appeal under s.12 is allowed, and if the ground or one of the grounds is that the finding of the jury ought not to stand and the CACD is of opinion that the proper verdict would have been that he was guilty of an offence of which the jury could have found him guilty, to substitute a verdict of guilty of that offence, and sentence him accordingly (s.13(4)); and

(c) on an appeal under s.12 it finds that there should have been a finding that the accused was under a disability, and that he did the act or made the omission charged against him, to make a hospital order (with or without a restriction order), a supervision order, an order for his absolute discharge.

3. Appeals against Sentence

General

7-006 Under CAA 1968 ss.9 and 10 an offender may appeal against a sentence:

(1) (not being a sentence fixed by law) passed upon him on his conviction on indictment, or passed upon him in subsequent proceedings; or

(2) (otherwise than on appeal from the magistrates' court) where:
   (a) he was committed by a magistrates' court to be dealt with for his offence by the Crown Court; or
   (b) having been given a suspended sentence or made the subject of:
      (i) an order for conditional discharge;
      (ii) a youth rehabilitation order; or
      (iii) a community order,
   appears before the Crown Court to be further dealt with.

Leave is required to appeal against sentence, whether under ss.9 or 10, either from the CACD or from the trial judge, or the judge who passed the sentence (s.11(1)A) (see 7-019).

Where the parent or guardian of a young person is ordered to pay a fine or enter into recognisances (under SA 2020 ss.128 or 376), he may appeal as if he had been convicted on indictment and the sentence passed on his conviction (SA 2020 ss.377 and 380).

The powers of the CACD, if it considers that an appellant should be sentenced differently for an offence for which he was dealt with by the court below, are (CAA 1968 s.11(3)):

- quash any sentence or order which is the subject of the appeal; and
- in place of it pass such sentence or make such order as it thinks appropriate for the case, and as the court below had power to pass or make when dealing with the offence,

but the court shall exercise its powers so that, taking the case as a whole, the appellant is not more severely dealt with on appeal than he was dealt with below.

Meaning of "sentence"

"Sentence" means any order made by a court when dealing with an offender including, in particular: **7-007**

(1) a hospital order under MHA 1983 Pt III with or without a restriction order;
(2) an interim hospital order under MHA 1983 Pt III;
(3) a hospital direction and a limitation direction under MHA 1983 Pt III;
(4) a recommendation for deportation;
(5) a confiscation order under POCA 2002 Pt 2 (but not a determination under POCA 2002 s.10A);
(6) an order which varies a confiscation order made under POCA 2002 Pt 2, if the varying order is made under ss.21, 22 or 29 (but not otherwise—see *R. v Ward* [2010] EWCA Crim 1932; [2011] 1 W.L.R. 766; an order for variation under s.23 is not a "sentence");
(7) a confiscation order under DTA 1994 other than one made by the High Court;
(8) a confiscation order under CJA 1988 Pt VI (proceeds of major crime);
(9) an order varying a confiscation order of a kind included in (7) or (8) above;
(10) an order made by the Crown Court varying a confiscation order made by the High Court by virtue of DTA 1994 s.19;
(11) a declaration of relevance, within the meaning of FSA 1989 s.23;
(12) an order for forfeiture or suspension of personal licence under s.129(2) of the Licensing Act 2003.

Meaning of "sentence"; other orders

The following have been recognised as a "sentence" for the purposes of appealing to the CACD: **7-008**

(1) an order for the payment of prosecution costs (*R. v Hayden* (1970) 30 Cr. App. R. 304);
(2) a compensation order (*R. v Thebith* (1970) 54 Cr. App. R. 35);
(3) a common law bind over order made on conviction (*R. v Williams* (1982) 75 Cr. App. R. 378);
(4) an order under PCC(S)A 2000 s.1, deferring sentence (*R. v L (Deferred Sentence)* [1999] 2 Cr. App. R. (S.) 7);
(5) a refusal under SOA 2003 s.110 to vary a sexual offences prevention order (*R. v Hoath* [2011] EWCA Crim 274; [2011] 4 All E.R. 306; *R. v Aldridge* [2012] EWCA Crim 1456);
(6) a financial reporting order under SOCA 2005 s.76(1) (*R. v Adams* [2008] EWCA Crim 914; [2008] 4 All E.R. 574);
(7) an anti-social behaviour order (*R. v P* [2004] EWCA Crim 287; [2004] 2 Cr. App. R. (S.) 63; see also *R. (on the application of Langley) v Preston Crown Court* [2008] EWHC 2623 (Admin); [2009] 3 All E.R. 1026, where it was suggested that the variation of an order would also fall within CAA 1968 s.50);
(8) an order in respect of the period under PCC(S)A 2000 s.82A in respect of

a discretionary life sentence (*R. v D* (1995) 16 Cr. App. R. (S.) 564), or failure to specify a period (*R. v Hollies* (1995) 16 Cr. App. R. 463);

(9) an order under CJCSA 2000 s.28 (disqualification from working with children);

(10) a statutory surcharge order (the words of the subsection are plainly wide enough to embrace a statutory surcharge order (*R. v Stone* [2013] EWCA Crim 723), although in a case in which no statutory surcharge order was imposed as it should have been, the CACD has no power to make such an order if the effect is to increase the ultimate overall penalty); and

(11) a sentence for contempt imposed upon an appellant, whether in respect of his conduct at the trial or for absconding from bail, is treated as a "sentence" for the purpose of appeal.

4. Substituted sentence under SA 2020 s.387

7-009 Both:

(1) an offender in respect of whom a reference is made under SA 2020 ss.387–388 (see DISCOUNTS ON SENTENCE); or

(2) the specified prosecutor who has made a reference to a judge of the Crown Court,

may, with the leave of the CACD, appeal to that court against the decision of the Crown Court, either to substitute, or not to substitute, a sentence under the provisions of the Act.

Procedure is in accordance with CrimPR 39. An appeal is initiated by serving an appeal notice on the Crown Court where sentence was reviewed within 28 days of the review.

5. Mandatory life sentences (minimum term)

7-010 An offender upon whom a mandatory life sentence was imposed before 18 December 2003 and who has had his minimum term set or reviewed by a judge of the High Court (see LIFE SENTENCES) may appeal to the CACD (CJA 2003 Sch.22 para.14).

(See also CJA 2003 (Mandatory Life Sentences: Appeals in Transitional Cases Order 2005 (SI 2005/2798) Pt 2 para.8).)

The procedure is under CrimPR 39 and is initiated by serving an appeal notice not more than 28 days after the decision appealed against.

Under CJA 2003 s.274(3) offenders sentenced to life imprisonment outside the UK and transferred to serve the sentence in England and Wales may appeal against the minimum term fixed by a High Court judge.

C. Initiating an appeal; CrimPR 39

1. General

7-011 In relation to those appeals set out above in 7-001 to 7-010, proceedings are initiated in accordance with CrimPR 39, the general provisions of CrimPR 36, and *CPD* IX. The procedure subsequent to the giving of notice is essentially in the hands of the Registrar, and the role of the Crown Court and its officers is confined to the acceptance, collation and transmission of documents (see 7-022), and in exceptional cases, the giving of a certificate of fitness to appeal (see 7-019) and the granting of bail (see 7-018).

The Guide to Commencing Proceedings in the CACD from 2008 has now been revised (July 2021) and may be consulted at *https://www.judiciary.uk/publications/the-court-of-appeal-division-guide-to-commencing-proceedings* [Accessed September 2022].

2. APPEAL NOTICE

An appeal notice must be served on the Registrar: **7-012**

(1) not more than 28 days after:
  (a) the conviction, verdict, or finding;
  (b) the sentence; or
  (c) the order, or the failure to make an order; or
  (d) the minimum term review decision under s.274(3) of, or paragraph 14 of Schedule 22 to, CJA 2003, about which the appellant wants to appeal.
(2) Not more than 15 business days after the order in a case in which the appellant appeals against a wasted or third party costs order;
(3) Not more than 20 business days after the Registrar serves notice that the CCRC has referred a conviction to the court.

(CrimPR 39.2)
As to extension of time, see 7-013.
Note that:

(1) CAA 1968 provides for a single appeal in respect of each case, but where, e.g. confiscation proceedings under POCA 2002 are postponed at the time sentence is passed, the offender may appeal against the sentence, and at the conclusion of the confiscation proceedings may bring a separate appeal against any order made (*R. v Neal* [1999] 2 Cr. App. R. (S.) 352);
(2) it will be inappropriate to seek to appeal against conviction until the Crown Court proceedings have been completed, which includes the passing of sentence; only in a rare case will the CACD entertain an appeal short of that stage (*R. v Drew* (1985) 81 Cr. App. R. 190); and
(3) for an appeal against conviction, time runs from the date of conviction (in the case of trial by jury from the date of verdict: *R. v Hawkins* [2010] EWCA Crim 2763; [2010] 9 Archbold Review 1).

As to appeal against conviction after a plea of guilty following the trial judge's direction, see *R. v Chalkley* [1998] 2 Cr. App. R. 79; *R. v Jefferies* [1998] 2 Cr. App. R. 79.

An appeal or application may be abandoned at any time before the hearing without permission by completing and lodging a notice of abandonment (CrimPR 36.13(2)(a)). An oral instruction or letter indicating a wish to abandon is insufficient. At the hearing, an application or appeal can only be abandoned with the permission of the court (CrimPR 36.13(2)(b)). Once abandoned, an appeal or application is treated as having been dismissed or refused by the full court, as the case may be (CrimPR 36.13(4)(c)) (Guide A17).

3. Extension of time limits; special cases

Extension of time

7-013 The CACD has power under CrimPR 36.3 to shorten a time limit or extend it (even after it has expired) unless that is inconsistent with other legislation.

A person who wants an extension of time within which to serve a notice or make an application must apply for that extension when serving the notice or making the application, giving the reasons for the application for an extension of time (CrimPR 36.4; see also Guide A6). Having arguable grounds of appeal will not necessarily result in an application, pursuant to s.18(3) of the Criminal Appeal Act 1968, for leave to appeal out of time, being granted. Leave will only be granted where justice requires it, and will involve consideration of a number of factors including the need for finality: *R. v Paterson* [2022] EWCA Crim 456; [2022] 4 WLUK 40.

Special cases

7-014 There are special rules for time limits in:

(1) dangerous offender cases, where a previous conviction has been subsequently set aside, or a previous sentence imposed has been modified by the CACD (see CJA 2003 s.231)—where the time limit is 28 days from the date on which the previous conviction was set aside or the previous sentence was modified;
(2) cases of mandatory minimum sentences depending on one or more previous convictions (under SA 2020 Pt 10 Ch.7), if a relevant previous conviction is set aside by the CACD, thus invalidating the mandatory sentence—where, again, the time limit is 28 days from the date on which the previous conviction was set aside;
(3) confiscation orders (whether made under CJA 1988, DTA 1994 or POCA 2002); a confiscation order is a sentence (CAA 1968 s.50). Where sentences are passed in separate proceedings on different dates there may be two appeals against sentence. Thus, there may be an appeal against the custodial part of a sentence and an appeal against a confiscation order (*R. v Neal* [1999] 2 Cr. App. R. (S.) 352).

4. Need for leave

7-015 Leave to appeal is required in all cases except where:

(1) the trial or sentencing judge has certified that the case is fit for appeal (see 7-019);
(2) the case has been referred by the CCRC (see 7-001); or
(3) the case is a "contempt" case under AJA 1960 s.13 (see 7-040).

In (2) the appellant must obtain leave to pursue grounds not related to the Commission's reasons for referral (CAA 1995 s.14(4B)).

5. Action by defence solicitors; service of notice

7-016 Where the defence advocate has advised an appeal, solicitors should forward the signed grounds of appeal direct to the Registrar accompanied by the appeal notice and such other forms as may be appropriate (e.g. applications for bail, leave to be present, leave to call fresh evidence, etc.) (Guide A2). The court must be provided with an appeal notice as a single document which sets out the grounds of appeal. Advocates should not provide the court with an advice addressed to lay or professional clients (CPD IX 39C.1).

Note that:

(1) the appeal notice and grounds of appeal are required to be served within the relevant time limit (see 7-013 and 7-014) in all cases, whether or not leave to appeal is required (e.g. where the trial judge or sentencing judge grants a certificate); but

(2) on a reference by the CCRC, if no Form NG and grounds are served within the required period, the reference will be treated as the appeal notice (CrimPR 39.5(2)).

In regard to applications to call fresh evidence, Form W and a s.9 statement from the witness, should be lodged in respect of each witness it is proposed to call. Form W should indicate whether there is an application for a witness order. The CACD will require a cogent explanation for the failure to adduce the evidence at trial. A supporting witness statement or affidavit from the appellant's solicitor should be lodged in this regard (*R. v Gogana, The Times,* 12 July 1999).

CrimPR 39.7 sets out the procedure to be followed where there is an application to introduce hearsay evidence, bad character evidence (etc.), or for the court to order the production of a document (etc.) or for the court to order a witness to attend.

In conviction cases, transcripts of the summing up and proceedings up to and including verdict are obtained as a matter of course. The transcript of the prosecution opening on a guilty plea and the judge's observations on passing sentence are usually obtained in sentence cases (Guide A7).

6. Grounds of appeal

Grounds must be settled with sufficient particularity to enable the Registrar, and subsequently the court, to identify clearly the matters relied upon. A mere formula such as "the conviction is unsafe" or "the sentence is in all the circumstances too severe" will be ineffective as grounds and time will continue to run against the applicant (Guide A3-1). **7-017**

The grounds of appeal should set out the relevant facts and nature of the proceedings concisely in one all-encompassing document, not separate grounds of appeal and advice. The intended readership of this document is the court, not the lay or professional client. Its purpose is to enable the single judge to grasp quickly the facts and issues in the case. In appropriate cases, draft grounds of appeal may be perfected before submission to the single judge (Guide A3-3, A3-4).

The mandatory contents of an appeal notice and of grounds of appeal are set out in CrimPR 39.3 (Guide A3-2).

Counsel should not settle or sign grounds unless they are reasonable, have some real prospect of success and are such that he is prepared to argue them before the court. He should not settle grounds he cannot support because he is "instructed" to do so by an accused.

For the obligations of counsel in appeals involving criticism of former counsel, see *R. v Achogbuo* [2014] EWCA Crim 567; [2014] 2 Cr. App. R. 7 and *R. v McCook* [2014] EWCA Crim 734; [2015] Crim. L.R. 350 (Guide A4-1 to 4-3).

The subsequent perfection of grounds of appeal is dealt with in the Guide at A8.

As to the Registrar's power to order service of a respondent's notice, see CrimPR 39.6 and the Guide at A9.

Applicants need to be aware that both the CACD and the single judge have a discretionary power under CAA 1968 s.29 to direct that part of the time during which the applicant is in custody after putting in his notice of application for leave to appeal should not count towards sentence (known as a "direction for loss of time") (see also the Guide A16).

7. Bail pending appeal

7-018 There is no statutory right to bail after conviction, but bail pending appeal, if sought, may be granted:

(1) by a single judge, or the full court of the CACD; or
(2) by a trial or sentencing judge who has certified the case fit for appeal.

The CACD may, subject to CJPOA 1994 s.25, if they think fit:

(a) grant bail pending determination of an appeal;
(b) revoke bail granted to an appellant by the Crown Court under SCA 1981 s.81(1)(f); or
(c) vary conditions of bail granted by the CACD or the Crown Court.

(CAA 1968 s.19)

For the application procedure, see CrimPR 39.8 and for rules concerning bail conditions see CrimPR 39.9. (Guide A13).

The Crown Court may, subject to CJPOA 1994 s.25, grant bail to any person to whom the Crown Court has granted a certificate under CAA 1968 ss.1(2) or 11(1)(a).

In practice, bail will usually only be granted where:

(a) it appears prima facie on cogent grounds that the appeal is likely to succeed; or
(b) where there is a risk that the sentence will have been served by the time the appeal is heard.

In short sentence cases, the CACD generally prefers to expedite the appeal and, if necessary, to list it at short notice (*R. v Walton* (1979) 68 Cr. App. R. 293).

The CACD may decline to treat an application as urgent if there is no good reason why the application was not made to the Crown Court.

As to bail with condition of surety in the CACD, see CrimPR 39.9; as to the forfeiture of recognisances in respect of failing to appear at the CACD, see CrimPR 39.10.

8. Application to Crown Court for leave; bail

7-019 The trial or sentencing judge may grant certificate of fitness for appeal; see CAA 1968 ss.2(b) and 11(1A). Certification should be reserved for exceptional cases. If the judge considers that there is no particular, cogent ground of appeal, there can be no certificate.

In particular, the trial judge should not grant a certificate with regard to sentence merely in the light of mitigation which he has already considered, nor should it be granted without seeking representations from the prosecutor. Before granting a

certificate in relation to a conviction, the judge should conclude that the chance of a successful appeal is substantial.
(*CPD* III 14H.1–6)

Procedure

An appellant who wishes the Crown Court judge to certify that a case is fit for appeal must either: 7-020

(1) apply orally, with reasons, immediately after:
 (a) the conviction, verdict or finding;
 (b) the sentence; or
 (c) the order, or the failure to make an order, about which the appellant wishes to appeal; or
(2) apply in writing and serve the application on the Crown Court officer not more than 10 business days after (a)–(c) above.

A written application must include the same information (with the necessary adaptations) as that required in an appeal notice (see 7-012).
(CrimPR 39.4)

The judge may think it right to hear an oral application in chambers and to invite the accused's advocate to submit, before the hearing of the application, a draft of the grounds of appeal which he is asking the judge to certify. The advocate for the Crown will be better able to assist the judge at the hearing if the draft grounds are sent beforehand to him also.

The judge:

(i) must first decide whether there exists a particular and cogent ground of appeal; if there is no such ground there can be no certificate;
(ii) should bear in mind that where he refuses a certificate, application may be made to the CACD for leave to appeal (and for bail);
(iii) should bear in mind that the length of time which may elapse before the hearing of the appeal is not relevant to the grant of a certificate, but if he grants a certificate, it may be a factor in the decision whether or not to grant bail.
 (*CPD* III 14H.3-6)

Where a person disqualified from holding or obtaining a driving licence appeals, or applies for leave to appeal, against his conviction or sentence, the Crown Court judge (or the CACD) may suspend the disqualification, if thought fit.

Bail on grant of certificate

The judge who tried the case (where the appeal is under CAA 1968 s.1 or s.9) or the judge who passed the sentence (in the case of an appeal under s.10) may grant bail, always provided that (*CPD* III 14H.5 and 6): 7-021

(1) the case is not one to which CJPOA 1994 s.25 (see BAIL) applies;
(2) the case is not one to which CAA 1968 s.12 (appeal against verdict of not guilty by reason of insanity), ss.15 or 16A (appeal against finding that the accused was under disability, or that he did the act or made the omission charged against him) apply;
(3) he gives a certificate under CAA 1968 ss.1(2) (question of fact or mixed law and fact) and 11(1A) (fit for appeal against sentence), or under SCA 1981

s.81(1B) that the case is fit for appeal on a ground which involves a question of law alone;

(4) the appellant has not made an application to the CACD for bail in respect of the offence or offences to which the appeal relates; and

(5) the power is exercised within 28 days from the date of the conviction appealed against, or from the date the sentence was passed where the appeal is against sentence, or in the case of an order made or treated as made on conviction, from the date of the making of the order.

9. Duties of Crown Court Officer

7-022 Where electronic arrangements have been made to receive and store documents for the Crown Court, the Crown Court officer must, as soon as practicable, ensure that all such material is available to the Registrar. The Crown Court officer must also provide the Registrar with any document, object or information for which the Registrar asks within such period as the Registrar may require (CrimPR 36.8(1)).

Where someone may appeal to the CACD, the Crown Court officer must keep any document or object exhibited in the proceedings in the Crown Court, or arrange for it to be kept by some other appropriate person until six weeks after the conclusion of those proceedings or the conclusion of any appeal proceedings that begin within that six weeks (CrimPR 36.8(2)).

Where CrimPR 39 applies (*appeal to CACD about conviction or sentence*), the Crown Court officer must as soon as practicable serve on or make available to the Registrar:

(a) the judge's certificate, if any, that the case is fit for appeal;
(b) the judge's decision on any application at the Crown Court centre for bail pending appeal;
(c) such of the Crown Court case papers as the Registrar requires; and
(d) such transcript of the Crown Court proceedings as the Registrar requires (CrimPR 36.8(5)).

Where CrimPR 37 applies (*appeal to CACD against ruling at preparatory hearing*), the Crown Court officer must as soon as practicable serve on the appellant a transcript or note of:

(a) each order or ruling against which the appellant wants to appeal; and
(b) the judge's decision on any application for permission to appeal (CrimPR 36.8(3)).

Where CrimPR 38 applies (*appeal to CACD against ruling adverse to the prosecution*), the Crown Court officer must as soon as practicable serve on the appellant a transcript or note of:

(a) each ruling against which the appellant wants to appeal;
(b) the judge's decision on any application for permission to appeal; and
(c) the judge's decision on any request to expedite the appeal (CrimPR 36.8(4)).

Where CrimPR 40 applies (*appeal to CACD regarding reporting or public access*) and an order is made restricting public access to a trial, the Crown Court officer must:

(a) immediately notify the Registrar of that order, if the appellant has given advance notice of intention to appeal; and

(b) as soon as practicable provide the applicant for that order with a transcript or note of the application (CrimPR 36.8(6)).

D. BEFORE CONCLUSION OF TRIAL; INTERLOCUTORY PROCEEDINGS

1. APPEALS AGAINST RULINGS AT PREPARATORY HEARINGS

General

Where a preparatory hearing is conducted under either CJA 1987 or CPIA 1996, either side may appeal from an order or ruling made by the judge (see CASE MANAGEMENT) on any: **7-023**

(1) question as to the admissibility of evidence;
(2) other question of law relating to the case; or
(3) question as to the joinder or severance of charges,

but only with the leave of the judge or the CACD. The CACD may confirm, vary or reverse the ruling (CJA 1987 s.9 and CPIA 1996 ss.31 and 35).

The right of appeal is restricted to the above matters (*Re Gunarwardena* (1990) 91 Cr. App. R. 55) and these do not include, e.g.:

(a) a ruling on a challenge to the prosecution case statement (*R. v Smithson* [1995] 1 Cr. App. R. 14);
(b) a decision refusing to quash counts on the indictment (*R. v Hedworth* [1991] 1 Cr. App. R. 421);
(c) a decision whether to order disclosure (*R. v H (Interlocutory application; Disclosure)* [2007] UKHL 7; [2007] 2 Cr. App. R. 6); or
(d) a refusal to stay an indictment as an abuse of process (*R. v VJA* [2010] EWCA Crim 2742).

In the case of a ruling given outside a preparatory hearing there is no general power of interlocutory appeal; the only avenue of appeal being that available to the Crown under CJA 2003 s.58 in the limited circumstances in which it is willing to give the undertaking stipulated for in s.58(8) that acquittal shall follow a failure of its appeal. Where the judge conducting a preparatory hearing simultaneously conducts a parallel hearing to exercise other powers (see CASE MANAGEMENT), a right of interlocutory appeal under s.9(11) arises only where the matters dealt with come within the scope of s.9(3) of the 1987 Act (and s.31(3) of the 1996 Act) (*R. v H (Interlocutory application; Disclosure)* [2007] UKHL 7; [2007] 2 Cr. App. R. 6).

The right to an interlocutory appeal is an exceptional right in Crown Court trials, and even where a question of law falling within the ambit of s.9(3)(c) is raised, the CACD may exercise its discretion in refusing to grant leave (*R. v VJA* [2010] EWCA Crim 2742).

Procedure is under CrimPR 37 and the general provisions of CrimPR 36 (Guide B1–B7).

Service of appeal notice

An appellant wanting to appeal under CJA 1987 s.9 or CPIA 1996 s.35(1) must serve an appeal notice on: **7-024**

(1) the Crown Court officer;

(2) the Registrar; and
(3) every party directly affected by the order or ruling against which the appellant wants to appeal,

not more than five business days after:

(a) the order or ruling against which he wants to appeal; or
(b) the Crown Court judge gives or refuses permission to appeal.

(CrimPR 37.2)

"Business day" means any day except Sunday, Christmas Day, Boxing Day, Good Friday, Easter Monday or a bank holiday.

A jury cannot be sworn (CJA 1987 s.9(13)) or the preparatory hearing concluded (CPIA 1996 s.25(2)) until the appeal is determined or abandoned. Where the trial date is imminent and the application urgent, the Registrar should be notified so that he may consider referring the application directly to the full court (Guide B3).

Form of appeal notice

7-025 The appeal notice must be in the form set out in *CPD*, and must:

(1) specify each order or ruling against which the appellant wants to appeal;
(2) identify each ground of appeal on which the appellant relies, numbering them consecutively (if there is more than one) and concisely outlining each argument in support;
(3) summarise the relevant facts;
(4) identify any relevant authorities;
(5) include or attach any application for the following, with reasons:
    (a) permission to appeal, if the appellant needs the court's permission;
    (b) an extension of time within which to serve the appeal notice;
    (c) a direction to attend in person a hearing that the appellant could attend by live link, if he is in custody;
(6) include a list of those on whom the appellant has served the appeal notice; and
(7) attach:
    (a) a transcript or note of each order or ruling against which the appellant wants to appeal;
    (b) all relevant skeleton arguments considered by the Crown Court judge;
    (c) any written application for permission to appeal that the appellant made to the Crown Court judge;
    (d) a transcript or note of the decision by the judge on any application for permission to appeal; and
    (e) any other document or thing that the appellant thinks the court will need to decide the appeal, and include or attach an electronic link to each such document that has been made available to the Registrar under CrimPR 36.8(1)(a).
(8) include or attach:
    (a) an electronic copy of any authority identified under para.(2)(d); or
    (b) if two or more such authorities are identified, electronic copies of each together in a single electronic document.

(CrimPR 37.3)

An appellant needs the permission of the CACD to appeal in every case to which CrimPR 37 applies unless the Crown Court judge gives permission.

Judge's permission to appeal

An appellant who wants the Crown Court judge to give permission to appeal must apply either: **7-026**

(1) orally, with reasons, immediately after the order or ruling against which he wants to appeal; or
(2) in writing, serving the application on:
  (a) the Crown Court officer; and
  (b) every party directly affected by the order or ruling, not more than two business days after that order or ruling.

A written application must include the same information (with the necessary adaptations) as an appeal notice (see 7-016).
(CrimPR 37.4)

Where no application is made to the trial judge, or the trial judge refuses leave, an application for permission may be made to the CACD (see 7-023).

For the Crown Court judge's power to give permission to appeal, see CJA 1987 s.9(11), CPIA 1996 s.35(1), CJA 2003 s.47(2).

Respondent's notice

A party on whom an appellant serves an appeal notice may serve a respondent's notice, and must do so if that party wants to make representations to the court or the court so directs, on: **7-027**

(1) the appellant;
(2) the Crown Court officer;
(3) the Registrar; and
(4) any other party on whom the appellant served the appeal notice,

not more than five business days after the appellant serves the appeal notice, or a direction to do so.

The respondent's notice must:

(a) give the date on which the respondent was served with the appeal notice;
(b) identify each ground of opposition on which the respondent relies, numbering them consecutively (if there is more than one), concisely outlining each argument in support and identifying the ground of appeal to which each relates;
(c) summarise any relevant facts not already summarised in the appeal notice;
(d) identify any relevant authorities;
(e) include or attach any application for the following, with reasons:
  (i) an extension of time within which to serve the respondent's notice;
  (ii) a direction to attend in person any hearing that the respondent could attend by live link, if the respondent is in custody;
(f) identify any other document or thing that the respondent thinks the CACD or the court will need to decide the appeal, and include or attach an electronic link to each such document that has been made available to the Registrar under CrimPR 36.8(1)(a);
(g) include or attach:

(i) an electronic copy of any authority identified under para.(5)(d); or
(ii) if two or more such authorities are identified, electronic copies of each together in a single electronic document.

(CrimPR 37.5)

2. Appeals against an order for trial of sample counts

7-028 Appeal lies by either side from an order made under DVA 2004 s.17, ordering that some, but not all, of the counts included in an indictment be tried without a jury (DVA 2004 s.18(5)).

The Act provides that CJA 1987 s.9(11) and CPIA 1996 s.35(1) in relation to appeals from preparatory hearings are to have effect. Procedure is therefore under CrimPR 37, and the general provisions of CrimPR 36 (7-023 to 7-027) (Guide D13).

3. Appeals against orders in relation to trials without a jury

7-029 Where the provisions of CJA 2003 Pt 7, relating to trials without a jury are in force (see TRIAL WITHOUT A JURY), appeal lies to the CACD from the judge's order under:

(1) s.46(3) (after discharging the jury) that the trial continue without a jury; or
(2) s.46(5) (after terminating the trial under s.46(4)) that any new trial that takes place shall be conducted without a jury,

but only with the permission of the judge or the CACD. On the termination of the appeal, the CACD may confirm or revoke the order (CJA 2003 s.47).

Procedure is that provided in relation to appeals from preparatory hearings under CrimPR 37 and the general provisions of CrimPR 36 (7-023 to 7-027) (Guide D14–15).

4. Prosecutor appealing judges' rulings under CJA 2003 Pt 9

General

7-030 CJA 2003 Pt 9 gives to a prosecutor a right of appeal to the CACD:

(1) generally, in regard to rulings made by the judge in relation to a trial on indictment (s.58), ("terminatory rulings"); and
(2) against certain evidentiary rulings made by the judge in the course of such a trial (s.62),

excepting that the prosecutor has no right of appeal under these provisions against a ruling:

(a) that the jury be discharged; or
(b) from which an appeal lies to the CACD by virtue of any other enactment (e.g. an appeal from a preparatory hearing against a ruling on the admissibility of evidence).

The first of these (CJA 2003 s.58) is in force in relation to criminal proceedings committed, transferred or sent for trial, or where a voluntary bill was preferred, after 4 April 2005.

The second (CJA 2003 s.62) is not yet in force, although there will be evidentiary rulings which will be susceptible to appeal under s.58 (*Prosecutor's Appeal (No.2 of 2008) R. v Y* [2008] EWCA Crim 10; [2008] 1 Cr. App. R. 34). See *R. v N Ltd* [2008] EWCA Crim 1223; [2007] 1 Cr. App. R. 3 (appeal against improper ruling of no case to answer); *R. v B* [2008] EWCA Crim 1997; [2009] 1 Cr. App. R. 19 (issue of separate trials where two of three accused were unfit to be tried).

An appeal under these provisions may be brought only with the leave of the judge who made the ruling.

Procedure is under CrimPR 38 and the general provisions of CrimPR 36.

Right of appeal

The prosecutor may (CJA 2003 s.58(2)) appeal in respect of a ruling made by the judge in relation to one or more offences included in the indictment at any time: **7-031**

(1) whether before or after the commencement of the trial;
(2) before the judge starts his summing-up; or
(3) would start his summing-up but for the making of an order under CJA 2003 Pt 7 (trial without a jury).

Note that:

(a) "ruling" here includes any decision, determination, direction, finding, notice, order, refusal, rejection or requirement; and
(b) the procedure covers the case both of a ruling which formally terminates a trial and a ruling which is in practice terminatory, since, in the absence of a right of appeal, the prosecutor would offer no further evidence.

The prosecutor may appeal under s.58 of the 2003 Act, a terminatory ruling in proceedings under s.4A of the Criminal Procedure (Insanity) Act 1964: *R. v Ahmed* [2021] EWCA Crim 927; [2022] Crim. L.R. 402.

A case management decision refusing to order an adjournment before trial or indeed at any time before the start of the summing-up may constitute a "terminatory" ruling against which a prosecutor may appeal (*R. v Clarke* [2007] EWCA Crim 2532; [2008] 1 Cr. App. R. 33).

Section 58 does not give the prosecutor a right of appeal from the dismissal of a charge or the quashing of a count in an indictment under the procedure provided by CDA 1998 s.51, Sch.3 para.2 (see SENDING FOR TRIAL) (*R. v Thompson* [2006] EWCA Crim 2849; [2007] 1 Cr. App. R. 15).

Although such rulings have come to be known as "terminatory", this expression does not appear in s.58, and there is no requirement that the prosecution case should be dealt a fatal blow by the ruling. What matters is the "acquittal agreement" (see 7-032), i.e. the critical condition that the prosecutor accepts that if the appeal fails, the accused must be acquitted. That is the price the prosecutor has to pay for bringing the appeal (*Prosecutor's Appeal (No.2 of 2008) R. v Y* [2008] EWCA Crim 10; [2008] 1 Cr. App. R. 34).

The judge's ruling has no effect whilst the prosecutor is able to take any steps under s.58(4), below.

Preconditions to appeal

The conditions precedent to the statutory right of appeal must be fulfilled if jurisdiction is to be conferred on the CACD. Both the prosecuting advocate and the judge need to be fully apprised of the provisions of the Act and the Rules concern- **7-032** ing terminating rulings, to avoid the sort of situation revealed in *R. v M* [2012] EWCA Crim 792; [2012] 2 Cr. App. R. 9.

Following the judge's ruling, the prosecuting advocate must (CJA 2003 s.58(4); CrimPR 38.2), if he is to appeal in respect of it:

(1) inform the judge, immediately after the ruling against which he wants to appeal, of his decision; or, alternatively
(2) immediately after the ruling, request an adjournment to consider whether he wants to appeal; and
(3) following that adjournment, if granted, inform the judge that he intends to appeal.

(CJA 2003 s.58(4))

The "ruling" which is referred to above is a formal ruling given in court (not an informal communication given by the judge by means of an email; *R. v F*, *The Times,* 19 June 2013). The prosecutor must also, at the time or before he informs the judge of his intention to appeal, undertake in open court that an acquittal will follow in respect of those offences that are the subject of the appeal, where either:

(a) he fails to obtain permission to appeal; or
(b) he abandons the appeal before it is determined by the CACD.

He must, under s.58(4), inform the court immediately after the ruling is given or after any period of adjournment allowed (*R. v Arnold* [2008] EWCA Crim 1084; [2008] 2 Cr. App. R. 37; see also *R. v N(T)* [2010] W.L.R. (D) 93; [2010] Crim. L.R. 411; also *Prosecutor's Appeal (No.2 of 2008) R. v Y* [2008] EWCA Crim 10; [2008] 1 Cr. App. R. 34). As to the interpretation of "immediately following the ruling", see *R. v M* [2012] EWCA Crim 792; [2012] 2 Cr. App. R. 9. See also *R. v Quillan* [2015] EWCA Crim 538; [2015] 2 Cr. App. R. 3 and *R. v C* [2017] EWCA Crim 2257; [2018] Crim. L.R. 564.

Either:

(i) an adjournment must be sought immediately; or
(ii) the decision to appeal and the acquittal agreement must be notified to the court immediately.

In any event, the acquittal agreement must be provided by, at latest, the time when a decision to intend to appeal is notified (*R. v M* [2012] EWCA Crim 792; [2012] 2 Cr. App. R. 9). As a general rule the judge should not require the prosecutor to decide there and then but should allow him until the next business day; see *R. v SA* [2019] EWCA Crim 144; [2020] 1 Cr. App. R. 5.

Where the ruling relates to two or more offences, any one or more of which may be the subject of an appeal, the prosecutor, when informing the judge that he intends to appeal, must, at the same time, inform him of the offence or offences which he seeks to make the subject of the appeal.

Where there is a ruling that there is no case to answer, the prosecutor may at the same time nominate one or more other rulings which relate to the offence(s) the subject of the appeal, and those other rulings will be treated as the subject of the appeal.

Application to trial judge preferred

7-033 Section 57 gives both the Crown Court judge and the CACD power to give permission to appeal, but applications should ordinarily be made to the trial judge.

A suspicion that the judge is likely to be hostile to the application is not a good reason for declining to make the application to him, nor is the belief that an application to the CACD is less likely to succeed if the trial judge refuses permission (*R. v F* [2009] EWCA Crim 1639).

In that case the CACD gave a number of reasons why it was good practice to first apply to the judge:

(1) the judge will be fully sighted of all the material factors regarding the issues involved so that the application would be likely to take very little time;
(2) he may already have concluded that the ruling raises issues fit for consideration by the CACD;
(3) the application involves the parties in no or minimal additional cost;
(4) he is involved in the process, since he may need to authorise an adjournment, and consider the question of expedition;
(5) the prosecutor is not disadvantaged if the application fails; he may still apply to the CACD;
(6) no harm is done if the prosecutor, having obtained permission, subsequently decides not to pursue the appeal; and
(7) application to the judge may accelerate the appeal process, enabling the trial to continue.

Application to the judge; permission to appeal

A prosecutor who wants the Crown Court judge to give permission to appeal must apply: **7-034**

(1) orally, with reasons, immediately after the ruling against which he wants to appeal; or
(2) in writing, and serve the application on the Crown Court officer and every accused directly affected by the ruling,

on the expiry of the time allowed under CrimPR 38.2 to decide whether to appeal.

The written application under (2) must include the same information (with any necessary adaptations) as an appeal notice, as to which see 7-016 (CrimPR 38.5(1)–(2)).

Except in the case of an appeal against a PII ruling (see DISCLOSURE), the judge must allow every accused directly affected by the ruling an opportunity to make representations (CrimPR 38.5(3); see also CrimPR 38.8(5)).

The general rule is that the judge should decide whether or not to give permission to appeal on the day that the application is made to him (CrimPR 38.5(4)), but he may adjourn for longer where there is a real reason for doing so (*R. v H* [2008] EWCA Crim 483).

Permission should be given only where the judge considers that there is a real prospect of success, not in an attempt to speed up the hearing of the appeal (*R. v Gilbert* [2006] EWCA Crim 3276).

Effect of ruling; continuation of proceedings

The judge's ruling effectively acquitting the accused, or otherwise terminating the trial, will not take effect in relation to the offence or offences which are the subject of the appeal whilst the appeal is pursued (CJA 2003 s.58(10)–(12)). **7-035**

The judge has no power to carry on regardless (*R. v SH* [2010] EWCA Crim

1931; [2011] 1 Cr. App. R. 14), because:

(1) any consequences of the ruling have no effect;
(2) the judge may not take any steps in consequence of it; and
(3) if he does, any such steps will be of no effect.

Where the trial involves more than one offence, or more than one accused, however, and the appeal does not apply to all the offences or all the accused, proceedings in respect of any offence which is not, or any accused who is not, the subject of an appeal may, at the discretion of the judge, be continued (*R. v SH* [2010] EWCA Crim 1931; [2011] 1 Cr. App. R. 14).

Any period during which proceedings for an offence are adjourned pending the determination of an appeal under Pt 9 is disregarded so far as the offence is concerned for the purposes of the overall time limit or the custody time limit (under POA 1985 s.22) which applies to the stage which the proceedings have reached when they are adjourned (CJA 2003 s.70).

CJA 2003 ss.71 and 72 provide for restrictions on reporting anything of the proceedings associated with the appeal until after the conclusion of the trial and create offences in respect of infringements of those restrictions. As of 28 June 2022, the wording of s.71 of the CJA 2003 was amended by replacing the word "hearing" in subss.(5)(a) and (6)(a) with the word "considering" (Judicial Review and Courts Act 2022 s.15(7)).

Expedited and non-expedited appeals

7-036 The Act places a mandatory obligation on the judge to consider the issue of expedition (CJA 2003 ss.59 and 60).

A decision has to be made (which in a long trial may have serious repercussions) whether:

(1) to await any decision of the CACD; or
(2) to abandon the trial with the risk that, if the appeal succeeds, the trial will have to start again (*R. v SH* [2010] EWCA Crim 1931; [2011] 1 Cr. App. R. 14).

At the time he informs the judge that he intends to seek leave to appeal against a ruling, the prosecutor must also make oral representations as to whether or not that appeal should be expedited under CJA 2003 s.59(1).

Before deciding whether or not the appeal should be expedited, the judge must allow every accused directly affected by the ruling an opportunity to make representations.

(CrimPR 38.6)

The court officer will provide a copy of the reasons given by the judge for his decision to the prosecutor, the accused and all interested parties.

Where the judge decides:

(a) to expedite the appeal, he may adjourn the trial;
(b) not to expedite the trial, he may either adjourn the trial or discharge the jury, if one has been sworn.

The judge may reverse his decision that the appeal should be expedited at any time before notice of appeal or application for leave to appeal is served on the Crown Court under CrimPR 38.6, providing reasons for that reversal in writing to the prosecutor, the accused and all interested parties.

A judge of the CACD may revoke the judge's decision to expedite an appeal.

Expedition does not impose time limits on the Registrar or the CACD. However, if leave has not been granted by the trial judge, the application may be referred to the full court by the Registrar to enable the application and appeal to be heard together to ensure that the matter is dealt with quickly (Guide C7).

Appeal to the CACD

Where permission is refused by the trial judge, application may be made to the CACD, where it may be granted by the single judge or by the court. 7-037

The prosecutor must serve an appeal notice on the Crown Court officer, the Registrar and every accused directly affected by the ruling against which he wants to appeal, not later than:

(1) the next business day (see 7-024) after telling the judge of the decision to appeal, if the judge expedites the appeal; or
(2) five business days after telling the judge of that decision, if the judge does not expedite the appeal.

(CrimPR 38.3)

This must include those matters set out in CrimPR 38.4(2), and in particular, include or attach any application (with reasons) for:

(a) permission to appeal, if the court's permission is needed;
(b) extension of time within which to serve the notice; or
(c) expedition of the appeal, or revocation of the judge's direction expediting the appeal,

and attaching any form of respondent's notice for an accused served with the appeal notice, who wants to complete one (see 7-038).

Respondent's notice

An accused on whom an appellant prosecutor serves an appeal notice may serve a respondent's notice, and must do so if: 7-038

(1) he wants to make representations to the CACD; or
(2) the CACD so directs.

(CrimPR 38.7(1))

He must serve his notice on the prosecutor, the Crown Court officer, the Registrar and any other accused on whom the prosecutor served the appeal notice, and he must serve the notice:

(a) not later than the next business day (see 7-024) after:
    (i) the prosecutor serves the appeal notice; or
    (ii) a direction to do so,
    if the Crown Court judge expedites the appeal; or
(b) not more than five business days after:
    (i) the prosecutor serves the appeal notice; or
    (ii) a direction to do so,
    if the Crown Court judge does not expedite the appeal.

(CrimPR 38.7(2)–(3))

The notice must state the matters set out in CrimPR 38.7(5). Any application for an extension of time within which to serve the notice, or a direction to attend in person any hearing that the respondent could attend by live link if the respondent is in custody, must be attached. Reasons must be specified.

Public Interest Immunity rulings (PII)

7-039 Where the prosecutor wants to appeal against a PII ruling, special provisions apply under CrimPR 38.8.

The prosecutor must not serve on any accused directly affected by the ruling:

(1) any written application to the Crown Court judge for permission to appeal; or
(2) an appeal notice,

if he thinks that to do so in effect would reveal something that he thinks ought not be disclosed, nor may he include in an appeal notice:

(a) the material that was the subject of the ruling; or
(b) any indication of what sort of material it is,

if he thinks that to do so would reveal something that he thinks ought not be disclosed.

In such cases he must serve on the Registrar with the appeal notice an Annex marked to show that its contents are only for the CACD and the Registrar, containing whatever he has omitted from the appeal notice, with reasons, and if relevant, explaining why he has not served the appeal notice.

In such cases CrimPR 38.5(3) and 38.6(2) (as to representations by the accused) do not apply.

E. Contempt cases

General

7-040 Appeal lies as of right to the CACD by any person dealt with by the Crown Court for contempt (AJA 1960 s.13). Most appeals concern persons wishing to appeal a sentence for failing to appear at the Crown Court which is treated as if it were a contempt. No leave to appeal is required; the appeal is as of right (*R. v Hourigan* [2003] EWCA Crim 2306; (2003) 147 S.J.L.B. 901).

Procedure is governed by CrimPR Pt 39 (see 7-011 and following). Proceedings are commenced by lodging an appeal notice at the Crown Court not more than 28 days after the order to be appealed. The Registrar may direct the service of a respondent's notice, or the prosecutor may serve one if he wishes to make representations to the CACD (Guide D5).

F. Appeals to the CACD under POCA 2002

1. Prosecutor's appeal regarding confiscation

Appeal by prosecutor

7-041 The prosecutor may appeal to the CACD where a judge of the Crown Court:

(1) makes a confiscation order under POCA 2002, in respect of the order; or
(2) decides not to make a confiscation order, against that decision, except in the case of an order or decision made by virtue of ss.10A (determination of extent of defendant's interest in property), 19, 20, 27 or 28 (reconsideration).

(POCA 2002 ss.31 and 32(1) and (4))

A decision to adjourn a confiscation application sine die is a decision under (2) above, and is subject to an appeal by the prosecutor (*R. v Hockey* [2007] EWCA Crim 1577; [2008] 1 Cr. App. R. (S.) 50). The amended provision gives the prosecutor a right of appeal from the judge's decision to stay confiscation proceedings as an abuse of process (*CPS (Durham) v N, CPS (Nottingham v P)* [2009] EWCA Crim 1573; [2010] Cr. App. R. (S.) 82).

In so far as the offender is concerned, a confiscation order is a "sentence" within CAA 1968 s.50(1) and appeal lies in the normal way under the ss.9 and 10. An order varying a confiscation order under POCA 2002 ss.21, 22 or 29 is also within CAA 1968 s.50, but not an order for variation under s.23 (*R. v Ward* [2010] EWCA Crim 1932; [2011] 1 W.L.R. 766).

The 2002 Act does not create a retrospective right for the prosecutor to appeal in respect of a decision under the 1988 Act (*R. v Moulden* [2008] EWCA Crim 2648; [2010] 1 Cr. App. R. 27).

Procedure is under CrimPR 42 (Guide D1–4). An appeal requires the leave of the CACD.

As to appeals to the CACD in respect of orders made by the Crown Court in relation to external requests or orders, see POCA 2002 (External Requests and Orders) Order 2005 (SI 2005/3181) Pt 2.

Prosecutor's notice of appeal

Where the prosecutor seeks to apply to the CACD for leave to appeal under POCA 2002 s.31, he must serve a notice of appeal on the Crown Court officer and on the accused within 28 days of the making of the ruling. Where an extension of time is required, reasons must be given (POCA 2002 (Appeals under Pt 2) Order 2003 (SI 2003/82)). **7-042**

The notice of appeal served upon the accused must be accompanied by a respondent's notice for him to complete and also a notice:

(1) informing him that the result of the appeal could be that the CACD would increase a confiscation order already imposed on him, make a confiscation order itself, or direct the Crown Court to hold a fresh hearing;
(2) informing him of his right under art.6 of the above order to be present at the hearing, even though he is in custody; and
(3) inviting him to serve notice on the Registrar if he wishes to apply for leave to be present, or to present any argument on the hearing of the application, and whether he wishes to present it in person or by means of a legal representative.

The notice must also draw to his attention CrimPR 42.4 (supply of documentary and other exhibits) and advise the accused to consult a solicitor as soon as possible.

The appellant must provide a Crown Court officer with a certificate of service stating that he has served the notice of appeal on the accused in accordance with the Rules, or explaining why he has been unable to effect service.

(CrimPR 42.11)

Respondent's notice

Where an accused is served with a notice of appeal under CrimPR 42.11 and wishes to oppose the application for leave to appeal, he must, not more than 10 busi- **7-043** ness days after the date on which he received the notice of appeal, serve on the Registrar and on the appellant a respondent's notice:

(1) stating the date on which he received the notice of appeal;
(2) summarising his response to the arguments of the appellant; and
(3) specifying any authorities which he intends to cite.

(CrimPR 42.12(1)–(2))

The time for giving notice may be extended by the Registrar, a single judge or by the CACD. If the Registrar refuses an extension of time, the accused is entitled to have his application determined by a single judge; if the single judge refuses the extension the accused is entitled to have his application determined by the court. (CrimPR 42.12(3)–(5))

Amendment and abandonment of appeal

7-044 The appellant may amend a notice of appeal served under CrimPR 42.11 or abandon an appeal under POCA 2002 s.31:

(1) without the leave of the CACD at any time before the hearing of the appeal has begun; or
(2) with the leave of the CACD after the hearing of the appeal has begun,

by serving notice in writing on the Registrar, and where the appellant abandons an appeal under (1) above he must send a copy of the notice to the accused, a court officer of the court of trial and the magistrates' court responsible for enforcing any confiscation order which the Crown Court has made (CrimPR 42.13(1)–(2)).

Where the appellant serves a notice amending a notice of appeal he must send a copy of it to the accused (CrimPR 42.13(3)).

Where an appeal is abandoned the application for leave to appeal or appeal will be treated, for the purposes of POCA 2002 s.85 (conclusion of proceedings), as having been refused or dismissed by the CACD (CrimPR 42.13(4)).

2. Appeals against determinations under POCA 2002 s.10A

7-045 POCA 2002 as amended by SCA 2015 confers a power on a judge of the Crown Court to determine the extent of an accused's interest in property for the purposes of confiscation proceedings (POCA 2002 s.10A; see CONFISCATION ORDERS). An appeal against such a determination lies to the CACD under POCA 2002 ss.31(4) and 32, at the instance of:

(1) the prosecutor; or
(2) any person who the CACD is satisfied is, or may be, a person holding an interest in the property, if that person was not given a reasonable opportunity to make representations when the determination was made; or if it appears to the CACD to be arguable that giving effect to the determination would result in a serious risk of injustice to that person.

An appeal will not lie where the CACD believes that an application under s.50 is to be made by the prosecutor for the appointment of a receiver, or where such an application has been made but has not yet been determined, or where a receiver has been appointed under s.50.

On an appeal under this provision the CACD will be able to confirm the determination, or make such order as it believes is appropriate.

3. Appeals against compliance orders under POCA 2002 s.13A

A judge making a confiscation order may make a "compliance order", which is such order as he believes is appropriate for the purpose of ensuring that that confiscation order is effective (POCA 2002 s.13A). If on an application under s.13A(3)(b) the Crown Court decides not to make a compliance order, the prosecutor can appeal to the CACD against the decision. If the judge decides to make an order, the prosecutor and any person affected by the order can appeal to the CACD in respect of that decision. **7-046**

On appeal under either provision the CACD can confirm the decision, or make such order as it believes is appropriate (POCA 2002 s.13B).

The relevant procedure is set out at CrimPR 42.14.

4. Appeals in relation to restraint orders

General

The accused has no right of appeal against the making of a restraint order. A person dissatisfied with the making of an order must apply to a judge of the Crown Court for its variation or discharge. See POCA 2002 s.43(1) and (2). **7-047**

Appeal does, however, lie to the CACD (Guide D3) by:

(1) the prosecutor or an accredited financial investigator from a refusal by the Crown Court to make an order, against that decision;

(2) the person who applied for an order, or any person affected by it, who applied to the Crown Court to vary or discharge it, against the judge's decision,

and the CACD may either confirm the order, or make such order as it believes appropriate.

The CACD's powers are wide enough to permit the court to suspend the effect of its final order pending a fresh application to the Crown Court (*Windsor v CPS* [2011] EWCA Crim 143; [2011] 2 Cr. App. R. 7).

Leave is required, and leave will be given only where the CACD considers that the appeal would have a real prospect of success or there is some other compelling reason why the appeal should be heard. An order giving leave may limit the issues to be heard and may be made subject to conditions (CrimPR 42.14).

As to procedure, see CrimPR 42.14–42.20 and 7-049.

As to appeals to the CACD in respect of orders made by the Crown Court in relation to external requests or orders, see POCA 2002 (External Requests and Orders) Order 2005 (SI 2005/3181) Pt 2.

Unless the CACD or the Crown Court orders otherwise, an appeal under s.43 will not operate as a stay of any order or decision of the Crown Court (CrimPR 42.18).

5. Appeals in relation to the appointment, etc. of receivers

Appeal lies to the CACD (Guide D4) where the Crown Court: **7-048**

(1) on an application for an order under any of ss.48–51, decides not to appoint a receiver, by the person who applied for the order, against that decision;

(2) appoints a receiver under any of ss.48–51, by the person who applied for the order or any person affected by it, against the decision;
(3) decides, on an application for an order under s.62, not to make a direction, by the person who applied for the order, against that decision;
(4) makes an order under s.62, giving directions to a receiver, by the person who applied for the order, any person affected by it and the receiver, in respect of the decision;
(5) decides, on an application under s.63, to vary or discharge a receivership order, by the person who applied for the order in respect of which the application was made, any person affected by the decision or the receiver, against the decision.

(POCA 2002 s.65)

Procedure is the same in each case, and the same as that in the case of an appeal under s.43, as to which see CrimPR 42.14–42.20 and 7-049.

On such an appeal the CACD may confirm the decision, or make such order as it believes is appropriate. See also the Proceeds of Crime Act 2002 (Appeals under Part 2) Order 2003 (SI 2003/82).

As to appeals to the CACD in respect of orders made by the Crown Court in relation to external requests or orders, see POCA 2002 (External Requests and Orders) Order 2005 (SI 2005/3181) Pt 2.

6. Procedure

Notice of appeal

7-049 Where a person wishes to apply to the CACD for leave to appeal under any of the provisions of POCA 2002 s.13B, s.43 or s.65 as set out above, he must serve a notice of appeal on the Crown Court officer (CrimPR 42.15).

Unless the Registrar, a single judge or the CACD directs otherwise, the applicant must serve the notice, accompanied by a respondent's notice for the respondent to complete as soon as practicable and in any event not later than five business days after the notice of appeal is served on the Crown Court, on:

(1) each respondent;
(2) any person who holds realisable property to which the appeal relates; and
(3) any other person affected by the appeal.

The documents which are to be served are set out in CrimPR 42.15(3). Where it is not possible to serve all of these documents the appellant must indicate which documents have not yet been served and the reasons why they are not currently available (CrimPR 42.15(4)).

The appellant must provide a Crown Court officer with a certificate of service stating that he has served the notice of appeal on each respondent in accordance with para.(2) and including full details of each respondent or explaining why he has been unable to effect service (CrimPR 42.15(5)).

An appeal may be abandoned without the leave of the CACD at any time *before* the CACD has begun hearing the appeal, or *with* its leave after the hearing of the appeal has begun, by serving notice in writing on the Registrar. The appellant must also serve copy of the notice to each respondent (CrimPR 42.17).

Respondent's notice

7-050 A respondent who wishes to ask the CACD to uphold the decision of the Crown Court for reasons different from or additional to those given by the Crown Court, must serve a respondent's notice on the Registrar.

The notice must be served on the Registrar not more than 10 business days after:

(1) the date the respondent is served with notification that the CACD has given the appellant leave to appeal; or
(2) the date the respondent is served with notification that the application for leave to appeal and the appeal itself are to be heard together.

Unless the Registrar, a single judge or the CACD directs otherwise, the respondent serving a respondent's notice must serve the notice on the appellant and any other respondent:

(a) as soon as practicable; and
(b) in any event not later than five business days after it is served on the Registrar.

(CrimPR 42.16)

G. References to the Court of Appeal by the Attorney General

1. On a point of law

7-051 Where a person tried on indictment has been acquitted (whether in respect of the whole or part of the indictment) the Attorney General may, if he desires the opinion of the CACD on a point of law which has arisen in the case, refer that point to the court for consideration and their opinion. In such a case, the court may hear argument:

(1) by, or by an advocate for, the Attorney General; and
(2) if the acquitted person desires to present argument, by an advocate on his behalf or, with leave, by the acquitted person himself.

If the CACD thinks fit, it may refer the matter to the Supreme Court.

The acquittal at the trial is not affected by the proceedings (CJA 1972 s.36). Furthermore the court must not allow anyone to identify the accused during the proceedings unless the accused gives permission (CrimPR 41.7).

2. Lenient sentences

General

7-052 Where it appears to the Attorney General that in the case of an offence:

(1) in which sentence is passed on a person for an offence triable only on indictment; or
(2) of a description specified in SI 2006/1116 as amended by SI 2012/1833 and SI 2014/1651 that:
    (a) the sentencing judge in a proceeding in the Crown Court has been unduly lenient; or
    (b) the trial judge has:
        (i) erred in law as to his powers of sentencing; or

(ii) failed to impose a mandatory sentence requirement listed in s.399(b) or (c) of the SA 2020,

the case may be referred to the CACD. The leave of that court is required (CJA 1988 ss.35(3), (9) and 36(1)).

Note that:

(a) "sentence" has the same meaning as in CAA 1968 save that it does not include an interim hospital order;
(b) "offence triable only on indictment" means an offence punishable only on conviction on indictment (CJA 1988 s.35(9)); and
(c) any two or more sentences are to be treated as passed in the same proceedings if they would be treated as such for the purposes of CAA 1968 s.10 (CJA 1988 s.36(3)).

A reference lies in respect of the specification of the minimum term in relation to a life sentence (*R. v Sullivan* [2004] EWCA Crim 1762; [2005] 1 Cr. App. R. 3).

As to certain transitional cases under CJA 2003, see SI 2007/1762.

Conduct of prosecutor

7-053 Where the prosecutor has been party to a bargain with the defence, or has acquiesced in a bargain between the court and the defence (see GOODYEAR INDICATION), it may be an abuse of process to refer a resulting sentence to the CACD, albeit that it was too lenient (e.g. *Attorney General's References (Nos 80 and 81 of 1999) (R. v Thompson)* [2000] 2 Cr. App. R. (S.) 138 CA; *Attorney General's Reference (No.44 of 2000) (R. v Peverret)* [2001] 1 Cr. App. R. 27 CA; *Attorney General's References (Nos 86 and 87 of 1999) (R. v Webb and Simpson)* [2001] 1 Cr. App. R. 141).

3. Procedure

The application

7-054 Where the Attorney General refers either a point of law under CJA 1972 s.36 or a sentencing case under CJA 1988 s.36, he must:

(1) serve on the Registrar and the defendant a notice of reference and any application for permission to refer a sentencing case; and
(2) with a notice of reference of point of law, give details of the offender affected, the date and place of the Crown Court decision and the verdict and sentence.

An application for permission to refer a sentencing case must be made within 28 days of the last of the sentences in that case. This deadline is prescribed by CJA 1988 Sch.3 para.1 and cannot be varied.

(CrimPR 41.2)

A notice of reference and application for permission to refer a sentencing case must be in the form set out in *CPD*. For details of the required contents of each document, see CrimPR 41.3.

Registrar's notice to accused/offender

7-055 The Registrar must serve on the accused the notice of reference and any application for permission to refer a sentencing case.

Where the Attorney refers a point of law he must notify the defendant that the outcome of the reference will not make any difference to the outcome of the trial and that the defendant may serve a respondent's notice.

Where the Attorney applies for permission to refer a sentencing case he must notify the defendant that the outcome of the reference may make a difference to that sentencing, and may result in a more severe sentence, and that the defendant may serve a respondent's notice.

(CrimPR 41.4)

Respondent's notice

An accused on whom the Registrar serves a reference or an application for permission to refer a sentencing case may serve a respondent's notice, and must do so if either he wants to make representations to the CACD, or if the CACD so directs. He must serve any respondent's notice on the Attorney-General and on the Registrar (CrimPR 41.4(1)–(2)). No particular form is prescribed. **7-056**

The respondent's notice must be served, where the Attorney General:

(1) refers a point of law, not more than 20 business days after either the Registrar serves the reference, or any direction to do so;
(2) applies for leave to refer a sentencing case, not more than 10 business days after the Registrar serves the application, or a direction to do so.

(CrimPR 41.4(3))

Where the Attorney General:

(a) refers a point of law, the respondent's notice must comply with CrimPR 41.4(4), including any application (with reasons) for an extension of time within which to serve his notice, leave to attend a hearing that he does not have a right to attend, or a direction to attend in person a hearing that the respondent could attend by live link, if he is in custody;
(b) applies for leave to refer a sentencing case, the respondent's notice must comply with CrimPR 41.4(5), including such applications as are mentioned in (a).

Variation/withdrawal of notice or application

Where the Attorney General wants to vary or withdraw a notice of reference or an application for permission to refer a sentencing case, he may vary or withdraw the notice or application without the leave of the CACD by serving notice on the Registrar and the accused before any hearing of the reference or application; but, at any such hearing, he may only vary or withdraw that notice or application with the court's leave (CrimPR 41.5). **7-057**

Right to attend hearing

A respondent who is in custody has a right to attend a hearing in public unless it is a hearing preliminary or incidental to a reference, including the hearing of an application for permission to refer a sentencing case. The court or the Registrar may direct that such a respondent is to attend a hearing by live link (CrimPR 41.6). **7-058**

Anonymity of accused on reference of point of law

7-059 Where the Attorney General refers a point of law, the CACD will not allow anyone to identify the accused during the proceedings unless the latter gives permission (CrimPR 41.7).

H. Appeal by way of case stated

7-060 Any order, judgment or other decision of the Crown Court, other than one relating to trial on indictment, may be questioned by any party to the proceedings, on the ground that it is:

(1) wrong in law; or
(2) in excess of jurisdiction,

by applying to the Crown Court to have a case stated by that court for the opinion of the High Court (SCA 1981 s.28).

The exclusion of matters relating to trial on indictment restricts this form of appeal to judgments and decisions of the Crown Court in its appellate jurisdiction. This section is concerned with its criminal jurisdiction and not its appellate jurisdiction in civil matters. The meaning of "relating to trial on indictment" is considered in detail at 7-067.

"Decision" means final decision; the High Court will not entertain an appeal unless the Crown Court has reached a final determination (*Loade v DPP* (1990) 90 Cr. App. R. 162; *Lycamobile Ltd v Waltham Forest LBC* [2014] EWHC 182 (Admin)).

Appeal by case stated or judicial review is not ordinarily an appropriate procedure for appealing against sentence (*Allen v West Yorkshire Probation Service* [2001] EWHC Admin 2; (2001) 165 J.P. 313).

On an appeal by way of case stated the court is concerned with the facts as stated "within the four corners of the case". There is no right to refer to other evidence, not stated in the case, without the agreement of the parties or on an application under SCA 1981 s.28A(2) to amend the case (*M v DPP* [2009] EWHC 752 (Admin); [2009] 2 Cr. App. R. 12).

Application to state a case

7-061 A party who wants the court to state a case for the opinion of the High Court must:

(1) apply in writing, not more than 21 days after the decision against which the applicant wants to appeal; and
(2) serve the application on the Crown Court officer and each other party,

specifying the decision in issue and the proposed question or questions of law or jurisdiction on which the opinion of the High Court will be asked, and indicating the proposed grounds of appeal.

Included or attached must also be any application for the following, with reasons:

(a) any extension of time within which to apply to state a case;
(b) bail pending appeal;
(c) the suspension of any driving disqualification imposed in the case, where the court can order such a suspension pending appeal.

A party wanting to make representations about the application must serve the representations on the Crown Court officer, and each other party, doing so not more than 10 business days after service of the application. The judge may determine the application without a hearing.

If the judge decides not to state a case, the court officer will serve on each party a notice of that decision, and the judge's written reasons for the decision, if not more than 15 business days later the applicant asks for those reasons.

(CrimPR 35.2)

Preparation of case stated

Where the judge decides to state a case for the opinion of the High Court, the Crown Court officer will serve on each party notice of the decision to state a case and any recognisance ordered by the court. **7-062**

Unless the judge otherwise directs, not more than 15 business days after the decision to state a case the applicant must serve a draft case on the Crown Court officer and each other party, specifying:

(1) the decision in issue;
(2) the question(s) of law or jurisdiction on which the opinion of the High Court will be asked;

and including a succinct summary of:

(a) the nature and history of the proceedings;
(b) the court's relevant findings of fact; and
(c) the relevant contentions of the parties.

If a question is whether there was sufficient evidence on which the court reasonably could reach a finding of fact, the draft must specify that finding, and include a summary of the evidence on which the court reached that finding, but except to that extent, the draft case must not include an account of the evidence received by the court.

A party who wants to make representations about the content of the draft case, or to propose a revised draft, must serve the representations or revised draft on the Crown Court officer and each other party, and do so not more than 15 business days after service of the draft case.

The court must state the case not more than 15 business days after the time for service of representations has expired.

The court officer will serve the case stated on each party.

(CrimPR 35.3)

For the procedure on appeal to the High Court, see Pt 52 of the Civil Procedure Rules 1998 and Practice Direction 52E.

Power to vary requirements

The court may shorten or extend (even after it has expired) a time limit under this part. A person who wants an extension of time must apply when serving the application, representations or draft case for which it is needed, and explain the delay. **7-063**

(CrimPR 35.5)

I. Judicial review

In relation to the jurisdiction of the Crown Court *other than its jurisdiction in relation to trial on indictment*, the High Court has jurisdiction to make: **7-064**

(1) a mandatory order to compel the Crown Court to exercise its proper jurisdiction;
(2) a prohibiting order, to restrain it from proceeding improperly; and
(3) a quashing order, to quash any order which has been made improperly.

(SCA 1981 s.29)

While judicial review provides a speedy and effective remedy in a proper case, it is a discretionary remedy (see *R. v Peterborough MC Ex p. Dowler* [1996] 2 Cr. App. R. 561; *R. v Hereford MC Ex p. Rowlands* [1997] 2 Cr. App. R. 340). Its ambit is restricted; in particular:

(1) the issue of these orders is reserved for simple and straightforward cases; the High Court will not attempt to resolve direct conflicts of evidence on material facts;
(2) the jurisdiction is confined essentially to matters of jurisdiction, thus the proper exercise of a discretion to admit or reject evidence in committal proceedings is not subject to control;
(3) the High Court will not permit the machinery of judicial review to be used as a means of appeal.

Application for permission

7-065 Procedure for judicial review is under CPR 1998 r.54. The permission of the High Court must be obtained before a claim for judicial review is made.

A claim is made by filing a claim form:

(1) promptly; and
(2) in any event not later than three months after the grounds to make the claim first arose (unless any other enactment specifies a shorter time limit), and this time limit may not be extended by agreement between the parties.

Where the decision of the Crown Court to dismiss an appeal is quashed, it is necessary for the case to be relisted before the Crown Court where it will be for a differently constituted court to determine the matter de novo (*R. v Leeds Crown Court Ex p. Barlow* [1989] R.T.R. 246).

Applications for judicial review are not usually an appropriate procedure for appealing against sentence (*Allen v West Yorkshire Probation Service* [2001] EWHC Admin 2; (2001) 165 J.P. 313).

Bail; RT disqualification; public funding

7-066 In relation to such proceedings, the Crown Court:

(1) may grant bail to a person who has applied for a quashing order, or who has applied for leave (so may the High Court);
(2) may not remove an RT disqualification pending the decision of the High Court (but the High Court may).

Jurisdiction; "relating to trial on indictment"

7-067 The meaning of the words "matters relating to trial on indictment" were considered by the House of Lords in *Re Smalley* [1985] A.C. 622; [1985] 80 Cr. App. R. 205 HL. It was held that these words included the "trial" of a person who pleads guilty on arraignment. Without offering a definition of a phrase which Parliament had chosen not to define, their Lordships held that the proper test was whether the relevant decision affected the conduct of a trial on indictment either in the course of a trial or pre-trial orders affecting the conduct of the trial. This guidance was considered by the House of Lords in *Re Ashton* [1994] 1 A.C. 9; [1993] 97 Cr. App. R. 203, and their Lordships declined to reconsider or depart from the guidance given therein.

The House of Lords further considered the position in *R. v Manchester Crown Court Ex p. DPP* [1994] 98 Cr. App. R. 461. Lord Browne-Wilkinson suggested (at 467) that a further helpful pointer might be to ask the question:

> "is the decision sought to be reviewed one arising in the issue between the Crown and the defendant formulated by the indictment (including the costs of such issue)? If the answer is 'yes', then to permit the decision to be challenged by judicial review may lead to delay in the trial: the matter is therefore probably excluded from review by the section. If the answer is 'no', the decision of the Crown Court is truly collateral to the indictment of the defendant and judicial review of that decision will not delay the trial: therefore, it may well not be excluded by the section."

The law as to what relates and does not relate to the Crown Court's jurisdiction on indictment has developed on a case by case basis within the parameters of the "pointers" expressed by the House of Lords. Some of the cases are not easily reconciled. In 2010 Law Com No.324 identified a number of cases that were shown:

(1) to have been held to relate to trial on indictment and therefore not reviewable, as:
- (a) a refusal to award an acquitted accused his costs out of central funds (*Re Meredith* (1973) 57 Cr. App. R. 451; *R. v Canterbury Crown Court Ex p. Regentford Ltd* [2000] All E.R. 2415; *R. v Harrow Crown Court Ex p. Perkins* (1998) 162 J.P. 527);
- (b) a refusal to award costs incurred as a result of an unnecessary or improper act or omission by, or on behalf of, another party to the proceedings (*R. (Commissioners for Customs and Excise) v Leicester Crown Court* [2001] EWHC Admin 33; *The Times,* 23 February 2001);
- (c) an order discharging a jury (*Ex p. Marlowe* [1973] Crim. L.R. 294);
- (d) an order in relation to the taking of steps to vet a jury panel (*R. v Sheffield Crown Court Ex p. Brownlow* (1980) 71 Cr. App. R. 19);
- (e) an order that an indictment lie on the file marked "not to be proceeded with without leave" (*Ex p. Raymond* (1986) 83 Cr. App. R. 94);
- (f) the judge's refusal to grant legal aid (*Ex p. Abodunrin* (1984) 79 Cr. App. R. 293);
- (g) the judge's decision to order a defence solicitor personally to pay the costs occasioned by the granting of a defence application for an adjournment (*Smith* [1974] 1 All E.R. 651 (see now Solicitors Act 1974 s.50(3));
- (h) a refusal to fix a date for trial until a certain event occurred, such as the trial of another matter (*Ex p. Ward* [1996] Crim. L.R. 123);
- (i) a decision to quash an indictment for want of jurisdiction to try an offence (*R. v Manchester Crown Court Ex p. DPP* (1994) 98 Cr. App. R. 461);
- (j) an order to stay criminal proceedings on the grounds of abuse of process (*Re Ashton* (1993) 97 Cr. App. R. 203 HL);

(k) the issue of a witness summons under CP(AW)A 1965 s.2(1) (*Ex p. Rees*, *The Times,* 7 May 1986);
(l) a decision pursuant to CP(AW)A 1965 s.4(3) to remand a witness in custody until such time as the court might appoint for receiving his evidence (*R. (on the application of TH) v Wood Green Crown Court* [2006] EWHC 2683 (Admin); [2007] Crim. L.R. 727);
(m) a refusal to grant a further extension of time in which to prefer a bill of indictment (*R. v Isleworth Crown Court Ex p. King* [1992] 1 WLUK 287; [1992] C.O.D. 298);
(n) a legal aid contribution order made at the conclusion of a trial (*Re Sampson* (1987) 84 Cr. App. R. 376);
(o) a decision not to dismiss a charge which had been sent for trial under CDA 1998 s.51 (*R. (on the application of Snelgrove) v Woolwich Crown Court* [2004] EWHC 2172 (Admin); [2005] 1 Cr. App. R. 18; *R. (on the application of O) v Central Criminal Court* [2006] EWHC 256 (Admin));
(p) a decision not to allow an individual to appear in person as prosecutor (*R. v Southwark Crown Court Ex p. Tawfick* [1995] Crim. L.R. 658);
(q) refusal of a representation order in the Crown Court for a confiscation hearing following the offender's conviction on indictment (*R. (on the application of Ludlam) v Leicester Crown Court* [2008] EWHC 2884 (Admin));
(r) failure to make a compensation order by reason of error of law (*R. (on the application of Faithfull) v Ipswich Crown Court* [2007] EWHC 2763 (Admin); [2008] 3 All E.R. 749);
(s) the designation of a local authority as the supervising authority in the course of sentencing (*R. (on the application of Kirklees MBC) v Preston Crown Court* [2001] EWHC Admin 510);
(t) an order in relation to bail once a trial on indictment has started (*R. (on the application of Uddin) v Leeds Crown Court* [2013] EWHC 2752 (Admin); [2014] 1 Cr. App. R. 13);

(2) to have been held *not* to relate to trial on indictment, which were therefore reviewable:
(a) an order for forfeiture of a surety's recognisance for bail where an accused failed to surrender to his trial at the Crown Court (*Re Smalley* (1985) 80 Cr. App. R. 205);
(b) a forfeiture order under MDA 1971 s.27 made against the owner of property who was not a defendant in the criminal proceedings (*R. v Maidstone Crown Court Ex p. Gill* (1987) 84 Cr. App. R. 96);
(c) an order committing an acquitted defendant to prison unless he agrees to be bound over (*R. v ILCC Ex p. Benjamin* (1987) 85 Cr. App. R. 267);
(d) following conviction, orders made under CYPA 1933 s.39 to protect the anonymity of a child who was an accused in the proceedings or an order discharging such an order (*R. v Manchester Crown Court Ex p. H* [2000] 1 Cr. App. R. 262);
(e) an order that an offender convicted on indictment whose legal representation was publicly funded should pay some or all of the costs of his representation (*R. v Patel* [2005] EWCA Crim 977);

(f) a bail decision "at an early stage of criminal proceedings" (*R. (on the application of M) v Isleworth Crown Court* [2005] EWHC 363 (Admin));
(g) a bail decision following conviction (*R. (on the application of Galliano) v Manchester Crown Court* [2005] EWHC 1125 (Admin); *R. (on the application of Groves) v Newcastle Crown Court* [2008] EWHC 3123 (Admin));
(h) a decision as to the manner in which the Crown Court deals with an application for bail (for example, whether or not to sit in public) (*R. (on the application of Malik) v Central Crown Court* [2006] EWHC 1539 (Admin); [2006] 4 All E.R. 1141);
(i) decisions and orders made following a finding of unfitness to plead (*R. v H, R. v M, R. v Kerr* [2001] EWCA Crim 2024; [2002] 1 Cr. App. R. 25; *R. v Grant* [2001] EWCA Crim 2611; [2002] 1 Cr. App. R. 38);
(j) a decision or order made without jurisdiction (*R. v Maidstone Crown Court, Ex p. Harrow LBC* [2000] 1 Cr. App. R. 117);
(k) the refusal of a judge to recuse himself on hearing a wasted costs application (*R. (on the application of AB) v X Crown Court* [2009] EWHC 1149 (Admin); [2010] Crim. L.R. 145);
(l) a third party application for a declaration (*R. (on the application of B) v Stafford Combined Court* [2006] EWHC 1645 (Admin); [2006] 2 Cr. App. R. 34);
(m) order imposing restrictions on reporting not a matter relating to trial on indictment where the trial had concluded (*R. (on the application of Wang Yam) v Central Criminal Court* [2014] EWHC 3558 (Admin); [2015] 1 Cr. App. R. 10);
(n) defendant's solicitors ordered to pay costs of third party which successfully resisted witness summons (*DLA Piper LLP v BDO LLP* [2013] EWHC 3970 (Admin); [2014] 1 W.L.R. 4425); and
(o) the making of an excepting direction under Youth Justice and Criminal Evidence Act 1999 s.45(5) (*R. v KL* [2021] EWCA Crim 200; [2021] 2 W.L.R. 1275).

Suspension of RT disqualification

Where a person ordered to be disqualified applies to the High Court for a quashing order to remove proceedings in the Crown Court, being proceedings in, or in consequence of which, he was convicted or his sentence was passed, or applies for leave to make such an application, the High Court may, if it thinks fit, suspend the disqualification on such terms as it thinks fit (RTOA 1988 s.40(1), (5)). **7-068**

Tainted acquittals

Under CPIA 1996 s.54 provision is made for a form of judicial review in a case where one person has been acquitted of an offence, and another person has been convicted of perverting the course of justice, intimidating witnesses, jurors, etc. under CJPOA 1994 s.51(1) or aiding, abetting, counselling, procuring, suborning or inciting the committing of an offence under s.1 of the Perjury Act 1911, involving interference or intimidation of a juror or a witness (or potential witness) in any proceedings which led to the acquittal. **7-069**

Where it appears to the court before which the person was convicted that there was a real possibility that, but for the interference or intimidation, the acquitted person would not have been acquitted, and that there is no doubt, because of lapse of time or any other reason, that it would not be contrary to the interests of justice to take proceedings against the acquitted person for the offence of which he was acquitted, the court must certify that fact (CPIA 1996 s.54(1), (2), (5)).

The prosecutor must apply in writing as soon as possible after conviction and serve the application on the court and on the acquitted defendant, if the court so directs. The application must give details of the conviction for interference or intimidation and details of the defendant's acquittal. It must explain why there is a real possibility that, but for the interference or intimidation, the defendant would not have been acquitted, and why it would not be contrary to the interests of justice to prosecute the defendant again, despite any lapse of time or other reason.

The judge may extend the time limit. He may allow an application to be made in a different form from that set out in *CPD* or to be made orally. He may determine the application at a hearing in private or in public, or without a hearing.

(CrimPR 27.2)

Where a court so certifies, it will be possible to make an application to the High Court for an order quashing the acquittal, and if such an order is made, it will be possible to take proceedings against the acquitted person for the offence of which he was acquitted (CPIA 1996 s.54(3) and (4)).

For the relevant procedure, see CrimPR 27.4–27.5.

The High Court will not be empowered to make such an order unless four conditions are fulfilled. The conditions are:

(1) it appears likely that, but for the interference or intimidation, the acquitted person would not have been acquitted;
(2) it does not appear that, because of lapse of time or for any other reason, it would be contrary to the interests of justice to take proceedings against the acquitted person for the offence of which he was acquitted;
(3) it appears to the court that the acquitted person has been given a reasonable opportunity to make written representations to the court;
(4) it appears that the conviction for the administration of justice offence will stand.

(CPIA 1996 s.55(1)–(4))

In applying the fourth condition the court will take into account all information before it but ignore the possibility of new factors coming to light. The fourth condition has the effect that the court will not make an order if (for instance) it appears that any time allowed for giving notice of appeal has not expired or that an appeal is pending.

(CPIA 1996 s.55(5)–(6))

Where an order is made quashing an acquittal and it is proposed to take proceedings against the acquitted person, any time limits within which, by statute, a prosecution must be commenced will run from the making of the order (CPIA 1996 s.56).

Powers of High Court to vary sentence

7-070 Where a person who has been sentenced for an offence by the Crown Court:

(1) after being convicted of an offence by a magistrates' court and committed for sentence; or

(2) on appeal against conviction or sentence,

applies to the High Court for a quashing order, then if the High Court determines that the Crown Court had no power to pass that sentence it may, instead of quashing the conviction, amend it by substituting any sentence which the magistrates' court in a case under (2) or the Crown Court in a case under (1) above, had power to impose.

(SCA 1981 s.43)

The High Court will, in an exceptional case, quash a sentence imposed by the Crown Court:

(a) where it is plainly demonstrated that in the process of sentencing an error of law has been perpetrated (*R. v Liverpool CC Ex p. Baird* (1985) 7 Cr. App. R. (S.) 437);
(b) which is harsh and oppressive and so far outside the normal sentence imposed for the offence as necessarily to involve an error of law (*R. v St Albans CC Ex p. Cinnamond* [1980] 2 Cr. App. R. (S.) 235; cf. *R. v Croydon CC Ex p. Miller* (1987) 85 Cr. App. R. 152; *R. (on the application of Sogbesan) v Inner London Crown Court* [2002] EWHC 1581 (Admin); [2003] 1 Cr. App. R. (S.) 79);
(c) which is irrational and truly astonishing (*R. v Acton Crown Court Ex p. Bewley* (1988) 10 Cr. App. R. (S.) 105; *R. v Chelmsford Crown Court Ex p. Birchall* (1989) 11 Cr. App. R. (S.) 510); and
(d) where the sentence imposed is "outside the broad area of the lower court's jurisdiction" [sic]: (*R. v Truro Crown Court Ex p. Adair* [1997] C.O.D. 296 DC; *R. v Southwark Crown Court Ex p. Smith* [2001] 2 Cr. App. R. (S.) 35).

Such sentence begins to run, unless the High Court directs otherwise, from the time when it would have started to run if passed in those proceedings, disregarding any time during which the offender was released on bail pending his application.

Where, on judicial review, the decision of the Crown Court to dismiss an appeal is quashed, it is necessary for the case to be relisted before the Crown Court, where it will be for a differently constituted court to determine the matter *de novo* (*R. v Leeds Crown Court Ex p. Barlow* [1989] R.T.R. 246).

J. Criminal Cases Review Commission

The Criminal Cases Review Commission, set up by CAA 1995 s.8, may refer to the CACD the conviction or sentence (not being one fixed by law) of a person convicted on indictment, a verdict of not guilty by reason of insanity and a finding of disability, where a finding that he did the act or made the omission was returned (CAA 1995 s.9; DVA 2004 s.58(1), Sch.10 para.31). Its powers and functions are reviewed in *R. v Criminal Cases Review Commission Ex p. Pearson* [2000] 1 Cr. App. R. 141 and *R. (on the application of Director of Revenue and Customs Prosecutions) v Criminal Cases Review Commission* [2006] EWHC 3064 (Admin); [2007] 1 Cr. App. R. 30. CAA 1995 s.14, as amended by CJA 2003 s.31, contains further provisions relating to such references. **7-071**

Powers of the CACD to order investigation

On an appeal against conviction, or an application for leave to appeal against conviction, the CACD (not a single judge) may direct the Commission to investigate and report on any matter if it appears that: **7-072**

(1) in the case of an appeal, the matter is relevant to the determination of the appeal, and ought, if possible, to be resolved before the appeal is determined;
(2) in the case of an application for leave to appeal, the matter is relevant to the determination of the application and ought, if possible, to be resolved before the application is determined;
(3) an investigation of the matter is likely to result in the CACD being able to resolve it; and
(4) the matter cannot be resolved by the CACD without an investigation by the Commission.

In due course the parties will be informed of the results, and the report and any statements, opinions and reports will be made available to them.
(CAA 1968 s.23A)

8. APPELLATE JURISDICTION

QUICK GUIDE

1. INTRODUCTION

The Crown Court exercises all appellate and other jurisdiction conferred on it by order under the provisions of the SCA 1981 or exercisable by it immediately before the commencement of that Act (SCA 1981 s.45(1)). CA 1971 s.8 Sch.1 vested in the Crown Court all jurisdiction formerly conferred on courts of quarter session or any committee of the same. Rights of appeal to the Crown Court are governed by MCA 1980 ss.108–110 and CrimPR 34. **8-001**

2. RIGHTS OF APPEAL

General

A general right of appeal to the Crown Court is given by MCA 1980 s.108(1) to a person convicted in a magistrates' court where he pleaded: **8-002**

(1) guilty, against his sentence; or
(2) not guilty, against his conviction and sentence.

Subject to the rare exceptional case (see 8-022), a plea of guilty in the magistrates' court is a bar to an appeal against conviction to the Crown Court (*R. v Birmingham Crown Court Ex p. Sharma* [1988] Crim. L.R. 741).

"Sentence" includes any "order made on conviction" by a magistrates' court except an order:

(a) for the payment of costs; or
(b) made in pursuance of an enactment under which the court has no discretion as to the making of the order or its terms,

and also includes a declaration of relevance under FSA 1989.

An invalid sentence does not nullify the conviction on which it is based, which remains a "conviction" entitling the Crown Court to entertain an appeal (*R. v Birmingham Justices Ex p. Wyatt* (1975) 61 Cr. App. R. 306).

"Orders made on conviction"

An "order made on conviction" is an order made as a consequence of the conviction for the particular offence. In consequence the following do not qualify: **8-003**

(1) an order which does not depend upon the fact of conviction (*R. v Hayden* (1975) 60 Cr. App. R. 304—a legal aid contribution order);
(2) an order sending a case to the Crown Court for trial (see *R. v London Sessions Appeals Committee Ex p. Beaumont* [1951] 1 K.B. 557); or

(3) an order committing an accused to the Crown Court for sentence under PCC(S)A 2000 s.3.

By statute the following may be appealed:

(a) a recommendation for deportation (which is treated as a "sentence") (IA 1971 s.6(5)(a));
(b) a guardianship or hospital order (MHA 1983 s.70);
(c) disqualification from driving under RTOA 1988 s.34 or s.35.

MCA 1980 s.108(3)(d) does not prevent an appeal to the Crown Court against a surcharge imposed under SA 2020 s.4 (see SURCHARGES) (MCA 1980 s.108(4)): *R. v Stone* [2013] EWCA Crim 723.

Other specific cases

8-004

Enactment	Appellant/subject of appeal	Notes
ABOOA 1956 s.1(1)	Person ordered, under JPA 1968 or otherwise, to enter into a recognisance, with or without sureties, to keep the peace or to be of good behaviour.	
ASBA 2014 s.15	Decision of youth court made under ASBA 2014 Pt I (Injunctions).	
B(A)A 1993 s.1	Prosecutor against the grant of bail to person charged with, or convicted of, offence punishable with imprisonment.	
CDA 1998 s.4(1) and (2)	Against the making of an ASBO or an ISO.	Repeal of s.4 by ASBA 2014 does not apply to an order made in proceedings begun before commencement (ASBA 2014 s.33).
CDA 1998 s.10(1)	Against the making of a parenting order under CDA 1998 s.8(1)(b).	A person in respect of whom an order is made under CDA 1998 s.8(1)(c) or 8A has rights of appeal under s.10(4).
CDA 1998 s.13D	Parent or guardian against the making of a parental compensation order under CDA 1998 s.13A in respect of activity by a child.	
SA 2020 Sch.10 para.14	Offender sentenced for the breach of a requirement of a community order.	

Enactment	Appellant/subject of appeal	Notes
CorJA 2009 s.79	Applicant where JP refuses application for investigation anonymity order.	
EA 2002 s.141F	Party or other person (with leave of the Crown Court) against the making or refusal to make an order lifting restrictions in relation to reporting allegations against teacher by pupil.	
FSA 1989 s.22(7)	Person aggrieved by making of a football banning order under FSA 1989 s.22.	
MCA 1980 s.108(2)	Offender sentenced for an offence in respect of which conditional discharge previously made.	
MCA 1980 s.108(3)	An offender against a declaration of relevance under FSA 1989 s.23.	A banning order made on conviction of a relevant offence will be quashed if the making of the declaration of relevance is reversed (FSA 1989 s.23(4)).
MHA 1983 s.45(1) (2)	Accused, or the parent or guardian of a juvenile, on the making of a hospital or guardianship order under s.37(3) without proceeding to conviction.	Same right of appeal as if made on conviction.
SA 2020 Sch.4 para.8	A juvenile offender dealt with for an offence on the revocation of a referral order made under SA 2020 ss.83–90.	
PCC(S)A 2000 s.61, Sch.5 paras.2(6), 4(4)	Juvenile sentenced in respect of breach of attendance centre order, or rules of centre.	
PCC(S)A 2000 s.137(6)	Parent or guardian ordered to pay the fine, compensation or costs of juvenile offender.	As to "parent or guardian" including a local authority, see s.137(8).
SA 2020 s.380	Parent or guardian ordered under SA 2020 s.380 to enter into a recognisance to ensure payment of outstanding sums owed by juvenile offender.	

Enactment	Appellant/subject of appeal	Notes
SA 2020 s.377	Parent or guardian ordered under SA 2020 s.376 to enter into recognisances to take proper care of, and exercise proper control over, relevant minor.	
POA 1985 s.22(7)	The accused against the extension, or further extension, of a custody or overall time limit, or the giving of a direction under POA 1985 s.22(6A).	See CrimPR 14.19 as to procedure.
POA 1985 s.22(8)	The prosecutor against the refusal to extend, or further extension, of a custody or overall time limit, or the giving of a direction under POA 1985 s.22(6A).	See CrimPR 14.19 as to procedure.
POCA 2002 s.299	Against the seizure or forfeiture of cash under POCA 2002 s.298.	
Policing and Crime Act 2009 s.46B	Appeal against decision of youth court in relation to gang-related injunctions.	CCA 2013 Sch.12.
PSIA 2001 s.11(4)	Individual or the Security Industry Authority against the refusal or the grant of a licence under the Private Security Industry Act 2001.	
SI 2004/2408 reg.7	Person against whom a third party costs order is made under POA 1985 s.19B.	
SOA 2003 s.101	Person in whose case a notification order has been made under SOA 2003 s.97, or an interim order under SOA 2003 s.100.	
SOA 2003 s.103H	Person against whom a sexual harm prevention order has been made under s.103A, or an interim order under s.103F or an order under s.103E making or refusing to make a variation, renewal or discharge.	
SOA 2003 s.110	Person against whom a sexual offences prevention order (SOPO) under SOA s.104, or	Repeal of s.110 by ASBA 2014 does not apply to an order made

Enactment	Appellant/subject of appeal	Notes
	an interim order under SOA s.109.	in proceedings begun before commencement (ASBA 2014 s.33).
SOA 2003 s.119	Person against whom a foreign travel order under SOA s.114 has been made or an order making or refusing to make an order under SOA s.118.	
SOA 2003 s.122G	Against the making of a sexual risk order under s.122A, an interim order, under s.122E or an order under s.122D, making or refusing to make a variation, renewal or discharge.	
SOA 2003 s.127	Person against whom a risk of sexual harm order (RSHO) under SOA s.123 has been made, or an interim order under SOA s.126.	Repeal of s.127 by ASBA 2014 does not apply to an order made in proceedings begun before commencement (ASBA 2014 s.33).
SOCPA 2005	Against the making of a financial reporting order under SOCPA 2005 s.76.	Repeal by SCA 2015 s.50 does not apply to an order made in proceedings before commencement (SCA 2015 s.86).
VCRA 2006 s.10(1)	Against the making of a drinking banning order under ss.3 or 6.	Repeal of s.10 by ASBA 2014 does not apply to an order made in proceedings begun before commencement (ASBA 2014 s.33).
YJCEA 1999 s.44(11)	Any party to the proceedings on the application, and "any other person", against an order making, or dispensing with or refusing to dispense with reporting restrictions in the case of a juvenile.	"Any other person" only with leave of the Crown Court.

Contempt of court

The effect of MCA 1980 s.108, combined with the CCA 1981 s.12(5), seems to give a right of appeal to a person sentenced in a magistrates' court for contempt against the sentence imposed and against the finding (*Haw v Westminster MC* [2007] EWHC 2960 (Admin); [2008] 2 All E.R. 326). **8-005**

The unsuccessful prosecutor

8-006 An unsuccessful prosecutor:

(1) has no right of appeal to the Crown Court against the dismissal of an information or an acquittal in the magistrates' court, unless conferred by statute, e.g. Commissioners for Revenue & Customs under CEMA 1979 s.147(2);

(2) has, by statute, a right of appeal to the Crown Court:
  - (a) against the refusal to extend, or further extend, the overall custody time limits, or a refusal to give a direction under POA 1985 s.22 (and see CUSTODY TIME LIMITS); and
  - (b) against the grant of bail, where B(A)A 1993 applies (see BAIL) (B(A)A 1993 s.1).

Reference by CCRC

8-007 Where a person has been convicted of an offence by a magistrates' court the Commission may refer to the Crown Court:

(1) the conviction; and
(2) (whether or not it refers the conviction), any sentence imposed on, or in subsequent proceedings relating to, the conviction.

(CAA 1995 s.11)

A reference of the:

(a) conviction is treated for all purposes as an appeal by the offender under MCA 1980 s.108(1) (whether or not he pleaded guilty); and
(b) sentence is treated for all purposes as an appeal by the offender under MCA 1980 s.108(1) against the sentence, and any other sentence imposed on, or in subsequent proceedings relating to, the conviction or to any related conviction.

On a reference of this nature, whether of the conviction or sentence, the Crown Court may not award any punishment more severe than that awarded by the court whose decision is referred.

3. Procedure on application

Application of CrimPR 34

8-008 CrimPR 34 applies where:

(1) a defendant wants to appeal under:
  - (a) MCA 1980 s.108 (general right of appeal);
  - (b) MHA 1983 s.45 (hospital or guardianship order made without convicting);
  - (c) SA 2020 Sch.5 para.10, Sch.7 paras 6(11) or 21(6), Sch.10 paras 10(11), 14(8), 23(6);
  - (d) CTA 2008 s.42 (finding of terrorist connection).

(2) the CCRC refers an accused's case to the Crown Court under CCA 1995 s.11;

(3) a prosecutor wants to appeal under:

(a) FSA 1989 s.14A(5A) (failure to make football banning order); and
(b) CEMA 1979 s.147(3) (any decision in proceedings for an offence under the Customs and Excise Acts).

(4) a person wants to appeal under:
(a) ABOOA 1965 s.1 (binding over order);
(b) CCA 1981 s.12(5) (detention for contempt of court, etc.);
(c) GR 1986 regs 3C (wasted costs order) or 3H (third party costs order);
(d) FSA 1989 s.22 (football banning order);
(e) CDA 1998 s.10(4) or 10(5) (parenting order);
(f) Offensive Weapons Act 2019 s.28(5)(b); or
(g) SA 2020 s.366(9).

Note that the Crown Court may, under CrimPR 34.10:

(1) shorten or extend (even after it has expired) a time limit;
(2) allow an appellant to vary an appeal notice that he has served;
(3) direct that an appeal notice be served on any person;
(4) allow an appeal notice or a notice of abandonment to be in a different form to one set out in *CPD* 2015, or to be presented orally.

Service of appeal notice and respondent's notice

An appellant must serve an appeal notice on: **8-009**

(1) the magistrates' court office; and
(2) every other party.

He must serve the appeal notice:

(a) as soon after the decision appealed against as he wants; but
(b) not more than 15 business days after:
  (i) sentence, or the date sentence is deferred, whichever is earlier, if the appeal is against conviction or against a finding of guilt;
  (ii) sentence, if the appeal is against sentence; or
  (iii) the order or failure to make an order about which the appellant wants to appeal, in any other case.

The appellant must serve with the appeal notice any application for:

(i) an extension of time if the appeal notice is late;
(ii) bail pending appeal, if the appellant is in custody; and
(iii) the suspension of any disqualification imposed or order made, where the magistrates court or the Crown Court can order such a suspension pending appeal.

Where both the magistrates court and the Crown Court can grant bail or suspend a disqualification or order pending appeal, an application must indicate by which court the appellant wants the application to be determined.

Where the appeal is against conviction or against a finding of guilt, unless the respondent agrees that the court should follow the appeal, the respondent must serve a respondent's notice on the Crown Court officer and the appellant not more than 15 business days after the service of the appeal notice.

(CrimPR 34.2)

The applicant has no right to an oral hearing in relation to an application for extension of time, though in a rare case the judge may, in his discretion, grant one

(*R. v Croydon Crown Court Ex p. Smith* (1983) 77 Cr. App. R. 277). The judge need give no reasons for his decision; he may grant an extension in respect of sentence only, if that is appropriate.

If the judge grants an extension, notice will be given to the parties and to the magistrates' court, see 8-017.

Form of appeal notice and respondent's notice

8-010 The appeal notice must:

(1) specify:
   (a) the conviction or finding of guilt;
   (b) the sentence; or
   (c) the order, or the failure to make an order,
   about which the appellant wants to appeal;
(2) summarise the issues;
(3) in an appeal against conviction or against a finding of guilt, to the best of the appellant's ability and to assist the court in fulfilling its duty under rule 3.2 (the court's duty of case management):
   (a) identify the witnesses who gave oral evidence in the magistrates' court;
   (b) identify the witnesses who gave written evidence in the magistrates' court;
   (c) identify the prosecution witnesses whom the appellant will want to question if they are called to give oral evidence in the Crown Court;
   (d) identify the likely defence witnesses;
   (e) give notice of any special arrangements or other measures that the appellant thinks are needed for witnesses;
   (f) explain whether the issues in the Crown Court differ from the issues in the magistrates' court, and if so how; and
   (g) say how long the trial lasted in the magistrates' court and how long the appeal is likely to last in the Crown Court;
(4) in an appeal against a sentence, order or failure to make an order:
   (a) identify any circumstances, report or other information of which the appellant wants the court to take account; and
   (b) explain the significance of those circumstances or that information to what is in issue;
(5) in an appeal against a finding that the appellant insulted someone or interrupted proceedings in the magistrates' court, attach:
   (a) the magistrates' court's written findings of fact; and
   (b) the appellant's response to those findings;
(6) say whether the appellant has asked the magistrates' court to reconsider the case; and
(7) include a list of those on whom the appellant has served the appeal notice.

A respondent's notice must:

(1) give the date on which the respondent was served with the appeal notice; and
(2) to assist the court in fulfilling its duty under rule 3.2:
   (a) identify the witnesses who gave oral evidence in the magistrates' court;
   (b) identify the witnesses who gave written evidence in the magistrates' court;

(c) identify the prosecution witnesses whom the respondent intends to call to give oral evidence in the Crown Court;
(d) give notice of any special arrangements or other measures that the respondent thinks are needed for witnesses;
(e) explain whether the issues in the Crown Court differ from the issues in the magistrates' court, and if so how; and
(f) say how long the trial lasted in the magistrates' court and how long the appeal is likely to last in the Crown Court.

If a party wants to reintroduce bad character evidence, hearsay evidence (etc.) or to renew an application for a witness summons, special measures (etc.) in the Crown Court, that party must include a notice to that effect in the appeal or respondent's notice, as the case may be.
(CrimPR 34.3)

Documents and exhibits

The magistrates' court officer must: **8-011**

(1) arrange for the magistrates' court to hear as soon as practicable any application to that court under rule 34.2(3)(c) (suspension of disqualification or order pending appeal); and
(2) as soon as practicable notify the Crown Court officer of the service of the appeal notice and make available to that officer:
  (a) the appeal notice and any accompanying application served by the appellant;
  (b) details of the parties including their addresses; and
  (c) a copy of each magistrates' court register entry relating to the decision under appeal and to any application for bail, or for the suspension of a disqualification or order pending appeal.
(3) Where the appeal is against conviction or against a finding of guilt, make available to the Crown Court officer as soon as practicable:
  (a) all material served on the magistrate's court officer to which applies:
    (i) Part 8 (Initial details of the prosecution case);
    (ii) Part 16 (Written witness statements);
    (iii) Part 17 (Witness summonses, warrants and orders);
    (iv) Part 18 (Measures to assist a witness or defendant to give evidence);
    (v) Part 19 (Expert evidence);
    (vi) Part 20 (Hearsay evidence);
    (vii) Part 21 (Evidence of bad character);
    (viii) Part 22 (Evidence of a complainant's previous sexual behaviour);
    (ix) Part 23 (Restriction on cross-examination by a defendant).
(4) Where the appeal is against sentence, make available to the Crown Court officer as soon as practicable any report received for the purposes of sentencing.
(5) Unless the magistrates' court otherwise directs:
  (a) must keep any document or object exhibited in the proceedings in the magistrates' court, or arrange for it to be kept by some other appropriate person, until at least:
    (i) 6 weeks after the conclusion of those proceedings; or

(ii) the conclusion of any proceedings in the Crown Court that begin within that 6 weeks; but

(b) need not keep such a document if:

(i) the document that was exhibited is a copy of a document retained by the party who produced it; and

(ii) what was in evidence in the magistrates' court was the content of that document.

(CrimPR 34.4)

Reference by CCRC

8-012 A reference by the CCRC must be served as soon as practicable by the Crown Court officer, on:

(1) the appellant;
(2) every other party; and
(3) the magistrates' court officer,

and the appellant may serve an appeal notice on the Crown Court officer and every other party not more than 15 business days later.

If the appellant does not serve an appeal notice, the Crown Court will treat the reference as the appeal notice.

(CrimPR 34.6)

Bail

8-013 A judge of the Crown Court may grant bail:

(1) to a person giving notice of appeal (as may the magistrates' court); and
(2) to a person whose conviction or sentence is referred to it by the CCRC.

The judge may alternatively find it expedient, following the practice of the CACD, to expedite the appeal hearing instead of granting bail (SCA 1981 s.81(1)(b)).

Any time during which such a person is released on bail does not count towards sentence.

Suspension of RT disqualification

8-014 If a person convicted of an offence and disqualified from holding or obtaining a driving licence appeals to the Crown Court, either:

(1) the magistrates' court; or
(2) the Crown Court,

may suspend the disqualification pending the appeal, on such terms as the court thinks fit (RTOA 1988 ss.39 and 40).

See also CrimPR 34.2(4) (8-009)

Interim hospital order

8-015 The fact that an appeal to the Crown Court is pending does not affect the power of the magistrates' court which has made an interim hospital order to:

(1) renew or terminate the order; or

(2) deal with the accused on its termination.

(SCA 1981 s.48(7))

Case management

In preparation for an appeal: **8-016**

(1) The Crown Court may conduct a preparation for appeal hearing (and if necessary more than one such hearing) where:
  (a) it is necessary to conduct such a hearing in order to give directions for the effective determination of the appeal; or
  (b) such a hearing is required to set ground rules for the conduct of the questioning of a witness or appellant.
(2) Where under rule 34.3(4) a party gives notice to reintroduce material or to renew an application first introduced or made in the magistrates' court:
  (a) no other notice or application to the same effect otherwise required by these Rules need be served; and
  (b) any objection served by the other party in the magistrates' court is treated as renewed unless within 15 business days that party serves notice withdrawing it.
(3) Where:
  (a) the appeal is against conviction or against a finding of guilt;
  (b) a party wants to introduce material or make an application under a Part of these Rules listed in rule 34.3(3); and
  (c) that party gives no notice of reintroduction or renewal under rule 34.3(4) (whether because the conditions for giving such a notice are not met or for any other reason), then such a party must serve the material, notice or application required by that Part not more than 15 business days after service of the appeal notice.

(CrimPR 34.7)

4. Hearings and decision

Public hearings; notice

The Crown Court must, as a general rule, hear any appeal or reference to which CrimPR 34 applies (see 8-009) in public, but: **8-017**

(1) may order any hearing to be in private; and
(2) where a hearing is about a public interest ruling, must hold the hearing in private.

The Crown Court officer will:

(a) give as much notice as is reasonably practicable of every hearing to the parties, any party's custodian and any other person whom the Crown Court requires to be notified;
(b) serve every decision on the parties, or on any other person whom the Crown Court requires to be served; and, where the decision determines an appeal, on the magistrates' court officer and the party's custodian, save that where a hearing or decision is about a public interest ruling, he will not give notice

of that hearing, or serve that decision, on anyone other than the prosecutor who applied for that ruling unless the court otherwise directs.

(CrimPR 34.8)

Where there is both an appeal against conviction and also a committal for sentence the Crown Court officer should ensure that the appellant/offender is informed of both hearings in one document: *R. (on the application of Bromley) v Secretary of State for Justice* [2010] EWHC 112 (Admin); [2010] A.C.D. 43.

Non-appearance

8-018 If the appellant fails to appear one of several courses may be adopted:

(1) if neither the appellant nor his advocate appears, and notice of hearing is proved, the appeal should not be treated as impliedly abandoned (*R. (on the application of Hayes) v Chelmsford Crown Court* [2003] EWHC 73 (Admin); [2003] Crim. L.R. 400);
(2) if an advocate appears on his behalf, the appeal may go on (*R. v Croydon Crown Court Ex p. Clair* (1986) 83 Cr. App. R. 202);
(3) if notice of appeal has been given, has not been withdrawn and no application to abandon is made, the appeal should be heard in the appellant's absence (*R. v Guildford Crown Court Ex p. Brewer* (1988) 87 Cr. App. R. 265).

The judge should not take it upon himself to conduct the respondent's case where an advocate fails to appear (*R. v Wood Green Crown Court Ex p. Taylor* [1995] Crim. L.R. 879). If the respondent does not appear, either personally or by advocate, and service of the notice, etc. is proved, any conviction or sentence appealed may be quashed (*R. v Croydon Crown Court Ex p. Clair* (1986) 83 Cr. App. R. 202), but before taking such a step, the judge ought to consider the position of any victim who may be deprived of compensation (*R. (on the application of Crown Prosecutor Service) v Portsmouth Crown Court* [2003] EWHC 1079 (Admin); [2004] Crim. L.R. 224).

Abandoning an appeal; bail; costs

8-019 An appellant:

(1) may abandon an appeal without the Crown Court's permission by serving a notice of abandonment on:
   (a) the magistrates' court officer;
   (b) the Crown Court officer; and
   (c) every other party before the hearing of the appeal begins;
(2) may only abandon the appeal after the hearing begins with the Crown Court's permission.

A notice of abandonment must be signed by or on behalf of the appellant.
(CrimPR 34.9)
Note that:

(i) where an appellant is allowed to abandon an appeal, the court has no power to increase the sentence (*R. v Gloucester Crown Court Ex p. Betteridge* [1998] Crim. L.R. 218); the judge has a discretion whether to make an order for costs on dismissing the appeal;

(ii) failure to appear when bailed to do so is not to be treated as an implied abandonment; provided service of the notice of hearing is proved the case may be treated as one of non-appearance (see 8-018); and

(iii) an appellant who has been on bail pending appeal, and who abandons his appeal must surrender to custody as directed by the magistrates' court officer, any conditions of bail applying until then (CrimPR 34.9(3)).

Notice of abandonment, deliberately given, is final; it cannot afterwards be withdrawn. It might be treated as a nullity only if the Crown Court found, after investigation, that it was given under a mistake or as a result of fraudulent inducement, so that there had been no real abandonment. There is no other jurisdiction to reinstate an abandoned appeal (*R. v Essex Quarter Sessions Appeals Committee Ex p. Larkin* [1961] 3 All E.R. 930; *R. v Knightsbridge Crown Court Ex p. Customs and Excise Commissioners* [1986] Crim. L.R. 324).

Once an appeal has commenced, a judge should only grant permission for the appeal to be abandoned in exceptional circumstances (*R. v Manchester Crown Court Ex p. Welby* (1981) 73 Cr. App. R. 248). The fact that an appeal has been called on and the appellant has been identified does not mean that the hearing has begun (*R. (on the application of Goumane) v Canterbury Crown Court* [2009] EWHC 1711 (Admin); [2010] Crim. L.R. 46).

Constitution of the court

On the hearing of an appeal: **8-020**

(1) the general rule is that the Crown Court must comprise:
  (a) a judge of the High Court, a Circuit Judge, a Recorder or a qualifying Judge Advocate; and
  (b) no less than two and no more than four justices of the peace, none of whom took part in the decision under appeal; and
(2) if the appeal is from a youth court, each justice of the peace must be qualified to sit as a member of a youth court.
(3) the Crown Court may include only one justice of the peace if:
  (a) the judge decides that otherwise the start of the appeal hearing will be delayed unreasonably; or
  (b) one or more of the justices of the peace who started hearing the appeal is absent.
(4) the Crown Court may comprise only a High Court judge, Crown Court judge, recorder or qualifying judge advocate sitting alone if:
  (a) the appeal is against conviction under MCA 1980 s.108; and
  (b) the respondent agrees that the court should allow the appeal under SCA 1981 s.48(2).

(SCA 1981 s.74 and CrimPR 34.11)

If the court conducts a hearing with only one justice, problems are likely to arise if the justice and the judge are unable to agree.

In so far as (3)(a) is concerned, the sole question under the law is whether there will be an unreasonable delay in the start of the appeal (*R. (on the application of Chinaka) v Southwark Crown Court* [2013] EWHC 3221 (Admin); (2013) 177 J.P. 683.

Objection to the constitution of the court needs to be taken not later than the time the proceedings are entered upon, or when the irregularity begins (SCA 1981 ss.8(2), 74(6)).

Case management decisions made before the hearing of the appeal can be made by a High Court judge, Crown Court judge, recorder or qualifying judge advocate sitting alone (CrimPR 34.11(3)).

Status of lay magistrates

8-021 Where a judge, Recorder or District Judge (Magistrates' Courts) sits with lay magistrates, he presides, and:

(1) the decision of the court may be by a majority;
(2) if the members are equally divided, the judge, District Judge or Recorder has a second and casting vote (SCA 1981 s.73(3));
(3) interlocutory decisions are taken by the court as a whole, though on questions of law the lay magistrates are likely to defer to the judge's views (*R. v Orpin* (1974) 59 Cr. App. R. 231);
(4) where the exercise of discretion arises, as where the admissibility of a confession is in issue (*R. v Orpin* (1974) 59 Cr. App. R. 231), or otherwise, the discretion falls to be exercised by the whole court, but where, as a matter of law, the discretion can only be exercised in one way, the lay magistrates are bound by the judge's decision (*Cook v DPP* [2001] Crim. L.R. 321).

Equivocal plea

8-022 An appellant may contend that he has a right of appeal against conviction because his plea of guilty in the magistrates' court was an equivocal one. To be "equivocal" the appellant must have added to his plea a qualification which, if substantiated, might show that he was not guilty of the offence (*Foster (Haulage) Ltd v Roberts* (1978) 67 Cr. App. R. 305 applied in *R. (on the application of Golrokhi) v Chelmsford Crown Court* [2013] EWHC 4343 (Admin)). It is an issue that the Crown Court must determine as a preliminary point (*R. v Durham Quarter Sessions Ex p. Virgo* [1952] 1 All E.R. 466).

The procedure to be followed is as follows (*R. v Marylebone Justices Ex p. Westminster City Council* [1971] 1 All E.R. 1025; *R. v Rochdale Justices Ex p. Allwork* (1981) 73 Cr. App. R. 319):

(1) evidence must be heard from or on behalf of the appellant as to the basis of the plea;
(2) if that evidence casts no doubt on the validity of the plea, or falls short of establishing that the plea was equivocal, the issue is resolved and the court proceeds to hear any appeal against sentence;
(3) if the evidence for the appellant does disclose prima facie that the plea in the magistrates' court was equivocal, help should be sought from the court below as to what happened at the hearing;
(4) the magistrate, chairman or legal adviser should be called upon to swear an affidavit as to what happened, and only after considering that evidence should the court determine the issue (and see *R. v Coventry Crown Court Ex p. Manson* (1978) 67 Cr. App. R. 315); and
(5) in appropriate circumstances, the case may be remitted to the magistrates for a fresh hearing.

Provided the Crown Court has made a proper enquiry before determining the issue, the remittal for a fresh hearing must be complied with by the court below (*R.*

v Plymouth Justices Ex p. Hart (1986) 83 Cr. App. R. 81). If a dispute arises as to whether there was a proper enquiry, the issue can only be resolved by the High Court on judicial review.

The fact that an unequivocal plea was entered below does not prevent an appellant putting forward a plea of autrefois *convict* or autrefois acquit at the hearing of the appeal (*Cooper v New Forest DC* [1972] Crim. L.R. 877). In exceptional circumstances an appellant may be permitted to appeal against conviction, even though his plea of guilty was unequivocal, where his plea was entered under duress (*R. v Huntingdon Crown Court Ex p. Jordan* (1981) 73 Cr. App. R. 194).

For the approach to be taken where an application is made long out of time following a guilty plea in the magistrates court, on the basis that the legal advice relied upon was erroneous, see *R. v Khalif* [2015] EWHC 917 (Admin); [2015] 4 Archbold Review 3.

Form of hearing

An appeal to the Crown Court is by way of rehearing (SCA 1981 s.79(3)). In an appeal against: **8-023**

(1) *conviction*:
   (a) the party seeking an order or conviction proves his case again;
   (b) there is no obligation on the prosecution to put its case in the same way as in the court below (*Hingley-Smith v DPP* [1998] 1 Arch. News 2 DC);
   (c) evidence is heard afresh;
   (d) the Crown Court does not "review" the decision of the lower court; it takes the place of the magistrates, forming its own view and substituting its opinion for that of the court below, in regard to conviction and/or sentence (*Drover v Rugman* [1950] 2 All E.R. 575; *Sagnata Ltd v Norwich Corp* [1971] 2 All E.R. 1441; *R. v Swindon Crown Court Ex p. Murray* (1998) 162 J.P. 36; *Hingley-Smith v DPP* [1998] 1 Arch. News 2 DC); and
   (e) it may find the case proved on a different basis from that found in the lower court (*Hingley-Smith v DPP* [1998] 1 Arch. News 2 DC);
(2) *sentence*:
   (a) there is a rehearing from conviction onwards; and
   (b) the Crown Court is not limited to considering whether the sentence imposed by the lower court was within its jurisdiction. The court goes through the sentencing process afresh, including, where appropriate, the inspection of driving licences, etc. (*Dyson v Ellison* (1974) 60 Cr. App. R. 191; *R. v Knutsford Crown Court Ex p. Jones* (1985) 7 Cr. App. R. (S.) 448), and the examination of any suggested "special reasons" for not disqualifying (*DPP v O'Connor* (1992) 95 Cr. App. R. 135);
(3) *binding over order*:
   (a) there is a rehearing; and
   (b) unless the appellant is prepared to admit the evidence which was before the magistrates, the facts must be proved by sworn evidence (*Shaw v Hamilton* (1982) 75 Cr. App. R. 288);
   (c) the issue is whether or not the court below was justified in making the

order, *not* whether the appellant is likely to repeat the conduct (*Hughes v Holley* (1988) 86 Cr. App. R. 130);

(4) *refusal of a firearms certificate* (see 8-030):
   (a) there is a rehearing; and
   (b) the views of the police being only one of the factors to be taken into consideration (*Cliff v MPC* (1973) 117 S.J. 855).

Special considerations govern appeals against local government decisions, e.g. *Stepney BC v Joffe* [1949] 1 All E.R. 256; *Northern Ireland Trailers Ltd v Preston Corp* [1972] 1 All E.R. 260.

The Crown Court is empowered to determine an appeal on a factual basis which differs from that adopted by the magistrates' court (see *Hingley-Smith v DPP* [1988] 1 Arch. News 2 DC). Any such question is determined in precisely the same way as on a plea to an indictment. The court is not bound by any finding of fact made in the magistrates' court which might limit its power of sentence.

If the Crown Court decides not to accept the express view of the court below on an appeal against sentence, it should explain that to the appellant and give him the opportunity to challenge the factual basis which the court proposes to adopt (*Bussey v DPP* [1999] 1 Cr. App. R. (S.) 125).

5. POWERS

In the course of the hearing

8-024 In the course of the hearing, the court may:

(1) correct any error or mistake in the order or judgment incorporating the decision which is the subject of the appeal; but
(2) *not* purport to amend the substance of the information on which the appellant was tried below (*Meek v Powell* [1952] 1 All E.R. 347; *Garfield v Maddocks* (1973) 57 Cr. App. R. 372; *Fairgrieve v Newman* (1986) 82 Cr. App. R. 60; *R. v Swansea Crown Court Ex p. Stacey* [1990] R.T.R. 183; *R. v Norwich Crown Court Ex p. Russell* [1993] Crim. L.R. 518);
(3) hear the appeal on the basis of the unamended information and may exercise the same jurisdiction as the court below, e.g. in the use of MCA 1980 s.123 (*R. v Swansea Crown Court Ex p. Stacey* [1990] R.T.R. 183).

On the termination of the hearing

8-025 On the termination of the hearing of an appeal the court may:

(1) In respect of the *decision* (SCA 1981 s.48(2) and (3)):
   (a) confirm, reverse or vary any part of the decision appealed against, including a determination not to impose a separate penalty;
   (b) remit the matter with its opinion thereon to the authority whose decision is appealed against; or
   (c) make such order in the matter as it thinks just, and by such order exercise any power which that authority might have exercised, subject to any enactment which expressly restricts or limits its powers;
(2) In respect of the *sentence* (SCA 1981 s.48(4)), whether the appeal was against conviction or sentence:
   (a) award any punishment, whether more or less severe than that awarded by the magistrates whose decision is appealed, provided it is a punish-

ment which those magistrates might have awarded at the time the appellant was sentenced by them (*R. v Portsmouth Crown Court Ex p. Ballard* (1990) 154 J.P. 109), save where the appeal is referred to the court by the CCRC (see 8-007);

(b) if the appeal is against one of several convictions on the same occasion, vary the sentences imposed for all the offences (*Dutta v Westcott* (1987) 84 Cr. App. R. 103).

The Crown Court should not increase sentence without giving a clear warning of its intention (e.g. *R. (on the application of Tottman) v DPP* [2004] EWHC 258 (Admin)).

"Sentence" includes any order made by a court when dealing with an offender, including a hospital order and a recommendation for deportation (SCA 1981 s.48(6)).

Interim hospital order

If, on the termination of an appeal, the Crown Court: **8-026**

(1) quashes an interim hospital order made by the magistrates, but does not pass any sentence or make any other order, it may direct the appellant to be kept in custody or released on bail pending his being dealt with by the magistrates; or

(2) makes an interim hospital order, the court below:
    (a) has the power to renew or terminate the order, and to deal with the accused on its termination; and
    (b) is to be treated for the purposes of absconding offenders (MHA 1983 s.31(8)) as the court which made the order.

(SCA 1981 s.48(7))

Forfeiture of cash under POCA 2002 s.298

An appeal by a party to proceedings in which a cash forfeiture order is made under POCA 2002 s.298 is by way of rehearing. The Crown Court may make any order it thinks appropriate, and if it upholds the appeal may order the release of the cash (POCA 2002 s.299). **8-027**

Requirement to give reasons

The judge presiding in the Crown Court is obliged to give reasons for the decision of the court, at least sufficient to demonstrate that the court has identified the main contentious issues in the case and how it has resolved them (*R. v Harrow Crown Court Ex p. Dave* (1994) 99 Cr. App. R. 114) and so that an appellant can know the reasons for the decision as soon as is reasonably possible, understand the nature of the criminality found and consider whether to appeal (*R. v Inner London Crown Court Ex p. Lambeth LBC* [2000] Crim. L.R. 303). Failure to do so may vitiate the decision, unless the reasons are obvious, the case is simple or the subject matter of the appeal unimportant (*R. v Kingston Crown Court Ex p. B* (2000) 164 J.P. 633). Reasons should be given contemporaneously with the decision (*R. v Snaresbrook Crown Court Ex p. Input Management Ltd* (1999) 163 J.P. 533; *R. v Inner London Crown Court Ex p. Lambeth LBC* [2000] Crim. L.R. 303). **8-028**

What is required to fulfil the duty will depend upon the circumstances of the particular case. Thus:

(1) it is insufficient merely to declare or announce that the appeal is dismissed; that does not amount to any substantive reasoning at all (e.g. *Pullum v CPS* [2000] C.O.D. 206); but
(2) a lengthy or elaborate judgment, such as might be given after a civil trial, will not usually be necessary or appropriate;
(3) where the determinative issue is factual, narrow and straightforward, a short judgment may suffice (*R. v Southwark Crown Court Ex p. Brooke* [1997] C.O.D. 81 at 82);
(4) where the issue turns on which witness is telling the truth, it is likely to be enough for the judge simply to say that he believes X rather than Y; indeed there may be nothing else to say, though it is often helpful to give a fuller explanation;
(5) in some cases the simple statement that the evidence of a particular witness is accepted may be enough (*R. v Harrow Crown Court Ex p. Dave* (1994) 99 Cr. App. R. 114); and
(6) the court must show that it has adopted a proper approach and has not misdirected itself, identifying the main issues in the appeal and how it determined them (*R. (on the application of Aitchison) v Sheffield Crown Court* [2012] EWHC 2844 (Admin); [2013] A.C.D. 7; see also *R. (Arthur) v Blackfriars Crown Court* [2017] EWHC 3416 (Admin); [2018] 2 Cr. App. R. 4).

6. COSTS AND ASSESSMENT

8-029 See COSTS AND ASSESSMENT

7. APPEALS UNDER THE FIREARMS ACT 1968

8-030 An appeal against a decision of a chief officer of police under FA 1968 ss.28A, 29, 30A, 30B, 30C, 34, 36, 37 or 38 lies to the Crown Court (FA 1968 s.44). It is determined on the merits and not by way of review (FA 1968 s.44(2)).

The procedure for initiating the appeal is similar to that for other appeals to the Crown Court, thus:

(1) notice of appeal must be given within 21 days after the date on which the appellant received notice of the decision of the chief officer of police by which he is aggrieved;
(2) the notice must be given both to the designated officer of the magistrates' court and to the chief officer, and must state the general grounds of his appeal;
(3) the Crown Court officer will give notice of the date and place of the hearing both to the appellant and to the chief officer, who is entitled to appear and be heard on the appeal; and
(4) the appellant may abandon his appeal at any time, not less than two clear days before the date fixed for the hearing, by giving notice in writing to the magistrates' court and to the chief officer.

On the hearing of the appeal, the court may consider any evidence or other matter, whether or not it was available when the decision of the chief officer was taken. The court must have regard to any guidance issued under s.55A that is relevant to the appeal (FA 1968 s.44(3)–(3A)).

The Crown Court may either dismiss the appeal or give the chief officer such directions as it thinks fit as respects the certificate or the register which is the subject of the appeal.

9. BAIL

Quick Guide

1. Jurisdiction of the Crown Court

(1) General

9-001 Bail may be granted in the Crown Court, subject to CJPOA 1994 s.25 (see 9-008), to any person:

(1) who has been sent in custody to the Crown Court for trial under CDA 1998 s.51 or s.51A;
(2) who is in custody pursuant to a sentence imposed by a magistrates' court and has appealed to the Crown Court against his conviction or sentence;
(3) who is in the custody of the Crown Court pending the disposal of his case by that court;
(4) who, after the decision of his case by the Crown Court, has applied to the court for a case to be stated for the High Court on that decision or is seeking a quashing order in respect of that decision;
(5) to whom a judge of the Crown Court has granted a certificate under CAA 1968 ss.1(2) or 11(1A), or SCA 1981 s.81(1B) that a case is fit for appeal (see APPEALS FROM THE CROWN COURT); or
(6) who has been charged with murder, the magistrates' court having no such jurisdiction (9-009).

(SCA 1981 s.81(1))

Where an accused is sent for trial to the Crown Court, the magistrates' bail ceases when he surrenders to the Crown Court, whether for arraignment or otherwise, and a judge, if releasing him again on bail, must consider afresh the appropriateness of any conditions, including the position of any surety (*R. v Kent Crown Court Ex p. Jodka* (1997) 161 J.P. 638).

As to granting bail during the trial, see 9-015. As to granting bail on application for leave to appeal to the CACD see APPEALS FROM THE CROWN COURT.

Where a young person is charged with a serious offence the judge ought to show that he has given sufficient and appropriate consideration to any suggested potential safeguards and the question of whether they provide sufficient protection against absconding or failing to surrender (*R. (on the application of Bailey) v CCC* [2010] EWHC 667 (Admin); [2010] Crim. L.R. 715).

HMCTS court staff must also ensure that the police, or the relevant Witness Care Unit, are notified as soon as possible of the outcome of bail hearings or a change in remand status (VC2, 19).

Challenging a Crown Court decision

9-002 CJA 2003 s.17 abolished the inherent power of the High Court to entertain an application in relation to bail where a judge has determined such an application under his general powers in criminal cases (BA 1976 s.3(8); SCA 1981 s.81(1)(a), (b), (c) or (g)).

Section 17(6), however, provided that nothing in the section should affect any other power of the High Court to grant or withhold bail (such as on an appeal by way of case stated), or to vary the conditions of bail, or any right of a person to apply for a writ of habeas corpus or any other prerogative remedy.

In *R. (on the application of Rozo) v Snaresbrook Crown Court* [2005] EWHC 75 (Admin) it was accepted that prerogative remedies in the context of s.17(6) embraced those set out in SCA 1981 s.29(1) (i.e. mandamus, prohibition and certiorari—now renamed). Following that case and *R. (on the application of F) v Southampton Crown Court* [2009] EWHC 2206 (Admin) the High Court has entertained applications for permission for judicial review of bail decisions in the Crown Court.

In some of those cases judicial review is granted because the refusal was thought to be irrational, and in others because the judge misdirected himself in law (*R. (on the application of JN) v Inner London Crown Court* [2008] EWHC 468 (Admin)). Procedural failings have also justified the grant of judicial review (*R. (on the application of Khan) v Leicester Crown Court* [2008] EWHC 1000 (Admin)). Once a trial on indictment has started the High Court does not have jurisdiction to make any order in respect of the Crown Court "in matters relating to trial on indictment" (*R. (on the application of Uddin) v Leeds Crown Court* [2013] EWHC 2752 (Admin); [2014] 1 Cr. App. R. 13).

Right to bail before conviction

9-003 Under the general provisions of BA 1976 but subject to CJPOA 1994 s.25 (see 9-008) a person who:

(1) appears or is brought before the Crown Court in the course of, or in connection with, proceedings for an offence, or applies to the Crown Court for bail in connection with the proceedings;
(2) has been convicted of an offence and whose case is adjourned for reports before sentence; or
(3) has been convicted of an offence and appears before the Crown Court under:
  (a) SA 2020 Sch.4 (referral orders: referral back to appropriate court);
  (b) SA 2020 Sch.5 (breach of reparation order);
  (c) SA 2020 Sch.7 (breach, revocation or amendment of youth rehabilitation orders);
  (d) SA 2020 Sch.10 Pt 2 (breach of requirements of a community order); or
  (e) the schedule to the Street Offences Act 1959 (breach of orders under s.1(2A) of that Act)

has a right to bail unless one of the exceptions under BA 1976 Sch.1 (see 9-004) is made out, and the judge exercises his discretion to withhold bail (BA 1976 s.4).

As to bail during the trial, see 9-015; as to bail on the expiry of a time limit under

POA 1985 and the Regulations made thereunder see CUSTODY TIME LIMITS. As to bail on a retrial under CJA 2003 Pt 10 see RETRIALS.

(2) Imprisonable offences triable on indictment or either-way

Exceptions to the right to bail; principal grounds

9-004 Quite apart from CJPOA 1994 s.25 (9-008) the judge may withhold bail from an accused (subject to expiry of the custody time limits) where, in the case of an imprisonable offence, triable on indictment or either way:

(1) there exist substantial grounds for the belief (*R. v Slough Justices Ex p. Duncan* (1982) 75 Cr. App. R. 384; cf. *R. v Mansfield Justices Ex p. Sharkey* [1985] 1 All E.R. 193) that if released on bail, whether subject to conditions or not, he will:
  (a) fail to surrender;
  (b) commit an offence while on bail; or
  (c) interfere with witnesses or otherwise obstruct the course of justice, whether in relation to himself or any other person;

(2) the offence is an indictable offence or an offence triable either-way, and it appears to the judge that the accused was on bail in criminal proceedings on the date of the offence;

(3) having previously been released on bail on or in connection with the proceedings, the accused has been arrested in pursuance of BA 1976 s.7;

(4) he is satisfied that the accused should be kept in custody for his own protection (or welfare in the case of a child (under 14) or young person (14 but under 18));

(5) the accused is already in custody in pursuance of the sentence of a court or a sentence imposed by an officer under the Armed Forces Act 2006;

(6) the judge is satisfied that there are substantial grounds for believing that the accused, if released on bail (whether subject to conditions or not) (see 9-017) would commit an offence while on bail by engaging in conduct that would, or would be likely to cause, physical or mental injury to an "associated person" (see below) or an associated person to fear physical or mental injury; or

(7) the judge is satisfied that it has not been practicable to obtain sufficient information for the purpose of taking the decisions in (1)–(3) above for want of time since the institution of proceedings against the accused.

(BA 1976 Sch.1 Pt 1 paras 2–6)

However, grounds (1), (2) and (3) above do not apply where the accused has:

(a) attained the age of 18;
(b) has not been convicted of an offence in those proceedings; and
(c) it appears to the judge that there is no real prospect that the accused will be sentenced to a custodial sentence in the proceedings.

(BA 1976 Sch.1 Pt 1 para.1A)

Detention of children and young persons for their own protection should be the exception. At the heart of any decision-making involving children must be the best interests of the child. The facts and circumstances relating to each individual decision to do so must be rigorously considered (*Archer v Commissioner of Police of the Metropolis* [2021] EWCA Civ 1662; [2022] Q.B. 401).

"Associated person" in (6) above means a person who is associated with the accused within the meaning of the Family Law Act 1996 s.62.

As to other reasons for withholding bail, see 9-008 to 9-014.

Exercise of discretion

Before the discretion to refuse bail arises: **9-005**

(1) the judge must be satisfied that one of the conditions in 9-004 is satisfied. With regard to (1) (in 9-004), it is the existence of substantial grounds for the belief, not the belief itself, which is the crucial factor (*R. v Slough Justices Ex p. Duncan*(1982) 75 Cr. App. R. 384);
(2) in deciding whether substantial grounds exist, the judge must act compatibly with ECHR art.5(3) which limits pre-trial custody; he must take into account all relevant considerations, including those relating to the character of the person involved, his morals, his home, his occupation, his assets, his family ties and all kinds of links with his community and country (*Letellier v France* (1992) 14 E.H.R.R. 83 R); and
(3) there should be evidence to support objections to bail, but it seems that the strict rules of evidence need not apply; evidence upon which the prosecution intend to rely in opposing bail should be disclosed (*Lamy v Belgium* (1989) 11 E.H.R.R. 529).

(3) Imprisonable offences to which Sch.1 Pt 1 does not apply

BA 1976 Sch.1 Pt IA applies to cases to which Sch.1 Pt I does not apply, i.e. those which are neither indictable only or triable either way. **9-006**

(4) Non-imprisonable offences

The seriousness of the offence is not to be treated as a conclusive reason for withholding bail from an unconvicted suspect (*Hurnam v State of Mauritius* [2005] UKPC 49; [2006] 1 W.L.R. 857, per Lord Bingham of Cornhill). **9-007**

In *Gault v United Kingdom* [2008] Crim. L.R. 476; *The Times*, 28 November 2007 ECHR regarded the fact that the prosecution did not object to bail as a "significant factor"; but see *R. (on the application of Burns) v Woolwich Crown Court* [2010] EWHC 129 (Admin) where it was made clear that decisions as to the grant of bail are a matter for the courts, not for the prosecutor.

Where the accused faces, or is convicted of, a non-imprisonable offence, bail need not be granted where (BA 1976 Sch.1 Pt II paras 2–5):

(1) the accused:
  (a) is a child or young person or has been convicted in the proceedings of an offence; and
  (b) having been previously granted bail in criminal proceedings, it appears that the accused has failed to surrender to custody in accordance with his obligation; and
  (c) the judge believes, in view of that failure, that the accused, if released on bail (whether subject to conditions or not), would fail to surrender to custody;
(2) the court is satisfied that the accused should be kept in custody for his own protection or, if he is a child, for his own welfare;

(3) the accused is in custody in pursuance of a sentence of a court or imposed by an officer under the Armed Forces Act 2006;
(4) the accused:
 (a) is a child or young person or has been convicted in the proceedings of an offence; and
 (b) having been released on bail in or in connection with the proceedings for the offence, he has been arrested in pursuance of BA 1976 s.7; and
 (c) the court is satisfied that there are substantial grounds for believing that the accused, if released on bail (whether subject to conditions or not) would fail to surrender, commit an offence on bail or interfere with witnesses or otherwise obstruct the course of justice (whether in relation to himself or anyone else);
(5) the accused:
 (a) having been released on bail in or in connection with the proceedings for the offence, has been arrested in pursuance of BA 1976 s.7; and
 (b) the judge is satisfied that there are substantial grounds for believing that if released on bail, (whether subject to conditions or not), he would commit an offence on bail by engaging in conduct that would, or would be likely to, cause physical or mental injury to an associated person or cause an associated person to fear physical or mental injury.

There is nothing to prevent conditions being imposed in such a case (*R. v Bournemouth MC Ex p. Cross* (1989) 89 Cr. App. R. 90 and see 9-017).

(5) Withholding bail

Previous convictions for certain serious offences

9-008 Where a person has been charged with or convicted of any of the following offences:

(1) murder;
(2) attempted murder;
(3) manslaughter;
(4) rape under the law of Scotland;
(5) an offence under SOA 1956 s.1 (rape);
(6) an offence under SOA 2003 s.1 (rape);
(7) an offence under SOA 2003 s.2 (assault by penetration);
(8) an offence under SOA 2003 s.4 (causing a person to engage in sexual activity without consent) where the activity involved penetration within s.4(4)(a)–(d);
(9) an offence under SOA 2003 s.5 (rape of a child under 13);
(10) an offence under SOA 2003 s.6 (assault of a child under 13 by penetration);
(11) an offence under SOA 2003 s.8 (causing or inciting a child under 13 to engage in sexual activity) where an activity involving penetration within s.8(3)(a)–(d) was caused;
(12) an offence under SOA 2003 s.30 (sexual activity with a person with a mental disorder impeding choice) where the touching involved penetration within s.30(3)(a)–(d);
(13) an offence under SOA 2003 s.31 (causing or inciting a person with a mental disorder impeding choice to engage in sexual activity) where an activity involving penetration within s.31(3)(a)–(d) was caused; and

(14) an attempt to commit an offence within any of the paras (4)–(13) above,

AND

he has previously been convicted of any offence in the list above or of culpable homicide (and, in the case of a previous conviction for manslaughter or culpable homicide, he was either then a child or young person and sentenced to long-term detention, or was not a child or young person and was sentenced to imprisonment or detention), he shall be granted bail in those proceedings only if the court is of the opinion that there are exceptional circumstances which justify it (CJPOA 1994 s.25).

Section 25 should be construed and applied essentially as a guide to the proper operation of BA 1976. Additionally it operates to disapply the ordinary requirement that bail should be granted automatically to anyone whose custody time limit has expired. There is an evidential burden on the accused to prove he should be released. If a person to whom s.25 applies, if granted bail, is likely to fail to surrender, to offend on bail or to interfere with witnesses or otherwise obstruct the course of justice, bail should not be granted. If, however, taking all the circumstances into consideration the accused does not create such an unacceptable risk, he is an exception to the norm and should be granted bail (*R. (on the application of O) v Harrow Crown Court* [2006] UKHL 42; [2007] 1 Cr. App. R. 9, affirmed by *O'Dowd v United Kingdom* (2012) 54 E.H.R.R 8).

Special cases: (1) murder

A person charged with murder (and this includes a person charged with murder and one or more other offences) may not be granted bail except by order of a judge of the Crown Court. **9-009**

Where a person appears or is brought before a magistrates' court charged with murder, a judge of the Crown Court will make a decision about bail in respect of that person:

(1) as soon as reasonably practicable; and
(2) in any event, within the period of 48 hours beginning with the day after the day on which the person appears or is brought before the magistrates' court.

(CorJA 2009 s.115)

In calculating the period of 48 hours referred to above, Saturdays, Sundays, Christmas Day, Good Friday and bank holidays are to be excluded.

Note that s.115(4) does not displace the power in CYPA 1969 s.23 (since repealed and replaced by LASPOA 2012 s.91; *R. (on the application of A) v Lewisham Youth Court* [2011] EWHC 1193 (Admin)).

Where the accused is charged with murder, and the Crown Court has not yet considered bail, the magistrates' court officer must arrange with the Crown Court officer for the Crown Court to consider bail as soon as practicable and in any event no later than the second business day after a magistrates' court sends the accused to the Crown Court for trial, or the first hearing in the magistrates' court, if the accused is not at once sent for trial (CrimPR 14.10).

Where an accused is charged with murder, he may not be granted bail unless the judge is of the opinion that there is no significant risk of his committing, while on bail, an offence that would, or would be likely to, cause physical or mental injury to any person other than the accused (BA 1976 Sch.1 para.6ZA).

Special cases: (2) drug users

9-010 There is a presumption against bail in the case of a person aged 18 or over, where that person is:

(1) charged with an imprisonable offence; and
(2) under arrangements in force in the court's area:
   (a) he tests positive for a specified (CJCSA 2000 Pt 3) Class A drug; and
   (b) he does not consent to:
      (i) undergo an assessment as to his dependency or propensity to use drugs; or
      (ii) following assessment, any relevant follow-up action recommended,

unless the judge is of the opinion that there is no significant risk of that person committing another offence while on bail (whether subject to conditions or not) (BA 1976 Sch.1 Pt 1 paras 6A–6C).

Before this provision applies, however, a sample (taken under PACE 1984 s.63B in connection with the offence, or under SA 2020 s.34A after conviction and before sentence) must have revealed the presence in that person's body of a specified Class A drug, and either:

- the offence must be one under MDA 1971 s.5(2) or (3), and relate to a specified Class A drug; or
- the judge must be satisfied that there are substantial grounds for believing that misuse by the accused of a specified Class A drug caused or contributed to the offence; or, even if it did not, the offence was motivated wholly or partly by his intended misuse of such a drug; and

if an assessment or a follow-up is proposed and agreed to, it must be a condition of bail that it be undertaken.

Special Cases: (3) breach of existing bail

9-011 Where the accused is aged 18 or over, and it appears that:

(1) he was on bail for an indictable offence or offence triable either way on the date of the offence; or
(2) having previously been released on bail in or in connection with the proceedings for the offence, he failed to surrender to custody,

he need not be granted bail (BA 1976 Sch.1 Pt 1 paras 2A, 6).

However, see 9-013 for further provisions applying to defendants under the age of 18.

Special cases: (4) extradition

9-012 Where the Home Secretary has given an undertaking in connection with a person's extradition to the UK which includes terms that that person be kept in custody until the conclusion of any proceedings against him for an offence, a judge may grant bail only if he considers that there are exceptional circumstances which justify it (EA 2003 s.154).

Statutory approach

In taking the decision whether to grant, withhold or vary bail in the case of a person accused or convicted of an *imprisonable offence*, the judge is bound to have regard to such of the following considerations as appear to be relevant (BA 1976 Sch.1 Pt 1 paras 9, 9AA, 9AB): **9-013**

(1) the nature and seriousness of the offence (or default) and the probable method of dealing with the accused for it (though see 9-007);
(2) the character, antecedents, associations and communities of the accused;
(3) the accused's record as respects the fulfilment of his obligations under previous grants of bail in criminal proceedings;
(4) except in the case of an accused whose case is adjourned for enquiries or a report, the strength of the evidence of his having committed the offence (or having defaulted);
(5) if the judge is satisfied that there are substantial grounds for believing that the accused, if released on bail (whether subject to conditions or not) would commit an offence while on bail, the risk that the accused might do so by engaging in conduct which would, or would be likely to, cause physical or mental injury to any person other than the accused,

as well as to any others which appear to be relevant.

If the accused is a child (under 14) or young person (14 but under 18) and it appears that he was on bail in criminal proceedings on the date of the offence, the court must give particular weight to that fact in deciding whether it is satisfied that there are substantial grounds for believing that the accused if released on bail would commit an offence while on bail.

If the accused is a child (under 14) or young person (14 but under 18) and it appears that:

(a) he was on bail in criminal proceedings on the date of the offence; or
(b) having been released on bail in, or in connection with, the proceedings for the offence, he failed, without reasonable cause, to surrender to custody; or
(c) having been released on bail in, or in connection with, the proceedings for the offence, he failed to surrender to custody but had reasonable cause for his failure, but failed to surrender as soon as reasonably practicable after the appointed time,

the judge must give particular weight to that factor in making his decision.

In making the decision, the considerations to which the judge must have regard, include, so far as is relevant, any misuse of controlled drugs by the accused (BA 1976 s.4(9)).

Common sense approach

It is common sense that: **9-014**

(1) the presumption of innocence, which is clearly a factor, is one which does not exclude competing factors which may be more formidable in the circumstances of the case;
(2) previous convictions per se should not be regarded as an automatic reason for refusing bail, but if there is a significance in the record and the nature of the charges, protection of the public needs to be considered;

(3) the allegation that at the time of the alleged commission of the offence the accused was in a position of trust to behave as a good citizen and not breach the law is an important factor; this may arise where, e.g. he is on bail in respect of another offence, subject to a community sentence, on licence or parole, or subject to a deferred sentence or a suspended sentence when, unless there are cogent reasons for deciding otherwise, bail ought to be refused; and

(4) vague or unspecified arguments that the police are still, after the case has been sent to the Crown Court for trial, making enquiries are hardly a good ground for refusing bail, but it is otherwise where the prosecutor can prove that it is in the interests of the public administration of justice that the accused be detained while those enquiries are made.

(6) Bail during the trial

9-015 Once a trial has begun, the further grant of bail, subject to BA 1976, whether during the short adjournment or overnight, is in the discretion of the trial judge (*CPD* III 14G.1–4).

In particular:

(1) it may be a proper exercise of that discretion to insist on the accused surrendering earlier and being released later than the times during which other persons are present, particularly in courts where no proper segregated refreshment facilities for jurors and witnesses are available (*Burgess v Secretary of State for the Home Department* [2001] 1 W.L.R. 93);

(2) an accused who was on bail while on remand should not be refused overnight bail during the trial unless in the judge's opinion there are positive reasons to justify the refusal; such reasons might include:

   (a) that a point has been reached where there is a real danger that the accused will abscond, either because the case is going badly for him, or for any other reason; or

   (b) that there is a real danger that he may interfere with witnesses, jurors or co-defendants;

(3) once the jury has returned a verdict a further renewal of bail should be decided in the light of the gravity of the offence, any friction between co-defendants and the likely sentence to be passed in all the circumstances of the case.

(7) Bail on remand for enquiries or reports

9-016 Where an offender's case is adjourned for enquiries or reports and the offence, or one of the offences, of which he is convicted in the proceedings is punishable with imprisonment, he need not be granted bail if it appears that it would be impracticable to complete the enquiries or make the report without keeping him in custody (e.g. the obvious case of the offender who has a history of non-cooperation) (BA 1976 Sch.1 Pt 1 para.7).

2. CONDITIONS AND REQUIREMENTS

(1) Imposing conditions

Bail in criminal proceedings is either: **9-017**

(1) unconditional; or
(2) subject to conditions.

A condition must not be imposed unless it appears to the judge necessary to do so for the purpose of:

(a) preventing a person's:
  (i) failure to surrender;
  (ii) commission of offences while on bail;
  (iii) interference with witnesses or obstruction of the course of justice, whether in relation to himself or anyone else;
(b) the accused's own protection, or, if he is a child or young person, for his own welfare or in his own interests; or
(c) an accused, in an appropriate case, making himself available for the purpose of enabling enquiries or a report to be made, and, in this case, only where it is necessary.

(BA 1976 s.3(1)–(6); Sch.1 Pt 1 para.8)

(2) Surety, security and requirements

As a general rule no security for his surrender is to be taken from an accused, nor is he required to provide a surety, nor is any other requirement to be imposed upon him as a condition of bail. **9-018**

Nevertheless, he may be required to:

(1) provide a *surety* or sureties; or
(2) give *security*, which may be given by himself or on his behalf,

before being released, to secure his surrender to custody (though neither of these provisions applies in the case of an accused granted bail on the expiry of a time limit under POA 1985 s.22); and he may also be required, before release on bail, or later, to comply with such *requirements* as appear to be necessary to secure the matters listed at (a)–(c) in 9-017 or before the time appointed for him to surrender to custody, to attend an interview with an authorised advocate or authorised litigator, as defined by CLSA 1990 s.119(1) (BA 1976 s.3(3)–(6)).

The obligation of a surety under the section is a personal obligation that cannot be delegated to another party. The surety is provided only to secure surrender to custody and not to secure performance of any other condition; it should be limited to that expressly identified in s.3 and for no other purpose. An exceptional case is that a parent or guardian may stand surety to secure that a child accused under 17 does not commit another offence (see BA 1976 s.3(7) at 9-020; *Shea v Winchester Crown Court* [2013] EWHC 1050 (Admin)).

As to the nature of the security envisaged by the Act, see *R. (on the application of Stevens) v Truro MC* [2001] EWHC Admin 558; [2002] 1 W.L.R. 144. As to drug users, see 9-025; as to murder cases, see 9-024. As to procedure for "taking" the surety, see 9-021.

The court should also notify sureties of the dates of the hearing at the Crown

Court at which the accused is ordered to appear in as far in advance as possible (see the observations of Parker LJ in *R. v Reading Crown Court Ex p. Bello* (1991) 92 Cr. App. R. 303).

Suitability of surety

9-019 In considering the suitability of any surety required, the judge needs to have regard, amongst other things, to the surety's:

(1) financial resources;
(2) character and previous convictions, if any; and
(3) proximity, whether in point of kinship, place of residence or otherwise, to the person for whom he seeks to stand surety.

(BA 1976 s.8(1) and (2))

In considering "financial resources":

(a) it is the resources of the surety, rather than of the principal, that are relevant; and
(b) in relation to the spouse of the principal, it is important to consider whether he/she has sufficient means to discharge the liability out of his/her separate property, and no account should be taken of any joint property or of the matrimonial home (*R. v Southampton Justices Ex p. Green* [1975] 2 All E.R. 1073).

There will be cases where a token investigation into the resources of the proposed surety will suffice; in appropriate cases it will be sensible to insist on examining bank accounts, building society books and other documents. Jewellery will seldom fetch the value suggested, nor is there likely to be an opportunity to sell a house or other immovable property.

Parent or guardian

9-020 Where the parent or guardian of a person under the age of 17 consents to be surety for the person for the purposes of this subsection, the parent or guardian may be required to secure that the person complies with *any requirement* imposed on him by virtue BA 1976 s.3(6), (6ZAA) or (6A) (as opposed only to securing his surrender to custody, as in the case of a person aged 17 or over; see 9-018), but:

(a) no requirement may be imposed on the parent or guardian by virtue of this subsection where it appears that the accused will attain the age of seventeen before the time to be appointed for him to surrender to custody; and
(b) the parent or guardian may not be required to secure compliance with any requirement to which his consent does not extend and shall not, in respect of those requirements to which his consent does extend, be bound in a sum greater than £50.

(BA 1976 s.3(7))

Taking the surety

9-021 The recognisance of any surety may be taken:

(1) forthwith, after enquiry into his suitability; or
(2) subsequently.

(BA 1976 s.8(3) and (4))

Where the accused cannot be released because no surety, or no suitable surety, is available, the judge must fix the amount of the surety, which may then be taken subsequently, in accordance with BA 1976 s.3(4), (5) and (6).

In such circumstances the recognisance may be entered into before an officer of the Crown Court, the governor of any prison or other place of detention in which the person granted bail is held, or those other persons specified in BA 1976 s.8(4).

In a case where the proposed surety resides in Scotland, the judge may, if satisfied of the suitability of the proposed surety, direct that arrangements be made for the surety to be entered into there, before a constable having charge at any police office or station there (BA 1976 s.8(5)).

Where a surety seeks to enter into a recognisance before one of those persons specified in BA 1976 s.8(4), and that person declines to take it because he is not satisfied of the surety's suitability, the proposed surety may apply:

(a) to the court which fixed the amount in which the surety was to be bound; or
(b) to a magistrates' court for the local justice area in which he resides,

for that court to take his recognisance, and that court will do so if satisfied of his suitability.

Where a recognisance is entered into before a court other than that which fixed the amount of the recognisance, the same consequences follow as if it had been entered into before the original court.

"Bail as before"

A judge granting "bail as before" needs to be careful with the procedure. Bail granted on a previous occasion ceases on the surrender of the accused, or offender, so that where the judge: 9-022

(1) contemplates granting bail on the same conditions as it was granted previously; and
(2) a surety was required on the previous occasion,

then, unless he proposes to remove the requirement of a surety he must consider the surety's position (*R. v Maidstone Crown Court Ex p. Jodka* (1997) 161 J.P. 638 and see *R. v Dimond* [2000] 1 Cr. App. R. 21).

Other requirements of bail

There can be no closed list of requirements which may be imposed, but common requirements are those as to residence, including sleeping every night at a named address, reporting periodically at a named police station between specified hours on specified days, observing a curfew between specified hours, residing in a specified hostel, surrender of passport and restrictions on entering or leaving certain defined areas, or approaching named persons. 9-023

Special conditions apply to bail pending appeal to the CACD (see APPEALS FROM THE CROWN COURT).

A requirement may be added that:

(1) before the time appointed for surrender to custody, the accused attend an interview with an advocate or authorised litigator as defined by CLSA 1990 s.119(1) (BA 1976 s.3(6)(e));
(2) where bail is granted pending reports, the offender attend on a probation officer or a medical practitioner, as directed;
(3) where one of the conditions imposed is residence in a bail or probation hostel, he comply with the rules of the hostel (BA 1976 s.3(6ZA));
(4) subject to s.3AA (see 9-026) in the case of a child or young person, s.3AB (see 9-027) in the case of other persons, and s.3AC (9-028), in all cases, he be subject to electronic monitoring requirements for the purpose of securing his compliance with any other requirement imposed on him as a condition of bail (BA 1976 s.3(6ZAB)); or
(5) "not to drive", but before imposing such a requirement, the judge ought to consider whether it may have possibly unjust results (*R. v Kwame* (1974) 60 Cr. App. R. 65); there is power to impose an interim disqualification under RTA 1991 on remanding an accused (see DRIVING DISQUALIFICATION).

Under CrimPR 14.14, where a judge imposes as a condition of bail a requirement for:

(1) a surety;
(2) a payment; or
(3) the surrender of a document or thing,

the judge may direct how such a condition must be met.

Unless the judge otherwise directs, if any such condition or direction requires a surety to enter into a recognisance, that recognisance must specify:

(a) the amount that the surety will be required to pay if the purpose for which the recognisance is entered is not fulfilled; and
(b) the date, or the event, upon which the recognisance will expire.

The surety must enter into the recognisance in the presence of the court officer, the accused's custodian, where the accused is in custody, or someone acting with the authority of either, and the person before whom the surety enters into the recognisance must at once serve a copy on the surety, and as appropriate, the Crown Court officer and the accused's custodian.

Unless the judge otherwise directs, if any such condition or direction requires someone to make a payment, or surrender a document or thing, that payment, document or thing must be made or surrendered to Crown Court officer, the accused's custodian where the accused is in custody; or someone acting with the authority of either; and the court officer or the custodian, as appropriate, must serve immediately on the other a statement that the payment, document or thing has been made or surrendered.

The custodian will release the accused when each requirement ordered by the court has been met.

Where an accused is released on bail with a condition of residence he must notify the prosecutor of the address at which he will live and sleep:

(i) as soon as practicable after the institution of proceedings, unless already done; and

(ii) as soon as practicable after any change of that address.

The prosecutor has a duty to help the court to assess the suitability of any address proposed as a condition of residence (CrimPR 14.11).

(3) Murder cases; medical reports

Where the judge grants bail to a person accused of murder, he must, unless he considers that satisfactory reports on his mental condition have already been obtained, impose as a condition of bail, a requirement that the accused: **9-024**

(1) is examined by two medical practitioners for the purpose of enabling reports to be prepared; and
(2) attend such institution or place as the judge directs, and comply with such other directions as may be given to him for the purpose by either of those medical practitioners.

(BA 1976 s.3(6A) and (6B))

Of those medical practitioners, at least one must be a practitioner approved for the purposes of MHA 1983 s.12 (see MENTALLY DISORDERED OFFENDERS). Failure to impose such a requirement renders the grant of bail a nullity (*R. v Central Criminal Court Ex p. Porter* [1992] Crim. L.R. 121).

(4) Drug users; assessment and follow-up

In relation to an accused to whom BA 1976 Sch.1 para.6B(1)(a)–(c) and (b) apply (see 9-010), and the court has been notified that arrangements for conducting a relevant assessment, or, as the case may be, providing relevant follow-up, have been made for the local justice area in which it appears that the relevant accused would reside if granted bail (and the notice has not been withdrawn), then if: **9-025**

(1) after analysis, he has been offered a relevant assessment or, if a relevant assessment has been carried out, he has had relevant follow-up proposed to him; and
(2) he has agreed to undergo the relevant assessment or, as the case may be, to participate in the relevant follow-up,

a condition *must* be imposed, if bail is granted, that he both undergo the relevant assessment and participate in any relevant follow-up proposed to him or, if a relevant assessment has been carried out, that he participate in the follow-up.

In this provision:

(a) "relevant assessment" means an assessment conducted by a suitably qualified person of whether that person is dependent upon or has a propensity to misuse any specified Class A drugs; and
(b) "relevant follow-up" means, in a case where the person who conducted the relevant assessment believes the accused to have such a dependency or propensity, such further assessment, and such assistance or treatment in connection with the dependency or propensity, as the person who conducted the relevant assessment (or conducts any later assessment) considers to be appropriate in his case.

(BA 1976 s.3(6C)–(6E))

In para.(a) above "Class A drug" and "misuse" have the same meaning as in

MDA 1971, and "specified" (in relation to a Class A drug) has the same meaning as in CJCSA 2000 Pt 3, as to both of which, see 9-010.

(5) Electronic monitoring requirement

Electronic monitoring requirement: (1) children and young persons

9-026 An electronic monitoring requirement may not be imposed on a child (under 14) or young person (14 but under 18) unless each of the following conditions is met:

(1) he has attained the age of 12 years;
(2) he is charged with, or has been convicted of:
  (a) a violent, sexual or terrorism offence; or
  (b) an offence punishable in the case of an adult with imprisonment for 14 years or more; or
  (c) one or more imprisonable offences which, together with any other imprisonable offences of which he has been convicted in any proceedings, amount, or would amount, if he were convicted of the offences with which he is charged, to a recent history of repeatedly committing imprisonable offences while remanded on bail or subject to a custodial remand (as defined in s.3AA(11) and (12);
(3) the judge is satisfied that the necessary provision for dealing with the person concerned can be made under arrangements for the electronic monitoring of persons released on bail that are currently available in each relevant local justice area;
(4) a Youth Offending Team has informed the court that in its opinion the imposition of electronic monitoring requirements will be suitable in the case of the child or young person.

(BA 1976 s.3AA)

The duties of the Crown Court officer in relation to the grant of bail on such a condition are set out in CrimPR 14.12.

As to his duties where the judge imposes as a condition of bail a requirement to reside in accommodation provided for that purpose by, or on behalf of, a public authority; or to receive bail support provided by, or on behalf of, a public authority, see CrimPR 14.13.

Electronic monitoring requirement: (2) other persons

9-027 An electronic monitoring requirement may not be imposed on a person who has attained the age of 18 unless each of the following conditions is met:

(1) the judge is satisfied that without the electronic monitoring requirement the person would not be granted bail; and
(2) the judge is satisfied that the necessary provision for dealing with the person concerned can be made under arrangements for the electronic monitoring of persons released on bail that are currently available in each relevant local justice area.

(BA 1976 s.3AB)

Electronic monitoring requirement: (3) responsible monitor

Where an electronic monitoring requirement is imposed as a condition of bail, it must include provision for making a person responsible for the monitoring. **9-028**

A person may not be made responsible for the electronic monitoring of a person on bail unless he is of a description specified in an order made by the Secretary of State.

For the purposes of ss.3AA or 3AB, a local justice area is a "relevant area" in relation to a proposed electronic monitoring requirement if the judge considers that it will not be practicable to secure the electronic monitoring in question unless electronic monitoring arrangements are available in that area (BA 1976 s.3AC).

3. Applications to the Crown Court

Notice of application to consider bail

Where a party wants a judge of the Crown Court to: **9-029**

(1) grant bail that has been withheld;
(2) withdraw bail that has been granted; or
(3) impose a new bail condition or to vary a present one,

he must apply in writing, serving the application on the court officer, the other party, and any surety affected or proposed, not less than two business days before any hearing in the case at which the applicant wants the court to consider it, if such a hearing is already due.

The application must:

(a) specify:
    (i) the decision that the applicant wants the court to make;
    (ii) each offence charged; and
    (iii) each relevant previous bail decision and the reasons given for each;
(b) if the applicant is an accused, explain:
    (i) as appropriate, why bail should not be withheld, or why a condition should be varied; and
    (ii) what further information or legal argument, if any, has become available since the most recent previous bail decision was made;
(c) if the applicant is the prosecutor, explain:
    (i) as appropriate, why bail should be withdrawn, or a condition imposed or varied; and
    (ii) what material information has become available since the most recent previous bail decision was made;
(d) propose the terms of any suggested condition of bail; and
(e) if the applicant wants an earlier hearing than required below, explain why it is needed.

A prosecutor who applies under this rule must serve on the accused, with the application, notice that the court has power to withdraw bail and, if the accused is absent when the court makes its decision, order his arrest.

A party who opposes an application must so notify the court officer and the applicant at once, and serve on each notice of the reasons for opposition.

Unless the court otherwise directs, the court officer will arrange for a judge to hear the application as soon as practicable and in any event, in the case of an application:

- to grant or withdraw bail, no later than the second business day after it was served; and
- to impose or vary a condition, no later than the fifth business day after it was served.

The court may vary or waive a time limit, allow an application to be in a different form to one set out in *CPD*, or to be made orally, and may, if CrimPR 14.2 allows, determine without a hearing an application to vary a condition.
(CrimPR 14.7)

Prosecutor's representations about bail

9-030 In any case where a judge can grant or withhold bail, it is the duty of the prosecutor:

(1) to provide the accused and the judge with all the information in his possession which is material to what the judge must decide;
(2) where he opposes the grant of bail, to specify:
 (a) each exception to the general right to bail on which he relies; and
 (b) each consideration that he thinks relevant; and
(3) if he wants a condition to be imposed on any grant of bail to:
 (a) specify each condition proposed; and
 (b) explain what purpose would be served by such a condition.

(CrimPR 14.5)

Exercise of court's powers under CrimPR 14

9-031 The judge may make a bail decision under CrimPR 14 at a hearing, in public or in private. An application to vary a condition of bail may be determined without a hearing if the parties to the application have agreed the terms of the variation proposed, or, on the application of an accused the judge determines the application no sooner than the fifth business day after the application was served.

The judge will not make a decision under CrimPR 14 unless:

(1) each party to the decision, and any surety directly affected by the decision, is present in person or by live link, or has had an opportunity to make representations;
(2) on an application for bail by an accused who is absent and in custody, the judge is satisfied that he has waived the right to attend, or was present when a court withheld bail in the case on a previous occasion and has been in custody continuously since then;
(3) on a prosecutor's appeal against a grant of bail, application to extend a custody time limit or appeal against a refusal to extend such a time limit, the judge is satisfied that an accused who is absent has waived his right to attend, or the judge is satisfied that it would be just to proceed even though the accused is absent; and
(4) he is satisfied that sufficient time has been allowed for the accused to consider information provided by the prosecutor under CrimPR 14.5(2), and for the court to consider the parties' representations and make the decision required.

The court may adjourn any determination if that is necessary to obtain information sufficient to allow the court to make the decision required.

At any hearing at which the court makes one of the following decisions, the judge must announce in terms the accused can understand (with help, if necessary), and by reference to the circumstances of the accused and the case, his reasons for:

(a) withholding bail, or imposing or varying a bail condition;
(b) granting bail, where the prosecutor opposed the grant; or
(c) where the accused is under 18, imposing or varying a bail condition when ordering him to be detained in local authority accommodation or ordering him to be detained in youth detention accommodation.

At a hearing at which the judge grants bail, he must tell the accused where and when to surrender to custody, or arrange for the court officer to give the accused that information as soon as practicable.

(CrimPR 14.2)

Reconsideration; subsequent applications

If a judge does not grant bail to an applicant, it is his duty to consider, at each subsequent hearing while the applicant is a person to whom the presumption under BA 1976 s.4 (see 9-003) applies and remains in custody, whether he ought to be granted bail: **9-032**

(1) at the first hearing after that at which the judge decided not to grant bail, the applicant may support his application with any argument as to fact or law which he desires, whether or not he has advanced that argument previously; and
(2) at subsequent hearings the judge need not hear arguments as to fact or law which he has heard previously.

(BA 1976 Sch.1 Pt IIA)

A decision based on BA 1976 Sch.1 para.5 (where it has not been practicable to obtain sufficient information to make the decision) is not a decision for these purposes (*R. v Calder Justices Ex p. Kennedy* (1992) 156 J.P. 716).

Where the judge, in reconsidering bail, refuses to withhold bail after hearing representations from the prosecution in favour of withholding bail, he must give reasons for refusing to withhold bail, and include a note of those reasons in the record of his decision, providing a copy to the prosecution if requested.

4. Record, variation and breach

Reasons and record; notification of recognisance, etc.

A judge: **9-033**

(1) granting or withholding bail; or
(2) varying conditions,

in relation to a person to whom the right to bail before conviction applies, must give his reasons. The court should include a note of its reasons in the record of its decision and give a copy of that note to the person in relation to whom the decision was taken, but does not need to give a copy of the note where the person has legal representation, unless his legal representative requests the court to do so.

(BA 1976 s.5(3)–(5))

It is the duty of the Crown Court officer:

(1) to arrange for a note or other record to be made of:
  (a) the parties' representations about bail; and
  (b) the judge's reasons for any decision:
    (i) to withhold bail, or to impose or vary a bail condition;
    (ii) to grant bail, where the prosecutor opposed the grant; or
    (iii) on an application to authorise extension of pre-charge bail (see CrimPR 14.19);
(2) to serve notice of any decision about bail on:
  (a) the accused (but only where his legal representative asks for such a notice, or where the accused has no legal representative);
  (b) the prosecutor (but only where the judge granted bail, the prosecutor opposed the grant and has asked for such a notice);
  (c) any party to the decision who was absent when it was made;
  (d) a surety who is directly affected by the decision;
  (e) the accused's custodian, where the accused is in custody and the decision requires the custodian to release the accused (or will do so, if a requirement ordered by the judge is met), or to transfer the accused to the custody of another custodian; or
  (f) the court officer for any other court at which the accused is required by that decision to surrender to custody.

Where the court postpones the date on which an accused who is on bail must surrender to custody, the court officer will serve notice of the postponed date on the accused and any surety.

Where the court determines without a hearing an application to which CrimPR 14.19 applies (application to authorise extension of pre-charge bail), the court officer must notify the applicant if the application is allowed, and notify the applicant and the accused if the application is refused.

(CrimPR 14.4)

Variation of conditions

9-034 On an application by or on behalf of a person to whom bail was granted, or by the prosecutor or a constable, a judge of the Crown Court may:

(1) if that court has granted bail; or
(2) a magistrates' court has committed a person to be sentenced or otherwise to be dealt with, or has sent that person for trial under CDA 1998 s.51 (see *R. v Lincoln Magistrates Court Ex p. Mawer* (1996) 160 J.P. 219),

vary any conditions of bail or impose conditions in respect of bail granted unconditionally.

(BA 1976 s.3(8))

Breach of condition or requirement

9-035 A person arrested under BA 1976 s.7(2) as being likely to abscond or to breach his conditions, or as having breached a condition of his bail (even where that bail was granted by the Crown Court) must be brought before a justice of the peace for the local justice area in which he is arrested (and not before the Crown Court) (BA 1976 s.7(4)–(6)). That justice has no power to send him to the Crown Court to be dealt with for the breach (see *Re Teesside Magistrates Court Ex p. Elliott*, *The Times*, 20 February 2000) but may remand him, or commit him to custody, or grant him bail on the same or different conditions, under the terms of BA 1976 s.7(4)–(6).

Note that:

(1) a Recorder of the Crown Court is not a justice for this purpose (*Re Marshall* [1994] Crim. L.R. 915); and
(2) a breach of condition, unlike failure to surrender, is not a contempt of court and should be dealt with under BA 1976 (*R. v Ashley* [2004] Crim. L.R. 297).

"Withdrawal" of surety

A surety, believing that his principal is about to abscond or has already absconded, has no right to "withdraw" his recognisance, unless the principal is before the court. He can make a complaint in writing at a police station, stating that the principal is unlikely to surrender, which empowers an officer to arrest the accused without warrant, but he remains bound if the police cannot find the principal to arrest him (*R. v Wood Green Crown Court Ex p. Howe* (1991) 93 Cr. App. R. 213). **9-036**

5. Failure to appear; absconding

What amounts to surrender

In the absence of special arrangements either particular to the court or particular to the individual case, surrender to the Crown Court for the purposes of s.6(1) is accomplished when: **9-037**

(1) the accused presents himself to the custody officer by entering the dock; or
(2) a hearing before the judge commences at which he is formally identified as being present.

If there has been no previous surrender, as ordinarily there will have been, it is also accomplished by arraignment (*R. v Central Criminal Court Ex p. Guney* [1996] 2 Cr. App. R. 352). Reporting to the court usher (either by the accused or his advocate) does not amount to surrender (*R. v Evans* [2011] EWCA Crim 2842; [2012] 2 Cr. App. R. 22).

Effect of failure to surrender

A person granted bail in criminal proceedings has a duty to surrender himself into the custody of the appropriate court at the time and place for the time being appointed for him to do so (BA 1976 ss.2(2), 3(1)–(2) and 6(1)). **9-038**

The failure of an accused to comply with the terms of his bail by not surrendering, or not doing so at the appropriate time, may undermine the administration of justice and may disrupt proceedings. The resulting delays impact on victims, witnesses and other court users and also waste costs. Failure to surrender affects not only the case with which the accused is concerned, but also the courts' ability to administer justice more generally by damaging the confidence of victims, witnesses and the public in the effectiveness of the court system and the judiciary.

It is most important, therefore, that accused persons who are granted bail appreciate the significance of the obligation to surrender to custody in accordance with the terms of their bail, and that judges take appropriate action if they fail to do so.

An accused who will be unable for medical reasons to attend court in accordance with his bail must obtain a certificate from his general practitioner or another appropriate medical practitioner such as the doctor with care of the accused at a hospital. This should be obtained in advance of the hearing and conveyed to the court through the accused's legal representative. In order to minimise the disruption to the court and to others, particularly witnesses if the case is listed for trial, the accused should notify the court through his legal representative as soon as his inability to attend court becomes known.

Guidance has been produced by the BMA and the CPS on the role and responsibilities of medical practitioners when issuing medical certificates in criminal proceedings. Judges and magistrates should seek to ensure that this guidance is followed. However, it is a matter for each individual court to decide whether, in any particular case, the issued certificate should be accepted. Without a medical certificate or if an unsatisfactory certificate is provided, the court is likely to consider that the defendant has failed to surrender to bail.

(*CPD* III 14B.1–3)

If an accused fails to surrender to his or her bail there are at least four courses of action for the judge to consider taking:

(1) imposing a penalty for the failure to surrender;
(2) revoking bail or imposing more stringent conditions;
(3) conducting the trial in the absence of the accused; and
(4) ordering that some or all of any sums of money lodged with the court as a security or pledged by a surety as a condition on the grant of bail be forfeited.

(*CPD* III 14B.4)

Absconding; a bail offence

9-039 A person granted bail in criminal proceedings, who:

(1) fails, without reasonable cause, to surrender to the appropriate court at the time and place for the time being appointed for him to do so; or
(2) having reasonable cause for such failure, then fails to surrender to custody at the appointed place as soon after the appointed time as is reasonably practicable,

commits an offence, which in the Crown Court is punishable as if it were a criminal contempt of court, and the offender is liable to imprisonment for up to 12 months or to a fine or both (BA 1976 s.6(1), (2), (5) and (7)).

An offender who fails to appear in answer to a summons issued as a result of an alleged failure to comply with a community order, but is not otherwise on bail, does not commit an offence under s.6 (*R. v Noble* [2008] EWCA Crim 1473; *The Times*, 21 July 2008).

Breach of bail by failing to surrender to the magistrates' court is not indictable; it may be dealt with in the Crown Court only where the magistrates commit the offender for sentence under BA 1976 s.6(6) (see COMMITTALS FOR SENTENCE).

The fact that such an offence is to be treated as if it were a criminal contempt does not alter the fact that it is an offence, and therefore:

(1) a person convicted in the magistrates' court of absconding and committed

under BA 1976 s.6(6) to the Crown Court for sentence is liable to the same penalties;
(2) an offender must be dealt with in respect of any suspended sentence on the ordinary principles; and
(3) as in the case of any other offence, the de minimis principle may be applied.

An accused who commits a bail offence commits an offence that stands apart from the proceedings in respect of which bail was granted. The seriousness of the offence may be reflected by an appropriate penalty being imposed for the bail offence. Thus:

(a) the fact that the accused is acquitted of the substantive offence for which he is being tried or dealt with, or the indictment is not proceeded with, does not preclude the court, in a proper case, from imposing an immediate custodial sentence for the offence of absconding (*R. v Kohli* (1983) 5 Cr. App. R. (S.) 175; *R. v Cockburn-Smith* [2008] EWCA Crim 3159; [2009] 2 Cr. App. R. (S.) 20);
(b) whilst the seriousness of the substantive offence does not of itself aggravate or mitigate the seriousness of the bail offence, its nature may be relevant in assessing the likelihood of harm caused by the failure to surrender;
(c) acquittal of the substantive offence does not mitigate the bail offence; and
(d) the fact that a fine is imposed on the substantive offence does not prevent a custodial sentence being imposed for the bail offence (*R. v Uddin* (1992) 13 Cr. App. R. (S.) 114).

The relevant sentencing guideline is the Definitive Guideline Failure to Surrender to Bail.

Dealing with the offence

The judge dealing with a bail offence, should do so as soon as is practicable, taking into account: **9-040**

(1) when the proceedings in respect of which bail was granted are expected to conclude;
(2) the seriousness of the offence for which the accused is already being prosecuted;
(3) the type of penalty that might be imposed for the bail offence and the original offence; as well as
(4) any other relevant circumstances.

At whatever stage the bail offence is dealt with, it should be noted that:

(a) the fact that it has proved possible to conclude the substantive proceedings in the absence of the accused has no bearing on his culpability for the bail offence, but may be relevant to the assessment of the harm caused;
(b) fleeing the jurisdiction is to be regarded as an aggravating feature (*R. v Cinar* [2011] EWCA Crim 524); and
(c) where, at the same time, determinate custodial sentences are imposed, both for the substantive offence and for the bail offence, the normal approach is for the sentences to be consecutive.

See *CPD* III 14C.5–10.

Execution of warrant; venue

9-041 The court at which the accused is produced should, where practicable and legally permissible, arrange to have all outstanding cases brought before it (including those from different courts) for the purpose of progressing matters and dealing with the question of bail. If the accused appears before a different court, for example because he is charged with offences committed in another area, and it is not practicable for all matters to be concluded by that court, then he may be remanded on bail or in custody, if appropriate, to appear before the first court for the outstanding offences to be dealt with.

(*CPD* III 14D.1)

Institution of proceedings

9-042 Where a person granted bail by a court subsequently fails to surrender to custody, he should normally, on arrest, be brought as soon as appropriate before the court at which the proceedings in respect of which bail was granted are to be heard. There is no requirement to lay an information within the time limit for the Bail Act offence where bail was granted by the court.

Given that bail was granted by the court, it is more appropriate that the court itself should initiate the proceedings by its own motion although the prosecutor may invite the court to take proceedings, if the prosecutor considers proceedings are appropriate.

(*CPD* III 14C.3–4)

As to procedure:

(1) where the judge is invited to take proceedings by the prosecutor, the prosecutor will conduct the proceedings, and, if the matter is contested, will call the evidence; absconding is a criminal charge which must be proved following the correct procedure (*R. v Davies* (1986) 8 Cr. App. R. (S.) 97; *R. v Woods* (1989) 11 Cr. App. R. (S.) 551; *R. v O'Boyle* (1991) 92 Cr. App. R. 202);
(2) where the judge initiates proceedings without such an invitation, the same role may be played by the prosecutor at the request of the judge, where this is practicable;
(3) the burden of proof is on the accused to prove that he had reasonable cause for his failure to surrender (BA 1976 s.6(3));
(4) the judge must give the accused the opportunity to explain himself; and invite submissions from the advocates; and
(5) the judge must make a finding of guilt or otherwise as the case may be.

(*CPD* III 14C.7–8)

An accused who commits an offence under BA 1976 s.6(1) or s.6(2) commits an offence that stands apart from the proceedings in respect of which bail was granted. The seriousness of the offence can be reflected by an appropriate penalty being imposed for the Bail Act offence. The Sentencing Council guideline must be followed unless it would be contrary to the interests of justice to do so. Where the appropriate penalty is a custodial sentence, consecutive sentences should be imposed unless there are circumstances that make this inappropriate (*CPD* III 14C.9–10).

When an accused has been convicted of a Bail Act offence, the judge should review the accused's remand status, including the conditions of that bail, in respect of all outstanding proceedings against him. Failure by the accused to surrender or a conviction for failing to surrender to bail in connection with the main proceedings will be significant factors weighing against the re-granting of bail.

Whether or not an immediate custodial sentence has been imposed for the Bail Act offence, the judge may, having reviewed the accused's remand status, also remand him in custody in the main proceedings.

(*CPD* III 14D.2–4)

6. Estreatment and forfeiture

Forfeiture of a recognisance given by a surety

Where the judge imposes as a condition of bail a requirement that a surety enter into a recognisance and, after the accused is released on bail: **9-043**

(1) the accused fails to surrender as required; or
(2) it appears to the judge that the surety has failed to comply with a condition or direction,

the Crown Court officer will serve notice on the surety and on each party to the decision to grant bail, of the hearing at which the court will consider the forfeiture of the recognisance. The judge will not forfeit the recognisance less than five business days after service of that notice.

(CrimPR 14.15)

The judge should not adjourn a decision on estreatment of sureties (or securities) until such time, if any, that the bailed accused appears before the court. It is possible that an accused who apparently absconds may have a defence of reasonable cause to the allegation of failure to surrender. If that happens, then any surety or security estreated will be returned. The reason for proceeding is that the accused may never surrender, or may not surrender for many years. The judge should still consider the sureties' obligations if that happens. Moreover, the longer the matter is delayed the more probable it is that the personal circumstances of the sureties will change.

The judge should follow the procedure at CrimPR 14.15. Before he makes a decision, he should give the sureties the opportunity to make representations, either in person, through counsel or by statement.

(*CPD* III 14F.3–4)

Approach to estreatment

Where an accused for whose attendance a person has stood surety fails to appear: **9-044**

(1) the court has discretion to forfeit the whole sum, part only of the sum, or to remit the sum;
(2) the starting point is that the surety should be forfeited in full;
(3) a defendant who absconds without forewarning his sureties does not thereby release them from any or all of their responsibilities;
(4) even if a surety does his best, he remains liable for the full amount, except at the discretion of the court;
(5) the presence or absence of culpability is a factor, but is not in itself a reason to reduce or set aside the obligations entered into by the surety;
(6) the means of the surety, and in particular changed means, are relevant; and
(7) the court should forfeit no more than is necessary, in public policy, to maintain the integrity and confidence of the system of taking sureties.

(*CPD* III 14F.5)

See *R. v Uxbridge Justices Ex p. Heward-Mills* [1983] 1 All E.R. 530 and *R. v Maidstone Crown Court Ex p. Lever* [1996] 1 Cr. App. R. 524.

What is reasonable in any given case depends on the circumstances of that case (*R. v York Crown Court Ex p. Coleman* (1988) 86 Cr. App. R. 151). The judge should look at the conduct of the surety to see whether there are mitigating circumstances (*R. v IL Crown Court Ex p. Springall* (1987) 85 Cr. App. R. 214; *R. v Reading CC Ex p. Bello* (1991) 92 Cr. App. R. 303; *R. v Wood Green Crown Court Ex p. Howe* (1991) 93 Cr. App. R. 213).

Where a wife's recognisance is estreated, the proceeds should come out of her own property and not out of her husband's, nor out of their joint property or the matrimonial home (*R. v Southampton Justices Ex p. Green* [1975] 2 All E.R. 1073).

Enforcement of estreated recognisances

9-045 A judge estreating a surety's recognisance:

(1) *must* make an order fixing a term of imprisonment in default if any sum which the surety is liable to pay is not duly paid or recovered, in which case:
   (a) the maximum default term is that set out in the table applicable to fines (see FINES); and
   (b) the restrictions as to immediate imprisonment or detention apply as they do in the case of a fine (see FINES);
(2) *may* make an order:
   (a) allowing time for payment of the amount due under the recognisance;
   (b) directing payment of the amount by instalments of such amounts and on such dates as may be specified in the order; or
   (c) discharging the recognisance or reducing the amount thereunder.

(PCC(S)A 2000 s.139)

Forfeiture of security (BA 1976 s.3(5))

9-046 Where:

(1) an accused has given security (under BA 1976 s.3(5)), before his release on bail; and
(2) the judge is satisfied that he has failed to surrender to custody, then, unless it appears that he had reasonable cause for failure, the judge may order the forfeiture of the security, or such amount less than the full value as he thinks fit.

Such order, unless previously revoked, takes effect at the end of 21 days beginning with the day on which it is made. If the security consists of money it is accounted for and paid in the same way as a fine imposed by the Crown Court. If it does not, it is enforced by such magistrates' court as is specified in the order.

The Crown Court officer will give notice of the decision to the person before whom security was given.

If the judge is subsequently satisfied on an application made by or on behalf of the person who gave security that he did, after all, have reasonable cause for his failure to surrender, he may:

(a) remit the forfeiture; or

(b) declare that the forfeiture extend to such an amount less than the full value as he sees fit to order.

An order for remission may be made before or after the original order has taken effect, but an application is not to be entertained unless the judge is satisfied that the prosecutor was given reasonable notice of the applicant's intention to make it.

Where an order for remission is made after the order for forfeiture has taken effect, any balance due to the person concerned will be repaid.

(BA 1976 s.5(7)–(9A))

Where security is provided to the accused by a third person, that person has no right to demand its return where the accused fails to appear (*R. (on the application of Stevens) v Truro Magistrates Court* [2001] EWHC (Admin) 558; [2002] 1 W.L.R. 144).

7. Bail appeals from magistrates' courts

(1) Appeal by accused

Apart from its jurisdiction to grant bail to an accused in its custody, the Crown Court may entertain an appeal by the person concerned in relation to certain specified situations where a case is still proceeding in the magistrates' court, as where the magistrates' court: **9-047**

(1) adjourns a case under:
   (a) MCA 1980 s.10;
   (b) MCA 1980 s.17C (intention as to plea: adjournment);
   (c) MCA 1980 s.18 (initial procedure on information against an adult for an offence triable either way);
   (d) MCA 1980 s.24C (intention to plead by child or young person);
   (e) CDA 1998 s.52(5) (cases sent for trial s.51); or
   (f) PCC(S)A 2000 s.11 (remand for medical examination); and
(2) the magistrates' court:
   (a) refuses to grant bail;
   (b) refuses to entertain an application by the accused for a rehearing; or
   (c) grants bail subject to the specified conditions set out below.

(BA 1976 s.5(6A))

In such circumstances the Crown Court must have a certificate in the prescribed form issued by the magistrates' court and stating that it has heard full argument on the application before refusing it (BA 1976 s.5(6A)).

Bail granted with conditions

Where the magistrates' court grants bail to a person on adjourning the proceedings in one of the situations set out in 9-048, the person concerned may appeal against any requirement: **9-048**

(1) that he resides away from a particular place or area;
(2) that he resides at a particular place other than a bail hostel;
(3) for the provision of a surety or sureties or the giving of security;
(4) that he remains indoors between certain hours; or
(5) imposed under BA 1976 s.3(6ZAA) (requirements with respect to electronic monitoring); or

(6) that he make no contact with another person provided that such appeal may not be brought unless the application to the magistrates' court under:
(a) BA 1976 s.3(8)(a);
(b) BA 1976 s.3(8)(b) (application by constable or prosecutor); or
(c) BA 1976 s.5B(1) (application by prosecutor).
was made and determined before the appeal was brought.

The judge, under this provision, may vary the conditions of bail. Where he determines such an appeal the person concerned may not bring a further appeal under the section in respect of the conditions of bail, unless an application or a further application to the magistrates' court under BA 1976 s.3(8)(a) is made and determined after the appeal (CJA 2003 s.16).

(2) Procedure: appeal by accused

9-049 Where an accused wants to:

(1) apply to the Crown Court for bail after a magistrates' court has withheld bail; or
(2) appeal to the Crown Court after a magistrates' court has refused to vary a bail condition as the accused wants,

an application must be made to the Crown Court in writing as soon as practicable after the magistrates' court's decision, and served on the Crown Court officer, the magistrates' court officer, the prosecutor, and any surety affected or proposed.

The application must:

(a) specify:
  (i) the decision that the applicant wants the Crown Court to make, and
  (ii) each offence charged;
(b) explain:
  (i) as appropriate, why the Crown Court should not withhold bail, or why it should vary the condition under appeal, and
  (ii) what further information or legal argument, if any, has become available since the magistrates' court's decision;
(c) propose the terms of any suggested condition of bail;
(d) on an application for bail, attach a copy of the certificate of full argument served on the accused under CrimPR 14.4(4); and
(e) if the applicant wants an earlier hearing than the rules provide for (see below) ask for that, and explain why it is needed.

The magistrates' court officer must as soon as practicable serve on the Crown Court officer a copy of the note or record made under CrimPR 14.4(1) in connection with the magistrates' court's decision, and the date of the next hearing, if any, in the magistrates' court.

A prosecutor who opposes the application must so notify the Crown Court officer and the accused at once and serve on each notice of the reasons for opposition. (CrimPR 14.8(1)–(5))

Before the Crown Court can deal with an application under CrimPR 14.8 by an accused after a magistrates' court has withheld bail, it must be satisfied that the magistrates' court has issued a certificate, under BA 1976 s.5(6A), that it heard full argument on the application for bail before it refused the application. The certificate is produced by the magistrates' court's computer system, Libra, as part of the

General Form of Order ("GENORD"). Two hard copies are produced, one for the defence and one for the prosecution. (Some magistrates' courts may also produce a manual certificate which will usually be available from the justices' legal adviser at the conclusion of the hearing; the GENORD may not be produced until the following day.)

Under CrimPR 14.4(4), the magistrates' court officer will provide the accused with a certificate. However, it is the responsibility of the defence, as the applicant in the Crown Court, to ensure that a copy of the certificate is provided to the Crown Court as part of the application (CrimPR 14.8(3)(e)). The applicant's solicitors should attach a copy of the certificate to the bail application form. If the certificate is not enclosed with the application form, it will be difficult to avoid some delay in listing.

Applications should be made to the court to which the accused will be, or would have been, sent for trial. In the event of an application in a purely summary case, it should be made to the Crown Court centre which normally receives Class 3 work (see ALLOCATION AND LISTING OF CASES). The hearing will be listed as a chambers matter, unless a judge has directed otherwise (*CPD* III 14A.2).

Arrangements for appeal

Unless the Crown Court otherwise directs, the court officer must arrange for a judge to hear the application or appeal as soon as practicable and in any event no later than the business day after it was served, though the Crown Court may vary any time limit under this rule (CrimPR 14.8(6)–(7)). **9-050**

The person concerned is entitled to be present at the hearing of the appeal (he is treated as so where he attends by a live link: CDA 1998 ss.57A, 57B; but note the amendments made by the Coronavirus Act 2020).

(3) Appeal by prosecutor

Where a magistrates' court grants bail to a person who is charged with, or convicted of, an offence punishable by imprisonment, the prosecution may appeal to a judge of the Crown Court against the granting of bail (B(A)A 1993 s.1). **9-051**

Such an appeal lies only where:

(a) in relation to offences punishable with less than a term of five years or more, the case was committed, transferred or sent, or a voluntary bill was preferred after 4 April 2005;
(b) the prosecution made representations that bail should not be granted; and
(c) such representations were made before it was granted.

As far as the prosecutor is concerned, oral notice of appeal must be given to the magistrates' court and to the person concerned at the conclusion of the proceedings in which such bail was granted, and before the release of the person concerned. The magistrates will remand the person concerned in custody (or, in the case of a person under 18, to local authority accommodation or youth detention accommodation under LASPOA 2012 Pt 3 Ch.3) until the appeal is determined or otherwise disposed of.

Oral notice must be followed by written notice within two hours of the conclusion of the proceedings, otherwise the appeal will be deemed to have been disposed of. If, having given oral notice of appeal, the prosecutor fails to serve written notice within the appropriate period, the person concerned will be released.

(B(A)A 1993 s.1(2)–(11))

(4) Procedure: Appeal by prosecutor

9-052 The prosecutor must serve an appeal notice on the court officer for the court which has granted bail and on the accused not more than two hours after telling that court of the decision to appeal.

The appeal notice must specify:

(a) each offence with which the accused is charged;
(b) the decision under appeal;
(c) the reasons given for the grant of bail; and
(d) the grounds of appeal.

Where written notice of appeal is served on the magistrates' court, the Crown Court officer will, as soon as is practicable, be provided with a copy of the appeal notice, the note or record made of the bail decision and notice of the date of the next hearing in the court which has granted bail.

If the Crown Court so directs, the Crown Court officer must arrange for the accused to be assisted by the Official Solicitor in a case in which he has no legal representative, and asks for such assistance.

On an appeal to the Crown Court, the Crown Court officer will arrange for a judge to hear the appeal as soon as practicable, and in any event no later than the second business day after the appeal notice was served.

The prosecutor may abandon an appeal to the Crown Court:

(i) before the hearing of the appeal begins without the court's permission, by serving a notice of abandonment, signed by or on behalf of the prosecutor, on the accused, the Crown Court officer, and the magistrates' court officer; but
(ii) after the hearing of the appeal begins, only with the judge's permission.

If the prosecutor fails to serve an appeal notice within time or he serves a notice of abandonment under this paragraph, the court officer for the court which has granted bail must instruct the accused's custodian to release the accused on the bail granted by that court, subject to any condition or conditions of bail imposed.

(CrimPR 14.9)

The appeal hearing must begin within 48 hours, excluding weekends and public holidays (construed as "two working days", see *R. v Middlesex Guildhall Crown Court Ex p. Okoli* [2001] 1 Cr. App. R. 1; see also *R. (on the application of Jeffrey) v Warwick Crown Court* [2003] Crim. L.R. 190).

Under B(A)A 1993 s.1, the appellate proceedings are expressly stated to be a rehearing, the judge having power to remand in custody or to release on bail on such conditions as he thinks fit. If the judge upholds the prosecutor's appeal, he must fix a date on which the accused is to appear before the magistrates in accordance with the magistrates' powers under MCA 1980 ss.128, 128A and 129, otherwise the accused will be unlawfully detained once the eight days of the remand have expired (*R. v Manchester Magistrates Court Ex p. Szakal* [2000] 1 Cr. App. R. 248; *Remice v Belmarsh Prison Governor* [2007] Crim. L.R. 796).

10. BIND OVER

QUICK GUIDE

General

A "bind over" requires a person to consent to enter into a recognisance, and, where appropriate, to provide a surety for refraining from a specified conduct or activity, for a specified period. **10-001**

That conduct or activity must be spelled out in the order. In light of the judgment in *Hashman v United Kingdom* (2000) 30 E.H.R.R. 241; [2000] Crim. L.R. 185, the judge should not bind an individual over "to be of good behaviour". Rather than binding an individual over to "keep the peace" in general terms, he should identify the specific conduct or activity from which the individual must refrain (*CPD* VII Sentencing J para.J.3). The terms of the order should be specified in a written order (*CPD* VII Sentencing J para.J.4).

The court's jurisdiction may be exercised over:

(1) an offender, at common law or under statute, principally JPA 1968;
(2) any other person under JPA 1968; or
(3) the parent or guardian of a convicted juvenile, under SA 2020 s.376. (Powers under the JPA 1361 and JPA 1968 are not affected by the SA 2020 s.378.)

Since there are technical distinctions applicable to the form of each order, it is important in making an order to specify which jurisdiction is being exercised (thus avoiding the difficulties arising in *R. v Finch* (1963) 47 Cr. App. R. 58 and *R. v Ayu* (1959) 43 Cr. App. R. 31).

As to binding over the parents or guardians of juveniles, see 10-010.

Note that:

(a) an offender must consent to the making of an order, and that consent is not vitiated by the fact that a custodial sentence is the only realistic alternative (*R. v Williams* (1982) 75 Cr. App. R. 378);
(b) the court cannot force a person to enter into recognisances, or treat him as bound where he declines to be; the remedy, where such person is over the age of 18 to commit him to prison until he agrees (*Veater v Glennon* (1981) 72 Cr. App. R. 331); but
(c) the court is powerless in respect of a person under 18 (*Veater v Glennon* (1981) 72 Cr. App. R. 331; *Howley v Oxford* (1985) 81 Cr. App. R. 246; *Surrey Chief Constable v Ridley* [1985] Crim. L.R. 725 unless that person consents (*Conlan v Oxford* (1984) 79 Cr. App. R. 157).

A. COMMON LAW BIND OVER; RESPITED JUDGMENT

Where judgment is pending, an appeal is pending, or in any other case where the circumstances make it expedient in the interests of justice, an offender may be required: **10-002**

(1) to enter into recognisances, with or without sureties, in a specific amount or amounts;
(2) to come up for judgment within a reasonable, specified period, if called upon to do so; and
(3) meanwhile to comply with certain stated conditions,

and the order needs to be carefully couched in these very terms (SCA 1981 s.79(2)(b)).

The judge should specify any conditions with which the individual is to comply in the meantime and not specify that he is to be of good behaviour. He should also, if the individual is unrepresented, explain the consequences of a breach of the binding over order in these circumstances (*CPD* VII Sentencing J paras J.17 and J.18).

Distinctive features

10-003 A common law bind over differs from one under JPA 1968 in that:

(1) a common law bind over ranks as a penalty, not as an ancillary order, and cannot therefore be combined with any other penalty such as a fine or imprisonment (*R. v Ayu* (1959) 43 Cr. App. R. 31);
(2) an offender called upon to come up for judgment is liable to be sentenced for the original offence, not merely to estreatment of recognisances; and
(3) a common law bind over ranks as a conviction, and even where no sentence is subsequently passed for the offence, appeal lies to the CACD (*R. v Abrahams* (1952) 36 Cr. App. R. 147; *R. v Williams* (1982) 75 Cr. App. R. 378).

Condition to leave jurisdiction

10-004 It may be a condition of a common law bind over (but not of an order under JPA 1968), provided the offender consents, that he leave the jurisdiction and not return for a specified period. The CACD has said that the power should be used very sparingly. Thus, in the following cases, the conditions listed below were imposed:

(1) *R. v Ayu* (1959) 43 Cr. App. R. 31 "to return to Nigeria forthwith and not to return to Great Britain during the period of the recognisance";
(2) *R. v Flaherty* [1958] Crim. L.R. 556 "to return to Ireland and not land again in this country for at least three years"; and
(3) *R. v Hodges* (1967) 51 Cr. App. R. 361 to attend a Carmelite organisation in the Republic of Ireland, which was prepared to accept the offender, and "not to return to England for ten years".

Only in exceptional circumstances should it be used to return an offender to a country of which he is not a citizen, and in which he does not habitually reside (*R. v Williams* (1982) 75 Cr. App. R. 378).

Appearing for judgment

10-005 An offender may be called upon to come up for judgment for something less than the commission of a further offence (*R. v McGarry* (1945) 30 Cr. App. R. 187). When he appears:

(1) the facts of any breach must be proved as if they were allegations of an offence;

(2) he must be given an opportunity to give evidence or call witnesses;
(3) if the matter of complaint is his failure to leave the country, the judge should enquire into whether that failure was a deliberate one (*R. v Philbert* [1973] Crim. L.R. 129); and
(4) he may be dealt with for the original offence; the judge is not limited to estreating any recognisances.

B. JUSTICES OF THE PEACE ACT 1968 s.1

General

A bind over under the Act is not dependent on conviction and, in a proper case, an acquitted accused may be bound over (*R. v ILCC Ex p. Benjamin* (1987) 85 Cr. App. R. 267), as where no evidence is offered. **10-006**

Jurisdiction extends beyond the offender, to any person who, or whose case, is before the court, requiring that person:

(1) to enter into recognisances, with or without sureties, in a specific sum;
(2) to refrain from some specific conduct or activity, for a specified period, which should not generally exceed 12 months; or
(3) in the case of an adult to go to prison if he does not comply.

For the distinctions between such a bind over and one at common law, see 10-003 (JPA 1968 s.1(7)).

Before imposing a bind over, the judge:

(a) must be satisfied that a breach of the peace involving violence or an imminent threat of violence has occurred, or that there is a real risk of violence in the future;
(b) should identify the specific conduct or activity from which the individual must refrain, and the details of that conduct or those activities should be specified in a written order served on the relevant parties; and
(c) should state his reasons for:
    (i) the making of the order;
    (ii) its length; and
    (iii) the amount of the recognisance.

(*CPD* VIII Sentencing J para.J.2)

The violence referred to in (a) may be perpetrated by the individual who will be subject to the order or by a third party as a natural consequence of that individual's conduct (*CPD* VII Sentencing J, para.J.2).

When making an order binding an individual over to refrain from specified types of conduct or activities, the details of that conduct or those activities should be specified in a written order, served on all relevant parties. The judge should state his reasons for the making of the order, its length and the amount of the recognisance. The length of the order should be proportionate to the harm sought to be avoided and should not generally exceed 12 months (*CPD* VII Sentencing J, para.J.4).

"Persons before the court"

RHOA 1974 s.7(5) excludes from a person's antecedents any order of the court "with respect to any person otherwise than on conviction". **10-007**

A "person before the court":

(1) includes a witness who gives evidence, whether for the Crown or for the accused (*Sheldon v Bromfield* [1964] 2 All E.R. 131); but
(2) does not include a person who is not a party and is not called as a witness (*R. v Swindon CC Ex p. Singh* (1984) 79 Cr. App. R. 137; *R. v Kingston CC Ex p. Guarino* [1986] Crim. L.R. 325; *R. v Lincoln CC Ex p. Jones*, *The Times*, 16 June 1989).

Evidence and procedure; burden of proof

10-008 Where the judge considers making an order, he should, in effect, apply the procedure prescribed for a magistrates' court under MCA 1980 ss.51–57, which include a requirement (s.53) to hear evidence and representations before making an order.

Thus, the judge should (even where there is an admission sufficient to found an order, and the person concerned consents to its being made):

(1) give:
 (a) the person who would be the subject of the order; and
 (b) the prosecutor,
 the opportunity to make representations, both as to the making of the order and as to its terms; and
(2) hear any admissible evidence the parties may wish to call (and which has not already been heard in the proceedings),

so as to satisfy himself that an order is appropriate in all the circumstances, and to be clear as to its terms (*CPD* VII Sentencing J para.J.5).

The judge should be satisfied:

(a) of the matters complained of, the burden of proof being on the prosecutor; and
(b) on the merits of the case, that an order is appropriate,

and should announce his decision before considering the amount of the recognisance.

The person made subject to the order should be told that he has a right of appeal (*CPD* VII Sentencing J para.J.10).

In fixing the amount of any recognisance, the judge should have regard to the person's financial resources and should hear representations either from him or his legal representatives, as to them (*CPD* VII Sentencing J para.J.11).

Enforcement and estreatment

10-009 If there is any possibility that a person will refuse to enter into a recognisance:

(1) the judge should consider whether there are any appropriate alternatives to a binding over order (for example, continuing with the prosecution); and
(2) where there are no appropriate alternatives and the person concerned continues to refuse to enter into the recognisance, the judge may use his common law power to commit that person to custody.

(*CPD* VII Sentencing J para.J.13)

Before the judge exercises a power to commit the individual to custody, the individual should be given the opportunity to see a duty solicitor or another legal representative and be represented in proceedings if the individual so wishes. Public funding should generally be granted to cover representation. The Judge may grant a Representation Order. In the event that the individual does not take the opportunity to seek legal advice, the judge must give him a final opportunity to comply with the request and must explain the consequences of a failure to do so (*CPD* VII Sentencing J paras J.14 and J.15).

A recognisance may be enforced only by estreatment (see BAIL), and committal to prison in default of payment. The judge must make such enquiries as are required before estreating the recognisance of a surety for bail (*R. v Marlow Justices Ex p. O'Sullivan* (1984) 78 Cr. App. R. 13).

Where there is an allegation of a breach of recognisance:

(a) the judge should be satisfied beyond reasonable doubt that a breach has occurred before making an order for estreatment, the burden of proof resting on the prosecutor;
(b) before such person is committed to custody, he must be given the opportunity to see a duty solicitor or another legal representative and be represented in the proceedings if he so wishes; public funding should generally be granted to cover such representation; and
(c) in the event that the person does not take the opportunity to seek legal advice, the judge must give him a final opportunity to comply with the request and must explain the consequences of a failure to do so.

C. Parents and guardians of juvenile offenders

Where a person under 18 is convicted of an offence, the judge: **10-010**

(1) *may*; and
(2) where the offender is under 16 when sentenced, *must*, if satisfied having regard to the circumstances of the case that it would be desirable in the interest of preventing the commission by him of further offences,

with the consent of that person, order the parent or guardian to enter into a recognisance to take proper care of him and exercise proper control over him, specifying the actions which the parent or guardian is to take and:

(a) if the parent or guardian refuses consent, and the judge considers that refusal unreasonable, order that person to pay a fine not exceeding £1,000; and
(b) where the judge has passed on the offender a sentence which consists of or includes a youth rehabilitation order, he may include in the recognisance a provision that the parent or guardian ensure that the offender complies with the requirements of the sentence.

Where he does not exercise his duty under (2) above, the judge must state in open court that he is not satisfied as mentioned in that paragraph, and why (SA 2020 ss.376(1) and (4); *CPD* VII Sentencing J para.J.19).

Amount and period of recognisances

In fixing the amount of a recognisance under these provisions, the court must take into account, among other things, the means of the parent or guardian so far as they appear or are known to him, and an order shall not require him to enter into a recognisance: **10-011**

(1) for an amount exceeding £1,000; or

(2) for a period exceeding three years or where the young person will attain the age of 18 in a shorter period, for a period exceeding that shorter period.

(SA 2020 s.376.)

A parent or guardian may appeal to the CACD against the making of such an order, as if he had been convicted on indictment and the order were a sentence passed on his conviction (SA 2020 s.377(2)).

The court may vary or revoke an order made by it if, on the application of the parent or guardian, it appears, having regard to any change in circumstances since the order was made, to be in the interests of justice to do so (SA 2020 s.377(3)).

11. CASE MANAGEMENT

Quick Guide

A. Introduction

1. General

The rules

Case management in criminal matters in the Crown Court is largely governed by the criminal procedure rules and various criminal practice directions. The 2020 Rules (SI 2020/759) replaced the 2015 Rules and the various amendments made since then and came into force on 5 October 2020 and together with various amendments made since 2020, the most recent of which (SI 2022/815) came into force from 3 October 2022, the work alongside the *Criminal Practice Directions (CPD)* (the most recent amendment (number 12) came into force on 24 March 2022). Forms are set out in Annex D to *CPD*. The ongoing review and amendments to the CrimPR and *CPD* bring into effect many of the recommendations made by Sir Brian Leveson, the then President of the QBD in his "*Review of Efficiency in Criminal Proceedings*" published on 23 January 2015. The changes seek to streamline case management and to further reduce ineffective and unnecessary hearings. There is a clear imperative on all to ensure that cases are managed effectively to make sure that cases are dealt with as expeditiously as is possible. **11-001**

The *CPD* 2015 [2015] EWCA Crim 1567 (handed down on 29 September 2015 and amended by *Amendment No.1* [2016] EWCA Crim 97 handed down on 23 March 2016, *Amendment No.2* [2016] EWCA Crim 1714 handed down on 16 November 2016, *Amendment No.3* [2017] EWCA Crim 30 handed down on 31 January 2017, *Amendment No.4* [2017] EWCA Crim 310 handed down on 28 March 2017, *Amendment No.5* [2017] EWCA Crim 1076 handed down on 26 July 2017), *Amendment No.6* [2018] EWCA Crim 516 handed down on 21 March 2018 and *Amendment No.7* [2018] EWCA Crim 1760 handed down on 26 July 2018, *Amendment No.8* [2019] EWCA Crim 495 handed down on 28 March 2019,

Amendment No.9 [2019] EWCA Crim 1603 handed down on 10 October 2019 and *Amendment No.10* [2020] EWCA Crim 605) consolidates the *CPD* given on 7 October 2013 [2013] EWCA Crim 1361; [2013] 1 W.L.R. 3164 with the four amendments to those directions ((i) [2013] EWCA Crim 2328; [2014] 1 W.L.R. 25; (ii) [2013] EWCA Crim 1569; [2014] 1 W.L.R. 35; (iii) [2015] EWCA Crim 430; [2015] 1 W.L.R. 1643; and (iv) [2015] EWCA Crim 1253) and replaces those directions. There have been further amendments issued with *Amendment No.11* [2020] EWCA Crim 1347 handed down on 29 October 2020, *Amendment No.12* [2022] EWCA Crim 367 handed down on 23 March 2022, *Amendment No.13* [2022] EWCA Crim 688 handed down on 25 May 2022 and *Amendment No.14* unreported, handed down on 19 August 2022. *Consolidated Criminal Practice Direction (PD)* Annexes D and E of the of 8 July 2002 as amended, which set out forms for use in connection with the CrimPR, continue to remain in force.

The *CPD* supplement many, but not all parts of the CrimPR. They include other directions about practice and procedure in the courts to which they apply. With the rearrangement of the CrimPR the *CPD* has also been arranged so as to correspond.

Civil matters in the Crown Court continue to be governed by the Crown Court Rules 1982, amended, in relation to case management, by SI 2009/3361.

In the case of heavy fraud and other complex criminal cases estimated to last more than four weeks, the Protocol reported at [2005] 2 All E.R. 429 should be followed (see 11-062), the full text of which is to be found in the Archbold Supplement at N1.

Local rules and practices

11-002 The Crown Court is a single court; its procedure and practice must be the same in all its locations, unless there is an objectively justifiable basis for such a practice based on local conditions. If a court considers that such a practice is required because of local conditions, then in these rare circumstances, details of the practice and the justification must be submitted to the office of the Lord Chief Justice before it is implemented. The Lord Chief Justice may, if appropriate, refer it to the Criminal Procedure Rule Committee (CPRC).

There are practices that are initiated in some courts with a view to improving the just and fair dispatch of the business of the Crown Court. Such initiatives are to be greatly welcomed and encouraged. However, to ensure such initiatives are looked at in the wider context that there is a single Crown Court, courts should inform the office of the Lord Chief Justice of such initiatives before embarking on them. The initiative can then be referred to the CPRC for consideration and monitoring. If the practice is beneficial, that benefit can be extended to the whole of the jurisdiction of England and Wales. If not, such a practice must cease (*R. v Baybasin* [2013] EWCA Crim 2357; [2014] 1 Cr. App. R. 19). The circumstances of that case, where balloting of jurors by numbers took place under a local rule have now been resolved by the insertion of CrimPR 25.6(5).

The "overriding objective"

11-003 The overriding objective of the CrimPR, is that criminal cases be dealt with justly (CrimPR 1.1) (see *SL (A Juvenile v DPP* [2001] EWHC (Admin) 882; [2002] 1 Cr. App. R. 32) and this overriding objective runs right through any application of the CrimPR. The judge must further the overriding objective, in particular when exercising any power given to him by legislation (including the CrimPR), applying any practice direction or interpreting any rule or practice direction (CrimPR 1.3). (See also *CPD* I General Matters 1A: The Overriding Objective).

Dealing with a case justly includes (CrimPR 1.1(2)):

(1) acquitting the innocent and convicting the guilty;
(2) dealing with the prosecution and the defence fairly;
(3) recognising the rights of the accused, particularly those under ECHR art.6;
(4) respecting the interests of witnesses, victims and jurors, and keeping them informed of the progress of the case;
(5) dealing with a case efficiently and expeditiously;
(6) ensuring that appropriate information is available to the judge when bail and sentence are considered; and
(7) dealing with the case in ways that take into account:
    (a) the gravity of the offence alleged;
    (b) the complexity of what is in issue;
    (c) the severity of the consequences for the accused and others affected; and
    (d) the needs of other cases.

Duties and burdens are imposed on all the participants in a criminal trial, including the judge. The preparation and conduct of trials is dependent on, and subject to, the CrimPR (*R. v K* [2006] EWCA Crim 724; [2006] Crim. L.R. 1012). The requirements of a fair trial for all accused, enshrined in ECHR art.6, are met by the proper application of the CrimPR (*R. v Musone* [2007] EWCA Crim 1237; [2007] 2 Cr. App. R. 29).

"It is no longer the role of the court simply to provide a level playing field and to referee whatever game the parties choose to play upon it. The court is concerned to ensure that judicial and court resources are appropriately and proportionately used in accordance with the requirements of justice." Per Lord Phillips MR in *Jameel v Dow Jones and Co* [2005] EWCA Civ 75; [2005] 2 W.L.R. 1614).

Duties imposed on parties

In the conduct of a criminal case anyone involved in any way with the case has a duty to: **11-004**

(1) prepare and conduct the case in accordance with the overriding objective (stated in 11-003);
(2) comply with the CrimPR, practice directions and directions made by the judge; and
(3) at once inform the judge, and all parties, of any "significant failure" (whether or not that participant is responsible for that failure) to take any procedural step required by the CrimPR, any practice direction or any direction of the court.

A failure is "significant" if it might hinder the court in furthering the "overriding objective" (CrimPR 1.2). "Practice direction" refers to the Lord Chief Justice's *Criminal Practice Directions* as amended, and "*Criminal Costs Practice Direction*" means the Lord Chief Justice's *Practice Direction (Costs in Criminal Proceedings, as amended)* (CrimPR 2.2).

Unless the context makes it clear that something different is meant, anything that a party may or must do under the CrimPR, may be done (CrimPR 46.1);

(a) by a legal representative on that party's behalf;
(b) by a person with the corporation's written authority, where that corporation is an accused;
(c) with the help of a parent, guardian or other suitable supporting adult where that party is an accused who is under 18, or whose understanding of what the case involves is limited.

A number of cases (see *R. v Phillips* [2007] EWCA Crim 1042) have emphasised the need for:

(1) judges to be robust in case management decisions;
(2) parties ordered to take steps, to take them; and
(3) case progression staff (11-006) to ensure compliance with management orders.

Nature of case management

11-005 While the presumption of innocence, and an adversarial process, are essential features of our legal tradition, and of the right of the accused to a fair trial, it is no part of a fair trial that questions of guilt and innocence should be determined by procedural manoeuvres. On the contrary, fairness is best served when the issues between the parties are identified as early and as clearly as possible (*CPD* 1 General Matters 1A.1 and 2).

Thus:

1. The object of a criminal trial is to convict the guilty and acquit the innocent.
2. It is not a game under which a guilty accused should be provided with a sporting chance.
3. The prosecution must prove its case.
4. An accused is not obliged to inculpate himself.
5. It is not for a party to obstruct or delay the preparation of a case for trial in order to secure some perceived procedural advantage, or to take unfair advantage of a mistake by someone else.

   If judges allow that to happen it damages public confidence in criminal justice. The CrimPR and the Practice Directions, taken together, make it clear that judges must not allow it to happen.
6. The right to a fair trial does not entitle either or both sides to take as much time as they like, or for that matter, as long as advocates and solicitors or the accused themselves think appropriate. Resources are limited. Time itself is a resource. It follows that the sensible use of time requires judicial management and control. In a postscript to the decision in *R. v TJC* [2015] EWCA Crim 1276, the LCJ stated:

   > "It is a regrettable feature of this case ... that despite the pre-trial hearings, counsel then representing the defendant had not raised any issue as to the adequacy of the way in which the prosecution had put its case. This was a failure that should not have occurred and resulted in three days of court time being wasted before the Recorder. This type of waste of resources must not be repeated. Those attending pre-trial hearings must give the proper attention to cases. If they do not, then it is open to the trial judge to proceed with the trial without entertaining applications of this type on the basis that they should have been made earlier; it will not matter that the advocate at the pre-trial hearing was different; it was the duty of

that advocate only to appear at the pre-trial hearing on the basis that the advocate was fully familiar with the case and had the requisite competence to do so."

Case Progression Officers (CPOs)

The CrimPR require each party, at the beginning of a case, unless the judge otherwise directs, to nominate an individual responsible for progressing the case, telling other parties and the judge who he is and how to contact him. A court officer will be appointed with a similar function. Such a person is called a "case progression officer". **11-006**

A CPO must (CrimPR 3.4(4)):

(1) monitor compliance with directions;
(2) make sure that the court is kept informed of events that may affect the progress of the case;
(3) make sure that he can be contacted promptly about the case during ordinary business hours;
(4) act promptly and reasonably in response to communications about the case; and
(5) if he will be unavailable, appoint a substitute to fulfil his duties and inform the other CPOs.

At, or as soon as possible after, any hearing the parties will be supplied with a copy of any directions made (CrimPR 3.14).

It is the primary duty of the parties to *comply* with the directions made.

It is the function of the Crown Court CPO to *monitor* compliance with the directions made, and to ensure that any failures which cannot be remedied, and which may affect the readiness of the case and the date for trial, are brought to the attention of the judge assigned to the case, if there is one, or to the Resident Judge (CrimPR 3.4).

The ambit of the judge's duty

The judge must further the "overriding objective" (11-001) by actively managing the case, that is by giving any direction appropriate to the needs of that case as early as possible (CrimPR 3.2(1)–(3)). **11-007**

"Active case management" includes (CrimPR 3.2(2)):

- the early identification of the *real issues*;
- the early identification of the *needs of witnesses*;
- achieving certainty as to what must be done, by whom, and when, in particular by the early setting of a *timetable* for the progress of the case;
- monitoring the *progress* of the case and compliance with directions;
- ensuring that *evidence*, whether disputed or not, is presented in the shortest and clearest way;
- *discouraging delay*, dealing with as many aspects of the case as possible on the same occasion, and avoiding unnecessary hearings;
- encouraging the participants to *co-operate* in the progression of the case; and
- making use of *technology* (11-076).

The judge has to strike a balance between the needs of everyone involved in the case and the need for justice to be done swiftly. He is responsible for controlling the timetable of the trial and may exercise his powers to ensure that the trial ends by a certain date. He should refuse an adjournment unless satisfied that it is necessary and justified.

The judge's case management powers

11-008 The judge may give any direction and take any step, actively to manage a case, unless that direction or step would be inconsistent with legislation, including the CrimPR (CrimPR 3.5(1)).

In particular, he may (CrimPR 3.5(2)):

(1) nominate a judge to manage the case;
(2) give a direction, on his own initiative or on application by a party;
(3) ask or allow a party to propose a direction;
(4) for the purpose of giving directions, receive applications and representations by letter, by telephone or by any other means of electronic communication, and conduct a hearing by such means;
(5) give a direction at a hearing, in public or in private, or without a hearing;
(6) fix, postpone, bring forward, extend, cancel or adjourn a hearing;
(7) shorten or extend (even after it has expired) a time limit fixed by a direction;
(8) require that issues in the case should be identified in writing, determined separately, and decide in what order they will be determined; and
(9) specify the consequences of failure to comply with a direction.

Any power to give a direction includes a power to vary or revoke that direction (11-020).

While the CrimPR do not refer explicitly to a power to require the attendance of appropriate legal representation, it is clear that this is implied by the broader case management powers to make directions or orders that will progress the case. Participation in case management is not a private arrangement between the client and the lawyers which the judge cannot affect. Were it otherwise, a client would be able to permit his lawyer to absent himself from part of a trial, irrespective of the views of the court.

There are many entirely appropriate reasons why a representative will not be able to attend court: other professional commitments, ill-health, personal tragedy are but a few and courts regularly make every allowance for these. In a case where the conduct of the advocate, amounts to willful and deliberate disobedience of the judge's order amounting to an act of defiance a finding of contempt of court may be appropriate, or, where that is not appropriate, a direction that counsel's conduct should be considered by the Bar Standards Board.

Alleged contempt by legal practitioners needs to be approached with care within the principles enunciated in CONTEMPT OF COURT.

The judge may deal with preliminary matters exclusively by reference to written submissions limited to a length specified by him if he thinks it right to do so.

Further:

(a) he is not bound to allow oral submissions, but if he does so he is entitled to put a time limit on them;
(b) the necessary public element of any hearing will be sufficiently achieved if the accused and representatives of the media in court are supplied with copies of written submissions if they wish to see them.

No particular method of approach is prescribed, as case management decisions are case specific (*R. v K* [2006] EWCA Crim 724; [2006] 2 All E.R. 552).

Note that:

(i) a magistrates' court may give a direction that will apply in the Crown Court if the case is to continue there; and conversely

(ii) a judge of the Crown Court may give a direction that will apply in a magistrates' court if the case is to continue there.

(CrimPR 3.5(3) and (4))

As to varying a direction given, see 11-020; as to varying a time limit set, see 11-021.

Sanctions for failure to comply

If a party fails to comply with a rule or a direction, the judge may (CrimPR 3.5(6)): **11-009**

(1) fix, postpone, bring forward, extend, cancel or adjourn a hearing; or
(2) exercise his powers to make a costs order; and
(3) impose such other sanction as may be appropriate.

Note that a costs order, where appropriate may be made under POA 1985 as follows:

(a) s.19 (costs incurred by reason of unnecessary or improper at or omission by or on behalf of a party);
(b) s.19A (costs incurred by improper etc., act or omission by legal representative); or
(c) s.19B (serious misconduct by third party),

as to which see COSTS AND ASSESSMENT.

An order for costs will not lie unless it is possible to identify whether and if so what costs have been wasted (*DPP v Radziwilowicz* [2014] EWHC 2283 (Admin)); see also *In Re West* [2014] EWCA Crim 1480). The difficulty, however, is that in many cases while it is clear that the court's time will have been engaged (with consequent costs), the parties are unlikely to have suffered financially, not least because of the way in which public funding is structured.

An even-handed approach

The authorities show (*R. v McDonagh* [2011] EWCA Crim 3238; *R. v Malcolm* [2011] EWCA Crim 2069; [2012] Crim. L.R. 238); *R. v Freeland* [2013] EWCA Crim 928) that: **11-010**

(1) it is an essential part of a judge's duty to exercise firm control over case management both pre-trial stage and throughout the trial;
(2) the objective is to achieve *greater efficiency* and better use of limited resources by closer identification of, and focus on, critical rather than peripheral issues;
(3) the judge must *keep the proceedings moving* and attempt to confine advocates *to relevant questioning*;
(4) he must ensure that a trial takes place where cards *are put on the table* and the CrimPR are followed (see *R. v Jisl* [2004] EWCA Crim 696; *The Times,* 19 April 2004).

However, CrimPR 1 requires the prosecution and the defence to be treated fairly and the rights of the accused, particularly under ECHR art.6, must be recognised. The judge may impose time limits on cross-examination (*R. v Chaaban* [2003] EWCA Crim 1012; [2003] Crim. L.R. 658; *R. v B* [2005] EWCA Crim 805; [2006] Crim. L.R. 54).

Amongst those rights, in effect declaratory of the common law, is the right to a trial by an impartial tribunal. Where the judge exercises his management functions, as where he seeks to ask an advocate why questions are being asked, or why cross-examination is not being progressed, or what the issues are, he must do so in an even-handed manner. If that does not work, the matter must be dealt with in the absence of the jury. It is not right for the judge persistently to criticise an advocate in severe terms in the presence of the jury.

The parties' duties

11-011 The judicial approach set out in 11-007 to 11-010 is mirrored by an obligation on the parties. Each party must (CrimPR 3.3) actively assist the judge in fulfilling his duty under CrimPR 3.2, without, or if necessary with, a direction; and must apply for a direction if needed to further the overriding objective (CrimPR 3.3).

It is no part of an advocate's duty "to raise untenable points at length or to embark on lengthy cross-examination on matters that are not in truth in issue". (*R. v Simmonds* (1967) 51 Cr. App. R. 316 at 326, approved in *R. v Kalia* (1974) 60 Cr. App. R. 200; see also the Bar Council statement of counsel's duties appended to the report of *R. v McFadden* (1976) 62 Cr. App. R 187).

The law of evidence requires that questions put, and evidence adduced is relevant. The advocate's task, in the proper performance of his duties to the client and to the court, is:

(1) to exercise judgment and discretion as to the way in which the client's case can best be presented;
(2) the fact that the client wishes a particular question to be asked, a point to be made or a witness to be called, does not mean that the question must be asked, the point made or the witness called (*R. v Hobson* [1998] 1 Cr. App. R. 31 at 35).

As to "ambush" attacks, see *McDonagh* [2011] EWCA Crim 3238.

2. Particular situations

Assignment of judge; continuity

11-012 In any complex case which is expected to last more than four weeks it is likely that the trial judge will be assigned under the direction of the Presiding Judges or the Resident Judge at the earliest possible moment.

In health and safety prosecutions at the Crown Court, at all events, when the matter is not the subject of an early plea, a judge may need to be appointed at an early stage to manage the case to trial. This should be done in all cases involving death or very serious injury and in any other cases where there is potential complexity (*R. v EGS Ltd* [2009] EWCA Crim 1942).

Note that:

(1) The ordinary rule is that the judge who has had conduct of a preparatory hearing should also conduct the trial, and absent compelling reason this should follow. (*R. v I(C)* [2009] W.L.R. (D) 286 CACD).

(2) Active steps must be taken in the planning of court business and judicial commitments to avoid wherever possible the necessity for a judge to find himself having to consider leaving a complex case between a case management or preparatory hearing and the trial.

As to the rank of judge appropriate for the trial of any particular class of offence, and the requirement for an authorised (or "ticketed") judge for the trial of specified classes of case, see ALLOCATION AND LISTING OF CASES.

Assignment of judge; clash of commitments

There will be cases where a judge is faced with a direct clash of commitments, which may only be resolved by the judge revising dates for trial or assignments of judges being changed. Such measures, while "administrative", are not to be compared to mere "operational convenience" considered in *R. v Southwark Crown Court Ex p. Customs and Excise Commissioners* (1993) 97 Cr. App. R. 266, which would not suffice. **11-013**

It does not help to apply the label "exceptional" to the circumstances which will justify such a course, save that:

(1) a decision not to conduct the trial is an exception to the general rule;
(2) there must be a sufficiently compelling cause to depart from the norm stated here, and the decision must be made by the judge, not, for example, by the listing officer;
(3) the decision must be made only after a hearing at which all parties have had an opportunity to make representations;
(4) before departing from the norm, the judge, if he is not the Resident Judge, ought to consult that judge;
(5) one of the circuit's Presiding Judges should be informed and consulted.

If, unusually, that necessity should arise at a preparatory hearing, the question to be resolved is not "a matter of law" but one of judgment for the judge (*R. v GH* [2010] Crim. L.R. 312).

Pruning; severance

Where the advocates have done their job properly, by narrowing the issues, pruning the evidence and so forth, it may be quite inappropriate for the judge to "weigh in" and start cutting out more evidence or more charges of his own volition. **11-014**

He should:

(1) not usurp the function of the prosecution; in pruning the indictment, bearing in mind that he will, at the outset, know less about the case than the advocates;
(2) make a careful assessment of the degree of judicial intervention which is warranted in the case.

There is, however, nothing to prevent him pruning the indictment by:

(a) persuading the prosecutor that it is not worthwhile pursuing certain charges and/or certain accused; or
(b) severing the indictment.

Severance for reasons of case management alone is perfectly proper, although the judge should have regard to any representations made by the prosecutor that severance would weaken his case.

Before using what may be seen as a blunt instrument the judge should insist on seeing full defence statements of all affected accused. Severance may be unfair to the prosecutor if, for example, there is a cut-throat defence in prospect.

(Complex Case Protocol para.3.vi(e) and (vii)).

Stopping a case; quashing an indictment

11-015 "Stopping" a case, quashing an indictment or otherwise preventing the continuation of a trial, is not an exercise of the power to manage; quashing an indictment brings a case to its end.

Provided he does so appropriately, the judge is perfectly entitled to express his views of a case and to encourage the prosecutor to reconsider the public interest; he must bear in mind, however, that the decision to institute or continue criminal proceedings is vested in the CPS by POA 1985 (*R. v FB* [2010] EWCA Crim 1857; [2010] 2 Cr. App. R. 35; *R. v SH* [2010] EWCA Crim 1931; [2011] 1 Cr. App. R. 14).

Expert evidence; surveillance

11-016 In relation to expert evidence, particularly in long and/or complex cases:

(1) identification of the subject matter of such evidence to be adduced by both sides should be made as early as possible, preferably at the directions hearing;

(2) following the exchange of such evidence, any areas of disagreement should be identified, and a direction should generally be made requiring the experts to meet and prepare, after discussion, a joint statement identifying points of agreement and contention, and areas where the prosecutor is put to proof on matters of which a positive case to the contrary is not advanced by the defence; and

(3) after the statement has been prepared it should be served on the court, the prosecutor and the defence; in some cases, it may be appropriate to provide it to the jury.

In relation to surveillance evidence where:

(a) a prosecution is based upon many months of observation or surveillance evidence; and

(b) it appears that it is capable of effective presentation based on a shorter period,

the advocates should be required to justify the evidence of such observations before it is permitted to be adduced, either substantially or in its entirety; schedules should be provided to cover as much of the evidence as possible and admissions sought.

(Complex Case Protocol para.3(viii) and (ix)).

Disclosure

11-017 Disclosure is important to the management of all cases. The *CPD* IV Disclosure 15A: Disclosure of Unused Material states:

> "Disclosure is a vital part of the preparation for trial, both in the magistrates' courts and in the Crown Court. All parties must be familiar with their obligations, in particular under the Criminal Procedure and Investigations Act 1996 as amended and the Code issued

under that Act, and must comply with the relevant judicial protocol and guidelines from the Attorney-General. These documents have recently been revised and the new guidance will be issued shortly as *'Judicial Protocol on the Disclosure of Unused Material in Criminal Cases'* and the *'Attorney General's Guidelines on Disclosure'*. The new documents should be read together as complementary, comprehensive guidance. They will be available electronically on the respective websites.

In addition, certain procedures are prescribed under CrimPR 15 of the Rules and these should be followed. The notes to Part 15 contain a useful summary of the requirements of the CPIA 1996 as amended."

See generally under DISCLOSURE.

Abuse of process

Applications to stay or dismiss for abuse of process are now a normal feature of feature of heavy and complex cases. **11-018**

Where such an issue arises:

(1) the arguments on both sides must be reduced to writing;
(2) the judge should direct full written submissions (rather than "skeleton arguments") in accordance with a timetable set by him, and these should identify any element of prejudice the accused is alleged to have suffered; and
(3) oral evidence will seldom be relevant.

See generally under ABUSE OF PROCESS.

Listing; venue

The following principles apply to listing in the Crown Court: **11-019**

(1) the judge is required, at the Plea and Trial Preparation Hearing (PTPH) (11-029) or earlier to make firm arrangements for the listing of cases;
(2) parties must comply with any directions and timetable then set so that a case is ready to be heard in accordance with the timetable;
(3) the case must commence promptly at the appointed hour in accordance with that timetable.

To avoid unnecessary and wasted hearings, the parties should be allowed adequate time to prepare the case, having regard to the time limits for applications and notices set by CrimPR and by other legislation. When those time limits have expired, the parties will be expected to be fully prepared.

The required forms and guidance notes can all be found in *CPD* Annex D. PDF and Word versions are available on the CrimPR pages of the Ministry of Justice website.

Once a trial date or window is fixed, it should not be vacated or moved without good reason. Under the CrimPR, parties are expected to be ready by the trial date. The listing officer may, in circumstances determined by the Resident Judge, agree to the movement of the trial to a date to which the defence and prosecution both consent, provided the timely hearing of the case is not delayed. The prosecution will be expected to have consulted the witnesses before agreeing to any change.

In all other circumstances, requests to adjourn or vacate fixtures or trial windows must be referred to the Resident Judge for his or her personal attention; the Resident Judge may delegate the decision to a named deputy (*CPD* XIII: Listing of trials; custody time limits and transfer of cases F.8–10).

Transfer between courts on the same circuit must be agreed by the Resident Judges of each court, subject to guidance from the Presiding Judges of the circuit. Transfer of trials between circuits must be agreed between the Presiding Judges and Delivery Directors of the respective circuits. Transfers may be agreed either in specific cases or in accordance with general principles agreed between those named (*CPD* XIII: Listing of trials, custody time limits and transfer of cases F.11-13).

Listing is a judicial responsibility and function. See as to its purpose and key principles, ALLOCATION AND LISTING OF CASES.

Conducting hearings by the use of live link or telephone

11-020 A new section was added with effect from 31 January 2017 to the *CPD* to make provision for hearings to be conducted by live link or by telephone (*CPD* I General Matters 3N: Use of Live Link and Telephone Facilities). The section has been the subject of updates in 2018 and 2020. The impact of the pandemic has led to courts making increasing use of remote hearings.

Where it is lawful and in the interests of justice to do so, courts should exercise their statutory and other powers to conduct hearings by live link or telephone (*CPD* 3N.1).

It is the duty of the court to make use of technology actively to manage the case (CrimPR 3.2(1), (2)(h)) and that includes an obligation to give directions for the use of live links and telephone facilities in the circumstances listed in CrimPR 3.2(4) and (5) (pre-trial hearings, including pre-trial case management hearings) (*CPD* 3N.2).

Where the court directs that evidence is to be given by live link, and especially where such a direction is given on the court's own initiative, it is essential that the decision is communicated promptly to the witness (CrimPR 18.4). None of those rules or other provisions require the renewal of a live link direction merely because a trial has had to be postponed or adjourned. Once made, such a direction applies until it is discharged by the court.

It is the duty of the parties to alert the court to any reason why live links or telephones should not be used where CrimPR 3.2 otherwise would oblige the court to do so; and, where a direction for the use of such facilities has been made, it is the duty of the parties as soon as practicable to alert the court to any reason why that direction should be varied (CrimPR 3.3(2)(e) and 3.6) (*CPD* 3N.3).

The word "appropriate" in CrimPR 3.2(4) and (5) is not a term of art. It has the ordinary English meaning of "fitting", or "suitable". Whether the facilities available to the court in any particular case can be considered appropriate is a matter for the court, but plainly to be appropriate such facilities must work, at the time at which they are required; all participants must be able to hear and, in the case of a live link, see each other clearly; and there must be no extraneous noise, movement or other distraction suffered by a participant, or transmitted by a participant to others. What degree of protection from accidental or deliberate interception should be considered appropriate will depend upon the purpose for which a live link or telephone is to be used. If it is to participate in a hearing which is open to the public anyway, then what is communicated by such means is by definition public and the use of links such as Skype or FaceTime, which are not generally considered secure from interception, may not be objectionable. If it is to participate in a hearing in private, and especially one at which sensitive information will be discussed—for example, on an application for a search warrant—then a more secure service is likely to be required (*CPD* 3N.4).

There may be circumstances in which the court should not require the use of live link or telephone facilities despite their being otherwise appropriate at a pre-trial hearing. In every case, in deciding whether any such circumstances apply, the court will keep in mind that, for the purposes of what may be an essentially administrative hearing, it may be compatible with the overriding objective to proceed in the defendant's absence altogether, especially if he or she is represented, unless, exceptionally, a rule otherwise requires. The principle that the court always must consider proceeding in a defendant's absence is articulated in CrimPR 3.9(2)(a). Where at a pre-trial hearing bail may be under consideration, the provisions of CrimPR 14.2 will be relevant (*CPD* 3N.5).

Such circumstances will include any case in which the defendant's effective participation cannot be achieved by his or her attendance by such means, and CrimPR 3.2(4) and (5) except such cases from the scope of the obligation which that rule otherwise imposes on the court. That exception may apply where (this list is not exhaustive) the defendant has a disorder or disability, including a hearing, speech or sight impediment, or has communication needs to which the use of a live link or telephone is inimical (whether or not those needs are such as to require the appointment of an intermediary); or where the defendant requires interpretation and effective interpretation cannot be provided by live link or telephone, as the case may be (*CPD* 3N.6).

Finally, that exception sometimes may apply where the defendant's attendance in person at a pre-trial hearing will facilitate communication with his or her legal representatives. The court should not make such an exception merely to allow client and representatives to meet if that meeting can and should be held elsewhere. However, there will be cases in which defence representatives reasonably need to meet with a defendant, to take his or her instructions or to explain events to him or her, either shortly before or immediately after a pre-trial hearing and in circumstances in which that meeting cannot take place effectively by live link (*CPD* 3N.7).

The Police, Crime, Sentencing and Courts Act 2022 s.200 expands the use of video and audio links in criminal proceedings. In July 2022 the LCJ issued guidance on the expansion of the links. As the guidance sets out, s.51 CJA 2003 (as substituted by the Police, Crime, Sentencing and Courts Act 2022 with effect from 28 June 2022) enables courts to require or permit a person to take part in eligible criminal proceedings through a live link ("a live link direction"), including at preliminary hearings, trials (whether summary or on indictment), sentencing, appeals and other identified types of hearing (see s.51(3)).

The LCJ's statutory guidance is provided pursuant to s.51(5) of the CJA 2003. It should be read with the Act, *CPD* 3N: Use of live link and telephone facilities and the extracts from the Judicial College, *Equal Treatment Bench Book* (Judicial College, 2021, revised July 2022) that deal with live links (available at *https://www.judiciary.uk/wp-content/uploads/2022/10/Equal-Treatment-Bench-Book-July-2022-revision-2.pdf* [Accessed November 2022]).

A live link direction may only be made in respect of those who are taking part in the proceedings (including counsel, solicitors, witnesses and defendants). It may not be made for those who are not taking part in the proceedings (e.g. public observers or journalists). Those who are not taking part in the proceedings are entitled to apply to observe the proceedings remotely under s.85A of the CA 2003. Separate guidance is in place in respect of such requests.

The court may only make a live link direction if:

(a) the parties to the proceedings (and where the defendant is under 18, the relevant youth offending team) have been given the opportunity to make representations; and

(b) the court is satisfied that it would be in the interests of justice.

In deciding whether the statutory criteria are met, the court must consider the guidance issued by the LCJ and all the circumstances of the case (s.51(5)). In particular, the court must consider (as appropriate to the circumstances of the individual case) (s.51(6)):

(a) the availability of the person to whom the direction would relate;
(b) any need for that person to attend in person;
(c) the views of that person;
(d) the suitability of the facilities at the place where that person would take part in the proceedings in accordance with the direction;
(e) whether that person would be able to take part in the proceedings effectively if the person took part in accordance with the direction;
(f) in the case of a direction relating to a witness:
  (i) the importance of the witness's evidence to the proceedings; and
  (ii) whether the direction might tend to inhibit any party to the proceedings from effectively testing the witness's evidence; and
(g) the arrangements that would or could be put in place for members of the public to see or hear the proceedings as conducted in accordance with the direction.

The process for seeking representations need not be elaborate. In some cases, the written request might make it clear that it is agreed, or might include the representations that all parties wish to make. In other cases, the parties (and, where appropriate, the youth offending team) can be asked by email from the court staff to submit any written representations. Where the request is made orally in the course of the hearing then oral representations from all parties can be obtained there and then.

It will not be in the interests of justice to make a live link direction unless live link facilities are available and are in working order, and will allow all participants to hear and (in the case of a video live link) see each other clearly, with no distractions, and the person attending by live link has the necessary technology available and is able to operate it. Nor is it likely to be in the interests of justice to make a live link direction unless a member of staff is available (without unreasonably impacting on other work) to set up the live link, test that it is working, and monitor its operation. In some instances, a participant in criminal proceedings may have a disorder or disability that prevents effective participation via live link. In those instances, too, it will not be in the interests of justice to make a live link direction.

The guidance then deals with the various participants and this is set out in 11-021 and 11-022.

There is guidance on jury attendance by live link (para.17). A live link direction may be made for the jury, but only if it is made for all members of the jury and only if all members of the jury are present at the same place (s.51(2)). It is likely to be very rare that live link directions are made for a jury. If, exceptionally, it is considered that a live link for the jury may be appropriate that should be raised with the Resident Judge before a decision is made.

Judge on the live link or phone

11-021 Nothing prohibits the member or members of a court from conducting a pre-trial hearing by attending by live link or telephone from a location distant from all the other participants. Despite the conventional view that the venue for a court hearing is the courtroom in which that hearing has been arranged to take place, the CPR define "court" as "a tribunal with jurisdiction over criminal cases. It includes a judge, recorder, District Judge (Magistrates' Court), lay justice and, when exercising their judicial powers, the Registrar of Criminal Appeals, a justices' clerk or assistant clerk." CrimPR 3.33 (Place of trial), which requires proceedings to take place in a courtroom provided by the Lord Chancellor, does not apply for the purposes of a pre-trial hearing and so there is no legal obstacle to the judge, magistrate or magistrates conducting it from elsewhere, with other participants assembled in a courtroom from which the member or members of the court are physically absent. In principle, nothing prohibits the conduct of a pre-trial hearing by live link or telephone with each participant, including the member or members of the court, in a different location (an arrangement sometimes described as a "virtual hearing"). This is dependent upon there being means by which that hearing can be witnessed by the public—for example, by public attendance at a courtroom or other venue from which the participants all can be seen and heard (if by live link), or heard (if by telephone). The principle of open justice to which para.3N.17 refers is relevant (*CPD* 3N.8). In 2020 with the impact of Coronavirus many more pre-trial hearings have taken place with the use of technology. In addition to the use of Skype, Teams and the phone, CVP (Cloud Video Platform) has been rolled-out to most courts and prisons to enable remote hearings to be facilitated. The press and public can be given access to hearings using this technology.

In the LCJ's July 2022 guidance, para.16 deals with judges. Members of the court may conduct a pre-trial hearing by live link from a location other than the court. It is unlikely to be in the interests of justice for a member of the court to attend the trial, or part of a trial, by live link, and it will only be appropriate for other hearings in exceptional cases. If, exceptionally, it is considered that a live link for the court may be appropriate that should be raised with the Resident Judge before a decision is made.

Vulnerable witnesses and defendants

Paragraphs I 3D to 3G inclusive of the *CPD* (Vulnerable people in the courts; **11-022**
Ground rules hearings to plan the questioning of a vulnerable witness or defendant; Intermediaries; Vulnerable defendants) contain directions relevant to the use of a live link as a special measure for a young or otherwise vulnerable witness, or to facilitate the giving of evidence by a defendant who is likewise young or otherwise vulnerable, within the scope of the YJCEA 1999. Defence representatives and the court must keep in mind that special measures under the 1999 Act and CrimPR Pt 18, including the use of a live link, are available to defence as well as to prosecution witnesses who meet the statutory criteria. Defence representatives should always consider whether their witnesses would benefit from giving evidence by live link and should apply for a direction if appropriate, either at the case management hearing or as soon as possible thereafter. A defence witness should be afforded the same facilities and treatment as a prosecution witness, including the same opportunity to make a pre-trial visit to the court building in order to familiarise himself or herself with it. Where a live link is sought as a special measure for a young or vulnerable witness or defendant, CrimPR 18.10 and 18.15 respectively require, among other things, that the applicant must identify someone to accompany that witness or defendant while they give evidence; must name the person, if possible; and must explain why that person would be an appropriate companion

for that witness. The court must ensure that directions are given accordingly when ordering such a live link. Witness Service volunteers are available to support all witnesses, prosecution and defence, if required (*CPD* 3N.11). CrimPR 3.9 deal with Ground rules hearings.

In the LCJ's guidance, paras 8–11 deal with the participation of defendants. The guidance sets out:

> "It may be in the interests of justice to allow or require a defendant to attend hearings (particularly preliminary hearings) by live link so as to avoid delays and disruption. As well as the parties' representations, the court will wish to take account of any mental health or other medical assessment before deciding if a live link is in the interests of justice. Pre and post court conferences between advocate and defendant may not be able to take place effectively by live link: where such conferences are desirable a live link is less likely to be in the interests of justice. Factors to consider in deciding whether the defendant should attend a sentencing hearing via live link include: the potential penalty; ensuring the explanations of sentence can be given satisfactorily for all participants and for the public; and the preferences of the maker of any Victim Personal Statement which is to be read. In the case of youths, arrangements must be made in advance of any live link hearing to enable the youth offending worker to be at the secure establishment where the youth is in custody. In the event that such arrangements are not practicable, the youth offending worker must have sufficient access to the youth via the live link booth before and after the hearing."

The guidance sets out:

> "It is rarely appropriate for a youth to be sentenced over a live link. Potentially, this may be acceptable where the youth is: (i) already serving a custodial sentence and either the sentence to be imposed is bound to be a further custodial sentence, or a non-custodial sentence is likely to be imposed which will have no material impact on the sentence being served; (ii) detained in a secure establishment a long way from court, and being produced would materially affect them; (iii) so disturbed their production would be a significant detriment to their welfare."

For witnesses: (para.15):

> "A live link may be used as a special measure under section 24 of the Youth Justice and Criminal Evidence Act 1999. Even when not used as a special measure, the court may allow a witness to give evidence by live link where that is in the interests of justice (for example to save a witness from a long journey to court where all parties agree the evidence can be given remotely, or to allow a medical expert witness (or any other witness) to give evidence without having to take the entire day off work). Where a live link direction is given for a witness, the witness must give evidence by the live link unless the live link direction is revoked (section 52(2), (4))."

Plea and sentence by link

11-023 Sections 57A to 57F of the CDA 1998 allow a defendant who is in custody to enter a plea by live link, and also for such a defendant who attends by live link to be sentenced. In appropriate circumstances, the court may allow a defendant who is not in custody to enter a plea by live link; but the same considerations as apply to sentencing in such a case will apply (see *CPD* 3N.13) (*CPD* 3N.9).

The CDA 1998 does not allow for the attendance by live link at a contested trial of a defendant who is in custody. The court may allow a defendant who wishes to do so to observe all or part of his or her trial by live link, whether she or he is in custody or not, but

(a) such a defendant cannot lawfully give evidence by such means unless he or she satisfies the criteria prescribed by s.33A of the YJCEA 1999 and the court so orders under that section (see also CrimPR 18.14–18.17);
(b) a defendant who is in custody and who observes the trial by live link is not present, as a matter of law, and the trial must be treated as taking place in his or her absence, she or he having waived the right to attend; and
(c) a defendant who has refused to attend his or her trial when required to do so, or who has absconded, must not be permitted to observe the proceedings by live link (*CPD* 3N.10).

Under ss.57A and 57D or 57E of the CDA 1998 the court may pass sentence on a defendant in custody who attends by live link. The court may allow a defendant who is not in custody and who wishes to attend his or her sentencing by live link to do so, and may receive representations (but not evidence) from her or him by such means. Factors of which the court will wish to take account in exercising its discretion include, in particular, the penalty likely to be imposed; the importance of ensuring that the explanations of sentence required in the Crown Court by CrimPR 25.16(7), can be given satisfactorily, for the defendant, for other participants and for the public, including reporters; and the preferences of the maker of any Victim Personal Statement which is to be read aloud or played pursuant to para.VII F.3(c) of these Practice Directions (*CPD* 3N.12).

The Police, Crime, Sentencing and Courts Act 2022 s.200 expands the use of video and audio links. In July 2022 the LCJ issued guidance (11-022) as to a live link to connect participants outside the UK (para.18). Where the participant is abroad, then (depending on the country concerned) the court will wish to consider whether a live link would risk damaging international relations so as to be contrary to the public interest. The factors to consider, and the checks that can be made, are set out in *Re Agbabiaka (Evidence from Abroad: Nare Guidance: Nigeria)* [2021] UKUT 286 (IAC); [2021] 10 WLUK 664.

Youth defendants

When a youth is appearing in the Crown Court, it will usually be appropriate for the youth to be produced in person at court. This is to ensure that the court can engage properly with the youth and that the necessary level of engagement can be facilitated with the YOT worker, defence representative and/or appropriate adult. The court should deal with any application for use of a live link on a case-by-case basis, after consultation with the parties and the YOT. Such hearings that may be appropriate include onward remand hearings at which there is no bail application, or case management hearings, particularly if the youth is already serving a custodial sentence (*CPD* 3N.13). **11-024**

It rarely will be appropriate for a youth to be sentenced over a live link. However, notwithstanding the court's duties of engagement with a youth, the overriding welfare principle and the statutory responsibility of the YOT worker to explain the sentence to the youth, after consultation with the parties and the YOT, there may be circumstances in which it may be appropriate to sentence a youth over the live link:

(a) If the youth is already serving a custodial sentence and the sentence to be imposed by the court is bound to be a further custodial sentence, whether concurrent or consecutive.
(b) If the youth is already serving a custodial sentence and the court is minded

to impose a non-custodial sentence which will have no material impact on the sentence being served.

(c) If the youth is being detained in a secure establishment at such a distance from the court that the travelling time from one to the other will be significant so as to materially affect the welfare of the youth.

(d) If the youth's condition—whether mental or otherwise—is so disturbed that his or her production would be a significant detriment to his or her welfare.

(*CPD* 3N.14)

Arrangements must be made in advance of any live link hearing to enable the YOT worker to be at the secure establishment where the youth is in custody. In the event that such arrangements are not practicable, the YOT worker must have sufficient access to the youth via the live link booth before and after the hearing (*CPD* 3N.15).

Conduct of participants

11-025 Where a live link is used, the immediate vicinity of the device by which a person attends becomes, temporarily, part of the courtroom for the purposes of that person's participation. That person, and any advocate or legal representative, custodian, court officer, intermediary or other companion, whether immediately visible to the court or not, becomes a participant for the purposes of CrimPR 1.2(2) and is subject to the court's jurisdiction to regulate behaviour in the courtroom. The substance and effect of this direction must be drawn to the attention of all such participants (*CPD* 3N.16).

In the LCJ's July 2022 guidance (see 11-020), as to advocates: (paras 12–14):

> "The interests of justice are wider than the circumstances of the individual case. They include the efficient despatch of business and the availability of judicial, staff, technical and other resources. So, provided that it would not cause any detriment to the individual case, it may well be in the interests of justice to allow an advocate to attend by live link if that will enable the advocate to undertake other work at another court centre on the same day. However, if the defendant is required to attend a hearing in person, then the interests of justice will usually require the defence advocate also to attend in person.
>
> Mentions, bail applications, ground rules hearings, CTL extensions, uncontested POCAs and hearings involving legal argument only will generally be suitable for remote attendance by all advocates. PTPHs will normally require advocates to attend, unless there has been sufficient engagement and preparation in advance. Sentencing hearings will require case-by-case consideration.
>
> Advocates must adopt the court dress and standards of conduct that would be applied if they were in the courtroom. The court must be able to communicate with all advocates throughout the time the list is being heard. Advocates must be ready and available as soon as the case is called on."

Open justice and records of proceedings

11-026 The principle of open justice to which CrimPR 6.2(1) gives effect applies as strongly where electronic means of communication are used to conduct a hearing as it applies in other circumstances. Open justice is the principal means by which courts are kept under scrutiny by the public. It follows that where a participant attends a hearing in public by live link or telephone then that person's participation must be, as nearly as may be, equally audible and, if applicable, equally visible to the public as it would be were he or she physically present. Where electronic means of communication are used to conduct a hearing, records of the event must be maintained in the usual way (CrimPR 5.4). This includes the recording of the proceedings (CrimPR 5.5) (*CPD* 3N.17).

Guidance

Guidance supplementing the *CPD* on the use of live link and telephone facilities to conduct a hearing or receive evidence in a criminal court is also set out in an annex to the *CPD*. **11-027**

Application to vary a direction

The power to give a direction under these provisions includes a power to vary or revoke that direction (CrimPR 3.5(5)). **11-028**

An application to vary a direction may be made if:

(1) the direction was given without a hearing;
(2) it was given at a hearing in the absence of the party; or
(3) circumstances have changed.

(CrimPR 3.6)

The judge may shorten or extend (even after it has expired) any time limit set by CrimPR 3 and allow an application or representations to be made orally. A person who wants an extension of time must apply when serving the application or representations for which it is needed explaining the delay (CrimPR 3.8).

The party applying to vary the direction must apply as soon as practicable after he becomes aware of the grounds for doing so; and give as much notice to the other parties as the nature and urgency of his application permits (CrimPR 3.6).

Agreement to vary a time limit fixed by a direction

The parties may agree to vary a time limit fixed by a direction but only if: **11-029**

(1) the variation will not:
    (a) affect the date of any hearing that has been fixed; or
    (b) significantly affect the progress of the case in any other way;
(2) the judge has not prohibited variation by agreement; and
(3) the court's case progression officer is promptly informed.

The court's case progression officer will refer the agreement to the judge if he doubts that the conditions in (l)(a) are satisfied (CrimPR 3.7).

3. Case preparation and progression

General

At every hearing (CrimPR 3.8): **11-030**

(1) if a case cannot be concluded there and then, the judge must give directions so that it can be concluded at the next hearing or as soon as possible after that (CrimPR 3.8(1));
(2) the court must, where relevant:
    (a) if the accused is *absent*, decide whether to proceed nonetheless;

(b) take the accused's *plea* (unless already done) or, if no plea can be taken, find out whether the accused is likely to plead guilty or not guilty;
(c) set, follow or revise a *timetable* for the progress of the case, which may include a timetable for any hearing including the trial or the appeal;
(d) in giving directions, ensure *continuity* in relation to the court and to the parties' representatives where that is appropriate and practicable; and
(e) where a *direction* has *not* been *complied with*, find out why, identify who was responsible, and take appropriate action;

(3) in order to prepare for a trial in the Crown Court, the judge must take every reasonable step to encourage and to facilitate the attendance of witnesses when they are needed, and to facilitate the participation of any person, including the accused (CrimPR 3.8(3)).

Facilitating the participation of the accused includes finding out whether he needs interpretation because either he does not speak or understand English or he has a hearing or speech impediment. Where the accused needs interpretation the court officer will arrange for interpretation to be provided at every hearing which the accused is due to attend (CrimPR 3.9(4)).

Note that where (CrimPR 3.8(5)):

(1) interpretation may be by an intermediary where the accused has a speech impediment, without the need for an accused's evidence direction;
(2) on application or on its own initiative, the court may require a written translation to be provided for the accused of any document or part of a document, unless:
(a) translation of that document, or part, is not needed to explain the case against the accused; or
(b) the accused agrees to do without and the judge is satisfied that the agreement is clear and voluntary and that the accused has had legal advice or otherwise understands the consequences.

On application by the accused, the judge must give any direction which he thinks appropriate, including a direction for interpretation by a different interpreter, where:

(1) no interpretation is provided;
(2) no translation is ordered or provided in response to a previous application by the defendant; or
(3) the accused complains about the quality of interpretation or of any translation.

Where a person is entitled or required to attend a hearing the court officer will give as much notice as is reasonably practicable to that person or his custodian (if any) (CrimPR 3.12(a)). The court will make available to the parties a record of any directions given (CrimPR 3.12(b)).

Readiness for trial (or appeal)

11-031 In relation to a party's preparation for trial (i.e. any hearing at which evidence will be introduced) or appeal, each party must (CrimPR 3.12(2)):

(1) comply with directions given by the judge;
(2) take every reasonable step to make sure his witnesses will attend when they are needed;

(3) make appropriate arrangements to present any written or other material; and
(4) promptly inform the court and the other parties of anything that may:
 (a) affect the date or duration of the trial or appeal; or
 (b) significantly affect the progress of the case in any other way.

The court may require a party to give a certificate of readiness.

Management of trial (or appeal)

In managing a trial (or an appeal), the judge: **11-032**

(1) must establish, with the active assistance of the parties, what are the disputed issues;
(2) must consider setting a timetable that:
 (a) takes account of those issues and of any timetable proposed by a party; and
 (b) may limit the duration of any stage of the hearing;
(3) may require a party to identify:
 (a) which witnesses that party wants to give evidence in person;
 (b) the order in which he intends those witnesses to give their evidence;
 (c) whether he requires an order compelling the attendance of a witness;
 (d) what arrangements, if any, he proposes to facilitate the giving of evidence by a witness;
 (e) what arrangements, if any, he proposes to facilitate the participation of any other person, including the accused;
 (f) what written evidence he intends to introduce;
 (g) what other material, if any, he intends to make available to the court in the presentation of the case;
 (h) whether he intends to raise any point of law that could affect the conduct of the trial or appeal; and
(4) may limit:
 (a) the examination, cross-examination or re-examination of a witness; and
 (b) the duration of any stage of the hearing.

(CrimPR 3.13)

The *CPD* VI Trial 25A (Identification for the jury of the issues in the case) and CrimPR 25.9(2)(b) and (c) provide for the prosecutor, on a plea of not guilty, summarising the prosecution case, concisely outlining the facts and the matters likely to be in dispute. Where there is a jury, to help the jurors to understand the case and resolve any issue in it, the court may invite the defendant concisely to identify what is in issue, if necessary in terms approved by the court. Where a defendant declines to do so, the court may direct that jurors are given copies of any defence statement served under CrimPR 15.4, edited of necessary to exclude inappropriate matters. As well as allowing for the early identification of the issues to a jury by the parties, there is an opportunity for the judge to give appropriate directions about the law at the same stage.

(*CPD* VI Trial 25A paras 25A.1–6)

The approach to procedural defects

The prevailing approach to procedural defects is to avoid determining cases on technicalities when they do not result in real prejudice and injustice but instead to **11-033** ensure that they are decided fairly on their merits. This approach is reflected in the CrimPR and, in particular, in the overriding objective.

Where a judge is confronted with procedural failure in the progress of an accused's case he should:

(1) ask himself whether the intention of the legislature was that anything done following that failure should be invalid;
(2) if the answer to that question is "no", go on to consider the interests of justice generally, and most particularly whether there is a real possibility that either the prosecution or the defence may suffer prejudice on account of the procedural failure; if there is such a risk, he must decide whether it is just to allow the proceedings to continue; and
(3) unless there is a clear indication that Parliament intended jurisdiction automatically to be removed following procedural failure, base his decision on a wide assessment of the interests of justice, with particular focus on whether there is a real possibility that the prosecution or the accused may suffer prejudice; if that risk is present he should then decide whether it is just to permit the proceedings to continue.

A procedural failure should result in a lack of jurisdiction only if this is necessary to ensure that the criminal justice system serves the interests of justice and thus the public, or where there is at least a real possibility of the accused suffering prejudice as a consequence of that procedural failure. It would be otherwise, of course, if a court acts without jurisdiction. In those circumstances the proceedings will usually be invalid (*R. v Soneji* [2005] UKHL 49; [2006] 2 Cr. App. R. 20; *R. v Knights* [2005] UKHL 50; [2006] 1 Cr. App. R. (S.) 80; *R. v Ashton* [2006] EWCA Crim 794; [2006] 2 Cr. App. R. 15; *R. v Clarke* [2008] UKHL 8; [2008] 2 Cr. App. R. 2; *R. (on the application of Bromley) v Secretary of State for Justice* [2010] EWHC 112 (Admin); [2010] A.C.D. 43.)

As to a judge rectifying defects by assuming the powers of a District Judge (Magistrates' Courts) under CA 2003 s.66, see JURISDICTION.

Notice to victims

11-034 HMCTS court staff must ensure wherever possible that the police or relevant Witness Care Unit are notified within:

(1) one working day of the decisions set out at (2)(a) to (c) below being made for victims of the most serious crime, persistently targeted, and vulnerable or intimidated victims (in cases in which the court staff have been notified that these categories of victims are involved); and
(2) three working days in cases involving all other victims of:
    (a) court dates in relation to all hearings;
    (b) the outcome of bail or change in remand status hearings and administrative special measures applications; and
    (c) adjournments and postponements of scheduled hearings.

(VC 2.19)

B. Preparation for Trial in the Crown Court

1. Pre-trial hearings

General rules

A judge of the Crown Court: **11-035**

(1) *may* and in some cases *must*, conduct a preparatory hearing where CrimPR 3.21 (see 11-049) applies;
(2) *must* conduct a PTPH;
(3) *may* conduct a further PTPH (and if necessary, more than one such hearing) only where:
  (a) the court anticipates a guilty plea;
  (b) it is necessary to conduct such a hearing in order to give directions for an effective trial; or
  (c) such a hearing is required to set ground rules for the conduct of the questioning of witness or defendant.

The PTPH must, as a general rule, be in public. The court can direct all or part of the hearing be in private. If it is to be in private, the decision to that affect must be in public. The hearing must be recorded in accordance with CrimPR 5.5. (CrimPR 3.21(2) and (3))

2. Case management—initial stage

General

As the CrimPR require cases to be dealt with efficiently and expeditiously (CrimPR 1.1(2)(e)) and the court is to further the overriding objective by active case management, both the magistrates' courts and the Crown Court are to proceed as set out in the *CPD* I General Matters 3A Case Management 3A.3–3A.28. The parties are expected to have prepared in accordance with CrimPR 3.3(1) to avoid unnecessary and wasted hearings. The parties will be expected to have communicated with each other by the time of the first hearing, to report to the court on that communication, and to continue thereafter to communicate with each other and with the court officer as set out in CrimPR 3.3(2) (*CPD* I General Matters 3A.2). **11-036**

The "Preparation for Effective Trial" form for use in the magistrates' courts, and the "Plea and Trial Preparation Hearing" form for the Crown Court (Annex E to the *CPD*) must be used as appropriate (*CPD* I General Matters 3A.3). Versions of both forms in pdf and Word format can be found on the CrimPR pages of the MoJ website. In 2019 a revised version of the PTPH form was issued, which came into effect as of 2 July 2019. Guidance on the completion of the forms is available on the judiciary website under guidance and resources.

In the magistrates' courts initial details of the prosecution case (IDPC) have to be served. If, immediately before the first hearing in the magistrates' court, the defendant was in police custody for the offence charged these include:

(1) a summary of the circumstances of the offence; and
(2) the defendant's criminal record.

If not in custody:

(1) a summary of the circumstances of the offence;

(2) any account of the defendant in interview, whether in that summary or another document;
(3) any written witness statement or exhibit available to the prosecutor which he considers material to plea, or to the allocation of the case for trial, or to sentence;
(4) the defendant's criminal record; and
(5) any available VPS or similar document on impact.

The details must include sufficient information to allow the defendant and the court at the first hearing to take an informed view: on plea; on venue for trial (if applicable); for the purposes of case management; or for the purposes of sentencing (including committal for sentence, if applicable) (*CPD* I General Matters 3A).

If the defendant is in custody and is charged with an offence that is indictable only or triable either way, at the first hearing the magistrates' court will proceed at once with the allocation of the case for trial. If that involves sending the defendant to the Crown Court, then that will be ordered. The magistrates' court will be expected to ask for and to record any indication of plea and issues for trial to assist the Crown Court (*CPD* I General Matters 3A.5).

If the defendant is on bail, and the prosecutor anticipates a guilty plea which is likely to be sentenced in the magistrates' court, the case is to be listed for a first hearing 14 days after charge, or the next available court date thereafter. Where it is anticipated there will be a not guilty plea, or the case is one likely to be sent or committed to the Crown Court for trial or sentence, then the first hearing must be 28 days after charge or the next available court date thereafter (*CPD* I General Matters 3A.7).

Where the matter is a summary only matter, or the case is allocated for summary trial, then depending on the plea, the magistrates' court will give such directions as are necessary for a trial or for sentencing. That will include consideration as to whether a pre-sentence report is necessary (*CPD* I General Matters 3A.6, 8).

In those cases where the magistrates' court is considering a committal for sentence or the defendant has indicated an intention to plead guilty in a matter to be sent to the Crown Court, the magistrates' court should request the preparation of a pre-sentence report if it considers that:

- there is a realistic alternative to a custodial sentence; or
- the defendant may satisfy the criteria as a "dangerous offender"; or
- there is some other appropriate reason.

Where a case is sent to the Crown Court and the defendant indicates an intention to plead guilty at the Crown Court, the magistrates' court must set a date for a PTPH at the Crown Court as set out in CrimPR 9.7(5)(a)(i) (*CPD* I General Matters 3A.10).

In those cases sent to the Crown Court where there is *no* indication of plea, the magistrates' court *must* set a date for a PTPH. That hearing must be within 28 days of sending, unless the standard directions of the Presiding Judges of the circuit direct otherwise. The magistrates' court may also give other directions appropriate to the needs of the case, in accordance with CrimPR 3.5(3), and in accordance with any standard directions issued by the Presiding Judges of the circuit (*CPD* I General Matters 3A.11).

Where a defendant is on bail and the prosecutor does not anticipate a guilty plea at the first hearing in the magistrates' court, it is essential that the initial details of the prosecution case provided for the first hearing are sufficient to assist the court to identify the real issues and to give appropriate directions for an effective trial—whether that be at the magistrates' court or the Crown Court. Unless there is good reason not to do so, the prosecution should make available the following material in advance of the first hearing in the magistrates' court:

(i) a summary of the circumstances of the offences including a summary of any account of the defendant in interview;
(ii) statements and exhibits identified by the prosecution as being of importance for the purpose of plea or initial case management, including any relevant CCTV that would be relied upon at trial and any Streamlined Forensic Report;
(iii) details of witness availability so far as known;
(iv) defendant's criminal record;
(v) VPS if provided;
(vi) an indication of any medical report or other expert evidence the prosecution is likely to adduce in relation to a victim or the defendant; and
(vii) any information as to special measures, bad character or hearsay, where applicable.

In addition to the material set out above (and see CrimPR 8) the information required by the "Preparation for Effective Trial" form (see above) *must* be available to be submitted at the first hearing, and the parties *must* complete that form, in accordance with the guidance. In those cases where there is to be a contested trial in the magistrates' court, the form includes directions and a timetable that will apply in every case unless the court otherwise orders (*CPD* I General Matters 3A.13).

The provisions of the *CPD* I General Matters 3A.12–13 do not preclude a court from taking a plea at the first hearing pursuant to CrimPR 3.21(2)(b) and to the court case managing the case as far as practicable under CrimPR 3 (*CPD* I General Matters 3A.14). The powers of the magistrates' court can be exercised by a single justice (*CPD* I General Matters 3A.15).

3. CASE PROGRESSION AND TRIAL PREPARATION IN THE CROWN COURT

Plea and trial preparation hearing (PTPH)

Where a magistrates' court has directed a PTPH, the period which elapses between sending for trial and the date of that hearing must be consistent within each circuit. In every case, the time allowed for the conduct of the PTPH must be sufficient for effective trial preparation. It is expected in every case that an indictment will be lodged at least seven days in advance of the hearing. A Note to the Practice Direction makes clear that the reference to "at least 7 days" in advance of the hearing is necessitated by the fact that, for the time being, different circuits have different timescales for the PTPH. Had this not been so, the paragraphs would have been drafted forward from the date of sending rather than backwards from the date of the PTPH (*CPD* I General Matters 3A.16 and the Note). **11-037**

In a case in which the defendant, not having done so before, indicates an intention to plead guilty to his representative after being sent for trial but before the PTPH, the defence representative will notify the Crown Court and the prosecution forthwith. The court will ensure there is sufficient time at the PTPH for sentence and a judge should at once request the preparation of a pre-sentence report if it appears to the court that either:

(a) there is a realistic alternative to a custodial sentence; or

(b) the defendant may satisfy the criteria for classification as a dangerous offender; or
(c) there is some other appropriate reason for doing so.

(*CPD* I General Matters 3A.17)

If at the PTPH the defendant pleads guilty and no pre-sentence report has been prepared, if possible the court should obtain a stand down report (*CPD* I General Matters 3A.18).

Where the defendant was remanded in custody after being charged and was sent for trial without initial details of the prosecution case having been served, then at least seven days before the PTPH the prosecutor should serve, as a minimum, the material identified in para.3A.12 of the *CPD* (see 11-036). If at the PTPH the defendant does not plead guilty, the court will be expected to identify the issues in the case and give appropriate directions for an effective trial. The Note to the Practice Direction about the seven days applies equally to this provision (*CPD* I General Matters 3A.19).

At the PTPH, in addition to the material required by para.3A.12 of the *CPD* (see 11-036), the prosecutor must serve sufficient evidence to enable the court to case manage effectively without the need for a further case management hearing, unless the case falls within para.3A.21 (see 11-038). In addition, the information required by the PTPH form must be available to the court at that hearing, and it must have been discussed between the parties in advance. The prosecutor must provide details of the availability of likely prosecution witnesses so that a trial date can immediately be arranged if the defendant does not plead guilty (*CPD* I General Matters 3A.20).

Further PTPH

11-038 In the light of CrimPR 3.21(1)(c) after the PTPH there will be no further case management hearing before the trial unless a condition listed in that rule is met and the court so directs, in order to further the overriding objective.

The directions to be given at the PTPH therefore may include a direction for a further case management hearing, but usually will do so only in one of the following cases:

(a) Class 1 cases;
(b) Class 2 cases which carry a maximum penalty of 10 years or more;
(c) cases involving death by driving (whether dangerous or careless), or death in the workplace;
(d) cases involving a vulnerable witness;
(e) cases in which the defendant is a child or otherwise under a disability, or requires special assistance;
(f) cases in which there is a corporate or unrepresented defendant;
(g) cases in which the expected trial length is such that a further case management hearing is desirable and any case in which the trial is likely to last longer than four weeks;
(h) cases in which expert evidence is to be introduced;
(i) cases in which a party requests a hearing to enter a plea;
(j) cases in which an application to dismiss or stay has been made;
(k) cases in which arraignment has not taken place, whether because of an issue relating to fitness to plead, or abuse of process or sufficiency of evidence, or for any other reason; and

(l) cases in which there are likely to be linked criminal and care directions in accordance with the 2013 Protocol.

If a further case management hearing is directed, a defendant in custody will not usually be expected to attend in person, unless the court otherwise directs (*CPD* I General Matters 3A.21).

Compliance hearing and compliance courts

A party that fails to comply with a case management direction may be required to attend the court to explain the failure. Unless the court otherwise directs a defendant in custody will not usually be expected to attend (*CPD* I General Matters 3A.23). **11-039**

To ensure effective compliance with directions of the courts made in accordance with the CrimPR and the overriding objective, courts should maintain a record whenever a party to the proceedings has failed to comply with a direction made by the court. The parties may have to attend a hearing to explain any lack of compliance. These hearings may be conducted by live link facilities or via other electronic means, as the court may direct. It will be for the Presiding Judges, Resident Judge and Justices' Clerks to decide locally how often compliance courts should be held, depending on the scale and nature of the problem at each court centre (*CPD* I General Matters 3A.26–3A.28).

Conduct of case progression hearings

As far as possible, case progression should be managed without a hearing in the courtroom, using electronic communication in accordance with CrimPR 3.5(2)(d). Court staff should be nominated to conduct case progression as part of their role, in accordance with CrimPR 3.4(2). To aid effective communication the prosecution and defence representative should notify the court and provide details of who shall be dealing with the case at the earliest opportunity (*CPD* I General Matters 3A.24). **11-040**

Completion of effective trial monitoring form

The *CPD* makes clear that it is imperative that the "Effective Trial Monitoring" form as devised and issued by His Majesty's Courts and Tribunals Service ("HMCTS") is accurately completed by the parties for all cases that have been listed for trial, and that advocates must engage with the process by providing the relevant details and completing the form (*CPD* I General Matters 3A.25). **11-041**

"Cards on the table"

Active case management at the PTPH is essential in order to reduce the number of ineffective, cracked and vacated trials, and delays during the trial caused by the need to resolve legal issues. **11-042**

The effectiveness of the hearing in a contested case depends in large measure upon preparation by all concerned and upon the presence of the trial advocate, or an advocate who is able to make decisions and give the court the assistance which the trial advocate could be expected to give. Resident Judges, in setting the listing policy, should ensure that list officers arrange cases as far as possible to enable the trial advocate to conduct case management hearings and the trial.

The position as it exists under the CrimPR is as follows:

(1) it is and remains the task of the prosecutor to establish a prima facie case and then to prove his case;
(2) the CrimPR require a "cards on the table" approach and give to the PTPH a central role as an integral part of the trial process;
(3) the hearing is not a formality—a rigorous examination is required of each case in which there is no guilty plea, to ensure that the trial can be fairly and expeditiously conducted in the interests of justice;
(4) the accused is required through his trial advocate, who must be present in person (or through a nominee whose informed decisions will bind the defence at trial), to identify the issues which will arise at trial;
(5) the trial advocate must also identify which part of the prosecutor's case will be challenged and which witnesses are required, the detailed timetable set for speeches, examination and cross-examination of witnesses; and
(6) the trial advocate must also provide all the other information required in the various Forms.

(*R. v Newell* [2012] EWCA Crim 650; (2012) 176 J.P. 273)

The accused must notify the Crown Court officer of the identity of the intended defence trial advocate as soon as practicable, and in any event no later than the case management hearing, and must notify him in writing of any change in the identity of the intended defence trial advocate as soon as practicable, and in any event not more than five business days after that change (CrimPR 3.27).

If an issue is not identified and subsequently raised, the judge has ample powers, including giving the prosecutor time to deal with that issue (*R. (on the application of DPP) v Chorley Magistrates Court* [2006] EWHC 1795 (Admin); *R. v Penner* [2010] EWCA Crim 1155; [2010] Crim. L.R. 936).

Rulings at the PTPH or PCMH

11-043 The judge may make rulings (see 11-067 and 11-068) which have binding effect (subject to being discharged or varied under CPIA 1996 s.40) as to:

(1) any question as to the admissibility of evidence; and
(2) any other question of law relating to the case concerned.

Where the defence are considering making an abuse of process application, the matter should be raised at the PTPH (*CPD* I General Matters 3C.1).

Note that:

(a) the extent to which the judge exercises the power to make such rulings at this hearing is a matter for him after considering representations;
(b) such directions as he does make must be easily understood by, and made available to, the CPOs; and
(c) time limits should normally be expressed by reference to a particular date rather than by the number of days allowed, to make the task of the CPO easier.

Except where otherwise required, a direction to "serve" material means serve on the other parties and file with the Crown Court. Where a direction requires a party to respond to a proposal (e.g. a proposed edited interview) the party responding will be expected to suggest a counter-proposal.

Defence trial advocate

The accused must notify the court officer of the identity of the intended defence trial advocate: **11-044**

(a) as soon as practicable, and in any event no later than the day of the PTPH; and
(b) in writing, or orally at the PTPH.

The accused must notify the court officer in writing of any change in the identity of the intended defence trial advocate as soon as practicable, and in any event not more than five business days after that change (CrimPR 3.27).

The defence statement

Due to the time provided for the service of a defence statement it may not be available before the PTPH. Clearly if it can be provided before the hearing that would be ideal and in the most straightforward of cases it may be feasible, but in many cases it will not be. **11-045**

Note that:

(1) under the previous regime if there was no defence statement by the time of the Plea and Case Management Hearing (PCMH) then the judge would normally require the trial advocate to see that such a statement was provided and not proceed with the PCMH until that was done. In the ordinary case the trial advocate may have been required to do that at a court, and the PCMH resume later that day to avoid delay and further costs; and
(2) at the PTPH the trial advocate should see it as part of his duty to assist the judge with the management of the case by setting out information on the PTPH Form, without the risk of the information so provided being used as a statement admissible in evidence against the accused.

Provided the case is conducted in accordance with the letter and spirit of the CrimPR, no information or statement written on the PTPH Form should, in the exercise of the judge's discretion under PACE 1984 s.78, be admitted in evidence as a statement that can be used against the accused. The information is provided to assist the court (*R. v Newell* [2012] EWCA Crim 650; (2012) 176 J.P. 273).

Children, young persons and vulnerable accused

If a vulnerable accused, especially one who is young: **11-046**

(1) is to be tried jointly with one who is not:
   (a) the judge should consider at the PTPH whether the vulnerable accused should be tried on his own; but
   (b) should only so order if satisfied that a fair trial cannot be achieved by use of appropriate special measures, or other support for the accused;
(2) is tried jointly with one who is not, the judge should consider whether any of the modifications set out in *CPD* I General Matters 3G (Vulnerable defendants) (see VULNERABLE ACCUSED AND WITNESSES) should apply in the circumstances of the joint trial and, so far as practicable, make orders to give effect to any such modifications.

Fixing trial dates

11-047 Cases will be listed for trial depending on the circumstances of each particular case in accordance with the listing practice determined by the Resident Judge. A trial date or trial window, will generally be fixed at, or immediately after, the PTPH.

Meeting the objectives of the listing practice set for the Crown Court when allocating dates or windows for hearings may require compromise. For example, where an accused is in custody and subject to CTLs, his needs should be considered carefully. The impact on individual witnesses of any delay in bringing the matter to trial and the impact on the accused of any change in the trial date must be balanced when considering timeliness (PD 2004, Annex F, saved by *CPD*). It is important that the mode of trial procedure is correctly followed at the hearing, carrying out the provisions of CDA 1998 Sch.3 paras 7–9 (see SENDING FOR TRIAL). Failure to do, while not necessarily nullifying subsequent proceedings, may result in the sort of problem which arose in *R. v Gul* [2012] EWCA Crim 1761; [2013] 1 Cr. App. R. 4 (where the accused was not given the right to be heard when the issue of venue was being addressed).

Under the regime set out in the CrimPR the parties are expected to provide an accurate estimate of the length of trial at the PTPH (or earlier) and accurate information about the availability of witnesses. Accurate information is essential. Experience has shown that dates on which an expert witness is available to attend the trial is sometimes the cause of difficulty.

Although the provision of accurate information is the responsibility of the parties, the listing officer or the CPO should try and ensure that this issue is addressed prior to the PCMH (PD 2004, Annex F, saved by *CPD*). As to maintaining custody time limits, see 11-048.

Custody time limits (CTL)

11-048 In so far as CTLs are concerned:

(1) at the PTPH in the Crown Court, the judge will ask the prosecution to inform the court when the time limit elapses;
(2) all efforts must be made to list the case within the time; it may be extended only in unusual or exceptional circumstances (see CUSTODY TIME LIMITS);
(3) if suitable, given priority and listed on a date not less than two weeks before the time limit expires, a case may be placed in a warned list; and
(4) the time limit should be kept under continual review by the parties, HMCTS and the Resident Judge; and if the time limit is at risk of being exceeded, an additional hearing should take place and should be listed before the Resident Judge or trial judge.

(Custody and Time Limits (CTL) (Revised Procedure) Protocol issued in December 2012, for which see CUSTODY TIME LIMITS, also in relation to applications for extension).

4. PREPARATORY HEARINGS

(1) General

Statutory provisions

By statute a preparatory hearing: 11-049

(1) *may* be ordered, either on application by the prosecutor or by an accused, or on the judge's own initiative, in two types of case, namely in:
  (a) *serious and complex fraud cases*, where, before the time when the jury are sworn, it appears to the judge that the evidence on the indictment reveals a case of fraud of such seriousness or complexity that substantial benefits are likely to accrue from such a hearing (CJA 1987 s.7 and 7(2A)); or
  (b) *cases other than serious fraud*, where, in relation to an offence:
    (i) an accused is sent for trial for the offence concerned; or
    (ii) proceedings for trial on the charge concerned are the subject of a notice under CDA 1998 s.51C; or
    (iii) a bill of indictment for the offences is preferred under AJ(MP)A 1933 s.2(2)(b) (voluntary bill) or (2)(ba) (deferred prosecution agreement); and
    (iv) a case of such complexity, or of such seriousness, is revealed, or a case whose trial is likely to be of such a length that substantial benefits are likely to accrue from a preparatory hearing before the time the jury are sworn (CPIA 1996 ss.28, 29 and 29(5));
(2) *must* be ordered to determine an application:
  (a) for a trial without a jury, under CJA 2003 s.44 (danger of jury tampering);
  (b) under DVA 2004 s.17 (sample counts by jury, and others by judge alone); or
  (c) under CPIA 1996 s.29 where s.29(1B) or (1C) applies (cases in which a terrorism offence is charged, or other serious cases with a terrorist connection).

The reference to the time the jury are sworn is to be read, in the case of a trial without a jury, as a reference to the time when, if the trial were conducted with a jury, the jury would be sworn (CJA 1987 s.7(2A); CPIA 1996 s.29(2)).

Special provisions apply to terrorist cases, as to which, see CPIA 1996 s.29(1B).

As to complex health and safety cases, see the observations of the CACD in *R. v EGS Ltd* [2009] EWCA Crim 1942.

The need for a preparatory hearing

For all practical purposes a judge of the Crown Court now has exactly the same powers of case management in a non-preparatory hearing as in one where a direction for a statutory preparatory hearing is given. Given the co-extensive powers of case management outside the preparatory hearing regime, (unless the holding of a hearing is mandatory), *judges ought to be very cautious about directing formal preparatory hearings* whether under CPIA 1996 or CJA 1987 (*R. v I* [2009] EWCA Crim 1793; [2010] 1 Cr. App. R. 10). Virtually the only reason for holding one is if the judge is going to give a ruling which ought to be the subject of an interlocu- 11-050 tory appeal. Such rulings are likely to be few and far between (*R. v CH* [2010] Crim. L.R. 312).

The mere desire of one party to test a ruling by interlocutory appeal is not a good enough reason for doing so, unless the point is one of the few which are genuinely suitable for such procedure and there is a real prospect of such appeal being both capable of resolution in the absence of evidence and avoiding significant wastage of time at the trial (*R. v I* [2009] EWCA Crim 1793; [2010] 1 Cr. App. R. 10).

Statutory purposes

11-051 The purposes of a statutory hearing are laid down as:

(1) identifying issues which are likely to be material to the determinations and findings which are likely to be required during the trial;
(2) if there is a jury, assisting their comprehension of those issues and expediting the proceedings before them;
(3) determining an application for trial without a jury;
(4) assisting the judge's management of the trial; and
(5) considering questions as to the severance or joinder of charges.

(CJA 1987 s.7(1); CPIA 1996 s.29(2))

The judge who is to conduct the hearing should be, save in the most exceptional cases, the judge who is to conduct the trial (*R. v Southwark Crown Court Ex p. Customs and Excise Commissioners* (1993) 97 Cr. App. R. 266, and 11-012 and 11-013).

A judge who is considering whether to hold such a hearing needs only to ask himself whether exercising any of his powers under s.9 at such a hearing, rather than at the trial when a jury has been sworn, is likely to result in substantial benefits. If so, he may order a preparatory hearing and exercise those of his powers under s.9 which he thinks likely to achieve those benefits (*R. v H (Interlocutory Application; Disclosure)* [2007] UKHL 7; [2007] 2 Cr. App. R. 6).

"Expediting the proceedings" (in (2) above) includes dealing with issues of evidence, and those questions which typically arise under PACE 1984 s.78 (*R. v Claydon* [2001] EWCA Crim 1359; [2004] 1 Cr. App. R. 36).

It should be emphasised that s.29(1) refers to an offence of *such* seriousness. The use of the intensifier "such" is plainly intended to convey a very high degree of gravity (*R. v R* [2013] EWCA Crim 708; [2014] 1 Cr. App. R. 5).

Restriction to statutory purposes

11-052 A preparatory hearing of this nature is restricted to the purposes specified in the statutory provisions set out in 11-051 not, e.g. merely to allow points of law to be decided and then tested by interlocutory appeal (*R. v Pennine Acute Hospitals NHS Trust* [2003] EWCA Crim 3436; [2004] 1 All E.R. 1324).

A preparatory hearing:

(1) needs to be distinguished from an informal pre-trial review (*Re Gunawardena* (1990) 91 Cr. App. R. 55); and
(2) is concerned with matters which will facilitate the trial, not with applications to prevent the trial taking place (*R. v Hedworth* [1997] 1 Cr. App. R. 421).

A ruling as to the scope of the indictment is a ruling as to its construction (*R. v G* [2002] Crim. L.R. 59).

As to the issue of separate trials where two of three accused were unfit to be tried, see *R. v B* [2008] EWCA Crim 1997; [2009] 1 Cr. App. R. 19. For preparatory hearings relating to decisions as to whether a particular defence may be advanced at the trial, see *R. v Quayle* [2005] EWCA Crim 1415; [2005] 2 Cr. App. R. 34; *R. v S Ltd* [2009] EWCA Crim 85; [2009] 2 Cr. App. R. 11. As to consideration of evidence and issues under PACE 1984 s.78, see *R. v Claydon* [2001] EWCA Crim 1359; [2004] 1 Cr. App. R. 36.

In relation to (1)(b) in 11-049 (i.e. cases other than serious fraud) there must be a case of such complexity, a case of such seriousness, or a case whose trial is likely to be of such a length that a preparatory hearing would be beneficial, as where, e.g.:

(a) the process of proper disclosure can be conducted;
(b) the marshalling of evidence can be prepared with direct reference to the live issues in the case; and
(c) issues as to the proper interpretation of the relevant legislation, and as to the directions to be given to the jury may be resolved,

but the power to make rulings on questions of law is confined to questions of law "relating to the case".

An application for disclosure under CPIA 1996 s.8 is not question of law "relating to the case" (*R. v Shayler* [2002] UKHL 11; [2002] 2 All E.R. 477).

Under CPIA 1996 s.8(2) the judge may determine such an application at any time, and nothing prevents him from dealing with it in parallel proceedings on the same occasion as he holds a preparatory hearing, though no interlocutory appeal will lie under CJA 1987 s.9(11) (*R. v H (Interlocutory Application; Disclosure)* [2007] UKHL 7; [2007] 2 Cr. App. R. 6).

The hearing

If a statutory preparatory hearing is ordered: **11-053**

(1) the trial starts with that hearing (*R. v H* [2005] EWCA Crim 2083; [2006] 1 Cr. App. R. 4), and arraignment takes place at the start of the hearing, if it has not taken place already;
(2) the judge must, therefore, bear in mind the effect on the CTLs of the decision to hold such a hearing (*Re Kanaris* [2003] UKHL 2; [2003] 2 Cr. App. R. 1);
(3) in most cases, the decision to hold a hearing should be in respect of all the accused joined in the same indictment (*Re Kanaris* [2003] UKHL 2; [2003] 2 Cr. App. R. 1); and
(4) any matter dealt with before the jury is sworn is to be treated as forming part of the hearing, provided that the purpose of dealing with it at that stage is one of the objects set out in the statute (*R. v Jennings* (1994) 98 Cr. App. R. 308).

(CJA 1987 s.8; CPIA 1996 s.30)

At the beginning of a preparatory hearing, the judge must announce that it is such a hearing; and take the accused's plea (unless already done) (CrimPR r.3.18).

The judge is not entitled to declare retrospectively there has been a preparatory hearing for the purposes of CPIA 1996 s.29 (*R. v C* [2010] EWCA Crim 2578; [2011] Crim. L.R. 396). Similarly it seems clear that it is not permissible, once a decision has been made to hold a preparatory hearing, for the judge in the course of his judgment to revoke that decision; the Act contains no such power. It is wrong in principle to allow the judge to take such a course which might prevent an appeal (*R. v YDG* [2012] EWCA Crim 2437; [2013] 1 Cr. App. R. 21).

As to reporting restrictions, see REPORTING AND ACCESS RESTRICTIONS.

Rulings and orders

11-054 At the hearing, the judge may determine:

(1) any question arising under CJA 1993 s.6 (relevance of external law to certain charges of conspiracy, attempt and incitement);
(2) any question as to the admissibility of evidence; and
(3) any other questions of law relating to the case, but note that:
    (a) he may not give a ruling which is tantamount to an order granting a stay or quashing the indictment (*R. v Hoogstraten* [2003] EWCA Crim 3642; [2004] Crim L.R. 498);
    (b) any ruling he gives has effect throughout the trial unless it appears to him, on application, that the interests of justice require him to vary or discharge it; and
    (c) he must be prepared to vary his rulings where required (*R. v Shayler* [2002] UKHL 11; [2002] 2 All E.R. 477).

(CJA 1987 s.9(3); CPIA 1996 s.31(3))

He may adjourn the hearing from time to time.

Parallel proceedings

11-055 While the only powers which the judge may exercise in a preparatory hearing are those set out in 11-054:

(1) where he is holding a parallel hearing at the same time, he may, in that other hearing, exercise other common law and statutory powers, although a right of interlocutory appeal arises under s.9(11) only where the matters come within s.9(3); and
(2) there is no reason in principle why the two hearings should not take place on the same occasion provided that the distinctions between the two hearings and the issues which the judge may determine in each, is kept clearly in mind (*R. v H (Interlocutory Application; Disclosure)* [2007] UKHL 7; [2007] 2 Cr. App. R. 6).

Where a judge orders a preparatory hearing and decides that orders under s.9(4) or (5) of the 1987 Act, or s.31(4)–(7) of the 1996 Act should be made before the hearing, he may make an order either before or at the hearing, and s.9(4)–(10) or s.31(4)–(7) respectively apply accordingly (CJA 1987 s.10, CPIA 1996 s.32).

An order or ruling made has effect during the trial unless it appears to the judge, on an application made to him during the trial, that the interests of justice require him to discharge it (CJA 1987 s.9(10), CPIA 1996 s.31(11)).

Disclosure by prosecutor

11-056 The judge may order the prosecutor:

(1) to supply the court and each accused with a written "case statement", of:
    (a) the principal facts of the prosecution case;
    (b) the witnesses who will speak to those facts;

- (c) any exhibits relevant to those facts;
- (d) any propositions of law on which the prosecutor intends to rely; and
- (e) the consequences in relation to any of the counts in the indictment which appear to him to flow from the matters stated in (a)–(d);

(2) to prepare his evidence and other explanatory material in such form as appears likely to aid the comprehension of a jury and to supply it in that form to the court and to each accused;

(3) to give the court and each accused notice of documents, the truth of the contents of which ought, in the prosecutor's view, to be admitted, and of any other matters which ought to be agreed; and

(4) to make any amendments to any case statement supplied that appear to the judge to be appropriate, having regard to any objections made by any accused.

(CJA 1987 s.9(10); CPIA 1996 s.31(4))

The judge may specify the time within which any requirements are to be complied with.

Disclosure by accused

Where the judge has ordered the prosecution to supply a case statement and the prosecutor has complied, the judge may order each accused to: **11-057**

(1) give the court and the prosecutor notice of any objections that he has to the case statement; and

(2) inform the court and the prosecution of any point of law (including points as to the admissibility of evidence) which he wishes to take, and any authority on which he intends to rely for that purpose; and in addition to the general provisions as to compulsory disclosure in criminal cases (as to which, see DISCLOSURE).

(CJA 1987 s.9(5); CPIA 1996 s.31(6) and (7))

The judge must, on making such an order, warn any accused of the possible consequences of not complying with it (see 11-049).

Note that the judge:

- (a) will, if he considers the reasons inadequate, inform the party concerned, and may require further or better reasons; and
- (b) may specify the time within which any requirement contained in it is to be complied with.

(CJA 1987 s.9(7) and (8); CPIA 1996 s.31(8), (9) and (10))

An order made under s.9(5) (or s.31(6) or (7)) should be clear, comprising short questions identifying matters upon which the prosecutor requires the accused's agreement. In the case of several accused each one's case should be the subject of individual orders (*Case Statements made under CJA 1987 s.9* (1993) 97 Cr. App. R. 417).

Case statements of no evidential value

Neither the prosecutor's case statement nor the defence statement has any evidential value, nor do they limit the respective parties in the evidence they may call. The object of ordering a case statement is to: **11-058**

(1) inform the other side of the case that is intended to be put forward;

(2) facilitate preparation for trial, and to avoid surprise; and
(3) enable comment to be made under CJA 1987 s.10 where there is a significant departure from the statement.

The judge should not permit a case statement to be put before the jury as a matter of course, as if it were particulars of the indictment (*R. v Mayhew* unreported 18 November 1991).

Departure from the case at trial

11-059 A party may depart from the case he disclosed in pursuance of a requirement under s.9 or s.31 (11-056, 11-057) respectively but where he:

(1) does so; or
(2) fails to comply with the requirement to disclose,

the judge, or with the judge's leave, any other party, may make such comment as appears appropriate, and the jury, or in the case of a trial without a jury, the judge, will be able to draw such inferences as appear proper, though no part of the case statement or any other information relating to the accused may be disclosed after the jury have been sworn without the consent of the accused concerned.

The judge, in doing anything under this provision, or in deciding whether to do anything under it, may have regard to such matters as the extent of any departure or failure and whether it is justified.

(CJA 1987 s.10; CPIA 1996 s.34)

(2) Procedure

General

11-060 Where a preparatory hearing:

(1) *may* be ordered under:
  (a) CJA 1987 s.7 (cases of serious or complex fraud); or
  (b) CPIA 1996 s.29 (other complex, serious or lengthy cases); or
(2) *must* be ordered, to determine an application for a trial without a jury, under:
  (a) CJA 2003 s.44 (danger of jury tampering); or
  (b) DVCVA 2004 s.17 (trial of sample counts by jury, and others by judge alone); or
(3) *must* be ordered under CPIA 1996 s.29, where s.29(1B) or (1C) applies (cases in which a terrorism offence is charged, or other serious cases with a terrorist connection).

The judge may decide whether to order a preparatory hearing:

(i) on an application or *on his own initiative*;
(ii) at a hearing (in public or in private), or without a hearing; and
(iii) in a party's absence, if that party applied for the order, or has had at least 14 days in which to make representations.

(CrimPR 3.22)

Making an application

11-061 A party who wants the judge to order a preparatory hearing must apply in writing as soon as reasonably practicable, and in any event not more than 14 days after the accused pleads not guilty, and serve the application on the court officer, and on each other party.

The applicant must:

(1) if relevant, explain what legislation requires the judge to order a preparatory hearing;
(2) otherwise, explain:
    (a) what makes the case complex or serious, or makes the trial likely to be long;
    (b) why a substantial benefit will accrue from a preparatory hearing; and
    (c) why the judge's ordinary powers of case management are not adequate.

A prosecutor who wants the court to order a trial without a jury must explain:

(1) where he alleges a danger of *jury tampering*:
    (a) what evidence there is of a real and present danger that jury tampering would take place;
    (b) what steps, if any, reasonably might be taken to prevent jury tampering; and
    (c) why, notwithstanding such steps, the likelihood of jury tampering is so substantial as to make it necessary in the interests of justice to order such a trial; or
(2) where he proposes *trial without a jury on some counts* on the indictment:
    (a) why a trial by jury involving all the counts would be impracticable;
    (b) how the counts proposed for jury trial can be regarded as samples of the others; and
    (c) why it would be in the interests of justice to order such a trial.

(CrimPR 3.23)

Application for non-jury trial; information withheld from accused

Where: **11-062**

(1) the prosecutor applies for an order for a trial without a jury because of a danger of *jury tampering*; and
(2) the application includes information that the prosecutor thinks ought not *be revealed* to an accused,

the prosecutor must:

(a) omit that information from the part of the application that is served on that accused;
(b) mark the other part to show that, unless the court otherwise directs, it is only for the court; and
(c) in that other part, explain why the prosecutor has withheld that information from that accused.

The hearing of the application will be in private, unless the judge otherwise directs; and if he so directs, may be, wholly or in part, in the absence of an accused from whom information has been withheld.

At the hearing of the general rule is that the court will receive, in the following sequence:

(a) representations first by the prosecutor and then by each accused in all the parties' presence; and then

(b) further representations by the prosecutor, in the absence of an accused from whom information has been withheld; but

the judge may direct other arrangements for the hearing.

Where, on an application to which this rule applies, the court orders a trial without a jury:

(a) the general rule is that the trial will be before a judge other than the judge who made the order; but
(b) the judge may direct other arrangements (CrimPR 3.24).

Representations in response to application

11-063 Representations against an application for an order must explain why the conditions for making it are not met (CrimPR 3.25).

Commencement of preparatory hearing

11-064 At the beginning of a preparatory hearing, the court must:

(1) announce that it is such a hearing; and
(2) take the accused's plea (under CrimPR 3.26 unless this has already been done).

(3) Reporting restrictions

11-065 See r.16 and REPORTING AND ACCESS RESTRICTIONS.

(4) Interlocutory appeals

Right of appeal

11-066 Appeal lies, but only with leave from that court, to the CACD, from:

(1) any order or ruling of a judge;
(2) made within the ambit of a preparatory hearing as defined in CJA 1987 s.7(1), or as the case may be, CPIA 1996 s.31(3); and
(3) involving a question of law within CJA 1987 s.9(3)(b) or (c).

(CJA 1987 s.9(13)–(14) and see APPEALS FROM THE CROWN COURT)

As to defence costs, see POA 1985 s.16(4A); CJA 2003 s.257. The judge may continue the preparatory hearing notwithstanding that leave has been granted to appeal, but the hearing is not to be concluded until any appeal has been determined or abandoned (see *R. v Y* [2001] Crim. L.R. 389). The CACD may confirm, vary or reverse the judge's decision.

C. PRELIMINARY HEARINGS; PRE-TRIAL RULINGS

Definitions

11-067 A pre-trial hearing is one which relates to a trial on indictment and takes place:

(1) after the accused has been sent for trial for the offence; or
(2) where the hearing relates to a trial to be held in pursuance of a bill of indictment preferred under AJ(MP)A 1933 s.2(2)(b) (a voluntary bill) or s.2(2)(ba) (a deferred prosecution agreement); and

(3) before the start of the trial.

(CPIA 1996 ss.39 and 71; CCA 2013 s.37(4))

The "start" of a trial on indictment (s.39(3)) occurs at the time when a jury are sworn or, if the judge accepts a plea of guilty *at* the time when a jury is sworn, when that plea is accepted (subject to s.30, and to CJA 1987 in relation to preparatory hearings).

In the case of a trial without a jury, the reference to the time the jury are sworn is to be read as a reference to the time when, if the trial were conducted with a jury, the jury would be sworn.

CDA 1998 s.57 permits the use of a TV link at such a hearing where such facilities exist, and the accused is in custody.

In terrorist cases (see ALLOCATION AND LISTING OF CASES), the judge will determine at a preliminary hearing whether the case is to remain in the terrorism list, and if so, will give directions setting the provisional timetable. The Legal Services Agency must attend the hearing by an authorised officer to assist the court (TerrPro 2007 paras 13 and 14).

Effect of pre-trial ruling

At such a hearing, the judge may, either on application by a party or of his own motion, make a ruling: **11-068**

(1) as to the admissibility of evidence; or
(2) on any question of law in the case.

That ruling has (subject to CPIA 1996 s.40(4)) immediate effect from the time it is made until the case against the accused is disposed of by acquittal or conviction or by the prosecutor deciding not to proceed.

(CPIA 1996 s.40)

It is desirable, where the judge is asked to decide whether the facts support a charge, for the facts on which the ruling is sought to be recorded (*R. v Marshall* [1998] 2 Cr. App. R. 282).

Under s.40(4) a judge, whether or not the judge who made the ruling, may, either on application or of his own motion, discharge, vary, or further vary it, if it appears to him to be in the interests of justice so to do, where there has been a change of circumstances since the ruling or the last application was made.

The judge may sometimes be asked, at the outset of a trial to:

(a) give a ruling whether on certain facts a particular defence would be open to the accused; or
(b) indicate how he would propose to direct the jury in relation to that issue,

with a view to the defence advocate giving advice to the accused about his plea (see *R. v Marshall* [1998] 2 Cr. App. R. 282). It is quite wrong for the judge to rule that there is no defence to a charge before the trial has even begun; that is to usurp the jury's function. The proper time for the judge to consider how to direct the jury in relation to a defence is after the evidence has been given (*R. v Asmeron* [2013] EWCA Crim 435; [2013] 2 Cr. App. R. 19).

Reporting restrictions

Reporting restrictions apply to proceedings and rulings under the section but the judge may lift the restrictions in certain circumstances (CJA 1996 ss.41 and 42). **11-069**

A ruling made under s.40(1) is not binding for the purposes of a retrial where the first jury disagreed. A judge may discharge or vary any ruling of his own motion if it appears to be in the interests of justice to do so.

D. HEAVY FRAUD AND OTHER COMPLEX CRIMINAL CASES

Introduction

11-070 The *Protocol for the Control and management of Heavy Fraud and other Complex Criminal Cases* [2005] 2 All E.R. 429:

(1) is primarily directed towards cases which are likely to *last eight weeks or longer*; but
(2) should also be followed in all cases estimated to last *more than four weeks*;
(3) applies to trials by jury, but many of the principles will be applicable where trials without a jury are permitted under CJA 2003 s.43 (see TRIAL WITHOUT A JURY); and,
(4) supplements the CrimPR, and summarises good practice which experience has shown may assist in bringing about some reduction in the length of trials of fraud and other crimes that result in complex trials.

Flexibility of application of this protocol according to the needs of each case is essential; it is designed to inform but not to prescribe.

The best handling technique for a long case is continuous management by an experienced judge nominated for the purpose.

The Judicial Protocol on the Disclosure of Unused Material in Criminal Cases (the Protocol) and the Attorney-General's Guidelines on Disclosure for Investigators, Prosecutors and Defence Practitioners (the Guidelines) (see further DISCLOSURE at 30-001) supersede s.4 of the Protocol for the Control and Management of Heavy Fraud and Complex Criminal Cases.

1. GENERAL

Contents

11-071 The Protocol is divided into a number of sections, relating to case management:

(1) during the investigation;
(2) before the trial; and
(3) at the trial.

In so far as the investigation is concerned, the Protocol provides for the creation of prosecution and defence teams, the channels of communication between those teams and the judge, particularly in relation to policy decisions, the level at which such decisions should be taken, and the involvement of the Legal Services Agency.

2. CASE MANAGEMENT

Objectives

11-072 The number, length and organisation of case management hearings will depend critically on the circumstances and complexity of the individual case. However, thorough, well-prepared and extended case management hearings will save court time and costs overall. Effective case management of heavy fraud and other complex criminal cases requires the judge to have a much more detailed grasp of the case than may be necessary for many other plea and case management hearings. (Protocol 3(i)(a))

A case management decision refusing to order an adjournment before trial or indeed at any time before the start of the summing-up may constitute a "terminatory" ruling against which a prosecutor may appeal (*R. v Clark* unreported 9 October 2007 CACD).

Fixing the trial date

Although it is important that the trial date should be fixed as early as possible, this may not always be the right course. There are two principal alternatives. **11-073**

The trial date should either:

(1) be fixed at the first opportunity, i.e. at the first (and usually short) directions hearing and from then on:
  (a) everyone must work to that date;
  (b) all orders and pre-trial steps will be timetabled to fit in with that date; and
  (c) all advocates and the judge should take note of this date, in the expectation that the trial will proceed on the date determined; or
(2) not be fixed until the issues have been explored at a full case management hearing, after the advocates on both sides have done some serious work on the case; only then can the length of the trial be estimated.

Which procedure is apposite must depend on the circumstances of each case, but the earlier it is possible to fix a trial date, by reference to a proper estimate and a timetable set by reference to the trial date, the better.

It is generally to be expected that once a trial is fixed on the basis of the estimate provided, that it will be *increased* if, and only if, the party seeking to extend the *time* justifies why the original estimate is no longer appropriate. (Protocol 3(ii))

The first hearing; initial directions

At the first opportunity the assigned judge should hold a short hearing to give initial directions. The directions on this occasion might well include: **11-074**

(1) that there should be a full case management hearing on, or commencing on, a specified future date by which time the parties will be properly prepared for a meaningful hearing and the defence will have full instructions;
(2) that the prosecution should provide an outline written statement of the prosecution case at least one week in advance of that case management hearing, outlining in simple terms:
  (a) the key facts on which it relies;
  (b) the key evidence by which the prosecution seeks to prove the facts;
(3) that a core reading list and core bundle for the case management hearing should be delivered at least one week in advance; and
(4) preliminary directions about disclosure.

In relation to (2) the statement must be sufficient to permit the judge to understand the case and for the defence to appreciate the basic elements of its case against each accused. The prosecution may be invited to highlight the key points of the case orally at the case management hearing by way of a short mini-opening. The outline statement should not be considered binding, but it will serve the essential purpose in telling the judge, and everyone else, what the case is really about and identifying the key issues.

(Protocol 3(iii))

The first case management hearing

11-075 At the first case management hearing:

(1) the prosecution advocate should be given the opportunity to highlight any points from the prosecution outline statement of case (which will have been delivered at least a week in advance); and
(2) each defence advocate should be asked to outline the defence.

If the defence advocate is not in a position to say what is, and what is not, in issue, then the hearing may be adjourned for a short and limited time and to a fixed date to enable the advocate to take instructions. Such an adjournment should only be necessary in exceptional circumstances, since:

(a) the defence advocate should be properly instructed by the time of the first case management hearing; and
(b) in any event he is under an obligation to take sufficient instructions to fulfil the obligations contained in CJA 2003 ss.33–39 (defence disclosure).

(Protocol 3(iv))

Real dialogue

11-076 At the hearing there should be a real dialogue between the judge and all advocates for the purpose of identifying:

(1) the focus of the prosecution case;
(2) any common ground; and
(3) the real issues in the case (see CrimPR 3.2).

As to the issues in health and safety cases, see *R. v EGS Ltd* [2009] EWCA Crim 1942.

The judge will try to generate a spirit of co-operation between the court and the advocates on all sides.

It may be noted that:

(a) the expeditious conduct of the trial and a focusing on the real issues must be in the interests of all parties;
(b) it cannot be in the interests of any accused for his good points to become lost in a welter of uncontroversial or irrelevant evidence;
(c) in many fraud cases the primary facts are not seriously disputed, the real issue being what each accused knew and whether that accused was dishonest.

Once the judge has identified what is, and what is not, in dispute, he is in a position to discuss with the advocate:

(i) how the trial should be structured;
(ii) what can be dealt with by admissions or agreed facts;
(iii) what uncontroversial matters should be proved by concise oral evidence;

(iv) what timetabling can be required under CrimPR 3.10; and
(v) other directions.

It is important that proper defence statements be provided as required by the CrimPR; judges will use the powers contained in CPIA 1996 ss.28–34 (and the corresponding provisions of CJA 1987 ss.33 and following) and the CrimPR to ensure that realistic defence statements are provided.

This objective may also be achieved by requiring the prosecution to serve draft admissions by a specified date and by requiring the defence to respond within a specified number of weeks.

The date of the next case management hearing should be fixed at the conclusion of the hearing so that there is no delay in fixing the date.

(Protocol 3(iv)(a)–(g))

Intensive case management

In particularly heavy fraud or complex cases the judge may possibly consider it necessary to allocate a whole week for a case management hearing. If that week is used wisely, many further weeks of trial time can be saved. In the gaps which will inevitably arise during that week (for example while the advocates are exploring matters raised by the judge) the judge can do a substantial amount of informed reading. The case has come "alive" at this stage. Indeed, in a really heavy fraud case, if the judge fixes one or more case management hearings on this scale, there will be need for fewer formal reading days. **11-077**

Moreover a huge amount can be achieved in the pre-trial stage, if all trial advocates are gathered in the same place, focusing on the case at the same time, for several days consecutively.

If one is looking at a trial which threatens to run for months, pre-trial case management on an intensive scale is essential.

(Protocol 3(iv)(e) and (v)(b))

Length of trial

Even intensive case management on the lines referred to at 11-069 may still be insufficient to reduce a potentially long trial to a manageable length. **11-078**

Generally a trial of three months should be the target, but there will be cases where a duration of six months or, in exceptional circumstances, even longer may be inevitable.

If the trial is not estimated to be within a manageable length, it will be necessary for the judge to consider what steps should be taken to reduce the length of the trial, whilst still ensuring that the prosecutor has the opportunity of placing the full criminality before the court.

To assist the judge in this task:

(1) the lead advocate for the prosecution should be asked to explain why the prosecution have rejected a shorter way of proceeding; he may also be asked to:
 (a) divide the case into sections of evidence;
 (b) explain the scope of, and the need for, each section;
(2) the lead advocates for the prosecution and for the defence should be prepared:
 (a) to put forward, in writing, if requested, ways in which a case estimated to last more than three months can be shortened; and

(b) to consider possible severance of counts or accused, the exclusion of sections of the case, or of evidence or areas of the case where admissions can be made.

(Protocol 3(vi))

Miscellaneous matters

11-079 Certain matters are as relevant to less complex cases as they are to heavy fraud cases, and these are dealt with elsewhere in this section. See, e.g.:

- "*pruning*" and *severance* (Protocol 3(vi)(e) and (vii) at 11-014);
- the rationalisation of *expert evidence*, and evidence of *surveillance* (Protocol 3(viii) and (ix) at 11-016);
- *disclosure* (Judicial Protocol on disclosure 2013 at 11-017); and
- *abuse of process* (Protocol 5(i)–(v) at 11-018).

3. The trial

Case management at the trial

11-080 The Protocol recognises that a heavy fraud or other complex trial has the potential to lose direction and focus:

(1) the jury may lose track of the evidence, thereby prejudicing both prosecution and defence;
(2) the burden on the accused, the judge and indeed all involved may become intolerable; and
(3) scarce public resources will be wasted.

In this situation, the judge needs to exercise firm control over the conduct of the trial at all stages; his role in a heavy fraud or other complex criminal case is different from his role in a "conventional" criminal trial.

So far as possible, he should be freed from other duties and burdens, so that he can give the high degree of commitment which a heavy fraud trial requires.

(Protocol 6(i) and (ii))

The Order of the Evidence

11-081 By the outset of the trial at the latest (and in most cases very much earlier) the judge must be provided with a schedule, showing the sequence of prosecution (and in an appropriate case defence) witnesses and the dates upon which they are expected to be called. This can only be prepared by discussion between prosecution and defence which the judge should expect, and say he expects, to take place (CrimPR 3.3).

The schedule should, in so far as it relates to prosecution witnesses, be developed in consultation with the witnesses, via the Witness Care Units, and with consideration given to their personal needs. Copies of the schedule should be provided for the Witness Service.

The schedule should be kept under review by the trial judge and by the parties. If a case is running behind or ahead of schedule, each witness affected must be advised by the party who is calling that witness at the earliest opportunity.

If an excessive amount of time is allowed for any witness, the judge can ask why.

The judge may probe with the advocates whether the time envisaged for the evidence-in-chief or cross-examination (as the case may be) of a particular witness is really necessary.
(Protocol 6(iii))

Case management sessions

There should be periodic case management sessions, during which the judge engages the advocates upon a stock-taking exercise, asking, amongst other questions, "where are we going?" and "what is the relevance of the next three witnesses?"; this will be a valuable means of keeping the case on track (CrimPR 3.10 will again assist the judge). **11-082**

"Case management notes" from the judge to the advocates, setting out the judge's tentative view on where the trial may be going off track, which areas of future evidence are relevant and which may have become irrelevant (e.g. because of concessions, admissions in cross-examination and so forth) together with written responses may, if cautiously used, provide a valuable focus for debate during the trial.

Controlling prolix cross-examination; interviews

Setting rigid time limits in advance for cross-examination is rarely appropriate, but the judge can and should indicate when cross-examination is irrelevant, unnecessary or time wasting, the judge may limit the time for further cross-examination of a particular witness (Protocol 3(v)). **11-083**

The judge should consider extensive editing of self serving interviews, even when the defence want the jury to hear them in their entirety; such interviews are not evidence of the truth of their contents but merely of the accused's reaction to the allegation (Protocol 3(vii)).

EPE and graphics

There is potential for saving time in fraud and other complex criminal trials, by: **11-084**

(1) electronic presentation of evidence (EPE), which should be used more widely; there should still be a core bundle of those documents to which frequent reference will be made during the trial;
(2) greater use of other modern forms of graphical presentations, wherever possible.

Problems have arisen when the legal aid authorities have declined to allow advocates or solicitors to do certain work; on occasions the matter has been raised with the judge managing or trying the case. Guidance has been provided to judges on how they can obtain information as to the reasons for such decisions; further information in relation to this can be obtained from the Complex Crime Unit, Legal Services Agency at present at Exchange House, 2 Harbour Exchange Square, London, E14 9GE.

Jury management

The jury: **11-085**

(1) should be informed as early as possible in the case as to what the issues are in a manner directed by the judge;

(2) must be regularly updated as to the trial timetable and the progress of the trial, subject to warnings as to the predictability of the trial process.

Legal argument should be heard at times that causes the least inconvenience to jurors.

It is useful to consider with the advocates whether written directions should be given to the jury and, if so, in what form (Protocol 3(viii)).

So-called "Maxwell hours" should be permitted only after careful consideration and consultation with the Presiding Judge.

Considerations in favour include:

(a) legal argument can be accommodated without disturbing the jury;
(b) there is a better chance of a representative jury;
(c) time is made available to the judge, advocates and experts to do useful work in the afternoons.

Considerations against include:

(i) the lengthening of the trial and the consequent waste of court time; and
(ii) the desirability of making full use of the jury once they have arrived at court.

E. RECORDS; TRANSCRIPTS

Duty to make records

11-086 For each case, as appropriate, the Crown Court officer will record, by such means as the Lord Chancellor directs:

(1) each charge or indictment against the accused;
(2) the accused's plea to each charge or count;
(3) each acquittal, conviction, sentence, determination, direction or order;
(4) each decision about bail;
(5) the power exercised where the court commits or adjourns the case to another court:
   (a) for sentence; or
   (b) for the offender to be dealt with for breach of a community order, a deferred sentence, a conditional discharge, or a suspended sentence order, imposed by that other court;
(6) the court's reasons for a decision, where legislation requires those reasons to be recorded;
(7) any appeal;
(8) each party's presence or absence at each hearing;
(9) any consent that legislation requires before the court can proceed with the case, or proceed to a decision;
(10) any request for assistance or other communication about the case received from a juror;
(11) the identity of:
   (a) the prosecutor;
   (b) the accused;
   (c) any of the applicants to whom the CrimPR apply;
   (d) any interpreter or intermediary;
   (e) the parties' legal representatives, if any;

(f) the judge or other person who made the order;
(g) where an accused is entitled to attend a hearing, any agreement by him to waive that right; and
(h) where interpretation is required for an accused any agreement by that accused to do without the written translation of a document.

(CrimPR 5.4)

As to arrangements for recording and transcription of proceedings where appeal may be brought to the CACD, see CrimPR 5.5. See as to the custody of case materials, CrimPR 5.6, and for the supply of information or documents about a case to the parties, members of the public and reporters, CrimPR 5.7–5.9.

12. CHILDREN AND YOUNG PERSONS

QUICK GUIDE

1. JUVENILES DEFINED

12-001 Young persons under 18 are commonly known as juveniles though the law distinguishes for some purposes between "children" (under 14) and "young persons" (14–18). Section 44(1) of CYPA 1933 provides that every court dealing with a child or young person brought before it, whether as an offender or otherwise, must have regard to the welfare of the child or young person who is brought before it, and shall, in a proper case, take steps for removing him from undesirable surroundings and seeing that proper provision is made for his education and training. As to the determination of the age of an offender, see AGE OF OFFENDER.

2. JUVENILES AS ACCUSED PERSONS

Jurisdiction

12-002 A juvenile appears in the Crown Court where:

(1) he is charged with an offence of homicide; or
(2) each of the requirements of SA 2020 s.311 and Sch.20 would be satisfied with respect to:
  (a) the offence; and
  (b) the person charged with it, if he were convicted of the offence;
(3) a minimum sentence under SA 2020 s.311 would apply if he were convicted of the offence;
(4) the offence is a "grave crime" such as is mentioned in SA 2020 s.259 and the magistrates' court considers that, if found guilty, it ought to be possible to sentence him in pursuance of that section, or where a sentence under the "dangerous offender" provisions is likely to be required;
(5) he is charged jointly with an adult and the magistrates' court considers it necessary in the interests of justice to commit the cases of both for trial, or to send the case or transfer the case to the Crown Court for trial;
(6) he is charged jointly with an adult; or
(7)
  (a) the charge arises out of circumstances connected with an offence with which an adult is charged;
  (b) an adult is charged with aiding and abetting or procuring an offence by a juvenile; or

(c) a juvenile is charged with aiding and abetting or procuring an offence by an adult; otherwise he will be tried in the youth court.

In (6) and (7) there is a discretion and it is for the lower court to determine whether the trial should be in the adult court or the youth court.

As to the manner in which juveniles are brought before the Crown Court, see SENDING FOR TRIAL.

Juveniles may be remitted to the youth court from the Crown Court, see 12-016.

3. TRIAL OF JUVENILES

In addition to the differences in the purposes of sentencing, juvenile offenders are generally dealt with in the youth court. Where they are tried on indictment there is no "juvenile assize court". They are tried in the Crown Court, generally where the juvenile is being tried with an adult, or where, due to the gravity of the offence it can only be tried at the Crown Court. A juvenile may be committed to the Crown Court for sentence (see COMMITTALS FOR SENTENCE). As to procedure, etc., see VULNERABLE ACCUSED AND WITNESSES. **12-003**

4. REMAND OF PERSONS UNDER 18

Remands of children otherwise than on bail

Where a judge deals with a child (i.e. under the age of 18) charged with, or convicted, of one or more offences: **12-004**

(1) by remanding the child; and
(2) that child is not released on bail,

then he must remand the child to local authority accommodation (see 12-005), but he may, instead, where the first or second set of conditions for such a remand (see 12-011 to 12-013) is met in relation to the child, remand him to youth detention accommodation (LASPOA 2012 s.91).

Section 157(2) PCSCA 2022 amends LASPOA 2012 ss.91, 98 and 102 to introduce a statutory duty for the court to consider the interests and welfare of the child before deciding whether to remand a child.

These provisions, detailed in this chapter, contained in LASPOA 2012 Pt 3 Ch.3 are of no effect in relation to proceedings in which a child is subject to a pre-commencement remand, that is a remand which commenced before 3 December 2012.

Remands to local authority accommodation

A remand to local authority accommodation is a remand to accommodation provided by or on behalf of a local authority. The court must designate the local authority that is to receive the child, which must be: **12-005**

(1) in the case of a child who is being looked after (see below) by a local authority, that authority; and
(2) in any other case, the local authority in whose area it appears that the child habitually resides, or the offence, or one of the offences, was committed.

(LASPOA 2012 s.92)

The designated authority is bound to receive the child, and provide, or arrange for the provision, of accommodation for the child whilst the child is remanded to local authority accommodation, and where the child is so remanded it is lawful for any person acting on behalf of the designated authority to detain the child.

A reference to a child who is being "looked after" by a local authority is to be construed in accordance with the Children Act 1989 s.22.

Conditions, etc., on remands to local authority accommodation

12-006 A child remanded to local authority accommodation may be required by the judge to comply with any conditions that could be imposed under BA 1976 s.3(6) (see BAIL) as if the child were then being granted bail, and may also be required to comply with any conditions imposed for the purpose of securing the electronic monitoring of the child's compliance with the conditions so imposed if the requirements in LASPOA 2012 s.94 are met.

The judge may impose on the designated authority requirements:

(1) for securing compliance with any conditions imposed on the child under s.93(1); or
(2) stipulating that the child must not be placed with a named person, but only after such consultation (if any) with the local authority as is reasonably practicable in all the circumstances of the case.

(LASPOA 2012 s.93)

Where the child has been remanded to local authority accommodation, "a relevant court" may:

(a) on the application of the designated authority, impose on that child any of the above conditions as if the court were then remanding the child to local authority accommodation;
(b) where it does so, impose on the authority requirements for securing compliance with the conditions imposed; and
(c) on the application of the designated authority or that child, vary or revoke any conditions or requirements imposed (including any previously varied under this subsection).

A judge who imposes conditions on a child under this section or varies conditions so imposed must explain to the child in open court and in ordinary language why the conditions are being imposed or varied.

"Relevant court" here, means the court by which the child was so remanded, or any magistrate's court that has jurisdiction in the place where the child is for the time being.

Requirements for electronic monitoring

12-007 For electronic monitoring to be imposed, the following conditions must be met:

(1) the child must have reached the age of 12;
(2) the offence mentioned in LASPOA 2012 s.91(1) (see 12-004), or one or more of those offences, is an imprisonable offence;
(3) the offence or one or more of those offences, must be either:
    (a) a violent offence (within SA 2020 Sch.18), a sexual offence (within SA 2020 Sch.19) or an offence punishable in the case of an adult with imprisonment for a term of 14 years or more; or

(b) together with any other imprisonable offences of which the child has been convicted in any proceedings, amount, or would amount if the child were convicted of that offence, or those offences, to a recent history of committing imprisonable offences while on bail, or subject to a custodial remand (see 12-008);

(4) the judge must be satisfied that the necessary provision for electronic monitoring can be made under arrangements currently available in the relevant local justice area; and

(5) a youth offending team has informed the court that, in its opinion, the imposition of an electronic monitoring condition will be suitable in the child's case.

(LASPOA 2012 ss.94 and 96)

A local justice area is a "relevant area" in relation to a proposed electronic monitoring condition if the judge considers that it will not be practicable to secure the electronic monitoring in question unless electronic monitoring arrangements are available in that area.

The reference (in (3)(b)) to a child being subject to a "custodial remand" is to the child being remanded to local authority accommodation or to youth detention accommodation or subject to a form of custodial detention in a country or territory outside England and Wales while awaiting trial or sentence, or during a trial, in that country or territory.

A reference to a child being remanded to local authority accommodation or youth detention accommodation includes a child being remanded to local authority accommodation under CYPA 1969 s.23, or being remanded to prison under s.23 as modified by CDA 1998 s.98 or under CJA 1948 s.27.

Where an electronic monitoring condition is imposed the condition must include a provision making a person responsible for the monitoring. A person who is made responsible in this way must be of a description specified in an order made by the Secretary of State.

Liability to arrest for breaking conditions of remand

A child may be arrested without warrant by a constable if: **12-008**

(1) he has been remanded to local authority accommodation;

(2) conditions under LASPOA 2012 s.93 have been imposed in respect of him; and

(3) a constable has reasonable grounds for suspecting that the child has broken any of those conditions.

A child thus arrested must be brought before a justice of the peace as soon as practicable, and in any event within the period of 24 hours beginning with his arrest, although if he was arrested during the period of 24 hours ending with the time appointed for him to appear before the court in pursuance of the remand, he must be brought before the court before which he was to have appeared.

In reckoning a period of 24 hours for these purposes no account is to be taken of Christmas Day, Good Friday or any Sunday. If a justice before whom the child is brought is:

(a) of the opinion that the child has broken any condition imposed under s.93 he must remand him; LASPOA 2012 s.91 (see 12-004) then applies to the child as if he was then charged with, or convicted of, the offence for which he had been remanded; or

(b) not of that opinion, he must remand the child to the place to which the child had been remanded at the time of his arrest, subject to the same conditions as those which had been imposed on him at that time.

(LASPOA 2012 s.97)

Remands to youth detention accommodation

12-009 A remand to youth detention accommodation is a remand to:

(1) a secure children's home;
(2) a secure college (as from 20 March 2015 CJCA 2015 s.38(3) Sch.9);
(3) a secure training centre;
(4) a young offender institution; or
(5) accommodation of a description specified by order under PCC(S)A 2000 s.107(1)(e) (for purposes of detention and training).

A "secure children's home" means accommodation which is provided in a children's home, within the meaning of the Care Standards Act 2000, in respect of which a person is registered under Pt 2 of that Act, and is approved by the Secretary of State for the purpose of restricting the liberty of children.

A child's detention in one of these kinds of accommodation pursuant to a remand to youth detention accommodation is lawful (LASPOA 2012 s.102).

Where a judge remands a child to youth detention accommodation, he must:

(i) state in open court that he has has considered subss.(3) and (4A) of s.91 and is of the opinion mentioned in LASPOA 2012 ss.98(4), 99(7), 100(4) or 101(7) (as the case may be); and
(ii) explain to the child in open court and in ordinary language why he is of that opinion.

Where a child is remanded to youth detention accommodation, the court must designate the local authority that is to receive the child, being:

(i) in the case of a child who is being looked after by a local authority, otherwise than by virtue of s.104(1), that authority; and
(ii) in any other case, but subject to s.102(7B), a local authority in whose area it appears to the court that the child habitually resides, or the offence or one of the offences was committed.

A child that is remanded to youth detention accommodation is to be treated as a child that is looked after by the designated authority. The designated authority must receive the child.

In a case to which (ii) applies, the judge must designate a local authority in whose area it appears to him that the child habitually resides (a "home authority") except where he:

- considers as respects the home authority, or each home authority, that it is inappropriate to designate such authority; or
- is unable to identify any place in England and Wales where the child habitually resides.

(LASPOA 2012 s.102(7A) and (7B))

If, in the latter case, the judge is not required by s.102(7A) to designate a home authority, but it appears to him that the offence was not, or none of the offences was committed in England and Wales, he must designate a local authority which he considers appropriate in the circumstances of the case.

Replacement designations

Where a child has been remanded to youth detention accommodation, the court which remanded him, or to which the child was remanded may designate a local authority for the child *in substitution for* the authority previously designated (whether that previous designation was made when the child was remanded or under this provision). **12-010**

Note further that:

(1) where a child has at any one time been subject to two or more remands to youth detention accommodation, a judge with jurisdiction to make such a replacement designation in connection with one or some of the remands, also has jurisdiction to make a replacement designation in connection with each of the other remands;
(2) where a replacement designation is made under s.102(7C) after the end of the period of the remand concerned, the substitution of a replacement designation has effect only for the purposes of regulations under s.103;
(3) where a replacement designation is made under s.102(7C) during the period of the remand concerned, the replacement designation has effect:
    (a) as respects the remainder of that period ending with the making of the replacement designation, only for the purposes of regulations under s.102; and
    (b) as respects the remainder of that period, for all of the purposes listed in s.102(6);
(4) a judge may make a replacement designation under s.102(7C) only if he considers that, had everything he knows been known by the court which made the previous designation that court would have made the substituted designation; and
(5) a judge who has jurisdiction to make a replacement designation under s.102(7C) may exercise that jurisdiction on an application by a local authority, or of his own motion.

(LASPOA 2012 s.102(7C)–(7J))

A replacement designation under s.102(7C) may be made in respect of a remand ordered before CCA 2013 s.19 comes into force, but a replacement order does not have any effect as respects any time before that section comes into force.

Remand to youth detention accommodation: first set of conditions

For a remand to youth detention accommodation (see 12-009) the first set of conditions in relation to a child is met if: **12-011**

(1) the child has reached the age of 12 (*the "age condition"*);
(2) the offence (mentioned in s.91(1) (see 12-004)), or one or more of those offences is:
    (a) a violent or sexual offence (see 12-007); or
    (b) is an offence punishable in the case of an adult with imprisonment for a term of 14 years or more (*the "offence condition"*);
(3) the judge is of the opinion, after considering all the options for the remand

of the child, that only remanding him to youth detention accommodation would be adequate:

(a) to protect the public from death or serious personal injury (whether physical or psychological) occasioned by further offences committed by the child; or

(b) to prevent the commission by the child of imprisonable offences (*the "necessity condition"*); and

that the risks posed by the child cannot be managed safely in the community;

(4) it appears to the court that it is very likely that the child will be sentenced to a custodial sentence for the offence or one or more of those offences; and

(5) the first or second *legal representation condition* (see 12-012) is met.

(LASPOA 2012 s.98)

The "first or second legal representation conditions"

12-012 The *first legal representation condition* that must be met under s.98 is that the child is legally represented before the court.

The *second legal representation condition* is that where the child is not legally represented before the court:

(1) representation was provided to the child under LASPOA 2012 Pt 1 for the purposes of the proceedings, but was withdrawn because:

(a) of the child's conduct; or

(b) it appeared that the child's financial resources were such that he was not eligible for such representation;

(2) the child applied for such representation and the application was refused because it appeared that his financial resources were such that he was not eligible for such representation; or

(3) having been informed of the right to apply for such representation and having had the opportunity to do so, the child refused or failed to apply.

(LASPOA 2012 s.98(5) and (6))

Remand to youth detention accommodation: second set of conditions

12-013 The second set of conditions for a remand to youth detention accommodation (s.91(4)(a)), is where in relation to the child each of the following is met:

(1) *the age condition,* i.e. that the child has reached the age of 12;

(2) *the sentencing condition,* i.e. it appears to the judge that it is very likely that the child will be sentenced to a custodial sentence for the offence, or for one or more of those offences;

(3) *the offence condition,* i.e. that the offence mentioned in s.91(1), or one or more of those offences, is an imprisonable offence;

(4) the *first or second history condition* or both (see 12-014);

(5) *the necessity condition* (see 12-011); and

(6) *the first or second legal representation condition* (see 12-012).

(LASPOA 2012 s.99)

A "custodial sentence" here means a sentence or order mentioned in PCC(S)A 2000 s.76(1).

References in this section to a child being remanded to local authority accommodation or youth detention accommodation include a child being remanded to local authority accommodation under CYPA 1969 s.23.

The "first or second history condition"

The *first history condition* is that: **12-014**

(1) the child has a recent and significant history of absconding while subject to a custodial remand and it appears to the court that the history is relevant in all the circumstances of the case; and
(2) the offence mentioned in s.91(1), or one or more of those offences, is alleged to be or has been found to have been committed while the child was remanded to local authority accommodation or youth detention accommodation (s.99(5)).

The *second history condition* is that the offence or offences mentioned in s.91(1), together with any other imprisonable offences of which the child has been convicted in any proceedings, amount or would, if the child were convicted of that offence or those offences, amount to a recent and significant history of committing imprisonable offences while on bail or subject to a custodial remand and this appears to the court relevant in all the circumstances of the case.

5. REMITTAL TO YOUTH COURT

Special provisions apply to juveniles in relation to punishment on conviction. As to the approach to sentencing juveniles, see Sentencing Council Guidelines Overarching Principles—Sentencing Youths and DEALING WITH AN OFFENDER. Custodial sentences are dealt with under DETENTION OF YOUNG OFFENDERS; Community sentences are dealt with under YOUTH REHABILITATION ORDERS. **12-015**

Remittal to youth court

Where a person under 18 is convicted in the Crown Court of an offence other than homicide, the judge, unless he is of opinion that the case is one which can properly be dealt with by: **12-016**

(1) an absolute or conditional discharge;
(2) a fine; or
(3) an order under SA 2020 s.376, requiring his parent or guardian to enter into recognisances,

is required to remit him to a youth court for sentence. This is unless the judge is satisfied that it would be undesirable to do so.

The appropriate youth court will be:

(a) if the offender was sent to the Crown Court under CDA 1998 s.51 or s.51A, a youth court acting for the place where he was sent to the Crown Court for trial; or
(b) in any other case, a youth court acting either for the same place as the Crown Court or for the place where the offender habitually resides.

The judge may, subject to CJPOA 1994 s.25 (restrictions on granting bail), give such directions as appear to be necessary with respect to the offender's custody or release on bail until he can be brought before the youth court. The appropriate certificate will be sent to the designated officer (SA 2020 s.25(9)).

An offender has no right of appeal against the order of remittal (SA 2020 s.26).

"Undesirable" to remit

12-017 Clearly, it may be "undesirable" to remit an offender to the youth court, where, for example:

(1) the judge who has presided over the trial is likely to be better informed as to the facts and circumstances of the case;
(2) there will be a risk of disparity in sentencing if co-accused are sentenced in different courts on different occasions;
(3) there is the risk of delay, duplication of proceedings and fruitless expense in such a procedure; or
(4) difficulties may be caused in seeking to challenge the proceedings, appeal from the conviction lying to the CACD, and against sentence to the Crown Court.

It may be desirable to remit where a report has been sought and the trial judge is likely to be unavailable when it is completed, though this situation can always be avoided by the magistrates who transfer the case to the Crown Court for trial giving directions for the preparation of reports (*R. v Lewis* (1984) 79 Cr. App. R. 94, per the Lord Chief Justice). A modern example of the approach is to be found in *R. v Akehurst* [2010] EWCA Crim 206.

It is suggested that the only occasion when remittal to a youth court is merited is where the judge has in mind the making of a supervision order, in which circumstances the magistrates may have a more complete knowledge of the local situation.

6. Penalties on conviction

Purposes, etc., of sentencing: offenders under 18

12-018 Where a judge is dealing with an offender aged under 18 in respect of an offence, he must have regard to:

(1) the principal aim of the youth justice system (which is to prevent offending (or re-offending) by persons aged under 18, see CDA 1998 s.37(1));
(2) in accordance with CYPA 1933 s.44, the welfare of the offender; and
(3) the purposes of sentencing mentioned; namely:
  (a) the punishment of offenders;
  (b) the reform and rehabilitation of offenders;
  (c) the protection of the public; and
  (d) the making of reparation by offenders to persons affected by their offences,

save that this provision does *not* apply:
  (i) to an offence the sentence for which is fixed by law; or
  (ii) to an offence the sentence for which falls to be imposed under:
    — SA 2020 s.312 (minimum sentence for offence of threatening with offensive weapon in public), SA 2020 s.311 (minimum sentence for certain firearms offences) SA 2020 ss.312 and 315 (minimum

sentence of or offence of threatening with article with blade or point or offensive weapon);
- — SA 2020 ss.312 and 315 (minimum sentences in certain cases of using someone to mind a weapon);
- — SA 2020 s.274 (detention for life for certain dangerous offenders); or
- — in relation to the making under MHA 1983 Pt 3 of a hospital order (with or without a restriction order); an interim hospital order, a hospital direction or a limitation direction.

(SA 2020 s.58)

Approach to sentence

A judge, in dealing with a child or young person who is brought before him, either as an offender or otherwise, must have regard to the welfare of the child or young person, and must, in a proper case, take steps for removing him from undesirable surroundings, and for securing that proper provisions is made for his education and training. **12-019**

This provision must be read with SA 2020 s.58 when it comes into force which require a court dealing with an offender aged under 18 also to have regard to the principal aim of the youth justice system and the specified purposes of sentencing.

Accordingly, in determining, in the case of an offender, whether he should take such steps as set out, the judge must also have regard to the matters mentioned in those paragraphs.

The SGC issued a definitive guideline on sentencing those under 18. Paragraph 4.9 suggests that the proper approach when sentencing a young offender is for the judge, within a sentence that is no more restrictive on liberty than is proportionate to the seriousness of the offence(s), to seek to impose a sentence that takes proper account of the matters to which a court must have regard by:

(1) confronting the offender with the consequences of his offending and helping him to develop a sense of personal responsibility;
(2) tackling the particular factors (personal, family, social, educational or health) that put him at risk of offending;
(3) strengthening those factors that reduce the risk that he will continue to offend;
(4) encouraging reparation to victims; and
(5) defining, agreeing and reinforcing the responsibilities of parents.

Financial penalties: (1) general

While fines, compensation and orders to pay costs may be made against juveniles in much the same way as against adults (see FINES and SURCHARGES), certain differences need to be noticed: **12-020**

(1) there is no statutory limit on the amount of a fine that may be imposed on a juvenile in the Crown Court, but where the court is limited to magistrates' court powers, the maxima are:
   (a) in the case of a young person under 18, £1,000; and
   (b) in the case of a child, £250, unless the maximum fine in the case of an adult is less, when that maximum applies; and
(2) a juvenile may not be committed to prison in default of payment of a fine

or compensation, though a magistrates' court enforcing a Crown Court fine may order him to attend at an attendance centre.

(MCA 1980 s.36)

Financial penalties: (2) responsibility of parent or guardian

12-021 Since few juveniles are likely to have the money available to pay fines, compensation or costs, where a person aged under 18 is convicted of an offence for which a fine, surcharge or an order for costs may be imposed or a compensation order made, and the judge is of the opinion that the case would best be met by such an order, whether or without any other punishment, the judge:

(1) *must*, in the case of an offender under 16; and
(2) *may*, in the case of an offender aged 16–17,

order the fine, surcharge, compensation or costs to be paid by the offender's parent or guardian unless:

(a) that person cannot be found; or
(b) it would be unreasonable, having regard to the circumstances, to make such an order.

(SA 2020 s.128)

This provision is extended to cover a case in which the judge would otherwise order a child or young person to pay a surcharge under SA 2020 ss.42 and 43 (see FINES and SURCHARGES).

A similar provision applies in a case where the judge is minded to impose a fine in respect of the breach of certain community and other orders (SA 2020 s.128).

An order should not be made unless the parent or guardian has been given an opportunity of being heard, or has been required to attend and has failed to do so (SA 2020 s.380).

Financial penalties: (3) purpose of section

12-022 In considering whether to make an order under these provisions, the judge should have regard to the purpose of SA 2020 s.128, which is that:

(1) parents should take some responsibility for their children's activities and they should take their duties seriously; though
(2) they cannot be held vicariously liable for every act of their child (*Lenihan v West Yorkshire Metropolitan Police* (1981) 3 Cr. App. R. (S.) 42); and
(3) it is unreasonable to make an order where a parent has done the best he or she can to keep their child from criminal ways (*R. v Sheffield Crown Court Ex p. Clarkson* (1986) 8 Cr. App. R. (S.) 454) and is in no position to control it (*TA v DPP* [1997] 1 Cr. App. R. (S.) 1).

If the judge observes the principle that compensation orders should be made only in simple and straightforward cases, orders are likely to be rare: see the complications outlined in *Bedfordshire Crown Court v DPP* [1996] 1 Cr. App. R. (S.) 322.

Where the judge orders a parent or guardian to pay the fine, etc. of a young offender, he does not "impose" the fine, and therefore no question of a default sentence under SA 2020 s.129 arises. Payment will be enforced by the magistrates' court under AJA 1970 s.41.

Financial penalties: (4) local authority as "parent or guardian"

References to a parent or guardian are to be construed as references to a local authority where the child or young person is: **12-023**

(1) one for whom that authority has parental authority; and
(2) in their care; or
(3) provided with accommodation by them in the exercise of any function (in particular those under CA 1989) which stands referred to their social services committee under the Local Authority Social Services Act 1970.

(SA 2020 s.128)

An order remanding a young person into local authority accommodation does not confer parental responsibility (*North Yorkshire County Council v Selby Youth Court Justices* [1994] 1 All E.R. 991).

Financial penalties: (5) orders against local authorities

The power of a local authority to restrain an offender in its care might be less than that of a parent. It has the same right to assert the unreasonableness of an order as has the parent. **12-024**

Where the authority has done everything it reasonably and properly can to protect the public from the offender, it is unreasonable to make an order against it (*D v DPP* (1995) 16 Cr. App. R. (S.) 1040).

Where the authority stands in loco parentis and the accused juvenile is acquitted, the authority is entitled to a defendant's costs order, where it would be appropriate in the case of the accused: *R. v Preston Crown Court Ex p. Lancashire CC* [1998] 3 All E.R. 765.

Financial penalties: (6) fixing the quantum

Similar provisions apply to an order against a parent or guardian as apply to financial orders in respect of offenders, and a parent or guardian, other than a local authority, may be required to comply with a financial circumstances enquiry (PCC(S)A 2000 s.138 (SA 2020 s.128)) (see FINES and SURCHARGES). **12-025**

Financial penalties: (7) parents, etc., as appellants

A parent or guardian may appeal to the CACD against an order made in the Crown Court as if he had been convicted on indictment and the order was a sentence passed on his conviction. **12-026**

(SA 2020 s.380(5))

7. EVIDENCE OF CHILDREN

Competency

A child, of whatever age, is like all other persons competent to give evidence in criminal proceedings unless it appears to the judge that he is not a person who is able to: **12-027**

(1) understand questions put to him as a witness; and
(2) give answers to them which can be understood.

(YJCEA 1999 s.53)

This section applies without the need for any gloss. Previous conceptions regarding children and their capacity to understand the nature and purpose of an oath and to give truthful and accurate evidence no longer apply and have no relevance (*R. v Barker* [2010] EWCA Crim 4; [2011] Crim. L.R. 233).

Note that:

(a) the questions are entirely "witness-specific";
(b) there are no presumptions or preconceptions;
(c) the witness need not understand the special importance of telling the truth; and
(d) need not understand every question or give a readily understood answer to every question.

Many competent adult witnesses would fail such a test. Provided the witness can understand the questions put to him and can give understandable answers, he is competent.

It is clear from s.53 that the age of the witness does not determine whether he is competent to give evidence. It cannot be said, therefore, that below a certain age a witness is too young to give evidence. The test set out in s.53(3) is whether the witness is able to understand the questions put to him and to give answers that can be understood (*R. v Powell* [2006] EWCA Crim 3; [2006] 1 Cr. App. R. 31).

There is a need, both for advocates' techniques and court processes to be adapted to enable the witness to give his or her best evidence. That will involve a degree of persistence and patience by all concerned. A witness found competent is entitled to have the best efforts made to adduce his or her evidence before the court, notwithstanding the difficulties that may exist (*R. v IA* [2013] EWCA Crim 1308).

It is for the judge to determine whether the child witness is competent, approaching the matter as set out in 12-028. It is a matter well within his capacity and he requires no expert evidence on the matter, though the Act provides for it if required.

Judge's approach

12-028 The judge's task in assessing the competence of the witness is to determine whether the child fulfils the conditions set out in 12-027. It may be said that:

(1) in the ordinary way the issue should be determined before the witness is sworn, usually as a preliminary issue at the start of the trial; although
(2) there may be cases where evidence emerges in the course of the trial which causes the judge to change his mind;
(3) the judge should watch the videotaped interview of the child witness and/or ask the child appropriate questions; and
(4) the burden of establishing competence lies on the party calling the witness, on a balance of probabilities.

The correct approach to competence is set out in *R. v MacPherson* [2005] EWCA Crim 3605; [2006] 1 Cr. App. R. 30; *R. v M* [2008] EWCA Crim 2751 (learning difficulties).

Where, as is frequently the case, the assessment is based, at least in part on the content of pre-recorded video interviews with the witness, it is important to bear in mind that it is the competence of the child at the time of the trial that is in issue, so that if the position has changed when his evidence is looked at as a whole, the question of competence should be reconsidered (*R. v Powell* [2006] EWCA Crim 3; [2006] 1 Cr. App. R. 3. See also *R. v M* [2008] EWCA Crim 2751).

Where a case depends on the evidence of a very young child, it is absolutely essential that the "achieving best evidence" ("ABE") interview takes place very soon after the event, and also that the trial, at which the child has to be cross-examined, takes place very soon thereafter (*R. v Powell* [2006] EWCA Crim 3; [2006] 1 Cr. App. R. 3—complainant not interviewed until nine weeks after the incident; trial did not take place for a further seven months). See also *R. v Malicki* [2009] EWCA Crim 365 (three-and-a-half-year-old child giving evidence nine months after the event).

Warning as to very young children

There is no longer any rule of law requiring corroboration of the unsworn evidence of a child, or any rule of practice to warn of the danger of convicting on such evidence, but it may be appropriate to warn the jury, if there is one, to take particular care with the evidence of a very young child. **12-029**

Evidence through TV link and by means of video recording

The special protection for child witnesses is dealt with in SPECIAL MEASURES DIRECTIONS. **12-030**

Restrictions on accused cross-examining in person

No person charged with an offence as is mentioned in this paragraph may cross-examine in person a witness who: **12-031**

(1) is alleged to be the person against whom the offence was or a witness to the offence; and
(2) is a child, or is to be cross-examined after giving evidence in chief by means of a video recording made or in any other way when he was a child.

(YJCEA 1999 s.35)

Section 35 applies to any offence under SOA 1956 ss.33–36, SOA 2003 Pt 1 or any relevant or superseded enactment (as to which see CJIA 2008 s.148, Sch.26 Pt 2 para.37), kidnapping, false imprisonment, or an offence under the Child Abduction Act 1984 ss.1 and 2, any offence under CYPA 1933 s.1 or any other offence which involves an assault on, or injury to, any person.

The prohibition applies not only to the offence to which s.35 applies, but also to any other offence of whatever nature with which that person is charged in the proceedings.

These restrictions should be explained to the accused by the judge as early in the proceedings as reasonably practicable.

Trial judge's duty

Where, under this restriction, an accused is prevented from cross-examining a witness in person, the judge must: **12-032**

(1) invite the accused to arrange for a legal representative to act for him for the purpose of cross-examining the witness; and

(2) require the accused to notify the court within seven days as to whether a legal representative is to act for him for that purpose and the details of that representative. The court is required to notify all parties of these details.

(YJCEA 1999 s.38(1), (2) and (3))

If the accused declines to be represented or fails to notify the court as required, the judge must consider whether it is necessary in the interests of justice to appoint a legal representative. If he does so, the court will notify all parties of the details of the appointment.

Where under this restriction the accused is prevented from cross-examining a witness in person, the judge must give an appropriate warning to the jury, if there is one, to ensure the accused is not prejudiced:

(a) by any inferences that might be drawn from the fact that the accused has been prevented from cross-examining the witness in person; or
(b) where the witness has been cross-examined by a legal representative appointed by the court, by the fact that this has happened rather than the witness being cross-examined by a person acting as the accused's own legal representative.

As to procedure, see generally CrimPR 31, and SPECIAL MEASURES DIRECTIONS.

Restrictions on publication

12-033 See REPORTING AND ACCESS RESTRICTIONS.

8. REPARATION ORDERS

12-034 Section 162 PCSCA 2022 abolishes reparation orders from 28 June 2022.

9. YOUTH OFFENDER PANELS

12-035 The power to refer a juvenile to a youth offender panel under SA 2020 ss.91–94 is reserved to the magistrates' courts. Jurisdiction will arise in the Crown Court only on appeal, or where an offender is subject to such an order at the time he was convicted in the Crown Court.

13. COMMITTALS FOR SENTENCE

Quick Guide

1. Jurisdiction and powers

Magistrates' powers

The powers of a magistrates' court to impose a sentence of imprisonment are restricted to the imposition of a sentence of: **13-001**

(1) six months in the case of a summary offence; or
(2) 12 months in the case of an offence triable either way.

(MCA 1980 s.12 as amended by CJA 2003, SA 2020 s.224 and Judicial Review and Courts Act 2022 s.13)

Special provisions apply to "schedule offences", i.e. those offences contained in MCA 1980 Sch.2 (i.e. criminal damage under CDA 1971 s.1 and aggravated vehicle taking under TA 1968 s.12A where no allegation is made other than damage, or where the damage involved does not exceed the prescribed limit).

As to fines, see SA 2020 ss.120–121, 124–127. The maximum fine available to a magistrates' court, save where statute provides otherwise is unlimited.

A magistrates' court may commit an offender to the Crown Court for sentence, or to be dealt with, where it considers that a sentence in excess of its powers is required, under the statutory framework.

The Crown Court, in hearing an appeal from a magistrates' court, has no power to commit the appellant to itself for sentence under SA 2020 s.14 in order to obtain enlarged powers of sentence, *R. v Bullock* (1963) 47 Cr. App. R. 288 (a decision on earlier legislation), but see *R. v Ashton* [2006] EWCA Crim 794; [2006] 2 Cr. App. R. 15.

As to the information to be provided to the Crown Court on committal, see CrimPR 28.10, and *CPD* VII Sentencing K Committal for Sentence: K.1.

Legal aid; public funding

For the purposes of legal aid in such proceedings the "interests of justice" criteria (see LEGAL AID; PUBLIC FUNDING) are deemed to be met: **13-002**

Note that:

(1) applicants who previously failed the means test are not able to resubmit their applications after conviction and obtain a non-means tested representation for their sentencing hearing at the Crown Court;

(2) applicants who did not submit an application for the magistrates' court proceedings will be subject to a means assessment for the sentencing hearing; if they are granted funding, the representation order will cover the sentencing hearing only; and
(3) the magistrates' court means test will extend to cover the sentence hearing at the Crown Court, and will determine whether the applicant is eligible for funding or not.

(*CLAM* 1.12.22)

Special rules apply in relation to persons who are deemed capable of paying privately, and for those who have failed the means test but may be unable to meet the costs of proceedings on committal for sentence (see LEGAL AID; PUBLIC FUNDING). Any applicant who has failed the means test continues to have access to the hardship provision should they find themselves unable to afford their case costs. (Further detail on the hardship process can be found at *CLAM* 1.12.22.)

Crown Court jurisdiction; procedure

13-003 The powers of the Crown Court will vary according to the statute under which the committal is made. Jurisdiction is exercisable by a judge of the Crown Court sitting alone. A judge hearing an appeal with justices should ensure, if there is a committal for sentence in the same case, that he sits alone when he comes to deal with it (SCA 1981 s.73(1)): *R. (on the application of Bromley) v Secretary of State for Justice* [2010] EWHC 112 (Admin); [2010] A.C.D. 43.

The Crown Court has no jurisdiction to hear an appeal from the offender as to his committal, though a case may be remitted to the magistrates where the committal is clearly invalid. Otherwise the committal will need to be challenged by judicial review (*R. v Sheffield Crown Court Ex p. DPP* (1994) 15 Cr. App. R. (S.) 768). Judicial review is dealt with in APPEALS FROM THE CROWN COURT.

Note that:

(1) the offender should be called on to admit his identity and the fact of conviction and committal;
(2) formal evidence of the conviction and committal should also be given (*R. v Jeffries* [1963] Crim. L.R. 559);
(3) it is sensible before embarking on committal proceedings to ensure that there is no appeal against the conviction on which the committal is based; if there is, the committal proceeding should be adjourned until the appeal has been determined (*R. v Faithful* (1950) 34 Cr. App. R. 220);
(4) the proceedings then follow those applicable on a plea of guilty on indictment; and
(5) care should be taken as to the age of the offender, since the statutory framework makes a sharp distinction between those under and over 18 years of age; the age at the date of conviction governs the *issue* (*R. v Robson* [2006] EWCA Crim 1414; [2007] 1 Cr. App. R. (S.) 54).

Advocates should always check the section under which the committal was made to identify the court's sentencing powers: *R. v Qayum* [2010] EWCA Crim 2237.

Basis of committal

13-004 It is important in relation to the judge's sentencing powers, to distinguish those cases committed under SA 2020 s.14 (Crown Court powers) and those committed under SA 2020 s.20 (magistrates courts' powers, see 13-006). A committal may still be valid even where the memorandum of conviction is inaccurate (*R. v Ayhan* [2011] EWCA Crim 3184; [2012] Crim. L.R. 299; *R. v Anderson* [2014] EWCA Crim 797). It is well established that in circumstances like these the essential question is not what power the memorandum of conviction records the magistrates court to have used, but the power actually used: *R. v Folkestone and Hythe Juvenile Court Justices Ex p. R (A Juvenile)* (1982) 74 Cr. App. R. 58, followed in *R. v Hall* (1982) 74 Cr. App. R. 67; *R. v Ayhan* [2011] EWCA Crim 3184; [2012] Crim. L.R. 299; and *R. v Morgan* [2012] EWCA Crim 1939; [2012] 176 JP 633. The correct approach, where an issue is raised, is for the judge to examine the question whether the magistrates' court was vested with the necessary jurisdiction. If it was, then an omission from, or an inaccuracy in, the memorandum of conviction about the statutory powers which were exercised, or which were available to be exercised, does not affect the validity of the committal.

Disputes as to the facts

It is the duty of the committing magistrates to ensure that the Crown Court is informed of the facts found, and the judge should sentence on the facts found by the magistrates' court and should not normally allow any dispute as to the facts to be reopened. Where: **13-005**

(1) an issue arises for the first time before the Crown Court, the judge should normally determine the issue on any necessary and available evidence; but
(2) if the offender claims to have raised the matter before the lower court, where the magistrates did not attempt to decide the issue, the judge will need to decide upon the course to be followed, taking into account all the circumstances, including:
  (a) the facts of the offence(s) as alleged by each party;
  (b) whether, on a balance of probabilities, he is satisfied that the offender raised the issue before the lower court;
  (c) the fact that the offender was committed because his record was considered serious enough to justify such a course; and
  (d) the delay which remittal to the magistrates' court will cause (*Munroe v DPP* [1988] Crim. L.R. 823).

The judge has a discretion to hold a *Newton* hearing (see GUILTY PLEAS) or further *Newton* hearing if there was one before the court below. In *R. (on the application of Gillan) v DPP* [2007] EWHC 380 (Admin); [2007] 2 Cr. App. R. 12 it was suggested that where there had been a *Newton* hearing at the magistrates' court, another should not be held at the Crown Court unless the offender could point to a significant new development.

See CrimPR 28.10 as to the material to be transmitted from the lower court to the Crown court.

Limitation of powers

The judge's powers vary according to the particular section of SA 2020 under which the offender is committed. **13-006**

He may deal with an offender:

(1) under *ss.14, 15 or 18*, in any way in which he could have dealt with him if he had just been convicted of the offence, on indictment (SA 2020 s.21), but

may not remit him to the magistrates' court (*R. v Isleworth Crown Court Ex p. Buda* [2000] 1 Cr. App. R. (S.) 538 (see 13-003–13-012));

(2) under *ss.16, 17 or 19*, in any way in which he could have dealt with him if he had just been convicted of the offence, on indictment (SA 2020 s.22) see (13-010–13-014);

(3) under *s.23*, in any way in which the magistrates' court could deal with him if it had just convicted him of the offence, save that:
   (a) if the offender is committed in respect of a suspended sentence, the powers in SA 2020 s.20 as limited by SA 2020 s.23(2) are exercisable; and
   (b) where the offender is committed in respect of an offence triable only on indictment in the case of an adult, but which was tried summarily because the offender was under 18 years of age, the judge's powers are to:
      (i) impose a fine not exceeding £5,000; or
      (ii) deal with the offender in respect of the offence in any way in which the magistrates' court could have dealt with him if it had just convicted him of an offence punishable with a term of imprisonment not exceeding twelve months.

(SA 2020 s.23 as amended)

Where magistrates commit a person to the Crown Court in respect of a breach of a suspended sentence imposed by the Crown Court they should consider carefully which of their statutory powers they should exercise in relation to any other offences listed before them. Their order should be clearly expressed and correctly recorded (*R. v Bateman* [2012] EWCA Crim 2158; [2013] 2 Cr. App. R. (S.) 26). As to committal under POCA 2002, see 13-015.

Any duty or power which would, apart from these provisions, fall to be discharged or exercised by the magistrates, must not be exercised, but instead, will be discharged or exercised by the judge of the Crown Court.

Ancillary orders; interim RT disqualification

13-007 Since committal to the Crown Court is an alternative to dealing with the offender, the magistrates' court is not empowered on committal to make any ancillary orders, save that where the magistrates' court:

(1) commits an offender under s.6 or any enactment to which that section applies; and
(2) does not exercise its power or duty to disqualify under RTOA 1988 ss.34, 35 or 36,

it may order him to be disqualified until the Crown Court has dealt with him in respect of the offence.

If the offender is not sentenced within six months of the date of committal, that disqualification lapses. On dealing with the offender, a judge of the Crown Court, if he imposes a disqualification, must reduce the period by the length of the interim disqualification (RTOA 1988 s.26(1), (4) and (10)).

2. ADULT'S CONVICTION OF EITHER-WAY OFFENCE (SA 2020 s.14)

13-008 On the summary trial of an offence, a magistrates' court may commit a person aged 18 or over, or a corporation, convicted of an offence triable either way (unless a "schedule offence" excluded by MCA 1980 s.17D), if of the opinion that the offence, or the combination of the offence with one or more other offences associated with it, is so serious that the Crown Court should have power to deal with the offender in any way it could deal with him if convicted on indictment.

Committal may be in custody or on bail to the Crown Court for sentence in accordance with SA 2020 s.21(2), and committal may be also in respect of certain other associated offences (see 13-016).

The power may be exercised where the magistrates consider that a financial penalty in excess of their powers (unlimited unless otherwise limited by the offence) ought to be imposed (*R. v N Essex Justices Ex p. Lloyd* [2001] 2 Cr. App. R. (S.) 15), where it was suggested that in such a case the magistrates' should inform the Crown Court of their reasons for committal. While the judge would not be bound by their statement, it would be extremely valuable for him to know why the committal was made.

The magistrates may also commit where they are of opinion that a restriction order under MHA 1983 is required (see MHA 1983 s.43(4); SA 2020 s.24(1)(c)).

A convicted corporation is treated as an individual aged 18 or over, but the custody and bail provisions do not apply.

If, on appearance before the Crown Court, it appears that the appellant pleaded guilty under a material mistake of fact, the court has a discretion to allow him to change his plea, and if, as a consequence, he pleads not guilty, he may be remitted to the magistrates' court: *R. v Isleworth Crown Court Ex p. Buda* [2000] 1 Cr. App. R. (S.) 538.

3. Dangerous adult (SA 2020 s.15)

Where, on the summary trial of a specified offence (within the meaning of SA 2020 s.306) triable either way, a person over 18 is convicted of the offence, the magistrates' court must, if it appears that the criteria for imposing a sentence under SA 2020 ss.266 or 279 would be met, commit the offender in custody or on bail for sentence in accordance with SA 2020 s.21(2) (SA 2020 s.15). **13-009**

It may also commit him under ss.3 (13-008) or 6 (13-016), where the provisions of those sections are satisfied.

4. Juvenile's indication of guilty plea (SA 2020 s.19)

A magistrates' court may commit: **13-010**

(1) a person under 18 brought before them on an information charging him with an offence mentioned in SA 2020 s.249(1)(a) or (b); where
(2) he or his representative indicates under MCA 1980 s.24A or, as the case may be, s.24B, that he would plead guilty if the offence were to proceed to trial; and
(3) proceeding as if MCA 1980 s.9(1) were complied with and he pleaded guilty under it, the magistrates convict him of the offence, and

the magistrates are of opinion that the offence or the combination of the offence and one or more offences associated with it is so serious that the Crown Court should, in their opinion have the power to deal with the offender as if the provisions of SA 2020 s.249 (detention for grave crimes) applied.

In such circumstances the offender may be committed:

(a) in custody or on bail to the Crown Court for sentence in accordance with SA 2020 s.22(2)); and

(b) in respect of certain other ancillary offences (see 13-016).

As to the power to commit where magistrates are of the opinion that a restriction order under MHA 1983 is required, see MHA 1983 s.43(4); SA 2020 s.24(1)(c).

5. DANGEROUS YOUNG OFFENDER (SA 2020 s.17)

13-011 A magistrates' court may commit a person under 18 where:

(1) he is convicted on summary trial of one of those offences specified in SA 2020 s.306); and

(2) it appears to the magistrates' court, in relation to the offence, that the criteria for the imposition of a sentence under SA 2020 s.254 would be met (see DANGEROUS OFFENDERS; PROTECTIVE SENTENCES).

The offender:

(a) must be committed in custody or on bail to the Crown Court for sentence in accordance with SA 2020 s.22(2); and

(b) may also be committed in respect of certain other ancillary offences (see 13-016),

though nothing prevents the court from committing a specified offence to the Crown Court for sentence under s.17 if the provisions of that section are satisfied. See as to the problems raised by conflicting legislation in this area *R. (on the application of Crown Prosecution Service) v South East Surrey Youth Court* [2005] EWHC 2929 (Admin); [2006] 2 Cr. App. R. (S.) 26.

6. ADULT'S INDICATION OF GUILTY PLEA (SA 2020 s.18)

13-012 The magistrates' court may commit a person aged 18 or over where:

(1) he appears or is brought before it on an information charging him with an offence triable either way (other than a "schedule offence");

(2) he, or, where applicable, his representative, indicates under MCA 1980 ss.17A, 17B or 20(7) that he would plead guilty if the offence were to proceed to trial; and

(3) the magistrates' court, proceeding under MCA 1980 s.91, convicts him of that offence.

Where:

(a) the magistrates have sent him to the Crown Court for one or more offences which, in their opinion are related to the offence, they may commit him in custody or on bail to the Crown Court, to be dealt with in respect of the offence in accordance with SA 2020 s.21(2); or

(b) that power is not exercisable but the court is still to determine whether to send the offender for trial under CDA 1998 s.51 or s.51A for one or more related offences:
   - (i) it must adjourn the proceedings relating to the offence until after it has made those determinations; and
   - (ii) if it sends the offender to the Crown Court for trial for one or more related offences, may then exercise that power.

13-013 In reaching their decision, or taking any step, under this provision:

(1) the magistrates' court is not bound by any indication of sentence given in

respect of the offence under MCA 1980 s.20 (mode of trial proceedings); and

(2) nothing the court does under this section may be challenged, or be the subject of any appeal in any court on the ground that it is not consistent with an indication of sentence.

If the magistrates' court does not, in committing under s.18, state that it has, in its opinion, power also to commit him under s.14(2) or, as the case may be, s.15(2), the Crown Court may act in accordance with s.20(1) unless he is convicted before it of one or more of the related offences.

7. JUVENILE'S INDICATION OF GUILTY PLEA; RELATED ANCILLARY OFFENCES (SA 2020 s.19)

Where: 13-014

(1) a person under 18 appears or is brought before a magistrates' court on an information charging him with an offence mentioned in SA 2020 s.249(1);
(2) he or his representative indicates under MCA 1980 s.24A, or as the case may be, s.24B, that he would plead guilty if the offence were to proceed to trial; and
(3) proceeding as if MCA 1980 s.9(1) were complied with and he pleaded guilty under it, the magistrates convict him of the offence,

then:

(a) if the magistrates have committed him to the Crown Court for one or more offences which, in their opinion are related to the offence, they may commit him in custody or on bail to the Crown Court, to be dealt with in respect of the offence in accordance with SA 2020 s.19(1); or
(b) if that power is not exercisable but the court is still to determine whether to send the offender for trial under CDA 1998 s.51 or 51A for one or more related offences:
    (i) it must adjourn the proceedings relating to the offence until after it has made those determinations; and
    (ii) if it sends the offender to the Crown Court for trial for one or more related offences, may then exercise that power.

Where the court under (a) commits the offender to the Crown Court to be dealt with in respect of the offence, and does not state that, in its opinion, it also has power to commit him under SA 2020 s.16(2), or as the case may be, SA 2020 s.17(2) will not apply unless he is convicted before the Crown Court of one or more of the related offences. Where s.17(2) does not apply, the Crown Court may deal with the offender in respect of the offence in any manner in which the magistrates' court could have dealt with him if it had just convicted him of the offence.

Where the magistrates' court commits a person in accordance with SA 2020 s.19, it may also commit him in respect of certain other ancillary offences.

8. POCA 2002

Where an offender is convicted of an offence by a magistrates' court, and the prosecutor asks the court to commit him to the Crown Court with a view to a confiscation order being considered under POCA 2002 s.6, the magistrates' court 13-015 must commit him to the Crown Court in respect of the offence, and may commit him in respect of any other offence where:

(1) the offender has been convicted of it by the magistrates' court or any other court; and
(2) the magistrates' court has power to deal with him in respect of it.

If a committal is made under this section in respect of an offence or offences, POCA 2002 s.6 applies accordingly, and the committal operates as a committal of the offender to be dealt with at the Crown Court in accordance with POCA 2002 s.71.

If a committal is made under this section in respect of an offence for which (apart from this section) the magistrates' court could have committed the offender for sentence under SA 2020 s.14, the court must state whether it would have done so.

A committal under this section may be in custody or on bail (POCA 2002 s.70).

Where an offender is committed to the Crown Court under s.70 in respect of an offence or offences, then (whether or not the court proceeds under s.6):

(a) in the case of an offence in respect of which the magistrates' court has stated under s.70(5) that it would have committed the offender for sentence, the judge at the Crown Court must inquire into the circumstances of the case, and may deal with the offender in any way in which he could deal with him if he had just been convicted of the offence on indictment before it; or
(b) in the case of any other offence the judge must inquire into the circumstances of the case, and may deal with the offender in any way in which the magistrates' court could deal with him if it had just convicted him of the offence.

(SA 2020 s.24)

9. Associated offences (SA 2020 ss.23 and 24)

13-016 Where magistrates commit an offender to the Crown Court under:

(1) the Vagrancy Act 1824 (incorrigible rogues);
(2) SA 2020 ss.14, 15 or 18 (see 13-008–13-014);
(3) PCC(S)A 2000 s.13(5) (conditionally discharged offender convicted of further offence); to be sentenced or otherwise dealt with in respect of an offence, then, if the relevant offence is:
    (a) an indictable offence, they may also commit him in respect of any other offence, in respect of which they have power to deal with him (being an offence of which he has been convicted by them or any other court); and
    (b) a summary offence, they may commit him in respect of any other offence of which they have convicted him, being either one punishable with imprisonment, or one in respect of which they have a power or a duty to disqualify him under RTOA 1988 ss.34, 35 or 36, or any suspended sentence in respect of which they have power to deal with him (under SA 2020 Sch.16);
(4) SA 2020 Sch.16 para.11(2) (offence committed during the operational period of a suspended sentence passed by the Crown Court), the magistrates may, if they think fit, commit him in custody or on bail to the Crown Court;

if they do not, they must give written notice of the conviction to the appropriate officer of the Crown Court.

(SA 2020 s.24)

If a person is to be committed to the Crown Court for sentence or to be dealt with it is clearly desirable that all outstanding matters should be dealt with by the court on the same occasion. The magistrates' court has power, therefore, exercising its primary power of committal, to commit the offender in respect of other "associated offences". The primary powers of committal for these purposes are those identified in s.6(4). Where the offence in respect of which the magistrates are exercising their primary power of committal (described in s.6(1) as the "relevant offence") is an indictable offence (a term which includes offences triable either-way) the power to commit associated offences is unrestricted (s.6(2)); if the relevant offence is a summary offence, the power is more limited (s.6(3)). (*R. v Bateman* [2012] EWCA Crim 2158; [2013] 2 Cr. App. R. (S.) 26 at 13-006.)

10. Table

The Table below seeks to identify the powers of the Crown Court in committals under differing provisions. **13-017**

Committal Powers		Category of Offender	Sentencing Powers	Sentencing Authority
(1)	SA 2020 s.14	Offender aged 18 or over indicating plea guilty to either-way offence committed because offence(s) so serious as to require Crown Court powers on indictment. A corporation may be committed for sentence and is treated as an individual of not less than 18.	Powers on indictment	SA 2020 s.21
(2)	SA 2020 s.15	Offender aged 18 or over convicted summarily of an offence under SA 2020 s.306 and categorised as a "dangerous offender".	Powers on indictment	SA 2020 s.21
(3)	SA 2020 s.19	Offender under 18 indicating plea of guilty to either-way offence committed because offence(s) so serious as to require Crown Court powers on indictment.	Powers on indictment	SA 2020 s.22

Committal Powers		Category of Offender	Sentencing Powers	Sentencing Authority
(4)	SA 2020 s.17	Offender under 18 convicted summarily of an offence and categorised as a "dangerous young offender" under SA 2020 s.249.	Powers on indictment	SA 2020 s.22
(5)	SA 2020 s.18	Accused not less than 18, charged with offence triable either-way, indicating plea of guilty if committed for trial, and accordingly convicted by magistrates, and committed for sentence.	Powers on indictment where magistrates certify power to commit under s.3 otherwise magistrates' powers	SA 2020 s.21
(6)	SA 2020 s.19	Accused under 18, charged with either-way offence and indicating plea of guilty, committed in respect "related offences".	Powers on indictment where magistrates certify power to commit under s.14 otherwise magistrates' powers	SA 2020 s.22
(7)	SA 2020 Sch.16 para.11(2)	Offender found by magistrates to be in breach of requirement of community order made by Crown Court.	May (a) add more onerous requirements; (b) powers on indictment; (c) in case of persistent failure by 18+ to comply in case of non–imprisonable offence, up to 51 weeks. If (b)—revocation	SA 2020 ss.20 and 23(2)
(8)	SA 2020 Sch.7 paras 22(2) and (4)	Offender found by magistrates to be in breach of relevant youth rehabilitation order made by the Crown Court.	Choice between (a) £1,000 fine; (b) making an attendance centre order; (c) making a curfew order;	SA 2020 s.24

Committal Powers		Category of Offender	Sentencing Powers	Sentencing Authority
			and (d) revocation and "as if order not made"	
(9)	SA 2020 Sch.7 para.6	Offender in respect of whom a relevant Crown Court youth rehabilitation order is in force, committed with a view to its revocation.	Revocation	SA 2020 s.24 and Sch.7 para.7, Sch.7 Pt 3 para.13
(10)	SA 2020 Sch.7 para.22(2) and (4)	Offender committed for sentence during currency of relevant youth rehabilitation order.	Choice between: (a) a simple revocation; and (b) "powers on indictment"	SA 2020 s.24(1)
(11)	SA 2020 s.20(2) or (4)(a)	Offender committed in respect of (1)–(6) and (17) also in respect of other joined offences.	Magistrates' powers in respect of ancillary cases	SA 2020 s.23
(12)	MHA 1983 s.43(1)	Offender 14 or over committed with a view to a restriction order being made under MHA 1983 s.41.	Choice between (a) making a restriction order; and (b) "magistrates' powers"	MHA 1983 s.43(2)
(13)	SA 2020 Sch.16 para.11	Offender committed in breach of Crown Court suspended sentence.	Powers under SA 2020 Sch.16 paras 8 and 9	SA 2020 s.24
(14)	BA 1976 s.6(6)	Bail absconder committed because greater punishment required; or more appropriate.	Imprisonment for not more than 12 months and/or a fine	BA 1976 s.6(7) and SA 2020 s.24(1)(d)
(15)	POCA 2002 s.70	Offender committed with a view to a confiscation order being made.	Powers on indictment	POCA 2002 s.71
(16)	SA 2020 Sch.2 para.5	Offender committed for breach of Crown Court conditional discharge.	Powers on indictment	SA 2020 s.24

14. COMMUNITY SENTENCES

Quick Guide

A. General principles

1. Powers to make orders

14-001 Where a person aged 18 or over is convicted of an offence, the judge may:

(1) where the sentence is not one prescribed by law (see 14-004); and
(2) none of the general restrictions on the making of such orders applies (14-005),

pass upon him a single generic "community order", imposing on him any one of the requirements set out in 14-002. Such orders, together with youth rehabilitation orders for offenders under 18 (see YOUTH REHABILITATION ORDERS), constitute "community sentences" (SA 2020 ss.200–205).

A community order is a composite package rather than an accumulation of sentences attached to different counts of the indictment. The judge should generally impose a single community order that reflects the overall criminality of the offending behaviour. Where it is necessary to impose more than one community order these should be ordered to run concurrently, and, for ease of administration, each of the orders should be identical (Sentencing Council Guideline: Totality).

In the case of an offence committed after 1 October 2012, the judge must order a surcharge to be paid by the offender (under SA 2020 ss.42 and 43). For offences committed on or after 14 April 2020 the amount is £22 in the case of an offender under 18, and of £95 in the case of an offender aged 18 or over. As to specific details in relation to age thresholds and computation of amounts, see FINES and SURCHARGES.

As to the threshold for such a community order, see 14-005.

The order must specify the end date not more than three years after the date of the order by which time all the requirements must have been complied with (SA 2020 s.209).

If the order imposes two or more different requirements it may also specify a date by which each of those requirements must have been complied with, and the last of those dates must be the same as the end date.

Subject to s.220 (duration of community order imposing unpaid work requirement) a community order ceases to be in force on the end date.

As to notification of the order, see 14-023.

As to the breach, revocation or amendment of orders, see 14-024; as to the transfer of orders to Scotland and Northern Ireland, see SA 2020 Sch.11.

2. The available requirements

The requirements which may be attached to a community order are those set out in the Table at 14-021. Details of those requirements are to be found in the sections referred to. The table sets out those requirements that can be made for offences committed on or after 1 February 2015. At the end of the table there is a reference to the position before that date. **14-002**

The provisions are subject to SA 2020 s.202 (not available where sentence fixed by law at 14-004) and availability of arrangements in local areas and to the following provisions of SA 2020 Sch.9 relating to particular requirements, namely:

- Sch.9 paras 1–3 in relation to unpaid work requirements;
- Sch.9 paras 4 and 5 in relation to rehabilitation activity requirements for offences committed on or after 1 February 2015;
- Sch. 9 para.6 in relation to programme requirements;
- Sch.9 paras 7 and 8 in relation to prohibited activity requirements;
- Sch.9 paras 9 and 10 in relation to curfew requirements;
- Sch.9 paras 11 and 12 in relation to exclusion requirements;
- Sch.9 paras 13 and 14 in relation to residence requirements;
- Sch.9 para.15 in relation to foreign travel prohibition requirements;
- Sch.9 paras 16–18 in relation to mental health requirements;
- Sch.9 paras 19–22 in relation to drug rehabilitation requirements;
- Sch.9 paras 23 and 24 in relation to alcohol treatment requirements; and
- Sch.9 paras 27 and 28 in relation to an attendance centre requirement (offender under 25); and
- Sch.9 paras 29–35 in relation to electronic monitoring requirements.

LASPOA 2012 s.76 inserted s.212A into CJA 2003 (alcohol abstinence and monitoring requirement) as a requirement of a community order (or suspended sentence). Section 76 was being brought into force for the purposes of a pilot in the South London local justice area for a period of 12 months by SI 2014/1777, which prescribes monitoring by means of a transdermal electronic tag which measures the level of alcohol contained in an offender's sweat. The relevant provisions for general application are set out in SA 2020 ss.201, 207 and Sch.9 paras 25 and 26.

In respect of those amendments made by LASPOA 2012, in respect of offences committed on or after 3 December 2012, where an offence is found to have been committed over a period of two or more days, or at some time during a period of two or more days, the offence is to be treated as having been committed on the last of those days (SI 2012/2906).

Punitive elements

14-003 Where the judge makes a community order, he must:

(1) include in the order at least one requirement imposed for the purpose of punishment (a rehabilitation activity requirement alone will not suffice, see *R. v Singh* [2021] EWCA Crim 1426; [2022] 1 Cr. App. R. (S.) 48); or
(2) impose a fine for the offence in respect of which the order is made; or
(3) comply with both of these provisions, but this provision does not apply where there are exceptional circumstances which:
 (a) relate to the offence or to the offender;
 (b) would make it unjust in all the circumstances for the judge to comply with (1) above in the particular case; and
 (c) would make it unjust in all the circumstances for him to impose a fine for the offence concerned.

(SA 2020 s.208(10))

Sentence fixed by law, etc.

14-004 Neither a community order (nor a youth rehabilitation order) may be made in respect of an offence for which the sentence:

(1) is fixed by law;
(2) falls to be imposed under SA 2020 ss.312, 315, 316 and 320 (PCA 1953 s.1A(5)) (minimum sentence for offence of threatening with offensive weapon in public), CJA 1988 s.139AA(7) (minimum sentence for offence of threatening with article with blade or point or offensive weapon), SA 2020 s.311 (FA 1968 s.51A(2)) (minimum sentence for certain firearms offences);
(3) falls to be imposed under SA 2020 ss.313, 314, 316–318 and 320 (required sentences for certain repeated offences committed by offenders aged 18 or over) (see IMPRISONMENT);
(4) falls to be imposed under SA 2020 ss.273 and 283 (life sentence for second listed offence for certain dangerous offenders); or
(5) falls to be imposed under SA 2020 ss.274 and 285 (requirement to impose imprisonment or detention for life) (see DANGEROUS OFFENDERS; PROTECTIVE SENTENCES).

(SA 2020 s.202)

In the case of an offender aged 18 or over, no community order under SA 2020 may be made in respect of an offence committed before 4 April 2005.

3. SENTENCE THRESHOLD

14-005 The judge must not impose a community order (or a youth rehabilitation order) on an offender unless he is of opinion that the offence, or the combination of the offence and one or more offences associated with it, is serious enough to warrant such a sentence, and, where he does pass such a sentence:

(1) the particular order or orders comprising or forming part of the sentence must be such as in his opinion is, or taken together are, the most suitable for the offender; and
(2) the restrictions on liberty imposed by the order or orders must be such as

in his opinion are commensurate with the seriousness of the offence, or the combination of the offence and the one or more offences associated with it, although (2) is subject to SA 2020 ss.179–183 (youth rehabilitation orders with intensive supervision and surveillance) and SA 2020 ss.204–205 (community orders, punitive elements (see 14-003)).

(SA 2020 s.204)

Before making a community order imposing two or more different requirements, the judge must consider whether, in the circumstances of the case, the requirements are compatible with each other (SA 2020 s.208(12)).

As far as practicable, any requirement imposed by a relevant order should be such as to avoid:

(a) any conflict with the offender's religious beliefs or with the requirements of any other relevant order to which he may be subject; and
(b) any interference with the times, if any, at which he normally works or attends school or any other educational establishment.

In determining the restrictions on liberty to be imposed by a community order (or a youth rehabilitation order) in respect of an offence, the judge may have regard to any period for which the offender has been remanded in custody (see s.205) in connection with the offence or any other offence the charge for which was founded on the same facts or evidence.

4. APPROACH TO COMMUNITY ORDER

The SC guideline on the Imposition of Community and Custodial Sentences for those sentenced on or after 1 February 2017 set out a number of general principles before addressing the appropriate levels of requirements that may comprise a community order. The principles are: **14-006**

- Community orders can fulfill all of the purposes of sentencing. In particular, they can have the effect of restricting the offender's liberty while providing punishment in the community, rehabilitation of the offender, and/or ensuring that the offender engages in reparative activities.
- A community order must not be imposed unless the offence is 'serious enough to warrant such a sentence'. Where an offender is being sentenced for a non-imprisonable offence, there is no power to make a community order.
- Sentencers must consider all available disposals at the time of sentence; even where the threshold for a community order has been passed, a fine or a discharge may be an appropriate penalty. In particular, a Band D fine may be an appropriate alternative to a community order.
- The court must ensure that the restriction on the offender's liberty is commensurate with the seriousness of the offence and that the requirements imposed are the most suitable for the offender.
- Sentencers should not necessarily escalate from one community order range to the next on each sentencing occasion. The decision as to the appropriate range of community order should be based upon the seriousness of the new offence(s) (which take into account any previous convictions).
- The court must ensure that the restriction on the offender's liberty is commensurate with the seriousness of the offence and that the requirements imposed are the most suitable for the offender.
- Sentencers should not necessarily escalate from one community order range

to the next on each sentencing occasion. The decision as to the appropriate range of community order should be based upon the seriousness of the new offence(s) (which take into account any previous convictions).

- Save in exceptional circumstances at least one requirement must be imposed for the purpose of punishment and/or a fine imposed in addition to the community order (SA 2020 s.208(10)–(11)). It is a matter for the court to decide which requirements are imposed for the purpose of punishment, but a rehabilitation activity requirement alone will not suffice (see *R. v Singh* [2021] EWCA Crim 1426; [2022] 1 Cr. App. R. (S.) 48).

Seriousness; the initial factor

14-007 The SC guidelines state that the seriousness of the offence should be the initial factor in determining which requirements to include. Offence specific guidelines refer to three levels within the community order band based on offence seriousness: low, medium and high. The culpability and harm present in the specific offence or offences should be considered so as to identify which of those three levels is the appropriate one. The guideline then goes on to set out some examples of the requirements that may be appropriate in each of those levels. At least one requirement must be imposed for the purpose of punishment and/or a fine imposed in addition to the community order unless there are exceptional circumstances which relate to the offence or the offender that would make it unjust in all the circumstances to do so (SA 2020 s.208(10)–(11)).

The primary purpose of a prohibited activity requirement or an exclusion requirement being not to punish the offender, but to prevent, or at least reduce, the risk of further offending, any such requirement must be proportionate to the risk of further offending (*R. v J* [2008] EWCA Crim 2002; (2008) 172 J.P. 513).

Information for the judge; reports

14-008 A pre-sentence report may be pivotal in helping the judge to decide whether to impose:

(1) a custodial sentence; or
(2) a community sentence; and if so, whether
(3) particular requirements, or a combination of requirements, are suitable for an individual offender.

If the judge reaches the provisional view that a community sentence is the most appropriate disposal, the judge should request a pre-sentence report, (whether written or verbal) unless it is of the opinion that such a report is unnecessary in all the circumstances of the case. It may be helpful for the judge to indicate to the National Probation Service the court's preliminary opinion as to which of the three sentencing ranges indicated in 14-010, is relevant and the purpose(s) of sentencing that that package of requirements is required to fulfil. Ideally a pre-sentence report should be completed on the same day to avoid adjourning the case (SCG Imposition of Community and Custodial Sentences).

The Sentencing Council guidelines state that the court must make clear to the offender that all sentencing options remain open including, in appropriate cases, committal for sentence to the Crown Court.

Judge's input; report unnecessary

If an adjournment cannot be avoided the information for the report writer should be provided in written form and a copy retained on the court file for the benefit of the sentencing court. If it is known that the same judge and the same defence advocate will be present on the day of sentence and a probation officer is present in court when the request is made, it may not be necessary to commit details of the request to writing. However, it is good practice to ensure that there is a clear record of the judge's request (SCG Imposition of Community and Custodial Sentences). **14-009**

There will be occasions when a report may be unnecessary, though these are likely to be infrequent.

The judge might consider dispensing with the need to obtain a presentence report for adult offenders, e.g. where:

(1) the offence falls within the *low* range of seriousness;
(2) he is minded to impose a single requirement, such as an exclusion requirement (where the circumstances of the case show that this would be an appropriate disposal without electronic monitoring); and
(3) the sentence will not require the involvement of the probation authorities.

Ranges of sentence: low, medium and high

Where the determination is that the sentencing level is "low", (offences only just cross the community order threshold, where the seriousness of the offence or the nature of the offender's record means that a discharge or fine is inappropriate), in general only one requirement will be appropriate and the length may be curtailed if additional requirements are necessary. Suitable requirements might include: any appropriate rehabilitative requirement(s), 40–80 hours of unpaid work, curfew requirement (e.g. up to 16 hours a day for a few weeks), exclusion requirement for a few months, prohibited activity requirement, or an Attendance Centre requirement where available. **14-010**

For those cases within "medium" (offences that obviously fall within the community order band), suitable requirements might include: any appropriate rehabilitative requirement(s), a greater number of hours of unpaid work (e.g. 80–150), curfew requirement (e.g. up to 16 hours a day for 2–3 months), exclusion requirement lasting in the region of 6 months, and a prohibited activity requirement.

"High" (offences only just fall below the custody threshold or the custody threshold is crossed but a community order is more appropriate in the circumstances), more intensive sentences which combine two or more requirements may be appropriate. Suitable requirements might include: any appropriate rehabilitative requirement(s), 150–300 hours of unpaid work, curfew requirement (e.g. up to 16 hours a day for 4–12 months), and an exclusion requirement lasting in the region of 12 months.

Nature and severity of the requirements imposed

The Sentencing Guideline also makes clear that in considering requirements consideration should be given to whether where there are two or more, they must be compatible with one another and must not be excessive. In addition that any requirement must not conflict with an offender's religious beliefs or with the requirements of any other order to which they may be subject and interference with attendance at work or educational establishment should also be avoided. **14-011**

The particular requirements imposed must be suitable for the individual offender and will be influenced by a range of factors, including: the stated purpose(s) of the sentence, the risk of re-offending, the ability of the offender to comply, and the availability of the requirements in the local area.

Recording the sentence; breach proceedings

14-012 The judge, in imposing sentence will wish to be clear about the "purposes" that the community sentence is designed to achieve when setting the requirements; "sharing" those purposes with the offender and the probation authorities will enable them to be clear about the goals that are to be achieved.

If the judge does not include in the order an express direction that any failure to comply with the requirements of the order is to be dealt with by a magistrates' court, the responsible officer will bring any breach proceedings in the Crown Court (SA 2020 s.211 and Sch.10).

Thus:

(1) a judge dealing with the matter thereafter will need to have full information about the requirements which were inserted into the community sentence imposed on the offender (including whether it was a low/medium/high level order), and about the offender's response;

(2) this information will enable the subsequent judge to consider the merits of imposing the same or different requirements as part of another community sentence.

The requirements should, therefore, be recorded in such a way as to ensure that they can be made available to another court if a further offence is committed.

Where an offender is required to serve a community sentence, the court records should be clearly annotated to show which particular requirements have been imposed.

Time spent on remand

14-013 If the judge is considering a community order in the case of an offender who has served time on remand, he must consider not just the punishment of the offender (including that already undergone by virtue of his period on remand) but also his rehabilitation and public protection (see SA 2020 ss.59, 60, 61 and 205).

Further, SA 2020 s.205 states that the judge imposing a community order

> "may have regard to any period for which the offender has been remanded in custody for the offence, or any other offence the charge for which was founded on the same facts or evidence."

While a judge imposing a community order will usually have regard to time spent by the offender on remand, the value of the community order in rehabilitative or public protective terms may still make such an order, even one with substantial restrictions, appropriate (*R. v Rakib* [2011] EWCA Crim 870; [2012] 1 Cr. App. R. (S.) 1) and see *R. v Price* [2013] EWCA Crim 1283; [2014] 1 Cr. App. R. (S.) 36.

5. Availability of arrangements in local area

14-014 The judge may not include in a relevant order, in respect of an offender:

(1) an *unpaid work requirement* unless satisfied that provision for the offender

to work under such a requirement can be made under the arrangements for persons to perform work under such a requirement which exist in the local justice area in which he resides or will reside;

(2) a *rehabilitation activity requirement* unless is satisfied that provision for the offender to participate in the activities proposed to be specified can be made under the arrangements for persons to participate in such activities which exist in the local justice area in which he resides or will reside;

(3) an *attendance centre requirement* unless:
  (a) notified by the Secretary of State that an attendance centre is available for persons of his description; and
  (b) the area in which the attendance centre proposed to be specified in the order is situated is an area in which there is an attendance centre which is available for persons of the offender's description and which the judge is satisfied is reasonably accessible to the offender;

(4) an *electronic monitoring requirement* unless the judge:
  (a) has been notified by the Secretary of State that electronic monitoring arrangements are available in the relevant areas (see (i)–(iii) below); and
  (b) is satisfied that the necessary provision can be made under those arrangements.

In the case of a relevant order:

(i) containing a curfew requirement or an exclusion requirement, the relevant area for the purposes of (4) above is the area in which the place proposed to be specified in the order is situated;
(ii) containing an attendance centre requirement, the relevant area for the purposes of (4) above is the area in which the attendance centre proposed to be specified in the order is situated; and
(iii) of any other kind, the relevant area for the purposes of (4) above is the local justice area proposed to be specified in the order.

In (i) above "place", in relation to an exclusion requirement, has the same meaning as in SA 2020, i.e. it includes "an area".

6. Adding an electronic monitoring requirement

Where the judge makes an order imposing: **14-015**

(1) a curfew requirement, or an exclusion requirement on a person aged 18 or over, he *must* also impose an electronic monitoring requirement (as defined by Sch.9 Pt 14 paras 29–35, unless either:
  (a) he is prevented from doing so by the non-consent of the proposed supervisor or the unavailability of facilities (Sch.9 Pt 14 para.33); or
  (b) in the particular circumstances of the case, he considers it inappropriate to do so;

(2) a requirement numbered (1)–(4), or (7)–(12) in the Table at 14-021, he *may* also impose an electronic monitoring requirement unless either;
  (a) he is prevented from doing so as outlined in (1)(a) or (b) above; or

(b) in the particular circumstances of the case, he considers it inappropriate to do so.

(SA 2020 s.208)
As to notification of the order, see 14-023.

7. ADMINISTRATIVE ARRANGEMENTS

Duties of responsible officer

14-016 Where a relevant order has effect, it is the duty of the responsible officer (as defined in SA 2020 s.213):

(1) to make any arrangements that are necessary in connection with the requirements imposed by the order;
(2) to promote the offender's compliance with those requirements; and
(3) where appropriate, to take steps to enforce those requirements.

(SA 2020 s.214)

Duty of offender to keep in touch with responsible officer

14-017 An offender in respect of whom a community order or a suspended sentence order is in force must keep in touch with the responsible officer in accordance with such instructions as he may from time to time be given by that officer. The obligation is enforceable as if it were a requirement imposed by the order (SA 2020 s.215).

Duty to obtain permission before changing residence

14-018 An offender in respect of whom a relevant order is in force must not change residence without permission given in accordance with this section by:

(1) the responsible officer; or
(2) a court.

The appropriate court may, on an application by the offender, give permission in a case in which the responsible officer has refused. A court may also give permission in any proceedings before it under Sch.10 (breach or amendment of orders, etc.).

The grounds on which the responsible officer or court may refuse an application for permission are that, in the opinion of the officer or court, the change in residence:

(a) is likely to prevent the offender complying with a requirement imposed by the relevant order; or
(b) would hinder the offender's rehabilitation.

The obligation imposed by subs.(1) is enforceable as if it were a requirement imposed by the relevant order.

This section does not apply if the relevant order includes a residence requirement imposed under s.216.

In this section "the appropriate court" has the same meaning as in Sch.10 (SA 2020 ss.209–212).

Transfer of orders to Scotland and Northern Ireland

Where the judge considering the making of an order is satisfied that the offender aged 18 or over resides, or will reside when the order comes into force, in Scotland or Northern Ireland, the provisions of SA 2020 s.219 and Sch.11 apply. **14-019**

Completion date

An order must specify a date, not more than three years after the date of the order by which time all the requirements in it must have been complied with. An order which imposes two or more requirements may also specify another date or dates in relation to compliance with any one or more of them (SA 2020 s.209). **14-020**

B. Table of available requirements

This table outlines the requirements available in relation to a community order. For more detailed provisions reference may be made to the appropriate section of SA 2020. The requirements are also available in respect of a suspended sentence order (see IMPRISONMENT). **14-021**

No.	Name	Requirements	SA 2020	Restrictions	Notes
1	Unpaid Work	To perform unpaid work for the number of hours work specified in the order at such times as the responsible officer may specify in instructions.	Sch.9 para.1	In the aggregate, for not less than 40 and not more than 300 hours. Subject to Sch.10 para.13(4) (extension of unpaid work requirement) the work required to be performed under such a requirement must be performed during the period of 12 months beginning with the day on which the order takes effect. Unless revoked, an order imposing an unpaid work requirement remains in force until the offender has worked under it for the number of hours specified in it. Where imposed by a suspended sentence supervision period does not extend beyond the operational period.	Not to be included unless arrangements for such work exist in the local justice area in which offender resides or will reside, after hearing probation officer judge is satisfied that offender is a suitable person to perform work under the order.
2	Rehabilitation Activity	To comply during the period the community order remains in force with any instructions given by the responsible office to attend appointments or participate in activities, or both.	Sch.9 paras 4–5	A relevant order imposing a rehabilitation activity requirement must specify the maximum number of days for which the offender may be instructed to participate in activities. Any instructions given by the	Where compliance with an instruction would require the co-operation of a person other than the offender, the responsible officer may give the instruction only if that person agrees.

No.	Name	Requirements	SA 2020	Restrictions	Notes
				responsible officer must be given with a view to promoting the offender's rehabilitation; but this does not prevent the responsible officer giving instructions with a view to other purposes in addition to rehabilitation. The activities that responsible officers may instruct offenders to participate in include: (a) activities forming an accredited programme (see para.6); and (b) activities whose purpose is reparative.	
3	Programme	To participate in accordance with instructions given by the responsible officer in the programme at the place or places from time to time specified in the order on the number of days so specified; and while at any of those places, to comply with instructions given by, or under the authority of, the person in charge of the programme.	Sch.9 para.6	No minimum or maximum period prescribed save for days specified in requirement.	
4	Prohibited activity	To refrain from participating in activities specified in the order,	Sch.9 paras 7 and 8		Such a requirement may be included only after consultation

No.	Name	Requirements	SA 2020	Restrictions	Notes
		on a specified day or days or during a specified period			with: (1) a member of a youth offending team; (2) an officer of a local probation board; or (3) an officer of a provider of probation services.
5	Curfew	To remain, for periods specified in the order, at a specified place.	Sch.9 paras 9 and 10	For an offence of which the offender was convicted on or after 28 June 2022: 2–20 hours in any 24 hours; maximum 112 hours in any period of 7 days beginning with the day of the week on which the requirement first takes effect; and maximum term 2 years; or For an offence of which the offender was convicted before 28 June 2022: 2–16 hours in any 24 hours; maximum term 12 months.	Only after the judge has obtained information about the place proposed to be specified in the order (including information as to the attitude of persons likely to be affected by the enforced presence there of the offender). Changes to the curfew requirements (set out to the left) were made by the Police, Crime, Sentencing and Courts Act 2022.
5A	Electronic monitoring	To submit to: (a) securing the electronic monitoring of the offender's compliance with other requirements imposed by the order during a period specified in the order, or determined by the responsible officer in accord-	Sch.9 paras 29–35	Must be imposed where: (1) a curfew requirement is imposed; or (2) an exclusion requirement is imposed, unless the judge: (a) in the particular circumstances of the case, considers it inappropriate to do so; or (b) is pre-	The order must provide for making a person responsible for the monitoring; and that person must be of a description specified by the Secretary of State. If there is a person (other than the offender) without whose coop-

No.	Name	Requirements	SA 2020	Restrictions	Notes
		ance with the relevant order; and (b) electronic monitoring of the offender's whereabouts (otherwise than for the purpose of monitoring the offender's compliance with any other requirements included in the order) during a period specified in the order. The offender must (in particular) submit, to being fitted, etc. with any necessary apparatus, and to its inspection or repair, and must not interfere with it, or with its working.		vented from including such a requirement in the order.	eration it will not be practicable to secure the monitoring, the requirement may not be included in the order without that person's consent. Not (under (a) in col.2) to be imposed for monitoring compliance with alcohol abstinence and monitoring requirement. Not to be included unless the court has been notified by the Secretary of State that electronic monitoring arrangements are available in the local justice area proposed to be specified in the order, and the judge is satisfied that: (a) the offender can be fitted with any necessary apparatus under the arrangements currently available and that any other necessary provision can be made under those arrangements; and (b) arrangements are generally operational throughout England and Wales (even if not always operational everywhere there) under which the offender's

No.	Name	Requirements	SA 2020	Restrictions	Notes
					whereabouts can be electronically monitored.
6	Exclusion	Prohibits the offender from entering a place specified in the order for a specified period. An exclusion requirement may: (1) provide for the prohibition to operate only during the periods specified in the order; and (2) may specify different places for different periods or days. "Place" includes an area.	Sch.9 para.11	The exclusion period must not be more than 2 years beginning with the day on which the requirement first takes effect. If the order specifies more than one exclusion period, each of the exclusion periods must fall within that 2-year period.	
7	Residence	A "residence requirement" is a requirement that, during the period specified in the order, the offender reside: (1) with an individual; or (2) at a place specified in the order.	Sch.9 paras 13–14	An order under (2) is referred to as "a place of residence requirement", and may not be included unless the offender was aged 16 or over at the time of conviction. If the order so provides, a place of residence requirement does not prohibit the offender from residing, with the prior approval of the responsible officer, at a place other than that specified in the order.	

No.	Name	Requirements	SA 2020	Restrictions	Notes
8	Foreign travel prohibition	To prevent offender from travelling on any specified day or days to countries or territories outside the British Islands.	Sch.9 para.15	May specify such countries or territories included or accepted or may specify all such. Period specified may not exceed 12 months beginning on the day the order is made, and a day must not fall outside the period of 12 months from making of order.	
9	Mental health treatment	To submit, during a specified period or periods to treatment by or under the direction of a registered medical practitioner or a chartered psychologist, (or both, for different periods) with a view to the improvement of the offender's mental condition.	Sch.9 paras 16–18	Treatment must be: (1) as a resident patient in an independent hospital or care home within the meaning of the Care Standards Act 2000 or a hospital within the meaning of MHA 1983, but not in hospital premises where high security psychiatric services within the meaning of that Act are provided; (2) as a non-resident patient at such institution or place as may be specified in the order; (3) by or under the direction of such registered.	Judge must be satisfied that the offender's mental condition is such as requires and may be susceptible to treatment but does not warrant the making of a hospital order or a guardianship order and also that arrangements can be made. Offender must consent.
10	Drug rehabilitation	To submit, during a specified period or periods to treatment by or under the direction of a specified person having the necessary qualifications or experi-	Sch.9 paras 19–22	Treatment must be: (a) as a resident in such institution or place as may be specified in the order; or (b) as a non-resident at such institution or place, and at such	Judge must be satisfied that the offender is dependent on, or has a propensity to misuse drugs, such as requires and may be susceptible to treatment Also

No.	Name	Requirements	SA 2020	Restrictions	Notes
		ence, with a view to the reduction or elimination of the offender's dependency on or propensity to misuse controlled drugs. To provide samples during the testing and treatment period, for the purpose of ascertaining whether he has samples in his body.		intervals, as may be so specified, but the order must not otherwise specify the nature of the treatment. The treatment and testing must be at least a 6 month period. Paragraph 22 provides for periodic reviews by the court.	that the requirement has been recommended by a probation officer, or, in the case of an offender under 18, youth offending team. Also that arrangements can be made. Offender must consent.
11	Alcohol treatment	To submit to treatment by or under the direction of a specified person having the necessary qualifications or experience, with a view to the reduction or elimination of the offender's dependency on alcohol.	Sch.9 paras 23 and 24	During the period specified in the order. Must be treatment: (1) as a resident in a specified place or institution; (2) as a non-resident; (3) by or under the direction of a specified person. The period must be not less than 6 months.	The judge must be satisfied that: (1) the offender is dependent on alcohol; (2) that his dependency requires and may be susceptible to treatment; and (3) offender consents.
12	Alcohol abstinence and monitoring	Subject to any specified exceptions, the offender must: (a) abstain from consuming alcohol or anything containing alcohol throughout a specified period; or (b) not consume alcohol so that during specified period no more than specified level of alcohol in his body; and (c) submit to	Sch.9 paras 25 and 26	Period under (a) must not exceed 120 days. Pilot scheme may precede bringing this provision into force.	Only where: (1) consumption of alcohol by the offender is an element of the offence for which the order is imposed, or an associated offence, or judge is satisfied that it was a factor that contributed to its commission; (2) judge is satisfied that offender is not dependent on alco-

No.	Name	Requirements	SA 2020	Restrictions	Notes
		monitoring as arranged. May be by electronic means.			hol (see No.11 above); (3) judge does not include order under No.11; (4) arrangements are available.
13	Attendance centre	To attend at an attendance centre (see CJA 2003 s.214) specified in the order for such number of hours as may be specified. It requires the offender to attend at the centre at the beginning of the period and during that period, to engage in occupation, or receive instruction, under the supervision of and in accordance with instructions given by, or under the authority of, the officer in charge, whether at the centre or elsewhere. The first time at which the offender is required to attend at the centre will be a time notified to the offender by the responsible officer. The subsequent hours will be fixed by the officer in charge of the centre.	Sch.9 paras 27 and 28	If: (1) the offender is aged 16 or over at the time of conviction, the hours specified must be no less than 12 and not more than 36; (2) the offender is aged 14 or over but under 16 at the time of conviction, they must be no less than 12 and not more than 24; (3) the offender is aged under 14 at the time of conviction, must not be more than 12. An offender may not be required under this requirement to attend at an attendance centre on more than one occasion on any day, or for more than three hours on any occasion.	Remain available in the case of offenders aged 16 and 17, in respect of offences committed before 9 November 2009, see AGE OF OFFENDER. Court must have been notified by the Secretary of State that: (1) an attendance centre is available for persons of the offender's description; and (2) the attendance centre at which the offender is required to attend is to be notified to the offender by the responsible officer from time to time. (3B) When choosing an attendance centre, the responsible officer must consider: (a) the accessibility of the attendance centre to the offender, having regard to the means of access available to the offender and any other circumstances; and (b) the description of persons for whom it is available.

As set out above, the table applies in those cases where the offences were committed on or after 1 February 2015. Where the offences pre-date 1 February, the court can order as part of the community order supervision, or a specified activity requirement, but not the rehabilitation activity.

C. Administrative

Copies of orders

14-022 The court by which any relevant order is made must forthwith provide copies of the order (SA 2020 s.212):

(1) to the offender;
(2) if the offender is aged 18 or over, to a probation officer assigned to the court; and
(3) where the order specifies a local justice area for which the court making the order does not act, to the appropriate provider of probation services acting for that area.

Where a relevant order imposes any requirement specified in the first column of CJA 2003 Sch.14 (SA 2020 Sch.9), the court by which the order is made must also forthwith provide the person specified in relation to that requirement in the second column of that Schedule with a copy of so much of the order as relates to that requirement.

Where a relevant order specifies a local justice area for which the court making the order does not act, the court making the order must provide to the magistrates' court acting for that area, a copy of the order, and such documents and information relating to the case as it considers likely to be of assistance to a court acting for that area in the exercise of its functions in relation to the order.

Duty of court officer

14-023 The Crown Court officer will notify:

(1) the offender of:
    (a) the requirement or requirements imposed; and
    (b) the name of the responsible officer or supervisor, and the means by which that person may be contacted; and
(2) the responsible officer or supervisor, of:
    (a) the offender's name, address and telephone number (if available);
    (b) the offence or offences of which the offender was convicted; and
    (c) the requirement or requirements imposed.

(CrimPR 28.2.2)

D. Breach, revocation and amendment

1. General

14-024 SA 2020 Sch.10 deals with the breach, revocation and amendment of community orders made under SA 2020 in respect of offenders aged 18 or over. Persons not coming within those provisions fall to be dealt with under SA 2020 s.218 which gives effect to Sch.10 on breach, revocation and amendment. As to youth rehabilitation orders, see YOUTH REHABILITATION ORDERS.

Process

Where a community order is made by the Crown Court it will generally include a direction that any failure to comply with the order be dealt with by a magistrates' court (see 14-012). **14-025**

Where, however, a community order made by the Crown Court does *not include such a direction* then if, at any time, it appears to a judge of the Crown Court that the offender has failed to comply with any of the requirements of the order, a summons may be issued, or if the information is on oath, a warrant, to bring him before the court. If he does not appear on a summons, a warrant may be issued (SA 2020 Sch.10 paras 8 and 9).

Any question whether the offender has failed to comply with the requirements of the order is to be determined by the judge and not by the verdict of a jury; the ordinary rules as to the presentation of the prosecution case apply (*R. v Gainsborough Justices Ex p. Green* (1983) 78 Cr. App. R. 9) (SA 2020 Sch.10).

The bare fact that an appeal has been lodged against conviction or sentence does not afford a reasonable excuse for failure to comply with the requirements of an order (*West Midlands Probation Board v Sutton Coldfield Magistrates Court* [2008] EWHC 15 (Admin); [2008] 3 All E.R. 1193).

In relation to breach proceedings in the Crown Court, directed to be heard at the Crown Court by the relevant prosecuting authority, applications for legal aid representation where there is time to instruct a litigator (any time prior to the date of the hearing), should be dealt with at the relevant magistrates' court; they are only subject to the "interests of justice" test (see LEGAL AID; PUBLIC FUNDING). If, on the day of the hearing at the Crown Court the accused is without representation, the judge has the discretion to grant an order for representation.

Powers of Crown Court

Where it is proved to the judge's satisfaction that an offender aged 18 or over has failed without reasonable excuse to comply with any of the requirements of the order, the judge *must* deal with him in respect of that failure in any one of the following ways, taking into account the extent to which the offender has complied with any of the requirements, namely: **14-026**

(1) by *amending* the terms of the order so as to impose more onerous requirements than those which he could impose if he were then making the order;
(2) by ordering the offender to pay *a fine* not exceeding £2,500;
(3) by *dealing with the offender* for the offence in respect of which the order was made in any way in which he could deal with him if he had just been convicted before the Crown Court of the offence; and
(4) in the case of the offender who has willfully and persistently failed to comply with the requirements of the order, the court may impose a sentence of imprisonment (or detention in a young offender institution even where the original offence was not punishable with imprisonment (SA 2020 Sch.10 para.11).

(SA 2020 s.218 and Sch.10)

Note that:

(a) in the case of (3) and (4) above, the judge must *revoke* the order if it is still in force;

(b) in dealing with an offender under (1) above (imposing more onerous terms), the judge may extend the duration of particular requirements (subject to any limit in respect of any individual time limits imposed in the Act), but may only amend the order to substitute a later date for that specified under s.177(5) in accordance with para.10(3ZA) and (3ZB), the effect of which is that a date substituted:
   (i) may not fall outside the period of six months beginning with the date previously specified under SA 2020 s.209; and
   (ii) subject to that, may fall more than three years after the date of the order.

(SA 2020 Sch.10 paras 11 and 13)

Note also that:

- the power to substitute a date may not be exercised in relation to an order if that power, or the power under para.13(2) to substitute a date, has previously been exercised in relation to that order (para.13(3)); and
- a date substituted under subpara.(3) is to be treated as having been specified in relation to the order under s.209.

Extension of unpaid work requirement

14-027 The appropriate court (see 14-032) may, on the application of the offender or of the responsible officer, amend a community order by substituting a later date for that specified under SA 2020 s.209.

A date substituted under subpara.(1):

(1) may not fall outside the period of six months beginning with the date previously specified under SA 2020 s.209; and
(2) subject to that, may fall more than three years after the date of the order.

(SA 2020 Sch.10 para.13)

Note that:

(a) the power under subpara.(1) may not be exercised in relation to an order if it has previously been exercised in relation to that order;
(b) a date substituted under subpara.(1) is to be treated as having been specified in relation to the order under SA 2020 s.209.

If the judge imposes a community work requirement which the original order did not contain, the minimum number of hours may be 20 rather than the 40 prescribed by SA 2020 s.209 and Sch.9 para.2.

As to failure to comply in respect of "treatment cases", see 14-029.

Approach to breach

14-028 The primary objective must be to ensure that the requirements of the original sentence are completed. A custodial sentence should be the last resort, where all reasonable efforts to ensure that an offender complete a community sentence have failed. If a custodial sentence is imposed, without adequate consideration being given to alternatives, the purposes identified originally as being important, may be undermined. The Sentencing Council have issued a definitive guideline on Breach of Community Orders. It applies to all offenders aged 18 and above sentenced on or after 1 October 2018, regardless of the date of the offence.

In approaching the alternatives set out in 14-026, the judge should take account the extent to which the offender has complied with the requirements of the order. In making that assessment the court should consider:

(1) the overall attitude and engagement with the order as well as the proportion of elements completed;
(2) the impact of any completed or partially completed requirements on the offender's behavior;
(3) the proximity of the breach to imposition of the order; and
(4) evidence of circumstances or offender characteristics, such as disability, mental health issues or learning difficulties which have impeded offender's compliance with the order.

Where a breach takes place towards the end of the operational period, and the judge is satisfied that the offender's appearance before the court is likely to be sufficient in itself to ensure future compliance, he should sentence in a way that enables the original order to be completed properly, for example, by a differently constructed community sentence that aims to secure compliance with the purposes of the original sentence. Where the judge decides to increase the onerousness of the order, he ought to:

(a) give careful consideration (with advice from the probation service), to the offender's ability to comply; and
(b) consider the impact on the offender's ability to comply, and the possibility of precipitating a custodial sentence for a further breach, and may consider:
    (i) extending the supervision or operational periods will be more sensible; or
    (ii) in other cases adding punitive or rehabilitative requirements instead,

being mindful, however, of the legislative restrictions on the overall length of community sentences and on the supervision and operational periods allowed for each type of requirement.

In dealing with an offender for breach of a requirement, (as opposed to dealing with him in respect of a new offence), non-compliance is not to be taken as an aggravation of the original offence; he must be sentenced on the facts upon which the original order was made (*R. v Clarke* [1997] 2 Cr. App. R. (S.) 163). If a driving disqualification was imposed at the time the relevant order was made, there is no power to impose a further disqualification if the order is revoked and the offender is re-sentenced (*R. v Coy* (1992) 13 Cr. App. R. (S.) 619).

Care needs to be taken where there are breaches of two orders, depending on whether they run concurrently (as in *R. v Butt* [2012] EWCA Crim 462, distinguishing *R. v Meredith* [1994] 15 Cr. App. R. (S). 5 (where they were expressed to run consecutively)).

Treatment cases

An offender who is required by: **14-029**

(1) a mental health treatment requirement;
(2) a drug rehabilitation requirement; or
(3) an alcohol treatment requirement,

to submit to treatment for his mental condition, or his dependency on, or propensity to misuse, drugs or alcohol, is not to be treated for these purposes as having failed to comply with that requirement on the ground only that he had refused to undergo any surgical, electrical or other treatment if, in the judge's opinion, his refusal was reasonable having regard to all the circumstances.

The judge may not, under these provisions, amend a mental health treatment requirement, a drug rehabilitation requirement or an alcohol treatment requirement unless the offender expresses his willingness to comply with the requirement as amended (CJA 2003 Sch.8 para.1).

2. REVOCATION WITH OR WITHOUT RE-SENTENCING

General

14-030 Where a community order is made by the Crown Court it will generally include a direction that any failure to comply with the order be dealt with by a magistrates' court (see 14-012), but where:

(1) an order, still in force, does not include such a direction; and
(2) the offender, or the responsible officer, applies to the Crown Court for the order, or for the offender to be dealt with in some other way for the offence in respect of which the order was made,

the judge may, if it appears to him to be in the interests of justice to do so, having regard to circumstances which have arisen since the order was made:

(a) *revoke* the order; or
(b) both *revoke* the order, *and deal with the offender* for the offence in respect of which the order was made, in any way in which he could deal with him if the offender had just been convicted of that offence by or before the court which made the order.

Note that:

- the circumstances in which an order may be revoked include the offender's making good progress or his responding satisfactorily to supervision or treatment, as the case requires;
- in dealing with an offender under this provision the judge must take into account the extent to which the offender has complied with the requirements of the order; and
- where the judge proposes to exercise his powers under this paragraph otherwise than on the application of the offender, the offender must be summoned to appear before the court and, if he does not appear in answer to the summons, a warrant may be issued for his arrest.

(SA 2020 s.218 and Sch.10)

Illness or disability

14-031 Where revocation is on the ground that the offender is unable to comply by reason of illness or disability, the imposition of a custodial sentence depends on the circumstances.

Thus, under the previous legislation it was held that:

(1) in general it should not be imposed (*R. v Fielding* (1993) 14 Cr. App. R. (S.) 494); particularly
(2) where the offender made it clear from the outset that there might be difficulties (*R. v Johnson* [2000] 1 Cr. App. R. (S.) 405); but
(3) it may well be appropriate where the offender failed to disclose any potential difficulties at the time the order was made (*R. v Hammon* [1998] 2 Cr. App. R. (S.) 202).

If the application is based on grounds which amount, in effect, to an alleged breach of the order, the judge should satisfy himself as to the grounds for revocation by hearing evidence, as if on a breach (*R. v Jackson* [1984] 6 Cr. App. R. (S.) 202; Crim. L.R. 573).

3. Amendment of order

The "appropriate court": summons or warrant

The "appropriate court" has wide powers to amend community orders made by the Crown Court. The Crown Court is the "appropriate court" where a community order made by the Crown Court does not include a direction that any failure to comply with the requirements of the order is to be dealt with by a magistrates' court. In relation to any other community order, the "appropriate court" is a magistrates' court acting in the local justice area concerned, or, in the case of an order imposing a drug rehabilitation requirement which is subject to review, the court responsible for the order (SA 2020 Sch.10 Pt 4). **14-032**

Where, therefore, no such direction has been included, and a judge is asked to exercise his powers of amendment, save for an amendment:

(1) cancelling a requirement;
(2) reducing the period of any requirement; or
(3) substituting a new local justice area, or a new place for the one specified in the order,

the offender must be summoned to appear, and if he does not appear in answer to the summons a warrant may be issued (SA 2020 Sch.10 Pt 4 para.18).

In practice, proceedings in the Crown Court in relation to amendments of this nature are generally a formality and, in the absence of any opposition are dealt with on the papers.

Change of residence

Where at any time while a community order is in force in respect of an offender: **14-033**

(1) he is given permission under s.216 to change residence; and
(2) the local justice area in which the new residence is situated ("the new local justice area") is different from the local justice area specified in the order,

if the permission is given by:

(a) a court, the court must amend the order to specify the new local justice area;
(b) the responsible officer, the officer must apply to the appropriate court to amend the order to specify the new local justice area, and the court must make that amendment:
    (i) in relation to a community order imposing a drug rehabilitation

requirement which is subject to review, the court responsible for the order;
(ii) in relation to a community order which was made by the Crown Court and does not include a direction that any failure to comply with the requirements of the order is to be dealt with by a magistrates' court, the Crown Court; and
(iii) in relation to any other community order, a magistrates' court acting in the local justice area specified in the order.

(SA 2020 s.218 and Sch.10 Pt 4 para.16)

Change of local justice area

14-034 Where at any time while a community order is in force in respect of an offender:

(1) a court amends the order (as to which see 14-032);
(2) the order as amended includes a residence requirement requiring the offender to reside at a specified place; and
(3) the local justice area in which that place is situated ("the new local justice area") is different from the local justice area specified in the order,

the court must amend the order to specify the new local justice area (SA 2020 Sch.10 Pt 4 para.16(2)).

4. AMENDMENT OF REQUIREMENTS

General

14-035 A judge of the Crown Court, being the appropriate court (see 14-032), may, on the application of the offender, or of the responsible officer, amend an order by:

(1) cancelling any of the requirements of the order; or
(2) replacing any of them with a requirement of the same kind, which the judge could include if he were then making the order,

provided that he may not amend, under this paragraph, a mental health treatment, a drug rehabilitation or an alcohol treatment requirement unless the offender consents to the requirement as amended.

Note that:

(a) no application may be made while an appeal against the order is pending, except in a case where it relates to a "mental health", "drug rehabilitation" or "alcohol treatment requirement", and the offender consents to comply with the requirement as amended; and
(b) the judge has the same powers in respect of a drug rehabilitation requirement which is subject to review, imposed by the Crown Court (see 14-032).

(SA 2020 s.218 and Sch.10 Pt 4 para.18)

If the offender fails to consent to the proposed amended requirement, the judge may revoke the community order and deal with the offender for the offence in respect of which the order was made, in any way in which he could deal with him if he had just been convicted in the Crown Court of the offence, taking into account the extent to which the offender has complied with the requirements of the order.

Where the order was made in respect of an offence punishable with imprisonment a custodial sentence may be imposed notwithstanding the restrictions imposed by SA 2020 s.230 (as to which see DEALING WITH AN OFFENDER).

Amendment of treatment requirements

Where the medical practitioner or other person by whom, or under whose direction, an offender is, in pursuance of: **14-036**

(1) "a mental health treatment requirement";
(2) "a drug rehabilitation requirement"; or
(3) "an alcohol treatment requirement",

being treated for his mental condition or his dependency on, or propensity to misuse, drugs or alcohol:

(a) is of the opinion:
  (i) that the treatment of the offender should be continued beyond the period specified;
  (ii) that the offender needs different treatment;
  (iii) that the offender is not susceptible to treatment; or
  (iv) that the offender does not require further treatment; or
(b) is for any reason unwilling to continue to treat or direct the treatment of the offender,

he must make a report in writing to that effect to the responsible officer and that officer will apply to the "appropriate court" (see 14-032) for the variation or cancellation of the requirement (SA 2020 Sch.10 Pt 4 para.19).

Review of drug rehabilitation requirement

Where the responsible officer is of the opinion that a community order imposing a drug rehabilitation requirement which is subject to review should be so amended as to provide for each subsequent periodic review (required by SA 2020 Sch.9 paras 21 and 22) to be made without a hearing instead of at a review hearing, or vice versa, he must apply to the court responsible for the order (which is the "appropriate court", see 14-032) for the variation of the order (SA 2020 Sch.10). **14-037**

Extension of unpaid work requirement

Where, in relation to any community order made by the Crown Court which does not include a direction that any failure to comply with any of the requirements of the order be dealt with by the magistrates' court, an unpaid work requirement is in force and, on the application of the offender or of the responsible officer it appears to the judge that it would be in the interests of justice to do so, having regard to circumstances which have arisen since the order was made, he may extend the period beyond the 12 months specified in SA 2020 Sch.9 para.1(1)(b) (SA 2020 Sch.10 para.21). **14-038**

5. TRANSFER TO SCOTLAND AND NORTHERN IRELAND

A judge of the Crown Court, being the "appropriate court" (see 14-032) may, where: **14-039**

(1) he is satisfied that an offender in respect of whom a community order is in force proposes to reside, or is residing, in Scotland, or Northern Ireland; and

(2) it appears that arrangements exist for persons to comply with such requirements in the locality in which the offender resides, or will be residing, and that provision can be made for him to comply with the requirements under those arrangements, and that suitable arrangements for his supervision can be made by the authorities there,

amend the order by requiring it to be complied with in Scotland or Northern Ireland, as the case may be, and requiring the offender to be supervised in accordance with arrangements made by the authorities there.

The requirements and formalities of such transfers are set out in SA 2020 s.219 and Sch.11.

E. Powers following subsequent conviction

Revocation and fresh sentence

14-040 Where an offender in respect of whom a community order is in force is:

(1) convicted of an offence in the Crown Court; or
(2) brought, or appears, before a judge of the Crown Court having been committed by a magistrates' court for sentence, and

it appears to the judge that it would be in the interests of justice to exercise the powers set out in (a) or (b) below, having regard to circumstances which have arisen since the community order was made, he may:

(a) revoke the order; or
(b) both:
    (i) revoke the order; and
    (ii) deal with the offender for the offence in respect of which the order was made, in any way in which the court which made the order could deal with him if he had just been convicted of that offence by or before the court which made the order,

    taking into account under (b)(ii) the extent to which the offender has complied with the requirements of the community order.

(SA 2020 Sch.10 Pt 3 paras 14 and 15)

The power to deal with the offender depends on the offender being convicted of the new offence while the community order is still in force; it does not arise where the offender is convicted after the expiry of the order, even if the offence was committed while the order was current (SA 2020 Sch.10 para.25(1)).

As to guidance by the Sentencing Council, see 14-006 and 14-007.

Sentence on the breach

14-041 In dealing with the offender for a breach the court must take into account the extent to which the offender has complied with the requirements of the relevant order (SA 2020 Sch.10 para.11(4)).

The fact that an offence committed during the currency of a relevant order is different in character from that or those for which the community order was passed, does not prevent the court revoking the order and dealing with the offender by imposing, for instance, a custodial sentence (*R. v Fleming* (1989) 11 Cr. App. R. (S.) 137). There is no binding principle that it can never be right to impose a consecutive term for an offence committed before offences for which a community sentence was passed; it depends in each case on what the interests of justice require (*R. v Newton* [1999] 2 Cr. App. R. (S.) 172).

The fact that a community sentence was originally imposed does not mean that the offence was not one qualifying for a custodial sentence. If the commission of a further offence destroys any mitigation there may have been, a custodial sentence may be appropriate.

The Sentencing Guideline: Breach of Community Orders provides guidance in relation to the exercise of powers following a conviction while serving a community sentence. Where an offender is convicted by a magistrates' court of an additional offence, the magistrates' court should ordinarily revoke the previous community order and sentence afresh for both the original and additional offence. Where convicted at the magistrates' court but the community order was made by the Crown Court, the magistrates' court may, and ordinarily should, commit the offender to the Crown Court so that the Crown Court can re-sentence for the original and additional offence. The sentencing court should consider the overall seriousness of the offending behavior taking into account the additional offence and the original offence. The court should consider whether the combination of associated offences is sufficiently serious to justify a custodial sentence. If it does not consider that custody is necessary, it should impose a single community order that reflects the overall totality of criminality. The court must take into account the extent to which the offender complied with the requirements of the previous order.

F. Administrative provisions; duties of court officer

On the making of an order revoking or amending a community order, the Crown Court officer must: **14-042**

(1) provide copies of the revoking or amending order to the offender and to the responsible officer;
(2) in the case of an amending order which substitutes a new local justice area, provide a copy of the amending order to:
    (a) the relevant probation officer; and
    (b) the magistrates' court acting for that area;
(3) in the case of an amending order which imposes or amends a requirement specified in the first column of SA 2020 Sch.10 Pt 6 para.27, provide a copy of so much of the amending order as relates to that requirement to the person specified in relation to it in the second column of the Schedule; and
(4) where (under subpara.(2)(b)) he provides a copy of an amending order to a magistrates' court acting for a different area, also provide to the court such documents and information relating to the case as he considers likely to be of assistance to a court acting for that area in the exercise of its functions in relation to the order.

(SA 2020 Sch.10 Pt 6 para.27(6))

Table SA 2020 Sch.11 Pt 6 para.27

14-043

Requirement	Person to whom copy of requirement is to be given
An exclusion requirement imposed for the purpose (or partly	The person intended to be protected.

Requirement	Person to whom copy of requirement is to be given
for the purpose) of protecting a person from being approached by the offender.	
A residence requirement relating to residence in an institution.	The person in charge of the institution.
A mental health treatment requirement.	The person specified under Sch.9 para.16(3)(b)(iii) (the registered medical practitioner or psychologist) or the person in charge of the institution or place specified under Sch.9 para.16(3)(b)(i) or (ii).
A drug rehabilitation requirement	The person in charge of the institution or place specified under Sch.9 para.19(5)(b) or (c).
An alcohol treatment requirement.	The person specified under Sch.9 para.23(5)(a) (the person having the necessary qualification or experience) or the person in charge of the institution or place specified under Sch.9 para.23(5)(c) or (d).
An electronic monitoring requirement.	Any person who by virtue of Sch.9 para.31(1) will be responsible for the electronic monitoring. Any person by virtue of whose consent the requirement is included in the order.

15. COMPANY DIRECTOR'S DISQUALIFICATION

General

An offender convicted before the Crown Court of: **15-001**

(1) an indictable offence (IA 1978 Sch.1);
(2) in connection with the promotion, formation, management or liquidation of a company; or
(3) with the receivership or management of a company's property;

may be disqualified from being:

(a) a director, liquidator or manager of a company;
(b) a receiver or manager of a company's property; or
(c) in any way, whether directly or indirectly, concerned, or taking part in, the promotion, formation or management of a company, without leave of the court, and may not act as an insolvency practitioner. (CDDA 1986 ss.1, 2)

As a discretionary order of a plainly punitive nature, such an order may not be combined with an absolute or conditional discharge (*R. v Young* (1991) 12 Cr. App. R. (S.) 29). See also DISCHARGE; ABSOLUTE AND CONDITIONAL.

There is no jurisdiction to limit a disqualification to the holding of a directorship in a public company. The judge should make it clear that the order applies to *all* the categories (a)–(c) (*R. v Ward* [2001] EWCA Crim 1648).

In (2) and (3) above "company" includes an overseas company (SBEEA 2015 Sch.7(1)).

Rationale behind disqualification

The rationale behind such an order is to protect the public from persons who, whether for reasons of dishonesty, naivety or incompetence, use or abuse their role as a company director to the detriment of the public (*R. v Millard* (1994) 15 Cr. App. R. (S.) 445; *R. v Edwards* (1998) 2 Cr. App. R. (S.) 213; *R. v Victory* (1999) 2 Cr. App. R. (S.) 102). **15-002**

In considering the appropriateness of a CDDO, the fact that the accused was a director only for a short time and/or derived little or no personal benefit from his dishonesty may have little relevance where substantial losses were incurred (*R. v Cobbey* (1993) 14 Cr. App. R. (S.) 82).

Where a defendant is convicted of strict liability regulatory offences, the judge must take care to identify the conduct which renders him unfit to be a company director. The defendant must be given proper notice of what allegations of personal misconduct he faces and an opportunity to make informed submissions (*R. v Chandler* [2015] EWCA Crim 1825; [2016] 1 Cr. App. R. (S.) 37).

In the absence of an application by the prosecutor, the judge should take the initiative and consider the making of an order. Where this is not done the CACD may later impose such an order (*Attorney General's References (Nos 88, 89, 90 and 91 of 2006)* [2006] EWCA Crim 3254; [2007] 2 Cr. App. R. (S.) 28).

If the prosecution do not specifically invite the court to make a CDDO, the judge should invite submissions before making an order (*R. v Ravjani* [2012] EWCA Crim 2519).

"Management of the company" defined

15-003 The words "management of the company" refer to the management of the company's affairs. There is no reason to differentiate between internal and external affairs (*R. v Corbin* (1984) 6 Cr. App. R. (S.) 17; *R. v Austen* (1985) 7 Cr. App. R. (S.) 214; *R. v Georgiou* (1988) 87 Cr. App. R. 207; *R. v Bond* [2015] EWCA Crim 634).

The correct test in deciding whether an offence is in connection with the management of a company is whether the offence has some relevant factual connection with the management of the company (see *R. v Goodman* [1993] 97 Cr. App. R. 210; *R. v Creggy* [2008] EWCA Crim 394; [2008] 3 All E.R. 91; *R. v Bond* [2015] EWCA Crim 634).

In *Re Keeping Kids Co* [2021] EWHC 175 (Ch); [2021] 2 WLUK 190, the High Court identified the general principles to be adopted in assessing whether someone is a "director" and a more favored "benevolent" approach to trustees of charities. There is no single test for when someone is a director but an important starting point is the company's corporate governance structure. The court is seeking to identify functions that were the sole responsibility of a director or board of directors, that is, the highest level of management of the company. Those who assume and exercise powers and functions that can only properly be exercised or discharged at that highest level of management will, consistent with the purpose of the disqualification legislation, be within its scope as de facto directors. The court observed that its benevolent approach towards charity trustees in circumstances where no dishonesty or wilful misconduct is alleged reflects the real risk that any other approach would deter individuals who would otherwise be well suited to becoming charity trustees from doing so.

Section 2 of the Rating (Coronavirus) and Directors Disqualification (Dissolved Companies) Act 2021 amends ss.6 and 7 of the Company Directors Disqualification Act 1986 to extend the powers of the Secretary of State under s.6 to investigate the conduct of former directors of dissolved companies which have not become insolvent and to allow the court to make disqualification orders against the former directors of dissolved companies. This entered into force on 15 February 2022.

Terms and length of disqualification

15-004 The order must contain a prohibition in respect of all the functions referred to in the section (*R. v Cole* [1998] B.C.L.C. 87). The maximum period of disqualification in the Crown Court is 15 years. Periods of disqualification of:

(1) over 10 years should be reserved for particularly serious cases, which may include those where there has been a previous disqualification;
(2) between 6 and 10 years should be reserved for intermediate cases; and
(3) between 2 to 5 years may be imposed in cases which are not particularly serious.

(*R. v Millard* [1994] 15 Cr. App. R. (S.) 445; *R. v Sheikh* [2010] EWCA Crim 921; [2011] 1 Cr. App. R. (S.) 12; *R. v Cadman* [2012] EWCA Crim 611; [2012] 2 Cr. App. R. (S.) 88)

The period of disqualification commences 21 days from the date of the order unless the court orders otherwise (CDDA 1986 s.1(2)).

A CDDO made against a person who is already the subject of a CDDO will run concurrently (CDDA 1986 s.1(3)).

A person acting in contravention of such an order is liable on conviction on indictment to imprisonment for not more than two years or to a fine, or both. The period of disqualification should reflect the level of risk to the public.

Compensation; confiscation

When a compensation order is made it is generally wrong in principle to inhibit a defendant from engaging in business activities which are necessary to fulfill the terms of the compensation order (*R. v Holmes* (1992) 13 Cr. App. R. (S.) 29). **15-005**

If an offender has been convicted of an offence of contravening an order under the Act, the questions to be asked in connection with confiscation are no different from those for any other offence. There is nothing in CDDA 1986 or in the confiscation legislation that suggests any different approach (*R. v Blatch* [2009] EWCA Crim 1303; [2010] 1 Cr. App. R. (S.) 60).

16. COMPENSATION ORDERS

General

16-001 A judge of the Crown Court may order the payment of compensation in a criminal case as a convenient and rapid means of avoiding the expense of civil litigation in the High Court or the county court provided the offender has the means to pay (*R. v Inwood* (1974) 60 Cr. App. R. 70). There is no limit on the amount.

Where a judge is dealing with an offender and a compensation order is available, the judge must give reasons if he does not make a compensation order (SA 2020 s.55).

He should not make an order where there is any doubt as to the liability to compensate or real doubt as to whether the offender can pay.

Sentence may be deferred (see DEFERRING SENTENCE) with a view to the making of reparation, without any formal order for compensation being made.

Power to make order

16-002 Where a person is convicted of an offence, the judge may, whether on application or otherwise, and subject to certain restrictions (set out below), make an order requiring him to:

(1) pay compensation for any personal injury, loss or damage resulting from the offence (or any offence taken into consideration on sentence—see SA 2020 s.145(2)); or
(2) make payments for funeral expenses or bereavement in respect of a death resulting from any such offence, other than a death due to an accident arising out of the presence of a motor vehicle on a road.

The judge may make a compensation order whether or not he also deals with the offender for the offence in any other way (SA 2020 s.134(2)).

"Personal injury" or "damage" include shock and anxiety directly occasioned by the offence (*Bond v Chief Constable of Kent* (1982) 4 Cr. App. R. (S.) 314). "Loss" includes the loss suffered by an innocent purchaser of stolen goods (*R. v Howell* (1978) 66 Cr. App. R. 179).

Offences taken into consideration; specimen charges

16-003 Where an offender is convicted on specimen charges, the amount of compensation which may be ordered is limited to that set out in the specimen charges (*R. v Crutchley* (1994) 15 Cr. App. R. (S.) 627). The fact that an offender freely admits to having made away with a certain sum does not alter the position, and does not, without the proper procedure for taking such offences into consideration being followed, mean that those offences are being taken into consideration for that purpose (*R. v Hose* (1995) 16 Cr. App. R. (S.) 682, applying *DPP v Anderson* (1978) 67 Cr. App. R. 185).

Damage: Theft Act and Fraud Act cases

16-004 In the case of an offence under TA 1968 or FrA 2006 where the property:

(1) is recovered, any damage to it occurring while it was out of the owner's possession is treated as having resulted from the offence, regardless of how the damage was caused and who caused it; but
(2) if it is not recovered, that presumption does not apply (*R. v Ahmad* (1992) 13 Cr. App. R. (S.) 212).

(SA 2020 s.137(2))

In a case of dishonest handling where the goods are recovered, no order may be made in respect of their permanent loss (*R. v Tyce* (1994) 15 Cr. App. R. (S.) 415).

Road accidents

An order may only be made in respect of injury or loss or damage which was due to a road accident (an accident arising out of the presence of a motor vehicle on a road) if it is in respect of: **16-005**

(1) loss suffered by a person's dependants in consequence of the person's death;
(2) damage which is treated by s.137 as resulting from an offence under the TA 1968 or FrA 2006; or
(3) uninsured harm.

(SA 2020 s.136(1)–(2), (5))

"Uninsured harm" means injury, loss or damage as respects which:

(a) the offender was uninsured in relation to the use of the vehicle in question; and
(b) compensation is not payable under any arrangements to which the Secretary of State is party.

(SA 2020 s.136(3))

Where an order is made in respect of such injury, loss or damage, the amount to be paid may include an amount representing all or part of any loss of, or reduction in, preferential rates of insurance attributable to the accident (SA 2020 s.136(4)).

Where sums are payable by the Motor Insurers' Bureau (MIB), the compensation payable is limited to the amount payable by MIB (*DPP v Scott* (1995) 16 Cr. App. R. (S.) 292).

A vehicle exempted from insurance under RTA 1988 s.144 is not "uninsured" for this purpose, nor is a driver uninsured who merely refuses to produce details, but is, in fact, covered (*McDermott v DPP* [1997] R.T.R 474).

Funeral expenses

A compensation order may be made for the benefit of anyone who incurred funeral expenses, except in respect of a death due to a road accident (SA 2020 s.138(1), (4), s.136(1)). **16-006**

An order in respect of bereavement may be made only for the benefit of a person for whose benefit a claim for damages for bereavement could be made under the Fatal Accidents Act 1976 s.1A (SA 2020 s.138(2)).

The amount of compensation must not exceed that specified in s.1A(3) of that Act (£12,980).

Compensation from Criminal Injuries Compensation Authority no bar

The fact that the victim may be able to get compensation from the Criminal Injuries Compensation Authority (CICA) set up under the Criminal Injuries **16-007**

Compensation Act 1995 (See website—*http://www.gov.uk/government/organisations/criminal-injuries-compensation-authority* [Accessed September 2022]) should not prevent the judge from making an order under s.135 in a proper case.

Compensation ordered by a criminal court is different from that which victims of crime may receive from CICA. Victims may apply to CICA and receive compensation whether or not the offender is detected or convicted. No award is made by CICA unless the appropriate amount exceeds £1,000.

Approach to making an order

16-008 Before making an order, the judge must:

(1) satisfy himself that injury, loss or damage has resulted from the offence of which the offender has been convicted or is having taken into consideration on sentence;
(2) settle the amount which the offender may be required to pay; and
(3) consider the means of the offender, giving him or his counsel the opportunity to be heard.

General principles

16-009 The general principles to be followed in making an order were restated in *R. v Miller* (1976) 68 Cr. App. R. 56. Those still relevant are:

(1) first and foremost, that an order should be made only where the legal position is clear (see16-010 and 16-011);
(2) the order must be precisely drawn and must be related to an offence of which the offender has been convicted, or which he has agreed to have taken into consideration;
(3) the judge must have regard to the offender's means (see 16-013);
(4) the order ought not to be oppressive (see 16-014); and
(5) the fact that the victim to whom compensation is payable has since died does not mean that an order is inappropriate (*Holt v DPP* (1996) 2 Cr. App. R. (S.) 314).

Causation

16-010 There must be a causal connection between the offence committed and the damage done or injury caused. The existence of civil liability is not a prerequisite to making an order in criminal proceedings (*R. v Chappell* (1984) 6 Cr. App. R. (S.) 214). The judge needs to ask himself whether loss or damage can fairly be said to have resulted to anyone from the offence (*R. v Rowiston* (1982) 4 Cr. App. R. (S.) 85, and see *R. v Taylor* (1994) 14 Cr. App. R. (S.) 276; *R. v Guertjens* (1992) 14 Cr. App. R. (S.) 280; *R. v Denness* [1996] 1 Cr. App. R. (S.) 159).

Real issue as to liability

16-011 Liability to pay compensation must be proved or admitted. Where there is a real issue as to the offender's liability to pay compensation, whether in respect of specific offences or specific victims:

(1) the question cannot be determined by argument;
(2) the judge will need to hear evidence; and

(3) it is for the prosecutor to put forward evidence, so that the offender may have an opportunity to test the basis on which the order is to be made (*R. v Horsham Justices Ex p. Richards* (1985) 7 Cr. App. R. (S.) 158; *R. v Halliwell* (1991) 12 Cr. App. R. (S.) 692).

Where issues may be unclear, as where, e.g.:

(a) up-to-date medical reports, photographs, etc., need to be provided (*R. v Cooper* (1982) Cr. App. R. (S.) 55);
(b) questions of loss of use arise, which in civil cases are "notoriously open to argument" (*R. v Donovan* (1981) 3 Cr. App. R. (S.) 192); or
(c) matters of set-off and contribution arise in social security benefit frauds (*Hyde v Emery* (1984) 6 Cr. App. R. (S.) 206),

such cases should generally be left to the civil courts or to the executive to deal with.

A line of authorities seeking to confine such orders to the "plainest and most straightforward situations" was reconsidered in *R. v Pola* [2009] EWCA Crim 655; [2010] 1 Cr. App. R. (S.) 6, where, upholding an order for compensation for personal injuries amounting to £90,000, the CACD noted that the courts had now developed expertise in financial matters as a result of experience of proceedings under POCA 2002. The judge had had the necessary evidence before him and had considered the JSB's *Guidelines for the Assessment of General Damages in Personal Injuries Cases*. Moses LJ observed that: "It may be that the very cautious approach adopted in the early cases needs some modification ...". However, in *R. v Stapylton* [2012] EWCA Crim 728; [2013] 1 Cr. App. R. (S.) 12 the CACD concluded that

> "because compensation orders are for straightforward cases, a court should not embark on a detailed enquiry as to the extent of any injury, loss or damage. If the matter demands such attention it is better left for civil proceedings" (at [11]).

See also *R. v Bewick* [2007] EWCA Crim 3297; [2008] 2 Cr. App. R. (S.) 31, where the CACD quashed a compensation order reflecting evaded tax because there were detailed and complex issues to be decided, involving the resolution of conflict between witnesses and the need to make arbitrary judgments, albeit based upon some evidence.

Amount of compensation payable; interest

The amount of compensation ordered to be paid must be such as the judge considers appropriate, having regard to the evidence, and to any representations made by or on behalf of the offender or the prosecutor. An order is not intended to be a precise evaluation of loss, such as takes place in a civil court when damages are awarded. The power to award compensation is a fairly blunt instrument. The remedy for the victim is intended to be speedy, efficacious and cost free (*R. v Williams* [2001] Cr. App. R. (S.) 500). **16-012**

Note that:

(1) the precise extent of the injury, loss or damage does not need to be established by evidence; but
(2) there should be some evidential basis from which the judge can determine what sum is appropriate; and
(3) where insufficient information is available or the evidence is unclear, the judge may adjourn until the necessary information is to hand.

The amount ought, in general, to be limited to the judge's assessment of the amount that might have been recovered in a civil action (*R. v Gateway Foodmarkets Ltd* [1997] 2 Cr. App. R. 40).

See also the Judicial College's *Guidelines on the Assessment of General Damages in Personal Injury Cases*. As to guidance offered by the Criminal Injuries Compensation Authority, see 16-007.

A sum may be added by way of interest equivalent to what the victim would be likely to recover if he proved his claim in the civil courts (*R. v Schofield* (1978) 67 Cr. App. R. 282).

Offender's means

16-013 In deciding whether to make an order, and in what amount, the judge is restricted by:

(1) SA 2020 s.135(3) which requires him to have regard to the means of the offender, in so far as they are known or appear to the court (as to whether funds held in a pension pot should be taken into account, see *R. v Sharif* [2022] EWCA Crim 215; [2022] 1 WLUK 470); and
(2) the principle set out in *R. v Webb* (1979) 1 Cr. App. R. (S.) 16 that an order should not be made in such an amount that the offender will have no prospect of paying it within the foreseeable future (*R. v Bradburn* (1973) 57 Cr. App. R. 948; *R. v Bagga* (1989) 11 Cr. App. R. (S.) 497; *R. v Olliver* (1989) 11 Cr. App. R. (S.) 10; *R. v Hewitt* (1990–91) 12 Cr. App. R. (S.) 466; *R. v Yehou* [1997] 2 Cr. App. R. (S.) 48).

Difficulties can be avoided if the judge indicates a provisional figure, and asks the defence advocate to provide information as to the offender's means (*R. v Phillips* [1988] 10 Cr. App. R. (S.) 419).

Note that:

(a) it is the offender's duty to put information as to his means before the court (any attempt to mislead entitles the judge to infer that he has assets (*R. v Bolden* (1987) 9 Cr. App. R. (S.) 83));
(b) it is the duty of his representatives to verify the accuracy of any statements (*R. v Roberts* (1987) 9 Cr. App. R. (S.) 275); and
(c) if the offender fraudulently claims to have means to pay, he has only himself to blame if an order is made (*R. v Dando* [1996] 1 Cr. App. R. (S.) 155).

Where the offender gives no evidence on the matter, and explanations given through counsel are "utterly unconvincing", the judge is entitled to act on the basis of any material put before him by the prosecutor, drawing appropriate inferences (*R. v Maisey* [2001] 1 Cr. App. R. (S.) 98).

The judge's view of the offender's means should be clearly set out in his sentencing remarks (*R. v Malik* [2019] EWCA Crim 1079).

Offender without means

16-014 Where an offender is clearly without means, a compensation order should not be made on the basis of:

(1) a promise to pay; and
(2) offers by friends and relatives to pay (*R. v Hunt* [1983] Crim. L.R. 250; *R. v Webb* [1979] 1 Cr. App. R. (S.) 16).

There are a number of authorities which state that a compensation order should not ordinarily be made on the basis of the proposed future sale of the matrimonial home (*R. v Harrison* (1980) 2 Cr. App. R. (S.) 313; *R. v Blackmore* (1984) 6 Cr. App. R. (S.) 244; *R. v Butt* (1986) 8 Cr. App. R. (S.) 216; *R. v Hackett* (1988) 10 Cr. App. R. (S.) 388), but there may be circumstances in which this is appropriate (*R. v McGuire* (1992) 13 Cr. App. R. (S.) 332; *R. v Martindale* [2014] EWCA Crim 1232). See 16-017 concerning the situation where compensation can be paid out of confiscation.

It is not unreasonable to require the offender to sell other items of property to enable him to pay the compensation (*R. v Workman* (1981) 3 Cr. App. R. (S.) 318), provided the judge takes steps to ascertain their value and a proper valuation can be made (*R. v Chambers* (1981) 3 Cr. App. R. (S.) 318).

It is not wrong in principle to make a compensation order where the defendant cannot immediately make payment from his own funds but could obtain funds by borrowing from a third party. However, no such order should be made unless there is evidence from which the court can conclude that there are sound prospects that the defendant will be able to repay the loan (*R. v Carrington* [2014] EWCA Crim 325; [2014] 2 Cr. App. R. (S.) 41).

Offender sentenced to custodial sentence

If a victim is entitled to compensation, an order obviates the necessity for civil proceedings. Before making an order against a person upon whom a custodial sentence is imposed, the judge must bear in mind that: **16-015**

(1) a custodial sentence will deprive the offender of his earning power;
(2) it may make it difficult for him to find work when he is released; and
(3) by the time he is released he might be in financial difficulty.

If the offender has sufficient assets, or will have reasonably assured earning capacity upon his release, it will often be appropriate to make an order (*R. v Love* [1999] 1 Cr. App. R. (S.) 75; *R. v Jorge* [1999] 2 Cr. App. R. (S.) 1). Whilst it may be undesirable for a compensation order to be hanging over the offender's head after release from a custodial sentence, there are exceptions, such as where it is clear that the offender has the means to pay, or where the sentence is comparatively short and the offender's job will still be open upon release (*R. v Gray* [2021] EWCA Crim 668; [2021] 4 WLUK 460).

Compensation preferred to fine

Where the judge considers it appropriate both: **16-016**

(1) to impose a fine; and
(2) to make a compensation order; but
(3) the offender has insufficient means to satisfy both an appropriate fine and appropriate compensation,

preference must be given to compensation, although a fine may be imposed as well (SA 2020 s.135(4)).

Compensation has priority over confiscation

While there is no objection to the judge imposing both a confiscation order (see CONFISCATION ORDERS) and a compensation order under this section where **16-017** the amount that may be realised is sufficient, the courts should always be at pains to ensure that so far as possible the victim is compensated, and compensation should be the first priority: *R. v Mitchell* [2001] 2 Cr. App. R. (S.) 29.

As regards the potential for double recovery and how it can be avoided, see *R. v Jawad* [2013] EWCA Crim 644; [2014] 1 Cr. App. R. (S.) 16.

POCA 2002 s.13(6) provides that, where the court makes a confiscation order and a "priority order" (which includes a compensation order), the court must direct that, if there are insufficient funds to satisfy both orders, the compensation order will be paid from the sum recovered under the confiscation order. This was considered in *R. v Parkinson* [2015] EWCA Crim 1448; [2016] 1 Cr. App. R. (S.) 6. The CACD held that there is no general principle that compensation orders would not generally be made in confiscation proceedings where they would require the sale of a family home. See also *R. v Reynolds* [2017] EWCA Crim 57.

Where the defendant has the means to satisfy both confiscation and compensation orders, the court has the power to make both orders but must be alert to the risk of double accounting and the risk of making a disproportionate confiscation order; *R. v Davenport* [2015] EWCA Crim 1731; [2016] 1 Cr. App. R. (S.) 41. Ordinarily, the court should not make a confiscation order in the full benefit sum where there had been actual restitution to the victims before the confiscation hearing. The court must examine with care assertions that restitution will be made after the confiscation hearing. If the court remains unsure that compensation would be paid, a confiscation order which included those sums would not ordinarily be disproportionate. The court must take a practical and realistic approach in deciding if restitution is assured. See also *R. v Jawad* [2013] EWCA Crim 644; [2013] 1 W.L.R. 3861.

Payment by parent or guardian

16-018 Where the offender is a juvenile, the judge *must* order his parent or guardian to pay the order (SA 2020 s.140), unless he is satisfied that:

(1) the parent or guardian cannot be found; or
(2) it would be unreasonable to so order, having regard to the circumstances of the case.

Where the offender has reached the age of 16, this provision has effect as if, instead of imposing a duty on a parent or guardian to pay, it confers a power on the court to make an order. In such a procedure it is the parent or guardian's means which need to be taken into account, not those of the juvenile.

Form of order: (1) joint orders

16-019 Where an offender is convicted of a number of offences:

(1) and a number of different victims are involved, a separate order must be made in respect of each offence, in respect of each amount (*R. v Oddy* (1974) 59 Cr. App. R. 66; *R. v Inwood* (1974) 60 Cr. App. R. 70);
(2) where there is only one victim, but several offences, one compendious order covering all the amounts, while not desirable, is not objectionable (*R. v Wharton* [1976] Crim. L.R. 320);
(3) where the offender's means are insufficient to meet claims by a number of victims, the amount of any compensation ordered should generally be apportioned pro rata among them, but there may be cases where there are good

reasons for departing from this general rule (*R. v Amey* (1983) 76 Cr. App. R. 206); and

(4) it is technically permissible, though undesirable, to make a joint order against two or more offenders; a separate order should be made in respect of each offender.

Form of order: (2) joint orders; several offenders

An order is not an additional penalty which gives rise to adjustment of sentence or to claims of disparity. An order may be made against one or more co-offenders who have assets, and yet not against a third who has none (*R. v Love* [1999] 1 Cr. App. R. (S.) 75). **16-020**

Where two or more offenders are charged jointly and one claimant establishes a claim against them with regard to one item, each ought, in general, to be ordered to pay in equal proportions, unless one of them is shown to be more directly responsible for the offence, or their ability to pay is markedly different (*R. v Grundy* [1974] 1 All E.R. 292; [1974] Crim. L.R. 128).

Where there are competing claims for limited funds, the total compensation available should normally be apportioned on a pro rata basis (*R. v Miller* [1976] Crim. L.R. 694).

Order made on appeal

Where an order is made on appeal, it is deemed, if it was made on an appeal brought from magistrates' court, to have been made by that court, and if it was made on appeal from the Crown Court or the CACD, to have been made by the Crown Court (SA 2020 s.143(7)). **16-021**

Enforcement of orders

In general, compensation is treated in the same way, for the purposes of enforcement, as a fine (see FINES). **16-022**

As with fines and other money payments due to the court, there is power to allow time for payment, or to order payment by instalments.

The superior courts have said that:

(1) an order ought to be sharp in its effect and not protracted by small amounts over a long period (*R. v Bradburn* (1973) 57 Cr. App. R. 948; *R. v Daly* (1974) 58 Cr. App. R. 333);

(2) where the offender is sentenced at the same time to a custodial term, the judge should direct the first of any instalments to be paid within a specified time of his release (*R. v Bradburn* (1973) 57 Cr. App. R. 948).

Despite a number of decisions to the contrary, the CACD said in *R. v Olliver* (1989) 11 Cr. App. R. (S.) 10 that there is no reason in principle why an order to pay a fine by instalments should not extend beyond a period of 12 months, even to a period of two or three years. See also *R. v Dickinson* [2010] EWCA Crim 2143; [2011] 1 Cr. App. R. (S.) 93 and *R. v Cooper* [2017] EWCA Crim 262.

No default sentence

The Crown Court does not fix any term of imprisonment in default, but may allow time to pay and payment of compensation by instalments. As enforcement is **16-023** carried out by the magistrates' court, the figures listed in Sch.4 to the MCA 1980 will apply. The maximum is 12 months. If the amount of the compensation order exceeds £20,000 and the Crown Court considers that the magistrates' courts terms are inadequate, the Crown Court may make an order that the maximum term of imprisonment should be a figure which reflects those in the table applicable to fines (see SA 2020 s.129).

(AJA 1970 s.41(8) and Sch.9).

Payment under order

16-024 The person in whose favour a compensation order is made is not entitled to receive any sum(s) due to him until the possibility of an appeal on which the order could be varied or set aside has expired, though the power of the Crown Court to give leave to appeal out of time is to be disregarded.

Where an order is made in respect of an offence taken into consideration on sentence, that order ceases to have effect if the offender successfully appeals against his conviction for the substantive offence(s), or if the CACD annuls the order.

An offender may appeal against an order as if it were part of the sentence imposed in respect of the offence(s) of which he was convicted (SA 2020 s.141).

Compensation out of forfeited property

16-025 Where the court makes an order under SA 2020 s.153 (see FORFEITURE AND DEPRIVATION ORDERS) in a case where:

(1) the offender has been convicted of an offence which has resulted in a person suffering personal injury, loss or damage; or
(2) any such offence is taken into consideration on sentence; and
(3) the judge is satisfied that, but for the inadequacy of the offender's means, he would have made a compensation order under which the offender would have been required to pay compensation of an amount not less than a specified amount,

he may also order that any proceeds which arise from the disposal of the property, and which do not exceed the sum specified, be paid to that person.

Such an order will not be effective:

(a) before the expiration of six months from the date on which the forfeiture order was made; or
(b) if a successful application is made under SA 2020 s.157 or s.1(1) of the Police (Property) Act 1897.

(SA 2020 s.159)

As to the position in relation to a confiscation order made under POCA 2002 Pt 1, see CONFISCATION ORDERS.

Review of order

16-026 At any time before the offender has paid into court the whole amount of any order made, and once there is no further possibility of an appeal, the court responsible for enforcing the order may, on the application of the offender, either discharge or reduce the amount remaining to be paid under the order if it appears that:

(1) the injury, loss or damage in respect of which it was made has been held in

civil proceedings to be less than it was taken to be for the purposes of the order;

(2) where the order is in respect of the loss of property, the property has been recovered by the victim;

(3) the offender's means are insufficient to satisfy in full the compensation order and any confiscation order, unlawful profit order or slavery and trafficking reparation order made in the same proceedings; or

(4) the offender has suffered a substantial reduction in his means which was not expected at the time the order was made, and that they are unlikely to increase for a considerable period (*R. v Palmer* (1994) 15 Cr. App. R. (S.) 550),

provided the consent of a judge of the Crown Court has been obtained (which will be unlikely to be withheld if the offender is unable to pay (*R. v Favell* [2010] EWCA Crim 2948)).

(SA 2020 s.143)

A copy of any application made by an offender to the enforcing magistrates' court, containing the information specified by CrimPR 28.5, will be served on the Crown Court officer, who will serve a copy on the person for whose benefit the compensation order was made. The magistrates' court must not vary or discharge the compensation order unless the offender and the person for whose benefit it was made have each had an opportunity to make representations at a hearing (whether or not either in fact attends); and where the order was made in the Crown Court, the Crown Court has notified its consent.

17. CONFISCATION ORDERS

QUICK GUIDE

1. GENERAL

The orders under POCA 2002

17-001 In respect of an offence committed after 24 March 2003 a judge of the Crown Court may make:

(1) *a confiscation order* (s.6) for the purpose of recovering from an offender:
   (a) having a "criminal lifestyle"—the benefit of his "general criminal conduct" (see 17-021); and
   (b) who has been convicted of particular offences—the benefit of his "particular criminal" conduct, (see 17-021); and

(2) *a restraint order* (s.41), prohibiting the dealing with property, where:
   (a) a criminal investigation has been started with regard to an offence; and
   (b) there is reasonable cause to believe that the alleged offender has benefited from his "criminal conduct".

He may also appoint a *receiver* to realise any property, and to apply the proceeds to discharging any sum due under a confiscation order (see RESTRAINT ORDERS).

Under POCA 2002 Pt 8 Ch.2 a judge also has powers to make a number of orders in connection with confiscation investigations (see INVESTIGATIVE ORDERS AND WARRANTS).

Jurisdiction

17-002 Where an offender is, in relation to offences committed on or after 24 March 2003:

(1) convicted of an offence or offences in proceedings (see *R. v Moulden* [2008] EWCA Crim 3561; [2009] 1 Cr. App. R. 27) before the Crown Court; or
(2) committed to the Crown Court for sentence; or
(3) committed to the Crown Court in respect of an offence or offences under POCA 2002 s.70 (committal with a view to a confiscation order being made);

and either:

(a) the prosecutor asks the court to proceed under this provision; or
(b) the judge believes it is appropriate to do so,

the judge *must* proceed to hold a "section 6 enquiry" for the purpose of investigating and deciding whether the offender has benefited from his criminal conduct.

Section 6 contains no definition of "prosecutor", but see POCA 2002 s.40(9) (b) which states that

> "references in this Part to the prosecutor are to the person the court believes is to have conduct of any proceedings for the offence."

Furthermore, the CACD held in *R. (on the application of Virgin Medilotd) v Zinga* [2014] EWCA Crim 52; [2014] 1 Cr. App. R. 27 that the term "prosecutor" is to be read throughout Pt 2 in that wide sense which must include all prosecutors including a private prosecutor.

Paragraphs (1)–(3) above are not satisfied if the accused absconds, but in such a case POCA 2002 s.27 may apply (see offender absconding at 17-054).

Date is of the essence; the provisions of POCA 2002 in relation to confiscation orders have no effect where the offence(s) were committed before March 24, 2003. If the prosecutor does not rely on a pre-commencement offence for the purpose of the confiscation proceedings, POCA 2002 applies (*R. v Aslam* [2004] EWCA Crim 2801; [2005] 1 Cr. App. R. (S.) 116). There may be cases (e.g. where there is more than one indictment) where more than one legislative framework may apply e.g. under CJA 1988 and POCA 2002 (e.g. *R. v Moulden* [2008] EWCA Crim 2561; [2009] 1 Cr. App. R. 27).

An offence committed over a period of two or more days (or during a period of days) is to be taken to have been committed on the first day. There is no limitation on the date of the commission of offences to be taken into consideration.

Where the criteria in s.6 are satisfied, the court is, subject to s.6(6), under a duty to make a confiscation order against an offender. Where s.6(6) applies (victim starting or intending to start proceedings in respect of loss, injury or damage), that duty is to be treated as a power.

An order must be made whether or not the offender receives a discharge, absolute or conditional (*R. v Varma* [2012] UKSC 42; [2013] 1 Cr. App. R. 8). In *R. v Waya* [2012] UKSC 51; [2013] 2 Cr. App. R. (S.) 20, the Supreme Court held that s.6(5)(b) should be read subject to the qualification "except insofar as such an order would be disproportionate and thus a breach" of art.1 of the First Protocol to ECHR (A1P1). SCA 2015 subsequently inserted into s.6(5)(b) the words

> "paragraph (b) applies only if, or to the extent that, it would not be disproportionate to require the defendant to pay the recoverable amount".

Procedure

CrimPR 33 sets out detailed procedures for the making of confiscation and other orders: **17-003**

(1) CrimPR 33.1–33.12: general rules applying to confiscation and related proceedings;
(2) CrimPR 33.13–33.27: rules applicable only to confiscation proceedings;
(3) CrimPR 33.32–33.50: general rules applicable to both restraint and receivership proceedings;

(4) CrimPR 33.51–33.55: rules applicable only to restraint proceedings;
(5) CrimPR 33.56–33.63: rules applicable only to receivership proceedings; and
(6) CrimPR 33.64–33.69: confiscation proceedings under CJA 1988 and DTA 1994.

It is important that confiscation hearings take place in good time after the offender is convicted or sentenced.

Applications for restraint orders should be determined by the Resident Judge, or a judge nominated by the Resident Judge, at the Crown Court location at which they are lodged.

In order to prevent possible dissipation of assets of significant value, applications under POCA should be considered urgent when lists are being fixed. In order to prevent potential prejudice, applications for the variation and discharge of orders, for the appointment of receivers, and applications to punish alleged breaches of orders as a contempt of court should similarly be treated as urgent and listed expeditiously.

(*CPD* XIII G.9–11)

Nature of order; proportionality

17-004 The term "confiscation" employed by the Act has a possible tendency to mislead. "It is not confiscation in the sense in which schoolchildren and others understand it" (per Lord Bingham in *R. v May* [2008] UKHL 28; [2008] 2 Cr. App. R. 28).

> "It does not in itself appropriate ownership of any assets. No property is escheat to the Crown; [it] is essentially an additional monetary penalty upon the offender. Unless an administration order is made, the means of enforcement of that penalty is assimilated to a fine" (per Lord Eassie in *Voudouri v HM Advocate* [2008] HCJAC 34; 2008 J.C. 431, a case under parallel Scots legislation).

Though draconian, the provisions are not penal in nature; their purpose is to deprive an offender of that which is not rightfully his. The benefit gained is the total value of the property or advantage obtained, not the net profit after deduction of expenses or any amount payable to co-conspirators (*R. v May* [2008] UKHL 28; [2008] 2 Cr. App. R. 28).

AIPI imports the requirement that there must be a reasonable relationship of proportionality between the means employed by the state in, inter alia, the deprivation of property as a form of penalty, and the legitimate aim which is sought to be realised by the deprivation (*R. v Waya* [2012] UKSC 51; [2013] 2 Cr. App. R. (S.) 20). Where, therefore, there is total restoration of the property obtained it should not be treated as "benefit". See also *R. v Axworthy* [2012] EWCA Crim 2889; *R. v Hursthouse* [2013] EWCA Crim 517; *R. v Jawad* [2013] EWCA Crim 644; [2014] 1 Cr. App. R. (S.) 16. SCA 2015 subsequently inserted into s.6(5)(b) the words

> "paragraph (b) applies only if, or to the extent that, it would not be disproportionate to require the defendant to pay the recoverable amount".

In *R. v Andrewes* [2022] UKSC 24, the Supreme Court held that where an offender had obtained remuneration through obtaining employment by false representations or non-disclosure, and where, through the performance of services, the offender had given full value for the earnings received, it would normally be disproportionate under the Proceeds of Crime Act 2002 Pt 2 s.6(5) to confiscate all the net earnings made. However, it would be proportionate to confiscate the difference between the higher earnings made as a result of the fraud and the lower earnings that the offender would have made had they not committed the fraud.

Where a finding of joint obtaining is made, whether against a single offender or more than one, the confiscation order against each offender should be made for the whole value of the benefit thus obtained, but should include a proviso that it is not to be enforced to the extent that a sum has been recovered by way of satisfaction of another confiscation order made *in relation to the same joint benefit*. A subsequent confiscation order made against a later-tried offender in relation to the same benefit may well be such an order. In theory a judge may therefore need to consider whether to stay the enforcement of a confiscation order made against one or more offenders to await the outcome of a later criminal trial against others in respect of the same criminal conspiracy. However, except perhaps when a second trial is imminent, it will not normally be appropriate bearing in mind the purpose of POCA 2002 and the statutory stipulation for a speedy hearing. Orders made on the basis of lifestyle assumptions will require special consideration on their facts (*R. v Ahmad* [2014] UKSC 36; [2014] 3 W.L.R. 23).

In *R. v Dad* [2014] EWCA Crim 2478; [2015] Crim. L.R. 356 the CACD held that an *Ahmad* proviso will not be required in every joint benefit case where the assumptions have been applied. Much will depend on the particular circumstances.

In *Collins v DPP* [2021] EWHC 634 (Admin); [2021] 1 W.L.R. 3391, the Divisional Court rejected the argument that in a case where confiscation orders have been made in respect of a benefit jointly obtained by two or more defendants (but with a direction that the orders are not to be enforced to the extent that a sum has been recovered by way of satisfaction of another confiscation order made in relation to the same joint benefit) credit should be given to each defendant for time served in default of payment by any of his or her accomplices.

The judge who assesses benefit is required to focus upon the property which the offender originally obtained. There is nothing in the wording of POCA which requires him to deduct the residual value of chattels after prolonged use. Nor does European jurisprudence require that such a deduction be made.

If an offender:

(1) obtains chattels as a result of his criminal conduct;
(2) uses them for a substantial period, thereby materially reducing their value; and
(3) those chattels are ultimately restored to their true owners,

the judge in assessing the offender's benefit should not give credit for the residual value of those chattels. Such an order is not disproportionate (*R. v Harvey* [2013] EWCA Crim 1104; [2014] 1 Cr. App. R. (S.) 46 reversed in part by *R. v Harvey* [2015] UKSC 73; [2016] 1 Cr. App. R. (S.) 60).

It is open for the prosecutor and the offender to agree a figure for realisable assets, but, consistent with his obligations to make a confiscation order under s.6, the judge cannot simply accept that figure without the offender disclosing, and the prosecutor accepting, the assets that make up the agreed valuation. Where there are "hidden assets" it is not open to the prosecutor and the offender to settle the amount to pay (*Telli v RCPO* [2007] EWCA Civ 1385; [2008] 2 Cr. App. R. (S.) 48).

See also *Jennings v CPS* [2008] UKHL 29; [2008] 2 Cr. App. R. 29; *R. v Green* [2008] UKHL 30; [2009] 1 Cr. App. R. 30; *R. v Sivaraman* [2008] EWCA Crim 1736; [2009] 1 Cr. App. R. (S.) 80.

2. Obligation to hold s.6 enquiry

Prosecutor's duty

17-005 Section 6 does not make confiscation proceedings automatic in every case where some benefit has been obtained by criminal conduct.

The prosecutor has a duty to decide in each case:

(1) whether to ask the judge to apply the provisions of s.6; and
(2) on what basis to put their claim, if they make one.

It is open to the judge:

(a) to permit confiscation proceedings to be withdrawn at any stage, or to permit them to be compromised; or
(b) as in any other criminal proceedings, to stay them where they amount to an abuse of the court's process.

The power to stay proceedings may be exercised where it would be oppressive to seek confiscation, or oppressive in the circumstances of the case, but that "oppression" must be real and the proceedings ought not to be stayed merely because the judge disagrees with the prosecutor's decision to seek confiscation (*R. v Shabir* [2008] EWCA Crim 1809; [2009] 1 Cr. App. R. (S.) 84; see also *R. v Parveez* [2017] EWCA Crim 873; [2017] Crim. L.R. 891). Abuse of process cannot be founded on the basis that the proper application of the legislative structure might produce an "oppressive" result with which the judge is unhappy; to conclude that proceedings taken in accordance with the statute constitute an abuse of process is tantamount to asserting a power to dispense with the statute, which, as a matter of principle, is impermissible (*CPS v Nelson* [2009] EWCA Crim 1573; [2010] 1 Cr. App. R. (S.) 82, applied in *R. v Beazley* [2013] EWCA Crim 567; [2013] 1 W.L.R. 3331).

Where the judge gives the offender an unequivocal representation (to which the prosecutor does not object) that confiscation proceedings will not proceed if the offender repays the benefit obtained from his criminal conduct and the offender has done so, it is an abuse of process for the court to proceed with the application. For the judge to give an offender an inducement and then renege on his indication after the offender has acted on that inducement to his disadvantage would damage the integrity of the process of criminal justice. See *R. (on the application of Secretary of State for Work and Pensions) v Croydon Crown Court* [2010] EWHC 805 (Admin); [2011] 1 Cr. App. R. (S.) 1; also *R. v LM* [2010] EWCA Crim 2327; [2011] 1 Cr. App. R. 12.

Postponement of the enquiry

17-006 The judge may either:

(1) proceed under s.6 before he sentences the offender (s.14(1)(a)); or
(2) postpone proceedings under s.6 for a specified period (s.14(1)(b)) where, e.g. he requires further information before proceeding.

The specified period referred to in (2) above, must not exceed two years from the date of conviction (see postponement at 17-037).

It is important if he "postpones" the proceedings in any way, that the judge indicates whether he is doing so under s.14(1)(a) or (b), to avoid the sort of problems which arose in *CPS Swansea v Gilleeney* [2009] EWCA Crim 193; [2009] 2 Cr. App. R. (S.) 80. Whether it is described as an adjournment or a relisting, a judicial decision to put the hearing back to a later date constitutes a postponement (*R. v Neish* [2010] EWCA Crim 1011; [2011] 1 Cr. App. R. (S.) 33, where the judge gave instructions to the listing officer and the listing officer carried out those instructions). An adjournment sine die amounts to a decision not to proceed under s.6 and confers a right of appeal on the prosecutor.

It is important that confiscation hearings take place in good time after the offender is convicted or sentenced (see 17-003). Where possible, the judge who conducted the trial or passed sentence should be the judge who conducts confiscation proceedings (see *R. v Knagg* [2009] EWCA Crim 1363; [2010] 1 Cr. App. R. (S.) 75).

When listing confiscation and related matters, court staff should consider the potential for such matters to encounter delay, and should take steps to ensure their swift listing and progression, and in particular have regard to the reasonable time requirement under ECHR art.6 which requires the total length of proceedings to be considered, not simply the time that elapses between hearings.

Where the judge proceeds under s.14(1)(b): **17-007**

(1) he must not, as part of that sentence include a fine, a financial order (other than a compensation order under SA 2020 s.133) or any of the forfeiture orders set out in 17-008 at (2); although; and
(2) if the offender is sentenced during the postponement period, the sentence may be varied by adding one of the prohibited orders, within 28 days starting with the last day of the period of postponement.

Section 14(8) provides that if proceedings are postponed for a period and an application to extend the period is made before it ends, the application may be granted even after the period ends.

Section 14(11) provides that a confiscation order must not be quashed only on the ground that there was a defect or omission in postponement.

Section 14(12) disapplies s.14(11) if, before the confiscation order was made, the court imposes a fine or a compensation order (etc.). In *R. v Guraj* [2015] EWCA Crim 305; [2015] 2 Cr. App. R. (S.) 21 the CACD took a strict view of s.14(12) and held that where the court had made a forfeiture order before making the confiscation order, s.14(12) prevented the prosecution from relying upon s.14(11). However this decision was reversed in *R. v Guraj* [2016] UKSC 65; [2017] 1 Cr. App. R. (S.) 32. The Supreme Court concluded that, irrespective of s.14(11), the correct approach to a failure to observe procedural provisions was to ask whether Parliament must have intended invalidity of the confiscation order even if there was no injustice or unfairness to the defendant. A failure to apply for a further postponement did not remove jurisdiction to make an order. The correct analysis was that a failure to follow the correct statutory procedure raised the very real possibility that it would be unfair to make an order, but jurisdiction to make an order remained. An order should not be made unless the court is satisfied that no substantial unfairness will ensue. Unfairness might ensue after a long period of inactivity, and is especially likely if the two-year period was exceeded without exceptional circumstances.

Relationship between order and sentence

17-008 The judge may pass sentence for the offence(s) of which the offender has been convicted either *before* making an order, as where he postpones his duty to conduct a s.6 enquiry (see 17-006), or *after* making an order.

If he knows that he will be carrying out fact-finding exercises in relation to the same offender at a later stage, the judge will need to take care in his sentencing remarks not to express himself in a manner that may sensibly be perceived to show that he is unlikely to believe anything the offender is likely to tell him. If remarks of that nature are pertinent to explaining his sentence, the judge will need to recuse himself from conducting any subsequent fact-finding exercise (*R. v Odewale* [2005] EWCA Crim 709; [2005] 2 Cr. App. R. (S.) 202).

The offender cannot rely in mitigation on the fact that a confiscation order has been made or will be made against him.

Where a confiscation is made *before* sentence the judge must take account of it before imposing:

(1) a fine, or any order involving payment by the offender, other than an order under SA 2020 s.46 (criminal courts charge) or a "priority order";
(2) a forfeiture order under MDA 1971 s.27; a deprivation order under SA 2020 s.153; or a forfeiture order under TerrA 2000 s.23 or s.23A.

(POCA 2002 ss.13(1)–(4))

Subject to the above, the judge must leave the confiscation order out of account in deciding the appropriate sentence for the offender (s.13(4)).

A "priority order" is:

(a) a compensation order under SA 2020 s.133;
(b) a surcharge order under SA 2020 s.42;
(c) an unlawful profit order under PSHFA 2013 s.4; and
(d) a slavery and trafficking reparation order under MSA 2015 s.8.

If the court makes a confiscation order and one or more priority orders, and the judge believes that the offender will not have sufficient means to pay them all in full, the court must direct that so much of the amount payable under the priority order(s) is to be paid out of any sums recovered under the confiscation order (POCA 2002 s.13(5)–(6)).

In *R. v Beaumont* [2014] EWCA Crim 1664; [2015] 1 Cr. App. R. (S.) 1 the CACD held that, where the court has made both a confiscation order and a compensation order, it was generally not appropriate to take the value of a family or matrimonial home into account in deciding whether to make an order under s.13(6). However, in *R. v Parkinson* [2015] EWCA Crim 1448; [2016] 1 Cr. App. R. (S.) 6 the CACD held that *Beaumont* was not authority for a general principle that a compensation order should not be made where the order would force the sale of the matrimonial home. See also *R. v Reynolds* [2017] EWCA Crim 57 for a recent application of *Parkinson*.

There is nothing to prevent the judge combining a confiscation order with a discharge, whether absolute or conditional, on the same count of an indictment; indeed where the criteria in s.6 are satisfied, subject to s.6(6), the judge has a duty to do so (see *R. v Varma* [2012] UKSC 42; [2013] 1 Cr. App. R. 8 at 17-002).

A sentence already imposed may be *varied* within 28 days of the last day of the postponement period (as set out in s.15(3)).

As to the *subsequent reconsideration* of an order, see 17-038.

Agreements by the offender to pay compensation

There is no power which enables the judge, in an appropriate case, to make a POCA confiscation order and to couple with it an order that compensation be paid to the loser out of it, save in the limited case of insufficient assets provided for by s.13(5) and (6) (as amended) (17-008). **17-009**

In *R. v Davenport* [2015] EWCA Crim 1731; [2016] 1 Cr. App. R. (S.) 41 the CACD provided step by step guidance on the approach to adopt where the defendant does have the means to satisfy both a confiscation order and a compensation order, interpreting *Jawad* [2013] EWCA Crim 644; [2014] 1 Cr. App. R. (S.) 16 in the light of *Waya*. In summary:

(1) the court is empowered to make both a confiscation order and a compensation order;
(2) however, the court should be alert to any risk of double counting and the risk of making a confiscation order which is disproportionate;
(3) the court ordinarily should not make both a compensation order and a confiscation order representing the full amount of the benefit where there has been actual restitution to the victims prior to the date of the confiscation hearing;
(4) where the defendant asserts that restitution will be made *after* the date of the hearing then the court should scrutinise very carefully the evidence and arguments raised in support of that assertion;
(5) if the court remains uncertain whether the victims will be repaid under the compensation order then a confiscation order which includes that amount will not ordinarily be disproportionate;
(6) however, mathematical certainty of restitution is not required. The court should approach matters in a practical and realistic way;
(7) restitution to the victims in the future is capable of properly being assessed as assured, depending on the particular circumstances, even if it will not be immediate. The longer the time frame the stronger the argument that restitution is not assured: but a prospective period of delay in realisation is not of itself necessarily a conclusive reason for proceeding to make a combination of such orders without adjusting the amount of the confiscation order;
(8) whilst a defendant who is truly intent on making restitution in full to his victims ordinarily should be expected to have arranged such restitution prior to the date of the confiscation hearing there may sometimes be cases where that is not possible. If, in such a case, the court has firm and evidence-based grounds for believing that restitution may nevertheless be forthcoming, albeit that cannot be taken as "assured" at the time of the hearing, the court has power in its discretion to order an adjournment; and

(9) each case must be decided on its own facts and circumstances.

3. ENFORCEMENT OF ORDER

Time for payment; interest

17-010 The amount ordered to be paid must ordinarily be paid on the day on which the order is made.

However, if the court is satisfied that the offender cannot pay the full amount on that day, it may specify the period within which the amount (or periods relating to specific amounts) must be paid, not exceeding three months from the date of the confiscation order.

Where the offender makes an application within the specified period, in which he demonstrates that he is unable to pay despite having made all reasonable efforts, the judge may extend the specified period to a maximum of six months from the date of the confiscation order.

(POCA 2002 s.11)

An order may be made after the expiry of the date originally specified, but not after the expiry of the six months from the date the order was made.

No extension may be granted unless the prosecutor is given an opportunity to make representations.

The period of time allowed for payment runs from the date the order is made, not from the determination of an appeal against the order. It would be wrong as a matter of principle for offenders to be encouraged to believe that the bringing of an appeal would be likely to lengthen the time allowed for payment (*R. v May* [2008] UKHL 28; [2008] 2 Cr. App. R. 28).

Where any amount required to be paid under the order is not paid when it is required to be paid, interest falls to be paid on that amount for the period for which it remains unpaid (at the rate for the time being specified in the Judgments Act 1838 s.17, in relation to civil debts), unless:

(a) an application has been made under s.11(4) for an extension of time;
(b) that application has not been determined by the court; and
(c) the period of six months starting with the day on which the order was made has not ended.

(POCA 2002 s.12)

The amount of the interest is to be treated as part of the amount to be paid under the confiscation order (and see *R. (on the application of Gibson) v Secretary of State for Justice* [2018] UKSC 2; [2018] 1 Cr. App. R. (S.) 51).

Compliance order

17-011 Where the court has made a confiscation order, it may make such order as it believes is appropriate for the purpose of ensuring that the confiscation order is effective. This is a "compliance order".

When the court makes the confiscation order, it must consider whether to also make a compliance order. Thereafter the court must consider any application for a compliance order made by the prosecutor.

(POCA 2002 s.13A)

In deciding whether to make such an order, the court must in particular consider whether any restriction or prohibition on travel outside the UK should be imposed.

A compliance order may be varied or discharged on application by the prosecutor or any person affected by the order.

In *R. v Pritchard* [2017] EWCA Crim 1267; [2017] 2 Cr. App. R. (S.) 54, the CACD provided some guidance on the power to make a compliance order. The wording of s.13A is that the court must believe it is appropriate to make a compliance order for ensuring the confiscation order is effective. That is not the same as it being "necessary". "Appropriate" does not require any gloss. An order should only be made if there is a proper reason for so doing, and that would depend on the facts and circumstances of the individual case. The determination of whether an order is justified involves considerations of proportionality. In considering a travel restriction, the court must strike a balance between ensuring the effectiveness of the confiscation order and the impact on the defendant. Indefinite travel restrictions should be the exception rather than the rule. The length of any travel restriction is matter for the judge, with relevant factors including the time left to be served under any custodial sentence and how much time was reasonably required to ensure the effectiveness of the confiscation order. It would be good practice to state expressly on the face of the order that the travel restriction would expire in any event on satisfaction in full of the confiscation order, and to refer expressly to the s.13A(5) right to apply for variation or discharge.

The procedure for applying for a compliance order is set out at CrimPR 33.14.

As to appeals against the making of a compliance order, see APPEALS FROM THE CROWN COURT.

Term of imprisonment in default

The judge must fix a term of imprisonment to be served in default of payment (POCA 2002 s.35). Sections 129(1)–(3) and (5) and 132(1)–(4) of the SA 2020 apply as if the amount ordered to be paid were a fine imposed on the defendant. The maximum terms are those set out in the table below: **17-012**

Amount	**Maximum term**
£10,000 or less	6 months
More than £10,000 but no more than £500,000	5 years
More than £500,000 but no more than £1 million	7 years
More than £1 million	14 years

The default term imposed should be within the permitted maximum so as to make clear to the offender that he has nothing to gain by failing to comply with the order (see *R. v Szrajber* (1994) 15 Cr. App. R. (S.) 821; *R. v French* (1995) 16 Cr. App. R. (S.) 841; *R. v Smith* [2003] EWCA Crim 344; *R. v Qema* [2006] EWCA Crim 1736; *R. v Liscott* [2007] EWCA Crim 1706; *R. v Howard* [2007] EWCA Crim 1489 considered in *R. v Pigott* [2009] EWCA Crim 2292; [2010] 2 Cr. App. R. (S.) 16).

The judge has a discretion up to the maximum period in the table; he is not bound to follow any arithmetical approach, but should consider the circumstances, bearing in mind that the purpose of the default sentence is to secure payment of the amount ordered (*R. v Pigott* [2009] EWCA Crim 2292; [2010] 2 Cr. App. R. (S.) 16, where the legislation is considered). The imposing of the sentence for the offence and the fixing of the default sentence are thus two separate exercises and the judge is not restrained by the "totality principle" in respect of the two terms; see *R. v Price* [2009] EWCA Crim 2918; [2010] 2 Cr. App. R. (S.) 44; also *R. v Aspinwell* [2010] EWCA Crim 1294; [2011] 1 Cr. App. R. (S.) 54.

Enforcement is as for a fine imposed by the Crown Court (see SA 2020 s.129(3)), with modifications disapplying MCA 1980 s.75 (allowing time to pay—see *CPS v Greenacre* [2007] EWHC 1193 (Admin)), s.81 (young offenders), s.85 (remittal) and s.87 (means enquiry).

In *Collins v DPP* [2021] EWHC 634 (Admin); [2021] 1 W.L.R. 3391, the Divisional Court rejected the argument that in a case where confiscation orders have been made in respect of a benefit jointly obtained by two or more defendants (but with a direction that the orders are not to be enforced to the extent that a sum has been recovered by way of satisfaction of another confiscation order made in relation to the same joint benefit) credit should be given to each defendant for time served in default of payment by any of his or her co-defendants.

The provisions of SA 2020 s.129(3) prevent immediate committal to prison. Where the offender serves a term of imprisonment or detention in default of paying any amount due under a confiscation order, his serving that term does not prevent the confiscation order from continuing to have effect so far as any other method of enforcement is concerned.

In *R. v Mills* [2018] EWCA Crim 944; [2018] 2 Cr. App. R. (S.) 32, the CACD confirmed that the prosecution cannot appeal against a default term, but observed that this was unsatisfactory, it being desirable for the prosecution to be able to challenge the default term where the judge had erred in his assessment.

Fixing the term

17-013 The following principles emerge from the authorities for the guidance of judges fixing the period of imprisonment to be served in default of payment of a confiscation order, in accordance with the appropriate scale (set out in 17-012).

The principles to be applied in setting the term in default were distilled in *R. v Castillo* [2011] EWCA Crim 3173; [2012] Crim. L.R. 401 (a case under CJA 1988 s.71) as follows:

(1) it is of the first importance to have in mind that the purpose of a default term is to secure payment of the confiscation order;
(2) it is not the judge's function to find an arithmetical match between the amount of the order and the length of the term, such that for any given band or bracket prescribed in the Act an order at the bottom of the band should attract a default term likewise at the bottom of the band, an order in the middle of the band should attract a term in the middle or an order at the top should attract a term at the top;
(3) the judge should not be influenced by the overall totality of the sentence passed for the crime plus the default term; but
(4) for any given band, he should have regard to the maximum amount of a confiscation order within the band and the maximum default term within the band; and
(5) given principle (4), and especially in a case falling within the top band (an amount exceeding £1m) where there is no maximum confiscation order but only a maximum default term—10 (now 14) years' imprisonment, regard must be had to the requirement of proportionality; though it should be noted that the demands of proportionality are much weaker here, where the

purpose of the default term is to secure satisfaction of the confiscation order, than where the judge is punishing the offender.

Enforcement as fine; receivers

Where a confiscation order is made, the court's functions as to fines and their enforcement (PCC(S)A 2000 ss.139(2)–(3) and (9) and 140(1)–(4); (SA 2020 s.129(1)–(3) and s.132(1)–(4))) apply as if the amount ordered to be paid were a fine imposed on the offender by the court making the order (POCA 2002 s.35(1)). **17-014**

In addition the judge:

(1) *may*, on the application of the prosecutor, appoint an enforcement receiver, where a confiscation is made and not satisfied (and is not subject to appeal) and confer on him the powers in s.51; and
(2) *must*, where a management receiver has been appointed under any restraint order, order him to transfer any property held by him to the enforcement receiver (POCA 2002 s.50).

There is nothing in POCA 2002 to prevent enforcement through the machinery available in civil law (see *Designated Officer for Sunderland Magistrates' Court v Krager* [2011] EWHC 3283 (Ch); [2012] 1 W.L.R. 1291).

4. SECTION 6 ENQUIRY: PROCEDURE

Enquiry is a precondition

A s.6 enquiry is a mandatory precondition to the making of a confiscation order. **17-015**
The judge may sentence an offender before making a confiscation order, but in relation to offences committed:

(1) *on or before 23 March 2003*, if he proceeds to sentence without ruling on whether or not there should be an enquiry, he may not make a confiscation order (*R. v Ross* [2001] Crim. L.R. 405);
(2) *on or after 24 March 2003*, he should consider whether to make an order or hold an enquiry before moving to sentence, and he must do so before he is entitled to impose a fine, compensation, forfeiture or deprivation of property.

Confiscation proceedings are not a criminal trial to which the presumption of innocence applies but part of the sentencing process in respect of a convicted offender (see *R. v Gavin* [2010] EWCA Crim 2727; [2011] 1 Cr. App. R. (S.) 126; *R. v Bhanji* [2011] EWCA Crim 1198). Following the principles set out in *R. v Jones* [2002] UKHL 5; [2002] Cr. App. R. 9, where an offender is absent from confiscation proceedings, otherwise than where he has absconded (as to which, see POCA 2002 ss.6(8), 27 and 28 (17-054)), the judge has a discretion to proceed in his absence, even where the absence is involuntary (e.g. due to chronic illness; *R. v Bhanji* [2011] EWCA Crim 1198; also *R. v Ali* [2014] EWCA Crim 1658; [2015] Crim L.R. 88).

As to the court's powers of postponement, see 17-037.

Confiscation proceedings are an extension of the sentencing hearing and are therefore criminal in nature although not proceedings to which the strict rules of evidence apply. In *R. v Clipston* [2011] EWCA Crim 446; [2011] 2 Cr. App. R. (S.) 101 the CACD opined that hearsay evidence is admissible, stating that where admissibility is contested, having regard to the nature of the proceedings and the need for fairness to both sides, the statutory provisions of CJA 2003 are the appropriate framework, not the provisions of CEA 1995.

In *Ihenacho v Croydon LBC* [2021] EWCA Crim 798; [2021] 5 WLUK 381 the CACD considered there to be clear authority that it is possible for a defendant to be unfit to plead in confiscation proceedings and, in certain circumstances, for the confiscation hearing to continue and statutory assumptions to apply. (Note: The cases cited—*R. v Gavin* [2010] EWCA Crim 2727; [2010] 10 WLUK 641 and *R. v Ali (Salah)* [2014] EWCA Crim 1658; [2015] 1 W.L.R. 841—were decided on the basis of the defendants' absence and the focus in those cases was therefore on whether proceedings were "fair").

Statement of information

17-016 Where the judge is to proceed under s.6 in a case where:

(1) asked by the prosecutor to do so, he will be given a statement of information within such period as he orders; and
(2) he proceeds of his own motion, he will order the prosecutor to give him a statement of information, and the prosecutor must do so within such period as the judge orders.

(POCA 2002 s.16(1)–(2))

Where the prosecutor:

(a) *believes the offender has a "criminal lifestyle"*, that statement will be a statement of the matters he believes are relevant in connection with deciding whether the offender has a criminal lifestyle, whether he has benefited from his general criminal conduct and his benefit from the conduct, and it will include such information as he believes is relevant in connection with the making by the judge of any required assumption under s.10 (see 17-032) and for the purpose of enabling him to decide if the circumstances are such that he must not make such an assumption; and
(b) *does not believe that the offender has a criminal lifestyle*, the statement will be a statement of matters he believes are relevant in connection with deciding whether the offender has benefited from his "particular criminal conduct", and the benefit from the conduct.

Such a statement must also contain the information prescribed in CrimPR 33.13.

POCA 2002 s.16(6A) provides that a statement of information must also include information which the prosecutor believes is or would be relevant in enabling the court to decide whether to make an order under s.10A and, if so, what determination to make. Section 10A provides that where the judge concludes that the offender holds property which is likely to be realised to satisfy the confiscation order, and a person other than the offender holds or may hold an interest in it, the judge may (if he thinks it appropriate to do so) determine the extent of the offender's interest in the property. Such a determination is conclusive for the purposes of realising property to satisfy the confiscation order. In cases where there is a claim by an interested party, the court should make clear whether or not it thought it appropriate to make a determination under s.10A and give reasons for that decision (*R. v Ghulam* [2018] EWCA Crim 1691; [2018] Crim. L.R. 926). Care should be taken in completing Forms 5050 and 5050A to reflect the court's conclusion.

In *R. v Moore* [2021] EWCA Crim 956; [2021] 4 W.L.R. 121 it was said that where there are complex issues concerning beneficial entitlement to property, it may be preferable to allow the issue to be litigated at the enforcement stage with an enforcement receiver rather than determine the third party's interest under s.10A of the 2002 Act. The CACD remarked (obiter) that the case raised concerns about the fairness of the requirement that issues concerning the beneficial entitlement to property (in the context of confiscation proceedings under the POCA 2002) should always be determined in the Crown Court, instead of there being at least an option to transfer the more complex cases into the business and property courts.

In *R. v Ruto* [2021] EWCA Crim 1669; [2021] 10 WLUK 490 it was said at [17]–[18], that the principle "to be borne firmly in mind" by a judge when considering a disputed issue under the POCA 2002 s.10A, is found in *R. v Forte* [2020] EWCA Crim 1455; [2021] 4 W.L.R. 26 at [12]. Whilst it was not necessary in every case to provide a long and complex ruling, it was necessary to make clear findings of fact and to explain why they were made.

If the judge decides to make a determination under s.10A, he can order a further statement of information to include specified information relevant to that determination (s.16(6B)).

If the prosecutor gives the court a statement of information, he may at any time give a further statement, and must do so if the judge so orders, and within the period ordered (s.16(6)).

If the judge makes an order under this section he may at any time vary it by making another (s.16(7)).

Offender's response to statement

Where a statement of information is given to the judge and a copy is served on the offender, the judge may order him: **17-017**

(1) to indicate, within the period ordered, the extent to which he accepts each allegation in it; and
(2) so far as he does not accept an allegation, to give particulars of any matters he proposes to rely on.

If the offender:

(a) accepts to any extent an allegation in the statement the judge may treat his acceptance as conclusive of the matters to which it relates for the purpose of deciding the issues referred to in ss.16(3) or (5), as the case may be; or
(b) fails in any respect to comply with such an order he may be treated as accepting every allegation in the statement apart from:
    (i) any allegation in respect of which he has complied with the requirement; or
    (ii) any allegation that he has benefited from his general or particular criminal conduct.

(POCA 2002 s.17)

CrimPR 33.13 requires that the offender's response be given in writing to the prosecutor and a copy be given to the court, and emphasises that the judge must satisfy himself that the offender understands the potential consequences of a failure to comply with a direction to serve a response, which include those set out above and also the drawing of such inferences from the failure as the judge believes to be appropriate.

No acceptance under this section that the offender has benefited from conduct is admissible in evidence in proceedings for an offence.

An allegation may be accepted or particulars may be given in a manner ordered by the judge. If he makes an order under this provision he may at any time vary it by making another.

An offender who pleads guilty without challenging in any way the evidence for the prosecution, is not debarred thereby from challenging the prosecution evidence for the purposes of confiscation proceedings (*R. v Knaggs* [2009] EWCA Crim 1363; [2010] 1 Cr. App. R. (S.) 75).

Offender providing information: s.18 orders

17-018 Where the judge is proceeding under s.6 in a case where:

(1) he has been asked by the prosecutor to do so; or
(2) he proceeds of his own motion, or he is considering whether to proceed,

he may, for the purpose of obtaining information to help him in carrying out his functions (including his functions under s.10A), at any time order the offender to give him specified information, and such an order may require all, or a specified part, of the information to be given in a specified manner and before a specified date (POCA 2002 s.18).

Note that under s.18A, the court can, in considering the exercise of its powers under s.10A, also order the provision of information by an "interested person". An interested person is a person other than the defendant who the court thinks is or may be holding an interest in property in which the offender also may hold an interest.

Such information must be given in writing, and a copy must be sent to the prosecutor (CrimPR 33.13).

In respect of both s.18 and s.18A, where:

(a) the offender or interested person fails, without reasonable excuse, to comply with an order, the judge, quite apart from any power he may have to deal with him in respect of a failure to comply with an order under this section, may draw such inference as he believes to be appropriate; and
(b) the prosecutor accepts to any extent an allegation made by the offender or interested person in giving information required by the judge's order, or in any other statement given to the court in relation to any matter relevant in deciding the available amount under s.9, the judge may treat the acceptance as conclusive.

An allegation may be accepted in any manner the judge may order.

If the judge makes an order under these provisions he may at any time vary it by making another.

No information provided pursuant to s.18 or s.18A is admissible in evidence in proceedings against the person providing it for an offence.

Aims of the enquiry

17-019 The amount of a confiscation order under POCA 2002 s.6 is determined by reference:

(1) to the offender's benefit from his "general criminal conduct" where he is shown on conviction to have a "criminal lifestyle"; or
(2) where he does not have such a lifestyle, to his benefit from his "particular criminal conduct".

The judge must therefore investigate and decide:

(a) whether the offender has "a criminal lifestyle" (within the meaning of s.75, as to which see below);
(b) if he decides that he does have a "criminal lifestyle", whether he has "benefited" from his "general criminal conduct" (see 17-022);
(c) if he does *not* have a "criminal lifestyle" whether he has benefited from his "particular criminal conduct" (see 17-023); and
(d) finally, if he has benefited, what is recoverable from him (the "recoverable amount", as to which see 17-035).

However, the duty to make a confiscation order must be treated as a power (s.6(6)–(6A)) where:

(i) the victim of the conduct has started or intends to start proceedings against the offender in respect of loss, injury or damage sustained in connection with the conduct; or
(ii) an order has been, or may be, made against the offender under s.4 of PSHFA 2013, or a person has started or intends to start proceedings under s.5 of PSHFA 2013.

Furthermore, a confiscation order should only be made if, or to the extent that, it would not be disproportionate to require the defendant to pay the available amount (s.6(5)(b)).

These are separate questions calling for separate answers. In addressing them the judge has first to establish the facts as best he can on the material available, relying, as appropriate, on the assumptions required to be made by the Act (see 17-032). In many cases the factual findings made will be decisive. In addressing them he needs to focus on the language of the statutory provision in question. Any judicial gloss or exegesis needs to be viewed with caution (*R. v May* [2008] UKHL 28; [2008] 2 Cr. App. R. 28). Considering similar provisions, HL pointed out in *R. v Briggs-Price* [2009] UKHL 19; [2009] 4 All E.R. 594, that the judge was not restricted to the mandatory application of the statutory assumptions, but might instead rely on the evidence given at the trial.

The judge must decide any question of benefit arising under (1) and (2) above on the balance of probabilities (s.6(7)).

"Criminal lifestyle"

An offender has a criminal lifestyle for the purposes of the Act, if the offence, or any of the offences of which he is convicted: **17-020**

(1) is a "lifestyle offence" specified in Sch.2;
(2) constitutes conduct forming part of a *course of criminal activity*; or
(3) is an offence committed over a period of at least six months and the offender has *benefited* from the conduct which constitutes the offence.

(POCA 2002 s.75(1)–(2))

The condition that an offence must be "committed over a period of at least six months" relates to the particular accused's part in an offence; where, therefore, the prosecutor fails to prove that the part played by the particular accused in a conspiracy lasted at least six months, even though the conspiracy itself lasted at least six, he cannot be said to have had a "criminal lifestyle" within s.75 (*R. v Bajwa* [2011] EWCA Crim 1093; [2012] 1 Cr. App. R. (S.) 23; applied in *R. v Molloy* [2013] EWCA Crim 682).

Where the offender has benefited from conduct which constitutes the offence (committed *after 24 March 2003*), such conduct forms part of a course of criminal activity in two circumstances, namely if where:

(a) in the proceedings in which he was convicted, he was also convicted of three or more other offences (i.e. at least four offences in the same proceeding), each of the three or more of them constituting conduct from which he has also benefited, committed *after 24 March 2003*; or
(b) in the period of six years ending with the day when those proceedings were started (or, if there is more than one such day, the earliest day) he was convicted on at least *two separate occasions* of an offence constituting conduct from which he has benefited notwithstanding that any of those offences were committed before *24 March 2003*,

and in either case the offender obtained "relevant benefit" of not less than £5,000 (POCA 2002 s.75(3)–(6)).

Definitions

17-021 *"Criminal conduct"* is conduct which constitutes an offence in England and Wales, or would constitute such an offence if it occurred in England and Wales (s.76(1)).

The *"general criminal conduct"* of an offender is *all* his criminal conduct, and it is immaterial whether:

(1) that conduct occurred before or after the passing of POCA 2002;
(2) property constituting a benefit from that conduct was obtained before or after the passing of the Act; or
(3) it formed the subject of criminal proceedings (s.76(2)).

The *"particular criminal conduct"* of the offender is his criminal conduct which constitutes:

(a) the offence or offences concerned;
(b) offences of which he was convicted in the same proceedings as those in which he was convicted of the offence or offences concerned; or
(c) offences which the judge will be taking into consideration in deciding his sentence for the offence or offences concerned,

but conduct which constitutes an offence which was committed *before 24 March 2003* is not particular criminal conduct (s.76(3)).

Assessing the offender's benefit

17-022 In deciding whether the offender has "benefited" from conduct, and in deciding the benefit from that conduct, the judge must take account of:

(1) conduct occurring up to the time he makes his decision; and
(2) property (see 17-026 and following) obtained up to that time.

Where:

(a) the conduct concerned is general criminal conduct; and
(b) a confiscation order has at an earlier time been made against the offender, and his benefit for the purposes of that previous order was benefit from his general criminal conduct,

then his benefit found at the time the last confiscation order (mentioned in (b) above) was made against him must be taken for the purposes of this section to be his benefit from his general criminal conduct at that time and must be deducted (POCA 2002 s.8(1)–(3)).

Definition of "benefit": particular criminal conduct

POCA 2002 s.76 provides: **17-023**

(1) a person "benefits" from conduct if he obtains property as a result of, or in connection with, the conduct;
(2) if he obtains a pecuniary advantage as a result of or in connection with conduct, he is to be taken to obtain as a result of or in connection with the conduct a sum of money equal to the value of the pecuniary advantage;
(3) references to "property" or a "pecuniary advantage obtained in connection with conduct" include references to property or a pecuniary advantage obtained both in that connection and some other; and
(4) if a person benefits from conduct his benefit is the value of the property obtained.

(POCA 2002 s.76(4)–(7))

It is important to bear in mind that:

(1) the purpose of the order is to deprive an offender of the product of his crime, not to operate by way of fine (see 17-004); and
(2) the question whether an offender has obtained an interest in property is not determined merely by the fact of temporary possession, nor is an offender to be deprived of what he never actually obtained but merely helped others to obtain (*Jennings v CPS* [2008] UKHL 29; [2008] 2 Cr. App. R. 29).

In the "Endnote" to his speech in *R. v May* [2008] UKHL 28; [2008] 2 Cr. App. R. 28 Lord Bingham emphasised that in determining whether an offender has obtained property or a pecuniary advantage and, if so, the value of any property or advantage so obtained, the judge should (subject to any relevant statutory definition) apply ordinary common law principles to the facts as found:

(a) the exercise of this jurisdiction involves no departure from familiar rules governing entitlement and ownership;
(b) an offender ordinarily obtains property if in law he owns it, whether alone or jointly, which will ordinarily connote a power of disposition or control, as where a person directs a payment or conveyance of property to someone else; he ordinarily obtains a pecuniary advantage if (among other things) he evades a liability to which he is personally subject; and
(c) mere couriers or custodians or other very minor contributors to an offence, rewarded by a specific fee and having no interest in the property or the proceeds of sale, are unlikely to be found to have obtained that property, though it may be otherwise with money launderers.

On this last point, an offender may play an important role in a conspiracy without "obtaining" property for the purpose of the test of benefit (*R. v Clark* [2011] EWCA Crim 15); [2011] 2 Cr. App. R. (S.) 55; see also *R. v Allpress* [2009] EWCA Crim 8; [2009] 2 Cr. App. R. (S.) 58 and *R. v Mehmet* [2015] EWCA Crim 797).

In *R. v Ryder* [2020] EWCA Crim 1110; [2020] 8 WLUK 176, it was held that the saving of costs (of removal of contaminated waste) otherwise required in an environmental context was capable of amounting to a pecuniary advantage.

Where co-accused jointly receive property as a result of criminal activity, each is liable to receive a confiscation order representing the entire value, as if he had acted alone, provided he has sufficient assets to meet the order (*R. v May* [2008] UKHL 28; [2008] 2 Cr. App. R. 28; but see also *R. v Ahmad* [2014] UKSC 36; [2014] 2 Cr. App. R. (S.) 75).

"Obtaining"; the test

17-024 It is necessary to look at the property coming to an offender which is his, and not what happens to the property subsequently. The judge is concerned with what the offender has obtained "so as to own it, whether alone or jointly, which will ordinarily connote a power of disposition or control" (*R. v May* [2008] UKHL 28; [2008] 2 Cr. App. R. 28; *Jennings v CPS* [2008] UKHL 29; [2008] 2 Cr. App. R. 29).

Profit (turnover less expenses) is not the test. "The offender's benefit is the property which he obtains from his criminal conduct even though he may then dispose of it for legitimate purposes" (*R. v del Basso* [2010] EWCA Crim 1119; [2011] 1 Cr. App. R. (S.) 41) but the costs or expenses incurred by the offender in committing the crime do not form part of his benefit (*R. v James* [2011] EWCA Crim 2991; [2012] 2 Cr. App. R. (S.) 44).

Under the previous legislation it was said in relation to DTA 1994 s.2(3) that a person's "proceeds" are his gross receipts rather than his net profits (e.g. *R. v Banks* [1997] 2 Cr. App. R. (S.) 110; *R. v Fadden, The Times* 26 January 1998).

However, in some cases where legitimate goods are supplied but the business or transaction in question is otherwise tainted, it may be appropriate to make a confiscation order in the amount of the defendant's profits, permitting him to deduct the expenses incurred in supplying the goods or services in question (*R. v Reynolds* [2017] EWCA Crim 1455; [2018] 4 W.L.R. 33). In cases where business has been obtained by corruption, prosecutors should be alert to the pecuniary advantage likely to have been obtained by market distortion and thus forming an additional benefit to the defendant, capable (if properly quantifiable) of increasing the amount of a confiscation order where the measure adopted has otherwise been limited to the defendant's profits.

In *R. v Lambert* [2012] EWCA Crim 421; [2012] 2 Cr. App. R. (S.) 23, the CACD, applying *R. v May* [2008] UKHL 28; [2008] 2 Cr. App. R. 28 and *Jennings v CPS* [2008] UKHL 29; [2008] 2 Cr. App. R. 29 decided that the total benefit obtained by offenders jointly operating a cannabis factory should not be apportioned between them, even if that meant that the total sum confiscated from them, together, was more than the total benefit actually received. However, in *R. v Ahmad* [2014] UKSC 36; [2014] 2 Cr. App. R. (S.) 75 the Supreme Court confirmed that where there had been a joint obtaining, confiscation orders had to be made against each defendant for the whole of the benefit obtained. However, each order had to provide that it was not to be enforced to the extent that any sum had been recovered in satisfaction of another confiscation order in respect of the same joint benefit.

The judge must ascertain the extent of the beneficial interests of the owners in a jointly owned asset (*R. v Gangar* [2012] EWCA Crim 1378; [2013] 1 Cr. App. R. (S.) 67).

Where an offender operates through a company which he controls the corporate veil may be lifted—see *R. v Sale* [2013] EWCA Crim 1306; [2014] 1 Cr. App. R.

(S.) 60, applying *Petrodel Resources Ltd v Prest* [2013] UKSC 34; [2013] 3 W.L.R; *R. v Boughton-Fox* [2014] EWCA Crim 2940; *R. v McDowell* [2015] EWCA Crim 173; [2015] 2 Cr. App. R. (S.) 14; *R. v Boyle Transport* [2016] EWCA Crim 19; [2016] 2 Cr. App. R. (S.) 11; and *R. v Powell* [2016] EWCA Crim 1043; [2016] Crim. L.R. 852.

Special instances of liability

Where a person benefits from conduct his benefit is the value of the property obtained (POCA 2002 s.76(7)). **17-025**

As to:

(a) the market value of property obtained by a thief or handler: see *R. v Stanley* [2007] EWCA Crim 2857; [2008] 2 Cr. App. R. (S.) 19; *CPS v Rose* [2008] EWCA Crim 239; [2008] 2 Cr. App. R. 15;

(b) liability in respect of unpaid tax: see *R. v Dimsey* [2000] 1 Cr. App. R. (S.) 497;

(c) the liability of smugglers evading duty on importation: see *R. v Bakewell* [2006] EWCA Crim 2; [2006] 2 Cr. App. R. (S.) 42 following *R. v Smith* [2002] 1 Cr. App. R. 35; see also *R. v Waller* [2008] EWCA Crim 2037; [2009] Cr. App. R. (S.) 76; *R. v White* [2010] EWCA Crim 978; *R. v Young* [2011] EWCA Crim 1176; [2011] Crim. L.R. 652;

(d) the "black market" value of drugs: for many years the courts considered that an importer of controlled drugs did not benefit because controlled drugs had no legitimate market value (for example, see *R. v Hussain* [2006] EWCA Crim 621). However, the House of Lords decided in *R. v Islam* [2009] UKHL 30; [2010] Cr. App. R. (S.) 42 that it was consistent with the statutory scheme to take account of the black market value of drugs when valuing the benefit obtained by an offender from their illegal importation. For applications of this principle see *R. v Kakkad* [2015] EWCA Crim 385; *R. v Hussain* [2014] EWCA Crim 1181; *R. v Elsayed* [2014] EWCA Crim 333 and *R. v Lister* [2014] EWCA Crim 2290;

(e) counterfeit goods: fact that goods are counterfeit is irrelevant for the purposes of calculating duty evaded; see *R. v Varsani* [2010] EWCA Crim 1938; [2011] 1 Cr. App. R. (S.) 96;

(f) dishonest mortgage applications: see *R. v Waya* [2012] UKSC 51; [2011] 1 Cr. App. R. (S.) 4; *R. v Oyebola* [2013] EWCA Crim 1052; [2014] 1 Cr. App. R. (S.) 58 (rental income); *R. v Odamo* [2013] EWCA Crim 1275; [2014] 1 Cr. App. R. (S.) 44;

(g) conspirators: see *R. v Siveraman* [2008] EWCA Crim 1736; [2009] 1 Cr. App. R. (S.) 80 (service station manager laundering diesel fuel—benefit equals duty and VAT avoided); *R. v Allpress* [2009] EWCA Crim 8; [2009] 2 Cr. App. R. (S.) 58 (couriers of cash from drug dealing—no benefit); *R. v Anderson* [2010] EWCA Crim 615 (pilot conspiring to facilitate illegal immigration, benefit—share of proceeds of conspiracy); the key question is whether a conspirator is an "equity" partner in the enterprise rather than a mere custodian, or baillee (see *R. v Clarke* [2011] EWCA Crim 15; [2011] 2 Cr. App. R. (S.) 55; also *R. v James* [2011] EWCA Crim 2991; [2012] 2 Cr. App. R. (S.) 44); *R. v Mackle* [2014] UKSC 5; [2014] 2 All E.R. 170 (offender in possession of dutiable goods where duty evaded has not necessarily benefited from his criminal activity); *R. v Chahal* [2015] EWCA Crim

816 (benefit was full value of fraudulent VAT reclaims where offender had passed sums on to the next link in the carousel chain);

(h) brothel keepers: the benefit is the share actually received, not the turnover (*R. v Worrall* [2012] EWCA Crim 1150);

(i) jointly owned property: the law on equitable interests in real property applies (*Jones v Kernott* [2011] UKSC 53; [2012] 1 All E.R. 1265), so the judge may have to determine who holds the beneficial interests;

(j) rental income from property: see *R. v Sumal & Sons (Properties) Ltd* [2012] EWCA Crim 1840; [2013] 1 W.L.R. 2078; *R. (on the application of Haringey LBC) v Roth (Boruch)* [2020] EWCA Crim 967;

(k) benefit from unlawful deposit of waste material is by reference to landfill tax, licence fees and other costs avoided through the unlawful operation: see *R. v Morgan* [2013] EWCA Crim 1307; see also *R. v Ryder* [2020] EWCA Crim 1110; [2020] 8 WLUK 176;

(l) VAT, income tax and corporation tax which has been accounted for: see *R. v Harvey* [2015] UKSC 73; [2016] 1 Cr. App. R. (S.) 60; and

(m) laundering money on a commission basis: *R. v Fulton* [2019] EWCA Crim 163.

The task in (i) above (equitable interests) must be undertaken in the Crown Court and does not have to be determined by a civil court (*R. v Harriott* [2012] EWCA Crim 2294). The burden is on the party seeking to show that the beneficial interests do not follow the legal estate (examples are to be found in *Re Ali* [2012] EWHC 2302; *R. v Perrey* [2011] EWCA Crim 2316; *CPS v Piper* [2011] EWHC 3570 (Admin); *Edwards v CPS* [2011] EWHC 1688 (Admin); *R. v Rowsell* [2011] EWCA Crim 1894; *R. v Ghori* [2012] EWCA Crim 1115; *R. v Alom* [2012] EWCA Crim 736). See also the comments of the CACD *R. v Moore* [2021] EWCA Crim 956; [2021] 4 W.L.R. 121 to the effect that where the case involves complex issues concerning beneficial entitlement to property, it may be preferable to allow the issue to be litigated at the enforcement stage with an enforcement receiver.

"Property"; general provisions

17-026 "Property" is all property wherever situated and includes:

(1) money;

(2) all forms of real or personal property; and

(3) things in action and other intangible or incorporeal property (as to inheritance and damages received from civil action, see *Maye v DPP Northern Ireland* [2008] UKHL 9; [2008] 1 W.L.R. 315).

(POCA 2002 s.150)

The following rules apply in relation to property:

(a) property is held by a person if he holds an interest in it;

(b) property is obtained by a person if he obtains an interest in it;

(c) property is transferred by one person to another if the first one transfers or grants an interest in it to the second;

(d) references to property held by a person include references to property vested in his trustee in bankruptcy (see *R. v Shahid* [2009] EWCA Crim 831; [2009] 2 Cr. App. R. (S.) 105), permanent or interim trustee (within the meaning of the Bankruptcy (Scotland) Act 1985) or liquidator;

(e) references to an interest held by a person beneficially in property include

references to an interest which would be held by him beneficially if the property were not so vested;
- (f) references to an interest, in relation to land in England and Wales or Northern Ireland, are to any legal estate or equitable interest or power;
- (g) references to an interest, in relation to land in Scotland, are to any estate, interest, servitude or other heritable right in or over land, including a heritable security; and
- (h) references to an interest, in relation to property other than land, include references to a right (including a right to possession).

"Criminal property" is defined in POCA 2002 s.340; see *R. v Loizou* [2005] EWCA Crim 1579; [2005] 2 Cr. App. R. 37; *R. v Amir* [2011] EWCA Crim 146; [2011] 1 Cr. App. R. 37; *R. v William* [2013] EWCA Crim 1262 (turnover of a business).

"Free" property

Property is free unless: **17-027**

- (a) an order is in force in respect of it under MDA 1971 s.27;
- (b) an order is in force in respect of it under Criminal Justice (Northern Ireland) Order 1994 (SI 19947/2795 (NI 15)) art.11 (deprivation orders);
- (c) an order is in force in respect of it under Proceeds of Crime (Scotland) Act 1995 Pt 2 (forfeiture of property used in crime);
- (d) an order is in force in respect of it under SA 2020 s.152 (deprivation orders);
- (e) an order is in force in respect of it under TerrA 2000 s.23, s.23A or s.111 (forfeiture orders);
- (f) an order is in force in respect of it under Anti-terrorism, Crime and Security Act 2001, paras 3(2), 6(2), 10D(1), 10G(2), 10J(3), 10S(2), 10Z2(3) of Sch.1;
- (g) an order is in force in respect of it under POCA 2002 ss.245A, 246, 255A, 256, 266, 295(2), 298(2), 303L(1), 303O(3), 303R(3), 303Z3 or 303Z14(4);
- (h) it has been forfeited under s.297ZA or s.303Z9;
- (i) it has been detained under ss.297C, 297D, 298(4) or 303O(9);
- (j) it is the forfeitable property in relation to an order under s.303Q(1);
- (k) it has been forfeited in pursuance of a cash forfeiture notice under para.5A of Sch.1 to the Anti-terrorism, Crime and Security Act 2001, or an account forfeiture notice under para.10W of Sch.1;
- (l) it is detained under paras 5B, 5C, 9A or 10G(7) of Sch.1; and
- (m) it is the forfeitable property in relation to an order under para.10I(1) of Sch.1.

(POCA 2002 s.82)

"Realisable" property

Realisable property is any free property held by the accused, and any "free" property held by the recipient of a "tainted gift" (see 17-030) (POCA 2002 s.83). **17-028**

In deciding what amounts to "realisable property", a distinction needs to be drawn between assets which are difficult, and those which are impossible, to realise. If an asset is impossible, and not merely difficult, to realise then it can be excluded from the ambit of realisable property (*R. v Chen* [2009] EWCA Crim 2669; [2010] 2 Cr. App. R. (S.) 34 as explained in *R. v Modjiri* [2010] EWCA Crim 829; [2011]

1 Cr. App. R. (S.) 20). It is otherwise where it is merely the case that a sale would encounter difficulties, which the judge applying the analysis in *R. v Modjiri* must disregard. See *Mundy v CPS* [2014] EWHC 819 (Admin) (property could not be sold until foreign court gave judgment) where the authorities are reviewed.

In a case where a life interest in one third of a trust fund was held to be free property and thus realisable, difficulties in predicting the income it would produce, coupled with the disproportionate costs of a possible adjournment to obtain expert evidence on its market value, meant that it was not in the public interest to prolong the proceedings, and so the quantum of the confiscation order was confirmed without reference to it (*R. v Walker* [2011] EWCA Crim 103; [2011] 2 Cr. App. R. (S.) 54).

Gifts and their recipients

17-029 Where the defendant transfers property to another person for a consideration the value of which is significantly less than the value of the property at the time of the transfer, he is to be treated as making a gift.

The property given is to be treated as such share in the property transferred as is represented by the fraction whose:

(1) numerator is the difference between the two values mentioned above; and
(2) denominator is the value of the property at the time of the transfer.

References to a recipient of a "tainted gift" are to a person to whom the defendant has made the gift.

(POCA 2002 s.78)

The "gift" provisions (of DTA 1994) have no bearing on a wife's share of the matrimonial home, for which she has given consideration by bringing up her children and looking after the family home, even though she has guilty knowledge of the source of her husband's wealth (*Gibson v RCPO* [2008] EWCA Civ 645; [2009] 2 W.L.R. 171, cf. *Customs and Excise Commissioners v A* [2003] Fam. 55; *CPS v Richard* [2006] 2 F.L.R. 1220).

In *R. v Usoro* [2015] EWCA Crim 1958; [2016] Crim. L.R. 349 the CACD held that where the defendant had made payments to the mother of his children for their maintenance, he was making payments of a sort he could in fact have been required to make in Family Court proceedings or via the Child Support Agency, and so the payments wholly or partly discharged his legal duty in respect of his children, and thus were not gifts.

Both these cases were distinguished in *R. v Hayes* [2018] EWCA Crim 682; [2018] 2 Cr. App. R. (S.) 27, where the defendant submitted that his wife's contribution as a housewife and mother should have been valued. The CACD held that the marriage and subsequent birth of their son could not involve consideration of "value" within s.78(1).

(1) the approach required under s.78 required the following steps:
    (i) first, placing a value on the property transferred at the time of transfer;
    (ii) secondly, assessing whether or not consideration had been provided by the recipient of the property and (if it had) assessing the value of the consideration provided;
    (iii) thirdly, assessing whether or not the value (if any) of that consideration (if any) was significantly less than the value of the property transferred at the time of transfer; and

(iv) fourthly, if there was found to be a significant difference applying the calculation prescribed in s.78(2); thereafter, also applying the provisions of s.81 as appropriate.

(2) Each of Steps (i), (ii) and (iii) above had always to be undertaken objectively and on an evidence-based approach. There was no room, in that context, for "plucking a figure out of the air".

(3) Where the consideration that was asserted to have been provided by the recipient of the property was not in the form of a direct financial contribution or contributions, it was necessary to examine the evidence rigorously and closely to see if the asserted consideration (whether by way of "services" or otherwise) was capable of being assessed as consideration of value and (if it was) to what extent.

(4) Any consideration that was asserted to have been provided had to be attributable to the transfer of property in question.

(5) Any consideration that was asserted to have been provided had, for the purposes of s.78(1), to be capable of being ascribed a value in monetary terms.

(6) Each case, ultimately, would depend on its own facts and circumstances ([58]).

"Tainted gifts"

Where a decision has *not* been made as to whether the accused has a criminal lifestyle, or a court has decided that *he has a criminal lifestyle*, a gift is said to *be tainted*: **17-030**

(a) where it was made by him at any time after "the relevant day"; and
(b) if it was made by him at any time and was of property:
  (i) which was obtained by him as a result of or in connection with his general criminal conduct; or
  (ii) which (in whole or part and whether directly or indirectly) represented in his hands property obtained by him as a result of or in connection with his general criminal conduct.

The "relevant day" is the first day of the period of six years ending with:

(a) the day when proceedings for the offence concerned were started against the accused; or
(b) if there are two or more offences and proceedings for them were started on different days, the earliest of those days.

Where the court has decided that the accused *does not have a criminal lifestyle*, a gift is said to be "tainted" if it was made by him at any time after:

(a) the date on which the offence concerned was committed; or
(b) if his particular criminal conduct consists of two or more offences and they were committed on different dates, the date of the earliest.

(POCA 2002 s.77(1)–(5))

Note that s.77(5) should be read as referring to *"any time after the commission of the offence"*, rather than *"any time after the date of the offence"*; *R. v Lehair* [2015] EWCA Crim 1324; [2016] 1 Cr. App. R. (S.) 2.

An offence which is a continuing offence is committed on the first occasion when it is committed. For the purposes of (2)(b) in the preceding paragraph, the accused's "particular criminal conduct" includes any conduct which constitutes offences which the court has taken into consideration in deciding his sentence for the offence or offences concerned (POCA 2002 s.77(6)–(9)). In *R. v Saroya* [2022] EWCA Crim 602; [2022] 5 WLUK 2 it was held that offence of dishonestly furnishing false material to a local authority, with a view to obtaining housing benefit, contrary to the Social Security Administration Act 1992 Pt VI s.111A(1)(b) was capable of being a continuing offence committed over an extended period for the purposes of the Proceeds of Crime Act 2002 s.75(2)(c) even where the representation is charged as having been made only on a single day.

A gift may be a "tainted gift" whether it was made before or after the passing of the Act. POCA 2002 s.81 prescribes how "tainted gifts" are to be valued; for the purposes of valuation it does not matter whether or not there is any likelihood of the gift being returned (*R. v Smith* [2013] EWCA Crim 502; [2013] 2 Cr. App. R. (S.) 77).

In *R. v Johnson* [2016] EWCA Crim 10; [2016] 2 Cr. App. R. (S.) 38 the CACD considered the impact of *Waya* on the tainted gift provisions. The CACD held that where the prosecution seeks to recover the value of a tainted gift which appears to be worthless at the date the confiscation order is made, the judge should carefully consider:

(a) The robustness of the evidence of the value of the tainted gift;
(b) The proportionality of making an order in the sum sought; and
(c) The appropriate term of imprisonment to be imposed in default; although there is an obligation to impose a term of imprisonment in default the court must consider all the circumstances of the case in accordance with *R. v Castillo* [2011] EWCA Crim 3173; where the court is affirmatively satisfied that enforcement is impossible that may be a reason to make a substantial reduction in the term imposed in default.

There must be clear and unassailable evidence that a tainted gift cannot be recovered before an order can be found to be disproportionate under s.6(5) (*R. v Box* [2018] EWCA Crim 542; [2018] Crim. L.R. 581).

In *R. v Waring* [2021] EWCA Crim 1369; [2021] 9 WLUK 263, the CACD accepted that the category of cases that are disproportionate is not closed, but the tainted gift regime "is a severe one designed to encourage or coerce those who dissipate the proceeds of crime into making good the losses thereby caused" (per Simler LJ at [31]).

Determination of extent of defendant's interest in property

17-031 Section 10A provides that where the judge concludes that the offender holds property which is likely to be realised to satisfy the confiscation order, and a person other than the offender holds or may hold an interest in it, the judge may (if he thinks it appropriate to do so) determine the extent of the offender's interest in the property. Such a determination is conclusive for the purposes of realising property to satisfy the confiscation order.

The "extent" of the accused's interest in property means the proportion that the value of his interest in it bears to the value of the property itself (POCA 2002 s.10A(5)).

In *R. v Moore* [2021] EWCA Crim 956; [2021] 4 W.L.R. 121 it was said that where the case involves complex issues concerning beneficial entitlement to property, it may be preferable to allow the issue to be litigated at the enforcement stage with an enforcement receiver.

Assumptions to be made in cases of "criminal lifestyle"

Where the judge decides that the offender has a "criminal lifestyle" he *must* make four assumptions (POCA 2002 s.10(1)–(7)) for the purpose of deciding whether the offender has benefited from his "general criminal conduct" (see 17-021) and deciding his benefit from that conduct. **17-032**

(POCA 2002 s.10(1)–(2))

The four assumptions are:

(1) *any property transferred* to the offender at any time after the "relevant day" is assumed to have been obtained by him:
   (a) as a result of his "general criminal conduct"; and
   (b) at the earliest time he appears to have held it;
(2) *any property held* by the offender at any time after the date of conviction is assumed to have been obtained by him:
   (a) as a result of his "general criminal conduct"; and
   (b) at the earliest time he appears to have held it;
(3) *any expenditure incurred* by the offender at any time after "the relevant day" was met from property obtained by him as a result of his "general criminal conduct"; and
(4) for the purpose of valuing any *property obtained* (or assumed to have been obtained) by the offender, it is assumed that he obtained it free of any other interests in it.

(POCA 2002 s.10(2)–(5))

These assumptions must be made unless:

(i) the assumption is shown to be incorrect; or
(ii) there would be a serious risk of injustice if the assumption were made.

(POCA 2002 s.10(6))

The prosecutor may adduce evidence of further offending, of which the offender was not convicted, in order to rebut his attempt to defeat the statutory assumptions (*R. v Bagnall* [2012] EWCA Crim 677; [2013] W.L.R. 207). Where the only question in the confiscation proceedings is the source of the assets held by the offender, the mere fact that the prosecutor has such evidence does not shift a criminal standard of proof onto the prosecution.

Note that the latter phrase "serious risk of injustice if the assumption were made" in s.10(6)(b):

(i) does not mean hardship to the offender by virtue of the order;
(ii) does not provide for the exercise of a discretion by the judge in determining whether it is fair to make an order; but
(iii) is to ensure a sensible calculation of the benefit and to ensure that the assumptions are not so unreasonable or unjust in respect of the particular offender that they should not be made (*CPS v Jones* [2006] W.L.R. (D.) 174).

The judge is not restricted to relying on the assumptions and may, instead, rely on the evidence given at the trial, but proof of criminal offences other than those charged on the indictment must be to the criminal standard (*R. v Briggs-Price* [2009] UKHL 19; [2009] 4 All E.R. 594, a decision on the similar provisions in DTA 1994 s.4; see also *R. v Whittington* [2009] EWCA Crim 1641; [2010] 1 Cr. App. R. (S.) 83) and *R. v Moss* [2015] EWCA Crim 713.

Where the judge does not make one or more of the required assumptions he must state his reasons (POCA 2002 s.10(7)); he must still decide whether the offender has benefited from his general criminal conduct and determine the recoverable amount, albeit without the assistance of those assumptions.

Note that the "relevant day" is the first day of the period of six years ending with:

- the day when proceedings for the offence concerned were started against the accused; or
- if there are two or more offences, and proceedings for them were started on different days, the earliest of those days,

but if a confiscation order mentioned in s.8(3)(c) has been made against the accused at any time during the period mentioned in s.10(8), then the "relevant day" is the day when the offender's benefit was calculated for the purposes of the last such confiscation order, and assumption (2) does not apply to any property which was held by him on or before the relevant day (POCA 2002 s.10(8)–(9)).

The "date of conviction" is the date on which the offender was convicted of the offence concerned, or if there are two or more offences and the convictions were on different dates, the date of the latest (POCA 2002 s.10(10)).

Offender having no criminal lifestyle

17-033 Where the judge decides that the offender does not have a *"criminal lifestyle"* he must go on to decide whether the offender has benefited from his *"particular criminal conduct"*, defined at 17-023. Conduct which constitutes an offence committed *on or before 23 March 2003* does not come within the definition.

Assessment of benefit

17-034 For the purpose of deciding the value at any time of property then held by a person, its value is the market value of the property at that time, but if at that time another person holds an interest in the property, its value in relation to such person is the market value of his interest at that time, ignoring any previous charging order made under the enactments referred to in POCA 2002 ss.79–81 (POCA 2002 s.79(1)–(4)).

Special rules apply to the valuation of property obtained from conduct (s.80), and to "tainted gifts" (see 17-030).

Where the court is considering the offender's general criminal conduct, the judge must, in order to avoid double counting, deduct the aggregate of any amounts ordered to be paid under a previous confiscation order which was also based upon his general criminal conduct. However, this does not apply to an amount which has previously been taken into account for the purposes of a deduction under this provision on an earlier occasion (POCA 2002 s.8(3)–(8)). See *R. v Chahal* [2014] EWCA Crim 101; [2014] 2 Cr. App. R. (S.) 35.

Deciding the "recoverable amount"

17-035 Once the judge has assessed the amount of the offender's benefit, he must make a confiscation order in that amount, unless:

(1) the offender shows that the "available amount" is less than that assessed benefit; in which case the amount subject to confiscation (the "recoverable amount") is the "available amount" (see 17-036), or a nominal amount, if the available amount is nil; or

(2) a victim of the offender's conduct has started or intends to start civil proceedings (s.6(6)), in which case the amount subject to confiscation is such amount as the judge believes is just, and which does not exceed the assessed benefit (POCA 2002 s.7).

A loser who takes advantage of his opportunity to invite the prosecutor to ask the court to make a compensation order cannot in any known sense of the word be said to have started, or to be intending to start, "proceedings" against the offender in respect of the loss. A compensation order, if made, is part of the orders made by the judge ancillary to sentence. He is under a duty to consider it whether the loser seeks it or not. The "proceedings" in which it is considered and, if appropriate, made, are the criminal proceedings brought by the Crown by way of indictment, not civil proceedings brought by the loser (*R. v Jawad* [2013] EWCA Crim 644; [2014] 1 Cr. App. R. (S.) 16).

In *CPS v Aquila Advisory Ltd* [2021] UKSC 49; [2021] 1 W.L.R. 5666, the Supreme Court upheld the decision of the CACD (see *CPS v Aquila Advisory Ltd* [2019] EWCA Civ 588) that where the directors of a company had been convicted of fraud, the rights of the company to recover the proceeds from its directors took precedence over the operation of a confiscation order made against those directors. The overarching principle of POCA 2002 is that neither a confiscation order under Pt 2, nor a civil recovery order under Pt 5, nor the money laundering provisions in Pt 7, should interfere with existing third party property rights (para.33).

In calculating the offender's benefit from the conduct concerned, any property:

(a) in respect of which a recovery order is in force under POCA 2002 s.266; or
(b) which has been forfeited in pursuance of a forfeiture notice under s.297A, or in pursuance of an account forfeiture notice under s.303Z9; or
(c) in respect of which a forfeiture order is in force under POCA 2002 ss.298(2), 303O(3), 303R(3), 303Z14(4); or
(d) which is the forfeitable property in relation to an order under s.303Q(1),

must be ignored.

"The available amount"

The "available amount" is the aggregate of: **17-036**

(1) the total of the values (at the time the confiscation order is made) of all the *"free property"* (see 17-027) then held by the offender;
(2) deducting the total amount payable in pursuance of *obligations* which then have priority; and
(3) adding the total of the values (at that time) of all "tainted gifts" (see 17-030).

(POCA 2002 s.9(1))

An obligation "has priority" if the offender has an obligation to pay:

(a) an amount due in respect of a fine or other order of a court which was imposed or made on conviction of an offence and at any time before the time the confiscation order is made; or
(b) a sum which would be included among the preferential debts (within the meaning of the Insolvency Act 1986 s.385) if the defendant's bankruptcy had commenced on the date of the confiscation order or his winding up had been ordered on that date.

(POCA 2002 s.9(2))

Where the judge decides the available amount, he must include in the confiscation order a statement of his findings as to the matters relevant for deciding that amount.

In *R. v Seed* [2021] EWCA Crim 1198; [2021] 1 W.L.R. 6033 it was held that the value of stolen property (jewellery) in the possession of police, but in relation to which the rightful owner had not been identified, was properly included in the assessment of the available amount for the purposes of s.9.

As to the value of a pension policy, see *R. v Chen* [2009] EWCA Crim 2669; [2010] 2 Cr. App. R. (S.) 34 and *R. v Hamid* [2014] EWCA Crim 2827. As to assessing the value of a life interest in trust property, see *R. v Walker* [2011] EWCA Crim 103; [2011] 2 Cr. App. R. (S.) 54.

Hidden assets

17-037 Where the offender asserts that the value of his assets is less than the benefit figure, the court is not bound to reject that assertion just because the court concludes that the offender has not revealed their true extent, or because the court has received no assistance from the offender; *R. v McIntosh* [2012] 1 Cr. App. R. (S.) 60; see also *R. v Mahmood* [2013] EWCA Crim 325; [2013] 1 W.L.R. 3146; *R. v Deny* [2015] EWCA Crim 69; *R. v Yu* [2015] EWCA Crim 1076; [2015] 2 Cr. App. R. (S.) 75 and *R. v Brooks* [2016] EWCA Crim 44. In *R. v Gricevicius* [2018] EWCA Crim 1061, the CACD held that, whilst *McIntosh* showed that a court should not make a precipitate leap from a failure to give evidence to an automatic order in the benefit figure, the instant case was not one where there was other evidence before the court which was relevant to the question of the available amount, and so the judge was entitled to find that the available amount equated to the benefit figure.

5. POSTPONEMENT OF MAKING ORDER

The act of postponement

17-038 Instead of proceeding under s.6 *before* sentencing the offender for his offence(s), the judge may, on the application of the offender or of the prosecutor, or indeed of his own motion (*R. v Zelzele* [2001] EWCA Crim 1763; [2001] 1 Cr. App. R. (S.) 62), postpone the s.6 proceeding, on one or more occasions, for up to "the permitted period", i.e.:

(1) a total of two years from the offender's conviction; or
(2) three months from the date on which any appeal against conviction is disposed of, if the three months ends more than two years after the date of conviction.

(POCA 2002 s.14(1)–(7))

The period of postponement may be extended beyond the expiry of the permitted period if there are exceptional circumstances. Where the application is made before the permitted period ends, it may be granted even after it ends.

(POCA 2002 s.14(8))

There is no limit to what may amount to exceptional circumstances (e.g. *R. v Jagdev* [2002] EWCA Crim 1326; [2003] 11 Cr. App. R. 2).

If two or more offences are involved, and they were on different dates, the date of the offender's conviction is the date of the latest.

A postponement may be granted without a hearing (*R. v Neish* [2010] EWCA Crim 1011; [2011] 1 Cr. App. R. (S.) 335).

It is not enough for the judge to adjourn the proceedings, he must postpone the confiscation hearing in terms. However:

(a) it is not necessary to specify the very date on which the substantive hearing is to begin, still less the day on which any order will be made; and
(b) it is sufficient if he gives directions for the service of statements and specifies a date on which the proceedings will next be listed, whether for disposal or for such other directions as may be necessary (*R. v Knights* [2005] UKHL 50; [2006] 1 Cr. App. R. (S.) 80).

6. Subsequent reconsideration

General

POCA 2002 provides for reconsideration of confiscation orders in five distinct situations: **17-039**

(1) where there was originally no s.6 enquiry, and so no order was made, but further evidence has become available (s.19);
(2) where the judge at the original proceedings decided that there was either no benefit from general criminal conduct or no benefit from particular criminal conduct, and so no order was made, but further evidence has become available (s.20);
(3) where a confiscation order was made, but further evidence concerning the benefit figure has become available (s.21);
(4) where a confiscation order was made and there is an application to recalculate the available amount (s.22); and
(5) where a confiscation order was made and the available amount calculated at the time is inadequate to satisfy the order (s.23).

An application by the prosecutor for reconsideration under ss.19, 20 or 21 is made in writing, giving, amongst other detail, the grounds for the application and an indication of the evidence available to support it. It must be lodged with the Crown Court, and must be served on the offender.

The application must include, where the parties are agreed on the terms of the proposed order, a draft order in the terms proposed and evidence of the parties' agreement.

The court can determine the application without a hearing where the parties are agreed on the terms of the order, but must determine the application at a hearing in any other case.

If there is to be a hearing of the application, the court officer must arrange for it to take place no sooner than the eighth day after it was served unless the court otherwise directs.

(CrimPR 33.15)

Statement of information

Where the judge holds a s.6 enquiry in reconsidering an earlier order (ss.19, 20), or the prosecutor applies for a reconsideration of the benefit calculated under the original order (s.21): **17-040**

(1) the prosecutor must give the court a statement of information (see 17-016) within the period the judge orders;

(2) s.16 (prosecutor's statement of information) applies accordingly with appropriate modifications where the prosecutor applies under s.21;
(3) s.17 (offender's response) (see 17-017) applies accordingly; and
(4) s.18 (provision of information by the offender) (see 17-018) also applies.

(POCA 2002 s.26)

Situation (1): no s.6 enquiry originally; fresh evidence now available (s.19 enquiry)

17-041 Where an offender was originally before the Crown Court in the circumstances obtaining under s.6(2) (see 17-015) but no s.6 enquiry took place, and:

(1) there is evidence which was not available to the prosecutor on the relevant date; and
(2) before the end of the period of six years starting with the date of conviction the prosecutor applies to a judge of the Crown Court to consider the evidence; and
(3) after considering the evidence the judge believes it is appropriate to proceed under s.6,

the judge must proceed to hold a confiscation enquiry ("a section 19 enquiry"). (POCA 2002 s.19(1)–(2))

Modifications to process for a s.19 enquiry

17-042 Where the judge embarks upon a s.19 enquiry, the basic confiscation process is modified as follows:

(1) If the offender has already been sentenced for the offence (or any of the offences) concerned, s.6 has effect as if his "particular criminal conduct" (see 17-023) included conduct which constitutes offences which the judge has taken into consideration in deciding his sentence for the offence or offences concerned.
(2) Section 8(2) (in relation to calculating the offender's benefit) does not apply; instead the judge must take account of:
 (a) conduct occurring before the "relevant date" (see below);
 (b) property obtained before that date; and
 (c) property obtained on or after that date if it was obtained as a result of, or in connection with, conduct occurring before that date.
(3) In relation to s.10 (the four assumptions; see 17-032):
 (a) assumptions (1) and (2) do not apply with regard to property first held by the offender on or after the relevant date;
 (b) assumption (3) does not apply with regard to expenditure incurred by him on or after that date; and
 (c) assumption (4) does not apply with regard to property obtained (or assumed to have been obtained) by him on or after that date.
(4) The "recoverable amount" for the purposes of s.6 is such amount as the judge believes is just, but does not exceed the amount found under s.7 (see 17-035).
(5) In arriving at the just amount the judge must have regard in particular to:
 (a) the amount found under s.7;

(b) any fine imposed on the offender in respect of the offence (or any of the offences) concerned;
(c) any order which falls within s.13(3) (see 17-008) and has been made against him in respect of the offence (or any of the offences) concerned and has not already been taken into account by the judge in deciding what is the free property held by him for the purposes of s.9; and
(d) any compensation order under SA 2020 s.133 or surcharge order under SA 2020 s.42 or order under PSHFA 2013 s.4 which has been made against him in respect of the offence (or any of the offences) concerned.

(6) If a compensation order or surcharge order or order under PSHFA 2013 s.4 has been made against the offender in respect of the offence or offences concerned, s.13(5) and (6) do not apply.

(POCA 2002 s.19(3)–(8))

Note that:

(i) the "relevant date" is, if the judge made a decision not to proceed under s.6, the date of the decision, and if he did not make such a decision, the date of conviction; and
(ii) the "date of conviction" is the date on which the offender was convicted of the offence concerned, or if there are two or more offences and the convictions were on different dates, the date of the latest.

(POCA 2002 s.19(10))

Situation (2): no benefit found originally; fresh evidence now available (s.20 enquiry)

If two conditions are satisfied the judge must make a fresh decision under s.6(4)(b) or (c) as to whether the offender has benefited from his general or particular criminal conduct (as the case may be), and may make a confiscation order under that section. **17-043**

(1) The first condition is that in the original s.6 enquiry the judge decided:
(a) that the offender had a criminal lifestyle but had not benefited from his general criminal conduct; or
(b) that he did not have a criminal lifestyle and had not benefited from his particular criminal conduct.

(2) The second condition is that:
(a) there is evidence which was not available to the prosecutor when the court decided that the offender had not benefited from his general or particular criminal conduct; and
(b) before the end of the period of six years starting with the date of conviction the prosecutor applies to the Crown Court to consider the evidence.

(3) After considering the evidence the judge concludes that he would have decided that the offender had benefited from his general or particular criminal conduct (as the case may be) if the evidence had been available to him.

(POCA 2002 s.20(1)–(5))

Modifications to process for a s.20 enquiry

17-044 Where the judge embarks upon a s.20 enquiry, the basic confiscation process is modified as follows:

(1) if the offender has already been sentenced for the offence (or any of the offences) concerned, s.6 has effect as if his particular criminal conduct included conduct which constitutes offences which the court has taken into consideration in deciding his sentence for the offence or offences concerned;
(2) s.8(2) (in relation to calculating the offender's benefit) will not apply, and instead the judge must take account of:
  (a) conduct occurring before the date of the original decision that the offender had not benefited from his general or particular criminal conduct;
  (b) property obtained before that date; and
  (c) property obtained on or after that date if it was obtained as a result of or in connection with conduct occurring before that date;
(3) in relation to s.10 (the four assumptions) (see 17-032):
  (a) assumptions (1) and (2) do not apply with regard to property first held by the defendant on or after the date of the original decision that he had not benefited from his general or particular conduct;
  (b) assumption (3) does not apply with regard to expenditure incurred by him on or after that date; and
  (c) assumption (4) does not apply with regard to property obtained (or assumed to have been obtained) by him on or after that date;
(4) "the recoverable amount" for the purposes of s.6 is such amount as the judge believes is just, but does not exceed the amount found under s.7 (see 17-035);
(5) in arriving at the just amount the judge must have regard in particular to:
  (a) the amount found under s.7;
  (b) any fine imposed on the offender in respect of the offence (or any of the offences) concerned;
  (c) any order which falls within s.13(3) (see 17-008) and has been made against him in respect of the offence (or any of the offences) concerned and has not already been taken into account by the judge in deciding what is the free property held by him for the purposes of s.9; and
  (d) any compensation order or surcharge order or order under PSHFA 2013 s.4 which has been made against him in respect of the offence (or any of the offences) concerned; and
(6) if a compensation order or surcharge order or order under PSHFA 2013 s.4 has been made against the offender in respect of the offence or offences concerned, ss.13(5) and (6) do not apply.

(POCA 2002 s.20(6)–(12))

Note that the "date of conviction" is the date on which the offender was convicted of the offence concerned, or if there are two or more offences and the convictions were on different dates, the date of the latest.

(POCA 2002 s.20(13))

Situation (3): order originally made: fresh evidence as to amount of benefit now available (s.21 enquiry)

Where the judge did make a confiscation order at the time, but there is evidence which was not available to the prosecutor at the relevant time, and the prosecutor believes that if the court were to find the amount of the offender's benefit in pursuance of this section it would exceed the relevant amount, then where: **17-045**

(1) before the end of the period of six years starting with the date of conviction the prosecutor applies to a judge of the Crown Court to consider the evidence; and
(2) after considering the evidence the judge believes it is appropriate for him to proceed under this provision,

he must make a new calculation of the offender's benefit from the conduct concerned.

(POCA 2002 s.21(1)–(2))

Modifications to process for a s.21 enquiry

Where the judge embarks upon a s.21 enquiry, the basic confiscation process is modified as follows: **17-046**

(1) if the offender has already been sentenced for the offence (or any of the offences) concerned, s.6 has effect as if his particular criminal conduct included conduct which constitutes offences which the judge has taken into consideration in deciding his sentence for the offence or offences concerned;
(2) s.8(2) (in relation to calculating the offender's benefit) does not apply, and the rules applying instead are that the judge must take account of:
    (a) conduct occurring up to the time it decided the offender's benefit for the purposes of the confiscation order;
    (b) property obtained up to that time; and
    (c) property obtained after that time if it was obtained as a result of or in connection with conduct occurring before that time;
(3) in applying s.8(5) as to aggregate (see 17-034) the confiscation order must be ignored;
(4) in relation to s.10 (the four assumptions) (see 17-032):
    (a) assumptions (1) and (2) will not apply with regard to property first held by the defendant after the time the court decided his benefit for the purposes of the confiscation order;
    (b) assumption (3) will not apply with regard to expenditure incurred by him after that time; and
    (c) assumption (4) will not apply with regard to property obtained (or assumed to have been obtained) by him after that time.

(POCA 2002 s.21(3)–(6))

Position where benefit exceeds relevant amount

If the amount found under the new calculation of the offender's benefit exceeds: **17-047**

(1) the relevant amount, the judge must make a new calculation of the recoverable amount for the purposes of s.6; and
(2) the amount required to be paid under the confiscation order, the judge may

vary the order by substituting for the amount required to be paid such amount as he believes is just.

In applying (1) above, the judge must:

(a) take the new calculation of the offender's benefit; and
(b) apply s.9 (see available amount, 17-036) as if references to the time the confiscation order is made were to the time of the new calculation of the recoverable amount and as if references to the date of the confiscation order were to the date of that new calculation.

In applying (2) above, the judge must have regard in particular to:

(i) any fine imposed on the offender for the offence (or any of the offences) concerned;
(ii) any order which falls within s.13(3) (see 17-008) and has been made against him in respect of the offence (or any of the offences) concerned, and has not already been taken into account by the judge in deciding what is the free property held by the defendant for the purposes of s.9; and
(iii) any compensation order or surcharge order or order under PSHFA 2013 s.4 which has been made against him in respect of the offence (or any of the offences), concerned,

but must *not* have regard to any compensation order or surcharge order or order under PSHFA 2013 s.4 if a court has made a direction under s.13(6) (see 17-008) that payment be made out of the confiscation order.
(POCA 2002 s.21(7)–(10))

Supplementary provisions

17-048 Note that:

(1) in deciding under this section whether one amount exceeds another the judge must take account of any change in the value of money;
(2) the relevant time is when the court calculated the offender's benefit for the purposes of the confiscation order, if this section has not applied previously, or when the court last calculated his benefit in pursuance of this section, if this section has applied previously;
(3) the relevant amount is the amount found as the offender's benefit for the purposes of the confiscation order, if this section has not applied previously, or the amount last found as his benefit in pursuance of this section, if this section has applied previously; and
(4) the "date of conviction" is the date on which the offender was convicted of the offence concerned, or if there are two or more offences and the convictions were on different dates, the date of the latest.

(POCA 2002 s.21(11)–(14))

Situation (4): order made: reconsideration of available amount

17-049 Where a court has made a confiscation order, and the amount required to be paid was the "available amount" as assessed under s.7(2) (see 17-035 and following), the prosecutor or a receiver appointed under s.50 may apply to the Crown Court to make a new calculation of the available amount (POCA 2002 s.22(1)–(4)).

The application:

(1) must be in writing, and may be supported by a witness statement;
(2) must identify any slavery and trafficking reparation order made by virtue of the confiscation order; and
(3) must include, where the parties are agreed on the terms of the proposed order, a draft order in the terms proposed and evidence of the parties' agreement.

The application and any other supporting documents must be lodged with the Crown Court, and must be served on the offender, on the receiver (if the prosecutor is making the application, and a receiver has been appointed under s.50), and/or on the prosecutor (if the receiver is making the application).

The court can determine the application without a hearing where the parties are agreed on the terms of the order, but must determine the application at a hearing in any other case.

If there is to be a hearing of the application, the court officer must arrange for it to take place no sooner than the eighth day after it was served unless the court otherwise directs.

(CrimPR 33.16)

On the hearing the judge must:

(1) make the new calculation; and in doing so
(2) apply s.9, in relation to the available amount, as if references to the time the confiscation order is made were a reference to the time of the new calculation and as if references to the date of the confiscation order were to the date of the new calculation.

If the amount found under the new calculation exceeds the relevant amount the judge may vary the order by substituting for the amount required to be paid such amount as he believes is just, but does not exceed the amount found as the defendant's benefit from the conduct concerned.

In deciding what is just he must have regard in particular to:

(a) any fine imposed on the offender for the offence (or any of the offences) concerned;
(b) any order which falls within s.13(3) (see 17-008) and has been made against him in respect of the offence (or any of the offences) concerned and has not already been taken into account in deciding what is the free property held by him for the purposes of s.9; and
(c) any compensation order or surcharge order which has been made against him in respect of the offence (or any of the offences) concerned; but

in deciding what is just regard must *not* be paid to any compensation order or surcharge order if a court has made a direction under s.13(6) that it be paid from the confiscation order.

(POCA 2002 s.22(3)–(6))

Note that:

(i) in deciding under this section whether one amount exceeds another the judge must take account of any change in the value of money;
(ii) the "relevant amount" is the amount found as the available amount for the purposes of the confiscation order, if this section has not been applied previously; or the amount last found as the available amount in pursuance of this section, if it has been applied previously; and
(iii) the amount found as the defendant's benefit from the conduct concerned

is the amount so found when the confiscation order was made; or, if one or more new calculations of his benefit have been made under s.21 (above), the amount found on the occasion of the last such calculation.

(POCA 2002 s.22(7)–(9))

See *R. v Padda* [2013] EWCA Crim 2330; [2014] 2 Cr. App. R. (S.) 22 for an example of the CACD approving a recalculation of the available amount from legitimate wealth later acquired. See also *R. v John* [2014] EWCA Crim 1240; [2014] 2 Cr. App. R. (S.) 73, where the CACD concluded that general damages awarded to the appellant after a road traffic accident cannot be excluded from a recalculation under s.22, but it would not be just to include special damages which reimbursed the appellant for sums he had already paid.

Situation (5): inadequacy of "available amount": variation of order

17-050 Where a judge has made a confiscation order, the offender, the prosecutor or a receiver appointed under s.50 may apply to a judge of the Crown Court to vary the order by substituting a lesser sum (POCA 2002 s.23).

The application:

(1) must be in writing, and may be supported by a witness statement;
(2) must identify any slavery and trafficking reparation order made by virtue of the confiscation order; and
(3) must include, where the parties are agreed on the terms of the proposed order, a draft order in the terms proposed and evidence of the parties' agreement.

The application and any other supporting documents must be lodged with the Crown Court, and must be served on the prosecutor, on the defendant (if the receiver is making the application), and/or on the receiver (if the defendant is making the application, and a receiver has been appointed under s.50).

The court can determine the application without a hearing where the parties are agreed on the terms of the order, but must determine the application at a hearing in any other case.

If there is to be a hearing of the application, the court officer must arrange for it to take place no sooner than the eighth day after it was served unless the court otherwise directs.

(CrimPR 33.17)

On such an application, the judge:

(1) must calculate the available amount, and in doing so he must apply s.9 as if references to the time the confiscation order is made were to the time of the calculation and as if references to the date of the order were to the date of the calculation; and
(2) if he finds that the available amount (so calculated) is inadequate for the payment of any amount remaining to be paid under the order, he may vary the order by substituting for the amount required to be paid, such smaller amount as he believes is just.

If a person has been adjudged bankrupt or his estate has been sequestrated, or if an order for the winding up of a company has been made, the judge must take into account the extent to which realisable property held by that person or that company may be distributed among creditors.

The judge may disregard any inadequacy which he believes is attributable (wholly or partly) to anything done by the offender for the purpose of preserving property held by the recipient of a tainted gift (see 17-030) from any risk of realisation under Pt 2 of the Act.

Where the Crown Court has made a finding that the offender had hidden assets, that finding cannot be re-litigated on an application by the offender under s.23 (*R. v Younis* [2008] EWCA Crim 2950; [2009] 2 Cr. App. R. (S.) 34).

The CACD has no jurisdiction to hear an appeal against a refusal by a Crown Court judge to vary a confiscation order on an application under s.23. An order made under s.23 varying a confiscation order is not included in the definition of "sentence" in CAA 1968 s.50(1) as amended (*R. v Ward (Barry)* [2010] EWCA Crim 1932; [2011] 1 W.L.R. 799).

Inadequacy of available amount: discharge of order

Where a judge has made a confiscation order, the designated officer of a magistrates' court may apply to a judge of the Crown Court for the discharge of the order if the amount remaining to be paid under the order is less than £1,000 (POCA 2002 s.24). **17-051**

The application must be in writing and must give details of the amount outstanding under the order and the grounds for the application. It must be served on the offender, the prosecutor and any receiver appointed under s.50. The judge may determine the application without a hearing unless one of those persons named above indicates, within seven days after the application was served on him, that he would like to make representations.

(CrimPR 33.18)

In dealing with the matter, the judge:

(1) must calculate the available amount, and in doing so must apply s.9 as if references to the time the confiscation order is made were to the time of the calculation and as if references to the date of the confiscation order were to the date of the calculation; and
(2) if he finds that the available amount (as so calculated) is inadequate to meet the amount remaining to be paid, and is satisfied that the inadequacy is due wholly to a specified reason or a combination of specified reasons as set out below, he may discharge the confiscation order.

The specified reasons are:

(a) in a case where any of the realisable property consists of money in a currency other than sterling, that fluctuations in currency exchange rates have occurred; and
(b) any reason specified by the Secretary of State by order.

The discharge of a confiscation order under s.24 does not prevent the making of an application under s.21(1)(d) or 22(1)(c). Where on such an application the court determines that the order should be varied under s.21(7) or 22(4), the court may provide that its discharge under s.24 is revoked (POCA s.24(6)–(7)).

Reconsideration, etc.: variation of prison term

Where a judge varies a confiscation order under POCA 2002 ss.21, 22, 23, 29, 32 or 33, the effect of the variation is to vary the maximum period applicable in relation to the order under POCA 2002 s.35(2A) and: **17-052**

(1) if the result is that that maximum period is less than the term of imprisonment or detention fixed in respect of the order under SA 2020 s.129(3), the judge must fix a reduced term of imprisonment or detention in respect of the confiscation order under SA 2020 s.129(3) in place of the term previously fixed; or
(2) if (1) is not the case, the judge may amend the term of imprisonment or detention fixed in respect of the confiscation order under SA 2020 s.129(3) (POCA 2002 s.39).

If the effect of s.12 is to increase the maximum period applicable in relation to a confiscation order, the prosecutor may apply to a judge of the Crown Court to amend the term of imprisonment or detention fixed in respect of the order under SA 2020 s.129(3) (POCA 2002 s.39(5)).

Application is made in writing giving the grounds for the application and details of the enforcement measures taken if any. On receipt of the application the court must at once send to the offender and the magistrates' court responsible for enforcing the order a copy of the application, and fix a date, time and place for the hearing and notify the same to the applicant and the offender.

If the judge makes an order increasing the default term, the court must at once send a copy of the order to the applicant, the offender, and the enforcing magistrates' court, and, if the offender is in custody at the time of the making of the order, the person having custody of him.

(CrimPR 33.21)

Small amount outstanding: discharge of order

17-053 Where a court has made a confiscation order, and the designated officer for a magistrates court applies to the Crown Court for the discharge of the order, and the amount remaining to be paid under the order is £50 or less, the judge may discharge the order.

(POCA 2002 s.25)

The discharge of a confiscation order under s.24 does not prevent the making of an application under s.21(1)(d) or 22(1)(c). Where on such an application the court determines that the order should be varied under s.21(7) or 22(4), the court may provide that its discharge under s.24 is revoked (POCA s.24(6)–(7)).

For the relevant procedure, see CrimPR 33.18.

Recovery from estate of deceased defendant impractical: discharge of order

17-054 Where a court has made a confiscation order and the offender dies before the order is satisfied and the designated officer for a magistrates court applies to the Crown Court for the discharge of the order, the court may discharge the order if:

(1) it is not possible to recover anything from the estate of the deceased for the purpose of satisfying the order to any extent; or
(2) it would not be reasonable to make any attempt or further attempt to recover anything from the estate of the deceased for that purpose.

(POCA 2002 s.25A)

7. Offender absconding

Offender convicted or committed

Where the offender: **17-055**

(1) absconds:

(a) before or after he is convicted of an offence or offences in proceedings before the Crown Court; or

(b) after he is committed to the Crown Court for sentence in respect of an offence or offences under SA 2020 ss.14–20; or

(c) after he is committed to the Crown Court in respect of an offence or offences under s.70 (committal with a view to a confiscation order being considered);

AND

(2) the prosecutor applies to the Crown Court to proceed under this section, and the judge believes it is appropriate for him to do so,

the judge must proceed under s.6 in the same way as he must proceed if the two conditions in s.6 are satisfied.

(POCA 2002 s.27(1)–(4))

However, if he proceeds under s.6 as applied by this section, a number of modifications are made to the process:

(i) any person the judge believes is likely to be affected by an order under s.6 is entitled to appear before him and make representations;

(ii) the judge must not make an order under s.6 unless the prosecutor has taken reasonable steps to contact the defendant;

(iii) s.6(9) as to the offences concerned applies as if the reference to s.6(2) is a reference to s.27(2);

(iv) ss.10 (assumptions), 16(4), 17 and 18 (as to statements of information) must be ignored; and

(v) ss.19, 20 and 21 (applications to reconsider the confiscation order) must be ignored while the defendant is still an absconder.

(POCA 2002 s.27(5))

An offender is not an "absconder" when he is deported by an act of the state (*R. v Gavin* [2010] EWCA Crim 2727; [2011] 1 Cr. App. R. (S.) 126).

(POCA 2002 s.27(7))

Once the defendant ceases to be an absconder:

(1) s.19 has a modified effect, such that it applies if:

(a) at a time when the first condition in s.27 was satisfied the judge did not proceed under s.6;

(b) before the end of the period of six years starting with the day when the accused ceased to be an absconder, the prosecutor applies to the Crown Court to proceed under s.6; and

(c) the judge believes it is appropriate for him to do so;

(2) s.20 has a modified effect, the second condition in s.20(4) being read as:

(a) before the end of the period of six years starting with the day the defendant ceased to be an absconder, the prosecutor applies to the Crown Court to reconsider whether the defendant has benefited from his general or particular criminal conduct (as the case may be); and

(b) the court believes it is appropriate for it to do so;

(3) s.21 has a modified effect, such that it applies if:

(a) a court has made a confiscation order;

(b) the prosecutor believes that if the court were to find the amount of the defendant's benefit in pursuance of this section it would exceed the relevant amount;

(c) before the end of the period of six years starting with the day when the defendant ceased to be an absconder, the prosecutor applies to the Crown Court to proceed under this section; and

(d) the court believes it is appropriate for it to do so;

(4) the modifications specified in s.27(5)(a)–(d) do not apply.

(POCA 2002 s.27(6))

Defendant neither convicted nor acquitted

17-056 Where:

(1) proceedings for an offence or offences are started against a defendant but are not concluded;

(2) he absconds;

(3) the period of three months (starting with the day the judge believes he absconded) has ended;

(4) the prosecutor applies to a judge of the Crown Court to proceed under this section; and

(5) the judge believes it is appropriate for him to do so,

he must proceed under s.6 in the same way as he is required to proceed if the two conditions in s.6 are satisfied.

However, if he proceeds under s.6 as applied by this section, a number of modifications are made to the process:

(a) any person the judge believes is likely to be affected by an order under s.6 is entitled to appear before him and make representations;

(b) the judge must not make an order under s.6 unless the prosecutor has taken reasonable steps to contact the defendant;

(c) s.6(9) as to the offences concerned applies as if the reference to s.6(2) were to s.27(2);

(d) ss.10 (assumptions), 16(4), 17 and 18 (statements of information) and 19 and 20 (reconsideration of case) must be ignored; and

(e) s.21 (reconsideration of benefit) must be ignored while the defendant is still an absconder.

(POCA 2002 s.28(1)–(5))

Once the defendant has ceased to be an absconder, s.21 applies where:

(a) a court has made a confiscation order;

(b) the prosecutor believes that if the court were to find the amount of the offender's benefit in pursuance of this section it would exceed the relevant amount;

(c) before the end of the period of six years starting with the day when the defendant ceased to be an absconder, the prosecutor applies to the Crown Court to proceed under this section; and

(d) the court believes it is appropriate for it to do so,

and the modifications to the process made by s.28(5)(a)–(d) (set out above) do not apply to the s.21 proceedings.

(POCA 2002 s.28(6))

If the judge makes an order under s.6 as applied by this section, and the defendant is later convicted in proceedings before the Crown Court of the offence (or any of the offences) concerned, s.6 does not apply so far as that conviction is concerned.

(POCA 2002 s.28(7))

Variation of order

Where: **17-057**

(1) the judge makes a confiscation order under s.6 as applied by s.28;
(2) the defendant ceases to be an absconder;
(3) he is convicted of an offence (or any of the offences) mentioned in s.28(2)(a);
(4) he believes that the amount required to be paid was too large (taking the circumstances prevailing when the amount was found for the purposes of the order);
(5) before the end of the relevant period he applies to the Crown Court to consider the evidence on which his belief is based; and
(6) the court considers the evidence and concludes that the defendant's belief is well founded,

the court must find the amount which should have been the amount required to be paid and it may vary the order by substituting such amount as it believes is just.

(POCA 2002 s.29(1)–(2))

The "relevant period" is the period of 28 days starting with:

(i) the date on which the defendant was convicted of the offence mentioned in s.28(2)(a); or
(ii) if there are two or more offences and the convictions were on different dates, the date of the latest.

But in a case where s.28(2)(a) applies to more than one offence the court must not make an order under this section unless it is satisfied that there is no possibility of any further proceedings being taken in relation to any such offence in respect of which the defendant has not been convicted.

(POCA 2002 s.29(3)–(4))

Application must be made in writing and must be supported by a witness statement giving details of the order made against him, any slavery and trafficking reparation order made by virtue of the confiscation order, the circumstances in which he ceased to be an absconder, his conviction of the offence or offences concerned and the reason why he believes the amount required to be paid under the order was too large.

The application and the statement must be lodged with the Crown Court and must be served on the prosecutor, at least seven days before the date fixed for the hearing unless the Crown Court specifies a shorter period.

(CrimPR 33.19)

Discharge of order

Where the judge makes a confiscation order under s.6 as applied by s.28, and the defendant is later tried for the offence or offences concerned and acquitted on all **17-058** counts, he may apply to the Crown Court to discharge the order, and in such a case the judge must discharge the order.

(POCA 2002 s.30(1)–(2))

Where the judge makes a confiscation order under s.6 as applied by s.28, and the defendant ceases to be an absconder, but has not been tried and acquitted of all counts, he may apply to the Crown Court to discharge the order.

The judge may discharge the order if he finds that:

(a) there has been undue delay in continuing the proceedings mentioned in s.28(2); or
(b) the prosecutor does not intend to proceed with the prosecution.

(POCA 2002 s.30(3)–(4))

Application for discharge is made in writing and must be supported by a witness statement giving details of the order made against him, the date on which he ceased to be an absconder, his acquittal, if he has been acquitted of the offence concerned, and if he has not been acquitted of the offence concerned:

(1) the date on which he ceased to be an absconder;
(2) the date on which the proceedings taken against him were instituted and a summary of the steps taken in the proceedings; and
(3) any indication by the prosecutor that he does not intend to proceed against him.

The application and the statement must be lodged with the Crown Court and must be served on the prosecutor at least seven days before the date fixed for the hearing unless the Crown Court specifies a shorter period.

(CrimPR 33.20)

8. FRESH PROCEEDINGS AFTER APPEAL

Crown Court proceeding afresh after appeal

17-059 Where the CACD orders the Crown Court to proceed afresh, a judge of the Crown Court must comply with any directions the CACD makes (POCA 2002 s.32(3)).

If the judge makes or varies a confiscation order under this section or in pursuance of a direction under this section he must have regard to:

(1) any fine imposed on the accused in respect of the offence (or any of the offences) concerned;
(2) any order which falls within s.13(3) (see 17-008) and has been made against him in respect of the offence (or any of the offences) concerned, unless the order has already been taken into account by a court in deciding what is the free property held by the accused for the purposes of s.9.

(POCA 2002 s.32(4))

Ancillary provisions

17-060 Where the Crown Court proceeds afresh under s.6 in pursuance of a direction by the CACD:

(1) if a court has already sentenced the defendant for the offence (or any of the offences) concerned, s.6 will have effect as if his particular criminal conduct

included conduct which constitutes offences which the court has taken into consideration in deciding his sentence for the offence or offences concerned;

(2) if a compensation order or a surcharge order or an order under PSHFA 2013 s.4 has been made against the defendant in respect of the offence (or any of the offences) concerned, the judge must have regard to it, and s.13(5) and (6) (see 17-008) do not apply;

(3) section 8(2) (in relation to benefit) does not apply, and the rules applying instead are that the judge must take account of:
 (a) conduct occurring before the relevant date;
 (b) property obtained before that date; and
 (c) property obtained on or after that date if it was obtained as a result of or in connection with conduct occurring before that date;

(4) in s.10 (the four assumptions; see 17-032):
 (a) assumptions (1) and (2) do not apply with regard to property first held by the defendant on or after the relevant date;
 (b) assumption (3) does not apply with regard to expenditure incurred by him on or after that date; and
 (c) assumption (4) does not apply with regard to property obtained (or assumed to have been obtained) by him on or after that date;

(5) section 26 (statement of information) applies as it applies in the circumstances mentioned in subs.(1) of that section.

The relevant date is the date on which the Crown Court decided not to make a confiscation order.

(POCA 2002 s.32(5)–(11))

Further appeal lies to the Supreme Court where similar provision in respect of a fresh order by a judge of the Crown Court apply (POCA 2002 s.33).

9. Commencement and conclusion of proceedings

Proceedings for an offence

Proceedings for an offence are *started* when: 17-061

(1) a magistrate issues a summons or warrant under MCA 1980 s.1 in respect of the offence;

(2) a relevant prosecutor issues a written charge and requisition or single justice procedure notice in respect of the offence;

(3) a person is charged with an offence after being taken into custody without a warrant; or

(4) a voluntary bill of indictment is preferred under AJ(MP)A 1933 s.2 in a case falling within subs.(2)(b) of that section (preferment by the CACD or a High Court judge) or subs.(2)(ba) of that section (preferment by a Crown Court judge following approval of deferred prosecution agreement).

If more than one time is found under the subsection in relation to proceedings they are started at the earliest of them.

Proceedings are *concluded*:

(a) if the defendant is acquitted on all counts in proceedings for an offence, when he is acquitted;

(b) if the defendant is convicted in proceedings for an offence and the conviction is quashed or the defendant is pardoned before a confiscation order is made, when the conviction is quashed or the defendant is pardoned;

(c) if a confiscation order is made against the defendant in proceedings for an offence (whether the order is made by the Crown Court or the CACD):
   (i) when the order is satisfied or discharged; or
   (ii) when the order is quashed and there is no further possibility of an appeal against the decision to quash the order;

(d) if the defendant is convicted in proceedings for an offence but the judge decides not to make a confiscation order against him:
   (i) if an application for leave to appeal under s.31(2) is refused, when the decision to refuse is made;
   (ii) if the time for applying for leave to appeal under s.31(2) expires without an application being made, when the time expires;
   (iii) if on appeal under s.31(2) the CACD confirms the judge's decision and an application for leave to appeal under s.33 is refused, when the decision to refuse is made;
   (iv) if on appeal under s.31(2) the CACD confirms the judge's decision and the time for applying for leave to appeal under s.33 expires without an application being made, when the time expires;
   (v) if on appeal under s.31(2) the CACD confirms the judge's decision and on appeal under s.33 the Supreme Court confirms the CACD's decision, when the latter confirms the decision;
   (vi) if on appeal under s.31(2) the CACD directs the Crown Court to reconsider the case, and on reconsideration the judge decides not to make a confiscation order against the defendant, when he makes that decision; and
   (vii) if on appeal under s.33 the Supreme Court directs the Crown Court to reconsider the case, and on reconsideration the judge decides not to make a confiscation order against the defendant, when he makes that decision.

In applying any one of the above provisions any power to extend the time for making an application for leave to appeal is to be ignored, as must the fact that a court may postpone making a confiscation order.

(POCA 2002 s.85)

Conclusion of applications

17-062 Applications are concluded as follows:

(1) under ss.19, 20, 27 or 28 in a case where:
   (a) the judge decides not to make a confiscation order against the defendant—when he makes the decision;
   (b) a confiscation order is made against him as a result of the application—when the order is satisfied or discharged, or when the order is quashed and there is no further possibility of an appeal against the decision to quash the order; and
   (c) the application is withdrawn—when the person who made the application notifies the withdrawal to the court to which the application was made;

(2) under s.21 or s.22:

(a) in a case where the judge decides not to vary the confiscation order concerned—when he makes the decision;

(b) in a case where the judge varies the confiscation order as a result of the application—when the order is satisfied or discharged, or when the order is quashed and there is no further possibility of an appeal against the decision to quash the order; and

(c) in a case where the application is withdrawn—when the person who made the application notifies the withdrawal to the court to which the application was made.

(POCA 2002 s.86)

Other interpretative provisions

A reference to "the offence (or offences)" concerned must be construed in accordance with s.6(9). **17-063**

A "criminal investigation" is an investigation which police officers or other persons have a duty to conduct with a view to it being ascertained whether a person should be charged with an offence.

A "defendant" is a person against whom proceedings for an offence have been started (whether or not he has been convicted).

A reference to "sentencing the defendant for an offence" includes a reference to dealing with him otherwise in respect of the offence.

(POCA 2002 s.88)

10. Seizure and forfeiture of cash

Detention of cash

POCA 2002 empowers an officer of HMRC, an SFO officer, an accredited financial investigator or a constable to seize any cash if he has reasonable grounds for suspecting that it is: **17-064**

(1) recoverable property; or
(2) intended by any person for use in unlawful conduct.

He may also seize cash if he suspects that *part* of it is recoverable property or is intended for use in unlawful conduct, if it is not reasonably practicable to seize only that part.

The amount of cash, or the part of it to which the officer's suspicion relates, must exceed £5,000.

There is nothing to prevent seizure under s.295 of money which has already been seized under, for instance, PACE 1984 s.19 (*Merseyside Chief Constable v Hickman* [2006] EWHC 451 (Admin), *The Times*, 7 April 2006).

(POCA 2002 s.294)

As to the meaning of "recoverable property", see POCA 2002 s.304(1); as to "unlawful conduct" see ss.241, 316(1).

While the officer of HMRC, an SFO officer, accredited financial investigator or constable continues to have reasonable grounds for his suspicions, the cash may be detained initially for a period of 48 hours (calculated in accordance with s.295(1A)–(1B)). The period may be extended on application, by any magistrates' court, or a single justice, but not beyond the period of six months beginning with the date of the order, or, in the case of any further order, not beyond a period of two years from the date of the first order.

On an application for detention, the court may make the order if satisfied that:

(1) there are reasonable grounds for suspecting that the cash is:
  (a) *recoverable property; or*
  (b) *intended to be used in unlawful conduct,*
AND
(2) in either case:
  (i) its continued detention is justified while its derivation is further investigated or consideration is given to bringing proceedings (in the UK or elsewhere) against any person for an offence with which the cash is connected; or
  (ii) the proceedings against any person for an offence with which the cash is connected have been started and have not been concluded.

Persons affected by the order must be notified of its making.

(POCA 2002 s.295)

Unless the cash, or part of it, is required as evidence, it must be paid into an interest-bearing account and any interest on it will be added to it on forfeiture or release.

(POCA 2002 s.296)

If, on application by the person from whom the cash was seized, a magistrates' court is satisfied that the conditions in s.295 for the detention of the cash are no longer met, it may order it to be released.

A constable, an SFO officer, an officer of Revenue and Customs or an accredited financial investigator, after notifying the magistrates' court, may release the whole or any part of the cash if satisfied that its detention is no longer justified.

(POCA 2002 s.297)

Forfeiture

17-065 Under s.297A a senior officer can serve a forfeiture notice if he is satisfied that the cash or part of it is recoverable property or is intended by any person for use in unlawful conduct. The content of such notices is prescribed by s.297B. Once the forfeiture notice has been given, if no objection is made within the specified period, the cash is forfeited (s.297C). If the notice lapses and the period for which cash detention was authorised has expired, the cash may be detained for a further 48 hours but must be released unless an application for further detention or forfeiture is made (s.297D). A person aggrieved by forfeiture in pursuance of a notice may apply for the forfeiture to be set aside, if he applies within 30 days of the period for objecting ending (s.297E).

Where an application for forfeiture is made under s.298, the court may order forfeiture of the cash or any part of it if satisfied that it is recoverable property or is intended by any person for use in unlawful conduct. Special provisions apply in relation to recoverable property belonging to joint tenants.

(POCA 2002 s.298)

Procedure in the magistrates' court is governed by the Magistrates' Courts (Detention and Forfeiture of Cash) Rules 2002 (SI 2002/2998).

There is no requirement that a court, whether the magistrates' court or the Crown Court in its appellate capacity, must, before exercising its power of forfeiture, be satisfied that when seized, there had been reasonable grounds to believe that the money was recoverable or had been used unlawfully (*Home Secretary v Tuncel* [2012] EWHC 402 (Admin); [2012] 1 W.L.R. 3355, approved by *R. (on the application of Campbell) v IPCC* [2017] EWCA Civ 1161).

Appeal against forfeiture

An appeal lies to the Crown Court *by any party to proceedings* for an order for forfeiture of cash under s.298 who is aggrieved by an order made or a decision not to make such an order. The appeal must be made before the end of the period of 30 days starting with the day on which the court made its order or decision. **17-066**

The Crown Court may make any order it thinks appropriate, and if it upholds the appeal, may order the release of the cash.

(POCA 2002 s.299)

The proceedings are civil in nature and by way of rehearing.

11. External requests; cross-border enforcement

The legislation

Foreign requests and orders are received by the Secretary of State and forwarded to the CPS or SFO to take court action. Those bodies have a discretion whether or not to proceed. Procedure is under POCA 2002 (External Requests and Orders) Order 2005 (SI 2005/3181) Pt 2, or, in regard to the former law, under the CJ(IC)A 1990 (Enforcement of Overseas Forfeiture Orders) Order 2005 (SI 2005/3180). **17-067**

The scheme

The procedure under both orders is similar. It provides for (inter alia) the registration of external forfeiture orders: **17-068**

(1) arising from a criminal conviction in the country from which the order is sent; and
(2) concerning relevant property in England and Wales.

Such an order must be an order made by a court in a designated country for the forfeiture and destruction, or the forfeiture and disposal of anything:

(a) in respect of which a "relevant offence" has been committed; or
(b) which was used or intended for use in connection with the commission of such an offence.

A "relevant offence" is defined as one that corresponds to or is similar to an offence under the law of England and Wales.

Such a request is channelled through the Secretary of State to the "relevant Director", being the DPP or DSFO.

An application by a relevant Director to a judge of the Crown Court must include a request to appoint the Director as the enforcement authority, and may be made to a judge in chambers without giving notice to the other party.

The judge's role

The judge must give effect to an external forfeiture order by registering it where he is satisfied that: **17-069**

(1) the order was made consequent on the conviction of the person named in the order and no appeal is outstanding in respect of that conviction;
(2) the order is in force and no appeal is outstanding in respect of it;
(3) giving effect to the order would not be incompatible with any of the Convention rights of any persons affected by it; and
(4) the property whose confiscation is specified is not subject to a charge.

Where the judge decides to give effect to an external forfeiture order he must:

(a) register the order in that court; provide for notice to be given to any person affected by it; and
(b) appoint the relevant Director as the enforcement authority for the order.

Only an order registered in the Crown Court may be implemented under the legislation.

There are provisions for cancelling or varying the order, appealing to the CACD and the Supreme Court and the appointment of enforcement receivers.

An order is satisfied when the property specified in it has been forfeited or disposed in accordance with the legislation.

Procedure

17-070 CrimPR 33 applies with the necessary modifications to proceedings under SI 2005/3181 as they apply to corresponding proceedings under POCA 2002 (CrimPR 33.12).

Cross-border enforcement

17-071 The enforcement in England and Wales of confiscation orders made under the Proceeds of Crime (Scotland) Act 1995 is governed by SI 2001/953.

As to the enforcement in England and Wales of restraint and receivership proceedings from Scotland and Northern Ireland, see SI 2002/3133 and RESTRAINT ORDERS; RECEIVERS.

12. PRODUCTION, ETC., ORDERS; SEARCH AND ACCESS

17-072 As to production etc. orders, and search and access under POCA 2002, see INVESTIGATIVE ORDERS AND WARRANTS.

13. APPEALS

17-073 As to appeals to the CACD in relation to matters under POCA 2002, both by the offender and the prosecutor, see APPEALS FROM THE CROWN COURT.

14. COMPENSATION FOLLOWING DEFAULT, VARIATION OR APPEAL

17-074 POCA 2002 provides for compensation to be paid to a person whose property has been affected by the enforcement of the confiscation legislation.

A judge of the Crown Court may order the payment of such compensation as he believes just:

(1) where, but only where:
   (a) a criminal investigation has been started with regard to an offence and proceedings are not started for the offence; or

(b) proceedings for an offence are started against a person and:
 (i) they do not result in his conviction for the offence; or
 (ii) he is convicted of the offence but the conviction is quashed or he is pardoned in respect of it;

(2) where (1)(a) above applies:
 (a) in the criminal investigation there has been a serious default by a person mentioned in subs.(9); and
 (b) the investigation would not have continued if the default had not occurred;

(3) where (1)(b) above applies, and:
 (a) in the criminal investigation with regard to the offence or in its prosecution there has been a serious default by a person who is mentioned in subs.(9); and
 (b) the proceedings would not have been started or continued if the default had not occurred; and

(4) an application is made by a person who held realisable property and has suffered loss in consequence of anything done in relation to it by or in pursuance of an order under Pt 2 of the Act.

Note that the offence referred to:

(i) in (1) above may be one of a number of offences with regard to which the investigation is started; and
(ii) in (2) above may be one of a number of offences for which the proceedings are started.

(POCA 2002 s.72(1)–(8))

Application is made in writing and may be supported by a witness statement. It must be lodged in the Crown Court, and served on both the person alleged to be in default and the person by whom the compensation would be payable at least seven days before the date fixed by the court for hearing the application, unless the court directs otherwise.

(CrimPR 33.22)

Source of payment

Compensation is payable to the applicant as follows. If the person in default was: **17-075**

(1) a member, or was acting as a member, of a police force, the compensation is payable out of the police fund from which the expenses of that force are met;
(2) a member of the CPS or was acting on its behalf, the compensation is payable by the DPP;
(3) a member of staff of the NCA the compensation is payable by the NCA;
(4) a member of the SFO, the compensation is payable by the Director of that office;
(5) an officer of the Commissioners of Inland Revenue, the compensation is payable by those Commissioners;
(6) an immigration officer, the compensation is payable by the Secretary of State; and

(7) an accredited financial adviser, and none of the above apply, the compensation is payable in accordance with POCA 2002 s.302(7A)(a), (c) or (da) or (e).

(POCA 2002 s.72(9))

Compensation on variation or discharge

17-076 Where the court varies a confiscation order under s.29 or discharges one under s.30, an application may be made to the Crown Court by a person who held realisable property and has suffered loss as a result of the making of the order, and the judge may order the payment of such compensation as it believes is just, to the applicant, by the Lord Chancellor.

(POCA 2002 s.73)

The application must be in writing, supported by a witness statement giving details of the order made under s.28, the variation or discharge under s.29 or s.30, the realisable property to which the application relates and the loss suffered by the applicant as a result of the making of the order.

These documents must be lodged with the Crown Court, and must be served on the prosecutor where he is appointed the enforcement authority, at least seven days before the date fixed for the hearing unless the Crown Court specifies a shorter period.

(CrimPR 33.23)

18. CONTEMPT OF COURT

QUICK GUIDE

1. GENERAL

Definition

Conduct that: 18-001

(1) denotes wilful defiance of, or disrespect towards, the court;
(2) wilfully challenges or affronts the authority of the court, or the supremacy of the law itself;
(3) disrupts the proceedings of the court; or
(4) interferes with the course of justice,

is punishable as contempt of court. The power to punish for contempt is inherent in the system of administration of justice (*Morris v Crown Office* [1970] 1 All E.R. 1079 per Lord Denning MR; see also *R. v Jales* [2007] EWCA Crim 393; [2007] Crim. L.R. 800).

In general, in the Crown Court, contempt may arise in three situations, i.e. where:

(1) such behaviour takes place, on the part of the accused or others, in the courtroom or its vicinity, or otherwise affecting the proceedings (see 18-004);
(2) there is disobedience to an order or direction of the court or other unlawful conduct (see 18-010 and 18-011); or
(3) statutory prohibitions under CCA 1981 (see 18-010 and REPORTING AND ACCESS RESTRICTIONS) are infringed.

In its minor forms, contempt of court may relate only to disciplinary matters of good order, such as where the accused, a juror or a witness is drunk or a spectator takes a photograph of the judge, accused or jury. In more serious cases there is a direct challenge to the authority of the court and the integrity of its proceedings; for example, where a witness refuses to take the oath or affirm, or a juror behaves improperly, or there is evidence of intimidation of a witness or juror. Contempt may also involve the commission of a crime such as breach of the peace or an attempt to pervert the course of justice.

Judge's response

The Crown Court, being a superior court of record (SCA 1981 s.45(4)) a judge has power to deal immediately with contempt in the face of the court. Procedure will depend on the nature of the contempt. 18-002

The judge will need to decide in each case whether to:

(1) adopt the "immediate summary" procedure of the type described at 18-012 and following;

(2) postpone the matter and adopt the "formal procedures" under CrimPR 48 (see 18-020 and 18-022);
(3) refer the matter to the prosecuting authorities for prosecution as a substantive offence; or
(4) refer the matter to the Attorney General for possible prosecution under RSC Ord.52.

The judge's response will depend on the circumstances, thus:

(a) a minor disruption can, of course, be ignored;
(b) selective deafness may be an advantage; and
(c) if the conduct cannot be ignored, he may simply accept an apology from the person and take no further action.

Again, he may:

(i) warn a person not to continue with the abusive or disruptive behaviour; or
(ii) order a person disrupting the proceedings to be removed from the court, even if that person is the accused.

There will be cases where a flexible, swift and efficient response will be needed, to enable the judge to control the proceedings, especially where the contempt is perceived by him (as in, e.g. *R. v Jones* [2011] EWCA Crim 3179).

A prompt, effective response may deter further contempt (see the discussion in *R. v Santiago* [2005] EWCA Crim 556; [2005] 2 Cr. App. R. 24, and the Scottish case of *Robertson v HM Advocate* [2007] HCJAC 63; 1907 SLT 1153).

In extreme cases the trial may proceed in the absence of the accused; this course of action does not preclude taking action against the accused for contempt (see *R. v Baker* [2008] EWCA Crim 334; [2008] All E.R. (D.) 191 (Apr)).

Where behaviour amounts to a criminal offence, as well as to contempt, the judge may, in his discretion, either deal with the matter by way of contempt or allow the prosecuting authority to take over the matter (*R. v S* [2008] EWCA Crim 138; [2008] Crim. L.R. 716, where the CACD listed factors relevant to the exercise of the discretion). In an appropriate case he may adjourn the matter until, for example, the end of the trial (*R. v Santiago* [2005] EWCA Crim 556; [2005] 2 Cr. App. R. 24; *R. v S* [2008] EWCA Crim 138; [2008] Crim. L.R. 716).

Where it is clearly inappropriate for the judge to deal with the contempt of his own motion, he may refer the proceedings to the Attorney General with a view to proceedings under RSC Ord.52.

Trials for contempt of court on indictment are now obsolete. Neither the Attorney General, nor the alleged contemnor, has any right to seek trial by jury on indictment (*Attorney General v Dallas* [2012] EWHC 156 (Admin); [2012] 1 Cr. App. R. 32).

The judge's powers of punishment

18-003 Penalties for contempt, (other than certain statutory forms, for which see 18-010) are governed by CCA 1981 s.14.

The judge may:

(1) impose a term of imprisonment which must be for a fixed term and may not exceed two years;
(2) impose a fine of an unlimited amount; or
(3) in cases of a mentally disordered contemnor make any order available as the

contemnor had been convicted of an offence (as to which see MENTALLY DISORDERED OFFENDERS).

The leading guidance on nature and length of sentence comes from *R. v Montgomery* [1995] 2 Cr. App. R. 23. The matters set out in *Montgomery* were considered in *Re Yaxley-Lennon (aka Tommy Robinson)* [2018] EWCA Crim 1856. See generally 18-031.

2. Species of contempt

(1) Contempt in the face of the court or otherwise affecting the proceedings

"In the face of the court"

A judge has power to punish immediately "contempt in the face of the court" where it is committed: **18-004**

(1) in the courtroom, witnessed by him;
(2) in the courtroom and reported to him; and
(3) beyond the courtroom, and even beyond the precincts of the court, where it:
 (a) is reported to him; and
 (b) relates to proceedings then in progress, or pending before the court.

The notion of what counts as being "in the face of the [Crown] court" has been construed broadly (see *Balogh* [1974] 3 All E.R. 283; *Attorney General v Butterworth* [1962] 3 All E.R. 326; *R. v Curtis* [2012] EWCA Crim 945; [2013] 1 Cr. App. R. (S.) 28). Contempt not witnessed by the judge is treated "as being constructively within the sight and hearing of the court itself".

CrimPR 48.5(1)(a) refers to conduct "in the courtroom or in its vicinity, or otherwise immediately affecting the proceedings". This is so, apparently, even where the contempt in the face of the court consists in not appearing at court.

Examples of conduct amounting to contempt in the face of the court include:

- assaulting or insulting persons in open court;
- insulting or threatening the judge, or a court officer, in court;
- throwing a missile at the judge, or court officer;
- directing insults at the jury;
- wearing offensive clothing, or none at all;
- creating a disturbance in adjacent parts of the building such that the court proceedings are disturbed;
- disruptive behaviour, including calling out or applauding in the public gallery;
- conducting a protest in court or distributing leaflets in the public gallery;
- witnesses and jurors duly summoned who refuse to attend court;
- witnesses duly sworn who refuse to answer proper questions when ordered to do so, unless the witness is protected by privilege;
- persons in or out of court who threaten those about to give evidence or who have given evidence; or
- persons in or out of court who threaten or bribe or attempt to bribe jurors or interfere with their coming to court.

Failure to comply with an order from the judge or bench designed to control conduct in court may amount to contempt in the face of the court.

Contempt of these kinds may well justify the use of the summary jurisdiction; but everything will depend upon the circumstances.

Contempt by accused

18-005 Where the accused disrupts the proceedings (*R. v Aquarius* (1974) 59 Cr. App. R. 165), or stages an outburst after sentence (*R. v Logan* [1974] Crim. L.R. 609), or abuses the trial judge (*R. v Hill* [1986] Crim. L.R. 457; *R. v McDaniel* (1990-91) 12 Cr. App. R. (S.) 44), the appropriate course is:

(1) to pass a sentence for contempt consecutive to that for the substantive offence; and
(2) not attempt to include a contempt element in the sentence for substantive offence.

Intimidation of witnesses

18-006 The most common situations are where witnesses are victimised or threatened, or attempts are made to influence or intimidate jurors. Here there is a "real need" for the judge to intervene:

(1) not only to safeguard the dignity of the court; but
(2) in the latter case to reassure other jurors waiting their call to court.

This sort of contempt is prevalent and calls for a deterrent sentence (*R. v Goult* (1983) 76 Cr. App. R. 140; *R. v Mulvaney* (1982) 4 Cr. App. R. (S.) 106; *R. v Maloney* (1986) 8 Cr. App. R. (S.) 123; *R. v Pittendrigh* (1985) 7 Cr. App. R. (S.) 221; *R. v Edmonds* [1999] 1 Cr. App. R. (S.) 475; *R. v Smith* [2001] 1 Cr. App. R. (S.) 66; *R. v Rogers* [2002] 1 Cr. App. R. (S.) 272).

Recalcitrant witnesses

18-007 The judge has both common law and statutory powers for dealing with misconduct by witnesses.

A number of potential situations may occur here:

(1) by statute, where failure to attend may be dealt with by warrant (see WITNESS SUMMONSES AND WARRANT);
(2) by CrimPR 48.5, for disobedience to a witness summons (see 18-015); or
(3) where a witness attends but declines to answer questions.

In the case of (3) it will be a question for the judge whether some positive action is called for in the circumstances. Refusal to answer a question may be dealt with by mere admonition, unless the answer to it is vital. The judge ought to approach penalty in (3) only after reflection. Unless there is good reason for dealing with the matter speedily, sentence should be postponed until the end of the trial, or at least to the end of the prosecution case, for proceedings under CrimPR 48.8 (*R. v Moran* (1985) 7 Cr. App. R. (S.) 101; *R. v Lewis* (1993) 96 Cr. App. R. 412), so that the witness has a chance to reconsider his position. Where the contempt proceedings arise in the course of a trial, the judge should ask the jury to withdraw before, e.g. having a witness arrested in court (*R. v Maguire* [1997] 1 Cr. App. R. 61).

Refusal to be sworn, or to answer questions may, alternatively, be treated as a contempt in the face of the court (see *R. v Phillips* (1984) 78 Cr. App. R. 88, *R. v Lewis* (1993) 96 Cr. App. R. 412). Note the special position of journalists under s.10 of the 1981 Act. It may be possible for the witness to plead duress out of fear: *R. v K* (1984) 78 Cr. App. R. 82.

"Prevarication" (as it is called in Scotland), i.e. the giving of evasive and equivocal answers, inconsistency in testimony, and feigned ignorance and lack of memory with respect to things which he must know, is not dealt with as contempt, but by means of the "hostile witness" procedure (see, for a recent example *R. v Welsh* [2013] EWCA Crim 409).

Where a witness disobeys a Crown Court summons without "just excuse" CP(AW)A 1965 s.3 provides that the witness is guilty of contempt and may be punished summarily by that court as if his contempt had been committed "in the face of the court". The maximum penalty is three months' imprisonment (s.3(2), and see *R. v Abbott* [2004] EWCA Crim 91; [2004] All E.R. (D.) 154 (Feb)).

Although the maximum penalty for common law contempt (at two years' imprisonment (CCA 1981 s.14)) is considerably higher than for the witness who disobeys a summons and does not attend, it was said in *R. v Montgomery* (see 18-031) that

> "whilst it is legitimate in the case of a witness refusing to testify, to have regard to the fact that the maximum sentence for failing to comply with a witness order is three months, that should not inhibit the court from imposing a sentence substantially longer than three months for a blatant contempt in the face of the court ...".

Contempt by jurors

It is an offence of both contempt and interference with the course of justice to impersonate a juror, and act in his or her stead (*R. v Levy* (1916) 32 T.L.R. 238; *R. v Clark* (1918) 82 J.P. 295). **18-008**

Note also that:

- where a jury reaches a verdict other than according to the evidence, a contempt may have been committed, e.g. leaving the verdict to chance (such as drawing lots, or tossing a coin);
- misusing the internet or electronic communications is always a serious irregularity and a custodial sentence for contempt is virtually inevitable (see *Attorney General v Fraill* [2011] EWHC 1629 (Admin); [2011] 2 Cr. App. R. 21);
- deception of the court by a juror is likely to lead to an immediate prison sentence for contempt (see *R. v Chapman* [2012] EWCA Crim 1011; [2013] 1 Cr. App. R. (S.) 22);
- it is not a contempt for jurors to decline to reach a verdict, or to reach a verdict which is perverse, providing that it is due to insufficiency of the facts; although
- a contumacious refusal to reach a verdict because of reluctance to judge another person, may, in an appropriate case, establish the actus reus of contempt (*R. v Schot* [1997] 2 Cr. App. R. 383), though it may be difficult or impossible to prove.

As to statutory offences by jurors, see 18-010.

The need to keep jurors' deliberations confidential in accordance with JA s.20D (previously CCA 1981 s.8 but as from 13 April 2015 s.8 was in effect repealed albeit the provisions are broadly similar), requires a judge to proceed with care if he needs to inquire into any irregularity in the way decisions have been reached. (See ss.20E–20G of the JA 1974 and also 18-010.) The approach to be adopted is set out by Lord Carswell in *R. v Smith* [2005] UKHL 12; [2005] 2 Cr. App. R. 10. In the context of an alleged contempt by, or affecting, a juror or jury, unless it is appropriate for the judge to deal summarily with the contempt of his own motion, which would be exceptional, such allegations should be dealt with by the Attorney General under RSC Ord.52 r.5 (Civil Procedure Rules 1998 Sch.1).

Juror misconduct may also amount to a statutory offence. If a juror fails to attend following a summons that may be dealt with as a contempt, or as a breach of the statutory provision (see 18-011).

Conduct of legal practitioners

18-009 The law of contempt is available to provide a fair trial, to ensure compliance with the court's orders and to protect the proper administration of justice, the sole purpose of the jurisdiction being

> "to give our courts the power effectively to protect the rights of the public by ensuring that the administration of justice shall not be obstructed or prevented" (per Salmon LJ in *Morris v Crown Office* [1970] 1 All E.R. 1079).

In the case of alleged contempt by legal practitioners it was made clear in the Privy Council case of *Izuora v The Queen* [1953] 1 All E.R. 827 that not every act of discourtesy to the court by counsel amounts to contempt, nor is conduct which involves a breach by counsel of his duty to his client necessarily in this category. In so far as the requisite intention is concerned, it was set out in *Attorney General v Newspaper Publishing Plc* [1987] 3 All E.R. 276 in this way:

> "the mens rea required is an intent to interfere with the course of justice. As in other branches of the criminal law, that intent may exist, even though there is no desire to interfere with the course of justice. Nor need it be the sole intent. It may be inferred, even though there is no overt proof. The more obvious the interference with the course of justice, the more readily will the requisite intent be inferred."

In *Weston v Central Criminal Court Courts Administrator* [1976] 2 All E.R. 875 (non-appearance, accompanied by an impertinent letter) the Court of Appeal set aside the order on the basis that there was nothing that the solicitor had done to interfere with the due administration of justice or to disobey an order of the court: the discourteous letter "did not interfere with the course of justice in the least". Applying *Izuora v The Queen* [1953] 1 All E.R. 827, he had, therefore, not "crossed the line dividing mere discourtesy and breach of duty to a client or the court from contempt".

In *Re West* [2014] EWCA Crim 1480, the CACD, accepting that not every failure to co-operate or refusal to attend court is a contempt, added that that is very different from saying that failure to co-operate or refusal to attend court could never be a contempt: it clearly can be. As where counsel failed: (a) to attend the adjourned preliminary hearing as directed; and (b) to assist with the case management requests that were made of him. In this case counsel's conduct constituted willful and deliberate disobedience of an order of the court as an act of defiance which is serious misconduct of a type that is wholly inimical to the proper discharge of his professional duties and, furthermore, in total disregard of his duty to the court.

ECtHR jurisprudence has emphasised that a distinction needs to be made between criticism and insult, also the forum in which it is made. A statement to the media made in court or its precincts might be a contempt in the face of the court, while if it is made away from the court and does not disrupt proceedings it would not be contempt in the face of the court.

(2) Statutory contempts

A judge of the Crown Court has power to punish as a contempt: **18-010**

(1) breaches of reporting restrictions under CCA 1981 ss.4 and 11 (see REPORTING AND ACCESS RESTRICTIONS);
(2) breaches of SO(A)A 1992 s.1 (see REPORTING AND ACCESS RESTRICTIONS);
(3) failure of a juror to answer a summons to attend court (JA 1974 s.19(1)) (see 18-015);
(4) misuse of sound recorders in court (CCA 1981 s.9) (see 18-015);
(5) CP(AW)A 1965 s.3 (disobeying a witness summons) (see 18-015);
(6) refusal to disclose sources of information (CCA 1981 s.10) (see REPORTING AND ACCESS RESTRICTIONS);
(7) publication relating to proceedings in private (CCA 1981 s.12) (see REPORTING AND ACCESS RESTRICTIONS);
(8) photography and sketching in court (CJA 1925 s.41) (see REPORTING AND ACCESS RESTRICTIONS);
(9) publication of any material relating to proceedings which is prejudicial to the administration of justice (see REPORTING AND ACCESS RESTRICTIONS);
(10) electronic communications from court other than in accordance with *Practice Guidance (Court Proceedings: Live text-based Communications)* (see REPORTING AND ACCESS RESTRICTIONS); and
(11) any other conduct with which the court can deal as, or as if it were, a criminal contempt of court (except failure to surrender to bail under BA 1976 s.6—see BAIL).

See as to the Lord Chancellor's power, with the concurrence of the Lord Chief Justice, to disapply provisions of (5) and (9) above, CCA 2013 s.32.

JA 1974 is amended by CJCA 2014 ss.42–44 to create a number of offences in relation to misconduct by a juror trying an issue before the court, including:

(a) research (JA 1974 s.20A) by intentionally seeking information when he knows, or ought reasonably to know that the information is or may be relevant to the case;
(b) sharing research with other jurors (JA 1974 s.20B) by intentionally disclosing information to another member the jury during the trial period, where he has contravened s.20A in the process of obtaining the information, and the information has not been provided by the court; and
(c) intentionally engaging in other prohibited conduct during the trial (JA 1974 s.20C), that is conduct from which it may reasonably be concluded that he intends to try the issue otherwise than on the basis of the evidence presented in the proceedings on the issue, whether or not he knows that the conduct is prohibited conduct.

A person guilty of such offences is liable, on conviction on indictment, to imprisonment for a term not exceeding two years or a fine (or both). Proceedings may only be instituted by or with the consent of the Attorney General.

Nothing in the above sections affects what constitutes contempt of court at common law.

JA 1974 s.20D also makes it an offence for a person intentionally to disclose information about statements made, opinions expressed, arguments advanced or votes cast by jury members in the course of their deliberations, or to solicit or obtain such information. There are a number of exceptions to s.20D set out in ss.20E–20G. Those exceptions cater for the investigation of potential irregularities. Section 20D replaced CCA s.8. The key distinction was to make the intentional disclosure of jury deliberations a specific criminal offence as opposed to another type of contempt.

(3) Contempt of court orders

18-011 A judge of the Crown Court has power to punish for contempt of court any person who:

(1) disobeys an order of the court (SCA 1981 s.45);
(2) uses disclosed prosecution material in contravention of CPIA 1996 s.17 (see DISCLOSURE);
(3) disobeys certain investigative orders to which rr.6.13 and 6.22 apply (see INVESTIGATIVE ORDERS AND WARRANTS); and
(4) disobeys a restraint order to which r.59.6 applies (see RESTRAINT ORDERS; RECEIVERS).

Where a person is accused in the Crown Court of such conduct (the respondent), the judge must not exercise his power to punish for contempt in his absence unless the respondent has had at least 14 days in which to make representations and introduce any evidence.

Procedure is under CrimPR 48.9 (at 18-022).

3. Procedures for contempt

(1) Summary or immediate procedure Summary or immediate process

18-012 The process by which the judge deals with contempt in the face of the court is usually described as "summary" or "immediate" (in *Balogh v St Albans Crown Court* [1974] 3 All E.R. 283 Lord Denning MR described it as summary and "draconian"). It must be distinguished from the situation where the judge postpones dealing with the matter, and the formal procedure under r.62.5 is followed (see 18-015) as in *R. v Santiago* [2005] EWCA Crim 556; [2005] 2 Cr. App. R. 24 and *R. v S* [2008] EWCA Crim 138; [2008] Crim. L.R. 716—see 18-002.

The authorities show that the immediate process should be exercised only where:

(1) the contempt is clearly proved, and nothing else will do to protect the ends of justice (see *R. v Tamworth Justices Ex p. Walsh* [1994] C.O.D. 277; *The Times,* 3 March 1994);
(2) it is necessary to act appropriately to ensure that the proceedings do not get out of order (*R. v Atkinson* [2011] EWCA Crim 1766. See, e.g. *R. v Pateley Bridge Justices Ex p. Percy* [1994] C.O.D. 453); and

(3) ensuring that a trial in progress or about to start can be brought to a proper and dignified end without disturbance and with a fair chance of a just verdict or judgment.

In *R. v Santiago* [2005] EWCA Crim 556; [2005] 2 Cr. App. R. 24 the CACD accepted that the threat of summary proceedings for contempt was likely to be more effective in preventing disruption than referring an alleged assault to the prosecuting authority for later prosecution. It must be left to the common sense of the judge to decide when he ought to resort to this power to deal with such contempt (*Balogh* [1974] 3 All E.R. 283 per Stephenson LJ).

The need for immediate action

The judge must make his own assessment of the need for taking immediate action to deal with an alleged contempt (*R. v Goult* (1983) 76 Cr. App. R. 140). **18-013**

He will need to distinguish between conduct:

(1) which involves disruption of the court, or threats to witnesses or jurors, which should be visited by immediate arrest; and, in contrast
(2) which is not likely to disturb the trial or affect the verdict, which can be dealt with under the formal procedure (under CrimPR 42.8), or referred to the prosecuting authorities.

The "urgency to act immediately" expressed in *Balogh* has been tempered by *Wilkinson v Lord Chancellor's Department* [2003] EWCA Civ 95; [2003] 2 All E.R. 184. See also *Rooney v Snaresbrook Crown Court* (1979) 68 Cr. App. R. 78.

As to the need not to act too hastily, and to give the contemnor an opportunity to apologise and to offer mitigation, see *R. v Phelps* [2009] EWCA Crim 2308; [2010] 2 Cr. App. R. (S.) 1 (and 18-015).

Where the contempt consists of abuse or vilification of the judge personally, the issue of contempt should be referred by him to another judge (see *Kyprianou v Cyprus (No.2)* [1907] 44 E.H.R.R. 44; *R. v Haslam* [2003] EWCA Crim 3444; *Wilkinson v Lord Chancellor's Department* [2003] EWCA Civ 95; *Robertson v HM Advocate* [2007] HCJAC 63; 1907 SLT 1153 and *R. v Santiago* [2005] EWCA Crim 556; [2005] 2 Cr. App. R. 24).

Where there is no dispute as to the essential facts it is open to the judge to deal with the matter himself since a fair-minded observer would not conclude there is a real possibility of bias (*Wilkinson v Lord Chancellor's Department* [2003] EWCA Civ 95).

In the case of a "formal enquiry" the court that conducts an enquiry:

(a) need not include the same member or members as the court that observed the conduct; but
(b) may do so, unless that would be unfair to the respondent.

(CrimPR 48.8(5))

Procedure sui generis

The immediate procedure described in 18-012 and 18-013 is a procedure sui generis (*R. v Griffin* (1989) 88 Cr. App. R. 63 per Mustill LJ). Thus there is: **18-014**

(1) no prosecutor;
(2) no requirement that the prosecutor or an injured party initiate the proceedings;

(3) no summons or indictment;
(4) no mandatory requirement for any written account of the accusation; and
(5) no preliminary procedure, and the proceedings are not adversarial.

When dealing in this manner with contempt:

(a) the judge may order the immediate arrest and detention of the alleged contemnor;
(b) the decision to try him summarily should be taken only when it is necessary to do so to preserve the integrity of the trial or the dignity of the court (see 18-012); and
(c) the decision should not be taken too quickly, time should always be allowed for reflection, if necessary overnight.

Procedure under CrimPR 48.5

18-015 CrimPR 48.5 specifies the procedure to be followed where the court observes, or has reported to it:

(1) obstructive, disruptive, insulting or intimidating conduct in or near the courtroom, or immediately affecting its proceedings;
(2) a contravention of:
  (a) CP(AW)A 1965 s.3 (disobeying a witness summons);
  (b) JA 1974 s.20 (disobeying a jury summons);
  (c) CCA 1981 s.8 (obtaining details of a jury's deliberations, etc.);
  (d) CCA 1981 s.9 (without the court's permission, recording the proceedings, etc.); or
  (e) any other conduct with which the court can deal as, or as if it were, a criminal contempt of court, (except failure to surrender to bail under BA 1976 s.6 (see BAIL)).

Unless the alleged contemnor's behaviour makes it impracticable to do so, the judge must explain, in terms he can understand (with help, if necessary):

(i) the conduct that is in question;
(ii) that the judge may impose imprisonment, or a fine, or both;
(iii) (where relevant) that the judge has power to order his immediate temporary detention, if in the judge's opinion that is required;
(iv) that the contemnor may explain the conduct;
(v) that he may apologise, if he so wishes, and that this may persuade the judge to take no further action; and
(vi) that he may take legal advice; and in this last case, allow him a reasonable opportunity to reflect, take advice, explain and, if he wishes, apologise.

The court may then:

- take no further action in respect of that conduct;
- enquire into the conduct there and then; or
- postpone the enquiry.

(CrimPR 48.5(1) and (2))

Older authorities

Observations in some of the older authorities would seem still to be apposite. **18-016**

The judge should enquire direct from the alleged contemnor whether he admits the conduct alleged against him and the fact that the conduct amounts to contempt of court (*R. v Moran* (1985) 81 Cr. App. R. 51; *R. v Grant* [1910] EWCA Crim 215).

No person should be found in contempt unless he distinctly admits it or, if he does not, unless it be proved against him beyond reasonable doubt—the criminal standard. An intention to disrupt the proceedings is not an essential element of contempt (*R. v Huggins* [2007] EWCA Crim 132; [2007] 2 Cr. App. R. 8).

> "The test for contempt [is] whether the [contemnor] knowingly did an act which he intended, and which was calculated, to interfere with the course of justice and was capable of having that effect" (*R. v Giscombe* (1984) 79 Cr. App. R. 79)

or foresaw the consequence without necessarily intending it (*R. v Schot* [1997] 2 Cr. App. R. 383 per Rose LJ). An intention to disrupt the proceedings or to show disrespect may be inferred from the act itself (e.g. *R. v Jones* [2011] EWCA Crim 3179).

By its nature the summary process needs to be used quickly or not at all, omitting, as it does, many of the safeguards to which the accused is ordinarily entitled (*R. v S* [2008] EWCA Crim 138; [2008] Crim. L.R. 716; *Wilkinson v Lord Chancellor's Department* [2003] EWCA Civ 95).

Where the contempt proceedings touch upon a trial in session, they must be in open court, and the defence advocate cannot be excluded (*R. v Cooledge* [1996] Crim. L.R. 749). The matter should not, however, be dealt with in the presence of the jury, nor should a recalcitrant witness be detained in their presence.

Temporary detention; review; bail

By reason of the jurisdiction conferred by SCA 1981 s.45 the judge has an inherent power, when dealing with obstructive, disruptive, insulting or intimidating conduct, to detain a contemnor temporarily, at least for the purpose of restoring order. **18-017**

> "In cases of criminal contempt (which include contempt in the face of the court ...), the superior courts have an inherent power of detention until the rising of the court on the day of the alleged contempt" (*Delaney v Delaney* [1996] 1 All E.R. 367 per Lord Bingham MR).

There is nothing in AJA 1960 s.13(1) to prohibit the grant of bail to an alleged contemnor.

Where contempt is alleged to have taken place outwith the presence of the judge, he has no power to remand the alleged contemnor into custody before the contempt is proved. Where he wishes to restrict the alleged contemnor's liberty during the further course of the trial he will have either to adjourn the trial and proceed to deal with the alleged contempt, or arrange for another judge to hear the allegation (*R. v Stevens*, *The Independent*, June 1997, QBD).

In a case in which the judge has ordered the contemnor's immediate temporary detention for conduct to which CrimPR 48.5 applies, the judge will review the case no later than the next business day (see 18-015).

On the review, the judge will:

(1) unless the contemnor is absent, repeat the explanations required by CrimPR 48.5(2)(a) (see 18-015); and
(2) allow him a reasonable opportunity to reflect, take advice, explain and, if he so wishes, apologise.

The judge may then:

(a) take no further action in respect of the conduct;
(b) enquire into the conduct there and then; or
(c) postpone the enquiry, and order the contemnor's release from such detention in the meantime.

(CrimPR 48.6)

It would seem that BA 1976 applies, since contempt proceedings are "proceedings for an offence" within the meaning of the above s.1(1). The likelihood of the alleged contemnor receiving a custodial sentence will be relevant (LASPOA 1912 s.90). There is a right of appeal against a refusal of bail in contempt proceedings (*R. v Serumaga* [2005] EWCA Crim 370; [2005] 1 W.L.R. 3366).

Legal representation

18-018 The judge ought to give the alleged contemnor the opportunity to have legal advice or representation or to prepare his defence (*R. v Selby Justices Ex p. Frame* [1991] 2 All E.R. 344; *R. v Haslam* [2003] EWCA Crim 3444; [2003] All E.R. (D.) 195 (Nov)). LASPOA 2012 ss.14(g) and 15 provide for advice and representation for contempt in the face of the court.

In *R. v Newbury Justices Ex p. Du Pont* (1984) 78 Cr. App. R. 255 at 260, May LJ distinguished between cases where an adjournment was appropriate, which allowed for legal advice, and cases where the court needed to deal with "a disruption obstructing the process of the court's business" and held that this distinction justified dispensing with legal representation in the latter kind of case but whether that would comply with ECHR jurisprudence has not yet been tested.

Postponement of enquiry

18-019 Where the judge postpones the enquiry (under (c) in 18-017):

(1) the court *must* arrange for the preparation of a written statement containing such particulars of the conduct in question as to make clear what the respondent appears to have done; and
(2) the court officer will serve on the respondent:
    (a) that written statement;
    (b) notice of where and when the postponed enquiry will take place; and
    (c) a notice that:
        (i) reminds the respondent that the court may impose imprisonment, or a fine, or both, for contempt; and
        (ii) warns him that the judge may pursue the postponed enquiry in his absence, if he does not attend.

(CrimPR 48.7)

(2) Formal procedure under CrimPR 48.8

General

In cases where the judge postpones dealing a matter of contempt and the formal procedure under CrimPR 48.8 is followed, this procedure is properly classified as a "summary process", but it is very different to the immediate procedure outlined in 18-012. It is more helpful to refer to this as a "formal procedure", since it involves: **18-020**

(1) the calling of witnesses by a prosecutor;
(2) the opportunity of examining them;
(3) the opportunity of the alleged contemnor to give evidence and call witnesses in his own evidence; and
(4) the provision of a reasoned judgment by the court against which an appeal lies to the CACD as of right.

CrimPR 48.8 applies to an enquiry and CrimPR 48.9 to the failure to comply with court orders.

The court must arrange for the preparation of a written statement containing such particulars of the conduct in question as to make clear what the respondent appears to have done, and the court officer must serve on the respondent:

- that written statement;
- notice of where and when the postponed enquiry will take place; and
- a notice that reminds the respondent that the judge can impose imprisonment, or a fine, or both, for contempt of court, and warns the respondent that the judge may pursue the postponed enquiry in the respondent's absence, if the respondent does not attend.

(CrimPR 48.7)

Any enquiry under CrimPR 48.8, or allegation under CrimPR 48.9, must be determined at a hearing, and the judge must not proceed in the respondent's absence unless:

(a) the respondent's behaviour makes it impracticable to proceed otherwise; or
(b) the respondent has had at least 14 days' notice of the hearing, or was present when it was arranged.

In *Re Yaxley-Lennon* [2018] EWCA Crim 1856 the Court considered strict adherence with the CrimPR. The Court noted that for much of the twentieth century, the courts took a rather mechanistic view of the consequences of any failure to comply with the rules relating to the procedure to be followed in cases of alleged contempt. Such rules existed in civil and family proceedings long before they were introduced into the CrimPR. In *M v P (Contempt of Court: Committal Order)* [1993] Fam. 167, the Court of Appeal sought to clarify the nature of the balance to be struck where the relevant rules have not been followed to the letter. Lord Donaldson identified the following principle at pp.178–9:

> "In all contempt cases, justice requires the court to take account of the interests of at least three categories of person, namely, (a) the contemnor (b) the 'victim' of the contempt and (c) other users of the court for whom the maintenance of the authority of the court is of supreme importance. The interests of the alleged contemnor require that he should have the right to be informed of the charges which he has to meet, to be advised and represented if he so wishes (subject to his being eligible for legal aid or otherwise able to finance his

defence), to be given a full and fair opportunity of meeting those charges and, if found guilty of contempt of court, to be informed in sufficiently clear terms of what has been found against him. In all these cases the court has been concerned to ensure that these fundamental requirements are met in the way in which, particularly in the case of the county courts, they are intended to be and should be met. However, we have tended to overlook the fact that they may in some circumstance be met in other ways. Whilst this court should always be quick to identify and condemn any departure from the proper procedures, the interests of the victim and of maintaining the authority of the courts require that in deciding what use to make of its powers under section 13(3) of the Act of 1960, this court should ask itself whether, notwithstanding such a departure, the contemnor has suffered any injustice. It does not follow that he has. Nor does it follow that the proper course is to quash the order. If he has not suffered any injustice, the committal order should stand, subject if necessary, to variation of the order to take account of any technical or procedural defects. In other cases it may be possible to do justice between the parties by exercising the court's power under section 13(3) by making 'such other order may be just.' If the circumstances are such that justice requires the committal order to be quashed amongst the options available is that of ordering a retrial …".

This was cited with approval in *Nicholls v Nicholls* [1997] 1 W.L.R. 314. Lord Woolf MR observed:

"The guidance which can be provided for future cases is as follows.

(1) As committal orders involve the liberty of the subject it is particularly important that the relevant rules are duly complied with. It remains the responsibility of the judge when signing the committal order to ensure that it is properly drawn and that it adequately particularises the breaches which have been proved and for which the sentence has been imposed.
(2) As long as the contemnor had a fair trial and the order has been made on valid grounds the existence of a defect either in the application to commit or in the committal order served will not result in the order being set aside except in so far as the interests of justice require this to be done.
(3) Interests of justice will not require an order to be set aside where there is no prejudice caused as a result of errors in the application to commit or in the order to commit. When necessary the order can be amended.
(4) When considering whether to set aside the order, the court should have regard to the interests of any other party and the need to uphold the reputation of the justice system.
(5) If there has been a procedural irregularity or some other defect in the conduct of the proceedings which has occasioned injustice, the court will consider exercising its power to order a new trial unless there are circumstances which indicate that it would not be just to do so."

In *Yaxley-Lennon* it was stated that it is this guidance which has been adopted and applied by the courts consistently over the last twenty years and, most recently at that time, in *Fort Locks Self Storage Ltd v William Deakin* [2017] EWCA Civ 404.

It was contended in *Yaxley-Lennon* that this is not the correct approach to the application of Pt 48 of CrimPR, any breach of which, it was argued, is fatal to the subsequent committal. In support of this, reliance was placed on the authority of *Re West* [2015] 1 W.L.R. 109 (CA (Crim Div)), a case in which a barrister was found to have acted in contempt of court in refusing unreasonably to attend a hearing in a criminal case when he had been ordered so to do. His punishment was a fine of £500. The Court of Appeal overturned the finding of contempt because the alleged contemnor had not been served with a notice in advance of the hearing as required by the CrimPR. Sir Brian Leveson P observed:

"34. While Mr West was thus made aware in advance of the hearing that contempt of court would be considered, the notices provided clearly fell short of the procedural requirements set out in the Crim PR. In the normal course, compliance with the strict provisions of the Crim PR can be waived by the parties or the court; in cases of alleged contempt, however, we have no doubt that strict observance of the provisions is essential. As Mr Cox observed, the contempt jurisdiction is a powerful tool which can directly impact on the liberty of the subject. Compliance with the Crim PR allows the "charge" to be fully formulated and beyond doubt; it provides a structure which forms the four corners of what is in issue and it avoids the very criticism that Mr Cox did advance in this case.

35. In the circumstances, given the significance of the jurisdiction of contempt of court, we have come to the conclusion that this failure of process invalidates the conclusion that the judge reached. We recognise that it is likely to have made little difference but we are not prepared to assert that; it is far more important to underline the vital importance, where issues of contempt arise in circumstances of this nature, of following the approach laid down by the Crim PR."

In *Yaxley-Lennon* it was held that notwithstanding this emphatic reminder of the particular importance of following the correct procedure in cases of alleged contempt, it was satisfied that the court in *West* did not intend to herald a departure from the approach set out in *Nicholls*:

"The inadequacy of the notice had not formed any part of the grounds of appeal raised on behalf of the contemnor in *West*. He sought to challenge the substance of the finding against him and there does not appear to have been any reference to authority on the point. The issue was raised by the court. Nonetheless, the language of the President does not support the proposition that any and every breach of the rules invalidates a finding of contempt; rather that was the position 'in the circumstances of that case'.

There is no justification for adopting a different approach to a failure to comply with the requirements of Part 48 of CrimPR from a failure to comply with parallel rules in the civil and family jurisdictions. They aim to achieve the similar outcome of fairness in the context of a process which can lead to a loss of liberty. Accordingly, we are satisfied that the approach to failures to follow rules of procedure identified in *Nicholls* should be applied to this and all cases subject to Part 48 of the Rules."

Procedure at hearing

At the enquiry, the judge must (CrimPR 48.8): **18-021**

(1) ensure that the respondent understands (with help, if necessary) what is alleged, if the enquiry has been postponed from a previous occasion;
(2) explain what the procedure will be; and
(3) ask whether the respondent admits the conduct in question.

If the respondent admits the conduct, the judge need not receive evidence; if he does not admit the conduct, the judge will receive any statement served under CrimPR 48.7, any other evidence of the conduct, and any evidence introduced by the respondent. He will also receive any representations by the respondent about the conduct.

If the respondent admits the conduct, or the judge finds it proved, the judge must:

(a) before imposing any punishment for contempt, give the respondent an opportunity to make representations relevant to punishment; and

(b) explain, in terms the respondent can understand (with help, if necessary):
   (i) the reasons for his decision, including his findings of fact; and
   (ii) the punishment he imposes, and its effect.

As to punishment, see generally 18-030.

(3) Procedure under CrimPR 48.9

By a party

18-022 Where:

(1) a party, or other person directly affected, alleges:
   (a) a failure to comply with an order to which CrimPR 33.70 (compliance order, restraint order or ancillary order), CrimPR 47.13 or CrimPR 47.22 (certain investigation orders) applies;
   (b) any other conduct with which the court may deal as a civil contempt of court; or
   (c) there is unauthorised use of disclosed prosecution material under CPIA 1996 s.17 (see below); or
(2) the judge deals on his own initiative with conduct to which (1) applies, such party or person as mentioned in (1) must:
   (a) apply in writing and serve the application on the court officer; and
   (b) serve on the respondent such application, and notice of where and when the judge will consider the allegation (not less than 14 days after service).

The application must:

- identify the respondent;
- explain that it is an application for the respondent to be dealt with for contempt of court;
- contain such particulars of the conduct in question as to make clear what is alleged against him; and
- include a notice warning him that the court may impose imprisonment, or a fine, or both, for contempt, and may deal with the application in his absence, if he does not attend the hearing.

Procedure is as under CrimPR 48.8 (at 18-020).

Judge acting on his own initiative

18-023 A judge who acts on his own initiative under para.(1)(b) (above) must:

(1) arrange for the preparation of a written statement containing the same information as in an application by a party (see 18-022); and
(2) arrange for the service on the respondent of that written statement, and notice of where and when the judge will consider the allegation (not less than 14 days after service).

(CrimPR 48.9(4))

Stay or adjournment; criminal trial pending

18-024 Where:

(1) there is an application to commit a person for contempt of court because he is in breach of a court order; and
(2) at the same time, a criminal trial is pending against the person accused of contempt,

the judge has a power to stay or adjourn the contempt proceedings until after the completion of the accused's criminal trial (*Harris v Crisp*, *The Times,* 12 August 1992), but the power to stay or adjourn should only be exercised exceptionally, where there is a "real risk of serious prejudice which may lead to injustice"; or, as it was put in *R. v Payton* [2006] EWCA Crim 1226; [2006] Crim. L.R. 997, "the issue was whether the fair trial of an [accused] would be prejudiced" (by the cash forfeiture proceedings in that case going ahead before the principal criminal trial).

If an application to stay or adjourn the contempt proceedings to await the outcome of a criminal trial is made, the judge will consider the issues that will arise on the contempt application and those that appear likely to arise at the criminal trial in the light of the prosecution case and the accused's case, so far as it is known at the time of the application (*R. v AA* [2010] EWCA Crim 2805).

He will have to consider also what evidence an accused might wish to give in the contempt hearing. He must form a judgment on whether, in holding the contempt hearing in which an accused may decide to give evidence, that would give rise to a real risk of serious prejudice to the accused in relation to his criminal trial which could thereby lead to injustice.

In forming that judgment, the judge must take account of all relevant factors and must disregard all those that are irrelevant.

Procedure on CrimPR 48.9 hearing

At the hearing of an allegation under CrimPR 48.9, the judge will: **18-025**

(1) ensure that the respondent understands (with help, if necessary) what is alleged;
(2) explain what the procedure at the hearing will be; and
(3) ask whether the respondent admits the conduct in question.

If the respondent admits the conduct, the judge need not receive evidence; if the respondent does not, the judge will consider:

(a) the application or written statement served under CrimPR 48.9;
(b) any other evidence of the conduct;
(c) any evidence introduced by the respondent; and
(d) any representations by the respondent about the conduct.

And the judge will, before imposing any punishment for contempt, give the respondent an opportunity to make representations relevant to punishment and will explain, in terms the respondent can understand (with help, if necessary) the reasons for his decision, including his findings of fact, and the punishment he imposes, and its effect (CrimPR 48.10).

Written witness statements or other hearsay

Where CrimPR 48.9 (above) applies, an applicant or respondent who wishes to introduce in evidence the written statement of a witness, or other hearsay, must: **18-026**

(1) serve a copy of the statement or notice of other hearsay on the court officer, and the other party; and

(2) do so when serving the application under CrimPR 48.9, in the case of an applicant or not more than seven days after service of that application or of the court's written statement, in the case of the respondent.

Such service is notice of that party's intention to introduce in evidence that written witness statement, or other hearsay, unless he otherwise indicates when serving it (CrimPR 48.11).

Note that:

(a) a party entitled to receive such notice may waive that entitlement (CrimPR 48.11(3));
(b) a written witness statement served under CrimPR 48.11 must contain a declaration by the person making it that it is true to the best of that person's knowledge and belief (CrimPR 48.12); and
(c) notice of hearsay, other than a written witness statement, served under CrimPR 48.11(2) must set out the evidence, or attach the document that contains it; and identify the person who made the statement that is hearsay (CrimPR 48.13).

Cross-examination of maker of written witness statement or other hearsay

18-027 Where a party wants the judge's permission to cross-examine a person who made a statement which another party wants to introduce as hearsay, then:

(1) the party who wants to cross-examine that person must:
  (a) apply in writing, with reasons; and
  (b) serve the application on the court officer and on the party who served the hearsay;
(2) a respondent who wants to cross-examine such a person must apply to do so not more than seven days after service of the hearsay by the applicant.

The judge may decide an application under this rule without a hearing, but must not dismiss such an application unless the person making it has had an opportunity to make representations at a hearing (CrimPR 48.14).

Credibility and consistency

18-028 Where a party wants to challenge the credibility or consistency of a person who made a statement which another party wants to introduce as hearsay, then:

(1) the party who wants to challenge the credibility or consistency of that person must:
  (a) serve a written notice of intention to do so on the court officer, and the party who served the hearsay; and
  (b) in that notice, identify any statement or other material on which he relies;
(2) a respondent who wants to challenge such a person's credibility or consistency must serve such a notice not more than seven days after service of the hearsay by the applicant, and must serve such a notice not more than three days after service of the hearsay by the respondent.

The party who served the hearsay may call that person to give oral evidence instead, and if so, must serve a notice of intention to do so on the court officer, and the other party, as soon as practicable after service of the notice under (1)(a) (above) (CrimPR 48.15).

Court's power to vary requirements of service

The judge may shorten or extend (even after it has expired) a time limit under CrimPR 48.11, 48.14 or 48.15. **18-029**

A person who wants an extension of time must apply when serving the statement, notice or application for which it is needed, and explain the delay (CrimPR 48.17).

4. Punishment

The judge's powers

Penalties for contempt (other than certain statutory forms of contempt) are governed by CCA 1981 s.14. **18-030**

The sanctions available to the Crown Court are:

(1) in the case of an adult:
  (a) imprisonment for a maximum of two years (SCA 1981 s.14(1)) and/or a fine of an unlimited amount;
  (b) in the case of a mentally disordered offender make any order available as if he had been convicted of an offence a hospital order (MHA 1983 s.14(4)); and
(2) in relation to young contemnors:
  (a) for those aged 18, 19 and 20, detention under PCC(S)A s.108 may be ordered, if appropriate;
  (b) in the case of those under 18, a fine is probably the only appropriate penalty, though an attendance centre order may be appropriate where the contemnor is over 17 (CCA 1981 s.14(2A)).

A custodial sentence may be:

(1) concurrent or consecutive to a period of custody imposed following a conviction (*R. v Stredder* [1997] 1 Cr. App. R. (S.) 199); or
(2) suspended (*Morris v Crown Office* [1970] 1 All E.R. 788).

There is no power to impose a community sentence, or make a probation order (*R. v Palmer* (1992) 95 Cr. App. R. 170) or indeed to impose any non-custodial punishment other than a fine.

The sentence for contempt may be consecutive to another term, even to a term imposed in a civil court (*R. v Anomo* [1998] 2 Cr. App. R. (S.) 269).

The statutory early release provisions apply to contemnors (CJA 2003 s.258).

Apart from a person who commits a bail offence (*R. v Tyson* (1979) 68 Cr. App. R. 314), a person adjudged guilty of contempt of court has not been "convicted of an offence" (*R. v Selby Justices Ex p. Frame* (1990) 12 Cr. App. R. (S.) 434).

Nature and length

The following general principles emerge (*R. v Montgomery* (1995) 16 Cr. App. R. (S.) 274): **18-031**

(1) an immediate term of imprisonment is the only appropriate sentence to impose on a person aged 18 or over who interferes with the administration

of justice, unless the circumstances are wholly exceptional (*R. v Owen* (1976) 63 Cr. App. R. 199);

(2) where victims of, or witnesses to, serious crime refuse to do their duty, or succumb to fear of reprisals by refusing to give evidence, there is a failure of law and order; when this occurs it is usually necessary to impose a custodial sentence to mark the gravity of the matter and to stiffen the resolve of other potential witnesses who may similarly be minded to default (*R. v Montgomery* (1995) 16 Cr. App. R. (S.) 274);

(3) while interference with jurors is often visited with higher sentences than refusal to give evidence, there is no rule or established practice to that effect; in the case of a recalcitrant witness while it is legitimate to have regard to the fact that the maximum sentence for failing to comply with a witness order is three months, this need not inhibit the judge from imposing a substantially longer sentence for a blatant contempt by a witness in the face of the court (*R. v Phillips* (1984) 78 Cr. App. R. 88; *R. v Jardine* (1987) 9 Cr. App. R. (S.) 41; and *R. v Samuda* (1989) 11 Cr. App. R. (S.) 471); in most cases, however a moderate term will suffice (*R. v Montgomery* (1995) 16 Cr. App. R. (S.) 274); and

(4) where the same conduct may amount to a contempt and to a specific statutory offence the judge must have some regard to the maximum for the offence but is not bound by it (*R. v Montgomery* (1995) 16 Cr. App. R. (S.) 274).

While there is no formal rule or guide the judge needs to have the proportionality of the punishment to the features of the case in mind (see *R. v Montgomery* (1995) 16 Cr. App. R. (S.) 274; *R. v Hardy* [2004] EWCA Crim 3397; [2005] 2 Cr. App. R. (S) 48 per Rose LJ).

There may be contempt which requires immediate action but not immediate imprisonment.

There may be cases punishable summarily where it would be appropriate to fine, or discharge, the contemnor or to take sureties for his good behaviour (see BIND OVER).

Any attempt to influence a juror, however subtle, is likely to be met with an immediate prison sentence, see *R. v Curtis* [2012] EWCA Crim 945; [2013] 1 Cr. App. R. (S.) 28.

Principal factors affecting length of sentence

18-032 The principal factors affecting sentence are set out in the guideline case of *R. v Montgomery* (1995) 16 Cr. App. R. (S.) 274, affirmed in *R. v Richardson* [2004] EWCA Crim 758.

They are:

(1) the gravity of the offence being tried;
(2) the effect upon the trial;
(3) the contemnor's reasons for, e.g. refusing to give evidence;
(4) whether the contempt is aggravated by impertinent defiance of the judge (as opposed to a simple refusal (*R. v Leonard* (1984) 6 Cr. App. R. (S.) 279));
(5) the scale of sentences in similar cases;
(6) the antecedents and personal circumstances of the contemnor (*R. v Palmer* (1992) 13 Cr. App. R. (S.) 595); and
(7) whether, for instance, a special deterrent is needed, as where at the begin-

ning of a series of trials it is becoming clear that witnesses are being threatened, or where there is a developing pattern of refusal in relation to certain types of offences or in particular parts of the country.

In the case of a witness refusing to testify, the importance of his evidence ought to be taken into account (*R. v Phillips* (1983) 5 Cr. App. R. (S.) 297).

In *Yaxley-Lennon* [2018] EWCA Crim 1856, the Court adapted the principles set out in *Montgomery* when dealing with the breach of an order under s.4(2) of the 1981 Act. They set out the following:

(a) the effect or potential consequences of the breach upon the trial or trials, and upon those participating in them;
(b) the scale of the breach, with particular reference to the numbers of people to whom the report was made, over what period and the medium or media through which it was made;
(c) the gravity of the offences being tried in the trial or trials to which the reporting restrictions applied;
(d) the contemnor's level of culpability and his or her reasons for acting in breach of the reporting restrictions;
(e) whether or not the contempt was aggravated by subsequent defiance or lack of remorse;
(f) the scale of sentences in similar cases, albeit each case must turn on its own facts;
(g) the antecedents, personal circumstances and characteristics of the contemnor; and
(h) whether or not a special deterrent was needed in the particular circumstances of the case.

Additionally, cases involving a breach of a s.4(2) postponement order will often give rise to the following potential consequences:

(a) trials may have to be abandoned irretrievably;
(b) juries may have to be discharged and retrials ordered with all the consequent delays and expense;
(c) witnesses, some of them perhaps vulnerable, may have to face the ordeal of giving evidence for a second time; and
(d) the trial judge's decision upon how to manage the trial in response to the contempt may form the subject matter of an appeal which, whether or not successful, will generate additional anxiety, delay and expense.

More generally, although there are no authoritative statutory guidelines relating to punishment for contempt because such punishment does not relate to criminal proceedings, we would, by analogy, draw specific attention to the need to give consideration to the twin elements of culpability and harm as identified in the Sentencing Council Guideline of 2004 relating to "Overarching Principles: Seriousness".

Notice of suspension of imprisonment

Where a judge exercises his power under SCA 1981 to suspend an order of **18-033**
imprisonment for contempt (whether on condition or for a period or both), and the respondent is absent when the court does so, the respondent must be served with notice of the terms of the court's order:

(1) by any applicant under CrimPR 48.9 (see 18-022); or
(2) by the court officer, in any other case.

(CrimPR 48.3)

Application to discharge an order for imprisonment

18-034 Where the judge has jurisdiction (by reason of SCA 1981 ss.15 and 45) to discharge an order for a respondent's imprisonment for contempt, and a respondent wants the court to discharge such an order, he must:

(1) apply in writing, unless the court otherwise directs, and serve any written application on the court officer, and on any applicant under CrimPR 48.9 on whose application the respondent was imprisoned; and
(2) in their application explain why it is appropriate for the order for imprisonment to be discharged, and give details of any appeal, and its outcome, and ask for a hearing, if the respondent wants one.

(CrimPR 48.4)

5. APPEALS

18-035 See APPEALS FROM THE CROWN COURT.

19. COSTS AND ASSESSMENT

Quick Guide

1. Introduction

General

The powers enabling a judge to award costs in criminal proceedings are primarily contained in POA 1985 ss.16, 17 and 18, AJA 1999 in relation to funded clients, LASPOA 2012 and in the Regulations made under those Acts, including GR 1986 (SI 1986/1335) as amended. The current approach to the award of costs in the Crown Court is to be found in *PDC 2015* which came into force on 5 October 2015 and was amended in March 2016. Procedure is governed by CrimPR 45. **19-001**

The judge has a much greater and more direct responsibility for costs in criminal proceedings than in civil proceedings and should keep the question of costs in the forefront of his mind at every stage of the case and ought to be prepared to take the initiative himself without any prompting from the parties (*PDC 2015* 4.2.2).

Principal power to award costs

POA 1985, by virtue of: **19-002**

(1) ss.16 and 16A makes provision for the award *of defence* costs out of central funds;
(2) s.17 provides for the award of costs *to private* prosecutors out of central funds;
(3) s.18 empowers the judge to order a convicted offender or unsuccessful appellant to pay costs to the prosecutor;
(4) s.19(1) and GR 1986 reg.3 provide for the award of costs between parties;
(5) s.19A provides for the court to disallow, or order a legal or other representative of a party to the proceedings to meet, wasted costs;
(6) s.19B provides for the court to make a "third party costs order" where there has been serious misconduct by a third party; and

(7) ss.21A–21C (inserted by CJCA 2014 s.31) make provision for the payment of a charge in respect of relevant court costs.

"Costs" in CrimPR 45.1 means:

(a) the fees payable to a legal representative;
(b) the disbursements paid by a legal representative; and
(c) any other expenses incurred in connection with the case.

In addition, a judge of the Crown Court has power under its inherent jurisdiction over officers of the court to order a solicitor personally to pay costs thrown away.

The judge has the same powers under ss.17 and 18 in relation to the award of costs on committals for sentence, and under s.16 for failure to comply with the conditions of a recognisance, as he has in relation to trials on indictment.

Other powers governed by CrimPR 45

19-003 The procedural provisions of CrimPR 45 govern these and certain other powers, such as awards of costs under:

(1) MCA 1980 s.109, SCA 1981 s.52, for the payment by an appellant of a respondent's costs on abandoning an appeal to the Crown Court (see CrimPR 45.6).
(2) SCA 1981 s.52, for the payment by a party of another party's costs on an appeal to the Crown Court in any case not covered by the above (see CrimPR 45.6).
(3) BBEA 1879 for the payment of costs by a party or by the bank against which an application for an order is made (see CrimPR 45.7).
(4) CP(AW)A 1965 s.2C(8), for the payment by the applicant for a witness summons of the costs of a party who applies successfully under CrimPR 17.7 to have it withdrawn (see CrimPR 45.7).
(5) FSA 1989 s.14H(5), for the payment by a defendant of another person's costs on an application to terminate a football banning order (see CrimPR 45.7).
(6) The Serious Crime Act 2007 (Appeals under Section 24) Order 2008 arts 14, 15, 16, 17, or 18 (see CrimPR 45.4–10).

For a complete list see the note underneath CrimPR 45.1.

General rules: (1) making the order

19-004 The court must not make an order about costs unless each party and any other person directly affected is present, or has had an opportunity to attend or to make representations. It may make an order about costs at a hearing in public or in private or without a hearing. In deciding what order, if any, to make about costs, the court must have regard to all the circumstances, including the conduct of all the parties and any costs order already made.

If the judge makes an order:

(1) about costs, he must specify who must, or must not, pay what, to whom, and must identify the legislation under which the order is made (where there is a choice of powers), giving reasons if he refuses an application for an order or rejects representations opposing an order;

(2) for the payment of costs the general rule is that the order will be for an amount that is sufficient reasonably to compensate the recipient for costs actually, reasonably and properly incurred, and reasonable in amount; but the judge may order the payment of:
   (a) a proportion of that amount;
   (b) a stated amount less than that amount;
   (c) costs from or until a certain date only;
   (d) costs relating only to particular steps taken; or
   (e) costs relating only to a distinct part of the case.

(CrimPR 45.2(1)–(6))

An order for the payment of costs takes effect when the amount is assessed, unless the judge exercises any power he has to order otherwise (CrimPR 45.2(9)).

General rules: (2) assessment

On an assessment of the amount of costs, relevant factors include: 19-005

(1) the conduct of all the parties;
(2) the particular complexity of the matter or the difficulty or novelty of the questions raised;
(3) the skill, effort, specialised knowledge and responsibility involved;
(4) the time spent on the case;
(5) the place where and the circumstances in which work or any part of it was done; and
(6) any direction or observations by the judge who made the order.

(CrimPR 45.2(7))

If the judge orders a party to pay costs to be assessed under CrimPR 45.2, he may order that party to pay an amount on account (CrimPR 45.2(8)).

Power to vary requirements

The judge may: 19-006

(1) extend a time limit for serving an application or representations under CrimPR 45.4–45.10 even after it has expired; and
(2) consider an application made:
   (a) in a different form to one set out in the Practice Direction; or
   (b) orally instead of in writing.

A person wanting an extension of time must apply when serving the application or representations for which it is needed, explaining the delay.

(CrimPR 45.3).

Note that the time limit for applying for a costs order may be affected by the legislation under which the order is made.

2. Costs out of central funds

Defence costs from central funds

Where a person: 19-007

(1) is not tried for an offence for which he has been indicted, or in respect of

which proceedings against him have been sent for trial or transferred for trial; or
(2) has been acquitted on any count in the indictment; or
(3) has been convicted in the magistrates' court and successfully appeals to the Crown Court,

the judge may make a defendant's costs order in his favour.

(POA 1985 s.16(2)–(3))

Whether to make such an order is a matter for the judge's discretion in the light of the circumstances of the particular case.

Note that:

(a) an order should normally be made whether or not an order for costs between the parties is made, unless there are positive reasons for not doing so; for example, where the accused's own conduct has brought suspicion on himself and has misled the prosecution into thinking that the case against him was stronger than it was;
(b) the judge, when declining to make a costs order, should explain, in open court, that the reason for not making an order does not involve any suggestion that the accused is guilty of any criminal conduct but the order is refused because of the positive reason that should be identified;
(c) where the judge considers that it would be inappropriate that the accused should recover all of the costs properly incurred, either the lesser amount must be specified in the order, or the judge must describe to the appropriate authority the reduction required.

(*PDC 2015* 2.2.1)

Where an offender is convicted of some count(s) in the indictment and acquitted on other(s) the judge may exercise his discretion to make a defendant's costs order but may order that only a proportion of the costs incurred be paid. He should make whatever order seems just having regard to the relative importance of the charges and the conduct of the parties generally. The proportion of costs allowed must be specified in the order (*PDC 2015* 2.2.2).

See generally CrimPR 45.4.

An acquitted accused assessed as ineligible for legal aid is able to receive legal costs from central funds—see the Costs in Criminal Cases (Legal Costs) (Exceptions) Regulations (SI 2014/130).

Extent of costs from central funds

19-008 Where the court may order the payment of costs out of central funds, costs include:

(1) on an appeal, costs incurred in the court that made the decision under appeal; and
(2) at a retrial, costs incurred at the initial trial and on any appeal;

but do not include costs met by legal aid (see LEGAL AID; PUBLIC FUNDING).

The judge may make an order on application by the person who incurred the costs or on his own initiative. A person wanting the judge to make an order must apply as soon as practicable, outlining the type of costs and the amount claimed, if he wants the judge to direct an assessment, or specifying the amount claimed, if he wants the judge to assess the amount himself.

The general rule is that an order must be made, but the judge may decline to make:

(a) a defendant's costs order if, for example:
   (i) the defendant is convicted of at least one offence; or
   (ii) the defendant's conduct led the prosecutor reasonably to think the prosecution case stronger than it was; and
(b) a prosecutor's costs order if, for example, the prosecution was started or continued unreasonably.

(CrimPR 45.4)

The general rule (under POA 1985 s.16(6)) is that any order will be of such amount as the judge considers reasonably sufficient to compensate him for any expenses incurred by him in the proceedings. Amendments made by LASPOA 2012, however, provide that where the judge considers that there are circumstances that make it inappropriate for the accused to recover the full amount, the order must be for the payment of such lesser amount as he considers just and reasonable (s.16(6A)).

If the judge makes an order, he may:

- direct an assessment, as applicable, under GR 1986 Pt III or the Serious Crime Act 2007 (Appeals under Section 24) Order Pt 3;
- assess the amount himself in a case in which either the recipient agrees the amount, or the judge decides to allow a lesser sum than that which is reasonably sufficient to compensate the recipient for expenses properly incurred in the proceedings.

An order for the payment of a defendant's costs which includes an amount in respect of fees payable to a legal representative, or disbursements paid by a legal representative, must include a statement to that effect.

If the judge directs an assessment, the order must specify any restriction on the amount to be paid that he considers appropriate.

(CrimPR 45.4(6)–(7))

Where the judge orders that the costs of a defendant, appellant or private prosecutor should be paid from central funds, the order will be for such amount as the court considers sufficient reasonably to compensate the party for expenses incurred by him in the proceedings; unless the court considers it inappropriate to allow the full amount in which event it will allow such lesser sum as it considers just and reasonable. This will include the costs incurred in the proceedings in the lower courts unless for good reason the court directs otherwise, but it cannot include expenses which do not directly relate to the proceedings themselves, e.g. loss of earnings. Where the party in whose favour the costs order is made is legally aided, he will only recover his personal costs: see POA 1985 s.21(4A)(a).

If a defendant's costs order includes legal costs (sums paid for advocacy, litigation services or experts' fees) the order must include a statement to that effect.

If the court does not fix the amount of costs to be paid out of central funds, the costs will be determined in accordance with GR 1986 by the appropriate authority, which will calculate the amount payable in respect of legal costs at such rates and scales as are prescribed by the Lord Chancellor. Where the court makes a defendant's costs order, or an order in favour of a private prosecutor, but considers it inappropriate that the recipient should recover the full amount of the costs, the court may assess and specify such lesser amount that it considers just and reasonable. If the court is not in a position to specify the amount payable, the Judge may make remarks which the appropriate authority will take into account as a relevant circumstance when determining the costs payable.

(*PDC 2015* 1.3.1–1.4.1)

Further considerations

19-009 Note that:

(1) it is not incompatible with the presumption of innocence for the judge to refuse to make an order because he considers that the accused brought suspicion on himself and misled the prosecutor into believing that the case against him was stronger than it was in reality (*R. v Guney* [2011] EWHC 767 (Admin); see also *R. (on the application of Monckton) v Carlisle Crown Court* [2015] EWHC 304 (Admin));

(2) in *Ashendon v United Kingdom* [2012] 54 E.H.R.R. 13 the ECtHR stated that their task was to consider whether the judge's reasons for not making an order indicated a reliance on suspicions that the acquitted applicant was in fact guilty. It was not incompatible with the presumption of innocence for a trial judge to refuse to make an order because he considered that the applicant had brought suspicion on himself and misled the prosecution into believing that the case against him was stronger than it actually was. This would also be the case where the applicant brought the case upon himself because he exercised his right to silence. The refusal to make an order did not amount to a penalty for exercising that right;

(3) the judge can also decline to order the costs of an acquitted person where he is sure that the person had perjured himself, or where the prosecution had been ambushed by the nature of the defence (*R. (on the application of Rees) v Snaresbrook Crown Court* [2012] EWHC 3879 (Admin)). However, where credibility is the reason for depriving a person of costs, the court must be sure of the matter, but should not express a view which might suggest that the person was guilty of the offence;

(4) where the prosecutor does not proceed because a witness is unavailable, an application for costs should normally succeed (*R. (on the application of Barrington) v Preston Crown Court* [2001] EWHC Admin 599);

(5) it does not necessarily follow that because a solicitor has claimed costs under a defendant's costs order that his client cannot make a claim for costs which he, the client, has incurred (*R. v Bedlington Magistrates Court Ex p. Wilkinson* (2000) 164 J.P. 156).

Payment of "legal costs"

19-010 A defendant's costs order may not require the payment out of central funds of an amount that includes an amount in respect of the accused's legal costs, save in certain circumstances.

"Legal costs" here means fees, charges, disbursements and other amounts payable in respect of advocacy services or litigation services including, in particular, expert witness costs.

Such costs may only be included where the accused is an individual and:

(1) the order is made under s.16(1), (3), or (4)(a)(ii) or (iii) or (d); or
(2) the legal costs were incurred in proceedings in a court below which were:
    (a) proceedings in a magistrates' court; or

(b) proceedings on an appeal to the Crown Court under MCA 1980 s.108 (right of appeal against conviction or sentence);

(3) the legal costs were incurred in proceedings before the Supreme Court; or

(4) the order is made under s.16(2) and a determination of financial ineligibility has been made.

Where the judge:

(i) makes an order requiring the payment of an amount that includes an amount in respect of legal costs, the order must include a statement to that effect;

(ii) fixes an amount in respect of legal costs incurred in the proceedings, the latter amount must not exceed an amount specified by regulations (POA 1985 s.16A).

Definitions:

"advocacy services" means any services which it would be reasonable to expect a person who is exercising, or contemplating exercising, a right of audience in relation to any proceedings, or contemplated proceedings, to provide;

"expert witness costs" means amounts payable in respect of the services of an expert witness, including amounts payable in connection with attendance by the witness at court or elsewhere;

"litigation services" means any services which it would be reasonable to expect a person who is exercising, or contemplating exercising, a right to conduct litigation in relation to proceedings, or contemplated proceedings, to provide.

In respect of proceedings commenced on or after 1 October 2012 legal costs may only be included in a defendant's costs order to an accused who is an individual and only in proceedings in a magistrates' court, appeals against conviction or sentence from a magistrates' court to the Crown Court, "relevant Crown Court proceedings", and certain appeals to the CACD (*PDC 2015* 1.4.2).

From 27 January 2014 (by virtue of amendments made by SI 2014/130) legal costs may be included in a defendant's costs order, provided that the accused is an individual, in "relevant proceedings" in the Crown Court if the Director of Legal Aid Casework has made a determination of financial ineligibility in relation to that accused.

The "relevant" proceedings are those:

- in which the accused has been sent by a magistrates' court to the Crown Court for trial;
- where a bill of indictment has been preferred (AJ(PM)A 1933 s.2(2)(b)); or
- following an order for a retrial made by the CACD or the Supreme Court.

(*PDC 2015* 1.4.3)

Where legal costs may be allowed, if the judge fixes the amount to be paid to a defendant under s.16(6C) of POA 1985 he must calculate any amounts to be allowed in respect of legal costs in accordance with the rates and scales prescribed. CrimPR 45.2(6) and (7) contain general rules about the amount of an award of costs that apply subject to any statutory limitation.

(*PDC 2015* 1.4.4–1.4.5)

Judge fixing the amount

19-011 When making a defendant's costs order, the judge will fix the amount to be paid out of central funds in the order if he considers it appropriate to do so and the accused agrees the amount, or s.16(6A) applies.

Where the judge does not fix the amount in the order:

(1) he must describe in the order any reduction required under s.16(6A); and
(2) the amount must be fixed by means of a determination made by or on behalf of the court in accordance with procedures specified in regulations made by the Lord Chancellor.

(POA 1985 s.16(6C)–(6D))

Where a person ordered to be retried is acquitted at his retrial, the costs which may be ordered to be paid out of central funds will include:

(a) any costs which, at the original trial, could have been ordered to be paid if that person had been acquitted; and
(b) if no order was made in respect of his expenses on appeal, any sums for the payment of which such an order could have been made.

(POA 1985 s.16(11))

Where the judge fixes an amount to be paid to the accused out of central funds in accordance with s.16(6C) he must, in relation to any amounts payable in respect of *legal costs*, calculate such amounts in accordance with the rates or scales or other provision made by the Lord Chancellor pursuant to reg.7(7) (below), whether or not that results in the fixing of an amount that the judge considers reasonably sufficient or necessary to compensate the accused.

(GR 1986 reg.4A; SI 2012/1804)

Determination of costs by appropriate authority

19-012 The appropriate authority will consider the claim and any further particulars, information or documents submitted by the applicant under reg.6(5), and will allow costs in respect of such work as appears to it to have been actually and reasonably done, and such disbursements as appear to it to have been actually and reasonably incurred.

In calculating such costs the appropriate authority will take into account all the relevant circumstances of the case including the nature, importance, complexity and difficulty of the work and the time involved. Any doubts which that authority may have as to whether the costs were reasonably incurred or were reasonable in amount must be resolved against the applicant. The costs awarded must not exceed the costs actually incurred.

In general, the appropriate authority will allow such legal costs as it considers reasonably sufficient to compensate the applicant for any expenses properly incurred by him in the proceedings, but where the subject of a costs order is an individual, and:

(1) the order was made under POA 1985 s.16(1), (3) or (4)(a)(ii), (iii) or (d);
(2) the order was made under s.16 and includes *legal costs* that were incurred in proceedings in a court below which were:
   (a) proceedings in a magistrates' court; or
   (b) proceedings on an appeal to the Crown Court under MCA 1980 s.108;

(3) the order was made under s.16(2) and a determination of financial ineligibility has been made,

the appropriate authority will calculate amounts payable out of central funds in respect of legal costs to the individual in accordance with the rates or scales or other provision made by the Lord Chancellor pursuant to reg.7(7), whether or not that results in the fixing of an amount that the appropriate authority considers reasonably sufficient or necessary to compensate the individual.

(GR 1986 reg.7)

Private prosecutor's costs

Subject to the exceptions set out below, the court may, in any proceedings in respect of an indictable offence (or any proceedings before a Divisional Court or the Supreme Court in respect of a summary offence), order the award of prosecution costs of such amount as the court considers reasonably sufficient to compensate the prosecutor for any expenses properly incurred by him in the proceedings. **19-013**

(POA 1985 s.17)

There is no power to order the payment out of central funds of any prosecutor who is a public authority, a person acting on behalf of a public authority or acting as an official appointed by a public authority as defined in the Act (POA 1985 s.17(2)).

In the limited number of cases in which a prosecutor's costs may be awarded out of central funds an application must be made by the prosecutor in each case and:

(1) an order should be made, save where there is good reason for not doing so, as where proceedings have been instituted or continued without good cause;
(2) the procedure applies to proceedings in respect of an indictable offence, or proceedings before the Administrative Court in respect of a summary offence; and
(3) GR 1986 reg.4(1) extends the provision to certain committals from a magistrates' court.

(*PDC 2015* 2.6.1)

Where the judge considers that there are circumstances that make it inappropriate for the prosecution to recover the full amount an order must be for the payment of such lesser amount as he considers just and reasonable (POA 1985 s.17(2A)).

The judge must fix the amount to be paid in the order if he considers it appropriate to do so and the prosecutor agrees the amount or s.17(2A) applies. Where he does not fix the amount to be paid in the order, he must describe in the order any reduction required under s.17(2A) and the amount will be fixed by means of a determination made by or on behalf of the court in accordance with procedures specified in regulations made by the Lord Chancellor (POA 1985 s.17(2B)).

For the purposes of an order under s.17 the costs of the prosecutor are taken to include the expense of compensating any witness for the expenses, travel and loss of time properly incurred in or incidental to his attendance (*PDC 2015* 2.6.3).

If there has been misconduct a private prosecutor should not be awarded costs out of Central Funds (*PDC 2015* 2.6.4).

Where the conduct of a private prosecution is taken over by the CPS the power to order payment of prosecution costs out of central funds extends only to the period prior to the intervention of the CPS (*PDC 2015* 2.6.5).

CrimPR 45.1 and 45.4 apply to the judge's power to award costs out of central funds.

There is no difference in relation to the rules on costs applicable in a private prosecution to a prosecution brought by the Crown. The legal principles applicable to public prosecutions apply straightforwardly to private prosecutions (*Asif v Ditta* [2021] EWCA Crim 1091; [2021] Crim. L.R. 984).

In *R. v Zinga (Costs)* [2014] EWCA Crim 1823; [2015] 1 Cr. App. R. 2 the CACD considered the proper approach to awarding costs to private prosecutors from central funds. The court should firstly ask whether it was proper and reasonable to instruct the solicitors and/or advocates actually instructed, and secondly, whether the costs were reasonable. In considering the first question, the court should consider what steps were taken to ensure that the terms on which the solicitors and advocates were engaged were reasonable. A private prosecutor will be expected to properly and reasonably examine the competition in the relevant market and seek tenders or quotations before selecting the lawyers to be instructed. See also *Ashgrove (Swansea) Ltd v Welsh Ministers* [2016] EWHC 3786 (Admin) and *Fuseon Ltd v Senior Courts Costs Office* [2019] EWHC 126 (Admin); [2020] 2 Cr. App. R. 2.

In *RSPCA v McCormick* [2016] EWHC 928 (Admin); [2016] 1 W.L.R. 2641, the High Court ordered that a proportion of the successful appellant's costs should be paid from central funds under s.17(1)(b), in recognition of the fact that the appeal had achieved some clarification and guidance on points of general public importance.

A private prosecutor is in principle entitled to recover from central funds his costs incurred in enforcing a confiscation order, even though the enforcement proceedings are governed by civil procedural law; *Mirchandani v Lord Chancellor* [2020] EWCA Civ 1260; [2021] 1 Cr. App. R. 7.

Witness, interpreter or medical evidence

19-014 The costs of the attendance of:

(1) a witness required by the accused or a private prosecutor or the court; or
(2) an interpreter required because of the accused's lack of English; or
(3) an intermediary required under YJCEA 1999 s.29 (see SPECIAL MEASURES DIRECTIONS); or
(4) an *oral* report by a medical practitioner,

are allowed out of central funds unless the judge otherwise directs (POA 1985 s.20(3); GR 1986 reg.16(1)).

In the case of a witness if, and only if, the court makes such a direction can the expense of the witness be claimed as a disbursement out of legal aid funds.

A "witness" includes any person properly attending to give evidence, whether or not he gives evidence or is called, but it does not include a character witness unless the judge has certified that the interests of justice require his attendance (see POA 1985 s.21(1)).

(*PDC 2015* 2.5.1)

The court may also order the payment out of central funds of such sums as appear to it to be reasonably sufficient to compensate any medical practitioner for the expenses, trouble, or loss of time properly incurred in preparing and making a report on the mental condition of a person accused of murder (see MH(A)A 1982 s.34(5)).

3. AWARDS OF COSTS AGAINST ACCUSED PERSONS

Award against offenders and appellants

A judge may make an order for costs: 19-015

(1) against a person convicted before him;
(2) in dealing with a person in respect of certain orders as to sentence specified in GR 1986 reg.14(3); or
(3) against an unsuccessful appellant; or
(4) against a person committed by a magistrates' court in respect of the proceedings specified in reg.14(1)–(2).

(POA 1985 s.18; *PDC 2015* 3.1)

Where he is satisfied that the offender or appellant has the means and ability to pay, he may make such order payable to the prosecutor as he considers just and reasonable (POA 1985 s.18(1)). The amount must be specified in the order.

An order under s.18 includes costs incurred under legal aid (POA 1985 s.21(4A)(b); *PDC 2015* 3.9).

An order:

(a) should be made only where the judge is satisfied that the accused or appellant has the means and the ability to pay;
(b) is not intended to be in the nature of a penalty which can only be satisfied on the offender's release from prison; and
(c) should not be made on the assumption that a third party might pay.

Whilst the judge should take into account any debt of the appellant or offender, where the greater part of those debts relates to the offence itself, the judge may still make an order for costs.

(*PDC 2015* 3.4)

Note that:

- where there are multiple accused the judge may make joint and several orders, but the costs ordered to be paid by an individual should be related to the costs in or about the prosecution of that individual;
- in a multi-handed case where some accused have insufficient means to pay their share of the costs, it is not right for that share to be divided among the other defendants; and
- where co-accused are husband and wife, the couple's means should not be taken together.

(*PDC 2015* 3.5)

The judge has a duty to consider the offender's means (see, e.g. *R. v Mountain* (1979) 68 Cr. App. R. 4 and *R. v Olaniregun* [2019] EWCA Crim 1294). If he allows time for payment he must ensure that the length of time would not be oppressive (*R. v Nuthoo* [2010] EWCA Crim 2383; [2011] Costs L.R. 87).

It is wrong in principle to make an order for the whole of the prosecution costs against an offender who is convicted on, e.g. three out of a total of seventeen counts (*R. v Splain* [2010] EWCA Crim 49; [2010] Costs L.R. 465); it is not necessary to take a mathematical approach, but the judge should take an overall view considering fairness and proportionality. The permissible balance between a costs order and a fine imposed for the same offence remains unclear. In *R. v Splain* (above) it was held that the fact that the amount of costs is disproportionate to any fines imposed is not the crucial factor; there may well be cases in which, in the totality of the sentencing process, the judge is justified in weighting the penalty on to the costs more than on to the fine. However, see *PDC 2015* 3.7, referring to *Balshaw v CPS* [2009] EWCA Crim 470 in which the CACD held that a costs order should not ordinarily be greatly at variance with any fine imposed. See also *R. v Dickinson* [2010] EWCA Crim 2143; [2011] 1 Cr. App. R. (S.) 93 in which the CACD held that an order for costs could not ordinarily be grossly disproportionate to a fine, although there was no requirement that the two sums had to stand in some arithmetical relationship. In *R. (on the application of Gray) v Aylesbury Crown Court* [2013] EWHC 500 (Admin); [2014] 1 W.L.R. 818 it was held that, although the normal rule is that costs should not be grossly disproportionate to a fine imposed for the same offences, there could be exceptions to the rule where justice required it. In that case the judge had been entitled to reject the submission that the costs should not be grossly disproportionate to the fine because he was obliged to make a balanced judgment in light of the factors set out at CrimPR 76.2 (now CrimPR 45.2).

There is no rule which prevents the judge from making a costs order payable solely from capital assets (*R. (on the application of Gray) v Aylesbury Crown Court* [2013] EWHC 500 (Admin); [2014] 1 W.L.R. 818).

In exceptional circumstances costs may be awarded against a non-party (*H Leverton Ltd v Crawford Offshore (Exploration) Services Ltd (in liquidation), The Times,* 22 November 1996) and see CrimPR 45.10).

Accused electing trial on indictment

19-016 In relation to an accused who elects trial on indictment:

(1) whilst costs should not be awarded against an offender in a way which appears to punish him for exercising his right to elect trial in the Crown Court, the exercise of that right is a material factor in deciding the appropriate sum to be ordered (*R. v Clelland* (1990–91) 12 Cr. App. R. (S.) 697; *R. v Hayden* (1974) 60 Cr. App. R. 304); and
(2) in a case which could conveniently have been tried summarily he may properly be ordered to pay costs on a scale appropriate to the Crown Court (*R. v Bushel* (1980) 2 Cr. App. R. (S.) 77; *R. v Boyle* [1995] 16 Cr. App. R. (S.) 927); but where an offender pleads guilty in the Crown Court to a summary offence, it is wrong to order him to pay more than would have been appropriate in the magistrates court (*R. v Sentonco* [1996] 1 Cr. App. R. (S.) 174).

Procedure

19-017 The judge may make an order under application by the prosecutor or on his own initiative (see 19-015). Where the prosecutor wants him to make an order he must apply as soon as practicable, and specify the amount claimed.

(CrimPR 45.5)

In so far as procedure is concerned:

- the prosecution should serve upon the defence, at the earliest time, full details of its costs so as to give the accused a proper opportunity to make representations upon them if appropriate;
- if an offender wishes to dispute all or any of the prosecution's claim for costs, he should, if possible, give proper notice to the prosecution of the

objections proposed to be made or at least make it plain to the court precisely what those objections are; and

- there is no provision for assessment of prosecution costs in a criminal case; such disputes have to be resolved by the judge, who must specify the amount to be paid (*R. v Associated Octel Ltd* [1996] EWCA Crim 1327; [1996] 4 All E.R. 846).

(*PDC 2015* 3.6)

The judge, when awarding prosecution costs, may award costs in respect of time spent in bringing the offences to light, even if the necessary investigation was carried out, for example, by an environmental health official. Generally it will not be just or reasonable to order a defendant to pay costs of investigation which the prosecutor itself will not satisfy.

The Divisional Court has held that there is a requirement that any sum ordered to be paid by way of costs should not ordinarily be greatly at variance with any fine imposed.

Where substantial research is required in order to counter possible defences, the judge may also award costs in respect of that work if he considers it to be justified. (*PDC 2015* 3.7)

Costs on appeal

CrimPR 45.6: **19-018**

(1) applies where the Crown Court (or magistrates' court or the Court of Appeal) may order a party to pay another person's costs on an appeal; and
(2) authorises the Crown Court, in addition to its other powers, to order a party to pay another party's costs on an appeal to that court, except on an appeal under MCA 1980 s.108 or MHA 1983 s.45.

In this rule, "costs" include costs incurred in the court that made the decision under appeal and costs met by legal aid.

The judge may make an order on application by the person who incurred the costs or on his own initiative. A person wanting the judge to make an order must apply as soon as practicable, notifying each other party and specifying the amount claimed, and against whom.

Where:

(a) an appellant abandons an appeal by serving a notice of abandonment, a person who wants the court to make an order must apply in writing not more than 10 business days later, and serve the application on the appellant and on the Crown Court officer;
(b) a party wants to oppose any application, he must make representations as soon as practicable, and where the application was under (a) serve representations on the applicant, and on the Crown Court officer, not more than 5 business days after it was served.

Where the application was under (a) above the Crown Court officer will submit it to the judge or serve it on the magistrates' court officer, for submission to the magistrates' court.

Where:

(i) the appellant abandons an appeal to the Crown Court; or

(ii) the Crown Court decides an appeal, (except an appeal under MCA 1980 s.108, or MHA 1983 s.45),

the judge, if he makes an order, may direct an assessment under CrimPR 45.11, or assess the amount himself.

If the judge makes an order in any other case, he must assess the amount himself.

Bank records, football banning orders, witness summonses

19-019 Where the judge may order a party to pay another person's costs in a case in which:

(1) he decides an application for the production in evidence of a copy of a bank record;
(2) he decides an application to terminate a football banning order;
(3) he allows an application to withdraw a witness summons; or
(4) he decides an application relating to a deferred prosecution agreement (breach/variation/lifting suspension of prosecution),

he may make an order either on application by the person who incurred the costs or on his own initiative.

A person wanting the court to make an order must apply as soon as practicable notifying each other party and specifying the amount claimed, and against whom.

A party who wants to oppose an order must make representations as soon as practicable.

If the judge makes an order, he may direct an assessment under CrimPR 45.11 or assess the amount himself.

(CrimPR 45.7)

4. COSTS INCURRED AS A RESULT OF UNNECESSARY OR IMPROPER ACT OR OMISSION

Costs resulting from unnecessary or improper act, etc.

19-020 A judge may order the payment of any costs incurred as a result of any unnecessary or improper act or omission by or on behalf of any party to the proceedings as distinct from his legal representative (POA 1985 s.19; GR 1986 reg.3).

The judge may find it helpful to adopt a three stage approach:

(1) Has there been an unnecessary or improper act or omission?
(2) As a result, have any costs been incurred by another party?
(3) If the answers to (1) and (2) are "yes", should he exercise his discretion to order the party responsible to meet the whole or any part of the relevant costs, and if so what specific sum is involved?

(*PDC 2015* 4.1.1)

Such an order is appropriate only where the failure is that of the prosecutor or the accused; where the failure is that of a legal representative, see *PDC 2015* 4.2 and 4.5 (see 19-022 and following).

There is no appeal to the CACD from the making of such an order.

Note that, under s.19(2) and GR 1986 reg.3, such an order can only be made "during the proceedings". Where an application is made after proceedings have concluded, the court is functus officio; *Quayum v DPP* [2015] EWHC 1660 (Admin).

The fact that a prosecution fails is not itself sufficient to satisfy the threshold criteria for a s.19 costs order; *R. v Cornish* [2016] EWHC 779 (QB); [2016] Crim. L.R. 560. A successful s.19 application would be very rare and should be restricted to those exceptional cases where the prosecution had made a clear and stark error as a result of which a defendant had incurred costs. In *R. (on the application of Holloway) v Harrow Crown Court* [2019] EWHC 1731 (Admin); [2020] 1 Cr. App. R. 8 it was held that the decision to prosecute *was* an improper act, because it was clear on any reasonable view that the prosecution could not succeed, and the prosecutor had failed to undertake an objective and independent analysis of the evidence before commencing the proceedings. See also *Evans v SFO* [2015] EWHC 263 (QB); [2015] W.L.R. 3595 and *R. (on the application of Haigh) v City of Westminster Magistrates' Court* [2017] EWHC 232 (Admin); [2017] 1 Costs L.R. 175.

Procedure

The judge may make an order on application by the party who incurred such costs or on his own initiative. A party wanting the judge to make an order must apply in writing as soon as practicable after becoming aware of the grounds for doing so, serving the application on the Crown Court officer and each other party, specifying: **19-021**

- the party by whom costs should be paid;
- the relevant act or omission;
- the reasons why that act or omission meets the criteria for making an order;
- the amount claimed; and
- those on whom the application has been served.

(CrimPR 45.8)

The judge will hear the parties and may then order that all or part of the costs so incurred by one party shall be paid to him by the other party (*PDC 2015* 4.1.2).

Before making such an order the judge may take into account any other order as to costs and the order must specify the amount of the costs to be paid. He is entitled to take such an order into account when making any other order as to costs in the proceedings (GR 1986 reg.3(2)–(4)).

The order can extend to costs met by legal aid incurred on behalf of any party (POA 1985 s.21(4A)(b); *PDC 2015* 4.1.3).

Where the judge considers making an order on his own initiative, he must identify the party against whom he proposes making the order, and specify:

(a) the relevant act or omission;
(b) the reasons why that act or omission meets the criteria for making an order; and
(c) with the assistance of the party who incurred the costs, the amount involved.

A party wanting to oppose an order must make representations as soon as practicable and, in reply to an application, serve representations on the applicant and on the Crown Court officer not more than 5 business days after it was served.

If the judge makes an order, he must assess the amount himself. However, to help him assess the amount the judge may direct an enquiry by the National Taxing Team (CrimPR 45.8(8)). CrimPR 45.8(9) sets out the criteria which the judge must have regard to in deciding whether to direct such an enquiry. See also *PDC 2015* 1.2.4.

5. COSTS AGAINST A LEGAL REPRESENTATIVE—WASTED COSTS

General

19-022 POA 1985 s.19A allows a judge to disallow costs or order the legal or other representative to meet the whole or any part of wasted costs.

The order may be made against any person exercising a right of audience or a right to conduct litigation (in the sense of acting for a party to the proceedings).

"Wasted costs" are:

(1) costs incurred by a party (which includes a publicly funded party) as a result of any improper, unreasonable or negligent act or omission on the part of any representative or his employee; or
(2) costs which, in the light of any such act or omission occurring after they were incurred, the judge considers it unreasonable to expect that party to pay.

(POA 1985 s.19A(3); POCA 2002 s.89(8); *PDC 2015* 4.2.1)

GR 1986 reg.3B requires the judge to specify the amount of the wasted costs and before making the order to allow the legal or other representative and any party to the proceedings to make representations (*PDC 2015* 4.2.3).

In making the order the judge may take into account any other orders for costs and may take the wasted costs order into account when making any other order as to costs. The judge should give reasons for making the order and any interested party (which includes the legal aid and Central Funds determining authorities) must be informed of the order and of the amount.

There has to be proved improper, unreasonable or negligent conduct (*Ridehalgh v Horsefield* [1994] Ch. 205; *Re Hickman & Rose*, *The Times,* 3 May 2000; and *Le Brocq v Liverpool Crown Court* [2019] EWCA Crim 1398; [2020] Crim. L.R. 565). Counsel is responsible for his clerk's errors, e.g. in not getting him to court, or missing the case in the list (*R. v Rodney (Wasted Costs Order)* [1997] 1 Arch. News 2).

As to the approach where the accused fails to appear and solicitor and advocate withdraw, see *Re Boodhoo* [2007] EWCA Crim 14; [2007] 1 Cr. App. R. 32.

See further *Re A Barrister (Wasted Costs Order) (No.1 of 1991)* (1992) 95 Cr. App. R. 288 and *Re P (A Barrister)* [2001] EWCA Crim 1728; [2002] 1 Cr. App. R. 19, set out in detail below.

R. v Carrigan; R. v Brown [2021] 10 Archbold Review 3: where there has been misconduct by a private prosecutor, not only will the court disallow an application by the prosecutor for costs from central funds, but the court will also consider whether wasted costs orders are appropriate.

Procedure

19-023 The judge may make an order on application by the party who incurred the costs, or on his own initiative. Costs include those met by legal aid.

A form of application is set out in *PDC 2015* Sch.5.

A party who wants the judge to make an order must apply in writing as soon as practicable after becoming aware of the grounds for doing so, serving the application on:

(1) the Crown Court officer;
(2) the representative responsible;

(3) each other party; and
(4) any other person directly affected,

specifying:

- the representative responsible;
- the relevant act or omission;
- the reasons why that act or omission meets the criteria for making an order;
- the amount claimed; and
- those on whom the application has been served.

Where the judge considers making an order on his own initiative, he will identify the representative against whom he proposes making the order and specify:

(a) the relevant act or omission;
(b) the reasons why that act or omission meets the criteria for making an order; and
(c) with the assistance of the party who incurred the costs, the amount involved.

A representative wanting to oppose an order must make representations as soon as practicable, and, in reply to an application, serve representations on the applicant and on the Crown Court officer not more than 5 business days after it was served.
(CrimPR 45.9)

Before making an order the judge must allow the legal or other representative and any party to the proceedings to make representations (*R. v Wiseman Lee (Solicitors) (Wasted Costs Order) (No.5 of 2000)* [2001] EWCA Crim 707). He will assess the amount himself, taking into account, where appropriate, any other order for costs, and notifying any interested party (which includes the Legal Aid Agency and central funds determining authorities) of the order and the amount.

In a case where a party's costs are met by legal aid, or are to be paid out of central funds, or there is to be an assessment under CrimPR 45.11, the judge may, instead of making an order, make adverse observations about the representative's conduct for use in an assessment.

If he makes an order, the general rule is that he will do so without waiting until the end of the case, but he may postpone making the order. *Film Lab Systems International v Pennington* [1994] 4 All E.R. 673 and *Medcalf v Mardell* [2002] UKHL 27; [2002] 3 All E.R. 721, both indicate the importance (at least in civil cases) of the judge dealing with the matter at the end of the case, avoiding the position where an advocate's conduct of the case is influenced by his self-interest.

The court may postpone the making of a wasted costs order to the end of the case if it appears more appropriate to do so, for example, because the likely amount is not readily available, there is a possibility of conflict between the legal representatives as to the apportionment of blame, or the legal representative concerned is unable to make full representations because of a possible conflict with the duty to the client.
(*PDC 2015* 4.2.7)

The court must assess the amount itself. However, to help him assess the amount the judge may direct an enquiry by the National Taxing Team (CrimPR 45.9(8)). CrimPR 45.9(9) sets out the criteria which the judge must have regard to in deciding whether to direct such an enquiry. See also *PDC 2015* 1.2.4.

The hearing

A judge contemplating making a wasted costs order should bear in mind the guidance given in *Re A Barrister (Wasted Costs Order) (No.1 of 1991)* (1992) 95 Cr. 19-024

App. R. 288, which should be considered together with all the statutory and other rules and recommendations set out by Parliament and in the practice direction:

(1) there is a clear need for the judge intending to exercise the wasted costs jurisdiction to formulate carefully and concisely the complaint and grounds upon which such an order may be sought; these measures are draconian and, as in contempt proceedings, the grounds must be clear and particular;
(2) where necessary, a transcript of the relevant part of the proceedings under discussion should be available and in accordance with the rules a transcript of any wasted cost hearing must be made; and
(3) an accused involved in a case where such proceedings are contemplated should be present if, after discussion with an advocate, it is thought that his interest may be affected and he should certainly be present and represented if the matter might affect the course of his trial.

CrimPR 45.9 requires that the judge must not make a costs order unless each party and any other person affected: (a) is present; or (b) has had an opportunity to attend or to make representations.
(*PDC 2015* 4.2.4)

A three stage approach

19-025 The same three stage test advocated at 19-020 is recommended when a wasted costs order is contemplated (*Re A Barrister (Wasted Costs Order) (No.1 of 1991)* (1992) 95 Cr. App. R. 288; see also *R. (on the application of B) v X CC* [2009] EWHC 1149 (Admin); [2010] Crim. L.R. 145).

It is inappropriate to propose any settlement that the representative might forgo fees. The complaint should be formally stated by the judge and the representative invited to make his own comments. After any other party has been heard the judge should give his formal ruling. Discursive conversations may be unfair and should not take place.
(*PDC 2015* 4.2.4)

The judge must specify the sum to be allowed or ordered.

Though the judge cannot delegate his decision to the appropriate authority, he may require the appropriate officer of the court to make enquiries and inform him as to the likely amount of costs incurred. By CrimPR 45.9(5) the judge is entitled to the assistance in this respect of the party who incurred the costs concerned.
(*PDC 2015* 4.2.6)

CACD Guidance

19-026 In *Re P (A Barrister)* [2001] EWCA Crim 1728; [2002] 1 Cr. App. R. 19 the CACD gave the following guidance:

(1) the primary object is not to punish but to compensate, albeit as the order is sought against a non-party, it can from that perspective be regarded as penal;
(2) the jurisdiction is a summary jurisdiction to be exercised by the judge who has "tried the case in the course of which the misconduct was committed";
(3) fairness is assured if the lawyer alleged to be at fault has sufficient notice of the complaint made against him and a proper opportunity to respond to it;
(4) because of the penal element a mere mistake is not sufficient to justify an order: there must be a more serious error;

(5) although the trial judge may decline to consider an application in respect of costs, for example on the ground that he is personally embarrassed by an appearance of bias, it will only be in exceptional circumstances that it will be appropriate to pass the matter to another judge, and the fact that, in the proper exercise of his judicial function, a judge has expressed views in relation to the conduct of a lawyer against whom an order is sought, does not of itself normally constitute bias or the appearance of bias so as to necessitate a transfer; and

(6) the normal civil standard of proof applies but if the allegation is one of serious misconduct or crime clear evidence will be required to meet that standard.

(*PDC 2015* 4.2.5)

Relevance of public funding

A wasted costs order should normally be made regardless of the fact that the client of the legal representative is legally aided. **19-027**

However, where the judge is minded to disallow substantial costs out of the legal aid fund, he may, instead of making a wasted costs order, make observations to the determining authority that work may have been unreasonably done (see 19-029). This practice should only be adopted where the extent and amount of the costs wasted is not entirely clear.

(*PDC 2015* 4.2.8)

Disallowance of legal aid costs

Where it appears to the judge, sitting in proceedings for which legal aid has been granted, that work may have been unreasonably done (e.g. if the represented person's case may have been conducted unreasonably so as to incur unjustifiable expense, or costs may have been wasted by failure to conduct the proceedings with reasonable competence or expedition), he may make observations to that effect for the attention of the appropriate authority. **19-028**

He should specify as precisely as possible the item, or items, which the determining officer should consider or investigate on the determination of the costs payable pursuant to the representation order. The precise terms of the observations must be entered in the court record.

(*PDC 2015* 4.3.1)

The Criminal Legal Aid (Remuneration) Regulations 2013:

- art.26 permits the appropriate officer to reduce any fee which would otherwise be payable by such proportion as the officer considers reasonable in the light of any adverse comments made by the judge; the power to make adverse comments co-exists with the power to disallow fees when making a wasted costs order; and
- art.27 allows the determining officer to disallow the amount of the wasted costs order from the amount otherwise payable to the litigator or advocate and allows for deduction of a greater amount if appropriate.

(*PDC 2015* 4.3.2)

Where the judge has in mind making such observations the litigator or advocate whose fees or expenses might be affected must be informed of the precise terms thereof and of his right to make representations to the appropriate authority and be given a reasonable opportunity to show cause as to why the observations or direction should not be made. Where such observations or directions are made the appropriate authority must afford an opportunity to the litigator or advocate whose fees might be affected to make representations in relation to them.

(*PDC 2015* 4.3.3–4.3.4)

Whether or not observations under *PDC 2015* 4.3.1 above have been made the appropriate authority may consult the judge or the court on any matter touching the allowance or disallowance of fees and expenses, but if the observations then made are to the effect mentioned in *PDC 2015* 4.3.1, the appropriate authority should afford an opportunity to the litigator or advocate concerned to make representations in relation to them.

(*PDC 2015* 4.3.5)

Very high cost cases

19-029 In proceedings which are classified as a very high cost case ("VHCC") as defined by the Criminal Legal Aid (Remuneration) Regulations 2013 reg.2:

- The representative of the funded person should be asked, at the earliest opportunity, whether the Lord Chancellor has been informed of the case in accordance with reg.12.
- If they have not been, the representative should be warned that he may not be able to recover his costs.

(*PDC 2015* 4.4.1)

Appeals against wasted costs orders

19-030 A party against whom a wasted costs order has been made may appeal against that order. In the case of an order made at first instance by the Crown Court, the appeal is to the CACD and the procedure is set out in CrimPR 39. The time limit for appeal is 21 days from the date of the order. Having heard the submissions, the appeal court may affirm, vary or revoke the order as it thinks fit and must notify its decision to the appellant, any interested party and the court which made the order.

(*PDC 2015* 4.2.9–4.2.10)

6. Award of costs against third parties

Power to make order

19-031 Under POA 1985 s.19B a Crown Court judge can make a third party costs order if there has been serious misconduct by the third party and the court considers it appropriate to make an order against him. See also GR 1986 regs 3E–3H.

Under CrimPR 45.10, where:

(1) there has been serious misconduct by a person who is not a party; and
(2) the judge can order that person to pay a party's costs (including legal aid costs),

the judge may make an order:

(a) on application by the party who incurred the costs; or

(b) on his own initiative.

When he makes an order, he may take into account any other order as to costs in respect of the proceedings, and may take the third party costs order into account when making any other order for costs in respect of those proceedings.
(*PDC 2015* 4.7.5)

There is no statutory definition of "serious misconduct" but

> "in this context [it] would include deliberate or negligent failure to attend to one's duties or falling below a proper standard in that regard" (*R. v Ahmati* [2006] EWCA Crim 1826).

The power extends to making such an order against a government department where there has been serious misconduct, including deliberate or negligent failure to attend to one's duties, or falling below a proper standard in that regard, but there is a higher threshold for liability than for a wasted costs order (above). As to the position of a person on contract (e.g. an interpreter) see *R. v Applied Language Solutions Ltd* [2013] EWCA Crim 326; [2013] 2 Cr. App. R. 16 and *Capita Translation and Interpreting Ltd, Re* [2015] EWFC 5; [2015] 2 F.L.R. 1269.

A party wanting the judge to make an order must (CrimPR 45.10(4)):

(i) apply in writing as soon as practicable after becoming aware of the grounds for doing so; and
(ii) serve the application on the court officer, the person responsible, each other party, and any other person directly affected.

In that application he must specify:

- the person responsible;
- the relevant misconduct;
- the reasons why the criteria for making an order are met;
- the amount claimed; and
- those on whom the application has been served.

Where the judge considers making an order on his own initiative, he must (CrimPR 45.10(5)):

(i) identify the person against whom he proposes making the order; and
(ii) specify:
  - the relevant misconduct;
  - the reasons why the criteria for making an order are met; and
  - with the assistance of the party who incurred the costs, the amount involved.

A person wanting to oppose an order must (CrimPR 45.10(6)):

(i) make representations as soon as practicable; and
(ii) in reply to an application, serve representations on the applicant and on the court officer not more than 5 business days after it was served.

If the judge makes an order the general rule is that he will do so at the end of the case. He should only make such an order during the case if there are good reasons to do so.
(*PDC 2015* 4.7.2)

He must assess the amount himself. However, to help him assess the amount the judge may direct an enquiry by the National Taxing Team (CrimPR 45.10(8)). CrimPR 45.10(9) sets out the criteria which the judge must have regard to in deciding whether to direct such an enquiry. See also *PDC 2015* 1.2.4.

The order must specify the amount of costs to be paid, and the court must notify the third party and any interested party of the order, and the amount ordered to be paid.
(*PDC 2015* 4.7.6)

Appeal by third party

19-032 A third party against whom the judge makes a third party costs order at first instance may appeal to the CACD:

(1) subject to an extension being granted, within 21 days of the order being made;
(2) by the appellant giving notice in writing to the court which made the order;
(3) stating the grounds of appeal; and
(4) serving a copy of the notice of appeal and grounds, including any application for extension of time in which to appeal, on any interested party (as defined in the regulations).

(GR 1986 reg.3H)

Procedure is under CrimPR 39. Leave is not required. The CACD may affirm, vary or revoke the order.

Note that:

(a) notice in writing (there is no specific form) must be served on the Crown Court within 15 business days of the order being made (unless an extension is granted by the CACD before or after it expires);
(b) stating the grounds of appeal.

The Registrar may serve a copy of the notice and grounds on any party directly affected by the appeal.

The registrar will notify the date of the hearing to any person directly affected and allow that party to make written or oral representations.

7. SOLICITORS; CROWN COURT'S INHERENT JURISDICTION

19-033 In addition to the power under:

(1) GR 1986 reg.3 to order that costs improperly incurred be paid by a party to the proceedings; and
(2) POA 1985 s.19A to make wasted costs orders,

a judge of the Crown Court, as a judge of one of the Senior Courts, may, in the exercise of his inherent jurisdiction over officers of the court, order a solicitor personally to pay costs thrown away by reason of a serious breach of his duty to the court, but:

(a) this power should be used only in exceptional circumstances not covered by the statutory powers; *R. v Smith* [1974] 1 All E.R. 651 and *Shaw Thew v Reeves (No.2)* [1982] 3 All E.R. 1086 emphasise that an order should be made only where the conduct of the solicitor is inexcusable and such as to merit reproof, not where mere mistake, error of judgment or negligence is disclosed; and
(b) no order may be made unless reasonable notice has been given to the solicitor of the matter alleged against him and he is given a reasonable opportunity of being heard in reply.

If the judge considers it necessary to hold such a hearing in chambers, a shorthand note should be kept.

(*PDC 2015* 4.6.1–4.6.3)

8. ASSESSMENT OF COSTS

Assessment of defence costs out of central funds

Where a legally aided accused wishes to claim out of pocket expenses or costs for work which has not been done under the representation order, the assessment of those costs should be carried out at the same time as the assessment of his solicitor's costs under the representation order and the solicitors should ensure that the two claims are submitted together for assessment (*PDC 2015* 5.1.1; *R. v Supreme Court Costs Office Ex p. Brewer* [2006] EWHC 1955 (Admin); [2007] Crim. L.R. 20). 19-034

Procedure following assessment: CrimPR 45.11

Where the judge directs an assessment under: 19-035

(1) CrimPR 33.48 (POCA 2002—rules applicable to restraint and receivership proceedings, assessment of costs);
(2) CrimPR 45.6 (costs on appeal); or
(3) CrimPR 45.7 (costs on an application),

the assessment will be carried out by the relevant assessing authority, namely, where the direction was given by a judge of the Crown Court, the Lord Chancellor.

The party in whose favour the court made the costs order ("the applicant") must:

(a) apply for an assessment, in writing, in any form required by the assessing authority, and not more than three months after the costs order; and
(b) serve the application on the assessing authority and the party against whom the court made the costs order ("the respondent").

The applicant must summarise the work done, specifying:

(i) each item of work done, giving the date, time taken and amount claimed;
(ii) any disbursements or expenses, including the fees of any advocate; and
(iii) any circumstances of which the applicant wants the assessing authority to take particular account.

The applicant must also supply receipts or other evidence of the amount claimed, and any other information or document for which the assessing authority asks, within such period as that authority may require.

A respondent wanting to make representations about the amount claimed must serve the representations on the assessing authority and on the applicant not more than 15 business days after service of the application.

The assessing authority must, if it seems likely to help with the assessment:

(i) obtain any other information or document;
(ii) resolve in favour of the respondent any doubt about what should be allowed; and
(iii) serve the assessment on the parties.

(CrimPR 45.11(1)–(6))

Re-assessment

19-036 Where either party wants the amount allowed re-assessed he must:

(1) apply to the assessing authority in writing and in any form required by that authority;
(2) serve the application on the assessing authority and on the other party not more than 15 business days after service of the assessment;
(3) explain the objections to the assessment;
(4) supply any additional supporting information or document; and
(5) ask for a hearing, if he wants one.

A party wanting to make representations about an application for re-assessment must do so in writing, serving the representations on the assessing authority, and on the other party, not more than 15 business days after service of the application, and asking for a hearing, if he wants one.

The assessing authority:

- will arrange a hearing, in public or in private, if either party asks for one;
- subject to that, may re-assess the amount allowed with or without a hearing;
- will reassess the amount allowed on the initial assessment, taking into account the reasons for disagreement with that amount and any other representations;
- may maintain, increase or decrease the amount allowed on the assessment;
- will serve the re-assessment on the parties; and
- will serve reasons on the parties, if not more than 15 business days later either party asks for such reasons.

Any time limit under this rule may be extended even after it has expired, by the assessing authority or by the Senior Costs Judge, if the assessing authority declines to do so.

(CrimPR 45.11(7)–(8))

As to appeal to a Costs Judge, see CrimPR 45.12, and to a High Court Judge, see CrimPR 45.13.

Appeals to a costs judge

19-037 A party dissatisfied with a costs assessment may apply to the relevant authority for a review of the assessment (GR 1986 reg.9 or CrimPR 45.11(7)). An appeal against a decision on such a review lies to the Senior Costs Judge of the Supreme Court Costs Office (CrimPR 45.12).

Written notice in the form set out in *PDC 2015* Sch.3 (adapted where appropriate) must be given within 21 days of receipt of the reasons for the assessment, or such longer time as the Costs Judge directs.

(*PDC 2015* 5.2)

9. CONTRIBUTION ORDERS

Contribution orders

19-038 In proceedings to which the Criminal Legal Aid (Contribution Orders) Regulations 2013 apply (see LEGAL AID; PUBLIC FUNDING) the funded accused may be liable to make payments under an income contribution order. If he is convicted or if the representation order is withdrawn, he may be required to pay the whole or part of the cost of the representation under a capital contribution order.

(*PDC 2015* 6.1.1)

If the trial judge considers that there are exceptional reasons, an accused who is acquitted may nevertheless be required to pay the whole or part of the costs of the representation in the Crown Court (reg.25(b)).

(*PDC 2015* 6.1.2)

Where an accused is convicted of one or more, but not all, offences he may apply in writing to the trial judge (or a judge nominated for that purpose by the Resident Judge) for an order that he pay proportion only of the costs of the representation in the Crown Court on the ground that it would be manifestly unreasonable that he pay the whole amount (reg.26). An application must be made within 21 days of the date on which the individual is dealt with. The judge may refuse the application or make an order specifying the proportion of costs which the defendant must pay.

(*PDC 2015* 6.1.3)

10. Costs in restraint, confiscation or receivership proceedings

The order for costs

Special provisions apply where a judge is deciding whether to make an order for costs in relation to restraint or receivership proceedings brought under POCA 2002 (confiscation proceedings are treated for costs purposes as part of the trial). **19-039**

The judge has a discretion as to whether costs are payable by one party to another, the amount of those costs and when they are to be paid.

The general rule is that if the judge decides to make an order about costs the unsuccessful party will be ordered to pay the costs of the successful party, but the judge may make a different order—CrimPR 33.47.

(*PDC 2015* 7.1.1)

Attention is drawn to the fact that in receivership proceedings the CrimPR provide that the Crown Court may make orders in respect of security to be given by a receiver to cover his liability for his acts and omissions as a receiver—CrimPR 33.60. The judge may also make orders in relation to determining the remuneration of the receiver—CrimPR 33.61 (*PDC 2015* 7.1.2).

In deciding what, if any, order to make about costs the judge is required to have regard to all the circumstances including the conduct of all the parties and whether a party has succeeded on part of an application, even if that party has not been wholly successful (*PDC 2015* 7.1.3).

The CrimPR set out the type of order which the court may make (the list is not exclusive):

- (a) a proportion of another party's costs;
- (b) a stated amount in respect of another party's costs;
- (c) costs from or until a certain date only;
- (d) costs incurred before proceedings have begun;
- (e) costs relating to particular steps taken in the proceedings;
- (f) costs relating only to a distinct part of the proceedings; and
- (g) interest on costs from or until a certain date including a date before the making of an order.

The judge is required, where it is practicable, to award a proportion (e.g. a percentage) of the costs, or costs between certain dates, rather than making an order relating only to a distinct part or issue in the proceedings. The latter type of order makes it extremely difficult for the costs to be assessed.

Where the judge orders a party to pay costs he may, in addition, order an amount to be paid on account by one party to another before the costs are assessed. Where he makes such an order, the order should state the amount to be paid and the date on or before which payment is to be made.

(*PDC 2015* 7.1.4–7.1.6)

Assessment of costs

19-040 Where the judge makes an order for costs in restraint or receivership proceedings he may make an assessment of the costs there and then (a summary assessment), or order assessment of the costs under CrimPR 45.11. If the judge neither makes an assessment of the costs nor orders assessment as specified above, the order for costs will be treated as an order for the amount of costs to be decided by assessment under CrimPR 45.11 unless the order otherwise provides.

Whenever the judge awards costs to be assessed he should consider whether to exercise the power to order the paying party to pay such sum of money as he thinks just, on account of those costs.

(*PDC 2015* 7.2.1–7.2.2)

In carrying out the assessment of costs the judge or the assessing authority is required to allow only costs which are proportionate to the matters in issue, and to resolve any doubt which he may have, as to whether the costs were reasonably incurred or were reasonable and proportionate in amount, in favour of the paying party.

(*PDC 2015* 7.2.3)

The judge or assessing authority carrying out the assessment should have regard to all the circumstances in deciding whether costs were proportionately or reasonably incurred or proportionate and reasonable in amount. Effect must be given to any orders for costs which have already been made.

The judge or the assessing authority should also have regard to:

(a) the conduct of all the parties, including in particular conduct before as well as during the proceedings;
(b) the amount or value of any property involved;
(c) the importance of the matter to all the parties;
(d) the particular complexity of the matter or the difficulty or novelty of the questions raised;
(e) the skill, effort, specialised knowledge and responsibility involved;
(f) the time spent on the case; and
(g) the place where and the circumstances in which work or any part of it was done.

(*PDC 2015* 7.2.4)

In applying the test of proportionality regard should be had to the objective of dealing with cases justly. Dealing with a case justly includes, so far as practicable, dealing with it in ways which are proportionate to:

- the amount of money involved;
- the importance of the case;
- the complexity of the issues; and

- the financial position of each party.

The relationship between the total of the costs incurred and the financial value of the claim may not be a reliable guide (*PDC 2015* 7.2.5–7.2.7).

In any proceedings there will be costs which will inevitably be incurred and which are necessary for the successful conduct of the case. Litigators are not required to conduct litigation at rates which are uneconomic, thus in a modest claim the proportion of costs is likely to be higher than in a large claim and may even equal or possibly exceed the amount in dispute. Where a hearing takes place, the time taken by the court in dealing with a particular issue may not be an accurate guide to the amount of time properly spent by the legal or other representatives in preparing for the trial of that issue (*PDC 2015* 7.2.6–7.2.7).

The CrimPR do not apply to the assessment of costs in proceedings to the extent that LASPOA 2012 s.26 (costs in civil proceedings) applies and statutory instruments made under that Act make different provision.

(*PDC 2015* 7.2.8)

Remuneration of a receiver

A receiver may only charge for his services if the Crown Court so directs and specifies the basis on which the receiver is to be remunerated (CrimPR 33.61(2)). The Crown Court (unless it orders otherwise) is required to award such sum as is reasonable and proportionate in all the circumstances. In arriving at the figure for remuneration the judge should take into account: **19-041**

- the time properly given by the receiver and his staff to the receivership;
- the complexity of the receivership;
- any responsibility of an exceptional kind or degree which falls on the receiver in consequence of the receivership;
- the effectiveness with which the receiver appears to be carrying out or to have carried out his duties; and
- the value and nature of the subject matter of the receivership.

The Crown Court may, instead of determining the receiver's remuneration itself, refer it to be ascertained by the assessing authority of the Crown Court.

In these circumstances CrimPR 45.11–45.13 (which deal with review by the assessing authority, further review by a Costs Judge and appeal to a High Court Judge) have effect.

(*PDC 2015* 7.3.1–7.3.2)

Procedure on appeal to the CACD

The Court of Appeal has no power to award costs on a prosecutor's appeal in relation to a confiscation order under s.31(1) or (2) of the Proceeds of Crime Act 2002 (*Barnet LBC v Kamyab* [2021] EWCA Crim 1209; [2022] 1 W.L.R. 57). **19-042**

The costs of, and incidental to, all proceedings on an appeal to the CACD against orders made in restraint proceedings, or appeals against or relating to the making of receivership orders, are in the discretion of the court (POCA 2002 s.89(4)). The court has full power to determine by whom and to what extent the costs are to be paid.

In any such proceedings the court may disallow or (as the case may be) order the

legal or other representative concerned to meet the whole of any wasted costs or such part of them as may be determined in accordance with the CrimPR.
(*PDC 2015* 7.4)

11. Advice on appeal to the CACD

19-043 In all cases the procedure set out in *A Guide to Proceedings in the Court of Appeal (Criminal Division)* published by the Criminal Appeal Office with the approval of the Lord Chief Justice should be followed, together with *PDC 2015* Pt 8.

12. VAT

19-044 For the proper approach to VAT on bills of costs lodged for determination or assessment, see *PDC 2015* Pt 9.

13. Enforcement and appeal

Search; time to pay; instalments

19-045 The enforcement of costs is a matter for the appropriate magistrates' court, but where a judge of the Crown Court makes an order against an accused for the payment of costs, he may:

(1) if the person against whom the costs have been awarded is present in court, order him to be searched and, unless the judge otherwise directs, any money found on him will be applied towards payment of the costs;
(2) allow time to pay the sum due under the order; or
(3) direct payment by instalments of such amounts and on such dates as he may specify.

(AJA 1970 s.41(1) and (2))

Payment by parent or guardian

19-046 Where a young person is found guilty of an offence, the judge must order any costs awarded to be paid by the parent or guardian (see CHILDREN AND YOUNG PERSONS).

Appeal against award of costs

19-047 An appeal lies to the CACD by an offender convicted on indictment and ordered to contribute towards the costs of the prosecution; no appeal lies by an accused tried on indictment and ordered to contribute towards the costs of his publicly funded defence (*R. v Hayden* (1974) 60 Cr. App. R. 304).

An order for costs made in relation to proceedings on indictment may not be challenged by a quashing order in the High Court.

19-048

14. Costs from central funds and relevant statutory authorities: PDC 2015 Sch.2

Proceedings	Court	Extent of Availability	Authority
Information not proceeded with	Magistrates'	Defendant	s.16(1)(a) POA 1985
Decision not to commit for trial	Magistrates'	Defendant	s.16(1)(b) POA 1985
Dismissal of information	Magistrates'	Defendant	s.16(1)(c) POA 1985
Person indicted or committed for trial but not tried	Crown	Defendant	s.16(2)(a) POA 1985
Notice of transfer given but person not tried	Crown	Defendant	s.16(2)(aa) POA 1985
Acquittal on indictment	Crown	Defendant	s.16(2)(b) POA 1985
Successful appeal to the Crown Court against conviction or sentence	Crown	Appellant	s.16(3) POA 1985
Successful appeal to the CACD against conviction or sentence or insanity/disability finding	CACD	Appellant	s.16(4) POA 1985
Appeal against order or ruling at preparatory hearing	CACD	Appellant	s.16(4A) POA 1985
Application for leave to appeal to Supreme Court	CACD	Appellant	s.16(5)(c) POA 1985
Attorney General reference to the CACD on point of law following acquittal	CACD, Supreme Court	Acquitted Defendant	s.36(5) CJA 1972
Attorney-General reference under s.36 CJA 1988 (lenient sentence appeals)	CACD	Convicted Defendant	Sch.3 para.11 CJA 1988
Determination of proceedings in a criminal cause or matter in Divisional Court	Divisional Court	Defendant in criminal proceedings	s.16(5)(a) POA 1985
Determination of appeal or application for leave to appeal from the CACD or DC	Supreme Court	Defendant in criminal proceedings	s.16(5)(b) and (c) POA 1985
Proceedings in respect of an indictable offence	Magistrates' and Crown	Private prosecutor	s.17(1)(a) POA 1985

Proceedings	Court	Extent of Availability	Authority
Proceedings before DC or Supreme Court (following summary offence)	Divisional Court and Supreme Court	Private prosecutor	s.17(1)(b) POA 1985
Criminal cause or matter	All	Defence or private prosecution witness, interpreter, intermediary and medical practitioner	s.19(3) POA 1985—there are restrictions on what may be paid (see regs 18, 19, 20, 21, 24 and 25 CCC (General) Regulations 1986)
Murder case	Crown	Medical practitioner	s.34(5) MH(A)A 1982
Criminal Procedure (Insanity) Act proceedings	Crown	Person appointed to put case for the defence	s.19(3)(d) POA 1985
Cross-examination of vulnerable witnesses	Magistrates' and Crown	Person appointed to cross-examine witness for the defence	s.19(3)(e) POA 1985
Compensation where a court refuses an application for a banning order	Magistrates' and Crown Court (on appeal where compensation refused by the magistrates' court)	Person against whom a banning notice has been given (limited to £5,000)	s.21D Football Spectators Act 1989
Compensation where loss results from closure notice or order or Part 1A closure notice or order	Magistrates' court and Crown Court on appeal	Person incurring financial loss	ss.10 and 11J Anti-Social Behaviour Act 2003
Costs where discharge ordered	Magistrates' court, High Court, Supreme Court	Person against whom Part 1 warrant issued	s.62 Extradition Act 2003

20. COURT SECURITY

QUICK GUIDE

1. COURT SECURITY OFFICERS

General

Court security officers may be appointed and designated by the Lord Chancellor. An officer must be readily identifiable as such (whether by means of his uniform or badge or otherwise), otherwise he is not to be regarded as acting in the execution of his duty. **20-001**

It is an offence (s.57) to assault (a fine on level 5), resist or wilfully obstruct (a fine on level 3) a court security officer acting in the execution of his duty (CA 2003 s.51).

Powers of search

A court security officer, acting in the execution of his duty may search: **20-002**

(1) any person who is in, or is seeking to enter, a court building; and
(2) any article in the possession of such a person,

such power does not authorise him to require a person to remove any of his clothing other than a coat, jacket, headgear, gloves or footwear.

"Court building", here, means any building where the business of any of the courts referred to in CA 2003 s.1, which includes the Senior Courts (formerly the Supreme Court), of which the Crown Court is one, is carried on, and to which the public has access (CA 2003 s.52).

Powers to exclude, remove or restrain persons

An officer acting in the execution of his duty may exclude or remove from a court building, or a part of a court building, any person who refuses: **20-003**

(1) to permit a search under s.52(1); or
(2) to surrender an article in his possession when asked to do so under s.54(1) (20-004); and may also:
    (a) restrain any person who is in a court building; or
    (b) exclude or remove any person from a court building, or a part of a court building,

if it is reasonably necessary to do so to:

(i) enable court business to be carried on without interference or delay;
(ii) maintain order; or
(iii) secure the safety of any person in the court building.

An officer acting in the execution of his duty may remove any person from a courtroom at the request of the court.

These powers include a power to use reasonable force, where necessary (CA 2003 s.53).

Surrender and seizure of articles

20-004 An officer acting in the execution of his duty, and reasonably believing that an article in the possession of a person who is in, or seeking to enter, a court building, ought to be surrendered on the ground that it may:

(1) jeopardise the maintenance of order in the court building (or a part of it);
(2) put the safety of any person in the court building at risk; or
(3) be evidence of, or in relation to, an offence,

must ask the person to surrender the article; if that person refuses to surrender the article, the officer may seize it (CA 2003 s.54).

Powers in relation to jurors' electronic communications devices

20-005 Where an order has been made under JA 1974 s.15A (surrender of electronic communications devices by jurors) in respect of the members of a jury (see JURY MANAGEMENT), a court security officer acting in the execution of his duty is able, if ordered to do so by a judge, to search a member of the jury in order to determine whether the juror has failed to surrender an electronic communications device in accordance with the order.

This provision does not, however, authorise the officer to require a person to remove clothing other than a coat, jacket, headgear, gloves or footwear.

If the search reveals a device which is required by the order to be surrendered:

(1) the officer must ask the juror to surrender the device; and
(2) if the juror refuses to do so, the officer may seize it.

"Electronic communications device" means a device that is designed or adapted for a use which consists of or includes the sending or receiving of signals that are transmitted by means of an electronic communications network (as defined in s.32 of the Communications Act 2003) (CA 2003 s.54A; CJCA 2015 s.70(2)).

Powers to retain articles surrendered or seized

20-006 An officer may retain an article which was:

(1) surrendered in response to a request under s.54(1); or
(2) seized under s.54(2),

until the time when the person who surrendered it, or from whom it was seized, is leaving the court building, but if he reasonably believes that the article may be evidence of, or in relation to, an offence, he may retain it until the time when the person who surrendered it, or from whom it was seized, is leaving the court building, or the end of the permitted period, whichever is later.

The "permitted period" is such period, not exceeding 24 hours from the time the article was surrendered or seized, as will enable the court security officer to draw the article to the attention of a constable (CA 2003 s.55).

In relation to articles seized from jurors under JA 1974 s.15A (electronic devices) a court security officer may retain an article which was:

(a) surrendered in response to a request under s.54A(4)(a); or

(b) seized under s.54A(4)(b),

until the end of the period specified in the relevant order under s.15A of JA 1974 the time specified in subss.(1) or (1A) (as appropriate) (CA 2003 s.55; CJCA 2015 s.70(3)).

2. Terrorist cases

In terrorist cases (see ALLOCATION AND LISTING OF CASES) the police service and the prison service will provide the Regional Listing Co-ordinator's Office with an initial joint assessment of the security risks associated with any court appearance by the accused within 14 days of charge. Any subsequent changes in circumstances or the assessment of risk which have the potential to impact upon the choice of trial venue will be notified to the Regional Listing Co-ordinator's Office immediately (*CPD* XIII Listing and Allocation, Annex 4: Protocol on the management of terrorism cases para.17). **20-007**

3. Armed police in the Crown Court

Guidance issued by Lord Chief Justice

CPD I General Matters: 3M Procedure for Applications for Armed Police Presence in Crown Courts and Magistrates' Courts Buildings (as substituted by the *Criminal Practice Directions 2015 (Amendment No.2)*, 16 November 2016 incorporates and revokes earlier guidance given by the Senior Presiding Judge for England and Wales on 1 November 2012. The *CPD* sets out the procedure for the making and handling of applications for authorisation for the presence of armed officers within the precincts of any Crown Court building at any time, including during the delivery of prisoners to court. The guidance applies to an application to authorise the carriage of firearms or Tasers in court. It does not apply to officers who are carrying CS spray or PAVA incapacitant spray which is included in the standard equipment issued to officers in some forces. **20-008**

Note that:

(1) the guidance does not apply when there is an emergency; in such circumstances the police must be able to respond in a manner which, in their professional judgment, is most appropriate; and
(2) applications may be made only in those designated Crown Court centres listed in the guidance.

Consideration of live link; preparatory work

Prior to the making of an application for armed transport of prisoners, or the presence of armed police officers in court buildings, consideration must be given to making use of prison video-link equipment to avoid the necessity of the prisoner's attendance at court for the hearing in respect of which the application is to be made. **20-009**

Notwithstanding his designation, each requesting officer must attend the relevant court before an application is made to ensure that there have been no changes to the premises and that there are no circumstances that might affect security arrangements.

Standard application

20-010 All applications should be made on the standard form attached to the guidance, directed to the Cluster Manager and should be sent by email if at all possible. Then:

(1) the Cluster Manager will notify the Presiding Judge on the Circuit by email, proving a copy of the form and any supporting evidence; the Presiding Judge may ask to see the senior police officer concerned;
(2) the Presiding Judge will consider the application; if it is refused the application fails and the police must be informed;
(3) if the Presiding Judge approves the application it should be forwarded to the secretary in the Senior Presiding Judge's office; the Senior Presiding Judge will make the final decision and the Presiding Judge will receive confirmation of that decision; and
(4) the Presiding Judge will notify the Cluster Manager, who will immediately inform the police by telephone of the decision; the decision will then be confirmed in writing to the police.

Urgent applications

20-011 If:

(1) the temporary deployment of armed police arises an urgent issue and a case would otherwise have to be adjourned; or
(2) the trial judge is satisfied that there is a serious risk to public safety,

then the Resident Judge will have a discretion to agree such deployment without having obtained the consent of the Presiding Judge or the Senior Presiding Judge. In such a case:

(a) the Resident Judge should assess the facts and agree the proposed solution with a police officer of at least the Superintendent level; that officer should approach the Firearms Division of the police;
(b) if the proposed solution involves the use of armed police officers, the Resident Judge must try to contact the Presiding judge and/or the Senior Presiding Judge by email and telephone; the Cluster Manager should be informed of the situation; and
(c) if the Resident Judge cannot obtain a response from the Presiding Judge or the Senior Presiding Judge, he may grant the application if satisfied that:
    (i) the application is necessary;
    (ii) without such deployment there would be a significant risk to public safety; and
    (iii) the case would have to be adjourned at significant difficulty or inconvenience.

21. CRIMINAL BEHAVIOUR ORDERS

QUICK GUIDE

A. MAKING AN ORDER

Powers

Where a person is convicted of an offence, a judge may: **21-001**

(1) in addition to any sentence which he imposes in respect of the offence; or
(2) in addition to an order for a conditional discharge; or
(3) on the application of the prosecutor,

make a CBO against the offender where he:

(a) is satisfied beyond reasonable doubt that the offender has engaged in behaviour that caused, or was likely to cause harassment, alarm or distress to any person; and
(b) considers that making the order will help in preventing the offender from engaging in such behaviour.

(SA 2020 s.331)

Whilst s.331(2)(a) requires the court to be satisfied to the criminal standard (that the offender has engaged in behaviour that caused or was likely to cause harassment etc.), SA 2020 s.331(2)(b) (whether the order will help in preventing the offender from engaging in such behaviour) does not expressly impose any burden of proof upon the prosecution. In *DPP v Bulmer* [2015] EWHC 2323 (Admin); [2016] 1 Cr. App. R. (S.) 12 at [48], Beatson LJ observed that:

> "whilst the court hearing an application for a Criminal Behaviour Order should proceed with a proper degree of caution and circumspection because such orders are not lightly to be imposed, satisfaction to the criminal standard is not required in what is an evaluative exercise".

Relevant factors in conducting this evaluative exercise include the following:

(1) where the evidence shows that a positive requirement would help prevent a person from engaging in anti-social conduct, the absence of such a requirement is a factor that can be taken into account in deciding whether to refuse to make an order, but it is impermissible to regard the absence of such a requirement as dispositive;
(2) the fact that a person has not responded to orders in the past is also a relevant factor but is not in itself a reason for deciding not to make a CBO; and
(3) the fact that the person is already subject to an ASBO may be relevant to a decision to refuse to make a CBO, but it must be remembered that one of

the purposes of such orders is to empower the police to take action before the anti-social behaviour they are designed to prevent takes place.

A CBO for the purpose of preventing the offender from engaging in behaviour that causes, or is likely to cause harassment, alarm or distress to any person:

(i) *prohibits* him from doing anything described in the order; and/or
(ii) *requires* him to do anything described in the order.

(SA 2020 s.330)

If the offender will be under the age of 18 when the application is made, the prosecutor must find out the views of the local youth offending team before applying for an order to be made.

"Local youth offending team" means the youth offending team in whose area it appears to the prosecution that the offender lives.

(SA 2020 s.331(5)–(6))

Like its predecessor, the ASBO, the CBO is designed for the protection of others and is not a penalty for an offence (*R. (on the application McCann) v Manchester Crown Court* [2002] UKHL 39; [2003] 1 Cr. App. R. 27). It cannot stand alone; it is an ancillary order which may be attached to any sentence imposed for an offence or to a conditional discharge. Unlike its predecessor, which might be initiated by the judge of his own motion, the new order requires an application by the prosecutor. Where it is shown that the conduct of an acquitted accused is, e.g. provocative and likely to be repeated, consideration may be given to imposing a bind over, or, in appropriate circumstances, a restraining order (see RESTRAINING ORDERS).

The judge should first sentence for the substantive offence, and then go on to consider whether an order should be made (albeit at the same hearing where that is appropriate).

As to the duration of an order, see 21-008.

Limitations on requirements

21-002 Prohibitions and requirements in a CBO must, so far as practicable, avoid:

(1) any interference with the times, if any, at which the offender normally works or attends school or any other educational establishment; and
(2) any conflict with the requirements of any other court order to which the offender may be subject.

(SA 2020 s.331(4))

In *R. v Khan (Kamran)* [2018] EWCA Crim 1472; [2018] 1 W.L.R. 5419 it was said that assessments of proportionality were intensively fact sensitive.

Applying for an order

21-003 CrimPR 31 sets out the procedure for all "behaviour orders", including CBOs.

Where the prosecutor wants the judge to make an order if the accused is convicted, he must serve a notice of intention to apply for such an order on the Crown Court officer, the accused against whom the order is sought and any person on whom the order would be likely to have a significant adverse effect, as soon as practicable (without waiting for the verdict) (CrimPR 31.3(2)).

The notice must summarise the relevant facts, identify the evidence on which he relies in support, attach any written statement that he has not already served, and specify the order he wants the judge to make; and the accused must then serve written notice of any evidence on which he relies, on the Crown Court officer and on the prosecutor (without waiting for the verdict) and in that notice identify the evidence and attach any written statement that has not already been served (CrimPR 31.3(3)). The defence must be given clear and comprehensive notice of any changes to the proposed application (*R. v Uddin* [2015] EWCA Crim 1918; [2016] 1 Cr. App. R. (S.) 57).

CDA 1998 s.1 (rather than s.1C) was considered by the House of Lords in *R. (on the application of McCann) v Manchester Crown Court* [2002] UKHL 39; [2003] 1 Cr. App. R. 27, which concluded that:

(i) the procedures for making an ASBO under CDA 1998 s.1 are *civil* rather than criminal in nature (and are not, therefore, subject to the rules of evidence applicable in criminal proceedings); but
(ii) the *criminal standard of proof* applies to proof of acts of anti-social behaviour alleged against the offender.

Whilst hearsay evidence is admissible in such proceedings, the judge still has to consider its weight and distinguish between hearsay that is cogent and that which is more properly to be regarded as unreliable. As to the procedure for admitting hearsay evidence, see CrimPR 31.6.

Need for hearing

The judge must not make an order unless the person to whom it is directed has had an opportunity: (i) to consider what order is proposed, and why, and the evidence in support; and (ii) to make representations at a hearing, whether or not the person in fact attends (CrimPR 31.2(1)). **21-004**

Furthermore,

(1) the terms of any order must be precise and capable of being understood by the accused, to whom they must be explained;
(2) the conditions in the order must be enforceable and workable in the sense that they allow a breach to be readily identified;
(3) the findings of fact giving rise to the making of the order must be recorded; and
(4) the exact terms of the order must be pronounced in open court, and explained to the offender, and the written order must accurately reflect the order as pronounced.

(*R. v Khan (Kamran)* [2018] EWCA Crim 1472; [2018] 1 W.L.R. 5419) (see also *R. v P* [2004] EWCA Crim 287; [2004] 2 Cr. App. R. (S) 65; *R. v Boness* [2005] EWCA Crim 2395; [2006] 1 Cr. App. R. (S.) 120; *R. v Douglas* [2011] EWCA Crim 2628 in relation to ASBOs).

Where an order is made at the time of the imposition of a prison sentence, the judge should have regard to the nature, length and likely effect of the sentence, the nature, length and actual effect of prior sentences, and the duration, conditions and likely effect of any period of licence (*R. v Barclay* [2011] EWCA Crim 32; [2011] 2 Cr. App. R. (S.) 67).

Proceedings on the hearing of the application

21-005 For the purpose of deciding whether to make a CBO the judge may consider evidence led by the prosecution and evidence led by the offender; it does not matter whether the evidence would have been admissible in the proceedings in which the offender was convicted. He may adjourn any proceedings on an application for a CBO even after sentencing the offender. It may not be appropriate for an adjourned application to be resolved before someone other than the sentencing judge (see *R. v Maguire* [2019] EWCA Crim 1193; [2019] 6 WLUK 656).

(SA 2020 s.332(1)–(3))

If the offender does not appear for any adjourned proceedings the judge may:

(1) further adjourn the proceedings;
(2) issue a warrant for the offender's arrest; or
(3) hear the proceedings in the offender's absence, but

may not act under para.(2) unless satisfied that the offender has had adequate notice of the time and place of the adjourned proceedings, and may not act under para.(3) unless satisfied that the offender:

(a) has had adequate notice of the time and place of the adjourned proceedings; and
(b) has been informed that if he does not appear for those proceedings the judge may hear the proceedings in his absence.

(SA 2020 s.332(4)–(6))

In proceedings in which a CBO is made against an offender who is under the age of 18:

- CYPA 1933 s.49 (restrictions on reports of proceedings in which children and young persons are concerned) does not apply in respect of the offender; and
- section 39 of that Act (power to prohibit publication of certain matters) does apply.

(SA 2020 s.332(7)–(8))

Requirements included in orders

21-006 An order that includes a requirement must specify the person who is to be responsible for supervising compliance with the requirement. That person may be an individual or an organisation.

Before including a requirement, the judge must receive evidence about its suitability and enforceability from the individual to be specified as above, if an individual is to be specified, or from an individual representing the organisation to be specified, if an organisation is to be specified.

Before including two or more requirements, the judge must consider their compatibility with each other.

It is the duty of a person specified under the above provision to:

(1) make any necessary arrangements in connection with the requirements for which that person has responsibility (the "relevant requirements");
(2) promote the offender's compliance with the relevant requirements; and
(3) inform the prosecution and the appropriate chief officer of police, if he considers that the offender:

(a) has complied with all the relevant requirements; or
(b) has failed to comply with a relevant requirement.

"The appropriate chief officer of police" means the chief officer of police for the police area in which it appears to the person specified that the offender lives.

An offender subject to a requirement in a CBO must:

(i) keep in touch with the person specified in relation to that requirement, in accordance with any instructions given by that person from time to time; and
(ii) notify the person of any change of address.

(SA 2020 s.333)

Duration of order

An order takes effect on the day it is made, save that if on the day a CBO (the new order) is made, the offender is subject to another CBO (the previous order), the new order may be made so as to take effect on the day on which the previous order ceases to have effect. **21-007**

An order must specify the period (the order period) for which it has effect.

In the case of a CBO made:

(1) before the offender has reached the age of 18, the order period must be a fixed period of:
 (a) not less than one year; and
 (b) not more than three years; and
(2) after the offender has reached the age of 18, the order period must be:
 (a) a fixed period of not less than two years; or
 (b) an indefinite period (so that the order has effect until further order).

The order may specify periods for which particular prohibitions or requirements have effect.

(SA 2020 s.334)

See *R. v Janes* [2016] EWCA Crim 676; [2016] 2 Cr. App. R. (S.) 27, where a 10 year order imposed following convictions for fraud was replaced with a three year order, with the CACD commenting on the need to put a restraint in place for the early years after the appellant's release from custody.

Form of order

A form of order is set out in *CPD* Annex D. **21-008**

The following points arising from the previous legislation may be of relevance in drawing up the order:

(1) the duration of the order ought to be for a *determinate period*: *R. v Vittles* [2004] EWCA Crim 1089; [2005] 1 Cr. App. R. (S.) 8;
(2) the order must be *tailor-made* for the individual offender, not designed on a word processor for use in every case (*R. (on the application of Lonergan) v Lewes Crown Court* [2005] 1 W.L.R. 2670; *R. v Boness* [2005] EWCA Crim 2395; [2006] 1 Cr. App. R. (S.) 120); most recently see *R. v Uddin* [2015] EWCA Crim 1918; [2016] 1 Cr. App. R. (S) 57;
(3) the judge must seek carefully to *match the prohibitions* in the order with the type of behaviour it is necessary to prohibit for the purposes in the Act (*R.*

v Uddin [2015] EWCA Crim 1918; [2016] 1 Cr. App. R. (S) 57; *CPS v T* [2006] EWHC 728 (Admin); [2006] 3 All E.R. 471); to ban the offender from "committing any criminal offence" is too wide and is unenforceable (*W v DPP* [2005] EWHC 1333 (Admin); (2005) 169 J.P. 435), as is a term "not to act in an antisocial manner in the City of Manchester" (*CPS v T* [2006] EWHC 728 (Admin); [2006] 3 All E.R. 471);

(4) the order must be substantially, not just formally, *prohibitory*; (a curfew order which imposes a restraint upon leaving or travelling between specified premises, or between particular times, was held to meet that test in *R. (on the application of Lonergan) v Lewes Crown Court* [2005] 1 W.L.R. 2670);

(5) it is not necessary that every condition imposed in the order run for the full term of the order; the test must be (using the new wording) "will it help in preventing the offender from engaging in such behaviour", and "what is *proportionate* in the circumstances" (*R. v Boness* [2005] EWCA Crim 2395; [2006] 1 Cr. App. R. (S.) 120);

(6) the judge's findings of fact in relation to the alleged anti-social behaviour should *be recorded* on the face of the order (*R. v Wadmore* [2006] EWCA Crim 686); and

(7) where an order is made at the time of the imposition of a prison sentence, the judge should have regard to the nature, length and likely effect of the sentence, the nature, length and actual effect of prior sentences, and the duration and likely effect of any period of licence (*R. v Barclay* [2011] EWCA Crim 32; [2011] 2 Cr. App. R. (S.) 67; see also *R. v P* [2004] EWCA Crim 287; [2004] 2 Cr. App. R. (S.) 65).

In *R. v Khan* [2018] EWCA Crim 1472; [2018] 2 Cr. App. R. (S.) 53, the CACD provided some general guidance on the consideration of applications for CBOs and the form of the order. As with any order of a criminal court with the characteristics of an injunction, it is essential that the guidance given in *R. v Boness (Dean)* [2005] EWCA Crim 2395, [2006] 1 Cr. App. R. (S.) 120 in relation to anti-social behaviour orders is borne in mind. The terms of the order must be precise and capable of being understood by the offender. The findings of fact giving rise to the making of the order must be recorded. The order must be explained to the offender. The exact terms of the order must be pronounced in open court and the written order must accurately reflect the order as pronounced. Because an order has to be precise and capable of being understood by the offender, a court should ask itself before making an order "are the terms of this order clear so that the offender will know precisely what it is that he is prohibited from doing?". Prohibitions should be reasonable and proportionate, realistic and practical, and be in terms which make it easy to determine and prosecute a breach. Exclusion zones should be clearly delineated (generally with the use of clearly marked maps) and individuals whom the defendant was prohibited from contacting or associating with should be clearly identified. In the case of a foreign national, translation might be required. Section 22 of the 2014 Act (SA 2020 s.331(2)(a)) might on a literal construction be said to apply to a high proportion of cases in the criminal courts. Many offences were committed in public places and caused a degree of alarm and distress either to the victims or to members of the public who observed them. However, it was not Parliament's intention that criminal behaviour orders should become a mere matter of box-ticking routine. Such orders were not to be imposed lightly; the court should proceed with a proper degree of caution and circumspection; the order had to be tailored to the specific circumstances of the person on whom it was to be imposed, and assessments of proportionality were intensively fact sensitive.

Interim orders

Where the judge adjourns the hearing of an application for a CBO he may make a CBO that lasts until the final hearing of the application or until further order (an interim order) if he thinks it just to do so. Section 331(1)(b), (3) and (5) and s.344(3)–(5) do not apply in relation to the making of an interim order. **21-009**

Subject to that, a court has the same powers whether or not the CBO is an interim order.

(SA 2020 s.335)

B. Variation and Discharge

A CBO may be varied or discharged by the court which made it on the application of either the offender or the prosecution. **21-010**

If an application by:

(1) the offender is dismissed, he may make no further application without the consent of the court which made the order, or the agreement of the prosecution;
(2) the prosecution is dismissed, the prosecution may make no further application under this section without the consent of the court which made the order, or the agreement of the offender.

The power to vary an order includes power to include an additional prohibition or requirement in the order or to extend the period for which a prohibition or requirement has effect. Section 333 applies to additional requirements included on a varied order as it applies to requirements included in a new order.

(SA 2020 s.336)

Procedure on Variation and Discharge

A person seeking variation or discharge of a CBO must apply in writing as soon as practicable after becoming aware of the grounds for doing so: **21-011**

(1) explaining what material circumstances have changed since the order was made, and why the order should be varied or revoked as a result; and
(2) serving the application on the court officer and, as appropriate, the prosecutor or accused, any other person protected or affected by the order and, if the court so directs, on any other person.

A party who wants the judge to take account of any particular evidence before making his decision must, as soon as practicable, serve notice in writing on the same persons identifying in that notice the evidence and attaching any written statement that has not already been served.

The judge may decide such an application with or without a hearing, but must not:

(a) dismiss an application unless the applicant has had an opportunity to make representations at a hearing (whether or not he in fact attends); or
(b) allow an application unless everyone required to be served, by this rule or by the court, has had at least 10 business days in which to make representations, including representations about whether there should be a hearing.

The Crown Court officer will serve the application on any person, if the judge so directs, and give notice of any hearing to the applicant, and to any person required to be served, by this rule or by the court.

(CrimPR 31.5)

C. REVIEW

Review of orders (person under the age of 18)

21-012 If:

(1) a person subject to a CBO will be under the age of 18 at the end of a review period (see below);
(2) the term of the order runs until the end of that period or beyond; and
(3) the order is not discharged before the end of that period,

a review of the operation of the order must be carried out before the end of that period.

The "review periods" are:

(a) the period of 12 months beginning with:
  (i) the day on which the order takes effect; or
  (ii) if, during that period the order is varied under s.336, the day on which it is varied (or most recently varied, if the order is varied more than once);
(b) a period of 12 months beginning with:
  (i) the day after the end of the previous review period; or
  (ii) if during that period of 12 months the order is varied under s.336, the day on which it is varied (or most recently varied, if the order is varied more than once).

A review must include consideration of:

- the extent to which the offender has complied with the order;
- the adequacy of any support available to the offender to help him or her comply with it; and
- any matters relevant to the question whether an application should be made for the order to be varied or discharged.

Those carrying out or participating in any such review must have regard to any relevant guidance issued by the Secretary of State when considering how the review should be carried out, what particular matters the review should deal with and what action (if any) it would be appropriate to take as a result of the findings of the review.

(SA 2020 s.337)

Carrying out and participating in reviews

21-013 A review under s.337 is to be carried out by the chief officer of police of the police force maintained for the police area in which the offender lives or appears to be living, acting in co-operation with the council for the local government area in which the offender lives or appears to be living and the council must co-operate in the carrying out of the review.

The chief officer may invite the participation in the review of any other person or body.

"Local government area" here means in relation to England, a district or London borough, the City of London, the Isle of Wight and the Isles of Scilly and in relation to Wales, a county or a county borough. The council for the Inner and Middle Temples is the Common Council of the City of London.

(SA 2020 s.338)

D. Breach of order

General

A person who without reasonable excuse: 21-014

(1) does anything he is prohibited from doing by a CBO; or
(2) fails to do anything he is required to do by a CBO,

commits an offence and is liable on conviction on indictment to imprisonment for a period not exceeding five years or to a fine, or to both.

If a person is convicted of such an offence it is not open to the judge before whom he is convicted to make an order for conditional discharge (SA 2020 s.339(3)).

In proceedings for such an offence, a copy of the original order, certified by the proper officer of the court which made it, is admissible as evidence of its having been made and of its contents to the same extent that oral evidence of those things is admissible in those proceedings.

Where proceedings for an offence are brought against a person under the age of 18:

(a) CYPA 1933 s.49 (restrictions on reports of proceedings in which children and young persons are concerned) does not apply in respect of the person; but
(b) YJCEA 1999 s.45 (power to restrict reporting of criminal proceedings involving persons under 18) does apply.

If the judge does exercise his power to give a direction under s.45 he must give his reasons for doing so.

(SA 2020 s.339)

Sentence on the breach

An offender in breach of an order commits an offence punishable on indictment with five years' imprisonment. In relation to the previous legislation, in *R. v Thomas* [2004] EWCA Crim 1173; [2005] 1 Cr. App. R. (S.) 9 and *R. v Braxton* [2004] EWCA Crim 1374; [2005] 1 Cr. App. R. (S.) 36, the CACD upheld terms of 18 months and three and a half years respectively. 21-015

In *R. v Lamb* [2005] EWCA Crim 3000; [2006] 2 Cr. App. R. (S.) 11 the CACD drew a distinction between mere breaches of the conditions of an order, which might be dealt with, e.g. by a community sentence, and a breach involving further anti-social behaviour which called for a more serious punishment.

Where the conduct constituting the breach also amounts to a distinct criminal offence the maximum sentence for which is prescribed by statute, while this should be borne in mind in the interests of proportionality, the sentence in respect of the breach is not limited to the statutory maximum for that offence, and the sentence should be commensurate with the breach (*R. v Lamb*; *R. v H* [2006] EWCA Crim 255; [2006] 2 Cr. App. R. (S.) 68).

The Sentencing Council's *Breach of a Criminal Behaviour Order Guideline* came into effect on 1 October 2018.

Procedure and evidence

21-016 In so far as procedure and evidence is concerned:

(a) a copy of the original order, certified as such by the proper officer of the court which made it, is admissible as evidence of its having been made and of its contents to the same extent that oral evidence of those things is admissible in those proceedings;
(b) whether or not the accused is in breach of the specific terms of the order is a question of fact (*R. v Doughan* [2007] EWCA Crim598; [2007] 171 J.P. 397);
(c) while questions as to the validity of the original order cannot found a defence, lack of clarity may be taken into account both in relation to reasonable excuse and to penalty (*CPS v T* [2006] EWHC 728 (Admin); [2006] 3 All E.R. 471); and
(d) where the accused is charged with breaching the terms of an order prohibiting him from engaging in behaviour "without reasonable excuse", the burden of proving absence of reasonable excuse, if it is raised, is on the prosecutor (*R. v Charles* [2009] EWCA Crim 1570; [2010] 1 Cr. App. R. 2).

See also *R. v Hunt* (1987) 84 Cr. App. R. 163; *R. v Evans* [2004] EWCA Crim 3103; [2005] 1 Cr. App. R. 32; *R. v Nicholson* [2006] EWCA Crim 1518; [2006] 2 Cr. App. R. 30.

The statute does not require the prosecutor to prove a specific mental element on the part of an offender at the time he committed the acts which constitute the breach.

E. SPECIAL MEASURES FOR WITNESSES

21-017 YJCEA 1999 Pt 2 Ch.1 (special measures directions in the case of vulnerable and intimidated witnesses) applies to CBO proceedings as it applies to criminal proceedings, but with the omission of the following provisions of that Act (which make provision appropriate only in the context of criminal proceedings), and any other necessary modifications.

Those provisions are:

- section 17(4)–(7) (witness eligible for assistance on ground of fear or distress about testifying);
- section 21(4C)(e) (child witness);
- section 22A (sexual offences);
- section 27(10) (video recorded evidence in chief); and
- section 32 (warning to jury).

YJCEA 1999 s.47 (restrictions on reporting special measures directions, etc.) applies with any necessary modifications:

(a) to a direction under s.19 of that Act (as to eligible witness) as applied by this section; and
(b) to a direction discharging or varying such a direction.

Sections 49 and 51 of that Act (offences) apply accordingly.

(SA 2020 s.340)

22. CUSTODY TIME LIMITS

Quick Guide

1. General

POA 1985 and the regulations made thereunder (Prosecution of Offences (Custody Time Limits) Regulations SI 1987/299 (as amended)) prescribe time limits during which an accused may be held in custody before being invited to tender pleas. See also the protocol between CPS and HMCTS *Amended Protocol for the Effective Handling of Custody Time Limit Cases in the Magistrates' and the Crown Court*, the latest version of which is dated 1 December 2014. The Regulations also limit the time during which the accused can be kept in custody. "Custody" includes remand, or committal to local authority accommodation. **22-001**

Subject to CJPOA 1994 s.25 (which disapplies these regulations—*R. (on the application of O) v Harrow Crown Court* [2006] UKHL 42; [2007] 1 Cr. App. R. 9) an accused is entitled to be released on bail where a custody time limit (CTL) (and any extension to it) expires, but his release requires an order of the court. Where the prosecution fails to act, the accused will need to apply for bail to the Crown Court or go to the High Court by way of judicial review (*Olotu v Home Office* [1997] All E.R. 385).

In every case where a defendant is released solely because an extension to the CTL application has been refused or no application to extend has been made, the release is in consequence of the expiry of the CTL and so the CTL comes to an end upon release. As a result, the CTL regime will not apply to any further period on remand (*R. (on the application of Jabbar) v Sheffield Crown Court* [2022] EWHC 516 (Admin); [2022] 3 WLUK 123).

Note that the expiry of a time limit does not necessarily give rise to a breach of ECHR art.5(3) in relation to trial within a reasonable time (*R. (on the application of O) v Harrow Crown Court* [2003] EWHC 868 (Admin); [2003] 1 W.L.R. 2756).

Under the regime set out in the CrimPR, at the hearing where the case is to be managed, the parties are expected to provide an accurate estimate of the length of trial, based on a detailed estimate of the time to be taken with each witness to be called, and accurate information about the availability of witnesses.

At the hearing the judge will ask the prosecution to clarify any CTL dates. The court clerk must ensure the CTL date is marked clearly on the court file or electronic file. When a case is subject to a CTL all efforts must be made at the first hearing to list the case within the CTL and the judge should seek to ensure this (*CPD* XIII F.2).

As legal argument may delay the swearing of a jury, it is desirable to extend the CTL to a date later than the first day of the trial (*CPD* XIII F.5).

2. Objectives

22-002 The objectives of the legislation are threefold:

(1) to ensure that any periods during which an unconvicted person is held in custody awaiting trial are as short as is reasonably and practicably possible;
(2) to oblige the prosecution to prepare its case for trial with all due diligence and expedition; and
(3) to invest the court with the power and duty to control any extension of the maximum period under the regulations for which such a person may be held in custody awaiting trial.

These are very important objectives, and a judge making a decision on the extension of CTLs (see 22-009) must be careful to give full weight to all three (*R. v Manchester Crown Court Ex p. McDonald* [1999] 1 Cr. App. R. 409).

The court has a statutory duty to ensure that:

(a) trials involving an unconvicted accused held in custody take place promptly and wherever possible within the original limit; and
(b) that a person is not detained beyond the expiry of the original limit unless it has been properly extended.

In order to help meet the challenges faced by criminal justice agencies in dealing with cases that have CTLs, a joint HMCTS CPS Protocol has been developed for the handling of these cases (see 22-001).

In the case of a retrial ordered by the CACD, the Crown Court must comply with the directions of the CACD and cannot vary those directions without reference to that court. In such circumstances, the CTL is 112 days starting from the date that the new indictment is preferred, i.e. from the date that the indictment is delivered to the Crown Court. Court centres should check that CREST has calculated the dates correctly and that it has not used 182 days on cases that have previously been "sent".

(*CPD* XIII F.6, F.7)

3. Crown Court limits

22-003 The maximum period of custody between the time when an accused is sent for trial and the start of the trial is 182 days. See further SI 1987/299 reg.5 as amended.

Where a case has been sent for trial and the indictment contains counts which allege offences which were sent on different occasions—the time limit applies to each count separately.

The "maximum period" laid down does not include the day on which custody commenced, and a CTL which would otherwise expire on a Saturday, Sunday, Christmas Day, Good Friday or a bank holiday is treated as expiring on the nearest preceding day which is not one of those days.

The prosecutor may apply to the judge before expiry for an extension to the CTL period (see 22-007).

The "start of the trial"

22-004 The "start of a trial" on indictment is taken to occur (subject to CJA 1988 s.8 and CPIA 1996 s.28 (preparatory hearings)) when:

(1) a jury is sworn and the accused is put in the charge of the jury;

(2) when a jury would have been sworn but for the making of an order under CJA 2003 Pt 7 (trials without a jury); or
(3) the judge accepts a guilty plea.

When the court is to consider fitness to plead, the trial starts when a jury is sworn, and not at the time when the court first begins to hear evidence (POA 1985 s.22(11), (11A) and (11B)). When DVA 2003 abolished trial by jury of an issue of unfitness to plead raised on arraignment it seems that POA 1985 s.22(11A), in respect of the start of a trial on indictment, was not amended.

If a preparatory hearing is ordered under CJA 1988 s.8, or CPIA 1996 s.28, the trial is deemed to start with that hearing, and arraignment takes place then if it has not taken place before (CJA 1988 s.8, CPIA 1996 s.31).

The CTLs still run when young offenders are remanded to the care of the local authority or to youth detention accommodation and in the case of transfers and remands under MHA ss.35 and 36.

In the event of a trial being aborted, the judge should be vigilant to take steps in fixing a speedy retrial, or, if there are difficulties about such a course, considering the grant of bail.

Where the limits do not apply

Where a person: **22-005**

(1) escapes from the custody of a magistrates' court or the Crown Court before the expiry of a limit which applies in his case; or
(2) having been released on bail in consequence of the expiry of a CTL (see 22-006), fails to surrender at the appointed time, or is arrested for breach of bail,

and is accordingly at large, the following periods, namely:

(a) the period for which the person is unlawfully at large; and
(b) such additional period (if any) as the court may direct, having regard to the disruption of the prosecution occasioned by:
    (i) that person's escape or failure to surrender; and
    (ii) the length of the period mentioned in (i) above,

must be disregarded so far as the offence in question is concerned for the purposes of the overall time limit which applies in his case in relation to the stage which the proceedings have reached at the time of the escape or, as the case may be, at the appointed time.

(POA 1985 s.22(5)–(6))

Once a person is brought back before the court because of a breach of bail or further offence, then the CTL clock restarts (*R. (on the application of Jabbar) v Sheffield Crown Court* [2022] EWHC 516 (Admin); [2022] 3 WLUK 123).

The fact that the accused is in custody for other matters does not prevent the time limit running (*R. v Peterborough Crown Court Ex p. L* [2000] Crim. L.R. 470).

(POA 1985 s.22(6A))

Where, following the initial charge(s) on which the accused first appeared before the magistrates, another charge is added, then irrespective of its nature, or when it was added, subject only to the accused being able to show abuse of process, a new CTL is created (*R. v Leeds Crown Court Ex p. Wardle* [2001] UKHL 12; [2001] 2 Cr. App. R. 20).

In relation to prosecution appeals (under CJA 2003 Pt 9) any period during which proceedings for an offence are adjourned pending the determination of an appeal will be disregarded for that offence for the purpose of the CTL which applies to the stage proceedings have reached when they are adjourned.

Expiry of time limit

22-006 On being notified that a CTL is about to expire, a judge of the Crown Court must grant that person bail in accordance with BA 1976 as modified for the purpose (see BAIL), with effect from the expiry of the limit, subject to a duty to appear before the Crown Court for trial. Where this situation arises, the prosecution will need to decide before the expiry of the limit, whether:

(a) to apply for an extension, or further extension, of the time limit; or
(b) to apply for conditions to be attached to the bail granted to the accused.

(SI 1987/299 reg.6(6))

4. Application for extension of period

22-007 An application by the prosecution for the extension, or further extension, of a time limit may be made orally or in writing:

(1) *before* the relevant time limit has expired (*R. v Peterborough Crown Court Ex p. L* [2000] Crim. L.R. 470);
(2) by giving, not less than five days before making the application, notice in writing to the accused or his representative, and to the Crown Court officer, of his intention to make the application; unless
(3) the accused or his representative informs the Crown that he does not require such notice; or
(4) a judge is satisfied on a balance of probabilities (*Re Craig* (1991) 91 Cr. App. R. 7) that it is not practicable for the prosecution to comply and directs either that the Crown need not comply, or specifies a lesser minimum period.

In the case of an application based on the length and complexity of the case, although reg.7 does not require it, it is good practice to give the grounds in the notice (*R. v Central Criminal Court Ex p. Marotta* [1998] 10 Arch. News 2). Bail Act considerations have no place under these provisions (*R. (on the application Eliot) v Reading Crown Court* [2001] EWHC 464 (Admin); [2002] 1 Cr. App. R. 3).

Where the prosecutor gives notice of application to extend a CTL, the Crown Court officer will arrange for a judge to hear that application as soon as practicable after the expiry of:

(a) five days from the giving of notice, in the Crown Court; or
(b) two days from the giving of notice, in a magistrates' court,

though the judge may shorten a time limit under this rule.
(CrimPR 14.18)

Successive applications

22-008 It is not:

(1) normally permissible, when an application is refused, for an application to

be made to a second judge on the same grounds, but see *R. v Bradford Crown Court Ex p. Crossling* [2000] 1 Cr. App. R. 463 (where the first judge may have acted on misleading information);

(2) permissible, where the High Court has reviewed a judge's decision, for a further application to be made to a judge of the Crown Court.

(*R. v Peterborough Crown Court Ex p. L* [2000] Crim. L.R. 470; cf. *R. v Leeds Crown Court Ex p. Wardle* [2001] UKHL 12; [2001] 2 Cr. App. R. 20)

5. Grounds for extension of period

22-009 A time limit may be extended or further extended by a judge of the Crown Court at any time before its expiry (*R. v Croydon Crown Court Ex p. Customs and Excise Commissioners* [1997] 8 Arch. News 1 DC), but not unless he is satisfied on the balance of probabilities:

(1) that the need for the extension is due to:
 (a) the illness or absence of the accused, a necessary witness, or a judge;
 (b) a postponement which is occasioned by the ordering by the court of separate trials in the case of two or more accused or two or more offences; or
 (c) some other good and sufficient cause; and
(2) that the prosecution has acted with all due diligence and expedition (POA 1985 s.22(3); see *R. v Norwich Crown Court Ex p. Parker and Ward* (1993) 96 Cr. App. R. 68; *R. v CCC Ex p. Behbehani* [1994] Crim. L.R. 352; *R. v CCC Ex p. Belle Lane* [1994] Crim. L.R. 352; *R. v Leeds CC Ex p. Briggs (No.2)* [1998] 2 Cr. App. R. 424).

"Good and sufficient cause" and "due diligence and expedition" are two distinct issues and require both separate consideration and a separate ruling. "Good cause" will not avail the Crown if they have not acted with "due expedition" (*R. v Central Criminal Court Ex p. Bennett*, *The Times,* 25 January 1999).

(1) "Good and sufficient cause"

22-010 The words are not susceptible to precise definition (*R. v Norwich Crown Court Ex p. Ricketts* [1990] Crim. L.R. 715). It will be a matter of fact in each case (*McKay White v DPP* [1989] Crim. L.R. 375). See also *R. v Norwich Crown Court Ex p. Cox* (1993) 97 Cr. App. R. 145; cf. *R. v Maidstone Crown Court Ex p. Schultz* (1993) 157 J.P. 601; *R. v Governor of Belmarsh Prison Ex p. Gilligan* [2000] 1 All E.R. 113 HL. Thus:

(1) an almost infinite number of matters may, depending on the facts, constitute such cause, but the seriousness of the offence, the need to protect the public and the fact that the extension sought is only a short one do not constitute good and sufficient cause (*R. v Manchester Crown Court Ex p. McDonald* [1999] 1 Cr. App. R. 409); and
(2) matters relevant to the granting or refusing of bail cannot of themselves provide good and sufficient cause for extending a time limit (*R. v Sheffield Crown Court Ex p. Headley* [2000] 2 Cr. App. R. 1).

The unavailability of a suitable judge or courtroom may, in special cases and on appropriate facts, amount to such a cause. See 22-012 and 22-013 under "listing difficulties".

(2) "Due diligence and expedition"

22-011 "Due diligence" is not the same as "due expedition". To fulfil the test of "due expedition" it is not enough to show that the prosecuting authorities "are doing their best". The test needs to be measured against some yardstick, or the object of the Act is defeated (*R. v Southampton Crown Court Ex p. Roddie* (1991) 93 Cr. App. R. 190; *R. v Sheffield MC Ex p. Turner* (1991) 93 Cr. App. R. 180. See also *R. v Central Criminal Court Ex p. Behbehani* [1994] Crim. L.R. 352).

"All due expedition" requires the diligence and expedition which would be shown by a competent prosecutor conscious of his duty to bring the case to trial as quickly and fairly as possible (*R. v Manchester Crown Court Ex p. McDonald* [1999] 1 Cr. App. R. 409).

Note that:

(1) delay on the part of an independent third party, such as a forensic laboratory (*R. v Central Criminal Court Ex p. Johnson* [1999] 2 Cr. App. R. 51) or an expert witness (*R. (on the application of Hadfield) v Manchester Crown Court* [2007] EWHC 2408 (Admin); *R. (on the application of Alexander) v Isleworth Crown Court* [2009] EWHC 85 (Admin); [2009] Crim. L.R. 583) is not directly relevant to the question whether the prosecutor has acted with "due expedition", though he should take every possible step to ensure that any relevant evidence was available on time (*R. (on the application of Clarke) v Lewes Crown Court* [2009] EWHC 805 (Admin));
(2) the reference to the Crown having acted "with all due expedition" refers to the time up to the making of the application to extend the limit, not to the issue of whether future delay may be caused by acceding to the application (*R. v Manchester Crown Court Ex p. McDonald* [1999] 1 Cr. App. R. 409); and
(3) lack of due diligence and expedition will not be fatal if it has no causal connection with the need for an extension (*R. (on the application of Gibson) v Winchester Crown Court* [2004] EWHC 361 (Admin); [2004] 2 Cr. App. R. 14).

(3) Listing difficulties

22-012 The superior courts have held (see *R. v Central Criminal Court Ex p. Abu-Wardeh* [1999] 1 Cr. App. R. 43; *R. v Manchester Crown Court Ex p. McDonald* [1999] 1 Cr. App. R. 409; *R. v Winchester Crown Court* [2004] EWHC 361 (Admin); [2004] 2 Cr. App. R. 14; *Kalonji v Wood Green Crown Court* [2007] EWHC 2804 (Admin)) that the unavailability of a suitable judge, or a suitable courtroom in which to try an accused in custody, is capable, in special cases, and on appropriate facts, of amounting to a "good and sufficient cause" for extending the time limits, though any such application should be rigorously examined.

In such circumstances:

(1) the judge should approach such grounds with great caution, as there is obviously a danger that the purposes of the statute will be undermined by too readily granting extensions on this basis;

(2) the fact that witnesses are professional investigators does not make their convenience, particularly with regard to other duties, irrelevant;
(3) where the application is made on the basis that the case clashes with another, the prosecutor will need to show why the other case requires priority (*R. v Stoke-on-Trent Crown Court Ex p. Marden* [1999] 1 Arch. News 2; *R. v Croydon YC Ex p. C* [2001] Crim. L.R. 40); and
(4) many of the problems which arise in this area can be obviated by fixing an early date for the trial.

The *Amended Protocol for the Effective Handling of Custody Time Limit Cases in the Magistrates' and the Crown Court* (1 December 2014) and *CPD* XIII F.4 provides the following guidance:

- The CPS must inform the court when the CTL elapses, and its expiry date should be announced at every hearing by the prosecution and agreed by the defence.
- If there is a risk that the CTL will be exceeded, an additional hearing should take place before the Resident Judge or another judge nominated by the Resident Judge.
- The list officer must consider whether other cases in which a defendant is on bail could be moved to accommodate a trial where the defendant is in custody.
- If suitable, given priority and listed on a date not less than two weeks before the CTL expires, a case may be placed in a warned list.
- If the case cannot be listed within the CTL, enquiries should be made with other courts across the cluster and, if need be, across the region and neighbouring regions.
- An application to extend the CTL in any case listed outside the CTL must be considered by the court whether or not it was listed with the express consent of the defence.
- Any application to extend must be considered as a matter of urgency and the reasons for the extension must be fully explained to the court.
- Where courtroom or judge availability is not in issue, but all parties and the court agree that the case will not be ready for trial before the expiry of the CTL, a date may be fixed outside the CTL. This may be done without prejudice to any application to extend the CTL or with the express consent of the defence; this must be noted on the papers.
- Where courtroom or judge availability is an issue, the court must itself list the case to consider the extension of the CTL; the senior manager or listing officer must provide the Delivery Director of the Circuit with a statement setting out in detail what has been done to try to accommodate the case within the CTL.

In *R. (on the application of McKenzie) v Leeds Crown Court* [2020] EWHC 1867 (Admin), it was held that where a trial could not commence within the CTL because the safety of all participants in the trial could not be secured because of the coronavirus pandemic, that could amount to good and sufficient cause. For an overview of the principles to be applied in determining CTL extension applications during the pandemic, and in particular what might amount to good and sufficient cause, see *R. (on the application of DPP) v Woolwich Crown Court* [2020] EWHC 3243 (Admin); [2021] 1 Cr. App. R. 11.

In *R. (on the application of Marten) v Lincoln Crown Court* [2022] EWHC 2283

(Admin); [2022] 9 WLUK 5 the Divisional Court rejected the submissions of the Crown that the continuing impact of the pandemic reduces the level of investigation necessary into whether a good reason, namely lack of a courtroom, is also a sufficient reason. The Court noted that in dealing with CTL applications it was "incumbent" upon judges to provide detailed information as to the availability of other locations, availability of judges, and budgetary allocation to the court in open court.

Note that the Coronavirus Crisis Protocol for the Effective Handling of Custody Time Limit Cases in the Magistrates' Court and the Crown Court introduced on 9 April 2020 was withdrawn with effect from 3 September 2020.

(4) Lack of resources; courtroom or judge availability

22-013 In these times of financial stringency, the unavailability of money by way of "sitting day allocation" may cause problems (see *R. (on the application of McAuley) v Coventry Crown Court* [2012] EWHC 680 (Admin); [2012] 1 W.L.R. 2766).

While lack of money provided by Parliament will rarely, if ever, justify an extension of a time limit, steps need to be taken to alleviate the situation. If an issue arises as to the availability of money concerning sitting day allocation, it must be referred to the Resident Judge before issues concerning the CTL arise. The Resident Judge is responsible for determining listing practice and prioritising cases. Where an application to extend a CTL is necessary because of insufficient sitting days, it must be heard in open court and accompanied by detailed evidence, which must be rigorously scrutinised. A detailed judgment must be given. The prosecution has to satisfy the court of the need to extend the CTL and it is incumbent upon HMCTS and the Resident Judge to provide proper evidence concerning the difficulties encountered in listing the case.

The judge must then subject the application and the evidence to that rigorous level of scrutiny that is required where a trial is to be delayed and a person confined to prison because of the lack of money to try the case. Although other considerations may apply to cases that are not routine, lack of money provided by Parliament will rarely, if ever, justify an extension of a time limit.

The judge hearing the application must give a full and detailed judgment.

In *R. v Crown Court at Lincoln* [2022] EWHC 2283 (Admin); [2022] 9 WLUK 5, the Administrative Court said that prosecution and defence advocates need to be adequately informed to advance their submissions to assist the court in the necessary rigorous scrutiny of whether there is a good and sufficient cause to extend the CTL. Where the judge hearing an application has been provided with information by the listing officer about the lack of availability of a court and/or a judge to try the case, it is incumbent on the judge to provide the detail of that information in open court, and to recognise that the application to extend the CTL is that of the prosecution and not that of the court.

In the overwhelming majority of cases, unavailability of a judge or courtroom will not constitute good and sufficient cause (*R. (on the application of Raeside) v Luton Crown Court* [2012] EWHC 1064 (Admin); [2012] 1 W.L.R. 2777). Only in cases of real complexity, or cases which require a particular judge (such as a High Court judge, or a judge authorised to try murder), will the unavailability of judge or courtroom be capable of going a long way to establishing good and sufficient cause.

In *R. (on the application of the DPP) v Crown Court at Bristol* [2022] EWHC 2415 (Admin); [2022] 9 WLUK 221, the Administrative Court (PQBD presiding) considered whether the impact of the strike by members of the Criminal Bar Association on the timely listing of trials could amount to a good and sufficient cause to extend the CTL. The court reviewed the leading authorities and reached the following conclusions:

- Adjournments made necessary by the absence of legal representation in the context of the CBA's indefinite action announced on 22 August 2022 could in principle constitute both a good and a sufficient cause for the purposes of s.22(3)(a)(iii) of the 1985 Act.
- However, if the situation remained unchanged, the relevant point at which the unavailability of legal representation could properly be described as chronic or routine was likely to be reached by the last week in November 2022 (by which time three months would have elapsed from the date when the CBA announced it would take indefinite action). Once that point was reached, the absence of legal representation in the context of the CBA action was unlikely to be capable of supplying a sufficient reason for extending custody time limits.
- The question whether an adjournment based on the unavailability of advocates due to the CBA action constituted a sufficient cause for extending the time limit was case-specific. Judges considering applications to extend custody time limits should consider (i) the likely duration of the delay before the trial; (ii) whether there has been any previous extension of the custody time limit; (iii) the age and antecedents of the defendant; (iv) the likely sentence in the event of a conviction; a defendant should rarely be kept in custody if he has served, or come close to serving the likely sentence were he convicted; (v) any particular vulnerabilities of the defendant which make remand in custody difficult; (vi) in a multi-handed trial where representation difficulties apply to one defendant but not others, whether delay could be reduced by separate trials. Judges should bear in mind that the burden is on the prosecution to satisfy the statutory criteria for the granting of an extension.
- In every case, judges should consider whether the public interests served initially by remanding the defendant in custody can now be served by stringent bail conditions. If so, this should be the preferred course.
- Any extension of a custody time limit should be for a relatively short period, generally not exceeding about three months, so that the court retains the power to review the position in the light of changing circumstances.
- Where a CTL has expired, there is no power in the Crown Court under s.22(3) of the 1985 Act or in this court under s.31(5)(b) of the 1981 Act to extend those limits.
- Where the DPP seeks to challenge by judicial review a decision to refuse to extend a custody time limit, a High Court judge sitting in the Administrative Court may in principle exercise the powers of the Crown Court under s.22(3) of the 1985 Act to grant a short extension of the custody time limit pending any substantive or rolled-up hearing. However, this power should only be exercised if the claim is strongly arguable and the prosecution has

shown that all the conditions in s.22(3) are met. In general, an oral hearing will be required.

6. Fixing a date

22-014 In *R. v Worcester Crown Court Ex p. Norman* [2000] 2 Cr. App. R. 33, it was said that there is a joint duty on the prosecutor and on the court to make early arrangements for the fixing of a trial date within the CTLs.

Ideally, the date should be fixed at the PTPH with the directions then being tailored to the date that has been fixed. If it is impossible to fix a date at the PTPH the judge should direct that the date be fixed on a date before the expiration of the CTL and that the matter should be re-listed in the event of a failure to agree such a date.

Trials should not be fixed on a date after the expiry of the CTL unless there has been proper and rigorous judicial consideration of the statutory questions: (i) whether there is good and sufficient cause for granting the CTL extension that would later be sought; and (ii) whether the prosecution has acted with all due diligence and expedition (*R. (on the application of Campbell-Brown) v Central Criminal Court* [2015] EWHC 202 (Admin); [2015] 1 Cr. App. R. 34). [NB: this case also deals with the narrow circumstances in which the convenience of counsel might constitute good and sufficient cause.]

As legal argument may delay the swearing in of a jury, it is desirable to extend CTLs to a date later than the first day of the trial.

7. The hearing of the application to extend

22-015 Bearing in mind the overriding purposes of the legislation (see 22-002) the judge:

(1) needs to be satisfied, on a balance of probabilities, that both the conditions in s.22(3) are made out, before exercising his discretion;
(2) must not abdicate his responsibility to address the issues by granting the application simply because the parties agree, or do not object (*R. v Manchester Crown Court Ex p. McDonald* [1999] 1 Cr. App. R. 409);
(3) should consider all matters directly and genuinely bearing on the preparation of the case for trial, bearing in mind that:
   (a) the time limit is a maximum not a target; and
   (b) the prosecutor is not required to show that every stage has been completed as quickly and efficiently as is humanly possible, although;
   (c) no attention should be paid to excuses such as staff shortages, sickness, etc.;
(4) may need to hear evidence or may, according to the circumstances of the case, be able to rely on information supplied by the advocates. It is for the prosecutor to decide which witnesses to call on the application, and the defence are not entitled to require specific witnesses to be called (*R. v Chelmsford Crown Court* [2001] EWHC 1115 (Admin); [2002] Crim. L.R. 485);
(5) may, if, but only if, he is so satisfied, exercise his discretion to extend the time limit. If he is not satisfied he may not. If he is satisfied, he may, but need not, extend the time limit (*R. v Manchester Crown Court Ex p. McDonald* [1999] 1 Cr. App. R. 409); and
(6) must give reasons for his ruling, indicating the way in which he has reached

his conclusions (*R. v Leeds Crown Court Ex p. Briggs* [1998] 2 Cr. App. R. 424). Some cases will require a detailed judgement (see *R. (on the application of McAuley) v Coventry Crown Court* [2012] EWHC 680 (Admin); [2012] 1 W.L.R. 2766).

Where the judge is considering a *further* extension, he has to consider those matters giving rise to that *further* extension. A defendant may only rely upon delay before the original extension if it is the root cause of the need to seek the *further* extension (*R. (on the application of Thomas) v Central Criminal Court* [2006] EWHC 2138 (Admin) [2007] 1 Cr. App. R. 7).

There may be cases where, even though there has been avoidable delay, an extension will not be refused.

8. Conditions of bail

If a CTL expires the accused has an immediate right to bail. The court can impose conditional bail but cannot impose a requirement that the accused provide a surety or give a security. **22-016**

An application by the prosecution for conditions to be attached to the bail granted to an accused where the time limits have expired is made:

(1) by giving notice in writing not less than five days before the expiry of the time limit, to the appropriate Crown Court officer and to the accused or his representative;
(2) stating whether or not it intends to ask the Crown Court to impose conditions, and, if it does, the nature of the conditions sought; and
(3) making arrangements for the accused to be brought before the Crown Court within the period of two days preceding the expiry of the time limit.

The prosecutor need not comply with: (1) above if it has given notice of its intention to apply for an extension, or further extension, of the limit; it need not comply with (2) if the judge so directs. If the judge is satisfied that it is not practicable, in all the circumstances, for the prosecution to comply with (1) he may so direct, or specify a lesser minimum period.

On receiving notice that the prosecution intends to ask the court to impose conditions on the grant of bail, the accused or his representative must:

(a) give notice in writing to the Crown Court officer and to the prosecution, that the accused wishes to be represented at the hearing of the application; or
(b) give notice to the appropriate officer, and to the prosecution, stating that the accused does not wish to oppose the application; or
(c) give to the appropriate officer, for the consideration of the Crown Court a written statement of the accused's reasons for opposing the application, sending a copy of the statement, at the same time, to the prosecution.

(SI 1987/299 reg.6)

9. Appeal to the Crown Court from the magistrates' court

An appeal brought: **22-017**

(1) by an accused under POA 1985 s.22(7) against a decision of the magistrates' court to extend or further extend a time limit imposed by the 1987 Regulations; or

(2) by the prosecution under POA 1985 s.22(8) against a decision refusing to extend or further extend such a time limit,

is commenced by the appellant's giving notice in writing of appeal:

(a) to the designated officer of the magistrates' court which took the decision;
(b) if the appeal is brought by the accused, to the prosecutor;
(c) if the appeal is brought by the prosecution, to the accused; and
(d) to the Crown Court officer.

(CrimPR 14.19)

22-018 The notice of appeal must be served as soon as practicable after the decision under appeal (and, in a prosecutor's appeal, before the expiry of the CTL) and must state:

(1) the date on which the time limit applicable to the case is due to expire; and
(2) if the appeal is brought by the accused under POA 1985 s.22(7), the date on which the time limit would have expired had the magistrates' court decided not to extend, or further extend, the time limit.

The Crown Court must arrange for the appeal to be heard as soon as possible and in any event not later than the second business day after the appeal notice was served.

An appellant may abandon an appeal under these provisions by serving a notice of abandonment on any person to whom the notice of appeal was required to be given before the hearing of the appeal begins. Once the hearing has begun, the appeal may only be abandoned with the permission of the court.

(CrimPR 14.19)

Judge's action on allowing appeal

22-019 Where:

(1) the prosecutor successfully appeals a grant of bail by the magistrates' court, the judge must stipulate a date (within the powers of the magistrates under MCA 1980 ss.128, 128A and 129) as a remand date on which the accused is to be brought before the magistrates' court (*R. v Manchester Magistrates Court Ex p. Szakal* [2000] 1 Cr. App. R. 248);
(2) the accused successfully appeals, and is admitted to bail by reason of the expiry of the CTL, the judge's powers to impose conditions on the grant are restricted—there is no power to require a surety or a security for his surrender under BA 1976 s.3(4), (5). He may be required, however, after his release, to comply with any other conditions of bail appropriate under s.3(6).

23. DANGEROUS OFFENDERS; PROTECTIVE SENTENCES

Quick Guide

1. Introduction

General

Certain violent or sexual offences, within the statutory categories of "specified", committed on or after 4 April 2005, attract the provisions of CJA 2003 ss.224–229, as modified by LASPOA 2012 and as now set out in SA 2020, namely: **23-001**

(1) a mandatory life sentence for a second listed offence (23-015);
(2) a life sentence for serious offences (23-017); or
(3) the "new" extended sentence (23-020).

These sentences are concerned with future risk and public protection as well as with punishment and are available only where the judge has assessed the offender as "dangerous" (SA 2020 s.308).

Note that:

(a) if, in relation to a dangerous offender, the requirements of MHA 1983 are satisfied, the judge may dispose of the case by means of a hospital order under the above, s.37 (see MENTALLY DISORDERED OFFENDERS); and
(b) presumably the former principle still applies that where an offender is to be sentenced for several offences, only some of which are "specified", the judge who imposes an extended sentence under ss.266–268 or ss.279–282 for the principal offences should generally impose shorter concurrent sentences for the other offences.

In 2015 the CJCA introduced special custodial sentences for certain offenders of particular concern. The aim was to ensure that those offenders who committed certain listed offences and received a custodial sentence, would not be automatically released at the half-way point of sentence and would only be released at the discretion of the Parole Board, and that they would also be subject to at least 12 months on licence on release from custody.

Legislative history

Protective sentences which exceed the normal determinate sentence of imprisonment were provided by both PCC(S)A 2000 and CJA 2003, for both dangerous and persistent offenders. The provisions are now set out in the SA 2020. **23-002**

LASPOA 2012 s.123 abolished the sentence of IPP (and the equivalent for juveniles (Detention for Public Protection)) and established a new sentencing framework.

Thus:

(1) under SA 2020 ss.273 and 283, after conviction for a second listed offence, the judge must pass a life sentence, unless the particular circumstances make it unjust;
(2) under SA 2020 s.285, a sentence of life imprisonment must be passed if the offender commits a serious offence, is dangerous and the seriousness of the offence is such as to justify the imposition of a life sentence; and
(3) a new form of extended sentence and significant changes to the early release provisions for extended sentences, are introduced.

The provisions leave untouched the discretionary life sentence under SA 2020 s.272 (see LIFE SENTENCES).

The abolition of those sentences is of no effect in relation to a person convicted before 3 December 2012, but see 23-003 for the saving in respect of an offender convicted of an offence before 3 December 2012, who had not been sentenced by that date.

References to protective sentences under PCC(S)A 2000 may be made to the 2007 edition; to IPPs and DPPs and the former extended sentences under CJA 2003, to the 2012 edition.

As to offences spanning the commencement date of the 2003 and 2012 provisions, see 23-003. As to consecutive sentences, see 23-004.

Offences spanning the commencement date

23-003 Where an offender falls to be sentenced for offences committed both before and after 4 April 2005, it will generally be preferable to pass sentence on the later offences by reference to the 2003 regime (as now set out in the SA 2020), imposing determinate sentences on the earlier offences, but this may not be possible if the later offences are less serious than the earlier ones.

Note that:

(1) where a count spans the commencement date, the provisions of CJA 2003 should not be applied unless the count specifies that at least one offence was committed after the qualifying date;
(2) care should be taken to ensure that a continuing offence which, as initially indicted, straddled 4 April 2005, is indicted, if necessary by amendment, so that sentence can properly be passed by reference to the 2003 and/or the pre-2003 regime as appropriate (see *R. v Harries* [2007] EWCA Crim 1622; [2008] 1 Cr. App. R. (S.) 47); and
(3) even where the judge is unsure if a qualifying offence was committed after the 2003 commencement date, offences before that date do not cease to be relevant, and may have some bearing on the question of "dangerousness" and on the minimum term to be specified: *R. v Harries* [2007] EWCA Crim 1622; [2008] 1 Cr. App. R. (S.) 47 following *R. v Howe* [2006] EWCA Crim 3147; [2007] 2 Cr. App. R. (S.) 11.

In relation to the modifications made by LASPOA 2012, it should be noted that:

(a) from 3 December 2012, the offences omitted from the 2003 Act, (i.e. IPPs and EPPs—see 2011 edition) will cease to be available in respect of any offences, whenever committed; but

(b) where an offender is convicted of an offence before 3 December 2012, but has not been sentenced by that date, an IPP or EPP remains available.

Consecutive sentences

Although there is no statutory prohibition on the imposition of: **23-004**

(1) consecutive sentences for dangerous offenders; or
(2) an extended sentence consecutive to another period of imprisonment,

for extended sentences providing there is at least one specified offence, the threshold requirement under SA 2020 ss.279 and 280 is reached if the total determinate sentence for all offences (specified or not) would be four years or more. The extended sentence should be passed either for one specified offence or concurrently on a number of them. Ordinarily either a concurrent determinate sentence or no separate penalty will be appropriate for the remaining offences (see *R. v Pinnell* [2010] EWCA Crim 2848).

Where consecutive sentences are considered appropriate or necessary:

(a) if one or more of those sentences are determinate sentences, the determinate sentences should be imposed first, and the extended sentence(s) expressed to be consecutive;
(b) in shaping the overall sentence, there is no obligation for the sentences to be expressed in historical date order; thus
(c) nothing prevents the sentence for the first offence in point of time being served consecutively to a sentence or sentences imposed for any later offence(s).

(*R. v O'Brien* [2006] EWCA Crim 1741; [2007] 1 Cr. App. R. (S.) 75; *Attorney General's Reference (No.55 of 2008)* [2008] EWCA Crim 2790; [2009] 2 Cr. App. R. (S.) 22 where the legislation and the authorities are reviewed.)

2. Definitions

For the purposes of SA 2020 s.306 an offence is: **23-005**

(1) a "*specified offence*" if it is:
  (a) a specified *violent offence*, that is an offence specified in SA 2020 Sch.18 Pt 1;
  (b) a specified *sexual offence*, that is an offence specified in SA 2020 Sch.18 Pt 2; or
  (c) a specified terrorism offence, that is an offence specified in SA 2020 Sch.18 Pt 3;
(2) an "*associated offence*" (SA 2020 s.400) provides that an offence is associated with another if the offender:
  (a) is convicted of it in proceedings in which he is convicted of the other offence, or (although convicted of it in earlier proceedings), is sentenced for it at the same time as he is sentenced for that offence; or
  (b) admits the commission of it in the proceedings in which he is sentenced for the other offence, and asks the judge to take it into consideration when sentencing him for that offence; and
(3) "*serious harm*" means death or serious personal injury, whether physical or psychological.

This last is a concept familiar since CJA 1991 s.2(2)(b), and pre-2004 decisions of the CACD continue to be relevant to its assessment. In *R. v Bowler* (1994) 15 Cr. App. R. (S.) 78 it was said that sexual assaults which are relatively minor physically may lead to serious psychological injury; and downloading indecent images of children may cause serious psychological injury to a child arising not only from what the child has been forced to do, but also from the knowledge that others will see what they were doing (see for instance *R. v Collard* [2004] EWCA Crim1664; [2005] 1 Cr. App. R. (S.) 34; *R. v Lang* [2005] EWCA Crim 2664; [2006] 2 Cr. App. R. (S.) 3).

"Specified offences"

23-006 SA 2020 Sch.18 sets out the various offences that are included with "specified" offences.

"*Members of the public*" seems to be an all-embracing term. It is wider than "others", which would exclude the offender himself. In *R. v Lang* [2005] EWCA Crim 2664; [2006] 2 Cr. App. R. (S.) 3, the CACD saw no reason to construe it so as to exclude any particular group, for example:

(a) prison officers or staff at mental hospitals, all of whom, like the offender, are members of the public; and
(b) in some cases, particular members of the public may be more at risk than members of the public generally, e.g. when an offender has a history of violence to co-habitees or of sexually abusing children of co-habitees, or, where the offender has a particular problem in relation to a particular woman.

This provision requires the judge to look beyond the instant offence (and any offences associated with it) in order to see whether there are aggravating factors which he should have in mind when assessing the seriousness of that instant offence.

When considering the seriousness of an offence SA 2020 ss.57, 59–62 and 63–65 require the judge:

(i) where an offender has previous convictions to treat each previous conviction as an aggravating factor if, in the case of that previous conviction, he considers that it can reasonably be so treated, having regard in particular to the nature of the offence to which the conviction relates and its relevance to the current conviction and the time that has elapsed since the conviction; and
(ii) to treat the commission of an offence on bail as an aggravating factor, when considering seriousness.

Listed offences: SA 2020 Schs 18 and 14

23-007 For convenience, the offences listed in Schs 18 and 14 are summarised here but reference should be made to the schedules themselves for completeness and accuracy.

Schedule 18 (specified offences) has three parts:

Part 1 (specified violent offences) includes the following:

Manslaughter; kidnapping; false imprisonment; soliciting murder; threats to kill; wounding (OAPA 1861 s.18 and s.20); other offences against the person (OAPA 1861 ss.21, 22, 23, 27, 28, 29, 30, 31, 32, 35, 37, 38 or 47); certain offences involving explosives; firearms offences (FA 1968 ss.16, 16A, 17(1) and (2), 18); cruelty to children and infanticide; certain Theft Act offences (robbery, burglary with intent and aggravated burglary and vehicle taking); arson and criminal damage; certain aviation offences; certain public order offences (riot, violent disorder and affray); racially or religiously aggravated assaults and harassment; causing death by dangerous driving, causing death by driving: disqualified drivers and causing death by careless driving when under the influence of drink or drugs; certain maritime and shipping offences; certain terrorist offences; offences relating to female genital mutilation; aiding, abetting, counselling, procuring or inciting the commission of, or conspiring, or attempting, to commit any of the offences listed.

Part 2 (specified sexual offences) includes the following:

Most offences under the SOA 1956 (ss.1–7, 9–11, 14–17, 19–29, 32, 33A); indecency with a child; burglary with intent to commit rape; offences concerning indecent photographs of children; most offences under the SOA 2003 (ss.1–19, 25, 26, 30–41, 47–50, 52, 53, 57–59, 61–67, 69, 70); aiding, abetting, counselling, procuring or inciting the commission of, or conspiring, or attempting, to commit any of the offences listed.

Part 3 (specified terrorism offences) includes the following:

Offences under TerrA 2000 ss.11, 12, 54, 56, 58, 58A, 58B or 59. Anti-terrorism Crime and Security Act 2001 ss.47, 50 or 113. Terrorism Act 2006 ss.1, 2, 5, 6, 10 or 11 as well as inchoate offences committed in relation to those listed above.

Schedule 14 also has three parts. Parts 2 and 3 deal with offences under service law and offences under the law of Scotland. Part 1 includes murder, manslaughter; soliciting murder; OAPA 1861 ss.18, 28 and 29; certain offences involving explosives; firearms offences (FA 1968 ss.16, 17(1) and 18; robbery where, at some time during the commission of the offence, the offender had in his or her possession a firearm or an imitation firearm within the meaning of the FA 1968; possession of indecent images of children under Protection of Children Act 1978; certain terrorist offences including TerrA 2000 ss.54, 56, 57 and 59; the Anti-terrorism Crime and Security Act 2001 ss.47, 50 and 113; the Terrorism Act 2006 ss.5, 6, 9, 10 and 11; most offences under the SOA 2003 (ss.1, 2, 4–12, 14, 15, 25, 26, 30, 31, 34, 35, 47–50 and 62 (with certain limitations on ss.25, 26, 30, 31, 34, 35, 47 and 62); DVCVA 2004 s.5; Modern Slavery Act 2015 ss.1 and 2; and an inchoate offence (s.398) in relation to an offence specified in Pt 1 of Sch.14.

3. General approach to sentencing where what was Chapter 5 of the CJA applies

In *Burinskas* [2014] EWCA Crim 334 the CACD considered it might be helpful, following their analysis of the new provisions to suggest an approach that the judge should take when considering whether to impose a sentence under the dangerous offender provisions of CJA 2003 Ch.5, as amended by LASPOA 2012 and now within SA 2020: **23-008**

(1) the *first question* to be considered in all cases where these provisions apply *is whether the offender is dangerous*; where ss.273 or 283 may be relevant there will be a temptation to move straight to a consideration of that provision; that temptation should be resisted, it may lead to the omission of this crucial first question;

(2) the *order* in which the judge should approach sentencing in a case of this type is this:

- (a) consider the question of dangerousness:
  - (i) if the offender is not dangerous and ss.273 or 283 do not apply, a determinate sentence should be passed;
  - (ii) if the offender is dangerous and the conditions in ss.273 or 283 are satisfied then (subject to s.2(a) and (b)), a life sentence must be imposed;
  - (iii) if the offender is dangerous, consider whether the seriousness of the offence and offences associated with it justify a life sentence;
- (b) if a life sentence is justified then the judge must pass a life sentence in accordance with ss.273 or 283; if either section applies, the judge should record that fact in open court; and
- (c) if a life sentence is not justified, then the judge should consider whether ss.273 or 283 applies; if it does then (subject to the terms of ss.273 or 283) a life sentence must be imposed.

If ss.273 or 283 do not apply the judge should then consider the relevant provisions on extended sentences. Before passing an extended sentence the judge should consider a determinate sentence.

4. "DANGEROUSNESS" AND ITS ASSESSMENT—S.308

General

23-009 Where a person has been convicted of a "serious offence" the judge has to assess under any of ss.255, 258, 267, 274, 280, or 285 whether there is a "significant risk" to members of the public of serious harm occasioned by the commission by the offender of further such offences.

Section 308 provides statutory direction on the approach to "dangerousness" which should be adopted by the judge, after taking into account all relevant matters. The word is intended as a convenient form of shorthand to describe the words, i.e. "a significant risk to members of the public of serious harm occasioned by the commission of further specified offences" (s.308(1)).

The assessment of dangerousness is a judicial responsibility based on a consideration of all the available information. Psychological assessments are not essential, and a finding of dangerousness may be made in appropriate circumstances even though the offender has no previous convictions. The seriousness of the offence(s) alone does not dictate that an offender is dangerous; the judge must still consider the issue of dangerousness within the context of s.229 (*R. v Cardwell* [2012] EWCA Crim 3030; [2013] Crim. L.R. 518).

The first question which arises for decision is whether the judge is of that opinion; absent such risk, no question of "dangerousness" arises.

In making his assessment, the judge:

1. *must* take into account all such "information" (see below) as is available to him about the nature and circumstances of the offence;
2. *may* take into account all such information as is available to him about the nature and circumstances of any other offences of which the offender has been convicted by a court anywhere in the world; and
3. *may* take into account any information which is before him about any pattern of behaviour of which any of the offences mentioned in (1) or (2) forms part; and
4. *may* take into account any information about the offender which is before him.

The reference in (2) to a conviction by a court includes a reference to a finding of guilt in service disciplinary proceeding and a conviction of a service offence within the meaning of the Armed Forces Act 2006 ("conviction" here including anything that under s.376(1) and (2) of that Act is to be treated as a conviction).

"Information" is not restricted to evidence; information bearing on the assessment of dangerousness which discloses previous offences committed by the offender may be considered even where the offender has not been charged or convicted of the offences (*R. v Considine* [2007] EWCA Crim 1166; [2008] 1 Cr. App. R. (S.) 41; *R. v Lavery* [2008] EWCA Crim 2499; [2009] 3 All E.R. 295).

It is clear from the SGC's definitive guideline on dangerous offenders, and the decisions of the CACD that the judge must apply the dangerousness provisions with particular care.

"Significant risk"

Significant risk must be shown in relation to the: **23-010**

(1) commission of further specified, but not necessarily serious, offences; and
(2) causing thereby of serious harm to members of the public.

If there is a significant risk of both, a life sentence must be imposed on an adult, which must be a life sentence if the offence is one for which the offender is liable to life imprisonment and the seriousness of the offence, or of the offence and one or more offences associated with it, is such as to justify imprisonment for life.

The issue is the risk to the public, not simply what the offender desired or intended. A reckless offender, or one with little or no insight into the consequences of his actions, may represent a significant risk to the public and a protective sentence may be fully justified notwithstanding that, in the broadest sense, the offender did not intend or desire the outcome of his actions. If the harm consequent on any individual offence was not intended or desired by the offender, then a determinate sentence of four years or more imprisonment is less likely to be appropriate.

On the other hand, a relatively minor offence may well re-ignite concern about the element of public danger posed by an offender. These considerations are all relevant to the judge's decision (see in relation to the previous provisions concerning indeterminate sentences *Attorney General's Reference (No.55 of 2008)* [2008] EWCA Crim 2790; [2009] 2 Cr. App. R. (S.) 22).

In relation to those under 18, there are similar provisions in relation to detention for life.

Factors in the assessment of dangerousness: R. v Lang

In *R. v Lang* [2005] EWCA Crim 2664; [2006] 2 Cr. App. R. (S.) 3 also in *R. v Pedley* [2009] EWCA Crim 846; [2010] 1 Cr. App. R. (S.) 24 the CACD considered that the following factors should be borne in mind where the judge is assessing significant risk: **23-011**

(1) the risk identified must be *significant*, this is a higher threshold than mere possibility of occurrence and can be taken to mean "noteworthy, of considerable amount or importance"; and
(2) in assessing the risk of further offences being committed, the judge should take into account:
    (a) the nature and circumstances of the current offence;

(b) the offender's *history of offending*, including not just the kind of offence but its circumstances and the sentence passed, details of which the prosecution must have available;
(c) whether the offending demonstrates *any pattern*; social and economic factors in relation to the offender including accommodation, employability, education, associates, relationships and drug or alcohol abuse; the offender's thinking, attitude towards offending and supervision and emotional state; and
(d) any pre-sentence or medical *report* which he calls for, which, together with the antecedents, will provide information on the matters mentioned in (c) above.

Further guidance was given in *R. v Johnson* [2006] EWCA Crim 2486; [2007] 1 Cr. App. R. (S.) 112.

The risk may arise out of a single set of convictions of an offender of previous good character where the offending is otherwise inexplicable (*Attorney General's Reference (No.5 of 2011)* [2011] EWCA Crim 1244; [2011] Crim. L.R. 730). As to the relevance of previous conviction, and the judge's duty to give reasons, see 23-013 and 23-014.

Where the judge has to assess future risk, he will be assisted in doing so in the great majority of cases by as much background as it is possible to have, and, in relation to factor (c) above, by the kind of discussion about behaviour and offending which a probation officer might have with an offender (see *R. v Lang*; *Attorney General's Reference (No.73 of 2010)* [2011] Crim. L.R. 571. But cf. *Attorney General's Reference (No.5 of 2011)* [2011] EWCA Crim 1244; [2011] Crim. L.R. 730).

As to the approach to such reports, see 23-012.

In relation to a particularly young offender, a protective sentence may be inappropriate even where a serious offence has been committed and there is a significant risk of serious harm from further offences (see *R. v D* [2005] EWCA Crim 2292; [2006] 1 Cr. App. R. (S.) 104).

Pre-sentence and other reports

23-012 The judge has an obligation under SA 2020 s.30 to obtain a report unless of the opinion that it is not necessary to do so (e.g. *Attorney General's Reference (No.145 of 2006)*, *The Times,* 20 March 2007). A pre-sentence report should usually be obtained before any sentence is passed which is based on significant risk of serious harm. The judge should guard against assuming there is a significant risk of serious harm merely because the foreseen specified offence is serious.

The judge:

(1) will be *guided*, but not bound by, the assessment of risk in any reports;
(2) should, if he contemplates differing from the assessment in such a report, give both advocates the opportunity of addressing the point; but
(3) will only in the rarest cases allow cross-examination of the author of the report (*R. v S* [2005] EWCA Crim 3616; [2006] 2 Cr. App. R. (S.) 35).

In a small number of cases, where the circumstances of the current offence or the history of the offender suggest mental abnormality on his part, a medical report may be necessary before risk can properly be assessed. If one is asked for it must address the risk of serious harm posed by the offender (above).

Relevance of previous convictions

It is not a prerequisite to a finding of dangerousness that the offender should have previous convictions. The judge may come to the conclusion that an offender with previous convictions, even for specified offences, does not necessarily satisfy the requirements of dangerousness. **23-013**

Note that:

(1) previous offences, not in fact specified for the purposes of s.308 are not disqualified from consideration; a pattern of minor previous offences of gradually escalating seriousness may be significant;
(2) the fact that no harm was actually caused both in the current and in any specified offence when examined for the purposes of s.308 (e.g. *R. v Isa* [2005] EWCA Crim 3330; [2006] 2 Cr. App. R. (S.) 29) may be fortuitous; it does not follow from the absence of actual harm caused by the offender to date that the risk that he will cause serious harm in the future is negligible (*R. v Shaffi* [2006] EWCA 418; [2006] 2 Cr. App. R. (S.) 92 does not suggest the contrary); and
(3) inadequacy, suggestibility or vulnerability may mitigate the offender's culpability; they may also serve to reinforce the conclusion that he is dangerous.

It is desirable, if not always practicable, for the prosecutor to give the facts of previous specified offences, but there is no reason why his failure to comply with good practice should render an adjournment obligatory or preclude the imposition of sentence; the defence advocate should have instructions sufficient to explain the circumstances, and if the prosecutor is unable to challenge those instructions, the judge may proceed to sentence on such information as he has (*R. v Lang* [2005] EWCA Crim 2664; [2006] 2 Cr. App. R. (S.) 3; *R. v Johnson* [2006] EWCA Crim 2486; [2007] 1 Cr. App. R. (S.) 112).

Spelling it out

The judge should usually, and in accordance with SA 2020 s.52, give reasons for all his conclusions, in particular: **23-014**

(1) whether there is or is not a significant risk of further offences or serious harm; and
(2) for not imposing an extended sentence under ss.255, 267 or 280.

He should, in giving reasons, briefly identify the information which he has taken into account.

The judge:

(a) does not need (*R. v Johnson* [2006] EWCA Crim 2486; [2007] 1 Cr. App. R. (S.) 112) to spell out all the details of the previous offences; but
(b) should not rely on a disputed fact in reaching a finding of dangerousness, unless the dispute can fairly be resolved adversely to the offender; and

(c) should explain in his sentencing remarks the reasoning which has led him to his conclusion.

5. SENTENCES FOR ADULT OFFENDERS

(1) Special custodial sentences for offenders of particular concern (SA 2020 ss.265 and 278)

23-015 SA 2020 ss.265 and 278 replace the provisions in CJCA 2015 for certain offenders of particular concern. Where a court imposes a sentence of detention in a young offender institution for an offence under Sch.13 and the offender was aged over 18 when the offence was committed and under 21 when convicted of the offence (s.265), and the court does not impose either an extended sentence under s.266 or a sentence of custody for life under s.272 for the offence (or for an offence associated with it), then the term of the sentence must be equal to the aggregate of the *appropriate custodial term* and a further period of 1 year for which the offender is subject to a licence. The aggregate terms must not exceed the maximum term of imprisonment with which the offence is punishable in the case of an offender aged 21 or over. The *appropriate custodial term* is the term that in the opinion of the court, ensures that the sentence is appropriate.

For those aged 18 or over when the offence was committed, and 21 or over when convicted of the offence, and the court does not impose either an extended sentence under s.279 or a sentence of imprisonment for life for the offence (or for an offence associated with it), then the same provisions as to aggregate sentence apply.

Schedule 13 lists various offences. These are OAPA 1861 ss.4, 28 or 29 where the offence has a terrorist connection; Explosive Substances Act 1883 ss.2, 3 or 4 where the offence has a terrorist connection; TA 2000 ss.11, 12, 54, 56, 57, 58, 58A, 58B or 59; Anti-terrorism Crime and Security Act 2001 ss.47, 50 or 113; Terrorism Act 2006 ss.1, 2, 5, 6, 8, 9, 10 or 11; Sexual Offences Act 2003 ss.5 or 6; an inchoate offence in relation to such an offence or murder (if it has a terrorist connection); and any offence that was abolished before 13 April 2005, and if committed on the day on which the offender was convicted of the offence, would have constituted a listed offence.

(2) Life sentence for a second listed offence (SA 2020 s.283)

General

23-016 A sentence of imprisonment for life *must* be imposed (SA 2020 s.283) where the following conditions apply:

(1) an offender aged 21 or over is convicted of an offence listed in SA 2020 Sch.15 Pt 1 (see 23-007);
(2) the second offence was committed on or after 3 December 2012; and
(3) both;
  (a) the "sentence condition"; and
  (b) the "previous conviction condition" are met,

unless the judge is of the opinion that there are particular circumstances which relate to the offence, the "previous offence" or to the offender, which would make it unjust in all the circumstances to do so.

The "*sentence condition*" is that, but for s.283, the court would impose a term of imprisonment or, for an offender aged 18–20, detention in a young offender institution, (disregarding any extension period imposed under s.273) of at least 10 years.

The "*previous offence condition*" is that:

(i) at the time the offence was committed the offender had been convicted of an offence listed in Sch.15; and
(ii) a "relevant" life sentence, sentence of imprisonment or detention for a determinate period had been imposed for it.

Note in relation to "relevance" that:

- a life sentence is "relevant" if the offender was not eligible for release during the first five years of the sentence, ignoring credit for any time spent on bail or in custody before sentence;
- an extended sentence is "relevant" where: (i) if it was imposed under SA 2020 (whether before or after the commencement of LASPOA 2012) the appropriate custodial term was at least 10 years; or (ii) in any other case, where the custodial term (ignoring credit for any time spent on bail or in custody before sentence) was at least 10 years;
- any other sentence of imprisonment or detention for a determinate period is "relevant" if it was for a period of at least 10 years (ignoring credit for any time spent on bail or in custody before sentence); and
- "relevant sentences" include certain equivalent sentences imposed in Scotland, Northern Ireland or states of the EU and as a result of the Armed Forces Act 2006.

In the case of an offence committed after 1 October 2012, the judge must order a *surcharge* to be paid by the offender (SA 2020 ss.42 and 43), of (for offences as from 14 April 2020) £190. As to specific details in relation to age thresholds and computation of amounts, see SURCHARGES. As to the payment of court costs, see COSTS AND ASSESSMENT.

An offence for which a sentence of life for a second listed offence is imposed under SA 2020 s.283 is not to be regarded as an offence, the sentence for which is fixed by law.

R. v Burinskas

In *R. v Burinskas* [2014] EWCA Crim 334 the CACD considered it helpful to make three observations about s.224A (though none of the cases before it directly raised its application): **23-017**

(1) for a life sentence to be imposed under s.224A (now SA 2020 s.283) there is no requirement of a finding that the offender is dangerous within the meaning of SA 2020, although it is likely that in most such cases he will be; it follows that the fact that an offender is not dangerous is not something that of itself will make it unjust to pass a life sentence under the section;
(2) s.225(2)(b) does not apply to the relevant offence in s.224A; there is no requirement to consider whether the "seriousness" threshold has been passed; and
(3) s.224A (now s.283) could lead (in cases that may be rare) to the imposition of a life sentence in respect of an offence.

(3) Life sentence for serious offences (SA 2020 ss.274, 285 and 307)

General

23-018 Where an offender aged 18 or over but under 21:

(1) is convicted of an *offence* (see 23-005, 23-006); and
(2) the *offence* is a Sch.19 offence; and
(3) the judge is of the opinion that there is a significant risk to members of the public (see 23-010 and following) of serious harm occasioned by the commission by him of further *specified offences* (see 23-005),

then if the judge considers that the seriousness of the offence, or of the offence and one or more offences associated with it, is such as to justify the imposition of a sentence of imprisonment for life, he *must* (SA 2020 s.274) impose a sentence of custody for life) (as to which see LIFE SENTENCES).

Where an offender is aged 21 or over, and is convicted of an offence in Sch.19, and the offence was committed on or after 4 April 2005, and the judge is of the opinion as set out at (3) above, then he *must* impose a sentence of imprisonment for life.

In the case of an offence committed after 1 October 2012, the judge must order a *surcharge* to be paid by the offender (SA 2020 ss.42 and 43), of £190. As to specific details in relation to age thresholds and computation of amounts, see FINES and SURCHARGES. As to the payment of court costs, see COSTS AND ASSESSMENT.

An offence, the sentence for which is imposed under SA 2020 s.274, is not to be regarded as an offence, the sentence for which is fixed by law.

The offences set out in Sch.19 include manslaughter; kidnapping; false imprisonment; OAPA 1861 ss.4, 18, 21, 22, 28, 29 or 32; the Explosive Substances Act 1883 ss.2, 3 and 4 (where committed on or after 13 April 2015); firearms offences (FA 1968 ss.16, 16A, 17(1) and (2), 18); cruelty to children and infanticide; certain Theft Act offences (robbery, burglary with intent and aggravated burglary and vehicle taking); arson and criminal damage; certain aviation offences; certain public order offences (riot, violent disorder and affray); racially or religiously aggravated assaults and harassment; death by dangerous driving and death by careless driving under the influence of drink or drugs; certain maritime and shipping offences; certain terrorist offences; offences relating to female genital mutilation; aiding, abetting, counselling, procuring or inciting the commission of, or conspiring, or attempting, to commit any of the offences listed.

Approach to sentence

23-019 In *R. v Burinskas* [2014] EWCA Crim 334 the CACD said that, taking into account the law prior to the coming into force of the CJA 2003 and the whole of the new statutory provisions, the question in s.225(2)(b) as to whether the seriousness of the offence (or of the offence and one or more offences associated with it) is such as to justify a life sentence requires consideration of:

(1) the *seriousness of the offence* itself, on its own or with other offences associated with it in accordance with the provisions of SA 2020 ss.59–62, 63; this is always a matter for the judgment of the court;
(2) the offender's *previous convictions* (in accordance with SA 2020 s.65);
(3) *the level of danger to the public* posed by the offender and whether there is a reliable estimate of the *length of time* he will remain a danger; and

(4) the *available alternative* sentences.

The CACD expressed the view that it was inevitable that the application of s.225 in its current form will lead to the imposition of life sentences in circumstances where previously the sentence would have been one of IPP. It is what Parliament intended and also ensures (as Parliament also intended), so far as is possible, the effective protection of the public.

The new statutory life sentence for a second listed offence is not a straight replacement for the former IPP, but provides a new route to imposing a life sentence. There are numerous authorities on the choice between a life sentence and IPP following the introduction of the latter sentence in 2003, given that the two sentences were very similar in their practical effect. These cases have had the effect of restricting the appropriate use of the discretionary life sentence to the most serious and grave cases where a life sentence would have a denunciatory value over and above IPP.

(The principal authorities are *R. v Kehoe* [2008] EWCA Crim 819; [2009] 1 Cr. App. R. (S.) 41; *R. v Wood* [2009] EWCA Crim 651; [2010] 1 Cr. App. R. (S.) 2; and *R. v Wilkinson* (also reported as *Attorney General's Reference (No.43 of 2009)* [2009] EWCA Crim 1925; [2010] 1 Cr. App. R. (S.) 100).)

There will be cases, however, where an offender who represents a danger to the public does not "qualify" for the statutory life sentence, yet, for some reason the imperative of public protection is not met by the new extended sentence. In such circumstances very long-term public protection must be provided by the imposition of a discretionary life sentence under SA 2020 s.274 (see also *R. v Saunders* [2013] EWCA Crim 1027).

The provisions of SA 2020 s.274 are mirrored in SA 2020 s.258 in relation to offenders under 18 at the time of conviction (see 23-021).

(The "road maps" in relation to protective sentences at 23-028 in relation to adults, and at 23-031 in relation to offenders under 18, may be found useful.)

Further considerations

It should be noted, in addition to the above, that: **23-020**

(1) SA 2020 s.231 provides that any custodial sentence must be for the shortest term (not exceeding the permitted maximum) that in the judge's opinion is commensurate with the seriousness of the offence, or the combination of the offence and one or more offences associated with it (see *Attorney General's Reference (No.55 of 2008)* [2008] EWCA Crim 2790; [2009] 2 Cr. App. R. (S.) 22); and

(2) where the offender has been convicted of, or has admitted, a number of offences, the length of the minimum term is governed by SA 2020 s.321, namely that the determination of the "tariff should reflect the seriousness of the offence, or the combination of the offence and one or more offences associated with it", but disregarding the credit which would normally be due for time already spent in custody.

See further LIFE SENTENCES.

(4) Extended sentence for violent or sexual offences: offenders 18 to 20 and offenders over 21 SA 2020 ss.266–268 and ss.279–282

General

23-021 An extended sentence of detention in a young offender institution or imprisonment *may* be imposed on an offender (SA 2020 ss.279–282) where:

(1) being aged 18 to 20 or over 21 he is convicted of a specified offence committed;
(2) the judge considers that there is a significant risk to members of the public of serious harm occasioned by the commission by the offender of further *specified offences*;
(3) the judge is not required by SA 2020 ss.283 or 285 to impose a sentence of imprisonment for life; and
(4) one of two conditions (conditions "A" or "B") is met: "*Condition A*" is that, at the time the offence was committed, the offender had been convicted of an offence listed in Sch.14 (see 23-007); "*Condition B*" is that, if the judge were to impose an extended sentence of imprisonment, the term that he would specify as the "appropriate custodial term" (taking into account any discount for plea—*R. v Fazli* [2009] EWCA Crim 939; 73 J.C.L. 463) would be at least four years.

The "appropriate custodial term" here means a term of imprisonment (not exceeding the maximum term permitted for the offence) that would be imposed.

Where an offender is convicted of an offence before 3 December 2012, but has not been sentenced by 3 December, an IPP or EPP under the previous provisions remains available. It should be noted that a life sentence under s.224A may not be imposed on such a person.

The provisions are mirrored in SA 2020 ss.254–257 in relation to offenders under 18 at the time of conviction (see 23-030).

As to the *surcharge* to be paid by the offender where imprisonment is imposed in respect of an offence committed after 1 October 2012 (SA 2020 ss.42 and 43), of £190, see IMPRISONMENT. As to specific details in relation to age thresholds and computation of amounts, see FINES and SURCHARGES. As to the payment of criminal court costs, see COSTS AND ASSESSMENT.

Further provisions

23-022 The judge must take care to identify the offence or offences to which the extended sentence is intended to apply (*R. v Pepper* [2005] EWCA Crim 1181; [2006] 1 Cr. App. R. (S.) 20).

Note that, in 23-018, para.(1), references to a specified offence, a specified violent offence and a specified sexual offence include an offence which:

(1) was abolished before 4 April 2005 and would have constituted such an offence had it been committed on the day the offender was convicted of the offence; and
(2) where the specified offence was committed before 4 April 2005 it remains eligible for an extended sentence, notwithstanding that CJA 2003 ss.224A or 225(2) did not apply to it.

The principle in *R. v O'Brien* [2006] EWCA Crim 1741; [2007] 1 Cr. App. R. (S.)

75 relating to indeterminate sentences (now abolished) presumably applies also to extended sentences, in that where the offender is to be sentenced for a number of associated offences none of which, individually, would justify an extended sentence, the judge may nevertheless aggregate the proposed sentences together in relation to one offence for the purpose of passing an extended sentence on that offence and passing concurrent sentences for the associated offences (assuming, of course, that the other statutory conditions are met) (*R. v Pinnell* [2010] EWCA Crim 2848; [2011] 2 Cr. App. R. (S.) 30).

Extended sentence: the length of extended term

An extended sentence of imprisonment is a sentence of imprisonment, the term of which is equal to the aggregate of: **23-023**

(1) the appropriate custodial term; and
(2) a further period ("the extension period") for which the offender is to be subject to a licence, and which is of such length as the judge considers necessary for the purpose of protecting members of the public from serious harm occasioned by the commission by him of further specified offences.

The extension period must:

(a) be for at least one year; and
(b) not exceed:
  (i) five years in the case of a specified *violent* offence; and
  (ii) eight years in the case of a specified *sexual* offence.

(SA 2020 ss.254–257)

The term of the extended sentence passed under s.226A in respect of an offence must not exceed the maximum term permitted for the offence (see *R. v Oldfield* [2011] EWCA Crim 2314). In *R. v Phillips* [2018] EWCA Crim 2008 the purpose of the extended licence period was considered. It should not be longer than necessary for the relevant purpose and it should be just and proportionate.

Nature of the extended term

The "*appropriate custodial term*" is the term of imprisonment that would (apart from s.254–257) be imposed in compliance with SA 2020 s.231(2) (i.e. must be the shortest term commensurate with the seriousness of the offence or the offence and other offences associated with it) (SA 2020 s.281). **23-024**

The extension period:

(1) must be of such length as the judge considers necessary to protect members of the public from serious harm by the commission of further specified offences by the offender; and
(2) must be at least a year; but
(3) must not exceed five years for a violent offence or eight years for a sexual offence; and
(4) may exceed a relevant sentencing guideline by reason of the clear distinction between the custodial term (which is the term actually served by the offender), and the extension period which is for the protection of the public (see *R. v Terry* [2012] EWCA Crim 1411; [2013] 1 Cr. App. R. (S.) 51),

and the term of an extended sentence must not exceed the maximum term permissible for the offence at the time it was committed.

Note that:

(a) it will not usually be appropriate to impose consecutive extended sentences, whether the principal offence is serious or merely specified (cf. *R. v Nelson* [2001] EWCA Crim 2264; [2002] 1 Cr. App. R. (S.) 134); and
(b) applying imprisonment to those aged 18 or over, the sentence for 18 to 20 year olds should continue to be expressed as "custody for life" or "detention in a young offender institution".

Totality; Sentencing Council Guideline

23-025 The Sentencing Council guideline on totality deals with using multiple offences to calculate the determinate term as follows:

(1) provided there is at least one specified offence the threshold requirement is reached if the total determinate sentence for all offences (specified or not) would be four years or more;
(2) the extended sentence should be imposed either for one specified offence or concurrently on a number of specified offences; and
(3) ordinarily, a concurrent determinate sentence, or (according to the CACD) "no separate penalty" will be appropriate for the remaining offences (*R. v Pinnell* [2010] EWCA Crim 2848; [2011] 2 Cr. App. R. (S.) 30).

The custodial period of an extended sentence must be adjusted for totality in the same way as a determinate sentence would be (see DEALING WITH AN OFFENDER). The extension period is measured by the need for protection of the public (*R. v Cornelius* [2002] EWCA Crim 138; [2002] 2 Cr. App. R. (S.) 69) and therefore does not require adjustment.

Release date: effect of 2012 and 2015 amendments

23-026 An extended sentence passed under the repealed sections of the sections of the CJA 2003 (ss.227 and 228) mean that the offender would be released once one half of the appropriate custodial term had been served.

The effect of ss.226A and 226B inserted by LASPOA 2012 was as follows (CJA 2003 s.246A (and as continued under the provisions of SA 2020)):

(1) the Secretary of State will release the offender on licence as soon as he has served *two-thirds* of the appropriate custodial term or, where he is serving two or more concurrent or consecutive sentences, the period calculated under CJA ss.263(2) and 264(2) ("the requisite custodial period"), *unless*:
   (a) the appropriate custodial term was at least 10 years; and
   (b) the sentence was imposed in respect of an offence listed in Sch.15 Pts 1–3; in which case
(2) the Secretary of State will refer the offender's case to *the Parole Board*, as soon as the offender has served "the requisite custodial period", and where the Board did not direct the offender's release under any previous reference under this provision, not later than the second anniversary of the disposal of that reference; and
(3) the Secretary of State will release the offender on licence as soon as he has:
   (a) served "the requisite custodial period"; and

(b) the Board has directed his release under this provision;

but

(4) the Parole Board will not direct the release of the offender unless:

(a) the Secretary of State has referred his case to it; and

(b) it is satisfied that it is no longer necessary for the protection of the public that the offender should be confined; and, in any event the Secretary of State will release the offender on licence as soon as he has served the appropriate custodial term unless he has previously been released on licence and recalled under CJA s.254.

With effect from 15 February 2015, as a result of the CJCA 2015 all extended determinate sentences will be referred to the Parole Board at the two-thirds stage of the sentence.

A three-stage approach to sentence

It was said in *R. v Nelson* [2001] EWCA Crim 2264; [2002] 1 Cr. App. R. (S.) 134 (though the judgment must be read in the light of the current provisions) that the judge should approach the imposition of an extended sentence in three stages: **23-027**

(1) decide on the sentence which would be *commensurate* with the offence;

(2) consider whether a *longer period* in custody was *necessary* to protect the public from serious harm from the offender; and

(3) consider whether the sentence was *adequate to protect the public* from the commission of further offences by the offender and impose an extended sentence.

It is not appropriate to reduce the custodial term because an extended licence period is imposed.

Multiple offences

In *R. v Pinnell* [2012] EWCA Crim 2848; [2011] 2 Cr. App. R. (S.) 30, the CACD issued guidance, (based upon the repealed provisions of s.227) and existing authorities, where an offender is convicted of multiple offences: **23-028**

(1) if, on ordinary principles, no single offence justifies a four-year custodial term, the seriousness of the aggregate offending must be considered;

(2) if a four-year custodial term results from aggregating the shortest terms commensurate with the seriousness of each offence, then that four-year term may be imposed in relation to the *specified offence*;

(3) if there is *more than one specified offence*, that aggregate term should be passed for the lead specified offence, or, if appropriate, concurrently on more than one specified offence;

(4) if appropriate, a *concurrent determinate term* may be imposed for other offences;

(5) there is no objection to imposing an extended sentence consecutive to another sentence, or (since the amendments made to the release provisions for extended sentences by the CJIA 2008) to imposing consecutive extended sentences, although this should be done only where there is a particular reason for doing so;

(6) the extension periods in the case of consecutive extended sentences will themselves be consecutive; and

(7) in a case of consecutive extended sentences, each offence must justify a custodial term of at least four years; and it is not possible to pass separate sentences of less than four years to meet this condition for the imposition of an extended sentence, even if their total is more than four years.

A recommended road map: (A) 18 to 20

23-029 In the case of an offender aged 18–20, the following approach may be recommended in the case of a dangerous offender where a protective sentence is contemplated:

Step 1. Has the offender been convicted of a "*specified offence*" listed in Sch.15?

If No: determinate sentence only.

If Yes: go to Step 2.

Step 2. Is the offender "*dangerous*", as defined in ss.308–310 (and see *R. v Lang* [2005] EWCA Crim 2664; [2006] 2 Cr. App. R. (S.) 3)?

If No: determinate sentence only.

If Yes: go to Step 3.

Step 3. Is the *seriousness* of the offence, or of the offence and at least one offence associated with it, such as to justify imprisonment (or for those aged 18–20 custody for life)?

If No: go to Step 4.

If Yes: a sentence of life imprisonment (or for those aged 18–20 custody for life) *must* be imposed.

Step 4. Has:

(a) the offender been convicted of an offence of an offence listed in Sch.15; and

(b) are both the "*sentence condition*" and the "*previous offence condition*" met?

If No: go to Step 5.

If Yes: a sentence of imprisonment for life *must* be imposed *unless* the judge considers that there are particular circumstances which:

(a) *relate to the offence*, the "previous offence" or the offender; and

(b) would make it *unjust* to do so in all the circumstances.

Step 5. If the judge is not required under the steps above to impose a sentence of imprisonment for life, are *Conditions "A"* or *"B"* in SA 2020 ss.254–257 met?

("A": at the time the offence was committed the offender had been convicted of an offence listed in Sch.15B; "B": an extended sentence would have at least four years as the minimum appropriate custodial term.)

If No: determinate sentence.

If Yes: an extended sentence under SA 2020 ss.254–257 *may* be imposed.

Step 6. Where appropriate, in the case of an offence committed after 1 October 2012, the appropriate surcharge must be ordered (SA 2020 ss.42 and 43). As to specific details in relation to age thresholds and computation of amounts, see FINES and SURCHARGES. As to the payment of court costs, see COSTS AND ASSESSMENT.

The CACD has said that in considering public protection, the judge should have in mind all the alternative and cumulative methods of providing the necessary public protection against any risk posed by the individual offender. There will be cases where a determinate sentence, or an extended sentence with appropriate conditions attached, might form part of the "total protection sentencing package" without imprisonment under s.225 being imposed (*Attorney General's Reference (No.55 of 2008)* [2008] EWCA Crim 2790; [2009] 2 Cr. App. R. (S.) 22).

6. Sentences for offenders under 18

Detention for life—SA 2020 ss.254–257

Where: **23-030**

(1) an offender aged under 18 is convicted of a serious offence committed after 3 December 2012; and
(2) the judge is of opinion that there is a significant risk to members of the public of serious harm occasioned by the commission by the offender of further specified offences,

then if the offence is one in respect of which the offender would apart from this section be liable to a sentence of detention for life under SA 2020 ss.250 and 258 and the judge considers that the seriousness of the offence, or of the offence and one or more offences associated with it, is such as to justify the imposition of a sentence of detention for life, he *must* impose a sentence of detention for life under that section (SA 2020 ss.254–257).

In the case of an offence committed after 1 October 2012, the judge must order a *surcharge* to be paid by the offender (SA 2020 ss.42 and 43), of £34. As to specific details in relation to age thresholds, computation of amounts and payment by parent or guardian, see FINES and SURCHARGES. As to the payment of court costs, see COSTS AND ASSESSMENT.

An offence the sentence for which is imposed under this provision is not to be regarded as an offence the sentence for which is fixed by law.

Extended sentence for violent, sexual or terrorism offences—SA 2020 s.255

An extended sentence of detention *may* be imposed where: **23-031**

(1) a person aged under 18 is convicted of a specified offence;
(2) the judge considers that there is a significant risk to members of the public of serious harm occasioned by the commission by the offender of further specified offences;
(3) the judge is not required by SA 2020 s.258(2) to impose a sentence of detention for life under SA 2020 ss.250 and 258; and
(4) if the judge were to impose an extended sentence of detention the term it would specify as the appropriate custodial term would be at least four years.

The "appropriate custodial term" here means a term of detention (not exceeding the maximum term permitted for the offence) which is the term that would (apart from s.226B) be imposed (taking into account any discount for plea—*R. v Fazli* [2009] EWCA Crim 939; 73 J.C.L. 463).

Similar provisions as to the length, nature and effect of such a sentence apply as they apply to the sentence in respect of an adult (see 23-020 to 23-025). In the case of an offence committed after 1 October 2012, the judge must order a *surcharge* to be paid by the offender (SA 2020 ss.42 and 43), of £34. As to specific details in relation to age thresholds, computation of amounts and payment by parent or guardian, see FINES and SURCHARGES. As to the payment of court costs, see COSTS AND ASSESSMENT.

As to the suggested three stage approach to this sentence, see 23-026.

Road map: (B) offenders under 18

23-032 In the case of an offender aged under 18 years, the following approach may be recommended in the case of a dangerous offender where a protective sentence is contemplated:

Step 1. Was the offender aged *under 18* when convicted of the current offence?

If No: go to road map "A" at 23-028.

If Yes: go to Step 2.

Step 2. Is the current offence, of which the offender has been convicted, a *specified offence* under Sch.15?

If No: impose either:

(a) a youth rehabilitation order with appropriate requirements; or

(b) an appropriate determinate sentence of detention.

If Yes: go to Step 3.

Step 3. Is the offender "*dangerous*", as defined in s.229 (and see *R. v Lang* [2005] EWCA Crim 2664; [2006] 2 Cr. App. R. (S.) 3)?

If No: impose either:

(a) a youth rehabilitation order with appropriate requirements; or

(b) an appropriate determinate sentence of detention.

If Yes: go to Step 4.

Step 4. Is: (a) the offence in respect of which the offender would, apart from s.258, be liable to a sentence of *detention for life* under SA 2020 ss.250 and 258; *and* (b) the *seriousness* of the offence, or of the offence and at least one offence associated with it, such as to justify a sentence of detention for life?

If No: go to Step 5.

If Yes: a sentence of detention for life *must* be imposed

Step 5. If the judge is not required under the steps above to impose a sentence of detention for life, if he were to pass an extended sentence would he specify *at least four years* as the minimum appropriate custodial term?

If No: impose either:

(a) a youth rehabilitation order with appropriate requirements; or

(b) an appropriate determinate sentence of detention.

If Yes: extended sentence of detention under s.255 *may* be imposed.

In the case of an offence committed after 1 October 2012, the judge must order the appropriate *surcharge* to be paid by the offender (under SA 2020 ss.42 and 43). As to specific details in relation to age thresholds, computation of amounts and payment by parent or guardian, see FINES and SURCHARGES.

As to the payment of court costs, see COSTS AND ASSESSMENT.

7. RECTIFICATION OF ERRORS

General

23-033 The regime for dangerous offenders requires the judge to carry out a careful step by step evaluation of the sentencing consequences of:

(1) the type of offence;
(2) the age of the offender; and
(3) the assessment of his dangerousness.

A common error is failure to appreciate that a "specified" offence is a "serious" offence.

In passing sentences the judge should bear in mind that if he wrongly imposes an extended sentence in respect of a serious offence, the CACD has no power to substitute an indeterminate sentence under ss.225 or 226 (*R. v Reynolds* [2007] EWCA Crim 538; [2007] 2 Cr. App. R. (S.) 27).

Rectification by the Crown Court

Where a mistake is made: **23-034**

(1) if it is identified quickly enough, the Crown Court may exercise the power under SA 2020 s.385 to vary the sentence within the period of 56 days beginning on the day on which the sentence or other order was imposed: such power:
    (a) would be properly exercised if the mistake was that the sentencing judge had failed to appreciate, e.g. that the specified offence was a "serious offence" and that the mandatory provisions of SA 2020 required a life sentence as opposed to an extended sentence; and
    (b) could be exercised where the mistake was a failure to recognise the offence as a "specified" offence, as a result of which an ordinary determinate sentence or other disposal had been imposed;
(2) if it is identified within the 56-day period, but for whatever reason the sentencing court is either:
    (a) unable to deal with the matter by way of variation within 56 days; or
    (b) considers that sentencing should be delayed beyond the 56-day period,

the sentencing judge should rescind the sentence; the sentencing court then being in the same position as it was at the time that the original sentence was imposed and accordingly having all the powers it had at that time, including the jurisdiction to adjourn sentence, if the justice of the case so required.

The Crown Court has power, after rescinding all or part of its original order, to adjourn the final sentence to a later date (*R. v Stillwell* (1992) 13 Cr. App. R. (S.) 253 not followed).

Rectification by the CACD

Where: **23-035**

(1) the judge concluded that an offender met the criteria of dangerousness, but has in some other way misunderstood or misapplied that consequence to the *offender's disadvantage*, the matter may be put right on appeal;
(2) the Attorney General seeks a reference under CJA 1988 s.36, the CACD has the power to put right any mistake.

Difficulties arise where an error *in favour of the offender* emerges as a result of an appeal by him.

If it becomes apparent during the course of the appeal that the sentencing judge has failed to appreciate that:

(a) a mandatory sentence should have been imposed; or

(b) a determinate sentence should have been passed;
(c) as opposed to an extended sentence,

the sentence is an unlawful sentence, but CAA 1968 s.11(3) precludes the CACD from interfering with such a sentence (*R. v Reynolds* [2007] EWCA Crim 538; [2007] 2 Cr. App. R. (S.) 87).

24. DEALING WITH AN OFFENDER

Quick Guide

General

CrimPR 25.16 provides a composite sequence of the procedure to be followed where, in respect of any count in the indictment the accused pleads guilty or is convicted. In such circumstances the judge may exercise his power where: **24-001**

1. the accused is an *individual*:
   - (a) to require a pre-sentence report (24-005);
   - (b) to commission a medical report (24-005); and
   - (c) to require a statement of the accused's financial circumstances (see FINES and SURCHARGES);
2. the accused is a corporation, to require such information as he directs about the accused's corporate structure and financial resources (see FINES and SURCHARGES).

He may adjourn sentence pending receipt of any such report, statement or information, or the verdict in a related case.

The prosecutor has a duty to:

- (i) summarise the prosecution case, if the sentencing judge has not heard evidence;
- (ii) identify in writing any offence that the prosecutor proposes should be taken into consideration in sentencing;
- (iii) provide information relevant to sentence, including any previous conviction of the accused, and the circumstances where relevant, and any statement of the effect of the offence on the victim, the victim's family or others; and
- (iv) identify any other matter relevant to sentence, including the legislation applicable, any sentencing guidelines, or guideline cases (see SENTENCING GUIDELINES), aggravating and mitigating features (see 24-039–24-042) affecting the accused's culpability and the harm which the offence caused, was intended to cause or might forseeably have caused (see VICTIM PERSONAL STATEMENTS), and the effect of such of the

information listed in (1) and (2) above as the judge may need to take into account.

Where the accused pleads guilty, the judge may (a) give directions for determining the facts on the basis of which sentence must be passed if the accused wants to be sentenced on a basis agreed with the prosecutor; or, (b) in the absence of such agreement, the accused wants to be sentenced on the basis of different facts to those disclosed by the prosecution case (see GUILTY PLEAS).

Where the judge has power to order the endorsement of the accused's driving licence, or power to order the disqualification of the accused from holding or obtaining one, if other legislation so permits, an accused who wants the judge not to exercise that power must introduce the evidence or information on which the defendant relies, the prosecutor may also introduce evidence and the parties may make representations about that evidence or information.

Before passing sentence:

- the court must give the accused an opportunity to make representations and introduce evidence relevant to sentence;
- where the accused is under 18, the judge may give his parents, guardian or other supporting adult, if present, such an opportunity as well; and
- if the judge requires more information, he may exercise its power to adjourn the hearing.

When the judge has taken into account all the evidence, information and any report available, he must as a general rule, pass sentence at the earliest opportunity, and when passing sentence:

- explain the reasons;
- unless the accused is absent his ill-health or disorderly conduct makes such an explanation impracticable, explain to him its effect, the consequences of failing to comply with any order or pay any fine, and any power that the court has to vary or review the sentence;
- give any such explanation in terms the accused, if present, can understand (with help, if necessary); and
- deal with confiscation, costs and any civil behaviour order.

(See 24-063 and following)

The general rule is subject to the judge's power to defer sentence for up to six months.

1. Some pre-sentencing requirements

Presence of offender

24-002 As a general rule the offender must be physically present in court where:

(1) he is sentenced to a custodial sentence; or
(2) a driving disqualification is imposed on him, unless, in this latter case:
  (a) the court has adjourned after conviction; and
  (b) he has been notified of the time and place for the resumption of the hearing, and the reason for the adjournment, and he fails to appear.

Where several offenders fall to be sentenced, it is desirable that they should all be sentenced by the same court. Where one pleads not guilty and his case is adjourned for trial, sentences on those who plead guilty should be adjourned to the conclusion of his trial (*R. v Weekes* (1982) 74 Cr. App. R. 161).

Care must be taken in dealing with a number of co-offenders to differentiate between them according to the mitigating or aggravating factors affecting each one of them.

As a consequence of the coronavirus pandemic in some cases the offender sentenced will be "present" in court through a prison video link, the CVP or some other form of live link. Whilst this approach may well work in many straightforward cases, there will be many situations where the case, public interest or pre-sentence preparation require the offender to be physically present.

Remittal, adjournment, deferment

An offender need not be dealt with on the very day of conviction, nor in every case by the judge before whom he appeared or was convicted. **24-003**

There is:

(1) a duty in certain circumstances to remit a juvenile offender to the appropriate youth court (see CHILDREN AND YOUNG PERSONS);
(2) a power to transfer an offender's case, administratively, from one court, or from one circuit, to another, where sentence or another trial is pending, in that court;
(3) a common law power to adjourn, which may be appropriate for:
  (a) the making of enquiries;
  (b) the provision of reports;
  (c) consolidating other outstanding charges, or other co-accused; or
  (d) the making of reparation by the offender (see COMPENSATION ORDERS);
(4) a statutory power to adjourn for the production of a driving licence (see DRIVING DISQUALIFICATION);
(5) certain statutory powers under MHA ss.35, 36 to remand to hospital for a medical examination and report (see MENTALLY DISORDERED OFFENDERS);
(6) power to postpone the making of a confiscation order under POCA 2002 ss.14, 15 (see CONFISCATION ORDERS); and
(7) a statutory power to defer passing sentence for a fixed period (see DEFERRING SENTENCE).

Outstanding indictments or offences

An accused who has a number of indictments, or counts, outstanding against him, should be sentenced on one occasion at the conclusion of all matters on which the Crown intend to proceed. Only in this way will consistency of sentencing be achieved. The problems caused by doing otherwise are obvious (*R. v Bennet* (1980) 2 Cr. App. R. (S). 96). **24-004**

In particular, where one offender has undertaken, after pleading guilty, to give evidence at the trial of his co-accused or other criminal confederates, while it is a matter for the judge to decide whether to sentence him before he gives evidence (*R. v Payne* (1950) 34 Cr. App. R. 43), it is generally more sensible to wait until he has given his evidence at the trial of the others (*R. v Weekes* (1982) 74 Cr. App. R. 161).

Reports; representation

24-005 In some cases a pre-sentence report may be required by statute; in other cases the judge may derive assistance from:

(1) a pre-sentence or other report; or
(2) a medical or psychiatric report,

as to which see REPORTS.

The latter may be mandatory where the judge has a mental health disposal in contemplation (see MENTALLY DISORDERED OFFENDERS).

It is unsafe to proceed to sentence unless the offender is represented (24-007).

Adjournment for reports—R. v Gillam: a potential trap

24-006 Where the judge adjourns for enquiries to be made or reports to be provided, he should be careful to observe the rules laid down in *R. v Gillam* [1980] 2 Cr. App. R. (S.) 267, and the numerous cases which have followed it.

The judge:

(1) must be careful not to say or do anything which might reasonably create in the offender's mind any expectation that he will adopt a particular option if the reports are favourable; and
(2) should state expressly that:
   (a) he is "keeping his options open"; and
   (b) that the grant of bail pending the preparation of a report is no indication of the nature of any sentence which he has in mind (*R. v Renan* (1994) 15 Cr. App. R. (S.) 722),

otherwise the CACD has indicated that a sense of injustice, "real or imagined," may be created in the offender's mind, though failure to warn the offender that the court is considering a custodial sentence does not vitiate any subsequent sentence (*R. v Woodin* (1994) 15 Cr. App. R. (S.) 307).

An indication that the judge does not intend to pass a "custodial sentence" includes a sentence of imprisonment which is suspended (*R. v Court* [2012] EWCA Crim 133; [2012] 1 Cr. App. R. 36).

Need for legal representation

24-007 A judge must not, on committal for sentence or on conviction on indictment:

(1) pass a sentence of imprisonment (other than a committal for contempt or any kindred offence);
(2) pass a sentence of detention under SA 2020 ss.250 or 259;
(3) pass a sentence of custody for life under SA 2020 s.272;
(4) pass a sentence of detention in a young offender institution; or
(5) make a detention and training order,

on a person who is not legally represented in that court, *and* has not been previously sentenced to that punishment by a court in any part of the UK unless he has the assistance of counsel or a solicitor to represent him in the proceedings in that court at some time after he is found guilty and before he is sentenced, except where:

(a) representation was made available to him for the purposes of the proceedings under LASPOA 2012 Pt 1 but was withdrawn because of his conduct or because it appeared that his financial resources were such that he was not eligible for such representation;

(b) he applied for such representation and the application was refused because it appeared that his financial resources were such that he was not eligible for such representation; or

(c) having been informed of his right to apply for such representation and having had the opportunity to do so, he refused or failed to apply.

(SA 2020 s.226; CrimPR 38.1(1) and (4))

Subject to any provision to the contrary contained in SA 2020 or any other enactment passed or instrument made under any enactment after 31 December 1967, a suspended sentence which has not taken effect is to be treated as a sentence of imprisonment, or in the case of a person aged at least 18 but under 21, a sentence of detention in a young offender institution for the purposes of all enactments and instruments made under enactments (SA 2020 s.289).

In respect of the previous sentence of imprisonment referred to in (1) a sentence which has been suspended and which has not taken effect under SA 2020 s.402 and Sch.16 or the legislation of Northern Ireland is to be disregarded (SA 2020 s.226).

As to representation in contempt cases, see *R. v Moran* (1985) 7 Cr. App. R. (S.) 101 and CONTEMPT OF COURT.

A breach of these provisions renders any subsequent sentence unlawful, and a nullity (*R. v Wilson* (1995) 16 Cr. App. R. (S.) 997).

Difficulties arise where an offender "sacks" his solicitor and/or counsel, or they withdraw between conviction and sentence. Under the representation order, an offender has the right to be represented by a solicitor and counsel of his choice and who are willing to act, unless and until that order is withdrawn (*R. v Kirk* (1983) 76 Cr. App. R. 194; *R. v Harris* [1985] Crim. L.R. 244; *R. v Dimech* [1991] Crim. L.R. 846; *R. v Stovell* [2006] EWCA Crim 27; [2006] Crim. L.R. 760).

Faced with a recalcitrant offender, the proper course is for the judge to revoke the representation order before proceeding to sentence (*R. v Wilson* (1995) 16 Cr. App. R. (S.) 997). (See also LEGAL AID; PUBLIC FUNDING.)

Antecedents

The accused's record should usually be provided in the following format: **24-008**

- Personal details and summary of convictions and cautions—Police National Computer (PNC) Court/Defence/Probation Summary Sheet.
- Previous convictions—PNC Court/Defence/Probation printout, supplemented by Form MG16 if the police force holds convictions not shown on PNC.
- Recorded cautions—PNC Court/Defence/Probation printout, supplemented by Form MG17 if the police force holds cautions not shown on PNC.

The defence representative should take instructions on the accused's record and if the defence wish to raise any objection to the record, this should be made known to the prosecutor immediately. It is the responsibility of the prosecutor to ensure that a copy of the accused's record has been provided to the Probation Service. Where following conviction a custodial order is made, the court must ensure that a copy is attached to the order sent to the prison.

The police should also provide brief details of the circumstances of the last three similar convictions and/or of convictions likely to be of interest to the court, the latter being judged on a case-by-case basis.

Here:

(1) the current alleged offence could constitute a breach of an existing sentence such as a suspended sentence, community order or conditional discharge; and

(2) if it is known that that sentence is still in force then details of the circumstances of the offence leading to the sentence should be included in the antecedents; the detail should be brief and include the date of the offence.

On occasions the PNC printout provided may not be fully up to date. It is the prosecutor's responsibility to ensure that all of the necessary information is available to the court and the Probation Service and provided to the defence. Oral updates at the hearing will sometimes be necessary, but it is preferable if this information is available in advance.

The antecedents should include dates of release from prior sentences and sentence expiry dates (*R. v Egan* [2004] EWCA Crim 630; *The Times,* 9 March 2004).

Bail or custody on adjournment

24-009 There is no general presumption in favour of bail after conviction, though it may be granted (subject to CJPOA 1994 s.25, see BAIL) where:

(1) the offender's case is adjourned for the purpose of enabling enquiries and a report to be made, to assist the court in dealing with him for the offence; or

(2) the offender appears or is brought before the court to be dealt with for breach of the requirements of a community order.

Where an offender's case is adjourned for enquiries or reports, and the offence, or one of the offences, of which he is convicted in the proceedings is punishable with imprisonment, he need not be granted bail if it appears that it would be impracticable to complete the enquiries or to make the report without keeping him in custody.

2. The statutory purposes of sentencing

Adult offenders

24-010 A judge dealing with an offender aged 18 or over in respect of his offence must, in every case, have regard to the following purposes of sentencing:

(1) the punishment of offenders;
(2) the reduction of crime (including its reduction by deterrence);
(3) the reform and rehabilitation of offenders;
(4) the protection of the public; and
(5) the making of reparation by offenders to persons affected by their offences.

(SA 2020 s.57)

The foundation of any sentence is SA 2020 s.57. The section, which is mandatory in effect, makes clear that whilst the punishment of an offender is one purpose of any sentence, it is not the only purpose. The rehabilitation of offenders and the protection of the public are other purposes to which the judge must have regard when considering sentence (*R. v Rakib* [2011] EWCA Crim 870; [2011] Crim. L.R. 570).

Consistent with the statutory provisions, the starting point for the sentencing decision should normally be assessed by reference to the guidance in force on the sentencing date. By SA 2020 s.59 the judge, when sentencing an offender, is required to follow any relevant guideline, unless satisfied that to do so would be contrary to the interests of justice (*R. v Hall* [2011] EWCA Crim 2753; [2012] 2 Cr. App. R. (S.) 21 and see SENTENCING GUIDELINES).

But as a matter of sentencing reality, whenever a gun is made available for use, as well as when a gun is used, public protection is the paramount consideration. Deterrent and punitive sentences are required and should be imposed (*R. v Olawaiye* [2009] EWCA Crim 1925; [2010] 1 Cr. App. R. (S.) 100).

Provisions (1)–(5), above, do not apply:

(a) in relation to an offender who is aged under 18 (as to which CJA 2003 s.142A will apply as and when brought into force) (note that from 1 December 2020 SA 2020 s.58 will come into force which states that nothing in the Sentencing Code affects the duties of the court to have regard to the principal aim of the youth justice system to have regard to the welfare and in certain circumstances to take steps in relation to surroundings and provision of education, etc.);
(b) to an offence the sentence for which is fixed by law; or
(c) to an offence the sentence for which falls to be imposed under PCA 1953 s.1A(5) (minimum sentence for offence of threatening with offensive weapon in public), FA 1968 s.51A(2) (minimum sentence for certain firearms offences), CJA 1988 s.139AA(7) (minimum sentence for offence of threatening with article with blade or point or offensive weapon), SA 2020 ss.311, 312, 313, 314 or 315 (required custodial sentences for certain repeat offences), or SA 2020 ss.258, 274, 285, 273 or 283 (life sentences); or
(d) in relation to the making, under MHA 1983 Pt 3, of a hospital order (with or without a restriction order), an interim hospital order, a hospital direction or a limitation direction.

"Sentence", in relation to an offence, includes any order made by a court when dealing with an offender in respect of his offence; and "sentencing" is to be construed accordingly.

As to those aged under 18, and children and young persons, see CHILDREN AND YOUNG PERSONS.

Sentencing regime applicable at date of sentence

An offender must be sentenced in accordance with the sentencing regime applicable at the date of sentence. If the offence was committed years earlier, contravening the criminal law in force at the date when it was committed, the offender is liable to be convicted of that offence and no other. In such a case, therefore, the sentence is limited to the maximum sentence then available for the offence of which he has been convicted. **24-011**

Thus:

(1) changes in the law which create new offences, or increase the maximum penalties for existing offences do not apply retrospectively to crimes committed before the change in the law;

(2) the offence of which the offender is convicted and the sentencing parameters (in particular, the maximum available sentence) applicable to that offence are governed not by the law at the date of sentence, but by the law in force at the time when the criminal conduct occurred; and
(3) judges cannot ignore statutory provisions which are currently in force. They apply to each and every sentencing decision, whenever the crime in question was committed, at the date of sentence.

As to "historic" cases, where an offender is brought to justice many years after his crimes were committed, particularly applicable, though not confined to, sexual crimes, see 24-012.

"Historic" or "cold" cases

24-012 In such cases, ignoring any express statutory provisions, such as those to be found in SA 2020 Schs 15 and 19 (mandatory life sentences) the following guidance is given in *R. v H* [2011] EWCA Crim 2753; [2012] 2 Cr. App. R. (S.) 21 (and see further 24-043):

(1) Sentence must be imposed at the date of the sentencing hearing:
  (a) on the basis of current legislative provisions; and
  (b) by measured reference to any definitive sentencing guidelines relevant to the situation revealed by the established facts;
(2) sentence must be limited to the maximum sentence at the date when the offence was committed; but
(3) it is wholly unrealistic to attempt an assessment of sentence by seeking to identify at the present day what the sentence for the individual offence was likely to have been if the offence had come to light at or shortly after the date when it was committed; and
(4) if maximum sentences have been reduced, as in some instances, e.g. theft, the more severe attitude to the offence in earlier years, even if it could be established, should not apply.

Provided sentences fall within or do not exceed the maximum sentence which could lawfully have been imposed at the date when the offence was committed, neither the retrospectivity principle (see *R. (on the application of Uttley) v Secretary of State for the Home Department* [2004] UKHL 38; [2005] 1 Cr. App. R. 15) nor art.7 of the European Convention are contravened.

3. A "Road Map" of Sentencing

24-013 For those steeped in criminal practice, much of the machinery of sentence will be well known, if not instinctive. For those coming from other disciplines, common law, commercial or family law, may find themselves assisted by the following "road map" useful in approaching the current maze of sentencing provisions, and deciding where the balance lies between the declared purposes of sentencing set out in 24-010.

Once the decision has been made to proceed to sentence and not to remit the offender to another court or judge for sentence (see 24-003), the following "step by step" approach may be useful for assessing:

(1) the seriousness of the offence;
(2) the culpability of the offender; and

(3) the level of actual, intended or foreseeable harm,

thus arriving at a proper and just disposal of the case.

The sentencing decision does not represent a mathematical exercise, nor does it result from an arithmetical calculation; the reality is that the judge must balance all the circumstances of the case to reach an appropriate sentence (*R. v Martin* [2006] EWCA Crim 1035; [2007] 1 Cr. App. R. (S.) 3).

There is nothing to prevent the judge from showing leniency in passing sentence provided that in his sentencing remarks he indicates that he is being merciful in the circumstances of the case and gives his reasons for being so.

The suggested steps, or stages, may be spelt out in brief as follows:

Step 1—The factual basis for sentence.
Step 2—Choice of disposal.
Step 3—Aggravating and mitigating features.
Step 4—TICs.
Step 5—Discounts.
Step 6—Credit of remand periods.
Step 7—Other factors.
Step 8—Following sentencing guidelines.
Step 9—Ancillary orders.
Step 10—Surcharge.
Step 11—Spelling it out.

Special considerations apply in relation to cases of corporate manslaughter and health and safety offences causing death, as to which see SGC 2010 para.37.

4. Step 1—The factual basis for sentence

General

As far as possible an offender should be sentenced on a basis which accurately reflects the facts of the individual case; a different set of circumstances is likely to arise depending upon whether there has been a trial or sentence follows a plea of guilty. A factual basis for sentence, (holding a *Newton* hearing where necessary—see GUILTY PLEAS) must be established, and also, in particular: **24-014**

(1) the offender's age—generally crucial to the sentencing process (see 24-052 and AGE OF OFFENDER); in general 18 is the watershed though, in the case of young offenders, a further breakdown may be necessary (see CHILDREN AND YOUNG PERSONS and DETENTION OF YOUNG OFFENDERS);
(2) the date of the commission of the offence—also crucial: SI 2005/643 brought into force most of the sentencing provisions of CJA 2003 and these apply to offences committed on or after 4 April 2005. Sentences for offences committed before that date continue to be governed by PCC(S)A 2000 (as repealed and replaced by provisions in SA 2020); certain specific orders are available only after certain stated dates;
(3) the number of offences to be dealt with—an offender may be sentenced only on the basis of the offences proved against him by admission or verdict, or which he has asked to be taken into consideration (see 24-045 to 24-047) (*R. v Canavan* [1988] 1 Cr. App. R. (S.) 243; *R. v Tovey* [2005] EWCA Crim

530; [2005] 2 Cr. App. R. (S.) 100); *R. v Oakes* [2012] EWCA Crim 2435; [2013] Crim. L.R. 252 (unconvicted of murder abroad);

(4) the seriousness of the offence(s) (24-026);
(5) the culpability of the offender;
(6) the harm caused to individuals, to the community or other types of harm (see, as to victims' views, VICTIM PERSONAL STATEMENTS);
(7) the prevalence of the offence(s) being dealt with (see 24-056); and
(8) any mental health considerations (24-036).

Crown's obligation to state facts in open court

24-015 To enable the public and the press to know the circumstances of an offence of which the accused has been convicted and for which he is being sentenced, in relation to each offence to which the offender has pleaded guilty, the prosecution must state the facts in open court before sentence is passed.

While he is not obliged to pass sentence on the least serious version of the facts (*R. v Solomon* (1984) 6 Cr. App. R. (S.) 120), the judge should give the offender the benefit of any doubt (see *R. v Stosiek* (1982) 4 Cr. App. R. (S.) 205). Other than in a case of murder reduced to manslaughter (see *R. v Frankum* (1983) 5 Cr. App. R. (S.) 259) it is inappropriate for the judge to take a "special verdict" (*R. v Larkin* [1943] K.B. 174).

At this stage, or immediately before sentence, the offender may ask for other admitted offences, not the subject of the indictment, or of committal from the magistrates' court, to be taken into consideration on sentence. As to the procedure for TICs, see 24-045.

Facts emerging following plea of guilty

24-016 Where sentence is passed following a plea of guilty, the basis for the sentence is to be derived from the prosecution case, which includes the facts disclosed in the witness statements of the prosecution and the facts outlined by the prosecution advocate, unless the plea is tendered and accepted on an agreed basis. As to the procedure in such a case, see GUILTY PLEAS. See also GOODYEAR INDICATION.

Facts emerging following trial

24-017 Where an offender is convicted after a trial:

(1) the factual basis for sentence may be derived from the evidence called at the trial; but
(2) the judge must be careful to sentence only for those offences:
    (a) to which the offender has pleaded guilty;
    (b) of which the offender has been convicted at the trial, or any other trial where sentence is pending and falls to be dealt with; or
    (c) which the offender formally asks to be taken into consideration (as to which see 24-045).

Where an issue arises as to sentence on which no evidence was called at the trial, the judge may hold a *Newton* hearing (see GUILTY PLEAS) to determine the matter (*R. v Finch* (1993) 14 Cr. App. R. (S.) 226).

Clearly, where the prosecution does not proceed on a count, the judge should enter a verdict of not guilty.

Interpreting the verdict

Problems may arise in interpreting the jury's verdict. In particular: **24-018**

(1) if the verdict can be explained only on one view of the facts the judge must adopt that view as the basis for sentence;
(2) if more than one view of the facts is consistent with the verdict, the judge may form his own view in the light of the evidence given; and
(3) if the verdict leaves open an important issue which may affect sentence, the judge must decide where the truth lies.

(*R. v Solomon* (1984) 6 Cr. App. R. (S.) 120; *R. v McGlade* (1991) 12 Cr. App. R. (S.) 105; *R. v Martin* [2006] EWCA Crim 1035; [2007] 1 Cr. App. R. (S.) 3)

5. Step 2—Choice of disposal

General

The form of sentence imposed on an offender will depend upon the factors outlined at Step 1, and the objective which the judge has in view, bearing in mind any restrictions placed upon his discretion by SA 2020. **24-019**

Where the judge seeks:

(1) to punish, the appropriate custodial sentence, be it imprisonment or one of those forms of detention provided for young offenders, as the case may be, will be apposite, or a financial penalty;
(2) merely to mark the conviction, and no more, an absolute discharge may be appropriate;
(3) to encourage the offender not to offend again, there are available four forms of preventive or conditional sentences:
    (a) a bind-over under JPA 1361, where breach involves forfeiture of a specific sum;
    (b) a common law bind-over, the breach of which may also involve a fresh sentence;
    (c) a conditional discharge, which permits a court to act on a breach, but does not involve a specific sentence on the breach; and
    (d) a suspended sentence of imprisonment;
(4) to rehabilitate the offender, he is likely to go for a community order to which a whole range of requirements may be added. Note that a detention and training order (see DETENTION OF YOUNG OFFENDERS), though punitive, is intended to have a regime which is, at the same time, "constructive", with an emphasis on discipline and education;
(5) to deal with a person who requires treatment for a specified mental disorder, hospital and guardianship orders under MHA 1983 may be made, or treatment requirements may be added to a community order (see MENTALLY DISORDERED OFFENDERS); or
(6) to keep dangerous offenders out of circulation, the appropriate provisions of PCC(S)A 2000 and CJA 2003 as modified by LASPOA 2012 and as are now repleaded and replaced by provisions in SA 2020 (see DANGEROUS OFFENDERS PROTECTIVE SENTENCES).

A good working rule is not to mix sentences which fall into established and different categories (*R. v McElhorne* [1983] Crim. L.R. 487).

Mandatory or discretionary?

24-020 The judge needs to know whether he is obliged by law to impose a certain sentence or whether the choice lies in his discretion.

A life sentence for murder is prescribed by law; in the case of other sentences, a minimum term may be prescribed in certain circumstances such as those which fall to be imposed under:

(1) SA 2020 s.311(2) (minimum sentence for offence of threatening with offensive weapon in public);
(2) SA 2020 s.311 (minimum term for offence of possession of a knife or offensive weapon);
(3) SA 2020 s.311(2) (minimum sentence for certain firearms offences);
(4) SA 2020 s.315(2) (minimum sentence for offence of threatening with article with blade or point or offensive weapon);
(5) SA 2020 ss.313(2) and 314(2) (required custodial sentences for certain repeat offences—Class A drug trafficking offences and "third" domestic burglary);
(6) SA 2020 s.315(2) (minimum sentences in certain cases of using someone to mind a weapon);
(7) SA 2020 ss.273 or 283 (life sentence for second offence by certain dangerous offenders);
(8) SA 2020 ss.274 or 285 (life sentence for dangerous offender); or
(9) SA 2020 s.258 (detention for life of person under 18 for serious offences).

Dangerous offenders

24-021 In relation to offenders sentenced after 3 December 2012 who qualify as "dangerous offenders" the judge may impose:

(1) a mandatory sentence of life imprisonment (or custody for life in the case of an offender under 18); or
(2) a discretionary extended sentence ("a new extended sentence") of imprisonment (or detention in the case of an offender under 18).

(See DANGEROUS OFFENDERS PROTECTIVE SENTENCES)

Where an offender does not qualify for a sentence under (1) or (2), a determinate custodial sentence or a community sentence may be imposed.

Thresholds

24-022 In considering the nature of the sentence to be imposed, it is necessary for the judge to consider whether:

(1) the case is "so serious" that it crosses the "custody threshold"? (24-024);
(2) if the case crosses the custody threshold, immediate custody is required;
(3) there are realistic alternatives to a custodial sentence, e.g. deferring sentence (see DEFERRING SENTENCE);
(4) if custody is not appropriate, the case is "serious enough" to cross the "community sentence" threshold (see 24-035);

(5) if it is a case for a community sentence penalty, which requirements should be attached to the order (see COMMUNITY SENTENCES in the case of an adult, YOUTH REHABILITATION ORDERS in the case of young offenders);
(6) if the community sentence threshold is not reached, a lesser sentence is appropriate, e.g. a fine (FINES), a compensation order (see COMPENSATION ORDERS), a conditional discharge (see DISCHARGE; ABSOLUTE AND CONDITIONAL) or a bind over (see BIND OVER);
(7) orders for deprivation or forfeiture of property (see FORFEITURE AND DEPRIVATION ORDERS) or restitution (see RESTITUTION ORDERS) are appropriate;
(8) a confiscation order under POCA 2002 is appropriate (see CONFISCATION ORDERS);
(9) any other ancillary order is called for (see ANCILLARY ORDERS);
(10) orders for prosecution and/or defence costs are appropriate (see COSTS AND ASSESSMENT).

Meaning of "custodial sentence"

Custodial sentences for the purposes of SA 2020 s.222 are, in relation to an offender: **24-023**

(1) a sentence of *imprisonment* other than a committal for contempt of court or any kindred offence;
(2) a sentence of *detention* under SA 2020 Pt 10 Ch.2;
(3) a sentence of *custody for life* under SA 2020 ss.272 or 275;
(4) a sentence of *detention in a young offender institution* under SA 2020 ss.262–263; or
(5) a *detention and training order* under SA 2020 s.233.

SA 2020 s.222 also refers to "pre-Code custodial sentence" which covers:

(i) a detention and training order under PCC(S)A 2000 s.100;
(ii) a sentence of detention imposed under PCC(S)A 2000 ss.90 or 91, CYPA 1933 s.53(1) or (3) or CJA 2003 ss.226B or 228;
(iii) a sentence of detention for public protection imposed under CJA 2003 s.226; or
(iv) a sentence of custody for life under PCC(S)A 2000 ss.93 or 94 or CJA 1982 s.8.

Different considerations govern different types of custodial sentence, but the imposition of any of them is subject to:

(a) the offence(s) "qualifying" for a custodial sentence (see 24-024);
(b) the offender's age (see AGE OF OFFENDER);
(c) unless unnecessary, the availability of a pre-sentence report (see REPORTS); and
(d) in general, the offender being legally represented (see 24-007).

So complex are many of the interlocking provisions governing the question of custodial sentences, that it is in this field particularly, that judges should not be slow to invite assistance from prosecuting counsel, nor should they be "affronted" where the latter offers such assistance on the relevant provisions and authorities (*Attorney General's Reference (No.7 of 1997)* [1998] 1 Cr. App. R. (S.) 268).

The Offender Rehabilitation Act 2014 became law on 1 June 2014. It amended the CJA 2003 and has flowed through to the SA 2020, when fully implemented, will radically alter the way in which offenders are supervised or managed under community orders, suspended sentence orders and on licence after release from custody. The provisions came into force on 1 February 2015. Sections 10 and 14 of the Act, together with Sch.4 and paras 4–7 of Sch.6, came into force in 2014. These changes have no impact on the courts.

The most important change is the imposition of a mandatory period of supervision and support for a full period of 12 months for all offenders given sentences of imprisonment or detention in a young offender institution of up to two years (see IMPRISONMENT; DETENTION AND YOUNG OFFENDERS).

The 12-month supervision period will include a "rehabilitation activity requirement" which, as well as standard conditions, may include participating in specified activities, and undergoing drug testing. Breach of one or more of these requirements will require the offender to be returned to court for the breach to be dealt with. The court may impose custody of up to 14 days, or a fine, or make a "supervision default order" upon breach. If the breach amounts to a new offence that will of course be dealt with separately.

While the arrangements for early release of an offender are not normally a matter to be taken into account on sentence, the important restructuring by this Act of the management of short sentences is a change which judges will need to be aware of, not least so that explanation of the practical effect of a custodial sentence (required to be given as part of the sentencing remarks) is clear and accurate (see 24-063).

Threshold for custodial sentences

24-024 Where a person is convicted of an offence committed on or after 4 April 2005, punishable with a custodial sentence, other than one:

(1) fixed by law; or
(2) a minimum sentence falling to be imposed under the provisions of SA 2020 ss.313, 314, 315 or 316–320,

the judge must not pass a custodial sentence on the offender unless he is of the opinion that the offence, or the combination of the offence, and one or more offences "associated" with it (24-025) is "so serious" (24-026) that neither a fine alone nor a community sentence can be justified for it.

Nothing, however, prevents the judge from passing a custodial sentence on an offender who fails to express his willingness to comply with a requirement which it is proposed to include in a community order, and which requires an expression of such willingness.

"Associated offences" for the purposes of SA 2020 s.400

24-025 "Associated" in relation to an offence is to be read in accordance with SA 2020 s.400. An offence is said to be "associated" with another for this purpose if:

(1) the offender is convicted of it in the proceedings in which he is convicted of the other offence, or, (although convicted of it in earlier proceedings) he is sentenced for it at the same time as he is sentenced for the other offence; or

(2) he admits the commission of it in the proceedings for which he is sentenced for that other offence and asks the judge to take it into consideration (see 24-045) in sentencing him for that offence.

It follows that:

(a) an offence in respect of which a suspended sentence was passed (*R. v Crawford* (1993) 14 Cr. App. R. (S.) 782), or a conditional discharge was made (*R. v Godfrey* (1993) 14 Cr. App. R. (S.) 804) on a previous occasion; or
(b) an uncharged offence, not represented by a sample count, and not taken into consideration on sentence,

are not "associated" offences.

"Seriousness" for the purposes of SA 2020 s.230

SA 2020 is silent as to when an offence is so "serious" that only a custodial sentence is justified; it is a subjective test. Obviously a crime which is deliberate and premeditated, and causes personal or mental injury, is usually more serious than one which is spontaneous and unpremeditated, causing only financial loss. Of course: **24-026**

(1) the judge is not bound to impose a custodial sentence just because the offence "qualifies"; he is still required to consider whether, having regard to mitigating circumstances, such a sentence is appropriate; and
(2) the fact that a court imposed a community sentence for an offence, does not prevent it "qualifying" for a custodial sentence if the offender is in breach of the order (*R. v Bray* (1991) 12 Cr. App. R. (S.) 705; *R. v Webster* (1990) 12 Cr. App. R. (S.) 760; *R. v Oliver* (1993) 96 Cr. App. R. 426).

In considering the seriousness of an offence, the judge:

(a) may take into account the offender's previous convictions, and/or any failure of his to respond to previous sentences;
(b) may take into account the prevalence of offences of a particular class, and public concern about them (*R. v Cunningham* (1993) 14 Cr. App. R. (S.) 444; *R. v Cox* (1993) 96 Cr. App. R. 464); and
(c) *must* treat as aggravating factors those matters stated at 24-039 to 24-041.

Custodial sentences: length—suspension

Where the judge decides on a custodial sentence he will need to consider: **24-027**

(1) How long that sentence should be (24-028) (as to joint conviction with juvenile see *R. v Tyre* (1984) 6 Cr. App. R. (S.) 247).
(2) Whether the sentence should be suspended (see 24-029) and if so whether:
    (a) for offences committed before 4 April 2005, there are "exceptional circumstances" justifying a suspended sentence; and
    (b) for offences committed after 4 April 2005, a suspended sentence order is appropriate.

(See IMPRISONMENT and SUSPENDED SENTENCE ORDERS.)

Length of discretionary sentence

24-028 In the case of a custodial sentence other than one fixed by law or falling to be imposed under CJA 2003 ss.225 or 226, for an offence committed on or after 4 April 2005, then, subject to minimum sentences:

(1) SA 2020 s.311 (firearms);
(2) SA 2020 ss.313 and 314 (required sentences for certain repeat offences); and
(3) SA 2020 ss.273, 274, 283, 285 and 307 (dangerous offenders); or
(4) SA 2020 s.315 (minding dangerous weapons); or
(5) SA 2020 s.312 (minimum sentence for offence of threatening with offensive weapon in public); or
(6) SA 2020 s.312 (minimum term for offence of possession of a knife or offensive weapon),

the custodial sentence must be for the shortest time (not exceeding the permitted maximum) that is, in the judge's opinion, commensurate with the seriousness of the offence, or the combination of the offence and one or more offences associated with it (CJA 2003 s.153).

(As noted above, from 1 December 2020 provisions in both acts are repealed and replaced by various provisions in SA 2020).

There will be cases where the maximum sentence is appropriate. Maximum sentences should not necessarily be reserved for cases where it is impossible to conceive of a worse example, they should, however, be reserved for cases of the utmost gravity (*R. v Foulger* [2012] EWCA Crim 1516).

Suspending a sentence of imprisonment

24-029 A judge passing a sentence of imprisonment, or, in the case of an offender aged at least 18 but under 21, detention in a young offender institution, for a term of at least 14 days but not more than two years in respect of an offence committed on or after 4 April 2005, in accordance with CJA 2003 s.189 may suspend the sentence and order:

(1) the offender to comply during a specified supervision period with one or more of the requirements falling within s.190(1) and specified in the order; and
(2) that the sentence of imprisonment will not take effect unless:
    (a) during the supervision period the offender fails to comply with a requirement imposed under (1) above; or
    (b) during the "operational period" specified in the order, the offender commits in Great Britain another offence (whether or not punishable with imprisonment).

(CJA 2003 s.189; see SUSPENDED SENTENCE ORDERS)

Offences not qualifying for custodial sentence

24-030 If none of the offences with which he is dealing qualifies for a custodial sentence in this sense, the judge can impose only a *financial penalty* or a *community sentence*. Where the offences with which he is dealing are of differing gravity, some "qualifying", others not:

(1) he is not prevented from passing custodial sentences in respect of the of-

fences not qualifying (*R. v Mussell* (1990) 12 Cr. App. R. (S.) 607; *R. v Oliver* (1993) 96 Cr. App. R. 426); but

(2) he ought not, in general, to pass consecutive sentences for such offences, or make the overall sentence longer by reference to them (*R. v Oliver* (1993) 96 Cr. App. R. 426).

Financial penalties

Where a person is convicted on indictment of any offence other than an offence: **24-031**

(1) for which the sentence is fixed by law; or
(2) falls to be imposed under SA 2020 ss.313 and 314 (required sentence for certain repeat offences); or
(3) falls to be imposed under any of the sections SA 2020 ss.273 and 283 (dangerous offenders),

the judge, if not precluded from sentencing an offender by his exercise of some other power, may impose a fine:

(a) instead of; or
(b) in addition to,

dealing with him in any other way in which he has power to deal with him, subject to any enactment requiring the offender to be dealt with in a particular way. As to surcharges, see SURCHARGES.

While judges may be reluctant to impose a fine, since fines are often not properly enforced by the magistrates' courts, recent statutory enactments have provided for a more rigorous approach to enforcement. If these prove to be effective, where an offender has means, a heavy fine may often be an adequate and appropriate punishment. If this is the case, CJA 2003 requires a fine to be imposed rather than a community sentence (*R. v Seed* [2007] EWCA Crim 254; [2007] 2 Cr. App. R. (S.) 69).

In relation to (1) above, the harm caused may, of course, be very long-standing harm, and in "historic cases" (see 24-012) the evidence may show that the impact of the crime years after it was committed is still disturbing and painful to the individual who is now an adult (*R. v H* [2011] EWCA Crim 2753; [2012] 2 Cr. App. R. (S.) 21).

Whilst previous convictions are a statutorily aggravating factor, the sentence must still be proportionate to the offence itself (see *R. v Neasham* [2012] EWCA Crim 542 (persistent domestic burglar) and *R. v Byrne* [2012] EWCA Crim 418 (persistent commercial burglars)).

Proper approach to a fine

The amount of any fine fixed must be such as, in the judge's opinion, reflects the seriousness of the offence, but in fixing the amount, he must: **24-032**

(1) in the case of an individual offender, inquire into his financial circumstances; and
(2) whether the offender is an individual or other person, take into account the circumstances of the case including, amongst other things, the financial circumstances of the offender, so far as they are known, or appear to him,

and (2) above applies whether it has the effect of increasing or reducing the amount of the fine.

The judge may, before sentencing, make a financial circumstances order under CJA 2003 s.162, and where the offender fails to comply or otherwise fails to co-operate in an enquiry into his financial circumstances, the judge may make such order as he thinks fit.

Community sentences

24-033 Community sentences, for the purposes of SA 2020 are, in relation to an offence committed on or after 4 April 2005, those which consist of:

(1) a community order, as defined by SA 2020 s.200 (see COMMUNITY SENTENCES); or
(2) a youth rehabilitation order under SA 2020 (see YOUTH REHABILITATION ORDERS).

A number of individual requirements may be added to such orders. Community sentences for offences committed before 4 April 2005 are dealt with under PCC(S)A 2000, and consist principally of a community rehabilitation order, a community punishment order and the combination of the two, to which additional requirements may be added (see COMMUNITY SENTENCES). (As noted above, from 1 December 2020 provisions in the various acts mentioned are repealed and replaced by various provisions in SA 2020).

No community sentence where sentence fixed by law, etc.

24-034 No community order or youth community order may be made in respect of an offence committed on or after 4 April 2005 for which the sentence:

(1) is fixed by law;
(2) falls to be imposed under SA 2020 s.311 (required sentences for certain firearms offences);
(3) falls to be imposed under SA 2020 ss.313 and 314 (required sentences for certain repeat offences);
(4) falls to be imposed under any of SA 2020 ss.273 and 283 (custodial sentences for dangerous offenders); or
(5) falls to be imposed under SA 2020 s.312 (required custodial sentence for minding a weapon).

(As noted above, from 1 December 2020 provisions in both acts are repealed and replaced by various provisions in SA 2020).

General restrictions on imposing community sentences

24-035 In relation to offences committed on or after 4 April 2005, the judge may not pass a community sentence on an offender unless he is of opinion that, subject to SA 2020 s.204(2), the offence, or the combination of the offence and one or more offences associated with it, was serious enough to warrant such a sentence, and where he does pass such a sentence:

(1) the particular requirement or requirements forming part of the community order must be such as in his opinion is, or taken together are, the most suitable for the offender; and
(2) subject to SA 2020 s.208, the restrictions on liberty imposed by the order

must be such as in his opinion are commensurate with the seriousness of the offence, or the combination of the offence and the one or more offences associated with it.

Where the judge passes a community sentence which consists of or includes one or more youth community orders:

(a) the particular order or orders forming part of the sentence must be such as in his opinion is, or taken together are, the most suitable for the offender; and

(b) the restrictions on liberty imposed by the order or orders must be such as in his opinion are commensurate with the seriousness of the offence, or the combination of the offence and the one or more offences associated with it.

As to the recommended approach to such an order see COMMUNITY SENTENCES.

Where an offender falls to be sentenced for two or more offences, one or more of which were committed before and some after 4 April 2005, sentences on the differing counts fall to be passed under different provisions and take differing forms, e.g. where the offender is to be sentenced for two such offences, one pre- and one post-commencement, and the judge seeks to deal with him by means of a community punishment order under the old law, he will need to make in respect of the post-commencement offence a community order under SA 2020 with a requirement for unpaid work.

Mental health disposal

In the case of an offender who is not so mentally disordered as to be absolved from criminal responsibility for his actions, but is nevertheless in need of psychiatric treatment, a judge may, in certain circumstances, remand to hospital for treatment accused persons who are waiting to be tried, as well as those waiting to be sentenced. Those who have been convicted may be: **24-036**

(1) sent to a hospital under an interim hospital order, or a hospital order;
(2) made the subject of a guardianship order; or
(3) made the subject of a community order with a mental health treatment requirement.

As to the procedure to a verdict of not guilty by reason of insanity or a finding of disability, see UNFITNESS TO PLEAD/INSANITY.

The judge in considering whether to make a hospital order or an interim hospital order, may ask the Regional Health Authority to assist in identifying an appropriate hospital for a particular offender. In some cases a hospital order may be made in conjunction with a restriction order (see generally MENTALLY DISORDERED OFFENDERS).

6. Step 3—Determining seriousness; aggravating and mitigating features

Judge's approach

In approaching the nature or length of any sentence; the judge should: **24-037**

(1) first determine the order, or the length of the custodial term which he has in mind; and

(2) then adjust it in the light of any mitigating (or aggravating) factors.

(*R. v Fraser* (1982) 4 Cr. App. R. (S.) 254)

Previous convictions and offences committed whilst on bail are treated as aggravating factors (see 24-038). Other aggravating and mitigating factors are dealt with from 24-039 to 24-043.

Determining seriousness

24-038 The judge must in relation to all offences, whether committed before or after 4 April 2005:

(1) consider the offender's culpability in committing the offence and any harm which the offence caused, was intended to cause or might foreseeably have caused; and
(2) when considering the seriousness of:
  (a) the current offence committed by an offender who has one or more *previous convictions*, to treat each previous conviction as an aggravating factor if, in the case of that conviction, he considers that it can reasonably be so treated having regard to the nature of the offence to which the conviction relates and its relevance to the current offence, and the time that has elapsed since the conviction;
  (b) an offence committed while the offender was *on bail*, to treat the fact that it was committed whilst he was on bail as an aggravating factor.

The principle remains, however, that the sentence must be in proportion to the offence itself, see *R. v Bailey* [2013] EWCA Crim 1779.

A "previous conviction" here, refers to one by a court in the UK, and a previous finding of guilt in service disciplinary proceedings, but the judge is not prevented from treating a previous conviction by a court outside the UK as an aggravating feature in any case where he considers it appropriate to do so.

Additional aggravating features

24-039 The nature and length of the sentence may be enhanced not only by the facts of the case but by aggravating features in addition to those mentioned in 24-038, such as:

(1) the number of offences;
(2) the period of offending;
(3) any racial or religious element in the offence (24-040);
(4) hostility based on the victim's sexual orientation or disability; or transgender identity (20-041);
(5) the impact of the offences on the community;
(6) planning and sophistication;
(7) offence(s) committed while the offender was subject to a community order (see COMMUNITY SENTENCES); and
(8) offence(s) committed in contravention of other court orders.

The effect of having offences taken into consideration (TICs) may be either aggravating or mitigating (see 24-045).

Increase racial or religious aggravation

In considering the seriousness of an offence, whether committed before or after 4 April 2005, other than one under CDA 1998 ss.29–32 (racially or religiously aggravated assaults, criminal damage, public order offences and harassment) if the offence was racially or religiously aggravated (within the meaning of CDA 1998 s.28) the judge must treat that as a factor which increases the seriousness of the offence, and must state in open court: **24-040**

(1) that it was so aggravated:
  (a) identifying the sentence which would have been appropriate in the absence of racial aggravation; and
  (b) adding an appropriate amount to reflect the element of racial aggravation; and
(2) indicating by how much the sentence has been enhanced to reflect the racial aggravation.

(SA 2020 s.66)

See *R. v Kelly* [2001] EWCA Crim 1751; [2002] 1 Cr. App. R. (S.) 85; *R. v Saunders* [2000] 1 Cr. App. R. (S.) 71, considered in *R. v Kelly*, though there may be cases where such an approach is inappropriate, e.g. *R. v O'Brien* [2003] EWCA Crim 302; [2003] 2 Cr. App. R. (S.) 66; *R. v Fitzgerald* [2003] EWCA Crim 2875; [2004] 1 Cr. App. R. (S.) 74.

The amount of the enhancement will depend on the circumstances of the particular case (*R. v Morrison* [2001] 1 Cr. App. R. (S.) 5).

As to what amounts to "racial" aggravation, contrast the cases of *R. v White* [2001] EWCA Crim 216; [2001] Crim. L.R. 576 and *DPP v Pal* [2000] Crim. L.R. 756. As to where it is not possible to identify which member of a group shouted racist slogans, see *R. v Davies* [2003] EWCA Crim 3700; [2004] 2 Cr. App. R. (S.) 29.

It is not open to the judge to sentence on the basis of racial aggravation unless the offender has been convicted on that basis (*R. v O'Callaghan* [2005] EWCA Crim 317; [2005] 2 Cr. App. R. (S.) 83; *R. v McGillivray* [2005] EWCA Crim 604; [2005] 2 Cr. App. R. (S.) 60), though in *R. v Lester* (1976) 63 Cr. App. R. 144 the prosecutor was allowed to adduce evidence of such aggravation, which was not adduced at the trial, in the course of a *Newton* hearing.

The judge should be careful not to draw any inference that the offence was so aggravated unless he gives notice to the offender and permits him to challenge the inference.

Aggravation due to disability, sexual orientation or transgender identity

Where the judge is considering the seriousness of an offence committed on or after 4 April 2005, in any of the following circumstances, namely that: **24-041**

(1) at the time of committing the offence, or immediately before or after doing so, the offender demonstrated towards the victim of the offence hostility based on:
  (a) the sexual orientation (or presumed orientation) of the victim;
  (b) a disability or presumed disability of the victim; or
  (c) the victim being (or being presumed to be) transgender; or
(2) that the offence was motivated (wholly or partly) by hostility towards persons who:

(a) are of a particular sexual orientation;
(b) have a disability or a particular disability; or
(c) are (in the case of an offence committed on or after 3 December 2012) transgender;

the judge must:

(i) treat the fact that the offence was committed in any of those circumstances as an aggravating factor; and
(ii) state in open court that the offence was committed in such circumstances.

(SA 2020 s.66)

There is no definition in the 2020 Act of "sexual orientation". In *R. v B* [2013] EWCA Crim 291; [2013] 2 Cr. App. R. (S.) 69, the CACD accepted the view expressed in MoJ Circular 2010/05, para.7, that "hatred on the grounds of sexual orientation" does not extend to "orientation based, for example, on a preference for particular sex acts or practices. It therefore covers only groups of people who are gay, lesbian, bisexual or heterosexual", and does not extend to paedophiles.

References to being transgender include references to being transsexual, or undergoing, proposing to undergo or having undergone a process or part of a process of gender reassignment.

It is immaterial for the purposes of (1) and (2) above whether or not the offender's hostility is also based, to any extent, on any other factor. "Disability" means any physical or mental impairment.

Where the prosecutor seeks to adduce evidence of such aggravation, which was not adduced at the trial, the evidence should be adduced after verdict at a *Newton* hearing. The judge should be careful not to draw any inference that the offence was so aggravated unless he gives notice to the offender and permits him to challenge the inference (see *R. v Lester* (1976) 63 Cr. App. R. 144). The same approach to sentence will apply as in 24-040.

Mitigating factors

24-042 The nature and length of the sentence may be reduced by mitigating factors such as:

(1) positive good character or lack of previous convictions;
(2) a plea of guilty and the application of the reduction principles (see DISCOUNTS ON SENTENCE, GUILTY PLEAS);
(3) the level of the offender's responsibility for the offence(s);
(4) whether the offender acted under pressure from others;
(5) clear evidence of contrition and remorse;
(6) the offender cooperating with the prosecutor (see DISCOUNTS ON SENTENCE);
(7) lapse of time between the commission of the offence and the date of sentence;
(8) credit of any remand period (see IMPRISONMENT);
(9) the offender's conduct during any remand period; and
(10) restorative justice factors (see *R. v Collins* [2003] EWCA Crim 1687; *R. v Barci* [2003] EWCA Crim 2816), and factors such as compensation (see COMPENSATION ORDERS).

"Historic" or "cold" cases

In "historic" or "cold" cases (see 24-012): **24-043**

(1) the particular circumstances in which the offence was committed and its seriousness must be the main focus; due allowance for the passage of time may be appropriate, thus:
  (a) the date may have a considerable bearing on the offender's culpability;
  (b) if, e.g. the offender was very young and immature at the time when the case was committed, that remains a continuing feature of the sentencing decision; and
  (c) similarly if the allegations had come to light many years earlier, and when confronted with them, the offender had admitted them, but for whatever reason, the complaint was not drawn to the attention of, or investigated by, the police, or was investigated and not then pursued to trial, these too would be relevant features;

(2) the circumstances in which the facts come to light varies, and careful judgment of the harm done to the victim is always a critical feature of the sentencing decision; equal care needs to be taken to assess the true extent of the offender's criminality by reference to what he actually did and the circumstances in which he did it;

(3) the passing of the years may demonstrate aggravating features if, for example, the offender has continued to commit sexual crime or he represents a continuing risk to the public; on the other hand, mitigation may be found in an unblemished life over the years since the offences were committed, particularly if accompanied by evidence of positive good character; and

(4) early admissions and a guilty plea are of particular importance in such cases. Just because they relate to facts which are long passed, the offender may be tempted to lie his way out of the allegations; it is greatly to his credit if he makes early admissions; even more powerful mitigation is available to the offender who out of a sense of guilt and remorse reports himself to the authorities. Considerations like these provide the victim with vindication, often a feature of great importance to them.

(*R. v H* [2011] EWCA Crim 2753; [2012] 2 Cr. App. R. (S.) 21)

Statutory saving for mitigation

In so far as offences committed on or after 4 April 2005 are concerned, nothing in relation to: **24-044**

(1) imposing community sentences (SA 2020 ss.200–201 and 220);
(2) imposing custodial sentences (SA 2020 ss.230 and 231);
(3) pre-sentence reports and other requirements (SA 2020 ss.30, 31 and 33);
(4) the fixing of fines (SA 2020 s.124);
(5) youth rehabilitation orders with intensive supervision and surveillance (SA 2020 ss.178 and 180); or
(6) youth rehabilitation with fostering (SA 2020 ss.178 and 180),

prevents the judge from mitigating an offender's sentence by taking into account any such matters as, in his opinion, are relevant in mitigation of sentence, including his power to mitigate:

(a) any penalty included in the offender's sentence by taking into account any other penalty included in that sentence; and
(b) the sentence of an offender convicted of one or more other offences, by applying the "totality principle" (see IMPRISONMENT).

In particular:

(i) SA 2020 s.230 does not prevent the judge, after taking into account such matters, from passing a community sentence, even though he is of opinion that the offence, or the combination of the offence and one or more offences associated with it, was so serious that a community sentence could not normally be justified for the offence; and
(ii) in the case of a person suffering from a mental disorder within the meaning of MHA 1983, nothing mentioned in (1)-(4) above is to be taken as requiring the judge to pass a custodial sentence, or any particular custodial sentence, or as restricting any power (whether under MHA 1983 or otherwise) which enables the judge to deal with an offender in the manner he considers to be most appropriate in all the circumstances.

(SA 2020 s.77)

7. STEP 4—TICS

General

24-045 The judge may, when passing sentence upon an offender for an offence, where:

(1) he is informed that there are outstanding charges against the offender; and
(2) the offender admits each of them and asks for them to be taken into consideration,

formally take them into consideration and pass a longer sentence than he would if he were dealing only with the counts on the indictment (*R. v Batchelor* (1952) 36 Cr. App. R. 64). Any sentence imposed is intended to reflect an offender's overall criminality (*R. v Miles* [2006] EWCA Crim 256; *The Times,* 10 April 2006).

There is no reason, therefore, in principle why an offence to be taken into consideration which is of a more serious nature than the one before the court should not result in a higher sentence than would otherwise have been the case (*R. v Lavery* [2008] EWCA Crim 2499; [2009] 3 All E.R.295) provided that the maximum term for these offences is not exceeded, and the whole sentence is proportionate.

As with other aspects of sentencing, the way in which the judge deals with such offences will depend on context:

(a) they may add nothing, or nothing very much, to the sentence he would otherwise have impose;
(b) they may aggravate the sentence and lead to a substantial increase, particularly where the offences show a pattern of criminal activity which suggests careful planning, or if the offences were committed on bail after an earlier arrest; or
(c) on the other hand, when assessing their significance, the judge is likely to attach weight to the demonstrable fact that the offender has assisted the police. Such co-operative behaviour may provide its own early indication

of guilt and will usually mean that no further proceedings need to be started (*R. v Miles* [2006] EWCA Crim 256; *The Times*, 10 April 2006).

Taking offences into consideration does not, technically, amount to a conviction of those offences, nor does the procedure found a subsequent plea of *autrefois convict*. It is perfectly feasible "as a matter of theoretical jurisprudence" to charge an offender with offences which have been taken into consideration. By convention it is not done, and where, perhaps in error, it is done, the judge dealing with the offences on the second occasion should see to it, without any doubt whatever, that no additional punishment is imposed on the offender on account of those offences.

Where offences should not be taken into consideration

In general, offences taken into consideration should be offences similar to that, or those, for which the judge is passing sentence on the indictment. The judge should not take an offence into consideration without the consent of the prosecutor; the public interest may require investigation, and a trial of that offence (*R. v McLean* (1912) 6 Cr. App. R. 26). **24-046**

The judge has no power to take into consideration:

(1) offences which he would have no jurisdiction to try (*R. v Simons* (1953) 37 Cr. App. R. 120); and
(2) offences committed outside the jurisdiction of the courts of England and Wales, such as offences committed in Scotland (see *Hilson v Easson* 1914 S.C. (J.) 99), or offences of a purely military disciplinary nature (*R. v Anderson* (1958) 42 Cr. App. R. 91), although where offences committed by members of the armed forces are "civil offences" within service legislation, there is nothing to prevent their being taken into consideration (*R. v Anderson*). SCEW guidelines on Offences to be Taken Into Consideration and Totality state that it is *undesirable* for TICs to be accepted where:
    (a) the TIC is likely to attract a greater sentence than the conviction offence;
    (b) it is in the public interest that the TIC should be the subject of a separate charge;
    (c) the offender will avoid a prohibition, ancillary order or similar consequence which it would have been desirable to impose on conviction (e.g. an offence involving RT disqualification—*R. v Simons* (1953) 37 Cr. App. R. 120) unless the offender is liable to such an order under offences of which he has been convicted (*R. v Collins* (1948) 32 Cr. App. R. 27; *R. v Jones* (1971) 55 Cr. App. R. 32);
    (d) the TIC constitutes the breach of an earlier sentence (*R. v Webb* (1953) 37 Cr. App. R. 82) which should be dealt with in the way prescribed for dealing with the breach of such orders;
    (e) the TIC is a "specified offence" for the purposes of SA 2020 (see DANGEROUS OFFENDERS; PROTECTIVE SENTENCES) and the conviction is not; or
    (f) the TIC is not founded on the same facts or evidence or part of a series of offences of the same or a similar character (unless the judge is satisfied that it is in the interests of justice to do so).

The SCEW Definitive Guideline suggests that the Crown Court may take summary-only offences into consideration provided the offences is founded on the same facts or evidence as the indictable offence, or is part of a series of offences of the same or similar character as the indictable conviction offence.

Under the Protection of Freedoms Act 2012 ss.92–101 a person may make a written application to the Secretary of State for a formal disregard of his convictions or cautions for certain behaviour which has been decriminalised. If the defence informs the judge that an application is going to be made:

(i) it will be up to the judge to decide how the case should proceed, and what note he should take of the fact; but
(ii) he is not under any obligation to make enquiries pro-actively, unless he considers it to be in the interests of justice to do so.

Approach to sentence

24-047 The guideline suggests that the sentence imposed on the offender should, in most circumstances, be increased to reflect the fact that other offences have been taken into consideration.

The judge should:

(1) determine the sentencing *starting point* for the conviction offence, referring to the relevant definitive sentencing guidelines; at this stage no regard should be had to the existence of the TICs;
(2) consider whether there are any aggravating or mitigating factors that justify an upward or downward adjustment from the *starting point*; the existence of TICs should be treated as an aggravating feature that generally justifies an upward adjustment from the *starting point*;
(3) where there are a large number of TICs it may be appropriate to move outside the category range, although this must be considered in the context of the case and subject to the principle of totality; the judge is limited to the statutory maximum for the conviction offence; then
(4) continue through the sentencing process including: applying any reduction for a guilty plea to the overall sentence, and bearing in mind the totality principle.

Ancillary orders may be considered in relation to any or all of the TICs, particularly compensation orders and restitution orders.

Ancillary orders

24-048 Where an offence is formally taken into consideration in this manner, ancillary orders such as:

(1) a compensation order (SA 2020 ss.133–134) (see COMPENSATION ORDERS); and
(2) a restitution order under SA 2020 ss.147–151 (see RESTITUTION ORDERS),

may be made in respect of them (see generally ANCILLARY ORDERS).

Procedural safeguards

24-049 The procedure involves an offender, convicted of one or more offences, being punished for other offences for which he has never been arraigned, tried or convicted and to which he has never pleaded guilty. It is essential, therefore, if justice is to be done, that the judge is satisfied in respect of each offence that the offender admits it and wishes it to be taken into consideration. In practice the police prepare a list of such offences, serving it, with the consent of his legal advisors, upon the offender and obtaining his signature to it, striking through such offences as are not admitted.

Thus, before being sentenced:

(1) the offender (not his advocate) should be asked in open court, whether he has received the list, and if so, whether:
  (a) he admits each of the offences (not struck out); and
  (b) whether he wishes each of them to be taken into consideration;
(2) on a committal for sentence, the fact that the magistrates indicate that they have taken certain offences into consideration, does not relieve the trial judge from ensuring that the accused still wishes them to be taken into consideration;
(3) if there is a lengthy schedule of offences, it is not normally necessary to take the accused through the document page by page; but
(4) if there is any doubt as to which offences the offender admits and wishes to have taken into consideration, the issue must be resolved in open court; and
(5) if the judge is not satisfied that the offender has had time to consider the list in detail, it may be necessary to adjourn (*R. v Marquis* (1951) 35 Cr. App. R. 33; *DPP v Anderson* (1978) 67 Cr. App. R. 185; *R. v Nelson* (1967) 51 Cr. App. R. 98; *R. v Davies* (1981) 72 Cr. App. R. 262).

As to compensation orders made in relation to offences taken into consideration, see COMPENSATION ORDERS.

8. Step 5—"Discounts" on sentence

A tract of cases developed by the CACD has given an offender the right to expect a discount on the otherwise appropriate sentence, where: **24-050**

(1) he pleads guilty to the indictment (*R. v Barnes* (1983) 5 Cr. App. R. (S.) 368); the position is now governed by statute (see DISCOUNTS ON SENTENCE);
(2) the judge considers that the offence would not have been committed but for the activities of an informer (*R. v Beaumont* (1987) 9 Cr. App. R. (S.) 342; *R. v Chapman* (1989) 11 Cr. App. R. (S.) 222; *R. v Tonnessen* [1998] 2 Cr. App. R. (S.) 328; *R. v Underhill* [1979] 1 Cr. App. R. (S.) 270); and
(3) the accused co-operates with the prosecuting authorities, not only by pleading guilty, but by giving information early enough for it to be potentially useful; this is also now covered by statute (see DISCOUNTS ON SENTENCE).

Such a discount should reflect the seriousness of the offence, the importance of the information, and the effect, where the informant gives evidence, on his future circumstances (*R. v Wood* [1996] Crim. L.R. 916) and the circumstances of the entrapment or other factors should be expressly mentioned in the judge's sentencing remarks (*R. v Mackey* (1993) 14 Cr. App. R. (S.) 53) save, obviously, in cases where the judge receives a "confidential text".

9. STEP 6—CREDIT OF REMAND PERIODS

24-051 As a consequence of CJA 2003 s.240, s.240ZA and SA 2020 ss.325–327, time spent in custody on remand is now credited administratively and does not require the order of the judge (see IMPRISONMENT).

As to time remanded on bail counting towards time served, the following steps for calculating the credit period:

(1) Add:
  (a) the day on which the offender's bail was first subject to the relevant conditions (and for this purpose a condition is not prevented from being a relevant condition by the fact that it does not apply for the whole of the day in question); and
  (b) the number of other days on which the offender's bail was subject to those conditions (but exclude the last of those days if the offender spends the last part of it in custody);

(2) deduct the number of days on which the offender, whilst on bail subject to the relevant conditions, was also:
  (a) subject to any requirement imposed for the purpose of securing the electronic monitoring of the offender's compliance with a curfew requirement; or
  (b) on temporary release under rules made under the Prison Act 1952 s.47;

(3) deduct from the remainder, the number of days during that remainder on which the offender has broken either or both of the relevant conditions; and

(4) divide the result by two, if necessary, rounding up to the nearest whole number.

In *R. v Hoggard* [2013] EWCA Crim 1024; [2013] Crim. L.R. 782 the CACD gave guidance as to the proper approach to be adopted:

(a) every court which imposed a curfew and tagging condition must use the relevant Court Service form which has to follow the accused from court to court;

(b) solicitors and counsel must ask the accused whether he has been subject to curfew and tagging and, if yes, find out, from the court record, for which periods;

(c) it is the responsibility of the CPS to have a system for ensuring that such information is available;

(d) consideration of Steps 1–3 of the calculation under SA 2020 s.325 and s.240A is part of the post-conviction proceedings and thus not subject to the invariable application of strict rules of evidence;

(e) the approach to admissibility of evidence, should be that identified in *R. v Clipston* [2011] EWCA Crim 446; [2011] 2 Cr. App. R. (S.) 101, with emphasis upon the procedures adopted to deal with Steps 1–3 being both flexible and fair;

(f) if there was a dispute, then the prosecution must prove contended non-deductions to the criminal standard but if the court considered that to resolve the dispute would amount to a disproportionate use of time and expense and the number of days involved was relatively modest, then the dispute should be resolved in the defendant's favour. The court would then perform the calculation required by Steps 4 and 5 and give the necessary direction; and

(g) the order should follow the formula which permitted an error to be corrected in the court office (*R. v Nnaji* [2009] EWCA Crim 468; [2009] 2 Cr. App. R. (S.) 107).

See also *R. v Leacock* [2013] EWCA Crim 1994; [2014] 2 Cr. App. R. (S.) 12.

10. Step 7—Other factors affecting sentence

Age

The age of the offender ought to be taken into account on sentence. In relation to a young offender, in addition to the distinctive range of penalties available for such, there is an expectation that, generally, he will be dealt with less severely than an adult, although this distinction diminishes as he approaches the age of 18. **24-052**

Young people are unlikely to have the same experience and capacity as adults to realise the effect of their actions on other people or to appreciate the pain and distress caused and because a young person is likely to be less able to resist temptation, especially where peer pressure is exerted (SGC(Y) 3.1) but:

(1) where deterrence may be a factor in the case of an adult, it is necessary to balance that aspect against the youth of the offender (*R. v Marriott* (1995) 16 Cr. App. R. (S.) 428); but
(2) in the case of very serious offences, however, the room for reduction is limited, indeed there may be none at all (*R. v Dodds, The Times,* 28 January 1997).

See generally AGE OF OFFENDER.

As to offenders of advanced age, see *R. v W (Sentencing: Age of defendant), The Times,* 26 October 2000.

Offender's ill-health

Questions of an offender's life expectancy or risks of his deterioration in prison will usually be a matter for the administrative authorities, thus: **24-053**

(1) if the offender is HIV positive or has otherwise a reduced life expectancy, this should not generally affect the sentence;
(2) the fact that the offender has a serious medical condition and is not easily treatable in prison does not automatically entitle him to a shorter sentence; but
(3) that does not, however, mean that a judge in sentencing must ignore the impact of ill-health on a man of a certain age.

(*R. v Bernard* [1997] 1 Cr. App. R. (S.) 135; *R. v Price* [2009] EWCA Crim 2918; [2010] 2 Cr. App. R. (S.) 44)

As to the wholly exceptional case in which it is claimed that the very fact of imprisonment may create a breach of ECHR art.3, see *R. v Qazi* [2010] EWCA Crim 2579; [2011] 2 Cr. App. R. (S.) 8; *R. v Hall* [2013] EWCA Crim 82; [2013] Crim. L.R. 426.

Cultural background

The cultural background of an offender is not necessarily relevant to sentence (*Attorney General's Reference (No.1 of 2011) (R. v A)* [2011] EWCA Crim 930; [2011] 2 Cr. App. R. (S.) 112). **24-054**

Foreign jurisdictions: deportation, etc.

24-055 The level of sentence which might be imposed in other jurisdictions is irrelevant (*R. v Maguire* [1997] 1 Cr. App. R. (S.) 130).

The fact that the offender will eventually be deported is not a matter which goes to reducing the length of a sentence of imprisonment. There are procedures at the end of a sentence for considering whether the Home Secretary will adopt a recommendation to deport (*R. v Chen* [2001] EWCA Crim 885; *The Times,* 17 April 2001).

As to foreign offenders serving sentences in English prisons, that is a comparatively small consideration where deterrent sentences are merited (see DEPORTATION).

Deterrence; prevalence of offence

24-056 Prevalence of a particular offence is a relevant factor, however:

(1) seriousness of a particular case should be judged on its own facts (see SGC Definitive Guideline, Overarching Principles: Seriousness) and an offender should not be further penalised for committing an offence of a particular type; and
(2) the court must have supporting evidence of local prevalence. *R. v Moss* [2010] EWCA Crim 1097; [2011] 1 Cr. App. R. (S.) 31.

Prevalence of an offence within the jurisdiction of a particular court is a more problematic matter. In *R. v Williamson* [2007] EWCA Crim 44 the CACD said it is justifiable in principle to include in appropriate cases a deterrent element in sentence to reflect local circumstances and needs, where those are either proved by evidence or well-known to the judge from local or regional knowledge, provided that any increase in sentence to reflect this element is proportionate; that is, should bear a reasonable relationship to the length of the sentence appropriate to the inherent seriousness of the offence.

The SGC Guidelines (held to be the proper course in *R. v Oosthuizen* [2005] EWCA Crim 1978; [2006] 1 Cr. App. R. (S.) 7; and *R. v Lanham* [2008] EWCA Crim 2450; [2009] 1 Cr. App. R. (S.) 105 and despite criticism in *R. v Stockdale* [2005] EWCA Crim 1582) emphasise the need for the judge both:

(a) to have supporting evidence from an external source to justify claims that a particular crime is prevalent in his area; and
(b) to be satisfied that there is a compelling need to treat the offence more seriously than elsewhere.

A community impact statement may be prepared by the police to make the court aware of particular crime trends in the local area and the impact of these on the local community.

Such statements:

- must be in proper form, that is a witness statement made under CJA 1967 s.9 or an expert's report; and served in good time upon the accused's solicitor or the accused, if he is not represented; and
- should be considered and taken into account by the judge prior to passing sentence; the statement should be referred to in the course of the sentencing hearing and/or in the sentencing remarks; subject to the judge's discre-

tion, the contents of the statement may be summarised or read out in open court.

The judge must pass what he considers to be the appropriate sentence having regard to the circumstances of the offence and of the offender, taking into account, so far as he considers it appropriate, the impact on the local community; opinions as to what the sentence should be are therefore not relevant. If, despite the advice, opinions as to sentence are included in the statement, the judge should pay no attention to them.

Except where inferences can properly be drawn from the nature of or circumstances surrounding the offence, the judge must not make assumptions unsupported by evidence about the effects of an offence on the local community.

It will not be appropriate for a Community Impact Statement to be made after disposal of the case but before an appeal.

(*CPD* VII Sentencing H. Community Impact Statements paras 1–7).

Amount and purity of drugs

With regard to assessing the amount and purity of drugs in reference to sentences for drugs offences, see *R. v Morris* [2001] 1 Cr. App. R. 25. **24-057**

Views of victim

As to the relevance of the views of victims of crime, see VICTIM PERSONAL STATEMENTS. **24-058**

Families of offenders

For the effect of sentence on innocent members of the offender's family, see *R. v Mills* [2002] EWCA Crim 26; [2002] 2 Cr. App. R. (S.) 52 followed in *R. v Bishop* [2011] EWCA Crim 1446 and *R. v Cerrone* [2011] EWCA Crim 2895. The CACD declined to accept a generalised submission that the application of an otherwise correct sentencing approach should be disregarded solely on the basis that there are young children from whom a defendant is the principal carer. This would nevertheless be a consideration. **24-059**

11. Step 8—Following sentencing guidelines

General

In passing sentence, the judge must follow any relevant sentencing guidelines, unless he is satisfied that it would be contrary to the interests of justice to do so. See SENTENCING GUIDELINES. **24-060**

Role of prosecutor

The advocate for the Crown ought not to be prevented from advising the judge on the legal aspects of any sentence that he might be contemplating, whether at the judge's invitation or otherwise. He should be immediately familiar with the maximum sentences for the offence(s) which are being dealt with, and with the preconditions for any form of sentence which the judge proposes to impose (see generally *Attorney General's Reference (No.7 of 1997)* [1998] 1 Cr. App. R. (S.) **24-061**

268; *R. (on the application of Inner London Probation Service) v Tower Bridge Magistrates Court* [2001] EWHC 401 (Admin); [2002] 1 Cr. App. R. (S.) 43). In particular he must bring to the judge's attention:

(1) any matters of law relating to sentence; and
(2) any sentencing guideline cases, making copies available to the judge.

(See *R. v Pepper* [2005] EWCA Crim 1181; [2006] 1 Cr. App. R. (S.) 29 where the authorities are reviewed.)

He also has functions in relation to disputed issues of fact (see GUILTY PLEAS) and as to the acceptance or otherwise of pleas, (see GOODYEAR INDICATION).

If the judge makes an error in sentencing, particularly in relation to his powers, the advocate, whether for the Crown or for the defence, should be alive to the possibility of rectifying the sentence under the slip rule (SA 2020 s.385 (see VARIATION OF SENTENCE)).

The DPP, on 22 February 2010, issued an updated edition of the Code for Crown Prosecutors.

12. Steps 9 and 10—Ancillary orders and surcharge

24-062 Consider whether any other additional ancillary order should be attached to the sentence. See ANCILLARY ORDERS.

Comply with the duty to order a surcharge (see SURCHARGES), and an order for the payment criminal court costs (see COSTS AND ASSESSMENT).

13. Step 11—Spelling it out

Duty to give reasons for and to explain effect of sentence

24-063 A judge passing sentence on an offender must:

(1) state in open court, in ordinary language and in general terms, his reasons for deciding on the sentence; and
(2) explain to the offender in ordinary language:
    (a) the effect of the sentence;
    (b) the effects of non-compliance with any order that the offender is required to comply with and that forms part of the sentence;
    (c) any power of the court to vary or review any order that forms part of the sentence; and
    (d) the effects of failure to pay a fine, if the sentence consists of or includes a fine.

He must also identify any definitive sentencing guidelines relevant to the offender's case and:

(i) explain how he discharged any duty imposed on it by SA 2020 ss.59–61 to follow guidelines (unless satisfied it would be contrary to the interests of justice to do so); and
(ii) where he is satisfied that it would be contrary to the interests of justice to follow the guidelines, state why.

Particular cases

24-064 Where:

(1) as a result of taking into account any matter referred to in CJA 2003 s.144(1) (guilty pleas), the judge imposes a punishment on the offender which is less severe than the punishment he would otherwise have imposed he must state that fact; or
(2) the offender is under 18 and the judge imposes a sentence that may only be imposed in the offender's case if the court is of the opinion mentioned in:
 (a) SA 2020 s.180 (youth rehabilitation order with intensive care and supervision or with fostering); or
 (b) SA 2020 s.230(2) (discretionary custodial sentence),

he must state why he is of that opinion.

Effect of custodial sentences

The judge should in passing a custodial sentence, explain the practical effect of the statutory provisions governing the particular term, and ensure that it is understood not only by the offender, but also by any victim and by any member of the public present in court, or "who reads a full report of the proceedings" (see *R. v Hennessey* [2000] Crim. L.R. 602). **24-065**

As to the general requirement to spell out the effect of an accused's plea of guilty, see DISCOUNTS ON SENTENCE.

Forms of words

In complying with the statutory requirements as to certain types of offences (24-064), forms of words were suggested both in former PD 2004 Annex C and in Sentencing—Forms of Words issued by the former JSB in the Crown Court Bench Book, the last edition of which is dated January 2006 and applied to pre-CJA 2003 sentences. There is a new Criminal Bench Book "The Crown Court Compendium" written by Sir David Maddison, Professor David Ormerod KC, HH Tonking and HH Wait. Part II: Sentencing deals with the changes to sentencing law arising from the ORA 2014, CJCA 2015 and other recent legislative changes. It sets out all of the sentences and orders commonly made in the Crown Court (though does not pretend to describe every possible order) and in most cases provides an example of sentencing remarks. The most recent version, updated to December 2020, has been edited by HHJ Picton, Professor David Ormerod KC (Hon), HHJ Lynn Tayton KC, HHJ Rajeev Shetty, HHJ Cooper, HHJ David Aubrey, HHJ Greg Dickinson KC, Recorder Andrew Smith KC and Lyndon Harris. **24-066**

14. Procedure after sentence

Suspending sentence pending appeal

There is no obligation on a court to suspend the operation of any sentence or order where an offender gives notice of appeal, but: **24-067**

(1) it is the usual practice not to enforce a fine pending the result of any appeal;
(2) there is a power, but no obligation, to suspend a driving disqualification (RTA 1988 s.39; MCA 1980 s.113(1)); and
(3) there is a power but no obligation, to grant bail to a person sentenced to a custodial term (see APPEALS FROM THE CROWN COURT).

A compensation order (see COMPENSATION ORDERS), and in certain cases, a restitution order (see RESTITUTION ORDERS), are suspended until the expiration of the time for appeal has expired, or, where notice is given, until the determination of the appeal.

Rescission and alteration

24-068 Ordinarily, a sentence imposed or other order made by the Crown Court when dealing with an offender, takes effect from the beginning of the day on which it is imposed, unless the judge otherwise directs, but:

(1) as a court of record, the Crown Court has an inherent jurisdiction to rectify mistakes in its record (*R. v Saville* [1981] Q.B. 12); and, more importantly
(2) a sentence or order may be varied or rescinded under SA 2020 subs.385(2) and (3), within the 56-day statutory time limit; and
(3) a reduced sentence passed in pursuance of an offender's agreement to give information to the authorities may be reviewed under SOCPA 2005 s.74.

(See VARIATION OF SENTENCE)

25. DEFERRED PROSECUTION AGREEMENTS

1. General

Introduction

CCA 2013 s.45 and Sch.17 introduced a procedure by which a "designated" prosecutor may enter into what is called a "deferred prosecution agreement" ("DPA") with a "person" whom he is considering prosecuting for an "alleged offence" of a specified nature, under which: **25-001**

(1) that person agrees to comply with the requirements imposed on him by the agreement; and, in return for which;
(2) the prosecutor agrees that, upon approval of the agreement by the court, the proceedings against that person for the alleged offence, are suspended.

The following are "designated prosecutors"—the DPP, the DSFO and any prosecutor designated by an order made by the Secretary of State (CCA 2013 Sch.17 para.3).

A designated prosecutor must exercise personally the power to enter into a DPA and, accordingly, any enactment that enables a function of a designated prosecutor to be exercised by a person other than the prosecutor concerned does not apply. If, however, the designated prosecutor is unavailable, the power to enter into a DPA may be exercised personally by a person authorised in writing by him.

Procedure is under CrimPR 11.

Prosecutors are required to have regard to the DPA Code issued on 11 February 2014 by the DPP and the DSFO, pursuant to CCA 2013 Sch.17 para.6(1).

The first DPA

The first DPA was approved on 30 November 2015 (see *SFO v Standard Bank Plc (Final)* 2015 WL 10460418; [2016] Lloyd's Rep. F.C. 102) following a preliminary hearing on 4 November 2015 (see *SFO v Standard Bank Plc (Preliminary)* 2015 WL 10382767; [2016] Lloyd's Rep. F.C. 91). The President of the QBD Sir Brian Leveson stated that this first DPA "should create the benchmark against which future such applications may fall to be assessed". **25-002**

The approved judgment for the preliminary hearing contains:

(1) a useful summary of the applicable law and procedure (paragraphs 1–7);
(2) a fact-specific analysis of how the interests of justice test should be applied (paragraphs 24-35); and
(3) a detailed consideration of the appropriateness of each term of the agreement (paragraphs 36-63); see also the approved judgment for the final hearing at paragraphs 12–20.

A second DPA was approved in July 2016 (*SFO v XYZ Ltd* [2016] Lloyd's Rep. F.C. 509) and the judgment of Sir Brian Leveson PQBD includes a summary of factors relevant to the interests of justice test (see 25-011).

In January 2017 a third DPA was approved (*SFO v Rolls Royce Plc* [2017] Lloyd's Rep. F.C. 249). The judgment includes a fact-specific analysis of the interests of justice test and the factors relevant to calculating the appropriate financial penalty.

In April 2017, the SFO entered into a DPA with Tesco Plc (*SFO v Tesco Stores Ltd* [2017] 4 WLUK 558; [2017] WL 10765126. In July 2019 a DPA was entered into with Serco Geografix Ltd *(SFO v Serco Geografix Ltd)* [2019] 7 WLUK 45; [2019] WL 02895020. In 2020 DPAs were entered into between the SFO and Airbus SE (*SFO v Airbus SE* [2020] 1 WLUK 435), between the SFO and G4S (*SFO v G4S Care and Justice Services (UK) Ltd* [2020] 7 WLUK 303), and between the SFO and Airline Services Ltd. The SFO entered into several further DPAs in 2021. In *Serious Fraud Office v Amec Foster Wheeler Energy Ltd* [2021] 6 WLUK 664; [2021] Lloyd's Rep. F.C. 353 the Crown Court approved a deferred prosecution agreement with a total financial sanction of around £99,910,423 plus costs of £3,367,088, in relation to the potential criminal liability of the respondent company for a number of counts of conspiracy to make corrupt payments and one count of failure to prevent bribery.

Persons who may enter into a DPA with a prosecutor

25-003 The "person" (P) who may be a party to a DPA may be a body corporate, a partnership or an unincorporated association, but may *not* be *an individual* (CCA 2013 Sch.17 para.4).

In the case of a DPA between a prosecutor and a partnership:

(1) the DPA must be entered into in the name of the partnership (and not in that of any of the partners); and
(2) any money payable under the DPA must be paid out of the funds of the partnership.

In the case of a DPA between a prosecutor and an unincorporated association:

(1) the DPA must be entered into in the name of the association (and not in that of any of its members); and
(2) any money payable under the DPA must be paid out of the funds of the association.

(CCA 2013 Sch.17 para.4)

A DPA is a discretionary tool created by the Act to provide a way of responding to alleged criminal conduct. The prosecutor may invite P to enter into negotiations to agree a DPA as an alternative to prosecution. In order to enter a DPA the prosecutor must apply an evidential stage and a public interest stage as provided by the DPA Code (see 25-001). The Code at para.2.1 makes it clear that an invitation to negotiate a DPA is a matter for the prosecutor's discretion. The proposed accused has no right to be invited to negotiate a DPA. The SFO and the CPS are first and foremost prosecutors and it will only be in specific circumstances deemed by their Directors to be appropriate that they will decide to offer a DPA instead of pursuing the full prosecution of the alleged conduct. In many cases, criminal prosecution will continue to be the appropriate course of action. An invitation to enter DPA discussions is not a guarantee that a DPA will be offered at the conclusion of the discussions.

Offences in relation to which a DPA may be entered into

The offences in relation to which a DPA may be entered, are the following (CCA 2001 Sch.17 Pt.2): 25-004

Common law offences

15 Conspiracy to defraud.

16 Cheating the public revenue.

Statutory offences

17 An offence under any of the following sections of the Theft Act 1968:

(a) s.1 (theft);
(b) s.17 (false accounting);
(c) s.20 (suppression, etc. of documents);
(d) s.24A (dishonestly retaining a wrongful credit).

18 An offence under any of the following sections of the Customs and Excise Management Act 1979:

(a) s.68 (offences in relation to exportation of prohibited or restricted goods);
(b) s.167 (untrue declarations, etc.);
(c) s.170 (fraudulent evasion of duty, etc.).

19 An offence under any of the following sections of the Forgery and Counterfeiting Act 1981:

(a) s.1 (forgery);
(b) s.2 (copying a false instrument);
(c) s.3 (using a false instrument);
(d) s.4 (using a copy of a false instrument);
(e) s.5 (offences relating to money orders, share certificates, passports, etc.).

20 An offence under s.450 of the Companies Act 1985 (destroying, mutilating, etc. company documents).

21 An offence under s.72 of the Value Added Tax Act 1994 (fraudulent evasion of VAT).

22 An offence under any of the following sections of the Financial Services and Markets Act 2000:

(a) s.23 (contravention of prohibition of carrying on regulated activity unless authorised or exempt);
(b) s.25 (contravention of restrictions on financial promotion);
(c) s.85 (prohibition of dealing etc. in transferable securities without approved prospectus);
(d) s.346 (provision of false or misleading statements to auditor or actuary);
(e) s.397 (misleading statements and practices);
(f) s.398 (misleading the FSA).

23 An offence under any of the following sections of POCA 2002:

(a) s.327 (concealing, etc. criminal property);
(b) s.328 (arrangements facilitating acquisition etc. of criminal property);
(c) s.329 (acquisition, use and possession of criminal property);
(d) s.330 (failing to disclose knowledge or suspicion of money laundering);
(e) s.333A (tipping off).

24 An offence under any of the following sections of the Companies Act 2006:

(a) s.658 (general rule against limited company acquiring its own shares);
(b) s.680 (prohibited financial assistance);
(c) s.993 (fraudulent trading).

25 An offence under any of the following sections of the Fraud Act 2006:

(a) s.1 (fraud);
(b) s.6 (possession, etc. of articles for use in fraud);
(c) s.7 (making or supplying articles for use in fraud);
(d) s.11 (obtaining services dishonestly).

26 An offence under any of the following sections of the Bribery Act 2010:

(a) s.1 (bribing another person);
(b) s.2 (being bribed);
(c) s.6 (bribery of foreign public officials);
(d) s.7 (failure of commercial organisations to prevent bribery).

27 An offence under reg.45 of the Money Laundering Regulations 2007 (SI 2007/2157).

Ancillary offences

28 Any ancillary offence relating to an offence specified in this Part.

Interpretation of this Part

29 "Ancillary offence", in relation to an offence, means:

(a) aiding, abetting, counselling or procuring the commission of the offence;
(b) an offence under SCA 2007 Pt 2 (encouraging or assisting crime) in relation to the offence;
(c) attempting or conspiring to commit the offence.

30 This Schedule applies in relation to conduct occurring before the commencement of this Schedule as if an offence specified in this Part included any corresponding offence under the law in force at the time of the conduct (and for the purposes of this paragraph, the common law offence of inciting the commission of another offence is to be treated as an offence corresponding to an offence under SCA 2007 Pt 2).

Transitional provision

25-005 Conduct constituting an alleged offence that occurred before the relevant commencement day may be taken into account for the purposes of these provisions. The "relevant commencement day" here means:

(1) in a case where the alleged offence is an offence that is specified in Pt 2 when this Schedule comes into force, the day on which this Schedule comes into force (24 February 2014);
(2) in a case where the alleged offence is an offence that is subsequently added to Pt 2 (whether by order under para.31 or otherwise), the day when the enactment adding that offence to Pt 2 comes into force.

(CCA 2013 Sch.17 para.39)

Effect of DPA on court proceedings

25-006 Proceedings in respect of the alleged offence are instituted by the prosecutor preferring a bill of indictment in the Crown Court charging the person with the alleged offence, in the nature of a voluntary bill (see AJ(MP)A 1933 s.2(2)(ba) (bill of indictment preferred with consent of Crown Court judge following DPA approval), and generally INDICTMENTS).

As to procedure, see 25-011 and following.

Cases coming before the court must be referred to the President of the King's Bench Division who will allocate the matter to a judge from a list of judges approved by the Lord Chief Justice. Only the allocated judge may thereafter hear any matter or make any decision in relation to that case (*CPD* XIII B.2).

As soon as proceedings are instituted they are to be automatically suspended and the suspension may only be lifted on an application to the Crown Court by the prosecutor; no such application may be made at any time when the DPA is in force.

At a time when such proceedings are suspended no other person may prosecute that person for the alleged offence.

(CCA 2013 Sch.17 para.2)

Content of DPA

A DPA must contain a statement of facts relating to the alleged offence, which may include admissions made by P. It must specify an expiry date, which is the date on which the DPA ceases to have effect if it has not already been terminated (CCA 2013 Sch.17 para.5). See also DPA Code 7.1. **25-007**

The requirements that a DPA may impose on P include, but are not limited to, the following:

- to pay to the prosecutor a financial penalty;
- to compensate victims of the alleged offence;
- to donate money to a charity or other third party;
- to disgorge any profits made by P from the alleged offence;
- to implement a compliance programme or make changes to an existing compliance programme relating to P's policies or to the training of P's employees or both;
- to cooperate in any investigation related to the alleged offence; and
- to pay any reasonable costs of the prosecutor in relation to the alleged offence or the DPA.

The DPA may impose time limits within which P must comply with the requirements imposed on it.

The amount of any financial penalty agreed between the prosecutor and P must be broadly comparable to the fine that a court would have imposed on conviction for the alleged offence following a guilty plea.

A DPA may include a term setting out the consequences of a failure by P to comply with any of its terms.

Any money received by a prosecutor, under a term of a DPA that provides for P to pay a financial penalty to the prosecutor or to disgorge profits made from the alleged offence, is to be paid into the Consolidated Fund.

In cases where neither limb of the evidential stage can be met by the conclusion of any DPA negotiations and it is not considered appropriate to continue the criminal investigation, the prosecutor may consider whether a Civil Recovery Order is appropriate, bearing in mind the Attorney General's guidance to prosecuting bodies on their asset recovery powers under the Proceeds of Crime Act 2002, issued 5 November 2009 (DPA Code 1.6).

Discontinuance of proceedings on expiry of DPA

25-008 If a DPA remains in force until its expiry date, then after the expiry of the DPA the proceedings instituted under Sch.17 para.2 will be discontinued by the Prosecutor giving notice. As to procedure see 25-023.

Where proceedings are discontinued in that manner, fresh criminal proceedings may not be instituted against P for the alleged offence. However, this does not prevent fresh proceedings from being instituted against P in a case where, after a DPA has expired, the prosecutor finds that, during the course of the negotiations for the DPA, P:

(1) provided inaccurate, misleading or incomplete information to the prosecutor; and
(2) knew or ought to have known that the information was inaccurate, misleading or incomplete.

A DPA is not to be treated as having expired for the above purposes if, on the expiry date specified in the DPA:

(a) an application made by the prosecutor under para.9 (breach of agreement; see 25-018) has not yet been decided by the court;
(b) following an application under para.9 the court has invited the parties to agree proposals to remedy any failure to comply, but the parties have not yet reached an agreement; or
(c) the parties have agreed proposals to remedy failure to comply following an invitation of the court under para.9(3)(a) but P has not yet complied with the agreement.

(CCA 2013 Sch.17 para.11(1)–(4))

Further provisions

25-009 In the case mentioned in Sch.17 para.11(4)(a) (see (a) of 25-008), if the judge:

(i) decides that P has not failed to comply with the terms of the DPA, or that it has failed to comply but he does not take action under para.9(3), the DPA is to be treated as expiring when the application is decided;
(ii) terminates the DPA, the DPA is to be treated as not having remained in force until its expiry date and 25-008 does not therefore apply;
(iii) invites the parties to agree proposals to remedy P's failure to comply, the DPA is to be treated as expiring when the parties have reached such an agreement and P has complied with it.

In the case mentioned in para.11(4)(b) (see (b) in 25-008), the DPA is to be treated as expiring when the parties have reached an agreement and P has complied with it.

In the case mentioned in para.11(4)(c) (see (c) in 25-008), the DPA is to be treated as expiring when P complies with the agreement.

(CCA 2013 Sch.17 para.11(5)–(8))

Where proceedings are discontinued under these provisions the prosecutor must publish the fact that the proceedings have been discontinued, and publish details of P's compliance with the DPA (unless he is prevented from doing so by an enactment or by an order of the court under para.12 (postponement of publication to avoid prejudicing proceedings), as to which see 25-017).

Use of material in criminal proceedings

Where a DPA between a prosecutor and P has been approved by a judge of the Crown Court, the statement of facts contained in the DPA is, in any criminal proceedings brought against P for the alleged offence, to be treated as an admission by it under CJA 1967 s.10. **25-010**

Where a prosecutor and P have entered into negotiations for a DPA but the DPA has not been approved by the judge, the material described below (drafts of the DPA, etc.) may only be used in evidence against P in the following circumstances:

(1) on a prosecution for an offence consisting of the provision of inaccurate, misleading or incomplete information; or
(2) on a prosecution for some other offence where in giving evidence the "person" concerned makes a statement inconsistent with the material.

Material may not, however, be used against that "person" by virtue of this provision unless evidence relating to it is adduced, or a question relating to it is asked, by or on behalf of that "person" in the proceedings arising out of the prosecution.

The "material" referred to is:

(a) material that shows that the "person" entered into negotiations for a DPA including in particular:
    (i) any draft of the DPA;
    (ii) any draft of a statement of facts intended to be included within the DPA; and
    (iii) any statement indicating that the "person" entered into such negotiations;
(b) material that was created solely for the purpose of preparing the DPA or statement of facts.

(CCA 2013 Sch.17 para.13)

2. PROCEDURE

General

Court approval of a DPA follows this two stage procedure: **25-011**

(1) a *preliminary hearing*, after the commencement of negotiations between the prosecutor and P in respect of an agreement, and before any terms are agreed, at which the prosecutor must apply for a declaration that:
    (a) entering into a DPA with P is likely to be in the interests of justice; and
    (b) the proposed terms of the DPA are fair, reasonable and proportionate; and
(2) a *final hearing*, when the prosecutor and P have agreed the terms of an agreement, at which the prosecutor must apply for a declaration that:
    (a) the DPA is in the interests of justice; and
    (b) the terms are fair, reasonable and proportionate,

but the prosecutor may not make this application unless the judge has made a declaration at a preliminary hearing.

A DPA only comes into force when it is approved by a judge of the Crown Court making a declaration at a final hearing.

(CCA 2013 Sch.17 paras 7(1), 8(1)–(3))

In *SFO v XYZ Ltd* [2016] Lloyd's Rep. F.C. 509 Sir Brian Leveson PQBD identified (at [15]) a number of factors relevant to the interests of justice test. These included:

- (i) the seriousness of the offence;
- (ii) the importance of incentivising the exposure and self-reporting of corporate wrongdoing;
- (iii) any history of similar conduct;
- (iv) the attention paid to corporate compliance before, during and after the offending;
- (v) the extent to which the entity had changed its culture and its personnel; and
- (vi) the impact of prosecution on employees and others innocent of any misconduct.

Application to approve a proposal to enter an agreement

25-012 A prosecutor wanting a judge to approve a proposal to enter an agreement must:

- (1) apply in writing *after* the commencement of negotiations between the parties *but before* the terms of agreement have been settled; and
- (2) serve the application on the Crown court officer and the accused.

The application must (CrimPR 11.3(3)):

- (a) identify the parties to the proposed agreement;
- (b) attach a proposed indictment setting out such of the offences listed in CCA 2013 Sch.17 Pt 2 as the prosecutor is considering;
- (c) include or attach a statement of facts proposed for inclusion in the agreement, which must give full particulars of each alleged offence, including details of any alleged financial gain or loss;
- (d) include any information about the accused that would be relevant to sentence in the event of conviction for the offence or offences;
- (e) specify the proposed expiry date of the agreement;
- (f) describe the proposed terms of the agreement, including details of any:
  - (i) monetary penalty to be paid by accused, and the time within which any such penalty is to be paid;
  - (ii) compensation, reparation or donation to be made by the accused, the identity of the recipient of any such payment and the time within which any such payment is to be made;
  - (iii) surrender of profits or other financial benefit by the accused, and the time within which any such sum is to be surrendered;
  - (iv) arrangement to be made in relation to the management or conduct of the accused's business;
  - (v) co-operation required of the accused in any investigation related to the offence or offences;
  - (vi) other action required of the accused;
  - (vii) arrangement to monitor the accused's compliance with a term;
  - (viii) consequence of the accused's failure to comply with a term; and
  - (ix) prosecution costs to be paid by the accused, and the time within which any such costs are to be paid;
- (g) in relation to those terms, explain how they comply with:
  - (i) the requirements of the DPA Code; and
  - (ii) any sentencing guidelines or guideline cases which apply;

(h) contain or attach the accused's written consent to the proposal; and
(i) explain why:
  (i) entering into an agreement is likely to be in the interests of justice; and
  (ii) the proposed terms of the agreement are fair, reasonable and proportionate.

If the proposed statement of facts includes assertions that the accused does not admit, the application must specify them and explain why that is immaterial for the purposes of the proposal to enter an agreement (CrimPR 11.3(4)).

See DPA Code 9.1.

Determination at a hearing; general

The judge must determine an application to which these provisions apply at a hearing, which: **25-013**

(1) must be in private, under CrimPR 11.3 (application to approve a proposal to enter an agreement);
(2) may be in public or private, under CrimPR 11.4 (application to approve the terms of an agreement), CrimPR 11.6 (application to approve a variation of the terms of an agreement)—25-021 or CrimPR 11.9 (application to postpone the publication of information by the prosecutor—25-020); and
(3) must be in public, under CrimPR 11.5 (application on breach of agreement—25-018) or CrimPR 11.7 (application to lift suspension of prosecution—25-022),

unless the judge otherwise directs.

If at a hearing in private to which CrimPR 11.4 or 11.6 applies the judge approves the agreement or the variation proposed, he must announce his decision and reasons at a hearing in public.

The judge will not determine an application under CrimPR 11.3, 11.4 or 11.6 unless:

(a) both parties are present;
(b) the prosecutor provides the court with a written declaration that, for the purposes of the application:
  (i) the investigator enquiring into the alleged offence(s) has certified that no information has been supplied which he knows to be inaccurate, misleading or incomplete;
  (ii) the prosecutor has complied with the prosecution obligation to disclose material to the accused; and
(c) the accused provides the court with a written declaration that, for the purposes of the application:
  (i) he has not supplied any information which he knows to be inaccurate, misleading or incomplete; and
  (ii) the individual through whom the accused makes the declaration has made reasonable enquiries and believes the accused's declaration to be true.

The judge will not determine an application under CrimPR 11.5 or 11.7 in the prosecutor's absence, or in the absence of the accused unless the latter has had at least 20 business days in which to make representations.

The judge must give reasons for his decision on whether or not to make a declaration; any declaration must be made in private, and his reasons must be given in private.

The prosecutor may make a further application for a declaration if, following the previous application, the judge declined to make a declaration (CCA 2013 Sch.17 para.7(2)–(4)).

If a judge approves a proposal to enter an agreement the general rule is that any further application to which CrimPR 11 applies must be made to the same judge, but the court may direct other arrangements (CrimPR 11.2(5)).

Determination at a hearing; adjournments

25-014 The judge may adjourn a hearing:

(1) if either party asks, or on his own initiative;
(2) in particular, if he requires more information about:
  (a) the facts of an alleged offence;
  (b) the terms of the proposal to enter an agreement, or of a proposed agreement or variation of an agreement; or
  (c) the circumstances in which the prosecutor wants him to decide whether the accused has failed to comply with the terms of an agreement.

The judge may:

(i) hear an application under CrimPR 11.4 immediately after an application under CrimPR 11.3, if the court approves a proposal to enter an agreement;
(ii) hear an application under CrimPR 11.7 immediately after an application under CrimPR 11.5, if the court terminates an agreement.

Application to approve the terms of an agreement

25-015 Where:

(1) the judge has approved a proposal to enter an agreement on an application under CrimPR 11.3 (25-012); and
(2) the prosecutor wants him to approve the terms of the agreement,

the prosecutor must (CrimPR 11.4(2)):

(a) apply in writing as soon as practicable after the parties have settled the terms; and
(b) serve the application on the Crown Court officer and the accused.

The application must (CrimPR 11.4(3)):

(i) attach the agreement;
(ii) indicate in what respect, if any, the terms of the agreement differ from those proposed in the application under CrimPR 11.3;
(iii) contain or attach the accused's written consent to the agreement;
(iv) explain why the agreement is in the interests of justice, and why the terms of the agreement are fair, reasonable and proportionate;
(v) attach a draft indictment, charging the accused with the offence or offences the subject of the agreement; and
(vi) include any application for the hearing to be in private.

See DPA Code 10.1.

The final hearing

A hearing at which an application is finally determined may be held in private. The judge must give reasons for his decision on whether or not to make a declaration. If he decides to approve the DPA and make a declaration, he must do so, and give his reasons, in open court. **25-016**

Upon approval of the agreement by the judge, the prosecutor must, unless he is prevented from doing so by any enactment or by an order of the judge under CJA 2003 Sch.17 para.12 (25-017), publish:

(1) the DPA;
(2) the judge's declaration at the preliminary hearing (see 25-012) and the reasons for his decision to make the declaration;
(3) in a case where the judge initially declined to make a declaration, his reasons for that decision; and
(4) the judge's final hearing declaration and the reasons for his decision to make the declaration.

(CJA 2003 Sch.17 para.8(4)–(7))

If the judge approves the agreement and the draft indictment, the court officer will endorse a copy of the indictment with a note to identify it as the indictment approved by the court and the date of the court's approval. The case must be treated as if it has been suspended by order of the court (CrimPR 11.4(4)).

Order postponing publication of information by prosecutor

The judge may (CCA 2013 Sch.17 para.12) order that the publication of information by the prosecutor under paras 8(7), 9(5), (6), (7) or (8), 10(7) or (8) or 11(8) be postponed for such period as he considers necessary if it appears to him that postponement is necessary for avoiding a substantial risk of prejudice to the administration of justice in any legal proceedings. **25-017**

3. Breach, amendment and revocation

Breach

If, at any time when a DPA is in force, the prosecutor believes that P has failed to comply with the terms of the agreement, he may make an application to the Crown Court for a judge to decide whether, on the balance of probabilities, P has failed to comply with the terms of the agreement (CCA 2013 Sch.17 para.9; see DPA Code 12.1). **25-018**

Where the prosecutor:

(1) believes that P has failed to comply with the terms of an agreement; and
(2) wants a judge to decide:
    (a) whether P has failed to comply; and
    (b) if so, whether to terminate the agreement, or to invite the parties to agree proposals to remedy that failure,

he must (CrimPR 11.5):

(i) apply in writing, as soon as practicable after becoming aware of the grounds for doing so; and
(ii) serve the application on the Crown Court officer and on P.

The application must (CrimPR 11.5(3)) specify each respect in which the prosecutor believes P has failed to comply with the terms of the agreement, explaining the reasons for his belief, and a copy of any document containing evidence on which he relies must be attached.

If P wants to make representations in response to the application, he must serve the representations on the Crown Court officer and on the prosecutor, not more than 20 business days after service of the application (CrimPR 11.5(4)).

If the judge finds that P has failed to comply with the terms of the agreement, he may either invite the prosecutor and P to agree proposals to remedy P's failure to comply, or terminate the agreement, giving reasons for his decision(s) (CCA 2013 Sch.17 para.9(3)).

Publication of decisions

25-019 Unless the prosecutor is prevented from doing so by an enactment or by an order of the court under para.12 (postponement of publication to avoid prejudicing proceedings; see 25-017), where:

(1) the judge decides that P has not failed to comply with the terms of the agreement, the prosecutor must publish the judge's decision and his reasons for that decision;
(2) the judge invites the prosecutor and P to agree proposals to remedy failure to comply, the prosecutor must publish the judge's decisions and the reasons for them;
(3) the judge terminates a DPA the prosecutor must publish the fact that the DPA has been terminated following a failure by P to comply with the terms of the DPA and the judge's reasons for his decisions; and
(4) the prosecutor believes that P has failed to comply with the terms of the DPA, but decides not to make an application to the Crown Court, he must publish details relating to that decision, including the reasons for his belief that P has failed to comply and the reasons for his decision not to make an application to the court.

(CCA 2013 Sch.17 para.9(5)–(8))

Application to postpone publication

25-020 Where the prosecutor:

(1) makes an application under CrimPR 11.4 (application to approve the terms of an agreement), 11.5 (application on breach of agreement) or 11.6 (application to approve a variation of the terms of an agreement); or
(2) decides not to make an application under CrimPR 11.5, despite believing that the accused has failed to comply with the terms of the agreement; or
(3) gives a notice under CrimPR 11.8 (notice to discontinue prosecution),

a party who wants the court to order that the publication of information by the prosecutor about the court's or the prosecutor's decision be postponed must (CrimPR 11.9(2)):

(a) apply in writing, as soon as practicable and in any event before such publication occurs, serving the application on the Crown Court officer and the other party; and

(b) in the application, specify the proposed terms of the order, and for how long it should last, and explain why an order in the terms proposed is necessary.

Variation

At any time when a DPA is in force, the prosecutor and P may agree to vary its terms (CCA 2013 Sch.17 para.10(1)) if: 25-021

(1) a judge has invited the parties to vary the DPA under para.9(3)(a); or
(2) variation is necessary to avoid a failure by P to comply with its terms in circumstances that were not, and could not have been, foreseen by the prosecutor or P at the time the DPA was agreed.

When the prosecutor and P have agreed to vary the terms of a DPA, the prosecutor must apply to a judge of the Crown Court for a declaration that the variation is in the interests of justice and the terms of the DPA as varied are fair, reasonable and proportionate (CCA 2013 Sch.17 para.10(2)).

The prosecutor must (CrimPR 11.6(2)) apply in writing, as soon as practicable after the parties have settled the terms of the variation and serve the application on the Crown Court officer and on the accused. A hearing at which an application under this paragraph is determined may be held in private. The judge must give reasons for his decision on whether or not to make a declaration; if he decides to approve the variation and make a declaration, he must do so, and give his reasons, in open court.

The application must (CrimPR 11.6(3)):

(a) specify each variation proposed;
(b) contain or attach the accused's written consent to the variation;
(c) explain why the variation is in the interests of justice, and why the terms of the agreement as varied are fair, reasonable and proportionate; and
(d) include any application for the hearing to be in private.

A variation only takes effect when it is approved by the judge making a declaration.

Where the judge decides not to approve the variation, the prosecutor must publish the judge's decision and the reasons for it, unless he is prevented from doing so by an enactment or by an order of the court under para.12.

Where the judge decides to approve the variation the prosecutor must publish:

(i) the DPA as varied; and
(ii) the judge's declaration under this paragraph and the reasons for his decision to make the declaration,

unless he is prevented from doing so by an enactment, or by an order of the court under para.12.

(CCA 2013 Sch.17 para.10(7)–(8))

See DPA Code 13.1.

In *SFO v Tesco Stores Ltd* [2017] 4 WLUK 558; [2019] WL 00295772, the acquitted defendants in a related prosecution of former employees applied for the Statement of Facts to be amended because it ascribed wrongdoing to them and was inconsistent with their acquittals. Sir Brian Leveson P ruled that he had no jurisdiction to modify the terms of the DPA or its supporting Statement of Facts. Having approved the DPA, the role of the court was limited to enforcing its terms.

Application to lift suspension of prosecution

25-022 Where:

(1) a judge terminates an agreement before its expiry date; and
(2) the prosecutor wants him to lift the suspension of the prosecution that applied when the terms of the agreement were approved,

the prosecutor must (CrimPR 11.7(2)) apply in writing, as soon as practicable after the termination of the agreement and serve the application on the Crown Court officer and the accused.

An accused who wants to make representations in response to the application must serve the representations on the Crown Court officer and on the prosecutor, not more than 20 business days after service of the application (CrimPR 11.7(3)).

Notice to discontinue prosecution

25-023 Where an agreement expires, whether on its expiry date, or on a date treated as its expiry date, without having been terminated by the court, the prosecutor must (CrimPR 11.8(2)):

(1) as soon as practicable give notice in writing discontinuing the prosecution on the indictment approved by the court under CrimPR 11.4 (application to approve the terms of an agreement); and
(2) serve the notice on the Crown Court officer and the accused.

Duty of court officer, recording, etc.

25-024 Unless the judge otherwise directs, the Crown Court officer must (CrimPR 11.10(1)):

(1) arrange for the recording of proceedings on an application to which CrimPR 11 applies;
(2) arrange for the transcription of such a recording if a party wants a transcript, or (subject to CrimPR 11.10(2) below) anyone else wants such a transcript.

Again, unless the court otherwise directs, a person who transcribes a recording of proceedings must not supply anyone other than a party with a transcript of a recording of:

(a) a hearing in private; or
(b) a hearing in public to which reporting restrictions apply,

but subject to that, must supply any person with any transcript for which that person asks in accordance with the transcription arrangements made by the Crown Court officer, and on payment by that person of any fee prescribed.

The Crown Court officer will not (CrimPR 11.10(3)) identify either party to a hearing in private under CrimPR 11.3 (application to approve a proposal to enter an agreement) or CrimPR 11.4 (application to approve the terms of an agreement) in any notice displayed in the vicinity of the courtroom or in any other information published by the Crown Court officer.

Judge's power to vary requirements

25-025 The judge may (CrimPR 11.11):

(1) shorten or extend (even after it has expired) a time limit under CrimPR 11;
(2) allow there to be made orally an application under:
  (a) CrimPR 11.4 (application to approve the terms of an agreement); or
  (b) CrimPR 11.7 (application to lift suspension of prosecution),

where the judge exercises his power under CrimPR 11.2(7) to hear one application immediately after another.

A party who wants an extension of time must (CrimPR 11.11(2)) apply when serving the application or notice for which it is needed and explain the delay.

26. DEFERRING SENTENCE

QUICK GUIDE

1. THE MACHINERY OF DEFERMENT

General

26-001 The judge may make a "deferment order" to defer passing sentence on an offender until such date as he may specify, not being more than six months after the date of deferment is announced, for the purpose of enabling him, or any other judge to whom it falls to deal with him, to have regard to:

(1) his conduct after conviction (including, where appropriate, his making reparation for his offence); or
(2) any change in his circumstances.

The power to defer is exercisable only:

(a) where the offender consents;
(b) the judge is satisfied, having regard to the nature of the offence and the character and circumstances of the offender that it would be in the interests of justice to exercise the power; and
(c) may impose requirements as to his conduct during the period of the deferment that the judge considers it appropriate to impose.

(SA 2020 ss.3–13)

In relation to (a) and (c) the judge should ask the offender expressly if he consents to the deferment, and undertakes to comply with such requirements as are proposed (*R. v McQuaide* (1974) 60 Cr. App. R. 239).

Nothing in these provisions affects the judge's power:

(i) to bind over an offender to come up for judgment (see BIND OVER); or
(ii) to defer passing sentence for any other purpose for which he may lawfully do so.

(SA 2020 s.12)

In order to avoid the problems that often arise from the exercise of the power to defer sentence the judge should, if he intends to exercise his power under s.3, use the word "defer"; if he intends to impose, e.g. a common law bind over, or merely to adjourn, he should avoid the use of the expression "defer" altogether (*R. v Fairhead* (1975) 61 Cr. App. R. 102).

Deferment does not imply that the offence or offences were "not so serious that a non-custodial sentence cannot be justified". The judge may consider that a custodial sentence is justified, and yet defer, having regard to the offender's circumstances (*R. v Bray* (1991) 12 Cr. App. R. (S.) 705).

Approach to deferment; guidelines

26-002 SGC (New Sentences: CJA 2003) S.1 Pt 2 para.1.2.6 suggests that a sentence is likely to be deferred in very limited circumstances. It does, however, enable the judge to review the conduct of the offender before passing sentence, having first prescribed certain requirements, and it also provides several opportunities for an offender to have some influence over the sentence passed on him, as it:

(1) tests his commitment not to re-offend;
(2) gives him an opportunity to do something where progress can be shown within a short period; and
(3) provides him with an opportunity to behave or refrain from behaving in a particular way that will be relevant to his sentence.

Given the power to require undertakings and the ability to enforce those undertakings before the end of the period of deferral, SGC (New Sentences: CJA 2003) S.1 Pt 2 para.1.2.7 recommends that the decision to defer sentence should be reserved predominantly for a small group of cases at either the custody or the community sentence thresholds where the judge considers that there would be particular value in giving the offender the opportunities listed because, if the offender complies with the requirements, a different sentence will be justified at the end of the deferment period, i.e. a community sentence instead of a custodial sentence or a fine or discharge instead of a community sentence.

A deferment of sentence involves the message that compliance with whatever is required of the offender during the period of deferment will lead to a lesser category of sentence; it is appropriate only if such a sentence is a proper and realistic possibility on the facts of the case (*Attorney General's Reference (No.101 of 2006) (R. v P)* [2006] EWCA Crim 3335).

The guidance in this paragraph, though given in regard to adults, applies equally to young offenders.

Spelling it out

Given the need for clarity in the mind of the offender and the possibility of sentence by another court, the judge should: **26-003**

(1) give a clear indication of the sentence he would be minded to impose if he had not decided to defer sentence;
(2) ensure that the offender understands the consequences of failure to comply with the requirements during the deferral period;
(3) make clear the consequence of not complying with any requirements; and
(4) indicate the type of sentence he would be minded to impose, although under the pre-2003 provisions it was said that only a judge who is sure that he will deal with the case on the date to which sentence is deferred should give any hint as to the probable outcome of the case (*R. v Johnson* (1981) 145 J.P. 491).

(SGC (New Sentences: CJA 2003) S.1 Pt 2 para.1.2.9)

A judge who sits regularly at a particular location should reserve to himself the duty of dealing with the case on the date to which it is deferred, otherwise he ought to leave a note of his reasoning, or arrange for a transcript to be available at the point of sentence (*R. v Jacobs* (1976) 62 Cr. App. R. 116).

Nature of the requirements

The judge may impose any conditions during the period of deferment that he considers appropriate. **26-004**

These may be:

(1) specific requirements as set out in the provisions for community sentences (see COMMUNITY SENTENCES); or
(2) requirements that are drawn more widely.

The latter should be specific, measurable conditions so that the offender knows exactly what is required of him, and the court can assess compliance; the restriction on liberty should be limited to ensure that the offender has a reasonable expectation of being able to comply whilst maintaining his social responsibilities (SGC (New Sentences: CJA 2003) S.1 Pt 2 para.1.2.8).

The requirements which may be imposed by virtue of (2) include requirements as to the offender's residence during the whole or any part of the period of deferment.

Participation in restorative justice activities

26-005 Without prejudice to the generality of SA 2020 s.5(1)(b) (see 26-001), the requirements that may be imposed under that paragraph include restorative justice requirements, that is requirements to participate in an activity where:

(1) the participants consist of, or include, the offender and one or more of the victims; and
(2) which aims to maximise the offender's awareness of the impact of the offending concerned on the victims.

A "victim" here means a victim of, or other person affected by, the offending concerned.

The imposition of such a requirement requires, in addition to the offender's consent and undertaking, the consent of every other person who would be a participant in the activity concerned. A supervisor appointed under s.8 does not count as a proposed participant (SA 2020 s.7).

(See Pre-sentence restorative justice (RJ) (*https://www.gov.uk/government/uploads/system/uploads/attachment_data/file/312426/pre-sentence-restorative-justice.pdf* [Accessed September 2022]) issued by the Secretary of State for Justice. While this guidance is not legally binding, it is intended to inform practice. It provides an overview of the processes involved in delivering pre-sentence restorative justice.

The Guideline suggests that the judge will only defer passing sentence to allow for restorative justice activity to take place, possibly alongside other requirements, if:

(a) the offender pleads guilty; and
(b) both the victim and offender consent to take part.

If the offender pleads guilty and initial consent has not already been obtained from all participants then initial consent must be obtained. This may take place on the day of the hearing or, alternatively, the judge may adjourn to allow for initial consent to be sought or for a full risk assessment to be made.

If the judge defers passing sentence to allow for such activity to take place the sentence hearing date will need to be set with enough time to allow for the activity to take place. In most cases only one period of deferment can be granted therefore if it is not possible to complete the activity or the outcomes of the activity within the deferment period the activity or outcomes may form part of a sentence plan.

See also the Restorative Justice Council's Best Practice Guidance for Restorative Practice.

Where such a requirement is imposed, the duty under SA 2020 s.5(3) (to give copies of order) extends to every person who would be a participant in the activity concerned. The amendment made by para.3 does not apply in respect of offences committed before the amendment comes into force (SA 2020 ss.5(1)(c) and 7).

Appointment of supervisor

Where an offender has agreed to comply with any such requirements as are mentioned at 26-004, the judge may appoint: **26-006**

(1) a probation officer; or
(2) any other person whom he thinks appropriate in relation to him, to act as a supervisor, provided that that person consents.

The supervisor's duty is to:

(a) monitor the offender's compliance with the requirements; and
(b) provide the court to which it falls to deal with the offender in respect of the offence in question with such information it may require relating to the offender's compliance with the requirements.

Administrative provisions

Where sentence is deferred under these provisions the appropriate officer will forthwith give a copy of the order, setting out any requirements imposed: **26-007**

(1) to the offender;
(2) where a probation officer or a provider of probation services has been appointed to act as his supervisor, to the board; and
(3) where any other person has been appointed to act as his supervisor, to that person.

(SA 2020 s.5(3))

No power to remand: process

No question of remand arises and therefore no question of bail. Where a "deferment order" is made, and it is proposed to deal with him on the date originally specified, then, if the offender does not appear on the day, a summons may be issued requiring him to appear before the court at a time and place specified, or a warrant may be issued to arrest him and bring him before the court at a time and place specified in the warrant (SA 2020 s.5(4) and s.6). **26-008**

Ancillary orders; RT disqualification

Deferment being, in effect, a species of adjournment, there is no power to make any other ancillary order, other than: **26-009**

(1) a restitution order; or
(2) a road traffic interim disqualification (*R. v Dwyer* (1974) 60 Cr. App. R. 39).

A court may impose a curfew as a condition, but it does not form part of the eventual sentence, and such a requirement may not specify periods which fall outside the period of six months beginning with the day on which it is made, see *R. v A* [2011] EWCA Crim 2747; (2012) 176 J.P. 1.

Appeal and review

26-010 Deferment of sentence ranks as a "sentence" for the purposes of CAA 1968 s.50 (*Attorney General's Reference (No.22 of 1992)* [1993] 14 Cr. App. R. (S.) 435; *Attorney General's Reference (Nos 36 and 38)* [1999] Crim. L.R. 236). As such it may be referred to the CACD by the Attorney General for review under CJA 1988 s.36(10) (see APPEALS FROM THE CROWN COURT) if it appears to him to be unduly lenient (see *Attorney General's Reference (No.22 of 1992)* [1993] 14 Cr. App. R. (S.) 435).

Further proceedings

26-011 An offender upon whom sentence was deferred at the Crown Court in terms of SA 2020 ss.3 and 11 may be dealt with subsequently in respect of:

(1) a breach of a *requirement* of the deferment (26-013); or
(2) a conviction of a *further offence* during the period of deferment.

Where it is necessary for the offender to be brought before the court to be dealt with, the Crown Court may issue:

(a) a summons, requiring him to appear; or
(b) a warrant to bring him,

before the court at a specified time and place.

2. Conviction of further offence

26-012 Where sentence has been deferred on an offender in respect of one or more offences, and, during the period of deferment the offender is convicted in England or Wales of any "later offence", then:

(1) whether or not the offender is sentenced for the later offence during the period of deferment;
(2) the judge who passes sentence on the offender for the later offence, may also (if this has not already been done) deal with him for the offence or offences for which the passing of sentence was originally deferred, provided that where he is dealing with a sentence deferred by a magistrates' court, the judge is restricted to passing a sentence which the magistrates could have passed.

(SA 2020 s.10)

A magistrates' court has no jurisdiction to deal with a sentence deferred by the Crown Court.

Commission of a further offence is not strictly a "breach" of the deferment; as to the breach of a requirement undertaken by the offender, see 26-013.

As to the judge's powers in such proceedings, see 26-014.

3. Breach of undertaking(s)

General

26-013 A judge may deal with an offender who appears, or is brought before, the Crown Court before the end of the period of deferment, where:

(1) sentence was deferred in respect of the offender, at the Crown Court;
(2) the offender undertook to comply with one or more requirements imposed under s.3(2) in connection with the deferment;
(3) a supervisor has reported to the court that the offender has failed to comply with one or more of those requirements; and
(4) the judge is satisfied that that is the case.

(SA 2020 s.9)

To bring the offender before the court, a summons may be issued requiring him to appear before the court at a specified time and place, or a warrant to arrest him and bring him before the court.

The judge's powers on the breach are those set out in 26-014.

4. JUDGE'S POWERS OF SENTENCING

Where the passing of sentence on an offender has been deferred, the power of the judge to deal with the offender: **26-014**

(1) at the end of the period of deferment;
(2) on breach of an undertaking (26-013); and
(3) on further conviction (26-012),

or of any other court which deals with him under SA 2020 s.10(2):

(a) is a power to deal with him, in respect of the offence for which passing of sentence has been deferred, in any way in which the original court could have dealt with him if it had not deferred passing sentence; and
(b) sentence may not be deferred again under s.3, although where sentence has been deferred in respect of one or more, and a magistrates' court has dealt with the offender by committing him to the Crown Court, the judge's power to deal with him does include the power of deferring sentence on him as if he had just been convicted of the offence or offences on indictment.

(SA 2020 s.11(4))

Approach to sentence

It is obviously desirable that the matter of sentence on the due date should be put before the judge who made the "deferment order" in the first place, but if that is not possible, the second judge should be fully apprised of the first judge's views (*R. v Gurney* [1974] Crim. L.R. 472). The judge deferring sentence will be wise to order a transcript of his remarks. Again, the advocate who represented the offender on the earlier occasion should, if possible, appear for him on the date when sentence is to be passed (*R. v Ryan* [1976] Crim. L.R. 508). **26-015**

The judge needs to remind himself, or ascertain, the purpose of the deferment, and to determine whether the offender has substantially conformed, or attempted to conform, with the proper expectations of the judge who made the order.

If the offender:

(1) has done so, he may legitimately expect that an immediate custodial sentence will *not* be imposed;
(2) has not done so, the judge should be careful to state precisely in what respects he has failed.

(*R. v George* (1984) 79 Cr. App. R. 26)

The judge may take into consideration the extent to which the offender has complied with any requirements undertaken at the time of deferment. He should not, however, be influenced by proceedings which are pending but incomplete (*R. v Aquarius* (1989) 11 Cr. App. R. (S.) 431).

The judge is bound to approach the matter on a fair consideration of the offender's progress, if any, during the period of deferment.

Thus:

(a) it is wrong to impose a custodial sentence if the offender has fulfilled that which was required of him (*R. v Gilby* (1975) 61 Cr. App. R. 112; *R. v Head* (1976) 63 Cr. App. R.157; *R. v Smith* (1979) 1 Cr. App. R. (S.) 339); and

(b) if the report made to the court is not unfavourable, a substantial custodial sentence is probably not appropriate.

27. DEPORTATION

General

The power of the Secretary of State to order the deportation of a person who is not a British citizen derives from IA 1971 s.5(1) which provides that **27-001**

> "where a person is under ss.3(5) or 3(6) liable to deportation the Secretary of State may make a deportation order against him".

Section 3(5) and (6) provide that such a person shall be liable to deportation if:

(1) the Secretary of State deems his deportation to be conducive to the public good (s.3(5)(a));
(2) another person to whose family he belongs is or has been ordered to be deported (s.3(5)(b)); or
(3) after he has attained the age of 17, he is convicted of an offence punishable by imprisonment and is recommended for deportation by a court empowered by the 1971 Act to do so (s.3(6)); that is by any court having power to sentence a person to whom s.3(6) applies unless the court commits him to be sentenced or further dealt with for the offence by another court (s.6(1)).

UKBA 2007 s.32(4) provides that "for the purpose of IA 1971 s.3(5)(a) (above) the deportation of a foreign criminal is conducive to the public good". Thus any "foreign criminal" is liable to deportation under s.3(5)(a) and *must* be deported under s.5(1) by virtue of s.32(5) of the 2007 Act. There is no need for a court to be involved in this process at all (*R. v Kluxen* [2010] EWCA Crim 1081; [2011] 1 Cr. App. R. (S.) 39, in which the principles are extensively reviewed; see also *R. v Gheorghiu* [2013] EWCA Crim 281; [2013] 2 Cr. App. R. (S.) 74).

Note that SA 2020 s.386 simply directs the reader to IA 1971 s.6.

Effect on sentencing process

In view of the duty imposed on the Secretary of State (above), it is no longer necessary or appropriate for a judge to recommend the deportation of an offender coming within the definition of "foreign criminal" in UKBA 2007 (see 27-003); no useful purpose is served by doing so, nor is it necessary for the judge to explain during his sentencing remarks that he is not recommending the deportation of a "foreign criminal" because the 2007 Act applies, although he may do so if he wishes. **27-002**

The judge retains the power under IA 1971 s.6 to recommend deportation only where the conditions in UKBA 2007 s.33 are not fulfilled (*R. v Kluxen* [2010] EWCA Crim 1081; [2011] 1 Cr. App. R. (S.) 39, and see 27-003).

The prosecutor is responsible for informing the judge at the stage of sentence if the offender is liable to automatic deportation.

The provisions described as "automatic deportation" in fact do not necessarily lead to the automatic deportation of an offender; they lead to a *liability* to deportation. Judges should not, therefore, pass a shorter sentence, or a sentence different in nature from one they would otherwise have passed, on the basis they have been informed that the offender is liable to automatic deportation (see *Attorney General's Reference (No.41 of 2013)* [2013] EWCA Crim 1729; [2014] 1 Cr. App. R. (S.) 80; *R. v Mintchev* [2011] EWCA Crim 499; [2011] 2 Cr. App. R. (S.) 81); *R. v Alkidar* [2019] EWCA Crim 330; [2019] 2 WLUK 571).

Definition of "foreign criminals"

27-003 UKBA 2007 provides that the Secretary of State must make a deportation order in respect of a "foreign criminal" (unless one of the exceptions in s.33 applies (see 27-004)).

A "foreign criminal" is defined as a person:

(1) who is not a British citizen or an Irish citizen;
(2) who is convicted in the UK of an offence; and
(3) to whom condition 1 or condition 2 applies.

Condition 1 (the more likely to arise in practice) is that the person is sentenced to a period of imprisonment of at least 12 months for a *single* offence (not consecutive sentences amounting in aggregate to 12 months or more—see *R. v Kluxen* [2010] EWCA Crim 1081; [2011] 1 Cr. App. R. (S.) 39).

Condition 2 is that the offence is one specified under the Nationality, Immigration and Asylum Act 2002 s.72(4)(a) and the person is sentenced to imprisonment.

A reference to a person sentenced to a term of imprisonment of at least 12 months includes a reference to an offender who is sentenced to:

(a) detention in an institution other than a prison (including in particular in a hospital or an institution for young offenders) for at least 12 months; or
(b) imprisonment or detention for an indeterminate period (provided that it may last for 12 months).

A suspended sentence of imprisonment does not attract automatic deportation at the time the sentence is passed, but will if a court subsequently orders the sentence to take effect.

(UKBA 2007 ss.32(1), (5), 38)

The exceptions

27-004 The Secretary of State is obliged to make a deportation order unless one or more of the exceptions specified in s.33 applies, and it is for the Secretary of State to decide whether any of those exceptions does apply.

The exceptions are where:

(1) the offender falls within IA 1971 ss.7 and 8 (Commonwealth or Irish citizens (as to which see 27-008) and other exemptions);
(2) removal would breach a person's Convention rights or the UK's obligations under the Refugee Convention;
(3) removal would breach the foreign criminal's rights under the Community Treaties;
(4) the offender was under 18 on the date of conviction;
(5) the offender is subject to proceedings under the Extradition Act 2003; or
(6) the offender is subject to an order under MHA 1983, or the relevant Scottish legislation.

(UKBA 2007 s.33)

Judge's remaining power to recommend

The judge retains the power under IA 1971 s.6 to recommend deportation only where the conditions in UKBA 2007 s.33 are not fulfilled. **27-005**

If an offender who is not a British citizen does not come within conditions 1 or 2 above, he is not a "foreign criminal" as defined in s.32, where, e.g.:

(1) he does not receive any single custodial sentence of 12 months or more; or
(2) he receives a non-custodial sentence,

and the question arises as to whether the judge should recommend his deportation. The approach was summarised in *R. v Kluxen* [2010] EWCA Crim 1081; [2011] 1 Cr. App. R. (S.) 39 as follows:

(a) in cases to which UKBA 2007 does not apply, it will rarely be appropriate to recommend the deportation of the offender concerned, whether or not the offender is a citizen of the EU;
(b) if the judge is, exceptionally, considering recommending deportation, he should apply the *Nazari* test (below) in tandem with the *Bouchereau* test (see 27-006) (there being no practical difference between the two); and this is so whether the offender is or is not a citizen of the EU; but
(c) the judge should not take into account the matters set out in 27-007.

No recommendation should be made without full enquiry.

The test to be applied

The test to be applied when deciding whether or not to make a recommendation has been expressed differently in different cases: **27-006**

(1) in *R. v Nazari* [1980] 2 Cr. App. R. (S.) 84 the test laid down was "whether the continued presence of the offender in the UK was to its detriment" (in that case none of the offenders were citizens of the EU); and
(2) in *R. v Bouchereau* [1978] 66 Cr. App. R. 202 (where the CACD was dealing only with citizens of the EU) it was said that the judge must consider whether the offender's conduct constituted "a genuine and sufficiently serious threat to the requirements of public policy affecting one of the fundamental interests of society".

The *Bouchereau* test was based on a European Directive which had since been replaced, but having considered the terms of the new Directive (Directive 2004/38), the CACD (in *R. v Kluxen* [2010] EWCA Crim 1081; [2011] 1 Cr. App. R. (S.) 39) concluded that the test had survived.

The two tests are substantially the same, and a judge considering recommending an offender's deportation should apply substantially the same test whether the offender is or is not a citizen of the EU.

In the view of the CACD in *R. v Kluxen* [2010] EWCA Crim 1081; [2011] 1 Cr. App. R. (S.) 39:

(a) both tests set at a high level the bar that must be cleared before a recommendation for deportation can be made;
(b) it will be rare for either test to be satisfied in the case of an offender, none of whose offences merit a custodial sentence of 12 months or more; and
(c) the test may conceivably be satisfied where an offender repeatedly commits minor offences or commits a single offence involving the possession

or use of false identity documents, for which he receives a custodial sentence of less than 12 months.

See *R. v Ul Haq* [2013] EWCA Crim 1478; [2014] 1 Cr. App. R. (S.) 52 for an example of a case where the *Nazari* test was met (series of five sexual offences for which the offender was sentenced to a total of 12 months' imprisonment).

The judge should warn counsel if they are considering making a recommendation and the court must give reasons if it does so (*R. v Carmona* [2006] EWCA Crim 508; [2006] 2 Cr. App. R. (S.) 102).

The recommendation is part of the sentence and SA 2020 s.52 applies to it, requiring the judge to give, in general terms, and in ordinary language, the reasons for his decision. The bald statement "that your continued presence in this country is contrary to the public interest" without giving reasons, may not be sufficient (see *R. v Ahsan* [2006] EWCA Crim 1793).

Matters not to be taken into account

27-007 According to the CACD in *R. v Kluxen*, the judge should not take account of:

(1) the rights of the offender under ECHR (for the reasons explained in *R. v Carmona* [2006] EWCA Crim 508; [2006] 2 Cr. App. R. (S.) 102: that the Secretary of State and the Asylum and Immigration Tribunal are better placed than the judge to consider the offender's Convention rights);
(2) the effect that a recommendation for deportation might have on innocent persons not before the court, such as members of the offender's family; and
(3) the political situation in the country to which the offender might be deported.

Commonwealth and Irish citizens

27-008 A Commonwealth citizen or citizen of the Republic of Ireland who was such a citizen at the coming into force of IA 1971 and was then ordinarily resident in the UK is not, on conviction of an offence, to be recommended for deportation under s.3(6) if, at the time of the conviction he has for the last five years been ordinarily resident in the UK and Islands.

"Ordinary residence" is a matter of fact and degree; mere temporary absence will not create a gap in "ordinary" residence; illegal residence ab initio, however, cannot amount to "ordinary residence" (*R. v Bangoo* [1976] Crim. L.R. 746).

Note that:

(1) the "last five years" before the material time is to be taken as a period amounting in total to five years excluding any time during which the person was serving a period of imprisonment or detention following conviction for an offence in the UK and Islands, and the period for which he was imprisoned or detained by virtue of the sentence amounted to six months or more; and
(2) for these purposes:
  (a) "sentence" includes any order made on conviction of an offence;
  (b) two or more sentences for consecutive (or partly consecutive) terms are treated as a single sentence; and
  (c) a person is deemed to be detained by virtue of a sentence:
    (i) at any time when he is liable to imprisonment or detention by virtue of the sentence, but is unlawfully at large; and

(ii) (unless the sentence is passed after the material time) during any period of custody by which under any relevant enactment the term to be served under the sentence is reduced.

Relevance of immigration status

R. v Benabbas [2005] EWCA Crim 2113; [2006] 1 Cr. App. R. (S.) 94 reviewed the cases in detail and restated the principle that where the offender's presence in this country: **27-009**

(1) is lawful and regular, the *Nazari* approach (above) involves a relatively straightforward exercise, i.e. balancing the aggravation of the offender's wrong-doing, present, past and potential against any mitigation which may be put forward;

(2) is illegal or irregular, the position may be more complicated, varying from:
   (a) a lawful entrant who overstays his permit;
   (b) an unlawful entrant who gains entry by fraudulent means;
   and also because the illegality or irregularity may be either:
   (i) the essence of the offence; or
   (ii) entirely irrelevant to it.

While a recommendation ought not to be made simply because of the irregularity or illegality of status, rather than on the *Nazari* principle, it is justified where, e.g. entry is by the use of a forged passport, since there is a detriment to the public interest which undermines confidence in the system (see also *R. v Junab* [2012] EWCA Crim 2660; [2013] 2 Cr. App. R. (S) 23; and *R. v Brown* [2010] EWCA Crim 1807; [2011] 1 Cr. App. R. (S.) 482(79)). It is clear from the cases of *Benabbas*, *Kluxen* and *Brown* that using false identification documents is an offence of such seriousness, in the sense of the detrimental effect the offender's continued presence will have on our society, that it can merit recommending deportation.

As to "sham" marriages for the purpose of establishing a right of abode, see *R. v Ahemed* [2005] EWCA Crim 1954; [2006] 1 Cr. App. R. (S.) 78 (in which a recommendation for deportation was upheld), distinguishing *R. v Aziz* [2004] EWCA Crim 1700.

28. DETENTION OF YOUNG OFFENDERS

QUICK GUIDE

1. INTRODUCTION

28-001 An offender under 18 years of age may not be sentenced to imprisonment nor may he be committed to prison for any reason other than that of:

(1) remanding him in custody;
(2) committing him in custody for sentence; or
(3) sending him for trial under CDA 1998 s.51 and following.

Note that:

(a) an offender's age is deemed to be that which it appears to the court to be on the date of conviction (*R. v Danga* (1992) 13 Cr. App. R. (S.) 408) after considering any available evidence (see AGE OF OFFENDER);
(b) it is not proper to adjourn after conviction for the purpose only of the offender reaching the age of 18 before being sentenced (*Arthur v Stringer* (1987) 84 Cr. App. R. 361);
(c) where an offender is convicted on a date before reaching a birthday relevant to his sentence, and is then sentenced on another date, after that "milestone" birthday has passed, he falls to be sentenced as if he were still under that age (*R. v Danga* (1992) 94 Cr. App. R. 252; *R. v Robinson* (1993) 14 Cr. App. R. (S.) 448); and
(d) a sentence will not be invalidated because it is later discovered that the offender is of a different age (*R. v Brown* (1989) 11 Cr. App. R. (S.) 263).

The CACD has said that CYPA 1933 ss.44(1) and 107(1) (regarding the welfare of the child) does not prevent the judge from considering other matters, such as general deterrence, but that a deterrent sentence should not be passed upon a juvenile unless the court has weighed most carefully in the balance, deterrence on one side and individual treatment for the rehabilitation of the offender on the other.

The Sentencing Council issued a guideline "Sentencing Children and Young People: Overarching Principles and Offence Specific Guidelines for Sexual Offences and Robbery" for those sentenced on or after 1 June 2017. The overarching principles deal with the general approach that a court should take including the welfare of the child or young person, the allocation of cases involving children and young people, parental responsibilities and the determination of the sentence. The Sentencing Council document then goes on to give guidance on the available sentences for courts dealing with children or young people. There is specific guidance on custodial sentences at paras 6.42–6.60.

Interval between date of offence and sentence

Where, between the date of: **28-002**

(1) the commission of the offence; and
(2) conviction,

the offender has crossed a relevant age threshold, the starting point in considering sentence is the sentence that he would have been likely to have received at the time of the commission of the offence. Whilst other factors may need to be considered, there would need to be good reason for departing from that starting point, although clearly, particularly where a long interval has elapsed between points (1) and (2) above, circumstances may have changed significantly, e.g. the offender may have revealed himself to be a dangerous criminal, or the tariff may have been increased.

The judge is entitled to take such factors into account and:

(a) may impose a sentence higher than that which would have been imposed at the date of the offence; but
(b) will seldom need to consider passing a sentence beyond the maximum which he could have passed on the date of the commission of the offence.

(*R. v Ghafoor* [2003] 1 Cr. App. R. (S.) 84; *R. v LM* [2002] EWCA Crim 3047; [2003] 2 Cr. App. R. (S.) 26; *R. v B* [2013] EWCA Crim 286)

2. Available custodial sentences

Custodial sentences for this age group, recognised and governed by PCC(S)A 2000 Pt V Ch.2, as amended by LASPOA 2012 and as from 1 December 2020 as set out by SA 2020, are eight in number, namely: **28-003**

(1) for offenders aged 18–20, the normal sentence in lieu of imprisonment is *detention in a young offender institution* under SA 2020 ss.262–263;
(2) for offenders under 18, the normal sentence is a *detention and training order* under SA 2020 ss.233–248;
(3) for offenders under 18 convicted of certain grave crimes, *detention* under SA 2020 ss.249 and 250;
(4) protective sentences for *dangerous offenders* under 18, in relation to *offences committed on or after 4 April 2005*, detention for life under SA 2020 ss.250, 258 and 260;
(5) protective sentences for offenders under 18, for specified violent, sexual or terrorism offences *committed on or after 4 April 2005*, and *extended sentence* under SA 2020 ss.254–257;
(6) in the case of a person under 18 convicted of murder, *detention during His Majesty's Pleasure* under SA 2020 ss.259, 260, 275, 322;
(7) in the case of an offender under 21 convicted of murder or any other offence the sentence for which is fixed by law (cf. (8) below) as life imprisonment, *custody for life* under SA 2020 s.276 unless he is liable to be detained under s.259 (above (6)); and
(8) in the case of an offender aged 18 but under 21, for which the sentence is not fixed by law (cf. (7) above) but for which a person aged 21 or over would be liable to imprisonment for life, if such a sentence is appropriate, *custody for life* under SA 2020 ss.262 and 263.

Different considerations govern different types of custodial sentence, but the imposition of any of them is subject, like any other custodial sentence:

(a) to the offence(s) "qualifying" for a custodial sentence (see DEALING WITH AN OFFENDER);
(b) to the offender's age (see AGE OF OFFENDER);
(c) unless unnecessary, to the availability of a pre-sentence report (see DEALING WITH AN OFFENDER); and
(d) the offender being legally represented (see DEALING WITH AN OFFENDER).

Spelling it out

28-004 Special care needs to be taken, in the case of young offenders, to indicate at the point of sentence the exact provisions which are being applied. In such cases, one of the most common reasons for appeals against sentence being allowed is the judge's failure to specify exactly what powers he is exercising (see *R. v Venison* (1993) 15 Cr. App. R. (S.) 624; *R. v Edgell* (1994) 15 Cr. App. R. (S.) 509; *R. v Anderson* (1991) 13 Cr. App. R. (S.) 325).

3. Detention in Young Offender Institution

28-005 The ordinary custodial sentence (i.e. leaving aside ss.259, 249 and 276) for an offender *aged at least 18 but under 21*:

(1) who is convicted of an offence punishable with imprisonment in the case of a person aged 21 or over; and
(2) where the prerequisites for a custodial sentence (see DEALING WITH AN OFFENDER) are present,

is detention in a young offender institution (SA 2020 s.262).

In the case of an offence committed after 1 October 2012, the judge must order a surcharge to be paid by the offender under SA 2020 ss.42 and 43. The amount payable varies according to the order made at sentence. For those aged 18 and under, where one or more offences are committed on or after 16 June 2022 the surcharge will be £41 for a suspended sentence order or a custodial sentence and £26 for a referral order or community order. Where all offences are committed on or after 14 April 2020 to 16 June 2022 the amounts are £34 and £22 respectively. In the case of an offender aged 18 or over, the surcharge in a case where the sentence is for a determinate period:

(a) of up to and including six months, is £128 where one or more offences are committed on or after 14 April 2020 up to 16 June 2022 and £154 where all offences are committed on or after 16 June 2022; and
(b) (b) of more than six months, is £156 where one or more offences are committed before 16 June 2022, and £187 where all offences are committed on or after 16 June 2022.

As to specific details in relation to age thresholds, computation of amounts and payment by parent or guardian, see FINES and SURCHARGES.

Length of term

28-006 As far as the length of the term is concerned:

(1) the maximum term is the same as the maximum term of imprisonment which the judge may impose for the offence; and
(2) the minimum term which may be ordered is 21 days, applying not to the totality, but to each separate sentence (*R. v Kent Youth Court Ex p. Kingwell* [1999] 1 Cr. App. R. (S.) 263).

(SA 2020 ss.262 and 263)

A discount would probably follow a plea of guilty (see DISCOUNTS ON SENTENCE).

As to prescribed minimum sentences for certain firearms offences, see 28-021 and IMPRISONMENT.

Consecutive sentences

Subject to the statutory maxima set out at 28-006, a young offender: **28-007**

(1) convicted of more than one offence for which he is liable to such a term; or
(2) serving such a term, and convicted of one or more further offences for which he is so liable,

may be sentenced to consecutive terms, as if they were sentences of imprisonment.

If he is:

(a) serving such a term;
(b) is aged 21 or over; and
(c) is convicted of one or more further offences for which he is liable to imprisonment,

he may be sentenced, subject to SA 2020 s.225 (restrictions on consecutive sentences for released prisoners), to imprisonment to run consecutively to the term(s) of detention (SA 2020 ss.269–271; see note (2) in 28-006).

Suspending a term

In the case of an offender aged 18 but under 21, in respect of an offence or offences committed on or after 4 April 2005, a term of detention in a young offender institution: **28-008**

(1) of at least 14 days; but
(2) no more than 12 months,

may be suspended.

See, generally, as to the imposition of suspended sentences, IMPRISONMENT.

In the case of an offence committed after 1 October 2012, the judge must order a surcharge to be paid by an offender under 18 (SA 2020 ss.42 and 43). For offences on or after 16 June 2022 the amount is £154 for six months or less, and £87 over six months.

As to specific details in relation to age thresholds, computation of amounts and payment by parent or guardian, see FINES and SURCHARGES.

4. DETENTION AND TRAINING ORDER

The ordinary custodial sentence (subject to SA 2020 ss.249, 250, 254–260, 275) to be passed on an offender *aged under 18* where: **28-009**

(1) he is convicted of an offence which is punishable with imprisonment in the case of a person aged 21 or over; and
(2) the judge is of opinion that SA 2020 s.230 (the general restriction on custodial sentences) applies, or the case falls within SA 2020 s.230(4) and (5) (persistent offender, see 28-010),

is a detention and training order, which provides a period of detention and training, followed by a period of supervision (SA 2020 ss.233–236).

In the case of an offence committed after 1 October 2012, the judge must order a surcharge to be paid by an offender under 18 (SA 2020 ss.42 and 43). For offences on or after 16 June 2022 the amount is £41. Where one or more offences are committed on or after 14 April 2020 and before 16 June 2022, it is £34.

As to specific details in relation to age thresholds, computation of amounts and payment by parent or guardian, see FINES and SURCHARGES.

The judge must not make a detention and training order in the case of an offender:

(a) under the age of 15 at the time of his conviction, unless he is of opinion that he is a persistent offender (*R. v L* [2012] EWCA Crim 1336); or
(b) under the age of 12 at that time, unless:
    (i) he is of opinion that only a custodial sentence would be adequate to protect the public from his further offending; and
    (ii) the offence was committed on or after such date as the Secretary of State may appoint.

The above paragraph applies with the omission of (i) in the case of offence the sentence for which falls to be imposed under:

- SA 2020 s.312 (minimum sentence for offence of threatening with offensive weapon in public); or
- SA 2020 s.315 (minimum sentence for offence of threatening with article with blade or point or offensive weapon).

The judge is entitled (by virtue of CYPA 1963 s.29(1)) to impose a detention and training order on an offender who was aged 17 at the date he committed an offence, even though he has attained the age of 18 by the date on which sentence is imposed (*Aldis v DPP* [2002] EWHC 403 (Admin); [2002] 2 Cr. App. R. (S.) 88). A young person aged 15 at the time of conviction may be sentenced to a detention and training order even though he was 14 at the time of the commission of the offence (*R. v BR (Sentencing: Extended Licences)* [2003] EWCA Crim 2199; [2004] 1 Cr. App. R. (S.) 59).

There is no power to impose an extended sentence under SA 2020 s.254 with a detention and training order—there is no licence period (*R. v B* [2005] EWCA Crim 312; [2005] 2 Cr. App. R. (S.) 87).

What amounts to a "persistent offender"?

28-010 "Persistent offender" is not defined in the Act, nor is it to be interpreted by reference to the government circular "Tackling Delays in the Youth Justice System" (*R. v Thomas* [2001] 1 Cr. App. R. (S.) 415). The currently understood meaning of the words should be applied to the facts of the case: *R. v S(A)* [2001] 1 Cr. App. R. (S.) 18 (a series of offences over two days).

Their application is best left to the good sense of the judge (*R. v Dexter* [2001] 1 Cr. App. R. (S.) 389).

Note that it is not necessary to come within the definition that:

(1) the offender should have previous convictions (*R. v Smith* [2001] 1 Cr. App. R. (S.) 62);
(2) he should have committed a string of offences, either of the same or a similar character (*R. v BR (Sentencing: Extended Licences)* [2003] EWCA Crim 2199; [2004] 1 Cr. App. R. (S.) 59); or
(3) his failure to address his offending behaviour arises by his failure to comply with previous orders (above); and

account may be taken of offences in respect of which he has been formally cautioned (*R. v D* [2001] Crim. L.R. 864), (and no doubt, reprimanded under CDA 1998 s.65) and of offences committed after the offence for which the offender is being sentenced (*R. v B* [2005] EWCA Crim 312; [2005] 2 Cr. App. R. (S.) 87 and see *R. v C* [2001] 1 Cr. App. R. (S.) 415, but note *R. v L* [2012] EWCA Crim 1336; [2013] 1 Cr. App. R. (S.) 56 (where two previous reprimands prior to a series of robberies were held not to amount to persistence)).

Term of order

The term of an order must: **28-011**

(1) be for 4, 6, 8, 10, 12, 18 or 24 months;
(2) not exceed 24 months, taking into account any period for which the offender has been remanded in custody in connection with the offence, or any other offence the charge for which was founded on the same facts or evidence; and
(3) not exceed the maximum term of imprisonment that the judge could, in the cases of an offender aged 21 or over, impose for the offence.

(SA 2020 s.236)

Consecutive terms may be imposed, each for one of the terms set out in (1) above, though the aggregate does not amount to one of those specified (*R. v Norris* [2001] 1 Cr. App. R. (S.) 116; cf. *R. v C* [2009] EWCA Crim 446), but it is not permissible to pass a number of shorter terms and aggregate them into a term of four months (*R. v Kent Youth Court Ex p. Kingwell* [1999] 1 Cr. App. R. (S.) 263).

Where the offence is a summary offence, and the maximum term of imprisonment that a court could (in the case of an offender aged 18 or over) impose for the offence is 51 weeks (see IMPRISONMENT) the term of detention and training must not exceed six months.

Discount for plea

When reflecting a plea of guilty (see DISCOUNTS ON SENTENCE) in the sentence, it is appropriate for the judge, where the offender is: **28-012**

(1) not liable to a term of detention under SA 2020 ss.249 and 250, to reduce the term of the detention and training order below the maximum available term, unless there are proper grounds for not allowing a discount (*R. v Kelly* [2002] 1 Cr. App. R. (S.) 11; [2001] EWCA Crim 1030; *R. v Marley* [2001] EWCA Crim 2779; [2002] 2 Cr. App. R. (S.) 21); and
(2) liable to such a term, the discount may properly be reflected by imposing a

detention and training order for the maximum term (*R. v March* [2002] 2 Cr. App. R. (S.) 98).

Time spent on remand

28-013 LASPOA 2012 omitted the former CJA 2003 s.240 and inserted a new s.240ZA, the effect of which was that time spent in custody on remand was automatically credited and does not require the order of the judge for imprisonment. For a DTO, time on remand taken into account in determining the length of the DTO (SA 2020 s.239).

As to time remanded on bail counting towards time served for imprisonment, see CJA 2003 s.240A; LASPOA 2012 s.109 (see IMPRISONMENT).

Consecutive terms

28-014 Where the offender:

(1) is convicted of more than one offence for which he is liable to an order; or
(2) is already subject to such an order and is convicted of one or more further offences for which he is liable to an order,

the judge has the same power to pass consecutive terms as if they were sentences of imprisonment, save that, while there is no requirement that the total term add up to one of the periods specified in s.101(1) (*R. v Norris* [2001] 1 Cr. App. R. (S.) 116):

(a) an order must not be made in respect of an offender the effect of which would be that he would be subject to detention and training orders for an aggregate which exceeds 24 months; and
(b) if the aggregate term to which he would otherwise be subject, does exceed 24 months, the excess will be treated as remitted.

(SA 2020 s.238)

The judge may, when imposing consecutive detention and training orders, whose individual terms are taken from the list in subs.(1), agree to an aggregate term taken from the list, i.e. any even number of months between 4 and 24. This gives him some measure of discretion in arriving at terms which reflect the varying culpability of different offenders involved in the same case (*R. v B* [2001] Crim. L.R. 80).

By statute a detention and training order may be ordered to take effect consecutively to a term of detention under SA 2020 ss.249 and 250 (cf. *R. v H (Grant) (A juvenile)* [2001] Cr. App. R. (S.) 31), or an extended sentence (see DANGEROUS OFFENDERS; PROTECTIVE SENTENCE; SA 2020 ss.250, 258, 260 and 254–257).

Improper combinations

28-015 A detention and training order may not be imposed to run concurrently with a term of detention under SA 2020 s.250 (SA 2020 s.235) (*R. v Hayward* [2001] 2 Cr. App. R. (S.) 31), and the converse also applies (*R. v Lang* [2001] 2 Cr. App. R. (S.) 39).

New offences during currency of the order

Where: **28-016**

(1) after his release and before the date on which the term of the order ends, the offender commits an offence punishable with imprisonment in the case of a person aged 21 or over; and

(2) whether before or after that date, he is convicted of that "new offence" the judge of the court by or before which he is convicted may, whether or not the judge passes any other sentence on him, order him to be detained in such secure accommodation as the Secretary of State may determine for the whole or any part of the period which:

   (a) begins with the date of the judge's order; and
   (b) is equal in length to the period between the date on which the new offence was committed, or the last of the days if it was committed over several, and the date on which the order would end.

The term will, as the judge directs, be served either before and be followed by, or concurrently with, any sentence imposed for the offence, and in either case will be disregarded in determining the appropriate length of that sentence.

(SA 2020 s.237)

5. Detention during His Majesty's Pleasure

Where a person convicted of murder, or of any other offence the sentence for which is fixed by law as life imprisonment, appears to the court to have been under 18 at the time the offence was committed, the judge must (notwithstanding anything in SA 2020 or any other Act) sentence him to be detained during His Majesty's Pleasure (SA 2020 s.259). The starting point for the minimum term is 12 years. **28-017**

See LIFE SENTENCES.

In the case of an offence committed after 1 October 2012, the judge must order a surcharge to be paid by an offender under 18 (SA 2020 ss.42 and 43). For offences on or after 16 June 2022 the amount is £41.

As to specific details in relation to age thresholds, computation of amounts and payment by parent or guardian, see FINES and SURCHARGES.

6. Offenders under 18—certain grave offences—SA 2020 ss.250–253

Where: **28-018**

(1) an offender under 18 is convicted on indictment of an offence:

   (a) punishable in the case of a person aged 21 or over with imprisonment for 14 years or more, not being an offence the sentence for which is fixed by law;
   (b) under SOA 2003 s.3 (sexual assault);
   (c) under SOA 2003 s.13 (child sex offences committed by children or young persons);
   (d) under SOA 2003 s.25 (sexual activity with a child family member); or
   (e) under SOA 2003 s.26 (inciting a child or family member to engage in sexual activity); or

(2)

   (a) an offender under 18 is convicted on indictment of an offence under the FA 1968 that is listed in s.51A(1A)(b), (e) or (f) of that Act and was committed in respect of a firearm or ammunition specified in s.5(1)(a), (ab), (aba), (ac), (ad), (ae), (af) or (c) or (1A)(a) (SA 2020 ss.249, 311 and Sch.20);

(b) the offence was committed after the commencement of VCRA 2006 s.30, and for the purposes of FA 1968 s.51A(3) at a time when he was aged 16 or over; and

(c) the judge is of the opinion mentioned in FA 1968 s.51A(2) (SA 2020 s.311 and Sch.20);

(3)

(a) an offender under 18 is convicted of an offence under VCRA 2006 s.28 (using someone to mind a weapon);

(b) s.29(3) of that Act applies (minimum sentences in certain cases); and

(c) the judge is of the opinion mentioned in s.29(6) (exceptional circumstances which justify not imposing the minimum sentence); and

(4) the judge is of the opinion that neither a youth rehabilitation order nor a detention and training order is suitable,

he may, subject to the general restrictions on passing custodial sentences set out in SA 2020 s.230, sentence the offender to be detained for such period as he may specify, not exceeding the maximum term of imprisonment with which the offence is punishable in the case of a person aged 21 or over (SA 2020 ss.249–253).

In the case of an offence committed after 1 October 2012, the judge must order a surcharge to be paid by an offender under 18 (SA 2020 ss.42 and 43). For offences on or after 16 June 2022 the amount is £41 where one or more offences are committed before 16 June 2022 but on or after 14 April 2020 it is £34.

As to specific details in relation to age thresholds, computation of amounts and payment by parent or guardian, see FINES and SURCHARGES.

In general:

(i) unless the offence merits a sentence *longer than two years*, and the criteria under s.91 are met, a term of detention and training should be imposed; and
(ii) if such is not permitted, then a non-custodial sentence should be passed (*R. (on the application of W) v Thetford Youth Court* [2002] EWHC 1252 (Admin); [2003] 1 Cr. App. R. (S.) 67).

Where SA 2020 ss.312 or 315 requires the imposition of a sentence of detention for a minimum term the sentence must be for the offender to be detained for at least the term so provided for, but not exceeding the maximum term of imprisonment with which the offence is punishable in the case of a person aged 21 or over.

Such an offender is liable to be detained in such place as the Secretary of State may direct or arrange.

Guideline cases

28-019 An order is primarily applicable to cases where the judge contemplates a sentence of at least two years; anything less than that should be dealt with by a detention and training order.

If the 24-month limit on detention and training orders is intended to ensure that offenders under 18 are not sentenced to lengthy periods of detention where this can be avoided, the judge ought to think long and hard before passing a sentence which exceeds this limit. However, the co-existence of the powers contained in s.91 recognise the "unwelcome but undoubted fact" that some crimes committed by offenders of this age merit sentences of detention in excess of 24 months.

The following principles are to be deduced from *R. v Fairhurst* (1987) 84 Cr. App. R. 19; *R. v Wainfur* [1997] 1 Cr. App. R. (S.) 43; *R. v Mills* [1998] 1 Cr. App. R. 43; and *R. v Manchester City Youth Court* [2001] EWHC (Admin) 860; [2002] 1 Cr. App. R. (S.) 135:

(1) a sentence of detention under s.91 should not be passed simply because a 24-months' term seems to be on the low side for the particular offence; the 24-month limit should not be exceeded unless the offence is clearly one calling for a longer sentence;
(2) if the judge is minded to impose a sentence of, e.g. four years under s.91, but is persuaded by mitigation that the circumstances justify a significant reduction to, e.g. two and a half years:
    (a) while he ought not to exceed the 24-month limit without careful thought;
    (b) if he concludes that a longer sentence, even if not a much longer sentence, is called for, he should impose what he considers the appropriate period under s.91;
(3) if, on a plea of guilty to an offence falling within s.91, the judge imposes a sentence of 24 months under s.100, where, but for the plea, detention under s.91 for a longer period would have been ordered, he should state this fact expressly.

The CACD has said that where an offender is convicted of a number of offences, for some of which detention under s.91 is available but for others it is not, the judge should sentence under s.91 where available and make the rather dubious order of "no separate penalty" (really a magistrates' courts order) in respect of those offences not qualifying (*R. v Carroll* [2004] EWCA Crim 1367; [2005] 1 Cr. App. R. (S.) 10).

Length of sentence

The offender may be sentenced to be detained for a determinate period not exceeding the maximum term of imprisonment with which the offence is punishable in the case of an offender of 21 or over, as may be specified in the order. **28-020**

Note that:

(1) the judge will need to have in mind the period during which danger is capable of arising from the offender's activities, without imposing a term which leaves the offender without hope (*R. v Storey* (1973) 57 Cr. App. R. 840; *R. v Bryson* (1974) 58 Cr. App. R. 464); and
(2) if the offence carries life imprisonment in the case of an offender of 21, and the doctors cannot indicate the period required, protection of the public should be secured by custody for life under s.94 (*R. v Nightingale* (1984) 6 Cr. App. R. (S.) 65).

The term should not exceed that which would be passed on an offender over 18, or over 21, for the same offence(s) (*R. v Burrowes* (1985) 7 Cr. App. R. (S.) 106).

In *R. v AM* [1998] 2 Cr. App. R. 57, the CACD upheld a single sentence of detention under s.91 in respect of one offence, making the length commensurate with the gravity of all the offences, and passing no separate penalty (a doubtful practice) for the other offences.

Prescribed minimum sentences for certain firearms offences

28-021 Where a person is convicted of certain offences under FA 1968 s.5, *committed on or after 4 April 2005*, the judge must impose in the case of an offender aged under 18 when convicted, a sentence of detention under SA 2020 s.250 for at least three years (with or without a fine), unless he is of opinion that there are exceptional circumstances relating to the offence or to the offender which justify his not doing so (FA 1968 s.51A and SA 2020 s.311 and Sch.20).

Where an offence is found to have been committed over a period of two or more days, or at some time during a period of two or more days, it is to be taken to have been committed on the last of those days.

Prescribed minimum sentences; SA 2020 s.312; PCA 1953; CJA 1988

28-022 Where a young offender is convicted of an offence under:

(1) PCA 1953 s.1A (threatening with article with blade or point or offensive weapon in public or on school premises); or
(2) CJA 1988 s.139AA (threatening with article with blade or point or offensive weapon);

an appropriate sentence, with or without a fine must be imposed unless the judge is of the opinion that there are particular circumstances relating to the offence or to the offender which would make it unjust to do so in all the circumstances.

An appropriate sentence in the case of a young offender is, in the case of an offender:

(a) aged 18 or over but under 21, a sentence of at least six months detention in a young offender institution; and
(b) aged at least 16 but under 18, a detention and training order of at least four months (SA 2020 ss.312 and 315).

Combination of sentences

28-023 It is generally undesirable that sentences of detention under s.250 and secure training orders under ss.233–248 be imposed, either consecutively to, or concurrently with, each other (*R. v Gaskin* (1985) 7 Cr. App. R. (S.) 28; *R. v McKenna* (1985) 7 Cr. App. R. (S.) 348).

However, it is not always possible to avoid this. Thus:

(1) terms of detention under s.250, and those under s.233, may be served in different establishments and it is generally undesirable to impose terms *concurrent* under both sections;
(2) the judge minded to impose *concurrent* terms under the two sections, should make sure that no administrative difficulty will result before doing so;
(3) where some of the offences fall within s.250 and others are "associated" but do not fall within the section, it will usually be preferable to impose a term under s.250 which takes account of the associated offence or offences, and to impose "no separate penalty" for the lesser offences; and
(4) there is no power to order a detention and training order to run consecutively

to a sentence under s.250 (*R. v H (Grant) (A juvenile)* [2001] 2 Cr. App. R. (S.) 31).

7. Dangerous offenders; protective sentences

The sentences created under CJA 2003 ss.224–227B, as amended by LASPOA 2012 Ch.5, as now set out by SA 2020 are dealt with in DANGEROUS OFFENDERS; PROTECTIVE SENTENCES. **28-024**

8. Custody for life

Sentences of custody for life under SA 2020 ss.250 and 258 (see 28-003) are within the definition of life sentences under SA 2020 and the principles relating to them are to be found in LIFE SENTENCES. **28-025**

The cases relating to the use of custody for life as a discretionary sentence indicate that the general principles relating to the use of imprisonment for life in relation to offenders aged 21 or over, apply.

In the case of an offence committed on or after 1 October 2012, the judge must order a surcharge to be paid by an offender (SA 2020 ss.42 and 43). For offences on or after 16 June 2022 the amount is £41 where under 18 and £187 where aged 18 or over. Where one or more offences are committed before 16 June 2022 and on or after 14 April 2020 it is £156.

As to specific details in relation to age thresholds, computation of amounts and payment by parent or guardian, see FINES and SURCHARGES.

29. DISCHARGE; ABSOLUTE AND CONDITIONAL

Quick Guide

1. General

29-001 A discharge, whether absolute or conditional, may be appropriate:

(1) generally, for any age of offender, provided that the offences is not one:
  (a) for which the sentence is fixed by law; or
  (b) which falls to be imposed under SA 2020 ss.313 and 314 (required minimum sentences for certain repeat offences); SA 2020 ss.312 and 315 (minimum sentence for offence of threatening with offensive weapon in public); SA 2020 s.311 and Sch.20 (minimum sentence for certain firearms offences); SA 2020 ss.312 and 315 (minimum sentence for offence of threatening with article with blade or point or offensive weapon); SA 2020 ss.258, 273, 274, 283 and 285 (sentences for public protection); or SA 2020 s.311 and Sch.20 (minimum sentences for using a person to mind a weapon); and

(2) specifically, where the nature of the offence and the character of the offender make the infliction of punishment inexpedient.

(SA 2020 ss.79 and 80)

A discharge is not a "community order" (SA 2020 ss.200 and 201).

2. Absolute discharge

29-002 An absolute discharge is appropriate where the judge considers no action is required beyond the mere finding of guilt, reflecting:

(1) the triviality of the offence (*R. v King* [1977] Crim. L.R. 627);
(2) the circumstances in which it came to be prosecuted (*Smedleys Ltd v Breed* [1974] Crim. L.R. 309); or
(3) factors relating to the offender (*R. v O'Toole* (1971) 55 Cr. App. R. 206).

It is not an order likely to be made frequently in the Crown Court.

3. Conditional discharge

General

29-003 The effect of an order is to discharge an offender subject to a *single condition* that he commit no offence during the "operational period" specified in the order, which may not exceed three years.

On making an order the court may, if it thinks it expedient for the purpose of the offender's reformation allow any person who consents to do so to give security for the good behaviour of the offender. If making such an order, the court should specify the type of conduct from which the offender is to refrain (SA 2020 s.80(6) and *CPD* Sentencing J para.J.20).

An order may *not* be made:

(1) where a person who has received two or more youth cautions is convicted of an offence committed within two years beginning with the date of the last of those cautions; or
(2) where a person who has received a youth conditional caution followed by a youth caution is convicted of an offence committed within two years beginning with the date of the youth caution, unless, in either case, the judge is of the opinion that there are exceptional circumstances relating to the offence or to the person that justify him doing so, and, if so, the judge must state so in open court and the reasons for that opinion;
(3) on the breach of a sexual harm prevention order (SOA 2003 s.103I(a); ASBA 2014 Sch.5) (see SEX OFFENDER ORDERS); or
(4) on the breach of an anti-social behaviour order.

(SA 2020 s.80(3) and s.330)

The judge should explain that:

(a) in view of the nature of the offence and any mitigating factors (including a plea of guilty) he does not propose to *punish* the offender;
(b) instead he proposes to discharge the offender conditionally for x months or years on condition that he commit no further offence during the period; and
(c) if he stays out of trouble for that period he will not be punished for the instant offence, but if he does commit another offence he may be brought back and sentenced in a different way, which might include a custodial sentence as well as being dealt with for the fresh offence.

In the case of an offence committed on or after 1 October 2012, the judge must order a surcharge to be paid by the offender (SA 2020 ss.42 and 43). For offences on or after 14 April 2020 the amount is £22 for an offender under 18, £17 in the case of an offender aged 18 or over, or a corporation.

As to specific details in relation to age thresholds, computation of amounts and payment by parent or guardian, see FINES and SURCHARGES.

4. Combining other orders

Since the whole basis for the imposition of a conditional discharge is that punishment is inexpedient, a *discretionary* order of a punitive nature (e.g. a fine—*R. v Sanck* (1990–91) 12 Cr. App. R. (S.) 155 or a company officer's disqualification order—*R. v Young* (1990–91) 12 Cr. App. R. (S.) 279) may not be combined with it on the same count of an indictment. It is otherwise where the order, albeit punitive (e.g. a confiscation order under POCA 2002, or a disqualification or endorsement under RTOA 1988) is *mandatory* (see *R. v Varma* [2012] UKSC 42; [2013] 1 Cr. App. R. 8) (SA 2020 s.80(7)). **29-004**

There is nothing to prevent the judge from combining with a discharge such orders as are set out in 29-005.

Ancillary orders

29-005 On making an order for discharge, the judge may:

(1) in the case of a conditional discharge, it is expedient for the purpose of the offender's reformation, to allow any person who consents to do so, to give *security for the offender's good behaviour*, specifying the type of conduct from which the offender is to refrain (as to which, see *CPD* Sentencing para.J.20);
(2) when discharging an offender absolutely or conditionally in respect of an offence:
   (a) impose any disqualification on him, make a compensation order (under SA 2020 s.133), a deprivation order (under SA 2020 s.152) or a restitution order (under SA 2020 s.147); and
   (b) make an order under SA 2020 s.46 for payment of a criminal courts charge, or of costs.
(3) where still appropriate make a recommendation for *deportation* (IA 1971 s.6(3); (SA 2020 s.82(2))); and
(4) when discharging an offender conditionally, make:
   (a) a *criminal behaviour order* (see CRIMINAL BEHAVIOUR ORDERS AND ISOs);
   (b) a *football banning order* (see FOOTBALL BANNING ORDERS); or
   (c) a *serious crime prevention order* (see SERIOUS CRIME PREVENTION ORDERS).

(SA 2020 ss.79(3) and 80(4))

The judge must consider making a compensation order under SA 2020 s.133 in any case where the section empowers the judge to do so, and if the judge does not do so, must explain why when explaining the sentence passed.

(SA 2020 ss.133–138)

In an appropriate case, the judge is under a duty to combine with a discharge any mandatory order, such as, e.g. disqualification or endorsement under RTOA 1988 s.46(1) or, where the criteria in POCA 2002 s.6 are satisfied (subject to subs.(6)), a confiscation order (see CONFISCATION ORDERS).

5. EFFECT OF DISCHARGE

29-006 A conviction of an offence for which an absolute or conditional discharge is made is deemed not to be a conviction for any purpose other than the purposes of the proceedings in which the order was made, or of any subsequent proceedings taken against the offender under s.402 for a breach (e.g. *R. v Longworth* [2006] UKHL 1; [2006] 2 Cr. App. R. (S.) 62, where the imposition of a conditional discharge was held not to activate the notification procedures of SOA 1997), though:

(1) where the offender was aged 18 or over at the time of his conviction of the offence in question, and is subsequently sentenced under s.402, this provision ceases to apply;
(2) the "deeming" provision does not affect:
   (a) any right of the offender to rely on his conviction in bar of any subsequent proceedings for the same offence;
   (b) the restoration of any property in consequence of his conviction; or
   (c) the operation in relation to him, of any enactment or instrument in

force on 1 July 1974, which is expressed to extend to persons dealt with under POA 1907 s.1(1) as well as to convicted persons;

(3) in any event, the conviction is to be disregarded for the purposes of an enactment or instrument which imposes any disqualification or disability on convicted persons, or authorises or requires the imposition of such; and

(4) the deeming provisions have effect subject to CAA 1968 s.50(1A) and MCA 1980 s.108(1A), and do not prevent an appeal against conviction, or otherwise.

(SA 2020 s.82)

6. Conviction of further offence

An offender convicted in any part of Great Britain of an offence committed during the "operational period" of a conditional discharge, and who is dealt with in respect of that further offence, is liable to be dealt with for the offence for which he was made the subject of the order. **29-007**

Where the original order was made by:

(1) the Crown Court, and the subsequent conviction is in a magistrates' court, the latter may commit him to the Crown Court, a judge of which, if satisfied of the breach, may deal with him for the offence for which the order was made in any way in which he could deal with him if he had just been convicted before him of that offence;

(2) the Crown Court, as is the subsequent conviction, a judge may deal with the offender as if he had just been convicted before him of the original offence; and

(3) a magistrates' court, and the subsequent conviction is in the Crown Court, or the offender is dealt with in the Crown Court after committal under para.(1) above:
   - (a) the judge's powers are limited to dealing with the offender in a manner in which the lower court could have dealt with him had he just been convicted before it; unless
   - (b) the original order was made when the offender was under 18, in respect of an offence triable only on indictment in the case of an adult, in which case the judge's powers in dealing with the original offence extend to a fine not exceeding £5,000, or the lower court's powers in relation to an offence punishable with imprisonment for a term not exceeding six months (see COMMITTALS FOR SENTENCE).

(SA 2020 s.402)

The relevant date for considering the appropriate sentencing option on the commission of a further offence is the date of subsequent sentence (*R. v Keelan* (1975) 61 Cr. App. R. 212).

7. Orders made on appeal

Where an order for conditional discharge has been made on appeal, for the purposes of s.402 (29-007), it is deemed: **29-008**

(1) if it was made on an appeal brought from a magistrates' court, to have been made by that magistrates' court; and

(2) if it was made on an appeal brought from the Crown Court or from the CACD, to have been made by the Crown Court.

(SA 2020 s.81 and Sch.2 para.2)

8. Procedure on the breach

29-009 In dealing with the alleged commission of a further offence during the operational period of a conditional discharge, the accused must be asked in terms whether:

(1) on the date specified he was convicted of the offence and made the subject of a conditional discharge;
(2) he admits that his subsequent conviction was within the operational period of that order; and
(3) he realises that he is liable to be dealt with for the original offence.

Should he dispute Paragraph (1) or (2) above, the issue falls to be determined by the judge, not by the verdict of a jury (SA 2020 s.81 and Sch.2 para.7).

While there is no statutory obligation to deal with an offender for breach of the order, failure to do so, save for good reason, renders the making of the original order pointless.

Generally, there should be a sentence which is more than nominal, though there is nothing to prevent the judge dealing with the breach by a fresh conditional discharge where the circumstances are exceptional and such a course is justified.

Termination of the order

29-010 If a person conditionally discharged under SA 2020 s.79, is sentenced for the offence in respect of which the order was made, the order ceases to have effect though a compensation order made when the original order was made remains in force (SA 2020 s.82(3); *R. v Evans* (1961) 45 Cr. App. R. 59).

30. DISCLOSURE

Quick Guide

A. General

Introduction

Disclosure remains one of the most important—as well as one of the most misunderstood and abused—of the procedures relating to criminal trials. The House of Lords stated in *R. v H* [2004] UKHL 3; [2004] 2 A.C. 134; [2004] 2 Cr. App. R. 10: **30-001**

> "Fairness ordinarily requires that any material held by the prosecution which weakens its case or strengthens that of the defendant, if not relied on as part of its formal case against the defendant, should be disclosed to the defence. Bitter experience has shown that miscarriages of justice may occur where such material is withheld from disclosure. The golden rule is that full disclosure of such material should be made." (p.147)

The Criminal Cases Review Commission has noted that failure to disclose material to the defence to which they were entitled remains the biggest single cause of miscarriages of justice (*JPD 2013* 1–2).

Historically, disclosure was viewed essentially as being a matter to be resolved between the parties, and the court only became engaged if a particular issue or complaint was raised. That perception is now wholly out of date. The regime established under CJA 2003 and the CrimPR gives judges the power—indeed, it imposes a duty on the judiciary—actively to manage disclosure in every case. The efficient, effective and timely resolution of these issues is a critical element in meeting the overriding objective of the CrimPR of dealing with cases justly (*JPD 2013* 56).

Protocols, Rules, Directions and Guidelines

The process of disclosure is now subject to parallel protocols applying to the judiciary and to the prosecution—the *Judicial Protocol on the Disclosure of Unused* **30-002**

Material in Criminal Cases (the JPD) and the Attorney General's *Guidelines on Disclosure for Investigators, Prosecutors and Defence Practitioners* (2022). The judicial protocol is prescribed for use by *CPD* IV 15A and applies in all criminal courts in England and Wales.

The *JPD* consolidates and replaces the following guidance:

- *Disclosure: a protocol for the Control and Management of Unused Material in the Crown Court*, issued by the CACD in 2006.
- Section 4, "Disclosure", of the Lord Chief Justice's *Protocol on the Control and Management of Heavy Fraud and Other Complex Criminal Cases*, 22 March 2005 (see CASE MANAGEMENT).
- The *Protocol for the Provision of Advance Information, Prosecution Evidence and Disclosure of Unused Material in the Magistrates' Courts*, 12 May 2006.

The tests for disclosure in law remain unchanged, depending on the appropriate regime governing disclosure. The Protocol enforces a rigorous application of the relevant test and emphasises that disclosure must be led by the prosecution with early judicial management.

The judge's role

30-003 While it is vital that obligations of disclosure are properly discharged by both the prosecution and the defence, the judge's active hands-on oversight of the process is an important safeguard against any potential miscarriages of justice.

The judge needs to have clearly in mind that:

(1) consideration of irrelevant unused material may consume wholly unjustifiable and disproportionate amounts of time and public resources, undermining the overall performance and efficiency of the criminal justice system; and
(2) unused prosecution material falls to be disclosed if, and only if, it satisfies the test for the disclosure regime applicable to the proceedings in question, subject to any overriding public interest considerations.

Disclosure is a vital part of the preparation for trial. All parties must be familiar with their obligations, in particular under CPIA 1996 and the Code issued under that Act, and must comply with *JPD 2013*. Active participation by the judge in the disclosure process is a critical means of ensuring that delays and adjournments are avoided, given that failures by the parties to comply with their obligations may disrupt or even frustrate the course of justice (*JPD 2013* 6).

However, it is also essential that the trial process is not overburdened or diverted by erroneous and inappropriate disclosure of unused prosecution material or by misconceived applications. Although the drafters of CPIA 1996 cannot have anticipated the vast increase in the amount of electronic material that has been generated in recent years, nevertheless the principles of that Act still hold true. Applications by the parties or decisions by judges based on misconceptions of the law or a general laxity of approach (however well-intentioned) which result in an improper application of the disclosure regime have, time and again, proved unnecessarily costly and have obstructed justice. The burden of disclosure must not be allowed to render the prosecution of cases impracticable (*JPD 2013* 3).

Application of regime; overarching principle

The overarching principle is that unused prosecution material will fall to be disclosed if, and only if, it satisfies the test for disclosure applicable to the proceedings in question, subject to any overriding public interest considerations. The test for disclosure will depend on the date the criminal investigation in question commenced, as this will determine whether the common law disclosure regime applies, or either of the two disclosure regimes under CPIA 1996 (*JPD 2013* 4). **30-004**

Where the particular criminal investigation commenced:

(1) before 1 April 1997 the common law applies, as set out in *R. v Keane* (1994) 99 Cr. App. R. 1;
(2) on or after 1 April 1997 but before 4 April 2005, the test under CPIA 1996 (before its amendment by CJA 2003) applies, with separate tests for disclosure of unused prosecution material at the primary and secondary stages (the latter following service of a defence statement by the accused), supported by the Code of Practice (SI 1999/1033) issued under CPIA 1996 s.23(1);
(3) on or after 4 April 2005, the "enhanced" provisions set out in CPIA 1996 (as amended by CJA 2003 Pt 5) apply, providing a single test for the disclosure of unused material, supported by the 2005 Code of Practice (SI 2005/985).

There may be circumstances where an investigation is commenced before 4 April 2005 and further offences are committed after that date. In such a situation the original disclosure scheme under the Act will apply to the original investigation and the enhanced provisions to the new offences.

As to the duties of the parties and the prosecutor's approach, see *R. v Olu* [2010] EWCA Crim 2795; [2011] 1 Cr. App. R. 33.

The concept of fairness

The concept of fairness recognises that: **30-005**

(1) there are interests other than those of the accused that need to be protected, including those of victims and witnesses who might otherwise be exposed to harm; the scheme of CPIA 1996 seeks to protect those interests;
(2) where there are fears for the safety of a prosecution witness, the prosecutor may be justified in not providing the defence with copies of audio and video tapes, but instead providing transcripts of the tapes and confining the defence to inspection of the tapes under controlled conditions (*R. v DPP Ex p. J* [2000] 1 All E.R.183 DC);
(3) material should not be disclosed which over-burdens the participants in the trial process, diverts attention from the relevant issues, leads to unjustifiable delay, and is wasteful of resources; and
(4) disclosure is a continuing process throughout the proceedings, up to the stage when any final appeal is determined.

In order to facilitate the extent of such disclosure, and to narrow the issues in respect of which it is necessary to call evidence, the accused is required to make advance disclosure of the general nature of his defence (30-015) and of any expert evidence (30-024) upon which he proposes to rely.

B. The application of the common law

30-006 The common law rules on disclosure as set out in *R. v Keane* (1994) 99 Cr. App. R. 1:

(1) continue to apply where a case does not fall within CPIA 1996;
(2) govern disclosure prior to the stage when the Act applies, i.e. to cases where the criminal investigation started before 1 April 1997 (30-004); and
(3) govern the judge's decision in relation to disclosure of sensitive material for which public interest immunity is claimed (30-049 and following).

C. The Criminal Procedure and Investigations Act 1996

Application of the Act

30-007 CPIA 1996 applies to cases reaching the Crown Court by any of the recognised channels set out in s.1(2), i.e. where:

- the matter has been sent to the Crown Court pursuant to CDA 1998 ss.51 or 51A;
- a matter has been added to the indictment in accordance with CJA 1988 s.40;
- a voluntary bill has been preferred under AJ(MP)A 1933 s.2(2)(b) or POA 1985 s.22B(3)(a); or
- following the preferment of a bill of indictment charging a person with an indictable offence under the authority of AJ(MP)A 1933 s.2(2)(ba) (bill of indictment preferred with consent of a Crown Court judge following approval of a deferred prosecution agreement), the suspension of the proceedings against the person under CCA 2013 Sch.17 para.2(2) is lifted under para.2(3) of that Schedule.

1. Initial duty of prosecutor to disclose

General

30-008 The disclosure process must be led by the prosecution so as to trigger comprehensive defence engagement, supported by robust judicial case management (*JPD 2013* 6). In relation to cases in which a criminal investigation began *after 4 April 2005*, CJA 2003 Pt 5 replaces the previous two-stage test with a new objective single test for the disclosure of unused prosecution material to the defence.

The former duty of secondary disclosure by the prosecutor is replaced with a revised continuing duty to disclose material that meets the new test, and he is specifically required to review the prosecution material on receipt of the defence statement, and to make further disclosure as required under his continuing duty.

In relation to criminal investigations begun before 4 April 2005, the former two-tier procedure applies.

Under the newer provisions the prosecutor is required (CPIA 1996 s.3) to:

(1) disclose to the defence any prosecution material which has not previously been disclosed to the accused and which might reasonably be considered capable of undermining the case for the prosecution against the accused, or of assisting the case for the accused; or

(2) give the accused a written statement that there is no such material, informing the Crown Court officer that he has done so.

The test for disclosure under s.3 of the CPIA 1996 as amended will be applicable in nearly every case and all those involved in the process will need to be familiar with it. Material fulfils the test if—but only if—it "might reasonably be considered capable of undermining the case for the prosecution … or of assisting the case for the accused" (*JPD 2013* 5).

"Prosecution material" for the purposes of both initial and continuing disclosure by the prosecution is defined as material which:

(a) is in the prosecutor's possession and came into his possession in connection with the case for the prosecution against the accused; or
(b) in pursuance of the Code of Practice, he has inspected in connection with the case for the prosecution against the accused.

The prosecutor and the defence are both under a duty to engage promptly in order to aid understanding of the defence case and the likely issues for trial at an early stage and regularly throughout proceedings (Attorney General's *Guidelines on Disclosure for Investigators, Prosecutors and Defence Practitioners* (2022), para.83).

Information affecting credibility of defence witness

At common law, information affecting only the credibility of a defence witness did not need to be disclosed (*R. v Brown* [1995] 1 Cr. App. R. 191) unless it also contained evidence favourable to the accused (*R. v Mills* [1998] 1 Cr. App. R. 43). As to the disclosure of previous convictions, see *R. v Vasilou* [2000] Crim. L.R. 845 and now the "bad character" provisions in CJA 2003; the fact that a witness giving evidence can expect to receive a reward at the conclusion of the trial ought to be disclosed (*R. v Allan* [2004] EWCA Crim 2236; [2005] Crim. L.R. 716). **30-009**

Time within which prosecutor must act

Although no specific time limit is prescribed, the prosecutor must (CPIA 1996 s.13(1)) act under this provision as soon as is "reasonably practicable" after the: **30-010**

(1) accused pleads not guilty;
(2) accused is committed or transferred for trial;
(3) accused is sent for trial under CDA 1998 s.51;
(4) court includes a count in the indictment; or
(5) bill of indictment is preferred,

depending on the manner in which the matter comes before the Crown Court.

When a case is sent to the Crown Court under CDA 1998 s.51, the rules allow the prosecutor 70 days from the date on which the case was sent, or 50 days where the accused is in custody, within which to serve the evidence on which the charge or charges are based (SI 2005/902). These time limits may be extended or varied at the court's direction.

Case management; enforcement of scheme

The Attorney General's *Guidelines on Disclosure for Investigators, Prosecutors and Defence Practitioners* (2022) state that any party who takes the view that **30-011** another party is not complying with their obligations under the disclosure regime should bring this to the attention of the court as soon as possible, and the *JPD 2013* makes it clear that the judge has a duty to enforce the statutory scheme.

He:

(1) should keep the timetable for prosecution and defence disclosure under review from the first hearing; and
(2) should as a matter of course ask the parties to identify the issues in the case, and invite the parties to indicate whether further disclosure is sought, and on what topics.

It is not enough for the judge to rely on the content of the PTPH form.

Proper completion of the disclosure process is a vital part of case preparation, and it may well affect the progress of the case:

(a) the judge will expect disclosure to have been considered from the outset;
(b) the prosecution and defence advocates need to be aware of any potential problems;
(c) substantive difficulties should be explained to the judge; and
(d) the parties should propose a sensible timetable.

Realism is preferable to optimistic but unachievable deadlines which may dislocate the court schedule and imperil the date of trial. It follows that judges should not impose deadlines for service of the case papers or disclosure until they are confident that the prosecution advocate has taken instructions from the individuals who are best placed to evaluate the work to be undertaken (*JPD 2013* 7).

Progress and review

30-012 The advocates—both prosecution and defence—must be kept fully informed throughout the course of the proceedings as to any difficulties which may prevent them from complying with their disclosure obligations. When problems arise or come to light after directions have been given, the advocates should notify the court and the other party (or parties) immediately rather than waiting until the date set by the court for the service of the material is imminent or has passed, and they must provide the court with a suggested timetable in order to resolve the problem (*JPD 2013* 8).

The progress of the disclosure process should be reviewed at every hearing. There remains no basis in practice or law for counsel to counsel disclosure (*JPD 2013* 8).

The judge should seize the opportunity to impose an early timetable for disclosure and to identify any likely problems, including issues concerning third party material and material that will require an application to the Family Court. In an appropriate case the court should consider holding a joint criminal/care directions hearing (*JPD 2013* 9).

Effectiveness of PTPH

30-013 Due to the time provided for the service of a defence statement it will only very rarely be available before the PTPH.

Note that:

(1) under the previous regime if there was no defence statement by the time of the PCMH the judge would normally require the trial advocate to see that

such a statement was provided and not proceed with the PCMH until that was done. In the ordinary case the trial advocate may have been required to do that at court, and the PCMH resumed later in the day to avoid delay and further costs;

(2) at the PTPH the trial advocate should see it as part of his duty to assist the judge with the management of the case by setting out information on the PTPH Form, without the risk of the information so provided being used as a statement admissible in evidence against the accused.

Provided the case is conducted in accordance with the letter and spirit of the CrimPR, no information or statement written on the PTPH Form should, in the exercise of the judge's discretion under PACE 1984 s.78, be admitted in evidence as a statement that can be used against the accused. The information is provided to assist the court (*R. v Newell* [2012] EWCA Crim 650; [2012] 2 Cr. App. R. 10; see also *Valiati v DPP* [2018] EWHC 2908 (Admin); [2019] 1 Cr. App. R. 17).

Engagement of parties

Questions of disclosure must be decided by the prosecutor, and the judge's assistance should only be sought if a question can properly be decided by him, most obviously where questions of public interest immunity are involved (*R. v B* [2000] Crim. L.R. 500). In *R. v Olu* [2010] EWCA Crim 2975; [2011] 1 Cr. App. R. 33, the CACD observed that disclosure under the CPIA 1996 regime must be carried out "thinkingly" and not as a "box-ticking exercise". It is the task of a prosecution lawyer to identify the issues in the case and for a police officer, who is not trained in that skill, to act under the guidance of the prosecutor. **30-014**

The judge should not allow the prosecution to avoid their statutory responsibility for reviewing the unused material by the expedient of permitting the defence to have access to (or providing the defence with copies of) the material listed in the schedules of non-sensitive unused prosecution material irrespective of whether it satisfies, wholly or in part, the relevant test for disclosure. Additionally, it is for the prosecutor to decide on the manner of disclosure, and it does not have to mirror the form in which the information was originally recorded (see per Rose LJ in *R. v CPS (Interlocutory Application under sections 35/36 CPIA)* [2005] EWCA Crim 2342) (see also CASE MANAGEMENT). Allowing the defence to inspect items that fulfil the disclosure test is also a valid means of providing disclosure (*JPD 2013* 13).

Note that:

(1) the larger and more complex the case, the more important it is for the prosecution to adhere to the overarching principle and ensure that sufficient prosecution attention and resources are allocated to the task; and

(2) handing the defendant the "keys to the warehouse" has been the cause of many gross abuses in the past, resulting in considerable expenditure by the defence without any material benefit to the course of justice (*JPD 2013* 14).

The circumstances relating to large and complex cases are outlined below at 36-039.

The judge will require the defence:

(a) to engage and assist in the early identification of the real issues in the case; and

(b) particularly in the larger and more complex cases, to contribute to the search terms to be used for, and the parameters of, the review of any electronically held material.

Any defence criticisms of the prosecution approach to disclosure should be timely and reasoned; there is no place for disclosure "ambushes" or for late or uninformative defence statements.

Admissions should be used so far as possible to narrow the real issues in dispute (*JPD 2013* 15).

A constructive approach to disclosure is a necessary part of professional best practice, for the defence and prosecution. This does not undermine the defendant's legitimate interests—it accords with his or her obligations under the CrimPR and it ensures that all the relevant material is provided.

Delays and failures by the prosecution and the defence are equally damaging to a timely, fair and efficient trial, and judges should be vigilant in preventing and addressing abuses. Accordingly, whenever there are potential failings by either the defence or the prosecution, judges, in exercising appropriate oversight of disclosure, should carefully investigate the suggested default and give timely directions (*JPD 2013* 16).

2. Compulsory disclosure by accused

General

30-015 In relation to criminal investigations begun after 4 April 2005, CJA 2003 Pt 5 requires the accused to provide a more detailed defence statement than was previously required.

Where the prosecutor has complied, or purported to comply, with the initial duty on him, the accused must give a defence statement both to the court and to the prosecutor (CPIA 1996 s.5(5)). The defence statement should:

(1) set out the nature of his defence (but see *R. v Tibbs* [2000] 2 Cr. App. R. 309; *R. v Wheeler* [2001] 1 Cr. App. R. 10);
(2) indicate the matters on which he takes issue with the prosecutor; and
(3) set out, in respect of each such matter, the reason why he takes issue with the prosecutor.

(CPIA 1996 s.6A)

Service of the defence statement is a most important stage in the disclosure process, and timely service is necessary to facilitate proper consideration of the disclosure issues well in advance of the trial date. The judge will expect a defence statement to contain a clear and detailed exposition of the issues of fact and law. Defence statements that merely rehearse the suggestion that the accused is innocent do not comply with the requirements of CPIA 1996 (*JPD 2013* 17).

As to the contents of such a statement, see 30-019. It must be served on the court officer and on the prosecutor (CrimPR 15.4).

Time limits

30-016 Timely service of the statement will allow for the proper consideration of disclosure issues well in advance of the trial date.

Defence disclosure must be:

(1) made within 28 days of the date upon which the prosecutor complies, or purports to comply, with the requirements of initial disclosure; and
(2) extended, if the judge so orders, by as many days as he (entirely at his own discretion) specifies.

Where the relevant period would end on a weekend, or on Christmas Day, Good Friday or a bank holiday, it is to be treated as expiring on the next day that is not one of those days.

There may be cases where it is not possible to serve a proper defence case statement within the 28-day time limit; well-founded defence applications for an extension of time under (2) above may be granted in a proper case.

The judge may extend the period only if an application is made by the accused before the end of the 28-day period which specifies the grounds for an extension and the length of the proposed extension (DDTLR 2011 reg.3(3)). The judge must be satisfied that it would be unreasonable to require the accused to provide a defence statement within the relevant period (DDTLR 2011 reg.3(2)). There is no limit on the number of applications that may be made.

Prosecutor's representations

The prosecutor should consider the defence statement carefully and promptly provide a copy to the disclosure officer, to assist the prosecution in its continuing disclosure obligations. The judge will expect the prosecutor to identify any deficiencies in the defence statement, and to draw these to the attention of the defence and the court; in particular in large and complex cases, it will assist the court if this is done in writing. **30-017**

Although the prosecution's ability to request, and the court's jurisdiction to give, an adverse inference direction under CPIA 1996 s.11 is not contingent on the prosecution having earlier identified any suggested deficiencies, nevertheless the prosecutor should provide a timely written explanation of its position.

Voluntary disclosure by accused

Where the prosecutor complies with his duty of initial disclosure under s.3 above, or purports to comply with it, the accused may give a defence statement to the prosecutor, and if he does so, must give one to the court. **30-018**

If the accused gives such a statement, he must give it during the period which is, by virtue of CPIA 1996 s.12, the relevant period (CPIA 1996 s.6, Sch.25 Pt 2 paras 20 and 26).

Contents of defence statement

A purported defence statement which is little more than reiteration of the accused's plea (i.e. an assertion that he is not guilty) is not a proper defence statement under the Act. A defence statement must comply with the requisite formalities set out in CPIA 1996 s.5(6) and (7) or s.6A as applicable (*R. v Bryant* [2005] EWCA Crim 2079 (per Judge LJ at [12])). **30-019**

Where the pre-April 2005 regime applies under CPIA 1996, the accused must, in his defence statement, set out the nature of his defence in general terms, indicating the matters upon which he takes issue with the prosecutor and setting out, in relation to each matter, why issue is taken. Any alibi defence relied upon must comply with the formalities in s.5(7)(a) and (b).

Where the enhanced requirements for defence disclosure apply under s.6A of the Act, i.e. where the case involves a criminal investigation commencing on or after 4 April 2005, the defence statement must (CPIA 1996 s.6A(1)):

(1) set out the nature of the accused's defence, including any particular defences on which he intends to rely;

(2) indicate the matters of fact on which he takes issue with the prosecution;
(3) where the criminal investigation commenced after 3 November 2008 set out the particulars of the matters of fact on which he intends to rely for the purposes of his defence;
(4) in the case of each such matter, set out why he takes issue with the prosecution; and
(5) indicate any point of law (including any point as to the admissibility of evidence) or abuse of process which he wishes to take, and any authority on which he intends to rely for that purpose.

Where an accused has no positive case to advance but declines to plead guilty, he is under no obligation to put into the statement an admission of guilt or a refusal to give instructions. However, the statement must say that:

(a) the accused does not admit the offence or relevant part of it; and
(b) the accused calls on the prosecutor to prove it, advancing no positive case,

because if he did advance a positive case he would have to give notice of it and it would have to appear in the statement (*R. v Rochford* [2010] EWCA Crim 1928; [2011] 1 Cr. App. R. 11 and see *R. v Malcolm* [2011] EWCA Crim 2069; [2012] Crim. L.R. 238).

A defence statement purporting to be given under ss.5, 6 or 6B above or a statement of the kind mentioned in s.6B(4) given on behalf of an accused by his solicitor will, unless the contrary is proved, be deemed to be given with the authority of the accused (CPIA 1996 s.6E).

Preparation of defence statements

30-020 In *R. v Rochford* [2010] EWCA Crim 1928; [2011] 1 Cr. App. R. 11 the CACD said of the requirements of the contents of defence statements under s.6A:

(1) the accused is not required to advance a positive case if he simply intends to put the prosecutor to proof, but the defence statement must say so;
(2) the accused is not required to breach his rights to legal professional privilege or to incriminate himself;
(3) the obligation to file a defence statement is a statutory obligation on the accused and it is not open to a lawyer to disobey his client's statutory obligation. If it were otherwise, it would be open to any accused at trial to put in evidence that he had been so advised, therefore resulting in no adverse comment, depriving s.11(5) of any effect; and
(4) if the accused refuses to plead but advances no positive case, his lawyer should go no further than to explain the nature and extent of the statutory obligation and to advise of the consequences of disobedience.

The judge must be alert to ensure that defendants do not suffer because of the failings of their lawyers, but there must be a clear indication to the professions that if justice is to be done, and if disclosure is to be dealt with fairly in accordance with the law, a full and careful defence case statement is essential.

Alibi defence

30-021 Where an alibi defence is relied upon:

(1) in relation to the pre-4 April 2005 regime, the particulars must comply with s.5(7)(a) and (b) of the Act; and

(2) in relation to the post-4 April 2005 regime, s.6A(2) of the Act applies and the defence statement must give particulars which include:
   (a) the name, address and date of birth of any witness the accused believes is able to give evidence in support of the alibi, or as many of those details as are known to the accused when the statement is given; and
   (b) any information in the accused's possession which might be of material assistance in identifying or finding any such witness in whose case any of the details mentioned in paragraph (a) are not known to the accused when the statement is given.

In *R. (on the application of Tinnion) v Reading Crown Court* [2009] EWHC 2930 (Admin); [2010] Crim. L.R. 733, it was said obiter that breach of this provision does not render the evidence of a witness inadmissible; the appropriate sanction is not that such a witness should not be called but that adverse comment may be made pursuant to CPIA 1996 s.11, and the court or jury may draw such inferences as appear proper from the failure to comply. See also *R. v Ullah* [2011] EWCA Crim 3275.

"Evidence in support of an alibi": definition

"Evidence in support of an alibi" is evidence tending to show that, by reason of the presence of the accused at a particular place or in a particular area at a particular time, he was not, or was unlikely to have been, at the place where the offence is alleged to have been committed at the time of its alleged commission (CPIA 1996 s.6A(3)). **30-022**

Insofar as an alibi defence is concerned, if at trial the accused said that he was located somewhere else at the material time or called evidence that he was somewhere else, he will have failed to comply if no notification has been given.

The statutory obligation to give the name and address of an alibi is triggered by the accused's belief that the witness is able to give evidence in support of the alibi. It is not necessary that the alibi witness can give such evidence let alone that he is also willing to do so (*Re Joseph Hill* [2013] EWCA Crim 775; [2013] 2 Cr. App. R. 20).

The judge's role

The judge must insist that the defence case statement is served by the due date, and he should then examine it with care to ensure that it complies with the formalities required by the Act (see 30-016 and 30-019) bearing in mind that: **30-023**

(1) if material does not weaken the prosecution case or strengthen that of the accused, there is no requirement to disclose it;
(2) for this purpose the parties' respective cases should not be restrictively analysed, but they must be carefully analysed, to ascertain the specific facts the prosecution seek to establish and the specific grounds on which the charges are resisted;
(3) the trial process is not well served if the defence are permitted to make general and unspecified allegations and then seek far-reaching disclosure in the hope that material may turn up to make them good; and
(4) neutral material or material damaging to the accused need not be disclosed and should not be brought to the attention of the court. (*R. v H* [2004] UKHL 3; [2004] 2 Cr. App. R. 10).

Where:

(a) no defence case statement is served, or an inadequate defence case statement is served within the relevant time limits, the judge should investigate the position;
(b) at a PTPH or FCMH there is no defence statement (even where an extension has been given or the time for filing has not yet expired), the defence should be warned in appropriate terms that pursuant to CPIA 1996 s.6E(2) an adverse inference may be drawn during the trial, and that this result is likely if there is no justification for the deficiency, and a note should be made that the warning has been given.

(*JPD 2013* 20)

Section 6E(2) (referred to in (b) above) provides that in relation to a criminal investigation begun after 4 April 2005, if it appears to the judge at a pre-trial hearing that an accused has failed to comply fully with ss.5, 6B or 6C, so that there is a possibility of comment being made or inferences drawn under s.11(5), he must warn the accused accordingly.

Any order by the judge to comply with the requirements of ss.5(5) and 6A of the Act to serve a defence statement in the required form is no more than an articulation of the provisions of the Act; he cannot invest himself with an extra-statutory power to punish non-compliance as a contempt of court. The sanctions are explicit in s.11 (*R. v Rochford* [2010] EWCA Crim 1928; [2011] 1 Cr. App. R. 11).

A lawyer is not permitted to advise an accused not to file a defence statement, or to omit from it something required by s.6A.

Notification of intention to call defence witnesses

30-024 In relation to cases reaching the Crown Court on or after 28 February 2011, an accused is required to serve on the court and on the prosecutor notice setting out:

(1) details of any witnesses whom he intends to call; and also
(2) details of all experts instructed, including those not called to give evidence.

(CPIA 1996 s.6C)

The notice must be served within 28 days of initial disclosure, unless the period is extended (DDTLR 2011 reg.2). A notice must be served even if it is not proposed to call any defence witnesses.

The Code of Practice for Interviews of Witnesses Notified by Accused (SI 2010/1223) governs the arrangement of police interviews with the defence witnesses disclosed.

Notification of names of experts

30-025 CPIA 1996 s.6D, which has not yet been brought into force, provides that if the accused instructs a person with a view to his providing any expert opinion for possible use as evidence for the trial of the accused, he must give to the court and the prosecutor, during the period specified in s.12, a notice specifying the person's name and address, unless that information has already been given under s.6C (30-024).

For rules governing the service of expert evidence, see CrimPR 19.

Disclosure by accused: copies to jury

The judge in a trial before a jury: **30-026**

(1) may, whether of his own motion or on application of a party, and where he is of opinion that seeing a copy of the defence statement would help the jury to understand the case or to resolve any issue in the case, direct that the jury be given a copy of any defence statement; and
(2) if he does so, may direct that it be edited so as not to include references to matters evidence of which would be inadmissible.

The reference here to "a defence statement" is a reference, where the accused has given:

(a) only an initial defence statement (that is, a defence statement given under ss.5 or 6), to that statement;
(b) both an initial defence statement and an updated defence statement (that is, a defence statement given under s.6B), to the updated defence statement; and
(c) both an initial defence statement and a statement of the kind mentioned in s.6B(4), to the initial defence statement.

(CPIA 1996 s.6E(4)–(6))

For an illustration of the exercise of this discretion, see *R. v Sanghera* [2012] EWCA Crim 16; [2012] 2 Cr. App. R. 17.

3. Continuing duty of prosecutor to disclose

At all times in relation to an alleged offence into which a criminal investigation has begun on or after 15 July 2005: **30-027**

(1) after the prosecutor has complied with s.3, or purported to comply with it; and
(2) before the accused is acquitted or convicted, or the prosecutor decides not to proceed with the case concerned,

the prosecutor must keep under review the question whether at any given time taking into account the state of affairs at that time (including the case for the prosecution as it stands at that time and, in particular, following the giving of a defence statement), there is prosecution material which:

(a) might reasonably be considered capable of undermining the case for the prosecution against the accused or of assisting the case for the accused; and
(b) has not been disclosed to the accused.

If there is, he must disclose it to the accused as soon as is reasonably practicable (or within the period mentioned in s.7A(5)(a), where that applies).

(CPIA 1996 s.7A, see also *JPD 2013* 22)

Where the accused gives a defence statement under ss.5, 6 or 6B, and if as a result of that statement:

(i) the prosecutor is required by this section to make any disclosure, or further disclosure, he must do so during the relevant period under s.12; but
(ii) he should only disclose material in response to such a request if the material meets the appropriate test for disclosure and if he declines to make disclosure he will during that period give to the accused a written state-

ment to that effect, and the matter must proceed to a formal hearing under s.8 (see 30-028).

(CPIA 1996 s.7A(5))

Subsections (3)–(5) of s.3 (methods by which prosecutor may make disclosure) apply equally to continuing disclosure.

Material must not be disclosed under this section to the extent that the court, on an application by the prosecutor, concludes it is not in the public interest to disclose it and orders accordingly, or to the extent that it is material the disclosure of which is prohibited by the Investigatory Powers Act 2016 s.56 (CPIA 1996 s.7A(8)–(9)).

Application by accused for disclosure: (1) notice

30-028 Where the accused has given a defence statement under ss.5 or 6 or 6B and the prosecutor has complied with s.7A(5) or has purported to comply with it or has failed to comply with it, if the accused has at any time reasonable cause to believe that:

(1) there is prosecution material which is required under s.7A to be disclosed to him; and
(2) that material has not been disclosed to him,

he may apply to the court for an order requiring the prosecutor to disclose such material to him.

(CPIA 1996 s.8)

The procedure for an application under s.8 is to be found in CrimPR 15.5.

The accused must serve notice on the Crown Court officer and on the prosecutor:

(i) describing the material that he wants the prosecutor to disclose;
(ii) explaining why he thinks there is reasonable cause to believe that:
  — the prosecutor has that material; and
  — it is material which CPIA 1996 requires the prosecutor to disclose; and
(iii) asking for a hearing, if he wants one, and explaining why it is needed.

Application by accused for disclosure: (2) nature of procedure

30-029 The judge should set a date as part of the timetabling exercise by which any application under s.8 is to be made, if this appears to be a likely eventuality.

The judge will require the s.8 application to be served on the prosecution well in advance of the hearing—indeed, prior to requesting the hearing—to enable the prosecutor to identify and serve any items that meet the test for disclosure.

Note that:

(1) service of a defence statement is an essential precondition for an application under s.8; and
(2) applications should not be heard or directions for disclosure issued in the absence of a properly completed statement.

In particular, blanket orders in this context are inconsistent with the statutory framework for disclosure laid down by the CPIA 1996 and the decision of the House of Lords in *R. v H* [2004] UKHL 3; [2004] 2 Cr. App. R. 10. It follows that defence requests for disclosure of particular pieces of unused prosecution material which are not referable to any issue in the case identified in the defence statement should be rejected.

The judge must ensure that the accused are not prejudiced by the failures of their legal representatives, and, when necessary, the professions should be reminded that if justice is to be done, and if disclosure is to be dealt with fairly in accordance with the law, a full and careful defence statement and a reasoned approach to s.8 applications are essential. In exploring the adequacy of the defence statement, a judge should always ask what the issues are and upon what matters of fact the accused intends to rely and with which matters of fact he takes issue (*JPD 2013* 24–27).

Application by accused: (3) dealing with the application

The judge may determine any such application at a hearing, in public or in private or without a hearing, but must not require the prosecutor to disclose material unless the prosecutor is present, or has had at least 14 days in which to make representations (CrimPR 15.5(4)–(5)). **30-030**

On an application by the prosecutor, the judge may give leave for the matter to be determined in the absence of the accused and his legal representative.

Note that a s.8 application is not a "question of law" under CJA 1987 s.9 or CPIA 1996 s.31(3)(c) and so does not fall to be decided within the scope of a preparatory hearing, although nothing prevents it being dealt with in parallel proceedings on the occasion of a preparatory hearing.

The consideration of detailed defence requests for specific disclosure (so-called "shopping lists") otherwise than in accordance with CrimPR 15.5 is wholly improper. Likewise, defence requests for specific disclosure of unused prosecution material in purported pursuance of CPIA 1996 s.8 and CrimPR 15.5, but which are not referable to any issue in the case identified by the defence case statement, should be rejected.

Application by accused for disclosure: (4) listing

Cases that raise particularly difficult issues of disclosure should be referred to the Resident Judge for directions (unless a trial judge has been allocated) and, for trials of real complexity, the trial judge should be identified at an early stage, prior to the PTPH if possible (see CASE MANAGEMENT). Listing officers, working in consultation with the Resident Judge and, if allocated, the trial judge, should ensure that sufficient time is allowed for judges to prepare and deal with prosecution and defence applications relating to disclosure, particularly in the more complex cases (*JPD 2013* 28 and 29). **30-031**

Methods of disclosure

Where disclosure by the prosecutor is required, and: **30-032**

(1) the material consists of information which has been recorded in any form:
   (a) the prosecutor discloses it by securing that a copy is made of it and that the copy is given to the accused; or
   (b) if, in the prosecutor's opinion, that is not practicable or is not desirable, by allowing the accused to inspect it at a reasonable time and a reasonable place, or by taking steps to secure that he is allowed to do so, and a copy may be in such form as the prosecutor thinks fit and need not be in the same form as that in which the information has already been recorded;
(2) the material consists of information which has not been recorded, the

(2) prosecutor discloses it by securing that it is recorded in such form as he thinks fit and taking either of the disclosure steps set out in (a) and (b) above;

(3) the material does not consist of information, the prosecutor discloses it by allowing the accused to inspect it at a reasonable time and a reasonable place or by taking steps to secure that he is allowed to do so.

(CPIA 1996 ss.3(3)–(5), 5)

The above provisions do not apply in relation to disclosure required by the Sexual Offences (Protected Material) Act 1997 ss.3, 7 or 9. Section 3(1) applies in relation to that disclosure (s.9(2)).

Material must not be disclosed under these provisions to the extent that it is:

(i) material the disclosure of which is prohibited by the Investigatory Powers Act 2016 s.56; or
(ii) material which a judge, on the application of the prosecutor, decides that it is not in the public interest for it to be disclosed (see 30-049 and following) and orders accordingly.

4. Default by prosecutor

30-033 Where the prosecutor:

(1) purports to act under s.3 *after* the end of the period which, by virtue of s.12 is the relevant period for ss.3 or 12; or
(2) purports to act under s.7A(5) *after* the end of the period which by virtue of s.12 is the relevant period for s.7A,

then this failure to act within the time limit concerned does not, on its own, constitute grounds for staying the proceedings for abuse of process (see ABUSE OF PROCESS), but his failure may constitute such grounds if it involves such delay by him that the accused is denied a fair trial (CPIA 1996 s.10).

5. Default by accused

30-034 The trial judge or any other party may make such comment as appears appropriate, and the judge or jury may draw such inferences as appear proper, in deciding whether the accused is guilty of the offence concerned, in three different sets of circumstances (CPIA 1996 s.11(5)).

The first set of circumstances

30-035 The first set of circumstances in which comments may be made is where the accused:

(1) fails to give an initial defence statement;
(2) gives an initial defence statement, but does so after the end of the period which is the relevant period for s.5 by virtue of s.12;
(3) is required by s.6B to give an updated statement or a statement of the kind mentioned in s.6B(4), but fails to do so;
(4) gives an updated statement, or a statement of the kind mentioned in s.6B(4), but does so after the end of the period which is the relevant period for s.6B by virtue of s.12;
(5) sets out inconsistent defences in his defence statement; or

(6) at his trial:
   (a) puts forward a defence which was not mentioned in his defence statement or is different from any defence set out in that statement;
   (b) relies on a matter (or any particular of any matter of fact) which, in breach of the requirements imposed by or under s.6A, was not mentioned in his defence statement [NB: no comment without leave of the court if the matter not mentioned was a point of law or an authority; see CPIA 1996 s.11(6)];
   (c) adduces evidence in support of an alibi without having given particulars of the alibi in his defence statement; or
   (d) calls a witness to give evidence in support of an alibi without having complied with s.6A(2)(a) or (b).

The second set of circumstances

The second set of circumstances in which comment may be made is where s.6 applies; that is, where the accused gives an initial defence statement, but: **30-036**

(1) gives the initial defence statement after the end of the period which, by virtue of s.12, is the relevant period for s.6; or
(2) does any of the things mentioned in paras (3)–(6) in 30-035 ("the first set of circumstances").

The third set of circumstances

The third set of circumstances in which comment may be made (and here any comment by another party under subs.(5)(a) may be made only with the leave of the court; see CPIA 1996 s.11(7)) is where the accused: **30-037**

(1) gives a witness notice but does so after the end of the period which, by virtue of s.12, is the relevant period for s.6C; or
(2) at his trial calls a witness not included, or not adequately identified, in a witness notice.

Where the accused puts forward a defence which is different from any defence set out in his defence statement, then in doing anything under subs.(5) or in deciding whether to do anything under it, the judge must have regard to:

(a) the extent of the difference in the defences; and
(b) whether there is any justification for it.

For a "perfectly correct and proper" judicial direction on discrepancies between the evidence of the accused and the contents of his defence statement, see *R. v Gregory* [2011] EWCA Crim 3276. But if the accused is cross-examined about discrepancies between his evidence and his defence statement the judge must give appropriate guidance to the jury—see *R. v Haynes* [2011] EWCA Crim 3281.

A person may not be convicted of an offence solely on an inference drawn under s.11(5) (CPIA 1996 s.11(10)).

Where the accused calls a witness whom he has failed to include, or to identify adequately, in a witness notice, in doing anything under s.11(5) or in deciding whether to do anything under it the judge must have regard to whether there is any justification for the failure (CPIA 1996 s.11(9)).

Interpretation

30-038 In these provisions (CPIA 1996 s.11(12)):

(1) "initial defence statement" means a defence statement given under ss.5 or 6;
(2) "updated defence statement" means a defence statement given under s.6B;
(3) a reference simply to an accused's "defence statement" is a reference:
   (a) where he has given only an initial defence statement, to that statement;
   (b) where he has given both an initial and an updated defence statement, to the updated defence statement;
   (c) where he has given both an initial statement and a statement of the kind mentioned in s.6B(4), to the initial defence statement;
(4) a reference to evidence in support of an alibi must be construed in accordance with s.6A(3); and
(5) "witness notice" means a notice given under s.6C.

D. Large and complex cases

30-039 Disclosure is a particular problem in larger and more complex cases, which require a scrupulous approach by the parties and robust case management by the judiciary (see CASE MANAGEMENT). *JPD 2013* (38–43) makes a number of recommendations in relation to such cases:

(1) the trial judge should be identified at the outset, if possible;
(2) legal representatives need to fulfil their duties in this context with care and efficiency, co-operating with the other party (or parties) and the judge;
(3) the judge and the other party (or parties) need to be informed of any difficulties as soon as they arise;
(4) the judge should be provided with an up-to-date timetable for disclosure whenever there are material changes in this regard;
(5) a disclosure management document, or similar, prepared by the prosecution will be of particular assistance to the court; and
(6) the judge should be prepared to give early guidance as to the prosecution's approach on disclosure, thereby ensuring early engagement by the defence.

Cases of this nature frequently include large volumes of digitally stored material. The Attorney General's *Guidelines on Disclosure for Investigators, Prosecutors and Defence Practitioners* (2022), and in particular *Annex A—Digital Material* are of particular assistance in this context.

The problems presented by vast quantities of digital files were recently considered in *R. v R* [2015] EWCA Crim 1941; [2016] 1 Cr. App. R. 20. The CACD held that:

(a) the prosecution has to take a grip on its case and disclosure requirements from the outset;
(b) the prosecution must adopt a considered and appropriately resourced approach to making initial disclosure—this must include the overall disclosure strategy, selection of software tools, identifying and isolating material that may be subject to LPP, and proposing search terms to be applied;
(c) the duty of making initial disclosure should not be rendered incapable of fulfilment through the physical impossibility of reading and scheduling each

and every item—the prosecution is entitled to use appropriate sampling and search terms, and its record keeping and scheduling obligations are modified accordingly;

(d) the judicial task of active and robust case management is not restricted to the secondary or subsequent stages of disclosure—the judge must also robustly manage initial disclosure, utilising the full range of case management powers;

(e) if the prosecution approach to initial disclosure is manifestly flawed, the court is entitled and obliged to give orders to address those flaws—the judge is not limited to exhortation and veiled warning as to later consequences;

(f) there can be no objection to the judge, after discussion with the parties, devising a bespoke approach to disclosure, but the scheme of CPIA 1996 must not be subverted; and

(g) the constant aim must be to make progress, if need be in parallel, from initial disclosure to defence statement, addressing requests for further disclosure.

See also *R. v Whale and West* [2016] EWCA Crim 742, in which the CACD held that the CPIA regime does apply to: (a) documentation created or received by a defendant himself; and (b) documents said to be required for memory refreshing.

See *R. v E* [2018] EWCA Crim 2426; [2019] Crim. L.R. 151 for an analysis of the circumstances in which a prosecution might properly be stayed as an abuse of process as a result of a conceded failure to pursue a line of enquiry when investigating allegations of sexual assault (text messages from complainant's mobile telephone). For guidance on the circumstances in which it is necessary for investigators to seek and disclose details of a witness's digital communications, see *R. v CB* [2020] EWCA Crim 790; [2020] 2 Cr. App. R. 20.

Applications for witness anonymity orders require particular attention; as the Court of Appeal noted in *R. v Mayers* [2008] EWCA Crim 2989; [2009] 1 Cr. App. R. 30, in making such an application, the prosecution's obligations of disclosure "go much further than the ordinary duties of disclosure".

If the judge considers that there are reasonable grounds to doubt the good faith of the investigation, he will be concerned to see that there has been independent and effective appraisal of the documents contained in the disclosure schedule and that its contents are adequate. In appropriate cases where this issue has arisen and there are grounds which show there is a real cause for concern, consideration should be given to receiving evidence on oath from the senior investigating officer at an early case management hearing.

E. Material held by third parties

General

Where material is held by a third party such as a local authority, a social services department, hospital or business, the prosecution may need to make enquiries of the third party, with a view to inspecting the material and assessing whether the relevant test for disclosure is met and determining whether any or all of the material should be retained, recorded and, in due course, disclosed to the accused. If access is granted, the prosecution will need to establish whether the custodian of the material intends to raise PII issues (see 30-049), as a result of which the material may have to be placed before the court for a decision. This does not obviate the need for the defence to conduct its own enquiries as appropriate. Speculative enquiries 30-040 without any proper basis in relation to third party material—whether by the prosecution or the defence—are to be discouraged, and, in appropriate cases, the judge will consider making an order for costs where an application is clearly unmeritorious and misconceived.

The revised Attorney General's *Guidelines on Disclosure for Investigators, Prosecutors and Defence Practitioners* (2022) identify a three step approach to accessing third party material (whether it is in the possession of the investigator or prosecutor or remains in the possession of the third party): (1) establishing a reasonable line of inquiry; (2) establishing relevance; and (3) balancing rights. A written record must be made of any decision to access third party material.

The *2013 Protocol and Good Practice Model: Disclosure of Information in Cases of Alleged Child Abuse and Linked Criminal and Care Directions Hearings* provides a framework and timetable for the police and CPS to obtain disclosable material from local authorities, and for applications to be made to the Family Court. It is applicable to all cases of alleged child abuse where the child is aged 17 years or under. It is not binding on local authorities, but it does represent best practice and therefore should be consulted in all such cases. Delays in obtaining this type of material lead to unacceptable delays to trials involving particularly vulnerable witnesses and every effort must be made to ensure that all disclosable material is identified at an early stage so that any necessary applications can be made and the defence receive material to which they are entitled in good time (*JPD 2013* 44 and 45).

Procedure

30-041 There is no specific procedure for disclosure of material held by third parties in criminal proceedings, although the procedure established under:

(1) CP(AW)A 1965 s.2; or
(2) MCA 1980 s.97,

is often used for this purpose. Both provisions require that the material in question is material evidence, i.e. immediately admissible in evidence in the proceedings (see *R. v Reading Justices Ex p. Berkshire CC* [1996] 1 Cr. App. R. 239; *R. v Derby Magistrates Court Ex p. B* [1996]1 Cr. App. R. 385 and *R. v Alibhai* [2004] EWCA Crim 681).

The revised Attorney General's *Guidelines on Disclosure for Investigators, Prosecutors and Defence Practitioners* (2022) provide that where a third party has refused access to material, and it is still believed that it is reasonable to seek production of the material and that the requirements of a witness summons are satisfied, where the material is sought pre-charge, investigators and prosecutors should request that the third party preserve the material and that request should be documented (para.43).

Further, where the third party in question declines to allow inspection of the material, or requires the prosecution to obtain an order before providing copies, the prosecutor will need to consider whether it is appropriate to obtain a witness summons under either of those sections. CrimPR 17 and paras 3.5 and 3.6 of the Code of Practice under the CPIA 1996 should be followed (*JPD 2013* 46).

Applications for third party disclosure must:

(a) identify the documents that are sought; and
(b) provide full details of why they are disclosable.

This is particularly relevant when access is sought to the medical records of those who allege they are victims of crime.

It should be appreciated that a duty to assert confidentiality may arise when a third party receives a request for disclosure, or the right to privacy may be claimed under ECHR art.8 (see in particular CrimPR 17.6). Victims do not waive the confidentiality of their medical records, or their right to privacy under art.8, by making a complaint against the accused.

The court, as a public authority, must ensure that any interference with the right to privacy under art.8 is in accordance with the law, and is necessary in pursuit of a legitimate public interest; general and unspecified requests to trawl through such records should be refused. Confidentiality rests with the subject of the material, not with the authority holding it. The subject is entitled to service of the application and has the right to make representations (CrimPR 17.5 and *R. (on the application of B) v Stafford Combined Court* [2006] EWHC 1645 (Admin); [2006] 2 Cr. App. R. 34). The 2013 Protocol and Good Practice Model at para.13 should be followed. It is likely that the judge will need to issue directions when issues of this kind are raised (e.g. whether enquiries with the third party are likely to be appropriate; who is to make the request; what material is to be sought, and from whom) and a timetable should be set (*JPD 2013* 47).

The judge will need to consider whether to take any steps if a third party fails, or refuses, to comply with a request for disclosure, including suggesting that either of the parties pursue the request and if necessary, make an application for a witness summons.

In these circumstances, the judge will need to set an appropriate timetable for compliance with CrimPR 17. Any failure to comply with the timetable must immediately be referred back to the court for further directions, although a hearing will not always be necessary. Generally, it may be appropriate for the defence to pursue requests of this kind when the prosecution, for good reason, decline to do so and the court will need to ensure that this procedure does not delay the trial (*JPD 2013* 48).

There are very limited circumstances in which information relating to Family Court proceedings (e.g. where there have been care proceedings in relation to a child who has complained to the police of mistreatment) may be communicated without a court order; see the Family Procedure Rules 12.73. Reference should be made to the 2013 Protocol and Good Practice Model. In most circumstances, a court order will be required and para.11 of the Protocol which sets out how an application should be made should be followed (*JPD 2013* 49).

Other Government Departments

Material held by other government departments or other Crown agencies will not be prosecution material for the purposes of CPIA 1996 ss.3(2) or 8(4) if it has not been inspected, recorded and retained during the course of the relevant criminal investigation. The CPIA Code of Practice and the Attorney General's Guidelines, however, impose a duty upon the prosecution to pursue all reasonable lines of inquiry and that may involve seeking disclosure from the relevant body (*JPD 2013* 50). **30-042**

Social services files

Where material is held by a third party such as a local authority, hospital or business, the prosecutor may seek to make arrangements to inspect the material with a view to applying the relevant test for disclosure to it and determining whether any **30-043** or all of the material should be retained, recorded and, in due course, disclosed to the accused. In considering the latter, the investigators and the prosecution will establish whether the holder of the material wishes to raise PII issues, as a result of which the material may have to be placed before the court.

CPIA 1996 s.16 gives such a party a right to make representations to the court. Where the third party in question declines to allow inspection of the material, or requires the prosecution to obtain an order before handing over copies of the material, the prosecutor will need to consider whether it is appropriate to obtain a witness summons under CP(AW)A 1965 s.2 (where the statutory requirements are satisfied and where the prosecutor considers that the material may satisfy the test for disclosure). *R. v Alibhai* [2004] EWCA Crim 681, makes it clear that the prosecutor has a "margin of consideration" in this regard.

Objections by third party

30-044 Where requests for disclosure are made by the prosecution, or anyone else, the third party may have a duty to assert confidentiality or the right to privacy under art.8 ECHR.

Where issues are raised in relation to allegedly relevant third party material, the judge must:

(1) ascertain whether enquiries with the third party are likely to be appropriate, and, if so, identify who is going to make the request, what material is to be sought, from whom the material is to be sought and within what time scale must the matter be resolved; and
(2) consider what action would be appropriate in the light of the third party failing or refusing to comply with a request, including inviting the defence to make the request on its own behalf and, if necessary, to make an application for a witness summons.

The judge should be aware that a summons can only be issued where the document(s) sought would be admissible in evidence.

While it may be that the material in question may be admissible in evidence as a result of the hearsay provisions of CJA 2003 ss.114–120, it is this that determines whether an order for production of the material is appropriate, rather than the wider considerations applicable to disclosure in criminal proceedings (see *R. v Reading Justices* [1996] 1 Cr. App. R. 239; *R. v Derby Magistrates Court* [1996] 1 Cr. App. R. 385).

Any directions made (for instance, the date by which an application for a witness summons with supporting affidavit under CP(AW)A 1965 s.2 should be served) should be put into writing at the time. Any failure to comply with the timetable must immediately be referred back to the court for further directions, although a hearing will not always be necessary.

Where the prosecution do not consider it appropriate to seek such a summons, the defence should consider doing so, where they are of the view (notwithstanding the prosecution assessment) that the third party may hold material which might undermine the prosecution case or assist that for the accused, and the material would be likely to be "material evidence" for the purposes of CP(AW)A 1965.

Relevance and use of material

30-045 The court, by issuing a witness summons to produce the documents, can only require disclosure of relevant or "material" documents.

On the authorities:

(1) to be "material" such documents must not only be relevant to the issues arising in the criminal proceedings, but must also be admissible in evidence;
(2) documents desired merely for the purpose of cross-examination are not admissible in evidence;
(3) the applicant must satisfy the court that there is a real possibility that the documents are likely to be material; and
(4) the procedure is not to be used as a fishing expedition (*R. v Reading Justices* [1996] 1 Cr. App. R. 239; *R. v Derby Magistrates Court* [1996] 1 Cr. App. R. 385).

It is then for the judge, conducting a balancing exercise, to decide whether the public interest in maintaining the confidentiality of those documents and the public interest in seeing that justice is done, requires the documents to be disclosed or withheld (*R. v Higgins* [1996] 1 F.L.R. 137).

Such documents are ordinarily to be used only for the purposes of taking instructions and putting matters contained within them to witnesses in the course of cross-examination; they are generally subject to public interest immunity, and the rights both of social services and of the persons who are the subject of the documentation must be respected.

The judge's order for disclosure does not, therefore, entitle either party to use the documents in any other way; where it is considered necessary by either party that wider use be made of the documentation or information, an application must be made to the judge to extend the use to which it may be put, so that the balance between the respective interests can properly be considered (*R. v J* [2010] EWCA Crim 385; [2010] 2 Cr. App. 2).

Procedure

An application must identify the documents sought and why they are said to be material evidence, particularly where attempts are made to access the medical reports of those who allege that they are victims of crime. Victims do not waive the confidentiality of their medical records, or their right to privacy under art.8 of the ECHR, by the mere fact of making a complaint against the accused. **30-046**

The procedure is as follows:

(1) the possessor of the documents must first decide whether or not they are relevant;
(2) the assistance of the judge should only be sought if a question can properly be decided by him, most obviously where questions of public interest immunity are involved (*R. v B* [2000] Crim. L.R. 50);
(3) if the judge is to be involved, it will be for him either to accept the assertion of the possessor or to look at the document himself. That decision is to be taken at his discretion, judicially exercised;
(4) the judge should be alert to balance the rights of victims against the real and proven needs of the defence. As a public authority, he must ensure that any interference with the ECHR art.8 rights of those entitled to privacy is in accordance with the law and necessary in pursuit of a legitimate public interest; general and unspecified requests to trawl through such records should be refused;
(5) if the possessor claims that the documents are irrelevant, suspect or

implausible, the judge will no doubt look at them himself, or he may regard assistance from an independent member of the Bar as being sufficient; and

(6) a verbatim record must be kept of any ex parte application. (*R. v Turner* (1995) 2 Cr. App. R. 94).

If material is held by any person in relation to family proceedings (e.g. where there have been care proceedings in relation to a child, who has also complained to the police of sexual or other abuse) then an application has to be made by that person to the family court for leave to disclose that material to a third party (see Family Procedure Rules 2010 Pt 7). This would permit, for instance, a local authority, in receipt of such material, to disclose it to the police for the purpose of a criminal investigation, or to the CPS, in order for the latter to discharge any obligations under CPIA 1996.

Costs

30-047 There is power to award costs in favour of local authorities out of public funds only where the court orders under CP(AWA) 1965 s.2C that the witness summons shall be of no effect (see WITNESS SUMMONSES AND WARRANTS).

International matters

30-048 The obligations of the Crown in relation to relevant third-party material held overseas are as set out in *R. v Flook* [2009] EWCA Crim 682; [2010] 1 Cr. App. R. 30:

(1) the prosecutor must pursue reasonable lines of enquiry; and
(2) if it appears there is relevant material, all reasonable steps must be taken to obtain it, whether formally or otherwise.

To a great extent, the success of these enquiries will depend on the laws of the country where the material is held and the facts of the individual case. It needs to be recognised that when the material is held in a country outside of the EU, the power of the Crown and the courts of England and Wales to obtain third-party material may well be limited (*JPD 2013* 51).

If informal requests are unsuccessful, the avenues are limited to the Crime (International Co-operation) Act 2003 and any applicable international conventions. It cannot, in any sense, be guaranteed that a request to a foreign government, court or body will produce the material sought. Additionally, some foreign authorities may be prepared to show the material in question to the investigating officers, whilst refusing to allow the material to be copied or otherwise made available (*JPD 2013* 51).

As the CACD observed in *R. v Khyam* [2008] EWCA Crim 1612; [2009] 1 Cr. App. R. (S.) 77 at [37]:

> "The prosecuting authorities in this jurisdiction simply cannot compel authorities in a foreign country to acknowledge, let alone comply with, our disclosure principles."

The obligation is therefore to take reasonable steps. Whether the prosecutor has complied with that obligation is for the courts to judge in each case (*JPD 2013* 52).

It is therefore important that the prosecution sets out the position clearly in writing, including any inability to inspect or retrieve any material that potentially ought to be disclosed, along with the steps that have been taken (*JPD 2013* 53).

F. Public interest immunity (PII)

1. Applications for Non-Disclosure in the Public Interest

(1) General

Introduction

There is provision in the Code of Practice for the police "disclosure officer" to list on a sensitive schedule any material which he believes it is not in the public interest to disclose, and the reasons for that belief. **30-049**

The schedule must include a statement that the disclosure officer believes the material is sensitive.

Examples are material:

(1) relating to national security;
(2) received from the intelligence and security agencies;
(3) relating to intelligence from foreign sources which reveals sensitive intelligence gathering methods, given in confidence;
(4) relating to the use of a telephone system and which is supplied to an investigator for intelligence purposes only;
(5) relating to the identity or activities of informants or undercover police officers or other persons supplying information to the police who may be in danger if their identities are revealed;
(6) revealing the location of any premises or other place used for police surveillance or the identity of any person allowing a police officer to use them for surveillance;
(7) revealing, directly or indirectly, techniques and methods relied on by a police officer in the course of a criminal investigation, e.g. covert surveillance techniques or other methods of detecting crime;
(8) disclosure of which might facilitate the commission of other offences or hinder the prevention and detection of crime;
(9) comprising internal police communications such as management minutes;
(10) upon the strength of which search warrants were obtained;
(11) containing details of persons taking part in identification parades;
(12) supplied to an investigator during a criminal investigation which has been generated by an official of a body concerned with the regulation or supervision of bodies corporate or of persons engaged in financial activities, or which has been generated by a person retained by such a body; or
(13) supplied to an investigator during a criminal investigation which relates to a child or young person and which has been generated by a local authority social services department, an Area Child Protection Committee or other party contacted by an investigator during the investigation.

Disclosure of an informant's identity (see (5) above) without his consent is one of those highly exceptional cases where the prosecution must apply to the court, and the court must carefully consider the issues and reach its own decision (*R. (on the application of WV) v CPS* [2012] Crim. L.R. 456 DC (considering, inter alia, *R. v H* [2004] UKHL 3; [2004] 2 Cr. App. R. 10)).

Disclosure to prosecutor

30-050 In exceptional circumstances, where an investigator considers that material is so sensitive that its revelation to the prosecutor by means of an entry on the sensitive schedule is inappropriate (e.g. where the material would be likely to lead directly to the loss of life or directly threaten national security) the existence of the material must be revealed to the prosecutor separately.

In such circumstances:

(1) the responsibility for informing the prosecutor lies with the investigator who knows the detail of the sensitive material;
(2) the investigator should act as soon as reasonably practicable after the file containing the prosecution case is sent to the prosecutor; and
(3) he must ensure that the prosecutor is able to inspect the material so that he can assess whether it needs to be brought before a court for a ruling on disclosure.

The judge's role

30-051 The judge:

(1) *must* give detailed consideration to the material sought to be withheld in the context of the prosecution and defence cases;
(2) *must* identify the public interest in question and assess the prejudice claimed to ensure that any derogation from the full disclosure rule is the minimum necessary to secure the required protection;
(3) *may* (CPIA 1996 ss.3(6), 7A(8), 8(5)) order that it is not in the public interest to disclose material, and if he does so, the material must not be disclosed by the prosecutor;
(4) *must* (CPIA 1996 s.15(3)–(4); CJA 2003 s.331, Sch.36 Pt 3 para.31), without the need for any application by the accused, keep under review throughout the trial the question whether, at any given time, it is still not in the public interest to disclose material affected by his order; and
(5) *must*, in making his decision, apply the decision-making framework set out at [36] of *R. v H* [2004] UKHL 3; [2004] 2 Cr. App. R. 10 (see also *CPD* 2013, AG's Guidelines 120).

The PII decision is sometimes described as a "balancing exercise" but this description is arguably misleading. The court has, in effect, a limited discretion to order non-disclosure of disclosable material where non-disclosure will not prevent a fair trial. If the disputed material may prove the accused's innocence or avoid a miscarriage of justice, then it must be disclosed (*R. v Keane* (1994) 99 Cr. App. R. 1). The cases were reviewed in *R. v H* [2004] UKHL 3; [2004] 2 Cr. App. R. 10.

Material damaging to the accused is not disclosable and should not be brought to the judge's attention (AG's Guidelines 115).

(2) Procedure

Prosecutor's application for public interest hearing

30-052 Where the prosecutor would, in the absence of a court order, have to disclose material, and wants the judge to decide whether it would be in the public interest to disclose it, the procedure is governed by CrimPR 15.3.

The prosecutor:

(1) *must* apply in writing, serving the application on the court officer, on any person who the prosecutor thinks would be directly affected by disclosure of the material and on the accused (but only to the extent that serving it on the accused would not disclose what the prosecutor thinks ought not be disclosed);

(2) the application *must*:

(a) describe the material, and explain why the prosecutor thinks that:

(i) it is material that the prosecutor would have to disclose;

(ii) it would not be in the public interest to disclose that material; and

(iii) no measure such as the prosecutor's admission of any fact, or disclosure by summary, extract or edited copy, would adequately protect both the public interest and the accused's right to a fair trial;

(b) *must* omit from any part of the application that is served on the accused anything that would disclose what the prosecutor thinks ought not be disclosed, in which case he must mark the other part to show that it is only for the court, and in that other part explain why the prosecutor has withheld it from the accused; and

(c) explain why, if no part of the application is served on the accused; unless already done, the judge may direct the prosecutor to serve an application on the accused or any other person whom the judge considers would be directly affected by disclosure of the material.

The hearing

30-053 The trial judge will determine the application at a hearing which will be in private, unless he otherwise directs, and if he so directs, may take place, wholly or in part, in the absence of the accused (CrimPR 15.3(6)). The judge that determines the public interest immunity application should continue to act as trial judge and keep the situation under review. There is no obligation on the judge to recuse himself from presiding at the trial because of knowledge acquired during the PII hearing, but he is entitled to do so if he considers that the interests of justice so require (*R. v Dawson* [2007] EWCA Crim 822). It must be remembered that material which is damaging to the accused should not be brought to the judge's attention at a PII hearing.

At the hearing, at which the accused is present, the general rule is that the judge will consider, in the following sequence:

(1) representations by the prosecutor and by any other person served with the application; and then

(2) by the accused, in the presence of them all; and then

(3) any further representations by the prosecutor and any such other person, in the absence of the accused, but

the judge may direct other arrangements (CrimPR 15.3(7)).

The judge will only determine the application if satisfied that he has been able to take adequate account of such rights of confidentiality as apply to the material, and the accused's right to a fair trial (CrimPR 15.3(8)).

Unless the judge otherwise directs, the Crown Court officer will not give notice to anyone other than the prosecutor of the hearing of an application unless the prosecutor served the application on that person, or of the judge's decision on the application, but may keep a written application or representations, or arrange for the whole or any part to be kept by some other appropriate person, subject to any conditions that the judge imposes.

The application, even if held in private or in secret, should be recorded. The judge should give some short statement of reasons; this is often best done document by document as the hearing proceeds.

The recording, copies of the judge's orders (and any copies of the material retained by the court) should be clearly identified, securely sealed and kept in the court building in a safe or locked cabinet consistent with its security classification, and there should be a proper register of the contents. Arrangements should be made for the return of the material to the prosecution once the case is concluded and the time for an appeal has elapsed (*JPD 2013* 55).

The trial judge's required approach

30-054 When any issue of derogation from the golden rule of full disclose arises, the judge must address a series of questions, as set out in *R. v H* [2004] UKHL 3; [2004] 2 Cr. App. R. 10:

(1) What is the material which the prosecution seek to withhold? This must be considered by the court in detail.

(2) Is the material such as may weaken the prosecution case or strengthen that of the defence? If No, disclosure should not be ordered. If Yes, full disclosure should (subject to (3), (4) and (5) below) be ordered.

(3) Is there a real risk of serious prejudice to an important public interest (and, if so, what) if full disclosure of the material is ordered? If No, full disclosure should be ordered.

(4) If the answer to (2) and (3) is Yes, can the defendant's interest be protected without disclosure or disclosure be ordered to an extent or in a way which will give adequate protection to the public interest in question and also afford adequate protection to the interests of the defence?

This question requires the court to consider, with specific reference to the material which the prosecution seek to withhold and the facts of the case and the defence as disclosed, whether the prosecution should formally admit what the defence seek to establish or whether disclosure short of full disclosure may be ordered. This may be done in appropriate cases by the preparation of summaries or extracts of evidence, or the provision of documents in an edited or anonymised form, provided the documents supplied are in each instance approved by the judge. In cases of exceptional difficulty the court may require the appointment of special counsel to ensure a correct answer to questions (2) and (3) as well as (4).

(5) Do the measures proposed in answer to (4) represent the minimum derogation necessary to protect the public interest in question? If No, the court should order such greater disclosure as will represent the minimum derogation from the golden rule of full disclosure.

(6) If limited disclosure is ordered pursuant to (4) or (5), may the effect be to render the trial process, viewed as a whole, unfair to the defendant? If Yes, then fuller disclosure should be ordered even if this leads or may lead the prosecution to discontinue the proceedings so as to avoid having to make disclosure.

(7) If the answer to (6) when first given is No, does that remain the correct answer as the trial unfolds, evidence is adduced and the defence advanced? It is important that the answer to (6) should not be treated as a final, once-and-for-all answer but as a provisional answer which the court must keep under review.

Notice and documentation

When the PII application is a Type 1 or Type 2 application, proper notice to the defence is necessary to enable the accused to make focused submissions to the court and the notice should be as specific as the nature of the material allows. In some cases only the generic nature of the material can be identified. In some wholly exceptional cases (Type 3 cases) it may be justified to give no notice at all. The judge should always ask the prosecution to justify the form of notice (or the decision to give no notice at all). **30-055**

JPD 2013 55 makes a number of points:

(1) The prosecution should be alert to the possibility of disclosing a statement in a redacted form by, for example, simply removing personal details. This may obviate the need for a PII application, unless the redacted material satisfies the test for disclosure.
(2) Except when the material is very short (for instance only a few sheets), or for reasons of sensitivity, the prosecution should supply securely sealed copies to the judge in advance, together with a short statement explaining the relevance of each document, how it satisfies the disclosure test and why it is suggested that disclosure would result in a real risk of serious prejudice to an important public interest; in undertaking this task, the use of merely formulaic expressions is to be discouraged.
(3) In any case of complexity a schedule of the material should be provided, identifying the particular objection to disclosure in relation to each item, and leaving a space for the judge's decision.

Appointment of special advocate

In *R. v H* [2004] UKHL 3; [2004] 2 Cr. App. R. 10 the House of Lords suggested that the power of the judge to appoint a special advocate to represent the accused on an application should be used only in exceptional cases where it might be necessary in the "interests of justice". Such an appointment ought not be ordered unless and until the judge was satisfied that no other course would adequately meet the overriding requirement of fairness to the accused. **30-056**

Other persons claiming interest

Where an application is made by the prosecutor under ss.7A(8) or 8(5), 14(2) or 15(4) and a person claiming to have an interest in the material: **30-057**

(1) applies to be heard by the court; and
(2) shows that he was involved (whether alone or with others) in the prosecutor's attention being brought to the material,

the judge must not make an order unless that person has been given an opportunity to be heard (CPIA 1996 s.16).

(3) Review

Review: (1) general

30-058 After a judge has made an order granting PII he must keep under review, until the accused is acquitted or the prosecutor decides not to proceed with the case, the question whether at any given time it is still not in the public interest to disclose material affected by the order (CPIA 1996 s.15(3)).

There is no need for any application, but the accused may apply to the judge for a review of the issue. If at any time the judge considers that it is in the public interest to disclose material to any extent, he will so order, and take steps to inform the prosecutor of his order (CPIA 1996 ss.15(4)–(5); see *R. v Giles* [2011] EWCA Crim 2259).

Review: (2) procedure on application

30-059 CrimPR 15.6 applies where:

(1) the judge has ordered that it is not in the public interest to disclose material that the prosecutor otherwise would have to disclose; and
(2) the accused wants the judge to review that decision, or the judge reviews that decision on his own initiative.

Where the accused wants the court to review that decision:

(a) he must serve an application on the Crown Court officer and on the prosecutor and in that application must describe the material that he wants the prosecutor to disclose, and explain why he thinks it is no longer in the public interest for the prosecutor not to disclose it; and
(b) the prosecutor must serve any such application on any person who he thinks would be directly affected if that material were disclosed, and the prosecutor and any such person must serve any representations on the Crown Court officer and on the accused, unless to do so would in effect reveal something that either thinks ought not be disclosed.

The judge may direct the prosecutor to serve any such application on any person whom the judge considers would be directly affected if that material were disclosed, and may direct the prosecutor and any such person to serve any representations on the accused.

Review: (3) the hearing

30-060 The judge will review a PII decision at a hearing which will be in private, unless he otherwise directs, and if he does so direct, the hearing may take place, wholly or in part, in the accused's absence.

At a hearing at which the accused is present the general rule is that the judge will receive, in the following sequence:

(1) representations first by the accused, and then by the prosecutor and any other person served with the application, in the presence of them all; and then
(2) further representations by the prosecutor and any such other person in the accused's absence,

but the judge may direct other arrangements for the hearing.

The judge may only conclude a review if satisfied that he has been able to take adequate account of such rights of confidentiality as apply to the material, and the accused's right to a fair trial (CrimPR 15.6(8)).

G. CONFIDENTIALITY

General

If an accused is given, or allowed to inspect, a document or other object under CPIA 1996 ss.3, 4, 7A, 14 or 15, or by virtue of an order under s.8, he must not disclose it or any information recorded in it (CPIA 1996 s.17), except: **30-061**

(1) in connection with the proceedings for whose purposes he was given the object or document, or allowed to inspect it; or
(2) with a view to the taking of further criminal proceedings (e.g. by way of appeal) in connection with the same matter, or in any such further criminal proceedings.

The accused may use or disclose:

(a) an object to the extent to which it has been displayed to the public in open court;
(b) information to the extent to which it has been communicated to the public in open court; or
(c) an object or information, with permission of the court, for the purpose, and to the extent specified, by the judge.

Where an accused wants the court's permission to use disclosed prosecution material otherwise than in connection with the case in which it was disclosed, or beyond the extent to which it was displayed or communicated publicly at a hearing, he must proceed under CrimPR 15.7.

Contravention

Any contravention by the accused of the restrictions on use or disclosure is a contempt of court, punishable in the Crown Court by imprisonment not exceeding two years or a fine or both (CPIA 1996 s.18). **30-062**

CrimPR 15.8(2) provides that where a person is accused of using disclosed prosecution material in contravention of CPIA 1996 s.17, any party who wants the court to exercise its power to punish that person for contempt of court must comply with the rules in CrimPR 48 (see CONTEMPT OF COURT).

The judge must not exercise his power to forfeit material used in contempt of court unless:

(1) the prosecutor; and
(2) any other person directly affected by the disclosure of the material is present, or has had at least 14 days in which to make representations.

(CrimPR 15.8(3))

31. DISCOUNTS ON SENTENCE

Quick Guide

1. General

31-001 Both at common law and by statute an offender has the right to expect a discount on the otherwise appropriate sentence, where:

(1) he pleads guilty timeously to the indictment (*R. v Barnes* (1983) 5 Cr. App. R. (S.) 368); the position is now governed by SA 2020 s.73 (see 31-002);

(2) the judge considers that the offence would not have been committed but for the activities of an informer (*R. v Beaumont* (1987) 9 Cr. App. R. (S.) 342; *R. v Chapman* (1989) 11 Cr. App. R. (S.) 222; *R. v Tonnessen* [1998] 2 Cr. App. R. (S.) 328; *R. v Underhill* [1979] 1 Cr. App. R. (S.) 270) (see 31-017); or

(3) the accused co-pleading guilty, but by giving information early enough for it to be potentially useful; this is now partially covered by SA 2020 ss.74 and 75 (see 31-019).

2. Reduction in sentence for a guilty plea

Statutory provisions

31-002 By SA 2020 s.73, in determining the sentence to be passed on an offender who has pleaded guilty to an offence, the judge must take into account:

(1) the stage in the proceedings at which the offender indicated his intention to plead guilty (and see *R. v Hussain* [2002] Crim. L.R. 327); and

(2) the circumstances in which this indication was given (and see *R. v Fearon* [1996] 2 Cr. App. R. (S.) 25; *R. v Aroride* [1999] 2 Cr. App. R. (S.) 406).

If the judge imposes a punishment on the offender which is less severe than he would otherwise have imposed, he must state in open court that he has done so (*R. v Hastings* [1996] 1 Cr. App. R. (S.) 167); if he withholds a discount he must explain why.

In *R. v Wendt* [2015] EWCA Crim 2241; [2016] 1 Cr. App. R. (S.) 53 sentence was deferred on the basis of an account given by the defendant for a PSR. When the defendant was to be sentenced at the end of the period of deferment, it emerged the account given was false. The sentencing court could not inflate the sentence as a result of false mitigation, but it was open to the court to reduce the credit for the plea to nothing.

The definition of "sentence" previously contained in CJA 2003 s.142(3) (now repealed and replaced by SA 2020 s.57) as including "any order made by a court when dealing with an offender in respect of his offence" would seem to suggest a discount not only on the principal sentence, but also in respect of ancillary orders. SA 2020 s.57 does not now include the words previously contained in CJA 2003 s.142(3). The Sentencing Council, *Reduction in Sentence for a Guilty Plea: Definitive Guideline* (Sentencing Council, July 2007) makes clear that it applies only to the punitive elements of the sentence and has no impact on ancillary orders including orders of disqualification from driving (Guideline B: Key Principles).

As to the attitude of the CACD where the judge fails to state that he has taken the plea into consideration, see *R. v Wharton* [2001] EWCA Crim 622; *The Times*, 27 March 2001, considering *R. v Bishop* [2000] 1 Cr. App. R. (S.) 432.

In relation to those offences mentioned below, the provisions in relation to mandatory minimum sentences do not prevent the judge, after taking into account:

(a) the stage in the proceedings for the offence at which the offender indicated his intention to plead guilty; and
(b) the circumstances in which this indication was given, from imposing in respect of an offence under the:
  - PCA 1953 s.1A(6)(a) (SA 2020 s.312 (minimum sentence for threatening with weapon or bladed article)) (38-040);
  - SA 2020 s.313 (minimum of seven years for third class A drug trafficking offence) (38-029);
  - SA 2020 s.314 (minimum of three years for third domestic burglary) (38-033); and
  - CJA 1988 s.139AA(8)(a) (SA 2020 s.315 (minimum sentence for repeat offence involving weapon or bladed article)) (see 38-041),

any sentence which is *not less than 80 per cent* of that specified in that provision (*R. v Gray* [2007] EWCA Crim 979; [2007] 2 Cr. App. R. (S.) 78; *R. v Fairclough* [2012] EWCA Crim 897), and in the case of an offence the sentence for which falls to be imposed in respect of an offence under the:

- PCA 1953 s.1A(6)(b) (SA 2020 s.312(3)); or
- CJA 1988 s.139AA(8)(b) (SA 2020 s.312(3))

any sentence that he considers appropriate.

Note that no reduction for a guilty plea is appropriate in relation to a minimum sentence for firearms offences committed under FA 1968 s.51A (*R. v Jordan* [2004] EWCA Crim 3291; [2005] 2 Cr. App. R. (S.) 44). In such cases the court is required to impose an appropriate sentence not less than the minimum term unless there are exceptional circumstances relating to the offence and/or the offender which justify not doing so. (SA 2020 s.311 and Sch.20). Note: s.124 of the Police, Crime, Sentencing and Courts Act 2022 amended SA 2020 ss.312–315 so as to require "exceptional circumstances" (not merely "particular circumstances") to avoid imposing minimum sentences for specified offences committed on or after 28 June and to which those provisions of the Code apply.

It is misleading to say that there is a maximum 20 per cent reduction. The section provides for that the final sentence must not be less than 80 per cent of minimum sentence. This is *not* the same thing (*R. v Gray* [2007] EWCA Crim 979; [2007] 2 Cr. App. R. (S.) 78). The appropriate discount must be applied to the total term imposed, provided that does not result in the sentence dropping below 80 per cent of the minimum term.

For the correct approach to sentencing in a minimum sentence case where the accused pleads guilty see *R. v Silvera* [2013] EWCA Crim 1764 and *R. v Nelson* [2013] EWCA Crim 2410.

Where the judge finds that it would be unjust to apply the minimum term the restriction on credit for plea to 80 per cent of the minimum does not apply (*R. v*

Darling [2009] EWCA Crim 1610; [2010] 1 Cr. App. R. (S.) 63; *R. v Flack* [2013] EWCA Crim 115; [2013] 2 Cr. App. R. (S.) 56).

Sentencing Council Guideline

31-003 The Sentencing Council, *Reduction in Sentence for a Guilty Plea: Definitive Guideline* (July 2007) makes a statement of purpose and sets out a recommended approach to the application of the principle, guidance on determining the level of reduction in an individual case and guidance on whether to withhold a reduction.

The guideline is also intended to assist judges when arriving at the appropriate minimum term for the offence of murder, applying SA 2020 Sch.21 (see LIFE SENTENCES).

The guideline applies regardless of the date of the offence to all individual offenders aged 18 and older and to organisations in cases where the first hearing is on or after 1 June 2017. It applies equally in the magistrates' courts and the Crown Court.

Sentencing Council: Statement of Purpose

31-004 The purpose of the Guideline is clearly stated under the heading "Key Principles":

The purpose of this guideline is to encourage those who are going to plead guilty to do so as early in the court process as possible. Nothing in the guideline should be used to put pressure on a defendant to plead guilty.

Although a guilty person is entitled not to admit the offence and to put the prosecution to proof of its case, an acceptance of guilt:

(a) normally reduces the impact of the crime upon victims;
(b) saves victims and witnesses from having to testify; and
(c) is in the public interest in that it saves public time and money on investigations and trials.

A guilty plea produces greater benefits the earlier the plea is indicated. In order to maximise the above benefits and to provide an incentive to those who are guilty to indicate a guilty plea as early as possible, this guideline makes a clear distinction between a reduction in the sentence available at the first stage of the proceedings and a reduction in the sentence available at a later stage of the proceedings.

The purpose of reducing the sentence for a guilty plea is to yield the benefits described above. The guilty plea should be considered by the court to be independent of the offender's personal mitigation:

- Factors such as admissions at interview, co-operation with the investigation and demonstrations of remorse should **not** be taken into account in determining the level of reduction. Rather, they should be considered separately and prior to any guilty plea reduction, as potential mitigating factors.
- The benefits apply regardless of the strength of the evidence against an offender. The strength of the evidence should **not** be taken into account when determining the level of reduction.
- The guideline applies only to the punitive elements of the sentence and has no impact on ancillary orders including orders of disqualification from driving.

Where an offence crosses the threshold for the imposition of a community or custodial sentence, application of the reduction principle may properly form the basis for imposing a fine or discharge, rather than a community sentence, or an alternative to an immediate custodial sentence. Where the reduction is applied in this way, the actual sentence imposed incorporates the reduction.

Sentencing Council: Application of the reduction principle

The Guideline at Section C sets out the approach a judge should take. The judge should follow five steps: **31-005**

(1) Determine the appropriate sentence for the offence(s) in accordance with any offence specific sentencing guideline.
(2) Determine the level of reduction for a guilty plea in accordance with this guideline.
(3) State the amount of that reduction.
(4) Apply the reduction to the appropriate sentence.
(5) Follow any further steps in the offence specific guideline to determine the final sentence.

Sentencing Council: Determining the level of reduction

The Sentencing Council guideline states that the maximum level of reduction in sentence for a guilty plea is one-third. Where a plea is indicated at the first stage of the proceedings a reduction of one-third should be made (subject to some exceptions set out below at 31-010). The first stage will normally be the first hearing at which a plea or indication of plea is sought and recorded by the court (Guideline D1). In *R. v Dale (Scott)* [2022] EWCA Crim 207; [2022] 1 WLUK 446 the CACD said that what was required to attract the one third discount was an unequivocal indication of a guilty plea at the first stage. However, what is meant by "unequivocal" is not determined by whether there is, or is not, to be a basis of plea. A plea of guilty is a plea to the offence, but not necessarily to all of the facts for which the prosecution contend. That is not equivocal in itself, and the basis need not necessarily be identified prior to entering or indicating a plea. If there is to be a basis of plea, the proper place to indicate that in the Better Case Management form is under the rubric of "real issues in the case". In *R v Johnstone (William)* [2021] EWCA Crim 1683; [2022] 2 Cr. App. R. (S.) 7, the CACD held that endorsing the words "likely guilty plea" on the BCM form was insufficient. However, the offender had been unrepresented and had made it clear in interview his intention to plead guilty; there was no evidence that anyone at the magistrates' court had explained the significance of the word "likely". Those were exceptional circumstances which made it unreasonable to expect the offender to have realised and understood that he needed to express an unequivocal intention to plead guilty in the magistrates' court. He was entitled to a full one-third reduction. **31-006**

Where a plea is indicated after the first stage of proceedings, a maximum reduction of one quarter (again subject to the exceptions below). The reduction applied should be decreased from one-quarter to a maximum of one-tenth on the first day of trial having regard to the time when the guilty first indicated to the court relative to the progress of the case and the trial date. The reduction should normally be decreased further, even to zero, if the guilty plea is entered during the course of the trial. The guideline notes that a trial is deemed to have started when the pre-recorded cross-examination has begun (Guideline D2).

Sentencing Council: Applying the reduction

31-007 The guideline makes clear that the reduction in sentence for a guilty plea can be taken into account by imposing one type of sentence rather than another; for example, by reducing a custodial sentence to a community sentence, or by reducing a community sentence to a fine. It also states that where a court has imposed one sentence rather than another in order to reflect the guilty plea, there should normally be no further reduction on account of the guilty plea. Where, however, the less severe type of sentence is justified by other factors, the appropriate reduction for the plea should be applied in the normal way (Guideline E1).

More than one summary offence

31-008 The guideline states that when dealing with more than one summary offence, the aggregate sentence is limited to a maximum of six months. Allowing for a reduction for each guilty plea, consecutive sentence might result in the imposition of the maximum six month sentence. The court may make a modest additional reduction to the overall sentence to reflect the benefits derived from the guilty pleas (Guideline E2).

Keeping an either way case in the magistrates' court

31-009 Reducing a custodial sentence to reflect a guilty plea may mean that the magistrates' court can retain jurisdiction of an either way offence rather than committing the case for sentence. The magistrates' court should apply the appropriate reduction to the sentence for the offence(s) arrived at by applying the offence specific guideline. If the resulting sentence is then within its jurisdiction, it should proceed to sentence (Guideline E3).

Exceptions

31-010 *Further information, assistance or advice necessary before indicating plea*
Where the sentencing court is satisfied that there were particular circumstances which significantly reduced the defendant's ability to understand what was alleged or otherwise made it unreasonable to expect the defendant to indicate a guilty plea sooner than was done, a reduction of one-third should still be made. In considering whether this exception applies, the guideline states that sentencers should distinguish between the cases in which it is necessary to receive advice and/or have sight of evidence in order to understand whether the defendant is in fact and law guilty of the offence(s) charged, and those cases in which a defendant merely delays guilty plea(s) in order to assess the strength of the prosecution evidence and the prospects of conviction or acquittal (Guideline F1).

Newton hearings and special reasons hearings

31-011 Where an offender's version of events is rejected at a Newton hearing the reduction which would have been available at the stage of proceedings the plea was indicated, should normally be halved. Where witnesses are called in such a hearing, it may be appropriate to further lower the reduction (Guideline F2).

Offender convicted of a lesser or different offence

31-012 Where a defendant is convicted of a lesser or different offence from that originally charged, and has earlier made an unequivocal indication of a guilty plea to this lesser or different offence to the prosecution and the court, the court should give the level of reduction that is appropriate to the stage in the proceedings at which this indication of plea (to the lesser or different offence) was made taking into account any other of these exceptions that apply. In the Crown Court where the offered plea is a permissible alternative on the indictment as charged, the offender will not be treated as having made an unequivocal indication unless the offender has entered that plea (Guideline F3).

Minimum sentence under s.51A of the Firearms Act 1968 (SA 2020 s.311 and Sch.20)

There can be no reduction for a guilty plea if the effect of doing so would be to reduce the length of sentence below the required minimum term (Guideline F4). **31-013**

In circumstances where an *appropriate* custodial sentence of at least six months falls to be imposed on a person aged 18 or over who has been convicted under ss.1 or 1A of the PCA 1953; or ss.139, 139AA or 139A of the CJA 1988 (SA 2020 ss.312 and 315) (certain possession of knives or offensive weapon offences) or a *prescribed* custodial sentence falls to be imposed under SA 2020 ss.313 and 314 (drug trafficking offences and burglary offences), the court may impose any sentence in accordance with this guideline which is not less than 80 per cent of the *appropriate* or *prescribed* custodial period (Guideline F5).

Mandatory life sentences for murder

The sentence for murder is different from all other sentences. By law, the sentence for murder is imprisonment (detention) for life and an offender will remain subject to the sentence for the rest of his life. **31-014**

Given the special characteristic of the offence of murder and the unique statutory provision in Sch.21 to the SA 2020 of starting points for the minimum term to be served by an offender, careful consideration has to be given to the extent of any reduction for a guilty plea and to the need to ensure that the minimum term properly reflects the seriousness of the offence. Whilst the general principles continue to apply (both that a guilty plea should be encouraged and that the extent of any reduction should reduce if the indication of plea is later than the first stage of the proceedings) the process of determining the level of reduction will be different (Guideline G).

Determining the level of reduction

Whereas a court should consider the fact that an offender has pleaded guilty to murder when deciding whether it is appropriate to order a whole life term, where a court determines that there should be a whole life minimum term, there will be no reduction for a guilty plea. In other circumstances: **31-015**

(i) the court will weigh carefully the overall length of the minimum term taking into account other reductions for which the offender may be eligible so as to avoid a combination leading to an inappropriately short sentence;

(ii) where it is appropriate to reduce the minimum term having regard to a plea of guilty, the reduction will not exceed one-sixth and will never exceed five years; and

(iii) the maximum reduction of one-sixth or five years (whichever is less) should only be given when a guilty plea has been indicated at the first stage of the proceedings.

Lesser reductions should be given for guilty pleas after that point, with a maximum of one-twentieth being given for a guilty plea on the day of trial. The exceptions outlined at F1 and F2 (31-010–31-014) apply to murder cases (Guideline G).

Deduction for Plea

31-016 The following tables reproduce figures for sentences *after* different fractional deductions as shown in columns 2–5. The first table shows sentences from 3 months to 15 years (expressed in months, then years), the second table shows sentences from 4 to 52 weeks (expressed in weeks). Note that the figures given are the result of simple arithmetic. Judges will doubtless wish to round figures either up or down.

Table 1: 3 months–15 years (in months)

Sentence	1/3	1/4	1/5	1/10
3 months	2	2.25	2.4	2.7
4 months	2.6	3	3.2	3.6
6 months	4	4.5	4.8	5.4
9 months	6	6.75	7.2	8.1
12 months (1 year)	8	9	9.6	10.8
15 months	10	11.25	12	13.5
18 months (1.5 years)	12	13.5	14.4	16.2
21 months	14	15.75	16.8	18.9
24 months (2 years)	16	18	19.2	21.6
30 months (2.5 years)	20	22.5	24	27
36 months (3 years)	24	27	28.8	32.4
42 months (3.5 years)	28	31.5	33.6	37.8
48 months (4 years)	32	36	38.4	43.2
54 months (4.5 years)	36	40.5	43.2	48.6
60 months (5 years)	40	45	48	54
72 months (6 years)	48	54	57.6	64.8
84 months (7 years)	56	63	67.2	75.6
96 months (8 years)	64	72	76.8	86.4

Sentence	1/3	1/4	1/5	1/10
108 months (9 years)	72	81	86.4	97.2
10 years	80	90	96	108
11 years	88	99	105.6	118.8
12 years	96	108	115.2	129.6
13 years	104	117	124.8	140.4
14 years	112	126	134.4	151.2
15 years	120	135	144	162

Table 2: 4–52 weeks

Sentence	1/3	1/4	1/5	1/10
4 weeks	2.66	3	3.2	3.6
6 weeks	4	4.5	4.8	5.4
10 weeks	6.66	7.5	8	9
12 weeks	8	9	9.6	10.8
15 weeks	10	11.25	12	13.5
18 weeks	12	13.5	14.4	16.2
20 weeks	13.3	15	16	18
24 weeks	16	18	19.2	21.6
26 weeks	17.33	19.5	20.8	23.4
30 weeks	20	22.5	24	27
36 weeks	24	27	28.8	32.4
42 weeks	28	31.5	33.6	37.8
48 weeks	32	36	38.4	43.2
52 weeks	34.66	39	41.6	46.8

3. Entrapment; informers

Where the judge takes the view that the offence would not have been committed save for the activities of an informer, he may, if he thinks fit, give a discount on sentence (*R. v Beaumont* (1987) 9 Cr. App. R. (S.) 342; *R. v Chapman* (1989) 11 Cr. App. R. (S.) 222; *R. v Tonnessen* [1998] 2 Cr. App. R. (S.) 328; *R. v Underhill* [1979] 1 Cr. App. R. (S.) 270). 31-017

Using test letters to establish the guilt of postal employees suspected of theft of mail does not come within this principle (*R. v Ramen* (1988) 10 Cr. App. R. (S.) 334); nor does the use of test purchases by undercover officers in relation to drug dealing (*R. v Springer* [1999] 1 Cr. App. R. (S.) 217; *R. v Mayeri* [1999] 1 Cr. App. R. (S.) 304).

The true relevance of official entrapment into the commission of crime is on the question of sentence, where it may be a substantial mitigating factor (*R. v Sang* (1979) 69 Cr. App. R. 282; HL; *R. v Beaumont* (1987) 9 Cr. App. R. (S.) 342; *R. v Mackey* (1993) 14 Cr. App. R. (S.) 53).

4. CO-OPERATION BY THE ACCUSED

(1) At common law

General

31-018 Offenders need to know that it is worth their while disclosing the criminal activities of others (*R. v Sivan* (1988) 10 Cr. App. R. (S.) 282). To this end, and within the limits specified below, the judge will need to tailor any sentence on any offender who has given such assistance to the authorities, punishing him for his offences, while also rewarding him for the help he has given.

Where the common law principles apply, i.e. where both the offence and the sentencing process took place before the coming into force of SOCPA 2005 Pt 2 Ch.2 (SA 2020 ss.74 and 75), information relevant to the agreement between the prosecutor, and such assistance given by the offender in pursuance of it, should be put before the judge in the form of a written document. There should be no need to see the judge in his private room (*R. v Z* [2007] EWCA Crim 1473; [2008] 1 Cr. App. R. (S.) 60).

In *R. v X* [1999] 2 Cr. App. R. (S.) 125 it was said that:

(1) except in very unusual circumstances, it will not be necessary or desirable for a document of this kind to contain details which will attract a public interest immunity application;
(2) if such a document does contain information which attracts a public interest immunity consideration, the usual rules about the conduct of such an application apply. It will be a case in which the defence could and should be told of the application;
(3) in the absence of any consideration of public interest immunity, a document of this kind should be shown to the defence, who will discuss its contents with the offender. An offender is entitled to see documents put before the judge. There should not normally be any question of evidence being given or of an issue being tried on the question of the extent of the information provided;
(4) if the offender wishes to disagree with the contents of such a document, it is not appropriate for there to be cross-examination of the police officers; he is not a Crown witness. It will be possible in an appropriate case for an offender to ask for an adjournment to allow further consideration to be given to the preparation of the document. Otherwise, his remedy is not to rely on it;
(5) the judge will normally disregard such a document if asked by the offender to do so. In such a case he is unlikely to entertain any submission that the offender has given valuable assistance to the police; and
(6) if the judge does take the documents into consideration, he should say no more than that he has taken into consideration all the information about the defendant with which he had been provided.

It is impossible to lay down any hard and fast rule as to the amount by which the sentence upon a large scale informer should be reduced by reason of the assistance which he gives to the police. It is a fact-specific decision (*R. v King* (1986) 82 Cr. App. R. 120).

The judge will:

(a) turn to the offences which the informer has admitted to assess their gravity and their number; that should enable him to arrive at a "starting figure";
(b) the "starting figure" then, once again, depend upon the number of cases involved and, e.g. property attacked was private dwelling-houses or business premises, and no doubt other features as well;
(c) then turn to the amount by which that starting figure should be reduced; that again will depend upon a number of variable features, such as the quality and quantity of the material disclosed by the informer, as well as its accuracy and his willingness or otherwise to confront other criminals and to give evidence against them in due course if required; and
(d) consider the degree to which the informer has put himself and his family at risk by reason of the information he has given; in other words the risk of reprisal.

No doubt there will be other matters as well.

See also *R. v Sivan* (1988) 87 Cr. App. R. 407; *R. v Bevens* [2009] EWCA Crim 2554; [2010] 2 Cr. App. R. (S.) 31.

Any discount should reflect the seriousness of the offence, the importance of the information, and the effect, where the informant gives evidence, on his future circumstances (*R. v Wood* [1996] Crim. L.R. 916) and the circumstances of the entrapment or other factors should be expressly mentioned in the judge's sentencing remarks (*R. v Mackey* (1993) 14 Cr. App. R. (S.) 53).

In *R. v ZTR* [2015] EWCA Crim 1427; [2016] 1 Cr. App. R. (S.) 15, the CACD held that the principle at common law allowing for an offender's sentence to be reduced to reflect assistance given to law enforcement authorities should not be altered to allow for a reduction in sentence for assistance provided after the time of sentence.

As to the obligation of the authorities to provide a text, and the safeguards where the offender believes the content to be inaccurate, see *R. v N* [2016] EWCA Crim 590; [2016] 2 Cr. App. R. (S.) 33.

Credit should also be given to the extent that an offender has given material assistance, even where that falls outside the Sentencing Code and "Text" regimes, but reductions would be confined to cases of very serious crime and the extent of assistance: *R. v Campbell* [2018] EWCA Crim 802; [2018] 2 Cr. App. R. (S.) 24.

(2) Statutory Agreements under SA 2020 ss.74 and 75 (formerly SOCPA 2005)

General

Under SA 2020 s.74, where an offender: **31-019**

(1) following a plea of guilty;
(2) is either convicted of an offence in proceedings in the Crown Court or is committed to the Crown Court for sentence; and
(3) has, pursuant to a written agreement made with a specified prosecutor (within the meaning of SOCPA 2005 s.71(4)), assisted, or offered to assist the investigator or prosecutor in relation to that or any other offence,

the judge may, in determining what sentence to pass on the offender, take into account the extent and nature of the assistance given or offered.

If he passes a sentence which is less than it would have passed but for the assistance given or offered, the judge:

(a) must state in open court:
  (i) that he has passed a lesser sentence than he would otherwise have passed; and
  (ii) what the greater sentence would have been; but
(b) need not do so if he thinks that it would not be in the public interest to disclose that the sentence has been discounted; but in such a case he must give written notice of the matters specified in (i) and (ii) above to both the prosecutor and the offender.

(SA 2020 s.74)

If s.74(3) does not apply by virtue of s.74(4) (i.e. the judge thinks it would not be in the public interest to disclose the discount on the sentence), then SA 2020 s.52(2) and s.322(4) (requirement to explain reasons for sentence or other order) do not apply to the extent that the explanation will disclose that a sentence has been discounted in pursuance of this provision.

Note that in this provision:

- a reference to a sentence includes, in the case of a sentence which is fixed by law, a reference to the minimum period an offender is required to serve, and a reference to a lesser sentence must be construed accordingly; and
- a reference to imprisonment includes a reference to any other custodial sentence within the meaning of SA 2020 s.222.

Each of the following is a specified prosecutor: the DPP, the DRCP, the DSFO, the DPP for Northern Ireland, and any prosecutor designated for the purpose by one of those.

An agreement with a specified prosecutor may provide for assistance to be given to that prosecutor or to any other prosecutor (SA 2020 ss.74 and 75).

Nothing in any enactment which:

(1) requires that a minimum sentence be passed in respect of any offence or an offence of any description, or by reference to the circumstances of any offender (whether or not the enactment also permits the court to pass a lesser sentence in particular circumstances); or
(2) in the case of a sentence which is fixed by law, requires the court to take into account certain matters for the purposes of making an order which determines, or has the effect of determining the minimum period of imprisonment which the offender must serve (whether or not the enactment also permits the court to fix a lesser period in particular circumstances),

affects the power of a court to act under this provision (SA 2020 ss.74 and 75).

If, in determining what sentence to pass on the offender, the judge takes into account the extent and nature of the assistance given or offered, that does not prevent the court from also taking account of any other matter which it is entitled by virtue of any other enactment to take account of for the purposes of determining the sentence, or in the case of a sentence which is fixed by law, any minimum period of imprisonment which an offender must serve (SA 2020 ss.74 and 75).

The essential feature of the new statutory framework is that the offender must publicly admit the full extent of his own criminality and must agree to participate in a formalised process. The legislation has not, however, abolished a well-understood feature of the sentencing process and there will be occasions when an offender has provided assistance to the police which does not fall within the new arrangements, and in particular the written agreement. He is not thereby deprived of whatever consequent benefit he should receive (*R. v P* [2007] EWCA Crim 2290; [2008] 2 Cr. App. R. (S.) 5).

Extent of Discount

The extent of the discount given will ordinarily depend on the value of the help given. Non-compliance with the written agreement is not a separate crime, nor an aggravating feature of the original offence; the penalty is that the offender is deprived of the reduction of sentence which would have been allowed if he had complied with the agreement. Unlike the common law arrangements by which discounts for a guilty plea should normally be reflective of the time when it was tendered, for the purposes of a review any discount should continue to reflect the extent and nature of the assistance given or offered (*R. v P* [2007] EWCA Crim 2290; [2008] 2 Cr. App. R. (S.) 5). Value is a function of quality and quantity. In dealing with such a case the judge must balance, on the information before him: **31-020**

(1) the nature and effect of the assistance given; if the information is:
  (a) unreliable, vague, lacking in practical utility or already known to the authorities, no identifiable discount need be given or, if given, may be minimal; or
  (b) is accurate, particularised, useful in practice and hitherto unknown to the authorities, enabling serious criminal activity to be stopped and serious criminals brought to book, the discount may be substantial;
(2) the degree of assistance provided, e.g. whether the offender is prepared to back up his information by testifying or expressing willingness to testify, or making a witness statement incriminating a co-accused, particularly where such conduct leads to the co-accused's conviction on his plea of guilty (see *R. v D* [2010] EWCA Crim 1485; [2011] 1 Cr. App. R. (S.) 69); and
(3) the degree of risk to which the offender exposes himself or his family to personal jeopardy.

Note that:

(a) there is no automatic entitlement, where an offender provides information of significant value and fulfils his side of the agreement, to a "normal" discount of between 50 and 66 per cent of the sentence that would have been passed after a trial;
(b) what the offender has earned by participating in the written agreement system under s.73 is an appropriate reward for the assistance provided to the administration of justice, and that is, in the end, fact-specific; and
(c) when it applies, the discount for a guilty plea is separate from, and additional to, the appropriate reduction for assistance provided by the offender.

Accordingly, the best course to adopt is to:

(i) go back to the starting point before any allowance is made for plea; then
(ii) discount that by the appropriate amount for the assistance given; and then
(iii) apply any discount for a plea of guilty to the resulting figure.

(*R. v P* [2007] EWCA Crim 2290; [2008] 2 Cr. App. R. (S.) 5; *R. v Newman* [2010] EWCA Crim 1566 3; [2011] 1 Cr. App. R. (S.) 68)

A large-scale police informer might expect a reduction in the proper sentence of between one-half and two-thirds according to the particular circumstances of the case, but no hard and fast rules apply (*R. v King* [1985] 6 WLUK 283; (1985) 7 Cr. App. R. (S.) 227). Only in the most exceptional case will the appropriate level of reduction exceed three-quarters of the total sentence which would otherwise be passed, and the normal level continues, as before, to be a reduction of somewhere between one-half and two-thirds of that sentence (*R. v P* [2007] EWCA Crim 2290; [2008] 2 Cr. App. R. (S.) 5).

R. v Dougall [2010] EWCA Crim 1048; [2011] 1 Cr. App. R. (S.) 37 is not to be taken as laying down a principle that anyone who enters into a s.73 agreement is entitled to expect a discount of 50 per cent from the sentence that would otherwise be correct after allowance for guilty plea (*R. v Ford* [2011] EWCA Crim 473; [2011] 2 Cr. App. R. (S.) 64).

5. INFORMATION GIVEN AFTER SENTENCE

31-021 The 2005 Act does not abolish the former common law procedure which may still be appropriate in certain circumstances (*R. v H* [2009] EWCA Crim 2485; [2010] 2 Cr. App. R. (S.) 18). It does not apply where information is given *after* sentence which is covered by the provisions of the Act. See *R. v A* [1999] 1 Cr. App. R. (S.) 52.

In the absence of a statutory agreement under the Act the former system obtains. Credit for information provided after sentence will be given by the CACD only in certain circumstances, as where, for one reason or another, the material was not put before the sentencing judge. An offender who, after sentence, seeks to provide information must either adopt the statutory agreement or seek to persuade the Secretary of State to exercise prerogative powers in his favour (*R. v H* [2009] EWCA Crim 2485; [2010] 2 Cr. App. R. (S.) 18; *R. v Emsden* [2015] EWCA Crim 2092; [2016] 1 Cr. App. R. (S.) 62).

6. REFERRAL BACK TO COURT

31-022 An offender receiving such a discounted sentence, and who either fails to any extent to give assistance in accordance with the agreement, or, having given the assistance in accordance with the agreement, in pursuance of another written agreement, gives or agrees to give further assistance, may have his sentence referred back to court, see CrimPR 28.11 and VARIATION OF SENTENCE.

32. DRIVING DISQUALIFICATION

Quick Guide

1. Introduction

General

An offender convicted of certain offences may be disqualified from driving a mechanically propelled vehicle and from holding or obtaining a driving licence. Disqualification: **32-001**

(1) to some extent serves a basic public protection purpose, where the offender's conduct has proved a danger to other road users; and

(2) in most cases, is intended to punish misuse, or careless use of, vehicles and to deter both the offender and others from indulging in it.

Disqualification is part of the basic penalty imposed by the court for the offence, but it is an ancillary order and must be attached to the sentence; it cannot stand alone (but see 32-011).

Where the judge decides not to order, where he can, the offender's disqualification from driving for the usual minimum period or at all, or to order the endorsement of his driving record, he must explain why he has not done so, when he explains the sentence that he has passed.

The judge must have regard to proportionality and consider whether the disqualification is broadly commensurate with any custodial sentence imposed (*R. v Backhouse* [2010] EWCA Crim 1111 and *R. v Knight* [2012] EWCA Crim 3019; [2013] 2 Cr. App. R. (S.) 45).

Length of disqualification

The law provides no limit to the length of a disqualification beyond any minimum prescribed period, but: **32-002**

(1) very long periods should be avoided unless the offender is a menace to other road users (*R. v Rickeard* [1975] R.T.R. 104; *R. v Davitt* [1974] Crim. L.R. 719), since such offenders are particularly likely to commit offences of driving while disqualified which they might not, were the term shorter;

(2) it is not desirable to prevent offenders of working age from driving for very long periods unless the public is in need of protection from bad driving (*R. v Zar* [2013] EWCA Crim 1897);

(3) with effect from 13 April 2015 for offences committed on or after that date,

when imposing a disqualification under ss.34 or 35 of the RTOA 1988 it *must* order an extension period as set out in s.35A(4) in addition to the period of disqualification. The intended effect is that the period of disqualification will not start until the defendant's release from the sentence (see 32-017); and

(4) as to disqualification for life, see *R. v Buckley* (1994) 15 Cr. App. R. (S.) 695.

As highlighted in the SGC Guideline on "Causing Death by Driving":

(a) all orders for disqualification imposed by the judge on the same date take effect immediately and cannot be ordered to run consecutively to one another;

(b) where an offender is convicted on the same occasion of more than one offence to which RTOA 1988 s.35(1) applies, only one disqualification must be imposed on him, although the judge must take into account all the offences when determining the disqualification period (RTOA 1988 s.34(1), (3));

(c) the judge should take into account all offences when determining the disqualification periods and should generally impose like periods for each offence; and

(d) as orders take effect immediately, it is generally desirable for the judge to impose a single disqualification order that reflects the overall criminality of the offending behaviour.

Situations in which disqualification arises

32-003 An offender may be disqualified:

(1) where a vehicle has been used for the purpose of crime (see 32-008);
(2) on conviction of any offence (32-011);
(3) on conviction of an RT offence attracting obligatory disqualification (32-013);
(4) on conviction of an RT offence attracting discretionary disqualification (32-021); and
(5) where RT disqualification is obligatory owing to the accumulation of penalty points for a series of offences (32-024), in addition to dealing with him in any other way, see 32-011.

The various systems of disqualification run parallel to each other and are not mutually exclusive (see *Jones v West Mercia Chief Constable* [2001] R.T.R. 8).

A magistrates' court, as part of its procedures for enforcing the payment of fines and other financial penalties may, under CJA 2003 s.30, instead of issuing a warrant of commitment, or proceeding under MCA 1980 s.81, order a defaulter to be disqualified for a period not exceeding 12 months.

The provisions of C(IC)A 2003 Pt 3 govern the recognition and enforcement of disqualifications imposed on persons normally resident in the UK by courts in EU Member States.

Endorsement

32-004 The particulars of all offences involving obligatory or discretionary disqualification must be endorsed on the offender's licence, where he holds one, unless there are special reasons for not doing so.

This is irrespective of whether he is disqualified or not. In the case of an offender who does not hold a licence, or a foreign driver, the court ordering endorsement with any particulars or penalty points must send notice of the order to the Secretary of State for endorsement of the offender's "driving record." (RTOA 1988 ss.44, 44A).

For reasons essentially connected with the imposition of fixed penalties (which cannot be issued to non-GB drivers), RSA 2006 introduces the concept of a "driving record" (defined in RTOA 1988 s.97A, inserted by RSA 2006 s.8) held by the Secretary of State.

The first stage of this procedure is introduced by s.9 and Sch.2 in relation to unlicensed and foreign drivers. The second stage, (s.10 and Sch.3) introduces a new system of endorsement of driving records for all drivers. The "counterpart" of a licence has no further function.

As to applications for removal of an endorsement, see RTOA 1988 s.45.

Conditional and absolute discharge

Where the judge makes an order of conditional or absolute discharge in respect **32-005** of an offence carrying obligatory or discretionary disqualification, he may also on that occasion exercise any power conferred, and must also exercise any duty imposed, on the court by RTOA 1988 ss.34, 35, 36 or 44 (RTOA 1988 s.46(1)).

Mechanics of disqualification: interim disqualification

In order to decide whether or not to exercise his power of disqualification, the **32-006** judge may take into consideration particulars of any previous conviction or disqualification endorsed on the offender's licence.

While, in general, a disqualification will be imposed at the time sentence is pronounced, which will normally follow upon conviction:

(1) there is nothing to prevent the judge from dealing with the substantive part of the sentence on the day of conviction and postponing ancillary questions of endorsement and disqualification until the licence is produced, and any other relevant information is to hand (*R. v Annesley* (1976) 62 Cr. App. R. 113);

(2) a judge who:

   (a) defers sentence in respect of an offence carrying obligatory or discretionary disqualification; or

   (b) adjourns after convicting an offender of such an offence, before dealing with him;

   may order him to be disqualified until he has been dealt with for the offence.

An order under (2) ceases to have effect on the expiry of six months from the date it is made, if the offender has not been dealt with before that and, when the court comes to deal with the offender, it is precluded from disqualifying him further in respect of the same offence or any offence in respect of which an order could have been made at the time the first order was made. Where the judge proposes to disqualify, he should draw this to the attention of counsel, so that the latter may deal with the point specifically (*R. v Powell* (1984) 6 Cr. App. R. (S.) 354).

Production of licence: suspension

32-007 Before making an order the court *must require* the offender, if he is the holder of a licence, (including an EU licence) to produce it, and if he has not caused it to be delivered to the court, or he does not produce it:

(1) he may be guilty of an offence; and
(2) the licence *must* be suspended until it is produced.

(RTA 1988 s.27(1), (3), (4))

2. Vehicle used for the purpose of crime

32-008 Where a person is convicted in the Crown Court or, having been convicted in the magistrates' court, is committed to the Crown Court for sentence under SA 2020 s.164:

(1) for an offence punishable with imprisonment for not less than two years on indictment;
(2) having been convicted in a magistrates' court of such an offence was committed to the Crown Court for sentence;
(3) is convicted by or before any court of common assault, or for any other offence involving an assault, including the aiding, abetting or procuring of such an offence; or
(4) the judge is satisfied that a vehicle was used by that person, or by anyone else, for the purpose of committing or facilitating the commission of the offence, including the taking of any steps after it was committed for the purposes of disposing of any property to which it related, or of avoiding apprehension or detection, or that the assault was committed by driving a motor vehicle,

he may disqualify that person for such period as he thinks fit. As to the appropriate mandatory extension in custody cases, see 32-017 (SA 2020 s.165).

The "offence" must be that, or one of those, of which he is convicted (*R. v Parrington* (1985) 7 Cr. App. R. (S.) 18).

Important considerations

32-009 A number of points needs to be noted in respect of the exercise, and the effect of exercising, this power:

(1) the power under SA 2020 s.164 is exercisable even though the offence committed does not attract endorsement under RTOA 1988;
(2) if the driving is only incidental to the offence, the power of disqualification under s.164 should not be used (*R. v Wilmot*, *The Times,* 24 January 1985);
(3) the fact that the offender did not himself drive the vehicle in the course of committing the offence does not protect him from disqualification; if one of several offenders uses a vehicle for the purposes of an offence, all or any of them may be disqualified (*R. v Wilmot*, *The Times,* 24 January 1985);
(4) the power should not be exercised without first giving the defence advocate an opportunity of dealing with it (*R. v Powell* (1984) 6 Cr. App. R. (S.) 354; *R. v Lake* (1986) 8 Cr. App. R. (S.) 69; *R. v Money* [1988] Crim. L.R. 626);
(5) the judge, in imposing a disqualification under s.147 (SA 2020 s.162),

should take account of the effect on the offender's employment prospects on his release (*R. v Wright* (1979) 1 Cr. App. R. (S.) 82; *R. v Davegun* (1985) 7 Cr. App. R. (S.) 110; *R. v Liddey* (1999) 2 Cr. App. R. (S.) 122);

(6) where a custodial sentence is imposed the length of disqualification should be equal to or slightly in excess of the period the offender will spend in custody (*R. v Bowling* [2008] EWCA Crim 1148; [2009] 1 Cr. App. R. (S.) 23; long periods are undesirable (*R. v Fazal* [1999] 1 Cr. App. R. (S.) 152) (see however, 32-017 and the effect of the "extension" period that must be passed for offences post April 2015);

(7) disqualification under s.164, does not "wipe the slate clean" of penalty points previously accumulated on the licence; nor is there any power, if the court declines to disqualify under s.165, to impose penalty points under RTOA 1988;

(8) there is no power to order a re-test under s.164 (*R. v Patel* (1995) 16 Cr. App. R. (S.) 756); and

(9) in dealing with a conspiracy, the only occasion on which an offender can be disqualified under s.164 is where the vehicle was used directly in the formation of the agreement: *R. v Gorry* [2018] EWCA Crim 1867 applying *R. v Riley* (1983) 5 Cr. App. R. (S.) 335.

Obligation to produce licence

A judge ordering a disqualification under s.164 must require the offender to produce: **32-010**

(1) any licence (defined in SA 2020 s.169);

(2) in the case where he holds a Northern Ireland licence, that licence; and

(3) in the case of a person holding an EU licence (as defined in RTA 1988 Pt III), his community licence.

(SA 2020 s.168)

3. Disqualification for any offence

The court before which a person is convicted of any offence committed after 31 December 1997 may: **32-011**

(1) provided the judge has been notified that he has that power;

(2) instead of, unless the sentence is fixed by law, or is one which falls to be imposed under various provisions of the SA 2020 on minimum sentences required for certain offences; or in addition to

(3) dealing with him in any other way,

order him to be disqualified for such period as he thinks fit, for holding or obtaining a driving licence (SA 2020 ss.162, 163 and 165).

As to the appropriate mandatory extension period in custody cases, see 32-018.

This power is wide-ranging; it is not limited to any particular offence, nor is it necessary that the offence be connected in any way with the use of a motor vehicle (*R. v Cliff* [2004] EWCA Crim 3139; [2005] 2 Cr. App. R. (S.) 22; see also *R. v Skitt* [2004] EWCA Crim 3141; [2005] 2 Cr. App. R. (S.) 22).

Obligation to produce licence

32-012 A judge ordering a disqualification under s.146 must require the offender to produce:

(1) any licence (defined in SA 2020 s.169);
(2) in the case where he holds a Northern Ireland licence, that licence; and
(3) in the case of a person holding an EU licence (as defined in RTA 1988 Pt III), his EU licence.

(SA 2020 s.168)

4. Obligatory disqualification for serious RT offences

32-013 An offender convicted of an offence involving obligatory disqualification must be disqualified for such period *not less than* the period specified in the fourth column of the table below as the judge thinks fit unless, for special reasons (see 32-034), he thinks fit to order him to be disqualified for a shorter period or not to order him to be disqualified at all. Where, for special reasons, the judge does not disqualify, the number of penalty points in the fifth column must be endorsed on the offender's licence.

Where there has been a conviction of a like offence within the ten years immediately preceding conviction (and an * appears against the number in the fourth column, there must be disqualification for a minimum of three years or six years where the offence is committed on or after 28 June 2022. Where a + appears against such a number, an extended re-test (RTOA 1988 s.36) must be ordered.

The offences listed under RTA 1988 ss.3, 4(1), 5(1)(a), 7(6), 7A(6) and 12 in square brackets are triable summarily only but may come before the Crown Court if sent there by the magistrates or may arise in the exercise of the Crown Court's appellate jurisdiction.

RTA 1988 s.	Offence	Code	Years	Penalty points
—	Motor manslaughter	DD60	2+	(3–11)
1	Causing death by dangerous driving	DD70	2+	(3–11)
1A	Causing serious injury by dangerous driving	DD10	2+	(3–11)
2	Dangerous driving	DD40	1+	(3–11)
2B	Causing death by careless or inconsiderate driving	CD80	1	(3–11)
2C	Causing serious injury by careless or inconsiderate driving		1	(3–11)
3	Careless and inconsiderate driving	CD10		(3–9)
3A	Causing death by careless driving:	CD40/ DG60	2*+	(3–11)

RTA 1988 s.	Offence	Code	Years	Penalty points
	(a) when under the influence of drink or drugs	CD50		
	(b) with excess alcohol concentration etc.	CD60		
	(c) and then failing to provide specimen for analysis	CD70		
3ZB	Causing death by driving by unlicensed, (*disqualified*) or uninsured driver (Disqualified drivers within s.3ZC for driving after 13 April 2015)	CD90		(3–11)
3ZC	Causing death by driving: disqualified drivers	BA40	2+	(3–11)
3ZD	Causing serious injury: disqualified drivers	BA60	2+	(3–11)
[4(1)	Driving or attempting to drive while unfit to drive through:			
	(a) drink, or (b) drugs	DR20 DR80	1* 1*	(3–11) (3–11)]
[5(1)(a), (b), (2)	Driving or attempting to drive with excess alcohol concentration	DR10	1	(3–11)]
[5A	Driving or attempting to drive with a concentration of specified controlled drug above the specified limit	DG10		(3–11)]
[7(6)	Failing without reasonable excuse to supply evidential specimen when driving or attempting to drive	DR30	*	(3–11)]
[7A(6)	Failing to allow a specimen to be subjected to laboratory test where the test would be for ascertaining ability to drive, or proportion of alcohol at the time offender was driving or attempting to drive		1*	(3–11)]
[12	Motor racing and speed trials on public way	MS50	1	(3–11)]
RTOA 1988 s.34	A person on whom more than one disqualification for a fixed period of 56 days or more has been imposed within the three			

RTA 1988 s.	Offence	Code	Years	Penalty points
	years immediately preceding the commission of the offence			
OAPA 3.35	Causing bodily harm by wanton or furious driving	DD90		(3–9)

As to the appropriate mandatory extension periods in custody cases, see RTOA 1988 s.35A, at 32-017.

Note also that:

(1) if, on conviction of any of the offences specified in the Table, the judge finds special reasons, and does not disqualify, he must order the offender's licence to be endorsed with 3–11 points; and
(2) if the judge exercises his power under RTOA 1988 ss.34 or 35 not to order any disqualification, or to order disqualification for a shorter period than would otherwise be required (or not to endorse the offender's licence under s.44) he must state the grounds for doing so in open court (RTOA 1988 s.47(1)).

Sentencing: offences under ss.1, 2B and 3A

32-014 The maximum period of imprisonment for causing death by dangerous driving and causing death by careless driving while under the influence of drink or drugs was increased to 14 years' imprisonment with the coming into force of CJA 2003 s.285 on 27 February 2004 (RTOA 1988 ss.1, 2B, 3A) and to life imprisonment as from 28 June 2022 for offences committed on or after that date (Police, Crime, Sentencing and Courts Act 2022 s.86).

Sentencing in such cases is now governed by the SGC's definitive guideline *Causing Death by Driving* for offenders sentenced on or after 4 August 2008 (see SENTENCING GUIDELINES). The previous guideline case, *R. v Cooksley* [2003] EWCA Crim 996; [2003] 2 Cr. App. R. 18 continues to provide some guidance on the length of any period of disqualification.

Manslaughter involving use of a motor vehicle

32-015 The maximum sentence for manslaughter is life imprisonment. The sentence for manslaughter involving the use of a motor vehicle, which involves an element of hostility, cannot be equated with other offences of causing death by driving, such as causing death by dangerous driving and causing death by careless driving, having consumed alcohol so as to be over the prescribed limit. The maximum sentence for these two offences has always corresponded has been 14 years (RTOA 1988 s.34A), but for offences committed on or after 28 June 2022 is also life imprisonment (Police, Crime, Sentencing and Courts Act 2022 s.86).

Reduced disqualification for offender attending course

32-016 Where a person is convicted by or before a court of a relevant drink offence, or a specified offence, and the court makes an order under RTOA 1988 s.34 disqualifying him for a period of not less than 12 months, it may order that the period of disqualification be reduced if, by a specified date, the offender satisfactorily completes an approved course specified in the order.

A "relevant drink offence" is an offence under the following provisions of RTA 1988:

- s.3A(1)(a)—causing death by careless driving when unfit to drive, etc.;
- s.3A(1)(b)—causing death by careless driving with excess alcohol;
- s.3A(1)(c)—failing to provide a specimen where required in connection with drink or the consumption of alcohol;
- s.4—driving or being in charge when under the influence of drink, committed by of unfitness through drink;
- s.5(1)—driving or being in charge with excess alcohol;
- s.7(6)—failing to provide a specimen committed in the course of an investigation into an offence within any of the above offences; and
- s.7A(6)—failing to allow a specimen to be subjected to a laboratory test in the course of an investigation into an offence within any of the above.

A "specified offence" means an offence under:

- RTA 1988 s.3—careless and inconsiderate driving;
- RTA 1988 s.36—failing to comply with a traffic sign;
- RTRA 1984 s.17(4)—misuse of special road; and
- RTRA 1984 s.89(1)—excess speed.

An order must not be made in the case of an offender convicted of a *specified offence* if the offender has, during the period of three years ending with the date on which the offence was committed, committed a specified offence and successfully completed an approved course (either under s.34A or under s.30A (totting up procedure), or the specified offence was committed during his probationary period (i.e. under Road Traffic (New Drivers) Act 1995 s.1)).

The court may make such an order only where:

(1) the offender appears to be 17 or over;
(2) it is satisfied that a place on a course is available for the offender;
(3) it informs the offender (orally or in writing and in ordinary language) of the effect of the order, and the fees payable and when they must be paid; and
(4) the offender agrees to the order being made.

Note that:

(a) the reduction must be of not less than three months nor more than one-quarter of the unreduced period (thus nine months in the case of a 12-month disqualification which is the usual period for a drink-driving offence, but, of course, it may be higher according to the alcohol level);
(b) the offender disqualified for two years, as is the case under RTA 1988 s.3A, will be eligible for a six-month reduction; and
(c) the date specified as the latest date for the completion of the course must be at least two months before the last day of the period of disqualification as reduced by the order.

Custody cases: extension period

Where a person is convicted of an offence for which the judge imposes a custodial sentence, other than a suspended sentence, and orders that person to be **32-017** disqualified under RTOA 1988 ss.34 or 35, or SA 2020 ss.162–165 the order *must* provide for the offender to be disqualified for:

(1) the *discretionary disqualification period*; being the period for which the judge would have imposed in the absence of s.35A; and
(2) an *appropriate extension period* as set out in s.35A(4), being where:
    (a) a *life sentence tariff determination* is made under SA 2020 s.321(2), a period equal to the part of the sentence specified in that order;
    (b) a *detention and training order* is made under SA 2020 s.233, a period equal to half the term of that order;
    (c) SA 2020 s.265 (*extended sentence* for certain violent or sexual offences: persons *18 or over*) applies in relation to the custodial sentence, a period equal to two-thirds of the term imposed pursuant to s.265(2); after that term has been reduced by any relevant discount; and
    (d) SA 2020 s.254 (*extended sentence* for certain violent or sexual offences: persons under 18) applies in relation to the custodial sentence, a period equal to two-thirds of the term imposed pursuant to s.254(b) after that term has been reduced by any relevant discount.

(RTOA 1988 s.35A)

In any other case, the appropriate extension period is a period equal to half the custodial sentence imposed, calculated after that sentence has been reduced by any relevant discount; that is the total number of days to count as time served as a result of crediting periods of remand in custody or on bail under SA 2020 s.166 (see DEALING WITH AN OFFENDER).

If a period determined under subs.(4) includes a fraction of a day, that period is to be rounded up to the nearest number of whole days.

Excluded sentences

32-018 The provisions at 32-017 do not apply where the judge has made an order under SA 2020 s.321(2) (determination of minimum term) in relation to a *mandatory life sentence; no early release* in relation to a custodial sentence.
(SA 2020 s.166)

Effect of custodial sentence in other cases

32-019 Where a person is convicted of an offence for which a judge proposes to order the person to be disqualified under ss.34 or 35, or under SA 2020 ss.162–165; and:

(1) the judge proposes to impose on the person a custodial sentence, (other than a suspended sentence) for another offence; or
(2) at the time of sentencing for the offence, a custodial sentence imposed on the person on an earlier occasion has not expired,

the judge must have regard, in determining the period for which the person is to be disqualified under ss.34 or 35, to the consideration below if and to the extent that it is appropriate to do so. That consideration is the diminished effect of disqualification as a distinct punishment if the person who is disqualified is also detained in pursuance of a custodial sentence (RTOA 1988 s.35B).

If the judge proposes to order the person to be disqualified under ss.34 or 35, and to impose a custodial sentence for the same offence, he may not in relation to that disqualification take that custodial sentence into account for the purposes of the first paragraph above.

(SA 2020 s.167)

Checklist

The Court of Appeal considered the effect of s.35A and s.35B in *R. v Needham* [2016] EWCA 416 and set out a helpful checklist. The checklist is as follows: 32-020

- *Step 1*

  Does the court intend to impose a "discretionary" disqualification under s.34 or s.35 for any offence?

  YES—go to Step 2.
- *Step 2*

  Does the court intend to impose a custodial term for that *same* offence?

  YES—s.35A applies and the court must impose an extension period (see s.35A(4)(h) for that *same* offence and consider Step 3).

  NO—s.35A does not apply at all—go on to consider s.35B and Step 4.
- *Step 3*

  Does the court intend to impose a custodial term for *another* offence (which is longer or consecutive) or is the defendant already serving a custodial sentence?

  YES—then consider what increase ("uplift") in the period of "discretionary disqualification" is required to comply with s.35B(2) and (3). In accordance with s.35B(4) ignore any custodial term imposed for an offence involving disqualification under s.35A.

  Discretionary period + extension period + uplift = total period of disqualification.

  NO—no need to consider s.35B at all

  Discretionary period + extension period = total period of disqualification.
- *Step 4*

  Does the court intend to impose a custodial term for *another* offence or is the defendant already serving a custodial sentence?

  YES—then consider what increase ("uplift") in the period of "discretionary disqualification" is required to comply with s.35B(2) and (3).

  Discretionary period + uplift = total period of disqualification.

Other points on extension periods.

In *Needham* (32-020) the Court of Appeal also gave consideration to allowance for time on remand or on a qualifying curfew. Where an interim disqualification is imposed and the defendant remanded in custody, no issue will arise as to credit for any time spent subject to curfew or on remand prior to sentencing against the period of disqualification imposed. (The Court of Appeal commented that in the light of the new legislation it may be inappropriate for an order of interim disqualification to be made where an offender is remanded in custody. Doing so would appear to run counter to the idea that disqualification should be served while the offender is at liberty. There may be unnecessary complications and courts should be hesitant before exercising this power on those remanded in custody.) 32-021

With time spent on remand, some of the original legislation was amended prior to enactment. As enacted the clear intention of Parliament is that time spent on remand will not count when calculating the extension period under s.35A. There is no corresponding provision for s.35B. The Court of Appeal stated:

> "... it is open to the court to avoid such injustice by permitting a court to take into account a significant remand period in determining the appropriate discretionary period under section 35A. Many of the offences to which section 35A applies involve obligatory minimum periods of disqualification. There can be no question of such a minimum period being reduced to take account of time spent on remand, but there may be scope for some reduction if the sentencer has in mind a longer period than the statutory minimum."

In *R. v Harkins* [2011] EWCA Crim 2227, it was observed that the point of the disqualification under s.147 is to punish and to deter. The order removes access to the lawful use of a vehicle used in commission of the offences for which the sentences were passed.

> "Thus, if the disqualification is to be effective at all, it is implicit that it must apply after release from custody and normally that will be a proportionate result provided it does not seriously impair rehabilitation ... Furthermore, proportionality is preserved by the general practice of keeping the period of disqualification broadly commensurate with the custodial sentence. That is not the same however as requiring the judge to fine tune the period of disqualification in order to accord with the precise calculation of release dates and periods spent on licence. Furthermore, it does not require the judge to have regard to any direction he has made for credit against the sentence for time spent on remand unless it would result in a gross disparity between the sentence passed and the period of disqualification."

This is the correct approach to the question of time spent on remand under s.35A.

> "If the time spent on remand would lead to a disproportionate result in terms of the period of disqualification, then the court has power in fixing the discretionary element to adjust that period to take account of time spent on remand."

It is not to be a precise arithmetical calculation taking place: the court should take a broad brush approach to the question of adjustment.

> "The scope for such adjustment would only arise (a) if there had been no interim disqualification, (b) if the period of remand was of such a nature that the term of disqualification would otherwise be disproportionate, and (c) would not reduce the discretionary term below the obligatory statutory minimum period of disqualification. A similar approach would apply when the court is assessing the correct period of disqualification under section 35B."

Minimum periods of disqualification

On obligatory minimum periods of disqualification, and whether that minimum period related to the discretionary period alone or to the discretionary period plus the extension period, the minimum term encompasses the discretionary period of disqualification alone (*R. v Needham* at [39]).

Early release arrangements

The length of the custodial term imposed for calculating the appropriate extension period under s.35A(4) relates to the term of custody pronounced by the court at the time of sentence and does not take account of the possibility of release earlier than the point identified in subs.(4), for example under the home detention curfew scheme.

Guilty plea

The SGC's definitive guideline on credit for a guilty plea states at para.2.6:

> "A reduction in sentence should only be applied to the punitive elements of a penalty. The guilty plea reduction has no impact on sentencing decisions in relation to ancillary orders, including orders of disqualification from driving."

Start of disqualification

Although the legislation has provided for the effects of disqualification to be felt after the release from custody, it has not altered the principle that disqualification starts from the day upon which it is pronounced by the court.

Extended re-test

See s.36(7) of the RTOA and *R. v Anderson* [2012] EWCA Crim 3060: the imposition of an extended retest is precluded where an order for such a test is already in force.

Impact on other provisions

Section 34A RTOA provides for a reduced disqualification period for drink drive offenders who have attended on a special course. There are provisions not yet in force and which make reference to the extension period under s.35A. As presently in force any reduction in the disqualification period for attendance on courses would come off the entire disqualification including the extension period under s.35A. If fully enacted, the reduction would only apply to the discretionary part of the disqualification. A similar situation applies to s.42 RTOA (removal of disqualification) in relation to the time which must elapse before an application can be made.

Impact on sentencing guidelines

The SGC guideline on causing death by dangerous driving provides at [31]: 32-022

> "When ordering disqualification from driving, the duration of the order should allow for the length of any custodial period in order to ensure that the disqualification has the desired impact. In principle, the minimum period of disqualification should either equate to the length of the custodial sentence imposed (in the knowledge that the offender is likely to be released having served half of that term), or the relevant statutory minimum disqualification period, whichever results in the longer period of disqualification."

In *Needham*, it was noted that this guidance itself appears to depart from guidelines given in *R. v Cooksley* [2003] 2 Crim App Rep 18. The Court noted that although the SGC approach went part of the way towards the subsequently enacted legislation, it fell short of the provisions now in force. If

> "... that guidance were now applied in the setting of the discretionary period with the new legislation then superimposed upon that, there would be a risk of double counting. Accordingly, in the light of the new legislation, we think that courts should focus on the legislation rather than [31] of the guideline. The court's approach should be to fix the discretionary term taking account of relevant factors including the need for protection of the public. There will often be close correlation between that factor and the levels of harm and culpability involved in the offence of causing death by dangerous driving. If the case is a section 35A case, then, as mandated, the court will fix a discretionary period plus an extension period. If the case is a section 35B case, then the court will apply section 35B as explained above."

Sentencing remarks must be clear so that others may identify the correct extension period pursuant to s.35A and any uplift pursuant to s.35B. Such information will be important for police, the courts, and DVLA. It will also be important to the

Court of Appeal. If, on appeal, a conviction on a count is quashed or a sentence is reduced, the court will need to know precisely by how much the period of disqualification was extended pursuant to s.35A or increased pursuant to s.35B so as to make appropriate adjustments to the disqualification imposed. Both s.34A (reduced disqualification for attendance on courses) and s.42 RTOA (removal of disqualification) would require identification of the extension period if certain provisions relating to them were brought into force. A judge sentencing under s.35A

> "should state the total period of disqualification but breaking that period down into the discretionary and extension periods. He should also give brief reasons for the length of the discretionary disqualification. When sentencing under section 35B the court should state the total period of disqualification imposed but then explain how the legislative steer of this section has been taken into account by indicating what the period of disqualification would have been but for section 35B and then indicating the period added by way of upward adjustment for the purposes of section 35B. Again, brief reasons should be given for the imposition of both these elements."

5. OFFENCES CARRYING DISCRETIONARY DISQUALIFICATION

32-023 Discretionary disqualification and obligatory endorsement apply to road traffic offences which are not, like those carrying obligatory disqualification, invariably grave matters, but which may still be serious enough to justify a period of disqualification. Where the court does not exercise its power of disqualification it *must*, in the absence of special reasons, endorse the licence with the appropriate number of penalty points. See TABLE at 32-041.

6. REPEATED OFFENCES—PENALTY POINTS

General

32-024 Under the penalty points system, an offender who commits a series of offences within a period of three years *must* be disqualified because of his repeated offending, whether or not the particular offence before the court would, in itself, justify disqualification (RTOA 1988 ss.28–31, 35).

It should be noted that:

(1) the system applies only to offences carrying obligatory disqualification in respect of an order made under RTOA 1988 s.34, as amended by RTA 1991 Sch.4 para.95 or to discretionary disqualification and obligatory endorsement as set out above;
(2) it applies in relation to an offence committed by aiding and abetting, etc. the commission of an offence such as is described in (1) above as if the offence involved discretionary disqualification;
(3) *if the court disqualifies the offender for his offence, no penalty points fall to be endorsed on his licence*; if he is not disqualified they are, unless there are special reasons for not doing so; where a driver is disqualified under RTOA 1988 s.34 and has to be dealt with on the same occasion for another road traffic offence carrying an obligatory endorsement, the endorsement under s.44 should be limited to the particulars of the conviction and should not include particulars of the offence or the penalty points attributable to the offence (*Martin v DPP* [2000] 2 Cr. App. R. (S.) 18);
(4) if the offender is convicted, whether on the same occasion or not, of two or

more offences committed on the same occasion and involving obligatory endorsement, *the total number of penalty points to be attributed to them is the number that would be attributed on a conviction for one of them (the most serious)*. Thus if the convictions are on separate occasions, the number to be attributed on later occasions is thereby restricted; but if (4) would ordinarily apply to two or more offences, the judge may still, if he thinks fit, decide that it will not apply to the offences, but must state his reasons for so doing in open court and enter those reasons in the record; and

(5) once an offender is disqualified, the "slate is wiped clean" of all penalty points accumulated up to the time of disqualification (see *R. v Brentwood Justices Ex p. Richardson* (1992) 95 Cr. App. R. 187) (see, in particular, *R. v Kent* (1983) 77 Cr. App. R. 120).

Reduced penalty points for attendance on course

Where a person is convicted of certain specified offences, and: 32-025

(1) penalty points are to be attributed to the offence and the court does not order him to be disqualified; and
(2) at least seven but no more than 11 penalty points are to be taken into account on the occasion of the conviction,

the court may order that three of the penalty points attributed to the offence (or all of them if three or fewer are so attributed) shall not be taken into account under s.29(1)(b) on the occasion of any conviction of an offence after the end of the period of 12 months beginning with the date of the order, if, by the relevant date, the offender completes an approved course (RTOA 1988 s.30A).

The specified offences are those under RTA 1988 s.3 (careless or inconsiderate driving), RTA 1988 s.36 (failing to comply with a traffic sign), RTRA 1984 s.17(4) (use of special roads) and RTRA 1984 s.89(1) (excess speed).

Repeated offences: disqualification

Disqualification under the penalty points system arises where the offender has, as a result of an offence committed within the three-year period, accumulated a total of 12 or more penalty points, including those to be endorsed on the instant occasion: 32-026

(1) if, taking the current offence into account, but disregarding any offence for which he is disqualified under RTOA 1988 s.34, the number of penalty points over the three-year period comes to 12 points or more, the disqualification is obligatory unless there are "mitigating circumstances";
(2) the qualifying date for both the earlier and the current offences is the *date of the offence*, not the date of conviction;
(3) where the offender is convicted on *the same occasion* of more than one offence involving obligatory or discretionary disqualification, *not more than one "totting up" disqualification may be imposed, and it must be allocated to a single offence*; and
(4) the *minimum period* for which such a person is to be disqualified varies according to whether he has been previously disqualified during the three years preceding the commission of the latest offence in respect of which penalty points are being taken into account. If:
    (a) there are no such disqualifications, the minimum period is *six months*;
    (b) if there is one—*12 months*; and

(c) if there are two or more, the minimum period is *two years*.

(RTOA 1988 s.35)

As to the appropriate mandatory extension period under RTOA 1988 s.35A, inserted by CorJa 2009 s.120, see 32-017.

Disqualifications by the Crown Court under SA 2020 s.164 or interim disqualifications by a magistrates' court pending committal to the Crown Court (RTOA 1988 s.26), are not included.

Mitigating circumstances

32-027 The judge may disqualify such an offender under the totting up provisions for a period below the minimum required under the system, or may decide not to disqualify at all, where he is satisfied that there are, *and states the grounds* for, mitigating the normal consequences of conviction, but may *not* do so where the offence is one carrying obligatory disqualification (see also *R. v Thomas* (1984) 78 Cr. App. R. 55).

"Mitigating circumstances" are not to be equated with "special reasons" (see 32-034). The former will, in the ordinary way, be largely circumstances pertaining to the offender, and concerned not with the gravity of the offence, but with the repetition of offences within a comparatively short period.

The statute expressly excludes from consideration any circumstances:

(1) that are alleged to make the offence(s) not serious;
(2) that show hardship, short of "exceptional hardship"; or
(3) which have been taken into consideration already on another occasion within the three years immediately preceding the conviction.

The test of "exceptional hardship" is not the same as that for "special reasons". The judge does not need to hear sworn evidence, although obviously it will usually be desirable to do so (*Owen v Jones* [1988] R.T.R. 102). Where an offender seeks to contend that mitigating grounds which he is putting forward are other and different from those put forward to some other court within the three-year period, it is for him to prove that they are different, by reference to that court's record or by calling evidence (*R. v Sandbach Justices Ex p. Pescud* (1983) 5 Cr. App. R. (S.) 177).

Where no mitigating circumstances exist the offender must be disqualified

32-028 This has been found by the CACD to be ignored or not sufficiently appreciated in the Crown Court (see, in particular, *R. v Kent* (1983) 77 Cr. App. R. 120).

Discretionary disqualification and totting up

32-029 Where an offender commits a motoring offence which attracts discretionary disqualification when he may also be liable for obligatory disqualification under the totting up provisions, the judge should use his discretion to consider:

(1) whether the offence itself should attract discretionary disqualification, in the light of the offender's whole record, for the repetition is an aspect of the offence, as are the facts of the case before him; and
(2) whether he should have a longer disqualification than the Act provides, then the judge may, instead of disqualifying him on the offence, add the appropri-

ate points to his licence, thus leading to a totting up disqualification under s.34: *Jones v DPP* [2001] R.T.R. 8.

7. Driving test order

General

Where: 32-030

(1) an offender:
  - (a) is disqualified on conviction of manslaughter, or of an offence under RTA 1988 ss.1 or 2;
  - (b) is disqualified under s.3A (death by careless driving whilst under the influence of drink or drugs) where the offence is committed on or after 31 January 2002;
  - (c) is disqualified under s.3ZB (causing death by driving unlicensed or uninsured driver), 3ZC (causing death by driving: disqualified drivers), or 3ZD (causing serious injury: disqualified drivers);
  - (d) is disqualified under RTA 1988 ss.34 or 35; or
  - (e) is convicted of such other offence involving obligatory disqualification as the Secretary of State may prescribe,

  the judge must (whether or not the offender has previously passed a test (*R. v Miller* (1994) 15 Cr. App. R. (S.) 505)) order him to be disqualified until he passes the "appropriate driving test"; and

(2) persons have been convicted of any other offence involving obligatory *endorsement* the court *may* make such an order (whether or not he has previously passed any test).

An "appropriate driving test" means:

(i) in such circumstances as the Secretary of State may prescribe, an extended driving test; and
(ii) otherwise, a test of competence to drive which is not an extended driving test.

The judge is bound, in deciding whether to make an order, to have regard to the safety of other road users.

Such a disqualification does not expire until proof of the passing of the test is delivered to the Secretary of State (RTOA 1988 s.36).

The superior courts have emphasised on a number of occasions (the most recent of which are *R. v Peat* (1984) 6 Cr. App. R. (S.) 311 and *R. v Lazzari* (1984) 6 Cr. App. R. (S.) 83), that such an order is *not* intended as a punishment, but to protect the public against incompetent drivers including those not having regard for other road users (*R. v Bannister* (1990–91) 12 Cr. App. R. (S.) 314).

Unless obligatory, the power should be exercised only where there is reason to doubt the offender's competence to drive, whether through age, infirmity or the circumstances of the offence.

When sentencing for aggravated vehicle taking it is inappropriate to order a passenger to take an extended driving test at the end of a period of disqualification (see *R. v Bradshaw* [2001] R.T.R. 4).

Notification of disability

32-031 Where, in any proceedings for an offence committed in respect of a motor vehicle, it appears to the judge that the accused may be suffering from any relevant disability, or prospective disability, within the meaning of RTA 1988 Pt III, he must notify the Secretary of State.

If there is evidence that an offender is liable to recurring bouts of an illness, such as hypomania, but is otherwise competent to drive, this is the course to take rather than to make a driving test order (*Hughes v Challes* (1983) 5 Cr. App. R. (S.) 374).

8. PROCEEDINGS AFTER DISQUALIFICATION; SUSPENSION; REMOVAL

General

32-032 The giving of notice of appeal does not operate to suspend the order of disqualification. If the order is to be suspended, it must be done by judicial act.

If an offender gives notice of appeal, or of his intention to apply for judicial review:

(1) the judge may, if he thinks fit, suspend any disqualification pending appeal; and
(2) any disqualification, whether obligatory or discretionary, may be suspended:
  (a) by the Crown Court, where the offender appeals to it against conviction or sentence;
  (b) by the CACD where the offender appeals, or applies for leave to appeal, against conviction or sentence;
  (c) by the High Court, where the offender applies to the magistrates to state a case under MCA 1980 s.87; or
  (d) by the High Court, where the offender applies, or applies for leave to apply, for a quashing order in respect of the proceedings before the magistrates' court.

Removal; procedure

32-033 A person disqualified by order of the court may apply to the court which made the order to remove it, provided that:

(1) two years have elapsed, if the disqualification was for less than four years;
(2) half the period has elapsed, if the disqualification was for not less than four and not more than ten years; or
(3) five years have elapsed in any other case.

The judge, as he thinks fit, having regard to the character of the applicant and his subsequent conduct, the nature of the offence and any other circumstances:

(a) may, by order, remove the disqualification from such date as he may specify; or
(b) may refuse the application; but
(c) must *not* add to it any conditions or additional requirements (*R. v Bentham* (1981) 3 Cr. App. R. (S.) 229).

(RTOA 1988 s.48)

Application should be made to the location of the Crown Court where the order of disqualification was made. An offender who wants the court to exercise the power of removal must apply in writing, no earlier than the date on which the court can exercise the power, serving the application on the Crown Court officer, specifying the disqualification that he wants the court to remove, and explaining why. The Crown Court officer will serve a copy of the application on the chief officer of police for the local justice area (CrimPR 29.2).

There is no power in removing a disqualification, to remove a driving test order.

If the application is granted, the applicant may be ordered to pay the whole or any part of the costs. Where the application is refused, a further three months must elapse before another is entertained.

These provisions do not differentiate between discretionary and obligatory disqualification, and there is nothing in law to prevent the court removing an obligatory disqualification although, if it thinks fit, the court may regard it as one which it is somewhat less ready to remove than a discretionary disqualification (*Damer v Davison* (1975) 61 Cr. App. R. 232).

9. Special reasons

General

Before the court can justify, for special reasons, not disqualifying for an offence where it is otherwise obligatory, or disqualifying for a period shorter than the statutory minimum, or for not ordering endorsement, four conditions must be fulfilled. These are that the facts advanced: **32-034**

(1) must amount to mitigating or extenuating circumstances;
(2) must *not* amount to a defence to the charge;
(3) must be directly connected with the commission of the offence; and
(4) must be matters which can properly be taken into account when imposing punishment (*R. v Wickens* (1958) 42 Cr. App. R. 236; *Myles v DPP* [2004] EWHC 594 (Admin); [2004] 2 All E.R. 902).

The judge *must state openly* any grounds for finding that special reasons exist for mitigating the statutory penalty.

Note that:

(a) the mere fact that the circumstances disclose a special reason does not, of itself, mean that the offender is entitled, as a matter of course, to escape disqualification; there is a serious burden on a court to decide, in its discretion, whether to refrain from disqualifying (*Taylor v Rajan* (1974) 59 Cr. App. R. 11) and that discretion should be exercised only in clear and compelling circumstances (*Vaughan v Dunn* [1984] R.T.R. 376; *DPP v Bristow* [1998] R.T.R. 100); and
(b) even where the above conditions are fulfilled, there may be some overriding factor which precludes the court from regarding as "special reasons" some circumstance which at first appeared to fall within the scope of the four preconditions (*Delaroy-Hall v Tadman* (1969) 53 Cr. App. R. 143).

In an excess alcohol case where the court found special reasons, and where it was not suggested that the actual driving undertaken or even attempted could have posed any appreciable risk of danger to anyone it would be hard to justify a period of disqualification in excess of the mandatory 12 months (*R. v St Albans Crown Court Ex p. O'Donovan* [2000] 1 Cr. App. R. (S.) 344 DC).

The court is concerned not with the special reason that caused the offender to take his car onto the road, but with the special reason for not disqualifying or for imposing a lesser disqualification.

Special to the offence

32-035 The need for the facts to be directly connected with the commission of the offence, means that the facts put forward as a special reason must be "special", in contrast with those that are general, and special to the *offence* rather than to the offender. It is because of this that special reasons are not to be found in the following circumstances (for example), that:

(1) the offender is a professional driver (*Whittal v Kirby* (1947) 111 J.P. 1), or has been driving for many years without complaint (*Lines v Hersom* [1951] 2 All E.R. 650), or is a careful person who would never have risked driving had he realised his condition (*Newnham v Trigg* [1970] R.T.R. 107);

(2) the offender is disabled and had no other means of getting home (*Mullarkey v Prescott* [1970] R.T.R. 296), or relies on his vehicle for transport (*R. v Jackson* (1969) 53 Cr. App. R. 341), or that disqualification will cause him serious hardship and/or hardship to his family (*Rennison v Knowler* [1947] 1 All E.R. 302; *Taylor v Austin* [1969] 1 All E.R. 544; *Reynolds v Roche* [1972] R.T.R. 282; *East v Bladen* (1986) 8 Cr. App. R. (S.) 186);

(3) the offender is a doctor, and the medical services in his area will deteriorate by reason of his being unable to drive (*Holroyd v Berry* [1973] R.T.R. 145), or a soldier on active service who must be in a position to drive (*Gordon v Smith* [1971] R.T.R. 52), or that the offender is a detective engaged in "undercover" activities which involve visiting public houses (*Vaughan v Dunn* [1984] R.T.R. 376);

(4) the offender has an idiosyncratic medical condition or diabetes (*R. v Wickins* (1958) 42 Cr. App. R. 236; *R. v Jackson* (1969) 53 Cr. App. R. 341; *Jarvis v DPP* (2001) 165 J.P. 15); or

(5) the offender has to drive because of his domestic situation (*Reynolds v Roche* [1972] R.T.R. 282).

Even less is it any sort of special reason that the court considers the penalty of disqualification too severe (*Williamson v Wilson* [1947] 1 All E.R. 306) or unfair (*Boliston v Gibbons* (1984) 6 Cr. App. R. (S.) 134). The fact that the offence is a trivial one is not a special reason for not *endorsing*, but the court is always entitled to take account of the minor nature of the offence, and the fact that any breach was unintentional (*Hawkins v Roots* [1976] R.T.R. 49). An incorrect statement by a police officer to the effect that failing to provide a specimen of blood or urine would not necessarily result in disqualification which misled the defendant into refusing to supply such a specimen, can amount to a special reason (*Bobin v DPP* [1999] R.T.R. 375).

Excess alcohol offences

32-036 The vast majority of cases in which offenders seek to put forward special reasons, are those relating to excess alcohol. In deciding whether special reasons exist and whether to exercise discretion the court should consider what would a sober, reasonable and responsible friend of the defendant advise: drive or not? Discretion should be exercised in favour of the driver only if there was a real possibility rather than a mere off-chance that the friend would advise the driver to drive (*DPP v Bristow*

[1998] R.T.R. 100). The views of the superior courts over a number of years, when analysed, are that in relation to such offences:

(1) in a case under RTA 1988, ss.4, 5 and 7(6), it must be borne in mind that a person who deliberately drives, knowing that he has consumed a considerable quantity of alcohol, presents a potential danger to the public, which no private crisis can lightly excuse;
(2) in a case under s.5, the amount of excess, however small, is not capable of amounting to a special reason—the Act lays down the prescribed statutory limit (*Delaroy–Hall v Tadman* (1969) 53 Cr. App. R. 143);
(3) the effect of lack of food, or the effect of drink on an empty stomach, is not capable of amounting to a special reason, whether under s.4 or s.5 (*Archer v Woodward* [1959] Crim L.R. 461; *Knight v Baxter* [1971] R.T.R. 270; *Kinsella v DPP* [2002] EWHC 545 (QB));
(4) the fact that an offender, unknown to him, was suffering from a disease which produced a greater degree of unfitness than would be present in a normal person, might amount to a special reason under s.4 (*R. v Wickins* (1958) 42 Cr. App. R. 236, but see *DPP v Jowle* (1999) 163 J.P. 85), as might the fact that he had inhaled industrial fumes at work (*Brewer v MPC* (1969) 53 Cr. App. R. 157), but such factors are irrelevant on a conviction under s.5 (*Goldsmith v Laver* [1970] R.T.R. 162); see also *DPP v Jowle* (1999) 163 J.P. 85 (mouthwash containing 26.9 per cent alcohol); cf. *R. v Cambridge Magistrates Court Ex p. Wong* [1992] R.T.R. 382; a motorist has a duty to enquire what he is drinking (*Robinson v DPP* [2003] EWHC 2718 (Admin); [2004] Crim. L.R. 670);
(5) the court should rarely, if ever, exercise its discretion in favour of an offender where the alcohol content exceeded 100mg per 100ml of blood (*Taylor v Rajan* (1974) 59 Cr. App. R. 11, 15; *Vaughan v Dunn* [1984] R.T.R. 376);
(6) the fact that the offender offered a specimen of urine when blood was required of him cannot be taken into account as a special reason (*Grix v Chief Constable of Kent* [1987] R.T.R. 193); and
(7) it is difficult to conceive of a special reason in relation to a contravention of s.7(6) (*R. v Jackson* (1969) 53 Cr. App. R. 341, but see *DPP v Kinnersley* (1993) 14 Cr. App. R. (S.) 516 (genuine fear of contracting AIDS by blowing into machine)).

A gloss on (4) above is provided by the cases of *Woolfe v DPP* [2006] EWHC 1497 (Admin); [2007] R.T.R. 16 where the offender suffered from a medical condition whereby alcohol was regurgitated from his stomach into his mouth, thereby making it possible that the reading was erroneous, and *O Sang Ng v DPP* [2007] EWHC 36 (Admin); [2007] R.T.R. 35, where the reading may have been affected by belching.

Sudden emergencies

A sudden emergency may amount to a special reason in cases under ss.4 and 5, **32-037** as where an unexpected situation arises in which a person who has been drinking but not intending to drive, is impelled to do so by a sudden medical necessity, or in answering an emergency call (*Aichroth v Cottee* [1954] 2 All E.R. 856; *Brown v Dyerson* (1968) 52 Cr. App. R. 630; *R. v Lundt-Smith* (1964) 128 J.P. 534; *R. v O'Toole* (1971) 55 Cr. App. R. 206).

A burglary at club premises where the driver was a keyholder has been held to be an emergency sufficient to justify a finding of special reasons (*DPP v Cox* [1996] R.T.R. 123 DC).

A threat by a woman to accuse a man of rape unless he drove to a cash point in order to give her money and then drove her home, amounted to special reasons (*DPP v Enston* [1996] R.T.R. 324). See also *DPP v Upchurch* [1994] R.T.R. 366; *DPP v Knight* [1994] R.T.R. 374; *DPP v Whittle* [1996] R.T.R. 154.

In dealing with such cases, the superior courts have said that the whole of the circumstances should be considered, including the nature and degree of the crisis or emergency which caused the offender to take his car onto the road, and:

(1) whether the emergency was sufficiently acute to justify the offender taking out his car;
(2) whether there were alternative means of transport available, or alternative means of dealing with the crisis;
(3) the manner of the offender's driving, the commission of traffic offences may be a consideration telling against exercise of the court's discretion; and
(4) whether the offender otherwise acted responsibly and reasonably.

These matters need to be considered objectively (*Taylor v Rajan* (1974) 59 Cr. App. R. 15; *DPP v Bristow* [1998] R.T.R. 100), and it is not for the court to put itself into the offender's position in assessing "reasonableness". A driver complaining of dizziness and blurred vision did not constitute a medical emergency sufficient to justify a finding of special reasons where the passenger, her husband, who was affected by drink, decided to take over the driving (*DPP v Whittle* [1996] R.T.R. 154 DC). There is a difference in a situation presented to a driver on the outward journey and that on the homeward journey after the emergency has been dealt with (*DPP v Waller* [1989] R.T.R. 112).

Where an emergency is relied on, the judge should ask himself whether a sober, reasonable and responsible friend of the accused present at the time (but himself unable to drive) would have advised the accused to drive. Critical factors that the friend would take account of would be:

(a) the amount the accused had had to drink;
(b) what threat he would pose to others if he did drive, having regard to the state of the roads and the distance he proposed to drive;
(c) the nature of the emergency; and
(d) what, if any, alternatives were open to him?

(*DPP v Heathcote* [2011] EWHC 2536 (Admin); (2011) 175 J.P. 530 considering, inter alia, *Jacobs v Reed* [1974] R.T.R. 81 and *DPP v Bristow* [1998] R.T.R. 100).

It is unlikely that merely travelling to a near relative because of some emotional need will ever be able to amount to a special reason (*Thompson v Diamond* [1985] R.T.R. 316).

"Laced drinks" case

32-038 It is often put forward in excess alcohol cases that the offender's drink had been "laced" by a third party, in order to found a special reason on the ground that the drink which the offender consumed was stronger or more potent than he had anticipated. It is not enough to show that the drink was stronger than he thought.

To be capable of amounting to a special reason:

(1) there must be an element of intervention or misleading by a third party, whereby the offender was induced to take stronger drink than he would normally have done by someone who misled him, or gave him false information; and

(2) it must be shown (*Pugsley v Hunter* [1973] R.T.R. 284; *Smith v Geraghty* [1986] R.T.R. 222) and the burden is on the offender to show, that the quantity of alcohol in his blood in excess of the prescribed limit:

   (a) is attributable to additional drink; and
   (b) was put into his glass without his knowledge—this will inevitably involve scientific evidence.

The judge must decide:

(i) whether the facts are capable of amounting to a special reason; and

(ii) additionally, whether the offender should have realised, when he came to drive, that he was not fit to do so by reason of the alcohol present in his body (*Pridige v Grant* [1985] R.T.R. 196; *DPP v Barker* [1990] R.T.R. 1; *Donahue v DPP* [1993] R.T.R. 156. See also *DPP v Connor* (1992) 95 Cr. App. R.135).

It is undesirable for the court to let itself be drawn into detailed scientific calculations, even where these are put before it by expert witnesses (*Smith v Geraghty* [1986] R.T.R. 222).

Factors to be considered

It was suggested in *Chatters v Burke* (1986) 8 Cr. App. R. (S.) 222 that there were seven factors to be considered and taken into account when deciding whether there were special reasons for mitigating the normal consequences of a conviction, namely: **32-039**

(1) how far was the vehicle driven?;
(2) in what manner was it driven?;
(3) the state of the vehicle;
(4) whether it was the offender's intention to go further;
(5) the conditions of road and traffic prevailing;
(6) the reason for the car being driven; and
(7) most importantly of all, whether there was a danger of the offender's coming into contact with pedestrians or other road users.

The mere fact that the offence occurred late at night, at a time and place where there were not many people about, or that the offender was merely re-parking, is not of itself capable of amounting to a special reason for not disqualifying. It might, however, amount to a special reason to show that the offender drove only a few yards in circumstances where his manoeuvres were unlikely to bring him into contact with other road users (*Mullarkey v Prescott* [1970] R.T.R. 296; *Coombs v Kehoe* [1972] 1 W.L.R. 797; and cf. *Haime v Walklett* (1983) 5 Cr. App. R. (S.) 165) but cf. *DPP v Humphries* [2000] R.T.R. 52, where the offender's intention was to drive some distance had he not been apprehended; see also *DPP v Conroy* [2003] EWHC 1674; [2004] 1 Cr. App. R. (S.) 37.

Proof of special reasons

32-040 The burden of proving circumstances amounting to a special reason lies upon the offender; the standard is that of a "balance of probabilities". The court should take into account any:

(1) relevant admissible evidence, given on oath;
(2) any admissions made in accordance with CJA 1967 s.10;
(3) any "expert reports" tendered and admissible by virtue of CJA 1988 s.30; and
(4) any submissions made by the Crown and/or defence counsel, but evidence from the offender as to what he has heard since the incident, does not qualify (*James v Morgan* [1988] R.T.R. 85).

10. NEW DRIVERS

32-041 The Road Traffic (New Drivers) Act 1995, provides that a person who has passed his driving licence test either under RTA 1988, or in certain countries abroad, is subject to a probationary period of two years beginning with the day on which he becomes a qualified driver.

If such a person:

(1) being the holder of a licence;
(2) is convicted of an offence involving obligatory endorsement;
(3) the penalty points to be taken into account under RTOA 1988 s.29 (32-025) on that occasion number six or more;
(4) the judge makes an order falling within RTOA 1988 s.44(1)(b) (32-004) in respect of the offence;
(5) the person's licence shows the date on which he became a qualified driver, or that date has been shown by other evidence in the proceedings; and
(6) it appears to the court, in the light of the order and the date so shown, that the offence was committed during the person's probationary period, the court must send to the Secretary of State:
    (a) a notice containing the particulars required to be endorsed on the counterpart of the person's licence in accordance with the order referred to in subs.(1)(d); and
    (b) on their production to the court, the person's licence and its counterpart.

The licence will then be revoked by the Secretary of State, and, with certain exceptions the driver will be required to take a further test before recovering his licence.

11. Disqualification table

Provision creating offence	General nature of offence	Maximum penalty	Disqualification	Penalty points	Code
RTRA 1984 s.16(1)	Contravention of temporary prohibition or restriction	Level 3	Discretionary in respect of speed restriction	3–6 or 3 (fixed penalty)	MW10
RTRA 1984 s.17(4)	Traffic regulation on special roads (motorways)	Level 4	Discretionary in certain circumstances; obligatory in respect of speed restriction	3–6 or fixed penalty in respect of speed limit, 3 in any other case	MW10
RTRA 1984 s.25(5)	Contravention of pedestrian crossing regulations	Level 3	Discretionary if committed in respect of motor vehicle	3	PC10
	(a) with moving vehicle				PC20
	(b) with stationary vehicle				PC30
RTRA 1984 s.28(3)	Not stopping at school crossing	Level 3	Discretionary if committed in respect of motor vehicle	3	TS60
RTRA 1984 s.29(3)	Contravention of order relating to street playground	Level 3	Discretionary if committed in respect of motor vehicle	2	MS30
RTRA 1984 s.89(1)	Exceeding speed limit	Level 3	Discretionary	3–6 or 3 fixed penalty	SP10
(a) goods vehicle speed limit					SP10
(b) for type of vehicle					SP20

Provision creating offence	General nature of offence	Maximum penalty	Disqualification	Penalty points	Code
(c) statutory speed limit on public road					SP30
(d) passenger vehicle speed limit					SP40
(e) motorway					SP50
RTA 1988 s.3	Careless and inconsiderate driving	Level 5	Discretionary	3–9	CD10 CD20 CD30
RTA 1988 s.4(2)	In charge of a motor vehicle when unfit to drive through drink or drugs	3 months or level 4 or both	Discretionary	10	DR90
RTA 1988 s.5(1)(b)	Being in a charge of a motor vehicle with excess alcohol in breath, blood or urine	3 months or level 4 or both	Discretionary	10	DR40
RTA 1988 s.5A(1)(b) and (2)	Being in charge of a motor vehicle with concentration of specified controlled drug above specified limit.	51 weeks or level 4 or both	Discretionary	10	DG40
RTA 1988 s.6(4)	Failing to co-operate with preliminary test	Level 3	Discretionary	4	DR70

Provision creating offence	General nature of offence	Maximum penalty	Disqualification	Penalty points	Code
RTA 1988 s.7A	Failing to allow specimen to be subjected to laboratory test	(a) Where the test would be for ascertaining ability to drive or proportion of alcohol at the time offender was driving or attempting to drive, 6 months or level 5 or both	Obligatory	3–11	
		(b) in any other case, 3 months or level 4 or both	Discretionary	10	
RTA 1988 s.12	Motor racing and speed trials on public ways	Level 4	Obligatory	3–11	MS50
RTA 1988 s.22	Leaving vehicle in dangerous position	Level 3	Discretionary if committed in respect of motor vehicle	3	MS10

Provision creating offence	General nature of offence	Maximum penalty	Disqualification	Penalty points	Code
RTA 1988 s.23	Carrying passenger on motor cycle contrary to s.23	Level 3	Discretionary	3	MS20
RTA 1988 s.35	Failing to comply with Traffic directions	Level 3	Discretionary if committed in respect of a motor vehicle by failure to comply with direction of constable or Traffic warden	3	TS40
RTA 1988 s.36	Failure to comply with Traffic sign	Level 3	Discretionary if committed in respect of a motor vehicle by failure to comply with signs specified in the regulations	3	
(a) Traffic lights					TS10
(b) double white lines					TS20
(c) stop signs					TS30
(d) others					TS50
RTA 1988 s.40A	Using vehicle in dangerous condition	Level 5 if committed in respect of a goods vehicle or vehicle adapted to carry more than 8 passengers	Obligatory if committed within 3 years of a previous conviction of the offender under s.40A Discretionary in any other case	3	CU20

Provision creating offence	General nature of offence	Maximum penalty	Disqualification	Penalty points	Code
		Level 4 in any other case			
RTA 1988 s.41A	Defective brakes, steering gear or tyres	Level 5 if committed in respect of goods vehicles or a vehicle adapated to carry more than 8 passengers	Discretionary	3	CU10
					CU30
					CU40
		Level 4 in any other case			
RTA 1988 s.41B	Breach of requirement as to weight, goods and passengers	Level 5	Discretionary	3	CU50
RTA s.41D	Breach of requirements as to control of vehicle, mobile telephones, etc.	Summarily	Discretionary	3	CU90
		(a) Level 4 on the stand-	Obligatory		

Provision creating offence	General nature of offence	Maximum penalty	Disqualification	Penalty points	Code
		ard scale if committed in respect of a goods vehicle or a vehicle adapted to carry more than 8 passengers. (b) Level 3 on the standard scale in any other case.			TS40 TS50
RTA 1988 s.87(1)	Driving otherwise than in accordance with licence	Level 3	Discretionary in a case where the offender's driving would not have been in accordance with any licence that could have been granted to him	3–6	LC10
RTA 1988 s.92(10)	Driving after making false declaration as to physical fitness	Level 4	Discretionary	3–6	LC30

Provision creating offence	General nature of offence	Maximum penalty	Disqualification	Penalty points	Code
RTA 1988 s.94(3A)	Driving after failing to notify SofS of onset of or deterioration in, relevant or prospective disability	Level 3	Discretionary	3–6	LC40
RTA 1988 s.94A	Driving after refusal, revocation, etc. of licence	6 months or level 5 or both	Discretionary	3–6	LC50
RTA 1988 s.96	Driving with uncorrected defective eyesight, etc.	Level 3	Discretionary	3	MS40
RTA 1988 s.103(1)(b)	Driving whilst disqualified	6 months or level 5 or both	Discretionary	6	BA10
					BA20
RTA 1988 s.143	Using motor vehicle while uninsured	Level 5	Discretionary	6–8	IN10
RTA 1988 s.170(4)	Failing to stop, report, after accident	6 months or level 5 or both	Discretionary	5–10	AC10
					AC20
					AC30
RTA 1988 s.172	Failure of keeper of vehicle to give information	Level 3	Discretionary if committed otherwise than by virtue of subss.(5) or (11)	6	MS90
OAPA 1861 s.35	Furious driving		Discretionary	3–9	DD90
	Stealing or attempting to steal a motor vehicle		Discretionary		UT20

Provision creating offence	General nature of offence	Maximum penalty	Disqualification	Penalty points	Code
TA 1968 s.12	Offence or attempt of taking conveyance, etc.		Discretionary		UT10
TA 1968 s.25	Going equipped, etc. committed with reference to the theft or taking of motor vehicles		Discretionary		UT30

33. FINES

1. General

Crown Court powers

Where a person is convicted on indictment, the judge may (SA 2020 s.120–121): **33-001**

(1) if not precluded from sentencing the offender by his exercise of some other power; and
(2) subject to any enactment requiring the offender to be dealt with in a particular way,

impose on him a fine, either instead of or in addition to dealing with him in any other way (SA 2020 s.120(1)).

The judge may not, however, impose a fine in the following circumstances (SA 2020 s.120(2)):

(a) where the offence is one in relation to which a mandatory sentence requirement applies by virtue of any of the following provisions of s.399—
   (i) paragraph (a) (life sentence for murder etc);
   (ii) paragraph (b) (other mandatory life sentences);
   (iia) paragraph (ba) (serious terrorism offences); or
   (iii) paragraph (c)(iv) (minimum sentence for third domestic burglary offence);
(b) is subject to any other enactment requiring the offender to be dealt with in a particular way; and
(c) does not apply if the court is precluded from sentencing the offender by its exercise of some other power.

There is no maximum level of fine in the Crown Court. The fine is fixed by reference to the seriousness of the fine (SA 2020 s.125(2)). Fines for certain offences are set by reference to the standard scale.

(2) The standard scale

Where reference is made to the "standard scale" of fines, the standard scale is as follows (SA 2020 s.122): **33-002**

Level on the scale	Amount of fine
1	£200
2	£500
3	£1,000
4	£2,500
5	£5,000

(3) Proper approach to financial penalty

33-003 SA 2020 s.57 sets out the duty of the judge in sentencing (see DEALING WITH AN OFFENDER). In considering the seriousness of the offence he must have regard to the culpability of the offender and the harm caused or which might foreseeably be caused (SA 2020 s.63).

If the judge decides to impose a fine he must have regard not only to the purposes of sentencing and the seriousness of the offence, but must also take into account the criteria set out in SA 2020 ss.124–125:

(1) before fixing the amount of the fine to be imposed on an individual, he must inquire into his financial circumstances;
(2) the amount of any fine fixed must in the judge's opinion reflect the seriousness of the offence; and
(3) in fixing the amount of any fine to be imposed on the offender (whether an individual or other person), he must take into account the circumstances of the case, including the financial circumstances of the offender so far as they are known or appear to the court, whether such financial circumstances have the effect of increasing or reducing the amount of the fine.

Note that:

(a) it is wrong to impose a fine upon an offender of substantial means for an offence for which an offender of lesser means would go to prison (*R. v Lewis* [1965] Crim. L.R. 121);
(b) conversely, it is wrong to imprison an offender because he is not able to pay a substantial fine (*R. v Reeves* (1972) 56 Cr. App. R. 366);
(c) the judge must not reduce the amount of a fine on account of any surcharge he orders to be paid under s.42 except to the extent that the offender has insufficient means to pay both (s.125(4));
(d) where separate fines are passed, care must be taken to avoid double counting; and
(e) if the judge aims to remove any illicit gains made by the offender, he should proceed by way of POCA 2002 s.6 (see CONFISCATION ORDERS) which must precede the making of a fine (cf. *R. v Kirtland* [2012] EWCA Crim 2127).

As to the approach to financial penalties for corporations, see 33-010. As to young offenders, see CHILDREN AND YOUNG PERSONS.

Ability to pay; means

33-004 The overriding principle in relation to the imposition of a fine is that the fine imposed should be within the offender's ability to pay.

It should be remembered that:

(1) it may be necessary to scale down an otherwise appropriate fine if the sum is more than the offender can be fairly required to pay within a reasonable time;
(2) there is no reason in principle why an order to pay a fine by monthly instalments should not extend for two or even three years or even longer (*R. v Olliver* (1989) 11 Cr. App. R. (S.) 10; *R. v Ganyo* [2011] EWCA Crim 2491; [2012] 1 Cr. App. R. (S.) 108 and *R. v Hossain* [2016] EWCA Crim 1099);

(3) an offender should not be fined more heavily merely because he has elected trial by jury; this is a matter which can be dealt with by an order for costs (*R. v Jamieson* (1974) 60 Cr. App. R. 318).

A fine should not be imposed on the basis that some person other than the offender is going to pay it on his behalf (*R. v Curtis* (1984) 6 Cr. App. R. (S.) 250; *R. v Rance* [2012] EWCA Crim 2023; [2013] 1 Cr. App. R. (S.) 123), let alone on the basis that the public should be reimbursed for any possible claim made on the Criminal Injuries Compensation Authority (*R. v Roberts* (1980) 2 Cr. App. R. (S.) 121).

Proportionality

In keeping with general sentencing principles, the total of the fine must be just and proportionate (see also *R. v Castillo* [2011] EWCA Crim 3173; [2012] 2 Cr. App. R. (S.) 36). If it is not, the judge ought to consider how to achieve such a result. **33-005**

Where there are:

(1) two or more offences arising out of the same incident; or
(2) multiple offences of a repetitive kind, especially when committed against the same person,

it will often be appropriate to impose for the most serious offence a fine which reflects the totality of the offending where this can be achieved within the maximum penalty for that offence and imposing "no separate penalty" for the other offences.

Where an offender is to be fined for two or more offences arising out of different incidents, it will often be appropriate to impose a separate penalty in respect of each case. The judge should then:

(1) add up the fines for each offence and consider if they are just and proportionate; and
(2) if the aggregate is not, the judge should consider whether all of the fines can be proportionately reduced.

Financial, etc. information required for sentencing

CPD VII Sentencing Q.1–6 supplements CrimPR 25.16, which set out the procedure to be followed where an offender pleads guilty, or is convicted, and is to be sentenced (see DEALING WITH AN OFFENDER). The directions are not concerned exclusively with corporate offenders, or with offences of an environmental, public health, health and safety or other regulatory character, but the guidance which they contain is likely to be of particular significance in such cases. **33-006**

The rules set out the prosecutor's responsibilities in all cases. Where the offence is of a character, or is against a prohibition, with which the sentencing court is unlikely to be familiar, those responsibilities are commensurately more onerous. The judge is entitled to the greatest possible assistance in identifying information relevant to sentencing.

In such a case, save where the circumstances are very straightforward, it is likely that justice will best be served by the submission of the required information in writing: see *R. v Friskies Petcare (UK) Ltd* [2000] 2 Cr. App. R. (S.) 401. Note that:

(1) though it is the prosecutor's responsibility to the court to prepare any such document, if the accused pleads guilty, or indicates a guilty plea, then it is

very highly desirable that such sentencing information should be agreed between the parties and jointly submitted;

(2) if agreement cannot be reached in all particulars, then the nature and extent of the disagreement should be indicated;

(3) if the judge concludes that what is in issue is material to sentence, then he will give directions for resolution of the dispute, whether by hearing oral evidence or by other means; and

(4) in every case, when passing sentence the judge must make clear on what basis sentence is passed: in fairness to the accused, and for the information of any other person, or court, who needs or wishes to understand the reasons for sentence (*CPD* VII.Q.1–3).

Provision of financial information

33-007 If so directed by or on behalf of the judge, an offender must supply accurate information about financial circumstances:

(1) In fixing the amount of any fine the judge must take into account, amongst other considerations, the financial circumstances of the offender (whether an individual or other person) as they are known or as they appear to be.

(2) Before fixing the amount of fine when the offender is an individual, the judge must inquire into his financial circumstances.

(3) Where the offender is an individual the judge may make a financial circumstances order in respect of him (SA 2020 s.35).

It is for the judge to decide how much information is required, having regard to relevant sentencing guidelines or guideline cases. However, by reference to those same guidelines and cases the parties should anticipate what the judge will require, and prepare accordingly.

In complex cases, and in cases involving a corporate offender, the information required will be more extensive than in others. In the case of a corporate defendant, that information usually will include details of the offender's corporate structure; annual profit and loss accounts, or extracts; annual balance sheets, or extracts; details of shareholders' receipts; and details of the remuneration of directors or other officers (*CPD* VII.Q.4).

In *R. v F Howe and Son (Engineers) Ltd* [1999] 2 Cr. App. R. (S.) 37 the CACD observed:

> "If a defendant company wishes to make any submission to the court about its ability to pay a fine it should supply copies of its accounts and any other financial information on which it intends to rely in good time before the hearing both to the court and to the prosecution. This will give the prosecution the opportunity to assist the court should the court wish it. Usually accounts need to be considered with some care to avoid reaching a superficial and perhaps erroneous conclusion. Where accounts or other financial information are deliberately not supplied the court will be entitled to conclude that the company is in a position to pay any financial penalty it is minded to impose. Where the relevant information is provided late it may be desirable for sentence to be adjourned, if necessary at the defendant's expense, so as to avoid the risk of the court taking what it is told at face value and imposing an inadequate penalty."

In the case of an individual, the judge is likewise entitled to conclude that the offender is able to pay any fine imposed unless he has supplied financial information to the contrary. It is his responsibility to disclose to the judge such information relevant to his or her financial position as will enable the judge to assess what he or she reasonably can afford to pay. If necessary, the judge may compel the disclosure of an individual offender's financial circumstances. In the absence of such disclosure, or where the judge is not satisfied that he has been given sufficient reliable information, he will be entitled to draw reasonable inferences as to the offender's means from evidence he has heard and from all the circumstances of the case (*CPD* VII.Q.6).

Parents and guardians

For the enforcement of fines in respect of juvenile offenders against parents and guardians, see CHILDREN AND YOUNG PERSONS. **33-008**

(4) Corporations; health and safety legislation; environmental offences

Position of corporations

The provisions of SA 2020 ss.120–125 are applicable to all offenders, including corporations. Thus, where a fine is to be imposed, the judge will first consider the seriousness of the offence and then the financial circumstances of the offender. **33-009**

In the case of a corporate offender, the court is not obliged to inquire into the means of the offender but must take them into account as far as they are known (*R. v Thames Water Utililties Ltd* [2015] EWCA Crim 960; [2015] 1 W.L.R. 4411). The fact that the offender is a corporation with a turnover in excess of £1 billion makes no difference to that basic approach (*R. v Sellafield Ltd* [2014] EWCA Crim 49 (per the Lord Chief Justice), where the effect of fines on corporations which provide a public service as opposed to those which operate for profit as ordinary commercial enterprises is considered).

Breaches of health and safety legislation where death or serious injury results are in a class of their own. In such a case the fine needs to be large enough to bring the message home not only to those that manage the corporation but also to its shareholders (*R. v F Howe & Son (Engineers) Ltd* [1999] 2 Cr. App. R. (S.) 37 at 44; *R. v Rimac Ltd* [2000] 1 Cr. App. R. (S.) 468). The fine may reflect public disquiet at the unnecessary loss of life.

The importance of the application of ss.124–125 in relation to corporate offenders is reflected in a number of the sentencing guidelines issued by the Sentencing Council, see for example the guidelines; *Corporate Manslaughter* (Sentencing Council, February 2016); *Organisations: Breach of duty of employer towards employees and non-employees/Breach of duty of self-employed to others/Breach of Health and Safety regulations* (Sentencing Council, February 2016); *Organisations: Breach of food safety and food hygiene regulations* (Sentencing Council, February 2016).

As to environmental offences, see *Organisations: Environmental Offences: Breach of duty of care* (Sentencing Council, July 2014) and *Organisations: Unauthorised or harmful deposit, treatment or disposal etc of waste/ Illegal discharges to air, land and water* (Sentencing Council, July 2014).

(5) Wealthy defendants

Where the defendant is a person of great personal wealth, the sentencing judge is entitled to take that into account, following the principles set out in *Sellafield* **33-010**

[2014] EWCA Crim 49 concerning fines to be imposed on companies of very significant size. In sentencing a defendant (whose wealth was estimated at £300 million) for an offence under the Wildlife and Countryside Act 1981, it was the judge's duty to impose a fine that would not only punish the defendant for what he had done for commercial gain but which would also deter others and protect the public interest, and so the fine had to be of sufficient size to achieve these objectives (*R. (on the application of Natural England) v Day* [2014] EWCA Crim 2683; [2015] 1 Cr. App. R. (S.) 53).

(6) Time to pay: instalments; default sentence

33-011 Where the judge imposes a fine he may (SA 2020 ss.129–130) make an order:

(1) allowing time for the payment of the amount of the fine;
(2) directing payment of that amount by instalments of such amounts and on such dates as may be specified in the order; and
(3) he *must* fix a term of imprisonment or detention in default of payment.

This period in default is designed to ensure that the offender pays the fine and gains nothing if he fails to comply with the order (*R. v Price* [2009] EWCA Crim 2918; [2010] 2 Cr. App. R. (S.) 44; *R. v Castillo* [2011] EWCA Crim 3173; [2012] 2 Cr. App. R. (S.) 36). The period in default is quite distinct and separate from any custodial sentence which may also be imposed. It may be made consecutive to any other term being served (SA 2020 s.129(6)).

An offender may not be committed to imprisonment or detention in default on the occasion when a fine is imposed upon him (i.e. he may not be refused time to pay) unless:

(a) in the case of an offence punishable with imprisonment, he appears to the judge to have sufficient means to pay forthwith (as to search of his person, see below);
(b) it appears to the judge that he is unlikely to remain long enough at a place of abode in the UK to enable the payment of the fine to be enforced by other methods; or
(c) on the occasion when the fine is imposed, the judge sentences him to an immediate prison sentence, custody for life, or detention in a young offender institution for that or another offence, or so sentences him for an offence in addition to forfeiting his recognisance, or he is already serving a sentence of custody for life or a term of imprisonment or detention.

(SA 2020 s.129(5))

Approach to order

33-012 When imposing a fine payable by instalments, with imprisonment in default, the proper course is for the judge to:

(1) impose the fine;
(2) fix an appropriate term in default of the whole amount; and
(3) if he thinks fit, make an instalment order.

(*R. v Cooper* (1982) 4 Cr. App. R. (S.) 55; *R. v Aitchison* (1982) 4 Cr. App. R. (S.) 404; *R. v Power* (1986) 8 Cr. App. R. (S.) 8)

Judges in the Crown Court will generally find it more useful to leave any question of instalments to the enforcing magistrate court. It will generally be useful to give the shortest reasonable period of time to pay, which will put the matter fairly and squarely into the hands of the enforcing court at the earliest opportunity.

(7) Maximum terms in default

The maximum periods of imprisonment or detention under SA 2020 s.129, are: **33-013**

An amount not exceeding £200	7 days
An amount exceeding £200 but not exceeding £500	14 days
An amount exceeding £500 but not exceeding £1,000	28 days
An amount exceeding £1,000 but not exceeding £2,500	45 days
An amount exceeding £2,500 but not exceeding £5,000	3 months
An amount exceeding £5,000 but not exceeding £10,000	6 months
An amount exceeding £10,000 but not exceeding £20,000	12 months
An amount exceeding £20,000 but not exceeding £50,000	18 months
An amount exceeding £50,000 but not exceeding £100,000	2 years
An amount exceeding £100,000 but not exceeding £250,000	3 years
An amount exceeding £250,000 but not exceeding £1 million	5 years
An amount exceeding £1 million	10 years

(SA 2020 s.129)

Custodial sentence and default terms

Where a person liable for the payment of a fine is sentenced to, or is serving, or is otherwise liable to serve a term of imprisonment, the judge may order that any default term shall not begin to run until after the end of the first-mentioned term, nor is this power restricted by any enactment authorising the Crown Court to deal with an offender in any way the magistrates might have dealt with him or could deal with him. **33-014**

(SA 2020 s.129(6)–(7))

(8) Coupling a fine with a custodial sentence

Combining an immediate custodial sentence with a fine is permissible, but: **33-015**

(1) it must be clear that the offender has the resources to arrange for payment even though he is to be in custody (*R. v Fairbairn* (1980) 2 Cr. App. R. (S.) 315);

(2) if this is not clear, then a fine ought not to be added (*R. v Maund* (1980) 2 Cr. App. R. (S.) 289); and

(3) it is appropriate if the general circumstances of the case show that the offender will continue to have access to the proceeds of his crime (*R. v Benmore* (1983) 5 Cr. App. R. (S.) 468).

In *R. v Channer* [2021] EWCA Crim 696; [2021] 4 WLUK 516, the CACD considered the Sentencing Council's Definitive Guideline: *Offences Taken into Consideration and Totality* (Sentencing Council, March 2012), and in particular the general principle that fines should not generally be imposed in combination with custodial sentences. A proper construction of the guideline indicated that if the court was imposing a suspended custodial sentence, which would not have any adverse effect on the offender's means, then it was more free to impose a fine in addition than it might otherwise have been, whereas if the custodial sentence was immediate, it would be necessary to look at the other relevant factors together to see whether, contrary to the general rule, a fine in addition to a custodial sentence should be imposed.

(9) Coupling a fine with an order for costs

33-016 The judge may both impose a fine and order the offender to pay the costs of the prosecution in an appropriate case. The principles governing such an order were reviewed in *R. v Northallerton Magistrates Court Ex p. Dove* [2000] 1 Cr. App. R. (S.) 136 (applied in *R. v Adedeji* [2019] EWCA Crim 804).

Note that:

(1) the judge must have regard to the means of the offender, and it is quite wrong to impose a very small fine and a very heavy order for costs—the two must go in step (*R. v Whalley* (1972) 56 Cr. App. R. 304; and see *R. v Firmston* (1984) 6 Cr. App. R. (S.) 189; *R. v Nottingham Justices Ex p. Fohmann* (1987) 84 Cr. App. R. 316; *R. v Jones* (1988) 10 Cr. App. R. (S.) 95; cf. *R. v Boyle* (1995) 16 Cr. App. R. (S.) 927); and

(2) while there is no requirement that the costs should stand in any arithmetical relationship to the fine, the costs should not in the ordinary way be grossly disproportionate to the fine.

(10) Personal search of offender

33-017 A judge of the Crown Court may, where:

(1) any person has been fined, or has had a recognisance forfeited;
(2) any person is made the subject of an order for costs, or compensation;
(3) a parent or guardian is ordered to pay a fine, costs or compensation;
(4) the Crown Court orders any person to pay a surcharge under SA 2020 s.42;
(5) an appellant from the magistrates' court is liable to pay any sum by virtue of an order made by the Crown Court or the magistrates' court,

order that person, if before him, to be searched, and any money found on him may be applied towards the payment of any sum owing, the balance being returned.

(PCC(S)A 2000 s.142 (referred to in SA 2020 s.131))

(11) Enforcement by magistrates' court

33-018 The enforcement of Crown Court fines is a matter for the appropriate magistrates' court.

(SA 2020 s.132)

34. FOOTBALL BANNING ORDERS

Introduction

Where an offender is: 34-001

(1) convicted before the Crown Court of a "relevant" offence (defined in Sch.1); or
(2) committed to the Crown Court for sentence for such an offence,

the judge may, in addition to:

(a) imposing a sentence in respect of the relevant offence; or
(b) discharging him conditionally (in spite of the provisions of SA 2020 ss.79, 80 and 82),

make a banning order in relation to him, and *must* make such an order if satisfied that there are reasonable grounds to believe that making a banning order would help to prevent violence or disorder (both of which expressions are defined in s.14(C)) at or in connection with any regulated football matches (FSA 1989 s.14A(2)).

If the judge is not so satisfied, he must state that fact in open court and give his reasons (FSA 1989 s.14A(3)). The prosecutor has a right of appeal against any refusal to make an order (see below) (FSA 1989 s.14A(5A)–(5C)).

An order is classified, with certain other orders, as a "civil behaviour order". Procedure in relation to such orders made after verdict or finding is governed by CrimPR 31 and is set out at CRIMINAL BEHAVIOUR ORDERS.

Period of ban

A banning order has effect for a period beginning with the day it is made, being neither more than the maximum nor less than the minimum. 34-002

Where:

(1) it is made under s.14A in addition to a sentence of imprisonment taking immediate effect, the maximum is ten years and the minimum six years; and
(2) in any other case where it is made under s.14A, the maximum period is five years and the minimum is three years.

(FSA 1989 s.14F)

Remand; bail

If the proceedings are adjourned, or further adjourned, the judge may remand the offender, who may be required by the conditions of his bail: 34-003

(1) not to leave England and Wales before his appearance before the court; and
(2) if the control period relates to a regulated football match outside the UK or to an external tournament which includes such matches, to surrender his passport to a police constable if he has not already done so.

(FSA 1989 s.14A(4BA), (4BB))

The preconditions

34-004 There are two main conditions for the making of an order. If those conditions are met, the making of an order is mandatory. The order is not designed as a punishment, although it will have that effect. It is designed as a preventative measure.

The two conditions are these:

(1) There must be a conviction for a relevant offence: s.14A(1) (see 34-005).
(2) The judge must be satisfied that there are reasonable grounds to believe that making a banning order would help to prevent violence or disorder at or in connection with any regulated football matches: s.14A(2); if the judge is not so satisfied, he must in open court state that fact and give his reasons: s.14A(3) (see 34-008).

Failure to address this second condition is fatal to the validity of the order (*R. v Doyle* [2012] EWCA Crim 995; [2013] 1 Cr. App. R. (S.) 36).

The offences which are "relevant" are listed in Sch.1. For the most part they become relevant not simply when a particular offence is committed, but only when it is committed in the circumstances stipulated in Sch.1. If the offence falls within Sch.1, then the second condition must also be met.

Once both conditions are satisfied then an order *must* be made.

The need for the second condition shows that it is not the law that an order will inevitably follow every conviction of a relevant offence (see *R. v Boggild* [2011] EWCA Crim 1928; [2012] 1 Cr. App. R. (S.) 81). There must be reasonable grounds to believe that making a banning order would help to prevent violence or disorder (both of which expressions are defined in s.14(C)) at or in connection with any regulated football matches.

The first condition: "relevant offences"

34-005 These are listed in Sch.1 (as amended). They may be categorised as follows (*R. v Doyle* [2012] EWCA Crim 995; [2013] Cr. App. R. (S.) 36):

(1) some offences listed in paras (a) and (p) are ipso facto relevant; they are, in essence, offences which of their nature are concerned with football;
(2) those listed under para.(b) must have been committed whilst entering or trying to enter the ground;
(3) those listed under paras (c)–(f) must have been committed during the period relevant to a football match (which means 24 hours either side of the match—see para.4(2)(b)) and when the offender was at, or entering or leaving, premises, although it would seem that the premises can be any premises and are not confined to football grounds; they might well, for example, be a public house; and
(4) those listed under paras (g)–(o) and (q) will be relevant if they are "related to football matches"; this calls for a judgment of the court declaring this to be so.

The decision under (4) is called in the Act a "declaration of relevance"; see s.23.

"Related to football matches"

34-006 The decision required in relation to offences listed under (g)–(o) and (q) in the Schedule is not an assessment of the legal character of the offence; it is a determination whether on the particular facts of the offence as it was committed on the occasion in question, the offence was "related to football matches".

Note that:

(1) although the test is expressed in terms of "matches" in the plural, it would appear that it would suffice if the behaviour was, on the particular facts, related to a single match;
(2) paras (g)–(o), although not (q), are all concerned with offences committed when the offender is on a journey to or from a football match at the stipulated level (essentially National League North or South or above), but the *mere* fact that offender was on a journey to or from a match is not enough. There must be another connection. The offence must be "related to football matches";
(3) the Act offers no definition of when this condition will be met. It is left to the judgment of the judge on the particular facts before him; and
(4) it would be wrong to attempt to define when the condition will be met. The facts which may occur will vary too much. It will not by itself be enough to make an offence "related to football matches" that it would not have occurred "but for" the fact that D was en route to or from a match.

An offence committed on a train while returning from a football match was held not to be "relevant" to the match in *R. v O'Keefe* [2003] EWCA Crim 2629; [2004] 1 Cr. App. R. (S.) 67, but see *DPP v Beaumont* [2008] EWHC 523 (Admin); [2008] 2 Cr. App. R. (S.) 98.

"Relevant to football matches" does not mean "relating to a football match". The fact that the offender has no history of misconduct in connection with football matches or that the act is an isolated incident does not prevent an order being made. The potential deterrent effect of the order on other spectators may be taken into account (*R. (on the application of White) v Blackfriars Crown Court* [2008] EWHC 510 (Admin); [2008] 2 Cr. App. R. (S.) 97; *Attorney General's Reference (No.14 of 2009* [2009] EWCA Crim 1143; [2010] 1 Cr. App. R. (S.) 93).

The CACD has said that it is instructive to identify the spark which caused the violence and whether it could be said to be wholly unrelated to the football. A fight between rival supporters may still relate to football even where their teams have not played against one another (see *R. v Parkes* [2010] EWCA Crim 2803; [2011] 2 Cr. App. R. (S.) 10).

Procedure relating to declaration

Ordinarily the judge is not entitled to make a declaration unless it is shown that the prosecutor gave notice to the offender at least five days before the first day of the trial that it proposed to relate the offence to football matches, to a particular football match or matches. However, in any particular case, he may make a declaration notwithstanding the fact that notice was not given as required, provided the accused consents to waive that notice or the judge is satisfied that the interests of justice do not require more notice (FSA 1989 s.23(1)–(2)). **34-007**

The making of a declaration ought to involve an express statement announced in open court and recorded in the memorandum of conviction (though failure in this regard will not invalidate the order provided it is shown that the judge considered the matter (*DPP v Beaumont* [2008] EWHC 523 (Admin); [2008] 2 Cr. App. R. (S.) 98)).

Appeal lies to the CACD against the making of a declaration of relevance, and if the declaration is reversed, the banning order will be quashed (FSA 1989 s.23(3)–(4). See *R. v Jelf* [2020] EWCA Crim 631; [2020] 2 Cr. App. R. (S.) 52, where a FBO was quashed but the CACD made a fresh order in the same terms as the order that had been quashed.).

The second condition (s.14A(2))

34-008 Whether this condition is met will in some cases be the key question. No doubt the more the offence is linked to football grievances or the group "culture" of a set of fans linked by their support for a team, the more likely it will be that an order will help prevent violence or disorder. The more there is a history of football related offending, the greater will be the likelihood that the condition will be met. However, it is clear that it is possible for this condition to be met by the commission of a single offence, of which the defendant has just been convicted.

It is important to remember that this condition clearly contemplates that there must be a risk of repetition of violence or disorder at a match before it is met. The test of reasonable grounds to believe that an order will help prevent violence or disorder at regulated matches does not set a high hurdle, but it is not automatically satisfied just because the instant offence was football-related. Many football-related offences will give rise to exactly this risk, but not all will; *R. v Boggild* [2011] EWCA Crim 1928; [2012] 1 Cr. App. R. (S.) 81 is an example of one which the judge determined did not.

The consequences of an order

34-009 The consequences of an order are considerable, and must be explained to the offender in ordinary language at the time the order is made (FSA 1989 s.14E(1)). They are usefully summarised in *R. v Doyle* [2012] EWCA Crim 995; [2013] 1 Cr. App. R. (S.) 36.

The order:

(1) prohibits the offender from attending any regulated football match anywhere in the UK (FSA 1989 s.14(4)(a)). That means all league matches at National League North and South level or above, plus cup matches except for preliminary rounds (it is not possible to make an order limited to particular matches or particular teams);
(2) requires the offender to report within five days to the police station, and to provide the police with all the names he uses, any address where he lives for more than four weeks and his passport details (FSA 1989 s.14E);
(3) then enables the enforcing authority (currently the UK Football Banning Order Authority) at its entire discretion, to direct him via the police as to how he must comply with the order; and
(4) also enables the authority, again at its discretion, to order him to report to a police station when told to do so, and to surrender his passport, in order to prevent him from travelling to a regulated football match outside the UK (FSA 1989 ss.14(4)(b) and 19).

During what is termed the control period for any foreign football match or tournament, the authority may prohibit the defendant from travelling out of the country at all (FSA 1989 s.19). This applies to all matches or tournaments in which a British team (national or club) has an interest, whether it is playing in any particular match or not. The control period starts five days before the match or tournament and ends only when the whole tournament ends.

If the offender wishes to avoid any of these prohibitions, the offender has to persuade the authority to grant an exemption (FSA 1989 s.20). That includes the case where he needs to travel abroad for a reason completely unconnected with football, such as work or a family wedding, to a country many miles away from the place where the match is happening; in this case also he must get special permission to go.

These components of an order are not optional but compulsory. Failure to comply with an order is a summary offence punishable with up to six months imprisonment (see 34-013).

Additional requirements

The Act permits additional requirements to be added by the court (FSA 1989 s.14G). These can be tailor made, but they must be requirements "in relation to any regulated football matches". See *R. v Doyle* [2012] EWCA Crim 995; [2013] 1 Cr. App. R. (S.) 36. These additional requirements are the only part of an order which is in the control of the court. Given the extent of the controls in the standard terms of an order, careful consideration ought to be given to whether any additional requirements sought are required. Where a draft order contains suggested additional requirements they should be scrutinised with care to ensure they are not disproportionate (see *R. v Irving* [2013] EWCA Crim 1932; [2014] 2 Cr. App. R. (S.) 6). **34-010**

Surrender of passport

In making a banning order the judge *must* impose a requirement as to the surrender, in accordance with the Act, in connection with regulated football matches outside the UK, of the offender's passport (FSA 1989 s.14E(3)). **34-011**

Appeals

The prosecution may appeal against the failure of the Crown Court to make a banning order (FSA 1989 s.14A(5A)). Appeal is to Civil Division of the Court of Appeal (*R. v Boggild* [2011] EWCA Crim 1928; [2012] 1 Cr. App. R. (S.) 81) and only where the CACD gives permission or the judge who decided not to make an order grants a certificate that his decision is fit for appeal. The court had constituted itself as the Civil Division of the Court of Appeal to hear the appeal. The court identified anomalies in the Act: there was no provision for the Criminal Division of the Court of Appeal to hear an appeal by the prosecution under s.14A(5A). Further, there was no provision empowering the court, on hearing the appeal, to make any order which the court below could have made. Also absent were the usual ancillary powers of the Criminal Division of the Court of Appeal relating to the reception of fresh evidence, the attendance of the accused and the making of a decision as to leave by a single judge. **34-012**

An order made on appeal under this section (other than one directing that an application be re-heard by the court from which the appeal was brought) is treated as if it were an order of the court from which the appeal was brought.

A defendant may appeal against the making of a declaration of relevance (FSA 1989 s.23(3)).

Failure to comply

34-013 Failure to comply with any requirement imposed by the order is a summary offence punishable with a fine not exceeding level 5 on the standard scale, or six months' imprisonment, or both (FSA 1989 s.14J). Offences committed under the comparable provisions of the Scottish legislation (Police, Public Order and Criminal Justice (Scotland) Act 2006 s.68(1)(a) or (c)) may be dealt with in England, carrying the same punishment (PCrA 2009 s.106).

Administrative provisions

34-014 The order will specify the police station at which the offender is to report initially and the Crown Court officer will:

(1) give a copy of the order to the offender and, as soon as reasonably practicable, send a copy to the enforcing authority and the officer responsible for the police station at which the offender is to report initially; and
(2) if the offender is sentenced to or is serving a custodial sentence, send a copy to the governor of the prison or other person to whose custody he is committed.

(FSA 1989 s.18(1), (2))

Application to terminate

34-015 The offender may apply to the court by which the order was made to terminate it, if it has had effect for at least two thirds of the specified period (FSA 1989 s.14H). On such an application the judge may:

(1) having regard to:
   (a) the offender's character;
   (b) his conduct since the order was made;
   (c) the nature of the offence which led to it; and
   (d) any other circumstances;
(2) terminate the order from a specified date; OR
(3) refuse the application; and
(4) order the offender to pay all or any part of the costs of the application.

Where an application is refused, no further application in respect of the order may be made within a period of six months beginning with the date of the refusal.

35. FORFEITURE AND DEPRIVATION ORDERS

Quick Guide

1. Deprivation order; SA 2020 s.152

Introduction

The scope of a deprivation order under SA 2020 s.152, which applies to all criminal offences, overlaps the narrower scope of specific orders available under other criminal statutes, to which reference should be made where appropriate. **35-001**

The general power

Subject to certain restrictions s.153 provides a general power to deprive an offender of his rights in property where he is convicted of an offence, and: **35-002**

(1) the judge is satisfied that any property which:
   (a) has been lawfully seized from him; or
   (b) was in his possession or under his control at the time when he was apprehended for the offence, or when the summons in respect of it was issued:
      (i) has been used for the purpose of committing, or facilitating the commission of, any offence; or
      (ii) was intended by him to be used for that purpose;

OR

(2) the offence (or an offence which the court has taken into consideration) consists of unlawful possession of property which:
   (a) has been lawfully seized from him; or
   (b) was in his possession or under his control at the time when he was apprehended for the offence, or when the summons in respect of it was issued.

"Facilitating the commission of an offence" includes the taking of any steps after the offence has been committed for the purpose of disposing of any property to which it relates or of avoiding apprehension or detection (SA 2020 s.153(4)).

A deprivation order may be made whether or not the judge also deals with the offender in any other way in respect of the offence of which he has been convicted, and without regard to any restrictions on forfeiture in any enactment contained in an Act passed before 29 July 1988 (SA 2020 s.153(6), s.155(2)).

Order only in straightforward cases

35-003 An order should be made only in the most straightforward of cases, and only upon the offender's admission or on a specific finding by the court (*R. v Troth* (1980) 71 Cr. App. R. 1; *R. v Kearney* [2011] EWCA Crim 826; [2011] 2 Cr. App. R. (S.) 106). It is desirable that the judge should make an express finding on the basis of which the order is made (*R. v Ranasinghe* [1999] 2 Cr. App. R. (S.) 366). The offender may be deprived only of such interest as he has in the property (see *Kearney*—motor vehicle encumbered by hire purchase; see also *R. v Thomas* [2012] EWCA Crim 1159 and *R. v Hall* [2014] EWCA Crim 2413). The judge must not make an order unless, prior to sentencing, he has made an enquiry as to the likely financial and other effects that the order is likely to have on the offender (*R. v Highbury Corner Magistrates Court Ex p. Di Matteo* (1991) 92 Cr. App. R. 263). There may be cases where the order will have a disproportionately severe effect on an offender and should not be made, particularly where forfeiture of a motor vehicle is concerned (*R. v Hamlett* [2015] EWCA Crim 1412; [2016] 1 Cr. App. R. (S.) 16; *R. v De Jesus* [2015] EWCA Crim 1118; [2015] 2 Cr. App. R. (S.) 44; however, see also *R. v Lee* [2012] EWCA Crim 2658; [2013] 2 Cr. App. R. (S.) 18 (deprivation of a van not disproportionate)).

Where a number of offenders are equally guilty, it is likely to be wrong to make an order in relation to one accused only (*R. v Ottey* (1984) 6 Cr. App. R. (S.) 163) but it may be fair and proper to do so in order to reflect differing levels of participation (*R. v Burgess* [2001] 2 Cr. App. R. (S.) 2).

Serious road traffic offences

35-004 Where a person commits an offence:

(1) under RTA 1988 which is punishable with imprisonment;
(2) of manslaughter; or
(3) under OAPA 1861 s.35 (furious or wanton driving),

and the offence consists of:

(a) driving, attempting to drive or being in charge of a vehicle;
(b) certain breathalyser offences; or
(c) failing, as the driver of a vehicle, to comply with RTA 1988 s.170(2) and (3) (duty to stop and give information or to report accident),

the vehicle is said to be regarded for the purposes of s.153 and s.157(3)(b) as used for the purpose of committing the offence, and for committing any offence of aiding, abetting, counselling or procuring the commission of the offence (SA 2020 s.154).

As to the power of a constable to seize and dispose of vehicles driven without a licence or insurance, see RTA 1988 ss.165A and 165B.

Effect of order

35-005 The effect of an order is that, apart from depriving the offender of his rights, if any, in the property, it enables the property to be taken into the custody of the police, if not already in their possession. The Police (Property) Act 1897 s.69 then applies, with certain modifications, leaving any third party or other claimant to make a claim within the six months under the Act (SA 2020 s.158).

Restrictions on use of s.143

As forfeited property has some financial value, the judge must, in considering whether to make an order, have regard to: 35-006

(1) the value of the property; and
(2) the likely financial and other effects on the offender (taken together with any other order the court contemplates making) (SA 2020 s.155(1)),

otherwise the order will be invalid (see *Trans Berckx BVBA v North Avon Magistrates Court* [2011] EWHC 2605 (Admin)).

Note also that:

(a) the power is applicable to all offences, including those to which a narrower specific statutory power applies (e.g. drugs and firearms, as to which see below) (*R. v O'Farrell* (1988) 10 Cr. App. R. (S.) 74);
(b) the power does not extend to depriving an offender of his rights in real property (*R. v Khan* (1983) 76 Cr. App. R. 29);
(c) the order is confined to the use, etc. of the property by the offender, not where it has been used by others to commit offences (e.g. by a person to whom drugs are supplied; see *R. v Slater* (1986) 83 Cr. App. R. 265); and
(d) the order is punitive in nature, and must be looked on as part of the sentence. The "totality principle" therefore applies and it may be necessary to adjust other parts of the sentence (*R. v Priestley* [1996] Crim L.R. 356).

Procedure and evidence

An order may be made only: 35-007

(1) where the Prosecutor proves that the requirements of the section are fulfilled (*R. v Kingston-upon-Hull Justices Ex p. Hartung* (1981) 72 Cr. App. R. 26; *R. v Pemberton* (1982) 4 Cr. App. R. (S.) 328); or
(2) on an admission by the accused or a precise finding of fact by the judge (*R. v Troth* (1980) 71 Cr. App. R. 1; *R. v Ball* [2002] EWCA Crim 2777; [2003] 2 Cr. App. R. (S.) 18);
(3) in the most straightforward cases, where the judge has given a warning of his intention, and a prior opportunity is given for representations to be made (*R. v Powell* (1984) 6 Cr. App. R. (S.) 354; *R. v Ball* [2002] EWCA Crim 2777; [2003] 2 Cr. App. R. (S.) 18); and
(4) in the case of a number of joint offenders, against all rather than against one only (*R. v Ottey* (1984) 6 Cr. App. R. (S.) 163).

As to the importance of the judge conducting a proper enquiry, including giving the defendant an opportunity to give evidence, see *R. v Jones* [2017] EWCA Crim 2192; [2018] 1 Cr. App. R. (S.) 35.

Application for benefit of victim

Where the judge makes an order in a case where: 35-008

(1) the offender has been convicted of an offence which has resulted in a person suffering personal injury, loss or damage; or
(2) any such offence is taken into consideration on sentence; and
(3) but for the inadequacy of the offender's means he would have made a

compensation order under which he would have been required to pay not less than a specified amount,

he may also order that any proceeds which arise from the disposal of the property and which do not exceed a sum he specifies, shall be paid to that person.

An order of this kind is not effective:

(a) before the end of the period specified in s.157(3)(a) (6 months); or
(b) if a successful application under the Police (Property) Act 1897 s.1(1) has been made.

(SA 2020 s.159)

Relationship with confiscation

35-009 A deprivation order should not be made until confiscation proceedings have been concluded (POCA 2002 s.13(2)–(3)). See also *R. v Guraj* [2016] UKSC 65; [2017] 1 Cr. App. R. (S.) 32.

2. FIREARMS OFFENCES; FA 1968 s.52(1)

35-010 An order as to the forfeiture or disposal of a firearm or ammunition found in the possession of an offender may be made where the offender:

(1) is convicted of an offence under FA 1968 (other than one under s.22(3) or an offence relating specifically to air weapons); or
(2) is convicted of an offence for which he is sentenced to imprisonment or detention in a young offender institution; or
(3) has been ordered to enter into a recognisance to keep the peace and/or be of good behaviour, a condition of which was that he should not carry a firearm; or
(4) is subject to a community order containing a requirement that he shall not possess, use or carry a firearm.

(FA 1968 s.52(1))

A "community order" means a community order within SA 2020 s.200, made in England and Wales, or a youth rehabilitation order within the meaning of SA 2020 s.173 (FA 1968 s.52(1A)). Where a firearm is forfeited, it may be seized and detained by a constable (FA 1968 s.52(3)).

3. DRUGS OFFENCES; MDA 1971 s.27

35-011 Where a person is convicted of an offence:

(1) under MDA 1971;
(2) specified in POCA 2002 Sch.2 para.1 (drug trafficking offences); or
(3) so far as it relates to that paragraph, Sch.2 para.10,

and anything is shown to the satisfaction of the judge to relate to the offence, the judge may order it to be forfeited and either destroyed or dealt with in such other manner as he may order (MDA 1971 s.27(1)).

If a person claiming to be the owner, or to be otherwise interested in the property, applies to be heard, an order must not be made unless an opportunity is given to him to be heard (MDA 1971 s.27(2)).

A number of broad principles were laid down in the cases of *R. v Cuthbertson*

(1980) 71 Cr. App. R. 148; *R. v Ribeyre* (1982) 4 Cr. App. R. (S.) 165; *R. v Marland* (1986) 82 Cr. App. R. 134; *R. v Churcher* (1986) 8 Cr. App. R. (S.) 94; *R. v Cox* (1986) 8 Cr. App. R. (S.) 384 and *R. v Llewellyn* (1985) 7 Cr. App. R. (S.) 225, thus:

(a) the order is concerned with forfeiture and not with restitution, compensation or the redress of unlawful enrichment;
(b) the order is apt to deal only with things which are tangible in the sense that physical possession may be taken of them by order of the court; "anything" includes money (*R. v Beard* [1974] 1 W.L.R. 1549) but not real property (*R. v Khan* (1983) 76 Cr. App. R. 29);
(c) it is necessary to connect the specific thing forfeited with a particular offence to which it relates (and see *R. v Morgan* [1977] Crim. L.R. 488); working capital for future deals may be forfeited under the general power in PCC(S)A 2000 s.143 (*R. v O'Farrell* (1988) 10 Cr. App. R. (S.) 74); and
(d) the offender ought to be permitted to adduce any material tending to show that the thing in question is not related to the offence.

A forfeiture order should not be made until confiscation proceedings have been concluded (POCA 2002 s.13(2)–(3)).

4. Public Order Act 1986 ss.25 and 29

Where a person is convicted of an offence under ss.19, 21, 23, 29B, 29C, 29E or 29G of the Act in relation to racial or religious hatred, or s.18 relating to the display of racially offensive written material, the court must order to be forfeited any written material or recording (as defined in s.29) produced and shown to be written material or a recording to which the offence relates (POrA 1986 ss.25 and 29). **35-012**

The order does not take effect until the ordinary time for appeal has expired, or, if an appeal is initiated, until it is finally determined or abandoned.

5. Protection of Children Act 1978

A Schedule to the Act, inserted by PJA 2006 s.39 Sch.11 makes provision for the forfeiture of photographs and pseudo photographs under the 1978 Act. **35-013**

6. MSA 2015; forfeiture of land vehicle, ship or aircraft

Where a person is convicted on indictment of an offence under MSA 2015 s.2, the judge may order the forfeiture of any land vehicle, ship or aircraft vehicle used, or intended to be used, in connection with the offence (MSA 2015 s.11) if the convicted person: **35-014**

(1) owned the vehicle, ship or aircraft at the time the offence was committed;
(2) was at that time a director, secretary or manager of a company which owned it;
(3) was at that time in possession of it under a hire purchase agreement;
(4) was at that time a director, secretary or manager of a company which was in possession of it under a hire-purchase agreement;
(5) in the case of a ship or aircraft, was the charterer; or
(6) was driving the land vehicle in the course of the commission of the offence, or committed the offence while captain of the ship or aircraft,

but in relation to a ship or aircraft to which (1) and (2) do not apply, forfeiture may be ordered only if, in the case of a ship, (a) or (b) below applies, or in the case of an aircraft (a) or (c) applies:

(a) where a person who, at the time the offence was committed, owned the ship or aircraft or was a director, secretary or manager of a company which owned it, knew or ought to have known of the intention to use it in the course of the commission of an offence under s.2;
(b) where the gross tonnage of a ship (not a hovercraft) is less than 500 tons; and
(c) where the maximum weight at which an aircraft may take off in accordance with its certificate of airworthiness is less than 5,700kg (MSA 2015 s.11).

Where a person who claims to have an interest in a land vehicle, ship or aircraft applies to the judge to make representations on the question of forfeiture, an order may not be made under this provision in respect of the vehicle, ship or aircraft, unless the person has been given an opportunity to make representations (MSA 2015 s.11(6)).

Release of seized vehicle, etc.

35-015 Where a land vehicle, ship or aircraft has been provisionally seized by a constable or senior immigration officer a person (other than the arrested person) may apply to the appropriate court for it on the grounds that:

(a) he owns the vehicle, ship or aircraft;
(b) he was, immediately before its detention, in possession of it under a hire-purchase agreement; or
(c) he is a charterer of the ship or aircraft.

The appropriate court will be, if the arrested person has not been charged, or he has been charged but proceedings for the offence have not begun to be heard, a magistrates' court, or, if he has been charged and proceedings for the offence are being heard, then the court hearing the proceedings.

The court to which an application is made may, on such security or surety being tendered as it considers satisfactory, release the vehicle, ship or aircraft on condition that it is made available to the court if the arrested person is convicted and an order for its forfeiture is made under s.11 (MSA 2015 s.12).

7. TERRORIST PROPERTY OFFENCES

Offences under TerrA 2000

35-016 The court by or before which a person is convicted of an offence under any of TerrA 2000 ss.15–18, may make a forfeiture order in accordance with the following provisions.

The judge may order the forfeiture, where a person is convicted of an offence:

(1) under ss.15(1), (2) or 16, of any money or other property which, at the time of the offence, the person had in his possession or under his control and which:
    (a) had been used for the purposes of terrorism; or
    (b) he intended should be used, or had reasonable cause to suspect might be used, for those purposes;

(2) under s.15(3), of any money or other property which, at the time of the offence, the person had in his possession or under his control and which:
   (a) had been used for the purposes of terrorism; or
   (b) which, at that time, he knew or had reasonable cause to suspect would or might be used for those purposes;
(3) under ss.17 or 18, of any money or other property which, at the time of the offence, the person had in his possession or under his control and which:
   (a) had been used for the purposes of terrorism; or
   (b) was, at that time, intended by him to be used for those purposes;
(4) under s.17, of the money or other property to which the arrangement in question related, and which:
   (a) had been used for the purposes of terrorism; or
   (b) at the time of the offence, the person knew or had reasonable cause to suspect would or might be used for those purposes;
(5) under s.18, of the money or other property to which the arrangement in question related;
(6) under s.17A, of any amount paid under, or purportedly under, the insurance contract [NB: s.23(5A) inserted by the Counter-Terrorism and Security Act 2015 s.42(2)]; and
(7) under any of ss.15–18, of any money or other property which wholly or partly, and directly or indirectly, is received by any person as a payment or other reward in connection with the commission of the offence.

(TerrA 2000 s.23)

Other terrorism offences; offences with a terrorist connection

The court by or before which a person is convicted of an offence to which TerrA 2000 s.23A applies may order the forfeiture of any money or other property in relation to which the following conditions are met: **35-017**

(1) that it was, at the time of the offence, in the possession or control of the person convicted; and
(2) that:
   (a) it had been used for the purposes of terrorism;
   (b) it was intended by that person that it should be used for the purposes of terrorism, or
   (c) the judge believes that it will be used for the purposes of terrorism unless forfeited.

The section applies to:

- any offence under TerrA 2000 ss.54 (weapons training), 57, 58 or 58A (possessing things and collecting information for the purposes of terrorism), 58B (entering or remaining in a designated area), 59, 60 or 61 (inciting terrorism outside the UK);
- any offence under TerrA 2006 Pt 1 ss.2 (dissemination of terrorist publications), 5 (preparation of terrorist acts), 6 (training for terrorism), 9–11 (offences involving radioactive devices or materials);
- any ancillary offence (as defined in CTA 2008 s.94) in relation to an offence listed in subs.(2); and
- an offence specified in CTA 2008 Sch.2 (offences where terrorist connection to be considered) as to which the court dealing with the offence has

determined, in accordance with SA 2020 s.69, that the offence has a terrorist connection.

(TerrA 2000 s.23A)

Supplementary provisions

35-018 Before making an order under ss.23 or 23A, the judge must give an opportunity to be heard to any person, other than the convicted person, who claims to be the owner or otherwise interested in anything which can be forfeited under that section.

In considering whether to make an order under those sections in respect of any property, the judge must have regard to:

(1) the value of the property; and
(2) the likely financial and other effects on the convicted person of the making of an order (taken together with any other order that the judge contemplates making).

(TerrA 2000 s.23B)
Schedule 4 makes further provision in relation to such forfeiture orders.

Interpretation

35-019 In these provisions, "forfeiture order" means an order made by a court in England and Wales under ss.23 or 23A, "forfeited property" means the money or other property to which a forfeiture order applies, and "relevant offence" means:

(1) an offence under any of ss.15–18;
(2) an offence to which s.23A applies; or
(3) in relation to a restraint order, any offence specified in SA 2020 s.69(4) or (5) applies (offences where terrorist connection to be considered).

(TerrA 2000 Sch.4 para.1)

Giving effect to the order

35-020 Where a judge makes a forfeiture order he may make such other provision as appears to him to be necessary for giving effect to the order, and in particular he may:

(1) require any of the forfeited property to be paid or handed over to the proper officer or to a constable designated for the purpose by the chief officer of police of a police force specified in the order;
(2) direct any of the forfeited property other than money or land to be sold or otherwise disposed of in such manner as he may direct and the proceeds (if any) to be paid to the proper officer;
(3) appoint a receiver to take possession, subject to such conditions and exceptions as may be specified by him, of any of the forfeited property, to realise it in such manner as he may direct and to pay the proceeds to the proper officer; and
(4) direct a specified part of any forfeited money, or of the proceeds of the sale, disposal or realisation of any forfeited property, to be paid by the proper officer to a specified person falling within s.23B(1).

In (2) and (4) a reference to the proceeds of the sale, disposal or realisation of property is a reference to the proceeds after deduction of the costs of sale, disposal or realisation.

A forfeiture order does not come into force until there is no further possibility of it being varied or set aside on appeal (disregarding any power of a court to grant leave to appeal out of time). MCA 1980 s.140 (disposal of non-pecuniary forfeitures) does not apply.

(TerrA 2000 Sch.4 para.2)

Meaning of "the proper officer"

35-021 "The proper officer" means, where the forfeiture order is made by the Crown Court and:

(1) the accused was sent to the Crown Court by a magistrates' court, the designated officer for the magistrates' court; and
(2) the proceedings were instituted by a bill of indictment preferred by virtue of AJ(MP)A 1933 s.2(2)(b) or (ba), the designated officer for the magistrates' court for the place where the trial took place.

The proper officer will issue a certificate in respect of a forfeiture order if an application is made by:

(a) the prosecutor in the proceedings in which the forfeiture order was made;
(b) the accused in those proceedings; or
(c) a person whom the judge heard under s.23B(1) before making the order.

The certificate will state the extent (if any) to which, at the date of the certificate, effect has been given to the forfeiture order.

(TerrA 2000 Sch.4 para.4)

Compensation to person suffering personal injury, loss or damage

35-022 Where a judge makes a forfeiture order in a case where:

(1) the offender has been convicted of an offence that has resulted in a person suffering personal injury, loss or damage; or
(2) any such offence is taken into consideration by the judge in determining sentence,

the judge may also order that an amount not exceeding a sum specified by him is to be paid to that person out of the proceeds of the forfeiture.

For this purpose the proceeds of the forfeiture means the aggregate amount of:

(a) any forfeited money; and
(b) the proceeds of the sale, disposal or realisation of any forfeited property, after deduction of the costs of the sale, disposal or realisation,

reduced by the amount of any payment under para.2(1)(d) or 3(1).

The judge may make an order only if he is satisfied that but for the inadequacy of the offender's means he would have made a compensation order under SA 2020 Pt 7 Ch.2 under which the offender would have been required to pay compensation of an amount not less than the amount specified.

(TerrA 2000 Sch.4 para.4A)

Definitions

35-023 For the purposes of these provisions proceedings for an offence are instituted when:

(1) a justice of the peace issues a summons or warrant under MCA 1980 s.1, in respect of the offence;
(2) when a person is charged with the offence after being taken into custody without a warrant; or
(3) a bill of indictment charging a person with the offence is preferred by virtue of AJ(MP)A 1933 s.2(2)(b) or (ba).

Where the application of this provision would result in there being more than one time for the institution of proceedings they shall be taken to be instituted at the earliest of those times.

Proceedings are concluded:

(a) when a forfeiture order has been made in those proceedings and effect has been given to it in respect of all the forfeited property; or
(b) when no forfeiture order has been made in those proceedings and there is no further possibility of one being made as a result of an appeal (disregarding any power of a court to grant leave to appeal out of time).

(TerrA 2000 Sch.4 para.11)

Relationship with confiscation

35-024 A forfeiture order under TerrA 2000 s.23 should not be made until confiscation proceedings have been concluded (POCA 2002 s.13(2)–(3)).

8. GAME ACT 1831

35-025 CJPOA 1994 Sch.9 para.4 contains provisions for forfeiting vehicles in the possession or under the control of poachers.

9. CONFISCATION ORDERS

35-026 These are governed by the provisions of POCA 2002; see CONFISCATION ORDERS.

10. FORFEITURE OF SEIZED CASH

35-027 As to forfeiture of seized cash, see CONFISCATION ORDERS.

11. ARMED FORCES ACT 2021

35-028 The Armed Forces Act 2006 is amended to introduce deprivation orders pursuant to the new s.177B–F. This system largely replicates that within the Sentencing Act 2020 for civilian offenders.

36. GOODYEAR INDICATION

Introduction

Prior to pleading guilty, it is open to an accused to request from the judge an indication of the maximum sentence that would be imposed if a guilty plea were to be tendered at that stage in the proceedings, in accordance with the guidance in *R. v Goodyear* [2005] EWCA Crim 888; [2005] 2 Cr. App. R. 20. The defence should give the court and the prosecution advance notice of the intention to seek an indication. **36-001**

Attention is drawn to the guidance set out in paras [53]–[78] of the judgment of *R. v Goodyear*.

The objective of the *Goodyear* guidance is to safeguard against the creation or appearance of judicial pressure on the accused. Any advance indication given should be the maximum sentence if a guilty plea were to be tendered at that stage of the proceedings only; the judge should not indicate the maximum possible sentence following conviction by a jury after trial. The judge should give a *Goodyear* indication only if one is requested by the accused, although the judge can, in an appropriate case, remind the defence advocate of the accused's entitlement to seek an advance indication of sentence.

Whether to give a *Goodyear* indication, and whether to give reasons for a refusal, is a matter for the discretion of the judge, to be exercised in accordance with the principles outlined by the CACD in that case (*CPD* VII Sentencing C: Indications of Sentence (R. v Goodyear) C.1–8).

Synopsis of Goodyear

The following are the important points to be gleaned from *Goodyear*: **36-002**

(1) The process of seeking an advance indication of sentence should be *initiated by the defence*; the defence advocate should have written instructions from the accused.
(2) An indication should not be sought while there is any uncertainty about an acceptable plea or the *factual basis* of sentencing.
(3) The judge should not give an advance indication unless one is sought by the accused.
(4) Hearings relating to such advance indications should normally take place in *open court*.
(5) The judge should *not* become *involved in discussions* which link the acceptable plea to the sentence which is likely to be imposed.
(6) Advance indications should not be given on *alternative bases*.
(7) The judge may give an advance indication of the *maximum sentence* which he would impose if a guilty plea was to be tendered at the stage the indication is sought.
(8) Once an advance indication of sentence is given, it is *binding* on the judge and any other judge who becomes responsible for the case.
(9) If the accused does not plead guilty within a reasonable time after the advance indication has been given, the indication ceases to have effect (*R. v Patel* [2009] EWCA Crim 67; [2009] 2 Cr. App. R. (S.) 16).

(10) The judge may *reserve his position* until he feels able to give an advance indication, for instance where reports on the accused are expected.

(11) The judge retains an *unfettered discretion to refuse* to give an advance indication.

(12) The right of the *Attorney General* to refer a sentence to the CACD on that it is unduly lenient is not affected by the giving of an advance indication of sentence.

The rules set out in *Goodyear* are quite specific. Deviation from these rules is likely to cause problems, see, e.g. *R. v Omole* [2011] EWCA Crim 1428; [2012] 1 Cr. App. R. 41 and *R. v Nightingale* [2013] EWCA Crim 405; [2013] 2 Cr. App. R. 7. See also *R. v Patel* [2009] EWCA Crim 67; [2009] 2 Cr. App. R. (S.) 16.

General provisions

36-003 The hearing will normally take place in open court, in the presence of the accused, with both sides represented and the proceedings being recorded in full. In particular:

(1) there should be no prosecution opening at this stage, nor any mitigation plea by the defence—these should be postponed until after the accused has pleaded guilty;

(2) the judge should not give an advance indication of sentence unless one has been sought by the accused, though he is always entitled, in an appropriate case, to remind the defence advocate that the accused is entitled to seek an advance indication;

(3) where appropriate, there must be an agreed, written basis of plea; unless there is, the judge should refuse to give an indication—otherwise he may become inappropriately involved in negotiations about the acceptance of pleas, and any agreed basis of plea;

(4) there should be little need for the judge to involve himself in discussions with the advocates, although he may wish to seek better information on any aspect of the case which is troubling him; and

(5) since the case may yet proceed as a trial, and if it does, no reference may be made to the request for a sentence indication, reporting restrictions should normally be imposed, to be lifted if and when the accused pleads or is found guilty. (See further REPORTING AND ACCESS RESTRICTIONS.)

Indication to be sought at earliest opportunity; procedure

36-004 A sentence indication should normally be sought at the PTPH. In cases "sent" to the Crown Court under CDA 1998 s.51, or transferred under CJA 1987 s.4 or CJA 1991 s.53, this is usually the first opportunity for the accused to plead guilty and therefore the moment when the maximum discount for the guilty plea will be available to him.

This does not, however, rule out the accused's entitlement to seek an indication at a later stage, or even, in a rare case, during the course of the trial itself.

Procedure is governed by CrimPR 3.31 and *CPD* VII Sentencing C: Indications of Sentence: *R. v Goodyear*. Where an accused wants the judge to give an indication of the maximum sentence that would be passed if a guilty plea were entered when the indication is sought, he must:

(1) apply in writing as soon as practicable; serving serve the application on the court officer, and the prosecutor; and
(2) the application must specify the offence or offences to which it would be a guilty plea, and the facts on the basis of which that plea would be entered; and
(3) include the prosecutor's agreement to, or representations on, that proposed basis of plea.

The prosecutor must:
(a) provide information relevant to sentence, including:
    (i) any previous conviction of the accused, and the circumstances where relevant; and
    (ii) any statement of the effect of the offence on the victim, the victim's family or others; and
(b) identify any other matter relevant to sentence, including:
    (i) the legislation applicable;
    (ii) any sentencing guidelines, or guideline cases; and
    (iii) aggravating and mitigating factors.

The hearing of the application may take place in the absence of any other accused, but; must be attended by the applicant accused's legal representatives (if any), and the prosecution advocate.

The fact that notice has been given, and any reference to a request for a sentence indication, or the circumstances in which it was sought, is inadmissible in any subsequent trial.

Limits on practice

Subject to the judge's power to give an appropriate reminder to the advocate for the accused: **36-005**

(1) the process of seeking a sentence indication should normally be started by the accused;
(2) whether or not the judge has given an appropriate reminder, the accused's advocate should not seek an indication without written authority, signed by his client, indicating that he wishes to seek an indication; and
(3) an unrepresented accused is entitled to seek a sentence indication of his own initiative.

There will be difficulties in (3) in either the judge or the prosecuting advocate taking any initiative and informing an unrepresented accused of this right. That might too readily be interpreted as, or subsequently argued, to have been improper pressure.

It must be understood that any indication given by the judge:
(a) reflects the situation at the time when it is given, and that if a "guilty plea" is not tendered in the light of that indication the indication will cease to have effect;
(b) relates only to the matters about which an indication is sought; certain steps, like confiscation proceedings, follow automatically, and the judge cannot dispense with them, nor, by giving an indication of sentence, create an expectation that they will be dispensed with; and

(c) remains subject to the right of the Attorney General, where it arises, to refer an unduly lenient sentence to the CACD.

The accused's right to apply for leave to appeal against sentence if, for example, insufficient allowance has been made for matters of genuine mitigation, remains unaffected.

R. v Goodyear makes it clear that:

- any advance indication of sentence should normally be confined to the maximum sentence if a plea of guilty were tendered at the stage that the indication was sought;
- that a judge should treat a request for a sentence indication, in whatever form it reached him, as if he were being asked to indicate the maximum sentence on the accused at that stage;
- the only other type of indication envisaged in *Goodyear*, should the judge see fit to give it, is an indication that the sentence or type of sentence to be imposed on the accused would be the same whether the case proceeded as a plea of guilty or went to trial, but *Goodyear* recognises that such an indication would be unusual; and
- the judge retains an unfettered discretion to refuse to give an indication at all or to reserve his position until a later stage, if he thinks it appropriate to do so (*R. v Omole* [2011] EWCA Crim 1428; [2012] 1 Cr. App. R (S.) 41).

No plea bargaining

36-006 The defence should not seek an indication while there is any uncertainty between the prosecution and the defence about:

(1) an acceptable plea or pleas to the indictment; or
(2) any factual basis relating to the plea.

Any agreed basis should be reduced into writing before an indication is sought. Where there is a dispute about a particular fact which counsel for the accused believes to be effectively material to the sentencing decision, the difference should be recorded, so that the judge can make up his own mind.

There should be no question of the judge giving a preliminary indication, followed by comments on it by the prosecution advocate, with the judge then reconsidering his indication, and perhaps raising it to a higher level, with the defence advocate then making further submissions to persuade the judge, after all, to reduce his indication.

The judge should not:

(a) be invited to give an indication on the basis of what would be, or what would appear to be, a "plea bargain";
(b) be asked or become involved in discussions linking the acceptability to the prosecution of a plea;
(c) be asked to indicate levels of sentence which he may have in mind depending on possible alternative pleas; or
(d) indicate the nature of any sentence he might pass if the accused were

convicted after a trial (see *R. v Patel* [2009] EWCA Crim 67; [2009] 2 Cr. App. R. (S.) 16).

Discretion to refuse indication

The judge retains an unfettered discretion to refuse to give an indication. It may be inappropriate. He may consider: 36-007

(1) that if he were to give an indication at the stage when it is sought, he would not properly be able to judge the true culpability of the accused, or the differing levels of responsibility between accused; this is a very important consideration;
(2) that, for a variety of reasons, the accused is already under pressure (perhaps from a co-accused), or is vulnerable, and that to give the requested indication, even in answer to a request, might create additional pressure;
(3) that the particular accused may not fully have appreciated that he should not plead guilty unless in fact he is guilty;
(4) in a case involving a number of accused, that an indication given to one, may itself create pressure on another; and
(5) that the application is nothing less than a "try on" by an accused who intends or is likely to plead guilty in any event, seeking to take a tactical advantage; in such a case he will probably refuse to say anything at all, and indeed, it may strike him as a plea tendered later than the first reasonable opportunity for doing so, with a consequent reduction in the discount for the guilty plea.

The judge may, instead of refusing to give an indication, reserve his position until such time as he feels able to give one, e.g. until a pre-sentence report is available. There will be cases where a psychiatric or other report may provide valuable insight into the level of risk posed by the accused, and if so, he may justifiably feel disinclined to give an indication at the stage when it is sought.

Again, the judge may not be sufficiently familiar with the case to give an informed indication, and if so, he may defer doing so until he is.

As to dangerous offenders cases, see 36-008.

"Dangerous offenders" cases

It is not necessarily inappropriate to give an indication merely because the accused is charged with a specified offence which attracts the mandatory dangerous offender provisions of CJA 2003, but there are dangers in doing so. 36-008

At the time when an indication is sought, the judge may not be in possession of the information necessary to enable him to make the assessment of risk required by the Act. Pre-sentence and other reports will not be available. In such cases it is a matter for the judge's discretion whether it is appropriate to give an indication; he is under no obligation to do so.

If the judge decides to give an indication:

(1) the prosecutor must make it clear that the offence is a specified offence to which the mandatory dangerous offender provisions apply, that the information necessary to make an assessment of dangerousness is not available;
(2) if the accused is later assessed not to be dangerous, the indication will relate to the maximum determinate sentence which will be imposed; and

(3) if the accused is later assessed as dangerous, the indication can relate only to the notional determinate term which will be used in the calculation of the minimum term to be served in conjunction with a sentence of life imprisonment, or the custodial term of an extended sentence (which could never be less than 12 months).

(*R. v Kulah* [2007] EWCA Crim 1701; [2008] 1 Cr. App. R. (S) 85; *R. v Seddon* [2007] EWCA Crim 3022; [2008] 2 Cr. App. R. (S.) 30)

Giving reasons

36-009 In a case:

(1) of an outright refusal, the judge will probably conclude that it is inappropriate to give his reasons; and
(2) where he has in mind to defer any indication, he may choose to explain his reasons, and further indicate the circumstances in which, and when, he would be prepared to respond to a request for a sentence indication.

If at any stage the judge refuses to give an indication (as opposed to deferring it) it remains open to the accused to seek a further indication at a later stage. Once the judge has refused to give an indication, however, he should not normally initiate the process, except, where it arises, to indicate that the circumstances had changed sufficiently for him to be prepared to consider a renewed application for an indication.

Binding effect of indication

36-010 An indication, once given, is binding ("as far as it goes"—*R. v Newman* [2010] EWCA Crim 1566; [2011] 1Cr. App. R. (S.) 68), and:

(1) remains binding on the judge who has given it; and
(2) binds any other judge who becomes responsible for the case.

If, after a reasonable opportunity to consider his position in the light of the indication, the accused does not plead guilty, the indication ceases to have effect (see *R. v Patel* [2009] EWCA Crim 67; [2009] 2 Cr. App. R. (S.) 16) and *R. v Utton* [2019] EWCA Crim 1341; [2020] 1 Cr. App. R. (S.) 7).

In straightforward cases, once an indication has been sought and given, there should not be an adjournment for the plea to be taken on another day, but:

(a) the judge who has given an indication, should, wherever possible, deal with the case immediately;
(b) if that is not possible, any subsequent hearings should be listed before him; and
(c) if that is not possible, and another judge deals with the case, while he has his own sentencing responsibilities, judicial comity as well as the expectation aroused in the accused that he will not receive a sentence in excess of that which the first judge indicated, requires that the subsequent judge should not exceed the earlier indication.

As to the judge rectifying an error, see *R. v Newman* [2010] EWCA Crim 1566; [2011] 1 Cr. App. R. (S.) 68.

In *R. v Davies* [2015] EWCA Crim 930; [2015] 2 Cr. App. R. (S.) 57 CA an indication was sought and given. The defendant pleaded guilty and then absconded before he was sentenced. The Court of Appeal held that the judge was bound (subject to any issues such as dangerousness) by the indication he had given on the primary offence.

The role of the Prosecutor

If an indication is sought, the prosecution advocate should ensure that the judge is in possession of, or has had access to, all the evidence relied on by the prosecution, including the antecedents and any personal impact statement from the victim of the crime (see VICTIM PERSONAL STATEMENTS). **36-011**

He may also need:

(1) to draw the judge's attention to any minimum or mandatory statutory sentencing requirements;
(2) to offer assistance with relevant guideline cases or to invite the judge to allow him to do so; and
(3) where applicable, to remind the judge that the position of the Attorney General to refer any eventual sentencing decision as unduly lenient is not affected.

If there has been no final agreement about the plea(s) or the basis of the plea(s), and the defence nevertheless seek an indication, which the judge appears minded to give, the prosecuting advocate ought to remind the judge of the guidance given in the preceding paragraphs that an indication of sentence should not normally be given until the basis of the plea has been agreed, or the judge has concluded that he can properly deal with the case without the need for a *Newton* hearing.

The prosecuting advocate should not say anything which may create the impression that the sentence indication has the support or approval of the Crown.

As to the acceptance of pleas by the Crown, see CCP 2004 para.19, *Attorney General's Guidelines on the Acceptance of Pleas*, updated to 21 October 2005 and the *Attorney General's Guidelines on Plea Discussions in Cases of Serious and Complex Fraud* (unreported) which came into force on 5 May 2009.

Effect on reference under CJA 1988 s.36

If the prosecution advocate has addressed his responsibilities, the discretion of the Attorney General to refer a sentence to the CACD as unduly lenient will be unaffected by the advance sentence indication. **36-012**

In particular:

(1) if a sentence indication has been given in accordance with these guidelines, before referring the eventual sentencing decision to the CACD, the Attorney General's decision will no doubt reflect that the accused had indeed pleaded guilty in response to the sentence indication, properly sought and given by the judge; and
(2) if the prosecuting advocate, to the contrary, has said or done anything which may indicate or convey support for, or approval of, the sentence indicated, the question whether the sentence should be referred to the CACD as unduly lenient, and the decision of the CACD whether to interfere with and increase it, will be examined on a case by case basis, in the light of everything said and done by the advocate for the Crown.

(See *Attorney General's Reference (Nos 80 and 81 of 1999)* [2000] 2 Cr. App.

R. (S.) 138; *Attorney General's Reference (Nos 86 and 87 of 1999)* [2001] 1 Cr. App. R. (S) 141; *R. v Mohammed* [2002] EWCA Crim 1607; [2003] 1 Cr. App. R. (S.) 57; but cf. *Attorney General's Reference (No.19 of 2004)* [2004] EWCA Crim 1239; [2005] 1 Cr. App. R. (S.) 18).

37. GUILTY PLEAS

Quick Guide

1. Introduction

A guilty plea will in, almost every case, attract a reduced sentence. The practice has now been formalised through the Sentencing Council's Guidelines Reduction in Sentence for a Guilty Plea (Sentencing Council 1). For the law and practice, see generally DISCOUNTS ON SENTENCE. See also GOODYEAR INDICATION. **37-001**

Where the accused pleads guilty to an offence and the judge is satisfied that the plea represents a clear acknowledgement of guilt, the court need not receive evidence unless CrimPR 25.16(4) applies (determination of facts for sentencing) (CrimPR 25.4).

As to the early guilty plea procedure, see CASE MANAGEMENT. The following overarching principles apply to guilty pleas:

(1) advocates must be free to perform their duty, namely, to give the accused the best advice possible and, if need be, in strong terms;
(2) that advice will often include advice that, in accordance with the relevant authorities and sentencing guidelines, the judge will normally reduce a sentence as a result of a guilty plea, and that the level of reduction will reflect the stage in the proceedings at which willingness to admit guilt was indicated;
(3) the advocate will, of course, emphasise that the accused must not plead guilty unless he is guilty of the offence(s) charged;
(4) the accused, having considered the advocate's advice, must have complete freedom of choice whether to plead guilty or not guilty; and
(5) where the accused pleads guilty, as where the court tries a case; the general rule is that the judge must not proceed if the accused is absent, unless satisfied that the accused has waived the right to attend, and the proceedings will be fair despite the accused's absence (CrimPR 25.2(b)(i), (ii)).

There must be freedom of access between advocate and judge; but any discussion must be between the judge and the advocates on both sides. If an advocate is instructed by a solicitor who is in court, he, too, should be allowed to attend the discussion.

This freedom of access is important because there may be matters calling for communication or discussion of such a nature that the advocate cannot, in the client's interest, mention them in open court, e.g. the advocate, by way of mitigation, may wish to tell the judge that reliable medical evidence shows that the accused is suffering from a terminal illness and may not have long to live.

Note that:

(a) it is imperative that, so far as possible, justice be administered in open court;
(b) advocates should, therefore, only ask to see the judge when it is felt to be really necessary; and
(c) the judge must be careful only to treat such communications as private where, in the interests of justice, this is necessary.

Where any such discussion takes place it should be sound-recorded.

Three routes

37-002 The three routes by which a plea of guilty may be put forward in the Crown Court, are:

(1) a plea of guilty to all or some of the charges on the basis of the prosecution case set out in the papers (37-003);
(2) a plea of guilty upon a basis of plea agreed by the prosecution and defence, or upon a basis of plea put forward by the defence and not contested by the prosecutor (37-004); and
(3) in cases involving serious or complex fraud conducted in accordance with a plea of guilty upon a basis of plea agreed by the prosecution and the defence, accompanied by joint submissions as to sentence (37-007).

Where the accused pleads guilty to an offence and the judge is satisfied that the plea represents a clear acknowledgement of guilt, evidence need not be received (CrimPR 25.4) unless CrimPR 25.16(4) applies (determination of facts for sentencing).

As to vacating a plea of guilty, see 37-021.

2. PLEA OF GUILTY ON THE BASIS OF THE PROSECUTION CASE

Procedure

37-003 In some cases, an accused will simply plead guilty to all charges on the basis of the facts as alleged and opened by the prosecutor, with no dispute as to the factual basis or the extent of offending. Alternatively, he may plead guilty to some of the charges brought. As to the position where the accused offers a plea to a lesser offence which is refused by the prosecutor, see *R. v Birt* [2011] EWCA Crim 2823; [2011] 2 Cr. App. R. (S.) 14, and *R. v Rainford* [2010] EWCA Crim 3220; [2011] 2 Cr. App. R. (S.) 15. See also *R. v Rawson* [2013] EWCA Crim 9; [2013] Crim. L.R. 430 (late plea to manslaughter following earlier offer refused by the prosecution, credit for plea of one eighth).

The admission comprised within the guilty plea is to the offence and not necessarily to all the facts or inferences for which the prosecution contends. The responsibility for determining the facts which inform the assessment of the sentence is that of the judge. In the normal course, when the contrary is not suggested, that assessment will be based on the prosecution facts as disclosed by the statements. If, however, the offender seeks to challenge that account, the onus is on him to do so and to identify the areas of dispute in writing, first with the prosecution and then with the court (*R. v Cairns* [2013] EWCA Crim 467; [2013] 2 Cr. App. R. (S.) 73).

When an accused pleads guilty as set out here, the judge will consider whether that plea represents a proper plea on the basis of the facts set out in the papers. Where the judge is satisfied that the plea is properly grounded, sentencing may take place (*CPD* VII Sentencing: Determining the factual basis of sentencing B.1).

Where the prosecution advocate is considering whether to accept a plea to a lesser charge:

(1) he may invite the judge to approve the proposed course of action, in which circumstances, the advocate must abide by the judge's decision; or
(2) if he does not invite the judge to approve the acceptance by the prosecution of a lesser charge, it is open to the judge to express his dissent with the course proposed and invite the advocate to reconsider the matter with those instructing him.

(*CPD* VII Sentencing: Determining the factual basis of sentencing B.3)

In any proceedings, where the judge is of the opinion that the course proposed by the advocate may lead to serious injustice, the proceedings may be adjourned to allow the following procedure to be followed:

(a) as a preliminary step, the prosecution advocate must discuss the judge's observations with the Chief Crown Prosecutor or the senior prosecutor of the relevant prosecuting authority, as appropriate, in an attempt to resolve the issue;
(b) where the issue remains unresolved, the DPP or the Director of the relevant prosecuting authority should be consulted; or
(c) in extreme circumstances the judge may decline to proceed with the case until the prosecuting authority has consulted with the Attorney General as may be appropriate.

(*CPD* VII Sentencing: Determining the factual basis of sentencing B.4)

Prior to entering a plea of guilty, an accused may seek a "Goodyear Indication" from the judge (see GOODYEAR INDICATION).

3. PLEA OF GUILTY ON AN AGREED BASIS OF PLEA

Principles

The prosecution may reach an agreement with an accused as to the factual basis on which the latter will plead guilty, often known as an "agreed basis of plea"; it is always subject to the approval of the judge who will consider whether it is fair and in the interests of justice. *R. v Underwood* [2004] EWCA Crim 2256; [2005] 1 Cr. App. R. 13 outlines the principles to be applied where the accused admits that he is guilty but disputes the basis of offending alleged by the prosecution. **37-004**

In such a case:

(1) the prosecutor may accept and agree the accused's account of the disputed facts or reject it in its entirety;
(2) if the prosecutor accepts the accused's basis of plea, he must ensure that the basis of plea is factually accurate and that it enables the judge to impose a sentence which appropriately reflects the justice of the case, it must not be agreed on a misleading or untrue set of facts and must take proper account of the victim's interests; in cases involving multiple accused, the bases of plea for each must be factually consistent with each other (*R. v Cairns* [2013] EWCA Crim 467; [2013] 2 Cr. App. R. (S.) 73);
(3) in resolving any disputed factual matters, the prosecutor must consider his primary duty to the court and must not agree with, or acquiesce, in an agreement which contains material factual disputes;

(4) if the prosecutor accepts the accused's basis of plea, it must be reduced to writing, be signed by the advocates for both sides, and made available to the judge prior to the prosecutor's opening;
(5) an agreed basis of plea which has been reached between the parties must not contain any matters which are in dispute;
(6) where the prosecutor lacks the evidence positively to dispute the accused's account, as where, e.g. the accused asserts a matter outside the knowledge of the prosecution, it does not mean that those assertions should be agreed; in such a case, the prosecutor should test the accused's evidence and submissions by requesting a *Newton* hearing (see 37-013);
(7) if an accused seeks to mitigate on the basis of assertions of fact outside the prosecutor's knowledge (for example as to his state of mind), the judge should be invited not to accept this version unless given on oath and tested in cross-examination by way of a *Newton* hearing (see 37-013); if evidence is not given in this way, then the judge may draw such inferences as he thinks fit from that fact (*R. v Cairns* [2013] EWCA Crim 467; [2013] 2 Cr. App. R. (S.) 73);
(8) if it is not possible for the parties to resolve a factual dispute when attempting to reach a plea agreement under this procedure, it is the responsibility of the prosecutor to consider whether the matter should proceed to trial, or to invite the judge to hold a *Newton* hearing as necessary; and
(9) where the prosecutor has not invited the judge to hold a *Newton* hearing, and the factual dispute between the prosecution and the defence is likely to have a material impact on sentence, and the defence does not invite the judge to hold a *Newton* hearing, the judge is entitled to reach his own conclusion on the facts of the evidence before him.

(*CPD* VII Sentencing: Determining the factual basis of sentencing B.6, 8)

A basis of plea should not normally set out matters of mitigation but there may be circumstances where it is convenient and sensible for the document outlining a basis to deal with facts closely aligned to the circumstances of the offending which amount to mitigation and which may need to be resolved prior to sentence. The resolution of these matters does not amount to a *Newton* hearing properly so defined and in so far as facts fall to be established the defence will have to discharge the civil burden in order to do so. The scope of the evidence required to resolve issues that are purely matters of mitigation is for the judge to determine.

(*CPD* VII Sentencing: Determining the factual basis of sentencing B.14)

Judge not bound by agreement

37-005 *R. v Underwood* makes it clear that, whether or not pleas have been "agreed", the judge is not bound by any such agreement and is entitled of his own motion to insist that any evidence relevant to the facts in dispute, or upon which the judge requires further evidence for whatever reason, should be called. Any view formed by the prosecutor on a proposed basis of plea is deemed to be conditional on the judge's acceptance of the basis of plea.

If the judge is minded not to accept the basis of plea in a case where that may affect sentence, he should say so. He is not entitled to reject an accused's basis of plea absent a *Newton* hearing unless he determines that the basis is manifestly false and as such does not merit examination by way of the calling of evidence or alternatively the accused declines the opportunity to engage in the process of the *Newton* hearing whether by giving evidence on his own behalf or otherwise.

(*CPD* VII Sentencing: Determining the factual basis of sentencing B.9, 10)

Procedure

Where the accused pleads guilty, but disputes the basis of offending alleged by the prosecutor, the following procedure should be followed: **37-006**

(1) the accused's basis of plea must be set out in writing, identifying what is in dispute and must be signed by the accused;
(2) the prosecution must respond in writing setting out their alternative contentions and indicating whether or not they submit that a *Newton* hearing is necessary;
(3) the judge may invite the parties to make representations about whether the dispute is material to sentence; and
(4) if the judge decides that it is a material dispute, he will invite such further representations or evidence as it may require and resolve the dispute in accordance with the principles set out in *R. v Newton* (1982) 77 Cr. App. R. 13.

(*CPD* VII Sentencing: Determining the factual basis of sentencing B.11)

Where the disputed issue arises from facts which are within the exclusive knowledge of the defendant and the defendant is willing to give evidence in support of his case, the defence advocate should be prepared to call the defendant. If the defendant is not willing to testify, and subject to any explanation which may be given, the judge may draw such inferences as appear appropriate.

(*CPD* VII Sentencing: Determining the factual basis of sentencing B.12)

The decision whether or not a *Newton* hearing is required is one for the judge.

Once the decision has been taken that there will be a *Newton* hearing, evidence is called by the parties in the usual way and the criminal burden and standard of proof applies. Whatever view has been taken by the prosecution, the prosecutor should not leave the questioning to the judge, but should assist the court by exploring the issues which the court wishes to have explored. The rules of evidence should be followed as during a trial, and the judge should direct himself appropriately as the tribunal of fact. Paragraphs 6–10 of *R. v Underwood* [2004] EWCA Crim 2256; [2005] 1 Cr. App. R. 13 provide additional guidance regarding the *Newton* hearing procedure.

(*CPD* VII Sentencing: Determining the factual basis of sentencing B.13)

The judge must always, if he does not accept the accused's version, inform him of that fact before proceeding to sentence, so that the accused may decide how to proceed (*R. v Lucien* [2009] EWCA Crim 2004; *The Times,* 13 July 2009).

The Attorney General has issued guidance for prosecutors regarding their duties when accepting pleas and during the sentencing exercise entitled Attorney General's Guidelines on the Acceptance of Pleas and the Prosecutor's Role in the Sentencing Exercise (30 November 2012).

4. Cases involving serious or complex fraud

General; definitions

This section applies when the prosecutor and the accused in a case involving al- **37-007** legations of serious or complex fraud have agreed a basis of plea and seek to make submissions regarding sentence.

Guidance for prosecutors regarding the operation of this procedure is set out in the Attorney General's Guidelines on Plea Discussions in Cases of Serious or Complex Fraud, in force from 5 May 2009.

Note that:

(1) "a plea agreement" here means a written basis of plea agreed between the prosecutor and the accused in accordance with the principles set out in *R. v Underwood* [2004] EWCA Crim 2256; [2005] 1 Cr. App. R. 13 supported by admissible documentary evidence or admissions under CJA 1967 s.10;
(2) "a sentencing submission" means sentencing submissions made jointly by the prosecutor and the defence as to the appropriate sentencing authorities and applicable sentencing range in the relevant sentencing guideline relating to the plea agreement; and
(3) "serious or complex fraud" includes, but is not limited to, allegations of fraud where two or more of the following are present:
   (a) the amount obtained, or intended to be obtained, exceeded £500,000;
   (b) there is a significant international dimension;
   (c) the case requires specialised knowledge of financial, commercial, fiscal or regulatory matters such as the operation of markets, banking systems, trusts or tax regimes;
   (d) the case involves allegations of fraudulent activity against numerous victims;
   (e) the case involves an allegation of substantial and significant fraud on a public body;
   (f) the case is likely to be of widespread public concern; or
   (g) the alleged misconduct endangered the economic well-being of the UK, e.g. by undermining confidence in financial markets.

(*CPD* VII Sentencing: Determining the factual basis of sentencing B.15–17)

Procedure

37-008 The procedure regarding agreed bases of plea outlined in 37-004–37-006, applies with equal rigour to the acceptance of pleas under this procedure. However, because under this procedure the parties will have been discussing the plea agreement and the charges from a much earlier stage, it is vital that the judge is fully informed of all relevant background to the discussions, the charges and the eventual basis of plea.

Where the accused:

(1) has not yet appeared before the Crown Court, the prosecutor must send full details of the plea agreement and sentencing submission(s) to the court, at least seven days in advance of the accused's first appearance;
(2) has already appeared before the Crown Court, the prosecutor must notify the court as soon as is reasonably practicable that a plea agreement and sentencing submissions under the Attorney General's Plea Discussion Guidelines are to be submitted. The court should set a date for the matter to be heard, and the prosecutor must send full details of the plea agreement

and sentencing submission(s) to the court as soon as practicable, or in accordance with the directions of the court.

(*CPD* VII Sentencing: Determining the factual basis of sentencing B.18–19)

Sufficiency of material

The provision of full details of the plea agreement requires sufficient information to be provided to allow the judge to understand the facts of the case and the history of the plea discussions, to assess whether the plea agreement is fair and in the interests of justice, and to decide the appropriate sentence. **37-009**

The material must include, but is not limited to:

(1) the plea agreement;
(2) the sentencing submission(s);
(3) all of the material provided by the prosecutor to the accused in the course of the plea discussions;
(4) relevant material provided by the accused, e.g. documents relating to personal mitigation; and
(5) the minutes of any meetings between the parties and any correspondence generated in the plea discussions.

The parties should be prepared to provide additional material at the request of the court.

The judge should at all times have regard to the:

(a) length of time that has elapsed since the date of the occurrence of the events giving rise to the plea discussions;
(b) the time taken to interview the accused; and
(c) the date of charge and the prospective trial date (if the matter were to proceed to trial),

so as to ensure that his consideration of the plea agreement and sentencing submissions does not cause any unnecessary further delay.

(*CPD* VII Sentencing: Determining the factual basis of sentencing B.20–21)

Status of plea agreement and joint sentencing submissions

Where a plea agreement and joint sentencing submissions are submitted, it remains entirely a matter for the judge how to decide how to deal with the case. He retains an absolute discretion to refuse to accept the plea agreement, and sentence otherwise than in accordance with the sentencing submissions made under the Attorney General's Plea Discussion Guidelines. **37-010**

Note that:

(1) sentencing submissions should draw the judge's attention to any applicable range in any relevant guideline, and to any ancillary orders that may be applicable; they should not include a specific sentence or agreed range other than the ranges set out in sentencing guidelines;
(2) prior to pleading guilty in accordance with the plea agreement the accused may apply to the judge for a *Goodyear* indication under the procedure set out in 37-012 and following; and
(3) in the event of the judge indicating a sentence or passing a sentence which

is not within the submissions made on sentencing, the plea agreement remains binding.

(*CPD* VII Sentencing: Determining the factual basis of sentencing B.22–25)

Accused not pleading guilty, or withdrawing plea

37-011 If the accused:

(1) does not plead guilty in accordance with the plea agreement; or
(2) having pleaded guilty in accordance with a plea agreement successfully applies to withdraw his plea under CrimPR 25.5, then:
   (a) the signed plea agreement may be treated as confession evidence, and may be used against him at a later stage in these or any other proceedings; and
   (b) any credit for a timely guilty plea may be lost.

The judge may, however, exercise his discretion under PACE 1984 s.78 to exclude any such evidence if it appears to him that, having regard to all the circumstances, including the circumstances in which the evidence was obtained, the admission of the evidence would have such an adverse effect on the fairness of the proceedings that the judge ought not to admit it.

Where an accused has failed to plead guilty in accordance with a plea agreement, e.g. in the circumstances set out here, the case is unlikely to be ready for trial immediately. The prosecution may have been commenced earlier than it otherwise would have been, in reliance upon the accused's agreement to plead guilty. This is likely to be a relevant consideration for the judge in deciding whether or not to grant an application to adjourn or stay the proceedings to allow the matter to be prepared for trial in accordance with the protocol on the *Control and Management of Heavy Fraud and other Complex Criminal Cases* (see CASE MANAGEMENT), or as required.

(*CPD* VII Sentencing: Determining the factual basis of sentencing B.26–27)

5. "GOODYEAR INDICATION"

Right to seek indication

37-012 Prior to pleading guilty by any of the routes set out in this chapter, it is open to an accused to request from the judge an indication of the maximum sentence likely to be imposed if a guilty plea is tendered at that stage in the proceedings, in accordance with the guidance in *R. v Goodyear* [2005] EWCA Crim 888; [2005] 2 Cr. App. R. 20; [2006] 1 Cr. App. R. (S.) 6 (see GOODYEAR INDICATION).

During the sentence indication process and during the actual sentencing hearing, the prosecution advocate is expected to assist the court in sentencing by providing, where appropriate, references to the relevant statutory powers of the court, relevant sentencing guidelines and authorities, and such assistance as the court is likely to require.

Whether to give such an indication is a matter for the discretion of the judge, to be exercised in accordance with the principles outlined in *Goodyear*. Such indications should normally not be given if there is a dispute as to the basis of plea unless the judge concludes that he can properly deal with the case without the need for a *Newton* hearing.

In cases where a dispute arises, the procedure in *R. v Underwood* should be followed prior to the court considering a sentencing indication further.

Following an indication of sentence, if an accused does not plead guilty, the indication will not bind the court (*CPD* VII Sentencing C: Indications of sentence: R. v Goodyear C.1).

6. Newton hearings

General

A *Newton* hearing (*R. v Newton* (1982) 77 Cr. App. R. 13) is the appropriate procedure by which a judge determines disputed issues of fact affecting sentence, where evidence of such facts was not called at a trial, or cannot be said to have been decided by a jury. **37-013**

The most common occasion for such a hearing is where, on a plea of guilty, there is a dispute as to the facts; it may also be an appropriate procedure after a jury trial, for the purpose of interpreting a jury's verdict (see 37-020).

Plea of guilty

Where an offender pleads guilty, the prosecution must state the facts in open court before sentence is passed. While he is not obliged to pass sentence on the least serious version of the facts (*R. v Solomon* (1984) 6 Cr. App. R. (S.) 120) the judge should give the offender the benefit of any doubt (see *R. v Stosiek* (1982) 4 Cr. App. R. (S.) 205). **37-014**

Unless a disputed fact is proved by the prosecution to the satisfaction of the judge, it ought not to count in passing sentence (*R. v Kerrigan* (1993) 14 Cr. App. R. (S.) 179). The judge will need to direct himself that the offender's account must be accepted unless it is proved to be untrue (*R. v Ahmed* (1984) 6 Cr. App. R. (S.) 391).

In *R. v Underwood* [2004] EWCA Crim 2256; [2005] 1 Cr. App. R. 13, the CACD re-stated the principles, and gave general guidance.

The court recognised three common scenarios, namely that the prosecutor might:

(1) accept and agree the offender's account of the disputed facts;
(2) reject the offender's version; or
(3) lack the evidence to dispute positively the offender's version.

Where there is a difference between the prosecution evidence and the factual basis on which the offender intends to plead guilty, responsibility for taking the initiative and alerting the prosecutor to the disputed areas rests with the defence. It will generally be sensible for the judge to agree to a request for a hearing when asked for one by any advocate, and not to indicate any provisional view formed on the papers.

Judge acting of his own motion

The judge is entitled, of his own motion, on a plea of guilty, to make known any concerns he may have about any matter revealed by the state of the evidence before him, and to insist on holding a *Newton* hearing to determine any disputed facts notwithstanding prior agreement between the prosecutor and the defence as to the facts (*R. v Beswick* [1996] 2 Cr. App. R. 427). **37-015**

Where appropriate, he may:

(1) decline to accept the plea, and in an appropriate case, direct trial by a jury;
(2) hear submissions, and then form his own view of the facts, in which case, if there is a substantial conflict, he is bound to accept the version given by the accused; or
(3) if he is not prepared to sentence on the accused's version, conduct a hearing, and after considering the evidence on both sides, if tendered, come to his own decision on the facts.

Where the judge considers the basis of the plea tendered by the accused to be "absurd or manifestly untenable" in the light of evidence given during a trial of a co-accused, he may resolve the issue against the accused without holding a hearing, provided he remains of the same view after hearing submissions from both sides, and gives a reasoned judgment (*R. v Taylor* [2006] EWCA Crim 3132; [2007] 2 Cr. App. R. (S.) 24).

The judge is not entitled to make findings of fact and pass sentence on a basis that is inconsistent with pleas to counts already approved by the court (see *R. v Yusuf* [2014] EWCA Crim 1586); particular care is needed in relation to a multi-count indictment involving one accused or an indictment involving a number of accused where there was joint enterprise. The judge, while reflecting the individual basis of pleas, must bear in mind the seriousness of the joint enterprise in which all were involved.

Where procedure inappropriate

37-016 There will be occasions when a *Newton* hearing will be inappropriate, as where:

(1) some issues, particularly where the accused denies committing a specific offence, will require a jury's verdict (see, e.g. *R. v Flack* [2013] EWCA Crim 115; [2013] 2 Cr. App. R. (S.) 56);
(2) if the difference between the two versions of fact is immaterial to sentence (in which event the accused's version must be adopted—*R. v Hall* (1984) 6 Cr. App. R. (S.) 321; *R. v Bent* (1986) 8 Cr. App. R. (S.) 19);
(3) the accused's account is manifestly false or wholly implausible—in such a case the judge is not obliged to hold a hearing (*R. v Hawkins* (1985) 7 Cr. App. R. (S.) 351; *R. v Bilinski* (1988) 86 Cr. App. R. (S.) 146; *R. v Walton* (1987) 9 Cr. App. R. (S.) 107; *R. v Mudd* (1988) 10 Cr. App. R. (S.) 22; *R. v Palmer* (1993) Cr. App. R. (S.) 123; cf. *R. v Satchell* [1996] 2 Cr. App. R. (S.) 258);
(4) the matters put forward by the accused do not contradict the prosecution case but constitute extraneous mitigation, where the judge is not bound to accept the truth of the matters put forward whether or not they are challenged by the prosecution (*R. v Broderick* (1994) 15 Cr. App. R. (S.) 46);
(5) it is sought to determine whether the accused has committed offences other than those to which he has pleaded guilty or has had taken into consideration (*R. v Huchison* (1972) 56 Cr. App. R. 307) or which were not included in the indictment (*R. v Eubank* [2001] EWCA Crim 891; [2002] 1 Cr. App. R. (S.) 4) and see *R. v Flack* [2013] EWCA Crim 115; [2013] 2 Cr. App. R. (S.) 56.

Matters of mitigation are not normally dealt with by way of a *Newton* hearing but it is always open to the judge to allow an offender to give evidence as to matters of mitigation (*R. v Underwood* [2004] EWCA Crim 2256; [2005] 1 Cr. App. R. 13).

Conduct of the hearing

After submissions, the judge must decide how to proceed; he is not bound by any agreement as to the plea and is entitled to insist that any evidence relevant to the facts in dispute be called. Whatever view may be formed by the prosecutor on any proposed basis of the plea is conditional on the judge agreeing to it (*R. v Underwood* [2004] EWCA Crim 2256; [2005] 1 Cr. App. R. 13, 37-014). **37-017**

The judge is entitled to expect the prosecuting advocate to assist him in reaching the true facts by testing the evidence and the prosecution is not bound by any agreement reached with the other side, which is merely conditional until it receives the judge's approval.

A decision to hold a hearing does not give rise to a ground for the offender to change his plea. Special provisions apply to committals for sentence (see 37-019).

Where necessary:

(1) relevant evidence should be called by the prosecution and by the defence (particularly where the issue arises from facts which are within the offender's exclusive knowledge);
(2) where the offender does not give evidence, then, subject to any explanation offered, the judge may draw such inference as he sees fit;
(3) the judge is entitled to take into account evidence which he has heard in the separate trials of co-accused (*R. v Smith* (1988) 87 Cr. App. R. 393) but should bear in mind that that evidence was not the subject of cross-examination by the accused who pleaded guilty (*R. v Winter* [1997] 1 Cr. App. R. (S.) 331 and *R. v Dudley* [2011] EWCA Crim 2805; [2012] 2 Cr. App. R. (S.) 15);
(4) the judge is not obliged to accept the version given by the accused and indeed he may draw adverse inferences from his conduct (*R. v Ghandi* (1986) 8 Cr. App. R. (S.) 391); and
(5) in coming to his decision, he may have regard to the accused's previous convictions (*R. v Walton* (1987) 9 Cr. App. R. (S.) 107).

The judge may reject the evidence called by the prosecution or by the accused or his witnesses, even if the prosecution has not called contradictory evidence; but his reasons should be explained in a judgment (*R. v Underwood* [2004] EWCA Crim 2256; [2005] 1 Cr. App. R. 13). Where the hearing involves the assessment of identification evidence, the judge must direct himself in accordance with the Turnbull guidelines. The criminal burden and standard of proof apply (*R. v Ahmed* (1984) 80 Cr. App. R. 295).

At the conclusion of any such hearing, in order to meet the requirements of the accused and the wider public, the judge should provide a reasoned decision as to his findings of fact and thereafter, following mitigation, proceed to sentence (*R. v Cairns* [2013] EWCA Crim 467; [2013] 2 Cr. App. R. (S.) 73).

Effect on credit for guilty plea

If: **37-018**

(1) the issues at the hearing are resolved entirely in the offender's favour, credit for his guilty plea should not be reduced;

(2) the offender is disbelieved, having required prosecution witnesses to be called (see, e.g. *R. v Stevens* (1986) 8 Cr. App. R. (S.) 297), or if he shows no insight into the consequences of his offence and no genuine remorse, the discount may be reduced.

There may be exceptional circumstances in which the entitlement to credit for his plea may be entirely dissipated as a result of a hearing, and in such a case the judge should explain why (*R. v Underwood* [2004] EWCA Crim 2256; [2005] 1 Cr. App. R. 13). He is entitled to withhold the full credit he might otherwise have given for a plea of guilty where the offender insists on a hearing and the victim of a sexual assault is compelled to give evidence (*R. v Stevens* (1986) 8 Cr. App. R. (S.) 297), but it is wrong for him to give the offender no credit at all for his plea (*R. v Hassall* [2000] 1 Cr. App. R. (S.) 67).

Even where the evidence against the offender is overwhelming, the accused should still be given credit for his early plea of guilty unless, in all the circumstances, the interests of justice do not require it (*R. v Wilson* [2012] EWCA Crim 386; [2012] 2 Cr. App. R. (S.) 77).

Committals for sentence

37-019 While a judge at the Crown Court has jurisdiction to hold a *Newton* hearing in the case of an offender committed for sentence, where it is in the interest of fairness and justice to do so, he should not necessarily accede to an application to do so in a case where it is apparent that the magistrates have already conducted such a hearing and made clear findings of fact as part of the decision-making process with regard to committing the offender for sentence.

The matter is one for the discretion of the judge, in the proper exercise of which he must be fully mindful of his obligation to carry out a proper inquiry into the circumstances of the case.

In the ordinary way, he ought not to exercise his discretion in favour of allowing an offender to reopen the magistrates' findings of fact unless the offender is able to point to some significant development or matter, such as the discovery of important further evidence having occurred since the lower court reached its decision on the facts (*Gillan v DPP* [2007] EWHC (Admin) 380; [2007] 2 Cr. App. R. 12).

7. INTERPRETING THE JURY'S VERDICT

37-020 The jury is not concerned with what may be described as the aggravating or mitigating circumstances which will be important in the event of a conviction, in relation to sentence. Only in very rare circumstances should the jury be asked questions supplementary to the verdict (one example being whether manslaughter has been proved as an involuntary act, by reason of diminished responsibility or because of loss of control).

After conviction following a trial, the judge is bound to honour the verdicts of the jury but, provided he does so, is entitled to form his own view of the facts in the light of the evidence. This is so even if the jury express an opinion on a matter going only to sentence: see *R. v Mills* [2003] EWCA Crim 2397; [2004] 1 Cr. App. R. (S.) 57. He has to determine the gravity of the offending and is both entitled and required to reach his own assessment of the facts, deciding what evidence to accept and what to reject. The conclusions must be clear and unambiguous not least so that both the offender and the wider public will know the facts which have formed the basis for the sentencing exercise.

They also inform the CACD should the offender seek to appeal the sentence as wrong in principle or manifestly excessive, or the Attorney General seeks to refer it as unduly lenient (*R. v Cairns* [2013] EWCA Crim 467; [2013] 2 Cr. App. R. (S.) 73).

If an issue not relevant to guilt but relevant to sentence has not been canvassed in the trial, a *Newton* hearing after verdict may be necessary (*R. v Finch* (1993) 14 Cr. App. R. (S.) 226 where "there was no evidence one way or the other"); and see *R. v Cairns* [2013] EWCA Crim 467; [2013] 2 Cr. App. R. (S.) 73.

Where a *Newton* hearing is held after a jury trial, for the purpose of interpreting a jury's verdict (see 37-013), the following points should be noted:

(1) if the verdict can be explained only on one view of the facts, the judge must adopt that view as the basis for sentence;
(2) if more than one view of the facts is consistent with the verdict the judge may form his own view in the light of the evidence given; and
(3) if the verdict leaves open an important issue which may affect sentence, the judge must decide where the truth lies.

(*R. v Solomon* (1984) 6 Cr. App. R. (S.) 120; *R. v McGlade* (1991) 12 Cr. App. R. (S.) 105; *R. v Martin* [2002] 2 Cr. App. R. (S.) 34; *R. v Mills* [2003] EWCA Crim 2397; [2004] 1 Cr. App. R. (S.) 57).

As to special verdicts, in *R. v Hopkinson* [2013] EWCA Crim 795; [2014] 1 Cr. App. R. 3, the CACD said that there will be occasions (very rare) where in the context of a trial for murder, where the alternative defences include, for example, diminished responsibility, loss of control, and lack of the necessary intent (see *R. v Larkin* (1944) 29 Cr. App. R. 18; *R. v Matheson* (1958) 42 Cr. App. R.145; *R. v Frankum* (1983) 5 Cr. App. R (S.) 259; *R. v Jones*, *The Times,* 17 February 1999) the judge may think it advisable to seek a special verdict, but even in the context of a murder trial a special verdict should continue to be a rarity (and see *R. v Bourne* (1952) 36 Cr. App. R. 125).

Without suggesting that the CACD were entitled to abolish the special verdict procedure, the court offered a shorthand way of suggesting that it did not expect special verdicts to be sought in other cases; and, at least, that the taking of special verdicts has fallen into virtual desuetude.

In particular it is inappropriate for a special verdict to be sought in the context of DVA 2004 s.5.

8. Change of plea

A plea of guilty may be changed, with leave of the judge, up to the moment of sentence (*R. (on the application of an infant) v Manchester City Recorder* [1969] 3 All E.R. 230) but not thereafter (*R. v Evans* [2011] EWCA Crim 2842; [2012] 2 Cr. App. R. 22). **37-021**

Where a party wants the court to vacate a guilty plea, he must (CrimPR 38.5):

(1) apply in writing, as soon as practicable after becoming aware of the grounds for doing so, and in any event, before the final disposal of the case, by sentence; or
(2) serve the application on the court officer, and on the prosecutor; and
(3) unless the judge otherwise directs, the application must:

(a) explain why it would be unjust for the guilty plea to remain unchanged;
(b) indicate what, if any, evidence the applicant wishes to call;
(c) identify any proposed witness; and
(d) indicate whether legal professional privilege is waived, specifying any material name and date.

Where an application to change plea is likely to involve a conflict between the accused and his former counsel it is good practice for the application to be heard by a judge from a different court centre (*R. v Oldfield* [2011] EWCA Crim 2910; [2012] 1 Cr. App. R. 17).

38. IMPRISONMENT

Quick Guide

1. General

Introduction

38-001 Immediate custody is the most commonly used disposal in relation to persons convicted of indictable offences at the Crown Court.

Before a sentence of imprisonment may be imposed:

(1) the offence must be punishable at common law or by statute by imprisonment;
(2) the offender must be aged 21 or over;
(3) the circumstances of the offence must have crossed the threshold for custodial offences; and
(4) the offender must have been represented, or have had the opportunity to be represented, between conviction and sentence (see generally DEALING WITH AN OFFENDER).

As to suspended sentences of imprisonment, see SUSPENDED SENTENCE ORDERS. As to custodial sentences for young offenders, see DETENTION OF YOUNG OFFENDERS. As to imprisonment and extended sentences for public protection, see DANGEROUS OFFENDERS; PROTECTIVE SENTENCES. As to life sentences, see LIFE SENTENCES.

As to the nature of the term, see 38-003; as to the length, see 38-007 and following.

Custody threshold

38-002 Apart from those cases where the sentence is fixed by law, or where required minimum sentences fall to be imposed on certain offenders by statute, an offender may not be sentenced to a term of imprisonment unless the judge is of the opinion that:

(1) the offence; or

(2) the combination of the offence and one or more offences "associated" with it,

is "so serious" that neither a fine alone, nor a community sentence, can be justified for it.

Nevertheless, nothing prevents the judge from passing a custodial sentence on an offender who fails to express his willingness to comply with a requirement which it is proposed to include in a community order, and which requires an expression of such willingness; or the definition of "imprisonment" in SA 2020 s.222 (interpretation), excludes a committal for contempt of court or any kindred offence.

As to offenders under 21, see CrimPR 38.1(1) and (4) and DETENTION OF YOUNG OFFENDERS. As to the need for a pre-sentence or medical report, and for legal representation, see DEALING WITH AN OFFENDER.

From 1 December 2020 the sentencing provisions of CJA 2003 (as modified by LASPOA 2012) or the PCC(S)A 2000 are repealed and replaced by various sections and schedules of SA 2020. The Sentencing Code makes no major substantive changes to the types of sentences or the ancillary provisions, it is simply a consolidation of existing sentencing procedure law. The SA 2020 does remedy some of the issues between those over 18 and under 21. References to the SA 2020 are set out in this chapter.

2. NATURE OF TERM

Date of commission of offence

38-003 The nature of a determinate sentence of imprisonment will depend crucially on whether the offence for which it is to be imposed was *committed before, or on or after, 4 April 2005*; in relation to life sentences (see LIFE SENTENCES) and mandatory minimum sentences (38-036) other dates may be crucial.

Categories of sentence

38-004 A sentence of imprisonment may be:

(1) a normal determinate sentence;
(2) a sentence fixed by law;
(3) a life sentence (see LIFE SENTENCES);
(4) a required minimum sentence under specified statutory provisions (see 38-027); or
(5) a public protection sentence under SA 2020 (see DANGEROUS OFFENDERS; PROTECTIVE SENTENCES).

As to the restricted power under PCC(S)A 2000 s.116 to return to prison a prisoner on licence, see 38-043. The power of a court to order that a defendant serve part of an earlier sentence when convicted of an offence committed after release from that sentence was not reproduced in the CJA 2003 and is not in the SA 2020.

A number of general topics relating to sentences of imprisonment are dealt with in DEALING WITH AN OFFENDER.

Length of term served relevance to sentence

38-005 CJA 1991 ss.32–39 abolished remission, and replaced it with a system under which all prisoners released before the end of their sentences remained at risk of having their sentences re-activated if they offended again. It replaced parole with a system of discretionary early release for those serving four years or more. It restricted an offender's liberty throughout the entire term imposed by the court to ensure that:

(1) at least half of that term was served in custody; and
(2) offenders sentenced to 12 months or more were supervised by a probation officer, whether or not they were granted parole.

CJA 2003 repealed CJA 1991 ss.32–51 and substituted for the division into sentences of less and those of more than four years, a division between those of less than 12 months, and those of 12 months and over.

With the coming into effect of CJA 2003 s.243A (LASPOA 2012 s.111) the former provisions, in CJA 1991, are, in effect, restored. Various changes to the release dates have taken place in 2019, 2020 (particularly where the offence has a terrorist connection) and 2022. (CTA 2008 s.30 and SA 2020 s.69.) In many cases now where an offender is sentenced to a lengthy custodial term, they will serve two-thirds rather than one-half.

Thus:

(a) a fixed-term prisoner sentenced to a determinate sentence of imprisonment or detention in a YOI for a term of less than seven years unless the offence is listed in CJA 2003 Sch.19ZA qualifies for release automatically after half his sentence has been served and serves the remainder of his sentence in the community on licence; he is liable to recall to custody throughout the whole period. For those sentences less than two years, then the prisoner will be subject to post-sentence supervision for 12 months (CJA 2003 s.256AA(4));
(b) a fixed-term prisoner sentenced to a term of imprisonment or detention in a YOI of seven years or more unless the offence is listed in SA 2020 Sch.15 with a maximum sentence of life imprisonment or listed in CJA 2003 Sch.19ZA is entitled to be released at the end of one-half of his sentence has been served and serves the remainder of his sentence in the community on licence; he is liable to recall to custody throughout the whole period;
(c) a fixed-term prisoner sentenced to a determinate sentence of imprisonment or detention in a YOI for a term of seven years or more where the offence is listed in SA 2020 Sch.15 with a maximum sentence of life imprisonment but is not listed in CJA 2003 Sch.19ZA is entitled to be released after two-thirds of his sentence has been served and serves the remainder of his sentence in the community on licence; he is liable to recall to custody throughout the whole period;
(d) a fixed-term prisoner sentenced to a sentence of imprisonment or detention in a YOI of any length where the offence is listed in CJA 2003 Sch.19ZA is eligible for release after serving two-thirds of the custodial term and entitled to be released at the expiry of the custodial term. If released he will serve the remainder of his sentence in the community on licence and liable to recall to custody throughout the whole period;
(e) for a prisoner of particular concern under SA 2020 ss.265 or 278 where the offence is not listed in CJA 2003 Sch.19ZA, then he is eligible for release after one-half of the custodial term and entitled to release at the expiry of the custodial term. If released he will serve the remainder of his sentence in the community on licence and liable to recall to custody throughout the whole period. There will be extended licence or post-sentence supervision

for 12 months after the expiry of the custodial term (SA 2020 ss.265(2)(b) or 278(2)(b));

(f) for a prisoner of particular concern under SA 2020 ss.265 or 278 where the offence is listed in CJA 2003 Sch.19ZA, then he is eligible for release after two-thirds of the custodial term and entitled to release at the expiry of the custodial term. If released he will serve the remainder of his sentence in the community on licence and liable to recall to custody throughout the whole period. There will be extended licence or post-sentence supervision for 12 months after the expiry of the custodial term (SA 2020 ss.265(2)(b) or 278(2)(b));

(g) for a prisoner subject to an extended sentence of imprisonment or detention in a YOI where the offence is not listed in CJA 2003 Sch.19ZA, then he is eligible for release after two-thirds of the custodial term has been served and entitled to release after expiry of the custodial term. If released he will serve the remainder of his sentence in the community on licence and liable to recall to custody throughout the whole period. There will be extended licence period as set out by the court at sentence of up to five or eight years but not less than one year (SA 2020 ss.268(4) or 281(4));

(h) for a prisoner subject to an extended sentence of imprisonment or detention in a YOI where the offence is listed in CJA 2003 Sch.19ZA, then he is eligible for release after two-thirds of the custodial term has been served and entitled to release after expiry of the custodial term. If released he will serve the remainder of his sentence in the community on licence and liable to recall to custody throughout the whole period. There will be extended licence period as set out by the court at sentence of up to five or eight years but not less than one year (SA 2020 ss.268(4) or 281(4)); and

(i) with effect from 28 June 2022, a new s.244ZA is inserted into the CJA Act 2003 by the Police, Crime, Sentencing and Courts Act 2022 s.130(1) and (3) so that for sentences imposed on or after 28 June 2022 of at least four years imposed for certain serious violent and sexual offences; and sentences of detention of at least seven years imposed for certain violent and sexual offences, the offender must serve two-thirds before release.

(CJA 2003 ss.243A, 244; ORA 2014 s.1)

For the special rules governing life sentences, see LIFE SENTENCES.

The Offender Rehabilitation Act 2014 (ORA), which came into force in early 2015 imposes a mandatory period of supervision and support for a full period of 12 months for all offenders given sentences of imprisonment or detention in a young offender institution of between 2 days and 24 months where the offences the offender is being dealt with occurred on or after 1 February 2015. The 12-month supervision period will include a "rehabilitation activity requirement" which, as well as standard conditions, may include participating in specified activities, and undergoing drug testing. Breach of one or more of these requirements will require the offender to be returned to court for the breach to be dealt with. The court will be able to impose custody of up to 14 days, or a fine, or make a "supervision default order" upon breach. If the breach amounts to a new offence that will of course be dealt with separately. The existing "rehabilitation requirement" and "activity requirement" will be abolished.

Commencement of sentence

Any sentence imposed, or other order made, by the Crown Court when dealing with an offender, takes effect from the beginning of the day on which it is imposed unless the judge otherwise directs (SA 2020 s.384). **38-006**

Note that:

(1) a sentence, or other order, varied under SCA 1981 s.47 (see VARIATION OF SENTENCE) takes effect from the beginning of the day on which it was originally imposed unless the judge otherwise directs; but
(2) the judge has no power under that section, or otherwise, to antedate the commencement of the sentence (*R. v Gilbert* (1974) 60 Cr. App. R. 220; *R. v Whitfield* [2001] EWCA Crim 3043; [2002] 2 Cr. App. R. (S.) 44).

3. LENGTH OF TERM; DISCRETIONARY SENTENCES

The general rule

Where a custodial sentence is appropriate: **38-007**

(1) it is a general principle that the offender may be sentenced only in respect of offences:
  (a) proved against him, whether by a plea of guilty, or by a guilty verdict on indictment; or
  (b) admitted by him, where he asks for them to be taken into consideration on sentence (see DEALING WITH AN OFFENDER; see also *R. v Canavan* [1998] 1 Cr. App. R. 79 as to specimen or sample counts);
(2) apart from a sentence which is:
  (a) fixed by law; or
  (b) falls to be imposed under SA 2020 ss.313 and 314 (required minimum sentences for certain repeat offences), SA 2020 ss.312, 315, 316 and 318 (minimum sentence for offence of threatening with offensive weapon in public), SA 2020 s.311 and Sch.20 (minimum sentence for certain firearms offences), SA 2020 ss.312, 315, 316 and 318 (minimum sentence for offence of threatening with article with blade or point or offensive weapon), SA 2020 ss.266–268 or ss.279–282 (sentences for public protection) or SA 2020 s.311 and Sch.20 (minimum sentences for using a person to mind a weapon) the term must be *commensurate with the seriousness* of the offence; but
(3) in the case of a "violent" or "sexual" offence, the sentence may be extended as to its licence period under SA 2020 ss.266–268 or ss.279–282 (see DANGEROUS OFFENDERS; PROTECTIVE SENTENCES).

In relation to (2) above, note that a sentence falls to be imposed under:

(i) SA 2020 s.312 (offensive weapons) (see 38-040); and
(ii) SA 2020 s.315 (bladed articles) (see 38-041).

(CJA 2003 s.305(4) (Interpretation of Pt 12); LASPOA 2012 Sch.26 para.22)

The judge *must* pay due regard to the statutory maxima, the regularly expressed views of the CACD, and the Sentencing Guidelines Council (SGC) established under CJA 2003 s.167 or the Sentencing Council for England and Wales (SCEW).

Where a judge passes a custodial sentence other than one of those mentioned in

(2) above, *the custodial term must be for the shortest term* (not exceeding the permitted maximum) that in the judge's opinion is commensurate with the seriousness of the offence, or the combination of the offence and one or more offences associated with it (SA 2020 s.231).

4. CONCURRENT OR CONSECUTIVE

General

38-008 There is no inflexible rule governing whether custodial sentences should be concurrent or consecutive. The overriding principle is that the overall sentence must be just and proportionate. The SCEW issued guidelines "Offences Taken Into Consideration and Totality" with effect from 11 June 2012 setting out the general principles and the general approach.

In passing sentence, the judge:

(1) must pass a separate sentence on each count of the indictment; it is wrong to impose a comprehensive sentence covering all of them together;
(2) has a general power to order that sentences run concurrently (*R. v Torr* (1966) 50 Cr. App. R. 73);
(3) may, subject to SA 2020 s.225 as to prisoners released on licence (38-010), order one term to commence at the expiration of a previous sentence imposed by any court in England and Wales, and this is so whether the sentences are passed in respect of separate counts contained in one indictment, or of counts in different indictments (*R. v Greenberg* (1944) 29 Cr. App. R. 51); and
(4) ought not to order one sentence to run *partly* concurrently and *partly* consecutively to another (*R. v Salmon* [2002] EWCA Crim 2088; [2003] 1 Cr. App. R. (S.) 85).

In relation to the release of prisoners, and their eligibility for home detention curfew, administrative problems may arise where one or more of the component sentences fall to be treated under the release provisions of CJA 1991 and one or more under the provisions of CJA 2003. The problem is highlighted in a note from the Senior Presiding Judge of 16 March 2009. See also *R. v Round* [2009] EWCA Crim 2667; [2010] 2 Cr. App. R. (S.) 94.

Special considerations apply to the combination of fixed term and extended sentences, see DANGEROUS OFFENDERS; PROTECTIVE SENTENCES.

R. v Ralphs [2010] 2 Cr. App. R. (S.) 30

38-009 The principles which ordinarily govern the imposition of consecutive terms of imprisonment, are conveniently summarised in *Attorney General's Reference (No.57 of 2009)*, also known as *R. v Ralphs* [2009] EWCA Crim 2555; [2010] 2 Cr. App. R. (S.) 30 and are these:

(1) consecutive terms should not normally be imposed for offences which arise out of the same incident or transaction (*R. v Noble* [2002] EWCA Crim 1713; [2003] 1 Cr. App. R. (S.) 65 considered);
(2) deciding whether the criminality could be regarded as a single incident is difficult and the fact that the offences were committed simultaneously is not necessarily conclusive (*R. v Fletcher* [2002] EWCA Crim 834; [2002] 2 Cr. App. R. (S.) 127 considered); and

(3) consecutive sentences may be justifiably imposed:
  (a) where distinct offences are committed in circumstances where they can properly be said to increase criminality; or
  (b) for offences committed on the same occasion when there are exceptional circumstances justifying a departure from the usual practice (*R. v Wheatley* (1983) 5 Cr. App. R. (S.) 417 considered).

The fact that offences were committed within a short, even a very short, span of time of each other is not necessarily conclusive. A close examination of the facts may reveal that distinct offences occurred, each independent of the other, and each calling for distinct punishment to reflect the offender's criminality where each of the two offences represented the most serious harm and high culpability (*R. v H* [2011] EWCA Crim 2753: [2012] 2 Cr. App. R. (S.) 21).

It is inappropriate for consecutive terms of imprisonment to be imposed as a way of compensating for what the judge believes to be an inadequacy in his sentencing powers (*R. v H*).

Restriction on consecutive sentences for released prisoners

Questions of release on licence and recall to prison are within the jurisdiction of the executive. The power of a judge of the Crown Court to return a prisoner on licence to custody under PCC(S)A 2000 s.116 was abolished by CJA 2003, though partially saved in respect of certain offences, (see 38-043) by SI 2005/950. **38-010**

A judge sentencing a person to a term of imprisonment may not order or direct that the term is to commence on the expiry of any other sentence of imprisonment from which he has been released under SA 2020 s.225.

"Sentence of imprisonment" here includes a sentence of imprisonment, detention in a YOI, or a sentence of detention under SA 2020 ss.250 and 254, CJA 2003 ss.226B or 228, PCC(S)A 2000 s.91, Children and Young Persons Act 1933 s.53(3). (SA 2020 s.225(3).)

Nor may the judge evade this prohibition by increasing a new concurrent sentence beyond what the offence merits, in order to ensure a sensible increase in the overall term (*R. v Costello* [2010] EWCA Crim 371; [2010] 2 Cr. App. R. (S.) 94 where the history and complexity of the section are considered).

General points; approach to sentence

A number of general points may be made in respect of consecutive sentences: **38-011**

(1) consecutive sentences should not ordinarily be imposed:
  (a) in respect of offences which arise out of a single incident (*R. v Jones* (1980) 2 Cr. App. R. (S.) 152) though there may be exceptional circumstances (see *R. v Wheatley* (1983) 5 Cr. App. R. (S.) 417; *R. v Dillon* (1983) 5 Cr. App. R. (S.) 439; *R. v Lawrence* (1989) 11 Cr. App. R. (S.) 580; *R. v Ralphs* [2009] EWCA Crim 2555; [2010] 2 Cr. App. R. (S.) 30); or
  (b) where offences form part of a series committed against the same victim over a short period of time;
(2) where there are convictions on two or more indictments, it is bad practice to make part of a sentence on the second indictment consecutive to a sentence on the first (*R. v Mills* (1969) 53 Cr. App. R. 294); and
(3) where a very long sentence is passed, no useful purpose is generally served

by imposing a short consecutive sentence for a different offence (*R. v Smith* (1981) 3 Cr. App. R. (S.) 201).

In approaching sentence, the judge should (Sentencing Council Guideline on Offences Taken into Consideration and Totality 2012):

(i) consider the sentence for each individual offence referring to the relevant sentencing guidelines;
(ii) determine whether the case calls for concurrent or consecutive sentences;
(iii) in the case of consecutive sentences, test the overall sentence(s) against the requirement that they be just and proportionate (the totality principle, see 38-016); and
(iv) consider whether the structure of the sentence is such as will best be understood by all concerned with it.

Spelling it out

38-012 Where the judge passes on an offender more than one term of imprisonment, he should state in the presence of the offender whether the terms are to be concurrent or consecutive. Should this not be done, the court clerk should ask the court, before the defendant leaves court, to do so.

If the offender is, at the time of sentence, already serving two or more consecutive terms of imprisonment and the judge intends to increase the total period of imprisonment, he should use the expression "consecutive to the total period of imprisonment to which you are already subject" rather than "at the expiration of the term of imprisonment you are now serving", as the offender may not then be serving the last of the terms to which he is already subject (*CPD* VII Sentencing E: Concurrent and Consecutive Sentences 1–3).

The SCEW definitive guideline on Totality should be consulted. Under CorJA 2009 s.125(1), for offences committed after 11 June 2012, that guideline must be followed unless it would be contrary to the interests of justice to do so.

Concurrent sentences

38-013 Concurrent offences will ordinarily be appropriate where:

(1) offences arise out of the same incident or facts; or
(2) there is a series of offences of the same or a similar kind, especially when committed against the same person.

The Totality Guidelines give examples.

Examples of (1) cited include:

- A single incident of dangerous driving resulting in injuries to multiple victims (*R. v Lawrence* (1989) 11 Cr. App. R. (S.) 580).
- Robbery with a weapon where the weapon offence is ancillary to the robbery and is not distinct and independent of it (*R. v Poulton* [2002] EWCA Crim 2487; [2003] 1 Cr. App. R. (S.) 116; *Attorney General's Reference (Nos 21 and 22 of 2003)* [2003] EWCA Crim 3089; [2004] 2 Cr. App. R. (S.) 13).
- Fraud and associated forgery.
- Separate counts of supplying different kinds of drugs of the same class as part of the same transaction.

Examples of (2) cited include:

- Repetitive small thefts from the same person, such as by an employee.
- Repetitive benefit frauds of the same kind committed in each payment period.

Where concurrent sentences are imposed the sentence should reflect the overall criminality involved. The sentence should be appropriately aggravated by the presence of the associated offences.

Examples cited include:

- A single incident of dangerous driving resulting in injuries to multiple victims and there are separate counts relating to each victim—the sentences should ordinarily be concurrent, but each sentence should be aggravated to take account of the harm caused.
- Repetitive offences of fraud or theft, the subject of separate counts should be properly considered in relation to the total amount obtained and the period over which the offending took place—the sentences should ordinarily be concurrent, each one reflecting the overall seriousness.
- Robbery with a weapon where the weapon offence is ancillary to the robbery and is not distinct and independent of it—the principal sentence for the robbery should properly reflect the presence of the weapon.

In this last example the judge must avoid double-counting and may consider it preferable for the possession of the weapon offence to run concurrently to avoid the appearance of under-sentencing in respect of the robbery (*Attorney General's Reference (Nos 21 and 22 of 2003)* [2003] EWCA Crim 3089; [2004] 2 Cr. App. R. (S.) 13).

Consecutive sentences

Consecutive sentences will ordinarily be appropriate where: **38-014**

(1) offences arise out of unrelated facts or incidents;
(2) offences are of the same or a similar kind, but the overall criminality will not sufficiently be reflected by concurrent sentences; or
(3) one or more offences qualifies for a statutory minimum sentence and concurrent sentences would improperly undermine the minimum.

Examples of (1) cited include:

- Theft on one occasion and an assault against a different victim on a separate occasion.
- An attempt to pervert the course of justice in respect of another offence charged (*Attorney General's Reference (No.1 of 1990)* [1990] 12 Cr. App. R. (S.) 245).
- A Bail Act offence (*R. v Millen* (1980) 2 Cr. App. R. (S.) 357).
- Any offence committed within the prison context.
- Offences that are unrelated because whilst they were simultaneously, they are distinct and there is an aggravated element that requires separate recognition, as:
  - — an assault on a constable committed to try and evade arrest for an offence also charged (*R. v Kastercum* (1972) 56 Cr. App. R. 298);
  - — a conviction for drug dealing and possession of a firearm where the firearm offence is not an intrinsic part of the drugs offence but requires separate recognition (*R. v Poulton* [2002] EWCA Crim 2487; [2003]

1 Cr. App. R. (S.) 116; *Attorney General's Reference (Nos 21 and 22 of 2003)* [2003] EWCA Crim 3089, [2004] 2 Cr. App. R. (S.) 13);

— threats to kill in the context of an indecent assault can be distinguished as a separate element (*R. v Fletcher* [2002] EWCA Crim 834; [2002] 2 Cr. App. R. (S.) 127).

Examples of (2) cited include:

- offences committed against different persons, such as repeated thefts involving attacks on several different shop assistants (*R. v Jamieson* [2008] EWCA Crim 2761; [2009] 2 Cr. App. R. (S.) 26);
- offences of domestic violence or sexual offences committed against the same individual.

An example of (3) is *R. v Raza* [2009] EWCA Crim 1413; [2010] 1 Cr. App. R. (S.) 56.

As to (c) it should be noted that it is not permissible to impose consecutive sentences for offences committed at the same time in order to evade the statutory maximum penalty (*R. v Ralphs* [2009] EWCA Crim 2555; [2010] 2 Cr. App. R. (S.) 30).

Where consecutive sentences are passed the aggregate must be just and proportionate.

If it is not, the judge should consider how to achieve such a result by, e.g.:

(a) in the case of similar offences, or offences of a similar level of severity, whether:

(i) all of the offences might be reduced (with particular reference to the category ranges within sentencing guidelines) and imposed consecutively; or

(ii) despite their similarity, the most serious offence(s) can be identified and the other sentences can all be reduced proportionately (with particular reference to the category ranges within sentencing guidelines) and passed consecutively in order that the sentence for the lead offence can be clearly identified;

(b) in the case of two or more offences of differing levels of seriousness whether:

(i) some offences are of such low seriousness in the context of the most serious offence(s) that they can be recorded as "no separate penalty" (for example technical breaches, or minor RT offences not involving mandatory disqualification); or

(ii) some of the offences are of lesser seriousness and are unrelated to the most serious offence(s) that they may be ordered to run concurrently so that the sentence for the most serious offence(s) can be clearly identified.

In any event the sentence ought to be structured in a way that will be best understood by all concerned with it.

Offender already serving a sentence

38-015 Where a new sentence falls to be imposed on an offender already serving a determinate sentence, then:

(a) if the offence being dealt with was committed before the original sentence—

the judge must consider what the length of the sentence would have been if the offence(s) had all been dealt with at the same time, and ensure that totality is just and proportionate in all the circumstances;

(b) if the offence being dealt with was committed after the original offence—the sentence will generally be consecutive, the total sentence to be served being just and proportionate;

(c) where the offender commits an act of violence in prison, any reduction is likely to be minimal (*R. v Ali* [1998] 2 Cr. App. R. 123); and

(d) if the offender is serving a determinate sentence but has been released from custody, SA 2020 s.284 prohibits the passing of a consecutive sentence—the new sentence should take into account the aggravating factor that the offence was committed on licence, but must not be artificially inflated with a view to ensuring that the offender serves a period additional to the recall period; this must be so even if the new sentence will, in consequence, add nothing to the period actually served (*R. v Costello* [2010] EWCA Crim 371; [2010] 2 Cr. App. R. (S.) 94).

As to an offender subject to a suspended sentence order, see SUSPENDED SENTENCE ORDERS.

As to extended sentences, see DANGEROUS OFFENDERS; PROTECTIVE SENTENCES.

The totality principle

Wherever consecutive sentences are imposed, while there is nothing to prevent the aggregate from exceeding the maximum for any one of them (*R. v Blake* (1961) 45 Cr. App. R. 292) it is the final duty of the judge to ensure that: **38-016**

(1) when sentencing for more than one offence, the total sentence imposed:
  (a) reflects all the offending behaviour before him; and
  (b) is just and proportionate, whether the sentences are structured as concurrent or consecutive;

(2) that since it is usually impossible to arrive at a just and proportionate sentence for multiple offences merely by adding together notional single terms, he addresses the offending behaviour, together with the factors personal to the offender, as a whole. (See the SCEW Offences Taken Into Consideration and Totality Definitive Guideline.)

5. CREDIT OF REMAND PERIODS

In relation to determinate sentences of imprisonment and detention imposed after 3 December 2012: **38-017**

(1) time spent in custody on remand is now automatically credited (under s.240ZA) and does not require the judge's direction; but

(2) time remanded on bail with certain restrictive conditions counts towards time served, but does require the judge's order (CJA 2003 ss.240ZA, 240A).

The position under (2) arises where the accused is remanded on bail by a court in the course of, or in connection with proceedings for the offence, or for any related offence, and his bail was subject to a qualifying curfew condition, and an electronic monitoring condition ("the relevant conditions"—*R. v Barrett* [2009] EWCA Crim 2213; [2010] 1 Cr. App. R. (S.) 87).

In such a case, subject to s.240A (3A) and (3B) (see 38-019) the judge must direct that the credit period is to count as time served by the offender as part of his sentence (SA 2020 ss.325–327).

LASPOA 2012 states that a suspended sentence "is to be treated as a sentence when it takes effect" (CJA 2003 ss.263, 264, 264AA, 264B).

The history of the matter is considered in detail in *R. v Leacock* [2013] EWCA Crim 1994; [2014] 2 Cr. App. R. (S.) 12, where the CACD emphasised that it is the duty of the advocate to check the position carefully at the time; the CACD will not correct errors unless an application is promptly made.

Definitions

38-018 The following definitions need to be noted:

(1) "curfew requirement" means a requirement (however, described) to remain at one or more specified places for a specified number of hours in any given day (provided that the requirement was imposed by a court or the Secretary of State and arises as a result of the conviction);

(2) "electronic monitoring condition" means any electronic monitoring requirements imposed under BA 1976 s.3(6ZAA) for the purpose of securing the electronic monitoring of a person's compliance with a qualifying curfew condition; and

(3) "qualifying curfew condition" means a condition of bail which requires the person granted bail to remain at one or more specified places for a total of not less than nine hours in any given day.

(CJA 2003 s.240A)

The "credit period" defined

38-019 The credit period is calculated by taking the following steps.

Step 1

Add:

(a) the day on which the offender's bail was first subject to the relevant conditions (and for this purpose a condition is not prevented from being a relevant condition by the fact that it does not apply for the whole of the day in question); and

(b) the number of other days on which the offender's bail was subject to those conditions (but exclude the last of those days if the offender spends the last part of it in custody).

Step 2

Deduct the number of days on which the offender, whilst on bail subject to the relevant conditions, was also:

(a) subject to any requirement imposed for the purpose of securing the electronic monitoring of the offender's compliance with a curfew requirement; or

(b) on temporary release under rules made under s.47 of the Prison Act 1952.

Step 3

From the remainder, deduct the number of days during that remainder on which the offender has broken either or both of the relevant conditions.

Step 4

Divide the result by two (CJA 2003 s.240A(3)).

Step 5

If necessary, round up to the nearest whole number.
Note that a day of the credit period counts as time served:

(a) in relation to only one sentence; and
(b) only once in relation to that sentence.

A day of the credit period is not to count as time served as part of any period of 28 days served by the offender before automatic release (see s.255B(1)).
(SA 2020 s.325, CJA 2003 s.240A(3A))

Although a judge might, in his discretion, give a modest period of credit for time spent on bail subject to such a condition before 3 November 2008, or time spent on bail before or after that date subject to conditions falling just short of the qualifying curfew (see *R. v Sherif* [2009] EWCA Crim 2653; [2009] 2 Cr. App. R. (S.) 235) no reduction in sentence should normally be given for a period spent on night-time curfew (*R. v Monaghan* [2009] EWCA Crim 2699; [2010] 2 Cr. App. R. (S.) 50).

Spelling it out

Where the judge gives such a direction, he must state, in open court: **38-020**

(a) the number of days on which the offender was subject to the "relevant conditions"; and
(b) the number of days (if any) which he deducted under Steps 2 and 3.

(CJA 2003 s.240A(8), (9) and (10) relating to cases in which the judge decides not to give a direction, are omitted by LASPOA 2012 s.109(5).)

Where the judge is minded to give a direction for such number of days less than that for which the offender was remanded, he ought to raise the matter with the defence advocate, who may wish to make representations (*R. v Barber* [2006] EWCA Crim 162; [2006] 2 Cr. App. R. (S.) 81; *R. v Metcalfe* [2009] EWCA Crim 374; [2009] 2 Cr. App. R. (S.) 85).

It is the duty of advocates to make proper enquiries to ensure that full and accurate information was before the court about qualifying periods of time spent on remand: see *R. v Hoggard* [2013] EWCA Crim 1024; [2014] 1 Cr. App. R. (S.) 42 (see 24-051 and *R. v Leacock* [2013] EWCA Crim 1994; [2014] 2 Cr. App. R. (S.) 12).

6. Ancillary orders

Custodial sentence combined with fine

It may be appropriate to combine a financial penalty with an immediate custodial sentence where: **38-021**

(1) there is reason to believe that the offender has assets which he has not disclosed (*R. v Michel* (1984) 6 Cr. App. R. (S.) 379; *R. v Benmore* (1983) 5 Cr. App. R. (S.) 468);
(2) there is reason to believe that a substantial amount of stolen property remains available for the offender's benefit on release (*R. v Chatt* (1984) 6 Cr. App. R. (S.) 75); and
(3) exceptionally, the maximum custodial term is not an adequate penalty (*R. v Garner* (1986) 82 Cr. App. R. 27).

7. Recommending licence conditions

General

38-022 Where a court sentences an offender to a term of imprisonment or a term of detention in a young offender institution of 12 months or more in respect of any offence, the court, may, when passing sentence, recommend to the Secretary of State (who is bound to have regard to such a recommendation), particular conditions which, in his view, should be included in any licence granted to the offender under Ch.6 of Pt 12 of the CJA 2003 on his release. Such a recommendation is not part of the sentence.

The conditions which may be recommended are those which impose on an offender:

(a) a requirement that he reside at a certain place;
(b) a requirement relating to his making or maintaining contact with a person;
(c) a restriction relating to his making or maintaining contact with a person;
(d) a restriction on his participation in, or undertaking of, any activity;
(e) a requirement that he participate in, or co-operate with, a programme, or set of activities, designed to further one or more of the purposes referred to in s.250(8) of the 2003 Act;
(f) a requirement that he comply with a curfew arrangement;
(g) a restriction on his freedom of movement (which is not a requirement referred to in subpara.(f));
(h) a requirement relating to his supervision in the community by a responsible officer.

(SA 2020 s.328)

Guidance as to licence conditions

38-023 In practice the judge is not likely to know with any certainty at the point of sentence:

(1) to what extent the offender's behaviour may have been addressed in custody; or
(2) what the offender's health and other personal circumstances may be on release,

so that it will be difficult, especially in the case of longer custodial sentences, for him to make an informed judgment about the most appropriate licence conditions to be imposed on release.

Although now archived on the SCEW website, the SGC New Sentence: CJA 2003 (at para.2.1.1–14) suggested that it might be helpful for the judge to:

(a) indicate any areas of an offender's behaviour about which he has the most concern; and
(b) make suggestions about the types of intervention whether this, in practice, will take place in prison or in the community.

A curfew, exclusion requirement or prohibited activity requirement might be suitable conditions to recommend for the licence period. The judge might also wish to suggest that the offender should complete a rehabilitation programme, e.g. for drug abuse, anger management, or improving skills such as literacy and could recommend that this should be considered as a licence requirement if the programme has not been undertaken or completed in custody.

The probation authorities need to have due regard to any such recommendations and the final decision on licence conditions will need to build upon any interventions during the custodial period and any other changes in the offender's circumstances.

The involvement of the probation authorities at the pre-sentence stage will clearly be pivotal. A recommendation on the likely post-release requirements included in a pre-sentence report will assist the judge in making his decision on the overall length of the sentence although any recommendation would still have to be open to review when release is being considered.

8. SENTENCES OF 12 MONTHS OR MORE

Length of term

Judges need to be aware that: **38-024**

(1) a fixed term custodial sentence of 12 months or more under the CJA 2003 framework (see 38-005) increased the sentence actually served, whether in custody or in the community, by one-third; and
(2) SGC recommended that in order to maintain consistency between the lengths of sentence under the pre- and post-CJA 2003 frameworks, a judge imposing a fixed term custodial sentence of 12 months or more for an offence committed on or after 4 April 2005, should consider reducing the overall length of the sentence that would have been imposed under the former provisions, by no more than one-quarter.

(SGC New Sentences: CJA 2003 para 2.1.7)

Spelling it out

The changes in the nature of custodial sentences for offences *committed on or after 4 April 2005* required changes in the way the sentence was pronounced (see DEALING WITH AN OFFENDER). **38-025**

The judge in imposing such a sentence (other than for a "dangerous offender" needs to spell out the practical implications of the sentence being imposed, so that offenders, victims and the public alike all understand).

He should state clearly, at the point of sentence:

(1) the way in which the sentence has been calculated;
(2) how it will be served;
(3) that the sentence is in two parts, one in custody and one under supervision in the community;

(4) that the sentence does not end when the offender is released from custody; and
(5) that non-compliance with licence requirements imposed in the second half of the sentence is likely to result in a return to custody.

(See CJA 2003 s.174, but there are no longer any prescribed forms of words to be used.)

9. Dangerous offenders

38-026 "Protective" sentences, or sentences for public protection, which exceed the normal determinate sentence of imprisonment provided both by PCC(S)A 2000 and CJA 2003 and as now set out by SA 2020, for both dangerous and persistent offenders. The former, which now apply only to offences committed before 4 April 2005, are no longer dealt with in this work. The regime under CJA 2003 has now been radically changed by LASPOA 2012, see DANGEROUS OFFENDERS; PROTECTIVE SENTENCES.

10. Mandatory minimum sentences

38-027 PCC(S)A 2000 introduced mandatory minimum sentences of:

(1) seven years for a third Class A drug trafficking committed since 30 September 1997;
(2) three years for a third domestic burglary committed since 30 November 1999; and
(3) an automatic life sentence for a second serious offence committed after 30 September 1997. This section was replaced from 4 April 2005 by the indeterminate sentence for public protection which has, itself, been abolished by LASPOA 2012.

CJA 2003 introduced a mandatory minimum sentence of five years (three years in the case of those aged 16 or 17) for certain offences under FA 1968 s.51A. Further firearms offences were added by VCRA 2006. LASPOA 2012 introduces mandatory minimum sentences of six months (four months detention and training in the case of those aged 16 or 17) for certain knife offences. The provisions are now set out in SA 2020 ss.311–315.

(1) Automatic life sentence

General

38-028 PCC(S)A 2000 introduced minimum terms for offenders who committed:

(1) a second serious offence (mandatory or "automatic" life sentence);
(2) a third Class A drug trafficking offence (minimum of seven years); and
(3) a third domestic burglary (minimum of three years).

The automatic life sentence under (1) applied only to offences committed after 1 October 1997 and before 4 April 2005, and was overtaken by the provisions of CJA 2003. It is no longer dealt with in this work, and reference should be made to the 2007 edition. Those sentences under (2) and (3) are dealt with at 38-029 and 38-033.

(2) Minimum seven years for third Class A drug trafficking offence

General

Where: **38-029**

(1) an offender is convicted of a Class A drug trafficking offence committed *after 1 October 1997*;
(2) at the time the offence was committed, the offender was 18 or over and had been convicted in any part of the UK of two other Class A drug trafficking offences; and
(3) one of those had been committed after he had been convicted of the other,
the judge *must* impose upon an offender an appropriate custodial sentence for a term of *at least seven years*, that is, in the case of:
   (a) an offender who is 21 or over, a sentence of at least seven years' imprisonment; or in the case of
   (b) an offender under 21, a sentence of at least seven years' detention in a young offender institution,

unless he is of opinion that there are particular circumstances relating to any of the offences or to the offender, which would make that sentence unjust in all the circumstances (SA 2020 s.313).

A hospital order may be made in respect of a mentally disordered offender as an alternative to such a sentence, or a hospital direction under MHA 1983 s.45A (inserted by CSA 1997 s.46) (MHA 1983 s.82(1)) and see MENTALLY DISORDERED OFFENDERS.

Definitions

"Class A drug trafficking offences", as the term implies, means a drug trafficking offence committed in respect of a Class A drug, and for this purpose "Class A drug" has the same meaning as in MDA 1971; "*drug trafficking offence*" means an offence which is specified in: **38-030**

(1) POCA 2002 Sch.2 para.1; or
(2) so far as it relates to that paragraph, para.10 of that Schedule.

(SA 2020 s.313(5))

The approach to "unjust"

In *R. v Harvey* [2000] 1 Cr. App. R. (S.) 368, the CACD rejected an approach to the section based on the contention that a sentence passed under the section which was manifestly excessive on the facts of the case was "unjust." Section 110 is intended to have a deterrent effect (see *R. v Lucas* [2011] EWCA Crim 1057; [2012] 1 Archbold Review 4 CA). The Guidelines issued by SGC on the seriousness of offences do not apply (*Attorney General's Reference (No.6 of 2006) (R. v Farish)* [2006] EWCA Crim 1043; [2007] 1 Cr. App. R. (S.) 12). **38-031**

As to the application of the "totality principle" to consecutive sentences, see 38-016.

Discount for plea

38-032 Nothing prevents the judge under this section, after taking into account any matters referred to in SA 2020 s.73(3)–(5), from imposing a sentence which is not less than 80 per cent of the minimum mandatory sentence (see *R. v Brown* [2000] 2 Cr. App. R. (S.) 435; *R. v Hickson* [2002] 1 Cr. App. R. (S.) 298). In *R. v Darling* [2009] EWCA Crim 1610; [2010] 1 Cr. App. R. (S.) 63 the CACD said that the discount was not restricted to the 20 per cent allowed by CJA 2003 s.144(2).

The correct interpretation of s.73 (reduction of sentence for guilty plea) is that the sentence imposed following application of the three strikes provision in ss.313 or 314 must, where there is a plea of guilty, be not less than 80 per cent of the required minimum sentence (*R. v Fairclough* [2012] EWCA Crim 897, following and applying *R. v Gray* [2007] EWCA Crim 979; [2007] 2 Cr. App. R. (S.) 78).

Section 313 is intended to have a deterrent effect. The Guidelines issued by SGC on the seriousness of offences do not apply (*Attorney General's Reference (No.6 of 2006) (R. v Farish)* [2006] EWCA Crim 1043; [2007] 1 Cr. App. R. (S.) 12).

And see generally DISCOUNTS ON SENTENCE.

(3) Minimum three years for third domestic burglary

General

38-033 Where:

(1) an offender is convicted of a domestic burglary (i.e. a burglary committed in respect of a building or part of a building which is a dwelling) committed *after 30 November 1999*;
(2) at the time when that burglary was committed, he was 18 or over and has been convicted in England or Wales of two other domestic burglaries; and
(3) one of those other burglaries was committed after he had been convicted of the other and both of them were committed after 30 November 1999,

the judge must (SA 2020 ss.314, 316–318 and 320) impose on an offender:

(a) who is 21 or over when convicted, a sentence of imprisonment;
(b) who is under 21 at that time, a sentence of detention in a young offender institution,

for a term of at least three years except where he is of the opinion that there are particular circumstances which:

(i) relate to any of the offences or to the offender; and
(ii) would make it unjust to do so in all the circumstances (as to which see DISCOUNTS ON SENTENCE).

Where an offence is found to have been committed over a period of two or more days, or at some time during a period of two or more days, it will be taken for the purposes of ss.311, 313, 314 and 315 to have been committed on the last of those days. (SA 2020 s.320.) As to persons convicted of corresponding offences under Service Law, see SA 2020 s.318.

In *R. v Stephens* [2000] 2 Cr. App. R. (S.) 320 failure to warn the offender of his liability to these provisions was held to be capable of amounting to an "exceptional circumstance".

The indictment must make clear that the building is a "dwelling" to found a sentence under this provision (*R. v Miller* [2010] EWCA Crim 809; [2011] 1 Cr. App. R. (S.) 12).

Attempted burglary is not burglary (*R. v Maguire* [2002] EWCA Crim 2689; [2003] 2 Cr. App. R. (S.) 10). As to conspiracy cases, see *Attorney General's Reference (Nos 48 and 49 of 2010)* [2010] EWCA Crim 2521; [2011] Crim. L.R. 169. For the correct approach to sentencing, see 38-034.

Prescribed sequence

The sequence of events required before an offender qualifies for such a sentence is as follows: **38-034**

(1) he must have committed a first offence of burglary;
(2) he must have been convicted of that offence; then
(3) he must have committed a second offence of burglary; and then
(4) he must have been convicted of that second offence; then
(5) he must have committed a third offence of burglary.

(*R. v Hoare* [2004] EWCA Crim 191; [2005] 2 Cr. App. R. (S.) 50)

The proper approach to sentencing (see *R. v Michael Andrews* [2013] 2 Cr. App R (S) 5; *R. v McKay* [2012] EWCA Crim 1900; *R. v Silvera* [2013] EWCA Crim 1764) is to have regard to the definitive SGC Guideline (on burglary) and then to ensure that the final sentence imposed is not less than the minimum sentence required by s.111. The three year minimum term is not the starting point; rather, the judge must go through the proper sentencing exercise in accordance with the guidelines and then cross-check to ensure that the sentence is no less than the minimum term required. In some circumstances it may be significantly more. Appropriate allowance for a plea of guilty may be made but the final sentence must not be less than 80 per cent of three years.

See also *R. v Nelson* [2013] EWCA Crim 2410 for observations of the CACD on how to deal with a minimum sentence case (burglary) within the early guilty plea scheme (see also DISCOUNTS ON SENTENCE).

As to the necessity of applying the "totality principle" (see 38-016), and the construction of the sentences to achieve this result, see *R. v Raza* [2009] EWCA Crim 1413; [2010] 1 Cr. App. R. (S.) 56; *R. v Sparkes* [2011] EWCA Crim 880; [2011] 2 Cr. App. R. (S.) 107.

A person convicted under Service Law, where the corresponding civil offence qualifies under SA 2020 ss.313–315, these provisions apply as if he had been convicted in England and Wales of the corresponding civil offence (SA 2020 s.318). See as to a Gilham situation *R. v Gibson* [2004] EWCA Crim 593; [2004] 2 Cr. App. R. (S.) 84.

In respect of qualifying offences, a certificate from the sentencing court is sufficient proof.

(SA 2020 s.317)

The approach to "unjust"

As to what may be "unjust" to impose the minimum mandatory sentence, the CACD in *R. v McInerney* [2002] EWCA Crim 3165; [2003] 2 Cr. App. R. (S.) 36 gave guidance on the operation of s.111. **38-035**

The CACD noted that:

(1) the object of the section was to require the courts to impose the mandatory sentence; but

(2) there would be occasions where it would be unjust to impose that sentence even where an offender would qualify; and
(3) s.314 (previously PCC(S)A 2000 s.111) gave the judge a fair degree of discretion to make a finding that it would be unjust for the full sentence to be imposed, always bearing in mind that he was required to be satisfied that there were particular circumstances relating to the offender, or the offence(s) or both.

See also *R. v Stone* [2011] EWCA Crim 2823; [2012] 2 Cr. App. R. (S.) 50; *R. v Flack* [2013] EWCA Crim 115; [2013] 2 Cr. App. R. (S.) 56; also *R. v Saw* [2009] EWCA Crim 1; [2009] 2 Cr. App. R. (S.) 367 (examples of exceptional cases, albeit not in the context of s.111 and mandatory minimum sentences). For an example of the interaction of sentencing guidelines with the minimum sentence provisions see *R. v Brinkley* [2013] EWCA Crim 760.

11. PRESCRIBED MINIMUM SENTENCES FOR CERTAIN FIREARMS OFFENCES

SA 2020 s.311 and Sch.20

38-036 Where a person is convicted of:

(1) an offence under FA 1968 s.5(1)(a), (ab), (aba), (ac), (ad), (ae), (af) or (c) committed *on or after 22 January 2004*;
(2) an offence under FA 1968 s.5(1A)(a) committed *on or after 22 January 2004*; or
(3) an offence under FA 1968 s.5(2A) committed in respect of a relevant firearm or relevant ammunition; or
(4) an offence committed *on or after 6 April 2007* in respect of a firearm or ammunition specified in s.5(1A)(a) under any provisions of FA 1968 ss.16, 16A, 17, 18, 19 and 20(1); and

the offence was committed at a time when he was aged 16 or over, the judge *must* impose a custodial sentence (detention under s.250, detention in a young offender institution or imprisonment), for at least a minimum term (with or without a fine) of three years for an offender aged under 18 when the offence was committed or five years for an offender aged 18 or over when the offence was committed unless he is of opinion that there are exceptional circumstances relating to the offence or to the offender which justify his not doing so (SA 2020 s.311(2) and (3)).

The offence must have been charged in the indictment; mere evidence of possession, without a count in the indictment is not enough (*Attorney General's Reference (No.114 of 2004)* [2004] EWCA Crim 2954; [2005] 2 Cr. App. R. (S.) 6).

Where an offence is found to have been committed over a period of two or more days, or at some time during a period of two or more days, it is to be taken to have been committed on the last of those days.

No reduction for a guilty plea is appropriate (see DISCOUNTS ON SENTENCE) in relation to a minimum sentence for firearms offences committed under FA 1968 s.51A (*R. v Jordan* [2004] EWCA Crim 3291; [2005] 2 Cr. App. R. (S.) 44).

Gun crime; the approach to the section

38-037 The theme that emerges from the judgments in *R. v Jordan* [2004] EWCA Crim 3291; [2005] 2 Cr. App. R. (S.) 44); *R. v Rehman* [2005] EWCA Crim 2056; [2006] 1 Cr. App. R. (S.) 77 and *R. v Wilkinson* [2009] EWCA Crim 1925; [2010] 1 Cr.

App. R. (S.) 100, is that the gravity of gun crime cannot be exaggerated. Guns kill and maim, terrorise and intimidate; that is why criminals want them, that is why they use them, and that is why they organise their importation and manufacture, supply and distribution.

Sentencing courts must address the fact that too many lethal weapons are too readily available, too many are carried, too many are used, always with devastating effect on individual victims and with insidious corrosive impact on the wellbeing of the local community.

In regard to sentencing, the judge needs to bear in mind that:

(1) possession of a firearm, without more, and without any aggravating features beyond the fact of such possession, is, of itself, a grave crime, and should be dealt with accordingly;
(2) Parliament intended that, for protection of the public against the dangers arising from the unlawful possession of firearms, considerations of retribution and deterrence should be given greater emphasis, and the personal circumstances of the offender less than would normally be the case (per Lord Nimmo Smith in the Scots case of *HMA v McGovern* 2007 HCJA 21; 2007 J.C. 145) unless these pass the "exceptional" threshold to which the section relates; and
(3) the Act, (unlike SA 2020 ss.313 and 314) does not permit a discount on the minimum sentence for a plea of guilty, unless the judge identifies "exceptional" circumstances.

Guidance in sentencing gun crime is to be found in *R. v Avis* [1998] 1 Cr. App. R. 120 updated by *R. v Wilkinson* [2009] EWCA Crim 1925; [2010] 1 Cr. App. R. (S.) 100. The minimum term provisions of FA 1968 are harsh, even Draconian, however their purpose is clear; it is to deter people from possessing firearms (*R. v Moses* [2009] EWCA Crim 2820). And see the observations of Judge LCJ in *R. v Wilkinson*; see also *Attorney General's Reference (No.6 of 2011)* [2012] EWCA Crim 86; [2012] Crim. L.R. 399.

"Exceptional circumstances"

If the judge identifies "exceptional circumstances": **38-038**

(1) the sentence is then at large, and the prescribed minimum sentence will be a factor which he can take into account (as he will the guideline case of *R. v Avis* [1998] 1 Cr. App. R. 120 and all available mitigation);
(2) he will then, but only then, take into account not only the "exceptional circumstances" themselves but also good character and any timely plea of guilt.

It is not appropriate for him to look at each circumstance separately and to conclude that it does not amount to an exceptional circumstance; a holistic approach is necessary. There will be cases where there is one single striking feature which relates either to the offence or to the offender, which causes the case to fall within the requirement of "exceptional circumstances". There will be other cases where no single factor by itself will amount to "exceptional" circumstances but the collective impact of all the relevant circumstances makes the case exceptional.

Cases in which exceptional circumstances can be said to arise are likely to be rare (*R. v Jordan* [2004] EWCA Crim 3291; [2005] 2 Cr. App. R. (S.) 44; *R. v McEneaney* [2005] EWCA Crim 431; [2005] Cr. App. R. (S.) 86; *R. v Evans* [2005]

EWCA 1811; [2006] 1 Cr. App. R. (S.) 64; *R. v Lashari* [2010] EWCA Crim 1504; [2011] 1 Cr. App. R. (S.) 72; *R. v Welsh* [2013] EWCA Crim 386, but see *R. v Blackall* [2005] EWCA Crim 1128; [2006] 1 Cr. App. R. (S.) 22 (paraplegic offender) and see *R. v Burton* [2012] EWCA Crim 1781; *R. v Mehmet* [2005] EWCA Crim 2074; [2006] 1 Cr. App. R. (S.) 75 (early plea, good character, no criminal intention, no ammunition) and *R. v Rehman* [2005] EWCA Crim 2056; [2006] 1 Cr. App. R. (S.) 77 (early plea, good character, cooperation with the authorities, public employment).

The circumstances are "exceptional" for the purposes of s.51A(2) if the minimum five-year term would be an arbitrary and disproportionate sentence (*R. v Rehman* [2005] EWCA Crim 2056; [2006] 1 Cr. App. R. (S.) 77). In *R. v Edwards* [2006] EWCA Crim 2833; [2007] 1 Cr. App. R. (S.) 111, the CACD emphasised that strong personal mitigation on its own is unlikely to be sufficient to amount to "exceptional circumstances". See also *R. v Ocran* [2010] EWCA Crim 1209; [2011] 1 Cr. App. R. (S.) 36; *R. v Boateng* [2011] EWCA Crim 861; *Attorney General's Reference (No.64 of 2010) (R. v Brunt)* [2010] EWCA Crim 2956; [2011] 2 Cr. App. R. (S.) 25; *R. v Shaw* [2011] 2 Cr. App. R. (S.) 65 (offender's poor health, age, guilty plea, lack of convictions, no evidence of weapons used in the commission of any crime, low risk of re-offending); *R. v Jones* [2011] EWCA Crim 1448; [2012] 1 Cr. App. R. (S.) 25 (offender of positive good character and exceptional talent/given much to the community/dedicated to caring for her sister with Down's Syndrome and the circumstances, though not giving rise to a defence of duress, were far removed from the possession of firearms by a willing volunteer); *R. v Burton* [2012] EWCA Crim 1781; [2013] 1 Cr. App. R. (S.) 84 (exceptional circumstances related to the offender's psychiatric problems and poor state of health) (but cf. *R. v Robinson* [2009] EWCA Crim 2600; [2010] 2 Cr. App. R. (S.) 20 where mental illness and depression were held not to be exceptional); *R. v Ramzan* [2012] EWCA Crim 2891; [2013] 2 Cr. App. R. (S.) 33 (offender, 29, no previous convictions) but cf. *R. v Downes* [2013] EWCA Crim 135; [2013] 2 Cr. App. R. (S.) 74 (61-year-old, married man, remorse, effective good character and depression not enough where he intended to sell the weapons).

The judge ought to accept the accused's account unless he is sure that it is not true (*R. v Lashari* [2010] EWCA Crim 1504; [2011] 1 Cr. App. R. (S.) 72).

Using someone to mind a weapon

38-039 Where an offender is guilty of an offence under VCRA 2006 s.28 (using someone to mind a weapon) and:

(1) at the time of the offence, the offender was aged 16 or over; and
(2) the dangerous weapon in respect of which the offence was committed was a firearm mentioned in FA 1968 s.5(1)(a)–(af) or (c) or FA 1968 s.51A (possession of a firearm which attracts a minimum sentence),

the judge *must* impose (with or without a fine) where the offender is:

(a) aged 18 or over at the time of conviction, a term of detention in a young offender institution or imprisonment of not less than five years; or
(b) under 18 at the time of conviction, a term of detention under SA 2020 s.250 of not less than three years,

unless, in either case he is of the opinion that there are "exceptional circumstances" relating to the offence which justify his not doing so.

Where:

(i) the judge is considering for the purposes of sentencing the seriousness of an offence under s.28; and
(ii) at the time of the offence the offender was aged 18 or over and the person used to look after, hide or transport the weapon was not,

he must treat the fact that that person was under the age of 18 at that time as an aggravating factor (that is to say, a factor increasing the seriousness of the offence), and must state in open court that the offence was so aggravated.

Where an offence under s.28 of using another person for a particular purpose is found to have involved that other person's having possession of a weapon, or being able to make it available, over a period of two or more days, or at some time during a period of two or more days, and on any day in that period, an age requirement was satisfied, the question whether s.29(3) applies or (as the case may be) the question whether the offence was aggravated under this section is to be determined as if the offence had been committed on that day. (SA 2020 s.311 and Sch.20 para.5.)

12. Prescribed minimum sentences; offensive weapons, blades and points

Prevention of Crimes Act 1953 (SA 2020 ss.312, 315, 316, 318 and 320)

Where a person is convicted of having an offensive weapon in a public place and: **38-040**

(1) unlawfully and intentionally threatening another person with the weapon; and
(2) doing so in such a way that there is an immediate risk of serious physical harm to that person,

the judge must (PCA 1953 s.1A(6)(a)) pass an appropriate custodial sentence, with or without a fine unless he is of the opinion that there are particular circumstances which:

(a) relate to the offence or to the offender; and
(b) would make it unjust to do so in all the circumstances.

In considering that opinion in the case of an offender under 18, the judge must have regard to CYPA 1933 s.44 (see CHILDREN AND YOUNG PERSONS).

An "appropriate custodial sentence" in this regard is, in the case of a person;

(i) aged 18 or over when convicted, detention in a young offender institution or imprisonment (but see below) for at least six months; or
(ii) aged at least 16 but under 18, when convicted, a detention and training order of at least four months.

The maximum term is six months on summary conviction, and four years on conviction on indictment, with or without a fine.

Note that:

- physical harm is "serious" if it amounts to grievous bodily harm under OAPA 1861; and

- "public place" and "offensive weapon" are defined in the Act (s.1).

CJA 1988 s.139AA (SA 2020 ss.312 and 315)

38-041 Where a person is convicted of having:

(1) in a public place, an article to which s.139 applies; or
(2) on school premises, an article to which s.139 applies or an offensive weapon; and
  (a) unlawfully and intentionally threatening another person with the article; and
  (b) doing so in such a way that there is an immediate risk of serious physical harm to that person,

the judge must (CJA 1988 s.139AA(8)(a)) pass, in the case of an offender aged 16 or over an appropriate custodial sentence, with or without a fine unless he is of the opinion that there are particular circumstances which relate to the offence or to the offender which would make it unjust to do so in all the circumstances.

In considering that opinion in the case of an offender under 18, the judge must have regard to CYPA 1933 s.44 (see CHILDREN AND YOUNG PERSONS).

An "appropriate custodial sentence" in this regard is, in the case of a person:

(i) aged 18 or over when convicted, detention in a young offender institution or imprisonment for at least six months; or
(ii) aged at least 16 but under 18, when convicted, a detention and training order of at least four months.

The maximum term is six months on summary conviction, and four years on conviction on indictment, with or without a fine.

The articles referred to in CJA 1988 s.139 are any article which has a blade or is sharply pointed, except a folding pocket knife. This last, to come within the Act if the cutting edge of its blade exceeds three inches.

Note that:

- physical harm is "serious" if it amounts to grievous bodily harm under OAPA 1861; and
- "public place" has the same meaning as in s.19, and "school premises" as in s.139A.

13. SPECIAL CUSTODIAL SENTENCE FOR OFFENDERS OF A PARTICULAR CONCERN

General

38-042 CJA 2003 s.236A, inserted by CJCA 2014 s.1 came into force for the sentencing of a person for an offence to which it applies from 13 April 2015. The provisions are now in SA 2020 s.278 (as amended by Police, Crime, Sentencing and Courts Act 2022):

(1) a person is convicted of an offence listed in SA 2020 Sch.13 (whether the offence was committed before or after this section comes into force);
(2) the person was aged 21 or over when the offence was committed; and
(3) the judge does not impose;
  (a) a sentence of imprisonment for life;
  (b) an extended sentence under SA 2020 s.279; or

(c) a serious terrorism sentence under s.282A.

Then, if the judge imposes a sentence of imprisonment for the offence, the term of the sentence must be equal to the aggregate of:

(i) the appropriate custodial term; and
(ii) a further period of one year for which the offender is to be subject to a licence.

Note that:

- The "appropriate custodial term" is the term that, in the opinion of the judge, ensures that the sentence is appropriate.
- The term of a sentence of imprisonment imposed under this provision for an offence must not exceed the term that, at the time the offence was committed, was the maximum term permitted for the offence.
- The references in (1) and (2) to a sentence imposed for the offence include a sentence imposed for the offence and one or more offences associated with it.

Offences under SA 2020 s.278

The offences to which SA 2020 s.278 applies are: **38-043**

Terrorism offences

1. An offence under OAPA 1861 s.4 (soliciting murder) that has a terrorist connection.
2. An offence under OAPA 1861 s.28 (causing bodily injury by explosives) that has a terrorist connection.
3. An offence under OAPA 1861 s.29 (using explosives etc. with intent to do grievous bodily harm) that has a terrorist connection.
4. An offence under the Explosive Substances Act 1883 s.2 (causing explosion likely to endanger life or property) that has a terrorist connection.
5. An offence under Explosive Substances Act 1883 s.3 (attempt to cause explosion, or making or keeping explosive with intent to endanger life or property) that has a terrorist connection.
6. An offence under Explosive Substances Act 1883 s.4 (making or possession of explosive under suspicious circumstances) that has a terrorist connection.
7. An offence under TerrA 2000 s.54 (weapons training).
8. An offence under TerrA 2000 s.56 (directing terrorist organisation).
9. An offence under TerrA 2000 s.57 (possession of article for terrorist purposes).
10. An offence under TerrA 2000 s.59 (inciting terrorism overseas).
11. An offence under the Anti-terrorism, Crime and Security Act 2001 s.47 (use, etc. of nuclear weapons).
12. An offence under Anti-terrorism, Crime and Security Act 2001 s.50 (assisting or inducing certain weapons-related acts overseas).
13. An offence under Anti-terrorism, Crime and Security Act 2001 s.113 (use of noxious substance or thing to cause harm or intimidate).
14. An offence under TerrA 2006 s.5 (preparation of terrorist acts).
15. An offence under TerrA 2006 s.6 (training for terrorism).
16. An offence under TerrA 2006 s.9 (making or possession of radioactive device or material).

17. An offence under TerrA 2006 s.10 (use of radioactive device or material for terrorist purposes, etc.).
18. An offence under TerrA 2006 s.11 (terrorist threats relating to radioactive devices, etc.).

Sexual offences

19. An offence under SOA 2003 s.5 (rape of a child under 13).
20. An offence under SOA 2003 s.6 (assault of a child under 13 by penetration).

Accessories and inchoate offences

21. (1) Aiding, abetting, counselling or procuring the commission of an offence specified in the preceding paragraphs of this Schedule (a "relevant offence").
    (2) An attempt to commit a relevant offence.
    (3) Conspiracy to commit a relevant offence.
    (4) An offence under SCA 2007 Pt 2 in relation to which a relevant offence is the offence (or one of the offences) which the person intended or believed would be committed.
22. An offence in the following list that has a terrorist connection:
    (a) an attempt to commit murder;
    (b) conspiracy to commit murder; and
    (c) an offence under SCA 2007 Pt 2 in relation to which murder is the offence (or one of the offences) which the person intended or believed would be committed.

Abolished offences

23. An offence that:
    (a) was abolished before the coming into force of s.236A, and CJCA 2014 (from 1 December 2020 and the enactment of the SA 2020, any offence abolished before 13 April 2015); and
    (b) if committed on the day on which the offender was convicted of the offence, would have constituted an offence specified in the preceding paragraphs of the Schedule.

Meaning of "terrorist connection"

24. For the purposes of the Schedule, an offence has a terrorist connection if a court has determined under CTA 2008 s.30 that the offence has such a connection.

(SA 2020 Sch.13 para.10)

In *R. v Lionel Rae Fruen* [2016] EWCA Crim 561, the CACD considered the application of s.236A. A helpful checklist is set out at [27] of the judgment.

a) Is the offence listed in Sch.13?
b) If the offence is a repealed historic sexual offence, did it involve rape or penetration of a child under 13?
c) Was the offender aged 18 or over when the offence was committed?
d) Sections 265 or 278 (formerly s.236A) cannot apply if the court imposes life or an extended sentence for the offence or an associated offence.

e) A sentence is to be expressed as a single term comprising the custodial element and a further one year period of licence.
f) Each offence qualifying for s.236A must be sentenced in the terms set out at e) above.
g) Are the s.236A sentences to run concurrently or consecutively to one another? If concurrently, the overall custodial term for those offences plus the one year further period of licence should be stated at the end of sentencing.
h) If consecutively, the total custodial term for those offences as well as the total further period of licence should be stated at the end of sentencing.

14. SUSPENDING A SENTENCE

See SUSPENDED SENTENCE ORDERS. **38-044**

39. INDICTMENTS

QUICK GUIDE

1. GENERAL

Introduction

39-001 Trial on indictment may be before a judge and jury or before a judge without a jury under CJA 2003 or under DVA 2004 (see TRIAL WITHOUT A JURY).

The statutory basis for the preferment, form and content of the indictment is IA 1915, AJ(MP)A 1933, supplemented by CrimPR 10 and *CPD* II 10A-B.

A valid indictment, not withdrawn, stayed or quashed, must be disposed of by the verdict(s) of a jury, or by the order of a judge, either entering a verdict of not guilty or by allowing it to lie on the file not to be proceeded with save with the leave of the court or the CACD.

Where the sole accused named in an indictment is proved before trial to have died, it is the practice for the judge to order the indictment to be endorsed "deceased".

Indictments Act 1915

39-002 IA 1915 s.3 provides for a statement of the offence or offences with which the accused is charged "together with such particulars as may be necessary for giving reasonable information as to the nature of the charge". The section further provides that an indictment would not be open to an objection if it were framed in accordance with the rules made under the 1915 Act.

Rules were contained in a schedule to the act which was repealed by the Indictment Rules 1971 which have been in turn replaced by CrimPR 10, supplemented by *CPD* 10A and 10B.

The present position

The current form of indictment is required to set out the matters alleged by the prosecution to justify the conviction of the accused. Draft indictments (or "bills" as they were formerly called) presented to the Crown Court are drawn by the CPS, or sometimes by counsel, often based upon specimens contained in the leading textbooks. However, practice is far from systematic. For many offences, there are no standard particulars. Among the existing forms there is considerable variation, ranging from forms which are little more than recitals of the legal elements of the offence, to others which are more fully particularised. In many cases, there is no discernible principle even within the count to explain the inclusion or exclusion of allegations corresponding to an element of the offence. **39-003**

By AJ(MP)A s.2(1) and 6ZA (as amended by CorJA 2009) a bill of indictment becomes an indictment once it is preferred before the Crown Court (*R. v PW* [2016] EWCA Crim 745; [2016] 2 Cr. App. R. 27 at [20]). In *R. v Jessemey* [2021] EWCA Crim 175, the CACD said that when a defendant is sent to the Crown Court for trial, a draft indictment will be served on the court by the prosecution, at which point it becomes a valid indictment. However, an indictment must be uploaded to the section of the Digital Case System reserved for indictments (section B); if the indictment is uploaded to a different section of the DCS that will not constitute a valid preferment and the document will remain a draft until added to the correct section.

An indictment does not have to be printed or signed, but for the potential benefit of the Criminal Appeal Office, any paper copy of the indictment should be endorsed with a note to identify as a copy of the indictment, and also with the date.

(CrimPR 10.2(7), *CPD* II 10A.2)

Duty of prosecutor

Where a case is to be tried on indictment, the prosecutor will need to present a draft indictment, though in cases of difficulty or where more than ordinary care is required in drafting it, counsel should be instructed (see *R. v Follett* (1989) 88 Cr. App. R. 310). The responsibility for the final correctness of the indictment at the trial rests on the prosecuting advocate (*R. v Newland* (1988) 87 Cr. App. R. 118; *R. v Moss* [1995] Crim. L.R. 828; but see also *R. v White* [2014] EWCA Crim 714; [2014] 2 Cr. App. R. 14 concerning the duties of the defence to act in accordance with the overriding objective). **39-004**

The prosecuting advocate at the trial may not be the same person who has had charge of the case at earlier stages. The indictment should be carefully scrutinised at the plea and trial preparation hearing and before arraignment of the accused. At all stages the prosecutor will need to check the indictment for the accuracy of the charges, their proper form, and potential overloading.

The role of the judge

As part of his case management duties the judge should scrutinise the indictment before trial. All too often, defects in the indictment which have gone unnoticed by the prosecutor result in "cracked" trials. **39-005**

It is sensible for the judge, before the start of the trial, to check that:

(1) if there is a time limit within which the prosecution must be brought, that it has not expired;
(2) if consent to prosecution is required, that consent has been obtained;
(3) the indictment is not overloaded, in that it contains too many counts;
(4) in the case of a multi-count indictment, whether one or more counts ought to be tried separately; and
(5) it is not an appropriate case for the indictment, or some of the counts in the indictment, to be tried without a jury (see TRIAL WITHOUT A JURY).

A judge is entitled to express his own view about whether the charge which an accused is facing is the appropriate one, provided that it is always appreciated that it is the prosecuting authority and not the judge which has the final say about whether someone should be prosecuted at all, and if so, what the appropriate charge should be. Even though an indictment would not have been amended but for the intervention of the judge, charge selection remains a matter for the prosecution. Judges may, however, in the interests of ensuring that the indictment is not defective in meeting the circumstances of the case, order amendment (IA 1915 s.5(1)), and in practice may need to test the prosecutor's commitment to the original decision (*R. v Wielgus* [2014] EWCA Crim 1047; see also *R. v Awoyemi* [2015] EWCA Crim 590).

2. THE REQUIREMENTS OF A VALID INDICTMENT

General

39-006 Every indictment must contain, and is sufficient if it contains, a statement of the specific offence or offences with which the accused is charged, together with such particulars as may be necessary for giving reasonable information as to the charge.
(IA 1915 s.3)

An indictment may be preferred only where:

(1) the person charged has been sent for trial for the offence under CDA 1998 s.51;
(2) the bill is preferred by the direction of the CACD, or by the direction, or with the consent, of a judge of the High Court (a "voluntary bill");
(3) the bill is preferred with the consent of a judge of the Crown Court following a declaration by the court under CCA 2013 Sch.17 para.8(1) (court approval of DPA); or
(4) the bill is preferred under POA 1985 s.22B(3)(a) (the reinstitution of proceedings),

provided that where the person charged has been sent for trial, the bill of indictment against him may include, either in substitution for, or in addition to, any count charging an offence for which he was sent for trial, any counts founded on material which was served on the person charged, being counts which may lawfully be joined in the same indictment.
(AJ(MP)A1933 s.2(2))

Form of Indictment

39-007 The Rules prescribe as follows:

(1) An indictment must be in writing and must be in one of the forms set out in *CPD*, unless it was generated electronically under CrimPR 10.3 or the court otherwise directs, and must contain, in a paragraph (a "count"):
  (a) a statement of the offence charged that:
    (i) describes the offence in ordinary language; and
    (ii) identifies any legislation that creates it; and
  (b) such particulars of the conduct constituting the commission of the offence as to make clear what the prosecutor alleges against the accused.
(2) More than one incident of the commission of the offence may be included in a count if those incidents taken together amount to a course of conduct having regard to the time, place or purpose of commission.
(3) The counts must be numbered consecutively.
(4) An indictment may contain:
  (a) any count charging substantially the same offence as one for which the accused was sent for trial;
  (b) any count contained in a draft indictment served with the permission of a High Court judge or at the direction of the CACD; and
  (c) any other count charging an offence that the Crown Court can try and which is based on the prosecution evidence already served.

(CrimPR 10.2(1)–(4), (6))

The previous iteration of CrimPR 10.2(2) included a further restriction on the counts which can be joined in the same indictment. That rule now appears, with a different emphasis, in CrimPR 3.29 (see 39-015).

For the purposes of AJ(MP)A 1933:

(i) a draft indictment constitutes a bill of indictment;
(ii) the draft or bill is preferred before the Crown Court and become the indictment
  - where CrimPR 10.3 applies (electronic indictment), immediately before the first or only count is read to or placed before the accused to take his plea (but see *R. v Jessemey* [2021] EWCA Crim 175, as to the need for the electronic copy to be added to the appropriate section of the digital case system);
  - where any of CrimPR 10.4 (draft indictment served by prosecutor after sending), 10.5 (draft indictment served with High Court judge's permission), 10.7 (draft indictment served on re-instituting proceedings) or 10.8 (draft indictment served at the direction of the CACD) applies, when the prosecutor serves a draft indictment on the Crown Court officer; and
  - where CrimPR 10.6 applies (draft indictment approved by the court with DPA), when the Crown Court approves the proposed indictment.

(CrimPR 10.2(5))

The purpose of CrimPR 10.2 is to enable the accused to know the case he has to meet and which statutory provisions apply. In *R. v Stocker* [2013] EWCA Crim 1993; [2014] 1 Cr. App. R. 18 the CACD held that a misstatement of the statute under which the count (rape) fell was "a pure technicality" and caused no prejudice; see also *R. v Wilson* [2013] EWCA Crim 1780; [2014] 1 Cr. App. R. 10 (where an environmental health offence was "mis-labelled"); *R. v Clarke* [2015] EWCA Crim 350; [2015] 2 Cr. App. R. 6 (where a "very, very poorly drafted" robbery indictment was held to be sufficient); *R. v Boateng* [2016] EWCA Crim 57; [2016] 2 Cr.

App. R. 5 (where the indictment wrongly referred to Immigration Act 1999 s.10 rather than Immigration Act 1971 s.3) and *R. v D* [2016] EWCA Crim 454; [2016] 2 Cr. App. R. 18 (where the indictment wrongly referred to SOA s.14 rather than s.15).

Stocker was applied in *R. v Walker* [2017] EWCA Crim 392; [2018] 1 Cr. App. R. 18. The CACD confirmed that the test was whether the error in the indictment was a purely technical defect or whether the count was fundamentally flawed because it breached CrimPR 10.2. The application of this test is particularly fact-sensitive. It is necessary to discern the true intention behind the drafting of the defective count and the effect of the error on the conduct of the trial. The court held that indicting an offence of gross indecency contrary to s.13 of the Sexual Offences Act 1956, where the prosecution of such an offence was time barred, was not a mere technicality, but a serious error of substance. See also *R. v Tonkin* [2019] EWCA Crim 393.

In *R. v P* [2022] EWCA Crim 690; [2022] 5 WLUK 270, the appellant argued that two counts were not sufficiently well particularised to distinguish the specific sexual acts alleged in those counts. The CACD dismissed the appeal. The Court accepted that the counts were not adequately particularised (having regard to CrimPR 10.2(1)(b)), however the prosecution and the judge had distinguished the counts and the jury could have had no doubt as to the specific sexual activity each count referred to.

Electronic indictments are dealt with in more detail in CrimPR 10.3, which applies unless the court otherwise directs before the defendant is arraigned.

Where:

(1) a magistrates' court has sent a defendant to the Crown Court;
(2) the magistrates court officer has served the notice required by CrimPR 9.5 on the Crown Court officer; and
(3) each allegation of an indictable offence, or an offence to which CJA 1988 s.40 applies, is presented electronically to the Crown Court as a count, then
    (a) each allegation constitutes a count;
    (b) the allegation or allegations together constitute a draft indictment;
    (c) before it is preferred under CrimPR 10.2(5)(b)(i), the prosecutor may substitute for any count an amended count to the same effect and charging the same offence;
    (d) before it is preferred under CrimPR 10.2(5)(b)(i), the prosecutor, if he has served copies of the evidence on which the prosecution case relies, may substitute or add:
        (i) any count charging substantially the same offence as one specified in the notice; and
        (ii) any other count charging an offence which the Crown Court can try and which is based on the prosecution evidence so served.

Any such added or substituted count must be served on the court and the accused. (CrimPR 10.3)

Before arraignment, the court must obtain the prosecutor's confirmation:

(i) that the indictment or draft indictment sets out a statement of each offence that the prosecutor wants the court to try and such particulars of the conduct constituting the commission of each offence as the prosecutor relies upon to make clear what is alleged; and
(ii) of the order in which the prosecutor wants the defendant's names to be

listed in the indictment, if the prosecutor proposes that more than one defendant should be tried at the same time.

(CrimPR 3.32)

Valid indictment

Thus a valid indictment must: **39-008**

(1) be properly preferred;
(2) be founded on a judicial proceeding, whether the act of a magistrates' court, or of a High Court judge granting a voluntary bill;
(3) include one or more counts, justiciable within the territorial and offence jurisdiction of the Crown Court, and based on the judicial proceedings on which it is founded or any other offences arising;
(4) be restricted to offences triable on indictment only or triable either way, save where the inclusion of summary offences is permitted by statute, such offences being offences known to the law; and
(5) be free from any suggestion of abuse of process.

The remedy for defects in requirements (1)–(4) is by means of a motion to quash the indictment as a whole, or a count of the indictment; the remedy for (5) is to apply for a stay of the proceedings (see ABUSE OF PROCESS).

The word "defective" in IA 1915 s.5(1) is to be given a liberal interpretation. It has been held to include, for example, the case where the indictment does not include as a defendant a person who might properly have been joined at the outset (*R. v Ismail* (1991) 92 Cr. App. R. 92) and also to cover the case where a single count indictment alleging conspiracy to defraud was amended after the prosecution opening by the addition of further counts to cater for the possibility that more than one conspiracy existed (*R. v Radley* (1973) 58 Cr. App. R. 394).

Multiple indictments

There is no rule of law or practice which prohibits two indictments being in existence at the same time for the same offence against the same person on the same facts, but the court will not allow the prosecution to proceed on both such indictments. Two or more indictments may be founded on a single sending (*R. v Follett* (1989) 88 Cr. App. R. 310); and there may be two indictments outstanding against an accused at any one time (*Poole v The Queen* [1960] 3 All E.R. 398). They cannot, however, be tried together and the court will insist that the prosecutor elect the one on which the trial shall proceed. **39-009**

Where different persons have been separately sent for trial for offences which can lawfully be charged in the same indictment it is permissible to join in one indictment the counts founded on the separate sendings despite the fact that an indictment in respect of one of them already exists (*CPD* II 10A.5).

Time limits and service

The prosecutor must serve a draft indictment on the Crown Court officer not more than 20 business days after: **39-010**

(1) service of copies of the documents containing the evidence on which the prosecution case relies, in a case where the accused is sent for trial (CrimPR 10.4);

(2) a High Court judge gives permission to serve a draft indictment (CrimPR 10.5); or
(3) the CACD orders a retrial (CrimPR 10.8).

The judge can extend any of these time limits even after it has expired (CrimPR 10.2(8)).

A failure to strictly comply with directions of the CACD (pursuant to s.8 of the Criminal Appeal Act 1968) in respect of the time within which arraignment should occur following an order for a retrial may invalidate the trial, see *R. v Llewelyn* [2022] EWCA Crim 154; [2022] 2 WLUK 533.

Unless the judge otherwise directs the Crown Court officer must:

(a) endorse any paper copy of the indictment made for the court with:
    (i) a note to identify it as a copy of the indictment; and
    (ii) the date on which the draft indictment became the indictment; and
(b) serve a copy on all parties.

(CrimPR 10.2(7))

Arraigning the accused on the indictment

39-011 In order to take the accused's plea, the court must:

(1) ensure that the accused is *correctly identified* by the indictment or draft indictment;
(2) satisfy itself that each allegation against the defendant has been explained to him, in terms the defendant can understand (with help, if necessary); and
(3) in respect of each count in the indictment:
    (a) *read* the count aloud to the accused, or arrange for it to be read aloud or placed before him in writing;
    (b) *ask* whether the accused pleads guilty or not guilty to the offence charged by that count; and
    (c) *take his plea.*

Where a count is read which is substantially the same as one already read aloud, then only the materially different details need be read aloud. Where a count is placed before the accused in writing, the court must summarise its gist aloud.

In respect of each count in the indictment:

- if the accused declines to enter a plea, the court must treat that as a not guilty plea unless CrimPR 25.10 applies (accused unfit to plead);
- if the accused pleads not guilty to the offence charged by that count but guilty to another offence of which the court could convict on that count, then if the prosecutor and the judge accept that plea, it must be treated as one of guilty of that other offence; otherwise it must be treated as one of not guilty; and
- if the accused pleads a previous acquittal or conviction of the offence charged by that count, he must identify that acquittal or conviction in writing, explaining the basis of that plea, and the judge must exercise his power to decide whether that plea disposes of that count.

(CrimPR 3.32)

3. STRUCTURE OF THE INDICTMENT

General

Whilst responsibility for the form and structure of the indictment is for the prosecutor, the judge has an inherent right to regulate the proceedings before him in the interests of justice and for case management purposes. Thus he may, in relation to an indictment or counts in an indictment: **39-012**

- stay them;
- split them;
- order separate trials of them;
- sever counts or accused; or
- join counts and accused.

Matters of practice and procedure may be dealt with by the judge on his own initiative and as part of case management, as in the case of:

(1) joinder of counts (39-015);
(2) joinder of summary offences (39-016);
(3) joinder of accused (39-017);
(4) specimen counts (39-018);
(5) multiple offending counts; more than one incident (39-019);
(6) multiple offending counts; trial by judge alone (39-020);
(7) overloaded and complex indictments (39-021);
(8) severance of counts (39-022);
(9) separate trials of accused (39-024);
(10) ordering additional particulars (39-026).

Minor or trivial offences

Good drafting practice includes: **39-013**

(1) the most serious offence disclosed on the papers should be charged in the indictment, e.g. wounding with intent to do grievous bodily harm rather than unlawful wounding;
(2) where the papers disclose evidence which is strong in respect of one offence and weak on another, only the offence in respect of which there is strong evidence should be included in the indictment; and
(3) where a serious offence is included in the indictment, trivial or comparatively minor offences should be omitted (where an accused is indicted for murder, there is little point in including a count for resisting arrest, for example).

No purpose is served by charging additional trivial offences.

> "Those who draft indictments should use common sense and should not put into indictments charges which are of a trivial nature. Not only is it unfair, but it also tends to impede the doing of justice on more important aspects of the indictment"

and "it is not fair to throw at an accused man 'everything except the kitchen sink'" (per Lawton LJ in *R. v Ambrose* (1973) 57 Cr. App. R. 538 at 540).

Length and complexity

39-014 It is undesirable that a large number of counts should be contained in one indictment.

Good working rules for the prosecutor include:

(1) do not include counts trivial in themselves, which merely detract from the really serious nature of the case, and add nothing to it (see *R. v Ambrose* (1973) 57 Cr. App. R. 538);
(2) charge a single count where the alleged criminality involved can be embraced satisfactorily in it (*R. v O'Meara, The Times*, 15 December 1989);
(3) do not include more counts than are necessary with a view to encouraging an accused to plead guilty to one or more; equally it is not appropriate to include a more serious count in the hope that this will encourage the accused to plead guilty to a less serious count; and
(4) in a case where there are a number of accused and there are complicated issues it may be appropriate for the case to be divided into two or more trials.

In *R. v Shillam* [2013] EWCA Crim 160 the CACD repeated the familiar warning that the prosecutor should always think carefully, before making use of the law of conspiracy, how to formulate the conspiracy charge or charges and whether a substantive offence or offences would be more appropriate.

Prosecution counsel and the judge should reflect carefully on the counts which should be presented to the jury. Unnecessary counts should be stripped out of the indictment which should reflect the realities of the case and not theoretical legal possibilities which could arise (count for false imprisonment unnecessary where rape charged (see *R. v N* [2010] EWCA Crim 941; [2010] 2 Cr. App. R. 14)).

Note that a plea offered to a lesser offence lapses if it is not accepted, so that a subsequent acquittal on the greater offence does not permit sentence to be imposed on the lesser. The plea to the lesser offence is treated as withdrawn, and a nullity (*R. v Yeardley* [2000] 2 Cr. App. R. 141; *R. v Al Tamimi* [2011] EWCA Crim 1123; *R. v Buttigieg* [2015] EWCA Crim 837; [2016] 1 Cr. App. R. 18). It is otherwise, of course, where the lesser offence forms an alternative left to the jury. The better course will usually be to add an extra count on that basis.

4. JOINDER OF COUNTS

39-015 The rule has been abolished which formerly required an indictment containing more than one count to include only offences founded on the same facts, or offences which constitute all or part of a series of the same or a similar character. However, if an indictment charges more than one offence, and if at least one of those offences does not meet those criteria, then CrimPR 3.21(4) cites that circumstance as an example of one in which the court may decide to exercise its power to order separate trials. It is for the court to decide which allegations, against whom, should be tried at the same time, having regard to the prosecutor's proposals, the parties' representations, the court's powers under the 1915 Act and the overriding objective. Where necessary the court should be invited to exercise those powers.

(*CPD* II 10A.3)

The rule is now that where the same indictment charges more than one offence, the court may exercise its power to order separate trials of those offences if it is of the opinion that:

(1) the defendant otherwise may be prejudiced or embarrassed in his or her defence (for example, where the offences to be tried together are neither founded on the same facts nor form or are part of a series of offences of the same or a similar character); or
(2) for any other reason it is desirable that the defendant should be tried separately for any one or more of those offences.

(CrimPR 3.29(4))
As to offences:

(1) founded on the same facts—the test is not to be interpreted too narrowly; the test is "do they have a common factual origin?" (*R. v Barrell* (1979) 69 Cr. App. R. 250);
(2) of the same or a similar character—the test was settled in *Ludlow v Metropolitan Police Commissioner* [1970] 54 Cr. App. R. 233.

Note that:

(a) two offences may constitute a "series"; but
(b) the offences must display a nexus between them, explained as "a feature of similarity which in all the circumstances enables the offences to be described as a series". The similarity may arise due to the same victim (*R. v C*, *The Times,* 4 February 1993) or similar facts (*R. v Baird* [1993] 97 Cr. App. R. 308), but the longer the interval between offences, the clearer the nexus must be (*R. O'Brien* [2000] Crim. L.R. 863); and
(c) the court must look at the true nature of the character of the offences. They do not have to be the same type of offence in law—the court is not concerned with legal characterisation or exact similarity (*R. v Williams* [2017] EWCA Crim 281; [2017] 2 Cr. App. R. 7, applied in *R. v J* [2018] EWCA Crim 2485; [2019] 1 Cr. App. R. 10).

Further counts can be added to the indictment on a retrial if further evidence comes to light since the original trial (*R. v F* [2012] EWCA Crim 720; [2012] 2 Cr. App. R. 13).

Where an indictment contains substantive counts and one or more related conspiracy counts, the court will expect the prosecutor to justify their joint trial. Failing justification, the prosecutor should be required to choose whether to proceed on the substantive counts or on the conspiracy counts. (*CPD* II 10A.4)

5. JOINDER OF SUMMARY OFFENCES

The Prosecution may include within the indictment a count charging certain offences otherwise triable only summarily under CJA 1988 s.40 if the charge: **39-016**

(1) is founded on the same facts or evidence as a count charging an indictable offence; or
(2) is part of a series of offences of the same or a similar character as an indictable offence charged,

but only if the facts or evidence relating to the offence have been disclosed to the accused.

(CJA 1988 s.40)
Section 40 applies to the following offences:

(a) common assault;

(b) assaulting a prisoner custody officer (CJA 1991 s.90(1));
(c) assaulting a secure training centre officer (CJPOA 1994 s.13(1));
(d) taking a motor vehicle without authority (TA 1968 s.12(1));
(e) driving whilst disqualified (RTA 1988 s.103(1)(b));
(f) assaulting a secure college custody officer (CJCA 2015 Sch.10 paras 14 and 24);
(g) criminal damage where triable only summarily; and
(h) any further offences as may be specified by statutory instrument.

But note *R. v Walton* [2011] EWCA Crim 2832 (handling stolen goods and assault following arrest did not arise out of the same facts).

Any such offence included in an indictment may be tried as if it were an indictable offence, save that the Crown Court's sentencing powers are limited to those of the magistrates' court.

Note that s.40 does *not* permit the prosecution otherwise to add any other summary-only charge to an indictment as an alternative to a count already included (for example to enable the accused to plead guilty to a lesser charge; see *R. v Hill* [2010] EWCA Crim 2999).

Where a count is improperly added to an indictment in breach of s.40(1), a conviction on the improperly joined count is a nullity, but the remainder of the indictment is not invalidated (*R. v McGrath* [2013] EWCA Crim 1261; [2014] Crim. L.R. 144). See also *R. v Maxwell* [2017] EWCA Crim 1233; [2018] 1 Cr. App. R. 5 and *R. v Merritt* [2019] EWCA Crim 1514.

6. Joinder of accused

39-017 Two or more accused may be joined in the same indictment or in the same individual count. However, the trial judge has an inherent discretion to order separate trials of accused who have properly been joined in an indictment. Where more than one accused is sent for trial for one or more offences, and there is no joint count, the prosecutor must show some nexus disclosed in the papers related by time and other factors before they or any of them can be joined in the same indictment or count. (See, further, severance of counts, 39-022.)

As to joining a new co-accused in an indictment on a retrial ordered by the CACD, see CAA 1968 s.7, also *R. v Hemmings* [2000] 1 Cr. App. R. 360 and *R. v Booker* [2011] EWCA Crim 7; [2011] 1 Cr. App. R. 26 (a previously absent co-conspirator can be tried with a conspirator subject to a retrial).

7. Specimen counts

39-018 Where a number of similar acts on different occasions is to be alleged, it is not open to the prosecution to charge one offence only as being representative of the whole course of conduct in order for the court to sentence for the whole of that course of conduct. The judge may sentence only on those offences in respect of which the accused has been convicted or which he has asked to be taken into consideration on sentence (*R. v Canavan* [1998] 1 Cr. App. R. 79).

In *R. v Hartley* [2011] EWCA Crim 1299; [2012] 1 Cr. App. R. 7 (and see also *R. v A* [2015] EWCA Crim 177; [2015] 2 Cr. App. R. (S.) 12) the CACD indicated three ways of dealing with this situation:

(1) to frame the counts in a form which complied with CrimPR 10.2(2) (see 39-019), which permits a count to allege a course of conduct; where this is

done, it will often be appropriate to include both a "course of conduct" count and a "single instance" count in relation to the same period;

(2) to take advantage of DVA 2004 ss.17–19, which, subject to strict conditions, permits trial by judge alone on outstanding allegations following conviction on representative counts; or

(3) to include sufficient counts so that the judge is enabled to impose sentence on a basis which sufficiently represents what had actually happened, but care is needed so as not to overload the indictment.

In *R. v Stewart*, *The Times*, 21 May 2012, it was held that where an indictment charged a specimen count of rape by reference to SOA 2003, it did not matter that the particulars of the offence specified a period beginning some weeks before, and continuing some weeks beyond, the coming into force of that Act. On the evidence, the jury must have been sure that there had been regular, continuing rapes, and the case was not analogous with those in which there was a single offence which might have been committed before, or after, the coming into force of the Act.

Where the prosecutor includes specimen counts in an indictment he must take care that the samples reveal to the defence:

(a) the case that the accused has to meet (*R. v Evans* [1995] Crim. L.R. 245);

(b) "with as much particularity as the circumstances admit" (*R. v Rackham* [1997] Crim. L.R. 592).

Where there is a realistic possibility that the jury could reach its verdict on a specimen count by focusing on different occasions, the jury must be directed that they need to be sure that the offence had been committed on the same occasion (*R. v Hobson* [2013] EWCA Crim 819; [2013] 2 Cr. App. R. 27; see also multiple offending counts, 39-019).

8. Multiple offending counts: more than one incident

CrimPR 10.2(2) allows a single count to allege more than one incident of the commission of an offence in certain circumstances. Each incident must be of the same offence. The circumstances in which such a count may be appropriate include, but are not limited to, the following: **39-019**

(1) the victim on each occasion was the same, or there was no identifiable individual victim as, for example, in a case of the unlawful importation of controlled drugs or of money laundering;

(2) the alleged incidents involved a marked degree of repetition in the method employed or in their location, or both;

(3) the alleged incidents took place over a clearly defined period, typically (but not necessarily) no more than about a year; and

(4) in any event, the defence is such as to apply to every alleged incident without differentiation. Where what is in issue differs between different incidents, a single "multiple incidents" count will not be appropriate, though it may be appropriate to use two or more such counts according to the circumstances and to the issues raised by the defence.

(*CPD* 10A.11)

Even in circumstances such as those set out above, there may be occasions on which a prosecutor chooses not to use such a count, in order to bring the case within POCA 2002 s.75(3)(a) (criminal lifestyle established by conviction of three or more offences in the same proceedings): for example, because s.75(2)(c) does not apply (criminal lifestyle established by an offence committed over a period of at least six months). Where the prosecutor proposes such a course, it is unlikely that Pt 1 of the Rules (the overriding objective) will require an indictment to contain a single "multiple incidents" count in place of a larger number of counts, subject to the general principles (set out at *CPD* II 10A.3).

(*CPD* II 10A.12)

Note that:

(a) for some offences, particularly sexual offences, the penalty for the offence may have changed during the period over which the alleged incidents took place; in such a case, additional "multiple incidents" counts should be used so that each count only alleges incidents to which the same maximum penalty applies;

(b) in other cases, such as sexual or physical abuse, a complainant may be in a position only to give evidence of a series of similar incidents without being able to specify when or the precise circumstances in which they occurred; in these cases, a "multiple incidents" count may be desirable;

(c) if on the other hand, the complainant is able to identify particular incidents of the offence by reference to a date or other specific event, but alleges that in addition there were other incidents which the complainant is unable to specify, then it may be desirable to include separate counts for the identified incidents and a "multiple incidents" count or counts alleging that incidents of the same offence occurred "many" times; and

(d) using a "multiple incidents" count may be an appropriate alternative to using "specimen" counts in some cases where repeated sexual or physical abuse is alleged; the choice of count will depend on the particular circumstances of the case and should be determined bearing in mind the implications for sentencing set out in *R. v Canavan* [1998] 1 Cr. App. R. 79; *R. v Shaw* [1998] 1 W.L.R. 604; [1998] 1 Cr. App. R. 79. In *R. v A* [2015] EWCA Crim 177; [2015] 2 Cr. App. R. (S.) 12 the CACD reviewed the circumstances in which a mixture of multiple incident and single incident counts might be appropriate where the prosecutor alleged sustained sexual abuse.

(*CPD* II 10A.13–14)

9. MULTIPLE OFFENDING COUNTS: TRIAL BY JURY AND THEN BY JUDGE ALONE

39-020 In the case of a large number of separate offences where the judge exercises the powers in the DVA 2004 ss.17–21 to direct a trial by a jury and then by a judge alone, the procedure directed in *CPD* II 10A.15–10A.20 should be followed (see TRIAL WITHOUT A JURY).

10. OVERLOADED AND COMPLEX INDICTMENTS

39-021 Where accused on trial have a variety of offences alleged against them, then, in the interests of effective case management it is the judge's responsibility to exercise his powers in accordance with the overriding objective set out in CrimPR 1.

Thus:

(1) the prosecution may be required to identify a selection of counts on which

the trial should proceed, leaving a decision to be taken later whether to try any of the remainder;
(2) where an indictment contains substantive counts and one or more related conspiracy counts, the court will expect the prosecution to justify the joinder;
(3) failing justification, the prosecution should be required to choose whether to proceed on the substantive counts or on the conspiracy counts; and
(4) in any event, if there is a conviction on any counts that are tried, then those that have been postponed can remain on the file marked "not to be proceeded with without the leave of the court or the Court of Appeal".

In the event that a conviction is later quashed on appeal, the remaining counts can be tried. Where necessary the court has power to order that an indictment be severed.

(*CPD* II 10A.3–4)

11. Severance of counts

Where, before trial, or at any stage of a trial, the judge is of the opinion that: **39-022**

(1) any accused may be prejudiced or embarrassed in his defence by reason of being charged with more than one offence in the same indictment; or
(2) for any other reason it is desirable to direct that the person should be tried separately for any one or more offences charged in an indictment,

he may order a separate trial of any count or counts of such indictment.

Where the judge concludes that the postponement of the trial of one accused is expedient as a consequence of the exercise of any power to amend an indictment or to order a separate trial of a count, the judge must make such order as to the postponement of the trial as appears necessary.

(IA 1915 s.5)

Where an order is made under IA 1915 s.5 for the postponement of a trial:

(a) if such an order is made during a trial the judge may discharge the jury from giving a verdict on the count or counts the trial of which is postponed or on the indictment, as the case may be;
(b) the procedure on the separate trial of a count will be the same in all respects as if the count had been found in a separate indictment, and the procedure on the postponed trial will be the same in all respects (if the jury has been discharged under (a) above) as if the trial had not commenced; and
(c) the judge may make such order as to granting the accused person bail and as to the enlargement of recognisances and otherwise as he thinks fit.

The power contained in s.5(3) to sever an indictment was held to apply only to valid indictments in *R. v Newland* (1988) 87 Cr. App. R. 118. But see *R. v Smith* [1997] 1 Cr. App. R. 390 and *R. v Taylor* [2016] NICA 10.

The intention of the Act

The manifest intention of IA 1915 s.5, is that: **39-023**

(1) charges founded on the same facts or related to a series of offences of the same or a similar character properly can, and normally should be, joined in

one indictment and a joint trial of the charges will normally follow, although the judge has a discretionary power to direct separate trials under s.5(3); and

(2) the judge has no duty to direct separate trials under s.5(3) unless in his opinion there is some special feature of the case which would make a joint trial of the several counts prejudicial or embarrassing to the accused and separate trials are required in the interests of justice.

In some cases the offences charged may be too numerous and complicated, or too difficult to disentangle, so that a joint trial of all the counts is likely to cause confusion and the defence may be embarrassed or prejudiced. As to the number and/or complexity of the counts in the trial of counts for sexual offences, see *DPP v Boardman* (1974) 60 Cr. App. R. 165; *R. v Scarrott* (1977) 65 Cr. App. R. 125.

In other cases objection may be taken to the inclusion of a count on the ground that it is of a scandalous nature and likely to arouse in the minds of the jury hostile feelings against the accused (*Ludlow v Commissioner of Police of the Metropolis* (1970) 54 Cr. App. R. 233). As to the scandalous nature of the evidence, see *R. v Laycock* [2003] EWCA Crim 1477; [2003] Crim. L.R. 803.

Where there is a multi-count indictment for some other type of offence, the principles in *Ludlow v Commissioner of Police of the Metropolis* (1970) 54 Cr. App. R. 233 apply. See also *DPP v P* (1991) 93 Cr. App. R. 267; *R. v Christou* [1996] 2 Cr. App. R. 360; *R. v Cannan* (1991) 92 Cr. App. R. 16.

The fact that the accused wishes to give evidence in his own defence on one of the counts but not on the others is not, in the normal case, a sufficient reason for severance, even though non-severance will oblige him to choose between not testifying at all and exposing himself to cross-examination about all the charges (*R. v Phillips* (1987) 86 Cr. App. R. 18).

The statutory regimes governing joinder/severance and cross-admissibility are entirely separate. In considering an application for severance, it is relevant to consider whether the evidence on one count will be cross-admissible in relation to the other counts, but it remains the case that severance should only be ordered if there is some special feature of the case which would make a joint trial of several counts prejudicial or embarrassing to the defendant and separate trials were required in the interests of justice (*R. v Powell* [2014] EWCA Crim 642; [2014] 2 Cr. App. R. 31).

In exercising his discretion, the trial judge should seek to achieve a fair resolution of the issues. This requires fairness to the accused but also to the prosecution.

An application to sever the indictment may be made on more than one occasion, as where it is made at a preliminary hearing and, being refused, is made again at the trial. The question for any subsequent judge will be whether there has been a sufficient change to justify reopening the question. If there has not, he is not obliged to hear the same point argued again (*R. v Wright* (1989) 90 Cr. App. R. 325).

The procedure for applications to sever counts from an indictment is set out below at 39-025.

12. SEPARATE TRIAL OF ACCUSED

39-024 The trial judge has an inherent discretion to order separate trials of accused who have properly been joined in an indictment, in accordance with the principles stated in *Ludlow v Commissioner of Police of the Metropolis* (1970) 54 Cr. App. R. 233; see also *R. v Assim* [1966] 50 Cr. App. R. 224. The manner in which the discretion is exercised does not ordinarily provide a successful ground of appeal. Guidance may, however, be drawn from the authorities, as follows:

(1) where the accused are charged in a joint count, the arguments in favour of a joint trial are very strong (see *R. v Lake* (1976) 64 Cr. App. R. 172; *R. v Josephs* (1977) 65 Cr. App. R. 253) and separate trials will not be ordered unless the circumstances are "very exceptional" (*R. v Miah* [2011] EWCA Crim 945; [2012] 1 Cr. App. R. (S.) 11, applied in *R. v Godber* [2013] EWCA Crim 2623). Thus:
   (a) severance will necessitate much or all of the prosecution evidence being given twice before different juries and increase the risk of inconsistent verdicts; and
   (b) even if the accused are expected to blame each other for the offence, the interests of the prosecution and the public in a single trial will generally outweigh the interests of the defence in not having to call each accused before the same jury to give evidence for himself which will incriminate the others (see *R. v Miah* [2011] EWCA Crim 945; [2012] 1 Cr. App. R. (S.) 11, applied in *R. v Godber* [2013] EWCA Crim 2623).

(2) where the prosecution case against one accused includes evidence that is admissible against him but not against his co-accused, there is no obligation to order severance simply because the evidence in question might prejudice the jury against the latter. However the judge should balance the advantages of a single trial against the possible prejudice to the second accused and should consider especially how far an appropriate direction to the jury is really likely to ensure that they take into account the evidence only for its proper purpose of proving the case against the first (see *R. v Lake* (1976) 64 Cr. App. R. 172 and *R. v B* [2004] EWCA Crim 1254; [2004] 2 Cr. App. R. 34).

This ground for separate trials is linked to the rule against overloading indictments (see 39-021). Where a joint trial of numerous accused would lead to a very long and complicated trial, the judge should consider whether a number of shorter trials, each involving only some of the accused, might make for a fairer and more efficient disposition of the issues. There may be a distinction to be drawn between cases where the accused are jointly charged in a single count and those where they are alleged to have committed separate offences which were nonetheless sufficiently linked to be put in one indictment. In the latter situation, the cases against the accused are unlikely to be as closely intertwined as when a joint offence is alleged, and the public interest argument in favour of a single trial is correspondingly less strong.

Application for joint or separate trials, etc.

Where a party wants a judge of the Crown Court to order: **39-025**

(1) the joint trial of:
   (a) offences charged by separate indictments; or
   (b) accused charged in separate indictments;

   OR

(2) separate trials of;
   (a) offences charged by the same indictments; or
   (b) accused charged in the same indictment;

OR

(3) the deletion of a count from an indictment,

such a party must:

(i) apply in writing:
- as soon as practicable after becoming aware of the grounds for doing so; and
- before the trial begins, unless the grounds for the application do not arise until trial;

(ii) serve the application on the court officer and on each other party; and

(iii) in the application specify the order proposed, and explain why it should be made.

A party wanting to make representations in response to the application must serve the representations on the court officer and on each other party not more than 10 business days after service of the application.

(CrimPR 3.29)

Where a judge makes an order on an application under CrimPR 3.29 or amending an indictment in any other respect, the court officer will, unless the judge otherwise directs, endorse any paper copy of each affected indictment with a note of the court's order and the date of that order (CrimPR 3.30).

13. Ordering additional particulars

39-026 It is open to the defence to ask for additional particulars of a count. One of the purposes of doing so is to anchor the prosecution to a particular means by which the charge may be made out (e.g. *R. v Landy* (1981) 72 Cr. App. R. 237; *R. v Hancock* [1996] 2 Cr. App. R. 554).

It may be helpful to the defence, and good practice, for the prosecution to be required to provide the defence (and also the jury, if appropriate) with a separate note explaining the indictment or a summary of the allegations in each count.

14. Objections to the indictment

The need for action

39-027 Issues arising from the preferment and form of the indictment may be raised by the advocates on either side, or the judge may, in an appropriate case, act on his own initiative.

The means by which defects in the indictment may be cured, or otherwise disposed of are by:

(1) demurrer (in theory), or plea to the jurisdiction;
(2) motion to quash; or
(3) application to amend.

The time for action

39-028 The proper time for raising objections to the indictment, or to individual counts of the indictment, is before arraignment.

In *R. v Gleeson* [2003] EWCA Crim 3357; [2004] 1 Cr. App. R. 29 the defence advocate chose to reserve until the close of the prosecution case a fundamental objection to the indictment. A number of observations were made by the CACD:

(1) the defence should have drawn attention to the proposed legal challenge at the PCMH and in the defence statement; had they done so they could have had no valid objection to the prosecutor correcting his error at that stage or certainly by the commencement of the trial;
(2) the proper determination of such difficulties when they arise was often fact-sensitive; it might not always be possible for amendments to be permitted with fairness to the accused at so late a stage, wherever the fault lay;
(3) just as an accused should not be penalised for errors by his legal representatives made in the course of the defence, so also a prosecution should not be frustrated by errors of the prosecutor unless such an error made a fair trial for the accused impossible;
(4) for a defence advocate to seek to take advantage of such errors by deliberately delaying identification of an issue of fact or law in the case until the last possible moment is no longer acceptable given the legislative and procedural changes to the criminal justice process in recent years; it is contrary to the requirement on an accused under CPIA 1996 s.5(6)(b) to indicate the matters on which he takes issue with the prosecutor, and to his professional duty to the court, and is not in the legitimate interests of the accused;
(5) the fact that an accused may prefer as a matter of tactics to keep his case close to his chest was not a valid reason for preventing a full and fair hearing on the issues canvassed at the trial; and
(6) requiring an accused to indicate in advance what he disputed about the prosecution case offended neither the principle that the prosecutor had to prove his case nor that an accused was not obliged to inculpate himself.

15. Demurrer and plea to the jurisdiction

If demurrer still survives it is most unlikely that it will arise at the present day. It had long been supposed to be obsolete, supplanted by a motion to quash the indictment, but made a brief re-appearance in *R. v Inner London Quarter Sessions Ex p. Commissioner of Police of the Metropolis* (1970) 54 Cr. App. R. 49; cf. *R. v Cumberworth* [1989] Crim. L.R. 591. **39-029**

Demurrer was a plea in bar of trial, being an objection to the form or substance of the indictment, apparent on its face. The plea, like other pleas in bar had to be tendered in writing by or on behalf of the accused, and lodged with the Crown Office, a copy being served on the prosecutor, preferably prior to arraignment. The issue was decided by the judge, who is not entitled to refer to the depositions or other committal statements for the purpose. If demurrer failed, as in the case of autrefois acquit and convict, the accused was entitled to plead over to the indictment (CLA 1967 s.6(1)).

Similar principles apply in the case of a plea to the jurisdiction. If the plea fails, the indictment will be put and the accused is entitled to plead not guilty to the general issue (CLA 1967 s.6(1)).

Pleas to the jurisdiction are probably obsolete. Objections to jurisdiction clear from the face of the indictment are better taken by a motion to quash.

16. Motion to quash

Defence motion

39-030 A motion to quash may be brought in a variety of circumstances, including where the indictment:

(1) is bad on its face (e.g. for duplicity or because the particulars of a count do not disclose an offence known to law);
(2) (or a count thereof) has been preferred otherwise than in accordance with the provisions of AD(MP)A 1933 s.2; such an indictment must be quashed because it is preferred without authority (see *R. v Lombardi* (1989) 88 Cr. App. R. 179);
(3) contains a count for an offence in respect of which the accused was not sent for trial and the documents do not disclose a case to answer for that offence (*R. v Jones* (1974) 59 Cr. App. R. 120; but see *R. v Thompson* [2011] EWCA Crim 102; [2012] 1 Cr. App. R. 12 where a new count was added based on a notice of additional evidence).

Where the indictment follows the charges on which the accused was sent for trial, and is properly drafted on its face, the defence cannot invite the judge to quash on the basis that the evidence disclosed in the papers did not, in fact, disclose a case to answer, and that therefore the accused was wrongly sent for trial (*London County QS Ex p. Downes* (1903) 37 Cr. App. R. 148). Where, however, the indictment contains a count on which the accused was not sent for trial, the normal rule is relaxed in respect of that count, since otherwise the accused would be put on trial for the offence without any prior opportunity of arguing that the evidence was insufficient.

Failure to apply at trial may show that there was no miscarriage of justice (e.g. *R. v Donnelly* [1995] Crim. L.R. 131).

Prosecutor's motion

39-031 The prosecutor may seek to quash his own indictment, or counts in it, where he realises that the indictment is defective or invalid. The effect of a successful application to quash is that the accused may not be tried on the indictment (or the particular count to which the motion relates). However, this does not mean that the accused is thereby acquitted.

Although the quashing of the indictment exhausts the effect of the committal proceedings on which it was founded (*R. v Thompson* (1975) 61 Cr. App. R. 108; *R. v Newland* (1988) 87 Cr. App. R. 118) the prosecution are not prevented from instituting fresh proceedings or applying for a voluntary bill.

The better course will usually be to ask the judge to stay (but not quash) the defective indictment and at the same time prefer a fresh indictment correcting the error in the original draft (see *R. v Follett* (1989) 88 Cr. App. R. 310). Care should be taken to arraign the accused on the fresh indictment before the original indictment is stayed.

17. Amending the indictment

Statutory provisions

39-032 Where, before trial, or at any stage of the trial, it appears to the judge that the indictment is defective, he must make such order or amendment of the indictment as he thinks necessary to meet the circumstances of the case, unless, having regard to the merits of the case, the required amendment cannot be made without injustice.

The power to amend may be exercised both:

(1) in respect of formal defects in the wording of a count, for example when the statement of offence fails to specify the statute contravened or when the particulars do not disclose an essential element of the offence; and
(2) in respect of substantial defects such as divergences between the allegations in the count and the evidence foreshadowed in the witness statements or called at trial.

(IA 1915 s.5)

Any alteration in matters of description, and probably in many other respects, may be made in order to meet the evidence in the case so long as the amendment causes no injustice to the accused (*R. v Pople* [1950] 34 Cr. App. R. 168). An indictment may be defective if it merely fails to allege an offence disclosed by the witness statements. "Defective", in the context of s.5(1), is not restricted to defects in form, but "has got a very much wider meaning" (*R. v Radley* (1973) 58 Cr. App. R. 394).

The power to amend may be exercised in respect of voluntary bills of indictment preferred on the direction of a High Court judge (see 39-037) just as it may be exercised in respect of other indictments (*R. v Alcock* (1999) 1 Cr. App. R. 227; *R. v Wells* [1995] 2 Cr. App. R. 417).

Limitation on power to amend

If the indictment is so defective as to be a nullity, it is not capable of amendment and there is a mistrial. An indictment is invalid from the outset in this way where, for example, it alleges an offence unknown to law. Where a count describes a known offence inaccurately, however, it is capable of amendment, subject to the usual considerations of prejudice to the defendant (*R. v McVitie* (1960) 44 Cr. App. R. 201; applied in *R. v Tyler* (1992) 96 Cr. App. R. 332). See also 39-007. **39-033**

Insertion of a new count

As well as enabling amendments to be made to existing counts, s.5(1) permits the insertion of an entirely new count into an indictment, whether in addition to or in substitution for the original counts (*R. v Johal* (1972) 56 Cr. App. R. 348). The prosecutor may apply to amend a count which is duplicitous by splitting it into two separate counts (*R. v Grout* [2011] EWCA Crim 299; [2011] 1 Cr. App. R. 38). Where the addition is made after arraignment, it will be necessary for the accused to be re-arraigned on the new counts. **39-034**

The amendment to an indictment may be so extensive that the question arises whether it amounts to the substitution of a fresh indictment (see *R. v Fyffe* [1992] Crim. L.R. 442).

With the abolition of committal proceedings, and the substitution of proceedings for dismissal in the Crown Court, it is a question whether any of the old cases relating to evidence disclosed on the papers (e.g. *R. v Osieh* [1996] 2 Cr. App. R. 144; *R. v Dixon* (1991) 92 Cr. App. R. 43; *R. v Hall* (1968) 52 Cr. App. R. 528) are still relevant. In *Hall* it was held that the issue really was "whether the amendment asked for ... was supported by evidence given at the committal proceedings".

In *R. v Thompson* [2011] EWCA Crim 102; [2012] 1 Cr. App. R. 12, a new count was properly added where it was based on a notice of additional evidence. See also *R. v F* [2012] EWCA Crim 720; [2012] 2 Cr. App. R. 13, where a new count was added on a retrial where further evidence had come to light.

Timing of amendment; risk of injustice

39-035 IA 1915 s.5(1), makes clear that an indictment may be amended at any stage of a trial, whether before or after arraignment—see *R. v Johal* (1972) 56 Cr. App. R. 348 (after arraignment but before empanelling the jury); *R. v Pople* [1950] 34 Cr. App. R. 168 (after the close of the prosecution case); *R. v Teong Sun Chuah* [1991] Crim. L.R. 463 (after a successful half time submission); and *R. v Collison* (1980) 71 Cr. App. R. 249 (after the jury had been out considering their verdict for over three hours).

Where a defendant pleaded guilty to a count of burglary which did not specify that the building in question was a dwelling, the court had the power to vacate the guilty pleas in the absence of an application by the defendant. Alternatively, the judge could have offered the defendant an opportunity to vacate his plea but allow his plea to stand as a plea to the amended indictment if he did not wish to vacate his plea (*R. v Love* [2013] EWCA Crim 257; [2013] 2 Cr. App. R. 4).

The later the amendment, the greater the risk of its causing injustice and therefore the less likely it ought to be allowed. However, an indictment may be amended even at the stage of retrial, provided that no injustice is done (*R. v Swaine* [2001] Crim. L.R. 166).

The principal consideration for the judge in deciding whether to allow an amendment is the risk of injustice. If the amendment cannot be made without injustice, it must not be made (IA 1915 s.5(1)). The timing of the amendment is a major factor in determining whether there will be injustice; see *R. v Gregory* (1972) 56 Cr. App. R. 441 (late amendment to the particulars by the deletion of the allegation as to ownership where that was the central issue in the case); *R. v O'Connor* [1997] Crim. L.R. 516 (amendment made at the close of the prosecution case allowing the prosecutor to shift his ground significantly).

In *R. v Foster* [2007] EWCA Crim 2869; [2008] 1 Cr. App. R. 38, the CACD commented on late amendments to an indictment where a lesser alternative was available to the jury, noting that the true purpose of an indictment is to specify the charges upon which the prosecution, *not the court*, is seeking a conviction or convictions. See also *R. v B(JJ)* [2012] EWCA Crim 1440; *The Times*, 8 May 2012.

When amendment is allowed, a notė of the order must be endorsed on the indictment (IA 1915 s.5(2) and CrimPR 3.30(2)).

In *R. v Stocker* [2013] EWCA Crim 1993; [2014] 1 Cr. App. R. 18; where the indictment in a trial for rape specified SOA 1956, rather than the 2003 Act, the CACD said the error (in the absence of any prejudice) was a pure technicality (see also *R. v Wilson* [2013] EWCA Crim 1780; [2014] 1 Cr. App. R. 10).

Where the prosecutor wishes to substitute or add counts to the indictment, or to invite the court to allow an indictment to be amended so that it charges offences which differ from those with which the defendant was first charged, the defendant should be given as much notice as possible of what is proposed in order to avoid delaying the proceedings (*CPD* II 10A.10).

If necessary, an adjournment may be granted to allow the parties (in particular the defence) to deal with the altered position (s.5(4)). Where the amendment comes during the course of a trial, there is power to discharge the jury from giving a verdict and to order a retrial on the indictment (s.5(5)).

18. CASES OF SERIOUS FRAUD

The *Protocol for the Control and Management of Heavy Fraud and other Complex Criminal Cases* [2005] 2 All E.R. 429 governs serious fraud and complex cases which are expected to last more than eight weeks, in conjunction with the CrimPR. In respect of matters concerning the indictment: **39-036**

(1) one course the judge may consider is pruning the indictment by omitting certain charges and/or by omitting certain accused. The judge must not usurp the function of the prosecution in this regard, and he must bear in mind that he will, at the outset, know less about the case than the advocates. The aim is to achieve fairness to all parties; and
(2) the judge has two methods of pruning available for use in appropriate circumstances:
   (a) persuading the prosecution that it is not worthwhile pursuing certain charges and/or certain accused; or
   (b) severing the indictment. Severance for reasons of case management alone is perfectly proper, although the judge should have regard to any representations made by the prosecution that severance would weaken their case. Before using what may be seen as a blunt instrument, the judge should insist on seeing full defence statements of all affected accused. Severance may be unfair to the prosecution if, for example, there is a cut-throat defence in prospect. For example, the defence of the principal accused may be that he relied on the advice of his accountant or solicitor that what was happening was acceptable. The defence of the professional may be that he gave no such advice. Against that background, it might be unfair to the prosecution to order separate trials of the two accused (see also CASE MANAGEMENT).

19. APPLYING FOR VOLUNTARY BILL

General

AJ(MP)A 1933 s.2(2)(b) and CDA 1998 Sch.3 para.2(6) allow the preferment of a bill of indictment by the direction or with the consent of a judge of the High Court. Bills so preferred are known as "voluntary bills". Applications for consent must comply with CrimPR 10.3 (*CPD* II 10B.2). The preferment of a voluntary bill is an exceptional procedure. Consent should only be granted where good reason to depart from the normal procedure is clearly shown and only where the interests of justice, rather than considerations of administrative convenience, require it (*CPD* II 10B.4). **39-037**

In *R. v Arfan* [2012] EWHC 2450 (QB); (2012) 176 J.P. 682, the CACD said that High Court judges should be very cautious about granting leave to prefer a voluntary bill against an accused. There is no exhaustive list of the circumstances in which it may be appropriate, but exceptional circumstances are called for.

In *SFO v Evans* [2014] EWHC 3803; [2015] 1 W.L.R. 3526 QBD stated that circumstances in which a voluntary bill might be granted following a dismissal of charges included:

(1) where charges had been dismissed on the basis of a technicality which the prosecution had reasonably failed to anticipate;
(2) where the judge had made a clear, obvious, basic and substantive error;
(3) where significant new evidence providing a sustainable basis for the charge had come to light after the dismissal hearing; and
(4) where there had been a serious procedural irregularity.

It might also be granted, sparingly, where the prosecution had changed its mind or to correct a prosecutorial mistake. However, it would not be granted where the prosecution had failed to identify the proper legal basis of the charges at the outset and had then repeatedly reformulated its case in an attempt to identify a sustainable legal basis. See also *Evans v SFO* [2015] EWHC 1525 (QB).

Procedure

39-038 Applications for a voluntary bill must be made following CrimPR 10.9. The prosecutor must serve a written application which:

(1) is served on the court and the defendant (unless the judge otherwise directs);
(2) attaches:
    (a) the proposed indictment;
    (b) copies of any documents containing the evidence upon which the prosecutor relies;
    (c) the indictment on which the defendant has already been arraigned; and
    (d) a list of any other offences for which the defendant has already been sent for trial (if not included in the existing indictment);
(3) requests a hearing, if the prosecutor wants one, and explains why it is needed;
(4) includes:
    (a) a concise statement of the circumstances of, and the reasons for, the application; and
    (b) a concise summary of the evidence attached to the application, cross referencing each passage in the evidence to the counts in the proposed indictment;
(5) contains (unless the application is made by the DPP or DSFO) a statement that to the best of the prosecutor's knowledge, information and belief:
    (a) the evidence relied upon will be available at trial; and
    (b) the allegations in the application are substantially true.

A proposed defendant served with an application who wishes to make representations must:

(i) serve the representations on the court and the prosecutor as soon as possible, or as directed; and
(ii) request a hearing, if the defendant wants one, and explain why it is needed.

The judge may determine the application without a hearing, or at a hearing in public or in private. He may receive oral evidence from any proposed witness, and may direct that any statement made in accordance with (5) must be repeated on oath or affirmation.

If permission is given to serve a draft indictment, the decision must be recorded in writing and endorsed on, or annexed to, the proposed indictment.

(CrimPR 10.9)

Any oral submissions should be made on notice to the other party and in open court, unless the judge directs otherwise (*CPD* II 10B.6). These requirements should be complied with in relation to each accused named in the indictment for which consent is sought, whether or not it is proposed to prefer any new count against him. (*CPD* II 10B.3)

20. Deferred prosecution agreements

See DEFERRED PROSECUTION AGREEMENTS. **39-039**

40. INVESTIGATIVE ORDERS AND WARRANTS

Quick Guide

A. Introduction

The legislation

40-001 A judge of the Crown Court may be asked to make a number of orders and warrants in relation to criminal investigations. These arise principally under the Police and Criminal Evidence Act 1984, the Proceeds of Crime Act 2002 and the Terrorism Act 2000. The conditions precedent to the making of such orders are to be found in the statute under which they arise. Procedure is governed by CrimPR.

A judge of the Crown Court may be asked to grant access to bankers' books under the Bankers Book Evidence Act 1879 (40-073), and to issue Letters of Request under the Criminal Justice Act 1988 (40-074). As to applications for the taking of evidence for overseas proceedings under the Crime (International Cooperation) Act 2003, see 40-076 and concerning Requests for Information about Banking Transactions for use in the UK, see 40-081.

An application requires of the judge;

(1) careful consideration and rigorous critical analysis;
(2) reasons for his decision, and in a complicated case, a short summary of the analytical processes undertaken by him in his scrutiny of the material presented.

(*R. (on the application of Rawlinson and Hunter Trustees) v Central Criminal Court* [2012] EWHC 2254 (Admin) and *R. v Zinga* [2012] EWCA Crim 2357; [2013] Crim. L.R. 226, where the cases are reviewed).

CPD emphasises (XI 47A.1) that the powers conferred by such orders are among the most intrusive that investigators can exercise. Every application must be carefully scrutinised with close attention paid to what the relevant statutory provision requires of the applicant and to what it permits.

The issuing of a warrant or the making of such an order is never to be treated as a formality and it is therefore essential that the judge considering the application is given, and must take, sufficient time for the purpose. The prescribed forms require the applicant to provide a time estimate, and listing officers should take account of these (*CPD* XI 47A.2).

Applicants for orders and warrants owe the court duties of candour and truthfulness; on any application made without notice to the respondent, and so on all applications for search warrants, the duty of frank and complete disclosure is especially onerous. The applicant must draw the judge's attention to any information that is unfavourable to the application; the existence of unfavourable information will not necessarily lead to the application being refused; it will be a matter for the judge what weight to place on each piece of information (*CPD* XI 47A.3).

The contents of any warrant must be clear and precise, identifying any suspects by name and any articles which are sought (*Van der Pijl v Kingston Crown Court* [2012] EWHC 3745 (Admin); [2013] A.C.D. 29; *R. (on the application of Anand) v HM Revenue and Customs Commissioners* [2012] EWHC 2989 (Admin)).

B. Procedure

General

The rules concerning investigative orders and warrants were overhauled by the Criminal Procedure (Amendment) Rules 2016, and further revisions were made by the Criminal Procedure (Amendment) Rules 2017, the Criminal Procedure (Amendment No. 3) Rules 2017, the Criminal Procedure (Amendment) Rules 2018 (SI 2018/132) and the Criminal Procedure (Amendment No. 2) Rules 2021 (SI 2021/849). **40-002**

The rules are now organised as follows:

(1) general rules applicable to all applications (CrimPR 47.1–47.3);
(2) general rules applicable to "investigation orders" (CrimPR 47.4–47.9);
(3) a set of highly prescriptive rules for each type of investigation order under each piece of legislation (CrimPR 47.10–47.23);
(4) general rules applicable to all "investigation warrants" (CrimPR 47.24–47.27);

(5) a set of highly prescriptive rules for each type of investigation warrant under each piece of legislation (CrimPR 47.28–47.34);
(6) rules concerning orders for the return or retention of property (CrimPR 47.35–47.40);
(7) rules concerning orders for the retention of fingerprints (CrimPR 47.41–47.44);
(8) rules concerning investigation anonymity orders under CorJA 2009 (CrimPR 47.45–47.49); and
(9) rules concerning investigation approval orders under RIPA 2000 (CrimPR 47.50–47.52).

CrimPR 47 must be followed, and the accompanying forms must be used. These are designed to prompt applicants, and the courts, to deal with all of the relevant criteria. The prescribed forms require the applicant to provide a time estimate, and listing officers should take account of these (*CPD* XI 47A.1).

The use of production orders and search warrants involves the use of intrusive state powers that affect the rights and liberties of individuals. It is the responsibility of the judge to ensure that those powers are not abused. To do so he must be presented with:

(1) a properly completed application, on the appropriate form;
(2) which includes a summary of the investigation to provide the context for the order;
(3) a clear explanation of how the statutory requirements are fulfilled; and
(4) full and frank disclosure of anything that might undermine the basis for the application.

Duties of applicant

40-003 The applicant should pay particular attention to the specific legislative requirements for the granting of such an application to ensure that the court has all of the necessary information, and, if the court might be unfamiliar with the legislation, should provide a copy of the relevant provisions. Applicants must comply with the duties of candour and truthfulness (see 40-001) and include in their application the declarations required by the CrimPR and must make disclosure of any unfavourable information to the court (*CPD* XI 47A.3).

Record and forms

40-004 Where an applicant supplements an application with additional oral or written information, on questioning by the judge or otherwise, it is essential that an adequate record is kept. What is needed will depend upon the circumstances. The CrimPR require that a record of the "gist" be retained. The purpose of such a record is to allow the sufficiency of the judge's reasons for his decision subsequently to be assessed. The gravity of such decisions requires that their exercise should be susceptible to scrutiny and to explanation by reference to all of the information that was taken into account (*CPD* XI 47A.4).

The forms that accompany CrimPR 47 provide for the frequently encountered applications; however, there are some hundreds of powers of entry, search and seizure, supplied by a corresponding number of legislative provisions. In any criminal matter, if there is no form designed for the particular warrant or order sought, the forms should still be used, as far as is practicable, and adapted as necessary (*CPD* XI 47A.5).

Exercise of court's powers: investigation orders

Subject to (1), (2) and (3) below, the judge may determine an application for an order, or to vary or discharge an order, at a hearing (which must be in private unless he otherwise directs), or without a hearing, and in the absence of the applicant, the respondent (if any), and any other person affected by the order, but: **40-005**

(1) he must not determine such an application in the applicant's absence if:
  (a) the applicant asks for a hearing; or
  (b) it appears to the judge that:
    (i) the proposed order may infringe legal privilege, within the meaning of PACE 1984 s.10 or of POCA 2002 ss.348 or 361 or art.9 of the Proceeds of Crime Act 2002 (External Investigations) Order 2014;
    (ii) the proposed order may require the production of excluded material, within the meaning of PACE 1984 s.11; or
    (iii) for any other reason the application is so complex or serious as to require the judge to hear the applicant.

(2) he must not determine such an application in the absence of any respondent or other person affected, unless:
  (a) the absentee has had at least two business days in which to make representations; or
  (b) the judge is satisfied that:
    (i) the applicant cannot identify or contact the absentee;
    (ii) it would prejudice the investigation if the absentee were present;
    (iii) it would prejudice the investigation to adjourn or postpone the application so as to allow the absentee to attend; or
    (iv) the absentee has waived the opportunity to attend.

(3) he must not determine such an application in the absence of a respondent who, if the order sought by the applicant was made, would be required to produce or give access to journalistic material, unless that respondent has waived the opportunity to attend.

The court officer must arrange for the application to be heard no sooner than two business days after it was served unless the court directs that no hearing need be arranged or the court gives other directions for the hearing.

If the judge so directs, parties may attend by live link or by telephone.

The judge must not make, vary or discharge an order unless the applicant states, in writing or orally, that to the best of the applicant's knowledge and belief:

(a) the application discloses all the information that is material to what the court must decide; and
(b) the content of the application is true.

Where the statement required is made orally it must be on oath or affirmation, unless the judge otherwise directs. The court must arrange for a record of the making of the statement.

(CrimPR 47.5)

The application: investigation orders

40-006 An applicant must:

(1) apply in writing and serve the application on the court officer;
(2) demonstrate that the applicant is entitled to make the application;
(3) provide an estimate of the time it will take the court to read and prepare for the hearing, and an estimate of the length of the hearing;
(4) attach a draft order;
(5) serve notice of the application on the respondent unless the court otherwise directs; and
(6) serve the application on the respondent to such extent, if any, as the court directs.

A notice served on the respondent must:

(a) specify the material or information in respect of which the application is made;
(b) identify the power the applicant invites the court to exercise; and
(c) identify the conditions for the exercise of that power.

The applicant must serve any order made on the respondent.
(CrimPR 47.6)
Where the application includes information that the applicant thinks ought only to be revealed to the court, the application must:

(i) identify that information; and
(ii) explain why it ought not to be served on the respondent or another person.

At the hearing the general rule is that the court must consider, in the following sequence:

(1) representations first by the applicant and then by the respondent and any other person, in the presence of them all, and then;
(2) further representations by the applicant, in the others' absence,

but the court may direct other arrangements.
(CrimPR 47.7)

Application to vary or discharge an order: investigation orders

40-007 An applicant, respondent or affected person who wants the court to vary or discharge an order must:

(1) apply in writing as soon as possible after becoming aware of the grounds for doing so;
(2) serve the application on the court officer and the respondent, applicant or person affected as applicable;
(3) explain why it is appropriate for the order to be varied or discharged;
(4) propose the terms of any variation; and
(5) ask for a hearing, if one is wanted, and explain why it is needed.

(CrimPR 47.8)

Application to punish for contempt of court: investigation orders

Where a person is accused of disobeying a relevant order, an applicant who wants the court to exercise its power to punish that person for contempt of court must comply with CrimPR 48. **40-008**
(CrimPR 47.9)

Power to vary requirements: investigation orders

The judge may: **40-009**

(1) shorten or extend (even after it has expired) a time limit;
(2) dispense with a requirement for service (even after service was required); and
(3) consider an application made orally instead of in writing.

A person who wants an extension of time must apply when serving the application for which it is needed and explain the delay.
(CrimPR 47.5)

Exercise of the court's powers: investigation warrants

(1) The court must determine an application for a warrant: **40-010**
   (a) at a hearing, which must be in private unless the court otherwise directs;
   (b) in the presence of the applicant; and
   (c) in the absence of any person affected by the warrant, including any person in occupation or control of premises which the applicant wants to search.
(2) If the court so directs, the applicant may attend the hearing by live link or telephone.
(3) The court must not determine an application unless satisfied that sufficient time has been allowed for it.
(4) The court must not determine an application unless the applicant confirms, on oath or affirmation, that to the best of the applicant's knowledge and belief:
   (a) the application discloses all the information that is material to what the court must decide, including any circumstances that might reasonably be considered capable of undermining any of the grounds of the application; and
   (b) the content of the application is true.
(5) If the court requires the applicant to answer a question about an application:
   (a) the applicant's answer must be on oath or affirmation;
   (b) the court must arrange for a record of the gist of the question and reply; and
   (c) if the applicant cannot answer to the court's satisfaction, the court may:
      (i) specify the information the court requires; and
      (ii) give directions for the presentation of any renewed application.
(6) If the court considers information to which rule 47.26(4) refers (information that the applicant thinks should be kept confidential), the court must so record.
(7) Unless to do so would be inconsistent with other legislation, on an application the court may issue—

(a) a warrant in respect of specified premises;
(b) a warrant in respect of all premises occupied or controlled by a specified person;
(c) a warrant in respect of all premises occupied or controlled by a specified person which specifies some of those premises; or
(d) more than one warrant—
  (i) each one in respect of premises specified in the warrant;
  (ii) each one in respect of all premises occupied or controlled by a person specified in the warrant (whether or not such a warrant also specifies any of those premises); or
  (iii) at least one in respect of specified premises and at least one in respect of all premises occupied or controlled by a specified person (whether or not such a warrant also specifies any of those premises).

The application: investigation warrants

40-011 CrimPR 47.26 provides that

(1) …
(2) The applicant must:
  (a) apply in writing;
  (b) serve the application on:
    (i) the court officer; or
    (ii) if the court office is closed, the court;
  (c) demonstrate that the applicant is entitled to apply, for example as a constable or under legislation that applies to other officers;
  (d) give the court an estimate of how long the court should allow:
    (i) to read and prepare for the application; and
    (ii) for the hearing of the application; and
  (e) tell the court when the applicant expects any warrant issued to be executed.
(3) The application must disclose anything known or reported to the applicant that might reasonably be considered capable of undermining any of the grounds of the application.
(4) Where the application includes information that the applicant thinks should be kept confidential, the applicant may:
  (a) set out that information in a separate document, marked accordingly; and
  (b) in that document, explain why the applicant thinks that that information ought not to be supplied to anyone other than the court.
(5) The application must include:
  (a) a declaration by the applicant that to the best of the applicant's knowledge and belief:
    (i) the application discloses all the information that is material to what the court must decide, including anything that might reasonably be considered capable of undermining any of the grounds of the application; and
    (ii) the content of the application is true; and
  (b) a declaration by an officer senior to the applicant that the senior officer has reviewed and authorised the application.

(6) The application must attach a draft warrant or warrants in the terms proposed by the applicant.

C. Orders under PACE 1984

General

By PACE 1984 s.9 and Sch.1 jurisdiction is conferred upon a Circuit Judge to entertain an application by an investigating officer to gain access to "special-procedure" and "excluded" material which cannot be achieved by means of a magistrates' warrant under s.8. The section makes no provision for access to legally privileged material, as to which see *R. v Inner London Crown Court Ex p. Baines* (1988) 87 Cr. App. R. 111 and *R. v Central Criminal Court Ex p. Francis* (1989) 88 Cr. App. R. 213). See also *Hallinan Blackburn Gittings & Nott (A Firm) v Middlesex Guildhall Crown Court* [2004] EWHC 2726 (Admin); [2005] 1 W.L.R. 766. **40-012**

The costs of any application under this procedure and of anything done or to be done in pursuance of an order made under it are in the discretion of the judge (PACE 1984 Sch.1 para.16). For an example of the application of para.16, see *HMRC v Financial Investment Advisers* [2009] Lloyd's Rep. F.C. 221.

An application under PACE 1984 (as opposed to one under POCA 2002 (see 40-027)) is appropriate where production of the material is sought for criminal investigation purposes to determine whether an offence has been committed, and, if so, to provide evidence of it (*R. v Southwark Crown Court* [1996] Cr. App. R. 436).

1. Production orders

If, on an application made by a constable, a judge is satisfied that one or other of the sets of access conditions set out below is fulfilled, he may make an order that the person who appears to be in possession of the material to which the application relates: **40-013**

(1) produce it to a constable for him to take away; or
(2) give him access to it, not later than the end of the period of seven days from the making of the order, or such longer period as he may specify.

(PACE 1984 s.9, Sch.1 paras 1, 4)

A computer and its hard disk are within the definition of "material" in PACE 1984 s.8(1) (*R. (on the application of Barclay) v Lord Chancellor and Secretary of State for Justice* [2008] EWCA Civ 1319; [2009] 2 W.L.R. 1205).

Where the material consists of information stored in any electronic form:

(a) an order under (1) has effect as an order to produce the material in a form in which it can be taken away and in which it is visible and legible, or from which it can readily be produced in a visible and legible form; and
(b) an order under (2) has effect as an order to give a constable access to the material in a form in which it is visible and legible.

(PACE 1984 Sch.1 para.5)

For the purposes of PACE 1984 ss.21 and 22 (access and copying, retention) material produced in pursuance of an order under (1) above is treated as if it were material seized by a constable (PACE 1984 Sch.1 para 6).

A person who fails to comply with an order may be dealt with by a judge as if he had committed contempt of the Crown Court, and enactments relating to contempt of that court have effect in relation to the matter (PACE 1984 Sch.1 para.15, and see CONTEMPT OF COURT).

Inter partes application

40-014 An application for an order that relates to material that consists of or includes journalistic material must be made inter partes (PACE 1984 Sch.1 para.7), after notice of application has been served (under para.8) (see *R. v Maidstone Crown Court Ex p. Waitt* [1988] Crim. L.R. 384). Notice of an application for such an order may be served on a person either by delivering it to him or by leaving it at his proper address or by sending it by post to him in a registered letter or by the recorded delivery service. The notice may be served on a body corporate, by serving it on the body's secretary or clerk or other similar officer; and on a partnership, by serving it on one of the partners (PACE 1984 Sch.1 paras 9, 10).

The application:

(1) must be accompanied by a document or documents containing a description of the material for which discovery is sought (*R. v Central Criminal Court Ex p. Adegbesan* (1987) 84 Cr. App. R. 219), though there may be occasions on which oral information is sufficient (*R. v Manchester Crown Court Ex p. Taylor* (1988) 87 Cr. App. R. 358);

(2) must state the general nature of the offence under investigation, though it is not necessary to state the precise section of any enactment (*R. v Manchester Crown Court Ex p. Taylor* (1988) 87 Cr. App. R. 358); and

(3) must state the address of the premises where the material is alleged to be.

As to service, see SERVICE OF DOCUMENTS.

Where notice of an application for such an order has been served on a person, he must not conceal, destroy, alter or dispose of the material to which the application relates except with the leave of a judge or with the written permission of a constable, until the application is dismissed or abandoned or he has complied with any order made on the application (PACE 1984 Sch.1 para.11).

Whatever material is given to the judge must be served upon the party against whom the order is sought; statements which have no substance, and which are to the prejudice of the party against whom the order is sought, ought to be ruled out by the judge (*R. v Inner London Crown Court Ex p. Baines & Baines* (1988) 87 Cr. App. R. 111).

The Act does not require the suspect to be given notice when the evidence sought is in the hands of a third party (*R. v Leicester Crown Court Ex p. DPP* (1988) 86 Cr. App. R. 243).

The "access conditions"

40-015 Before granting an order, the judge must be satisfied that one or other of the access conditions contained in Sch.1 paras 2 and 3 are made out (PACE 1984 s.11); it is not enough that the applicant believes them to be satisfied (*R. v Central Criminal Court* [2002] Crim. L.R. 65). Although the strict rules of evidence do not apply to a hearing there must be evidence that the relevant set of access conditions has been fulfilled.

"The first set of access conditions"

The "first set of access conditions" is fulfilled if: 40-016

(1) there are reasonable grounds for believing:
  (a) that an indictable offence has been committed;
  (b) that there is material which consists of "special procedure material" (see 40-019), or includes such material and does not also include "excluded material" (see 40-018) on premises specified in the application;
  (c) that the material is likely to be of substantial value (whether by itself or together with other material) to the investigation in connection with which the application is made; and
  (d) that the material is likely to be relevant evidence;
(2) other methods of obtaining the material:
  (a) have been tried without success; or
  (b) have not been tried because it appeared that they were bound to fail; and
(3) it is in the public interest, having regard:
  (a) to the benefit likely to accrue to the investigation if the material is obtained; and
  (b) to the circumstances under which the person in possession of the material holds it,

that it should be produced or that access should be given to it.

(PACE 1984 Sch.1 para.2)

Where the first set of access conditions is made out, the judge may make a production order even where it might infringe the privilege against self-incrimination (*R. v Central Criminal Court Ex p. Bright* [2001] 2 All E.R. 244), though in exercising his discretion, he should consider the implications of self-incrimination.

"The second set of access conditions"

The "second set of access conditions" is fulfilled if: 40-017

(1) there are reasonable grounds for believing that there is material which consists of or includes "excluded material" or "special procedure material on premises specified in the application;
(2) but for s.9(2) of the Act a search of the premises for that material could have been authorised by the issue of a warrant to a constable under an enactment; and
(3) the issue of such a warrant would have been appropriate.

(PACE 1984 Sch.1 para.3)

"Excluded material"; "journalistic material" defined

Excluded material is defined in PACE 1984 as: 40-018

(1) personal records which a person has acquired or created in the course of any trade, business, profession or other occupation, or for the purposes of any paid or unpaid office and which he holds in confidence; and

(2) human tissue or tissue fluid which has been taken for the purpose of diagnosis or medical treatment and which a person holds in confidence; and
(3) "journalistic material" (see below) which a person holds in confidence and which consists of documents or records other than documents.

A person holds material other than "journalistic material" in confidence for these purposes if he holds it subject:

(a) to an express or implied undertaking to hold it in confidence; or
(b) to a restriction on disclosure or an obligation of secrecy contained in any enactment, including an enactment contained in an Act passed after PACE 1984.

A person holds "journalistic material" in confidence for those purposes if:

(i) he holds it subject to such an undertaking, restriction or obligation; and
(ii) it has been continuously held (by one or more persons) subject to such an undertaking, restriction or obligation since it was first acquired or created for the purposes of journalism.

(PACE 1984 s.11)

"Journalistic material" is defined as material acquired or created for the purposes of journalism, but for the purposes PACE 1984, only if it is in the possession of a person who acquired or created it for the purposes of journalism. A person who receives material from someone who intends that the recipient shall use it for the purposes of journalism is to be taken to have acquired it for those purposes (PACE 1984 s.13).

"Special procedure material" defined

40-019 "Special procedure material" is defined in the Act as "journalistic material" (see 40-018), other than "excluded material" (see 40-018) and, material, other than items subject to legal privilege (see 40-020) and "excluded material" (see 40-018), in the possession of a person who:

(1) acquired or created it in the course of any trade, business, profession or other occupation or for the purpose of any paid or unpaid office; and
(2) holds it subject to an express or implied undertaking to hold it in confidence or to a restriction or obligation such as is mentioned in s.11(2)(b).

Where material is:

(a) acquired by an employee from his employer and in the course of his employment by a company from an associated company, it is only "special procedure material" if it was special procedure material immediately before the acquisition;
(b) created by an employee in the course of his employment, it is only "special procedure material" if it would have been special procedure material had his employer created it;
(c) created by a company on behalf of an associated company, it is only "special procedure material" if it would have been special procedure material had the associated company created it.

(PACE 1984 s.14)

"Items subject to legal privilege"

"Items subject to legal privilege" are defined in PACE 1984 s.10 as: **40-020**

(1) communications between a professional legal adviser and his client or any person representing his client, made in connection with the giving of legal advice to the client;
(2) communications between a professional legal adviser and his client or any person representing his client or between such an adviser or his client or any such representative and any other person, made in connection with or in contemplation of legal proceedings and for the purposes of such proceedings; and
(3) items enclosed with or referred to in such communications and made:
    (i) in connection with the giving of legal advice; or
    (ii) in connection with or in contemplation of legal proceedings and for the purposes of such proceedings,

when they are in the possession of a person who is entitled to possession of them, unless they are held with the intention of furthering a criminal purpose when they are not items subject to legal privilege.

Procedure

As well as complying with the general rules in CrimPR 47.6, every application for a PACE 1984 production order must also comply with the strict requirements of CrimPR 47.10. **40-021**

2. Search warrants

Where, on an application made by a constable, a Circuit Judge is satisfied: **40-022**

(1) that either set of access conditions set out in 40-016 and 40-017 is fulfilled; and
(2) that:
    (a) it is not practicable to communicate with any person entitled to grant entry to the premises to which the application relates; or
    (b) it is practicable to communicate with such person, but not with any person entitled to grant access to the material; or
    (c) the material contains information subject to a restriction or obligation of confidentiality (defined in s.11(2)(b) of the Act) and which is likely to be disclosed in breach of it if a warrant is not issued; or
    (d) that service of a notice of application for an access order might seriously prejudice the investigation,

he may issue a warrant authorising entry to and search of the premises under that warrant; anything for which a search has been authorised may be seized and retained.

(PACE 1984 Sch.1 paras 12–14)

Where, on an application made by a constable, a Circuit Judge is satisfied that:

1. the second set of access conditions is satisfied; and
2. an order under para.4 for a production order has not been complied with,

he may issue a warrant authorising entry to and search of the premises under that warrant; anything for which a search has been authorised may be seized and retained.

(PACE 1984 Sch.1 para.12(b) and 13)

The judge may not issue an all premises warrant unless satisfied:

(i) that there are reasonable grounds for believing that it is necessary to search premises occupied or controlled by the person in question which are not specified in the application, as well as those which are, in order to find the material in question; and
(ii) that it is not reasonably practicable to specify all the premises which he occupies or controls which might need to be searched.

(PACE Sch.1 para.12A)

There will be cases where a production order is likely to be obstructed and so only a search warrant will be appropriate, but an application under PACE 1984 Sch.1 para.12 must not become a matter of common form. Where such a search is authorised the High Court has said that the reason for authorising it ought to be made clear (*R. v Maidstone Crown Court Ex p. Waitt* [1988] Crim. L.R. 384); *R. v Leeds Crown Court Ex p. Switalski* [1991] Crim. L.R. 559). In *R. (on the application of Faisaltex Ltd) v Preston Crown Court* [2008] EWHC 2832 (Admin.); [2009] 1 Cr. App. R. 37 DC a search warrant for the offices of a reputable firm of solicitors was quashed where there was no basis upon which the judge could conclude that the issue of a production order might seriously prejudice the investigation.

Approach to application

40-023 An application is made ex parte. The authorities show that since the issue of a warrant is a very serious interference with the liberty of the subject:

(1) it should be issued only after the "most mature careful consideration of all the facts of the case" (*Williams v Summerfield* (1972) 56 Cr. App. R. 597);
(2) the responsibility for ensuring that the procedure is not abused lies with the judge, who should be scrupulous in discharging that responsibility (*R. v Maidstone Crown Court Ex p. Waitt* [1988] Crim. L.R. 384); and
(3) in a case of complexity, it should not go through "on the nod", but the judge ought to give his reasons for granting the warrant, showing that he has taken the appropriate matters into account (*R. v Southwark Crown Court Ex p. Sorsky Defries* [1996] C.O.D. 117; see also *R. (Newcastle United Football Club Ltd) v The Commissioners of HMRC* [2017] EWHC 2402 (Admin); [2017] 4 W.L.R. 187 on the importance of giving reasons).

The authorities emphasise the importance of strictly adhering to the proper procedure by which a warrant is obtained. See for example *R. (on the application of S) v Chief Constable of the BTP* [2013] EWHC 2189 (Admin); [2014] 1 W.L.R. 1647; see also. *R. v Lewes Crown Court Ex p. Hill* (1991) 93 Cr. App. R. 60; *Wood v North Avon MC* [2009] EWCH 3614 (Admin); (2010) 174 J.P. 157; *R. (on the application of G) v Commissioner of Police of the Metropolis* [2011] EWHC 3331 (Admin).

In considering the application, the judge is not restricted to considering material that could be disclosed to the subject of the warrant. The judge may consider material which could not be disclosed to the subject of the warrant and can restrict what could be disclosed, even if what fell to be disclosed could not, without more, support the conclusions necessary for the warrant to be granted (*R. (on the applica-*

tion of Haralambous) v St Albans Crown Court [2016] EWHC 916 (Admin); [2016] 2 Cr. App. R. 17).

Procedure

40-024 As well as complying with the general rules in CrimPR 47.24–47.27, every application for a PACE 1984 warrant must also comply with the strict requirements of CrimPR 47.28.

D. Orders under POCA 2002

1. General

Orders available

40-025 Under POCA 2002 a judge may be called upon to make orders in relation to confiscation, money laundering and detained cash proceedings, as follows:

(1) a *production order* (40-027) requiring a person to produce any relevant material which is in his possession or under his control;
(2) an *order to grant entry* (40-030);
(3) a *disclosure order* (40-034) requiring persons to give the appropriate person any relevant information;
(4) a *customer information order* (40-038) requiring a financial institution to provide information relating to the affairs of a customer;
(5) an *account monitoring order* (40-043) requiring a financial institution to provide details of transactions on a particular account over a specified period of time; and
(6) a *search and seizure warrant* (40-047) where a production order is not complied with or the requirements for the issue of a production order are not available.

Applications for the purpose of a civil recovery investigation are reserved to a judge of the High Court. Applications for unexplained wealth orders and interim freezing orders, which were introduced by the Criminal Finances Act 2017, are also reserved to the High Court.

Applications under these provisions are most often made where the dominant purpose of the application is to determine in respect of a criminal offence whether, and, if so to what extent, a person has benefitted from it, or the whereabouts of any proceeds (*R. v Guildford Crown Court Ex p. Bowles* [1997] Cr. App. R. 436).

Applications for one of those orders numbered (1)–(5) above are governed by CrimPR 47.

Applying for an order

40-026 An applicant wanting a judge to make one of the orders listed (1)–(5) in 40-025 must follow the general rules at CrimPR 47.6, the rules specific to applications under POCA 2002 in CrimPR 47.17 and the rules specific to the particular order sought in CrimPR 47.18–47.22.

2. Production orders

General

40-027 A production order requires either that:

(1) the person the application specifies as appearing to be in possession or control of material produce it to an appropriate officer for him to take away; or

(2) the person gives an appropriate officer access to the material, within the period stated in the order.

(POCA 2002 s.345(4))

A judge may, on an application made to him by an appropriate officer, make a production order if satisfied that each of the requirements for the making of it (set out at 40-029) is fulfilled (POCA 2002 s.345(1), (5)).

The period stated in a production order must be a period of seven days beginning with the day on which the order is made unless it appears to the judge that a longer or shorter period would be appropriate in the particular circumstances (POCA 2002 s.345(5)).

Disobedience to an order is contempt of court.

Whilst the court has a discretion to order immediate production, the default position is that production is to be made within seven days. The court can only depart from that period if, on a sound evidential basis, it had good grounds for doing so. An immediate order might be appropriate if the order was directed at someone who might disclose the investigation or dispose of the documents sought. However, where the order was directed at a professional in respect of whom there was no evidence of wrongdoing, an immediate order would be wrong without any such evidential basis (*R. (on the application of Chatwani) v National Crime Agency* [2015] EWHC 1284 (Admin)).

Making an application

40-028 An applicant must follow the general rules at CrimPR 47.6, the rules specific to applications under POCA 2002 in CrimPR 47.17 and the rules specific to POCA 2002 production orders in CrimPR 47.18.

An application for variation or discharge is made under CrimPR 47.8.

Requirements for making an order

40-029 Before making an order the judge must be satisfied that there are reasonable grounds for:

(1) suspecting that:
   (a) in the case of a *confiscation investigation*, the person specified in the application as being subject to the investigation has benefited from his criminal conduct;
   (b) in the case of a money *laundering investigation*, the person specified in the application as being subject to the investigation has committed a money laundering offence;
   (c) in the case of a detained cash investigation into the *derivation of cash*, the property specified in the application as being subject to the investigation, or part of it, is "recoverable property";

(d) in the case of a detained cash investigation into the *intended use of cash*, the property specified in the application as being subject to the investigation, or part of it, is intended to be used by any person in unlawful conduct; and

(e) in the case of a detained property investigation into the *derivation of property*, the property specified in the application as being subject to the investigation, or part of it, is "recoverable property";

(f) in the case of a detained property investigation into the *intended use of property*, the property specified in the application as being subject to the investigation, or part of it, is intended by any person to be used in unlawful conduct;

(g) in the case of a frozen funds investigation into the *derivation of money* held in a frozen account, the property specified in the application as being subject to the investigation, or part of it, is "recoverable property";

(h) in the case of a frozen funds investigation into the *intended use of money* held in a frozen account, the property specified in the application as being subject to the investigation, or part of it, is intended by any person to be used in unlawful conduct;

and

(2) believing that the person specified in the application as appearing to be in possession or control of the material so specified is in *possession or control* of it;

(3) believing that the material is likely to be of *substantial value* (whether or not by itself) to the investigation for the purposes of which the order is sought;

(4) believing that it is in the *public interest* for the material to be produced or for access to it to be given, having regard to:

(a) the benefit likely to accrue to the investigation if the material is obtained;

(b) the circumstances under which the person specified in the application as appearing to be in possession or control of the material holds it.

(POCA 2002 s.346)

Addition of order granting entry

Where the judge makes a production order requiring a person to give an appropriate officer access to material on any premises, he may, on application by an appropriate officer specifying the premises, make an order to grant entry in relation to the premises. **40-030**

Such an order requires any person who appears to an appropriate officer to be entitled to grant entry to the premises to allow him to enter the premises to obtain access to the material.

(POCA 2002 s.347)

An applicant must follow the general rules at CrimPR 47.6, the rules specific to applications under POCA 2002 in CrimPR 47.17 and the rules specific to orders granting entry in CrimPR 47.19.

Privileged material

A production order: **40-031**

(1) does not require a person to produce, or give access to:
   (a) privileged material, i.e. material which the person would be entitled to refuse to produce on grounds of legal professional privilege in proceedings in the High Court;
   (b) "excluded material" (see 40-018); but
(2) has effect in spite of any restriction on the disclosure of information (however imposed).

(POCA 2002 s.348(1)–(4))

Retention of material

40-032 An "appropriate officer" may take copies of any material which is produced, or to which access is given, in compliance with the order, and material produced in compliance with the order may be retained for so long as it is necessary to retain it (as opposed to copies of it) in connection with the investigation for the purposes of which the order was made.

But if an appropriate officer has reasonable grounds for believing that:

(1) the material may need to be produced for the purposes of any legal proceedings; and
(2) it might otherwise be unavailable for those purposes,

it may be retained until the proceedings are concluded (POCA 2002 s.348(5)–(7)).

Special provisions apply under s.349 to computer information and under s.350 to government departments.

Discharge and variation

40-033 An application to discharge or vary a production order or an order to grant entry may be made to a judge of the Crown Court by:

(1) the person who applied for the order; or
(2) any person affected by the order,

and the judge may discharge or vary the order (POCA 2002 s.351(3)–(4)).

If an appropriate officer (or accredited financial investigator of a particular description) applies for a production order or an order to grant entry, an application to discharge or vary the order need not be by the same appropriate officer or investigator, but must be made by an appropriate officer or investigator of the same description (POCA 2002 s.351(5)–(5A)).

The procedure is under CrimPR 47.8.

3. Disclosure orders

General

40-034 A disclosure order is an order authorising an appropriate officer to give to any person he considers has relevant information a notice in writing requiring him, with respect to any matter relevant to the investigation for the purposes of which the order is sought, to:

(1) answer questions, either at a time specified in the notice or at once, at a specified place;

(2) provide information specified in the notice, by a specified time and manner; and
(3) produce documents, or documents of a description, specified in the notice, either at or by a specified time or at once, and in a specified manner.

(POCA 2002 s.357(4))

A judge may, on the application of the "relevant authority" (see 40-036), make a disclosure order for the purposes of a confiscation investigation if satisfied that each of the requirements for the making of the order is fulfilled (POCA 2002 s.357(1)).

For the making of a disclosure order there must be reasonable grounds:

(a) for suspecting that, in the case of a confiscation investigation, the person specified in the application for the order has benefited from his criminal conduct;
(b) for suspecting that, in the case of a money laundering investigation, the person specified in the application for the order has committed a money laundering offence;
(c) for believing that information which may be provided in compliance with a requirement imposed under the order is likely to be of substantial value (whether or not by itself) to the investigation for the purpose for which the order is sought;
(d) for believing that it is in the public interest for the information to be provided, having regard to the benefit likely to accrue to the investigation if the information is obtained.

(POCA 2002 s.358)

A disclosure order does not confer the right to require a person to answer any privileged question, provide any privileged information or produce any privileged document, except that a lawyer may be required to provide the name and address of a client of his. A privileged question is a question which the person would be entitled to refuse to answer on grounds of legal professional privilege in proceedings in the High Court. Privileged information is any information which the person would be entitled to refuse to provide on grounds of legal professional privilege in proceedings in the High Court.

A disclosure order does not confer the right to require a person to produce excluded material.

The order takes effect in spite of any restrictions on the disclosure of information, however imposed (s.361(6)).

Restrictions are imposed on the use of such statements by s.360.

A disclosure order can only be made in respect of a person within the jurisdiction; *SOCA v Perry* [2012] UKSC 35; [2013] 1 Cr. App. R. 6.

The application

An applicant must follow the general rules at CrimPR 47.6, the rules specific to applications under POCA 2002 in CrimPR 47.17 and the rules specific to disclosure orders in CrimPR 47.20. **40-035**

The application must state that:

(1) a person specified in the application is subject to a confiscation investigation which is being carried out by an appropriate officer and the order is sought for the purposes of the investigation; or

(2) a person or property specified in the application is subject to a civil recovery investigation and the order is sought for the purposes of the investigation; or
(3) a person specified in the application is subject to a money laundering investigation which is being carried out by an appropriate officer and the order is sought for the purposes of the investigation; or
(4) a person specified in the application is subject to an exploitation proceeds investigation and the order is sought for the purposes of the investigation.

(POCA 2002 s.357(3))
An application for variation or discharge is made under CrimPR 47.8.

Definitions

40-036 The term *relevant authority* means "an appropriate officer" in respect of confiscation and money laundering investigations.
(POCA 2002 s.357(7))

Variation and discharge

40-037 An application to discharge or vary a disclosure order (other than one made for the purposes of a civil recovery investigation or an exploitation proceeds investigation) may be made to a judge by:

(1) the person who applied for the order; or
(2) any person affected by the order, and

the judge may discharge, or vary the order.

If an appropriate officer (or accredited financial investigator of a particular description) applies for a production order or an order to grant entry, an application to discharge or vary the order need not be by the same appropriate officer or investigator, but must be made by an appropriate officer or investigator of the same description. An appropriate officer may not make an application for a disclosure order, or an application to discharge or vary such an order, unless he is a senior appropriate officer or is authorised to do so by a senior appropriate officer.
(POCA 2002 s.362)
An application for variation or discharge is made under CrimPR 47.8.

4. Customer information orders

Nature of order

40-038 A customer information order is an order that a financial institution covered by the application for the order must, on being required to do so by notice in writing given by an appropriate officer, provide any such customer information as it has relating to the person specified in the application, in such manner, and at or by such time, as the officer requires. If the institution requires the production of evidence of authority to give the notice, it is not bound to comply with the requirement unless evidence of the authority has been produced to it.
(POCA 2002 s.363(5)–(7))

A judge may, on the application of an appropriate officer, make a customer information order for the purposes of a confiscation investigation or a money laundering investigation, if he is satisfied that each of the requirements for the making of the order (see 40-041) is fulfilled. No application for a customer information order may be made in relation to a detained cash investigation, a detained property investigation or a frozen funds investigation (POCA 2002 s.363(1)–(1A)).

"Customer information" defined

"Customer information", in relation to a person and a financial institution, is information whether the person holds, or has held, an account or accounts at the financial institution (whether solely or jointly with another) and (if so) information as to: **40-039**

(1) if the person is an individual:
  (a) his account number(s), his full name and date of birth, his most recent address and any previous addresses, and the date on which he began to hold the account or accounts and, if he has ceased to hold the account or any of the accounts, the date or dates on which he did so;
  (b) such evidence of his identity as was obtained by the financial institution under or for the purposes of any legislation relating to money laundering;
  (c) the full name, date of birth and most recent address, and any previous addresses, of any person who holds, or has held, an account at the financial institution jointly with him; and
  (d) the account number or numbers of any other account or accounts held at the financial institution to which he is a signatory and details of the person holding the other account or accounts.

(2) if the person is a company or limited liability partnership or a similar body incorporated or otherwise established outside the UK:
  (a) the account number or numbers, the person's full name, a description of any business which the person carries on;
  (b) the country or territory in which it is incorporated or otherwise established and any number allocated to it under the CA 2006 or corresponding legislation of any country or territory outside the UK, also any number assigned to it for the purposes of VAT in the UK;
  (c) its registered office, and any previous registered offices, under CA 2006 (or corresponding earlier legislation) or anything similar under corresponding legislation of any country or territory outside the UK; also its registered office, and any previous registered offices, under the LLPA 2000, or anything similar under corresponding legislation of any country or territory outside Great Britain;
  (d) the date or dates on which it began to hold the account or accounts and, if it has ceased to hold the account or any of the accounts, the date or dates on which it did so;
  (e) such evidence of its identity as was obtained by the financial institution under or for the purposes of any legislation relating to money laundering;
  (f) the full name, date of birth and most recent address and any previous addresses of any person who is a signatory to the account or any of the accounts.

(POCA 2002 s.364(1)–(3))

Making an application

40-040 An applicant must follow the general rules at CrimPR 47.6, the rules specific to applications under POCA 2002 in CrimPR 47.17 and the rules specific to customer information orders in CrimPR 47.21.

Requirements for making order

40-041 For the making of a disclosure order there must be reasonable grounds:

(1) for suspecting that in the case of a confiscation investigation, the person specified in the application for the order has benefited from his criminal conduct;
(2) in the case of a money laundering investigation, there must be reasonable grounds for suspecting that the person specified in the application for the order has committed a money laundering offence;
(3) in the case of *any* investigation, for believing that information which may be provided in compliance with a requirement imposed under the order is likely to be of substantial value (whether or not by itself) to the investigation for the purposes for which the order is sought;
(4) in the case of *any* investigation, for believing that it is in the public interest for the information to be provided, having regard to the benefit likely to accrue to the investigation if the information is obtained.

(POCA 2002 s.365)

The order takes effect in spite of any restrictions on the disclosure of information, however imposed (s.368). Restrictions are imposed on the use of statements made in response to an order (s.367).

Discharge or variation

40-042 An application to discharge or vary a customer information order may be made to a judge by:

(1) the person who applied for the order; or
(2) any person affected by the order,

and the judge may discharge or vary the order.

If an appropriate officer (or accredited financial investigator of a particular description) applies for a production order or an order to grant entry, an application to discharge or vary the order need not be by the same appropriate officer or investigator, but must be made by an appropriate officer or investigator of the same description. An appropriate officer may not make an application for a disclosure order, or an application to discharge or vary such an order, unless he is a senior appropriate officer or is authorised to do so by a senior appropriate officer.

(POCA 2002 s.369)

An application for discharge or variation must be made in accordance with CrimPR 47.8.

5. ACCOUNT MONITORING ORDERS

Nature of order

40-043 An account monitoring order is an order that the financial institution specified in the application for the order must, for the period stated in the order, provide account information of the description specified in the order to an appropriate officer in the manner, and at or by the time or times, stated in the order. The period stated in an order must not exceed the period of 90 days beginning with the day on which the order is made.

Account information is information relating to an account or accounts held at the financial institution specified in the application by the person so specified (whether solely or jointly with another).

(POCA 2002 s.370(4)–(7))

A judge may, on an application made to him by an appropriate officer, in respect of a confiscation investigation or a money laundering investigation, make an account monitoring order if he is satisfied that each of the requirements set out in 40-045 is fulfilled (POCA 2002 s.370(1)). No application for an account monitoring order may be made in relation to a detained cash investigation, a detained property investigation or a frozen funds investigation (POCA 2002 s.370(1A)).

Account monitoring orders have effect as if they were orders of the court (POCA 2002 s.375(6)). Disobedience to an order is contempt of court.

Making an application

An application must state that: **40-044**

(1) a person specified in the application is subject to a confiscation investigation, an exploitation proceeds investigation or a money laundering investigation; and
(2) the order is sought for the purposes of the investigation, or is sought against the financial institution specified in the application in relation to account information of the description specified.

(POCA 2002 s.370 (2))

It may specify information relating to:

(a) all accounts held by the person specified in the application at the financial institution so specified;
(b) a particular description, or particular descriptions, of accounts so held; or
(c) a particular account, or particular accounts, so held.

(POCA 2002 s.370(5))

An applicant must follow the general rules at CrimPR 47.6, the rules specific to applications under POCA 2002 in CrimPR 47.17 and the rules specific to account monitoring orders in CrimPR 47.22.

An application for variation or discharge is made under CrimPR 47.8.

Requirements for making the order

Before the judge can make an account monitoring order, there must be, in the case of: **40-045**

(1) a confiscation investigation, reasonable grounds for suspecting that the person specified in the application has benefited from his criminal conduct;
(2) a money laundering investigation, reasonable grounds for suspecting that the person specified in the application order has committed a money laundering offence.

There must also be, in the case of any investigation, reasonable grounds:

(a) for believing that information which may be provided in compliance with a requirement imposed under the order is likely to be of substantial value (whether or not by itself) to the investigation for the purposes of which the order is sought; and
(b) for believing that it is in the public interest for the information to be provided, having regard to the benefit likely to accrue to the investigation if the information is obtained.

(POCA 2002 s.371)

Variation and discharge

40-046 An application to discharge or vary an account monitoring order may be made to a judge by:

(1) the person who applied for the order; or
(2) any person affected by the order,

and the judge may discharge or vary the order.

If an appropriate officer (or accredited financial investigator of a particular description) applies for a production order or an order to grant entry, an application to discharge or vary the order need not be by the same appropriate officer or investigator, but must be made by an appropriate officer or investigator of the same description.

(POCA 2002 s.375)

An application for variation or discharge is made under CrimPR 47.8.

6. Search and seizure warrants

General

40-047 A search and seizure warrant is a warrant authorising an "appropriate person":

(1) to enter and search the premises specified in the application for the warrant; and
(2) to seize and retain any material found there which is likely to be of substantial value (whether or not by itself) to the investigation for the purposes of which the application is made.

A judge may, on an application made to him by an appropriate officer, issue a search and seizure warrant if satisfied that either of the requirements for the issuing of the warrant is fulfilled, namely that:

(a) a production order made in relation to material has not been complied with and there are reasonable grounds for believing that the material is on the premises specified in the application for the warrant; or
(b) that s.353 is satisfied in relation to the warrant.

(POCA 2002 s.352(1), (6))

An application for a search and seizure warrant must state that:

(i) a person specified in the application is subject to a confiscation investigation, a civil recovery investigation, an exploitation proceeds investigation, or a money laundering investigation; or
(ii) property specified in the application is subject to a civil recovery investiga-

tion or a detained cash investigation, a detained property investigation or a frozen funds investigation; and also

(iii) that the warrant is sought:
- for the purposes of the investigation;
- in relation to the premises specified in the application;
- in relation to material specified in the application, or that there are reasonable grounds for believing that there is material falling within s.353(6), (7), (7A), (7B), or (8) on the premises.

(POCA 2002 s.352(2)–(3))

A search and seizure warrant does not confer the right to seize privileged material, that is any material which a person would be entitled to refuse to produce on grounds of legal professional privilege in proceedings in the High Court. Nor does it confer the right to seize excluded material (POCA 2002 s.354).

An "appropriate person" is defined in s.352(5).

On the need for the applicant to give the judge a full and clear picture of what lies behind the application and to inform the judge of material that might tell against it, and for the judge to take time to subject the application to rigorous scrutiny, see *R. (on the application of Golfrate Property Management Ltd) v Southwark Crown Court* [2014] EWHC (Admin); [2014] 2 Cr. App. R. 12; see also *R. (on the application of Mills) v Sussex Police* [2014] EWHC 2523 (Admin); [2014] 2 Cr. App. R. 34.

Requirements where production order not available

A search and seizure warrant may be issued where (although a production order is not available/appropriate) there are reasonable grounds for suspecting that: **40-048**

(1) in the case of *a confiscation investigation*, the person specified in the application has benefited from his criminal conduct; or
(2) in the case of *a money laundering investigation*, the person specified in the application has committed a money laundering offence; or
(3) in the case of a detained cash investigation into the *derivation of cash*, the property specified in the application, or part of it, is recoverable property; or
(4) in the case of a detained cash investigation into the *intended use of cash*, the property specified in the application, or part of it, is intended to be used by any person in unlawful conduct; or
(5) in the case of a detained property investigation into the *derivation of property*, the property specified in the application or part of it, is recoverable property; or
(6) in the case of a detained property investigation into the *intended use of property*, the property specified in the application, or part of it, is intended by any person to be used in unlawful conduct; or
(7) in the case of a frozen funds investigation into the *derivation of money* held in a frozen account, the property specified in the application, or part of it, is recoverable property; or
(8) in the case of a frozen funds investigation into the *intended use of money* held in a frozen account, the property specified in the application, or part of it, is intended by any person to be used in unlawful conduct; or
(9) in the case of an exploitation proceeds investigation, the person specified in the application is within s.346(2A); and

(10) either the first or the second set of conditions (see 40-049 and 40-050) is complied with.

(POCA 2002 s.353(1), (2))

40-049 *The first set of conditions* is that there are reasonable grounds for believing that:

(1) any material on the premises specified in the application for the warrant is likely to be of substantial value (whether or not by itself) to the investigation for the purposes of which the warrant is sought;
(2) it is in the public interest for the material to be obtained, having regard to the benefit likely to accrue to the investigation if the material is obtained; and
(3) it would not be appropriate to make a production order for any one or more of the following reasons, namely that:
  (a) it is not practicable to communicate with any person against whom a production order could be made;
  (b) it is not practicable to communicate with any person who would be required to comply with an order to grant entry to the premises; or
  (c) the investigation might be seriously prejudiced unless an appropriate person is able to secure immediate access to the material.

(POCA 2002 s.353(3), (4))

40-050 *The second set of conditions* is that:

(1) there are reasonable grounds for believing that there is material on the premises specified in the application and that the material falls within subss.(6), (7), (7A), (7B), (7C), (7D), (7E), (7F), (8) or (8A) (set out below); and
(2) there are reasonable grounds for believing that it is in the public interest for the material to be obtained, having regard to the benefit likely to accrue to the investigation if the material is obtained; and
(3) any one or more of the requirements in subs.(9) is met, i.e. that:
  (a) it is not practicable to communicate with any person entitled to grant entry to the premises;
  (b) entry to the premises will not be granted unless a warrant is produced;
  (c) the investigation might be seriously prejudiced unless an appropriate person arriving at the premises is able to secure immediate entry to them.

(POCA 2002 s.353(5)–(9))

POCA 2002 s.353 provides the following clarification concerning "material" (subss.(6), (7A), (7B), (7C), (7D), (7E), (7F), (8) or (8A)):

(6) In the case of *a confiscation investigation*, material falls within this subsection if it cannot be identified at the time of the application but it:
  (a) relates to the person specified in the application, the question whether he has benefited from his criminal conduct or any question as to the extent or whereabouts of his benefit from his criminal conduct, or of realisable property available for satisfying a confiscation order made in respect of him; and
  (b) is likely to be of substantial value (whether or not by itself) to the investigation for the purposes of which the warrant is sought.

(7A) In the case of a detained cash investigation into the *derivation of cash*, material falls within this subsection if it cannot be identified at the time of the application but it:

(a) relates to the property specified in the application, the question whether the property, or a part of it, is recoverable property or any other question as to its derivation; and

(b) is likely to be of substantial value (whether or not by itself) to the investigation for the purposes of which the warrant is sought.

(7B) In the case of a detained cash investigation into the *intended use of cash*, material falls within this subsection if it cannot be identified at the time of the application but it:

(a) relates to the property specified in the application or the question whether the property, or a part of it, is intended by any person to be used in unlawful conduct; and

(b) is likely to be of substantial value (whether or not by itself) to the investigation for the purposes of which the warrant is sought.

(7C) In the case of a detained property investigation into the derivation of property, material falls within this subsection if it cannot be identified at the time of the application but it:

(a) relates to the property specified in the application, the question whether the property, or a part of it, is recoverable property or any other question as to its derivation; and

(b) is likely to be of substantial value (whether or not by itself) to the investigation for the purposes of which the warrant is sought.

(7D) In the case of a detained property investigation into the intended use of property, material falls within this subsection if it cannot be identified at the time of the application but it:

(a) relates to the property specified in the application or the question whether the property, or a part of it, is intended by any person to be used in unlawful conduct; and

(b) is likely to be of substantial value (whether or not by itself) to the investigation for the purposes of which the warrant is sought.

(7E) In the case of a frozen funds investigation into the derivation of money held in a frozen account, material falls within this subsection if it cannot be identified at the time of the application but it:

(a) relates to the property specified in the application, the question whether the property, or a part of it, is recoverable property or any other question as to its derivation; and

(b) is likely to be of substantial value (whether or not by itself) to the investigation for the purposes of which the warrant is sought.

(7F) In the case of a frozen funds investigation into the intended use of money held in a frozen account, material falls within this subsection if it cannot be identified at the time of the application but it:

(a) relates to the property specified in the application or the question whether the property, or a part of it, is intended by any person to be used in unlawful conduct; and

(b) is likely to be of substantial value (whether or not by itself) to the investigation for the purposes of which the warrant is sought.

(8) In the case of *a money laundering investigation*, material falls within this subsection if it cannot be identified at the time of the application but it:

(a) relates to the person specified in the application or the question whether he has committed a money laundering offence; and
(b) is likely to be of substantial value (whether or not by itself) to the investigation for the purposes of which the warrant is sought.

(8A) In the case of *an exploitation proceeds investigation*, material falls within this subsection if it cannot be identified at the time of the application but it:

(a) relates to the person specified in the application, the question whether exploitation proceeds have been obtained from a relevant offence in relation to that person, any question as to the extent or whereabouts of any benefit as a result of which exploitation proceeds are obtained or any question about the person's available amount; and
(b) is likely to be of substantial value (whether or not by itself) to the investigation for the purposes of which the warrant is sought (This subsection is to be construed in accordance with CorJA 2009 Pt 7 (criminal memoirs etc.).

Making the application

40-051 An applicant must follow the general rules at CrimPR 47.6, the rules specific to applications for investigation warrants in CrimPR 47.24–47.27 and the rules specific to POCA 2002 search warrants in CrimPR 47.32.

E. Orders under Terrorism Act 2000

1. Production Order; "Excluded" or "Special Procedure" material

General

40-052 For the purposes of a terrorist investigation, an appropriate officer may apply to a Circuit Judge for an order to produce or give access to particular material, or material of a particular description, which consists of, or includes, excluded material (see 40-018) or "special procedure" material (see 40-019), within the meaning of PACE 1984.

Such an order may require a specified person to:

(1) produce to an appropriate officer within a specified period for seizure and retention any material which he has in his possession, custody or power and to which the application relates;
(2) give an appropriate officer access to any material of the kind mentioned in (1) within a specified period; and
(3) state to the best of his knowledge and belief the location of material to which the application relates if it is not in, and it will not come into, his possession, custody or power within the period specified under (1) or (2).

(TerrA 2000 Sch.5 para.5(1)–(3))

For the purposes of this provision:

(a) an order may specify a person only if he appears to the judge to have in his possession, custody or power any of the material to which the application relates; and
(b) a period specified in an order must be the period of seven days beginning

with the date of the order unless it appears to the judge that a different period would be appropriate in the particular circumstances of the application.

(TerrA 2000 Sch.5 para.5(4))

Where the judge makes an order under (2) above in relation to material on any premises, he may, on the application of a constable, order any person who appears to the judge to be entitled to grant entry to the premises to allow any constable to enter the premises to obtain access to the material.

(TerrA 2000 Sch.5 para.5(5))

An appropriate officer is a constable or a counter-terrorism financial investigator.

(TerrA 2000 Sch.5 para 5(6))

Such an order has effect as if it were an order of the Crown Court (TerrA 2000 Sch.5 paras 4, 10).

Preconditions for order

The judge may grant such an application if satisfied: **40-053**

(1) that the material to which the application relates consists of or includes excluded material or special procedure material;
(2) that it does not include items subject to legal privilege (see 40-020); and
(3) that the two conditions set out below are satisfied in respect of that material.

The first condition is that:

(a) the order is sought for the purposes of a terrorist investigation; and
(b) there are reasonable grounds for believing that the material is likely to be of substantial value, whether by itself or together with other material, to a terrorist investigation.

The second condition is that there are reasonable grounds for believing that it is in the public interest that the material should be produced or that access to it should be given having regard to:

(a) the benefit likely to accrue to a terrorist investigation if the material is obtained; and
(b) to the circumstances under which the person concerned has any of the material in his possession, custody or power (TerrA 2000 Sch.5 para.6).

If the order is sought by a counter-terrorism financial investigator, the first condition is satisfied only to the extent that the terrorist investigation mentioned relates to terrorist property (TerrA 2000 Sch.5 para.6).

Material not yet available

An order may be made in relation to: **40-054**

(1) material consisting of or including excluded or special procedure material which is expected to come into existence within the period of 28 days beginning with the date of the order;
(2) a person whom the judge thinks is likely to have any of the material to which the application relates in his possession, custody or power within that period.

Where an order is made in these circumstances by virtue of this paragraph, para.5(3) (at 40-052) will apply with these modifications:

(a) the order will require the specified person to notify a named appropriate officer as soon as is reasonably practicable after any material to which the application relates comes into his possession, custody or power;
(b) the reference in para.5(3)(a) to material which the specified person has in his possession, custody or power is to be taken as a reference to the material referred to in (a) above which comes into his possession, custody or power; and
(c) the reference in para.5(3)(c) (40-052) to the specified period is to be taken as a reference to the period of 28 days beginning with the date of the order.

Where an order is made by virtue of this paragraph, para.5(4) (40-052) will not apply and the order:

(i) may only specify a person falling within subpara.(1)(b); and
(ii) must specify the period of seven days beginning with the date of notification required under subpara.(2)(a) unless it appears to the judge that a different period would be appropriate in the particular circumstances of the application.

(TerrA 2000 Sch.5 para.7)

Miscellaneous

40-055 An order under para.5 (40-052):

(1) does not confer any right to production of, or access to, items subject to legal privilege (40-020); and
(2) has effect notwithstanding any restriction on the disclosure of information imposed by statute or otherwise.

Where the material to which the application relates consists of information contained in a computer:

(a) an order under para.5(3)(a) has effect as an order to produce the material in a form in which it can be taken away and in which it is visible and legible; and
(b) an order under para.5(3)(b) has effect as an order to give access to the material in a form in which it is visible and legible.

An order may be made in relation to material in the possession, custody or power of an authorised government department (for the purposes of the Crown Proceedings Act 1947), in which case it must be served as if the proceedings were civil proceedings against the department, and it may require any officer of the department, whether named in the order or not, who may for the time being have in his possession, custody or power the material concerned, to comply with the order. (TerrA 2000 Sch.5 para.8)

Process of application for a production order

40-056 An applicant must follow the general rules at CrimPR 47.6, the rules specific to applications for investigation orders in CrimPR 47.11 and the rules specific to TerrA production orders in CrimPR 47.12.

2. "Excluded" or "Special Procedure" material: search

Application for warrant

A constable may apply to a Circuit Judge for the issue of a warrant for the purposes of a terrorist investigation. 40-057

The warrant will authorise any constable to:

(1) enter the premises mentioned below;
(2) search the premises and any person found there; and
(3) seize and retain any relevant material which is found on the search,

but must not authorise:

(a) the seizure and retention of items subject to legal privilege;
(b) a constable to require a person to remove any clothing in public except for headgear, footwear, an outer coat, a jacket or gloves.

For the purposes of (3) above, material is relevant if the constable has reasonable grounds for believing that it is likely to be of substantial value, whether by itself or together with other material, to a terrorist investigation.

The premises referred to in (1) above are:

(i) one or more sets of premises specified in the application (in which case the application is for a "specific premises warrant"); or
(ii) any premises occupied or controlled by a person specified in the application, including such sets of premises as are so specified (in which case the application is for an "all premises warrant").

(TerrA 2000 Sch.5 para.11)

Preconditions to grant of warrant

The judge may grant an application for: 40-058

(1) a specific premises warrant under para.11 if satisfied that:
  (a) a production order (para.5) in relation to material on the premises specified in the application has not been complied with; or
  (b) that there are reasonable grounds for believing that:
    (i) there is material on premises specified in the application which consists of or includes excluded material or special procedure material but does not include items subject to legal privilege; and
    (ii) the conditions set out below are satisfied;
(2) an all premises warrant under para.11 if satisfied that:
  (a) a production order (para.5) has not been complied with, and that the person specified in the application is also specified in the order; or
  (b) there are reasonable grounds for believing that:
    (i) there is material on premises to which the application relates which consists of or includes excluded material or special procedure material but does not include items subject to legal privilege; and
    (ii) the first and second conditions set out below are met.

The first condition is that the warrant is sought for the purposes of a terrorist investigation, and the material is likely to be of substantial value, whether by itself or together with other material, to a terrorist investigation.

The second condition is that it is not appropriate to make a production order in relation to the material because:

- it is not practicable to communicate with any person entitled to produce the material;
- it is not practicable to communicate with any person entitled to grant access to the material or entitled to grant entry to premises to which the application for the warrant relates; or
- a terrorist investigation may be seriously prejudiced unless a constable can secure immediate access to the material.

(TerrA 2000 Sch.5 para.12)

Process of application for a search warrant

40-059 An applicant must follow the general rules at CrimPR 47.6, the rules specific to applications for investigation warrants in CrimPR 47.24–47.27 and the rules specific to TerrA search warrants in CrimPR 47.31.

3. Explanation order

General

40-060 A constable may apply to a Circuit Judge for an order requiring any person specified in the order to provide an explanation of any material seized in pursuance of a warrant under paras 1 or 11, produced or made available to a constable under para.5.

A counter-terrorism financial investigator may apply to a Circuit Judge for an order requiring any person specified in the order to provide an explanation of any material produced or made available to a designated financial investigator under para.5.

Such an order does not require any person to disclose any information which he would be entitled to refuse to disclose on grounds of legal professional privilege in proceedings in the High Court, but a lawyer may be required to provide the name and address of his client.

A statement by a person in response to a requirement imposed by an order under this paragraph may be made orally or in writing. It may be used in evidence against him only on a prosecution for an offence under para.14 of the Act (giving misleading information).

Such an order has effect as if it were an order of the Crown Court.

(TerrA 2000 Sch.5 para.13)

Content of application

40-061 An applicant must follow the general rules at CrimPR 47.6, the rules specific to applications for TerrA investigation orders in CrimPR 47.11 and the rules specific to TerrA explanation orders in CrimPR 47.14.

4. Customer information order

General

40-062 An order may be made by a Circuit Judge, on the application of a police officer of at least the rank of superintendent, where the judge is satisfied:

(1) the order is sought for the purposes of a terrorist investigation;
(2) the tracing of terrorist property is desirable for the purposes of the investigation; and
(3) the order will enhance the effectiveness of the investigation,

under which a constable or counter-terrorism financial investigator named in the order may require a financial institution (as defined in para.6 of the Schedule) to which the order applies to provide customer information for the purposes of the investigation. The order may provide that it applies to all financial institutions, a particular description or particular descriptions of financial institutions, or a particular financial institution or particular financial institutions.

(TerrA 2000 Sch.6 paras 1, 5)

"Customer information" here means:

(a) information whether a business relationship exists or existed (as defined) between a financial institution and a particular person ("a customer");
(b) the customer's account number, full name, date of birth and address or former address;
(c) the date on which a business relationship between a financial institution and a customer begins or ends;
(d) any evidence of a customer's identity obtained by a financial institution in pursuance of or for the purposes of any legislation relating to money laundering; and
(e) the identity of a person sharing an account with a customer.

The information must be provided;

- in such manner and within such time as the constable or counter-terrorism financial investigator may specify; and
- notwithstanding any restriction on the disclosure of information imposed by statute or otherwise.

An institution which fails to comply with such a requirement commits a summary offence, although it is a defence for an institution charged with such an offence to prove that the information required was not in the institution's possession, or that it was not reasonably practicable for the institution to comply with the requirement.

(TerrA 2000 Sch.6 paras 1, 2, 7)

Content of application

An applicant must follow the general rules at CrimPR 47.6, the rules specific to applications for TerrA investigation orders in CrimPR 47.11 and the rules specific to TerrA customer information orders in CrimPR 47.15. **40-063**

5. ACCOUNT MONITORING ORDERS

General

An account monitoring order is an order that the financial institution specified in the application must, for the period specified in the order, in the manner so specified, at or by the time or times so specified and at the place or places so specified, provide information of the description specified in the application to an appropriate officer. **40-064**

The period stated in the order must not exceed the period of 90 days beginning with the day on which the order is made.

A Circuit Judge may, on an application made to him by an appropriate officer, make such an order if satisfied that:

(1) the order is sought for the purposes of a terrorist investigation;
(2) the tracing of terrorist property is desirable for the purposes of the investigation; and
(3) the order will enhance the effectiveness of the investigation.

An appropriate officer is a police officer or counter-terrorism financial investigator.

(TerrA 2000 Sch.6A paras 1, 2)

Making an application

40-065 An application for an account monitoring order may be made ex parte to a judge in chambers.

An application must state that the order is sought against the financial institution specified in the application in relation to information which:

(1) relates to an account or accounts held at the institution by the person specified in the application (whether solely or jointly with another); and
(2) is of the description so specified.

The application may specify information relating to:

(a) all accounts held by the person specified in the application for the order at the financial institution so specified;
(b) a particular description, or particular descriptions, of accounts so held; or
(c) a particular account, or particular accounts, so held.

(TerrA 2000 Sch.6A paras 2, 3)

Content of application

40-066 An applicant must follow the general rules at CrimPR 47.6, the rules specific to applications for TerrA investigation orders in CrimPR 47.11 and the rules specific to TerrA account monitoring orders in CrimPR 47.16.

Discharge or variation

40-067 An application to discharge or vary an account monitoring order may be made to the Crown Court by:

(1) the person who applied for the order; or
(2) any person affected by the order.

If the application for the account monitoring order was made by one police officer or counter-terrorism financial investigator, an application to discharge or vary the order may be made by a different officer.

A judge may vary or discharge the order.

An account monitoring order has effect as if it were an order of the Crown Court.

(TerrA 2000 Sch.6A para.4)

An application for variation or discharge is made under CrimPR 47.8.

6. DISCLOSURE ORDERS

General

The Criminal Finances Act 2017 Sch.2 inserted into TerrA 2000 Sch.5A which provides for disclosure orders. **40-068**

A disclosure order is an order authorising an appropriate officer to give, to any person the officer considers has relevant information, notice in writing requiring the person to answer questions, provide information or produce documents, with respect to any matter relevant to the terrorist financing investigation concerned.

A Circuit Judge may, on an application made to him by an appropriate officer, make such an order if satisfied that:

(1) there are reasonable grounds for suspecting that a person has committed an offence under any of sections 15 to 18 or that the property specified in the application is terrorist property;
(2) there are reasonable grounds for believing that information which may be provided in compliance with a requirement imposed under the order is likely to be of substantial value (whether or not by itself) to the terrorist financing investigation concerned; and
(3) there are reasonable grounds for believing that it is in the public interest for the information to be provided, having regard to the benefit likely to accrue to the investigation if the information is obtained.

(TerrA 2000 Sch.5A, para.9)

Making an application

An application must state that a person or property specified in the application is subject to a terrorist financing investigation and the order is sought for the purposes of the investigation. **40-069**

(TerrA 2000 Sch.5A para.9(2))

Content of application

An applicant must follow the general rules at CrimPR 47.6, the rules specific to applications for TerrA investigation orders in CrimPR 47.11 and the rules specific to TerrA disclosure orders in CrimPR 47.13. **40-070**

F. WARRANT UNDER CJA 1987 s.2

For the procedure governing applications for warrants under CJA 1987 s.2, see the rules concerning applications for investigation warrants in CrimPR 47.24–47.27 and the rules specific to applications for CJA 1987 s.2 warrants in CrimPR 47.29. **40-071**

G. ORDER UNDER CJPA 2001 s.59

The Crown Court has jurisdiction under CJPA 2001 s.59 to entertain an application by the police, or other investigating authority, to retain material that has been unlawfully seized under search warrants pending an application for a fresh search **40-072** warrant (*R. (on the application of Panesar) v Central Criminal Court* [2014] EWHC 2821 (Admin)).

The procedure is now set out in CrimPR 47.35–47.36 and 47.38–47.40.

In considering a s.59 application, the judge is not restricted to considering material that could be disclosed. The judge may consider material which could not be disclosed to the subject of the warrant and could restrict what could be disclosed, even if what fell to be disclosed could not, without more, support the conclusions necessary for the warrant to be granted (*R. (on the application of Haralambous) v St Albans Crown Court* [2016] EWHC 916 (Admin.); [2016] 2 Cr. App. R. 17). See CrimPR 47.39 for the rules specifically concerning such applications.

An application under s.59(6) CJPA 2001 to authorise the continued retention of property unlawfully seized is not limited to domestic cases and can be made in relation to foreign cases where there is no question of a domestic criminal trial (*Heilligger v Westminster Magistrates' Court* [2022] EWHC 1056 (Admin); [2022] 5 WLUK 59).

H. ORDER UNDER BBEA 1879

40-073 A judge may, on the application of any party to a legal proceeding, order that such party be at liberty to inspect and take copies of any entries in a banker's book for any of the purposes of such proceedings.

An order may be made either with or without summoning the bank or other party, and must be served on the bank three clear days before the same is to be obeyed, unless the judge otherwise directs (Sunday, Christmas Day, Good Friday, and any bank holiday being excluded from the computation) (BBEA 1879 ss.7, 11).

An application for an order, or to withdraw an order is made under CrimPR 17. Although the Act provides for an ex parte application "there is much to be said for notice being given" (*R. v Marlborough St MC Ex p. Simpson* 79 Cr. App. R. 291).

The expressions "bank", "banker" and "bankers' books" are defined in BBEA 1879 s.9. "Legal proceeding", "court" and "judge" are defined in s.10.

Note that:

(1) before making the order the judge should satisfy himself that the application is not solely a "fishing expedition" to find material on which to hang a charge, but should consider whether the prosecution, who normally make such an application, have in their possession other evidence against the accused (*Williams v Summerfield* (1972) 56 Cr. App. R. 597);
(2) the order ought to be limited to a certain specific period, and ought not to be oppressive (*Ex p. Simpson* (1980) 70 Cr. App. R. 291); and
(3) the mere fact that the accused has given notice of intention to plead guilty is not a reason for refusing an order (*Owen v Sambrook* [1981] Crim. L.R. 329).

The costs of any application to the judge under or for the purposes of the Act, and the costs of anything done or to be done under an order are in the discretion of the court or judge, who may order the same, or any part, to be paid to any party by the bank where the same have been occasioned by any default or delay on the part of the bank. Any such order against a bank may be enforced as if the bank was a party to the proceeding.

(BBEA 1879 s.8)

I. LETTERS OF REQUEST

General

Where, on an application made to him by a designated prosecuting authority, it appears to a judge that: **40-074**

(1) an offence has been committed or that there are reasonable grounds for suspecting that an offence has been committed; and

(2) proceedings in respect of the offence have been instituted, or that the offence is being investigated;

he may request assistance in obtaining outside the UK any evidence specified in his request for use in the proceedings or investigation.

(C(IC)A 2003 s.7)

Prosecutors are "designated" by SI 2004/1034 as amended.

J. OVERSEAS PRODUCTION ORDERS

The Crime (Overseas Production Orders) Act 2019 allows a Crown Court judge to make, at the request of an investigator, an order against a person or corporation in another jurisdiction requiring them to produce or give access to electronic data likely to be of substantial value to the investigation here (s.1). **40-075**

Section 3 enables law enforcement officers and prosecutors to make a request for communications data that is "comprised in, included as part of, attached to or logically associated with electronic data" sought through an overseas production order.

For the requirements for making an order, see s.4, for the contents of an order, see s.5, and for the effect of an order see s.6.

For the relevant procedure, see CrimPR 47.67 and 47.68.

K. EVIDENCE FOR USE OVERSEAS

Where a request under the Crime (International Co-operation) Act 2003 for assistance in obtaining evidence in England and Wales is received, the Secretary of State may nominate the Crown Court to receive any evidence to which the request relates which appears appropriate to that court for the purpose of giving effect to the request (C(IC)A 2003 s.15). **40-076**

"Evidence" is not confined to direct evidence for use at trial, and may extend to information which might lead to the discovery of evidence (*R. v Home Secretary Ex p. Fininvest Spa* [1997] 1 Cr. App. R. 257), a decision under the 1990 Act. As to references to the DSFO, see *R. (on the application of Evans) v Director of the Serious Fraud Office* [2002] EWHC 2304 (Admin); [2003] W.L.R. 299 as to the application of "section 2 notices" (under CJA 1988 s.2).

In such proceedings the judge has the like powers for securing the attendance of a witness as he has for the purposes of other proceedings before the court (see WITNESS SUMMONSES AND WARRANTS) (C(IC)A 2003 Sch.1 para.1). Subject to any question of privilege the court may take evidence on oath (C(IC)A 2003 Sch.1 para.3).

The nominated court may determine who may appear or take part in the proceedings, and whether a party to the proceedings is entitled to be represented, and the public may be excluded from the proceedings if the judge thinks it is necessary to do so in the interests of justice.

(CrimPR 49.4)

The Crown Court officer must enter the details required by CrimPR 49.5 in an overseas record.

As to evidence by live link or telephone link, see below.

The evidence received by the nominated court must be given to the court or authority that made the request or to the Secretary of State for forwarding to the court or authority that made the request, so far as may be necessary in order to comply with the request.

Where the evidence consists of:

(1) a document, the original or a copy must be provided;
(2) any other article, the article itself, or a description, photograph or other representation of it, must be provided.

(C(IC)A 2003 Sch.1 para.6)

No order as to costs may be made (C(IC)A 2003 Sch.1 para.9).

Note that BBEA 1879 (40-073) applies to the proceedings as it applies to other proceedings before the court (C(IC)A 2003 Sch.1 para.7).

Witness not to be compelled

40-077 A person cannot be compelled to give any evidence which he could not be compelled to give:

(1) in criminal proceedings in the part of the UK in which the nominated court exercises jurisdiction; or
(2) in criminal proceedings in the country from which the request for the evidence has come;

but this does not apply unless the claim of the person questioned to be exempt from giving the evidence is conceded by the court or authority which made the request.

Where the person's claim is not conceded, he may be required to give the evidence to which the claim relates (subject to the other provisions of this paragraph), but the evidence may not be forwarded to the court or authority which requested it if a court in the country in question, on the matter being referred to it, upholds the claim.

Without prejudice to the generality of (1) above, a person cannot be compelled to give any evidence if his doing so would be prejudicial to the security of the UK (a certificate signed by or on behalf of the Secretary of State to that effect being conclusive evidence of that fact).

A person cannot be compelled to give any evidence in his capacity as an officer or servant of the Crown (C(IC)A 2003 Sch.1 para.5(7). Subparas (4) and (6) are without prejudice to the generality of subpara.(1)).

Hearing witnesses in the UK through television links

40-078 Where the Secretary of State receives a request from an external authority for a person in the UK to give evidence through a live television link in criminal proceedings before a court in a country outside the UK, the Secretary of State will, unless he considers it inappropriate to do so, by notice in writing nominate a court in the UK where the witness may be heard in the proceedings in question through a live television link.

Any statement made on oath by a witness giving evidence in pursuance of this provision is treated for the purposes of the Perjury Act 1911 s.1 as made in proceedings before the nominated court. Anything done by the witness in the presence of the nominated court which, if it were done in proceedings before the court, would constitute contempt of court is to be treated for that purpose as done in proceedings before the court. Subject to that, evidence given pursuant to this section is not to be treated for any purpose as evidence given in proceedings in the UK (C(IC)A 2003 s.30).

The nominated court has the like powers for securing the attendance of the witness to give evidence through the link as it has for the purpose of proceedings before the court (C(IC)A 2003 Sch.2 para.1). The witness is to give evidence in the presence of the nominated court (para.3). The nominated court is to establish the identity of the witness (para.4). The nominated court is to intervene where it considers it necessary to do so to safeguard the rights of the witness (para.5). The evidence is to be given under the supervision of the court of the country concerned (para.6). The evidence is to be given in accordance with the laws of that country and with any measures for the protection of the witness agreed between the Secretary of State and the authority in that country which appears to him to have the function of entering into agreements of that kind (para.7).

(1) The witness cannot be compelled to give any evidence which he could not be compelled to give in criminal proceedings in the part of the UK in which the nominated court exercises jurisdiction.
(2) The witness cannot be compelled to give any evidence if his doing so would be prejudicial to the security of the UK.
(3) A certificate signed by or on behalf of the Secretary of State or, where the court is in Scotland, the Lord Advocate to the effect that it would be so prejudicial for that person to do so is to be conclusive evidence of that fact.
(4) The witness cannot be compelled to give any evidence in his capacity as an officer or servant of the Crown.
(5) Subparagraphs (2) and (4) are without prejudice to the generality of subpara.(1) (para.9).

Hearing witnesses in the UK by telephone

Where the Secretary of State receives a request, from an external authority, for **40-079** a person in the UK to give evidence by telephone in criminal proceedings before a court, giving the name and address of the witness and stating that the witness is willing to give evidence by telephone in the proceedings before that court, the Secretary of State will, unless he considers it inappropriate to do so, by notice in writing nominate a court in the UK where the witness may be heard in the proceedings in question by telephone. The same provisions apply as in the second paragraph of 40-078.

The nominated court must notify the witness of the time when and the place at which he is to give evidence by telephone (C(IC)A 2003 Sch.2 para.11). The nominated court must be satisfied that the witness is willingly giving evidence by telephone (para.12). The witness is to give evidence in the presence of the nominated court (para.13). The nominated court is to establish the identity of the witness (para.14). The evidence is to be given under the supervision of the court of the participating country (para.15). The evidence is to be given in accordance with the laws of that country (para.16).

Interpreter: television or telephone link

40-080 Where a court is nominated under C(IC)A 2003 s.30(3) or s.31(4) to hear a witness over a television or telephone link and it appears to the Crown Court officer that the witness to be heard in the proceedings is likely to give evidence in a language other than English, he will make arrangements for an interpreter to be present at the proceedings to translate what is said into English.

Where it appears to the Crown Court officer that the witness to be heard is likely to give evidence in a language other than that in which the proceedings of the external court will be conducted, he will make arrangements for an interpreter to be present at the relevant proceedings to translate what is said into the language in which the proceedings of the external court will be conducted.

Where the evidence in the proceedings is either given in a language other than English or is not translated into English by an interpreter, the court shall adjourn the proceedings until such time as an interpreter can be present to provide a translation into English.

Where a court in Wales understands Welsh:

(a) paragraph (2) does not apply where it appears to the justices' clerk or Crown Court officer that the witness in question is likely to give evidence in Welsh;
(b) paragraph (4) does not apply where the evidence is given in Welsh; and
(c) any translation which is provided pursuant to paragraph (2) or (4) may be into Welsh instead of English (CrimPR 49.6).

L. Requests for information about banking transactions for use in the UK

Information about a person's bank account abroad

40-081 A judge entitled to exercise the jurisdiction of the Crown Court, on an application made by a specified prosecuting authority, may request assistance from a participating country under C(IC)A 2003 s.43 if satisfied that:

(1) a person is subject to an investigation in the UK into serious criminal conduct (i.e. conduct which constitutes an offence to which para.3 of art.1 (request for information on bank accounts) of the 2001 Protocol applies);
(2) the person holds, or may hold, an account at a bank which is situated in a participating country; and
(3) the information which the applicant seeks to obtain is likely to be of substantial value for the purposes of the investigation.

The following information may be requested:

(a) information as to whether the person in question holds any accounts at any banks situated in the participating country;
(b) details of any such accounts; and
(c) details of transactions carried out in any period specified in the request, in respect of any such accounts.

Any request made must:

(i) state the grounds on which the judge making the request thinks that the person in question may hold any account at a bank which is situated in a participating country and (if possible) specify the bank or banks in question;

(ii) state the grounds on which the judge considers that the information sought to be obtained is likely to be of substantial value for the purposes of the investigation; and

(iii) include any information which may facilitate compliance with the request.

For the purposes of s.43 a person holds an account if the account is in his name or is held for his benefit, or he has a power of attorney in respect of the account (C(IC)A 2003 s.43(7)).

Monitoring banking transactions

If it appears to a judge entitled to exercise the jurisdiction of the Crown Court, on an application made by a prosecuting authority designated by the Secretary of State, that the information which the applicant seeks to obtain is relevant to an investigation in the UK into criminal conduct, the judge may request assistance in obtaining from a participating country details of transactions to be carried out in any period specified in the request in respect of any accounts at banks situated in that country (C(IC)A 2003 s.44). **40-082**

Sending requests for assistance

A request for assistance under C(IC)A 2003 ss.43 or 44 above, is sent to the Secretary of State for forwarding to a court specified in the request and exercising jurisdiction in the place where the information is to be obtained, or to any authority recognised by the participating country in question as the appropriate authority for receiving requests for assistance of the kind to which this section applies, although in cases of urgency the request may be sent to the court (C(IC)A 2003 s.45). **40-083**

M. External Investigations

General

The Proceeds of Crime Act 2002 (External Investigations) Order SI 2014/1893, which came into force 13 August 2014, has effect for the purpose of enabling an appropriate officer to assist an external investigation by obtaining orders and warrants from the Crown Court. An "external investigation" for the purposes of the Order is an investigation by an overseas authority into whether property has been obtained as a result of or in connection with criminal conduct (POCA 2002 s.447(3)). It does not apply to an external investigation into whether a money laundering offence has been committed. **40-084**

The powers conferred are exercisable only if the appropriate officer believes that the external investigation relates to a criminal investigation or criminal proceedings in the country or territory of the overseas authority carrying out the external investigation. "Criminal proceedings" include proceedings to remove from a person the benefit of that person's criminal conduct following that person's conviction for an offence or offences.

The Secretary of State may refer to the Director General of the NCA, a constable or an officer of HMRC a request for assistance in relation to an external investigation, and the Director General of the NCA, a constable or an officer of HMRC may, on receipt of the request for assistance, act under the Order.

In addition to the offences prescribed by POCA 2002 for breach of individual orders, art.5 of the Order provides for offences of prejudicing an external investigation. This broadly corresponds to s.342 of the 2002 Act. The article makes it an offence to prejudice an external investigation by making a disclosure about it or by tampering with evidence relevant to the external investigation.

The provisions of the Order are in broadly similar terms to those of POCA 2002. Thus, as the Explanatory Note accompanying the statutory instrument indicates:

Production, etc. orders

40-085 Articles 6 and 7 (*making an order*) correspond to POCA 2002 ss.345 and 346;

Article 8 (*order to grant entry*) broadly corresponds POCA 2002 s.347;

Article 9 (*privileged, excluded material*) broadly corresponds to POCA 2002 s.348;

Article 10 (*material contained in a computer*) broadly corresponds to POCA 2002 s.349;

Article 11 (*material held by an authorised government department*) broadly corresponds to POCA 2002 s.350; and

Article 12 (*application without notice*) broadly corresponds to POCA 2002 s.351.

Search and seizure warrants

40-086 Article 13 (*issue of warrant*) broadly corresponds to POCA 2002 s.352;

Article 14 (*conditions for issuing warrant*) broadly corresponds to POCA 2002 s.353; and

Article 15 (*execution of warrant*) broadly corresponds to POCA 2002 ss.354 and 356. The judge may make the warrant subject to such conditions as he sees fit.

Disclosure orders

40-087 Article 16 (*making an order*) broadly corresponds to POCA 2002 s.357; unlike the other orders covered by this instrument, which have to be applied for separately on each occasion, once a disclosure order has been made there is a continuing power of investigation.

Article 17 (*requirements of order*) broadly corresponds to POCA 2002 s.358;

Article 18 (*offences*) broadly corresponds to POCA 2002 s.359;

Article 19 (*statements in response*) broadly corresponds to POCA 2002 s.360; and

Articles 20 and 21 (*further provisions*) broadly correspond to POCA 2002 ss.361 and 362.

Customer information orders

40-088 Article 22 (*nature of order*) broadly corresponds to POCA 2002 s.363; art.28(6) requires in certain circumstances the prior authorisation of a senior appropriate officer before an appropriate officer can make an initial or variation application for a customer information order. An appropriate officer who is also a senior appropriate officer may apply for the order and variations themselves without requiring further and separate authorisation.

Articles 23 and 24 (*definitions and requirements*) broadly correspond to POCA 2002 ss.364 and 365;

Article 25 (*offences*) broadly corresponds to POCA 2002 s.366;

Article 26 (*statements in response*) broadly corresponds to POCA 2002 s.367; and

Articles 27 and 28 (*further provisions*) broadly correspond to POCA 2002 ss.368 and 369.

Account monitoring orders

Article 29 (*making an order*) broadly corresponds to POCA 2002 s.370; 40-089

Article 30 (*requirements of order*) broadly corresponds to POCA 2002 s.371; it is anticipated that it will need to be shown that an account monitoring order lasting over a period of time (rather than a one-off production order) is necessary;

Article 31 (*statements in response*) broadly corresponds to POCA 2002 s.372; and

Articles 32 to 34 (*further provisions*) broadly correspond to POCA 2002 ss.373–375.

Codes of Practice

Article 35 provides that the Codes of Practice established under the Proceeds of Crime Act 2002 (Investigations in England, Wales and Northern Ireland: Code of Practice) Order 2008 (SI 2008/946) and the Proceeds of Crime Act 2002 (Investigative Powers of Prosecutors in England, Wales and Northern Ireland: Code of Practice) Order 2008 (SI 2008/1978) apply in relation to confiscation proceedings. 40-090

41. JURISDICTION

Introduction

41-001 The Crown Court is part of the Senior Courts of England and Wales; it is a superior court of record.

Its jurisdiction is exercised by:

(1) any judge of the High Court;
(2) any Circuit judge, Recorder, qualifying judge advocate or District Judge (Magistrates' Courts); or
(3) subject to and in accordance with SCA 1981 ss.74 and 75(2), a judge of the High Court, Circuit Judge, Recorder or qualifying judge advocate, sitting with not more than four justices,

and any such persons when exercising the jurisdiction of the Crown Court are judges of the Crown Court.

The jurisdiction of the Crown Court exercisable by a qualifying judge advocate by virtue of subs.(1) is the jurisdiction of the Court in relation to any criminal cause or matter other than an appeal from a youth court.

A person who is or has been a judge of the Court of Appeal, or who is or has been a puisne judge of the High Court may sit in the Crown Court at the request of the appropriate authority (SCA 1981 ss.8, 9).

Note that:

(a) a justice of the peace is not disqualified from acting as a judge of the Crown Court merely because the proceedings are not at the place within the local justice area to which he is assigned or because the proceedings are nor related to that area in any other way (SCA 1981 s.8(2)); and
(b) when the Crown Court sits in the City of London it is known as the Central Criminal Court, and the Lord Mayor of the City and any Alderman of the City is entitled to sit as a judge of the Central Criminal Court and any judge of the High Court, Circuit Judge, Recorder or District Judge (Magistrates' Courts) (SCA 1981 s.8(3)).

Judges, etc., as justices of the peace

41-002 A Circuit judge, a Deputy Circuit Judge, a Deputy Judge of the High Court, a Judge of the High Court, and a Recorder have the powers of a justice of the peace who is a District Judge (Magistrates' Courts) in relation to criminal causes and matters. Each of the holders of such office is qualified to sit as a member of a youth court (CA 2003 s.66(2), (3)).

SCA 1981 amended by the Armed Forces Act 2011 Sch.2, allows qualifying judge advocates, who conduct military courts, to sit also as judges of the Crown Court.

CCA 2013 Sch.14 contains a list of those members of the judiciary by whom jurisdiction in the Crown Court is exercisable, by the amendment of SCA 1981 s.8.

From the explanatory notes to CA 2003 s.66 it was clearly envisaged that the power was intended to enable a judge of the Crown Court to deal with a summary offence attached to an indictment. The power is clearly wider than that and has been used by judges in the Crown Court to rectify errors of procedure. See, e.g. *R. v Ashton* [2006] EWCA Crim 794; [2006] 2 Cr. App. R. 15 where a judge acting as a District Judge (Magistrates' Courts) quite properly: (a) conducted mode of trial proceedings where these had been omitted; and (b) committed an accused to the Crown Court for sentence where that was appropriate. In the latter case, it was held that there was no statutory impediment to prevent him in his capacity as a judge of the Crown Court from passing sentence on an accused so committed.

Considerable care needs to be taken to avoid falling into error when a judge of the Crown Court exercises powers under CA 2003 s.66. In *R. v Gould* [2021] EWCA Crim 447; [2021] 1 W.L.R. 4812 the CACD set out the scope of a judge's power to use s.66. See too *R. v Cummins* [2022] EWCA Crim 124; [2022] 1 WLUK 432 as to the importance of the judge making clear when they purport to exercise powers under s.66; and

R. v Iles [2012] EWCA Crim 1610; (2012) 176 J.P. 601 (and SENDING FOR TRIAL) on the dangers of the judge sitting as a district judge to deal with summary matters sent with the indictment. See also *R. v Chalk (Thomas Paul)* [2022] EWCA Crim 433; [2022] 4 W.L.R. 55 as to the risk of falling into error when attempts are made by a judge to solve technical problems by sitting as a DJ(MC) under s.66.

Any matter required to be recorded in the magistrates' court's register, should be recorded by the clerk in the Crown Court records, ensuring that there is an accurate and accessible record of any decision or other important feature of the proceedings (*R. v Ashton* [2006] EWCA Crim 794; [2006] 2 Cr. App. R. 15).

In *R. v Ashton* the CACD stressed that in most instances when there has been a procedural failure, it will be unnecessary for s.66 to be used to carry out a process of rectification. Instead, the matter should be approached on the principles set out in *Soneji* and *Knights* (see 11-033) which will normally obviate the need to go through such procedural steps.

See also *R. v Miller* [2010] EWCA Crim 809; [2011] 1 Cr. App. R. (S.) 12 where the accused was wrongly committed for sentence.

General jurisdiction

Subject to the provisions of SCA 1981, the Crown Court exercises: **41-003**

(1) all such appellate and other jurisdiction as is conferred upon it by that or any other Act; and
(2) all such jurisdiction as was exercisable by it immediately before the commencement of that Act (i.e. 1 January 1972),

and its jurisdiction includes all such powers and duties as were exercisable by it, or fell to be performed by it, immediately before that date.

(SCA 1981 s.45(2), (4))

The Crown Court is a creature of statute, it lacks inherent jurisdiction (e.g. *R. (on the application of Trinity Mirror Plc) v Croydon Crown Court* [2008] EWCA Crim 50; [2008] 2 Cr. App. R. 1).

CA 1971 s.8 and Sch.1 conferred on the Crown Court all appellate and other jurisdictions conferred on courts of quarter session, or on any committees of such courts.

Subject to CP(AW)A 1965 s.8, the Crown Court has, in relation to the attendance and examination of witnesses, any contempt of court, the enforcement of its orders and all other matters incidental to its jurisdiction, the like powers, rights, privileges and authority of the High Court. As to the meaning of "incidental" see *R. (on the application of Trinity Mirror Plc) v Croydon Crown Court* [2008] EWCA Crim 50; [2008] 2 Cr. App. R. 1.

Jurisdiction on indictment; practice and procedure

41-004 All proceedings on indictment are brought before the Crown Court, and its jurisdiction with respect to such proceedings includes jurisdiction:

(1) in proceedings on indictment in England and Wales for offences wherever committed; and in particular
(2) in proceedings on indictment for offences within the jurisdiction of the Admiralty of England.

(SCA 1981 s.46(1))

The rules as to service of the indictment are contained in CrimPR 10, but note that a signature is no longer required to convert a draft indictment into an indictment (see generally INDICTMENTS). See *R. v Jessemey* [2021] EWCA Crim 175, as to the need to ensure that a draft indictment is added to the correct section of the digital case system.

SCA 1981 continues in effect all enactments and rules relating to procedure in connection with indictable offences, and in particular preserves:

(a) the practice by which, on any one indictment, the taking of pleas, the trial by jury and the pronouncement of judgment may respectively be by or before different judges;
(b) the release, after respite of judgment, of a convicted person on recognisance to come up for judgment if called on, but meanwhile to be of good behaviour;
(c) the manner of trying any question relating to the breach of a recognisance; and
(d) the manner of execution of any sentence on conviction, or the manner in which any other judgment or order given in connection with trial on indictment may be enforced.

(SCA 1981 s.79(1), (2))

The provisions of the Act relating to the Crown Court's appellate jurisdiction are dealt with under APPELLATE JURISDICTION. The court's powers to grant bail are dealt with under BAIL.

Sittings of the Crown Court

41-005 In relation to the business of the Crown Court:

(1) any business may be conducted at any place in England or Wales, and the sittings of the court at any place may be continuous or intermittent or occasional;
(2) judges may sit simultaneously to take any number of different cases in the same or different places, and may adjourn cases from time to time; and
(3) the places at which the court sits and the days and times at which the court sits at any place are matters to be determined in accordance with directions given by the Lord Chancellor after consulting the Lord Chief Justice.

(SCA 1981 s.78)

The Crown Court is a single court and those who sit in it sit merely from time to time as judges of the court. There is nothing which prevents a case which is part-heard at one location or before one judge, from being adjourned to a later date in contemplation of its being reheard before a different court. There is no principle which retains a case within the so-called "seisin" of an individual judge (*R. v Dudley Crown Court Ex p. Smith* (1974) 58 Cr. App. R. 184).

Composition of the Crown Court

All proceedings in the Crown Court are heard and disposed of before a single judge of the court, except in relation to courts including lay magistrates. Where a judge of the High Court, a Circuit Judge, a Recorder or a District Judge (Magistrates' Courts) or a qualifying Judge Advocate sits with lay magistrates, he presides, and: **41-006**

(1) the decision of the Crown Court may be by a majority; and
(2) if the members of the court are equally divided, the presiding judge, Recorder, etc. has a second and casting vote.

Where a situation arises during the course of the proceedings which involves an interlocutory decision, it must be dealt with by the court as then constituted, i.e. including the magistrates (SCA 1981 s.73(1), (3)).

On a question of law, the magistrates will obviously defer to the views of the presiding judge (*R. v Orpin* (1974) 59 Cr. App. R. 231). See generally APPELLATE JURISDICTION.

Business in chambers

A judge of the Crown Court may exercise the following jurisdiction, sitting in chambers: **41-007**

(1) hearing applications for bail;
(2) issuing a summons or warrant;
(3) hearing any application relating to procedural matters preliminary or incidental to criminal proceedings in the Crown Court, including applications relating to CDS funding;
(4) jurisdiction under:
    (a) CrimPR 3.13(2)(a) (listing first appearance of accused sent for trial);
    (b) CrimPR 17.2 (application for witness summons); and
    (c) CrimPR 34.8(1)(a) (an appeal, or any hearing in relation to an appeal against decision of magistrates' court);
(5) hearing an application under YJCA 1999 s.41(2) (evidence of complainant's sexual history);
(6) hearing applications under POA 1985 s.22(3) (extension or further extension of a custody time limit);
(7) hearing an appeal brought by an accused under POA 1985 s.22(7) against a decision of the magistrates' court to extend or further extend a time limit, or by the prosecution under s.22(8) against the magistrates' refusal to extend or further extend such a limit;
(8) hearing an appeal under B(A)A 1993 s.1 (against grant of bail by the magistrates' court) (CrimPR 19); and
(9) hearing appeals under CJA 2003 s.16 (against condition of bail imposed by the magistrates' court).

Note that in relation to applications for bail, except in the case of an application made by the prosecutor or a constable under BA 1976 s.3(8), the applicant is not entitled to be present on the hearing of the application unless the Crown Court gives him leave to be present.

An application to vary the place of trial (see ALLOCATION AND DISTRIBUTION OF CASES) must be heard in open court.

Hearings in camera

41-008 As to trials in camera, see REPORTING AND ACCESS RESTRICTION (CrimPR 6.6).

42. JURY MANAGEMENT

QUICK GUIDE

1. QUALIFICATIONS FOR JURY SERVICE

Statutory qualifications

The qualifications for jury service are set out in JA 1974 s.1, and Sch.1, as amended by CJA 2003 and subsequently. Those eligible are: **42-001**

(1) those aged 18–75; and
(2) registered voters in the UK who have been resident here for at least five years.

The principal exclusions are:

(a) the mentally disabled; and
(b) those who are on bail, or have been sentenced, in criminal proceedings.

The Lord Chancellor is responsible for the system of summoning jurors (JA 1974 s.2) in which a trial judge has no power to interfere.

There remains the statutory power, which may be exercised in exceptional circumstances by a trial judge to summon a person within the vicinity of the court without the need for a formal notice to serve as a juror (JA 1974 s.6 and *CPD* VI 39F.1). In practice this is rarely used and the better course, where there is a shortage of eligible jurors, will usually be to adjourn the trial to allow the court's jury-summoning officer to find a fresh panel. In a routine case a panel of at least 14 jurors is regarded as a necessary and workable minimum.

Jury vetting, in accordance with the Attorney General's Guidelines is permissible (*R. v Mason* [1981] 71 Cr. App. R. 157).

CPD VI Trial 26A Juries: introduction 26A.1 emphasises that jury service is an important public duty which individual members of the public are chosen at random to undertake.

The duty to serve

The normal presumption is that everyone, unless mentally disordered or otherwise disqualified, is required to serve when summoned to do so, but the legislative changes brought about by CJA 2003 have meant an increase in the number of jurors with professional and public service commitments, and the judge needs to **42-002** be alert to the need to exercise his discretion to adjourn a trial, or excuse or discharge a juror should the need arise.

2. Excusal and deferment

Application for excusal or deferment before trial

42-003 A person summoned for jury service may, subject to JA 1974 s.9A, show to the satisfaction of the Crown Court officer that there is good reason why:

(1) his attendance should be excused, in which case the Crown Court officer may excuse him; or
(2) his attendance should be deferred, in which case that officer may defer his attendance,

though in a case under (2), if an application has been granted or refused, the powers may not be exercised again in respect of the same summons.

Special provisions apply to serving naval, military or air force personnel, both in relation to excusal (under s.9(2A) and (2B)) and deferment (under s.9A(2A) and (2B)).

HMCTS has issued written guidance under JA 1974 s.9AA, entitled *Guidance for Summoning Officers when considering deferral and excusal applications* (updated 18 June 2009).

The guidance is reproduced in *Archbold* (London: Sweet & Maxwell), para.4-285–4-287.

A person may appeal to a judge against the officer's refusal (see 42-008).

At any time before a juror completes the oath or affirmation, the judge may, of his own initiative, or where the court officer refers the juror to him, and after enquiry of the juror, exercise the power to excuse the juror from service for lack of capacity to act effectively as a juror because of an insufficient understanding of English.

(CrimPR 26.2; see also JA 1974 s.10.)

Eligibility to serve: (1) general

42-004 The widening of the eligibility to serve under CJA 2003 means that more individuals are eligible to serve as jurors. Judges need to be vigilant to the need to exercise their discretion to adjourn a trial, excuse or discharge a juror if the need arises. Whether or not an application has been made to the court jury-summoning officer for excusal or deferment a person summoned may apply to the judge to be excused. Such applications must be considered with common sense and according to the interests of justice.

An explanation should be required for an application being much later than necessary.

Eligibility to serve: (2) competence; disability

42-005 Where it appears to the Crown Court officer that a juror attending may be unable to serve on account of insufficient understanding of English, he may refer the matter to a judge who will determine whether or not he should be excused (and see *R. v Osman* [1996] 1 Cr. App. R. 126, where the prospective juror was profoundly deaf and unable to follow the proceedings) (*CPD* VI 26 C (Juries: eligibility) C.1, 2).

At any time before a juror completes the oath or affirmation, the judge may exercise his power to excuse him or her from jury service for lack of capacity to act effectively as a juror because of an insufficient understanding of English:

(1) on the judge's own initiative; or
(2) where the court officer refers the juror to him; and
(3) after enquiry of the juror.

CrimPR 26.2. See also *CPD* VI 26C.3, and guidance issued by the SPJ on 19 October 2018 on jurors with a disability which deals with the judge's discretion to "stand down" a juror who is not competent to serve by reason of personal disability, questions of reasonable adjustment and the requirement for a fair trial.

Provisions in the Police, Crime, Sentencing and Courts Act 2022 make amendments to s.9 JA 1974 so that a deaf juror can have the services of a British Sign Language [BSL] interpreter or interpreters so as to enable a person to be capable of acting effectively as a juror. A BSL interpreter approved by the trial judge may remain with the jury in the course of their deliberations, but the interpreter must not interfere in or influence the deliberations. The 2022 Act also cater for extending a number of provisions on jurors to interpreters (challenge for cause, surrender of electronic communication devices) and the scope of juror offences (see 42-030) as well as a specific provision creating a new offence of interpreters interfering in or influencing jury deliberations.

Eligibility to serve: (3) police officers, prison officers, employees of prosecuting agencies and the judiciary

A judge should always be made aware at the stage of jury selection if any juror in waiting falls within any one of these categories (and see *R. v Khan* [2008] EWCA Crim 531; [2008] 2 Cr. App. R. 13). The juror summons warns jurors in these categories that they will need to alert court staff. **42-006**

Police officers: In the case of a serving police officer, an inquiry by the judge will have to be made to assess whether a police officer may serve as a juror. Regard should be paid to:

- whether evidence from the police is in dispute in the case and the extent to which that dispute involves allegations made against the police;
- whether the potential juror knows or has worked with the officers involved in the case; and
- whether the potential juror has served or continues to serve in the same police units within the force as those dealing with the investigation of the case, or is likely to have a shared local service background with police witnesses in a trial.

A serving police officer can serve where there is no particular link between the court and the station where the police officer serves.

Prison officers: In the case of a serving prison officer, the judge will need to inquire whether the individual is employed at a prison linked to that court or is likely to have special knowledge of any person involved in a trial.

Prosecutors: In the case of employees of prosecuting authorities, the judge will need to ensure that they do not serve on a trial prosecuted by the prosecuting authority by which they are employed. They can serve on a trial prosecuted by another prosecuting authority (*R. v Abdroikov* [2007] UKHL 37; [2008] 1 Cr. App. R. 21; *Hanif v United Kingdom* [2011] ECHR 2247; (2012) 55 E.H.R.R. 16; *R. v L* [2011] EWCA Crim 65; [2011] 1 Cr. App. R. 27).

Potential jurors falling into these categories should be excused from jury service unless there is a suitable alternative court/trial to which they can be transferred. (*CPD* VI 26C.6–10)

As to challenges to such persons, see below 42-016 and following.

The judiciary: Written guidance to members of the judiciary summoned for jury service was given by Lord Woolf CJ, in a letter dated 15 June 2004 which referred to the Lord Chancellor's *Guidance for Summoning Officers when considering deferral and excusal applications* (*Archbold*, para.4-287—see para.18 for reference to the judiciary).

Excusal in the course of the trial

42-007 As to where a juror may be excused for personal reasons once the trial has commenced see 42-038.

Right of appeal

42-008 Where a person summoned for jury service in the Crown Court wants to appeal against a refusal:

(1) to excuse him from such service; or
(2) to postpone the date on which he is required to attend for such service,

he must appeal to the court to which he has been summoned, applying in writing, as soon as reasonably practicable; and serving the application on the court officer.

The application must:

(a) attach a copy of the jury summons, and the refusal to excuse or postpone, which is under appeal; and
(b) explain why the court should excuse him from jury service, or postpone its date, as appropriate.

The court to which the appeal is made:

(i) may extend the time for appealing, and may allow the appeal to be made orally;
(ii) may determine the appeal at a hearing in public or in private, or without a hearing; and
(iii) may adjourn any hearing of the appeal; but

must not determine an appeal unless the appellant has had a reasonable opportunity to make representations in person (CrimPR 26.1; see also JA 1974 ss.9 and 9A).

Where a person summoned for jury service:

(i) fails to attend as required; or
(ii) after attending as required, when selected under r.38.6 is not available, or is unfit for jury service by reason of drink or drugs,

that conduct may be punished as if it were a contempt of court (JA 1974 s.20).

The maximum penalty which may be imposed is a fine of £1,000.

3. MAKE UP OF JURY

Principle of a random jury

42-009 The residual discretion of a judge at common law to discharge a juror in order to ensure a fair trial has never been held to include a discretion to influence the overall composition of the jury, as by discharging a jury drawn from a particular section of the community (see *R. v Tarrant* [1990] Crim. L.R. 342). Fairness, in relation to this aspect of the trial, is achieved by the principle of random selection (see JA 1974 s.11).

The judge's residual discretion may be exercised:

(1) even in the absence of objection by either party;
(2) on grounds that would found a challenge for cause;
(3) for instance, where a juror is not likely to be able or willing to perform his duties (e.g. through an inadequate command of English); and
(4) for instance, where a juror is infirm, hard of hearing, or whose attendance at a long trial would be burdensome (*R. v Mason* (1980) 71 Cr. App. R. 157).

Information about jurors

The court may invite each member of a panel of jurors to provide such information, by such means and at such a time as the court directs, about; **42-010**

(1) that juror's availability to try a case expected to last for longer than the juror had expected to serve; and
(2) any association of that juror with, or any knowledge by that juror of a party or witness, or any other person, or any place, of significance to the case.

Where jurors provide information under this rule, the court may postpone the selection of the jury to try a case to allow each juror an opportunity to review and amend that information before that selection.

Using that information, the court may exercise its power to excuse a juror from selection as a member of the jury to try a case, but the court must not:

(a) excuse a juror without allowing the parties an opportunity to make representations; or
(b) refuse to excuse a juror without allowing that juror such an opportunity.

(CrimPR 26.4)

Precautionary measures before swearing the jury

The judge should consult the advocates as to the questions, if any, it may be appropriate to ask potential jurors before they are empanelled and sworn. **42-011**

Topics to be considered include:

- the availability of jurors for the duration of a trial which may run beyond the usual period for which jurors are summoned (generally two weeks);
- whether any juror knows the accused or parties to the case;
- whether potential jurors are so familiar with any locations that feature in the case that they may have, or come to have, access to information not in evidence; and
- in cases where there has been any significant local or national publicity, whether any questions should be asked of potential jurors.

(*CPD* VI Trial 26D: Juries: Precautionary measures before swearing 39 D.1)

Judges should however exercise caution. At common law a judge has a residual discretion to discharge a particular juror who ought not to be serving, but this discretion can only be exercised to prevent an individual juror who is not competent from serving. It does not include a discretion to discharge a jury drawn from particular sections of the community or otherwise to influence the overall composition of the jury. If there is a risk that there is widespread local knowledge of the accused or a witness, the judge may, after hearing submissions from the advocates, decide to exclude jurors from particular areas to avoid the risk of jurors having or acquiring personal knowledge of the defendant or a witness (*CPD* VI 26 D.2).

Length of trial

42-012 Where the trial is estimated to be significantly longer than the normal period of jury service, it is good practice for the trial judge to enquire whether the potential jurors on the jury panel foresee any difficulties with the length and if the judge is satisfied that the jurors' concerns are justified, he may say that they are not required for that particular jury. This does not mean that the judge must excuse the juror from sitting at that court altogether, as it may well be possible for the juror to sit on a shorter trial at the same court (*CPD* VI 39 D.3).

Juror with potential connection to the case or parties

42-013 Where a juror appears on a jury panel, it will be appropriate for a judge to excuse the juror from that particular case where the potential juror is personally concerned with the facts of the particular case, or is closely connected with a prospective witness. Judges need to exercise due caution (*CPD* VI 39D.4).

Police and prison officers; prosecutors; the judiciary

42-014 Particular difficulties may arise where a prospective juror works within the criminal justice system. As to those who are, or have been, police officers, prison officers or members of the prosecuting authority, see 42-006 and *R. v Abdroikov* [2007] UKHL 37; [2008] 1 Cr. App. R. 21; *R. v Khan* [2008] EWCA Crim 531; [2008] 2 Cr. App. R. 13; *R. v GC* [2008] Crim. L.R. 984. For a useful illustration see *R. v L* [2010] EWCA Crim 65; [2011] 1 Cr. App. R. 27 (conviction quashed where jury included two police officers (one retired) and an employee of CPS). See also *Hanif v United Kingdom* [2011] ECHR 2247; (2012) 55 E.H.R.R. 16 (where a police juror was personally acquainted with a police witness in the trial).

The mere presence of a police officer on a jury is not a breach of ECHR art.6. Each case is fact specific. It is reasonably to be expected, for example, that a police officer who works out of the same police station as one of the police witnesses in the trial might readily be excused or stood down, whereas merely being a member of the same county constabulary would not be.

As to members of the judiciary, see the written guidance given by Lord Woolf CJ, in a letter dated 15 June 2004 which referred to the Lord Chancellor's *Guidance for Summoning Officers when considering deferral and excusal applications* (*Archbold*, para.4–285—see para.18 for reference to the judiciary).

Racial, religious, etc. cases

42-015 Applications are sometimes made to the trial judge where the case involves an accused of a particular racial or ethnic group, and where it is suggested that the jury should consist, either wholly or partly, of that same particular racial or ethnic group. The trial judge has no discretion to interfere in that way with the composition of the panel, or of an individual jury (see *R. v Danvers* [1982] Crim. L.R. 680; *R. v Broderick* [1970] Crim. L.R. 155; *R. v Ford* (1989) 89 Cr. App. R. 278).

Note, however, that the judge may excuse, or discharge, a juror who has an insufficient understanding of English (see JA 1974 s.10 and *CPD* VI 26C.1–2).

A conscientious objection arising from religious beliefs is unlikely, itself, to amount to a good reason for excusal unless, possibly, it would prevent the potential juror from properly fulfilling his duties (see *R. v Guildford Crown Court Ex p. Siderfin* (1990) 90 Cr. App. R. 192).

Note that:

(1) the mere fact that a juror is, for instance, of a particular race, or holds a particular religious belief, cannot be made the basis for a challenge for cause on the ground of bias, or on any other ground;
(2) there is no principle of the criminal law that a jury should be racially balanced (*R. v McCalla* [1986] Crim. L.R. 335); and
(3) the trial judge's residual discretion, in the absence of any challenge, to exclude from the jury a person who is obviously incompetent to act through personal disability (*R. v Mason* (1980) 71 Cr. App. R. 157), is not to be exercised so as to undermine the random nature of the jury, or to influence its overall composition (*R. v Ford* (1989) 89 Cr. App. R. 278).

4. CHALLENGES TO JURORS

Attorney General's Stand by Guidelines

The Attorney General has issued an updated *Jury Vetting: Right of Stand by Guidelines* (with effect from 27 November 2012) on the exercise by the Crown of their right to stand a juror by (see *https://www.gov.uk/guidance/jury-vetting-right-of-stand-by-guidelines--2* [Accessed 18 September 2022]). **42-016**

The circumstances in which it would be proper for the Crown to exercise its right to stand by a member of a jury panel are:

(1) where a jury check authorised in accordance with the Attorney General's Guidelines on Jury Checks reveals information justifying exercise of the right to stand by in accordance with para.11 of the guidelines and the Attorney General personally authorises the exercise of the right to stand by; or
(2) where a person is about to be sworn as a juror who is manifestly unsuitable and the defence agree that, accordingly, the exercise by the prosecution of the right to stand by would be appropriate.

An example of the sort of exceptional circumstances which might justify stand by is where it becomes apparent that a juror selected for service to try a complex case is in fact illiterate.

A prosecutor who exercises the prosecution right without giving reasons to prevent the court selecting an individual juror must announce the exercise of that right before the juror completes the oath or affirmation.
(CrimPR 25.8)

Types of Challenge

A challenge may be made for cause: **42-017**

(1) to the panel or part panel; or, more usually
(2) to an individual juror.

The judge should require the advocate to make plain immediately which form of challenge he is pursuing and must decide whether to hear the challenge in chambers, in camera, or in open court. The advocate should identify clearly the objection to the juror serving. A record should be made of all proceedings, and in every case the fact of the challenge and the court's decision on it should be entered in the court record.

(1) Objecting to jurors

42-018 A party who objects to:

(1) the *panel* of jurors must serve notice explaining the objection on the court officer and on the other party before the first juror's name or number is drawn;
(2) the selection of an *individual juror* must:
  (a) tell the court of the objection;
  (b) after the juror's name or number is announced; and
  (c) before the juror completes the oath or affirmation; and
  (d) explain the objection.

A prosecutor who exercises the prosecution right without giving reasons to prevent the court selecting an individual juror must announce the exercise of that right before the juror completes the oath or affirmation.

The judge will determine an objection under paragraph (1) or (2) at a hearing, in public or in private; and in the absence of the jurors, unless he otherwise directs. (CrimPR 25.8)

Prima facie grounds

42-019 If it appears to the judge that there are prima facie grounds on which the challenge could be supported, the summoning officer should be asked to appear and answer the challenge. If the grounds are contested, the judge must determine, after hearing evidence, whether it is borne out, the burden being on the challenger to satisfy the judge on a balance of probabilities.

Result of determination

42-020 If the challenge is:

(1) overruled, the jury should be called into court in the normal way, and the judge should make no further reference to the challenge; or
(2) upheld, the trial should be adjourned until a new panel can be produced.

Challenge to individual juror

42-021 A challenge is made to an individual juror when 12 jurors have been empanelled by being called into the jury box:

(1) at the time when the juror is sworn (*R. v Morris* (1991) 93 Cr. App. R. 102); but
(2) before he is sworn.

A party who objects to the selection of an *individual juror* must tell the court of the objection after the juror's name or number is announced, and before the juror completes the oath or affirmation, and explain the objection (CrimPR.25.8(2)).

An accused will be informed of his right of challenge by the Crown Court officer.

Resolving the challenge informally

If a challenge is indicated and the advocate can state the grounds of challenge without prejudicing his client in the eyes of the other jurors, or embarrassing the juror concerned, the judge may be able to deal with the matter in open court, briefly and informally. **42-022**

If the challenge succeeds, another juror will be called from the panel. Subsequent challenges will be dealt with in the same manner. All 12 jurors will then be sworn in the presence of each other.

Resolving the challenge formally; need for hearing

Where it is not possible to deal with the matter informally, the sworn jurors should be asked to retire to their room in the charge of the jury bailiff, and the remainder of the panel should be asked to leave court for the time being; the challenged juror should be kept outside, in the care of an usher, but close by in case it is necessary to question him. **42-023**

The judge will decide whether:

(1) to hear the challenge in open court; or
(2) to exclude the public and press.

If the grounds of the challenge make it desirable in the interests of justice, and of the challenged juror, to close the court, the judge should announce that that court will sit "as in chambers" and the public and press should be asked to leave the court. Challenges should not be heard in the judge's room.

If the ground of challenge appears prima facie valid and the facts are contested, the judge must decide the facts. The burden of proof is on the party challenging, on a balance of probabilities.

The judge may:

(1) hear evidence on the voir dire;
(2) question the juror; and
(3) permit advocates to ask questions directed to the particular ground of challenge alleged.

Before he questions the juror the judge might be well advised to discuss with the advocates what he has in mind to ask the juror as well as what they wish to ask.

Before there can be any right under (3) to question a juror, a prima facie foundation of fact must be laid (*R. v Chandler (No.2)* (1964) 48 Cr. App. R. 143; *R. v Broderick* [1970] Crim. L.R. 155; cf. *R. v Kray* (1969) 53 Cr. App. R. 412).

The questioning of jurors, whether orally or in a witness questionnaire, where there is no suggestion that they might have an interest in the case, should be avoided save in the most exceptional circumstances (*R. v Andrews* [1999] Crim. L.R. 156). Speculative questions, seeking to establish the basis for challenge on different grounds, are not permissible.

Decision on the facts

42-024 If the challenge is:

(1) allowed, the juror should be discharged and a fresh juror called to take his place when the remainder of the jury return; or
(2) disallowed, the judge should caution the juror not to disclose to the others any of the matters considered at the hearing of the challenge, and not to allow the fact of the challenge to influence him in any way.

At the end of the process all 12 jurors will have been sworn in the presence of one another.

Where a challenge, or an objection, to a juror arises once the jury has been sworn and the trial has commenced, different considerations apply. For questions relating to the discharge of jurors see 42-038.

Order under CCA 1981, s.4(2)

42-025 Where matters raised in the challenge might prejudice the trial, the judge should consider making a postponement order under CCA 1981 s.4(2) (see REPORTING AND ACCESS RESTRICTIONS) restricting publication until the end of the trial.

5. SELECTING THE JURY

General

42-026 CrimPR 25.6 applies where:

(1) the accused pleads not guilty;
(2) the accused declines to enter a plea and the court treats that as a not guilty plea; or
(3) the court determines that the accused is not fit to be tried.

It does not apply where the judge orders a trial without a jury because of a danger of jury tampering or where jury tampering appears to have taken place, or he tries without a jury counts on an indictment after a trial of sample counts with a jury.

The general provisions of the rule require the court to select a jury to try the case from the panel, or part of the panel, of jurors summoned by the Lord Chancellor to attend at that time and place.

Where it appears that too few jurors to constitute a jury will be available from among those so summoned, the court may exercise its own power to summon others in the court room, or in the vicinity, up to the number likely to be required, and add their names to the panel summoned by the Lord Chancellor; but the parties must be if they are absent when that power is exercised.

The court must select the jury by drawing at random each juror's name from among those so summoned and either:

(a) announcing each name so drawn; or
(b) where the court is satisfied that that is necessary because of a risk of interference with the jury, announcing an identifying number assigned by the court officer to that person.

If too few jurors to constitute a jury are available from the panel after all their names have been drawn, the court may exercise its own power to summon others in the court room, or in the vicinity, up to the number required; and again, announce the name of each person so summoned, or an identifying number assigned by the court officer to that person, where the court is satisfied that that is necessary because of a risk of interference with the jury.

The jury selected:

- *must* comprise no fewer than 12 jurors; or
- *may* comprise as many as 14 jurors to begin with, where the court expects the trial to last for more than four weeks.

Where the court selects a jury comprising more than 12 jurors, the court must explain to them that the purpose of selecting more than 12 jurors to begin with is to fill any vacancy or vacancies caused by the discharge of any of the first 12 before the prosecution evidence begins; any such vacancy or vacancies will be filled by the extra jurors in order of their selection from the panel. The court will discharge any extra juror or jurors remaining by no later than the beginning of the prosecution evidence; any juror who is discharged for that reason then will be available to be selected for service on another jury, during the period for which that juror has been summoned.

Each of the 12 or more jurors the court selects:

(i) must take an oath or affirm; and
(ii) becomes a full jury member until discharged.

The oath or affirmation must be in these terms, or in any corresponding terms that the juror declares to be binding on him or her, namely:

> "I swear by Almighty God [or I do solemnly, sincerely and truly declare and affirm] that I will faithfully try the defendant and give a true verdict according to the evidence."

The usual procedure for empanelling a jury is to ballot from those assembled by calling out the names of the jurors in open court in the presence of the accused. As each person's name is called, that person steps into the jury box and is sworn. In this way everyone in court knows the names of the jurors who are to try the accused. The position was considered in *R. v Comerford* [1998] 1 Cr. App. R. 235, where the jury were balloted by numbers. No juror was identified in court by name. The CACD held that this procedure was lawful as it had no material and adverse effect on the fairness of the trial. However

> "it is highly desirable that in normal circumstances the usual procedure for empanelling a jury should be 'nobble' a jury, it is reasonably thought to be desirable to withhold juror's names, we can see no objection to that course provided the accused's right of challenge is preserved."

See, however, *R. v Baybasin* [2013] EWCA Crim 2357; [2014] 1 Cr. App. R. 19.

6. JUDGE'S ROLE AT TRIAL; GUIDANCE AND WARNINGS

General

It is almost invariably sensible for the trial judge, at the start of any but the most simple trial, to give the jury a brief indication of their functions, and the process of a criminal trial together with any other guidance appropriate to the particular court or trial. 42-027

Jurors can be expected to follow instructions given to them diligently (*R. v Taylor* [2013] UKPC 8; [2013] 1 W.L.R. 1144).

Helpful general guidance was given by Lord Judge CJ, in *R. v Thompson* [2010] EWCA Crim 1623; [2010] 2 Cr. App. R. 27. And see *CPD* VI 39G.3–4.

The court will also arrange for each juror to receive:

1. general information about jury service and about a juror's responsibilities;
2. written notice of the prohibitions against discussion of a case with someone who is not a member of the jury, and enquiry into the circumstances of a case, or into the parties, beyond what is described in evidence; and
3. a written warning that breach of those prohibitions is a contempt of court, and the judge has power to impose imprisonment, or a fine, or both, for contempt of court.

(CrimPR 26.3)

CPD sets out a form of notice for use in connection with this rule.

Preliminary instructions to jurors

42-028 After the jury has been sworn and the defendant has been put in charge the judge will want to give directions to the jury on a number of matters.

Trial judges should instruct the jury on general matters which will include the time estimate for the trial and normal sitting hours. The jury will always need clear guidance on the following:

- the need to try the case only on the evidence and to remain faithful to their oaths or affirmations;
- the prohibition on internet searches for matters related to the trial, any issues arising or the parties;
- the importance of not discussing any aspect of the case with anyone outside their own number or allowing anyone to talk to them about it, whether directly, by telephone, through internet facilities such as *Facebook* or *Twitter* or in any other way;
- the importance of taking no account of any media reports about the case;
- the collective responsibility of the jury in ensuring that the conduct of each member is consistent with the jury oath and that the directions of the trial judge are followed; and
- the need to bring any concerns, including concerns about the conduct of other jurors, to the attention of the judge at the time, and not to wait until the case is concluded. The point should be made that, unless that is done while the case is continuing, it may not be possible to deal with the problem at all.

Judges should consider reminding jurors of these instructions as appropriate at the end of each day and in particular when they separate after retirement.

(*CPD* VI 26G: Juries: Preliminary instructions to jurors 26.1–4)

In those Crown Courts where the scheme is in operation each member of the jury must be provided with a copy of the notice "Your Responsibilities as a Juror". The note sets out in words and diagrams what is required of jurors whilst serving on a jury. The notice is designed to reinforce the preliminary directions given by the judge. Jurors are advised that they should keep the notice with their summons and at the end of the trial they are allowed to retain it.

(*CPD* VI 26G.5)

Further or other guidance

What judges may choose to say further is a matter of personal practice and particular to the court or to the trial in prospect. Some judges address the jury at the outset of a trial before the case is opened, others do so at the first midday or overnight adjournment. Other judicial indications often given include: **42-029**

- that the jury may take any notes but that part of the judge's task in summing-up is to remind them of the evidence and that they need to focus on the witnesses and the delivery, as well as the content, of their evidence;
- that the jury should keep an open mind until they have seen and heard all the witnesses and the evidence and the addresses from the advocates;
- that it is for them collectively to bring their common sense and knowledge of the world and of other people to bear on their task;
- that they have no need, and should not, make a point of undertaking their own research into the subject matter of the case, or of visiting any places which may feature; they are jurors not investigators;
- that the jury may communicate with the judge through questions or notes but that they should not be too quick to ask a question about the evidence because the answer to their question may be answered by a witness, or an advocate, at a later stage in the evidence, or the case, generally; and
- the overwhelming importance of their acting together as a group, and the confidentiality of their discussions whilst together.

Judges (as well as advocates) may find it helpful to be familiar with the contents of the leaflet Your Guide to Jury Service sent to those summoned for jury service by HMCTS and the DVD, *Your Role as a Juror*, played to them on their first attendance at court as to the information which they will already have received.

7. JURY IRREGULARITIES AND MISCONDUCT

General

Where an incident arises concerning the jury which may affect the integrity of the trial it may, or may not, involve an allegation of impropriety by a juror or within the jury. The *CPD* makes clear that a jury irregularity is: **42-030**

> "anything that may prevent one or more jurors from remaining faithful to their oath or affirmation to 'faithfully try the defendant and give a true verdict according to the evidence.' Jury irregularities take many forms. Some are clear-cut such as a juror conducting research about the case or an attempt to suborn or intimidate a juror. Others are less clear-cut—for example, when there is potential bias or friction between jurors".

(*CPD* VI Trial 26M: Juries: Jury irregularities)

Irregularities were addressed in a document issued in November 2012 by the President of the Queen's Bench Division, entitled Jury Irregularities in the Crown Court: a Protocol [2013] 1 W.L.R. 486. That protocol has now been revised and consolidated in *CPD* VI 26M: Juries: Jury irregularities.

A jury irregularity is anything which may hinder a juror, or the jury, from returning a true verdict according to the evidence by compromising their independence or by introducing something extraneous into their deliberations.

Under the previous version of the *CPD*, the Crown Court required approval from the Vice President of the Court of Appeal (Criminal Division) (the CACD) prior to providing a juror's details to the police for the purposes of an investigation into a jury irregularity. Such approval is no longer required. Provision of a juror's details to the police is now a matter for the Crown Court (*CPD* VI: 26M.4).

Surrender of electronic communications devices

42-031 A judge dealing with an issue will be able (CJCA 2014 s.40) to order the members of a jury trying the issue to surrender any electronic communications devices for a period, but only where he considers that:

(1) the order is necessary or expedient in the interests of justice; and
(2) the terms of the order are a proportionate means of safeguarding those interests.

An order may only specify a period during which the members of the jury are:

(a) in the building in which the trial is being heard;
(b) in other accommodation provided at the judge's request;
(c) visiting a place in accordance with arrangements made by the court; or
(d) travelling to or from a place mentioned in (b) or (c).

An order may be made subject to exceptions.

It will be a contempt of court for a member of a jury to fail to surrender an electronic communications device in accordance with an order under this section, but proceedings for a contempt of court under this section may only be instituted on the motion of a court having jurisdiction to deal with it.

"Electronic communications device" means a device that is designed or adapted for a use which consists of or includes the sending or receiving of signals that are transmitted by means of an electronic communications network (as defined in s.32 of the Communications Act 2003).

As to powers of search, see COURT SECURITY.

Irregularities during the course of the trial

42-032 An irregularity may take one of many forms, from a juror searching for material on the internet to friction between individual jurors or improper pressure by one juror on another: The primary concern of the judge should be the impact on the trial.

The trial judge must be notified of any irregularity at once, in the absence of the jury. When the judge becomes aware of a jury irregularity he should follow the procedure set out in the *CPD* VI Trial 26M: Juries: Jury irregularities. Seven steps are identified in the process the judge is to adopt:

STEP 1:	Consider isolating juror(s)
STEP 2:	Consult with advocates
STEP 3:	Consider appropriate provisional measures (which may include surrender/seizure of electronic communications devices and taking defendant into custody)
STEP 4:	Seek to establish basic facts of jury irregularity

STEP 5:	Further consult with advocates
STEP 6:	Decide what to do in relation to conduct of trial
STEP 7:	Consider ancillary matters (contempt in face of court and/or commission of criminal offence)

(1) Step 1: isolating juror(s).

The judge should consider whether the juror(s) concerned should be isolated from the rest of the jury, particularly if the juror(s) may have conducted research about the case. If two or more jurors are concerned, the judge should consider whether they should also be isolated from each other, particularly if one juror has made an accusation against another.

(2) Step 2: consulting with advocates.

The judge should consult with the advocates and invite submissions about appropriate provisional measures (Step 3) and how to go about establishing the basic facts of the jury irregularity (Step 4). Unless there is good reason not to do so, the consultation should be conducted in open court; in the presence of the defendant; and with all parties represented. If the jury irregularity involves a suspicion about the conduct of the defendant or another party, there may be good reason for the consultation to take place in the absence of the defendant or the other party. There may also be good reason for it to take place in private. If so, the proper location is in the court room, with DARTS recording, rather than in the judge's room. If the jury irregularity relates to the jury's deliberations, the judge should warn all those present that it is an offence to disclose, solicit or obtain information about a jury's deliberations (s.20D(1) JA 1974—and see 39M.35–39M.38 of the *CPD* regarding the offence and exceptions). This would include disclosing information about the jury's deliberations divulged in court during consultation with the advocates (Step 2 and Step 5) or when seeking to establish the basic facts of the jury irregularity (Step 4). The judge should emphasise that the advocates, court staff and those in the public gallery would commit the offence by explaining to another what is said in court about the jury's deliberations.

(3) Step 3: consider appropriate provisional measures.

Surrender/seizure of electronic communications devices.

The judge should consider whether to make an order under s.15A(1) JA 1974 requiring the juror(s) concerned to surrender electronic communications devices, such as mobile telephones or smart phones. Having made an order for surrender, the judge may require a court security officer to search a juror to determine whether the juror has complied with the order. Section 54A of the CA 2003 contains the court security officer's powers of search and seizure. Section 15A(5) JA 1974 provides that it is contempt of court for a juror to fail to surrender an electronic communications device in accordance with an order for surrender (see 39M.29–39M.30 regarding the procedure for dealing with such a contempt).

Any electronic communications device surrendered or seized under these provisions should be kept safe by the court until returned to the juror or handed to the police as evidence.

Taking defendant into custody.

If the defendant is on bail, and the jury irregularity involves a suspicion about the defendant's conduct, the judge should consider taking the defendant into custody. If that suspicion involves an attempt to suborn or intimidate a juror, the defendant should be taken into custody.

(4) Step 4: Seek to establish basic facts of jury irregularity.

The judge should seek to establish the basic facts of the jury irregularity for the purpose of determining how to proceed in relation to the conduct of the trial. The judge's enquiries may involve having the juror(s) concerned write a note of explanation and/or questioning the juror(s). The judge may enquire whether the juror(s) feel able to continue and remain faithful to their oath or affirmation. If there is questioning, each juror should be questioned separately, in the absence of the rest of the jury, unless there is good reason not to do so.

In accordance with 39M.10–39M.13, the enquiries should be conducted in open court; in the presence of the defendant; and with all parties represented unless there is good reason not to do so.

(5) Step 5: Further consult with advocates.

The judge should further consult with the advocates and invite submissions about how to proceed in relation to the conduct of the trial and what should be said to the jury (Step 6). In accordance with 39M.10–39M.13, the consultation should be conducted in open court; in the presence of the defendant; and with all parties represented unless there is good reason not to do so.

(6) Step 6: Decide what to do in relation to the conduct of the trial.

When deciding how to proceed, the judge may take time to reflect. Considerations may include the stage the trial has reached. The judge should be alert to attempts by the defendant or others to thwart the trial. In cases of potential bias, the judge should consider whether a fair minded and informed observer would conclude that there was a real possibility that the juror(s) or jury would be biased (*Porter v Magill* [2001] UKHL 67; [2002] 2 A.C. 357).

(*CPD* VI 26M7–25)

Options

42-033 The options open to the judge will include:

(1) to *take no action* (perhaps with a reassuring explanation to the jury that nothing untoward has occurred as concerns them) and *continue with the trial* with a reminder to the jury, taking care to avoid any pressure on them, that their verdict will be a decision of them, as a body;

(2) *discharge the juror(s) concerned* with thought to what explanation (if any) should be given to those discharged as well as to the remaining jurors;

(3) *discharge the whole jury and either continue with the trial without a jury or re-list* the trial, with a warning to the discharged jurors not to discuss the case; or

(4) *order a new trial with, or without, a jury*, if jury tampering has occurred.

(*CPD* VI 26M.26)

Ancillary matters

42-034 Step 7 of the process set out in the *CPD* requires the court to consider ancillary matters.

A jury irregularity may also involve contempt in the face of the court and/or the commission of a criminal offence. The possibilities include the following:

(i) Contempt in the face of the court by a juror.

If a juror commits contempt in the face of the court, the juror's conduct may also constitute an offence. If so, the judge should decide whether to deal with the juror summarily under the procedure for contempt in the face of the court or refer the matter to the Attorney General's Office or the police (see 39M.31 and 39M.33).

In the case of a minor and clear contempt in the face of the court, the judge may deal with the juror summarily. The judge should follow the procedure in s.2 of Pt 48 of the CrimPR. The judge should also have regard to the practice direction regarding contempt of court issued in March 2015 (Practice Direction: Committal for Contempt of Court—Open Court), which emphasises the principle of open justice in relation to proceedings for contempt before all courts.

If a juror fails to comply with an order for surrender of an electronic communications device (see 39M.15–39.M18), the judge should deal with the juror summarily following the procedure for contempt in the face of the court (*CPD* VI M: 28–30).

(ii) An offence by a juror or a non-juror under the JA 1974.

Offences that may be committed by jurors are researching the case, sharing research, engaging in prohibited conduct or disclosing information about the jury's deliberations (ss.20A–20D JA 1974). Non-jurors may commit the offence of disclosing, soliciting or obtaining information about the jury's deliberations (s.20D JA 1974).

If it appears that an offence under the JA 1974 may have been committed by a juror or non-juror (and the matter has not been dealt with summarily under the procedure for contempt in the face of the court), the judge should contact the Attorney General's Office to consider a police investigation, setting out the position neutrally. The officer in the case should not be asked to investigate. Contact details for the Attorney General's Office are set out at the end of the practice direction.

If relevant to an investigation, any electronic communications device surrendered or seized pursuant to an order for surrender should be passed to the police as soon as practicable (*CPD* VI M: 31–32).

(iii) An offence by juror or a non-juror other than under the JA 1974.

A juror may commit an offence such as assault or theft. A non-juror may commit an offence in relation to a juror such as attempting to pervert the course of justice—for example, if the defendant or another attempts to suborn or intimidate a juror.

If it appears that an offence, other than an offence under the JA 1974, may have been committed by a juror or non-juror (and the matter has not been dealt with summarily under the procedure for contempt in the face of the court), the judge or a member of court staff should contact the police setting out the position neutrally. The officer in the case should not be asked to investigate.

If relevant to an investigation, any electronic communications device surrendered or seized pursuant to an order for surrender should be passed to the police as soon as practicable (*CPD* VI M: 33–34).

Other matters to consider

42-035 The *CPD* then sets out various other matters for the judge to consider.

(i) Jury deliberations

In light of the offence of disclosing, soliciting or obtaining information about a jury's deliberations (s.20D(1) JA 1974), great care is required if a jury irregularity relates to the jury's deliberations. During the trial, there are exceptions to this offence that enable the judge (and only the judge) to: Seek to establish the basic facts of a jury irregularity involving the jury's deliberations (Step 4); and Disclose information about the jury's deliberations to the Attorney General's Office if it appears that an offence may have been committed (Step 7).

With regard to seeking to establish the basic facts of a jury irregularity involving the jury's deliberations (Step 4), it is to be noted that during the trial it is not an offence for the judge to disclose, solicit or obtain information about the jury's deliberations for the purposes of dealing with the case (ss.20E(2)(a) and 20G(1) JA 1974).

With regard to disclosing information about the jury's deliberations to the Attorney General's Office if it appears that an offence may have been committed (Step 7), it is to be noted that during the trial: It is not an offence for the judge to disclose information about the jury's deliberations for the purposes of an investigation by a relevant investigator into whether an offence or contempt of court has been committed by or in relation to a juror (s.20E(2)(b) JA 1974); and a "relevant investigator" means a police force or the Attorney General (s.20E(5) JA 1974).

(ii) Minimum number of jurors

If it is decided to discharge one or more jurors (Step 6), a minimum of nine jurors must remain if the trial is to continue (s.16(1) JA 1974).

(iii) Preparation of statement by judge

If a jury irregularity occurs, and the trial continues, the judge should have regard to the remarks of Lord Hope in *R. v Mirza* [2004] UKHL 2; [2004] 1 A.C. 1118; [2004] 2 Cr. App. R. 8 at [127] and [128], and consider whether to prepare a statement that could be used in an application for leave to appeal or an appeal relating to the jury irregularity (*CPD* VI M: 35–40).

Allegations of misconduct—cases that pre-date the most recent CPD

42-036 Where an allegation of serious misconduct by a juror arises the judge cannot ignore the allegation. However, it would be quite unreasonable for him to discharge the jury simply because such an allegation has been made. He will need to investigate it, as best he can, given the confidentiality of jury deliberations, with the only people who could know whether any jurors were indeed expressing themselves in discreditable language or approaching their responsibilities in dereliction of their duty—*R. v Momodou* [2005] EWCA Crim 177; [2005] 2 Cr. App. R. 6.

As to the nature of any investigation see the *CPD* set out at 42-034.

The principles to be drawn from the leading cases (*R. v Smith* [2005] UKHL 12; [2005] 2 Cr. App. R. 10; and *R. v Momodou* [2005] EWCA Crim 177; [2005] 2 Cr. App. R. 6) indicate that in matters arising during the trial, and before verdict, the judge has a discretion either: (1) to discharge the jury; (2) to deal with the matter by giving the jury directions, or further directions tailored to the circumstances.

A *Watson* direction (*R. v Watson* (1988) 87 Cr. App. R. 1) may be sufficient by re-emphasising their duty to carry out their discussion with proper give and take. The terms must be cautious because the overriding principle is that pressure must not be placed upon a juror to reach a verdict contrary to that which his conscience and assessment of the evidence dictate (*R. v Pinches* [2010] EWCA Crim 2000).

Some recent illustrations of the handling of jury irregularities include—*R. v JC* [2013] EWCA Crim 368; [2013] Crim. L.R. 854 (note indicating irregularities within the jury does not necessarily call for automatic discharge of the jury); *R. v Gifford* unreported (2013) (both advocates agreeing on the approach adopted); *R. v Burland* [2013] EWCA Crim 518 (dissent within the jury before any evidence is called—the judge should enquire of the jury whether each juror could undertake his work in accordance with his oaths and, as may be necessary, investigate further); *R. v Dicks* [2013] EWCA Crim 429 (inadmissible prejudicial information inadvertently revealed to the jury—the test is whether a fair-minded and informed observer would conclude that there was a real danger of prejudice against the accused).

See also *R. v Baybasin* [2013] EWCA Crim 2357; [2014] 1 Cr. App. R. 19 (in the absence of other strong or compelling evidence the CACD will not order inquiries into cases where a juror raises a complaint of jury impropriety after the verdict); *R. v Mole* [2013] EWCA Crim 2420 (inappropriate communication between jury bailiff and jury); *R. v Hazell* [2013] EWCA Crim 2526 (juror approached in public area of the court but jury convicted before matter could be investigated by the judge).

After verdicts have been returned

The trial judge has no jurisdiction in relation to irregularities that come to light after the end of the trial (i.e. delivery of verdicts or jury discharge). **42-037**

Thus:

(1) if information about an irregularity comes to light after verdict, but before sentence, then the judge should proceed to sentence (unless there is good reason not to do so), and pass the information to the Registrar;

(2) if, after a trial, a juror contacts the judge about it, the communication should be referred to the Registrar to consider what steps may be appropriate, including seeking the direction of the Vice President, or a nominated judge, of the CACD;

(3) if the communication suggests any issue of contempt or a criminal offence, the Registrar will inform the Attorney General; if it suggests a possible ground of appeal, the accused's legal representatives will be informed; where it raises no issues of legal significance, the Registrar will explain that no action is required;

(4) if the prosecution become aware of an irregularity that might form a basis for an appeal, they should notify the defence; if the defence become aware of an irregularity that might form an arguable ground of appeal, they may wish to lodge an appeal; and

(5) if an application for leave to appeal relates to an alleged jury irregularity,

then the registrar may refer the case to the CACD for it to consider whether to direct the CCRC to conduct an investigation (before or after leave is granted) under the CAA 1968 s.23A; the CCRC will report back to the CACD.

(*CPD* VI 26M Jury irregularity after jury discharged: M 41–58)

As to the discharge of jurors, or of the jury, see 42-038 and 42-039. As to where contempt is suspected, contempt by jurors should generally be dealt with by the Attorney General; however it may be appropriate for the trial judge to deal with a very minor and clear contempt in the face of the court admitted by the juror. The procedure in such a case is provided for in CrimPR 48. See further for contempt by jurors under CONTEMPT OF COURT.

8. DISCHARGE OF JURORS

Discharge of individual juror(s)

42-038 The trial judge has an inherent discretion to discharge a juror, or jurors, in the course of the trial (provided the number of jurors does not fall below nine) (JA 1974 s.16):

(1) through illness or incapacity of continuing to act (*R. v Hambery* (1977) 65 Cr. App. R. 233; *R. v S* [2009] EWCA Crim 104);

(2) in a case where, after enquiry, it is shown that a juror has been approached (*R. v Blackwell* [1995] 2 Cr. App. R. 625; *R. v Oke* [1997] Crim. L.R. 898; *R. v Appiah* [1998] Crim. L.R. 134);

(3) where it is alleged that dissension is being caused in the jury room (*R. v Orgles* (1994) 98 Cr. App. R. 185; *R. v Farooq* [1995] Crim. L.R. 169); or

(4) where a juror was insufficiently proficient in the English language (*R. v M* [2012] EWCA Crim 2056; [2013] 1 Cr. App. R. 5 but where, as in that case, the same panel was reselected and sworn with an additional juror care needs to be taken to avoid infringing the principle of random selection under JA 1974 s.11).

Where it is alleged that a juror, or jurors, is, or are, unable to fulfil their duty, the particular juror may be questioned outwith the presence of the jury as a whole in which case the juror should be kept separate from the other jurors until the matter is resolved by the judge through discharge of the juror (which may take place without the entire jury being present) or otherwise, but where dissension is alleged, and therefore the inability of the jury as a whole to fulfil their duty, the whole jury ought to be present.

While discharge is a matter within the discretion of the judge, it is sensible, and good practice, to canvass their views on the matter (*R. v Richardson* (1979) 69 Cr. App. R. 235; *R. v Bryan* [2001] EWCA Crim 2550; [2002] Crim. L.R. 240 and *R. v McGrady* [2011] All E.R. (D.) 144).

Where a member of the jury is discharged at any stage of the trial it is not incumbent on the judge to direct the remaining members to ignore any views expressed by the discharged juror (*R. v Carter* [2010] EWCA Crim 201; [2010] 2 Cr. App. R. 33).

Discharge of a juror for personal reasons

42-039 Where a juror unexpectedly finds himself in difficult professional or personal circumstances during the course of the trial, he should be encouraged to raise such problems with the trial judge. This may apply, for example, to a parent whose childcare arrangements unexpectedly fail or a worker who is engaged in the provision of services the need for which can be critical or a Member of Parliament who has deferred his jury service to an apparently more convenient time, but is unexpectedly called back to work for a very important reason. Such difficulties will normally be raised through a jury note in the normal manner.

In such circumstances the judge must:

(1) exercise his discretion according to the interests of justice and the requirements of each individual case; and
(2) decide for himself whether the juror has presented a sufficient reason to interfere with the course of the trial; if the juror has presented a sufficient reason.

(*CPD* VI Trial 26H: Juries: Discharge of a juror for personal reasons 1–3)

In longer trials it may well be possible to adjourn for a short period in order to allow the juror to overcome the difficulty; in shorter cases it may be more appropriate to discharge the juror and to continue the trial with a reduced number of jurors; the power to do this is implicit in JA 1974 s.16(1).

In unusual cases (such as an unexpected emergency arising overnight) a juror need not be discharged in open court.

The good administration of justice depends on the co-operation of jurors who perform an essential public service. All applications for excusal should be dealt with sensitively and sympathetically and the trial judge should always seek to meet the interests of justice without unduly inconveniencing any juror.

Offences by jurors

JA 1974 is amended by CJCA 2014 ss.42–44 to create a number of offences in relation to misconduct by a juror (including any BSL interpreter appointed) trying an issue before the court, including: **42-040**

(1) *research* (JA 1974 s.20A) by intentionally seeking information, when he knows or ought reasonably to know that the information is or may be relevant to the case;
(2) *sharing research* with other jurors (JA 1974 s.20B) by intentionally disclosing information to another member of the jury during the trial period, where he has contravened s.20A in the process of obtaining the information, and the information has not been provided by the court; and
(3) intentionally engaging in *other prohibited conduct* during the trial (JA 1974 s.20C), that is conduct from which it may reasonably be concluded that he intends to try the issue otherwise than on the basis of the evidence presented in the proceedings on the issue, whether or not he knows that the conduct is prohibited conduct.

There is also an offence for an interpreter appointed under s.9C(2) intentionally to interfere in or influence the deliberations of the jury in proceedings before a court.

A person guilty of such offences is liable, on conviction on indictment, to imprisonment for a term not exceeding two years or a fine (or both). Proceedings may only be instituted by or with the consent of the Attorney General.

Nothing in the above sections affects what constitutes contempt of court at common law.

Discharge of jury as a whole

42-041 The trial judge has a discretion to discharge the whole jury from giving a verdict. This position may be reached in a number of ways:

(1) where it clear that the jury is not able to arrive at a verdict;
(2) where there is a "real danger", from anything said or done in the course of the trial, that the jury may be prejudiced against the accused (*R. v Sawyer* (1980) 71 Cr. App. R. 283; *R. v Spencer* (1986) 83 Cr. App. R. 277; *R. v Gough* (1992) 95 Cr. App. R. 433);
(3) in the case of an irregularity as where:
  (a) an accused's bad character is inadvertently disclosed (cf. *R. v Weaver* (1967) 51 Cr. App. R. 77; *R. v Blackford* (1989) 89 Cr. App. R. 239);
  (b) where one accused pleads guilty and the prosecution propose to continue the trial of co-accused (*R. v Fredrick* [1990] Crim. L.R. 403); or
  (c) the judge deals with a recalcitrant witness for contempt before the trial is completed (*R. v Maguire* [1997] 1 Cr. App. R. 61);
(4) in the case of impropriety by a juror or the jury; or
(5) where a juror's personal knowledge of the accused emerges in the course of the trial (*R. v Hood* (1968) 52 Cr. App. R. 265).

The judge's decision on these issues is not simply a case management decision. If the judge were to conclude that there were "real grounds for doubting the ability" of the jury to bring "an objective judgment to bear" on the issues, the jury should be discharged. The decision requires a balanced judgment of the things said to create the risk of bias in the jury, while simultaneously taking account of the directions available to be given by the trial judge to address and extinguish the risk. The ultimate question is fact- or case-specific in the context of the trial process as a whole (*R. v Azam* [2006] EWCA Crim 161; [2006] Crim. L.R. 776).

As to the position where there is contempt by the accused in a deliberate attempt to abort the trial, *R. v Russell* [2006] EWCA Crim 470; [2006] Crim. L.R. 862.

Procedure for discharging jurors

42-042 The judge may exercise his power to discharge a juror at any time after the juror completes the oath or affirmation and before he discharges the jury.

No later than the beginning of the prosecution evidence, if the jury then comprises more than 12 jurors the court must discharge any in excess of 12 in reverse order of their selection from the panel.

The judge may exercise his power to discharge the jury (as a whole) at any time after each juror has completed the oath or affirmation and before the jury has delivered its verdict on each offence charged in the indictment.

The judge will exercise his power to discharge the jury when, in respect of each offence charged in the indictment, either the jury has delivered its verdict on that offence or the judge has discharged the jury from reaching a verdict (CrimPR 25.7).

9. Separation of jury whilst in deliberation

Separation of jury during consideration of verdict

42-043 The judge has an unfettered discretion to allow the jury to separate at any time, whether before or after they have been directed to consider their verdict (JA 1974 s.13).

If they are allowed to separate during consideration of their verdict, e.g. where they are sent home, or to arranged accommodation at the end of the day, the judge should give them a direction along the following lines:

(1) they must decide the case on the evidence and arguments they have seen and heard in court and not on anything they may have seen or heard or may or hear outside the court;
(2) that the evidence has been completed and it would be wrong for any juror to seek for, or to receive, further evidence or information of any sort about the case;
(3) that they must not talk to anyone about the case save to other members of the jury and then only when they are deliberating in the jury room; and that they must not allow anyone to talk to them about the case unless that person is a juror and he or she is in the jury room deliberating about the case; and
(4) that when they leave court they should try to set the case they are trying on one side until they return to court and retire to their jury room to resume their deliberations.

(*R. v Oliver* [1996] 2 Cr. App. R. 514; *R. v Hunt* [1998] Crim. L.R. 343)

Where the jury separates in contravention of the judge's order, the judge should ask both the court clerk and the usher who has witnessed any incident to "articulate in open court in front of the accused and the advocates precisely what has transpired" in order that he might receive informed submissions as to the approach to be adopted with the jury (*R. v B* [2011] EWCA Crim 1183).

10. NO ENQUIRY INTO VERDICT

Where there has been no ambiguity, procedural defect or dissent at the time when the verdict is delivered, an inquiry into that verdict will not be authorised on the basis, e.g. of a subsequent allegation by one of the jurors that the verdict was not in fact unanimous: *R. v Lewis*, *The Times*, 26 April 2001 (*Gregory v United Kingdom* (1997) 25 E.H.R.R. 577 and *Sanders v United Kingdom* (2000) 8 B.H.R.C. 279 distinguished). **42-044**

The CACD will not inquire as to what went on in the jury room (CCA 1981 s.8(1); *R. v Miah* [1997] 2 Cr. App. R. 12; followed in, *R. v Qureshi* [2001] EWCA Crim 1807; [2002] 1 Cr. App. R. 33). Also *R. v Thompson* [2010] EWCA Crim. 1623; [2010] Cr. App. R. 27. The authorities establishing this principle are not affected by the implementation of HRA 1998 (*R. v Young* [1995] 2 Cr. App. R. 379; *Ellis v Deheer* [1922] 2 K.B. 113; *Nanan v Trinidad and Tobago* (1986) 83 Cr. App. R. 292; *R. v Lewis* [2001] EWCA Crim 749 considered).

The trial judge, in dealing with such a matter, must apply his mind to the correct principles laid down by European authority. For him to accept what the jurors say without determining whether it is correct, or hearing the accused's account which disputes the jurors' account, is a failure to ascertain the circumstances and to consider whether a fair-minded observer would conclude that there was a real possibility of bias (*R. v Brown* [2001] EWCA Crim 2828; [2002] Crim. L.R. 409; following *R. v Medicaments (No.2)* [2001] 1 W.L.R. 700).

In the absence of other strong or compelling evidence the CACD will not order inquiries into cases where a juror raises a complaint of jury impropriety after the verdict (*R. v Baybasin* [2013] EWCA Crim 2357; [2014] 1 Cr. App. R. 19).

Rule of admissibility

42-045 The rule against any investigation or inquiry into jury deliberations is a rule of admissibility (*R. v Mirza* [2004] UKHL 2; [2004] 2 Cr. App. R. 8) and evidence about the deliberations of a jury is therefore inadmissible, subject to two narrow exceptions:

(1) where there are serious grounds for believing a complete repudiation of the oath taken by the jurors to try the case on the evidence (as by resorting to use of a Ouija board) has taken place; or
(2) where extraneous material has been introduced into the jury deliberations (e.g. papers mistakenly admitted to the jury room, discussions with outsiders and information derived from research on the internet), the CACD will enquire into it.

Where a juror communicated with her fiancé, who had been present in the public gallery, by text message during the trial, it was said that the correct test to be applied was whether a fair-minded, independent and informed observer would have considered there to be a real risk that the jury had received information or views which it could not put out of its mind (*R. v Mears* [2011] EWCA Crim 2651; (2011) 108(45) L.S.G. 21).

11. RECTIFICATION OF VERDICT

Judge's discretion to rectify mistake in verdict

42-046 Where the jury have made a mistake, and the interests of justice so require, the trial judge has a discretion to set aside the discharge of the jury before they have separated, or seen, or heard anything which they should not have seen or heard, in order to let them deliberate further. This is provided that the mistake is brought to his notice without delay. *Igwemma v Chief Constable of Greater Manchester* [2001] EWCA Civ 935; [2001] 4 All E.R. 751; cf. *R. v Tantram* [2001] EWCA Crim 1364; [2001] Crim. L.R. 82.

43. LEGAL AID; PUBLIC FUNDING

Scope of this chapter

An exhaustive explanation of the current regime governing the provision of legal aid in the Crown Court is beyond the scope of this chapter. The aim here is to provide an overview of the regime and then focus upon those areas which may require determination by the Crown Court. **43-001**

For a detailed practical explanation of the operation of the scheme, see the *Criminal Legal Aid Manual: Applying for legal aid in criminal cases in the magistrates' and Crown Court*, published by the LAA and last updated in May 2021 (*CLAM* 2021).

Overview of LASPOA 2012

Sections 13–20 of LASPOA 2012 concern criminal legal aid: **43-002**

- Advice and assistance for individuals in custody (s.13).
- The definition of "criminal proceedings" (s.14).
- Advice and assistance for criminal proceedings (s.15).
- Representation for criminal proceedings (s.16).
- Qualifying for representation (s.17).
- Determinations by the Director (s.18).
- Determinations by the court (s.19).
- Provisional determinations (s.20).

Section 27 concerns choice of provider of services. The duty to secure the availability of criminal legal aid under s.1(1) does not include a duty to secure that, where services are made available to a person, they are made available by a provider selected by the person (s.27(3)), but this is qualified by s.27(4)–(10) which provide that the person may select any representative willing to act for him, subject to regulations, and specify the circumstances in which this may be restricted.

Overview of the Criminal Legal Aid (General) Regulations 2013 (SI 2013/9)

These regulations concern determinations whether a person qualifies for criminal legal aid under LASPOA 2012. **43-003**

Regulation 9 lists the "other proceedings" which are criminal proceedings for the purpose of LASPOA 2012 s.14(h).

Regulations 19 and 20 list proceedings which are, respectively, "to be regarded as incidental" and "not to be regarded as incidental" to the criminal proceedings from which they arise.

Regulation 21 states that, for the purposes of a determination under s.16, making representation available to a person for the purposes of criminal proceedings is taken to be "in the interests of justice" when the proceedings are before:

(a) the Crown Court, to the extent that such proceedings do not relate to an appeal to the Crown Court;
(b) the High Court;
(c) the CACD; or

(d) the Supreme Court.

Some proceedings automatically meet the interests of justice criteria:

(i) where a person is committed, sent or transferred to the Crown Court for trial;
(ii) where a voluntary bill has been laid;
(iii) where a retrial has been directed by the CACD; and
(iv) where a person has been committed for sentence.

Applications for appeals to the Crown Court are still subject to the interests of justice test.

Where the Director makes a determination under s.16 that a person qualifies, he must issue a representation order and send a copy to the individual and any provider named in the representation order (reg.23(1)(a)–(b)). Where he makes a determination that a person does not qualify, the person must be provided with written reasons and details of any review or appeal available (reg.23(3)(a)–(b)).

A person determined to be eligible for representation in the magistrates' court is eligible for representation in the Crown Court in relation to those proceedings (reg.24).

A determination *must* be withdrawn if the director is satisfied that the interests of justice no longer require representation (reg.26(1)). It *may* be withdrawn where:

(a) the person declines to accept the determination in the terms offered;
(b) the person requests that the determination is withdrawn; or
(c) the provider named in the representation order declines to continue to represent the person (reg.26(2)).

Applications for review are set out in reg.27.

Under reg.28, where a person remains dissatisfied following such a review, he may appeal to a court in accordance with regs 29 (magistrates court) and 30 (Crown Court) against a decision that the interests of justice do not require, or no longer require, representation to be made available.

Regulation 30 provides that, in cases of Crown Court representation, the appeal lies to an officer of the Crown Court. The officer may refer the appeal to a Crown Court judge. The officer or the judge may:

(i) affirm the determination; or
(ii) decide that the interests of justice require representation to be made available, or to continue to be made available.

The Director must then make a determination reflecting that decision.

Overview of the Criminal Legal Aid (Determination by a Court and Choice of Representative) Regulations 2013 (SI 2013/614)

Determination by the Crown Court

43-004 The Criminal Legal Aid (Determinations by a Court and Choice of Representative) Regulations 2013 (SI 2013/614) make provision for determinations by a court under LASPOA 2012 Pt 1 in relation to whether an individual qualifies for criminal legal aid, and in relation to the right under reg.27(4) of an individual who qualifies for legal aid to select a representative of his choice.

Part 2 of the Regulations makes provision in relation to the power of the Crown Court to make a determination under LASPOA 2012 s.16 as to whether an individual qualifies for representation for criminal proceedings, and also makes provision about the form and content of applications for a determination, the requirements placed on courts in making such determinations and about the withdrawal of a determination.

Part 3 of the Regulations makes provision about the right of an individual under LASPOA 2012 s.27(4) to select a representative of his choice.

An application to the Crown Court for a determination must be made orally (reg.4(1)).

The power to make a determination may be exercised by the court or an officer of the court (reg.5(2)).

Regulation 6 provides that the Crown Court may make a determination under s.16 as to whether a person qualifies for representation for the purposes of criminal proceedings before the Crown Court only where:

(a) those proceedings are described in s.14(g) (contempt in the face of the court);
(b) those proceedings arise out of an alleged failure to comply with an order of the Crown Court and it appears that there is no time to instruct a provider; or
(c) where the person is brought to the court in pursuance of a warrant issued by the Crown Court.

Regulation 9 sets out the circumstances in which the court can withdraw a determination.

Choice of representative

43-005 Regulation 12 sets out the restrictions on the right of choice provided by s.27(4), namely that the provider must be either employed by the Lord Chancellor to provide criminal legal aid, or be permitted to do so.

Regulation 13 provides that where there are co-defendants, the right of choice in s.27(4) does not include the right to select a provider who is not also instructed by the co-defendant, or one of them, unless the court or the Director determines that:

(1) there is a conflict of interest between those defendants; or
(2) there is likely to be a conflict of interest.

This does not apply where the provider in question is an advocate.

Such a determination must be applied for in writing in accordance with reg.11.

Change of provider

43-006 The right to choose in s.27(4) does not include a right to select a provider in place of the original provider (reg.14(1)).

The court can determine that a replacement provider can be selected where:

(1) the court determines that:
    (a) there has been a breakdown in the relationship between the person and the provider such that effective representation can no longer be provided; or
    (b) there is *some other compelling reason* why effective representation can no longer be provided;

    OR
(2) the court determines that:

(a) the original provider:
   (i) considers there to be a duty to withdraw from the case in accordance with his rules of professional conduct; or
   (ii) is no longer able to represent the person through circumstances outside the provider's control; and
(b) the original provider has provided the court with details as to:
   (i) the nature of any such duty to withdraw from the case; or
   (ii) the particular circumstances which render the provider unable to represent the person.

Procedure in making a "change of provider" determination

43-007 The application of this test is now governed by CrimPR 46.3. Where a defendant who has legal aid wishes to change his representative, he must:

(1) apply in writing as soon as practicable after becoming aware of the grounds for doing so; and
(2) serve the application on the court and the legal representative named in the legal aid representation order.

The application must:

(a) explain what the case is about, including what offences are alleged, what stage it has reached and what is likely to be in issue at trial;
(b) explain how and why the applicant chose the legal representative named in the legal aid representation order;
(c) if an advocate other than that representative has been instructed for the applicant, explain whether the applicant wishes to replace that advocate;
(d) explain, giving relevant facts and dates:
   (i) in what way, in the applicant's opinion, there has been a breakdown in the relationship between the applicant and the current representative such that neither the individual representing the applicant nor any colleague of his or hers any longer can provide effective representation; or
   (ii) what other compelling reason, in the applicant's opinion, means that neither the individual representing the applicant nor any colleague of his or hers any longer can provide effective representation;
(e) give details of any similar previous application made by the applicant;
(f) state whether the applicant:
   (i) waives LLP in respect of communications with his current representative, so as to enable that representative to respond to the application; or
   (ii) declines to waive LLP and acknowledges that, as a result, the court may draw such inferences as it thinks fit;
(g) explain how and why the applicant has chosen the proposed new representative;
(h) include or attach a statement from the proposed new representative:
   (i) confirming his eligibility and willingness to conduct the case;
   (ii) confirming that he can meet the current timetable for the case including any set hearing dates; and
   (iii) explaining what dealings he has had with the applicant before the present case;

(i) ask for a hearing, if the applicant wants one, and explain why it is needed.

The current representative must:

(a) respond in writing no more than five business days after service of the application; and
(b) serve the response on the court, the applicant and the proposed new representative.

The response must:

(a) explain which, if any, of the matters set out in the application the current representative disputes;
(b) explain, giving relevant facts and dates:
   (i) whether, and if so in what way, in the current representative's opinion, there has been a breakdown in the relationship with the applicant such that neither the individual representing the applicant nor any colleague of his or hers any longer can provide effective representation;
   (ii) whether, in the current representative's opinion, there is some other compelling reason why neither the individual representing the applicant nor any colleague of his or hers any longer can provide effective representation, and if so what reason;
   (iii) whether the current representative considers there to be a duty to withdraw from the case in accordance with professional rules of conduct, and if so the nature of that duty;
   (iv) whether the current representative no longer is able to represent the applicant through circumstances outside the representative's control, and if so the particular circumstances that render the representative unable to do so;
(c) explain what, if any, dealings the current representative had had with the applicant before the present case; and
(d) ask for a hearing, if the current representative wants one, and explain why it is needed.

The general rule is that the application will be determined without a hearing. There is a widespread and mistaken view that if a written application is refused the application can be renewed at a hearing. However, the CrimPR envisage a single, final determination, made without a hearing unless there is a specific reason that a hearing is necessary.

Unless the court directs otherwise, any hearing will be:

(i) in private; and
(ii) in the absence of each other party and their representatives and advocates.

If the court allows the application, then as soon as practicable:

(a) the current representative must make available to the new representative such documents in the current representative's possession as have been served on the applicant party; and

(b) the new representative must serve notice of appointment on each other party.

Considering an application

43-008 In *R. (on the application of Sanjari) v Birmingham Crown Court* [2015] EWHC 2037 (Admin); [2015] 2 Cr. App. R. 30 (DC), Thomas LCJ provided emphatic guidance on the purpose and practical application of the Regulations:

(1) Judges must subject applications under reg.14 to rigorous and searching scrutiny.
(2) Defendants cannot be permitted to unnecessarily delay and complicate proceedings by the device of changing their representatives. Judges must be astute to guard against this risk.
(3) A defendant's unhappiness or disagreement with realistic legal advice is not a ground which will permit the transfer of the representation order.
(4) Judges must also be astute to the risk that a defendant may be induced to try to change his representation for commercial reasons.
(5) The court is entitled to expect the grounds for the application to be advanced with objectivity, independent judgment and a high standard of professional conduct.

The court cited with approval the judgment of HH Judge Wakerley QC in the case of *R. v Khan (Ashgar)* unreported July 2001, in which HH Judge Wakerley was considering regulations which were not materially different from the 2013 Regulations. He stated that there must be strict compliance with the Regulations. The "substantial compelling reason" needs to be specified. It will not generally be sufficient to allege a lack of care or competence of existing representatives. Only in extremely rare cases, and where full particulars are given in the application, will a general ground of loss of confidence or incompetence be entertained. It is not sufficient to say that there has been a breakdown in the relationship—many breakdowns are imagined rather than real or are the result of proper advice. See also *R. v Ulcay* [2007] EWCA Crim 2379; [2008] 1 Cr. App. R. 27.

Withdrawal of legal aid

43-009 Regulation 9 provides that the court may withdraw legal aid if:

(1) the defendant declines to accept legal aid in the terms which are offered;
(2) the defendant requests that legal aid is withdrawn; or
(3) the current representative declines to continue to represent the defendant.

Regulation 15(2) of the Criminal Legal Aid (Determinations by a Court and Choice of Representative) Regulations 2013, provides that where a determination is withdrawn but a subsequent determination is made that the defendant qualifies for representation, the defendant does not have a right to choose a different provider from that named in the original representation order. Under reg.15(3) the court can determine that the person can select a different provider from that named in the original representation order if there are good reasons why a different provider should be selected.

The purpose of reg.15 is to prevent a defendant from defeating the effect of an unsuccessful application for a change of provider under reg.14 (by making a fresh legal aid application following a withdrawal of legal aid).

CrimPR 46.3(9)–(10) provides that if the court refuses the application for a change of representative, and:

(1) the applicant declines further representation by the current representative or asks for legal aid to be withdrawn; or
(2) the current representative declines further to represent the applicant; and
(3) the court withdraws the applicant's legal aid;

the court must serve notice of the withdrawal of legal aid on the applicant and the current representative.

King's Counsel and multiple advocates

A determination that a person is entitled to select a King's Counsel or more than one advocate may be made by the assigned trial judge, a High Court judge, a resident judge or a judge nominated by a resident judge. All such determinations, except those made by a High Court judge, must be approved by the presiding judge of the circuit or a judge nominated by him (reg.19). **43-010**

Ordinarily, in relation to any criminal proceedings that are not before a magistrates' court, the right of an individual conferred by s.27(4) of the Act does not include a right to select a King's Counsel or more than one advocate, but under reg.18 the relevant court may determine that an individual can select:

(a) a King's Counsel if that individual's case involves substantial novel or complex issues of law or fact which could not be adequately presented except by a King's Counsel, and either:
   (i) the "exceptional condition" is met; or
   (ii) the "counsel condition" is met.

The relevant court may determine that an individual can select:

(b) two junior advocates if that individual's case involves substantial novel or complex issues of law or fact which could not be adequately presented by a single advocate, including a King's Counsel alone, and either:
   (i) the "exceptional condition" is met; or
   (ii) the "prosecution condition" is met;
(c) a King's Counsel and a junior advocate if that individual's case involves substantial, novel or complex issues of law or fact which could not be adequately presented except by a King's Counsel assisted by a junior advocate and either:
   (i) the "exceptional condition" is met; or
   (ii) the "counsel condition" and the "prosecution condition" are met; and
(d) three advocates if the proceedings relate to a prosecution brought by the SFO and the court determines that three advocates are required to represent the individual.

In the case of (d) above, the Crown Court must also determine that the individual's case involves substantial novel or complex issues of law or fact which could not be adequately presented by two junior advocates, or by a King's Counsel assisted by a junior advocate, and either:

(i) the "exceptional condition" is met; or
(ii) the "prosecution condition" is met.

Nothing in reg.18, above, permits an individual to select more than one King's Counsel ((SI 2013/614) regs 18 and 20).

The meaning of the conditions referred to above is as follows:

- "the counsel condition" means, in relation to particular criminal proceedings, that a King's Counsel or senior Treasury Counsel has been instructed on behalf of the prosecution;
- "the exceptional condition" means, in relation to particular criminal proceedings, that the individual's case is exceptional compared with the generality of cases involving similar offences;
- "the prosecution condition" means, in relation to particular criminal proceedings, any of the following circumstances:
  - — only where the court is satisfied that the individual will be prejudiced, or is likely to be prejudiced, if he is not represented by two or more advocates in circumstances in which the prosecution has two or more advocates (Amendment of the 2013 Regulations reg.18(3), by The Criminal Legal Aid (Determinations by a Court and Choice of Representative) (Amendment) Regulations 2013 (SI 2013/2814));
  - — the number of prosecution witnesses exceeds 80;
  - — the number of pages of prosecution evidence exceeds 1000; and
- "prosecution evidence" means all witness statements, documentary and pictorial exhibits and records of interview with the individual and with any other accused which form part of the served prosecution documents or are included in any notice of additional evidence.

For the purposes of making a determination under reg.18, the relevant court may require from any advocate already assigned to the individual a written opinion on the representation needed to adequately present the case (SI 2013/614 reg.21).

Noting juniors

43-011 The right of an individual conferred by s.27(4) of the Act does not include a right to select:

(1) *two junior advocates*, unless the relevant court determines that the individual could not be adequately represented by a junior advocate; and a noting junior;

(2) *a King's Counsel assisted by a junior advocate*, unless the relevant court determines that the individual could not be adequately represented by a King's Counsel assisted by a noting junior;

(3) *three junior advocates*, unless the relevant court determines that the individual could not be adequately represented by two junior advocates and a noting junior;

(4) *two junior advocates and a noting junior*, unless the relevant court determines that the individual could not be adequately represented by a junior advocate and two noting juniors;

(5) *a King's Counsel assisted by two junior advocates*, unless the relevant court determines that the individual could not be adequately represented by a King's Counsel assisted by a junior advocate and a noting junior; or

(6) *a King's Counsel assisted by a junior advocate and a noting junior*, unless the relevant court determines that the individual could not be adequately represented by a King's Counsel assisted by two noting juniors.

The term "noting junior" means a junior advocate whose instructions include (but are not limited to) taking a note of the proceedings.

(SI 2013/614 reg.23)

King's Counsel; multiple advocate determinations by the Director

The Director may, upon the committal, transfer or sending for trial of an individual, determine that the individual can select a King's Counsel without a junior advocate if the proceedings are a trial for murder. He may also, upon receipt of a notice of an individual's case under CDA 1998 s.51B, determine that the individual can select a King's Counsel with one junior advocate if the prosecution is brought by the SFO (SI 2013/614 reg.22). **43-012**

Recovery of defence costs orders

The Criminal Legal Aid (Recovery of Defence Costs Orders) Regulations 2013 (SI 2013/511) set out the circumstances in which the represented person is required to make a payment towards the cost of his representation under LASPOA 2012 s.23 in respect of criminal proceedings before any court other than the magistrates' court and the Crown Court. **43-013**

Financial resources and eligibility

The Criminal Legal Aid (Financial Resources) Regulations 2013 (SI 2013/471) (as amended) set out the criteria for financial eligibility for legal aid. Their practical application and effect is set out in the *CLAM* 2021. **43-014**

The financial eligibility of legal persons for criminal (and civil) legal aid is governed by the Legal Aid (Financial Resources and Payment for Services) (Legal Persons) Regulations 2013 (SI 2013/512).

Contribution orders and apportionment

The Criminal Legal Aid (Contribution Orders) Regulations 2013 (SI 2013/483), as amended by the Criminal Legal Aid (Contribution Orders) (Amendment) Regulations 2013 (SI 2013/2792) govern the circumstances in which a person who has the benefit of a representation order may be liable to make contributory payments, following an assessment of their financial resources. **43-015**

There are two issues which may arise for determination by a Crown Court judge:

(1) whether an acquitted person should be liable to make payments; and
(2) whether a person who has been convicted of some but not all offences should pay a proportion of the cost of their representation ("apportionment").

An acquitted person must make payments under a contribution order for the cost of their representation in the Crown Court if the trial judge considers that there are exceptional reasons why the person should be liable to do so (reg.25(b)).

Under reg.26, where a person is:

(a) charged with more than one offence; and
(b) convicted of one or more, but not all, such offences,

the person may apply in writing to the judge for an order that he pay a proportion of the amount of the cost of representation in the Crown Court, on the ground that it would be manifestly unreasonable to pay the whole amount. The application must be made within 21 days of the date on which the person is sentenced or otherwise dealt with following conviction.

The trial judge, or when he is not available, a judge nominated by the Resident Judge, will consider the application and grant or refuse it.

See also *PDC* 2015 6.1.3 and *CLAM* 2021 Appendix L.

In considering apportionment, the following approach is suggested. As a general principle, a decision to apportion an offender's costs should not be based solely upon any concerns the trial judge may have about the prosecution's conduct of the case, but should be a fair reflection of the outcome for the offender.

A situation may, however, arise where, at the end of the trial process, the judge is satisfied that the prosecution's conduct of the case has contributed significantly to an unfair financial outcome for the offender. If, having taken all the factors of the trial process into account, the judge reaches such a conclusion, it may inform his decision about whether apportionment is appropriate.

Cases can and do change following sending to the Crown Court, and for a variety of reasons, e.g. a review of the evidence based on subsequent developments; a reluctance of a witness to appear; or the willingness of the victim to agree at a late stage to a plea to a lesser charge.

The judge may consider that the offender's own conduct during the investigation contributed to the framing of particular charges, and that it was reasonable for the prosecution to continue to pursue those charges until events took a different turn.

If, after consideration, the judge is satisfied that apportionment is the reasonable way forward, then the amount that is considered appropriate should be expressed as a percentage of the total amount payable under the terms of a contribution order, rather than a defined amount of money.

44. LICENSED PREMISES EXCLUSION ORDER

General

Where any court by or before which a person is convicted of an offence committed on licensed premises is satisfied that, in committing that offence, he resorted to violence or offered or threatened to resort to violence, the judge *may, in addition* to: 44-001

(1) any sentence which is imposed in respect of the offence of which he is convicted; or
(2) an order discharging him conditionally or absolutely,

make an *exclusion order* (LPEO) prohibiting him from entering those premises (or any other licensed premises which the court may specify by name and address) without the express consent of the licensee, his servant or agent. The order must be for a period of not less than three months but less than two years. Such an order cannot stand alone.

The order continues in force for the period specified unless it is terminated earlier.
(LP(E)A 1980 s.1)
Note that:

(a) the LPEO is designed for those who make a nuisance of themselves in public houses to the annoyance of other customers and the danger of the landlord, not for persons of otherwise clean record (*R. v Grady* [1990] 12 Cr. App. R. (S.) 152);
(b) there is no need for an application to be made—the trial judge may make an order of his own motion;
(c) if there is to be an application it is undesirable that it should be made by a person who is not a victim or a party in the case—an interested third party ought to make representations to the prosecuting authority (*R. v Penn* [1996] 2 Cr. App. R. (S.) 214); and
(d) the order can specify all licensed premises in a particular area but must include the name of each relevant premises because a copy must be sent to the licensee of each premises (*R. v Arrowsmith* [2003] EWCA Crim 701; [2003] 2 Cr. App. R. (S.) 46). To avoid uncertainty such an order must specify a geographical boundary such as a borough or parish rather than the name of a town or village (*R. v Lomas* [2007] EWCA Crim 1792).

Penalties for non-compliance

A person who enters premises in breach of an LPEO commits an offence and is liable on summary conviction to a fine of £1,000 or to imprisonment for one month or both. A court before which a person is so convicted must consider whether the order should continue in force and may, if it thinks fit, terminate the order, or vary it by deleting the name of any specified premises, but the order is not otherwise affected by a person's conviction for such an offence. 44-002
(LP(E)A 1980 s.2)

45. LIFE SENTENCES

QUICK GUIDE

A. INTRODUCTION

Life sentence—meaning

45-001 A life sentence means:

(1) a sentence of imprisonment for life;
(2) a sentence of detention during His Majesty's pleasure; and
(3) a sentence of custody for life.

A life sentence may be *mandatory* as where on conviction for murder, an offender aged:

(a) 21 years or over *must* be sentenced to *life imprisonment*;
(b) 18–20 *must* be sentenced to *custody for life*; and
(c) 18 or under at the date of the offence *must* be sentenced to *detention at His Majesty's pleasure*,

or it may be, in the circumstances outlined in section C, a *discretionary life sentence*.

For those convicted after 3 December 2012, as a result of the provisions in LASPOA 2012 s.123, a sentence of imprisonment for public protection (IPP) created for serious offences by s.225(1) and (3) of the 2003 Act is no longer available.

Where appropriate

45-002 For those offenders convicted after 3 December 2012 there are four situations in which a life sentence arises for consideration, namely (*R. v Saunders* [2013] EWCA Crim 1027):

(1) a *mandatory life sentence* (the sentence fixed by law (in the case of an offender aged 21 or over convicted of murder));
(2) a *statutory life sentence* where, following conviction for a second listed offence under SA 2020 ss.273 and 283, a sentence of life imprisonment "must" be passed unless the particular circumstances would make it unjust;
(3) a *discretionary life sentence* under SA 2020 s.272 following conviction for an offence, where the conditions set out in s.272 are established (this sentence is also statutory but may be imposed only if justified by reference to the seriousness of the offence and the protection of the public (SA 2020 ss.274, 284 and 285)); and
(4) *a second form of discretionary life sentence* where the case does not fall within (2) or (3) (above); it is the maximum sentence which the judge may impose where there is evidence that the offender is likely to commit grave offences in the future (*R. v Bellamy* [2001] 1 Cr. App. R. (S.) 34; *R. v Saunders* [2013] EWCA Crim 1027; [2014] 1 Cr. App. R. (S.) 45; *R. v Burinskas* [2014] EWCA Crim 334).

The sentences under (2) and (3) are more conveniently dealt with under DANGEROUS OFFENDERS; PROTECTIVE SENTENCES.

It is unsuitable to impose on an offender:

(a) already serving a custodial term, a life sentence to commence on the expiry of that term—it should take effect immediately (*R. v Jones* (1962) 46 Cr. App. R. 129);
(b) disproportionate fixed terms for other offences, to run concurrently with a life sentence, thus restricting the chances of the offender's release (*R. v Nugent* (1984) 6 Cr. App. R. (S.) 93; *R. v Daniels* (1984) 6 Cr. App. R. (S.) 8);
(c) a determinate sentence to run consecutively to a life sentence (*R. v Foy* (1962) 46 Cr. App. R. 290).

The court vis-à-vis the Parole Board

The release of an offender serving a life sentence is a matter for the Parole Board; there is a clear division of functions in relation to such sentences. **45-003**

Thus:

(1) the judge specifies the period which the offender should serve by way of punishment and deterrence (the "minimum term"); and
(2) the Parole Board decides whether the offender continues to represent a danger to the public.

An offender serving a life sentence is not considered for parole until he has served the minimum term.

SA 2020 s.322 empowers the judge to set the minimum term to be served by a person convicted of murder, determined by reference to the statutory framework set out in SA 2020 Sch.21 (47-004). The minimum term in all other life sentences is set by application of SA 2020 s.321 (see 45-005).

As to the transitional arrangements for sentence where the offence was committed before 18 December 2003, see *CPD* VII Sentencing N Transitional arrangements for sentences where the offences was committed before 18 December 2003: N1-8; for the purposes of sentences where the murder was committed after 31 May 2002 and before 18 December 2003, the judge should apply the Practice Statement handed down on 31 May 2002 reproduced at paras N.10–N.20.

Once the minimum term has expired, the Parole Board will consider the offender's suitability for release and, if appropriate, direct his release. See generally *R. v Sullivan* [2004] EWCA Crim 1762; [2004] 1 Cr. App. R. 3.

B. MANDATORY LIFE SENTENCES

General

The statutory scheme enacted by Parliament for sentencing an adult guilty of murder committed on or after 18 December 2003, is set out in the M(ADP)A 1965, SA 2020 and CCA 1997. **45-004**

The trial judge must:

(1) under s.1 of the 1965 Act, impose a life sentence for murder;
(2) under SA 2020 ss.275, 321 and 322 decide whether to make:
    (a) a minimum term of a fixed number of years; or

(b) a whole life order.

If a fixed minimum term order is made, the Parole Board has the power under the provisions of s.28 of the 1997 Act, "the early release provisions", to direct release of the offender after the expiry of any minimum term for a fixed number of years set by the trial judge; it considers in essence the risk to the public if release is ordered. However, the Parole Board has no such power where a whole life order is made. A power of release is given under CCA 1997 s.30 to the Secretary of State, if there are exceptional circumstances which justify release on compassionate grounds (*R. v McLoughlin* [2014] EWCA Crim 188; [2014] Crim. L.R. 471).

Setting the minimum term

45-005 SA 2020 s.321, a judge passing a mandatory life sentence must announce in open court either:

(1) the minimum term the offender must serve before the Parole Board can consider release on licence under the provisions of CSA 1997 s.28; or
(2) that the seriousness of the offence is so exceptionally high that the early release provisions should not apply at all (a "whole life order").

In setting the minimum term, the judge must (*CPD* VII Sentencing: Mandatory Life Sentences M.3) set the term he considers appropriate taking into account the seriousness of the offence.

In considering the seriousness of the offence, the court must have regard to the general principles set out in Sch.21, as amended, supplemented by *CPD* VII Sentencing: Mandatory Life Sentences M and any SGC and Sentencing Council guidelines relating to offences in general which are relevant to the case and not incompatible with the provisions of Sch.21. Although it is necessary to have regard to such guidance, it is always permissible not to apply the guidance if a judge considers there are reasons for not following it. It is always necessary to have regard to the need to do justice in the particular case. However, if a court departs from any of the starting points given in Sch.21, the court is under a duty to state its reasons for doing so. (SA 2020 s.322(4).)

The judge's task involves a three-step approach, namely:

(1) the first step; choosing one of the five starting points (45-006);
(2) the second step; considering aggravating and mitigating factors (45-007); and
(3) the third step; taking into account previous convictions (45-008).

In setting the minimum term, the judge must set the term he considers appropriate taking into account the seriousness of the offence. In considering the seriousness of the offence, he must have regard to the general principles set out in SA 2020 Sch.21 and any guidelines relating to offences in general which are relevant to the case and not incompatible with the provisions of Sch.21.

Schedule 21 states that the first step is to choose one of five starting points: "whole life", 30 years, 25 years, 15 years or 12 years.

Schedule 21 has been amended in relation to those aged under 18 as at the date when an offence was committed, but where they are convicted of the offence on or after 28 June 2022 so as to amend the 30, 25 and 15 year start points and also so as to permit whole life orders for those aged 18, 19 or 20 in addition to those aged 21 and over. Paragraph 5A is inserted so that the following are the starting points for minimum terms:

Age of offender when offence committed	Starting point for para.3(1) [30 years] had the offender been under 18	Starting point for para.4(1) [25 years] had the offender been under 18	Starting point for para.5(1) [15 years] had the offender been under 18
17	27 years	23 years	14 years
15 or 16	20 years	17 years	10 years
14 or under	15 years	13 years	8 years

The 12 year start point for minimum terms will continue to apply for those aged under 18 when the offence was committed and where they are convicted before 28 June 2022.

Where the judge makes an order under SA 2020 s.322(4)(a) and (b) above, he must state, in open court, in ordinary language, his reason for deciding on the order made.

In complying with his general duty to state his reasons for doing so, he must, in particular, state:

(a) which of the starting points in Sch.21 (45-006) he has chosen; and
(b) his reasons for any departure from that starting point.

The first step; choosing the starting point

45-006 The "minimum term", in relation to a mandatory life sentence, means the part of the sentence to be specified in an order under s.322(2). A detailed scheme of general principles for determining the minimum term is to be found in SA 2020 Sch.21.

Schedule 21 states that the first step is to choose one of the five starting points set out in it, that is:

(1) "whole life";
(2) 30 years;
(3) 25 years;
(4) 15 years; or
(5) 12 years.

Where the 15-year starting point has been chosen, judges should have in mind that this starting point encompasses a very broad range of murders. In *R. v Sullivan* the CACD, they found it should not be assumed that Parliament intended to raise all minimum terms that would previously have had a lower starting point, to 15 years (*CPD* VII Sentencing M: Mandatory Life Sentences: M.4).

(1) A *whole life order* (Sch.21 para.2(2)) will be appropriate where:
  (a) *the offender was aged 21 or over when he committed the offence*; and
  (b) the judge considers that the seriousness of the offence (or the combination of the offence and one or more offences associated with it) is so grave that the offender ought to spend the rest of his life in prison.

The effect of such an order is that the early release provisions in CSA 1997 s.28 will not apply (*CPD* VII M.5). Paragraph 2(2) sets out examples of cases where it would normally be appropriate to take the "whole life order" as the appropriate starting point, namely:

(i) the murder of two or more persons, where each murder involves any of the following:
- — a substantial degree of premeditation or planning;
- — the abduction of the victim; or
- — sexual or sadistic conduct;

(ii) the murder of a child (i.e. under 18) if involving the abduction of the child or sexual or sadistic motivation;

(iii) the murder of a police officer or prison officer in the course of his or her duty, where the offence was committed on or after 13 April 2015;

(iv) a murder done for the purpose of advancing a political, religious, racial or ideological cause; or

(v) a murder by an offender previously convicted of murder,

but the judge must consider all the material facts before concluding that a very lengthy finite term is not a sufficiently severe penalty (*R. v Jones* (1962) 46 Cr. App. R. 129). In *Oakes* [2012] EWCA Crim 2435; [2013] Crim. L.R. 252 the compatibility of whole life orders with ECHR art.3 was considered. A whole life order is reserved for the most exceptional cases, and while the CACD did not suggest that it can be imposed only where there has been murderous violence, such an order will inevitably be very rare indeed. The making of a whole life order requires detailed consideration of the individual circumstances of each case. It is likely to be rare that the circumstances will be such that such an order is required. Such an order does not amount to inhuman and degrading treatment contrary to ECHR art.3, *R. v McLoughlin* [2014] EWCA Crim 188; [2014] Crim. L.R. 471 (disagreeing with the judgment of the Grand Chamber of the European Court in *Vintner v United Kingdom (No.2), The Times,* 13 July 2013).

In *R. v Stewart* [2022] EWCA Crim 1063; [2022] 7 WLUK 418 the CACD considered four cases concerned with whole life orders. The LCJ set out those cases where the application of the statutory framework has been considered: *R. v Peters* [2005] EWCA Crim 605; [2005] Cr. App. R. (S.) 101; *Re Jones* [2005] EWCA Crim 3115; [2006] 2 Cr. App. R. (S.) 19; *R. v Height (John)* [2008] EWCA Crim 2500; [2009] 1 Cr. App. R. (S.) 117; *R. v Wilson* [2009] EWCA Crim 999; [2010] 1 Cr. App. R. (S.) 11; *R. v Oakes* [2012] EWCA Crim 2435; [2013] Q.B. 979; *R. v McLoughlin* [2014] EWCA Crim 188; [2014] 1 W.L.R. 3964; *R. v Reynolds* [2014] EWCA Crim 2205; [2015] 1 Cr. App. R. (S.) 24; *Hutchinson v United Kingdom* [2017] 1 WLUK 173; 43 B.H.R.C. 667 and *R. v McCann* [2020] EWCA Crim 1676; [2021] 4 W.L.R. 3, before then dealing with each of the four sets of facts it had to consider. The judgement then helpfully sets out the general principles from the provisions and authorities:

(i) For offences committed before 28 June 2022, a whole life order may only be considered where a sentence of life imprisonment is imposed on an offender who is over the age of 21 (SA 2020 s.321(3)(a)). Section 126 of the Police, Crime, Sentencing and Courts Act 2022 extends the availability of a whole life order to offenders aged 18, 19 and 20 from that date.

(ii) A whole life order may only be imposed if the court considers that the seriousness of the offence(s) is such that it should not make a minimum term order (SA 2020 s.321(3)(b)).

(iii) "A whole life order should be imposed where the seriousness of the offending is so exceptionally high that just punishment requires the offender to be kept in prison for the rest of his or her life. Often, perhaps usually, where such an order is called for the case will not be on the borderline. The facts of the case, considered as a whole, will leave the judge in no doubt that the offender must be kept in prison for the rest of his or her life. Indeed, if the judge is in doubt this may well be an indication that a finite minimum term which leaves open the possibility that the offender may be released for the final years of his or her life is the appropriate disposal. To be imprisoned for a finite period of thirty years or more is a very severe penalty. If the case includes one or more of the factors set out in [the schedule] it is likely to be a case that calls for a whole life order, but the judge must consider all the material facts before concluding that a very lengthy finite term will not be a sufficiently severe penalty." *Jones* at [10]

(iv) It is "a sentence of last resort for cases of the most extreme gravity" which is "reserved for the few exceptionally serious cases" where "the judge is satisfied that the element of just punishment requires the imposition of a whole life order"—*Wilson* at [14], *Reynolds* at [5(iv)]. In a borderline case, if the judge is in any doubt as to whether this standard is reached, a minimum term order is likely to be the appropriate disposal—*Jones* at [10], *Reynolds* at [5(ii)].

(v) The statutory scheme "does not shut the door" on the possibility of a whole life order where a discretionary sentence of life imprisonment is imposed for a crime other than murder, but such a case would be "wholly exceptional"—*McCann* at [89]. All bar one of those currently serving whole life orders were convicted of murder and, in most cases, more than one offence of murder.

(vi) In assessing whether the seriousness of the offence(s) warrants a whole life order, the court must have regard to the general principles set out in Sch.21 (SA 2020 s.322(3)). Each case will depend critically on its particular facts. The sentencing judge must undertake a careful analysis of all the relevant facts as "justice cannot be done by rote"—*Peters* at [5], *Reynolds* at [5(i)], *Jones* at [6]. Schedule 21 must be applied in a flexible, not rigid, way to achieve a just result—*Height* at [29]. Because each case depends on its own facts, comparison with other cases is unlikely to be helpful. It is the application of the principles to a careful assessment of the relevant facts of the case that is important.

(vii) The court must first identify the appropriate starting point. Where the seriousness of the offence(s) is exceptionally high, then the starting point is a whole life order. Where the seriousness of the offence(s) is "particularly high" the starting point is a minimum term of 30 years. Otherwise, the starting point will be 15 or 25 years depending on the circumstances.

(viii) Cases of murder involve taking human life where the offender intended to kill or cause really serious harm. All murders are necessarily extremely serious crimes. For that reason, they attract the mandatory life sentence. The requirement for the seriousness to be "exceptionally high" before a whole life order is made arises in that context. The case must be exceptionally serious, even in the context of murder. The period that an offender is required to serve, in the case of a minimum term before the parole board can consider release, encompasses every type of murder from true mercy killings at one end of the spectrum to the most evil at the other.

(ix) The period that a murderer must serve does not reflect the value the life taken away and does not attempt to do so.

(x) Paragraphs 2(2) and 3(2) of Sch.21 list the types of case where the seriousness is "normally" to be regarded as "exceptionally high" or "particularly high". These are not exhaustive lists. The legislation does not exclude the possibility that other cases might reach the indicted level of seriousness, though such cases are "probably rare"—*Height* at [28]. The same applies in reverse: a case that nominally comes within the ambit of paras 2(2) or 3(2) may not reach that level of seriousness because of the particular facts—*Height* at [28]. The conclusion in *Height* was that it will be rare for a case that does not come directly within the scope of para.2(2) to be regarded as being exceptionally serious.

(xi) Having determined the appropriate starting point, the court must consider the aggravating and mitigating factors. These may result in a departure from the starting point. If the starting point is a whole life order, then the balance of mitigating factors and aggravating factors might result in the imposition of a minimum term order. That balance is not struck by listing aggravating and mitigating factors and then considering which list is the longer. Both aggravating and mitigating factors may vary in potency. The statutory factors which indicate that a whole life order should be considered would themselves normally be aggravating factors. Care must be taken not to double count. Conversely, if the starting point is a minimum term order, then the balance of aggravating factors and mitigating factors might result in the imposition of a whole life order.

(xii) A plea of guilty is relevant when determining whether the seriousness of a case is exceptionally high and requires a whole life order—*Jones* at [15], *Reynolds* at [5(iii)].

(xiii) If the test in SA 2020 s.321(3) is satisfied, then a whole life order must be imposed. Otherwise, a sentence of life imprisonment must be subject to a minimum term order (s.321(2)).

(xiv) A whole life order means that the statutory early release provisions do not apply. It does not preclude the possibility of release by the Home Secretary on compassionate grounds. A decision whether to release on compassionate grounds may be challenged in judicial review proceedings. The Grand Chamber of the European Court of Human Rights has confirmed (in agreement with this court's decision in *McLoughlin*) that "the whole life sentence ... [is] in keeping with Article 3 of the Convention"—*Hutchinson* at [72].

(xv) The assessment of seriousness is for the sentencing judge. On an appeal, or a reference by the Law Officers, this court will not substitute its own assessment for that of the sentencing judge. On an appeal against the imposition of a whole life order or a reference by the Attorney or Solicitor General this court will interfere only if the sentence was manifestly excessive or unduly lenient, as the case may be: *Peters* at [9].

(2) *30 years* will be the appropriate starting point where:

(a) (Paragraph 3(2)(h)) *the offender is aged 18 to 20* and commits a murder that is so serious that it would require a whole life order if committed by an offender aged 21 or over (*CPD* VII M.6); or

(b) (Paragraph 3(1)) case is not so serious as to require a "whole life order" but where the seriousness of the offence is particularly high and *the offender was aged 18 or over* when he committed the offence (para.3(1)). Paragraph 3(2) sets out examples of cases where a 30 year starting point would normally be appropriate (if they do not require a "whole life order") (*CPD* VII M.7) namely:

- (i) in the case of an offence committed before 13 April 2015, the murder of a police or prison officer in the course of his duty;
- (ii) a murder involving the use of a firearm or explosive;
- (iii) a murder done for gain (such as a murder done in the course or furtherance of robbery or burglary, done for payment or done in the expectation of gain as a result of the death);
- (iv) a murder intended to obstruct or interfere with the course of justice;
- (v) a murder involving sexual or sadistic conduct;
- (vi) the murder of two or more persons;
- (vii) a murder that is racially or religiously aggravated or aggravated by sexual orientation disability or transgender identity; or
- (viii) a murder falling within para.2(2) committed by an offender who was aged under 21 when he committed the offence.

As to what amounts to sadism, see *R. v Bonellie* [2008] EWCA Crim 1417; [2009] 1 Cr. App. R. (S.) 55. Sadism need not be sexual to justify a 30-year term (*Attorney General's Reference (Nos 108 and 109 of 2005)* [2006] EWCA Crim 513; [2006] 2 Cr. App. R. (S.) 80). See also *R. v Davies* [2008] EWCA Crim 1055; [2009] 1 Cr. App. R. (S.) 15. The standard of proof that the judge should apply when deciding whether aggravating features exist for lifting the starting point from 15 to 30 years is the same as that to be applied by a jury when reaching its verdict (*R. v Davies*). Cases that (if not falling within Sch.21 para.4(1) above) would normally fall within para.2 include:

(3) The above criteria, suggesting a starting point of 30 years, are not exhaustive of the cases which fall into that category, and do not exclude the possibility that in some cases, probably rare, the seriousness may be such as to justify a 30-year starting point even when the express criteria normally required for that purpose and set out above are absent (*R. v Height* [2005] EWCA Crim 2500; [2009] 1 Cr. App. R. (S.) 117; *R. v Herbert* [2008] EWCA Crim 2501; [2009] 2 Cr. App. R. (S.) 9). The schedule should not be applied mechanically; the factors listed in para.5(2) are not exhaustive of what a judge may determine to be of "particularly high" seriousness (*R. v Griffiths* [2012] EWCA Crim 2012; [2013] Crim. L.R. 436). See, as a further illustration, *Attorney General's Reference (No.73 of 2012)* [2012] EWCA Crim 2924; [2013] Crim. L.R. 440.

(4) *25 years* will ordinarily be the appropriate starting point (Sch.21 para.4) where the case does not fall within 2 or 3 (above) but:
(a) the murder was committed on or after 2 March 2010;
(b) *the offender was aged 18 or over when the murder was committed*; and he took a knife or other weapon to the scene intending:
(i) to commit any offence; or
(ii) have it available as a weapon; and
(iii) used that knife or weapon in committing the murder (*CPD* VII M.8).

The difficulties arising from the interpretation of this section were examined in *R. v Kelly* [2011] EWCA Crim 1462; [2012] 1 Cr. App. R. (S.) 56. The CACD pointed out that its application was not confined to murders committed with the use of a knife which had been taken out and used in public; a murder committed with a knife in the home of the offender or victim might still engage Sch.21 para.5A if the knife had been brought to the property for that purpose. Problems would always arise in the context of defining what was meant by "the scene" (*Attorney General's Reference (No.103 of 2011) (R. v Thomson)* [2012] EWCA Crim 135). In *R. v Dillon* [2015] EWCA 3 the CACD set out three points emerging from various cases on "taking a knife or other weapon to the scene": (i) a knife taken from the kitchen to another part of the same flat or house, including a balcony will not normally be regarded as having taken to the scene, even if a door is forced open; (ii) a knife taken out of the house or flat into the street, or into another part of the premises, or on to a landing outside a flat, will normally be regarded as take to the scene; and (iii) a starting point is not the same as a finishing point—important to avoid major differences in sentence based on fine distinctions.

(5) *15 years* will be the appropriate starting point (Sch.21 para.5) where *the offender was aged 18 or over when he committed the offence* and the case does not fall within paras 2, 3 or 4 above (*CPD* VII M.9). Note that:
   (a) 18–20 year olds convicted before the coming into force of s.126 of the Police, Crime, Sentencing and Courts Act 2022 on 28 June 2022 are the subject only of the 30-year, 25-year and 15-year starting points (*CPD* VII M.10), for those convicted after that date, they can be made subject of whole life orders as well.
   (b) The appropriate starting point when setting a sentence of detention during His Majesty's pleasure for offenders aged under 18 when they committed the offence and they are convicted before 28 June 2022 when s.127 of the Police Crime, Sentencing and Courts Act 2022 came into force is 12 years (para.6) (*CPD* VII M.11).

The second step; aggravating and mitigating factors

45-007 The second step after choosing a starting point is to take account of any aggravating or mitigating factors which would justify a departure from the starting point. Additional aggravating factors (other than those specified in paras 2(2), 3(2) and 4(2) are listed at para.9 of Sch.21. Examples of mitigating factors are listed at para.10. Taking into account the aggravating and mitigating features, the court may add to or subtract from the starting point to arrive at the appropriate punitive period (*CPD* VII M.12).

Aggravating factors (additional to those mentioned in Sch.21 paras 2(2), 3(2) and 4(2)) that may be relevant to the offence of murder include:

(1) a significant degree of planning or premeditation;
(2) the fact that the victim was particularly vulnerable because of age or disability;
(3) mental or physical suffering inflicted on the victim before death;
(4) the abuse of a position of trust;
(5) the use of duress or threats against another person to facilitate the commission of the offence;
(6) the fact that the victim was providing a public service or performing a public duty; and
(7) concealment, destruction or dismemberment of the body.

Mitigating factors that may be relevant to the offence of murder include:

(1) an intention to cause serious bodily harm rather than to kill;
(2) lack of premeditation;
(3) the fact that the offender suffered from any mental disorder or mental dis-

ability which (although not falling within MHA 1959 s.2(1)), lowered his degree of culpability;
(4) the fact that the offender was provoked (for example, by prolonged stress) in a way not amounting to a defence of provocation;
(5) the fact that the offender acted to any extent in self-defence;
(6) a belief by the offender that the murder was an act of mercy; and
(7) the offender's age.

The starting points at (2)–(4) above, provide the judge with guidance as to the range within which the sentence is likely to fall having regard to the salient features of the case. It will often be impossible to divorce the choice of starting point from a consideration of aggravating and mitigating circumstances. Detailed consideration of these circumstances may result in a minimum term of *any* length (whatever the starting point) or in the making of a whole life order.

Nothing in these provisions restricts the application of SA 2020 s.65 (previous convictions), s.64 (bail), or s.73 (guilty plea).

The third step; previous convictions

The third step is that the judge should consider the effect of SA 2020: **45-008**

(1) s.65 in relation to previous convictions;
(2) s.64 where the offence was committed whilst the offender was on bail; and
(3) s.73 where the offender has pleaded guilty.

(Sch.21 para.11)

He should then take into account what credit the offender would have received for a remand in custody under SA 2020 s.240 or s.240ZA of the 2003 Act and/or for a remand on bail subject to a qualifying curfew condition under s.240A, but for the fact that the mandatory sentence is one of life imprisonment. Where the offender has been thus remanded in connection with the offence or a related offence, the judge should have in mind that no credit will otherwise be given for this time when the offender is considered for early release. The appropriate time to take it into account is when setting the minimum term. The judge should make any appropriate subtraction from the punitive period it would otherwise impose, in order to reach the minimum term (*CPD* VII M.13).

Calculation of the minimum term

Following the three steps set out at 45-006 to 45-008, the judge should have arrived at the appropriate minimum term to be announced in open court (see 45-010 and 45-018). As Sch.21 para.8 makes clear, the judge retains the ultimate discretion and he may arrive at any minimum term from any starting point. The minimum term is subject to appeal by the offender under CJA 2003 s.271 and subject to review on a reference by the Attorney General under s.272 (*CPD* VII M.14). **45-009**

Schedule 21 cannot be applied mechanistically; para.3(2) is in no sense an exhaustive list of the kinds of case which a judge may determine to be of particularly high seriousness. A mechanical application of the Schedule is apt to create absurd anomalies, such as that corrected in *R. v Height* [2008] EWCA Crim 2500; [2009] 1 Cr. App. R. (S.) 117.

Nor can the Schedule be applied in an arithmetical manner, by adding or subtracting years attributable to separate features of the case: that was demonstrated to be unworkable in *R. v Peters* [2005] EWCA Crim 605; [2005] 2 Cr. App. R. (S.) 101

at 627. As was observed in *R. v Jones* [2005] EWCA Crim 3414; [2006] 2 Cr. App. R. (S.) 18 at 117, the very large gaps between the starting points identified in the Schedule present the judge with considerable difficulties in his quest to match the penalty to the infinitely variable circumstances of crime.

Announcing the minimum term

45-010 Having gone through the three steps outlined, the judge is then under a duty (SA 2020 s.322(4)), to state in open court, in ordinary language, his reasons for deciding on the minimum term or for passing a whole life order (*CPD* VII Sentencing P: Procedure for announcing the minimum term in open court P.1).

In order to comply with this duty, the judge:

(1) should state clearly the minimum term he has determined;
(2) should state, in doing so, which of the starting points he has chosen and his reasons for doing so;
(3) must state, where he has departed from that starting point due to mitigating or aggravating features, the reasons for that departure and any aggravating or mitigating features which have led to that departure;
(4) should, at that point, also declare how much, if any, time is being deducted for time spent in custody and/or on bail subject to a qualifying curfew condition; and

should then explain that the minimum term is the minimum amount of time the offender will spend in prison, from the date of sentence, before the Parole Board can order early release. If it remains necessary for the protection of the public, the prisoner will continue to be detained after that date. The judge should also state that where the offender has served the minimum term and the Parole Board has decided to direct release, the offender will remain on licence for the rest of his life and may be recalled to prison at any time (*CPD* VII P.2).

Where the offender was 21 or over when he committed the offence and the judge considers that the seriousness of the offence is so exceptionally high that a "whole life order" is appropriate, he should state clearly his reasons for reaching this conclusion. He should also explain that the early release provisions will not apply (*CPD* VII P.3).

C. Discretionary life sentences

The power

45-011 The new statutory life sentence has not replaced IPP. Many offenders who represent a danger to the public may not "qualify" for the statutory life sentence. Yet, for some offenders, the imperative of public protection continues undiminished, and is not wholly met by the "new" extended sentence. Very long-term public protection is therefore to be provided by the imposition of a discretionary life sentence (*R. v Saunders* [2013] EWCA Crim 1027; [2014] 1 Cr. App. R. (S.) 45).

In *R. v Saunders*, Lord Judge CJ expressed the view of the CACD that discretionary life sentences could still be passed other than under what is now SA 2020 ss.274 and 285. Some commentators have questioned that view in the light of the provisions of the CJA 2003. The CACD has observed that such questioning runs contrary to the Sentencing Council Sexual Offences Guideline, where it is expressly stated that:

"Life imprisonment is the maximum for the offence [of rape]. Such a sentence may be imposed either as a result of the offence itself where a number of aggravating factors are present, or because the offender meets the dangerousness criterion."

Criteria

The criteria governing the imposition of a *discretionary* life sentence are essentially the same whether the form of such a sentence is one of imprisonment, custody for life under SA 2020 s.275 or detention for life under SA 2020 s.250. **45-012**

A discretionary life sentence should be reserved for cases of the utmost gravity, where the culpability of the offender is particularly high or where the offence itself is particularly grave (*R. v Kehoe* [2009] 1 Cr. App. R. (S.) 9; and *R. v Wilkinson* [2009] EWCA Crim 1925; [2010] 1 Cr. App. R. (S.) 100; *R. v Wood* [2010] 1 Cr. App. R. (S.) 2; *R. v McCloud* [2011] EWCA Crim 1516; [2012] 1 Cr. App. R. (S.) 35). Cases decided before CJA 2003 came into force no longer offer guidance on when a life sentence should be imposed (*R. v Kehoe*). It is neither possible nor desirable to set out all those circumstances in which such a sentence might be desirable.

Offender eligible for hospital order

Where the pre-conditions for a hospital order (see MENTALLY DISORDERED OFFENDERS) are satisfied, and a bed is available in a secure hospital, the judge should make a hospital order instead of imposing a discretionary life sentence (*R. v Mitchell* [1997] 1 Cr. App. R. (S.) 90; *R. v Fleming* (1993) 14 Cr. App. R. (S.) 151 to be disregarded) unless, in abnormal circumstances the judge decides to impose a life sentence in such a case, where he considers the offender's culpability so great that a hospital order cannot be justified (*R. v Fairhurst* [1996] 1 Cr. App. R. (S.) 242). **45-013**

It is not proper to impose a life sentence merely to frustrate the offender's premature release by a Mental Health Review Tribunal.

Where an offender is judged to be dangerous, imprisonment rather than a mental health order should follow having regard to the judge's power to direct that the offender should be removed from prison to hospital under MHA 1983 s.45A (*R. v Jenkin* [2012] EWCA Crim 2557; [2013] Crim. L.R. 246). See *R. v IA* [2005] EWCA Crim 2077; [2006] 1 Cr. App. R. (S.) 91.

The minimum term

While the length of the minimum term for offenders sentenced to a mandatory life sentence is set by operation of SA 2020 s.322 and Sch.21 (see 45-009), the minimum term in all other life sentences is set by application of SA 2020 s.323. **45-014**

SA 2020 s.323 empowers the judge when passing a sentence of life imprisonment, where such a sentence is not fixed by law (i.e. not a mandatory life sentence under Pt B) to specify by order such part of the sentence ("the relevant part") as shall be served before the offender may require the Secretary of State to refer his case to the Parole Board. This is applicable to offenders under the age of 18 years as well as to adult defendants (*CPD* VII Sentencing L: Imposition of life sentences L.1).

Thus the discretionary life sentence falls into two parts:

(1) the relevant part, which consists of the period of detention imposed for punishment and deterrence, taking into account the seriousness of the offence; and

(2) the remaining part of the sentence, during which the offender's detention will be governed by consideration of risk to the public.

(*CPD* VII L.2)

The minimum term is the part of the sentence the judge considers appropriate taking into account:

(a) the seriousness of the offence, or of the combination of the offence and one or more offences associated with it;
(b) the effect of any direction which it would have given under CJA 2003 s.240ZA (crediting period of remand in custody) if it had sentenced him to a term of imprisonment; and
(c) the early release provisions as compared with s.244 of the CJA 2003.

The judge is not obliged by statute to make use of the provisions of s.82A when passing a discretionary life sentence. However, he should do so, save in the very exceptional case where he considers that the offence is so serious that detention for life is justified by the seriousness of the offence alone, irrespective of the risk to the public. In such a case, he should state this in open court when passing sentence (*CPD* VII L.3).

Where an offender is 21 or over the judge may, because of the seriousness of the offence or of the combination of the offence and one or more offences associated with it, direct that there be no minimum term and that the early release provisions shall not apply (see SA 2020 s.323). There has not been a case where that course has ever been taken where a discretionary life sentence has been passed.

Where an offender is 21 or over the judge may, because of the seriousness of the offence or of the combination of the offence and one or more offences associated with it, direct that there be no minimum term and that the early release provisions shall not apply (see SA 2020 s.323). There has not been a case where that course has ever been taken where a discretionary life sentence has been passed.

Approach to the minimum term

45-015 The effect of SA 2020 s.323 is to require the judge to identify the sentence that would have been appropriate had a life sentence not been justified and to reduce that notional sentence to take account of the fact that had a determinate sentence been passed the offender would have been entitled to early release.

When imposing a discretionary life sentence the practice is for the judge to reduce the notional sentence by one half to reach the minimum term. That approach was endorsed in *R. v Szczerba* [2002] EWCA Crim 440; [2002] 2 Cr. App. R. (S.) 86, although the court said there might be cases in which, exceptionally, the reduction might be less than one half. When *Szczerba* was decided any prisoner serving a sentence of four years or more (a "long term prisoner") was eligible for release at the halfway point of his sentence, but not entitled to release until the two-thirds point. The courts did not change their approach when, by operation of s.244(1) and s.249(1) of the CJA 2003 all prisoners serving determinate sentences became entitled to release at the halfway point of their sentences. In *R. v Burinskas* the CACD noted that PCC(S)A 2000 s.82A(3A)–(3C) (now SA 2020 s.323) permit the judge to reduce the notional determinate term by less than one half in some cases. These provisions inserted by CJIA are not yet in force.

In cases where the judge is to specify the relevant part of the sentence under SA 2020 s.323, he should permit the advocate for the accused to address him as to the appropriate length of the relevant part. Where no relevant part is to be specified, the advocate for the accused should be permitted to address the court as to the appropriateness of this course of action (*CPD* VII L.4).

In specifying the relevant part of the sentence, the judge should have regard to the specific terms of s.323 and should indicate the reasons for reaching his decision as to the length of the relevant part (*CPD* VII L.5).

He is not obliged to, though there is no reason why he should not, have regard to the provisions of SA 2020 Sch.21 (above 46-009) in relation to the tariff in respect of mandatory life sentences (*R. v McNee* [2007] EWCA Crim 1529; [2008] 1 Cr. App. R. (S.) 24).

Reduction for plea of guilty

There are important differences between the usual fixed term sentence and the minimum term set following the imposition of the mandatory life sentence for murder. The most significant of these is that a reduction for a plea of guilty in the case of murder will have double the effect on time served in custody when compared with a determinate sentence. This is because: **45-016**

(1) a determinate sentence provides, in most circumstances, for the release of the offender on licence half way through the total sentence; whereas
(2) in the case of murder, a minimum term is the period in custody before consideration is given by the Parole Board to whether release is appropriate.

Given this difference, the special characteristic of the offence of murder and the unique statutory provision of starting points, careful consideration needs to be given to:

(a) the extent of any reduction; and
(b) the need to ensure that the minimum term properly reflects the seriousness of the offence.

Whilst the general principles continue to apply (both that a guilty plea should be encouraged and that the extent of any reduction should reduce if the indication of plea is later than the first reasonable opportunity), the process of determining the level of reduction is different. (See *R. v Last* [2005] EWCA Crim 106; [2005] 2 Cr. App. R. (S.) 64; *R. v Peters* [2005] EWCA Crim 605; [2005] 2 Cr. App. R. (S.) 101.)

The crediting of periods of remand in custody is dealt with administratively (see SA 2020 s.323 and CJA 2003 s.240ZA; as to crediting periods spent on bail under certain conditions, see CJA 2003 s.240A under IMPRISONMENT.

Approach to reduction

The Sentencing Council Definitive Guideline on Reduction in Sentence for a Guilty Plea F, recommends the following approach: **45-017**

(1) where the judge determines that there should be a *whole life* minimum term, there will be no reduction for a guilty plea.

However, the judge should bear in mind the fact that the offender has pleaded guilty when deciding whether it is appropriate to order a whole life term—this applies also to other matters of mitigation (*R. v Jones* [2005] EWCA Crim 3115; [2006] 2 Cr. App. R. (S.) 19);

(2) in other circumstances:

(a) the judge must weigh carefully the overall length of the minimum term taking into account other reductions for which offenders may be eligible so as to avoid a combination leading to an inappropriately short sentence;
(b) where it is appropriate to reduce the minimum term having regard to a plea of guilty, the maximum reduction will be one sixth and should never exceed five years;
(c) the maximum reduction of one-sixth or five years (whichever is less) should only be given when a guilty plea has been indicated at the first stage of the proceedings. Lesser reductions should be given for guilty pleas after that point, with a maximum of one-twentieth being given for a guilty plea on the day of trial.

As the Guideline makes clear the general exceptions on reductions for plea relating to further information, assistance or advice necessary before indicating plea, and the situation following a Newton hearing or a special reasons hearing, will also apply. (F1 and F2 Reduction in Sentence for a Guilty Plea).

Announcing the minimum term

45-018 When a judge gives in public his decision as to the minimum term an offender is required to serve, he should:

(1) make clear how that term is calculated;
(2) normally commence by indicating what he considers would be the appropriate determinate sentence suitable for punishment and deterrence;
(3) then explain that it is necessary to calculate a minimum term so that it will be known when his case should be referred to the Parole Board; and finally
(4) explain that if a prisoner is released on licence, still, for the remainder of his life, he can be recalled to prison if he does not comply with the terms of his licence.

In specifying the relevant part of the sentence, the judge should have regard to the specific terms of SA 2020 s.323 and should indicate the reasons for reaching his decision as to the length of the relevant part.

46. LIVE LINKS

Quick Guide

Nature of live link

A "live link" enables a person to give evidence, usually by means of CCTV from a place outside the courtroom or the court building instead of having to attend court in the usual manner. It needs to be distinguished from recordings of evidence given as a witness's examination-in-chief. A "live link" and telephone facilities can also be used to conduct hearings (see CASE MANAGEMENT). **46-001**

Provision is made for this procedure to be adopted in a number of different situations under various statutes:

(1) by a witness, under YJCEA 1999 s.24 by means of a special measures direction (see SPECIAL MEASURES DIRECTIONS);
(2) by a witness other than the accused under CJA 2003 ss.51–56 (see 46-002);
(3) by a witness other than the accused who is outside the UK, under CJA 1988 s.32 (see 46-009);
(4) under CDA 1998 ss.57B, 57D and 57E (inserted by PJA 2006 s.45) permitting the presence of the accused at preliminary hearings and in relation to sentencing hearings by means of live link (see 46-010); and
(5) in relation to a vulnerable accused under YJCEA 1999 ss.33A and 33B (inserted by PJA 2006 s.47) (see 46-014).

In terrorist cases (see ALLOCATION AND LISTING OF CASES) all Crown Court hearings prior to the trial will be conducted by video link for all accused in custody, unless a judge otherwise directs (TerrPro 2007 para.17).

A "live link" must enable the person in relation to whom a direction is made to see and hear a person at the place where the proceedings are being held and to be seen and heard by the accused, where appropriate, the judge and the jury (if there is one), legal representatives acting in the proceedings, and any interpreter or other person appointed by the court to assist the witness, disregarding for this purpose the extent (if any) to which such a person is unable to see or hear by reason of any impairment of eyesight or hearing.

Nothing in the statutory provisions is to be regarded as affecting any power of a judge:

(a) to make an order, give directions or give leave of any description in relation to any witness (including the accused); or

(b) to exclude evidence at his discretion (whether by preventing questions being put or otherwise).

1. Witnesses other than the accused: CJA 2003

General

46-002 A witness (other than the accused) may, if the judge so directs, give evidence through a live link in:

(1) an appeal to the Crown Court arising out of a summary trial;
(2) a trial on indictment; and
(3) a hearing before the Crown Court which is held after the accused has entered a plea of guilty; and

the judge may give such a direction either on an application by a party to the proceedings, or of his own motion, but may authorise such a course only where:

(a) he is satisfied that it is in the interests of the efficient or effective administration of justice for the witness to give evidence in the proceedings through a live link, e.g. from his place of work;
(b) he has been notified that suitable facilities are available in the area in which it appears that the proceedings will take place.

The responsibility for ensuring that facilities are in place is that of the prosecutor. The withdrawal of any such a notification will not affect a direction given under this provision before that withdrawal (CJA 2003 s.51(1)–(5)).

Exercise of court's powers

46-003 The judge may decide whether to give or discharge a live link direction:

(1) at a hearing, in public or in private, or without a hearing;
(2) in a party's absence, if that party:
   (a) applied for the direction or discharge; or
   (b) has had at least 14 days in which to make representations in response to an application by another party.

(CrimPR 18.23)

Content of application

46-004 An applicant for a live link direction must:

(1) unless the judge otherwise directs, identify the place from which the witness will give evidence;
(2) if that place is in the UK, explain why it would be in the interests of the efficient or effective administration of justice for the witness to give evidence by live link;
(3) if the applicant wants the witness to be accompanied by another person while giving evidence:
   (a) name that person, if possible; and
   (b) explain why it is appropriate for the witness to be accompanied;

(4) ask for a hearing, if the applicant wants one, and explain why it is needed.

(CrimPR 18.24)

A form of application is set out in the *CPD*.

The procedure under CrimPR 18.24 applies equally to cases under CJA 1988 s.32 (see 46-009, but not to cases under YJCEA 1999 s.24 as to which see SPECIAL MEASURES DIRECTIONS).

Representations in response

46-005 Where a party wants to make representations about:

(1) an application for a live link direction;
(2) an application for the discharge of such a direction; or
(3) a direction or discharge that the court proposes on its own initiative, he must:
    (a) serve the representations on:
        (i) the Crown Court officer; and
        (ii) each other party; and
    (b) do so not more than 14 days after, as applicable:
        (i) service of the application; or
        (ii) notice of the direction or discharge that the judge proposes; and
    (c) ask for a hearing, if that party wants one, and explain why it is needed.

Representations against a direction or discharge must explain, as applicable, why the conditions prescribed by CJA 1988 or CJA 2003 are not met (CrimPR 18.26).

In deciding whether to give a direction, the judge must consider all the circumstances of the case. Those circumstances include in particular:

(1) the availability of the witness;
(2) the need for the witness to attend in person;
(3) the importance of the witness's evidence to the proceedings;
(4) the views of the witness;
(5) the suitability of the facilities at the place where the witness would give evidence through a live link; and
(6) whether a direction might tend to inhibit any party to the proceedings from effectively testing the witness's evidence.

The judge must state in open court his reasons for refusing an application for a direction under the section (CJA 2003 s.51(6)–(8)).

Application to discharge a live link direction

46-006 A party who wants the judge to discharge a live link direction must:

(1) apply in writing, as soon as reasonably practicable after becoming aware of the grounds for doing so; and
(2) serve the application on:
    (a) the Crown Court officer; and
    (b) each other party, and must:
        (i) explain what material circumstances have changed since the direction was given;
        (ii) explain why it is in the interests of justice to discharge the direction; and

(iii) ask for a hearing, if the applicant wants one, and explain why it is needed.

Effect of direction; rescission

46-007 Where the judge gives a direction for a witness to give evidence through a live link, the witness must give all his evidence through the live link unless the direction is rescinded. The judge may rescind a direction if it appears to him to be in the interests of justice to do so, on an application by a party to the proceedings, or of his own motion, but no application may be made by a party unless there has been a material change of circumstances since the direction was given, e.g. where problems arise with the technology after a direction has been given.

Where the judge does rescind the order, the witness ceases to be able to give evidence through the live link, but this does not prevent the judge from giving a further direction under CJA 2003 s.51 in relation to him (CJA 2003 s.52(1) and (2)).

The judge must state in open court his reasons for rescinding a direction, or for refusing an application to do so (CJA 2003 s.52(7)).

Warning to jury

46-008 Where, as a result of a direction under CJA 2003 s.51, evidence has been given through a live link, the judge may give the jury (if there is one) such directions as he thinks necessary to ensure that the jury give the same weight to the evidence as if it had been given by the witness in the courtroom or other place where the proceedings were held (CJA 2003 s.54).

2. Witnesses outside the UK: CJA 1988

General

46-009 With the leave of the judge, a person other than the accused, who is outside the UK, may, in a trial on indictment for certain specified proceedings, give evidence through a live television link.

A statement made on oath by a witness outside the UK and given in evidence through such a link is treated for the purposes of s.1 of the Perjury Act 1911 as having been made in the proceedings in which it is given in evidence.

The proceedings to which such procedure applies are:

(1) proceedings for murder, manslaughter or any other offence consisting of the killing of any person;

(2) proceedings being conducted by the Director of the Serious Fraud Office under CJA 1987 s.1(5); and

(3) proceedings (other than those falling within (2)) in which a notice of transfer has been given CJA 1987 s.4 by any of the designated authorities.

(CJA 1988 s.32; SI 1990/2084)

3. Accused's attendance at certain preliminary and sentencing hearings: CDA 1998 Pt 3A

Introduction

46-010 CDA 1998 Pt 3A applies to preliminary hearings and sentencing hearings in the course of proceedings for an offence and enforcement proceedings relating to confiscation orders, enabling the judge, in the circumstances provided for by ss.57B, 57C, and 57E (and a magistrates' court under s.57F), to direct the use of a live link for securing the accused's attendance at a hearing to which it applies. The accused is treated as present in court when, by virtue of such a live link direction, he attends the hearing through a live link (CDA 1998 s.57A).

"Confiscation order" here means an order made under CJA 1988 s.71, an order made under DTA 1994 s.2, or an order made under POCA 2002 s.6.

Preliminary hearings

In relation to a preliminary hearing, where the accused is in custody and it appears to the judge before which the preliminary hearing is to take place that the accused is likely to be held in custody during the hearing, he may give a live link direction in relation to the attendance of the accused at the hearing, but he must not give (or rescind) such a direction (whether at a hearing or otherwise) unless he has given the parties to the proceeding an opportunity to make representations. **46-011**

Note that:

(1) such a direction is a direction requiring the accused, if he is being held in custody during the hearing, to attend it through a live link from the place at which he is being held; and
(2) if a hearing takes place in relation to the giving or rescinding of such a direction, the judge may require or permit a person attending the hearing to do so through a live link.

(CDA 1998 s.57B)

Continued use at sentencing hearing

Where a live link under ss.57B or 57C is in force and: **46-012**

(1) the accused is convicted of the offence in the course of that hearing (whether by virtue of a guilty plea or an indication of an intention to plead guilty); and
(2) the judge proposes to continue the hearing as a sentencing hearing in relation to the offence,

the accused may continue to attend through the live link by virtue of the direction if:

(a) the hearing is continued as a sentencing hearing in relation to the offence; and
(b) the judge is satisfied that the accused continuing to attend through the live link is not contrary to the interests of justice.

The accused may not, however, give oral evidence through the live link during the continued hearing unless the judge is satisfied that it is not contrary to the interests of justice for him to give it in that way (CDA 1998 s.57D).

Use of live link in sentencing hearings

If it appears to the judge by or before whom the accused is convicted that it is likely that the accused will be held in custody during any sentencing hearing for the **46-013** offence, he may give a live link direction in relation to that hearing, being a direction requiring the accused, if he is being held in custody during the hearing, to attend through a live link from the place at which he is being held.

Such a direction may be given:

(1) by the judge of his own motion or on an application by a party; and
(2) in relation to all subsequent sentencing hearings before the court or to such hearing or hearings as may be specified or described in the direction; but

the judge may not give such a direction unless he is satisfied that it is not contrary to the interests of justice to give the direction.

The judge may rescind such a direction at any time before or during a hearing to which it relates if it appears to him to be in the interests of justice to do so (but this does not affect his power to give a further live link direction in relation to the offender).

The judge may exercise his power of his own motion or on an application by a party.

The court must state in open court its reasons for refusing an application for, or for the rescission of, a live link direction under this section.

The offender may not give oral evidence while attending a hearing through such a live link unless the judge is satisfied that it is not contrary to the interests of justice for him to give it in that way (CDA 1998 s.57E).

This section applies to hearings in proceedings relating to a reference under SOCPA 2005 s.74 as it applies to sentencing hearings (PJA 2006 Sch.15 para.62).

Definitions

46-014 Note that:

(1) "custody" includes local authority accommodation or youth detention accommodation to which a person is remanded under LASPOA 2012 s.91, but does not include police detention (CDA 1998 s.57A(3); LASPOA 2012 Sch.12 para.39);
(2) "live link" means an arrangement by which a person (when not in the place where the hearing is being held) is able to see and hear, and to be seen and heard by, the court during a hearing (and for this purpose any impairment of eyesight or hearing is to be disregarded); (The definition of "live link" is amended by the Criminal Procedure (Amendment No.2) (Coronavirus) Rules 2020 (SI 2020/417) so that (i) "live video link" means a live television link or other arrangement by which a person taking part in a hearing can see and hear, and be seen and heard by, everyone else who is taking part and who is not in the same place as that person; and (ii) "live audio link" means a live telephone link or other arrangement by which a person taking part in a hearing can hear, and be heard by, everyone else who is taking part and who is not in the same place as that person. This definition will apply until the coronavirus amendments are repealed;
(3) "police detention" has the meaning given by PACE 1984 s.118(2);
(4) "preliminary hearing" means a hearing in the proceedings held before the start of the trial (within the meaning of subss.(11A) or (11B) of s.22 of POA 1985) including, in the case of proceedings in the Crown Court, a preparatory hearing held under CJA 1987 s.7 (cases of serious or complex fraud) or CPIA 1996 s.29 (other serious, complex or lengthy cases); and

(5) "sentencing hearing" means any hearing following conviction which is held for the purpose of proceedings relating to the giving or rescinding of a direction under s.57 and sentencing the offender or determining how the court should deal with him in respect of the offence.

4. Evidence of vulnerable accused: YJCEA 1999

General

In any proceedings against a person for an offence the judge may, on the application of the accused, give a live link direction if he is satisfied: **46-015**

(1) that specified conditions (below) are met in relation to the accused; and
(2) that it is in the interests of justice for the accused to give evidence through a live link.

Such a direction is a direction that any oral evidence to be given before the court by the accused is to be given through a live link.

The specified conditions are that, in the case of an accused who:

(a) is aged under 18 when the application is made, and:
  (i) his ability to participate effectively in the proceedings as a witness giving oral evidence in court is compromised by his level of intellectual ability or social functioning; and
  (ii) use of a live link would enable him to participate more effectively in the proceedings as a witness (whether by improving the quality of his evidence or otherwise);
(b) has attained the age of 18 at that time, and:
  (i) he suffers from a mental disorder (within the meaning of MHA 1983) or otherwise has a significant impairment of intelligence and social function;
  (ii) he is for that reason unable to participate effectively in the proceedings as a witness giving oral evidence in court; and
  (iii) use of a live link would enable him to participate more effectively in the proceedings as a witness (whether by improving the quality of his evidence or otherwise).

While a live link direction has effect, the accused may not give oral evidence before the court in the proceedings otherwise than through a live link.

The judge may discharge a live link direction at any time before ordering any hearing to which it applies if it appears to him to be in the interests of justice to do so (but this does not affect the power to give a further live link direction in relation to the accused).

The judge may exercise his power of his own motion or on an application by a party, and must state in open court its reasons for:

(1) giving or discharging a live link direction; or
(2) refusing an application for or for the discharge of a live link direction.

(YJCEA 1999 s.33A)

Interpretation

For the purposes of these provisions a "live link" means an arrangement by which the accused, while absent from the place where the proceedings are being held, is **46-016** able to see and hear a person there, and to be seen and heard by the persons mentioned below (and for this purpose any impairment of eyesight or hearing is to be disregarded) being:

(1) the judge and the jury (if there is one);
(2) where there are two or more accused in the proceedings, each of the other accused;
(3) legal representatives acting in the proceedings; and
(4) any interpreter or other person appointed by the court to assist the accused.

Nothing in these provisions affects:

(a) any power of a court to make an order, give directions or give leave of any description in relation to any witness (including an accused); or
(b) the operation of any rule of law relating to evidence in criminal proceedings.

(YJCEA 1999 ss.33B and 33C)

46-017 Section 200 of the Police, Crime, Sentencing and Courts Act 2022 expands the use of video and audio links in criminal proceedings. In July 2022 the LCJ issued guidance on the expansion of the links. As the guidance sets out, s.51 CJA 2003 (as substituted by the Police, Crime, Sentencing and Courts Act 2022 with effect from 28 June 2022) enables courts to require or permit a person to take part in eligible criminal proceedings through a live link ("a live link direction"), including at preliminary hearings, trials (whether summary or on indictment), sentencing, appeals and other identified types of hearing (see s.51(3)). See under CASE MANAGEMENT and 11-020. In addition in relation to taking evidence from a location outside the UK and live links see *R. v Kadir* [2022] EWCA Crim 1244.

47. MAJORITY VERDICT

Introduction

When complying with JA 1974 s.17, a uniform practice should be adopted. It is inadvisable for the judge, in summing up, or indeed the advocates, in addressing the jury, to attempt an explanation of the section, for fear that the jury will be confused. Before the jury retire, the judge should direct them in some such words as the following: **47-001**

> "As you may know, the law permits me, in certain circumstances, to accept a verdict which is not the verdict of you all. Those circumstances have not as yet arisen, so that when you retire, I must ask you to reach a verdict upon which each one of you is agreed. Should, however, the time come when it is possible for me to accept a majority verdict, I will give you a further direction."

(*CPD* VI Trial 26: Majority verdicts Q.1)

An alternative form of words is contained in the Crown Court Compendium Pt I at 21-4.

Taking the verdict

It is not generally desirable that the jury be told the actual time which must elapse before they may return a majority verdict (*R. v Porter* [1996] Crim. L.R. 126). The practice should be as follows: **47-002**

(1) Should the jury return *before* two hours and ten minutes since the last member of the jury left the jury box to go to the jury room (or such longer time as the judge thinks reasonable) has elapsed (see s.17(4)), they should be asked, in respect of each count separately:
  (a) "Have you reached a verdict upon which you are all agreed? Please answer 'yes' or 'no'."
  (b)
    (i) if unanimous, or on those counts where it is unanimous, this verdict to be accepted;
    (ii) if not unanimous, or on those counts where not unanimous, the jury should be sent out again for further deliberation with a further direction to arrive, if possible, at a unanimous verdict.

(2) Should the jury return (whether for the first time or subsequently) or be sent for *after* the two hours and ten minutes (or the longer period) has elapsed, then questions (a) and (b) above should be put to them, and if it appears that they are not unanimous, they should be asked to retire once more and told that they should continue to endeavour to reach a unanimous verdict but that, if they cannot, the judge will accept a majority verdict (as in s.17(4)), i.e. the verdict on which at least 10 out of 12, or 10 out of 11, or 9 out of 10 jurors are agreed.

(3) When the jury *finally* return, they should be asked, separately on each count:
  (a) "Have at least 10 (or 9 as the case may be) of you agreed upon your verdict?"

(b) If "yes", "What is your verdict? Please answer only 'Guilty' or 'Not Guilty'."
(c) If "Not Guilty", accept the verdict without more ado.
(d) If "Guilty", "is that the verdict of you all, or by a majority?"
(e) If "Guilty by a majority", "How many of you agreed to the verdict and how many dissented?"

(*CPD* VI: Majority verdicts 26 Q.2–Q.4)

A majority verdict which does not comply with the statutory language is not a proper majority verdict (*R. v Bateson* (1970) 54 Cr. App. R. 11; *R. v Barry* (1975) 61 Cr. App. R. 172; *R. v Austin* [2003] Crim. L.R. 426).

Recording the time; further deliberations

47-003 At whatever stage the jury return, before question (a) (47-002), is asked, the Crown Court officer present will state in open court, for each period when the jury was out of court for the purpose of considering their verdict(s), the time at which the last member of the jury left the jury box to go to the jury room, and the time of their return to the jury box, and will additionally state in open court the totals of such periods (*CPD* VI: Majority verdicts 26 Q.5).

If there is an error in procedure, e.g. in timing, the judge may correct that error by a further direction (*R. v Shields* [1997] Crim. L.R. 758).

Multiple count indictment

47-004 Where there are several counts (or alternative verdicts) left to the jury, the practice will need to be adapted to the circumstances.

Thus:

(1) the procedure will have to be repeated in respect of each count (or alternative verdict);
(2) the verdict should be accepted in those cases where the jury is unanimous;
(3) the further direction in VI: Majority verdicts 26 Q.2 should be given in cases in which it is not unanimous; and
(4) should the jury in the end be unable to agree on a verdict by the required majority (i.e. if the answer to the question in para.46.4(a) is in the negative) the judge in his discretion will either ask them to deliberate further or discharge them (*R. v Noah* (2004) S.J. 1249).

(*CPD* VI: Majority verdicts 26 Q.7–Q.8)

Application to other verdicts

47-005 JA 1974 s.17 applies also to verdicts other than "Guilty" or "Not Guilty", e.g. to:

(1) special verdicts under the CP(I)A 1964;
(2) special verdicts on findings of fact.

Accordingly, in such cases the questions to jurors will have to be suitably adjusted. (*CPD* VI: Majority verdicts 26 Q.9)

The CACD has said on several occasions that a *Watson* direction should not be given before, or at the same time as, a majority verdict direction, see *R. v Arthur*

[2013] EWCA Crim 1852; [2014] Crim. L.R. 229; *R. v Scully* [2013] EWCA Crim 2288.

(*CPD* VI: Majority verdicts 26 Q.9)

48. MENTALLY DISORDERED OFFENDERS

QUICK GUIDE

1. INTRODUCTION

48-001 Faced with an accused or an offender who is not so mentally disordered as to be absolved from criminal responsibility for his actions, but is nevertheless in need of treatment, a judge has power:

(1) for the purpose of informing his sentencing decision, to remand that person to hospital for a medical report (48-004), or treatment (48-006) or to make an interim hospital order (48-007);
(2) to divert the offender from punishment by ordering treatment in a hospital instead of in prison (48-009 and following);
(3) to combine hospital treatment with a prison sentence, by making a hospital direction (48-020);
(4) to make an offender the subject of a guardianship order (48-021); or
(5) to make an offender the subject of a community order, or a youth rehabilitation order, with a requirement that he undergo psychiatric treatment (48-022).

Where appropriate, a hospital order may be made in conjunction with a restriction order (see 48-012).

Although offenders do receive treatment in prison, the judge has no control over the allocation of offenders to prisons which are able to provide treatment, nor is it correct sentencing practice to pass a sentence of imprisonment on the assumption that the offender will receive psychiatric treatment in prison. In *Vowles* (see 48-021) the Court of Appeal said that courts could bear in mind the Secretary of State's powers under s.47 MHA to transfer to hospital.

The position in relation to the judge's powers on a special verdict being returned that the accused is not guilty by reason of insanity, or findings being recorded that the accused is under a disability and that he did the act or made the omission charged against him, are dealt with under UNFITNESS TO PLEAD/INSANITY.

The Secretary of State can direct the transfer to hospital of prisoners under sentence in certain circumstances under s.47 MHA 1983. There are similar powers under s.48 MHA 1983 (as amended by the MHA 2007) for those detained in a prison or remand centre but not serving a sentence, those on remand by a magistrates' court, civil prisoners and those detained under the Immigration Act 1971.

Transfers in both cases are based on referrals by the Mental Health Team at the prison to the NHS provider. This will be determined by GP registration, or if unregistered, then by address, and should the person have neither, on the basis of where the alleged offence took place.

Referrals from prison are sent to the relevant regional secure unit and admissions are managed by panels at the relevant hospitals and not by individual clinicians. A doctor from the unit will visit the prison and carry out an assessment, write a report and make a recommendation to the panel for a final decision. The prison will receive a copy of that report and a letter from the panel confirming acceptance or rejection of the referral. Alternatives to admission to the regional secure unit which offers medium security is either a High Secure Hospital or low secure locked ward also known as Psychiatric Intensive Care Unit [PICU].

Any decision to admit must have the agreement of the Mental Health Case Work Section (MHCS) at the Prison and Probation Service (HMPPS). They will review the case summary, charges and previous convictions to consider risk. If concerned by the proposed level of security, they may insist on a High Secure assessment. This will delay the process of transfer as this will normally require the High Secure service to carry out their own assessment and review any proposal through their own admissions panel.

Once there is agreement with the MHCS for a transfer there will be two medical recommendations sent to the MHCS when a bed is available. When received, the MHCS will issue a transfer warrant to the prison mental health team who will arrange transport. The warrant gives a 14-day period in which the defendant must be admitted to hospital. No information on proposed dates for admission will be given publicly.

Once transferred and admitted the normal period of assessment and treatment is 12 weeks. At the end of the period of assessment no report will be provided to the court unless the court specifically requests a report or those representing the defendant make an approach to instruct the responsible clinician. Some clinicians will only accept instructions from the court.

Courts have powers under s.51 MHA 1983 to bring to an end a s.48 transfer. This can occur where a hospital produces a defendant at the end of a period of assessment and wishes the defendant to be returned to prison. In addition, transfers will come to an end if the court disposes of the case.

General

It should be noted that: **48-002**

(1) the psychiatric facilities which the courts may use for their purposes are the same as those provided by the NHS for treatment of non-offender patients;
(2) with the exception of those "medical hospitals" which provide treatment in conditions of the highest security, any given psychiatric hospital will, as a general rule, admit patients only from a particular catchment area, from which each prospective patient must come, or with which he must have some connection;
(3) different hospitals specialise in the treatment of different forms of mental disorder, so that in respect of any one catchment area there are likely to be at least two hospitals, one providing treatment for mental illness, and one providing treatment for mental handicap; for this reason the consent of the hospital is required before the judge may order admission;
(4) where the judge has in mind making a hospital order, the Integrated Care Board (or the Local Health Board in Wales for the area in which the of-

fender resides), the National Health Service Commissioning Board (NHS), (or the National Assembly for Wales) or any other Integrated Care Board is required to assist in identifying an appropriate hospital for a particular offender; and

(5) where a judge is considering a mental health disposal, they must be satisfied that treatment is available and will continue to be available and funded for the duration of the order. If the treatment proposed is not within an NHS hospital, courts should take particular care to confirm the proposed hospital/treatment centre has the appropriate level of security and specialist staff to address the offending behaviour in addition to treating the mental disorder. Courts should always be very cautious before passing a hospital order or mental health treatment order in any case in which the cost of treatment would be met from non-NHS funds. This may result in wholly inadequate safeguarding processes. It should also be noted that probation will not monitor privately funded mental health treatment requirements. (Sentencing Council Sentencing offenders with mental disorders para.28). It should be noted that it will be routine for some private sector regional secure unit beds to be funded by the NHS.

Definition of "mental disorder"

48-003 "Mental disorder" means any disorder or disability of the mind, and "mentally disordered" is to be construed accordingly. MHA 2007 substitutes this single test for the four categories contained in the 1983 Act.

A person with learning disability is not to be considered by reason of that disability to be suffering from mental disorder for the purposes of those orders dealt with in this section (i.e. orders under ss.35–38, 45A, 47, 48 and 51) unless that disability is associated with abnormally aggressive or seriously irresponsible conduct on his part (MHA 1983 s.1).

A person is not to be treated under mental health powers *solely* on grounds of dependence on alcohol, though a person dependent on alcohol is not excluded where he suffers from another mental disorder, even if that other mental disorder is associated with alcohol or drug abuse (MHA 2007 s.3).

The Sentencing Council guidelines, *Sentencing Offenders with mental disorders, developmental disorders, or neurological impairments* that came into force on 1 October 2020 set out at Annex A the main classes of mental disorders and presenting features.

2. Remand for reports

Remand to hospital for reports

48-004 The judge may remand to hospital, for a report on his mental condition, a person who:

(1) is awaiting trial for an offence punishable with imprisonment; or
(2) has been arraigned for such an offence but has not yet been sentenced or otherwise dealt with for that offence, provided that this power is not to be exercised in the case of an offender convicted of an offence for which the sentence is fixed by law.

Before doing so, however, the judge must:

(a) be satisfied on the written or oral evidence of an approved clinician, that there is reason to suspect that the person is suffering from mental disorder (see 48-003);
(b) be of the opinion that it would be impracticable for a report on his mental condition to be made if he were remanded on bail; and
(c) be satisfied on the oral or written evidence of the approved clinician who would be responsible for making the report (or of some other person representing the managers of the hospital) that arrangements have been made for his admission to that hospital within the seven days beginning with the date of the remand (MHA 1983 s.35(1)–(4)).

The judge may ask for evidence of the availability of age-appropriate hospital facilities for offenders under the age of 18. The Sentencing Council guidelines, *Sentencing Offenders with mental disorders, developmental disorders, or neurological impairments* that came into force on 1 October 2020 set out at Annex B some helpful information on seeking reports. CrimPR 28.8 set out directions for commissioning medical reports for sentencing purposes.

Remand conditions; absconding

When a person is remanded to hospital under these provisions: 48-005

(1) the remand, or further remand, must be for not more than 28 days at a time, or for more than 12 weeks in all, and the Crown Court may terminate the remand at any time if it appears appropriate to do so;
(2) the Crown Court may further remand, beyond the 28 days, if it appears, on the written or oral evidence of the approved clinician, that a further remand is warranted; such further remand may be granted without the need for the patient to be brought before the court, provided he is represented by an advocate who is given an opportunity of being heard; and
(3) the patient is entitled to obtain, at his own expense, an independent medical report, and to apply to the judge, on the basis of it, for his remand to be terminated (MHA 1983 s.35(5)–(7)).

If a person absconds from a hospital to which he has been remanded, or while being conveyed to or from that hospital, he may be arrested and brought before the court that remanded him. A judge may thereupon terminate the remand and deal with him in any way in which he would have dealt with him if he had not been remanded.

Remand to hospital for treatment

The judge may, instead of remanding in custody: 48-006

(1) a person in custody awaiting trial before the court for an offence punishable with imprisonment (other than an offence for which the sentence is fixed by law); or
(2) a person who, at any time before sentence, is in custody in the course of a trial before that court for such an offence,

remand him to a specified hospital if he is satisfied, on the written or oral evidence:

(a) of two registered medical practitioners that he is suffering from mental disorder of a nature or degree which makes it appropriate for him to be detained in a hospital for medical treatment, and that appropriate medical treatment is available for him;

(b) of the approved clinician who would have overall responsibility for his case or a representative of the hospital managers, that arrangements have been made for his admission within a period of seven days beginning with the date of the remand (MHA 1983 s.36(1)–(3)).

It should be noted that:

(i) where the judge has remanded under these provisions, he may further remand if it appears on the written or oral evidence of the responsible clinician that a further remand is warranted;

(ii) the power of further remand may be exercised without that person being brought before the court, provided he is represented by an advocate who is given an opportunity of being heard;

(iii) a person must not be remanded, or further remanded under these provisions, for more than 28 days at a time, or for more than 12 weeks in all; a judge may at any time terminate the remand if it appears appropriate to do so; and

(iv) a person remanded under these provisions is entitled to obtain, at his own expense, an independent medical report from a medical practitioner (or an approved clinician) chosen by him, and to apply to the court on the basis of it, for his remand to be terminated.

As with a remand for reports, the judge requires evidence of arrangements to admit the person to hospital within seven days of the remand. That evidence may come from the approved clinician who would have overall responsibility for his case, or anyone representing the hospital managers. If the judge does not have the requisite evidence to make a remand for treatment under s.36, an alternative is to remand in custody and rely on the Secretary of State to use his power under s.48 to direct the accused's transfer to hospital.

The same provisions in relation to an absconder apply as they do under s.35(9) and (10). (See 48-005; MHA 1983 s.36(4)–(7)).

Interim hospital order

48-007 Where a person is convicted before the Crown Court of an offence punishable with imprisonment (other than an offence the sentence for which is fixed by law), and the judge is satisfied, on the written or oral evidence of two registered medical practitioners, at least one of whom is employed at the hospital which is to be specified in the order that:

(1) the offender is suffering from mental disorder (see 48-003);

(2) there is reason to suppose that the mental disorder from which the offender is suffering is such that it may be appropriate for a hospital order to be made in his case; and

(3) the judge is satisfied on the written or oral evidence of the approved clinician who would have overall responsibility for his case, or of some other representative of the hospital managers, that arrangements have been made for his admission within the period of 28 days beginning with the date of the order,

he may, before making a hospital order, or dealing with him in some other way, make an interim hospital order authorising the offender's admission to such hospital as is specified and his detention there.

An interim hospital order remains in force for such period not exceeding 12 weeks as the judge may specify in making the order, but may be renewed for further periods of not more than 28 days at a time, if it appears, on the written or oral evidence of the responsible clinician, that such continuation is warranted. No order may continue in force for more than 12 months in all, and the judge must terminate the order:

(a) if he makes a full hospital order in respect of the offender; or
(b) after considering the written or oral evidence of the responsible medical officer, he decides to deal with the offender in some other way.

The power of renewing an interim hospital order may be exercised without the offender being brought before the court if he is represented by counsel who is given an opportunity of being heard. (Some courts have adopted the process of accepting that "being heard by the defence advocate" includes receiving representations by email, and where there is no objection from the parties, the court has renewed the order accordingly using in part, an administrative process, and on occasions the judge has read the decision into the public record without the parties attending. Although this has been in respect to s.38, it could probably equally apply to s.35.)

The same provisions apply in relation to persons absconding from hospital, etc. as apply in the case of ss.35 and 36 (see 48-005; MHA 1983 ss.38(1), (3), (4) and 54(1)). Where an interim hospital order is in place, the court may make a hospital order without the offender being brought to court if he is represented by an authorised person who is given an opportunity of being heard. (MHA 1983 s.38(2)).

As to obtaining information from health authorities as to the availability of places, see 48-024.

3. The sentencing stage

Approach to sentence

The judge, at the sentencing stage, unless he makes a guardianship order, is faced with the choice of: 48-008

(1) passing an appropriate sentence of imprisonment and either:
    (a) relying on the Secretary of State's power to direct transfer to hospital for treatment; or
    (b) exercising his own power to direct treatment by adding a hospital direction (48-020); or
(2) diverting the offender from punishment by making a hospital order (48-009), and if he does so:
    (a) delegating decisions on management and discharge to the care team, based on clinical criteria, by means of an unrestricted hospital order under MHA 1983 s.37 (48-009); or
    (b) requiring the Secretary of State to oversee the risk management of the case in the interests of protection of the public, by means of a restriction order under MHA 1983 s.41 (48-012); or
(3) where appropriate, making a community order (48-022), or, if the offender is under 18, a youth rehabilitation order with a treatment requirement.

The CACD has said that in approaching sentence in a case involving a degree of mental disorder the judge should take the following steps (*R. v Birch* (1990) 90 Cr. App. R. 78 at 87):

- if a period of compulsory detention is not, or may not, be apposite, he should consider the possibility of a community order, or a youth rehabilitation order, with a requirement of in- or outpatient treatment;
- otherwise, he will need to satisfy himself that the preconditions for making a hospital order are satisfied; here he acts on the evidence of the doctors, and if left in doubt may use the provisions of ss.38 and 39 to make an interim order;
- if he is satisfied that the preconditions for a hospital order are made out, he will have to decide whether to make such an order or whether "the most suitable way of disposing of the case" is to impose a sentence of imprisonment (see 48-019);
- he must then consider whether the further condition imposed by s.41 (see 48-012 and Pt 5, restriction order) is satisfied, in which case he may make a restriction order; he is not obliged to do so, and may again consider sending the offender to prison, either for life or for a fixed term (*R. v Speake* (1957) 41 Cr. App. R. 222);
- if he decides to make a restriction order, he must make one without limit of time; and
- he must choose between an order without restriction, which may enable the author of a serious act of violence to be at liberty within months of the making of the order, and a restriction order which may lead to the offender being detained, in some cases, for a longer period than if he had been given a custodial sentence; it is, moreover, a choice which depends upon the prognosis, the ultimate responsibility for which is left to the judge.

The decision whether to make a hospital order instead of imposing a sentence of imprisonment is discretionary, and fulfilment of the pre-conditions in s.37 does not give rise to a presumption that an order will be made. Whilst the welfare of the offender is an important matter to be taken into consideration, it must be assessed in the light of the seriousness of the offence. Where there are other co-offenders, it is not wrong to take account of parity of sentencing (*R. v Khelifi* [2006] EWCA Crim 770; [2006] 2 Cr. App. R. (S.) 100).

The gravity of the offence committed is not material save that it may indicate a need for special treatment (*R. v Eaton* [1976] Crim. L.R. 390).

An offender should always be represented where the court is contemplating such an order (*R. v Blackwood* (1974) 59 Cr. App. R. 170).

The Sentencing Council guidelines, *Sentencing Offenders with mental disorders, developmental disorders, or neurological impairments* that came into force on 1 October 2020 set out a number of notes to sentencers at para.4:

- some mental disorders can fluctuate and an offender's state during proceedings may not be representative of their condition at the time the offence was committed;
- care should be taken to avoid making assumptions. Many mental disorders, neurological impairments or developmental disorders are not easily recognisable;
- no adverse inference should necessarily be drawn if an offender had not previously either been formally diagnosed or willing to disclose an impairment or disorder;

- offenders may be unaware or unwilling to accept they have an impairment or disorder and may fear stigmatisation if they disclose it;
- it is not uncommon for people to have a number of different impairments and disorders. This is known as "co-morbidity";
- drug and/or alcohol dependence can be a factor, and may mask an underlying disorder;
- difficulties of definition and classification in this field are common. There may be differences of expert opinion and diagnosis in relation to the offender or it may be that no specific disorder can be identified;
- a formal diagnosis is not always required; and
- where a formal diagnosis is required, a report by a suitably qualified expert will be necessary.

The Sentencing Council guidelines reinforce the importance of psychiatric and psychological reports being forwarded to the prison for welfare reasons where there are custodial sentences. This is also consistent with CrimPR 28.9.

4. Hospital order

General

Where a person is convicted before the Crown Court of an offence punishable with imprisonment, other than an offence for which the sentence is fixed by law, the judge may make a hospital order authorising his admission to, and detention in, a specified hospital. In the case of an offence the sentence for which would otherwise fall to be imposed under: 48-009

(1) PCA 1953 s.1A(5) (SA 2020 ss.312 and 315) (minimum sentence for offence of threatening with offensive weapon in public), FA 1968 s.51(2) (SA 2020 s.311 and Sch.20) (minimum sentence for certain firearms offences), CJA 1988 s.139AA(7) (SA 2020 ss.312 and 315) (minimum sentence for offence of threatening with article with blade or point or offensive weapon);
(2) PCC(S)A 2000 ss.110 and 111 (SA 2020 ss.313 and 314) (required minimum sentences for certain repeat offences);
(3) CJA 2003 ss.224A, 226A(4) or 226B(3) (SA 2020 ss.258, 273, 274, 283 and 285) (sentences for public protection); or
(4) VCRA 2006 s.29(4) or (6) (minimum sentences for using a person to mind a weapon),

(read in accordance with CJA 2003 s.305(4) (SA 2020 s.311 and Sch.20)) there is nothing to prevent the judge from making a hospital order.

(MHA 1983 s.37(1) (note that from 1 December 2020 the provisions in PCA 1953, FA 1968, CJA 1988, PCC(S)A 2000, CJA 2003 and VCRA 2006 are repealed and replaced by provisions of the SA 2020)).

As to the position where the judge faces a choice between a hospital order and a custodial sentence, see 48-019. As to the effect of a hospital order, see 48-011.

Preconditions for hospital order

Before a hospital order may be made, the judge must be: 48-010

(1) dealing with an offender for an imprisonable offence;
(2) satisfied on the written or oral evidence of two medical practitioners (at least one of whom is approved for the purposes of s.12 of the 1983 Act) that:

(a) the offender is suffering from mental disorder; and

(b) the mental disorder from which the offender is suffering is of a nature or degree which makes it appropriate for him to be detained in a hospital for medical treatment and appropriate treatment is available for him;

(3) satisfied, on the written or oral evidence of the approved clinician who would have overall responsibility for the offender's case or of some other person representing the managers of the hospital, that arrangements have been made for his admission within 28 days; and

(4) of the opinion, having regard to all the circumstances, including the nature of the offence and the character and antecedents of the offender, and to other available methods of dealing with him, that the most suitable method of disposing of the case is by means of a hospital order (see, e.g. *R. v IA* [2005] EWCA Crim 2077; [2006] 1 Cr. App. R. (S.) 91) (MHA 1983 s.37(2)).

As to the improper combination of such a sentence with other orders, see 48-023.

In view of (4), even where the other criteria are met, the judge has a duty to decide whether a hospital order is the most suitable method of disposing of the case, or whether there ought to be a custodial sentence, see 48-019.

Effect of order

48-011 Once the offender is admitted to hospital pursuant to such an order, unless it is accompanied by a restriction order under s.41, his position is almost exactly the same as if he were a civil patient. In effect he passes out of the penal system and into the hospital regime; neither the judge nor the Secretary of State has any say in his disposal. Thus:

(1) he becomes a patient to be managed at the discretion of his responsible clinician;

(2) he can be discharged at any time by the responsible clinician, the question informing the decision to discharge being whether his disorder, and the risk arising from it, justifies his continuing detention for medical treatment;

(3) the order will lapse after six months, if it has not already been discharged, unless renewed by the responsible clinician;

(4) from the point where renewal is made, the patient is entitled to seek review of his detention by the Mental Health Review Tribunal, as is his nearest relative; and

(5) the responsible clinician may discharge him into the community subject to conditions, under a community treatment order, which will include conditions that the patient be available to his care team as directed to ensure that he receives the treatment he requires, or for purposes of assessment; he may be recalled to hospital by the responsible clinician if that becomes necessary, to ensure that he receives the treatment he needs, for his own health and safety or for the protection of others. Community Treatment Orders may be used in the following sections: 37, 45A, 47, 48 and 51.

The community treatment order lapses after six months unless renewed and can be lifted at any time by the responsible clinician or the Tribunal. Unless a community treatment order is made, discharge from hospital signals the end of any obligation on the patient to accept treatment. His responsible clinician, or the

Tribunal, can discharge him absolutely at any time. He can also apply for a discharge by the hospital managers. These reviews are in practice delegated to volunteers who may have no legal or clinical knowledge but are nonetheless empowered to override the opinion of the responsible clinician.

It is thus essential, where doubt in relation to future risk exists at the time of sentencing, for the judge to make a restriction order, since otherwise a patient under a hospital order may be discharged without regard to the criteria which his clinical supervisor would have to apply.

The decision whether to make a hospital order is one for the judge's discretion. There is no kind of presumption that where an offender meets the conditions specified in s.37(2) a hospital order will be made (*R. v Khelifi* [2006] EWCA Crim 770; [2006] 2 Cr. App. R. (S.) 100).

The Tribunal has discretion to discharge the patient from hospital even where the criteria for detention are met, and must do so if it is not satisfied that he remains mentally disordered to a nature or degree which justifies his continuing detention in hospital for medical treatment; or if it is not satisfied that his detention is not necessary for his own health or safety or for the protection of others. It has no power to discharge subject to a community treatment order, thus a discharge by the tribunal invariably terminates an unrestricted hospital order absolutely.

The Sentencing Council guidelines, *Sentencing Offenders with mental disorders, developmental disorders, or neurological impairments* that came into force on 1 October 2020 set out at Annex C the criteria and release provisions for hospital orders. There is also a section in the same annex setting out the effect of the orders and the release provisions.

5. Restriction order

General

A restriction order is an order under MHA 1983 s.41 which accompanies a hospital order in cases where the judge considers that for the protection of the public from serious harm, the offender should not be released from hospital without careful consideration by either the Secretary of State or by the Tribunal. The order prevents the offender from being discharged, granted leave of absence or transferred to another hospital without the approval of the Secretary of State. In certain circumstances a restricted patient may be discharged by the Tribunal (MHA 1983 s.41; HO 1990). **48-012**

Preconditions

The judge may, where he makes a hospital order in respect of an offender, also make a restriction order, ordering that the offender be subject to special restrictions, provided that: **48-013**

(1) having regard to the nature of the offence, the antecedents of the offender, and the risk of his committing offences if set at large, he considers it necessary for the protection of the public from serious harm to do so; and
(2) at least one of the medical practitioners whose evidence is taken into account has given evidence orally before the court (MHA 1983 s.41).

Under the amendments effected by MHA 2007, all restriction orders are now to be made without limit of time. In the ordinary case, where punishment as such is not intended and the object is that the offender should receive treatment and be at large again as soon as he can safely be discharged, a restriction order is not appropriate (*R. v Morris* (1961) 45 Cr. App. R. 185); but a restriction order ought to be made, where the judge considers that the public needs to be protected:

(a) in cases of violence or the more serious sexual offences, particularly if the offender has a record of involving violent behaviour (*R. v Gardiner* (1967) 51 Cr. App. R. 187; *R. v Birch* (1989) 11 Cr. App. R. (S.) 202);

(b) in the case of the anti-social pest who requires treatment under a hospital order (*R. v Toland* (1974) 58 Cr. App. R. 453; *R. v Royse* (1981) 3 Cr. App. R. (S.) 58); and

(c) where doubt in relation to future risk exists at the time of sentencing.

The section places the responsibility of making a restriction order on the judge if, in his opinion, it is necessary for the protection of the public; the fact that all the medical witnesses advise against it does not mean that it is wrong in principle, but there must be evidence on which to base such an order (*R. v Courtney* (1987) 9 Cr. App. R. (S.) 404).

Effect of restriction order

48-014 In marked contrast with the regime under the ordinary hospital order, is an order coupled with a restriction on discharge pursuant to s.41. Such an order is not a separate means of disposal; it has no existence independently of the hospital order to which it relates. It does, however, fundamentally affect the circumstances in which the patient is detained.

Where the judge imposes a restriction order, he is still ordering treatment as a substitute for punishment. The distinction from the unrestricted order is that he has concluded, in the light of the circumstances of the offender and the offence that decisions on liberty should not be left to clinical discretion. The patient's management will still be determined by clinical assessment of his mental disorder and the risks arising from it, but the Secretary of State for Justice becomes responsible for the risk assessment informing decisions to grant greater liberty and, consequently for taking those decisions. The making of a restriction order has a number of significant effects on the hospital order. Thus:

(1) it converts it into an order of indefinite duration; it does not require regular renewal to prevent it from lapsing, but remains in force indefinitely until it is discharged by the responsible clinician with the agreement of the Secretary of State under s.23, or s.42 or by the Tribunal under ss.73 or 75;

(2) nearest relatives have no powers in respect of restricted patients; nor can a restricted patient be discharged by hospital managers, unless the Secretary of State for Justice agrees;

(3) restrictions relieve the responsible clinician of ultimate responsibility for protecting the public from further harm, by requiring him to obtain the Secretary of State's agreement to certain decisions; his agreement is required before the patient can be given leave in the community, can be transferred to a different hospital or discharged into the community;

(4) a restricted patient may be, and usually is, discharged into the community subject to conditions; this is to ensure that the patient continues to receive the medical treatment he needs, and to protect the public; he may be made subject to supervision by social and psychiatric supervisors, charged with

keeping the Secretary of State informed of the patient's progress and behaviour in the community;

(5) the patient may be recalled to hospital by the Secretary of State at any time if he decides it is necessary for the protection of the public, and provided he has current medical evidence of mental disorder; and

(6) the conditionally discharged patient remains liable to detention in hospital, and consequently to recall, unless and until the Secretary of State lifts his restrictions under s.42(1), or the Tribunal orders absolute discharge from his restrictions under s.75.

The Tribunal is required to order the discharge of a patient if not satisfied that the nature or degree of his disorder, on the day of the hearing, justifies his liability to detention in hospital. It cannot sanction continuing detention of the patient simply because he is dangerous. A restricted hospital order will be absolutely discharged in the great majority of cases well within the offender's lifetime, when his mental disorder is assessed as insufficiently serious to justify continuing liability to detention. Unlike the life or indeterminate sentence, a restricted hospital order is not, therefore, a device which can invariably protect the public from further harm for the offender's lifetime. Restrictions can, however, remain in place for as long as all parties, including the Tribunal, assess that they are necessary in the light of risk arising from the offender's mental disorder.

Approach to restriction order

The judge is required to assess not the seriousness of the risk that the accused will re-offend, but the risk that if he does so the public will suffer serious harm. In *R. v Birch* (1990) 90 Cr. App. R. 78 where the principles were reviewed, the CACD was of the opinion that: **48-015**

(1) the harm need not be limited to personal injury;

(2) the harm need not relate to the public in general, it suffices if a single person or category of persons is at risk; and

(3) the potential harm must however be serious; a high possibility of a recurrence of minor offences is not enough.

The decision whether to make an order is one for the judge; he may make an order even where the medical witnesses do not advise it (*R. v Royse* (1981) 3 Cr. App. R. (S.) 58; cf. *R. v Reynolds, The Times,* 1 November 2000). The seriousness of the offence is only one of the factors which he is required to take into consideration.

A minor offence by an offender who is shown to be mentally disordered and dangerous may be the subject of a restriction order; conversely, a serious offence committed by an offender adjudged to have a low risk of re-offending may lead to a restriction order being made (*R. v Courtney* (1987) 9 Cr. App. R. (S.) 404; *R. v Khan* (1987) 9 Cr. App. R. (S.) 455).

A restriction order should not be imposed merely to mark the gravity of the offence (though this is a factor in the assessment of risk), or as a means of punishment, since a hospital order is not intended for that purpose.

Restriction order after committal by magistrates

Where an offender is committed to the Crown Court by a magistrates' court, with a view to a restriction order being made, the judge must enquire into the circumstances of the case, and: **48-016**

(1) if he has power under s.41 to do so, and the offence is punishable on summary conviction with imprisonment, he may make a hospital order with or without a restriction order (see *R. v Avbunudje* (1999) 2 Cr. App. R. (S.) 189); or

(2) if he does not make such an order, he may deal with the offender in any other manner in which the magistrates could have dealt with him (MHA 1981 s.43(1) and (2)).

The Crown Court has the same powers to make orders under ss.35, 36 and 38 as in the case of a person convicted before it.

Restriction order: naming a hospital unit

48-017 Where the judge makes a restriction order, he may direct that the patient be detained in hospital at a level of security that he deems necessary to ensure protection of the public; he may do the same in the case of a hospital direction.

The majority of hospital trusts manage accommodation ranging from medium secure to locked wards or unlocked wards. A hospital order directing admission to clinical commissioning group or a Local Health Board in Wales or a major psychiatric hospital, will give to the hospital managers a discretion over the level of security under which the patient is detained. The judge may wish to specify a level of security if the offender has been found to present a risk of serious harm to others, where he presents a serious escape or absconding risk, or where his hospital admission is attached to a life, or indeterminate sentence under a hospital direction.

Note that:

(1) naming a hospital unit allows the judge to require that the patient be detained under the level of security he deems appropriate;

(2) the unit named may be any unit of an individual hospital which the judge chooses to name;

(3) the intention is that it should be a ward or secure unit which offers a specific level of security, so that in naming it, the judge is directing the offender's detention under that category of security; if the judge does not have adequate knowledge of the levels of security available in the hospital to which it wishes to order admission, MHA 1983 s.39 (see 48-024) may serve to acquire that information;

(4) while clinicians who will be responsible for the patient's care are likely to be ready to advise the judge on the naming of hospital units, the discretion lies with the judge; and

(5) the practical effect of naming a hospital unit is that the Secretary of State's authority is required to move the offender to a different level of security, whether in a different hospital or the one to which the offender was admitted (MHA 1983 s.43(1) and (3)).

The Secretary of State may agree, in due course, to remove the requirement to detain within a named unit, allowing the offender to be managed more flexibly within the hospital. This would happen after a risk assessment had concluded that the offender's management could safely be managed without the constraints of a named unit.

Restriction order; ancillary provisions

Where a restriction order is made, the judge should ascertain that the hospital to which the offender is to be admitted has the facilities for his safe custody (*R. v Cox* (1968) 52 Cr. App. R. 106). "Place of safety" is defined in s.55 MHA 1983 (as amended in 2007) as: **48-018**

"in relation to a person who is not a child or young person, means any police station, prison or remand centre, or any hospital the managers of which are willing temporarily to receive him, and in relation to a child or young person has the same meaning as in the CYPA 1933."

In addition:

(1) arrangements may be made for his admission to hospital in any part of the country where a vacancy exists; and
(2) the judge may give such directions as he thinks fit for his conveyance to a place of safety and his detention there, pending his admission to hospital within 28 days (*R. v Marsden* (1968) 52 Cr. App. R. 301).

The Sentencing Council guidelines, *Sentencing Offenders with mental disorders, developmental disorders, or neurological impairments* that came into force on 1 October 2020 set out at Annex C the criteria and release provisions for restriction orders. There is also a section in the same annex setting out the effect of the orders and the release provisions.

Custodial sentence as an alternative

Where the offences committed pass the custody threshold (see DEALING WITH AN OFFENDER), the judge is bound to consider whether a custodial sentence or a hospital order (if necessary with a restriction order) is more appropriate (*R. v Drew* [2003] UKHL 25; [2003] 2 Cr.App. R. 24). **48-019**

A custodial sentence may be chosen by a judge as an alternative to a hospital order either because:

(1) the offender is dangerous and no suitable secure hospital accommodation is available; or
(2) there is an element of culpability in the offence which merits punishment, as may happen where there is no connection between the mental disorder and the offence, or where the offender's responsibility for the offence is reduced but not wholly extinguished.

In such a case, where appropriate, the judge should:

(a) decide whether a period of compulsory detention is apposite; if the answer is that it is not, or may not be, the possibility of a probation order with a condition of in- or outpatient treatment should be considered;
(b) ask himself whether the conditions contained in s.37(2)(a) for the making of a hospital order are satisfied; here the judge acts on the evidence of the doctors (if left in doubt, he may avail himself of the provisions of ss.38 and 39 to make an interim hospital order, giving him and the doctors further time to decide between hospitals with or without restrictions and some other disposal, and to require the relevant authority to furnish information on arrangements for the admission of the offender);

(c) if he concludes that the conditions empowering him to make an order are satisfied, consider whether to make such an order, or whether "the most suitable method of disposing of the case" (s.37(2)(b)) is to impose a sentence of imprisonment; and

(d) finally, consider whether the further condition imposed by s.41(1) is satisfied; if it is, he may make a restriction order; but he is not obliged to do so, and may again consider sending the offender to prison, either for life or for a fixed term; if he does decide on a restriction order, he must then choose between an unlimited order, or one for a fixed term.

(*R. v Birch* (1989) 11 Cr. App. R. (S.) 202 and see the analysis by the CACD of how the judge should determine where the balance between prison and hospital falls in *Attorney General's Reference (No.54 of 2011)* [2013] EWCA Crim 2276; [2012] 1 Cr. App. R. (S.) 106 (prison) and in *R. v Fort* [2013] EWCA Crim 2332 (hospital)).

Where an offender is judged to be dangerous, imprisonment rather than a mental health order should follow (*R. v Jenkin* [2012] EWCA Crim 2557; [2013] Crim. L.R. 246).

Special considerations apply where the custodial sentence contemplated is a life sentence (see *R. v IA* [2005] EWCA Crim 2077; [2006] 1 Cr. App. R. (S.) 91; *R. v Beatty* [2006] EWCA Crim 2359; *R. v Simpson* [2007] EWCA Crim 2666; [2008] 1 Cr. App. R. (S.) 111; *R. v Hughes* [2010] EWCA Crim 1026); [2010] M.H.L.R. 188).

6. Hospital direction; s.45A

General

48-020 Where an offender convicted of an offence before the Crown Court, the sentence for which is not fixed by law, and the judge:

(1) considers making a hospital order in respect of him before deciding to impose a sentence of imprisonment ("the relevant sentence");

(2) is satisfied, on the written or oral evidence of two registered medical practitioners, that:
  (a) the offender is suffering from a mental disorder;
  (b) that the mental disorder is of a nature or degree which makes it appropriate for him to be detained in a hospital for medical treatment; and
  (c) such medical treatment is available for him,

he may (MHA 1983 s.45A) give both of the following directions:

(i) a *hospital direction* that the offender, instead of being removed to and detained in prison, be removed to and detained in a specified hospital; and

(ii) a *limitation direction*, that the offender be subject to the special restrictions imposed by s.41 (48-011),

but the latter direction should not be given unless one of the medical practitioners has given oral evidence before the court.

(See *R. v M* [2014] EWCA Crim 1641. The Court of Appeal made clear that s.45A(3) does not incorporate into it the conditions set out in s.41(1) for a restriction order as a prerequisite for the making of a restriction direction.)

Similar provisions as to admission, etc. apply as in the case of a hospital order (48-017).

These directions must not be given unless the judge is satisfied on the oral or written evidence of the approved clinician who would have overall responsibility for his case, or of some other person representing the hospital managers, that arrangements have been made for the patient's admission within 28 days.

Effect of s.45A direction

A hospital direction enables the judge to combine the effects of an order for treatment in hospital with the tariff associated with a prison sentence. Under the 1997 Act, a hospital direction could only be made for offenders categorised as psychopathically disordered; under the 2007 Act, there is no sub-categorisation of mental disorder, and a hospital direction is available in respect of any offender who receives a prison sentence, except where the sentence is fixed by law. **48-021**

Section 45A thus gives the judge who is considering the imposition of a "sentence of imprisonment" on an offender (as opposed to hospital orders under both ss.37 and 41 of the MHA):

(1) the power to sentence the offender to imprisonment; but
(2) at the same time, to give a direction for the offender's removal to hospital for treatment; together with
(3) a limitation direction which is the equivalent of a restriction order under s.41 of the MHA; provided that
(4) the conditions set out in s.45A(2) are fulfilled.

An order made under this section is to be contrasted with the situation where a court has imposed a sentence of imprisonment and then there is a pause and then the Secretary of State makes an order for a transfer to a hospital under s.47.

In *R. v Cooper* [2010] EWCA Crim 2335; [2010] M.H.L.R. 240 the court dealt with the origins of s.45A, to be found in the White Paper, *Protecting the Public*, published in 1999, which included the following analysis proposed a "hybrid order" for certain mentally disordered offenders, for whom the present form of hospital order is unsatisfactory, particularly those who are considered to bear a significant degree of responsibility for their offences. The order would enable the judge, in effect, to pass a prison sentence upon an offender and at the same time his immediate admission to hospital for medical treatment. See also *R. v Staines* [2006] EWCA Crim 15; [2006] 2 Cr. App. R. (S.) 61.

In *R. v Lucinda Vowles* [2015] EWCA Crim 45 further consideration was given to the differing regimes under s.37 and 41 of the MHA and indeterminate sentences. The decision for release is made by the Parole Board under the latter whereas the First-tier Tribunal (Health, Education and Social Care Chamber) (Mental Health) make the decision under the s.37/41 route.

The court set out the approach to be adopted. A judge must consider, where the conditions of s.37(2)(a) MHA are met, what is the appropriate disposal. The matters to be considered include: (1) the extent to which the offender needs treatment for the mental disorder from which the offender suffers; (2) the extent to which the offending is attributable to the mental disorder; (3) the extent to which punishment is required; and (4) the protection of the public including the regime for deciding release and the regime after release. There must always be sound reasons for departing from the usual course of imposing a penal sentence and the judge must set these out.

It is also stated that the fact that two psychiatrists are of the opinion that a hospital order with restrictions under s.37/41 is the right disposal is never a reason on its own to make such an order. The judge must first consider all the relevant circumstances, including the four matters set out in the previous paragraph and then consider the alternatives in order.

In a case where (1) the evidence of medical practitioners suggests that the offender is suffering from a mental disorder; (2) that the offending is wholly or in significant part attributable to that disorder; and (3) treatment is available, and it considers in the light of all the circumstances, that a hospital order (with or without a restriction) may be an appropriate way of dealing with the case, consider the matters in the following order:

(i) As the terms of s.45A(1) of the MHA require, before a hospital order is made under s.37/41, whether or not with a restriction order, a judge should consider whether the mental disorder can appropriately be dealt with by a hospital and limitation direction under s.45A.
(ii) If it can, then the judge should make such a direction under s.45A(1). This consideration will not apply to a person under the age of 21 at the time of conviction as there is no power to make such an order.
(iii) If such a direction is not appropriate the court must then consider, before going further, whether, if the medical evidence satisfies the condition in s.37(2)(a) (that the mental disorder is such that it would be appropriate for the offender to be detained in a hospital and treatment is available), the conditions set out in s.37(2)(b) would make that the most suitable method of disposal. It is essential that a judge gives detailed consideration to all the factors encompassed within s.37(2)(b). For example, in a case where the court is considering a life sentence under the Criminal Justice Act 2003 as amended in 2012 (following the guidance given in *Attorney General's Reference (No.27 of 2013); R. v Burinskas* [2014] 1 W.L.R. 4209), if (1) the mental disorder is treatable; (2) once treated there is no evidence he would be in any way dangerous; and (3) the offending is entirely due to that mental disorder, a hospital order under s.37/41 is likely to be the correct disposal.
(iv) Although the Court of Appeal set out the general circumstances to which a court should have regard but, as the language of s.37(2)(b) makes clear, the court must also have regard to the question of whether other methods of dealing with a defendant are available. This includes consideration of whether the powers under s.47 for transfer to hospital for treatment would, taking into account all the other circumstances, be appropriate.

In *R. v Ahmed* [2016] EWCA Crim 670 the court considered the decision in *Vowles*. Both cases were the subject of further consideration in *R. v Edwards* [2018] EWCA Crim 595. In *Edwards* the court set out a summary of the principles extracted from the statutory framework and the case law:

(i) the first step is to consider whether a hospital order may be appropriate;
(ii) if so, the judge should then consider all his sentencing options including a s.45A order;
(iii) in deciding on the most suitable disposal the judge should remind him or herself of the importance of the penal element in a sentence;
(iv) to decide whether a penal element to the sentence is necessary the judge should assess (as best he or she can) the offender's culpability and the harm caused by the offence. The fact that an offender would not have com-

mitted the offence but for their mental illness does not necessarily relieve them of all responsibility for their actions;

(v) a failure to take prescribed medication is not necessarily a culpable omission; it may be attributable in whole or in part to the offender's mental illness;

(vi) if the judge decides to impose a hospital order under s.37/41, he or she must explain why a penal element is not appropriate; and

(vii) the regimes on release of an offender on licence from a s.45A order and for an offender subject to s.37/41 orders are different but the latter do not necessarily offer a greater protection to the public, as may have been assumed in Ahmed and/or or by the parties in the cases before us. Each case turns on its own facts.

In *R. v Westwood* [2020] EWCA Crim 598 the CACD quashed an extended sentence and a s.45A direction with orders under s.37/41 as a better way of protecting the public.

The Sentencing Council guidelines, *Sentencing Offenders with mental disorders, developmental disorders, or neurological impairments* that came into force on 1 October 2020 set out at Annex C the criteria and release provisions for s.45A orders. There is also a section in the same annex setting out the effect of the orders and the release provisions. The facts and individual circumstances of cases will clearly vary. In *R. v Cleland* [2020] EWCA Crim 906; [2020] 7 WLUK 209 (and in *R. v Nelson* [2020] EWCA Crim 1615; [2020] 12 WLUK 8) the CACD returned to the topic of the relationship as between ss.37, 41 and 45A and the importance, unless it would be contrary to the interests of justice, to follow the SC Guideline.

Section 45A not available where offender under 21

An order under s.45A cannot be made in respect of an offender who is under 21 at the time of conviction and is thus being considered for a sentence of custody for life, as opposed to a sentence of imprisonment, as would be the case on a person over 21 at the date of conviction (*Attorney General's Reference (No.54 of 2011)* [2013] EWCA 2276; [2012] 1 Cr. App. R. (S.) 106; *R. v Fort* [2013] EWCA Crim 2332). **48-022**

An offender under 21 cannot lawfully be sentenced to a term of imprisonment even if he attains 21 by the time he is sentenced (PCC(S)A 2000 s.89; *R. v Danga* (1992) 94 Cr. App. R. 252).

Where:

(1) an offender aged between 18 and 21 is convicted of an offence for which the sentence is not fixed by law; and

(2) for which, if he were over 21 he would be liable to imprisonment for life,

the judge "shall, if it considers that a sentence for life would be appropriate" sentence the offender to "custody for life" (PCC(S)A 2000 s.94).

That is not a sentence of imprisonment, as is clear from the provisions of PCC(S)A 2000 s.95 which stipulates that a person who is sentenced to custody for life will be detained in a young offender institution unless the Secretary of State orders that he is to be detained in a prison or remand centre.

The Sentencing Council guidelines, *Sentencing Offenders with mental disorders, developmental disorders, or neurological impairments* that came into force on 1 October 2020 set out at Annex C the criteria and release provisions for s.45A orders.

There is also a section in the same annex setting out the effect of the orders and the release provisions.

7. GUARDIANSHIP ORDER

48-023 An alternative to a community order under CJA 2003 Pt 12, or a youth rehabilitation order within the meaning of CJIA 2008 Pt 1, with a requirement of treatment may be, in some cases, a guardianship order which places the offender under the guardianship either of the local authority social services department, or of some person approved by the local authority (such as a relative). The conditions for the making of a guardianship order are essentially the same as those for a hospital order.

The judge will need to be satisfied:

(1) in the case of an offender who has attained the age of 16, that the mental disorder is of a nature or degree which warrants his reception into guardianship; and
(2) that the local authority or other person is willing to receive him into guardianship.

The order gives the guardian power to require the offender to live at a specified place, to attend specified places at specified times for treatment, occupation, education or training, and to allow access to any doctor, approved social worker or other person specified. The disadvantage is that there is no sanction available to the court in the event of non-compliance as there is in the case of a community order, or a youth rehabilitation order.

The Sentencing Council guidelines, *Sentencing Offenders with mental disorders, developmental disorders, or neurological impairments* that came into force on 1 October 2020 set out at Annex C the criteria and release provisions for guardianship orders. There is also a section in the same annex setting out the effect of the orders and the release provisions.

8. COMMUNITY ORDER WITH MEDICAL TREATMENT REQUIREMENT

48-024 Where imprisonment is inexpedient, the court may consider making a community order with a requirement of medical treatment (see COMMUNITY SENTENCES) or a youth rehabilitation order with a similar requirement (see YOUTH REHABILITATION ORDERS). Where the judge:

(1) requests a medical examination of the accused and a report; or
(2) requires information about the arrangements that could be made for the accused where he is considering:
    (a) a hospital order; or
    (b) a guardianship order,

unless the judge otherwise directs, the court officer must, as soon as practicable, serve on each person from whom a report or information is sought a note that:

(i) specifies the power exercised by court;
(ii) explains why the court seeks a report or information from that person; and

(iii) sets out or summarises any relevant information available to the court.

9. Miscellaneous

Improper combination of sentence

When making a hospital or guardianship order, the judge may not, in addition: **48-025**

(1) pass a sentence of imprisonment, impose a fine, or make a community order within the meaning of CJA 2003 Pt 12, or a youth rehabilitation order within the meaning of CJIA 2008 Pt 1;
(2) make an order under PCC(S)A 2000 s.150, binding over the parent or guardian of a juvenile offender; or
(3) if the order is a hospital order, make a referral order within the meaning of PCC(S)A 2000 in respect of the offence.

Information from Health Authorities

Where a court is minded to make a hospital order, or an interim hospital order, in respect of any person, it may request the Integrated Care Board or the Local Health Board for the region in which that person resides or last resided, or the National Health Service Commissioning Board (NHS England), the National Assembly for Wales or any other Integrated Care Board or Local Health Board any that seems to the court to be appropriate to furnish the court with such information as it has, or can reasonably obtain, with respect to the hospital or hospitals in its region or elsewhere at which arrangements could be made for the admission of that person. **48-026**

In the case of a person who has not attained the age of 18, this provision has effect as if reference to the making of a hospital order included a remand under ss.35 or 36, or the making of an order under s.44. In the case of such a person, the information which may be requested may include information about the availability of age-appropriate accommodation or facilities.

In Wales, such a request should be addressed to the Secretary of State.

Adding a sexual harm prevention order (SHPO)

Where a judge deals with an offender: **48-027**

(1) in respect of an offence listed in SOA 2003 Schs 3 or 5; or s.104
(2) in respect of a finding that:
  (a) he is not guilty of such an offence by reason of insanity; or
  (b) he is under a disability and has done the act charged against him in respect of such an offence; and
(3) the judge is satisfied that it is necessary to make such an order, for the purpose of protecting the public, or any particular member of the public, from serious harm from the offender,

he may make a sexual harm prevention order in respect of him, as to which see SEX OFFENDER ORDERS (SOA 2003 s.103A).

Reports by medical practitioners

The registered practitioner whose evidence is taken into account under s.35(3)(a) and at least one of the registered medical practitioners whose evidence is taken into **48-028** account under ss.36(1), 37(2)(a), 38(1), 45A(2) and 51(6)(a) and whose reports are taken into consideration under ss.47(1) and 48(1) must be a practitioner approved for the purpose by the Secretary of State as having special expertise in the diagnosis or treatment of mental disorder.

Where, for the purposes of provision of this Part of MHA 1983 under which a judge may act on the written evidence of any person, a report in writing purporting to be signed by that person may be received in evidence without proof of:

(1) the signature of that person; or
(2) of his having the requisite qualifications or approval or authority or of being of the requisite description to give the report,

but the judge may require the signatory of any such report to attend and give oral evidence.

Where, in pursuance of a direction of the court, any such report is tendered in evidence otherwise than by or on behalf of the person who is the subject of the report then:

(a) if that person is represented by an advocate or solicitor, a copy of the report must be given to that advocate or solicitor;
(b) if that person is not represented, the substance of the report must be disclosed to him or, if he is a child or young person, to his parent or guardian if present in court; and
(c) except where the report relates only to his admission to hospital, that person may require the signatory of the report to be called to give oral evidence and evidence to rebut that contained in the report may be called by or on behalf of that person.

See REPORTS. As to the expenses of any such practitioner, see COSTS AND ASSESSMENT.

Information to be supplied on admission to hospital or guardianship

48-029 Where the judge:

(1) orders the accused's detention and treatment in hospital; or
(2) makes a guardianship order,

unless the judge otherwise directs, the court officer will, as soon as practicable, serve on (as applicable) the hospital or the guardian:

(a) a record of the court's order;
(b) such information as the court has received that appears likely to assist in treating or otherwise dealing with the accused, including information about:
    (i) the accused's mental condition;
    (ii) his other circumstances; and
    (iii) the circumstances of the offence.

(CrimPR 28.9)

48-030 There is guidance providing an overview of the restricted patient system in England and Wales and the role of the Secretary of State for Justice and the MHCS in HMPPS produced by the MoJ. (Mentally disordered offenders—the restricted patient system—Background Briefing V1 issued December 2017). The briefing sets out the different types of restriction order and directions and transfers. The briefing makes clear that for determinate or fixed term sentences, where the prisoner remains in hospital, the restrictions will expire at the point of the automatic release date and they will then be managed solely by doctors with no input from the Secretary of State as an unrestricted patient.

(Sometimes referred to as "notional s37s"). For indeterminate sentences the restrictions will remain in place for so long as the patient remains detained in hospital. Someone hospitalised through the criminal justice system should be identified as a "MAPPA" case. The Multi-Agency Public Protection Arrangements are a vital part of safeguarding.

49. OATHS AND FORMALITIES

QUICK GUIDE

A. Oaths and Affirmations

1. Legal requirements

49-001 An oath is taken, or an affirmation is made, by a witness prior to giving evidence and by a juror following empanelment. If an oath is taken it may be taken in the manner, and with the effect, prescribed by the Oaths Act 1978 ss.1–6:

(1) the person swearing shall hold the New Testament, or, in the case of a Jew, the Old Testament, in his uplifted hand and shall say or repeat after the officer administering the oath the words "I swear by Almighty God that" followed by the words of the oath prescribed by law;
(2) unless the person to be sworn objects, or is incapable of taking the oath, it shall be administered as in (1) above;
(3) in the case of a person who is neither a Christian nor a Jew, the oath shall be administered in any lawful manner; it is for the person swearing to specify the holy book on which, or the manner by which, he wishes to be sworn;
(4) any person who objects to taking an oath may instead make a solemn affirmation which has the same force and effect as an oath. The form is "I do solemnly, sincerely and truly declare and affirm that";
(5) any person desiring to swear with uplifted hand, in the form and manner used in Scotland, is permitted to do so (s.3); and
(6) where an oath has been taken the fact that the person taking it had, at the time, no religious belief, does not affect the validity of the oath (s.4).

Where an oath is to be taken by a child or young person, the Oaths Act 1978 s.1 has effect so that the words "I promise before Almighty God" are used instead of the words "I swear by Almighty God". The oath taken in either form is deemed to have been duly taken (CYPA 1963 s.28(1)).

It is customary for Sikhs and Muslims to be sworn on vernacular editions of their own Books.

2. The effect of the oath or affirmation

49-002 Failure to comply with the words prescribed in the Oaths Act 1978 will not necessarily invalidate the oath or affirmation, so long as it was taken or made in such a way as was binding, and intended to be binding, on the conscience of the taker (*R. v Chapman* [1980] Crim. L.R. 42, where the witness failed to take the testament in his hand). Similarly, the lawfulness of an oath depends not on the intricacies of the witness's religion but on whether:

(a) the oath taken appeared to the court to be binding on the conscience of the witness; and
(b) the witness himself considered his conscience to be bound (*R. v Kemble* [1990] 91 Cr. App. R. 178).

A witness may not usually be questioned as to the form of his oath but where a witness desires to affirm when he is reasonably expected to take the oath on a holy book, see *R. v Mehrban* [2001] EWCA Crim 2627; [2002] 1 Cr. App. R. 40; see also *R. v Mahmood* [2012] EWCA Crim 3107 concerning the circumstances in which cross-examination may be permissible and the appropriate direction to the jury.

3. Children and young persons aged 14 and over

No witness in criminal proceedings may be sworn unless: **49-003**

(1) he has attained the age of 14 years; and
(2) he has a sufficient appreciation of the solemnity of the occasion and of the particular responsibility to tell the truth which is involved in taking an oath.

A person, if he is able to give intelligible testimony, is presumed to have a sufficient appreciation of those things unless any party adduces evidence to show the contrary and, if such evidence is adduced, the burden is on the party seeking to have the witness sworn to prove the matters in (1) and (2) above.

A person is able to give intelligible testimony if he is able to:

(a) understand questions put to him as a witness; and
(b) give answers to them which can be understood.

(YJCEA 1999 s.55)

If, by virtue of YJCEA 1999 s.55(2), a person is not permitted to be sworn for the purpose of giving evidence on oath, his evidence shall be given unsworn. No conviction, verdict or finding in proceedings in which such a person gave evidence may be taken as unsafe for the purposes of CAA 1968 ss.2(1), 13(1) and 16(1); YJCEA 1999 s.56(1), (2) and (5).

Where a child is aged 14 or over and his evidence has been admitted by means of a pre-recorded interview under YJCEA 1999 s.27 (see SPECIAL MEASURES), he should take the oath prior to cross-examination (*R. v Simmonds* [1996] Crim. L.R. 816).

4. Children aged under 14

For the evidence of children generally see CHILDREN AND YOUNG PERSONS. **49-004**

5. Jurors

The wording of the affirmation to be made by jurors is set out in *CPD* VI 26E. **49-005**
The precise wording of an oath to be taken on a Holy Book will depend on the juror's faith as indicated to the court.

B. Oaths and Formalities: wording

49-006 The following are commonly used forms of wording.

(1) *Arraignment*

"A .... B .... you stand indicted for that you, on the .... day of .... (e.g. stole) .... How say you A .... B .... are you guilty or not guilty?"

(2) *Challenge to jurors*

"A .... B ...., the names that you are about to hear called are the names of the jurors who will try you. If, therefore, you wish to object to them, or to any of them, you must do so as they come to the Book to be sworn and before they are sworn, and your objection shall be heard."

(3) *Jurors' oath or affirmation*

(a) *On trial*

(i) The oath to be taken by jurors is:

"I swear by Almighty God that I will faithfully try the defendant(s), and give a true verdict according to the evidence."

(ii) The words of affirmation are:

"I do solemnly, sincerely and truly declare and affirm that I will faithfully try the defendant(s), and give a true verdict according to the evidence."

(b) *Defendant standing mute*

"I swear by Almighty God [or, "I solemnly, sincerely and truly declare and affirm"] that I will well and truly try whether A .... B ...., the defendant, who stands charged with ...., is mute of malice, or will not answer directly to the indictment wilfully and of malice, or by the Visitation of God, and, give a true verdict according to the evidence."

(4) *Putting the jury in charge*

"Members of the Jury, the defendant A .... B .... stands indicted for that he, on the .... day of .... (e.g. stole) .... To this indictment he has pleaded not guilty, and it is your charge to say, having heard the evidence, whether he be guilty or not guilty."

(5) *Witness's oath or affirmation*

"I swear by Almighty God [or "I solemnly, sincerely and truly declare and affirm"] that the evidence I shall give shall be the truth, the whole truth, and nothing but the truth."

(6) *Witness under 18*

"I promise (before Almighty God) to tell the truth, the whole truth, and nothing but the truth."

(7) *Interpreter's oath or affirmation*

"I swear by Almighty God [or "I solemnly, sincerely and truly declare and affirm"] that I will well and faithfully interpret, and true explanation make, of all such matters and things as shall be required of me, according to the best of my skill and understanding." (For the form of the oath in Welsh, see Welsh Courts (Oaths & Interpreters) Rules 1943 (S R & O 1943/683), as amended by SI 1959/1507 and SI 1972/97.)

(8) *Jury retiring: bailiff's oath*

"I shall keep this jury together in some private and convenient place; I shall suffer none to speak to them, neither shall I speak to them myself, concerning the trial here this day, without leave of the court, unless it be to ask them if they are agreed upon their verdict."

(9) *Voir dire*

"I swear by Almighty God [or "I solemnly, sincerely and truly declare and affirm"] that I will true answer make to all such questions as may be asked of me."

(10) *Intermediary declaration*

"I swear by Almighty God [or "I solemnly, sincerely and truly declare"] that I will well and faithfully communicate questions and answers and make true explanation of all matters and things as shall be required of me according to the best of my skill and understanding." (See further SPECIAL MEASURES DIRECTIONS.)

(11) *Person accompanying witness into Live Link TV room*

"I swear by almighty God [or "I solemnly, sincerely and truly declare and affirm"] that I will adhere to the instructions given by the learned judge and observe them fully." (For procedure see SPECIAL MEASURES DIRECTIONS.)

As to the use of the Welsh language in courts in Wales, see *CPD* 3J and 3K (and see further WELSH LANGUAGE CASES).

50. REPORTING AND ACCESS RESTRICTIONS

Quick Guide

1. Approach to reporting restrictions

The principle of open justice

50-001 The general rule is that:

(1) open justice is an essential principle in the criminal courts but the principle is subject to some statutory restrictions; these restrictions are either automatic or discretionary (*CPD* I 6B.1);

(2) the media have a right to attend all court hearings and are entitled to report those proceedings fully and contemporaneously.

The public has the right to know what takes place in the criminal courts and the media in court act as the eyes and ears of the public, enabling it to follow court proceedings and to be better informed about criminal justice issues:

> "It is impossible to over-emphasize the importance to be attached to the ability of the media to report criminal trials ... this represents the embodiment of the principle of open justice in a free country". (*Re Trinity Mirror Plc* [2008] EWCA Crim 50; [2008] Q.B. 770; [2008] 2 Cr. App. R. 1 per Sir Igor Judge P)

Exceptions are rare and must be justified on the facts. Any such exceptions must be necessary and proportionate. No more than the minimum departure from open justice will be countenanced (*Guardian News And Media Ltd v Incedal* [2014] EWCA Crim 1861; [2015] 1 Cr. App. R. 4). See that case also as to national security considerations.

Updated guidance on *Reporting Restrictions in the Criminal Courts* ("RRG") was published in April 2015 by the Judicial College, the News Media Association, the Society of Editors and the Media Lawyers Association. A revised version was released in May 2016. It is intended to provide a single useful reference point for courts and the media. The guidance summarises the automatic and discretionary reporting restrictions and states where the law permits exceptions to the open justice principle. A checklist sets out the points to consider before any restriction upon press access or reporting is made. Each section concludes with a bullet point summary of the key principles. It also includes "ready reference guides" to automatic and discretionary reporting restrictions.

As to access to court documents and material presented in open court, the presumption is generally in favour of open justice, see 50-052.

The effect of the general rule

50-002 The effect of the general rule stated in 50-001 is that:

(1) proceedings must be heard in public;
(2) evidence must be communicated publicly; and
(3) fair, accurate and contemporaneous media reporting of proceedings should not be prevented by any action of the court unless there are exceptional circumstances laid down by statute or the common law.

Thus where the court tries a case or the accused pleads guilty, the general rule is that the trial must be in public, but that is subject to the judge's power to:

(a) impose a restriction on reporting what takes place at a public hearing, or public access to what otherwise would be a public hearing;
(b) withhold information from the public during a public hearing; or
(c) order a trial in private.

(CrimPR 6.1–6.2)

A judge must not, therefore:

(i) order or allow the exclusion of the press or public from court for any part of the proceedings;
(ii) permit the withholding of information from the open court proceedings; or
(iii) impose a permanent or temporary ban on the reporting of the proceedings or any part of them, including anything that prevents the proper identification, by name and address, of those appearing or mentioned in the course of the proceedings,

save in well-established circumstances or as specifically permitted by statute (see below).

Particular rights are given to the press to give effect to the open justice principle so that they can report court proceedings to the wider public even if the public is excluded.

If a judge is asked to exclude the media or prevent them from reporting anything, however informally, he should not agree to do so without:

- first checking whether the law permits him to do so;
- considering whether he ought to do so;
- inviting submissions from the media or their legal representatives.

The prime concern is the interests of justice.

Checking the legal basis

In checking the legal basis for any proposed restriction, the judge needs to: **50-003**

(1) check whether there is any statutory power which allows departure from the open justice principle;
(2) check the precise wording of the statute;
(3) decide whether the terms of the statute are relevant to the particular case; and
(4) determine, where it is suggested that the power for the requested departure from the open justice principle is derived from common law and the court's inherent jurisdiction to regulate its own proceedings, if the authorities support that contention.

Where a restriction is automatic no order can or should be made in relation to matters falling within the relevant provisions. However, the court may, if it considers it appropriate to do so, give a reminder of the existence of the automatic restriction. The court may also discuss the scope of the restriction and any particular risks in the specific case in open court with representatives of the press present. Such judicial observations cannot constitute an order binding on the editor or the reporter although it is anticipated that a responsible editor would consider them carefully before deciding what should be published. It remains the responsibility of those reporting a case to ensure that restrictions are not breached (*CPD* I 6B.2).

The interests of justice

50-004 In the case of discretionary restrictions, the judge needs to decide whether action is necessary in the interests of justice.

Thus:

(1) automatic statutory restrictions upon reporting may already apply; or
(2) there may be restrictions on reporting imposed by the media's own codes, or as a result of an agreed approach.

Further questions are whether:

(a) the applicant has adduced the factual evidence necessary for the judge's assessment of his application; and
(b) any derogation from the open justice principle is really necessary.

Before exercising his discretion to impose a restriction the judge must follow precisely the statutory provisions under which the order is to be made, paying particular regard to what has to be established, by whom and to what standard. Certain general principles apply to the exercise of his discretion:

- he must have regard to CrimPR 6 and 18 (see below);
- he must keep in mind the fact that every order is a departure from the general principle that proceedings shall be open and freely reported;
- before making any order he must be satisfied that the purpose of the proposed order cannot be achieved by some lesser measure, e.g. the grant of special measures, screens or the clearing of the public gallery (usually subject to a representative/s of the media remaining);
- the terms of the order must be proportionate so as to comply with ECHR art.10 (freedom of expression); and
- no order should be made without giving other parties to the proceedings and any other interested party, including any representative of the media, an opportunity to make representations.

(*CPD* I 6B.3–4)

Criminal Procedure Rules Pt 6

50-005 Part 6 governs the imposition of reporting restrictions.

The judge must have regard to the importance of dealing with criminal cases in public and allowing a public hearing to be reported to the public.

He may determine an application at a hearing, in public or in private or without a hearing, but he must not exercise a power to which the rule applies unless each party and any other person directly affected:

(1) is present; or

(2) has had an opportunity to attend, or to make representations.

(CrimPR 6.2)

Judge's general power to vary requirements

The judge has general powers to: **50-006**

(1) shorten or extend (even after it has expired) a time limit;
(2) require an application to be made in writing instead of orally;
(3) consider an application or representations made orally instead of in writing; and
(4) dispense with a requirement to give notice, or to serve a written application.

Someone who wants an extension of time must apply when making the application or representations for which it is needed, and explain the delay.
(CrimPR 6.3)

Making an application

Where a judge can: **50-007**

(1) impose a restriction on:
    (a) reporting what takes place at a public hearing;
    (b) public access to what otherwise would be a public hearing; or
(2) withhold information from the public during a public hearing,

he may do so on application by a party or on his own initiative.
A party who wants the judge to do so must:

(a) apply as soon as reasonably practicable;
(b) notify:
    (i) each party; and
    (ii) such other party (if any) as the court directs;
(c) specify the proposed terms of the order, and for how long it should last;
(d) explain:
    (i) what power the judge has to make the order; and
    (ii) why an order in the terms proposed is necessary; and
(e) where the application is for a reporting direction in respect of a witness under YJCEA 1999 s.45A or s.46 (see 50-033, 50-034 and SPECIAL MEASURES DIRECTIONS) explain:
    (i) how the circumstances of the person whose identity is concerned meet the conditions prescribed by that section, having regard to the factors which that section lists; and
    (ii) why a reporting direction would be likely to improve the quality of the witness's evidence, or the level of cooperation the witness gives the applicant in connection with the preparation of the applicant's case.

(CrimPR 6.4)

Varying or removing restrictions; application

Where a judge can vary or remove a reporting or access restriction, unless other legislation otherwise provides, he may do so on application by a party or person directly affected, or on his own initiative. **50-008**

A party or person who wants the judge to do so must:

(1) apply as soon as reasonably practicable;
(2) notify:
  (a) each other party; and
  (b) such other person (if any) as the court directs;
(3) specify the restriction; and
(4) explain, as appropriate, why it should be removed or varied.

(CrimPR 6.5)

Media representations

50-009 Where relevant, the judge should invite:

(1) oral or written representations by the media or their representatives; and
(2) legal submissions on the applicable law from the prosecutor;

in addition to any legal submissions and any evidence which the law may require in support of an application for reporting restrictions from a party.

He should:

(a) invite media representations at the time he is first considering an order; and
(b) if an order is imposed, hear media representations as to whether any restriction imposed should be lifted or varied.

Committing the order to writing

50-010 If an order is made, the judge should make it clear in open court that a formal order has been made and its precise terms. It may be helpful to suggest at the same time that the judge would be prepared to discuss any problems arising from the order with the media in open court, if they are raised by written note.

The order should be in precise terms, stating:

(1) its legal basis;
(2) its precise scope; and
(3) its duration and when it will cease to have effect if appropriate.

Note that:

(a) any order should provide for any interested party who has not been present or represented at the time of the making of the order to have permission to apply within a limited period, e.g. 24 hours;
(b) the wording of the order is the responsibility of the judge making the order: it must be in precise terms and, if practicable, agreed with the advocates;
(c) the order must be in writing and must state the power under which it is made, its precise scope and purpose and the time at which it shall cease to have effect, if appropriate; and
(d) the order must specify, in every case, whether or not the making or terms of the order may be reported or whether this itself is prohibited. Such a report could cause the very mischief which the order was intended to prevent.

The court officer is responsible for:

(i) recording the decision of the court; and

(ii) arranging for a notice of the decision:
— to be prominently displayed near the courtroom; and
— communicated to reporters by such other arrangements as the Lord Chancellor directs.

(*CPD* I 6B.4)

A copy of the order should be provided to any person known to have an interest in reporting the proceedings and to any local or national media who regularly report proceedings in the court.

Court staff should be prepared to answer any enquiry about a specific case, but it is and will remain the responsibility of anyone reporting a case to ensure that no breach of any order occurs and the onus rests on such person to make enquiry in case of doubt.

(*CPD* I 6B.4–7)

Review of order

The judge should exercise his discretion to hear media representations against the imposition of any order under consideration or as to the lifting or variation of any reporting restriction as soon as possible. **50-011**

2. Hearings from which the public are excluded

General

The public are generally excluded from proceedings held in private (in camera) and from those held in Chambers. This section is concerned with trials and associated hearings (e.g. for sentencing or confiscation). The presumption is always in favour of open justice. Hearings in chambers are routinely held for some case management purposes (e.g. PII applications) and even bail applications. The judge always has a discretion to permit outsiders to be present at a hearing in chambers. **50-012**

Proceedings in private (in camera)

The court has an inherent power to regulate its own proceedings and may, in exceptional circumstances, hear a case, or part of a case, in secret. **50-013**

Note that:

(1) the only exception to the open justice principle at common law justifying hearings in camera is where the hearing of the case in public would frustrate or render impracticable the administration of justice (*Attorney General v Leveller Magazine* (1979) 68 Cr. App. R. 342); and
(2) the test is one of necessity.

The necessity test requires that even where the judge concludes that part of a case should be heard in camera, he must give careful consideration as to whether other parts of the same case can be heard in public and should adjourn into open court as soon as exclusion of the public ceases to be necessary.

(RRG 2.1)

In *Re Guardian News and Media Ltd* [2016] EWCA Crim 11; [2016] 1 Cr. App. R. 13, the CACD held that the DPP, the party applying for a trial in camera, had to make a very clear case. Where the reasons for the application relate to national security, the court will pay the highest regard to what is stated by the Secretary of

State, and, so long as there is an evidential basis for it, the court should not depart from the view of the Secretary of State on national security issues. However, it is for the court alone to decide whether the evidence should be heard in camera. Although the circumstances will be rare, the court is free to depart from the Secretary of State's views as to the weight to be attached to national security interests. The prosecutor's view that the case will not continue if the evidence is to be heard in public is not determinative, because that would remove the court's proper function and does not satisfy the test of necessity.

Adopting alternative measures

50-014 Since hearing a case in secret has a severe impact upon the public's right to know about court proceedings, permanently depriving it of the information heard in secret, it follows that if the judge can prevent the anticipated prejudice to the trial process by adopting a lesser measure he should adopt that course.

Such measures may include:

(1) a discretionary reporting restriction such as a postponement order under CCA 1981 s.4(2) (50-036);
(2) allowing a witness to give evidence from behind a screen (see SPECIAL MEASURES DIRECTIONS);
(3) a reporting direction under YJCEA 1999 ss.45, 45A or 46 (see SPECIAL MEASURES DIRECTIONS);
(4) a witness anonymity order under CorJA 2009 s.86 (see SPECIAL MEASURES DIRECTIONS); or
(5) ordering that a witness shall be identified by a pseudonym (such as by a letter of the alphabet) and prohibiting publication of the witness's true name by an order under CCA 1981 s.11 thus removing the need to exclude the public (see 50-037).

Where only a small part of the witness's evidence is sensitive, it is permissible to allow that part to be written down and not shown to the public or media in court.

However, alternative measures such as these are also exceptional and stringent tests must be satisfied before they are adopted.

(RRG 2.1)

Circumstances justifying proceedings in private

50-015 Circumstances which may justify hearing a case in camera include situations where the nature of the offence, if made public, would cause harm to national security, e.g. by:

(1) disclosing sensitive operational techniques; or
(2) identifying a person whose identity for strong public interest reasons should be protected, such as an undercover police officer.

Any application to proceed in camera should be supported by relevant evidence and the test to be applied in all cases is whether proceeding in private is necessary to avoid the administration of justice from being frustrated or rendered impracticable.

Disorder in court may also justify an order that the public gallery be cleared (see also CONTEMPT OF COURT). Again, the exceptional measure should be no greater than necessary. Representatives of the media (who are unlikely to have participated in the disorder) should normally be allowed to remain.

(RRG 2.1)

Procedure

Where the judge can order a trial in private, a party who wants the court to do so must: 50-016

(1) apply in writing not less than five business days before the trial is due to begin, serving the application on the Crown Court officer, and on each other party, explaining the reasons for the application, how much of the trial the applicant proposes should be in private; and
(2) explaining why no measures other than trial in private will suffice, such as:
   (a) reporting restrictions;
   (b) an admission of facts;
   (c) the introduction of hearsay evidence;
   (d) a direction for a special measure under YJCEA 1999 s.19 (see SPECIAL MEASURES DIRECTIONS);
   (e) a witness anonymity order under CorJA 2009 s.86 (see SPECIAL MEASURES DIRECTIONS); or
   (f) arrangements for the protection of a witness.

Where the application includes information that the applicant thinks ought not be revealed to another party, the applicant must omit that information from the part of the application that is served on that other party, mark the other part to show that, unless the judge otherwise directs, it is only for the court and in that other part, explain why the applicant has withheld that information from that other party.

The Crown Court officer will at once display a notice of the application somewhere prominent in the vicinity of the courtroom, and will give notice of the application to reporters by such other arrangements as the Lord Chancellor directs.

(CrimPR 6.6(1)–(5))

Determination at a hearing

The application must be determined at a hearing which: 50-017

(1) must be in private, unless the judge otherwise directs;
(2) if he so directs, may be, wholly or in part, in the absence of a party from whom information has been withheld; and
(3) must be after the accused is arraigned but before the jury is sworn.

At the hearing of the application:

(a) the general rule is that the judge must consider, in the following sequence:
   (i) representations first by the applicant and then by each other party, in all the parties' presence; and then
   (ii) further representations by the applicant, in the absence of a party from whom information has been withheld; but
(b) the judge may direct other arrangements for the hearing.

The trial in private will not be held until the business day after the day on which such trial is ordered, or the disposal of any appeal against, or review of, any such order, if later.

(CrimPR 6.6(6)–(8))

Representations in response

50-018 Where a party, or a person directly affected, wants to make representations about an application, he must serve the representations on the Crown Court officer, the applicant, each other party, and such other person (if any) as the judge directs, and do so as soon as reasonably practicable after notice of the application, asking for a hearing, if that party or person wants one, and explaining why it is needed, specifying any alternative terms proposed.

(CrimPR 6.7)

Order about restriction or trial in private

50-019 Where the judge orders, varies or removes a reporting or access restriction or orders a trial in private, the Crown Court officer will:

(1) record the court's reasons for the decision; and
(2) as soon as reasonably practicable, arrange for a notice of the decision to be displayed somewhere prominent in the vicinity of the courtroom, and communicated to reporters by such other arrangements as the Lord Chancellor directs.

(CrimPR 6.8)

3. Automatic Reporting Restrictions

(1) Youth Court proceedings

Proceedings emanating from youth courts (CYPA 1933 s.49)

50-020 In so far as proceedings in the Crown Court are concerned:

(1) on appeal from a youth court; or
(2) in proceedings on appeal from a magistrates' court under SA 2020 Sch.7 (proceedings for breach, revocation or amendment of youth rehabilitation orders),

no report may be published which reveals the name, address or school of any child or young person concerned in the proceedings, whether as the subject of those proceedings or as a witness, or which includes any particulars likely to lead to his identification (a similar ban applies to pictures) and it is the duty of the judge to announce in the course of the proceedings that this prohibition applies (otherwise it does not).

These automatic reporting restrictions may be lifted in three specific circumstances, i.e. where:

(a) the judge is satisfied that it is appropriate to do so for avoiding injustice to the child or young person;
(b) to assist in the search for a missing, convicted or alleged young offender who has been charged with, or convicted of, a violent offence, a sexual offence, a terrorism offence or an offence punishable with a prison sentence of 14 years or more in the case of a 21-year-old offender; and

(c) in relation to a child or young person who has been convicted, if the judge is satisfied that it is in the public interest to do so.

The judge must offer the parties an opportunity to make representations and take these into account before lifting the restrictions.

YJCEA 1999 s.44 (not yet in force) will create an automatic reporting restriction that prohibits the publication of any matter likely to identify a child or young person who is the subject of a criminal investigation and which lasts until the commencement of proceedings. The Act also makes a number of amendments to CYPA 1933 s.49.

(2) Special measures and other directions

The publication of any matter relating to: **50-021**

(1) the use of a live link for an accused (s.19) and directions prohibiting an accused from cross-examining a witness in person (ss.33A and 36), an order discharging, or in the case of an order under s.19, varying such a direction; or

(2) proceedings:
   (a) on an application for such a direction or order; or
   (b) where a judge acts of his own motion to determine whether to give or make any such order or direction,

may not be reported before they are determined, either by conviction or otherwise, or are abandoned.

These automatic restrictions may, however, be lifted by the judge and lapse automatically when proceedings against the accused are determined or abandoned (YJCEA 1999 s.47).

(3) Indecent material calculated to injure public morals

The Judicial Proceedings (Regulation of Reports) Act 1926 s.1 prohibits the publication in relation to any judicial proceedings of any indecent medical, surgical or physiological details which would be calculated to injure public morals. **50-022**

(4) Alleged offences by teachers

Where allegations are made against a person who is employed or engaged as a teacher at a school that: **50-023**

(1) the person is or may be guilty of a criminal offence; and
(2) the allegation is made by or on behalf of a registered pupil at the school,

no matter relating to that person may be included in any publication if it is likely to lead members of the public to identify the person as the teacher who is the subject of the allegation. However, any person may make an application to a magistrates' court for an order dispensing with those restrictions, which the court may make, to the extent specified in the order, if it is satisfied that it is in the interests of justice to do so, having regard to the welfare of:

(a) the person who is the subject of the allegation; and
(b) the victim of the offence to which the allegation relates.

The restrictions will cease to apply if the person concerned allows to be published what would otherwise have been prohibited under the section (EA s.141F(12)). Breach of the restrictions is a criminal offence (see ss.141G and 141H) (EA 2002 s.141F).

Appeal lies to the Crown Court against a decision to make or to refuse to make a dispensing order (see APPELLATE JURISDICTION).

A person wanting to appeal must:

- serve an appeal notice on the Crown Court officer, and each other party;
- serve on the Crown Court officer, with the appeal notice, a copy of the application to the magistrates' court;
- serve the appeal notice not more than 15 business days after the magistrates' court's decision against which the appellant wants to appeal; and
- in the appeal notice, explain, as appropriate, why the restriction should be maintained, varied or removed.

(CrimPR 6.5(4)–(5))

(5) Specified sexual offences

Anonymity of victims of certain sexual offences

50-024 SO(A)A 1992 s.1 imposes restrictions on the identification of complainants in the majority of sexual offences (listed in s.2).

Where:

(1) an allegation has been made that an offence listed in s.2 has been committed against a person, no matter relating to that person shall during that person's lifetime be included in any publication if it is likely to lead members of the public to identify that person as the person against whom the offence is alleged to have been committed; and

(2) a person is accused of such an offence, no matter likely to lead members of the public to identify a person as the person against whom the offence is alleged to have been committed ("the complainant") shall during the complainant's lifetime be included in any publication.

Section 1:

(a) does not apply in relation to a person by virtue of the above at any time after a person has been accused of the offence; and

(b) in its application in relation to a complainant by virtue of (2) above has effect subject to any direction given by a judge under s.3 (50-025 below).

The matters relating to a person in relation to which the restrictions imposed by (1) or (2) above apply, include in particular:

(i) the person's name;

(ii) the person's address;

(iii) the identity of any school or other educational establishment attended by the person;

(iv) the identity of any place of work; and

(v) any still or moving picture of the person.

Nothing in this provision prohibits the inclusion in a publication of matter consisting only of a report of criminal proceedings other than proceedings at, or intended to lead to, or on an appeal arising out of, a trial at which the accused is charged with the offence.

Contravention of any of the provisions of s.1 is a criminal offence (s.5).

The right to anonymity does not apply to the reporting of a trial or appeal where the sexual offences of which complaint has been made are not the subject of the charges before the court (*R. v Musharraf* [2022] EWCA Crim 678; [2022] 5 WLUK 197).

Judges' power to lift prohibition

If, before the commencement of a trial at which a person is charged with an offence to which s.2 applies, he or another person against whom the complainant may be expected to give evidence at the trial, applies to the judge for a direction under this subsection and satisfies the judge: **50-025**

(1) that the direction is required for the purpose of inducing persons who are likely to be needed as witnesses at the trial to come forward; and
(2) that the conduct of the applicant's defence at the trial is likely to be substantially prejudiced if the direction is not given,

the judge must direct that the provisions in 50-024 shall not, by virtue of the accusation alleging the offence in question, apply in relation to the complainant.

If at a trial the judge is satisfied:

(a) that the effect of s.1 is to impose a substantial and unreasonable restriction upon the reporting of proceedings at the trial; and
(b) that it is in the public interest to remove or relax the restriction,

he must direct that that section shall not apply to such matter as is specified in the direction (but such a direction must not be given by reason only of the outcome of the trial) (SO(A)A 1992 s.3).

Similar provisions apply to the case of a person who has been convicted of an offence and has given notice of appeal against the conviction, or notice of an application for leave to appeal.

A direction given under s.3 does not affect the operation of s.1 at any time before the direction is given.

Section 1 confers lifelong anonymity on complainants in the cases to which the 1992 Act applies. It does not confer on the trial judge any express power to make an order restricting publication of the defendant's name in order to protect or enforce a complainant's right to anonymity. The only express power to make an order impacting on the complainant's right to anonymity under s.1 is conferred by s.3, which provides that the judge may give a direction which lifts the anonymity of the complainant in a number of carefully defined situations where the interests of justice so require.

Decisions about what should or should not be published in a newspaper, or for that matter in the media generally, are left to editors and reporters; if s.1 is contravened, they face criminal prosecution (*R. (on the application of Press Association) v Cambridge Crown Court* [2012] EWCA Crim 2434; [2013] 1 Cr. App. R. 16).

(6) Victims of female genital mutilation

Section 71 of the Serious Crime Act 2015 introduced a new reporting restriction for the victims of female genital mutilation ("FGM"). **50-026**

Where an allegation has been made that an FGM offence has been committed against a person, no matter which is likely to lead members of the public to identify the person as the person against whom the offence is alleged to have been committed may be published during the person's lifetime.

The court can relax or remove the restriction if satisfied that it would cause substantial prejudice to a person's defence at trial, or if it imposes a substantial and unreasonable restriction on the reporting of the proceedings and it is in the public interest to do so.

(7) Rulings at pre-trial hearings

50-027 Pre-trial rulings on the admissibility of evidence or on points of law are subject to automatic reporting restrictions by virtue of CPIA 1996 s.41. The restrictions automatically cease to apply when the trial has concluded. They can be lifted before the conclusion of the trial on the application of any person if the court is satisfied that it is in the interests of justice to do so.

(8) Preparatory hearings

50-028 Preparatory hearings under CPIA 1996 and CJA 1987 are subject to automatic reporting restrictions (CPIA 1996 s.37 and CJA 1987 s.11). There are limited categories of factual information which may be reported. The restrictions automatically cease to apply when the trial has concluded. They can be lifted before the conclusion of the trial on the application of any person if the court is satisfied that it is in the interests of justice to do so.

(9) Dismissal applications

50-029 Unsuccessful dismissal applications under CDA 1998 are subject to automatic reporting restrictions (CDA 1998 Sch.3 para.3). The restrictions automatically cease to apply when the trial has concluded. They can be lifted before the conclusion of the trial on the application of any person if the court is satisfied that it is in the interests of justice to do so. Successful dismissal applications may be fully reported.

(10) Prosecution appeals against rulings

50-030 Automatic reporting restrictions apply when the prosecution informs the court of its intention to appeal against the court's ruling, and to the court's subsequent decisions concerning adjourning the trial or discharging the jury. For details of the limited categories of information which may be reported, see CJA 2003 s.71. The restrictions automatically cease to apply when the trial has concluded. They can be lifted before the conclusion of the trial on the application of any person if the court is satisfied that it is in the interests of justice to do so.

4. DISCRETIONARY REPORTING RESTRICTIONS

(1) Approach

General

50-031 Before imposing a discretionary reporting restriction, the judge should check that no automatic reporting restriction already applies which would make a discretionary restriction unnecessary.

The following are the principal discretionary restrictions:

(1) in the case of a *child under 18* as an accused, witness or victim, the media may be ordered not to publish anything likely to lead to the child being identified as being concerned in the proceedings (YJCEA 1999 s.45);
(2) in the case of a *child under 18* as a witness or victim (not the accused), the media may be ordered not to publish anything likely to lead to the child being identified as being concerned in the proceedings during their lifetime (YJCEA 1999 s.45A); and
(3) in the case of an *adult* witness (other than the accused) in the proceedings, the quality of whose evidence or whose co-operation with the preparation of the case is likely to be diminished by reason of fear or distress in connection with being identified, the media may be ordered not to publish any matter relating to the witness during his lifetime if it is likely to lead members of the public to identify him as being a witness in the proceedings (YJCEA 1999 s.46).

Procedural safeguards

The following procedural safeguards are common to all discretionary reporting restrictions: **50-032**

- care should be taken to ensure that the statutory conditions for imposing a discretionary reporting restriction are met;
- where the statutory conditions are met, the judge should balance the need for the reporting restriction against the public interest in open justice and freedom of expression;
- the need for an order should be convincingly established by clear and cogent evidence;
- the terms of the order should go no further than is necessary to meet the statutory objective;
- the media should be given an opportunity to attend or make representations about a discretionary reporting restriction;
- the order should be put in writing as soon as possible; and
- the media should be put on notice as to the existence and terms of the order.

(RRG 4.1)

(2) Protection of under-18s

Reporting restrictions under YJCEA 1999 s.45

YJCEA 1999 s.45 replaces CYPA 1933 s.39 in relation to all criminal proceedings, but s.39 continues to apply to civil and family proceedings and to Criminal Behaviour Orders. **50-033**

The court may direct that no matter relating to any person under the age of 18 (victim, witness or accused) shall be published if it is likely to lead to their identification as a person concerned in the proceedings (YJCEA 1999 s.45(3)).

The court must have regard to the welfare of the person in deciding whether to make an order (YJCEA 1999 s.45(6)).

Examples of matters that may be included in a s.45 reporting restriction as likely to lead to the identification of the person (etc.) are set out at s.45(8).

YJCEA 1999 s.63 sets out the definition of "publication", which includes any speech, writing, relevant programme or other communication in whatever form, which is addressed to the public at large or any section of the public. It thus covers print media, broadcast media and social media such as Twitter and Facebook. It expressly does not include indictments or other documents prepared for use in particular legal proceedings.

A s.45 reporting restriction ceases to have effect when the person reaches the age of 18 (but see s.45A reporting restrictions, below; see also *JC v Central Criminal Court* [2014] EWHC 1041 (Admin); [2014] 2 Cr. App. R. 13).

Much of the case law concerning the application of CYPA 1933 s.39 will continue to be of some relevance. Some of it is set out below.

There must be good reason, apart from age alone, for making such an order and the onus is on the applicant to show cause for restricting publicity (*R. v Central Criminal Court Ex p. W* [2001] 1 Cr. App. R. 2).

In deciding whether to make an order under s.39 the judge must balance the interests of the public in the full reporting of criminal proceedings against the desirability of not causing harm to a child. Where the child is an accused the judge should give considerable weight to the age of the offender and the potential damage to any young person of public identification as a criminal before having the burden or benefit of adulthood (*R. v Inner London Crown Court Ex p. Barnes* [1996] C.O.D. 17) and having regard to the statutory need to take into account his welfare under CYPA 1933 s.44.

In *R. v Winchester Crown Court Ex p. B (A Minor)* [2000] 1 Cr. App. R. 11, Simon Brown LJ listed a number of principles distilled from the authorities:

(a) whether there are good reasons for naming the accused;
(b) the age of the accused and the potential damage to him of public identification;
(c) his welfare as directed by CYPA 1933 s.44;
(d) the deterrent effect of naming on the accused (if convicted) and on others;
(e) the public interest in open justice;
(f) the weight to be attributed to different factors may shift during the proceedings, especially after a verdict or plea of guilty; and
(g) the making of an appeal may be relevant.

The issue is not what the need for identifying the child or young person is, but rather whether it is necessary to restrict his identification (*R. v Jolleys Ex p. Press Association* [2013] EWCA Crim 1135; [2014] 1 Cr. App. R. 15).

The judge has complete discretion as to who to hear on any application (*R. v Central Criminal Court Ex p. Crook* [1995] 2 Cr. App. R. 212, and see *Re R. (a Minor) (Wardship) Restrictions on Publication* [1994] 2 F.L.R. 637).

The court may dispense with or vary a s.45 reporting restriction if it is satisfied that:

(1) doing so is necessary in the interests of justice; or
(2) the restrictions impose a substantial and unreasonable restriction on reporting and it is in the public interest to relax or remove them.

(YJCEA 1999 s.45(4)–(5))

In making any such "excepting direction" the court must have regard to the welfare of the person.

(YJCEA 1999 s.45(6))

In considering the public interest the court should have regard to the matters identified in YJCEA 1999 s.52, which include the public interest in open reporting, the welfare of the child or young person and the views of the child or young person.

For analysis of the exceptional circumstances in which the High Court can order lifetime anonymity for a child offender after their 18th birthday, see *RXG v Ministry of Justice* [2019] EWHC 2026 (QB) and *DXB v Persons Unknown* [2020] EWHC 134 (QB).

Reporting restrictions under YJCEA 1999 s.45A

Section 45A brings the law for juvenile witnesses and victims into line with that for adults under s.46. **50-034**

Under s.45A, the court may direct that no matter relating to any person under the age of 18 (a victim or witness but not the accused) shall be published during that person's lifetime if it is likely to lead to their identification as a person concerned in the proceedings (YJCEA 1999 s.45A(2)).

The s.63 definition of publication (see 50-033) applies to s.45A orders.

Examples of matters that may be included in a s.45A reporting restriction as likely to lead to the identification of the person (etc.) are set out at s.45A(4).

A s.45A order may only be made if the court is satisfied that:

(1) the quality of any evidence given by the person; or
(2) the level of co-operation given by the person to any party in the proceedings in connection with that party's preparation of its case,

is likely to be diminished by reason of fear or distress on the part of the person in connection with being identified as a person concerned in the proceedings.

Section 45A(6) sets out a list of factors that the court must take into account:

(1) the nature and alleged circumstances of the offence to which the proceedings relate;
(2) the age of the person;
(3) any of the following if they appear to be relevant:
    (a) the social and cultural background and ethnic origins of the person;
    (b) the domestic, educational and employment circumstances of the person; and
    (c) any religious beliefs or political opinions of the person;
(4) any behaviour towards the person by:
    (a) an accused;
    (b) members of the family or associates of the accused; or
    (c) any other person who is likely to be an accused or a witness in the proceedings.

The court must also take into account any views expressed by the person in respect of whom the order may be made and, if that person is under the age of 16, any appropriate person other than an accused (YJCEA 1999 s.45A(7)).

The court must additionally have regard to:

(1) the welfare of the person;
(2) whether it would be in the interests of justice to make the direction; and

(3) the public interest in avoiding the imposition of substantial and unreasonable restrictions on reporting (YJCEA 1999 s.45A(8)).

The power to make an excepting direction under s.45A are identical to those under s.45 (see 50-033).

(3) Protection of adult witnesses

Reporting restrictions under YJCEA s.46

50-035 The judge may prohibit the publication of matters likely to identify an adult witness in criminal proceedings (other than the accused) during his lifetime.

He must:

(1) be satisfied that the quality of the witness's evidence, or his co-operation with any party to the proceedings in connection with that party's preparation of the case, is likely to be diminished by reason of fear or distress in connection with his identification by the public as a witness;
(2) in determining (1), take into account the factors listed at s.46(4) (which are identical to those under s.45A(6) (50-034));
(3) be satisfied that giving a reporting direction is likely to improve the quality of the witness's evidence, or his co-operation with any party to the proceedings in connection with that party's preparation of the case;
(4) take into account any views expressed by the witness; and
(5) in exercising his discretion, balance the interests of justice against the public interest in not imposing a substantial and unreasonable restriction on reporting of the proceedings, taking into account the factors in s.52.

(YJCEA 1999 s.46)

The court may dispense with or vary a s.46 reporting restriction if it is satisfied that:

(1) doing so is necessary in the interests of justice; or
(2) the restrictions impose a substantial and unreasonable restriction on reporting and it is in the public interest to relax or remove them.

In *R. v ITN News* [2013] EWCA Crim 773; [2013] 2 Cr. App. R. 22, the CACD dismissed an appeal against the judge's order under s.46 postponing publication of photographs of the wife of the accused and their children; she was a key witness against him. The judge had held that publication of the photographs would have affected the quality of her evidence, through the risk of identification of the children, even though her name and their names had been changed and she had changed her appearance and gave evidence from behind a screen.

The topic is dealt with in further detail in SPECIAL MEASURES DIRECTIONS.

(4) Postponement of fair and accurate reports

General

50-036 In certain exceptional circumstances a judge has the power to order that court reporting be postponed. This power is created by CCA 1981 s.4(2) and only arises where such reporting creates a substantial risk of prejudice to the proceedings in question or to other imminent or pending proceedings (*R. v Marine A* [2013] EWCA Crim 2637; [2014] 1 Cr. App. R. 26, per the Lord Chief Justice).

Section 4(2) provides that in respect of any legal proceedings held in public, the judge may, where it appears to be necessary for avoiding a substantial risk of prejudice to the administration of justice in:

(1) those proceedings; or
(2) any proceedings pending or imminent,

order that the publication in good faith of a fair, accurate and contemporaneous report of the proceedings, or any part of the proceedings, be postponed for such period as he thinks necessary for the purpose.

"Substantial" does not have the meaning of "weighty" but means rather "not insubstantial" or "not minimal" (*Attorney General v Newsgroup Newspapers Ltd* [1987] Q.B. 1, per Sir John Donaldson MR).

The order, which must be put into writing, must be formulated in precise terms, and must be communicated to the press.

It must include:

(a) the order's precise scope;
(b) the time at which the order will cease to have effect; and
(c) the specific purpose for which it is made.

The judge must balance the competing interests of ensuring a fair trial and open justice. He should approach the matter in three stages, considering:

(i) whether the reporting of the proceedings would give rise to a substantial risk of prejudice to the administration of justice; if not that is an end of the matter;
(ii) if there is a substantial risk, whether an order would eliminate that risk; if not there can be no necessity for an order;
(iii) even if satisfied that the order would achieve the objective, whether the risk can be overcome by less restrictive means; and

even if there is no other way of eliminating the perceived risk of prejudice, it still does not follow necessarily that an order has to be made; that requires a value judgement (*R. v Sarker* [2018] EWCA Crim 1341; [2019] 1 Cr. App. R. 3).

Note that:

- the risk has to be assessed at the time of the application (*R. v George* [2002] EWCA Crim 1923; [2003] Crim. L.R. 282);
- the relevant risk is as to the administration of justice and not to other matters, such as community hostility towards witnesses (*Re MGN Ltd* [2011] EWCA Crim 100; [2011] 1 Cr. App. R. 31); and
- the test under s.4(2) does not require serious prejudice (cf. s.2(2)).

If the judge comes to the conclusion that there is a substantial risk of prejudice he should consider whether, in the light of the competing public interests, it is necessary for avoiding that risk to make the order, whether in his discretion he should make the order, and if so, with all or only some of the restrictions sought (*R. v Central Criminal Court Ex p. The Telegraph Plc* (1994) 98 Cr. App. R. 91, per Lord Taylor CJ).

In *Re MGN Ltd* [2011] EWCA Crim 100; [2011]1 Cr. App. R. 31 it was said that an order under s.4(2) should be regarded as a last resort. The CACD added that the use of s.4(2) for the purposes of alleviating the difficulties of giving evidence, even if evidence had to be given in more than one trial, was rarely appropriate. If the conditions for an order under s.4(2) are established in the case of a particular witness or witnesses so that the order is justified in accordance with principle, then the order should be made; but in essence the protection of witnesses is more appropriately secured by statutory measures designed for that purpose (see further SPECIAL MEASURES DIRECTIONS), or any further legislation designed to enable witnesses to give their best.

In order to comply with ECHR art.10, an order must be proportionate and should be limited to those specific matters that create a substantial risk of prejudice to the administration of justice if published contemporaneously.

The procedure is regularly invoked in cases involving sequential trials, with the aim of postponing the reporting of specific parts of the evidence in the first trial to prevent prejudice to the accused in the second trial. It is generally not appropriate to invoke this power in relation to matters that form part of the evidence in both trials because in those cases prejudice is unlikely to arise.

An order imposing an indefinite prohibition is not valid under the section (*R. (on the application of Press Association) v Cambridge Crown Court* [2012] EWCA Crim 2434; [2013] 1 Cr. App. R. 16).

For consideration of the circumstances in which an order under s.4(2) may be lifted, see *Khuja v Times Newspapers Ltd* [2017] UKSC 49; [2018] 1 Cr. App. R. 1, and *R. (on the application of Rai) v Winchester Crown Court* [2021] EWCA Civ 604; [2021] 2 Cr. App. R. 20.

(5) Withholding names and other matters

50-037 Where the judge, if he has power to do so, allows a name or any other matter to be withheld from the public in criminal proceedings, he may make such directions prohibiting the publication of that name or matter in connection with the proceedings as are necessary. Section 11 does not itself confer any power upon courts to allow "a name or other matter to be withheld from the public in proceedings before the court", but it applies in circumstances where such a power has been exercised either at common law or statute. The purpose of s.11 is to support the exercise of such a power by giving the court a statutory power to give ancillary directions prohibiting the publication, in connection with the proceedings, of the name or matter which has been withheld from the public in the proceedings themselves. The directions which the court is permitted to give are such as appear to it to be necessary for the purpose for which the name or matter was withheld (*In re Guardian News and Media Ltd* [2010] UKSC 1; [2010] 2 All E.R. 799; *A v British Broadcasting Corporation (Scotland)* [2014] UKSC 25; [2014] 2 All E.R. 1037). The suggestion that no order may be made under s.11 unless members of the public had been present in the courtroom and had had a name or other matter withheld from them is an unduly narrow construction of the provision.

As to combining trial in camera with the anonymisation of the accused, see *Guardian News and Media Ltd v Incedal* [2014] EWCA Crim 1861; [2015] 1 Cr. App. R. 4.

A choice may have to be made between the competing interests of ECHR arts 8 (family life) and 10 (freedom of expression) (*Attorney General's Ref. (No.3 of 1999) (Re BBC's Application to Set Aside or Vary a Reporting Restriction Order)* [2009] UKHL 34; [2010] 1 A.C. 145) and *Re Guardian News and Media Ltd* [2010] UKSC 1; [2010] 2 A.C. 697.

Note the power under YJCEA 1999 s.46 to make a special measures direction to protect the identity of a witness (see 50-035).

In *Marine A* [2013] EWCA Crim 2637; [2014] 1 Cr. App. R. 26 it was reiterated that an accused must be named save in rare circumstances where necessary and proportionate. Following the test in *Ex p. Telegraph* [2001] EWCA Crim 1075; [2001] 1 W.L.R. 1983, the judge must ask himself:

(1) Would reporting give rise to a substantial risk of prejudice to the administration of justice in the proceedings?
(2) Is the order necessary to eliminate the risk or is there a less drastic means of achieving that objective?
(3) Is the degree of risk contemplated tolerable in the sense of being the lesser of two evils?

Thus, in a case involving a threat to life the question is whether there is a real and immediate threat. In other cases a balance has to be struck to establish whether there is a sufficient public interest in identifying the defendant having regard to the impact on his and his family's private life.

Section 11 does not arise for consideration unless the judge, having the power to do so, withholds the name or other matter from the public in the proceedings before him (see *R. v Arundel Justices Ex p. Westminster Press Ltd* [1985] 2 All E.R. 390; (1985) 149 J.P. 299, and *Re Trinity Mirror Plc* [2008] EWCA Crim 50; [2008] 2 Cr. App. R. 1). It is a pre-condition to the making of an order on the basis of s.11 that the name of the accused should have been withheld throughout the proceedings (see *R. (on the application of Press Association) v Cambridge Crown Court* [2012] EWCA Crim 2434; [2013] 1 Cr. App. R. 16).

An order should be made only where the nature or circumstances of the proceedings are such that hearing all the evidence in open court would frustrate or render impracticable the administration of justice.

It is not appropriate to invoke s.11, e.g.:

(a) for the benefit of an accused's feelings;
(b) to comfort, or to prevent financial damage or damage to reputation resulting from proceedings concerning a person's business;
(c) to prevent identification and embarrassment of the accused's children, because of his public profile (see *Re Trinity Mirror Plc* [2008] EWCA Crim 50; [2008] 2 Cr. App. R. 1),

but it is properly employed to safeguard the identity of children and young persons, complainants in rape cases, witnesses who might later be exposed to violence or blackmail, or the revelation of someone's identity where it might prejudice national security.

Note, however, the decision in *Z v News Group Newspapers Ltd* [2013] EWHC 1150 (Fam); [2013] Fam. Law 1130 (above) where an order was made in the Family Division restraining identification of the accused's children under the inherent jurisdiction.

Where the ground for seeking a s.11 order is that the identification of a witness will expose that person to a risk to his life, engaging the state's duty to protect life under ECHR art.2, the judge ought to take into consideration that person's subjective fears and the extent to which those fears are objectively justified.

It will ordinarily be necessary for an application under s.11 to be made in camera (*R. v Tower Bridge MC Ex p. Osbourne* (1989) 88 Cr. App. R. 28). The provisions of *CPD* 6B.4 apply equally to orders under s.11 as to orders under s.4(2) (see 50-036 above).

The judge is required to hear representations from the media about making an order. In cases of urgency, a temporary order should be made and the media should be invited to attend on the next convenient date.

The media have a right of appeal against a s.11 order made in the Crown Court (CJA 1988 s.159; see APPEALS FROM THE CROWN COURT).

In *R. v Abdulaziz* [2016] EWCA Crim 887; [2016] 2 Cr. App. R. 28, the CACD upheld an order under s.11 restricting publication of a judge's explanation for an order, where publication of the reasons for the order would have undermined the order itself. The Court offered guidance on the proper approach to what may be said in court about hearings in camera.

(6) Injunctions

50-038 In relation to the attendance and examination of witnesses, any contempt of court, the enforcement of its orders and all other matters incidental to its jurisdiction, the Crown Court has the same powers as the High Court (SCA 1981 s.45).

In *HTV Cymru (Wales) Ltd, Ex p.* [2002] E.M.L.R. 11, Aikens J held that whilst the Crown Court has no general power to issue injunctions, it does possess a limited power to grant an injunction to restrain a threatened contempt of court. He made an order under SCA 1981 s.45 prohibiting the media from contacting or interviewing any witness who had given or was likely to give evidence for the Crown.

Similarly, in *R. v Harwood* [2012] EW Misc 27 (CC), Fulford J (as he then was) issued an injunction to restrain a threatened contempt by directing various named internet service providers, website operators, search engines and other online operators to remove certain material concerning the accused until the conclusion of the trial. The judge had held that proceedings were "active" under the strict liability rule (CCA 1981 s.2(3)) and continuing publication of the material on the internet was a potential contempt. He accepted that an order under CCA 1981 s.4(2) would not have been open to him because the material in question had already been published and was not a contemporaneous report. He concluded that an order under SCA 1981 s.45 was necessary and proportionate, and not incompatible with art.10(1).

In *R. v F* [2016] EWCA Crim 12; [2016] 2 Cr. App. R. 13, the CACD held that an order under SCA 1981 s.45, directing various websites to remove content and disable the facility for users to post comments, was appropriate to protect the integrity of the trial.

However, in *R. (on the application of Trinity Mirror Plc) v Croydon Crown Court* [2008] EWCA Crim 50; [2008] 2 Cr. App. R. 1, the CACD held that the Crown Court had no jurisdiction to make an order restraining the identification of a convicted offender in order to protect his children because such an order was not incidental to its jurisdiction as it did not relate to his trial, conviction or sentence, and so did not fall within the ambit of s.45.

(7) Quashing of acquittal and retrial

50-039 If necessary in the interests of justice, the CACD may make an order to prevent the inclusion of any matter in a publication which appears to give rise to a substantial risk of prejudice to the administration of justice in a retrial (CJA 2003 s.82).

Before the prosecution has given notice of its application for an acquittal to be quashed and a case to be retried, such an order may only be made on the application of the DPP and only where an investigation has commenced.

After such notice has been given, the order may be made either on the application of the DPP or of the CACD's own motion. The order may apply to a matter which has been included in a publication published before the order takes effect (but such an order applies only to later inclusion of the matter in a publication, and does not otherwise affect the earlier publication).

Unless an earlier time is specified, the order will automatically lapse when there is no longer any step that could be taken which would lead to the acquitted person being tried pursuant to an order made on the application, or, if he is so tried, at the conclusion of the trial.

(8) Prohibition of derogatory assertions in mitigation

SA 2020 s.39 provides that where an assertion is made in a speech in mitigation, or in a submission relating to sentence on appeal, the court may make a derogatory assertion order where there are reasonable grounds for believing: **50-040**

(1) that the assertion is derogatory to a person's character; and
(2) that the assertion is false or that the facts asserted are irrelevant to sentence.

The effect of the derogatory assertion order is that the assertion must not be published in Great Britain in a written publication available to the public, or included in a relevant programme for reception in Great Britain.

The order ceases to have effect at the end of the period of 12 months beginning with the day on which it was made, but can be revoked at any time by the court which made it.

An interim order can be made where it appears to the court that there is a real possibility that a derogatory assertion order will be made in relation to an assertion. (SA 2020 s.39)

The prosecution advocate is under a duty to challenge any assertion by the defence in mitigation which is derogatory to a person's character and which is either false or irrelevant to proper sentencing considerations. If the defence advocate persists, the prosecutor should invite the judge to consider holding a *Newton* hearing to determine the issue (*Attorney General's Guidelines on Acceptance of Pleas and the Prosecutor's Role in the Sentencing Exercise* (reissued 2012)).

(9) Criminal behaviour orders

In relation to any proceedings for an offence under SA 2020 s.339 (breach of a criminal behaviour order) that are brought against a person under the age of 18: **50-041**

(1) CYPA 1933 s.49 (see 50-020) (restricting reports of proceedings in which children and young persons are concerned) does not apply in respect of the person; and
(2) YJCEA 1999 s.45 (power to restrict reporting of criminal proceedings involving persons under 18) does apply.

If, in such proceedings the judge exercises his power to give a direction under YJEA 1999 s.45, he must give his reasons for doing so.
(SA 2020 s.339(5)–(6))

(10) Deferred prosecution agreements

Order postponing publication of information by prosecutor

The judge may (CCA 2013 Sch.17 para.12) order that the publication of information by the prosecutor under paras 8(7), 9(5), (6), (7) or (8), 10(7) or (8) or 11(8) **50-042** be postponed for such period as he considers necessary if it appears to him that postponement is necessary for avoiding a substantial risk of prejudice to the administration of justice in any legal proceedings.

5. Miscellaneous

(1) Sound recording of court proceedings

Use of sound recording devices

50-043 Apart from the making or use of sound recordings for the purposes of official transcription of proceedings, it is a contempt of court:

(1) to use in court, or bring into court for use, any tape recorder or other instrument for recording sound, except with the leave of the court;
(2) to publish a recording of legal proceedings made by means of any such instrument, or any recording derived directly or indirectly from it, by playing it in the hearing of the public or any section of the public, or to dispose of it or any recording so derived, with a view to such publication; and
(3) to use any such recording in contravention of any conditions of leave granted under (1) above.

(CCA 1981 s.9(1))

Leave under (1) may be granted or refused at the discretion of the court, and if granted, may be granted subject to such conditions as the court thinks proper with respect to the use of any recording made pursuant to the leave; and where leave has been granted the court may withdraw or amend it either generally or in relation to any particular part of the proceedings.

Without prejudice to any other power to deal with an act of contempt under (1) above, the judge may order the instrument, or any recording made with it, or both, to be forfeited; and any object so forfeited shall (unless the court otherwise determines on application by a person appearing to be the owner) be sold or otherwise disposed of in such manner as the court may direct (CCA 1981 s.9(3)).

Under CCA 2013 s.32 the Lord Chancellor has power to provide for exceptions (and see further CONTEMPT OF COURT).

Applying for permission

50-044 Where the judge can give permission to:

(1) bring into a hearing for use, or use during a hearing, a device for recording sound, or communicating by electronic means; or
(2) publish a sound recording made during a hearing,

he may give such permission on application or on his own initiative (CrimPR 6.9(2)).

These provisions do not apply to the making or use of sound recordings for purposes of official transcripts of the proceedings, upon which the Act imposes no restriction whatever.

A person who wants the court to give such permission must apply as soon as reasonably practicable, notifying each party, and such other person (if any) as the judge directs, and explaining why the judge should permit the use or publication proposed (CrimPR 6.9(3)).

The discretion given to the judge to grant, withhold or withdraw leave to use equipment for recording sound or to impose conditions as to the use of the recording is unlimited, but the following factors may be relevant to its exercise:

(a) the existence of any reasonable need on the part of the applicant for leave, whether a litigant or a person connected with the press or broadcasting, for the recording to be made;
(b) the risk that the recording could be used for the purpose of briefing witnesses out of court; and
(c) any possibility that the use of the recorder would disturb the proceedings or distract or worry any witnesses or other participants.

(*CPD* I 6A.2)

As a condition of the applicant using such a device, the judge may direct arrangements to minimise the risk of its use in:

(i) contravening a reporting restriction;
(ii) disrupting the hearing; or
(iii) compromising the fairness of the hearing, for example by affecting the evidence to be given by a witness, or the verdict of a jury.

Such a direction may require that the device is used only:

- in a specified part of the courtroom;
- for a specified purpose;
- for a purpose connected with the applicant's activity as a member of a specified group, for example representatives of news-gathering or reporting organisations at a specified time, or in a specified way.

(CrimPR 6.9(4)–(5))

Consideration should always be given as to whether conditions as to the use of a recording made pursuant to leave should be imposed. The identity and role of the applicant for leave and the nature of the subject matter of the proceedings may be relevant to this. The particular restriction imposed by CCA 1981 s.9(1)(b) (contempt of court) applies in every case, but may not be present in the mind of every applicant to whom leave is given. It may therefore be desirable on occasion for this provision to be drawn to the attention of those to whom leave is given (*CPD* I 6A.3-4).

The transcript of a permitted recording is intended for the use of the person given leave to make it and is not intended to be used as, or to compete with, the official transcript mentioned in CCA 1981 s.9(4) (*CPD* I 6A.5).

Breach; forfeiture of unauthorised sound recording

Where a contravention of CCA 1981 s.9(1) is alleged, the procedure in CrimPR 48.2 (contempt of court) should be followed. Furthermore, s.9(3) of the 1981 Act permits the court to "order the instrument, or any recording made with it, or both, to be forfeited" and the procedure is set out at CrimPR 6.10 (see also *CPD* I 6A.6). **50-045**

Where someone without the judge's permission:

(1) uses a device for recording sound during a hearing; or
(2) publishes a sound recording made during a hearing,

the judge may exercise his power to forfeit the device or recording, whether on application by a party or on his own initiative. He may make a provisional order to allow time for representations.

A party who wants the judge to forfeit a device or recording must:

(a) apply as soon as reasonably practicable;
(b) notifying, as appropriate, the person who used the device, or who published the recording, and each other party, explaining why the judge should exercise that power.

(2) Photography and sketching in court; films etc.

Photography and sketching

50-046 Under CJA 1925 s.41 it is an offence:

(1) to take or attempt to take in any court, a photograph, or with a view to publication make or attempt to make in any court any portrait or sketch of any person, being a judge of the court or a juror or a witness in or a party to any proceedings before the court; or
(2) publish any photograph, portrait or sketch taken or made in contravention of such provisions or any reproduction of it.

The prohibition covers those in, or entering or leaving, the court building and its precincts (s.41(2)(c)). The police are not exempt (*R. v Loveridge* [2001] EWCA Crim 973; [2001] 2 Cr. App. R. 29).

CCA s.32 was brought into force in July 2013 and gives the Lord Chancellor power to make exceptions to CJA 1925 s.41. Section 41 has now been disapplied in respect of certain proceedings in the Court of Appeal (see The Court of Appeal (Recording and Broadcasting) Order 2013 (SI 2013/2786)) and the test recording of sentencing remarks in the Crown Court (see the Crown Court (Recording) Order 2016 (SI 2016/612)).

(3) Jury deliberations

50-047 It is a contempt of court to disclose or solicit any details of statements made, opinions expressed, arguments advanced or votes cast by members of a jury in the course of their deliberations in any legal proceedings. The prohibition on disclosure binds both the jurors themselves and the media in relation to the publication of any such disclosure.

Jury deliberations are confidential except with the authority of the trial judge during the trial, or the CACD after the verdict. Enquiries into jury deliberations are "forbidden territory" (*R. v Adams* [2007] EWCA Crim 1; [2007] 1 Cr. App. R. 449(34) CA), the rule being one of admissibility (*R. v Mirza* [2004] UKHL 2; [2004] 2 Cr. App. R. 8) and evidence about the deliberations of a jury is therefore inadmissible, subject to two narrow exceptions:

(1) where there has been a complete repudiation of the oath taken by the jurors to try the case on the evidence (as by resorting to the use of a ouija board); if there are serious grounds for believing such a repudiation of the oath has taken place, the CACD will inquire into it, and may hear evidence *de bene esse*, including from the jurors themselves, to decide whether it has happened; and
(2) where extraneous material has been introduced into the jury deliberations; examples include papers mistakenly admitted to the jury room, discussions with outsiders and, more recently, information derived from research

on the internet; where this has occurred, the CACD will examine the evidence to ascertain the facts.

(*R. v Thompson* [2010] EWCA Crim 1623; [2010] 2 Cr. App. R. 27)

(4) Text-based messages, etc. from court

Introduction

The Practice Guidance issued by the Lord Chief Justice in November 2011 has now been subsumed into the 2015 *CPD*. **50-048**

The guidance is consistent with the legislative structure which:

(1) prohibits:
  (a) the taking of photographs in court (CJA 1925 s.41); and
  (b) the use of sound recording equipment in court unless the leave of the judge has first been obtained (CCA 1981 s.9);
(2) requires compliance with the strict prohibition rules created by CCA 1981 ss.1, 2 and 4 in relation to the reporting of court proceedings.

General Principles

The following general principles apply: **50-049**

(1) the judge has an overriding responsibility to ensure that proceedings are conducted consistently with the proper administration of justice, and to avoid any improper interference with its processes;
(2) a fundamental aspect of the proper administration of justice is the principle of open justice; fair and accurate reporting of court proceedings forms part of that principle;
(3) that principle is, however, subject to well-known statutory and discretionary exceptions; two such exceptions are the prohibitions on photography in court and on making sound recordings of court proceedings;
(4) the statutory prohibition on photography in court is absolute; and
(5) sound recordings are also prohibited unless, in the exercise of its discretion, the judge permits such equipment to be used; in criminal proceedings, some of the factors relevant to the exercise of that discretion are contained in *CPD* I 6A.2.

(*CPD* I 6C.2–5)

General Considerations

The normal, indeed almost invariable, rule has been that mobile phones must be turned off in court. There is however no statutory prohibition on the use of live text-based communications in open court. **50-050**

Thus:

(1) where a member of the public, who is in court, wishes to use live text-based communications during court proceedings, an application for permission to activate and use (in silent mode) a mobile phone, small laptop or similar piece of equipment, solely in order to make live, text-based communications of the proceedings will need to be made; the application may

be made formally or informally (for instance by communicating a request to the judge through court staff);

(2) it is presumed that a representative of the media or a legal commentator using live, text-based communications from court does not pose a danger of interference to the proper administration of justice in the individual case; this is because the most obvious purpose of permitting the use of live, text-based communications would be to enable the media to produce fair and accurate reports of the proceedings; as such, a representative of the media or a legal commentator who wishes to use live, text-based communications from court may do so without making an application to the court;

(3) when considering, either generally on its own motion, or following a formal application or informal request by a member of the public, whether to permit live, text-based communications, and if so by whom, the paramount question for the judge will be whether the application may interfere with the proper administration of justice;

(4) in considering the question of permission, the factors identified in *CPD* I 6A.2 are likely to be relevant;

(5) without being exhaustive, the danger to the administration of justice is likely to be at its most acute in the context of criminal trials, e.g. where witnesses who are out of court may be informed of what has already happened in court and so coached or briefed before they then give evidence, or where information posted on, for instance, Twitter, about inadmissible evidence may influence members of a jury;

(6) it may be necessary for the judge to limit live, text-based communications to representatives of the media for journalistic purposes but to disallow its use by the wider public in court; that may arise if it is necessary, for example, to limit the number of mobile electronic devices in use at any given time because of the potential for electronic interference with the court's own sound recording equipment, or because the widespread use of such devices in court may cause a distraction in the proceedings;

(7) subject to these considerations, the use of an unobtrusive, handheld, silent piece of modern equipment for the purposes of simultaneous reporting of proceedings to the outside world as they unfold in court is generally unlikely to interfere with the proper administration of justice; and

(8) permission to use live, text-based communications from court may be withdrawn by the court at any time.

(*CPD* I 6C.6–6C.14)

(5) Taking notes in court

50-051 As long as it does not interfere with the proper administration of justice, anyone who attends court may take notes on paper or on an electronic device. The permission of the court is not required.

However, where there is reason to suspect that the taking of notes may be for an unlawful purpose, or that it may disrupt the proceedings, it is entirely proper for court staff to make appropriate enquiries. The court can prohibit note taking by a specified individual or individuals if that is necessary and proportionate to prevent unlawful conduct (for example, where there were grounds for believing that the notes would be used to brief another witness who had yet to give evidence).

The existence of a reporting restriction is not, without more, a sufficient reason to prohibit note taking, although it may need to be made clear to those taking notes that the reporting restriction will affect how much, if any, of what they note may be communicated to anyone else.

See *CPD* I 6D.1-3 and *Ewing v Cardiff and Newport Crown Court* [2016] EWHC 183 (Admin); [2016] 1 Cr. App. R. 32.

6. Access to court documents and material

In a case where documents have been placed before a judge and referred to in the course of the proceedings, the default position is that access by non-parties should be permitted on the common law principle of open justice, and where access is sought for a proper journalistic purpose, the case for allowing it will be particularly strong. However, there may be countervailing reasons. It is not sensible or practical to look for a standard formula for determining how strong the grounds of opposition need to be in order to outweigh the merits of the application; the judge has to carry out a proportionality exercise, which will be fact-specific. Central to the judge's evaluation will be the purpose of the open justice principle, the potential value of the material in advancing that purpose and, conversely, any risk of harm which access to the documents may cause to the legitimate interests of others (*R. (on the application of Guardian News and Media Ltd) v City of Westminster Magistrates' Court* [2012] EWCA Civ 420; [2013] Q.B. 618; and see also *Marine A* [2013] EWCA Crim 2367; [2014] 1 Cr. App. R. 26 and *R. v Blackman* [2017] EWCA Crim 326 where still and video recordings were withheld). **50-052**

In *Re Guardian News and Media Ltd* [2016] EWCA Crim 58, the CACD held that the judge had been wrong to refuse to allow media access to video footage which had been played extensively in open court.

Where a member of the public, including a reporter, wants information about a case from the court officer, they must apply in accordance with CrimPR 5.8. Certain categories of information, such as the nature of the offences and pleas entered, or the court's decisions made at any public hearing, must be provided upon request, subject to certain restrictions. Other information about the case, or access to documents, must be applied for in writing (unless the court otherwise directs) and the provision of the information or document is at the discretion of the court. For further details of the application process, see CrimPR 5.7–5.8 and *CPD* I 5B.

CPD I 5B.1 to 5B.36 sets out detailed guidance about the provision of information in general and the provision of particular classes of material, such as documents read aloud in their entirety, jury bundles, witness statements etc.

7. Appeals

General

A person aggrieved may appeal to the CACD, if the CACD gives leave, against an order restricting the access of the public to the whole or any part of a trial on indictment or to any proceedings ancillary to such a trial (CJA 1988 s.159(1)). There is no appeal against refusal to make such an order (*R. v S* [1995] 2 Cr. App. R. 347). **50-053**

Appeal pursuant to s.159 CJA 1988 does not confer a right of appeal against a decision refusing an application for an excepting direction under s.46(9) of the Youth Justice and Criminal Evidence Act 1999. Challenge to such a decision must be by way of judicial review (*Re Pembrokeshire Herald* [2021] EWCA Crim 1165; [2021] 2 Cr. App. R. 23).

Persons who may be aggrieved include both media representatives and the accused (*Re A* [2006] 1 W.L.R. 1351).

Since this avenue of appeal does not extend to proceedings in the magistrates' courts, it is not available in respect of proceedings in the Crown Court in the exercise of its appellate jurisdiction (*R. v Malvern Justices Ex p. Evans* (1988) 87 Cr. App. R. 19).

Procedure is governed by CrimPR 40. The proceedings being civil in nature, there is no power to grant representation under legal aid.

The CACD may:

(1) stay any proceedings in any other court until after the appeal is disposed of;
(2) confirm, reverse or vary the order complained of; and
(3) make such order as to costs as it thinks fit (CJA 1988 s.159(5)(c)) but not out of central funds (*Holden v CPS* (1993) 97 Cr. App. R. 376).

Service and form of appeal notice

50-054 A person wanting to appeal must serve an appeal notice on the Crown Court officer, the Registrar, the parties and any other person directly affected by the order, not later than:

(1) the next business day after an order restricting public access to the trial; or
(2) ten business days after an order restricting reporting of the trial.

The notice must include, with reasons, an application for leave to appeal, and, where relevant, an application for an extension of time within which to serve the notice, and any applications in relation to attendance at the hearing or the introduction of evidence.

(CrimPR 40.3)

The person applying for the order will also need to serve on the Registrar, as soon as practicable after service of the notice, a transcript or note of the application for the order and any other document he thinks the court will need to decide the appeal.

(CrimPR 40.5)

Advance notice

50-055 Where advance notice of an order restricting public access is given, an appellant may serve advance written notice of an intention to appeal against any such order if it is made on the Crown Court officer, the Registrar, the parties and any other person who will be directly affected by the order against which he intends to appeal, if it is made not more than five business days after the Crown Court officer displays notice of the application for the order.

The notice must give the same information (with any necessary adaptations) as the appeal notice. If the order is made, the court will treat the advance notice as the appeal notice.

(CrimPR 40.4)

Respondent's notice

50-056 Where an appellant wants to appeal against an order restricting the reporting of a trial, a person on whom an appellant serves an appeal notice may, and must if that person wants to make representations to the CACD or if the CACD directs, serve on the appellant (etc.), within three business days, a notice containing those matters set out in CrimPR 40.6(6), in particular summarising any relevant facts not already summarised in the appeal notice.

51. REPORTS

Quick Guide

1. General

51-001 For the purposes of forming any such opinion as is mentioned in SA 2020:

- SA 2020 s.204 (threshold for community sentences);
- SA 2020 s.230 (threshold for custodial sentence); or
- SA 2020 s.231 (length of custodial sentence); or
- SA 2020 s.180 (certain forms of youth rehabilitation orders),

the judge is obliged to take into account all such information as is available to him about the circumstances of the offence, and the offence or offences associated with it including any aggravating or mitigating factors. In forming such opinion as is mentioned in SA 2020 s.208(4) (suitability of community requirements), he may take into account any information about the offender which is before him.

Under the Offender Rehabilitation Act 2014 the entire provision of probation services was restructured. The 35 probation trusts were abolished and replaced by a National Probation Service (NPS). Some 21 Community Rehabilitation Companies (CRC) were set up, with the aim that they would be responsible for about 70 per cent of the supervision of the community sentences and shorter prison sentences, through sub-contracting with the private sector, charities and independent organisations. The remaining supervision work, on higher risk offenders, will be managed by the National Probation Service. It is expected, of course, that the NPS and CRC will work closely together. From the point of view of sentencing procedure, all advice to the court in the form of pre-sentence reports will continue to be provided by the NPS, as will offender risk assessments. In May 2019 the then Lord Chancellor, David Gauke, set out plans for all offender management to be brought under the NPS. This process was completed with effect from July 2021.

2. Pre-sentence reports

Statutory provisions

51-002 The judge must, unless in the circumstances of the case he is of the opinion that it is unnecessary to do so, obtain and consider a presentence report before:

(1) in the case of a custodial sentence, forming any such opinion as is mentioned in SA 2020:
- s.230(7) (51-001);
- s.231(8) (51-001);
- s.283 or s.273 (qualification for life sentence or custody for life for second listed offence);
- s.274 or s.285 (life sentence for serious offences—"dangerousness");
- s.258 (detention for life—"dangerousness");
- s.255 (extended sentence—"dangerousness"); or

(2) in the case of a community sentence, forming any such opinion as is mentioned in:
- SA 2020 ss.204 or 180 (51-001); or
- any opinion as to the suitability for the offender of the particular requirement or requirements to be imposed by the community order or youth rehabilitation order.

(SA 2020 s.30)

See also *Attorney General's Reference (Nos 73 and 75 of 2010 and No.3 of 2011)* [2011] EWCA Crim 633; [2011] 2 Cr. App. R. (S.) 100.

Nature of report

A "pre-sentence report" is defined by statute, and differs from other reports, such as those of providers of probation services and members of youth offending teams (as to which see 51-012). The term is restricted to reports which: **51-003**

(1) are made or submitted by an appropriate officer (as defined), with a view to assisting the court in determining the most suitable method of dealing with the offender; and
(2) contain information as to such matters as may be prescribed by rules.

A pre-sentence report that:

(a) relates to an offender aged under 18; and
(b) is required to be obtained and considered before the court forms an opinion mentioned in the sections set out in 51-002, must be in writing.

Otherwise, subject to any rules made under the section, the judge may accept a pre-sentence report given orally in open court.

(SA 2020 s.31)

Offenders under 18

In a case where: **51-004**

(1) an offender is aged under 18;
(2) the offence is not triable only on indictment; and
(3) there is no other offence associated with it which is triable on indictment only, the judge is not entitled to say it is unnecessary to obtain a report, unless:
    (a) there exists a previous report, or reports; and
    (b) he considers the information contained in that report or the most recent, if there is more than one.

(SA 2020 s.30(2) and (3))

In *R. v Atkins* [2001] EWCA Crim 2804; *The Times,* 14 January 2002, it was suggested that it might be desirable to require a pre-sentence report in all cases involving young offenders, even if a custodial sentence was inevitable.

Necessity for report

Quite apart from statute, in all cases where a judge is contemplating sending an offender to prison for the first time, other than perhaps for an extremely short period of time, it should be the invariable practice that a pre-sentence report be obtained. **51-005**

R. v Gillette, *The Times,* 3 December 1999 suggests that is always necessary, but in *R. v Armsaramah* [2001] 1 Cr. App. R. (S.) 133 the CACD disagreed and see *R. v ILCC Ex p. Mentesh* [2001] Cr. App. R. (S.) 467. *Gillette* does not need to be followed in every case.

No report; effect

51-006 A custodial sentence is not invalidated by a breach of the provisions, but any court dealing with an appeal will need to obtain and consider a report if one were not obtained in the court below unless it is satisfied that the lower court was justified in finding it unnecessary, or itself finds it unnecessary to do so.

(SA 2020 ss.30(4) and 33)

The same caveat applies in relation to offenders under 18 (SA 2020 s.30(4)), respecting disclosure of pre-sentence reports.

Adequacy and availability

51-007 It is for the judge to decide whether a report available to him is adequate for sentencing purposes, and constitutes compliance with SA 2020 ss.30 and 31, and if he considers a further report necessary he may call for one (see *R. v Okinikan* (1993) 96 Cr. App. R. 431).

A degree of care, it is suggested, needs to be taken in the assessment of pre-sentence reports, since great importance is likely to be given to them, especially by inexperienced judges. Much of the material contained in them offends the cardinal rules of criminal evidence.

There is a deal of self-serving information contributed by the offender and his family, frequent hearsay drawn from former reports by other officers and other material on the file, and opinion evidence contributed by persons not necessarily qualifying as "experts" on the required level. There tends to be a bias towards non-custodial recommendations, and sometimes there is prejudice created by incompatibility between the officer reporting and the offender.

National guidelines seek to correct a frequently found lack of objectivity (see, e.g. *R. v James* (1981) 3 Cr. App. R. (S.) 233).

Note that:

(1) the judge is not obliged to ensure that every detail advanced by the defence is checked and confirmed; but
(2) where "fresh and highly relevant" material is raised for the first time in the report, the judge ought to discuss the implications with both parties (*R. v Cunnah* [1996] 1 Cr. App. R. (S.) 393), and there may be need for a *Newton* hearing (see GUILTY PLEAS); and
(3) where the defence seek to treat an account given in the report as a basis for sentence, the advocate should expressly draw the judge's attention to the material, and the prosecutor should be warned in advance (*R. v Tolera* [1999] 1 Cr. App. R. (S.) 25).

Disclosure of report

51-008 Where the court obtains a pre-sentence report, other than a report given orally in court (51-003), a copy must be given to:

(1) the offender or his advocate or solicitor;

(2) any parent or guardian of an offender under 18, who is present in court; and
(3) to the prosecutor, that is to say, the person having conduct of the proceedings in respect of the offence.

Note that:

(a) if the offender is aged under 18 and it appears to the judge that the disclosure to the offender or to any parent or guardian of his of any information contained in the report would be likely to create a risk of significant harm to the offender, a complete copy of the report need not be given to the offender or, as the case may be, to that parent or guardian;
(b) if the prosecutor is not of a description prescribed by order made by the Secretary of State, a copy of the report need not be given to him if the judge considers that it would be inappropriate for him to be given it; and
(c) in relation to an offender aged under 18 for whom a local authority has parental responsibility and who is in its care, or is provided with accommodation by it in the exercise of any social services functions, references to his parent or guardian are to be read as references to the authority.

The Pre-Sentence (Prescription of Prosecutors) Order 1998 (SI 1998/191) prescribes a Crown Prosecutor, any other person acting on behalf of the Crown Prosecution Service or a person acting on behalf of the Commissioners of Revenue and Customs, the Secretary of State for Social Security, and the Director of the Serious Fraud Office.

3. Mentally disordered offenders

Statutory provisions

Before sentencing an offender who is, or appears to be, mentally disordered within the meaning of MHA 1983 (see MENTALLY DISORDERED OFFENDERS) to a custodial sentence, other than one fixed by law, the judge must, in addition to the requirements as to pre-sentence reports: **51-009**

(1) obtain and consider a medical report, made orally or in writing by a medical practitioner approved for the purpose under MHA 1983 s.12, unless he is of opinion that it is unnecessary to do so; and
(2) consider any information before the court relating to his mental condition (whether given in a medical report, a pre-sentence report or otherwise), and the likely effect of such a sentence on that condition and on any treatment which may be available for it.

Nothing in SA 2020 ss.204, 230, 231 (restrictions on sentence):

(a) requires the judge to pass a custodial sentence, or any particular custodial sentence, on a mentally disordered offender; or
(b) restricts his power to deal with such an offender in a more appropriate way under MHA 1983 or otherwise, to deal with such an offender in the manner he considers to be the most appropriate in all the circumstances.

(SA 2020 s.232)

Where the judge requests a medical examination of an accused and a report, or requires information about the arrangements that could be made for the accused where he is considering making a hospital or guardianship order (see MENTALLY DISORDERED OFFENDERS), the court must:

(a) identify each issue in respect of which the court requires expert medical opinion and the legislation applicable;
(b) specify the nature of the expertise likely to be required for giving such opinion;
(c) identify each party or participant by whom a commission for such opinion must be prepared, who may be:
  (i) a party (or party's representative) acting on that party's own behalf;
  (ii) a party (or party's representative) acting on behalf of the court; or
  (iii) the court officer acting on behalf of the court;
(d) where there are available to the court arrangements with the National Health Service under which an assessment of a defendant's mental health may be prepared, give such directions as are needed under those arrangements for obtaining the expert report or reports required;
(e) where no such arrangements are available to the court, or they will not be used, give directions for the commissioning of an expert report or expert reports, including:
  (i) such directions as can be made about supplying the expert or experts with the defendant's medical records;
  (ii) directions about the other information, about the defendant and about the offence or offences alleged to have been committed by the defendant, which is to be supplied to each expert; and
  (iii) directions about the arrangements that will apply for the payment of each expert;
(f) set a timetable providing for:
  (i) the date by which a commission is to be delivered to each expert;
  (ii) the date by which any failure to accept a commission is to be reported to the court;
  (iii) the date or dates by which progress in the preparation of a report or reports is to be reviewed by the court officer; and
  (iv) the date by which each report commissioned is to be received by the court; and
(g) identify the person (each person, if more than one) to whom a copy of a report is to be supplied, and by whom.

(3) A commission addressed to an expert must:
  (a) identify each issue in respect of which the court requires expert medical opinion and the legislation applicable;
  (b) include:
    (i) the information required by the court to be supplied to the expert;
    (ii) details of the timetable set by the court; and
    (iii) details of the arrangements that will apply for the payment of the expert;
  (c) identify the person (each person, if more than one) to whom a copy of the expert's report is to be supplied; and
  (d) request confirmation that the expert from whom the opinion is sought:
    (i) accepts the commission; and
    (ii) will adhere to the timetable.

(CrimPR 28.8 as substituted by the Criminal Procedure (Amendment No.2) Rules 2018)

A new section was added to the *CPD* on Medical Reports for Sentencing Purposes with effect from October 2018. There are general observations on the procedure to be followed and what is expected of the expert. The provisions of the practice direction mirror those in the CrimPR (*CPD* VII Sentencing R: R1, 2, 3 and 4). There are provisions on timetable for the commissioning, preparation and consideration of any report (R5). CrimPR 3.28 requires the court to set a timetable for the preparation and reception of a report. The timetable must be incorporated within the trial preparation timetable. The fact that a medical report is to be obtained, whether commissioned at the instigation of a party or by the court, is never a reason to postpone a PTPH or to decline to give the directions needed for trial. A trial date must be set and other directions given in the usual way. (*CPD* VII R5–10). In terms of commissioning a report reference is made to Good practice guidance: commissioning, administering and producing psychiatric reports for sentencing prepared for and published by the MoJ and HMCTS in September 2010. (*http://www.ohrn.nhs.uk/resource/policy/GoodPracticeGuidePsychReports.pdf* [Accessed October 2021]) which includes standard forms of letters of instruction and other documents. (*CPD* VII R11–13).

In relation to funding arrangements, where a medical report has been, or is to be, commissioned by a party then that party is responsible for arranging payment of the fees incurred, even though the report is for the court's use. That must be made clear in that party's commission. Where requested by the court and commissioned by the court or by court staff, the commission must confirm that fees will be paid by HMCTS as well as details of how, and to whom, to submit an invoice or claim for fees as well as notice of the prescribed rates of fees. (*CPD* VII R14 and 15).

4. Rules governing experts' reports

Contents of report

An expert's report must: **51-010**

(1) give details of the expert's qualifications, relevant experience and accreditation;
(2) give details of any literature or other information which he has relied on in making the report;
(3) contain a statement setting out the substance of all facts given to the expert which are material to the opinions expressed in the report, or upon which those opinions are based;
(4) make clear which of the facts stated in the report are within the expert's own knowledge;
(5) say who carried out any examination, measurement, test or experiment which the expert has used for the report and:
  (a) give the qualifications, relevant experience and accreditation of that person;
  (b) say whether or not the examination, measurement, test or experiment was carried out under the expert's supervision; and
  (c) summarise the findings on which the expert relies;
(6) where there is a range of opinion on the matters dealt with in the report:
  (a) summarise the range of opinion; and
  (b) give reasons for his own opinion;
(7) if the expert is not able to give his opinion without qualification, state the qualification;
(8) include such information as the judge may need to decide whether the expert's opinion is sufficiently reliable to be admitted in evidence;

(9) contain a summary of the conclusions reached;
(10) contain a statement that the expert understands his duty to the court, and has complied and will continue to comply with that duty; and
(11) contain the same declaration of truth as a witness statement.

(CrimPR 19.4)

Where more than one party wants to introduce expert evidence on an issue the judge may direct that the evidence on that issue be given by one expert only (see CrimPR 19.7; as to instructions to such joint expert, see CrimPR 19.8).

As to service of expert evidence, see CrimPR 19.3. As to the notice required to be served before expert evidence is called by a party, see DISCLOSURE.

Pre-hearing discussion of expert evidence

51-011 Where more than one party wants to introduce expert evidence, the judge may direct the experts to:

(1) discuss the expert issues in the proceedings; and
(2) prepare a statement for the court of the matters on which they agree and disagree, giving their reasons.

Except for that statement, the content of that discussion must not be referred to without the judge's permission.

A party may not introduce expert evidence without the judge's permission if the expert has not complied with a direction under this rule.

(CrimPR 19.6)

5. OTHER REPORTS

51-012 Where a report by an officer of a provider of probation services or a member of a youth offending team is made to any court (other than to a youth court) with a view to assisting the court in determining the most suitable method of dealing with any person in respect of an offence, and the report does not qualify as a pre-sentence report (see 51-003), a copy of the report must be given:

(1) to the offender or his advocate or solicitor; and
(2) if the offender is aged under 18, to any parent or guardian of his who is present in court.

In relation to an offender under 18:

(a) where it appears to the judge that disclosure to the offender or to any parent or guardian of his of any information contained in the report would be likely to create a risk of significant harm to the offender, a complete copy of the report need not be given to the offender, or as the case may be, to that parent or guardian;
(b) for whom a local authority have parental responsibility and who is in their care, or is provided with accommodation by them in the exercise of any social services functions, references in this section to his parent or guardian are to be read as references to the authority.

52. RESTITUTION ORDERS

General

A restitution order may be made where: 52-001

(1) goods have been stolen and a person is convicted with reference to the theft (whether or not stealing is the gist of the offence); or
(2) the court takes such an offence into consideration in determining sentence.

(SA 2020 s.148)

References to the words "stolen" and "theft" refer also to goods which have been obtained by blackmail and fraud (within the meaning of the Fraud Act 2006).

"Goods" includes, unless the context otherwise requires, money and all kinds of property within the meaning of TA 1968 except land, and includes things severed from the land by stealing.

An order may be made in respect of money owed by the Crown.

(SA 2020 s.151(2), (4) and (5))

A restitution order where goods have been stolen should be made only where the title to property is abundantly clear. If there is any doubt that the property from which it is proposed to make an order belongs to the defendant, an order should not be made and the applicant should be left to pursue his remedies in the civil courts (*R. v Ferguson* [1970] 1 W.L.R. 1246; (1970) 54 Cr. App. R. 410).

Nature of order

Whether or not the passing of sentence is deferred in other respects, the judge may make an order: 52-002

(1) requiring any person having possession or control of the goods to restore them to a person entitled to recover them from him;
(2) requiring any other goods representing the stolen goods to be transferred or delivered to any person entitled to recover those other goods from the offender;
(3) requiring payment of a sum out of any removed money to any person who would be entitled to recover the stolen goods from the offender if they were in the offender's possession; or
(4) requiring payment of a sum out of any removed money to:
    (a) any person to whom the offender has sold the stolen goods; or
    (b) any person from whom the offender has borrowed money on the security of the stolen goods.

Orders under (2) and (3) above may be combined provided the person in whose favour the orders are made does not thereby recover more than the value of the goods.

Orders made under (4) above can only be made if the court has made an order under (1) above (SA 2020 s.148(3)).

The judge can only make a restitution order under s.147(1)(d) if he is satisfied that the purchaser purchased the goods in good faith, or the lender acted in good faith in lending money on the security of the goods.

(SA 2020 s.149(2), (6), and (7))

Procedure

52-003 A victim of theft who wants the court to order restitution must apply in writing as soon as practicable, without waiting for the verdict. The application must be served on the Crown Court and must identify the goods and explain why the applicant is entitled to them. The Crown Court will serve a copy of the application on each party. The judge will not determine the application unless the applicant and each party has had an opportunity to make representations at a hearing (whether or not each in fact attends). The judge may extend the above time limit, even after it has expired, and may allow an application to be made orally (CrimPR 28.7).

No order should be made unless, in the judge's opinion, the relevant facts sufficiently appear from:

(1) evidence given at the trial;
(2) any written statements or admissions made for use as, and admissible as, evidence at the trial;
(3) any documents served on the offender in pursuance of regulations made under CDA 1998 Sch.3 para.1 (sending for trial); and
(4) admissions made by or on behalf of any person in connection with any proposed exercise of the powers to make a restitution order.

(SA 2020 s.149(2))

The court cannot hear additional evidence in support of the application after the conclusion of the trial (*R. v Church* (1971) 55 Cr. App. R. 65).

53. RESTRAINING ORDERS AND DOMESTIC ABUSE PROTECTION ORDERS

Quick Guide

1. Restraining orders on conviction

Making of restraining order on conviction

A judge sentencing or otherwise dealing with an offender convicted of an offence may: 53-001

(1) as well as sentencing him or dealing with him in any other way;
(2) make a restraining order, for the purpose of protecting the victim of the offence, or any other person mentioned in the order, from conduct which:
    (a) amounts to harassment; or
    (b) will cause fear of violence,

by prohibiting the offender from doing anything described in the order, for a specified period or until further order.

(SA 2020 ss.359 and 360)

Apart from what is in SA 2020 s.364 (references to harassing a person include alarming the person or causing the person distress), the Sentencing Code contains no definition of harassment. In construing s.1 of the PHA 1997, however, one must have regard to what the ordinary person would understand by harassment. It does not follow that because references to harassing a person include alarming a person or causing a person distress (SA 2020 s.364), *any* course of conduct which causes alarm or distress therefore amounts to harassment (*Thomas v News Group Newspapers* [2001] EWCA Civ 1233 at [29]). In *R. v Curtis* [2010] EWCA Crim 123; [2010] 1 Cr. App. R. 31 the court referred to the definition of "harass" in the *Concise Oxford Dictionary*, 10th edn (Oxford: Oxford University Press), as meaning to "torment by subjecting to constant interference or intimidation". Essentially, it involves persistent conduct of a seriously oppressive nature, either physically or mentally, targeted at an individual and resulting in fear or distress (*Thomas v News Group Newspapers* at [30]).

It is clear that for an order to be made under SA 2020 s.360 (or PHA 1997 s.5A) the offence in respect of which the accused is convicted (or acquitted) does not need to have been an offence under the 1997 Act itself (*R. v R* [2013] EWCA Crim 591; [2013] 2 Cr. App. R. 12).

There is no reason in principle why a restraining order should not be made to protect a company or a group of persons from harassment (*R. v Buxton* [2010] EWCA Crim 2925; [2011] 2 Cr. App. R. (S.) 23).

A restraining order is classified as a "civil behaviour order". Procedure in relation to such orders made after verdict or finding is governed by CrimPR 31 and is set out in CRIMINAL BEHAVIOUR ORDERS.

Both the prosecution and the defence may lead, as further evidence, any evidence that would be admissible in proceedings for an injunction under PHA 1997 s.3 (SA 2020 s.362).

Any person mentioned in the order is entitled to be heard.

As to the requirements of an order, see 53-004.

As to variation or discharge, see 53-007.

Breach of the order without reasonable excuse is an offence punishable on conviction on indictment with five years' imprisonment (SA 2020 s.363).

2. Orders following acquittal

Making order following acquittal

53-002 An order may be made even where an accused is acquitted of an offence where:

(1) there is clear evidence that the victim needs protection; but
(2) insufficient evidence to convict of the particular charges before the court; and
(3) the judge considers that it is *necessary* to make an order to protect a person from harassment by him ("fear of violence" present in s.5, is omitted from s.5A).

(PHA 1997 s.5A)

Note that by PHA 1997 s.5A(2), s.5(3)–(7) apply to an order under s.5A as they apply to an order under s.5. The order may have effect for a specified period or until further order. Both prosecution and defence may lead further evidence.

A person found by a jury to be "not guilty by reason of insanity" (i.e. by a special verdict under the Trial of Lunatics Act 1883 s.2) has been acquitted of the offence; that is what a finding of "not guilty" is, whatever the basis upon which that verdict is returned (*R. v R* [2013] EWCA Crim 591; [2013] 2 Cr. App. R. 12). The CACD left open the question of the effect of a finding of unfitness to be tried where a jury has subsequently determined under CP(I)A 1964 s.4A that the accused "did the act ... charged against him". However, in *R. v Chinegwundoh* [2015] EWCA Crim 109; [2015] 1 Cr App. R. 26, the CACD concluded that where a defendant was unfit to be tried, and was found to have committed the acts charged against him in a hearing under the Criminal Procedure (Insanity) Act 1964, that did not amount to a criminal conviction. It could not be regarded as an acquittal either. The court therefore had no power to impose a restraining order on the defendant under PHA 1997.

A court can impose a restraining order where the prosecution has offered no evidence (*DPP v Christou* [2015] EWHC 4157 (Admin); [2016] 2 Cr. App. R. 16).

The fact that a jury is not sure that the conduct alleged amounted to harassment is not necessarily a ground for concluding that there is no risk of harassment in the future. Section 5A is silent as to the standard of proof required but the order is a civil order so the ordinary civil standard of proof applies. The evidence does not have to establish that there had been harassment on the balance of probabilities; it is enough if the evidence establishes conduct which falls short of harassment but which might well, if repeated in the future, amount to harassment and so make an order necessary (*R. v Major* [2010] EWCA Crim 3016; [2011] 1 Cr. App. R. 25; see also *R. v Thompson* [2010] EWCA Crim 2955; [2011] 2 Cr. App. R. (S.) 24). The CACD has emphasised the importance of scrupulous adherence to the terms of s.5A and the requirement of *necessity* for an order (*R. v Smith* [2012] EWCA Crim 2566;

[2013] 2 Cr. App. R. (S.) 28; *R. v Taylor* [2017] EWCA Crim 2209; [2018] 1 Cr. App. R. (S.) 39); and *R. v Baldwin* [2021] EWCA Crim 703; [2021] 5 WLUK 166).

3. Procedure

General

Procedure is governed by CrimPR 31 (see CRIMINAL BEHAVIOUR ORDERS). **53-003**

Where the judge is considering making an order, whether under SA 2020 s.360, or PHA 1997 s.5A, he should, of his own initiative, consider adjourning the hearing to enable:

(1) the parties to serve notice in writing identifying any evidence they wish him to take account of, in compliance with CrimPR 31.4(2); and
(2) compliance with the rules relating to hearsay (CrimPR 31.6–31.8),

even if he is minded to exercise the discretion open to him under CrimPR 31.9 (which allows the court to shorten or extend a time limit, allows a notice or application to be given in a different form, or presented orally, and allows a requirement for service to be dispensed with, even after service was required).

It is a fundamental principle of CrimPR 31 that any person facing the imposition of a restraining order should be given proper notice of what is sought and the evidential basis for the application, and should be allowed a proper opportunity to address the evidence and make informed representations as to the appropriateness of an order (see CrimPR 31.2(1)).

Where the prosecutor applies for a restraining order (whether the defendant is convicted or acquitted), the prosecutor must serve draft order on the court officer and the defendant as soon as practicable (without waiting for the verdict). The draft order must specify:

(a) those prohibitions which, if the defendant is convicted, the prosecutor proposes for the purpose of protecting a person from conduct which amounts to harassment or will cause fear of violence; or
(b) those prohibitions which, if the defendant is acquitted, the prosecutor proposes as necessary to protect a person from harassment by the defendant.

(CrimPR 31.3(6))

Where the judge is contemplating making an order immediately following a trial, provided the accused's representative has had an opportunity to address all relevant issues, consideration can properly be given to exercising the discretion contained in CrimPR 31.9 (*R. v K* [2011] EWCA Crim 1843; [2012] 1 Cr. App. R. (S.) 88).

If the judge is considering making a restraining order under s.5A of the Protection from Harassment Act 1997 of his own motion in a case where there has been no trial and no evidence has been offered, it will be necessary to consider carefully what evidence is relevant to the issue of the making of the restraining order and to consider which parts of that evidence are agreed or disputed. This needs to be identified fairly so that the defendant may respond. Witness statements are admissible, but the judge is likely to need to hear oral evidence to resolve relevant disputes of fact. In giving judgment, the judge will also need to identify the evidence justifying the necessity for making the order (*R. v Baldwin* [2021] EWCA Crim 703; [2021] 5 WLUK 166). He must also consider carefully the requisite length of the order, ensuring that it is proportionate (*R. v Brough* [2011] EWCA Crim 2802; [2012] 2 Cr. App. R. (S.) 8).

In *R. v Picken* [2006] EWCA Crim 2194 it was said that an order should not be made without finding out the views of the potential victim.

Terms of order

53-004 In making an order the judge should:

(1) bear in mind that the purpose of an order is to prohibit particular conduct with a view to protecting the persons mentioned in the order from harassment;
(2) ensure that the order is expressed and drawn up in clear and precise terms so that there is no doubt as to what the offender is prohibited from doing;
(3) tailor any order to the precise requirements of the individual case;
(4) expressly identify the persons in respect of whom the order is made;
(5) have regard to considerations of proportionality when considering the terms of the order i.e. whether any term is proportionate and necessary to achieve the aim set out in (1); and
(6) clearly identify the period specified in the order.

(*R. v Debnath* [2005] EWCA Crim 3472; [2006] 2 Cr. App. R. (S.) 25; *R. v Pearson* [2021] EWCA Crim 784; [2021] 5 WLUK 305)

The order may be expressed to be for a specified term or until further order (SA 2020 s.359(2)).

The judge is required to identify the factual basis for imposing an order (*R. v Major* [2010] EWCA Crim 3016; [2011] 1 Cr. App. R. 25; *R. v Buxton* [2010] EWCA Crim 2925; [2011] 2 Cr. App. R. (S.) 23).

In *R. v Smith* [2012] EWCA Crim 2566; [2013] 2 Cr. App. R. (S.) 28 the CACD said that an order under s.5A must identify a victim. An order is for the protection of a particular vulnerable person, or possibly an identifiable group of vulnerable persons not (as the judge had intended) for the protection of the world at large.

In the case of a group of persons the group must be sufficiently defined so that they know who they are and those against whom the order is made also know which persons are included and which are not (*R. v Buxton* [2010] EWCA Crim 2925; [2011] 2 Cr. App. R. (S.) 23).

See also *R. v AD* [2019] EWCA Crim 1339; [2020] 1 Cr. App. R. (S.) 21, in which a restraining order prohibiting any unsupervised contact with any child under the age of 16 was held to be too wide, the court observing that a restraining order should not be used as a means of imposing, in the context of non-sexual offending, the wide restrictions permitted by the SHPO provisions under the Sexual Offences Act 2003 s.103A.

4. Breach and Sentence

Breach

53-005 Where a breach is alleged, and any issue of reasonable excuse is raised, the burden of proving absence of reasonable excuse is on the prosecutor (*R. v Evans* [2004] EWCA Crim 3102; [2005] 1 Cr. App. R. 32. See also *R. v Nicholson* [2006] EWCA Crim 1518; [2006] 2 Cr. App. R. 30; *R. v Charles* [2009] EWCA Crim 1570; [2010] 1 Cr. App. R. 2; and *B v DPP* [2012] EWHC 72 (Admin); [2012] 2 Cr. App. R. 2).

Sentence

In sentencing for a breach, the judge should consider: 53-006

(1) whether there is a history of disobedience to court orders;
(2) the seriousness of the particular conduct proved;
(3) whether there has been persistent misconduct or a solitary instance of misbehaviour;
(4) the effect on the victim;
(5) the degree of future risk and whether the victim requires protection;
(6) the offender's mental health; and
(7) any plea of guilty, remorse shown, etc.

(*R. v Liddle* [2000] 1 Cr. App. R. (S.) 131; *R. v Gardner* [2010] EWCA Crim 2154; [2011] 1 Cr. App. R. (S.) 103)

As to relevant applicable sentencing guidelines, see the Sentencing Council's Breach of a Protective Order definitive guideline, and the Breach Offences definitive guideline.

5. Variation and discharge

General

The prosecutor, the accused or any other person mentioned in the order may apply to the court which made the order for it to be varied or discharged by a further order; any person mentioned in the order is entitled to be heard on the hearing of such application (SA 2020 s.361). 53-007

A court dealing with a person for an offence may vary or discharge the order by further order (SA 2020 s.363(6)). Procedure on variation and discharge is governed by CrimPR 31.5 (as to which see CRIMINAL BEHAVIOUR ORDERS).

6. Appeals

Appeal; order made after acquittal

A person made subject to such an order after an acquittal has the same right of appeal against the order as if: 53-008

(1) he had been convicted of the offence in question before the court which made the order; and
(2) the order had been made under s.5.

Thus he has a right of appeal under CAA 1968 ss.9 and 10 (see APPEALS FROM THE CROWN COURT). Procedure is governed by CrimPR 36 and 39.

Where the CACD allows an appeal against conviction, it has power to remit the case to the Crown Court to consider whether an order ought to be made (PHA 1997 s.5A(5)).

7. Domestic Abuse Protection Orders

From a date to be appointed, the Domestic Abuse Act 2021 makes provision for the imposition of Domestic Abuse Protection orders (DAPO). These may be made by criminal courts upon conviction or acquittal, or against a person whose appeal 53-009 against conviction has been allowed by the Crown Court (DAA 2021 s.31). A DAPO may prohibit a person from doing things described in the order, or require the person to do the things described in the order, for the purpose of preventing him from being abusive towards a person aged 16 or over to whom the person is personally connected (DAA 2021 s.27). The conditions for making a DAPO are set out in s.32. Matters to be considered before making an order are set out in s.33. DAA 2021 ss.35–36 contains examples of requirements that may be included in the DAPO.

A DAPO has effect for a specified period, until the occurrence of a specified event, or until further order (DAA 2021 s.38).

For breach of a DAPO see s.39. For variation and discharge of a DAPO see ss.44–45.

54. RESTRAINT ORDERS; RECEIVERS

QUICK GUIDE

A. RESTRAINT ORDERS

1. POCA 2002

General

A restraint order under POCA 2002 s.41 prohibits a specified person from dealing with any "realisable property" (as defined in s.83) held by him. "Dealing with property" includes removing it from England and Wales. The order is analogous to a *Mareva* injunction (now known as a "freezing" order). The object of the order, like that of a *Mareva* injunction, is to strike a balance at an interlocutory stage between: **54-001**

(1) preventing the dissipation of realisable property which may be subject to a confiscation order; and
(2) meeting the reasonable requirements of its owner in the meantime.

(*Re Peters* [1988] 3 All E.R. 46 per Nourse LJ at [51])

The enforcement in England and Wales of restraint and receivership proceedings from Scotland and Northern Ireland is governed by SI 2002/3133.

Where an accused in criminal proceedings is said to have breached a restraint order made under POCA 2002 by making prohibited transactions, a judge of the Crown Court has jurisdiction to try an application made by the prosecutor for the accused to be committed for contempt (*R. v M* [2008] EWCA Crim 1901; [2009] 1 Cr. App. R. 17). As to sentence, see *R. v Roddy* [2010] EWCA Crim 671; [2010] 2 Cr. App. R. (S.) 107; *R. v Baird* [2011] EWCA Crim 459; [2011] 2 Cr. App. R. (S.) 78 and *R. v Patel* [2017] EWCA Crim 820. A breach of a restraint order under s.41 is a civil, not a criminal contempt (*Director of the Serious Fraud Office v O'Brien* [2014] UKSC 23; [2014] A.C. 1246).

A breach of a restraint order is *capable*, without more (i.e. involving no illegality beyond the breach of the order itself) of constituting the offence of perverting the course of justice (*R. v Kenny* [2013] EWCA Crim 1; [2013] 1 Cr. App. R. 23; see also *R. v Norman* [2013] EWCA Crim 1397).

Nature of order

A restraint order, unlike a confiscation order (see CONFISCATION ORDERS) is not a final order made on conviction of an offender; it is pre-emptive and provisional in operation, and is intended to prevent the dissipation of assets until **54-002** the court is in a position, if satisfied that it is right to do so, to make a confiscation order.

Thus:

(1) provided one of the conditions set out in POCA 2002 s.40 (54-004) is satisfied, an order may be made at a stage before there has been any determination of whether or not the person in respect of whose property it is made has been guilty of criminal conduct, let alone whether or not he has benefited from such conduct;
(2) the judge is concerned solely with the preservation of realisable assets at a time when it cannot be known whether an accused will be convicted or not, thus he must seek to strike the balance referred to in 54-001;
(3) it need not be shown that the respondent has property rights in the property to be restrained; any of the fraudsters in a fraudulent scheme has a beneficial interest in money retained in the execution of the fraud;
(4) the grant of an order is discretionary; the judge must proceed on the basis of statements made ex parte on behalf of the prosecutor; he cannot assume that a confiscation order under the Act will be made in due course; and
(5) the order takes effect immediately, before intimation to the specified person.

Where there are several accused it may be appropriate to make orders in respect of each to protect, as against each other, the whole sum which is said to represent the proceeds of the offence(s) (*Re Peters* [1988] 3 All E.R. 46; *Jennings v CPS* [2008] UKHL 29; [2008] 2 Cr. App. R. 14).

The application

54-003 An order may be made on an ex parte application made in chambers by the prosecutor or by an accredited financial investigator (accredited in accordance with POCA 2002 s.3) (POCA 2002 s.42(1) and (2)).

The application may be made without notice if it is urgent or if there are reasonable grounds for believing that giving notice would cause the dissipation of realisable property which is the subject of the application. It must be made in writing and must be supported by a witness statement giving the grounds for the application, and:

(1) to the best of the witness's ability, full details of the realisable property in respect of which the applicant is seeking the order, specifying the person holding that property;
(2) the proposed terms of the order;
(3) the grounds for, and full details of, any application for any ancillary order under s.41(7) for the purpose of ensuring that the restraint is effective; and
(4) where the application is made by an accredited financial investigator, a statement that he is authorised under POCA 2002 s.68 to make the application.

(CrimPR 33.51)

An application for the appointment of a management receiver or an enforcement receiver under CrimPR 33.56 may be joined with an application for a restraint order or an application for the conferral of powers on a receiver (CrimPR 33.33).

Hearings should be listed some days before the day on which any arrests are to be made.

The fact that such applications are made ex parte, and the potential seriousness of the consequences for defendants (at this stage presumed to be innocent) and for potential third parties, mean that there is a special burden both on the prosecution and on the court. Hughes LJ spelt this out plainly and emphatically in *Re Stanford International Bank Ltd* [2010] EWCA Civ 137; [2011] 1 Ch. 33 at [191], in a passage (cited in *An Informer v A Chief Constable* [2012] EWCA Civ 197; [2012] 3 All E.R. 601) repeated and endorsed in *Barnes v The Eastenders Group* [2014] UKSC 26; [2014] 2 Cr. App. R. 19 (see in particular [118]–[124] under the heading "Lessons for the future") and in *Ashford v Southampton City Council* [2014] EWCA Crim 1244). In summary, Hughes LJ said:

1. It is essential that the duty of candour laid upon any applicant for an order without notice is fully understood and complied with.
2. It is not limited to an obligation not to misrepresent; it consists in a duty to consider what any other interested party would, if present, wish to adduce by way of fact, or to say in answer to the application, and to place that material before the judge.
3. That duty applies to an applicant for a restraint order under POCA in exactly the same way as to any other applicant for an order without notice; even in relatively small value cases, the potential of a restraint order to disrupt other commercial or personal dealings is considerable.
4. The prosecutor may believe that the defendant is a criminal, and he may turn out to be right, but that has yet to be proved; an application for a restraint order is emphatically not a routine matter of form, with the expectation that it will routinely be granted.
5. The fact that the initial application is likely to be forced into a busy list, with very limited time for the judge to deal with it, is a yet further reason for the obligation of disclosure to be taken very seriously.
6. In effect the prosecutor seeking an ex parte order must put on his defence hat and ask himself what, if he were representing the defendant or a third party with a relevant interest, he would be saying to the judge, and, having answered that question, that is what he must tell the judge.

A material failure to observe the duty of candour as explained above may well be regarded as serious default within the meaning of POCA 2002 s.72 because of its potential to cause serious harm (*Barnes v The Eastenders Group* [2014] UKSC 26; [2014] 2 Cr. App. R. 19). Subsequent applications to:

(i) vary or discharge a restraint order;
(ii) appoint a management receiver; or
(iii) commit the accused or an affected third party for contempt of court in respect of an alleged breach of a restraint order,

should, where possible, be heard by the judge who made the restraint order.

On an application to discharge a restraint order on the basis of non-disclosure by the authority that obtained the order, the Crown Court should determine whether the non-disclosure was material to the making of the order, and if so, whether the public interest required the order to remain in place nonetheless (see *Director of the Serious Fraud Office v A* [2007] EWCA Crim 1927; (2007) 151 S.J.L.B. 1058; *Malabu Oil and Gas Ltd v DPP* [2015] 12 WLUK 424; [2016] Lloyd's Rep. F.C. 108).

Particulars for order

54-004 A judge of the Crown Court may make a restraint order prohibiting any specified person from dealing with any "realisable property" held by him, where any of the preconditions prescribed by s.40 (set out below) are satisfied.
(POCA 2002 s.41(1))

"Realisable property" is defined (in s.83) as any free property (see s.82) held by the accused and any free property held by the recipient of a tainted gift (see s.77). "Property" is all property wherever situated (s.84(1)). "Dealing with property" includes removing it from England and Wales (s.41(9)).

The preconditions to be satisfied are any of the following:

(1) a criminal investigation has been started in England and Wales with regard to an offence, and there are reasonable grounds to suspect that the alleged offender has benefited from his criminal conduct;
(2) proceedings for an offence have been started in England and Wales and not concluded, and there is reasonable cause to believe that the defendant has benefited from his criminal conduct;
(3) an application by the prosecutor (for subsequent reconsideration of an order) has been made under POCA 2002 ss.19, 20, 27 or 28 and not concluded, or the judge believes that such an application is to be made, and there is reasonable cause to believe that the defendant has benefited from his criminal conduct;
(4) an application by the prosecutor has been made under s.21 (for a reconsideration of benefit) and not concluded, or the judge believes that such an application is to be made, and there is reasonable cause to believe that the court will decide under that section that the amount found under the new calculation of the offender's benefit exceeds the relevant amount (as defined in that section); or
(5) an application by the prosecutor has been made under s.22 (for a reconsideration of the available amount), and not concluded, or the judge believes that such an application is to be made, and there is reasonable cause to believe that the court will decide under that section that the amount found under the new calculation of the available amount exceeds the relevant amount (as defined in that section).

Note that condition (2) is not satisfied if the judge believes that there has been undue delay in continuing the proceedings, or that the prosecutor does not intend to proceed, and the same applies if an application as mentioned in conditions (3), (4) and (5) has been made.

If condition (1) is satisfied:

(a) references here to the defendant (or offender) are to the "alleged" offender;
(b) references to the "prosecutor" are to the person the judge believes is to have conduct of any proceedings for the offence; and
(c) section 77(9) has effect as if proceedings for the offence had been started against the offender when the investigation was started.

(POCA 2002 s.40)

The judge should examine whether there is a real risk of dissipation of assets by the accused or anyone else prior to satisfaction of a confiscation order, should a restraint order not be made. There will rarely be direct evidence of the risk, but he may infer such risk from the circumstances.

Where dishonesty is alleged there will usually be reason to fear that realisable assets will be dissipated (*Jennings v CPS* [2008] UKHL 29; [2008] 2 Cr. App. R. 29; cf. *Re B (Restraint Order)* [2008] EWCA Crim 1374; [2009] 1 Cr. App. R. 14 where there was no such evidence).

If a restraint order is made, and the applicant for the order applies to the judge to do so (whether as part of the application for the restraint order, or at any time afterwards), the judge may make such order as he believes to be appropriate for ensuring that the restraint order is effective. See, e.g. *DPP v Scarlett* [2000] 1 W.L.R. 515, a decision under DTA 1994 s.26. Paragraph 89 of the Explanatory Notes to POCA confirms that this may include a Disclosure Order (see INVESTIGATIVE ORDERS AND WARRANTS).

(POCA 2002 s.41(6) and (7))

Particulars of the order

The order: 54-005

(1) may provide that it applies to:
  (a) all realisable property held by the specified person whether or not the property is described in the order;
  (b) realisable property transferred to the specified person after the order is made;
(2) may be made subject to other exceptions, and an exception, in particular:
  (a) *may* make provision for reasonable living expenses and reasonable legal expenses (see 54-008);
  (b) *may* make provision for the purpose of enabling any person to carry on any trade, business, profession or occupation; and
(3) *must* be made subject to an exception enabling relevant legal aid payments to be made (a legal aid exception).

(POCA 2002 s.41(2)–(3))

A relevant legal aid payment is a payment that the specified person is obliged to make under regulations made under LASPO 2012, and in connection with services provided in relation to an offence which falls within s.41(5), whether the obligation to make payment arises before or after the restraint order is made.

Where an exception to a restraint order is made under s.41(3), (2)(a) and (b) above it must not make provision for any legal expenses which relate to an offence which falls within s.41(5) and are incurred by the accused or by a recipient of a tainted gift.

(POCA 2002 s.41(4))

The offences falling within s.41(5) are:

(i) the offences mentioned in s.40(2) or (3) if the first or second condition, as the case may be, is satisfied; and
(ii) the offence, or any of the offences, concerned if the 3rd, 4th or 5th condition is satisfied.

A legal aid exception:

- must be made subject to prescribed restrictions (if any) on the circumstances in which payments may be made, or the amount of the payments that may be made, in reliance on the exception;
- must be made subject to other prescribed conditions (if any); and

- may be made subject to other conditions.

Any other exception to a restraint order may be made subject to conditions. (POCA 2002 s.41(5)–(5A))

Legal aid exceptions are not subject to a restriction introduced by The Restraint Orders (Legal Aid Exception and Relevant Legal Aid Payments) Regulations 2015 (SI 2015/868) reg.2, which states that relevant legal aid payments cannot be made unless the offence to which those payments has resulted in a confiscation order which has been discharged or satisfied.

If the court:

(a) makes a restraint order; and
(b) receives an application to make an order under subs.(7),

the court may make such order as it believes is appropriate for the purpose of ensuring that the restraint order is effective.

Where the court makes a restraint order by virtue of the first condition (above: a criminal investigation has been started, etc.), the court must:

(i) include a requirement for the applicant to report to the court on the progress of the investigation at such times and in such manner as the court may specify (a "reporting requirement"); and
(ii) discharge the order if proceedings for the offence are not started within a reasonable time (whether or not an application to discharge is made).

If the judge decides that a reporting requirement should not be imposed, he must give reasons for that decision, and may at any time vary the order to include a reporting requirement (whether or not an application to vary is made).

In considering whether to make an order under subs.(7), the court must in particular consider whether any restriction or prohibition on the defendant's travel outside the UK ought to be imposed.

(POCA 2002 s.41(6)–(7D))

The judge to whom an application for a restraint order is made must look at it carefully and with a critical eye:

(a) the power to impose restraint and receivership orders is an important weapon in the battle against crime but if used when the evidence on objective analysis is tenuous or speculative, it is capable of causing harm rather than preventing it;
(b) where third parties are likely to be affected, even if the statutory conditions for making the order are satisfied, the judge must still consider carefully the potential adverse consequences to them before deciding whether on balance the order should be made and, if so, on what conditions; and
(c) a judge who is in doubt may always ask for further information and require it to be properly vouched.

See *Ashford v Southampton City Council* [2014] EWCA Crim 1244 and the cases cited there.

An order must include a statement that disobedience of the order, either by a person to whom it is addressed, or by any other person, may be contempt of court, and details of the possible consequences of being held in contempt must be included. It is the duty of the applicant to serve copies of the order and of the witness statement made in support, on the defendant and any person prohibited from dealing with realisable property by the order, and to notify any person whom he knows to be affected by the order, of its terms (CrimPR 33.52).

Charges; seizure

Charging orders are abolished by POCA 2002 but s.41(8) provides that a restraint order is not to affect property for the time being subject to a charge under: **54-006**

(1) DTA 1986 s.9;
(2) CJA 1988 s.78;
(3) CJ (Confiscation) (NI) Order 1990 (SI 1990/2588 (NI 17)) art.14;
(4) DTA 1986 s.27;
(5) Proceeds of Crime (NI) Order 1996 (SI 1996/1299 (NI 9)) art.32.

(POCA 2002 s.41(8))

Restraint orders: power to retain seized property etc.

A restraint order may include provision authorising the detention of any property to which it applies if the property: **54-007**

(1) is seized by an appropriate officer under a relevant seizure power; or
(2) is produced to an appropriate officer in compliance with a production order under s.345.

In particular such provision may relate to:

(a) specified property, to property of a specified description or to all property to which the restraint order applies; and
(b) property that has already been seized or produced or to property that may be seized or produced in future.

(POCA 2002 s.41A)

"Appropriate officer" here means an accredited financial investigator, a constable, an officer of Revenue and Customs, an NCA officer, an immigration officer, or a member of staff of the relevant director (within the meaning of s.352(5A)). "Relevant seizure" power means a power to seize property which is conferred by, or by virtue of, ss.47C, 352, or Pt 2 or 3 of PACE 1984 (including as applied by order under PACE 1984 s.114(2)).

Order subject to exceptions

The judge may make a restraint order subject to exceptions including, but not limited to exceptions for: **54-008**

(1) reasonable living expenses;
(2) reasonable legal expenses; and
(3) the purpose of enabling any person to carry on any trade, business or occupation.

An exception to a restraint order may be made subject to conditions.
(CrimPR 33.52)

The terms of any exception need careful consideration, since an order may cause serious hardship. Save in exceptional cases, its terms should not go beyond what is required to prevent dissipation of the assets; the order properly does not prevent the meeting of ordinary and reasonable expenditure (*Re Peters* [1988] 3 All E.R. 46). The courts have generally insisted upon adequate provision being made in the order for the specified person's reasonable living expenses.

In relation to reasonable living expenses:

(a) an order ought, ordinarily, from the moment it is granted on the ex parte application, to contain a provision for such expenses unless good reason is shown why this should not be done in the particular case;
(b) it may be convenient for the prosecutor, when applying for the order, to insert such an exception into the draft order sought; or, if he does not, he should come before the judge prepared to explain why, in the circumstances of the case, it would be inappropriate to include such a provision; and the circumstances relied upon ought to be set out in the application;
(c) it will generally be appropriate to put a limit in the order;
(d) consistent with the principle that a person not convicted of any offence should not unreasonably be made to incur expenditure in coming to court, the limit should err on the side of generosity, though at the ex parte stage it may not be possible to fix the appropriate limit with any accuracy;
(e) the applicant may, of course, once the order is granted, attempt to reach agreement with the specified person as to the appropriate level of expenditure to be permitted by the exception to the order; if agreement is reached, the order may be varied by consent; if not, either party may apply to the court;
(f) the expression "reasonable living expenses" may cover the payment of ordinary debts as they fall due, though a separate exception may be required here; if there is any uncertainty about this, an application may be made to the court; and
(g) as to policing the exception, s.41(3)(c) permits the judge to impose conditions. He might require the specified person, as a condition of making an exception allowing payment of reasonable living expenses, to take certain steps designed to enable the prosecutor to be aware of the level and type of expenditure and apply to the court if he considers that it goes beyond what is permissible. There might be a condition to require the specified person to identify the accounts from which he habitually makes payment of his ordinary living expenses. There may be other appropriate conditions. Alternatively, the specified person might be required to establish a separate account into which certain sums can be paid and from which payments can be made consistent with the order.

In a case where it is known that the specified person carries on a trade, business, profession or occupation, a similar approach should be taken, in line with the provisions in s.41(3)(b) of the Act.

The order must not make an exception for legal expenses where this is prohibited by POCA 2002 s.41(4). The fact that recipients of tainted gifts are also excluded from the provision of legal expenses by s.41(4)(b) means that the provision is not directed simply at excluding legal expenses in connection with the defendant's criminal proceedings, but also the restraint proceedings themselves (see *Re S (Restraint Order: Release of Assets for Legal Representation)* [2004] EWCA Crim 2374; [2005] 1 Cr. App. R. 17; see also *R. v AP* [2007] EWCA Civ 3128; [2008] 1 Cr. App. R. 39; cf. *HMRC v Robert William Briggs-Price* [2007] EWCA Civ 568).

In *R. v Luckhurst (Andrew John)* [2020] EWCA Crim 1579; [2021] 1 W.L.R. 1807, the Court identified at [33] a non-exhaustive list of factors that may be potentially relevant to what constitutes "reasonable living expenses": (1) whether the payment is necessary or desirable to improve or maintain the value of assets available to meet a confiscation order; (2) the extent of D's assets set against the size of any likely confiscation order; (3) affordability: D's means at the time of the restraint order or variation application; (4) the period of the restraint; (5) whether there is a prima facie case that the existing standard of living is the result of criminal activity; and if so, what standard of living would be enjoyed but for such criminal activity; and (6) whether the amount to be expended was unreasonable in an absolute sense. The court may make an exception to discharge a debt incurred in respect of reasonable living expenses (at [36]).

The CACD certified the following point of law for the Supreme Court:

> "Does section 41(4) of POCA preclude an exception to a restraint order to make provision for reasonable legal expenses incurred by the defendant or the recipient of a tainted gift where those expenses incurred by the defendant or the recipient of a tainted gift are in respect of civil proceedings founded on the same or similar allegations, alleged facts and/or evidence as those of the offence(s) (within the meaning of section 41(5)) which gave rise to the making of the restraint order?"

The Supreme Court answered the certified question in the negative. On the correct interpretation of s.41(4), legal expenses in respect of civil proceedings for causes of action (such as for torts or equitable wrongs) are not precluded but are controlled by the courts' discretion in the same way as, for example, living expenses.

An allowance for ordinary living expenses cannot be used to pay a contribution to the Legal Services Commission (*CPS v Campbell* [2009] EWCA (Crim) 997; [2010] 1 W.L.R. 650).

General procedural provisions

CrimPR 33 contains a number of general provisions concerning restraint and receivership proceedings: **54-009**

(1) applications in restraint and receivership proceedings are dealt with without a hearing, unless the judge orders otherwise; proceedings may be heard in chambers (CrimPR 33.34–33.35); and

(2) as far as evidence in the proceedings is concerned:

  (a) the judge may control the evidence by giving directions as to the issues on which he requires evidence, the nature of the evidence necessary to decide those issues and the way in which it is to be placed before him; he may exclude evidence that would otherwise be admissible, and may limit cross-examination (CrimPR 33.36);

  (b) any fact which needs to be proved by the evidence of a witness may be proved, unless the judge orders otherwise, by his evidence in writing; a party may apply for leave to cross-examine, and if it is granted and the witness fails to attend, his evidence may not be used without the judge's permission (CrimPR 33.37);

  (c) a party may apply to the court to issue a witness summons requiring a witness to attend or to produce documents to the court; CrimPR 17.3 applies (CrimPR 33.38); and

  (d) hearsay evidence may be admitted without the duty to give notice required by CEA 1995 s.2(1) (CrimPR 33.39).

Every order must be drawn up by the Crown Court unless:

(i) the Crown Court orders a party to draw it up;
(ii) a party, with the permission of the Crown Court, agrees to draw it up; or
(iii) the order is made by consent under CrimPR 33.42.

For the rules concerning consent orders, see CrimPR 33.42.

The Crown Court may direct that an order drawn up by a party be checked by the Crown Court before it is sealed, or that before an order is drawn up by the Crown Court, the parties lodge an agreed statement of its terms.

Where an order is to be drawn up by a party, he must lodge it with the Crown Court no later than seven days after the date on which the court ordered or permitted him to draw it up so that it can be sealed by the Crown Court. If he fails to lodge it within that period, any other party may draw it up and lodge it.

The Crown Court is not required to accept a document which is illegible, has not been duly authorised, or is unsatisfactory for some other similar reason (CrimPR 33.46). As to costs in such proceedings, see CrimPR 33.47–50.

Hearsay evidence

54-010 Evidence must not be excluded in restraint proceedings on the ground that it is hearsay (of whatever degree). Sections 2–4 of CEA 1995 apply in relation to restraint proceedings as those sections apply in relation to civil proceedings (POCA 2002 s.46).

Note that for the purposes of this section:

(1) "restraint proceedings" are proceedings for a restraint order; for the discharge or variation of such an order; and on an appeal under ss.43 or 44; and
(2) "hearsay" is a statement which is made otherwise than by a person while giving oral evidence in the proceedings and which is tendered as evidence of the matters stated. Nothing in s.46 affects the admissibility of evidence which is admissible apart from that section.

Obligations in relation to exercise of powers

54-011 In relation: (a) to the powers conferred on a judge by ss.41–59 and 62–67D; (b) to the powers of a receiver appointed under ss.48, 50; and (c) the powers conferred on appropriate officers and senior officers, there is a general obligation to exercise them:

(1) with a view to the value for the time being of realisable property being made available (by the property's realisation) for satisfying any confiscation order that has been or may be made against a defendant;
(2) in a case where a confiscation order has not been made, with a view to securing that there is no diminution in the value of such property; and
(3) without taking account of any obligation of the defendant or a recipient of a tainted gift if the obligation conflicts with the object of satisfying any confiscation order that has been or may be made against the defendant.

[Note that where the restraint order contains a legal aid exception, in considering (1) and (3) above the powers must be exercised with a view to satisfying any obligation to make relevant legal aid payments in connection with the relevant offence; see The Restraint Orders (Legal Aid Exception and Relevant Legal Aid Payments) Regulations 2015 (SI 2015/868) reg.5.]

The powers may be exercised in respect of a debt owed by the Crown, subject to the following rules:

(a) the powers must be exercised with a view to allowing a person other than the defendant or a recipient of a tainted gift to retain or recover the value of any interest held by him;
(b) in the case of realisable property held by a recipient of a tainted gift, the powers must be exercised with a view to realising no more than the value for the time being of the gift; and
(c) in a case where a confiscation order has not been made against the defendant, property must not be sold if the judge so orders.

The judge may order that property is not to be sold if, on an application by the defendant or by the recipient of a tainted gift, he decides that the property cannot be replaced. Such an order may be revoked or varied.

(POCA 2002 s.69(1)–(5))

As to the position where it is sought to pay a debt to a third-party creditor from the restrained assets, see *SFO v Lexi Holdings Plc* [2008] EWCA Crim 1443; [2009] 1 Cr. App. R. 23.

Discharge and variation; breach

An application to discharge or vary a restraint order or an order under s.41(7) may be made to the Crown Court by the person who applied for the order or by any person affected by it, and on such application the court may discharge the order, or vary it. **54-012**

Where the condition in s.40 which was satisfied was that proceedings were started or an application was made, the judge must:

(1) discharge the order on the conclusion of the proceedings or of the application (as the case may be); unless
(2) the proceedings are concluded by the defendant's conviction being quashed but the CACD has ordered a retrial or the prosecution has applied for a retrial.

But the court must discharge the order if the CACD declines to order a retrial, or if a retrial is ordered but the proceedings for the retrial are not started within a reasonable time, or otherwise on the conclusion of the retrial proceedings.

[Note that where the restraint order contains a legal aid exception, in considering (1) above the order should be discharged only if the person has satisfied their obligation to make relevant legal aid payments in connection with the relevant offence; see The Restraint Orders (Legal Aid Exception and Relevant Legal Aid Payments) Regulations 2015 (SI 2015/868) reg.5.]

Where the condition in s.40 which was satisfied was that an investigation was started, the judge must discharge the order:

(a) if proceedings for the offence are not started within a reasonable time; or
(b) on the conclusion of the proceedings.

Where the condition in s.40 which was satisfied was that an application was to be made, the court must discharge the order:

(a) if the application is not made within a reasonable time; or

(b) on the conclusion of the proceedings.

(POCA 2002 s.42(3)–(8))

Procedural rules for an application for:

(a) discharge or variation by a person affected by the order are set out at CrimPR 33.53;
(b) variation of the order by the person who applied for the order are set out at CrimPR 33.54; and
(c) discharge of the order by the person who applied for it are set out at CrimPR 33.55.

Breach of a restraint order is a civil, not a criminal, contempt (*OB v DSFO* [2012] EWCA Crim 67; [2012] 3 All E.R. 999) and where there are aggravating features may constitute an offence of perverting the course of justice, though prosecutors should not charge an offender in breach with the offence unless it is necessary to do so (for example where there were aggravating features which would make punishment for a contempt inadequate (see *R. v Kenny* [2013] EWCA Crim 1; [2013] 1 Cr. App. R. 23)).

Appeal to the CACD

54-013 There is no appeal against the making of a restraint order. A person dissatisfied with the making of an order must apply to the Crown Court for its variation or discharge.

Appeal does, however, lie to the CACD in the following circumstances:

(1) if on an application for a restraint order the judge decides not to make one, the person who applied for the order may appeal to the Court of Appeal against the decision; and
(2) if an application is made under s.42(3) in relation to a restraint order or an order under s.41(7), the person who applied for the order or any person affected by the order may appeal to the Court of Appeal.

In either situation, the CACD may confirm the decision or make such order as it believes appropriate (POCA 2002 s.43).

Leave is required and will only be given where the CACD considers that the appeal would have a real prospect of success or there is some other compelling reason why the appeal should be heard. An order giving leave may limit the issues to be heard and may be made subject to conditions (CrimPR 42.14).

As of 4 April 2022, CrimPR 42.8 (notice of determination), CrimPR 42.11 (notice of appeal), CrimPR 42.12 (respondent's notice), and CrimPR 42.13 (amendment and abandonment of appeal), were amended by r.11(a)–(d) of the Criminal Procedure (Amendment) Rules 2022 (SI 2022/45).

Detention of property pending appeal

54-014 Where a restraint order:

(1) includes provision under s.41A authorising the detention of property, and the restraint order is discharged under ss.42(5) or 43(3)(b); or
(2) includes provision under s.41A authorising the detention of property, and the restraint order is varied under ss.42(5) or 43(3)(b) so as to omit any such provision,

the property may be detained until there is no further possibility of an appeal against the decision to discharge or vary the restraint order, or any decision made on an appeal against that decision (POCA 2002 s.44A).

Registration

The Registration Acts, as defined in s.47(2) apply in relation to: **54-015**

(1) restraint orders as they apply in relation to orders which affect land and are made by the court for the purpose of enforcing judgments or recognisances; and
(2) applications for restraint orders as they apply in relation to other pending land actions,

but no notice may be entered in the register of title under the Land Registration Act 2002 in respect of a restraint order.

The person applying for a restraint order is treated for the purposes of s.57 of the Land Registration Act 1925 (inhibitions) as a person interested in relation to any registered land to which the application relates, or a restraint order made in pursuance of which the application relates (POCA 2002 s.47).

2. Terrorism Act 2000

Restraint orders; serious default

The power to make a restraint order under TerrA 2000 Sch.4 paras 5–8 is reserved to the High Court, as is the power to order compensation in respect of serious default (TerrA 2000 Sch.4 para.9). **54-016**

B. Receivers

1. POCA 2002

A judge of the Crown Court is empowered under the provisions of POCA 2002 to appoint receivers of property in two instances: **54-017**

(1) "*management receivers*" manage property pending a defendant's conviction (and sometimes afterwards); and
(2) "*enforcement receivers*" dispose of such property to satisfy a confiscation order.

The appointment of a receiver before trial is essentially to safeguard the defendant's realisable assets rather than to maximise the amount which may be available to meet any future confiscation order (*Re Peters* [1988] 3 All E.R. 46).

A receiver is entitled to be recompensed in respect of his costs, expenses and remuneration out of the assets in his hands as receiver (*Capewell v Customs and Excise Commissioners* [2007] UKHL 2; [2007] 2 All E.R. 370). See also *CPS v The Eastenders Group* [2012] EWCA Crim 2436; [2013] 1 Cr. App. R. 24 where the issues are discussed in detail. As to the need for proportionality, see *CPS v Eastenders Group* [2014] UKSC 26; [2014] 2 Cr. App. R. 19.

As to procedure, see 54-022.

(1) Management receivers

54-018 Where:

(1) a restraint order is made; and
(2) the applicant for that order applies to a judge for an order (whether as part of the application for the restraint order or at any time afterwards),

the judge may by order appoint a receiver in respect of any realisable property to which the restraint order applies.

(POCA 2002 s.48)

On the application of the person who applied for the restraint order, the judge may confer on the receiver, in relation to any such property to which the restraint order applies, powers to:

(a) take possession of the property;
(b) manage or otherwise deal with it;
(c) commence, carry on or defend any legal proceedings in respect of it; and
(d) realise so much of it as is necessary to meet the receiver's remuneration and expenses,

provided the property is not for the time being subject to a charge under any of those provisions mentioned at 54-006.

The judge may also by order confer on the receiver power to enter any premises in England and Wales and to:

(i) search for or inspect anything authorised by the judge;
(ii) make or obtain a copy, photograph or other record of anything so authorised; and
(iii) remove anything which the receiver is required or authorised to take possession of in pursuance of a court order.

(POCA 2002 s.49(1)–(3))

As to procedure, see CrimPR 33.56–33.57, which are set out at 54-022 in the section dealing with enforcement receivers.

The judge may also by order authorise the receiver, for the purpose of the exercise of his functions, to hold property, enter into contracts, sue and be sued, employ agents, execute powers of attorney, deeds or other instruments and take any other steps the judge thinks appropriate.

(POCA 2002 s.49(4))

An application to appoint a management receiver should, where possible, be heard by the judge who made the restraint order(s).

Persons having possession of realisable property

54-019 The judge may order any person who has possession of realisable property to which the restraint order applies to give possession of it to the receiver.

(POCA 2002 s.49(5))

The judge may:

(1) order a person holding an interest in realisable property to which the restraint order applies to make to the receiver such payment as the court specifies in respect of a beneficial interest held by the defendant or the recipient of a tainted gift; and

(2) may (on payment being made) by order transfer, grant or extinguish any interest in the property,

provided that the property is not for the time being subject to a charge under any of those provisions mentioned at 54-006.

(POCA 2002 s.49(5)–(7))

The judge must not:

(a) confer the power to manage the property under s.49(2)(b) or to realise property to meet the receiver's expenses under s.49(2)(d); or
(b) exercise the power conferred on it under (1) above in respect of property,

unless he gives persons holding interests in the property a reasonable opportunity to make representations to it but this does not apply to property which is perishable or ought to be disposed of before its value diminishes.

(POCA 2002 s.49(8)–(8A))

The judge may order that any power conferred under this section be subject to such conditions and exceptions as he specifies.

(POCA 2002 s.49(9)

"Managing or otherwise dealing with property" includes:

(i) selling it, or any part of it or interest in it;
(ii) carrying on or arranging for another person to carry on any trade or business the assets of which are or are part of the property; and
(iii) incurring capital expenditure in respect of the property.

(POCA 2002 s.49(10))

Under POCA 2002 s.49(9) a receivership order may be made subject to such conditions and exceptions as the judge specifies. The conditions attached to receivership orders appear to have become largely standard, but the making of a receivership order should never be a rubber stamping exercise. The court has a responsibility to consider what conditions it should contain. In *Re Pigott* [2010] EWCA Civ 285; [2010] C.P. Rep. 31 it was suggested that in an appropriate case a management receivership order might be made subject to a special term that, if it should be shown in due course that the property subject to the order was not "realisable property" of the defendant but wholly in the legal and beneficial ownership of a third party, then the costs of the management receivership should be borne, not by the property, but, in the absence of any other source, by the prosecutor. There may indeed be cases in which such a condition would be appropriate, particularly cases in which the court can see the possibility that payment of the receiver's expenses and remuneration out of the relevant assets might infringe a person's A1P1 rights (*Barnes v The Eastenders Group* [2014] UKSC 26; [2014] 2 Cr. App. R. 19). See also *Re Smith* [2017] EWHC 3332 (Comm), where a modified *Pigott* condition was imposed.

(2) Enforcement receivers

In the case of a confiscation order made but not satisfied, and not subject to appeal (e.g. an order falling to be enforced in the magistrates' court) a judge may, on the application of the prosecutor, appoint an enforcement receiver in respect of realisable property. 54-020

(POCA 2002 s.50)

If he does so he may, on the prosecutor's application, by order confer on the receiver:

(1) in relation to the realisable property, the powers to:
   (a) take possession of it;
   (b) manage or otherwise deal with it;
   (c) realise it in such manner as the judge may specify; and
   (d) commence, carry on or defend any legal proceedings in respect of it; provided it is not for the time being subject to a charge under any of the enactments set out at 54-006;
(2) the power to enter any premises in England and Wales and:
   (a) search for or inspect anything authorised by the judge;
   (b) make or obtain a copy, photograph or other record of anything so authorised; and
   (c) remove anything which the receiver is required or authorised to take possession of in pursuance of a court order.

The judge may also authorise the receiver, for the purpose of the exercise of his functions to hold property, enter into contracts, use and be used, employ agents, execute powers of attorney, deeds or other instruments and take any other steps the court thinks appropriate.

(POCA 2002 s.51(1)–(5))

"Managing or otherwise dealing with property" includes:

(i) selling the property or any part of it or interest in it;
(ii) carrying on or arranging for another person to carry on any trade or business the assets of which are or are part of the property; and
(iii) incurring capital expenditure in respect of the property.

(POCA 2002 s.51(10))

The court may order that a power conferred by an order under this section is subject to such conditions and exceptions as it specifies.

(POCA 2002 s.51(9))

As to procedure, see CrimPR 33.56–33.57 (see 54-022 below).

Persons having possession of realisable property

54-021 The judge may order any person who has possession of realisable property to give possession of it to the receiver, and may:

(1) order a person holding an interest in realisable property to make to the receiver such payment as he specifies in respect of a beneficial interest held by the defendant or the recipient of a tainted gift; and
(2) (on payment being made) by order transfer, grant or extinguish any interest in the property, unless the property is for the time being subject to a charge under any of the enactments set out at 54-006.

The judge must not:

(a) confer the power to manage or to realise property; or
(b) exercise the power conferred on him by (1) and (2) above, in respect of property,

unless he gives persons holding interests in the property a reasonable opportunity to make representations. He is not obliged to do that where the property is perishable, or ought to be disposed of before its value diminishes.

Representations that a person is entitled to make do not include representations that are inconsistent with a determination under s.10A, unless the person was not given a reasonable opportunity to make representations when the determination was made and has not appealed it, or it appears that there would be a serious risk of injustice if the court was bound by the determination. If either of these qualifications apply, the determination does not bind the court.
(POCA 2002 s.51(8)–(8B))

(3) Procedure

Appointment of receiver

An application for the appointment of a management receiver under s.48(1) or an enforcement receiver under s.50(1) is made as follows under CrimPR 33.56. 54-022

The application may be made without notice if:

(1) the application is joined with an application for a restraint order under CrimPR 33.51;
(2) the application is urgent; or
(3) there are reasonable grounds for believing that giving notice would cause the dissipation of realisable property which is the subject of the application.

It must be in writing and must be supported by a witness statement giving:

(a) the grounds for the application;
(b) full details of the proposed receiver;
(c) to the best of the witness's ability, full details of the realisable property in respect of which the applicant is seeking the order, and specifying the person holding that realisable property;
(d) where the application is made by an accredited financial investigator, a statement that he has been authorised to make the application under s.68; and
(e) if the proposed receiver is not a person falling within POCA 2002 s.55(8) (a constable, an accredited financial investigator, etc.) and the applicant is asking the court to allow the receiver to act:
    (i) without giving security; or
    (ii) before he has given security or satisfied the court that he has security in place,

explain the reasons why that is necessary.

Where the application is for the appointment of an enforcement receiver, the applicant must provide the Crown Court with a copy of the confiscation order made against the defendant.

The application and witness statement must be lodged with the Crown Court, and except where notice of the application is not required to be served, the application and witness statement must be lodged with the Crown Court and served on the defendant, any person who holds realisable property to which the application relates, and any other person whom the applicant knows to be affected by the application, at least seven days before the date fixed by the court for hearing the application, unless the Crown Court specifies a shorter period.

If the court makes an order for the appointment of a receiver, the applicant must serve copies of the order and of the witness statement made in support of the application on such persons.

(CrimPR 33.56)

Conferral of powers

54-023 An application to the court for the conferral of powers on a management receiver under s.49(1) or on an enforcement receiver under s.51(1) is made as follows under the procedure in CrimPR 33.57.

The application may be made without notice if the application is to give the receiver power to take possession of property and:

(1) the application is joined with an application for a restraint order under CrimPR 33.51;
(2) the application is urgent; or
(3) there are reasonable grounds for believing that giving notice would cause the dissipation of the property which is the subject of the application.

The application must be made in writing and supported by a witness statement which must:

(a) give the grounds for the application;
(b) give full details of the realisable property in respect of which the applicant is seeking the order and specifying the person holding that realisable property;
(c) where the application is made by an accredited financial investigator, include a statement that he has been authorised to make the application under s.68; and
(d) (if the application is for power to start, continue or defend legal proceedings in respect of the property) explain what proceedings are concerned, in which court, and what powers the receiver will ask that court to exercise.

Where the application is for the conferral of powers on an enforcement receiver, the applicant must provide the Crown Court with a copy of the confiscation order made against the defendant.

The application and witness statement must be lodged with the Crown Court, and except where notice of the application is not required to be served, the application and witness statement must be served on the defendant, any person who holds realisable property in respect of which a receiver has been appointed or in respect of which an application for a receiver has been made, any other person whom the applicant knows to be affected by the application, and the receiver (if one has already been appointed), at least seven days before the date fixed by the court for hearing the application, unless the Crown Court specifies a shorter period.

If the judge makes an order for the conferral of powers on a receiver, the applicant must serve copies of the order on those persons.

(CrimPR 33.57)

Miscellaneous

54-024 As to the giving of security by a receiver see CrimPR 33.60; as to non-compliance by receiver, see CrimPR 33.63. As to the judge's power to order a receiver to prepare and serve accounts, see CrimPR 33.62.

(4) Application of sums received

By enforcement receivers

Sums in the hands of an enforcement receiver (s.50), being the proceeds of the realisation of property (under s.51), or other sums in which the defendant holds an interest, must be applied: 54-025

(1) in payment of such expenses incurred by a person acting as an insolvency practitioner as are payable by virtue of s.432;
(2) in making any payments directed by the Crown Court; and
(3) on the defendant's behalf towards satisfaction of the confiscation order.

[NB: where the order contains a legal aid exception, The Restraint Orders (Legal Aid Exception and Relevant Legal Aid Payments) Regulations 2015 (SI 2015/868) reg.5 substitute in (3) (above) for the words "confiscation order" the words "the obligation … to make a relevant legal aid payment … in relation to the relevant offence".]

If the amount payable under the confiscation order has been fully paid and any sums remain in the receiver's hands, he must distribute them among such persons who held, or hold, interests in the property concerned (i.e. the proceeds of realisation and other sums mentioned above) as the Crown Court directs, and in such proportions as it directs.

Before making any direction, the judge must give persons who held, or hold, interests in the property concerned a reasonable opportunity to make representations.

The receiver will apply sums towards satisfaction of the confiscation order by paying them to the designated officer of the magistrates' court responsible for enforcing the confiscation order, as if the amount ordered to be paid were a fine, on account of the amount payable under the order.

(POCA 2002 s.54(1)–(7))

By the magistrates' court

Where the designated officer of the magistrates' court receives sums on account of the amount payable under a confiscation order (whether the sums are received under s.54 or otherwise), receipt reduces the amount payable under the order, but he must apply them in payment of such expenses incurred by a person acting as an insolvency practitioner as are payable under s.432, and are not already paid under ss.54(2)(a) or 67D(2)(a). 54-026

If he received the sums under ss.54 or 67D he must next apply them in payment of the remuneration and expenses:

(1) of any management receiver (s.48), to the extent that they have not been met by virtue of the exercise by that receiver of a power conferred under s.49(2)(d); and
(2) of the enforcement receiver appointed under s.50; or
(3) to which an "appropriate officer" is entitled by virtue of s.67B.

It is immaterial in the case of (3) whether he is a permanent or temporary member or he is on secondment from elsewhere.

If a direction was made under s.13(6) for an amount payable under a priority order to be paid out of sums recovered under the confiscation order, he will next apply the sums in payment of that amount.

If any amount remains after he makes those payments, the amount will be treated for the purposes of Courts Act 2003 s.38 as if it were a fine imposed by a magistrates' court.

(POCA 2002 s.55)

Seized money

54-027 Where money is held by a person:

(1) in an account maintained by him with a bank or a building society; or
(2) which has been seized by a constable under a relevant seizure power by a constable or another person lawfully exercising the power, and is being detained in connection with a criminal investigation or an investigation referred to in s.341; and

a confiscation order is made against the person holding money to which this section applies, and a receiver has not been appointed under s.50 in relation to the money, a magistrates' court may order the bank, building society, or person on whose authority the money is detained, to pay the money to the designated officer of the magistrates' court on account of the amount payable under the confiscation order.

A person applying for such an order must give notice to the bank or buildings society with which the account is held.

Where the money is held in an account not maintained by the person against whom the confiscation order is made, the magistrates court may make the order only if the extent of the person's interest has been determined under s.10A, and must have regard to that determination in deciding the appropriate order to make. Failure to comply with an order may result in the defaulting bank or building society being fined; for the purposes of MCA 1980, the sum will be treated as adjudged to be paid by a conviction of the court.

(POCA 2002 s.67)

(5) Application for directions

54-028 A receiver appointed under ss.48 or 50 may apply to a judge of the Crown Court for an order giving directions as to the exercise of his powers, as may any person affected by action taken by the receiver and any person who may be affected by action the receiver proposes to take. On such an application, the judge may make such order as he believes is appropriate.

(POCA 2002 s.62)

The application must be made in writing and lodged with the Crown Court. It must also be served on the following persons (except where they are the person making the application):

(1) the person who applied for appointment of the receiver;
(2) the defendant;
(3) any person who holds realisable property in respect of which the receiver has been appointed;
(4) the receiver; and
(5) any other person whom the applicant knows to be affected by the application,

at least seven days before the date fixed by the court for hearing the application, unless the Crown Court specifies a shorter period.

If the judge makes an order for the discharge or variation of an order relating to a receiver under s.63(2), the applicant must serve copies of the order on any persons whom he knows to be affected by the order.

(CrimPR 33.58)

(6) Discharge and variation

Variation and discharge of orders

The following persons may apply to a judge of the Crown Court to vary or discharge an order made under any of ss.48–51: **54-029**

(1) the receiver;
(2) the person who applied for the order; and
(3) any person affected by the order.

The procedure is under CrimPR 33.58.

On such application, the judge may discharge or vary the order, but, in the case of an order under ss.48 or 49 in relation to management receivers:

(a) if the condition in s.40 which was satisfied was that proceedings were started or an application was made, the judge must discharge the order on the conclusion of the proceedings or of the application (as the case may be); [Note that where the restraint order contains a legal aid exception, the order should be discharged only if the person has satisfied their obligation to make relevant legal aid payments in connection with the relevant offence; see The Restraint Orders (Legal Aid Exception and Relevant Legal Aid Payments) Regulations 2015 (SI 2015/868) reg.5]; and
(b) if the condition which was satisfied was that an investigation was started or an application was to be made, the court must discharge the order if, within a reasonable time, proceedings for the offence are not started or the application is not made (as the case may be).

(POCA 2002 s.63)

As to when applications and other proceedings are commenced or concluded, see CONFISCATION ORDERS.

Management receivers: discharge

Where: **54-030**

(1) a management receiver stands appointed under s.48 in respect of realisable property; and
(2) a judge appoints an enforcement receiver under s.50,

he must order the management receiver to transfer to the other receiver all property held by him by virtue of the powers conferred on him by s.49, other than that which he holds by virtue of the exercise by him of his power under s.49(2)(d).

Where the management receiver complies with the order he is discharged from his appointment under s.48, and from any obligation under the Act arising from his appointment.

Where this section applies the judge may make such a consequential or incidental order as he believes appropriate.

Where the amount payable under a confiscation order has been fully paid, the receiver must make an application to the court under CrimPR 33.59 as to any sums still in his hands.

(POCA 2002 s.64)

(7) Restrictions on dealing with property

Restraint orders

54-031 Where a restraint order is made:

(1) no distress may be levied (and no power to use the procedure in Sch.12 to TCEA 2007 (taking control of goods) may be exercised) against any realisable property to which the order applies except with the leave of a judge of the Crown Court and subject to any terms he may impose;
(2) if the order applies to a tenancy of any premises, no landlord or other person to whom rent is payable may exercise any right of forfeiture by peaceable re-entry in relation to the premises in respect of any failure by the tenant to comply with any term or condition of the tenancy, except with the leave of a judge and subject to any terms he may impose; and
(3) if any court in which proceedings are pending in respect of any property is satisfied that a restraint order has been applied for or made in respect of the property, that court may either stay the proceedings or allow them to continue on any terms it thinks fit, provided it gives an opportunity to be heard to the applicant for the restraint order, and any receiver appointed in respect of the property under ss.48 or 50.

(POCA 2002 s.58)

Enforcement receivers

54-032 Where an enforcement receiver is appointed under s.50 in respect of any realisable property:

(1) no distress may be levied (and no power to use the procedure in Sch.12 to TCEA 2007 (taking control of goods) may be exercised) against any property to which the order applies except with the leave of a judge of the Crown Court and subject to any terms he may impose;
(2) if the order applies to a tenancy of any premises, no landlord or other person to whom rent is payable may exercise any right of forfeiture by peaceable re-entry in relation to the premises in respect of any failure by the tenant to comply with any term or condition of the tenancy, except with the leave of a judge and subject to any terms he may impose; and
(3) if any court in which proceedings are pending in respect of any property is satisfied that an order under s.50 appointing a receiver in respect of the property has been applied for or made, the judge may either stay the proceedings or allow them to continue on any terms he thinks fit, but before exercising any such power must give an opportunity to be heard to the prosecutor, and the receiver (if the order under s.50 has been made).

(POCA 2002 s.59)

(8) Appealing POCA receivership orders

Appeal to the CACD

Where an application is made for an order under any of ss.48–51 and the court decides not to make one, the person who applied may appeal to the CACD against the decision. **54-033**

If the court makes an order under any of those sections, the person who applied for the order or any person affected by the order may appeal to the CACD.

If an application is made for an order under s.62 and the court decides not to make one, the person who applied may appeal to the CACD.

If the court makes an order under s.62, the person who applied for the order, any person affected by the order or the receiver may appeal to the CACD.

Appeal to the CACD against a decision of the court on an application under s.63 may be made by the person who applied for the order, any person affected by the order or the receiver.

On any such appeal, the CACD may confirm the decision or make such order as it believes is appropriate.

(POCA 2002 s.65)

See further APPEALS FROM THE CROWN COURT.

Financial investigators; applications and appeals

In relation to applications under ss.41, 42, 48, 49 or 63, or appeals under ss.43, 44, 65 or 66, an accredited financial investigator must not make such an application or bring such an appeal unless he is one of the following, or is authorised for the purpose by one of the following: **54-034**

(1) a police officer who is not below the rank of superintendent;
(2) an officer of Revenue and Customs who is not below such grade as is designated by the Commissioners for Revenue and Customs as equivalent to that rank; and
(3) an accredited financial investigator who falls within a description specified in an order made for the purposes of this paragraph by the Secretary of State or the Welsh Ministers under s.453.

If such an application is made or appeal brought by an accredited financial investigator any subsequent step in the application or appeal or any further application or appeal relating to the same matter may be taken, made or brought by a different accredited financial investigator who falls within subs.(3).

If:

(a) an application for a restraint order is made by an accredited financial investigator; and
(b) a court is required under s.58(6) to give the applicant for the order an opportunity to be heard, the court may give the opportunity to a different accredited financial investigator who falls within subs.(3).

(POCA 2002 s.68)

Definitions

A reference to the offence (or offences) concerned must be construed in accordance with s.6(9). **54-035**

A "criminal investigation" is an investigation which police officers or other persons have a duty to conduct with a view to it being ascertained whether a person should be charged with an offence.

A "defendant" is a person against whom proceedings for an offence have been started (whether or not he has been convicted).

A reference to "sentencing the defendant for an offence" includes a reference to dealing with him otherwise in respect of the offence.

(POCA 2002 s.88)

2. Terrorism Act 2000

Appointment of receiver

54-036 Where a judge makes a forfeiture order (see FORFEITURE AND DEPRIVATION ORDERS) under TerrA 2000, he may make such other provision as appears to him to be necessary for giving effect to the order, in particular:

(1) requiring any of the forfeited property to be paid or handed over to the proper officer or to a constable designated for the purpose by the chief officer of police of a police force specified in the order;
(2) directing any of the forfeited property other than money or land to be sold or otherwise disposed of in such manner as he may direct and the proceeds (if any) to be paid to the proper officer; and
(3) directing a specified part of any forfeited money, or of the proceeds of the sale, disposal or realisation of any forfeited property, to be paid by the proper officer to a specified person falling within s.23B(1).

He may also appoint a receiver to take possession, subject to such conditions and exceptions as may be specified by him, of any of the forfeited property, to realise it in such manner as he may direct and to pay the proceeds to the proper officer.

A reference to the proceeds of the sale, disposal or realisation of property is a reference to the proceeds after deduction of the costs of sale, disposal or realisation.

(TerrA 2000 Sch.4 para.2)

Receivers

54-037 A receiver appointed under para.2 is entitled to be paid his remuneration and expenses by the proper officer out of the proceeds of the property realised by the receiver and paid to the proper officer. If, and in so far as those proceeds are insufficient, the receiver is entitled to be paid his remuneration and expenses by the prosecutor.

He is not liable to any person in respect of any loss or damage resulting from action:

(1) which he takes in relation to property which is not forfeited property, but which he reasonably believes to be forfeited property;
(2) which he would be entitled to take if the property were forfeited property; and
(3) which he reasonably believes that he is entitled to take because of his belief that the property is forfeited property,

but this does not apply in so far as the loss or damage is caused by the receiver's negligence.

(TerrA 2000 Sch.4 para.3)

C. External Requests

The legislation

POCA 2002 (External Requests and Orders) Order 2005 (SI 2005/3181) (as amended by LASPOA 2012 (Consequential, Transitional and Saving Provisions) Regulations 2013 (SI 2013/534) and by the Proceeds of Crime Act 2002 (External Requests and Orders) (Amendment) Order 2015 (SI 2015/1750) and the Proceeds of Crime Act 2002 (External Requests and Orders) (Amendment) Order 2016 (SI 2016/662)), and in regard to the former law, CJ(IC)A 1990 (Enforcement of Overseas Forfeiture Orders) Order 2005 (SI 2005/3180), make provision for "restraint orders" on dealing with property situated in England and Wales specified in a request by an overseas authority. **54-038**

Articles 6, 7, 8 and 8A of the POCA 2002 (External Requests and Orders) Order 2005 provide a scheme to make a restraint order in response to an external request only in respect of property in England and Wales.

There is no power to make such an order in respect of property outside the jurisdiction, e.g. in Scotland (*King v SFO* [2009] UKHL 17; [2009] 2 Cr. App. R. 2).

Such a request is channeled through the Secretary of State to the "relevant Director" being the DPP or DSFO.

The scheme

The procedure under both orders is similar. On an application by a relevant Director, a judge of the Crown Court, on being satisfied that: **54-039**

(1) a relevant property in England and Wales is identified in the request (other than property already subject to a charge);
(2) a criminal investigation or proceedings for an offence have been started in the country from which the request is made; and
(3) it appears to the judge that there are reasonable grounds for believing that as a result of the investigation or those proceedings an external forfeiture order may be made against the person named in the request,

may make a restraint order, prohibiting any specified person from dealing with relevant property which is identified in the request and specified in the order, other than property subject to a charge (see 54-006).

The order may be made subject to exceptions and be made subject to conditions. When the judge makes an order, and the applicant applies to him either then or afterwards, he may also make such further orders for the purpose of ensuring that the restraint order is effective. There is also power, on application, to discharge or vary a restraint order, a right of appeal by either side to the CACD and the Supreme Court, and a power to appoint a management receiver.

Procedure

CrimPR 33 and 42 apply with the necessary modifications to proceedings under SI 2005/3181 as they apply to corresponding proceedings under POCA 2002 (CrimPR 33.12). **54-040**

D. Compensation for serious default

54-041 POCA 2002 s.72 provides for compensation to be paid to a person whose property has been affected by the enforcement of the confiscation legislation.

A judge of the Crown Court may order the payment of such compensation as he believes just:

(1) where, but only where:
  (a) a criminal investigation has been started with regard to an offence and proceedings are not started for the offence; or
  (b) proceedings for an offence are started against a person and:
    (i) they do not result in his conviction for the offence; or
    (ii) he is convicted of the offence but the conviction is quashed or he is pardoned in respect of it;
(2) where (1)(a) above, applies:
  (a) in the criminal investigation there has been a serious default by a person mentioned in subs.(9); and
  (b) the investigation would not have continued if the default had not occurred;
(3) where (1)(b) above, applies, and:
  (a) in the criminal investigation with regard to the offence or in its prosecution there has been a serious default by a person who is mentioned in subs.(9); and
  (b) the proceedings would not have been started or continued if the default had not occurred; and
(4) an application is made by a person who held realisable property and has suffered loss in consequence of anything done in relation to it by or in pursuance of an order under Pt 2 of the Act.

Note that the offence referred to:

(i) in (1) above may be one of a number of offences with regard to which the investigation is started; and
(ii) in (2) above may be one of a number of offences for which the proceedings are started.

Application is made in writing and may be supported by a witness statement. It must be lodged in the Crown Court, and served on both the person alleged to be in default and the person by whom the compensation would be payable.

(CrimPR 33.22)

In *Bhandal v Revenue and Customs Commissioners* [2015] EWHC 538 (Admin); [2015] Lloyd's Rep. F.C. 343 QBD, the court considered the concept of "serious default" in s.76(2) of the CJA 1988. The court held that it did not require any deliberate action or inaction that was known to be wrong; negligence or even inadvertence, provided that it could properly be considered serious, would suffice. The question was whether anything done or omitted by a person (mentioned in s.72(9) of the 2002 Act) was not in the circumstances reasonable; where the person concerned acted on the advice of counsel, he would be likely to establish that there was no default, provided of course that counsel was not misled by any omissions in the information given to him.

Source of payment

Compensation is payable to the applicant as follows. If the person in default was: **54-042**

(1) a member, or was acting as a member, of a police force, the compensation is payable out of the police fund from which the expenses of that force are met;

(2) a member of the CPS or was acting on its behalf, the compensation is payable by the DPP;

(3) an officer of NCA, the compensation is payable by the NCA;

(4) a member of the SFO, the compensation is payable by the DSFO;

(5) an officer of the Commissioners of Inland Revenue, the compensation is payable by those Commissioners;

(6) an immigration officer, the compensation is payable by the Secretary of State; or

(7) an accredited financial investigator, and none of (1)–(6) above apply, the compensation is payable in accordance with paras (a), (c), (da) or (e) of s.302(7A) (as the case may require).

(POCA 2002 s.72(9))

Compensation on variation or discharge

Where the court varies a confiscation order under s.29 or discharges one under s.30, an application may be made to the Crown Court by a person who held realisable property and has suffered loss as a result of the making of the order, and the judge may order the payment of such compensation as it believes is just, to the applicant, by the Lord Chancellor. **54-043**

(POCA 2002 s.73)

The application must be in writing, supported by a witness statement giving details of the order made under s.28, the variation or discharge under s.29 or s.30, the realisable property to which the application relates and the loss suffered by the applicant as a result of the making of the order.

These documents must be lodged with the Crown Court, and must be served on the prosecutor at least seven days before the date fixed for the hearing unless the Crown Court specifies a shorter period.

(CrimPR 33.23)

55. RETRIALS

QUICK GUIDE

General

55-001 It is a commonplace, where a jury has failed to reach a verdict in a criminal trial for there to be a retrial before another jury. No particular provisions apply in such circumstances. Whether a retrial, particularly a second retrial, is in the interests of justice (which require a fair trial in circumstances which are neither oppressive nor unjust) is ultimately a question for the trial judge (*R. v Bell* [2010] EWCA Crim 3; [2010] 1 Cr. App. R. 27). A second retrial should, however, be confined to the small number of cases in which the jury are being invited to address a crime of extreme gravity, which has undoubtedly occurred, and in relation to which the evidence that the accused committed the crime remains powerful.

The "interests of justice" test is not a hard-edged concept. A decision as to what the interests of justice require calls for an exercise of judgment in which a number of relevant factors have to be taken into account and weighed in the balance. In difficult borderline cases, there may be scope for legitimate differences of opinion (*R. v Maxwell* [2010] UKSC 48; [2011] 2 Cr. App. R. 31, per Lord Dyson—a case concerning the exercise of discretion by the CACD to order a retrial pursuant to CAA 1968 s.7(1)).

There is a convention that if the prosecutor fails to secure a conviction on two occasions he will not seek a further retrial (*R. v Henworth* [2001] EWCA Crim 120; [2001] 2 Cr. App. R. 4; *DPP v Edgar* (2002) 164 J.P. 471; *R. v Bell* [2009] EWCA Crim 3; [2010] 1 Cr. App. R. 27). As to the matters to be considered see *R. v Hussein* [2013] EWCA Crim 707; [2013] 1 Cr. App. R. (S.) 112.

As to when such a proceeding might amount to an abuse of process, see ABUSE OF PROCESS.

There are, however, certain specialties of evidence and procedure which apply to retrials ordered by the CACD under CAA 1968 s.7 (see 55-002) and those concerning serious offences under CJA 2003 Pt 10 (see 55-007).

A. RETRIAL UNDER CAA 1968 s.7

Arraignment

55-002 In a case where the CACD has ordered that an appellant should be re-tried:

(1) the appellant must be arraigned on a new indictment, preferred at the direction of the CACD within the time limit specified by that court, being within two months of the order (see CAA 1968 s.8);
(2) the Registrar will write to the court manager of the Crown Court immediately when a retrial has been ordered and send with the letter a copy of the draft judgment; his letter is copied to the prosecuting authority and the defence; and

(3) the Registrar will send a copy of the approved judgment of the court as soon as it is available.

The CACD will normally order that the venue of the re-trial be determined by the Presiding Judge of the circuit where the original trial took place. The court manager or listing officer should therefore contact the regional listing coordinator immediately so that the Presiding Judge can make the decision as to venue.

Immediately after the decision of the Presiding Judge as to the location of the trial is made the listing officer of the court nominated by the Presiding Judge, or the listing officer's staff, should:

(a) contact the prosecutor to ask when the indictment will be delivered; and
(b) list the case for arraignment as soon as possible within the time period directed by the Court of Appeal.

These cases must be given sufficient priority so that the case is listed for arraignment in the period between receipt of the indictment and expiry of the time limit. In cases where a retrial is ordered by the CACD the custody time limit is 112 days starting from the date that the new indictment is preferred, i.e. from the date that the indictment is delivered to the Crown Court.

The Crown Court must comply with the directions given by the CACD and may not vary those directions without reference to that court. In cases where a retrial is ordered by the CACD the custody time limit is 112 days starting from the date that the new indictment is preferred, i.e. from the date that the indictment is delivered to the Crown Court. Court centres should check that the systems in place have calculated the dates correctly and that it has not used 182 days on cases that have previously been "sent for trial" (*CPD* XIII Listing: F Listing of trials, custody time limits and transfer of cases: F.6, F.7).

Ancillary orders

In relation to: **55-003**

(1) *Bail*, CrimPR 39.8 sets out the process where a party wants to make an application for bail pending appeal or retrial. The application has to be served on the Registrar and the other party. Applications must not be decided upon without giving the other party an opportunity to make representations (CrimPR 39.8(1)–(3)). Conditions of bail pending retrial are set out in CrimPR 39.9.
(2) *Legal aid*, the CACD has no power to make a representation order and the original Crown Court representation order does not cover the retrial; an application for a representation order must be made, clearly indicating that the application relates to a retrial ordered by the CACD; process for administering such applications is the same as for indictable offences (see LEGAL AID; PUBLIC FUNDING).
(3) *Publicity*, an order under CCA 1981 s.4(2) (see CONTEMPT OF COURT) will ordinarily be made.

As to joining a new co-accused see CAA 1968 s.7, also *R. v Hemmings* [2000] 1 Cr. App. R. 360; *R. v Booker* [2011] EWCA Crim 7; [2011] 1 Cr. App. R. 26. As to the joinder of further courts to the indictment, see *R. v F* [2012] EWCA Crim 720; [2012] 2 Cr. App. R. 13. Special rules apply in relation to persons subject to mental health procedures (see CAA 1968 s.8(3) and (3A)). The CACD may make orders as to the custody of the exhibits pending the retrial.

Arraignment at the Crown Court

55-004 After the end of two months from the date of the order, such person:

(1) may not be arraigned on an indictment preferred in pursuance of such a direction unless the CACD gives leave; and
(2) may to apply to the CACD to set aside the order and to direct the trial court to enter a judgment of acquittal of the offence for which he was ordered to be retried.

The CACD will not give leave to arraign in these circumstances unless satisfied that:

(a) the prosecutor has acted with all due expedition (*R. v Coleman* (1992) 95 Cr. App. R. 345; *R. v Horne*, *The Times,* 27 February 1992); and
(b) there is good and sufficient cause for a retrial in spite of the lapse of time since the order under s.7 was made.

The words "with all due expedition" are not to be equated with "all due diligence and expedition" required under POA 1985 (see CUSTODY TIME LIMITS); the former is a less exacting test (*R. v Jones* [2002] EWCA Crim 2284; [2003] 1 Cr. App. R. 20). See also *R. v Smith* [2007] EWCA Crim 519; *R. v Dales* [2011] EWCA Crim 134.

Evidence

55-005 Evidence at a retrial ordered by the CACD must be given orally if it was given orally at the original trial, unless:

(1) all the parties to the retrial agree otherwise;
(2) CJA 2003 s.116 applies (admissibility of hearsay evidence where a witness is unavailable); or
(3) the witness is unavailable to give evidence:
    (a) for reasons outwith those in s.116; and
    (b) CJA 2003 s.114(d) applies (admission of hearsay evidence under residual discretion).

(CAA 1968 Sch.2 paras 1 and 1A)

The fact that a witness refuses to give evidence on a retrial will not necessarily mean that he is to be considered "unavailable". The trial judge will have to consider with care the circumstances of refusal, just as he will in the other situation where a witness is not physically unavailable, namely fear. Among the circumstances to be considered will be whether all reasonable efforts have been made to obtain oral evidence from the witness at the retrial, the reasons for the refusal, whether either party has contributed to the situation leading to the refusal, and whether the judge is satisfied that it is in the interests of justice for the evidence to be admitted, having regard to all relevant factors, including those identified in CJA 2003 s.114(2) (*R. v R* [2013] EWCA Crim 708; [2014] 1 Cr. App. R. 5, per Treacy LJ).

The prosecution may be permitted to adduce evidence on a retrial of statements made on oath by the accused at the original trial, to show that he had lied (*R. v Binham* [1991] Crim. L.R. 774).

Sentence

Where a person ordered to be retried is convicted again, the judge may pass in respect of the offence any sentence authorised by law: 55-006

(1) not being a sentence of greater severity than that passed on the original conviction; and
(2) notwithstanding that, on the date of conviction on retrial, the offender has ceased to be of an age at which such a sentence could otherwise be passed.

(See *R. v Skanes* [2006] EWCA Crim 2309)

A sexual offences prevention order (now a sexual harm prevention order) (see SEX OFFENDER ORDERS) cannot be increased on retrial from five years to seven in length (*R. v Robson* [2007] EWCA Crim 1472).

Where imprisonment or other detention is imposed in such a case, the sentence begins to run from the time when a like sentence passed at the original trial would have begun to run; but in computing the term of his sentence or the period for which he may be detained thereunder, the judge must have regard to any time:

(a) before the offender's conviction on retrial which would have been disregarded in computing that term or period if the sentence had been passed at the original trial and the original conviction had not been quashed; and
(b) during which he was released on bail under CAA 1968 s.8(2).

(CAA 1968 Sch.2 para.2)

The crediting of periods of remand in custody is dealt with automatically (see CJA 2003 s.240ZA; LASPOA 2012 s.108); as to crediting periods spent on bail subject to certain conditions, see CJA 2003 s.240A under IMPRISONMENT.

B. RETRIAL FOR SERIOUS OFFENCES UNDER CJA 2003 PT 10

General

Where: 55-007

(1) a person has been acquitted, whether before or after the passing of CJA 2003:
    (a) of a "qualifying offence" in proceedings:
        (i) on indictment in England and Wales;
        (ii) on appeal against conviction, verdict or finding on indictment in England and Wales; or
        (iii) on appeal from a decision of such an appeal; or
    (b) in proceedings elsewhere than in the UK of an offence under the law of the place where the proceedings were held, if the commission of the offence as alleged would have amounted to, or included, the commission in the UK or elsewhere of a "qualifying offence";
(2) there is new and compelling evidence, within the meaning of s.78 that that person is guilty of the qualifying offence; and
(3) in all the circumstances it is in the interests of justice for such an order to be made, then, with the written consent of the DPP, the prosecutor may apply to the CACD, in the case of: (1) for an order quashing that person's acquittal in England and Wales and ordering his retrial for the qualifying offence, and in the case of; (2) for a determination whether the acquittal is a

bar to that person being retried in England and Wales for the offence, and if it is, for an order that it should not be a bar.

Not more than one application may be made in relation to an acquittal.
(CJA 2003 ss.75 and 76)

Definitions

55-008 A person acquitted of an offence in proceedings under these provisions is treated for the purposes of that provision as also acquitted of any qualifying offence of which he could have been convicted in the proceedings because of the first-mentioned offence being charged in the indictment, except an offence:

(1) of which he has been convicted;
(2) of which he has been found not guilty by reason of insanity; or
(3) in respect of which, in proceedings where he has been found to be under a disability (as defined by CP(I)A 1964 s.4), a finding has been made that he did the act or made the omission charged against him.

"Qualifying offences" are those set out in CJA 2003 Sch.5 Pt 1, but do not include references to an offence which, at the time of the acquittal was the subject of an order under s.77(1) or (3).

Conduct punishable under the law in force elsewhere than in the UK is an offence under that law for the purposes of s.62(4) however it is described in that law.
(CJA 2003 s.75(2)–(5))

Consent of DPP

55-009 The written consent of the DPP is required before any application may be made to the CACD. He may give his consent only if satisfied that:

(1) there is evidence as respects which the requirements of s.65 (as to new and compelling evidence) appear to be met; and
(2) it is in the public interest (within the meaning of s.65) for the application to proceed.

(CJA 2003 s.76(3) and (4))

Determination by the CACD

55-010 A retrial will be ordered only where the CACD is satisfied that the requirements of:

(1) s.78 as to new and compelling evidence; and
(2) s.79 as to the interests of justice,

are met, otherwise the application will be dismissed.

Where the CACD determines that the acquittal is a bar to the person being tried for the qualifying offence, it must, if satisfied that the provisions of ss.78 and 79 are met, make the order applied for, or otherwise make a declaration to the effect that the acquittal is a bar to the person being tried for the offence.
(CJA 2003 s.77)

Where the CACD determines that the acquittal is not a bar to the person being tried for the qualifying offence, it will make a declaration to that effect (e.g. *R. v Dunlop* [2006] EWCA Crim 1354; [2007] 1 Cr. App. R. (S.) 8).

"New and compelling" evidence

The quashing of an acquittal is an exceptional step and can only be ordered if the statutory requirement in relation to the reliability of the new evidence is clearly established, in relation to "new and compelling" evidence that the acquitted person is guilty of the qualifying offence: **55-011**

(1) evidence is "new" if it was not adduced in the proceedings in which the person was acquitted (nor, if those were appeal proceedings, in earlier proceedings to which the appeal related); and
(2) evidence is "compelling" if:
  (a) it is reliable (e.g. *R. v Miell* [2007] EWCA 3130; [2008] 1 Cr. App. R. 23);
  (b) it is substantial; and
  (c) in the context of the outstanding issues, it appears highly probative of the case against the acquitted person.

(CJA 2003 s.78(1)–(7))

To be "compelling" evidence does not have to be irresistible, nor is absolute proof of guilt required (*R. v Dobson* [2011] EWCA Crim 1255, above, applying *R. v G (G)* [2009] EWCA Crim 1207; [2009] Crim. L.R. 738). The legislative structure does not suggest that availability of a realistic defence argument, which might serve to undermine the reliability or probative value of the new evidence, precludes an order quashing the acquittal. Provided the new evidence is reliable, substantial and appears to be highly probative, then for the purposes of s.78, it is "compelling".

(See further as to these requirements *R. v B(J)* [2009] EWCA Crim 1036; [2009] Crim. L.R. 736; *R. v G(G)* [2009] EWCA Crim 1207; [2009] Crim. L.R. 738 and *R. v A* [2008] EWCA Crim 2908; [2009] 1 Cr. App. R. 25.)

Note that:

(i) "the outstanding issues" are the issues in dispute in the proceedings in which the person was acquitted and, if those were appeal proceedings;
(ii) any other issues remaining in dispute from earlier proceedings against the acquitted person;
(iii) for the purpose of this provision, it is irrelevant whether any evidence would have been admissible in earlier proceedings against the acquitted person.

The "interests of justice"

The "interests of justice" for the purposes of these provisions, are to be determined having regard, in particular, to: **55-012**

(1) whether existing circumstances make a fair trial unlikely;
(2) for the purposes of that question and otherwise, the length of time since the qualifying offence was allegedly committed;
(3) whether it is likely that the new evidence would have been adduced in the earlier proceedings against the acquitted person but for a failure by an officer or a prosecutor to act with due diligence; and
(4) whether, since those proceedings or, if later, since the commencement of CJA 2003 Pt 10 any officer or prosecutor has failed to act with due diligence or expedition.

(CJA 2003 s.79)

The interests of justice test contained in s.79 require attention to be focused on the express statutory criteria provided in that section. Those criteria, however, whilst wide ranging, are not exhaustive. However, compelling the new evidence may be, it is elementary that any second trial should be a fair one (*R. v Dobson* [2011] EWCA Crim 1255, above).

A reference to an "officer or prosecutor" includes a reference to a person charged with corresponding duties under the law in force elsewhere than in England and Wales, and where the earlier prosecution was conducted by a person other than officer or prosecutor, (3) above applies in relation to that person as well as in relation to a prosecutor.

Application by the prosecutor

55-013 The prosecutor may apply under s.76(1) for the quashing of an acquittal in England and Wales, or under s.76(2) in the case of a person acquitted elsewhere than in the UK, for a determination that that acquittal is no bar to a trial in England and Wales, or if it is, for an order that it should not be such a bar.

The double jeopardy bar does not ordinarily apply to cases which have been discontinued for reasons other than acquittal.

A prosecutor seeking to make a s.76 application must (CrimPR 27.4) serve notice of that application in the form set out in *CPD* Annex D on the Registrar and the acquitted person and that notice must be accompanied by:

(1) witness statements relied upon as new and compelling evidence of guilt of the acquitted person as well as any relevant documents from the original trial including the offences and evidence given; and
(2) any other document or thing that the prosecutor thinks the court will need to decide the application;

and file with the Registrar a witness statement or certificate of service which exhibits a copy of that notice (CrimPR 27.4).

Response of the acquitted person

55-014 An acquitted person seeking to oppose a s.76 application must serve a response in the form set out in *CPD* Annex D on the Registrar and the prosecutor which:

(1) indicates if he is also seeking an order under s.80(6) of the Criminal Justice Act 2003 for:
   (a) the production of any document, exhibit or other thing; or
   (b) a witness to attend for examination and to be examined before the CACD; and
(2) exhibits any relevant documents.

The acquitted person must serve that response not more than 28 days after receiving notice under CrimPR 27.4, although the CACD may extend the period for service either before or after that period expires (CrimPR 27.5).

Examination of witnesses or evidence by the CACD

55-015 An application may be made to the CACD by a party at least 14 days before the day of the hearing of the s.76 application, in the form set out in *CPD* Annex D for an order under s.80(6) for:

(1) the production of any document, exhibit or other thing which in the prosecutor's opinion is necessary for the determination of the application;
(2) a witness who would be a compellable witness at the trial the prosecutor wants the court to order,

sending it to the Registrar with a copy sent to each party to the application.

Such application will need to set out the details, with relevant facts and dates, of the defendant's acquittal and explaining what new and compelling evidence there is against the defendant, and why in all the circumstances it would be in the interests of justice for the court to make the order sought.

The written witness statements on which the prosecutor relies as new and compelling evidence, the relevant documents from the trial when the defendant was acquitted, including a record of the offences and the evidence given along with any other document or thing that the prosecution thinks the court will need to decide the application must be attached to the notice (CrimPR 27(3)).

Reporting restrictions

CJA 2003 s.82 provides for restrictions on reporting anything done under s.77, and creates offences (s.83) in respect of infringements of those proceedings. **55-016**

An application by the DPP under s.82 for restrictions on publication:

(1) must be in the form set out in *CPD* Annex D and be served on the Registrar and the acquitted person;
(2) if notice of a s.76 application has not been given and the DPP has indicated that there are reasons why the acquitted person should not be notified of the application for restrictions on publication, the CACD may order that service on the acquitted person is not to be effected until notice of a s.76 application is served on that person; and
(3) if the CACD makes an order for restrictions on publication of its own motion or on application of the DPP, the Registrar will serve notice and reasons for that order on all parties, unless (2) applies (CrimPR 27.3).

See *R. v D (Acquitted person; Retrial)* [2006] EWCA Crim 828; [2006] 2 Cr. App. R. 18 as to the appropriate way to proceed.

Effect of determination

Where the CACD: **55-017**

(1) quashes an acquittal under CJA 2003 s.77(1); or
(2) declares an acquittal to be no bar to a prosecution, under CJA 2003 s.77(3),

any subsequent trial will be on an indictment preferred by direction of the CACD, and arraignment must take place within two months from the date of the order, unless the CACD allows a longer period.

The CACD will not extend the period unless satisfied that:

(a) the Crown has acted with due expedition (see 55-002 in relation to retrial under CAA 1968 s.7); and
(b) there is good and sufficient cause for trial despite the lapse of time since the order under s.77 was made.

(CJA 2003 s.84(1), (2) and (3))

The determination of the application may be given at the conclusion of the hearing, or may be reserved. Notice will be given by the Registrar to the parties. Where the CACD orders a retrial, the Registrar will, as soon as practicable, serve notice on the Crown Court officer at the appropriate place of trial (CrimPR 36.7).

Where the accused is not arraigned within the time limits, he may apply to the CACD in the form set out in the Practice Direction, to set aside the order and:

(i) for any direction required for restoring an earlier judgment and verdict of acquittal of the qualifying offence (CJA 2003 s.84(4)); or
(ii) in the case of a person acquitted elsewhere than in the UK, for a declaration to the effect that the acquittal is a bar to his being tried for the qualifying offence (CJA 2003 s.84(5)).

The prosecutor must ensure that arraignment takes place within two months of the date which the CACD ordered a retrial. If the acquitted person has not been arraigned before the end of two months after that date, the prosecutor may apply, by serving the form set out in *CPD* Annex D on the Registrar, for leave to arraign. The acquitted person may apply to the CACD to set aside the order.

An indictment under (1) or (2) may relate to more than one offence, or more than one person, and may relate to an offence which, or a person who, is not the subject of an order or declaration under s.77 (CJA 2003 s.84(6) and (7)).

Evidence on retrial

55-018 The trial will take account of all the evidence in the case. The evidence given must be given orally if it was given orally at the original trial, unless:

(1) all the parties to the trial agree otherwise;
(2) CJA 2003 s.116 (witness unavailable) applies; or
(3) the witness is unavailable to give evidence, otherwise than as mentioned in CJA 2003 ss.116(2) and 114(1)(d) (interests of justice).

At a trial pursuant to an order under s.77(1) CDA 1998 Sch.3 para.5 (use of depositions) does not apply to a deposition read as evidence at the original trial.

The prosecution may be permitted to adduce evidence on a retrial of statements made on oath by the accused at the original trial, to show that he had lied (*R. v Binham* [1991] Crim. L.R. 774).

C. Bail under CJA 2003 Pt 10

Bail and custody before application

55-019 The Act recognises that it may take some time for the police and the Crown to formulate the case for the CACD, but this time should not be disproportionate. The power to remand in custody or on bail is given to the Crown Court.

Where a person appears or is brought before the Crown Court in accordance with s.88(1) or (2), the judge may either:

(1) grant bail for him to appear, if notice of application is served on him under s.80(2), before the CACD at the hearing of that application; or
(2) remand him in custody to be brought before the Crown Court under s.89(2).

Where bail is granted under this provision, it may be revoked, and the person may be remanded in custody as referred to in (2).

(CJA 2003 s.88(4) and (5))

If, at the end of the "relevant period" that is:

(a) the period of 42 days beginning with the day on which he is granted bail or remanded in custody; or
(b) that period as extended or further extended under s.88(8),

no notice of application under CJA 2003 s.76(1) or (2) in relation to that person has been given under s.80(1), that person:

(i) if on bail subject to a duty to appear, ceases to be under that duty and to any conditions of that bail; or
(ii) if in custody on remand under s.88(4)(b) or (5) must be released immediately without bail.

(CJA 2003 s.88(6) and (7))

As to applications for bail, see CrimPR 41.7.

Procedure; hearing in the Crown Court

Where a person is to appear, or be brought, before the Crown Court pursuant to CJA 2003 ss.88 or 89, CrimPR 19 (see CrimPR 41.5) applies as to bail. **55-020**

Where a person is to appear or be brought before the Crown Court pursuant to ss.88 or 89 the judge may order that the person shall be released from custody on entering into a recognisance, with or without sureties, or giving other security before the Crown Court officer, or any other person authorised by virtue of MCA 1980 s.119(1) to take a recognisance where a magistrates' court having power to take the recognisance has, instead of taking it, fixed the amount in which the principal and his sureties, if any, are to be bound.

The court officer will forward a copy of any record made in pursuance of BA 1976 s.5(1) to the Registrar.

Extension of the "relevant period"

A judge may, on the application of the prosecutor, extend or further extend the "relevant period" until a specified date, but only where he is satisfied that: **55-021**

(1) the need for the extension is due to some good and sufficient cause; and
(2) the prosecutor has acted with all due diligence and expedition.

(As to "good and sufficient cause" and "diligence and expedition" see ABUSE OF PROCESS.)

The prosecutor may apply to extend or further extend the relevant period and that application must be served on the Crown Court officer and the acquitted person (CrimPR 27.2(4)).

Bail and custody before hearing

Where notice of application is given under CJA 2003 s.80(1), then in relation to the person to whom that application relates, if he: **55-022**

(1) is in custody under s.88(4)(b) or (5) he must be brought before a judge of the Crown Court as soon as practicable and, in any event within 48 hours after the notice is given;
(2) is not in custody under s.88(4)(b) or (5) the Crown Court may, on application by the prosecutor, issue:

(a) a summons requiring him to appear before the CACD at the hearing of the application; or
(b) a warrant for his arrest,

and a warrant may be issued at any time even though a summons has previously been issued.

The summons, or a subsequent direction of the Crown Court, may specify the time and place at which that person must appear, and the time and place may be varied from time to time by a direction of the Crown Court.

A prosecutor's application for a summons or a warrant under s.89(3)(a) or (b) must be served on the court officer (27.6).

(CJA 2003 s.89(1), (2), (3), (4) and (5))

Appearance before the Crown Court

55-023 A person arrested under a warrant under s.89(3)(b) must be brought before a judge of the Crown Court as soon as practicable and in any event within 48 hours after his arrest (and SCA 1981 s.81(5) giving the magistrates' court as an alternative, does not apply).

The judge must, where a person is brought before him under either s.89(2) or (6) either:

(1) remand him in custody to be brought before the CACD at the hearing of the application; or
(2) grant bail for him to appear before the CACD at the hearing.

(CJA 2003 s.89(6), (7), (8) and (9))

Bail granted by the Crown Court may be revoked, and the person remanded in custody in accordance with s.89(7)(b).

Revocation of bail

55-024 Where bail is revoked under CJA 2003 Pt 10 and the person concerned is not before the Crown Court when his bail is revoked, a judge must order him to surrender himself forthwith to the custody of the court, and where he surrenders in compliance with that order, the judge must remand him in custody.

(CJA 2003 s.91(1) and (2))

56. SENDING FOR TRIAL

Quick Guide

1. Allocation

Guidelines

56-001 Magistrates' Courts must follow the Sentencing Council's guideline on allocation (mode of trial) (the revised version which came into effect on 1 March 2016) when deciding whether or not to send accused charged with "either-way" offences for trial in the Crown Court under CDA 1998 s.51(1).

(*CPD* II 9A.1)

The guideline refers to the factors to which a court must have regard in accordance with MCA 1980 s.19. Section 19(2)(a) permits reference to previous convictions of the accused.

The guideline lists four factors that the court must also have regard to. No examples or guidance are given. However, the following could be a consideration when applying the factors: that where cases involve complex questions of fact or difficult questions of law, including difficult issues of disclosure of sensitive material, the court should consider sending for trial.

General observations

56-002 Certain general observations can be made:

(1) the court should never make its decision on the grounds of convenience or expedition;

(2) the fact that the offences are alleged to be specimens is a relevant consideration (although it has to be borne in mind that difficulties can arise in sentencing in relation to specimen counts; see *R. v Clark* [1996] 2 Cr. App. R. 282; [1996] 2 Cr. App. R. (S.) 351; *R. v Canavan* [1998] 1 W.L.R. 604; [1998] 1 Cr. App. R. 79; [1998] 1 Cr. App. R. (S.) 243 and *R. v Oakes* [2012] EWCA Crim 2435; [2013] 2 Cr. App. R. (S.) 22);

(3) the fact that the offender, if convicted, will be asking for other offences to be taken into consideration is not a relevant consideration;

(4) the court may give an indication of the likely sentence in the event of a guilty plea for young defendants prior to sending for trial in the Crown Court or ordering trial in the youth court (CrimPR 9.13); and

(5) a defendant may be sent for trial in the Crown Court in the defendant's absence if the defendant is represented in cases where a case must be sent to the Crown Court (CrimPR 9.7).

2. MAGISTRATES' COURTS PROCEDURE

Adults and corporations sent for trial

56-003 Adults (i.e. accused aged 18 and over) and corporations may be sent for trial in respect (CDA 1998 s.51(2) and (11)) of:

(1) indictable only offences other than those in respect of which notice has been given under CDA 1998 ss.51B or 51C (see 56-006 and 56-007); but also of:
(2) either-way offences where the magistrates' court is required under MCA 1980 ss.20(9)(b), 21, 23(4)(b) or (5) or 25(2D) to proceed in accordance with (1); and
(3) cases in which notice is given under ss.51B or 51C in respect of the offence under s.51(1) and (2).

The offences for which such a person is sent to the Crown Court may include:

(a) any either-way offence appearing to be related to (1) above; and
(b) any summary offence appearing to be related to the offence in (1) above and punishable with imprisonment or a discretionary RT disqualification (CDA 1998 s.51(7)–(9)).

A child or young person charged jointly with the adult with an indictable offence for which the adult is sent for trial, or an indictable offence which appears to the court to be related to that offence, may also, subject to MCA 1980 ss.24A and 24B (which provide for certain cases involving children and young persons to be tried summarily where considered necessary in the interests of justice) be sent with the adult for trial for the indictable offence, and the same rules as to either-way and summary offences apply.

Special procedures apply where an accused is charged with low-value shoplifting, as defined by MCA 1980 s.22A.

Sections 51 and 51A of the Crime and Disorder Act 1998 provides that indictable offences can be sent to the Crown Court without a first hearing in the magistrates' court.

Section 46ZA of the Senior Courts Act 1981 provides the Crown Court with a power to remit a person back to a magistrates' court for trial. This power may only be exercised in respect of either way offences and with the consent of the defendant.

CrimPR 9.16 provides that where s.46ZA SCA 1981 or para.6 of Sch.3 to CDA 1998 applies, then the Crown Court may exercise its power to send back:

- at a hearing, in public or in private, or without a hearing;
- in the defendant's absence, but only if the defendant consents to being absent on its exercise; and
- in the prosecutor's absence, but only if the prosecutor has had at least five business days in which to make representations.

If a defendant is under 18 the Crown Court must:

- consider sending the defendant back; and
- explain why, if it does not do so.

Children and young persons

56-004 Children and young persons (i.e. those aged under 18) may be sent to the Crown Court subject to MCA 1980 ss.24A and 24B (which provide for certain offences involving children or young persons to be tried summarily), where:

(1) the offence is one of homicide;
(2) each of the requirements of SA 2020 s.311 (FA 1968 s.51A—minimum sentences in respect of certain firearms offences) would be satisfied with respect to the offence and the person charged with it if he were convicted of the offence;
(3) VCRA 2006 s.29(3) (minimum sentences in certain cases of using someone to mind a weapon) would apply if he were convicted of the offence;
(4) the offence is one of those grave offences mentioned in SA 2020 s.249 (other than one mentioned in (6) below) in relation to which the court considers that if he is found guilty of the offence it ought to be possible to sentence him under SA 2020 s.251;
(5) the offence is such as is mentioned in SA 2020 s.252A(1)(a) and the court considers that if he is found guilty it ought to be possible to sentence him under that section to a term of detention of more than two years;
(6) notice is given to the court under ss.51B or 51C below in respect of the offence; or
(7) the offence is a specified offence (within the meaning of SA 2020 s.306) and it appears to the court that if he is found guilty of the offence the criteria for the imposition of a sentence under SA 2020 s.255(1) (dangerous offenders) would be met.

(CDA 1998 s.51A(1)–(3))

Where the court sends a child or young person for trial under s.51A(2), it may at the same time send him to the Crown Court for trial for any indictable offence or summary offence with which he is charged and which (if it is an indictable offence) appears to be related to the offence for which he has been sent, or (if it is a summary offence) if it appears to be related to the offence for which he has been sent, or to the indictable offence, and is punishable with imprisonment or involves obligatory or discretionary disqualification from driving.

(CDA 1998 s.51A(4))

Where a child has been sent for trial, and subsequently appears before a magistrates court charged with an indictable or summary offence, the court may send that offence to the Crown Court where (if it is an indictable offence) it appears to be related to the offence for which he has been sent, or (if it is a summary offence) it appears to be related to the offence for which he has been sent, or to the indictable offence, and is punishable with imprisonment or involves obligatory or discretionary disqualification from driving.

(CDA 1998 s.51A(5))

Presumption against sending young offenders to the Crown Court

There is a strong presumption against sending young offenders to the Crown Court unless it is clearly necessary and the case is so serious that a sentence above two years is required. 56-005

When such a situation arises:

(1) the general policy of the legislation is that offenders under 18 and particularly those under 15 should, wherever possible, be tried by the youth court;
(2) it is a further purpose of the legislation that generally speaking first time offenders aged 12–14 and offenders under 12 should not be detained in custody and in deciding on jurisdiction the court should have regard to the

fact that the exceptional power to detain for grave offences should not be used to water down the general principle; those under 15, who rarely attract a period of detention, and even more rarely those under 12, should not be detained in custody; and

(3) in each case the magistrates are required to consider whether there is a real prospect, having regard to the accused's age, that he might require a sentence of, or in excess of, two years, or alternately whether, although the sentence might be less than two years, there was some unusual feature which entitled them to decline jurisdiction (*R. (on the application of H) v Southampton Youth Court* [2004] EWHC 2912 (Admin); [2005] 2 Cr. App. R. (S.) 30; see also *R. (on the application of BH (A Child)) v Llandudno Youth Court* [2014] EWHC 1833 (Admin)).

An adult charged jointly with a juvenile with an indictable offence for which the juvenile is sent for trial, or an indictable offence which appears to the court to be related to that offence, may also be sent for trial for the indictable offence and any related indictable or summary only offence (CDA 1998 s.51A(4), (6), (7)).

CrimPR 9.16 provides that where s.46ZA SCA 1981 or para.6 of Sch.3 to CDA 1998 applies and the defendant is under 18, the Crown Court must:

- consider sending the defendant back; and
- explain why, if it does not do so.

Serious or complex fraud cases

56-006 Serious or complex fraud cases involving an indictable offence may be sent to the Crown Court where the designated authority (see below) is of the opinion that the evidence of the offence charged:

(1) is sufficient for the person charged to be put on trial for the offence;
(2) reveals a case of fraud of such seriousness or complexity that it is appropriate that the management of the case should without delay be taken over by the Crown Court; and
(3) notice is given to the magistrates' court at which the person charged appears, or before which he is brought, before any summary trial begins,

the effect of which is that the functions of the magistrates' court in relation to the case cease except:

(a) for the purposes of selecting the place of trial (s.51D);
(b) in relation to defence public funding, as provided by LASPOA 2012 s.19; and
(c) in connection with remanding the person charged (whether in custody or on bail).

A "designated authority" includes the DPP, the DSFO and the Secretary of State. The decision to give notice of transfer is not subject to appeal, or liable to be questioned in any court.

(CDA 1998 s.51B)

Certain cases involving children

56-007 A case may be sent to the Crown Court under CDA 1998 s.51C where notice is given by the DPP to a magistrates' court at which a person charged appears or is brought, and before any summary trial begins, in respect of an offence:

(1) which involves an assault on, or injury, or a threat of injury to, a person;
(2) under CYPA 1933 s.1 (cruelty to persons under 16);
(3) under SOA 1956, the Protection of Children Act 1978, or SOA 2003;
(4) of kidnapping or false imprisonment, or an offence under the Child Abduction Act 1984 ss.1 or 2;
(5) under MSA 2015 s.1 or s.2; or
(6) which consists of attempting or conspiring to commit, or of aiding, abetting, counselling, procuring or inciting the commission of such an offence,

where he is of the opinion (to be certified in the notice) that:

(a) the evidence of the offence charged is sufficient for the person charged to be put on trial for the offence;
(b) a child would be called as a witness at the trial; and
(c) for the purpose of avoiding any prejudice to the welfare of the child, the case should be taken over and proceeded with without delay by the Crown Court.

The provisions of s.51B(4), (5) and (6) (above) in relation to serious or complex frauds then apply.

"Child" here means:

(i) a person who is under the age of 17; or
(ii) any person of whom a video recording was made when he was under the age of 17 with a view to its admission as his evidence-in-chief in the trial of a person charged with the offence which is the subject of the notice.

(CDA 1998 s.51C)

Content of notices; place of trial

56-008 The magistrates' court will specify in a notice:

(1) the offence or offences for which a person is sent for trial under s.51 or s.51A; and
(2) the place at which he is to be tried (which, if a notice has been given under s.51B, must be the place specified in that notice),

and a copy of the notice will be served on the accused and given to the Crown Court sitting at that place.

In a case where a person is sent for trial under s.51(1) or s.51A for more than one offence and the court includes any further offence in the notice, the court will specify in the notice the offence to which the further offence appears to the court to be related.

In selecting the place of trial, the magistrates will have regard to:

(a) the convenience of the defence, the prosecution and the witnesses;
(b) the desirability of expediting the trial; and
(c) any direction given by or on behalf of the Lord Chief Justice under SCA 1981 s.75(1) (see ALLOCATION AND LISTING OF CASES).

(CDA 1998 s.51D)

Terrorist cases

56-009 The procedure to be adopted in terrorism cases was set out in the *Protocol on the case management of Terrorism Cases*, issued in December 2006 by the President of the QBD, but this has been replaced by Annex 4 to *CPD* XIII.

The sending magistrate's court should ordinarily direct that the PTPH should take place about 14 days after charge. The sending magistrates' court should contact the Regional Listing Coordinator's Office who will be responsible for notifying the magistrates' court as to the relevant Crown Court to which to send the case.

In all terrorism cases, the magistrates' court case progression form for cases sent to the Crown Court under CDA 1998 s.51 should not be used. Instead of the automatic directions set out in that form, the magistrates' court must make the following directions to facilitate the preliminary hearing at the Crown Court:

(1) Three days prior to the preliminary hearing in the terrorism cases list, the prosecution must serve upon each defendant and the Regional Listing Co-ordinator:
   (a) a preliminary summary of the case;
   (b) the names of those who are to represent the prosecution, if known;
   (c) an estimate of the length of the trial; and
   (d) a suggested provisional timetable which should generally include:
      (i) the general nature of further enquiries being made by the prosecution;
      (ii) the time needed for the completion of such enquiries;
      (iii) the time required by the prosecution to review the case;
      (iv) a timetable for the phased service of the evidence;
      (v) the time for the provision by the Attorney General of his consent if necessary;
      (vi) the time for service of the detailed defence case statement;
      (vii) the date for the case management hearing; and
      (viii) estimated trial date;
   (e) a preliminary statement of the possible disclosure issues setting out the nature and scale of the problem including the amount of unused material, the manner in which the prosecution seeks to deal with these matters and a suggested timetable for discharging their statutory duty; and
   (f) any information relating to bail and custody time limits.

(2) One day prior to the preliminary hearing in the terrorist cases list, each accused must serve in writing on the Regional Listing Co-ordinator and the prosecution:
   - the proposed representation;
   - observations on the timetable; and
   - an indication of plea and the general nature of the defence.

When a terrorism case is so sent the case will go into the terrorism list and be managed by a judge as described in para.(1) above.

(*CPD* XIII Annex 4))

3. Crown Court procedure

Sending for trial; service of prosecution case

56-010 Where:

(1) under CrimPR 9.10 or 9.13 a magistrates' court allocates a case to the Crown Court for trial;
(2) under CrimPR 9.11 an accused does not agree to trial in a magistrates' court; or
(3) under CrimPR 9.12 a magistrates' court grants a prosecutor's application for Crown Court trial,

the magistrates' court will:

(a) invite the prosecutor to make representations about any ancillary matters, including bail and directions for the management of the case in the Crown Court;
(b) invite the accused to make any such representations; and
(c) exercise its powers to:
  (i) send the defendant to the Crown Court for trial; and
  (ii) give any ancillary directions.

(CrimPR 9.14)

The prosecutor will serve on the accused copies of the documents containing the evidence on which the prosecution relies, and will at the same time serve copies of those documents on the Crown Court officer.

(CrimPR 3.19)

CDA 1998 (Service of Prosecution Evidence) Regulations 2005 reg.2 requires service of the prosecution evidence not more than 50 days after sending for trial where the accused is in custody, and not more than 70 days where the accused is on bail.

Dismissal; no case to answer

Any person sent for trial on any charge or charges may, at any time: **56-011**

(1) after he has been served with copies of the documents containing the evidence on which the charge or charges are based; and
(2) before he is arraigned (and whether or not the indictment has been preferred against him),

apply orally, or in writing, to the Crown Court sitting at the place specified in the notice served upon him (under s.51D(1)) for the charge, or any of the charges in the case, to be dismissed.

The judge must dismiss a charge (and quash any count relating to it in any indictment preferred against the applicant) if it appears to him that the evidence against the applicant would not be sufficient for him to be properly convicted.

(CDA 1998 s.52(6) and Sch.3 para.2(1)–(2))

The question for decision is the sufficiency of the evidence.

The criteria to be applied on consideration of an application are those ordinarily applied to a submission of "no case to answer" (for which see *R. v X* [1989] Crim. L.R. 726).

Where the evidence is largely documentary, the judge must assess the inferences which the prosecutor proposes to ask the jury to draw from the documents and decide whether it appears to him that such inferences might properly be drawn (*R. (on the application of IRC) v Kingston Crown Court* [2001] 4 All E.R. 721).

Reporting restrictions are imposed (CDA 1998 Sch.3 para 3; see REPORTING AND ACCESS RESTRICTIONS).

Result of dismissal or amendment

56-012 The result of the above proceedings before the judge may be that:

(1) the indictment no longer contains any indictable only offence; or
(2) any remaining offences triable either-way may not be, in the judge's opinion, suitable for trial on indictment;
(3) there are summary offences remaining to be dealt with.

No main offence remaining

56-013 Where a person has been sent for trial under s.51 or s.51A, but has not been arraigned, and is charged on an indictment which, as a result of amendment, or a successful application to dismiss, or for any other reason, no longer includes any "main offence", as defined below, the procedure is as follows:

(1) each remaining count of the indictment charging an offence triable either-way is read to the accused;
(2) he is informed that in relation to each of those offences he may indicate whether, if the court were to proceed to trial, he would plead guilty or not guilty, and that if he pleads guilty he will be treated as if he had pleaded guilty on arraignment;
(3) he is then asked whether, if the offence in question were to proceed to trial, he would plead guilty or not guilty;
(4) if he indicates that he would plead guilty, the judge proceeds as if he had been arraigned on the count in question and had pleaded guilty; and
(5) if he indicates that he would plead not guilty, or fails to indicate how he would plead, the judge will decide whether the offence is more suitable for summary trial or for trial on indictment.

Where, in the exceptional case, the judge considers that because of the accused's disorderly conduct before the court, it is not practicable for the proceedings to be conducted in his presence, and he considers that the proceedings should be conducted in his absence, then provided that the accused is legally represented:

(a) the judge will cause each count of the indictment charging an either-way offence to be read to the representative;
(b) that representative will be asked whether, if the offence were to proceed to trial, the accused would plead guilty or not guilty; and
(c) depending on the representative's answer, the ordinary procedure (outlined above) will apply.

(CDA 1998 s.52(6) and Sch.3 paras 7, 8 and 9; CJA 2003 s.41 and Sch.3 para.20(7))

Definition of "main offence"; adults

56-014 A "main offence" for the purposes of the above provisions is:

(1) an offence for which the person has been sent to the Crown Court for trial under s.51(1); or
(2) an offence:
    (a) for which the person has been sent to the Crown Court for trial under s.51(5) or s.51A(6) ("the applicable subsection"); and

(b) in respect of which the conditions for sending him to the Crown Court for trial under the applicable subsection (as set out in s.51(5)(a)–(c) or s.51A(6)(a) and (b)) continue to be satisfied.

(CDA 1998 Sch.3 para.7(9))
As to children and young persons, see 56-018.

Summary trial or trial on indictment

Before deciding the question whether an offence is more suitable for summary trial or for trial on indictment, the judge must give: 56-015

(1) the prosecutor an opportunity to inform the court of the accused's previous convictions in Great Britain (if any); and
(2) the accused an opportunity to make representations as to whether summary trial or trial on indictment would be more suitable.

In deciding the question, the judge must consider:

(a) whether the sentence which a magistrates' court would have power to impose for the offence would be adequate; and
(b) any representations made by the prosecution or the accused,

and must have regard to any allocation guidelines, or revised allocation guidelines, issued as definitive guidelines under CorJA 2009 s.122 (see ALLOCATION AND LISTING OF CASES).

It has to be emphasised, however, that the responsibility for deciding whether any counts to which the accused has pleaded not guilty, or is treated as if he has so pleaded, are more suitable for summary trial or trial on indictment is vested exclusively in the judge. The entitlement of the accused is to make submissions in support of summary trial if he wishes to do so, but he does not enjoy an entitlement to summary trial. The ultimate decision must be made by the judge (*R. v Gul* [2012] EWCA Crim 1761; [2013] 1 Cr. App. R. 4).

Where:

(i) the accused is charged on the same occasion with two or more offences; and
(ii) it appears to the judge that they constitute or form part of a series of two or more offences of the same or a similar character,

then (a) above has effect as if references to the sentence which a magistrates' court would have power to impose for the offence are a reference to the maximum aggregate sentence which a magistrates' court would have power to impose for all of the offences taken together.

(CDA 1998 s.52(6) and Sch.3 para.9(4))

Special provisions apply (see Sch.3 para.14) in the case of "schedule offences" (i.e. those offences of criminal damage and aggravated vehicle taking set out in MCA 1980 Sch.2).

Offence more suitable for summary trial

Where the judge decides that such an offence is more suitable for summary trial: 56-016

(1) he will explain to the accused that:
 (a) it appears to him more suitable for the accused to be tried summarily for the offence;

(b) he can either consent to be so tried or, if he wishes, be tried on indictment; and
(c) in the case of a "specified offence" (within the meaning of SA 2020 s.306) that if he is tried summarily and is convicted by the magistrates' court, he may be committed for sentence to the Crown Court under SA 2020 s.15 if the committing court is of such opinion as is mentioned in subs.(1)(b) of that section (see COMMITTALS FOR SENTENCE);

(2) he will then ask the accused whether he wishes to be tried summarily or on indictment;
(3) if the accused indicates that he wishes to be tried summarily, the judge will remit him for trial to a magistrates' court acting for the place from which he was sent for trial; and
(4) if the accused does not give such an indication, the Crown Court will retain its functions and proceed accordingly.

If the judge decides that the case is more suitable for summary trial, only then does the accused have the right to elect trial by jury; he has no corresponding right to elect summary trial (*R. v Gul*, see 56-015).

(CDA 1998 s.52(6) and Sch.3 para.10)

Offence more suitable for trial on indictment

56-017 Where the judge considers that the offence is more suitable for trial on indictment:

(1) he will tell the accused that he has so decided; and
(2) the Crown Court will retain its functions and proceed accordingly.

(CDA 1998 s.52(6) and Sch.3 para.11)

Children and young persons

56-018 Where a child or young person has been:

(1) sent for trial under s.51 or s.51A but has not been arraigned; and
(2) is charged on indictment which (following amendment, or for any other reason) includes no "main offence" (see below),

then, instead of following paras 7–12 of the Schedule (i.e. 56-013–56-017), the judge must remit the child or young person for trial to a magistrates' court acting for the place where he was sent to the Crown Court for trial.

A "main offence" for the purposes of this provision is:

(a) an offence for which the child or young person has been sent to the Crown Court for trial under s.51A(2); or
(b) an offence:
  (i) for which the child or young person has been sent to the Crown Court for trial under s.51(7); and
  (ii) in respect of which the conditions for sending him to the Crown Court for trial under that subsection (as set out in paras (a) and (b) of that subsection) continue to be satisfied.

(CDA 1998 s.52(6) and Sch.3 para.13)

Summary offence included in indictment

Where the magistrates' court has sent a person for trial under ss.51 or 51A for offences which include a summary offence, the procedure at the Crown Court is as follows. **56-019**

If:

(1) that person is convicted on indictment, the judge will consider whether the summary offence is "related" to the indictable offence for which he was sent for trial, or, as the case may be, any of the indictable offences for which he was so sent; and
(2) he finds that it is, the substance of the offence will be put to the accused and he will be asked to plead to it;
(3) the accused pleads guilty, he will be convicted, the judge's powers of sentencing being limited to those of the lower court;
(4) the accused does not plead guilty, the Crown Court ceases to have powers in the matter unless the prosecutor informs the judge that he does not wish to offer any evidence on the charge, in which case the judge may dismiss it.

(CDA 1998 s.52(6) and Sch.3 para.6)

In *R. v X* [2012] EWCA Crim 1610, the CACD noted the developing practice of magistrates' courts to adjourn summary-only matters, knowing the offender is due to appear at the Crown Court on other matters, and to invite the Crown Court to enable the summary cases to be dealt with at the same time by the expedient of arranging for a circuit judge to sit as a district judge. The CACD observed that while such a practice had advantages, there were also dangers.

A judge of the Crown Court who is invited to deal with two sets of proceedings in this way must:

(a) decide whether it is appropriate in the light of submissions from both the prosecution and the defence, keeping firmly in mind that when sentencing as a district judge the sentence is imposed by the magistrates' court; and
(b) remember that as regards the magistrates' court matters, he is limited to the powers of a magistrates' court, powers which must be carefully checked by the advocates, and also that in the case of any sentence that he imposes when sitting as a magistrates' court there is a different route of appeal from that applicable to sentences imposed by him when sitting in the Crown Court.

If the invitation is accepted, then consideration must again be given to these dangers at the stage of deciding what sentence should be imposed by the judge when sitting as a magistrates' court.

Power to proceed in absence of accused

The judge may deal with any of the procedures under paras 7–11 of Sch.3 (see 56-013–56-017) in the absence of the accused, provided the accused is legally represented by a representative who signifies to the court the accused's consent to such a course, and the judge is satisfied that there is good reason for proceeding in the accused's absence. **56-020**

(CDA 1998 s.52(6) and Sch.3 para.15)

In such a case, any explanations and questions to, and any consents to be given by the accused, will be given to and answered by the legal representative.

4. APPLICATION TO DISMISS; PROCEDURE

Application

56-021 Where an accused wants the Crown Court to dismiss an offence sent for trial there, he must:

(1) apply in writing:
  (a) not more than 20 business days after service of the prosecution evidence; and
  (b) before his arraignment;
(2) serve the application on the Crown Court officer, and each other party; and
(3) in the application:
  (a) explain why the prosecution evidence would not be sufficient for the accused to be properly convicted;
  (b) ask for a hearing, if he wants one, and explain why it is needed;
  (c) identify any witness whom he wants to call to give evidence in person, with an indication of what evidence the witness can give;
  (d) identify any material already served that he thinks the court will need to determine the application; and
  (e) include any material not already served on which he relies.

(CrimPR 3.20(1)–(2))

Prosecutor's reply

56-022 A prosecutor who opposes the application must:

(1) serve notice of opposition, not more than 10 business days after service of the accused's notice, on the Crown Court officer, and each other party; and
(2) in the notice of opposition:
  (a) explain the grounds of opposition;
  (b) ask for a hearing, if he wants one, and explain why it is needed;
  (c) identify any witness whom he wants to call to give evidence in person, with an indication of what evidence the witness can give;
  (d) identify any material already served that he thinks the court will need to determine the application; and
  (e) include any material not already served on which he relies.

(CrimPR 3.20(3))

Determination of application; supplementary

56-023 The court may determine an application under this rule:

(1) at a hearing, in public or in private, or without a hearing;
(2) in the absence of the accused who made the application, and the prosecutor, if the latter has had at least 10 business days in which to serve notice opposing the application.

The court may:

(a) shorten or extend (even after it has expired) a time limit under CrimPR 3.20;
(b) allow a witness to give evidence in person even if that witness was not identified in the defendant's application or in the prosecutor's notice.

Note that the power to extend the time limit within which a defendant must serve notice of his application to dismiss (not more than 20 business days after service of the prosecution evidence and before arraignment) does not mean that the defendant can apply to dismiss the charges after he has been arraigned. See also *R. v Thompson* [2006] EWCA Crim 2949; [2007] 1 Cr. App. R. 15 and *R. v N Ltd* (2008) EWCA Crim 1223; (2009) 1 Cr. App. R. 3.

(CrimPR 3.20(4)–(5))

As to reporting restrictions, see REPORTING AND ACCESS RESTRICTIONS.

57. SENTENCING GUIDELINES

QUICK GUIDE

1. INTRODUCTION

57-001 Sentencing in any case is subject to:

(1) any guideline judgment of the CACD;
(2) any definitive guideline of the Sentencing Council for England and Wales ("SCEW");
(3) any helpful indications from other reported cases, relevant to sentencing the offender.

The SCEW was established by s.118(1) of the CorJA 2009 and came into existence on 6 April 2010.

The duty of the court is now set out in SA 2020 ss.59–62.

This chapter does not attempt to set out sentencing guidelines in detail. Reference should be made to *http://www.sentencingcouncil.org.uk* [Accessed September 2022]. The Sentencing Council strongly encourages use of the online versions of the guidelines to ensure that reference is made to the current version.

The duty

57-002 The judge:

(1) must, in sentencing an offender, follow any sentencing guidelines which are relevant to the offender's case;
(2) must, in exercising any other function in relation to the sentencing of offenders, follow any sentencing guidelines which are relevant to the exercise of that function, *unless* it would be contrary to the interests of justice to do so;
(3) must, in following a guideline, impose a sentence within the offence range (subject to reduction for a guilty plea, assistance given, totality); and
(4) must, in following a guideline, decide which of the categories most resembles the case they are dealing with in order to identify the sentence starting point (but not if none of the categories sufficiently resembles the case).

However, there is no separate duty to impose a sentence within the category range.

(SA 2020 ss.59–60)

There is no restriction on any power which enables a court to deal with a mentally disordered defendant in the manner it considers to be most appropriate in all the circumstances (SA 2020 s.59(3)).

Approach to guidelines

57-003 There is now a duty to "follow" rather than merely "have regard to", any sentencing guideline issued by the SCEW. That duty includes a duty to impose a sentence within the category range unless it would be unjust to do so. A judge must give reasons for the sentence imposed by reference to any relevant guidelines and to explain why, if it be the case, they have decided not to follow a relevant guideline in the interests of justice.

Note that:

(1) a "guideline" is no more than a guideline. It does not affect the judge's powers as set out in the legislation; it merely indicates how those powers might be exercised. It does not alter the law (*R. v Peters* [2005] EWCA Crim 605; [2005] 2 Cr. App. R. (S.) 101);
(2) there will be cases where there is good reason to depart from a guideline; justice may require a more merciful sentence than a guideline level might indicate, sometimes a more severe one; sometimes the individual case will not fit into the structure of any definitive guideline (*Attorney General's Reference (No.8 of 2007)* [2007] EWCA Crim 922; [2008] 1 Cr. App. R. (S.) 1; *Attorney General's References (Nos 8, 9 and 10 of 2009)* [2009] EWCA Crim 1636; [2010] 1 Cr. App. R. (S.) 66);
(3) preliminary documents produced by the SCEW (e.g. consultation documents) are of very limited value (*Attorney General's References (Nos 61, 62 and 63 of 2011)* [2011] EWCA Crim 2619; see also *Attorney General's References (Nos 82 to 96 and 104 to 109 of 2011)* [2012] EWCA Crim 155; [2012] 2 Cr. App. R. (S.) 56);
(4) a judge should only depart from guidelines for good reason, which will generally be specific to the offence or offender under consideration; he is not entitled to depart from them because he disagrees with them. Reconsideration of guidelines is a matter for the Sentencing Council, not for a trial judge (*R. v Heathcote-Smith* [2011] EWCA Crim 2846; [2012] Cr. App. R. (S.) 25);
(5) where the judge decides not to apply a relevant sentencing guideline, he must explain why he has not done so when he explains the sentence he has passed (CrimPR 28.1(a)) but CorJA 2009 s.125 does not require him to state in terms that the interests of justice require him to go outside the guidelines, as if reciting a mantra—see *R. v Sharma* [2013] EWCA Crim 175; and
(6) it is the duty of the advocates to bring any relevant guidelines to the attention of the judge.

2. SGC AND SCEW GUIDELINES

Definitive Guidelines of the SCEW are to be found at: *http://www.sentencingcouncil.org.uk* [Accessed September 2022]. Current guidelines are listed on the website under "Offences" and "Overarching Guidelines", the former has a useful search facility. **57-004**

Recent additions and amendments to sentencing guidelines include:

- Terrorism: The Sentencing Council has published updated sentencing guidelines for terrorism offences in England and Wales following consultation. The new guidelines, which will come into effect on 1 October 2022, update the current guidelines published in 2018 to reflect changes brought in by the Counter-Terrorism and Border Security Act 2019 and the Counter-Terrorism and Sentencing Act 2021.
- Child Sexual Offences: The Sentencing Council published revised sentenc-

ing guidelines for child sexual offences where no child exists or is harmed. The changes came into effect on 31 May 2022.

- Burglary: Revised sentencing guidelines for domestic, non-domestic and aggravated burglary offences in England and Wales, came into effect on 1 July 2022.
- Importation of firearm offences: new guideline for sentencing offenders convicted of firearms importation offences in England and Wales, following consultation which applies to adult offenders sentenced in the magistrates' court or the Crown Court on or after 1 January 2022.
- Modern Slavery Offences: sentencing guideline came into effect on 1 October 2021.
- Revised sentencing guidelines for assault offences including attempted murder and common assault, and new guidance for assaults on emergency workers were published following wide consultation and came into effect on 1 July 2021.
- Trademark Offences: The new guidelines, which apply to using a trademark without the owner's consent contrary to s.92 of the Trade Marks Act 1994, came into effect on 1 October 2021.
- Breach of a sexual harm prevention order (SHPO): clarifying that when the court is dealing with such a breach, it does not have a standalone power to make a fresh order or to vary the order.
- Compensation: adding wording relating to giving reasons if compensation is not awarded in all relevant guidelines.
- Confiscation: providing fuller information on confiscation in all relevant guidelines.
- Racially or religiously aggravated offences: making the uplift for racial/religious aggravation a separate step and consistent across guidelines for these offences.
- Domestic abuse overarching guideline: revising the definition of domestic abuse in the light of the Domestic Abuse Act 2021 and expanding it to include a wider range of relationships.

58. SERIOUS CRIME PREVENTION ORDERS

QUICK GUIDE

1. OVERVIEW

Powers

A Serious Crime Prevention Order ("SCPO") can be made by the High Court in certain circumstances, or by the Crown Court where a defendant has been convicted of a "serious offence". This chapter deals only with SCPOs made in the Crown Court. **58-001**

Where a judge of the Crown Court is dealing with a person aged 18 or over who (SCA 2007 s.2(1)–(3)):

(1) has been convicted by or before a magistrates' court of having committed a serious offence in England and Wales and has been committed to the Crown Court to be dealt with; or
(2) has been convicted by or before the Crown Court of having committed a serious offence in England and Wales,

he may, in addition to dealing with that person in relation to the offence, make a SCPO, if he has reasonable grounds to believe that the order would protect the public by preventing, restricting or disrupting involvement by that person in serious crime in England and Wales (SCA 2007 s.19(1)–(2)).

Such an order is ancillary and may be made only:

(a) in addition to a sentence imposed in respect of the offence concerned; or
(b) in addition to an order discharging the person conditionally (SCA 2007 s.19(7)).

The order may contain such prohibitions, restrictions or requirements and such other terms, as the judge considers appropriate for the purpose of protecting the public in the manner set out above, subject to the safeguards set out below at 58-007 to 58-011.

Section 19 does not provide a jurisdictional time limit in relation to the making of such an application, nor does it require that the court must still be otherwise dealing with an offender when an application is made (*R. v Adams* [2021] EWCA Crim 1525; [2022] 1 W.L.R. 1736).

Procedure is governed by CrimPR 31 (see CRIMINAL BEHAVIOUR ORDERS).

As to legal aid, proceedings before the Crown Court in relation to such orders under ss.19, 20, 21 and 24, are criminal proceedings within the meaning of the Criminal Legal Aid (General) Regulations 2013 reg.9 (see LEGAL AID; PUBLIC FUNDING).

Preconditions

58-002 The first precondition for making a SCPO is that the defendant has been convicted of a "serious offence" (SCA 2007 s.2(1)–(2)). A "serious offence" means an offence under the law of England and Wales which, at the time when the court is considering the matter in question:

(a) is specified, or falls within a description specified, in Pt 1 of Sch.1 to the Act (as amended by SCA 2015 s.47 and MSA 2015 s.57(1)); or
(b) is one which, in the particular circumstances of the case, the judge considers to be sufficiently serious to be treated for the purposes of the application or matter as if it were so specified.

The second precondition is that an application must be made by the DPP or DSFO.

The application requires the name and address of the prosecutor and prosecuting authority by which the application is brought (*R. v Shirley (James)* [2022] EWCA Crim 475; [2022] 4 W.L.R. 64).

The third precondition is that the court must have reasonable grounds for believing that an order would protect the public by preventing, restricting or disrupting involvement by the defendant in serious crime. The court is concerned here with future risk, which must be a real or significant risk (not a bare possibility) that the defendant would commit further offences (*R. v Hancox* [2010] EWCA Crim 102; [2010] 2 Cr. App. R. (S.) 74; see also *R. v Carey* [2012] EWCA Crim 1592 and *R. v Hall* [2014] EWCA Crim 2046; [2015] 1 Cr. App. R. (S.) 16). The principles set out in *R. v Mee* [2004] EWCA Crim 629; [2004] 2 Cr. App. R. (S.) 8 in the context of Travel Restriction Orders apply equally to SCPOs. Orders must be proportionate. The provisions of the order must be commensurate with the risk. They must be clearly and precisely expressed so that the offender and any police officer contemplating enforcement can readily understand what the offender can and cannot do. They must be practicable and enforceable. SCPOs are not an additional alternative form of sentence; they are not designed to punish.

An order is not restricted to violent or sexual crimes and can apply to offences of dishonesty (*R. v Batchelor* [2010] EWCA Crim 1025; [2011] 1 Cr. App. R. (S.) 25).

Types of provision that may be made

58-003 The Act sets out examples of the type of provision that may be made by an order, but does not limit the type of provision that may be made. The examples of prohibitions, restrictions or requirements that may be imposed by such orders can apply in relation to places other than England and Wales.

Examples of prohibitions, etc. that may be imposed on:

(1) individuals (including partners in a partnership) by an order, include prohibitions or restrictions on, or requirements in relation to:
   (a) an individual's financial, property or business dealings or holdings;
   (b) an individual's working arrangements;
   (c) the means by which an individual communicates or associates with others, or the persons with whom he communicates or associates;
   (d) the premises to which an individual has access;
   (e) the use of any premises or item by an individual; and
   (f) an individual's travel (whether within the UK, between the UK and other places or otherwise);

(2) bodies corporate, partnerships and unincorporated associations by an order, include prohibitions or restrictions on, or requirements in relation to:
(a) financial, property or business dealings or holdings of such persons;
(b) the types of agreements to which such persons may be a party;
(c) the provision of goods or services by such persons;
(d) the premises to which such persons have access;
(e) the use of any premises or item by such persons; and
(f) the employment of staff by such persons.

(SCA 2007 s.5)

Any provision must be proportionate to the risk foreseen (see 58-002). The provisions must be expressed in terms which the offender and any officer contemplating arrest or other means of enforcement can readily know what he may or may not do (*R. v Hancox* [2010] EWCA Crim 102; [2010] 2 Cr. App. R. (S.) 74).

Examples of requirements that may be imposed on any persons by an order include:

(1) a requirement on a person to answer questions, or provide information, specified or described in an order:
(a) at a time, within a period or at a frequency;
(b) at a place;
(c) in a form and manner; and
(d) to a law enforcement officer or description of law enforcement officer,

notified to the person by a law enforcement officer specified or described in the order;

(2) a requirement on a person to produce documents specified or described in an order:
(a) at a time, within a period or at a frequency;
(b) at a place;
(c) in a manner; and
(d) to a law enforcement officer or description of law enforcement officer,

notified to the person by a law enforcement officer specified or described in the order.

The prohibitions, etc. that may be imposed on individuals by an order include prohibitions, restrictions or requirements in relation to an individual's private dwelling (including, for example, prohibitions or restrictions on, or requirements in relation to, where an individual may reside).

Note that:

- "document" means anything in which information of any description is recorded (whether or not in legible form);
- "a law enforcement officer" means:
  (i) a constable;
  (ii) an NCA officer who is for the time being designated under CCA 2013 ss.9 or 10;
  (iii) an officer of Revenue and Customs; or
  (iv) a member of the SFO; and
- "premises" includes any land, vehicle, vessel, aircraft or hovercraft.

(SCA 2007 s.5(5), (6) and (7))

2. FAILURE TO COMPLY

58-004 A person who fails to comply with an order without reasonable excuse commits an offence (SCA 2007 s.25), punishable:

(1) on summary conviction, with imprisonment for a term not exceeding 12 months or to a fine not exceeding the statutory maximum or to both; and
(2) on conviction on indictment, to imprisonment for a term not exceeding five years or to a fine or to both.

The court before which a person is convicted of such an offence may order the forfeiture of anything in his possession at the time of the offence which the judge considers to have been involved in the offence, provided that before making such an order he gives an opportunity to make representations to any person (in addition to the convicted person) who claims to be the owner of that thing or otherwise to have an interest in it (SCA 2007 s.26(1)–(2)).

Where a forfeiture order is made it may include such other provisions as the judge considers necessary for giving effect to the forfeiture, including provision relating to the retention, handling, destruction or other disposal of what is forfeited (SCA 2007 s.26(4)–(5)).

The forfeiture order must not be made so as to come into force before there is no further possibility (ignoring any right to appeal out of time) of the order being varied or set aside on appeal (SCA 2007 s.26(3)).

(SCA 2007 ss.25 and 26)

3. GENERAL SAFEGUARDS IN RELATION TO ORDERS

58-005 An individual under the age of 18 may not be the subject of an order (nor may a person be the subject of an order if he falls within a description specified by order of the Secretary of State).

An order may be made only on an application by the DPP or the DSFO.

A judge must, on an application by a person, give the person an opportunity to make representations in the proceedings before him arising by virtue of ss.19, 20 or 21 if he considers that the making or variation of the order concerned (or a decision not to vary it) would be likely to have a significant adverse effect on that person.

Any court considering an appeal in relation to an order must, on an application by a person, give the person an opportunity to make representations in the proceedings if that person was given an opportunity to make representations in the proceedings which are the subject of the appeal.

(SCA 2007 s.14)

Notice requirements

58-006 The subject of an order is bound by it (or a variation of it) only if:

(1) he is represented (whether in person or otherwise) at the proceedings at which the order or the variation is made; or
(2) a notice setting out the terms of the order or the variation has been served on him.

The notice may be served on him by delivering it to him in person, or sending it by recorded delivery to him at his last-known address (whether residential or otherwise).

(SCA 2007 s.10)

For the purposes of delivering such a notice to him in person, a constable or a person authorised for the purpose by the relevant applicant authority may, if necessary by force, enter any premises where he has reasonable grounds for believing the person to be and search those premises for him.

4. Information safeguards

Oral answers and LPP

An order may not require: **58-007**

(1) a person to answer questions, or provide information, orally; or
(2) a person:
  (a) to answer any privileged question;
  (b) to provide any privileged information; or
  (c) to produce any privileged document.

A "privileged question" is defined as a question which the person would be entitled to refuse to answer on grounds of legal professional privilege in proceedings in the High Court; "privileged information" being information which the person would be entitled to refuse to provide on grounds of legal professional privilege in such proceedings. A "privileged document" is a document which the person would be entitled to refuse to produce on grounds of legal professional privilege in such proceedings.

(SCA 2007 ss.11 and 12)

However, this does not prevent an order from requiring a lawyer to provide the name and address of a client of his.

Excluded material and banking information

An order may not require a person: **58-008**

(1) to produce any excluded material as defined by PACE 1984 s.11; or
(2) to disclose any information or produce any document in respect of which he owes an obligation of confidence by virtue of carrying on a banking business, unless one of two conditions is met, namely:
  (a) the person to whom the obligation of confidence is owed consents to the disclosure or production; or
  (b) the order contains a requirement:
    (i) to disclose information, or produce documents, of this kind; or
    (ii) to disclose specified information which is of this kind or to produce specified documents which are of this kind.

(SCA 2007 s.13)

Restrictions relating to other enactments

An order may not require a person: **58-009**

(1) to answer any question;
(2) to provide any information; or
(3) to produce any document,

if the disclosure concerned is prohibited under any other enactment, as defined.
(SCA 2007 s.14)

Restrictions on use of the information obtained

58-010 A statement made by a person in response to a requirement imposed by a SCPO may not be used against him in any criminal proceedings unless condition A or B is met:

(1) Condition A is that the criminal proceedings relate to an offence under SCA 2007 s.25 (failure to comply); and
(2) Condition B is that:
  (a) the criminal proceedings relate to another offence;
  (b) the person who made the statement gives evidence in the criminal proceedings;
  (c) in his evidence the person makes a statement inconsistent with the statement he made in compliance with the SCPO; and
  (d) evidence relating to the statement made in compliance with the SCPO is adduced, or a question about it is asked, by the person or on his behalf.

(SCA 2007 s.15)

58-011 Section 5A of SCA 2007 permits onward disclosure of information provided in response to an information requirement in an SCPO in order to check its accuracy or for the prevention and detection of crime.

5. Duration, variation and discharge of orders

Duration of orders

58-012 An order must specify when it is to come into force and when it is to cease to be in force. With the exception detailed below, it is *not to be in force for more than five years* beginning with its coming into force. It may specify different times for the coming into force, or ceasing to be in force, of different provisions of the order.

Where an order specifies different times, it:

(1) must specify when each provision is to come into force and cease to be in force; and
(2) is not to be in force for more than five years beginning with the coming into force of the first provision of the order to come into force.

The fact that an order, or any provision of an order, ceases to be in force does not prevent the court from making a new order to the same or similar effect. A new order may be made in anticipation of an earlier order or provision ceasing to be in force.

(SCA 2007 s.16)

A SCPO can be extended in certain limited circumstances. Where the subject of the SCPO is charged with a serious offence or an offence under SCA 2007 s.25 (failure to comply), the relevant applicant authority may apply to the Crown Court for the SCPO to continue in effect until:

(1) following the person's conviction, the order is varied or replaced or discharged;

(2) the person is acquitted;
(3) the charge is withdrawn; or
(4) proceedings are discontinued or the charge is ordered to lie on the file.

The order continues in effect until one of these events even if it would otherwise have ceased to have effect before then.

The extension can only be made if the SCPO is still in force at the time of the application and the court has reasonable grounds for believing that the order would protect the public by preventing, restricting or disrupting involvement by the person in serious crime.

(SCA 2007 s.22E)

Power to vary order on conviction

Where a judge is dealing with a person who: **58-013**

(1) has been convicted by or before a magistrates' court of having committed a serious offence in England and Wales and has been committed to the Crown Court to be dealt with; or
(2) has been convicted by or before the Crown Court of having committed a serious offence in England and Wales,

he may in the case of a person who is the subject of a SCPO in England and Wales, and in addition to dealing with the person in relation to the offence, vary the order if he has reasonable grounds to believe that the terms of the order as varied would protect the public by preventing, restricting or disrupting involvement by the person in serious crime in England and Wales.

A variation may be made only on an application by the relevant applicant authority and, as in the case of an original order, only:

(a) in addition to a sentence imposed in respect of the offence concerned; or
(b) in addition to an order discharging the person conditionally.

(SCA 2007 s.20)

A variation may include an extension of the period during which the order, or any provision of it, is in force (subject to the original limits imposed on the order by s.16(2) and (4)(b) (see 58-014)).

Power to vary or replace orders on breach

Where a judge is dealing with a person who: **58-014**

(1) has been convicted by or before a magistrates' court of having committed an offence under SCA 2007 s.25 in relation to a serious crime prevention order and has been committed to the Crown Court to be dealt with; or
(2) has been convicted by or before the Crown Court of having committed an offence under s.25 in relation to a serious crime prevention order,

he may, in addition to dealing with that person in relation to the offence, vary or replace the order, if he has reasonable grounds to believe that the terms of the order as varied would protect the public by preventing, restricting or disrupting involvement by that person in serious crime in England and Wales.

An order may be varied or replaced under this section only on an application by the relevant applicant authority, and only:

(a) in addition to a sentence imposed in respect of the offence concerned; or

(b) in addition to an order discharging the person conditionally.

A variation may include an extension of the period during which the order, or any provision of it, is in force (subject to the original limits imposed on the order by s.16(2) and (4)(b)).

"Replacing" a SCPO means making a new SCPO and discharging the existing one.

(SCA 2007 s.21)

Inter-relationship between different types of orders

58-015 Serious crime prevention orders may also be made, on application, by the High Court. It should be noted that:

(1) the fact that an order has been made or varied by the High Court does not prevent it from being varied by the Crown Court in accordance with this Part;
(2) the fact that an order has been made or varied by the Crown Court does not prevent it from being varied or discharged by the High Court in accordance with this Part;
(3) a decision by the Crown Court not to make an order does not prevent a subsequent application to the High Court for an order under s.1 in consequence of the same offence; and
(4) a decision by the Crown Court not to vary an order under ss.20 or 21 does not prevent a subsequent application to the High Court for a variation of the order in consequence of the same offence.

(SCA 2007 s.22)

6. Nature of proceedings

General

58-016 Proceedings before the Crown Court arising by virtue of ss.19, 20 or 21 are civil proceedings. This has three consequences:

(1) the standard of proof to be applied in such proceedings is the civil standard of proof;
(2) the court is not restricted to considering evidence that would have been admissible in the criminal proceedings in which the person concerned was convicted; and
(3) the judge may adjourn any proceedings in relation to an order even after sentencing the person concerned.

The Crown Court, when exercising its jurisdiction under this Part of the Act, remains a criminal court for the purposes of CJA 2003 Pt 7 in relation to procedure rules and practice directions.

Note also that:

(a) an order may be made as mentioned in SCA 2007 s.19(7)(b) in spite of anything in PCC(S)A 2000 ss.12 and 14 (SA 2020 ss.79, 80 and 82) which relate to orders discharging a person absolutely or conditionally and their effect; and

(b) a variation of an order may be made as mentioned in ss.20(6)(b) or 21(6)(b) in spite of anything in those sections of PCC(S)A 2000.

(SCA 2007 s.36)

Procedure is governed by CrimPR 31.

7. Appeal to the CACD

An appeal against a decision of the Crown Court in relation to a SCPO may be made to the CACD by: **58-017**

(1) the person who is the subject of the order; or
(2) the relevant applicant authority.

In addition, an appeal may be made to the CACD in relation to a decision of the Crown Court:

(a) to make an order; or
(b) to vary, or not to vary, such an order,

by any person who was given an opportunity to make representations in the proceedings concerned by virtue of s.9(4).

Appeal lies only with the leave of the CACD, or, without such leave, where the judge who made the decision grants a certificate that the decision is fit for appeal (see APPEALS FROM THE CROWN COURT).

(SCA 2007 s.24(1) and (2))

59. SERVICE OF DOCUMENTS

Application of CrimPR Pt 4

59-001 Part 4 of the CrimPR applies to the service of every document in a case to which the CrimPR applies, subject to any special rules in other legislation (including other Parts of the CrimPR or in the *CPD* (CrimPR 4.1)). The court may treat a document as served if the addressee responds to it even if it was not served in accordance with the CrimPR. The court may specify the time as well as the date by which a document must be:

(1) served under CrimPR 4.3 or CrimPR 4.8; or
(2) transmitted by fax, email or other electronic means if it is served under CrimPR 4.6.

(CrimPR 4.11)

The person who serves a document may prove that by signing a certificate explaining how and when it was served (CrimPR 4.12). As to date of service, see 59-011.

Methods of service

59-002 A document may be served by any of the methods described in CrimPR 4.3–4.6, below (subject to CrimPR 4.7), or in CrimPR 4.8, i.e. by:

(1) handing over a document (CrimPR 4.3 (see 59-003));
(2) by leaving or posting a document (CrimPR 4.4 (see 59-004));
(3) through a document exchange (DX) (CrimPR 4.5 (see 59-005));
(4) electronic means (CrimPR 4.6 (see 59-006));
(5) by persons in custody (CrimPR 4.8 (see 59-007)); or
(6) by other methods (CrimPR 4.9 (see 59-008)).

Where a document may be served by electronic means, the general rule is that the person serving it must use that method (CrimPR 4.2(2)).

CrimPR 4.7 (see 59-009) *restricts the method of service* in the case of certain specified documents.

Handing over a document

59-003 A document may be served on:

(a) an *individual* by handing it to him or her;
(b) a *corporation* by handing it to a person holding a senior position in that corporation;
(c) an individual or corporation who is *legally represented* in the case by handing it to that representative;
(d) the *prosecution* by handing it to the prosecutor or to the prosecution representative;
(e) the *court officer* by handing it to a court officer with authority to accept it at the relevant court office; and

(f) the *Registrar* of Criminal Appeals by handing it to a court officer with authority to accept it at the Criminal Appeal Office.

(CrimPR 4.3(1))

If an individual is under 18, a copy of a document served under para.(a) must be handed to his or her parent, or another appropriate adult, unless no such person is readily available (CrimPR 4.3(2)).

[Note. Certain legislation treats a body that is not a corporation as if it were one for the purposes of rules about service of documents. See, e.g. the Adoption and Children Act 2002 s.143.]

Leaving or posting a document

A document may be served by addressing it to the person to be served and leaving it at the appropriate address for service under CrimPR 4 or by sending it to that address by first class post or by the equivalent of first class post (CrimPR 4.4(1)). **59-004**

The *address for service* on:

(a) an *individual*, is an address where it is reasonably believed that he or she will receive it;
(b) a *corporation*, is its principal office in England and Wales, and if there is no readily identifiable principal office, then any place in England and Wales where it carries on its activities or business;
(c) an individual or corporation who is *legally represented* in the case, is that representative's office;
(d) the *prosecution*, is the prosecutor's office;
(e) the *court officer*, is the relevant court office; and
(f) the *Registrar* of Criminal Appeals is the Criminal Appeal Office, Royal Courts of Justice, Strand, London WC2A 2LL.

(CrimPR 4.4)

Service outside England and Wales may be allowed under other legislation, as under CLA 1977 s.39 (service of summons, etc. in Scotland and N. Ireland); CA 2006 s.1139(4) (service of copy summons, etc. on registered office in Scotland and N. Ireland); Crime (International Cooperation) Act 2003 (service of summons, etc. outside the UK CrimPR 49.1 and 49.2; and CA 2006 s.1139(2) (service on overseas corporation).

Service through a document exchange

A document may be served by document exchange (DX) where: **59-005**

(1) the person to be served:
 (a) has given a DX box number; and
 (b) has not refused to accept service by DX; or
(2) the person to be served is legally represented in the case and the representative has given a DX box number.

A document may be served by addressing it to that person or representative, as appropriate, at that DX box number it the document exchange at which the addressee has that DX box number or a document exchange at which the person serving it has a DX box number (CrimPR 4.5). Where the person to be served is the court officer, the address for service is the relevant court office (CrimPR 4.5(3)).

Service by electronic means

59-006 A document may be served by transmitting it by electronic means to a person, or representative, as appropriate, at his given address where:

(1) the person to be served:
  (a) has given an electronic address, or is given access to an electronic address at which a document may be deposited; and
  (b) has not refused to accept service by that method; or
(2) the person to be served is legally represented in the case and the representative has given an electronic address or is given access to an electronic address at which a document may be deposited.

Where a document is served under this rule the person serving it need not provide a paper copy as well (CrimPR 4.6(4)).

Service by person in custody

59-007 A person in custody may serve a document by handing it to the custodian addressed to the person to be served. Such custodian must then:

(a) endorse it with the time and date of receipt;
(b) record its receipt; and
(c) forward it promptly to the addressee.

(CrimPR 4.8)

Service by another method

59-008 The court may allow service of a document by a method:

(1) other than those described in CrimPR 4.3–4.6 and in CrimPR 4.8;
(2) other than one specified by CrimPR 4.7, where that rule applies.

An order allowing service by another method must specify:

(a) the method to be used; and
(b) the date on which the document will be served.

(CrimPR 4.9)

Documents that must be served by specified methods

59-009 An application or written statement, and notice under CrimPR 48.9 alleging contempt of court may be served:

(1) on an *individual*, only under CrimPR 4.3(1)(a) (by handing it to him or her);
(2) on a *corporation*, only under CrimPR 4.3(1)(b) (by handing it to a person holding a senior position in that corporation).

For the purposes of s.12 of the RTOA 1988, a notice of a requirement under s.172 of the RTA 1988 or under s.112 of the RTRA 1984 to identify the driver of a vehicle may be served:

(1) on an *individual*, only by post under CrimPR 4.4(1) and (2)(a);

(2) on a *corporation*, only by post under CrimPR 4.4(1) and (2)(b).

Documents that may not be served on a legal representative

Unless the court otherwise directs, these documents are, in so far as they affect the Crown Court: **59-010**

(a) a summons or a witness summons;
(b) notice of an order under RTOA 1988 s.25;
(c) any notice or document served under CrimPR 14 (BAIL and CUSTODY TIME LIMITS);
(d) notice under CrimPR 24.16(a) of when and where an adjourned hearing will resume;
(e) notice under CrimPR 28.5(3) of an application to vary or discharge a compensation order;
(f) notice under CrimPR 28.10(2)(c) of the location of the sentencing or enforcing court;
(g) an application or written statement, and notice, under CrimPR 48.9 alleging contempt of court.

(CrimPR 4.10)

Date of service

A document served under CrimPR 4.3 (59-003) or CrimPR 4.8 (59-007) is served on the day it is handed over. **59-011**

Unless something different is shown, a document served on a person by any other method is served:

(a) in the case of a *document left at an address*, on the next business day after the day on which it was left;
(b) in the case of a *document sent by first class post* or by the equivalent of first class post, on the second business day after the day on which it was posted or despatched;
(c) in the case of a *document served by document exchange*, on the second business day after the day on which it was left at a document exchange allowed as CrimPR 4.5;
(d) in the case of a *document transmitted by electronic means*, on the day on which it was sent under CrimPR 4.6(2)(a) if that day is a business day and if it was sent by no later than 14.30 that day, on the day on which notice of its deposit is given under CrimPR 4.6(2)(b), if that day is a business day and if that notice is given by no later than 14.30 that day, or otherwise on the next business day after it was sent or such notice was given; and
(e) in any case, on the day on which the *addressee responds to it if* that is earlier.

(CrimPR 4.11(1) and (2))

Unless something different is shown, a *document produced by a court computer* system for dispatch by post is to be taken as having been sent by first class post or by the equivalent of first class post to the addressee on the business day after the day on which it was produced (CrimPR 4.10(3)).

In the CrimPR, unless the context makes it clear that something different is meant "business day" means any day except Saturday, Sunday, Christmas Day, Boxing Day, Good Friday, Easter Monday or a bank holiday (CrimPR 2.2(1)).

Where a document is served on, or by, the court officer, "business day" does not include a day on which the court office is closed (CrimPR 4.11(4)).

Proof of service

59-012 The person who serves a document may prove that by signing a certificate explaining how and when it was served (CrimPR 4.12).

Court's power to give directions about service

59-013 The court may specify the time and date by which a document must be served under CrimPR 4.3 (handing over) or CrimPR 4.8 (service on person in custody). Similarly it may specify the time and date by which a document must be sent or deposited by electronic means. The court may treat a document as served if the addressee responds to it even if it was not served in accordance with the rules.

(CrimPR 4.13)

60. SEX OFFENDER ORDERS

QUICK GUIDE

A. INTRODUCTION

The SOA 2003: **60-001**

(1) repealed SOA 1997 Pt I relating to the registration of sex offenders;
(2) abolished restraining orders under SOA 1997 s.5A;
(3) retained the sexual offences prevention order (ss.104–122); and
(4) abolished sex offender orders under CDA 1998; but retained the "disqualification from working with children order" under CJCSA 2000 Pt 2; that order was abolished by the Vulnerable Groups Act 2006.

The ASBA 2014 Sch.5 para.3 abolished sexual offences prevention orders, and by the insertion into SOA 2003 of s.103A and following, created a new order, a sexual harm prevention order (SHPO). It applies where a defendant falls to be sentenced on or after 8 March 2015 for an offence listed in Schs 3 or 5 of SOA 2003. From 1 December 2020 the provisions in SOA 2003 and ASBA 2014 are repealed and replaced by equivalent provisions in the SA 2020 Pt 11 Ch.2 ss.343–358.

A judge of the Crown Court is now left with:

(a) a *duty* to certify the facts in relation to a certificate under the notification provisions of SOA 2003 Pt 2;
(b) the power to make a *sexual harm prevention order*;
(c) (during the transitional period) the obligation to *disqualify an offender from working with children*, under CJCSA 2000 s.28 (*R. v C* [2011] EWCA Crim 1872; [2012] 1 Cr. App. R. (S.) 89 reversing the decision in *Att. Gen.'s Reference (No.18 of 2011)* [2011] EWCA Crim 1300; [2012] 1 Cr. App. R. (S.) 27); and
(d) *the obligation to notify* an offender in certain circumstances that he will be barred from working with children or vulnerable adults by the Independent Safeguarding Authority ("ISA") established under the 2006 Act (with effect from 1 December 2012 the ISA was abolished and its functions are transferred to the Disclosure and Barring Service—see 60-013).

Where, on a conviction, sentence or order, legislation requires an offender:

(i) to notify information to the police; or
(ii) to be included in a barred list,

the judge must tell him that such requirements apply and under what legislation.

B. CERTIFICATION

For the purposes of the notification requirements in SOA 2003 Pt 2, a certificate **60-002**
is required in the case of any person:

(1) convicted of an offence listed in Sch.3;
(2) found not guilty of such an offence by reason of insanity; or
(3) found to be under a disability and to have done the act charged against him, in respect of such an offence.

(SOA 2003 s.92) (It is also required where a person is cautioned in respect of such an offence (s.80(1).)

The judge should certify those facts in open court, either at the time of sentence or subsequently that:

(a) on that date he was convicted, found not guilty as in (2) above, or found to be under a disability in the circumstances stated in (3) above;
(b) that the offence in question is an offence listed in Sch.3; and
(c) that he is so certifying (*R. v G (Sex Offender) (Registration)* [2002] 2 Cr. App. R. (S.) 79),

so that the certificate may be used as evidence in later proceedings (see also *R. v Rawlinson, The Times,* 14 October 1999).

The whole term of an extended sentence imposed under SA 2020 ss.279–282 or 266–268 is the relevant period for the purposes of determining the notification period (and the same would seem to apply for extended sentences under CJA 2003 ss.227 or 228) see *R. (on the application of Minter) v Chief Constable of Hampshire* [2011] EWHC 1610 (Admin); [2012] 1 W.L.R. 1157).

The court officer will give notice to the offender of the requirement to register with the police, and of the duration of such requirement, which, in the case of:

(i) custodial sentences of 30 months or more, runs for life, 6-30 months, runs for 10 years, 6 months or less, runs for 7 years;
(ii) custodial sentences of more than 6 months but less than 30 months, runs for 10 years;
(iii) custodial sentences of 6 months or less, runs for 7 years;
(iv) a conditional discharge, runs for the period of the conditional discharge;
(v) any other description, runs for 5 years; and
(vi) a hospital order runs for 7 years, or where a restriction order is imposed, indefinitely,

though adjustments will be made where there are two or more notification requirements in existence (SOA 2003 s.82).

If the offender is under 18 the periods are halved.

The Sexual Offences Act 2003 (Notification Requirements) (England and Wales) Regulations 2012 introduce new requirements in relation to all offenders subject to the notification requirements of SOA 2003.

C. Sexual Harm Prevention Order (SHPO)

General

60-003 A judge may make a "sexual harm prevention order" in respect of an accused (SA 2020 s.345) where, in respect of an offence listed in SOA 2003 Schs 3 or 5 he deals with him in respect of:

(1) such an offence;
(2) a finding that he is not guilty of such an offence by reason of insanity; or

(3) a finding that he is under a disability and has done the act charged against him in respect of such an offence, and

the judge is satisfied that it is necessary to make a such an order, for the purpose of:

(a) protecting the public or any particular members of the public from sexual harm from the accused; or
(b) protecting children or vulnerable adults generally, or any particular children or vulnerable adults, from sexual harm from the accused outside the UK.

A sexual harm prevention order prohibits the defendant from doing anything described in the order. Subject to SA 2020 s.348(1), a prohibition contained in it has effect for a fixed period, specified in the order, of at least five years, or until further order (any order made for a period of less than five years will be unlawful (*R. v R* [2010] EWCA Crim 907)).

Breach of the order is an offence carrying five years imprisonment on indictment (SA 2020 s.354).

Nature and extent of prohibitions

An order may specify: **60-004**

(1) that some of its prohibitions have effect until further order and some for a fixed period;
(2) different periods for different prohibitions.

The only prohibitions that may be included in an order are those *necessary* for the purpose of:

(a) protecting the public or any particular members of the public from sexual harm from the accused; or
(b) protecting children or vulnerable adults generally, or any particular children or vulnerable adults, from sexual harm from the accused outside the UK.

As to the definitions of "the public", "sexual harm", "child" and "vulnerable adult" each has the meaning given in SA 2020 s.358 (see 60-003).

Where the judge makes a sexual harm prevention order in relation to a person who is already subject to such an order (whether made by that court or another), the earlier order ceases to have effect (SA 2020 ss.343–349).

Prohibitions on foreign travel

A "prohibition on foreign travel" means: **60-005**

(1) a prohibition on travelling to any country outside the UK named or described in the order;
(2) a prohibition on travelling to any country outside the UK other than a country named or described in the order; or
(3) a prohibition on travelling to any country outside the UK.

A prohibition on foreign travel contained in a sexual harm prevention order must be for a fixed period of not more than five years, but this does not prevent the prohibition from being extended for a further period (of no more than five years each time) under SA 2020 s.350.

A sexual harm prevention order that contains a prohibition under (3) above must require the accused to surrender all of his passports at a police station specified in the order on or before the date when the prohibition takes effect, or within a specified period. Any passports surrendered will be returned as soon as reasonably practicable after that person ceases to be subject to a sexual harm prevention order containing a prohibition within (3) (unless the person is subject to an equivalent prohibition under another order). There are exceptions in relation to a passports issued by or on behalf of the authorities of a country outside the UK if the passport has been returned to those authorities, passports issued by or on behalf of an international organisation if the passport has been returned to that organisation.

"Passport" means:

(a) a UK passport within the meaning of the IA 1971;
(b) a passport issued by or on behalf of the authorities of a country outside the UK, or by or on behalf of an international organisation; or
(c) a document that can be used (in some or all circumstances) instead of a passport.

(SA 2020 s.348)

Notification requirements

60-006 Where a sexual harm prevention order is made in respect of:

(1) an accused who was a relevant offender immediately before the making of the order, and he would (apart from this provision cease to be subject to the notification requirements while the order (as renewed from time to time) has effect, he remains subject to the notification requirements;
(2) an accused who was not a relevant offender immediately before the making of the order,

the order causes him to become subject to the notification requirements from the making of the order until the order (as renewed from time to time) ceases to have effect.

The "relevant date" is the date of service of the order.

Where:

(i) a sexual harm prevention order is in effect in relation to a relevant sex offender (within the meaning of s.88A); and
(ii) by virtue of ss.88F or 88G the relevant sex offender ceases to be subject to the notification requirements of this Part,

the sexual harm prevention order ceases to have effect (SA 2020 s.352).

Width and scope of restriction: "necessary" and "proportionate"

60-007 In relation to the former sexual offences prevention order it was held that not only the order, but also the restrictions and prohibitions contained in it must be necessary and proportionate (*R. v R* [2010] EWCA Crim 907). The fact that an order was "appropriate" was not sufficient (*R. v Halloren* [2004] EWCA Crim 233; [2004] 2 Cr. App. R. (S.) 57). Each prohibition must be necessary and proportionate (*R. v Mortimer* [2010] EWCA Crim 1303).

SOA 2003 s.107(2) stated in terms that the only prohibitions that may be included in the order are those necessary for the purpose of protecting the public or any particular members of the public from serious sexual harm from the accused. Section 103A(3) is in the same terms as is SA 2020 s.346. It was said in relation to the earlier section that no order should be drawn wider than is necessary to achieve its stated purpose and the terms should be:

(1) tailored to fit the exact circumstances of the case although that should not lead to inventiveness in drafting which was likely to store up trouble for the future;
(2) sufficiently clear on their face so that the offender, those who had to deal with him in ordinary daily life and those responsible for enforcement know what he can, and cannot, do without difficulty or the need for legal advice; and
(3) such that any risk of unintentional breach was avoided.

(*R. v Hemsley* [2011] EWCA Crim 1772; [2011] Crim. L.R. 967; *R. v Smith* [2009] EWCA Crim 1795)

In the absence of evidence or inference which could properly be drawn, normal activities should not be prohibited or restrained (*R. v Buchanan* [2010] EWCA Crim 1316).

As to prohibitions on the use of the internet, and restrictions on contact with children and young persons, see *R. v Smith* [2009] EWCA Crim 1795.

In deciding whether the facts alleged require an order, it was desirable that the standard of proof, though theoretically the civil standard, should be the equivalent of the criminal standard (*Cleveland Chief Constable v Haggas* [2009] EWHC 3231 (Admin); [2010] 3 All E.R. 506, applying *R. (on the application of McCann) v Manchester Crown Court* [2002] UKHL 39; [2003] 1 Cr. App. R. 27).

The approach was considered in *R. v Parsons and Morgan* [2017] EWCA Crim 2163. No order should be made unless it is necessary to protect the public from sexual harm. If an order is necessary, then the prohibitions imposed must be effective. The prohibitions must be clear and realistic and capable of simple compliance and enforcement. Any SHPO must be tailored to the facts. There is no one size that fits all of the many factual scenarios. Terms must not be oppressive and must be proportionate. See also *Atttorney General's Reference (R. v NC)* [2016] EWCA Crim 1448; [2017] 1 Cr. App. R. (S.) 13 CA, and the guidance in relation to SOPOs in *R. v Smith (Steven); R. v Clarke (Wayne); R. v Hall (Bryan); R. v Dodd (Jonathan) (Practice Note)* [2011] EWCA Crim 1772, which, subject to the points made in *Parsons and Morgan*, was said to be in general, essentially sound and should continue to be followed. *R. v Choung* [2019] EWCA Crim 1650; [2020] 1 Cr. App. R. (S.) 13 deals with the position with computer-generated works or Hentai images and sexual harm. If those images were the only ones that a defendant possessed or was likely to possess, as they did not involve any actual sexual harm to any actual children, there would be no risk of sexual harm and no need for a SHPO.

Procedure

Procedure is governed by CrimPR 31 (behaviour orders after verdict or finding) as to which see CRIMINAL BEHAVIOUR ORDERS. **60-008**

If a person is convicted of a qualifying offence and presents a significant risk of harm to children:

(1) the defence advocate should be alert to the possibility, if not the likelihood, of an order being made when sentence is finally passed; and
(2) the prosecutor should be in a position, when asked by the judge, to submit

draft proposals for incorporation into the order both to the judge and to the defence in good time for the hearing; and
(3) if there is insufficient time for the defence advocate and the offender to consider the contents or terms of such proposed order because of late service, application should be made to the judge for the hearing to be put back in order for instructions to be taken (*R. v Buchanan* [2010] EWCA Crim 1316).

Where the judge forms a provisional view as to the imposition of an order (subject, of course, to the assessment of risk), it will be helpful if he directs the preparation of a pre-sentence report and a consideration of the assessment of dangerousness, to invite the probation authorities to consider whether the management of the risk could be assisted by the imposition of an order and, if so, the restrictions which might be appropriate. The burden is squarely on prosecuting counsel, as to whose duties, see *R. v Jackson* [2012] EWCA Crim 2602; (2013) 177 J.P. 147.

The prosecutor must:

(a) serve a draft order on the court officer and on the accused not less than two business days before the hearing at which the order may be made; and
(b) in the draft order, specify those prohibitions which he proposes as necessary for the purpose of protecting the public or any particular members of the public from serious sexual harm from the offender.

Orders in relation to siblings

60-009 In relation to sexual offences prevention orders, it was said that where the judge was considering making an order to protect from abuse within the family, particularly a sibling of the abused person, it might be desirable, to draft the order in terms that provide a link with the court's family jurisdiction.

Where the victim has a sibling living in the same family, it was said that the judge ought to conduct a risk assessment and consider:

(1) the likelihood of the offender committing a further Sch.3 offence; and
(2) the sibling being caused serious physical or psychological harm as a result, even if the offence was not directed against him.

Where the judge considered that there was a risk that the offender would in future commit one or more Sch.3 offences which, unless the sibling was protected by an order, would cause him SA 2020 s.350, the persons who may apply a variation of the order do not include a sibling or anyone acting on his behalf. There may be occasions when an order is made to protect a child of the offender where the family court's jurisdiction should be reflected in the order because of the additional flexibility that it provides. The judge has jurisdiction to make an order in the following terms:

> "[the offender] shall not, without the order of a judge exercising jurisdiction under the Children Act 1989, communicate or seek to communicate, whether directly or indirectly with [the sibling] whilst he remains under the age of 16 years."

In that way the child's interest in a possibly changing situation can better be met than through the blunt instrument of the SOPO alone (*R. v D* [2005] EWCA Crim 3660; [2006] Cr. App. R. (S.) 32).

Variation, renewal and discharge of order

In relation to an order made by the Crown Court, under SA 2020 s.350: **60-010**

(1) the offender;
(2) the chief officer of police for the area in which he resides; or
(3) a chief officer of police who believes that the offender is in, or is intending to come to, his police area,

may apply to the Crown Court for an order varying, renewing or discharging the order.

On application, the judge, after hearing the applicant and (if they wish to be heard), the other persons mentioned in this paragraph, may make any order, varying, renewing or discharging the order, that he considers appropriate.

Additional prohibitions may be imposed on the offender only if it is necessary to do so for the purpose of protecting the public, or any or any particular members of the public from sexual harm from the offender or of protecting children or vulnerable adults generally, or any particular children or vulnerable adults, from sexual harm from the offender outside the UK.

Any renewed or varied order may contain only such prohibitions as are necessary for this purpose.

The judge must not discharge an order before the end of five years beginning with the day on which it was made, without the consent of the offender and:

(a) where the application is made by a chief officer of police, that chief officer; or
(b) in any other case, the chief officer of police for the area in which the offender resides.

Procedure on variation, renewal or discharge is governed by CrimPR 31 (see CRIMINAL BEHAVIOUR ORDERS).

Breach of order

A person commits an offence punishable with a maximum of five years imprisonment if he breaches an order. Significant sentences are necessary in respect of serious breaches (see *R. v Byrne* [2009] EWCA Crim 1555; [2010] 1 Cr. App. R. (S.) 65 where the authorities are reviewed). **60-011**

It is not open to the judge to impose a conditional discharge (SA 2020 s.354(5)).

For breaches where sentence takes place on or after 1 October 2018, the Sentencing Council definitive guideline on breach offences will apply. The breach of a SHPO, a foreign travel order and a failure to comply with notification requirements are covered by specific guidelines with the overall definitive guideline.

Appeals

Appeal lies to the CACD from the making of an order under: **60-012**

(1) 60-003 (1) as if the order were a sentence passed on the offender for an offence; and under
(2) 60-003 (2) and (3) as if the accused had been convicted of the offence and the order were a sentence passed on the accused for that offence.

(SA 2020 s.353)

An appeal lies to the CACD against the variation of an order, or the refusal to make such an order, where made by the Crown Court.

Procedure is governed by CrimPR Pts 36 and 39.

On appeal the CACD may quash the order and make another appropriate order (since it is an appeal against sentence) (*R. v Hoath* [2011] EWCA Crim 274; [2011] 4 All E.R. 306).

D. Disqualification from working with vulnerable groups

General

60-013 Until 10 September 2012, the judge was required, under the Safeguarding Vulnerable Groups Act 2006 Sch.3 para.25 to inform an offender convicted of an offence or who received an order which leads to automatic barring by the Independent Safeguarding Authority ("ISA") that they will be barred by the ISA, whether or not the conviction or order allows the person to make representations to the ISA against their bar.

With effect from 10 September 2012, under changes introduced by the Protection of Freedoms Act 2012 (see SI 2003/2234), those offenders convicted of an offence, or who receive an order (i.e. some disqualification which leads to automatic barring):

(1) *without* the right to make representations, should continue to be told that they *will* be barred;
(2) *with* the right to make representations should now be told that they *may* be barred.

Representations will now be made before a person is barred, rather than after it (as has previously been the case), so some such people will not be barred. In addition, the ISA will now bar those people who have the right to make representations against their bar only if they have been, are or might in future be engaged in regulated activity, as set out in the SVGA Sch.4 (as amended). The list of automatic barring offences is set out in SI 2009/37 (as amended) indicating the offences which bring the right to make representations and those which do not.

With effect from 1 December 2012 the ISA was abolished and its functions are transferred to the Disclosure and Barring Service. For the avoidance of doubt, the former power (under CJCSA 2000) of the court to disqualify an offender has been abolished as from 17 June 2013 by PFA 2012 s.83 but judges are still required to spell out the consequences of conviction to the offender.

61. SHERIFF'S AWARDS; COMMENDATIONS

A judge of the Crown Court may, where a person appears to have been active in or towards the apprehension of a person later charged with an indictable offence, order the sheriff of the county in which the offence was committed, to pay a reward of such sums as seem to the judge be just and reasonable (CLA 1826 ss.28, 29). **61-001**

This is an important power and the Senior Master has previously commented as follows:

(1) there are no fetters on this power; any suggestions that there is no money in the budget etc. ought to be discounted; the 1826 Act does not allow for such intervention by the executive;
(2) an award is not intended to be compensatory but to be sufficient to reflect the public's appreciation of the recipient's bravery;
(3) many of the awards made are, in the light of modern day standards, extremely modest; it is suggested that a sum of £350 might be a minimum save for small children, and that an award of £500 would not be over-generous; and
(4) once an award is made, a cheque is ordinarily drawn by the Crown Court officer and sent to the High Sheriff for presentation.

The Crown Court also issues from time to time a certificate of commendation, where the judge identifies a person who has merited commendation for conduct not coming within CLA 1826. Such certificates are intended to supplement the existing system.

62. SPECIAL MEASURES DIRECTIONS

Quick Guide

62-001 The first parts of this chapter are concerned with those "special measures" introduced by YJCEA 1999 for the purpose of assisting a witness or accused to give evidence in criminal proceedings. A "witness" is defined in CrimPR 18.2 as anyone (other than an accused) for whose benefit an application, direction or order is made.

Conveniently, the section includes a number of linked topics: restrictions on cross-examination by the accused in person, anonymity of witnesses and witness preparation; pre-recorded cross-examination and re-examination added to which is restraint of the accused, which does not fit comfortably under any other title.

Procedure differs according to the nature of the proceedings.

For measures attending the accused, see VULNERABLE ACCUSED AND WITNESSES.

A. General procedure in relation to directions or orders

General procedural rules

General procedural rules are contained in CrimPR 18.3–18.5 in relation to applications for a court direction or order. Further rules applying particularly to special measures directions are contained in CrimPR 18.8–18.13; those in relation to a defendant's evidence directions in CrimPR 18.14–18.17, and those in relation to witness anonymity orders in CrimPR 18.18–18.22. **62-002**

Once it is established that a witness is eligible for assistance by way of special measures, s.19(2) of the YJCEA provides that:

(1) it is for the trial judge to determine whether any of the special measures available would be likely to improve the quality of the evidence given by a witness; and
(2) if the judge so concludes, it is for him to decide which of the special measures, or which combination of them, would be likely to maximise so far as practicable the quality of the particular witness's evidence.

In deciding this matter, the judge is required by s.19(3) to consider all the circumstances of the case including any view expressed by the witness and whether the measure or measures might inhibit the effective testing of evidence.

It should be borne in mind, however, that as part of his general responsibilities, the trial judge is expected to deal with specific communication problems faced by accused persons or witnesses as part and parcel of his ordinary control of the judicial process. This overall responsibility for the fairness of the trial is not altered because of the wide band of possible special measures enshrined in statute (*R. v Cox* [2012] EWCA Crim 549; [2012] 2 Cr. App. R. 6).

However, assisting a vulnerable witness to give evidence is not merely a matter of ordering the appropriate measure. Further directions about vulnerable people in the courts, ground rules hearings and intermediaries are to be found in VULNERABLE ACCUSED AND WITNESSES. Special measures need not be considered or ordered in isolation. The needs of the individual witness should be ascertained, and a combination of special measures may be appropriate. For example, if a witness who is to give evidence by live link wishes, screens can be used to shield the live link screen from the defendant and the public, as would occur if screens were being used for a witness giving evidence in the court room (*CPD* V Evidence 18A: Measures to assist a witness or defendant to give evidence 18A.1, 2).

VC3.3 and 3.4 impose a duty on HMCTS court staff to:

(1) ensure that:
    (a) any special measures required by a victim are available if the judge has ordered them;
    (b) victims are able to enter the court through a different entrance and are seated in a separate waiting area from the suspect where possible; and
    (c) there is a contact point for victims so they are able to find out what is happening in their case whilst it is being heard in court; and
(2) ensure wherever possible that:
    (a) victims giving evidence do not have to wait more than two hours; and

(b) contact details for all victims who are witnesses are taken so they are able to leave the court precincts and be contacted when necessary.

B. SPECIAL MEASURES DIRECTIONS UNDER YJCEA 1999

1. ELIGIBILITY FOR SPECIAL MEASURES

General

62-003 A witness is eligible for a special measures direction under YJCEA 1999 if, at the time the judge makes a determination, the witness:

(1) is under 18 (i.e. a "child witness" or a "qualifying witness"); or
(2) the judge considers the quality of the evidence given by the witness is likely to be diminished by reason of the fact that the witness:
  (a) suffers from mental disorder within the meaning of MHA 1983 (see MENTALLY DISORDERED OFFENDERS);
  (b) otherwise has a significant impairment of intelligence and social functioning; or
  (c) has a physical disability or is suffering from a physical disorder.

(YJCEA 1999 s.16(1) and (2))

In determining whether a witness falls within (2) above, the judge must consider any views expressed by the witness (YJCEA 1999 s.76(4)).

A "child witness" is a witness under 18; a "qualifying witness" is one who was a child witness when interviewed (YJCEA 1999 ss.21 and 22).

By the Special Measures for Child Witness (Sexual Offences) Regulations 2013 (SI 2013/2971), a complainant of a "relevant" (in effect a sexual) offence is presumed to be under the age of 18 if there are reasons to believe that he is so.

References to the "quality" of a witness's evidence are to its quality in terms of completeness, coherence and accuracy, and for this purpose "coherence" refers to a witness's ability in giving evidence to give answers which address the questions put to him and can be understood both individually and collectively.

In all special measures permitted, it is important that the judge direct the jury that they should not prejudice the accused (see 62-029).

Witness in fear or distress

62-004 Also eligible for assistance is a witness, other than the accused, in "relevant proceedings" (see below) if the judge is satisfied that the quality of evidence (see 62-003) given by the witness is likely to be diminished by reason of fear or distress on his part in connection with giving evidence in the proceedings (YJCEA 1999 s.17(1) and (2)).

"Relevant proceedings" are those listed in YJCEA 1999 Sch.1A.

In making his determination as to whether a witness is so eligible, the judge must take into account, in particular:

(1) the nature and alleged circumstances of the offence;
(2) the witness's:
  (a) age;
  (b) social and cultural background, and ethnic origins;
  (c) domestic and employment circumstances;
  (d) religious beliefs or political opinions; and

(3) any behaviour towards the witness on the part of the accused or his associates or members of his family, or of any other person likely to be an accused or witness in the proceedings,

to the extent that these matters appear to him to be relevant, and he must also, in determining the question, consider any views expressed by the witness.

It is open to the judge to determine the issue on (1) above, alone, and he may do so notwithstanding the fact that the witness is neither young nor particularly vulnerable (*R. v Brown* [2004] Crim. L.R. 1034).

Complainant in sexual case

Where the complainant in respect of a sexual offence is a witness in proceedings relating to that offence (or to that offence and any other offences) the witness is eligible for assistance in relation to those offences unless the witness has informed the court of his wish not to be eligible (YJCEA 1999 s.17(4)). **62-005**

Offences involving weapons

A witness in proceedings relating to an offence involving the weapons listed in CorJA 2009 Sch.1A (or to such an offence and any other offences) is eligible for assistance in relation to those proceedings unless the witness has informed the court of his wish not to be so eligible (YJCEA 1999 s.17(5) and (6)). **62-006**

2. Available special measures

General

The special measures set out below may be adopted only where the court has been notified by the Secretary of State that relevant arrangements may be made available in the area in which the proceedings will take place. **62-007**

The following are "special measures":

(1) screening the witness from the accused (s.23);
(2) evidence by live link (s.24);
(3) permitting evidence to be given in private (s.25);
(4) removal of wigs and gowns (s.26);
(5) video recorded evidence in chief (s.27);
(6) examination of witness through intermediary (s.29); and
(7) aids to communication (any appropriate device to assist in overcoming communication problems due to a witness's disability, disorder or impairment).

(YJCEA 1999 s.18(2))

Each of these measures is dealt with separately at 62-022 to 62-028.

Two further special measures introduced by YJCEA 1999, namely video recorded cross-examination and re-examination (s.28) and examination of the accused through an intermediary (s.33AB) are now in force in relation to proceedings at all locations of the Crown Court. Initially these measures were limited to witnesses eligible for assistance under s.16(1), but in case of s.16(1)(a) only if the witnesses under 16 at the time of the hearing. More recently these measures have also been rolled out to cover those cases where witnesses are eligible under s.17(4) in cases of modern slavery and sexual offences.

Witnesses under 18, or those who suffer from disabilities or disorders may be eligible for all the measures set out above, those suffering from fear or distress may be considered only for those numbered (1)–(5).

3. Procedure in relation to special measures directions

General

62-008 The judge may decide whether to give, vary or discharge a special measures direction:

(1) at a hearing in public or in private, or without a hearing; and
(2) in a party's absence if that party:
  (a) applied for the direction, variation or discharge; or
  (b) has had at least 14 days in which to make representations.

(CrimPR 18.8)

Content of application

62-009 An applicant for a special measures direction must:

(1) explain how the witness is eligible for assistance;
(2) explain why special measures would be likely to improve the quality of the witness's evidence;
(3) propose the measure or measures that in the applicant's opinion would be likely to maximise so far as practicable the quality of that evidence;
(4) report any views that the witness has expressed about:
  (a) his eligibility for assistance;
  (b) the likelihood that special measures would improve the quality of his or her evidence; and
  (c) the measure or measures proposed by the applicant;
(5) in a case in which a child witness or a qualifying witness does not want the primary rule to apply, provide any information that the judge may need to assess the witness's views;
(6) in a case in which the applicant proposes that the witness should give evidence by live link:
  (a) identify someone to accompany the witness while the witness gives evidence;
  (b) name that person, if possible; and
  (c) explain why that person would be an appropriate companion for the witness, including the witness's own views;
(7) in a case in which the applicant proposes the admission of video recorded evidence, identify:
  (a) the date and duration of the recording;
  (b) which part the applicant wants the court to admit as evidence, if the applicant does not want the court to admit all of it;
(8) attach any other material on which the applicant relies; and
(9) if the applicant wants a hearing, ask for one, and explain why it is needed.

(CrimPR 18.10)

CPD 2015 V 21A sets out a form of application in Annex D for use in connection with this rule.

Application containing information withheld from another party

Where an applicant serves an application for a direction (or for its variation or discharge) and the application includes information that he thinks should not be revealed to another party, he must: 62-010

(1) omit that information from the part of the application that is served on that other party;
(2) mark the other part to show that, unless the judge otherwise directs, it is only for the court; and
(3) in that part, explain why he has withheld that information from that other party.

(CrimPR 18.12)

Hearing an application

Any hearing will be in private unless the judge otherwise directs, and if he so directs may be wholly or in part in the absence of a party from which information has been withheld. 62-011

In general, on a hearing the judge will consider in sequence:

(1) representations first by the applicant and then by each other party, in all the parties' presence; and then
(2) further representations by the applicant in the absence of a party from whom information has been withheld, but the judge may direct other arrangements.

(CrimPR 18.12(3) and (4))

Representations in response

Where a party wishes to make representations in respect of an application for a direction (its variation or discharge) or a direction (variation or discharge) that the judge proposes to make of his own initiative, he must: 62-012

(1) serve the representations on the Crown Court officer and each other party;
(2) do so not more than 14 days after the service of the application, or notice of the direction (variation or discharge) which the judge proposes; and
(3) ask for a hearing, if he wants one and explain why it is needed.

Where representations include information that the person making them thinks ought not to be revealed to another party, he must take the steps indicated in 62-010.

Representations against a direction must explain:

(a) why the witness is not eligible for assistance; or
(b) if he is eligible, why:
    (i) no special direction would be liable to improve the quality of his evidence;
    (ii) the proposed measure(s) would not be likely so far as practicable to maximise the quality of his evidence; or
    (iii) the proposed measure(s) might tend to inhibit the effective testing of that evidence.

Representations against the variation or discharge of a direction must explain why it should not be varied or discharged (CrimPR 18.13).

Determination of application

62-013 Where the judge determines that a witness is eligible for assistance by virtue of either s.16 or s.17 he must then determine:

(1) whether any of the special measures available in relation to the witness (or any combination of them) would, in his opinion, be likely to improve the quality (see 62-003) of the evidence given by the witness; and
(2) if so:
  (a) determine which would in his opinion be likely to maximise as far as is practicable, the quality of such evidence; and
  (b) give a direction for the measure or measures to apply to the evidence given by the witness.

(YJCEA 1999 s.19(2))

Status of directions; reasons

62-014 A special measure direction is binding until the proceedings are determined or abandoned in relation to each accused. A direction may be varied or discharged in the interests of justice, by the judge of his own initiative, or on application by a party where there has been a material change of circumstances.

The judge must state in open court the reasons for all his determinations relating to special measures directions (YJCEA 1999 s.20(1) and (2)).

4. "CHILD WITNESSES"

General

62-015 A witness under 18 is a "child witness" for the purposes of these provisions whether or not he is eligible for special measures under any other provisions of YJCEA 1999.

Where the judge in making a determination under s.19(2) (see 62-003) determines that a witness is a child witness, he must:

(1) first have regard to the rules as to child witnesses set out in 62-016 to 62-017 (s.21(3)–(4C); and
(2) then determine which, if any, of the available forms of special measure is appropriate (s.19(2)) as to which see 62-003,

and for the purposes of s.19(2), as it then applies to the witness, any special measures required to be applied to him are treated as if they were determined, pursuant to s.19(2)(a) and (b)(i), to be ones that (whether on their own or with any other special measures) would be likely to maximise so far as practicable the quality of his evidence (YJCEA 1999 s.21(1) and (2)).

The primary rule as to child witnesses

62-016 The primary rule in the case of a child witness or a "qualifying witness" (62-003), is that the judge *must give a direction* in relation to which provides for his evidence being admitted:

(1) under s.27 by means of a video of an interview with the witness in place of his examination-in-chief; and
(2) after that evidence which is not given by means of a video recording, whether in chief or otherwise by means of a live link in accordance with s.24; or
(3) if one or both of those measures are not taken, for the witness when giving evidence to be screened from seeing the accused, *unless*:
  (a) the witness does not want the rule to apply and the judge is satisfied that to omit a measure usually required would not diminish the quality of the witness's evidence; or
  (b) the judge is satisfied that compliance with it would not be likely to maximise the quality of the witness's evidence.

(YJCEA 1999 s.21(3) and (4))

Limitations on primary rule

There are limitations on the primary rule for child witnesses, namely: **62-017**

(1) the requirement in (1) of 62-013 is subject to the availability of the special measure in question;
(2) the requirement in (1) of 62-013 is subject to s.27(2), i.e. that a special measure may not provide for a video recording, or part of it, to be admitted, if the judge is of opinion that, in all the circumstances of the case, in the interests of justice, that recording, or part of it, should not be admitted;
(3) if the witness informs the judge of his wish that the rule should not apply or should apply only in part, the rule does not apply to the extent that the judge is satisfied that not complying with the rule would not diminish the quality of the witness's evidence; and
(4) the primary rule does not apply to the extent that the judge is satisfied that compliance with it would not maximise the quality of the witness's evidence so far as practicable (whether because any other special measure available would have that effect or otherwise).

(YJCEA 1999 s.21(4))

Factors to be taken into account

In making his decisions under the above provisions, the judge must take into account (together with any other factors he considers relevant): **62-018**

(1) the ability of the witness to understand the consequences of giving evidence otherwise than in accordance with the primary rule;
(2) the relationship (if any) between the witness and the accused;
(3) the witness's social and cultural background and ethnic origins; and
(4) the nature and alleged circumstances of the offence to which the proceedings relate.

The above provisions (s.21) are extended to witnesses other than the accused who do not qualify as child witnesses at the time of the hearing, but were under 18 when a relevant recording was made. The provisions of s.21(2)–(4) and (4C) so far as relating to the giving of a direction complying with the requirement contained in s.21(3)(a), apply to *a qualifying witness* in respect of the relevant recording as they apply to a child witness (within the meaning of that section) (YJCEA 1999 s.21(4C)).

Consequences of disapplication

62-019 Where, as a consequence of all or part of the primary rule stated in the preceding paragraph being disapplied under (C), a witness's evidence, or any part of it, would fall to be given as testimony in court, the judge must give a special measures direction making such provision as is described in s.23 for the evidence or that part of it.

The requirement in subs.(4A) is subject to the following limitations:

(1) if the witness informs the court of his wish that the requirement in subs.(4A) should not apply, the requirement does not apply to the extent that the judge is satisfied that not complying with it would not diminish the quality of the witness's evidence; and
(2) the requirement does not apply to the extent that the court is satisfied that making such a provision would not be likely to maximise the quality of the witness's evidence so far as practicable whether because the application to that evidence of one or more other special measures available in relation to the witness would have that result or for any other reason.

(YJCEA 1999 s.21(4B) and (4C))

Duty of applicant

62-020 A party who wants to introduce the evidence of a "child" or "qualifying" witness (62-003) must, as soon as reasonably practicable:

(1) notify the court that the witness is eligible for assistance;
(2) provide the judge with any information that he may need to assess the witness's views, if the latter does not want the primary rule to apply; and
(3) serve any recorded evidence on the Crown Court officer and each other party.

The contents of such an application are stated in CrimPR 18.9 and 18.10 and an appropriate form is to be found in *CPD* Annex D.

Where the application is for variation or discharge of a direction, the applicant must:

(a) explain what material circumstances have changed since the direction was given (or last varied);
(b) explain why the direction should be varied or discharged; and
(c) ask for a hearing, if he wants one, and explain why it is needed.

(CrimPR 18.11)

5. SPECIAL PROVISIONS RELATING TO SEXUAL OFFENCES

General

62-021 Where in criminal proceedings in the Crown Court relating to a sexual offence (or to a sexual offence and other offences):

(1) the complainant in respect of that offence is a witness in the proceedings; and

(2) is not an eligible witness by reason of s.16(1)(a) (62-003) (whether or not he is an eligible witness by reason of any other provision of ss.16 or 17),

then, if a party to the proceedings makes an application for a special measures direction in relation to the complainant, he may request that the direction provide for any relevant recording to be admitted under s.27 (video recorded evidence-in-chief).

A "relevant recording" in relation to a complainant, is a video recording of an interview of him made with a view to its admission as the evidence-in-chief of the complainant.

If:

(a) a party to the proceedings makes such a request with respect to the complainant; and
(b) the judge determines that the complainant is eligible for assistance by virtue of ss.16(1)(b) or 17,

the judge must:

(i) firstly have regard to s.22A(7)–(9); and
(ii) then (under s.19(2)) determine which, if any, of the special measures is appropriate; and

any special measure required to be applied in relation to the complainant will be as if it were a measure determined by the judge pursuant to s.19(2)(a) and (b)(i), to be one that (whether on its own or with any other special measures) would be likely to maximise, so far as practicable, the quality of the complainant's evidence (YJCEA 1999 s.22A).

Subject to s.27(2) the judge *must* give a special measures direction in relation to the complainant that provides for any relevant recording to be admitted under s.27, *except that* that requirement does not apply to the extent that the judge is satisfied that compliance with it would not be likely to maximise the quality of the complainant's evidence so far as practicable (whether because the application to that evidence of one or more other special measures available in relation to the complainant would have that result or for any other reason).

6. Types of special measure

(1) Screening witness from accused

A special measures direction may provide for the witness, while giving testimony or being sworn in court, to be prevented by means of a screen or other arrangement from seeing the accused, but the screen or other arrangement must not prevent the witness from being able to see, and to be seen by the judge and the jury, if there is one, legal representatives acting in the proceedings and any interpreter or other person appointed (in pursuance of the direction or otherwise) to assist the witness. **62-022**

Where two or more legal representatives are acting for a party to the proceedings, the provision is satisfied in relation to those representatives if the witness is able at all material times to see and be seen by at least one of them. See *R. v Brown* [2004] Crim. L.R. 1034, as to a direction to the jury (YJCEA 1999 s.23).

(2) Evidence by live link

A special measures direction may provide for the witness to give evidence by means of a live link. Such a direction may also provide for a specified person to ac- **62-023** company the witness while the witness is giving evidence by live link. In determining who that person is the judge will have regard to the wishes of the witness.

Where a direction provides for a witness to give evidence by that means he may not give evidence in any other way without the permission of the judge, which permission may be given if it appears to the judge to be in the interests of justice to do so, in which case he may do so:

(1) on the application of a party to the proceedings if there has been a material change of circumstances since the time the direction was made, or since any previous application; or
(2) on his own initiative.

(YJCEA 1999 s.24)

The presence of a supporter is designed to provide emotional support to the witness, helping reduce the witness's anxiety and stress and contributing to the ability to give best evidence. It is preferable for the direction to be made well before the trial begins and to ensure that the designated person is available on the day of the witness's testimony so as to provide certainty for the witness.

Note that:

(a) an increased degree of flexibility is appropriate as to who can act as supporter. This can be anyone known to and trusted by the witness who is not a party to the proceedings and has no detailed knowledge of the evidence in the case. The supporter may be a member of the Witness Service but need not be an usher or court official. Someone else may be appropriate (*CPD* V 18B.1–5);
(b) the usher should continue to be available both to assist the witness and the witness supporter, and to ensure that the court's requirements are properly complied with in the live link room;
(c) in order to be able to express an informed view about special measures, the witness is entitled to practise speaking using the live link (and to see screens in place). Simply being shown the room and equipment is inadequate for this purpose; and
(d) if, with the agreement of the judge, the witness has chosen not to give evidence by live link but to do so in the court room, it may still be appropriate for a witness supporter to be selected in the same way, and for the supporter to sit alongside the witness while the witness is giving evidence.

(*CPD* V 18B.1–5)

(3) Evidence to be given in private

62-024 In a case where:

(1) the proceedings relate to a sexual offence; or
(2) it appears to the judge that there are reasonable grounds for any person (other than the accused) to has sought to, or will, intimidate the witness in connection with testifying in the proceedings, a special measures direction may provide for the exclusion from the court during the giving of the witness's evidence, of persons specified in it, provided that the persons excluded do not include the accused, legal representatives acting in the

proceedings or any interpreter or other person appointed in pursuance of the direction to assist the witness.

(YJCEA 1999 s.25)

Special provisions are made in s.25(3) for the press.

(4) Video recorded evidence-in-chief

A special measure direction may provide for a video recording of an interview of a witness to be admitted as evidence-in-chief of that witness, unless the judge is of the opinion, having regard to all the circumstances of the case, that in the interests of justice the recording, or part of it should not be so admitted. **62-025**

In determining that question, the judge:

(1) *must* consider whether any prejudice to the accused which might result from that part being admitted is outweighed by the desirability of showing the whole or substantially the whole of the recording; and

(2) *may*, if he gives such a direction, subsequently direct that it is not to be admitted if:

(a) the witness will not be available for cross-examination (whether conducted in the ordinary way or in accordance any such direction);

(b) the parties to the proceedings have not agreed that there is no need for the witness to attend; or

(c) any rule requiring disclosure of the circumstances in which the recording was made have not been complied with.

Where a recording, or part of a recording, is admitted, the witness must be called by the party tendering it in evidence unless either a direction provides for his cross-examination to be given otherwise than by testimony in court, or the parties have agreed that there is no need for him to be available. The witness may not, without the permission of the judge, give evidence-in-chief otherwise than by means of the recording, as to any matter which in the judge's opinion is dealt with in the witness's recorded testimony.

The judge may give such permission, either on the application of a party, if there has been a change of circumstances, or on his own initiative, if it appears to him to be in the interests of justice to do so. In giving such permission, the judge may direct that evidence in question be given by the witness by means of a live link, in which case s.24(5) (62-023) will apply (YJCEA 1999 s.27).

Giving evidence is not a memory test and the speculative possibility that a witness might say something when giving live evidence in chief which is different from what she said in a pre-recorded interview and, thereby, deprive the defence of the opportunity of cross-examining on those differences is not, in itself, an adequate reason for refusing to allow the playing of an interview (*R. v Davies* [2011] EWCA Crim 1177; [2011] Crim. L.R. 732).

The procedure for making an application for leave to admit into evidence video recorded evidence-in-chief is given in CrimPR Pt 18.

Where the judge, on application by a party to the proceedings or of his own motion, grants leave to admit a recording under s.27, he may direct that any part of the recording be excluded (s.27(2) and (3)). When such direction is given, the party who made the application to admit the video recording must edit the recording in accordance with the judge's directions and send a copy of the edited recording to the appropriate officer of the Crown Court and to every other party to the proceedings.

Where a recording is to be adduced during proceedings, it should be produced and proved by the interviewer, or any other person who was present at the interview with the witness at which the recording was made. The applicant should ensure that such a person will be available for this purpose, unless the parties have agreed to accept a written statement in lieu of attendance by that person.

Once a trial has begun, if, by reason of faulty or inadequate preparation or for some other cause, the procedures set out above have not been properly complied with and an application is made to edit the video recording, thereby necessitating an adjournment for the work to be carried out, the court may, at its discretion, make an appropriate award of costs (*CPD* V Evidence 16B: Video recorded evidence in chief 16B.1–4).

Witnesses are entitled to refresh their memory from their statement or visually recorded interview. *CPD* V Evidence 18C: Visually Recorded Interviews: Memory Refreshing and Watching at a Different Time from the Jury makes provision for memory refreshing and the viewing of interviews at a time other than when the jury or court are viewing it.

Decisions about how, when and where refreshing should take place should be court-led and made on a case-by-case basis in respect of each witness. General principles include venue for viewing, monitoring the viewing, whether to see it more than once and arrangements for when it is to be seen. [*CPD* V Evidence 18C: C1–3].

There is no legal requirement that the witness should watch the interview at the same time as the court. Increasingly, this is arranged to occur at a different time. [*CPD* V Evidence 18C: C4 and 5].

(5) Pre-recorded cross-examination and re-examination

62-026 Section 28 of the YJCEA 1999 is now operating through most areas of England and Wales. As and when brought into force by SI for a particular Crown Court, a witness will be eligible for this form of special measure, if he or she is under 18 at the time of the special measures hearing or he or she suffers from a mental disorder within the meaning of the MHA 1983, or has a physical disability or a physical disorder, and the quality of his or her evidence is likely to be diminished as a consequence or where the complainant in respect of a sexual offence or an offence under ss.1 or 2 of the Modern Slavery Act 2015 is a witness in proceedings relating to that offence (or to that offence and any other offences) (s.17(4) YJCEA 1999) (*CPD* V Evidence 18E.1).

Amendment No.12 of the *CPD* sets out an amended detailed practice direction on s.28 and covers the first hearing in the magistrates' court and then the process in the Crown Court before and at the PTPH (18E.12–28), the process before a Ground Rules Hearing (18E.29–33) and at the hearing itself (18E.34–39). The *CPD* deals with the recording of the cross-examination and re-examination, the process after the recording and preparation for the trial (18E.40–56). There is an annex to the *CPD* that is designed to assist all advocates in their preparation for the cross-examination of vulnerable witnesses (*CPD 2015 Amendment No.5* [2017] EWCA Crim 1076).

(6) Examination of witness through intermediary

62-027 A special measures direction may provide for any examination of a witness (however and wherever conducted) to be conducted through an intermediary, that is an interpreter or other person approved for the purpose by the judge. See, e.g. *R. v Watts* [2010] EWCA Crim 1824; [2011] Crim. L.R. 68. While intermediaries make a valuable contribution to the administration of justice in appropriate cases, that does not mean that whenever the process would be improved by the availability of an intermediary it is mandatory for one to be made available (*R. v Cox* [2012] EWCA Crim 549; [2012] 2 Cr. App. R. 65 per Judge LCJ).

The overall responsibility of the trial judge for the fairness of a trial has not been altered because of the increased availability of intermediaries, or indeed the wide band of available special measures. In the context of an accused with communication problems, when every sensible step taken to identify an available intermediary has been unsuccessful, the next stage is not for the proceedings to be stayed, which may represent a gross unfairness to the complainant, but for the judge to make an informed assessment of whether the absence of an intermediary would make the trial unfair.

The intermediary's function is to communicate to the witness questions put to him, and to the person asking such questions the answers given by the witness in reply, and to explain those questions and answers so far as is necessary to enable them to be understood.

Any such examination of the witness must take place in the presence of such persons as the Rules, or the judge's direction, may provide, but in such circumstances in which:

(1) the judge and legal representatives acting in the proceedings are able to see and hear the examination of the witness and to communicate with the intermediary; and
(2) (except in the case of a video recorded examination) the jury (if there is one) are able to see and hear the examination of the witness.

Where two or more legal representatives are acting for a party to the proceedings, (2) above is to be regarded as satisfied in relation to those representatives, if at all material times it is satisfied in relation to at least one of them (YJCEA 1999 s.29).

The intermediary must not act in a particular case except after making the appropriate oath or declaration (see OATHS AND FORMALITIES).

Note that these provisions do not apply to an interview of the witness which was recorded by means of a video recording (see 62-025) with a view to its admission as the witness's evidence-in-chief, although a special measures direction may provide for such a recording to be admitted under s.27 if that interview was conducted through an intermediary, provided that:

(a) the intermediary made the statutory declaration before the interview began; and
(b) the judge's approval for the purposes of these provisions (i.e. s.29) is given before the direction is given.

The judge ought to give an explanation of the role of the intermediary to the jury, stressing that the intermediary:

- is not an expert;
- is independent;
- is present to assist with two-way communication in court; and
- will only intervene if a communication issue is identified.

Any particular health problems of the witness should be identified.

Care must be taken in permitting juries to have a transcript of a witness's interview (*R. v Popescu* [2010] EWCA Crim 1230; [2011] Crim. L.R. 227). (See VULNERABLE ACCUSED AND WITNESSES).

(7) Aids to communication

62-028 A special measures direction may provide for a witness while giving evidence (whether in testimony in court or otherwise) to be provided with such aids to communication as the judge considers appropriate with a view to enabling questions or answers to be communicated to or by the witness despite any disability or disorder or other impairment which he has or suffers from (YJCEA 1999 s.30).

(8) Status and weight of statements made; jury warning

62-029 Where a statement made by a witness is not, in accordance with a special measures direction, made in direct oral testimony in court but forms part of the witness's evidence in the proceedings, that statement is to be treated as if made by the witness in direct oral testimony and accordingly:

(1) it is admissible evidence of any fact of which such testimony from the witness would be admissible; but
(2) is not capable of corroborating any other evidence given by the witness,

and this provision applies to a statement admitted under s.27 (62-025) which is not made on oath even if it would have been required to be given on oath if made by the witness in direct oral testimony in court.

In estimating the weight, if any, to be attached to such a statement, the judge must have regard to all the circumstances from which an inference can reasonably be drawn as to the accuracy of the statement or otherwise (YJCEA 1999 s.31).

Where, in a trial on indictment with a jury a statement has been given in accordance with a special measures direction, the judge must give the jury such warning, if any, as he considers necessary to ensure that the fact that the direction was given to the witness does not prejudice the accused (YJCEA 1999 s.32).

C. Reporting direction; adult witnesses

General

62-030 On the application of any party to the proceedings, the judge may make a reporting direction in respect of any witness in the proceedings, other than the accused, who has attained the age of 18.

A reporting direction is a direction that no matter relating to the witness may, during the witness's lifetime, be included in any publication if it is likely to lead members of the public to identify him as being a witness in the proceedings.

The judge may give such a direction only where he determines that:

(1) the witness is eligible for protection (see 62-032); and
(2) giving a reporting direction in relation to him is likely to improve:
    (a) the quality of his evidence (see 62-031); or
    (b) the level of co-operation given by him to any party to the proceedings in connection with that party's preparation (see 62-031) of its case.

(YJCEA 1999 s.46(1)–(5) and (8))

Definitions

Note that in 62-030: 62-031

- "quality" refers to the quality of the evidence in completeness, coherence and accuracy, and for this purpose;
- "coherence" refers to the witness's ability, in giving evidence, to give answers which address the questions put to him and can be understood both individually and collectively.

References to a party's *preparation* of the case, include, in the case of the prosecutor, the carrying out of investigations into any offence at any time charged in the proceedings (YJCEA 1999 s.46(12)).

For the purposes of this provision a witness is "*eligible for protection*" if the judge is satisfied that:

(1) the quality of evidence given by the witness; or
(2) the level of co-operation given by the witness to any party to the proceedings in connection with that party's preparation of its case,

is likely to be diminished by reason of fear or distress on the part of the witness in connection with being identified by members of the public as a witness in the proceedings (YJCEA 1999 s.46(3)).

Eligibility; matters to be taken into account

In determining whether a witness is eligible for protection under these provisions the judge must take into account, in particular: 62-032

(1) the nature and alleged circumstances of the offence to which the proceedings relate;
(2) the age of the witness;
(3) such of the following matters as appear to the judge to be relevant, namely:
    (a) the witness's social and cultural background and ethnic origins;
    (b) the witness's domestic and employment circumstances; and
    (c) the witness's religious beliefs or political opinions (if any);
(4) any behaviour towards the witness on the part of:
    (a) the accused, members of the family or associates of the accused; or
    (b) any other person who is likely to be an accused or a witness in the proceedings, and, in determining that question the judge must, in addition, consider any views expressed by the witness.

In determining whether to give a reporting direction the judge must consider whether it would be in the interests of justice to do so, and the public interest in avoiding the imposition of a substantial and unreasonable restriction on the reporting of the proceedings (YJCEA 1999 s.46(4)).

See *R. v ITN News* [2013] EWCA Crim 773; [2013] 2 Cr. App. R. 22 where the judge made an order postponing publication of photographs of the wife of the accused and their children (she was a key witness against him) on the grounds that publication of the photographs would have affected the quality of her evidence, through the risk of identification of the children (even though she and their names had been changed and she had changed her appearance and she gave evidence from behind a screen).

Matters to which restrictions apply

62-033 The matters in relation to which the restrictions imposed by a reporting direction apply if their inclusion in any publication is likely to lead members of the public to identify him as being a witness in the proceedings (see 62-030) include:

(1) the witness's name;
(2) his address;
(3) the identity of any educational establishment attended by him;
(4) the identity of any place of work; and
(5) any still or moving picture of him.

(YJCEA 1999 s.46(7))

Exception; revocation

62-034 The judge (or an appellate court) may, by an excepting direction, dispense to any extent specified in it, with the restrictions imposed by a reporting direction if:

(1) he is satisfied that it is necessary in the interests of justice to do so; or
(2) he is satisfied that:
   (a) the effect of those restrictions is to impose a substantial and unreasonable restriction on the reporting of the proceedings; and
   (b) it is in the public interest to remove or relax that restriction,

but no excepting direction may be given under (2) by reason only of the fact that the proceedings have been determined in any way or have been abandoned.

Note that:

(i) a *reporting direction* may be revoked by the judge (or by an appellate court); and
(ii) an *excepting direction* may be given at the time the reporting direction is given or subsequently; and may be varied or revoked by the judge (or by an appellate court).

(YJCEA 1999 s.46(9)–(11))

Applying for a reporting direction; procedure

62-035 An application for a reporting direction in relation to a witness is made in the form set out at *CPD* Annex D, or orally under r.16.3. Procedure is governed by rr.16.4 and 16.5, as to which see REPORTING AND ACCESS RESTRICTIONS.

D. RESTRICTIONS ON CROSS-EXAMINATION BY ACCUSED IN PERSON

General

62-036 No accused may cross-examine in person:

(1) the complainant in a sexual offence with which he is charged, or in connection with any other offence (of whatever nature) with which he is charged in the proceedings;
(2) child complainants and certain child witnesses in relation to certain named offences; or
(3) where (1) and (2) do not apply, if it appears to the judge:

(a) that the quality of evidence given by the witness on cross-examination:
   (i) is likely to be diminished if the cross-examination (or further cross-examination) is conducted by the accused in person;
   (ii) would be likely to be improved if a direction were given under the section; and
(b) that it would not be contrary to the interests of justice to give such a direction.

(YJCEA 1999 ss.34–36)

Procedure

Where an accused in person is prevented from cross-examining a witness by virtue of YJCEA 1999 ss.34, 35 or 36 (62-036): **62-037**

(1) the judge must explain to the accused, as early in the proceedings as is reasonably practicable, that he is prevented from cross-examining a witness in person, and should arrange for a legal representative to act for him for the purpose of cross-examining the witness;
(2) the accused must then notify the Crown Court officer in writing, within seven days of the judge giving his explanation, or within such other period as the judge may in any particular case allow, of the action, if any, that he has taken;
(3) where the judge gives his explanation to the accused, either within seven days of the day set for the commencement of any hearing at which a witness in respect of whom a prohibition under ss.34, 35 or 36 applies may be cross-examined, or after such a hearing has commenced, the period of seven days will be reduced in accordance with any directions issued by the judge;
(4) where the accused has arranged for a legal representative to act for him, the notification must include details of the name and address of the representative, and the Crown Court officer will notify all other parties to the proceedings of the name and address of the person, if any, appointed to act for the accused; and
(5) where at the end of the period of seven days or such other period as the judge has allowed, the court has received no notification from the accused, the judge may grant the accused an extension of time, for such period as is considered appropriate in the circumstances of the case, whether of his own motion or on the application of the accused.

Before granting of an extension, the judge may hold a hearing, at which all parties to the proceedings may attend and be heard.

Any decision as to the grant of an extension of time will be notified to the parties by the Crown Court officer (CrimPR 23.2).

Appointment of legal representative

Applications for legal aid will be subject to means testing. **62-038**
If:

(1) the applicant fails to choose an advocate;
(2) his application for legal aid was refused in the magistrates' court (see LEGAL AID; PUBLIC FUNDING); or
(3) he appears unrepresented in the Crown Court,

the judge will consider whether he ought to appoint a solicitor or advocate. If he appoints a representative, payment will be made via Central Funds (*CLAM* Annex 13).

Where the court decides in accordance with YJCEA 1999 s.38(4) to appoint a qualified legal representative, the Crown Court officer will notify all parties to the proceedings of the name and address of the representative. Such an appointment, except to the extent as the judge may in a particular case determine, terminates at the conclusion of the cross-examination of the relevant witness or witnesses (CrimPR 23.2).

Appointment arranged by the accused

62-039 The accused may arrange for the legal representative appointed by the court to be appointed to act for him for the purpose of cross-examining any witness in respect of whom a prohibition applies.

Where such an appointment is made:

(1) both the accused and the legal representative appointed must notify the court of the appointment;
(2) the legal representative must, from the time of his appointment, act for the accused as though the arrangement had been made under s.38(2)(a) of the 1999 Act and will cease to be the representative of the court under s.38(4); and
(3) where the court receives notification of the appointment, either from the legal representative or from the accused, but not from both, it will investigate whether the appointment has been made, and if it concludes that the appointment has not been made, the representative will continue as if appointed by the court.

(CrimPR 23.2)

An accused may, notwithstanding an appointment by the court under s.38(4) of the 1999 Act, arrange for a legal representative to act for him for the purpose of cross-examining any witness in respect of whom a prohibition under ss.34, 35 or 36 of the 1999 Act applies.

Where the accused arranges for, or informs the court of his intention to arrange for a legal representative to act for him, he must notify the court, within such period as the court may allow, of the name and address of any person appointed to act for him.

The required notifications will be made to the parties by the Crown Court officer.

Prosecutor's application

62-040 An application by the prosecutor for the court to give a direction under YJCEA 1999 s.36 in relation to any witness must:

(1) be sent to the Crown Court officer and, at the same time, a copy must be sent by the applicant to every other party to the proceedings; and
(2) state why, in the prosecutor's opinion:
    (a) the evidence given by the witness is likely to be diminished if cross-examination is undertaken by the accused in person;
    (b) the evidence would be improved if a direction were given under s.36(2); and

(c) it would not be contrary to the interests of justice to give such a direction.

On receipt of the application, the Crown Court officer will refer it if the trial has started, to the trial judge, or if the trial has not started when the application is received, to the judge who has been designated to conduct the trial, or if no judge has been designated for that purpose, to such judge who may be designated for the purposes of hearing that application.

Where a copy of the application is received by a party to the proceedings more than 14 days before the date set for the trial to begin, that party may make observations in writing on the application to the Crown Court officer, but any such observations must be made within 14 days of the receipt of the application and be copied to the other parties to the proceedings (CrimPR 23.4).

Party seeking to oppose order

A party to whom such an application is sent, who wishes to oppose the application, must give his reasons for doing so to the Crown Court officer and the other parties to the proceedings. Those reasons must be notified: **62-041**

(1) within 14 days of the date the application was served on him, if that date is more than 14 days before the date set for the trial to begin;
(2) if the trial has begun, in accordance with any directions issued by the trial judge; or
(3) if neither subpara.(1) or (2) applies, before the date set for the trial to begin.

Where the application is made before the date set for the trial to begin and it:

(a) is not contested by any party to the proceedings, the court may determine the application without a hearing;
(b) is contested by a party to the proceedings, the court must direct a hearing of the application.

Where the application is made after the trial has begun, the application may be made orally giving reasons why the application was not made before the trial commenced, and providing the court with the information set out in 62-040; the trial judge may give such directions as he considers appropriate to deal with the application.

Where a hearing is to take place, the court officer will notify each party to the proceedings of the time and place of the hearing, and a party notified in accordance may be present at the hearing and be heard.

The Crown Court officer will, as soon as possible after the determination of the application, give notice of the decision and the reasons for it to all the parties to the proceedings (CrimPR 23.5, 23.6, 23.7).

E. Witness Anonymity

1. General

CE(WA)A 2008 enacted new provisions in relation to witness anonymity orders, abolishing the rules of the common law, but it remains a fundamental principle that, save in the exceptional circumstances permitted by the legislation, an accused person is entitled to know the identity of witnesses who incriminate him. The legislation seeks to preserve the balance between the accused's rights, including his **62-042** entitlement to a fair trial and a public hearing and to examine the witnesses against him (*R. v Mayers* [2008] EWCA Crim 2899; [2009] 1 Cr. App. R. 30). With the coming into force of CorJA 2009 Pt 3 Ch.2, the provisions of CE(WA)A 2008 ss.1–9 and 14 have ceased to have effect.

While anonymous witnesses ought not to be called as a matter of routine, now that witness intimidation has become a feature of contemporary life, orders should not be confined to cases of terrorism and gangland killings (*R. v Powar* [2009] EWCA Crim 594; [2009] 2 Cr. App. R. 8).

Nothing in the legislation diminishes the overriding responsibility of the trial judge to ensure that the proceedings are conducted fairly.

A witness anonymity order should be regarded as a special measure of last resort and is, by its nature, exceptional. For a case where the prosecution failed in their duty of full and frank disclosure and witness anonymity orders were quashed see *R. v Donovan* [2012] EWCA Crim 2749.

Nothing in the provisions affects the common law rules as to the withholding of information on the grounds of public interest immunity. The common law principles relating to PII are expressly preserved (*R. v H* [2004] UKHL 3; [2004] 2 Cr. App. R. 10 remains authoritative).

Disclosure must be complete, in accordance with the Attorney General's guidelines and other guidance.

Thus:

(1) the prosecutor must comply with his duties in relation to full and frank disclosure, and must be proactive, focusing closely on the credibility of the anonymous witness and the interests of justice; and
(2) defence statements complying with CJIA 2008 s.60, providing for broader identification by the defence of the issues, are crucial.

The obligations of the prosecutor in the context of witness anonymity go much further than the ordinary duties of disclosure. A prosecutor must ask himself what, if he were representing the accused, he would be saying to the court. The judge requires the assistance of the prosecution to ensure that the effect of any anonymity order, following a hearing at which the accused is neither present nor represented, will not result in proceedings which would or might be unfair (see *R. v Donovan* [2012] EWCA Crim 2749).

Where the judge entertains reservations about the good faith of the efforts made by the prosecution investigation into any relevant consideration bearing on the question of witness anonymity, an application for an order is likely to be met with a blank refusal (*R. v Mayers* [2008] EWCA Crim 2899; [2009] 1 Cr. App. R. 30). Procedure is governed by CrimPR Pt 18 and *CPD* V Evidence 18D: Witness Anonymity Orders.

2. NATURE OF ORDER

62-043 A "witness anonymity order" is an order made by a court that requires such measures as may be specified in the order to be taken in relation to a witness in criminal proceedings, as the judge considers appropriate to ensure that the identity of the witness is not disclosed in, or in connection with, the proceedings.

The kind of measures that may be required to be taken in relation to a witness include (but is not limited to) measures for securing one or more of the following:

(1) that the witness's name and other identifying details be withheld, or removed from materials disclosed to any party to the proceedings;

(2) that the witness use a pseudonym;
(3) that the witness be not asked questions of any specified description that might lead to the identification of the witness;
(4) that the witness be screened to any specified extent; and
(5) that the witness's voice be subjected to modulation to any specified extent, although

nothing in this provision authorises the judge to require the witness to be screened to such an extent that the witness cannot be seen by the judge or other members of the court (if any), or the jury (if there is one); nor the witness's voice to be modulated to such an extent that the witness's natural voice cannot be heard by such persons (CorJA 2009 s.86).

3. Case management; service

Where such an application is proposed, with the parties' active assistance the court should set a realistic timetable, in accordance with the duties imposed by CrimPR 3.2 and 3.3 (see CASE MANAGEMENT) and CrimPR 18.18–18.22. **62-044**

Where possible, the trial judge should determine the application, and any hearing should be attended by the parties' trial advocates.

Where the prosecutor proposes an application for such an order, it is not necessary for the application to have been determined before the proposed evidence is served. In most cases an early indication of what that evidence will be if an order is made will be consistent with a party's duties under CrimPR 1.2 and 3.3.

The prosecutor should serve with the other prosecution evidence a witness statement setting out the proposed evidence, redacted in such a way as to prevent disclosure of the witness's identity (as permitted by s.87(4) of the Act). Likewise the prosecutor should serve with other prosecution material disclosed under CPIA 1996 any such material appertaining to the witness, similarly redacted (*CPD* V Evidence 18D Witness anonymity orders D.3 and 4).

4. Making an application

An application for a witness anonymity order to be made in relation to a witness in criminal proceedings may be made to the court by the prosecutor or by the accused (CorJA 2009 s.87). **62-045**

An application should be made as early as possible and within the period for which CrimPR 18.8 provides. The application, and any hearing of it, must comply with the requirements of that rule and with those of CrimPR 18. In accordance with CrimPR 19.19 and 3.3 the applicant must provide the court with all available information relevant to the considerations to which the Act requires a court to have regard (*CPD* V Evidence 18D.5).

Where an application is made:

(1) by the prosecutor, he:
 (a) must (unless the judge directs otherwise) inform the court of the identity of the witness; but
 (b) is not required to disclose in connection with the application:
  (i) the identity of the witness; or
  (ii) any information that might enable the witness to be identified, to any other party to the proceedings or his or her legal representatives;

(2) by the accused, he:
   (a) must inform the court and the prosecutor of the identity of the witness; but
   (b) (if there is more than one accused) is not required to disclose in connection with the application:
      (i) the identity of the witness; or
      (ii) any information that might enable the witness to be identified, to any other accused or his legal representatives.

Accordingly, where the prosecutor or the accused proposes to make an application under this section in respect of a witness, any relevant material which is disclosed by or on behalf of that party before the determination of the application may be disclosed in such a way as to prevent the identity of the witness, or any information that might enable the witness to be identified, from being disclosed except as required above.

"Relevant material" in this context, means any document or other material which falls to be disclosed, or is sought to be relied on, by or on behalf of the party concerned in connection with the proceedings or proceedings preliminary to them. The judge must give every party to the proceedings the opportunity to be heard on an application under this section, he is not prevented from hearing one or more parties in the absence of an accused and his legal representatives, if it appears to him to be appropriate to do so in the circumstances of the case (CorJA 2009 s.87(2)–(8)).

The Crown Court officer will notify the DPP of an application, unless the prosecutor is, or acts on behalf of, a public authority (CrimPR 18.20).

5. Content and Conduct of Application

62-046 An applicant for a witness anonymity order must include in the application nothing that might reveal the witness's identity, but must describe the measures proposed by the applicant, and explain how the proposed order meets the conditions prescribed by CorJA 2009 s.88 and explain why no measures other than those proposed will suffice, such as:

(1) an admission of the facts that would be proved by the witness;
(2) an order restricting public access to the trial;
(3) reporting restrictions, in particular under YJCEA 1999 s.46 or under CYPA 1933 s.39;
(4) a direction for a special measure under YJCE 1999 s.19;
(5) introduction of the witness's written statement as hearsay evidence under CJA 2003 s.116; or
(6) arrangements for the protection of the witness.

The applicant must also attach to the application:

(a) a witness statement setting out the proposed evidence, edited in such a way as not to reveal the witness's identity;
(b) where the prosecutor is the applicant, any further prosecution evidence to be served, and any further prosecution material to be disclosed under CPIA 1996, similarly edited; and

(c) any defence statement that has been served, or as much information as may be available to the applicant that gives particulars of the defence, and

must ask for a hearing, if he wants one (CrimPR 18.21).

6. Representations in response

All parties must have an opportunity to make oral representations to the judge on an application for an order (s.87(6) of the Act). However, a hearing may not be needed if none is sought (CrimPR 18.22), see the examples given in *CPD* V Evidence 18D Witness Anonymity orders D8. **62-047**

A party upon whom an application for an order is served must serve a response on the other parties and on the court. To avoid the risk of injustice a respondent must actively assist the court. If not already done, a respondent defendant should serve a defence statement under CPIA 1996 ss.5 or 6 (see DISCLOSURE) so that the judge is fully informed of what is in issue. The prosecutor's continuing duty to disclose material (under CPIA 1996 s.7A) may be engaged by a defendant's application for a witness anonymity order, therefore a prosecutor's response should include confirmation that that duty has been considered.

Nothing disclosed under the 1996 Act by a respondent prosecutor to a respondent defendant should contain anything that might reveal the witness's identity. A respondent prosecutor must provide an applicant defendant and the court with all available information relevant to the considerations to which the Act requires a court to have regard, whether or not that information falls to be disclosed under the 1996 Act (*CPD* V Evidence 18D Witness Anonymity orders D6, D7).

Where a party or, where the case is over, a witness, wants to make such representations about:

(1) an application for a witness anonymity order;
(2) an application for the variation or discharge of such an order; or
(3) a variation or discharge the judge proposes on his own initiative,

he must serve the representations on the Crown Court officer, and on each other party, and do so not more than 14 days after, as applicable, service of the application, or notice of the variation or discharge that the court proposes, asking for a hearing, if that party or witness wants one.

Where representations include information that the person making them thinks might reveal the witness's identity, that person must:

(a) omit that information from the representations served on an accused;
(b) mark the information to show that it is only for the court (and for the prosecutor, if relevant); and
(c) with that information include an explanation of why it has been withheld.

Representations against a witness anonymity order must explain why the conditions for making the order are not met, and representations against the variation or discharge of such an order must explain why it would not be appropriate to vary or discharge it, taking account of the conditions for making an order.

A prosecutor's representations in response to an application by an accused must include all information available to the prosecutor that is relevant to the conditions and considerations specified by CorJA 2009 ss.88 and 89 (CrimPR 18.22).

7. Conditions for making order

62-048 Where an application is made for a witness anonymity order to be made in relation to a witness in criminal proceedings, the judge may make such an order only if he is satisfied that the following conditions, A–C, are met:

(1) Condition A is that the proposed order is necessary in order to:
  (a) protect the safety of the witness or another person or to prevent any serious damage to property; or
  (b) prevent real harm to the public interest (whether affecting the carrying on of any activities in the public interest or the safety of a person involved in carrying on such activities, or otherwise).
(2) Condition B is that, having regard to all the circumstances, the effect of the proposed order would be consistent with the accused receiving a fair trial.
(3) Condition C is that the importance of the witness's testimony is such that in the interests of justice the witness ought to testify and:
  (a) the witness would not testify if the proposed order were not made; or
  (b) there would be real harm to the public interest if the witness were to testify without the proposed order being made.

In determining whether the proposed order is "necessary" for the purpose mentioned in (1) above, the judge must have regard (in particular) to any reasonable fear on the part of the witness, that he or another person would suffer death or injury, or that there would be serious damage to property, if the witness were to be identified.

No order may be made unless all three of the above conditions are satisfied. The fact that a witness provides the sole or decisive evidence against the accused is not, of itself, conclusive as to whether conditions A–C are met. Condition C (interests of justice) should be considered first. In relation to Condition A (safety of witness) it matters not whether the risk to the safety of the witness is attributable to the actions of the accused personally; it may be established if and when the safety of the witness is under threat from any source. Condition B (fair trial) is fact-specific (*R. v Mayers* [2008] EWCA Crim 2899; [2009] 1 Cr. App. R. 30) (CorJA 2009 s.88).

Relevant considerations

62-049 When deciding whether Conditions A–C in 62-048 are met in the case of an application for a witness anonymity order, the judge must have regard to the considerations mentioned below, and such other matters as he considers relevant.

The considerations are:

(1) the general right of a person accused in criminal proceedings to know the identity of a witness in the proceedings;
(2) the extent to which the credibility of the witness concerned would be a relevant factor when the weight of his evidence comes to be assessed;
(3) whether evidence given by the witness might be the sole or decisive evidence implicating the accused;
(4) whether the witness's evidence could be properly tested (whether on grounds of credibility or otherwise) without his identity being disclosed;
(5) whether there is any reason to believe that the witness:
  (a) has a tendency to be dishonest; or
  (b) has any motive to be dishonest in the circumstances of the case, hav-

ing regard (in particular) to any previous convictions of the witness and to any relationship between the witness and the accused or any associates of the accused; and

(6) whether it would be reasonably practicable to protect the witness by any means other than by making a witness anonymity order specifying the measures that are under consideration by the judge.

(CorJA 2009 s.89)

This list is not to be seen as being in any order of priority. None of them is conclusive of whether the accused can have a fair trial (and that applies to the question whether the evidence is the sole or decisive evidence against the accused) (*R. v Mayers* [2008] EWCA Crim 2899; [2009] 1 Cr. App. R. 30).

8. Evaluation of evidence

The judge should examine whether the anonymous evidence is supported extraneously, or whether there were a number of witnesses who incriminated the accused. If numerous witnesses are to give evidence anonymously it will be advisable to investigate any link between them, although there is no corroboration requirement. **62-050**

Witnesses who come forward before there would be an opportunity to manufacture a case incriminating the accused are likely to be treated with less suspicion than witnesses who come forward later out of the blue.

In relation to police witnesses, particularly those working undercover, it may be accepted that there are often sound reasons for maintaining their anonymity. The judge will normally be entitled to follow the unequivocal assertion by such a witness that without an anonymity order, he would not be prepared to testify (*R. v Mayers* [2008] EWCA Crim 2899; [2009] 1 Cr. App. R. 30).

9. The need for a hearing

The judge may decide whether to make, vary or discharge an order at a hearing (which will be in private, unless he otherwise directs), or without a hearing (unless any party asks for one) and in the absence of an accused (CrimPR 18.18). **62-051**

A hearing may not be needed if none is sought. Where, for example:

(1) the witness is an investigator who is recognisable by the defendant but known only by an assumed name, and there is no likelihood that the witness's credibility will be in issue, then the judge may indicate a provisional decision and invite representations within a defined period, usually 14 days, including representations about whether there should be a hearing; in such a case, where the parties do not object the judge may make an order without a hearing; or

(2) the judge provisionally considers an application to be misconceived, an applicant may choose to withdraw it without requiring a hearing.

Where confidential supporting information is presented to the judge before the last stage of the hearing, he may prefer not to read that information until that last stage.

The judge may adjourn the hearing at any stage, and should do so if his duty under CrimPR 3.2 so requires.

Where the judge directs a hearing of the application then he should allow adequate time for service of the representations in response (*CPD* V Evidence 18D Witness Anonymity orders D8–D11).

Nothing in the statute permits the giving of hearsay evidence from an anonymous witness (*R. v Ford* [2010] EWCA Crim 2250; [2011] Crim. L.R. 475).

10. DETERMINATION OF THE APPLICATION

62-052 The judge must not exercise his power to make, vary or discharge such an order, or to refuse to do so:

(1) before or during the trial, unless each party has had an opportunity to make representations;
(2) on an appeal by the accused to which r.63 (appeal to the Crown Court) applies unless in each party's case that party has had an opportunity to make representations, or the appeal court is satisfied that it is not reasonably practicable to communicate with that party;
(3) after the trial and any such appeal are over, unless in the case of each party and the witness, each has had an opportunity to make representations, or the court is satisfied that it is not reasonably practicable to communicate with that party or witness.

(CrimPR 18.18(2))

At the hearing, the general rule is that the judge will consider, in the following sequence:

(a) representations, first by the applicant and then by each other party in all the parties' presence; and then
(b) information withheld from the defendant, and further representations by the applicant, in the absence of any, or any other defendant,

but the judge may direct other arrangements.

(CrimPR 18.19(3))

During the last stage of the hearing it is essential that the judge test thoroughly the information supplied in confidence in order to satisfy himself that the conditions prescribed by the Act (see 62-048) are met. At that stage, if the judge concludes that this is the only way in which it can satisfy itself as to a relevant condition or consideration, exceptionally he may invite the applicant to present the proposed witness to be questioned by him. Any such questioning should be carried out at such a time, and the witness brought to the court in such a way, as to prevent disclosure of his or her identity (*CPD* V Evidence 18D Witness Anonymity orders D13).

Before the witness gives evidence, the applicant must identify the witness to the judge, if not already done, and without revealing his name, to any other party or person, unless, at the prosecutor's request the judge orders otherwise (CrimPR 18.19(4)).

On a prosecutor's application, the court is likely to be assisted by the attendance of a senior investigator or other person of comparable authority who is familiar with the case (*CPD* V Evidence 18D Witness Anonymity orders D12).

11. APPOINTMENT OF SPECIAL COUNSEL

62-053 The judge may ask the Attorney General to appoint special counsel to assist. However, it must be kept in mind that:

"Such an appointment will always be exceptional, never automatic; a course of last and never first resort. It should not be ordered unless and until the trial judge is satisfied that no other course will adequately meet the overriding requirement of fairness to the accused." (*R. v H* [2004] UKHL 3; [2004] 2 Cr. App. R. 10)

Whether to accede to such a request is a matter for the Attorney General, and adequate time should be allowed for the consideration of such a request (*CPD* V Evidence 18D Witness Anonymity orders D14).

12. Nature and announcement of order

Where the court makes a witness anonymity order it is essential that the measures to be taken are clearly specified in a written record of the order approved by the judge and issued on his behalf. The written record of the order must not disclose the identity of the witness to whom it applies, however, it is essential that there be maintained some means of establishing a clear correlation between witness and order, and especially where in the same proceedings witness anonymity orders are made in respect of more than one witness, specifying different measures in respect of each. **62-054**

Careful preservation of the application for the order, including any confidential information presented to the court, ordinarily will suffice for this purpose (*CPD* V Evidence 18D Witness Anonymity orders D17, D18).

The judge should announce his decision on an application in the parties' presence and in public. He should give such reasons as it is possible to give without revealing the witness's identity. He will be conscious that reasons given in public may be reported and reach the jury. Consequently, he should ensure that nothing in his decision or his reasons can undermine any warning he may give to jurors under s.90(2) of the Act (see 62-058); the announcement of those reasons will be recorded (*CPD* V Evidence 18D Witness Anonymity orders D16).

13. Recording the proceedings

A recording of the proceedings will be made, in accordance with CrimPR 5.5. The Crown Court officer should treat such a recording in the same way as the recording of an application for a public interest ruling. **62-055**

14. Discharge or variation of the order

The judge may discharge or vary a witness anonymity order on application, if there has been a material change of circumstances since the order was made, or since any previous variation of it, or of his own initiative. **62-056**

CrimPR 18.21 allows the parties to apply for the variation of a pre-trial direction where circumstances have changed.

The judge should keep under review the question of whether the conditions for making an order are met. In addition, consistently with their duties under CrimPR 1.2 and 3.3 (see CASE MANAGEMENT) it is incumbent on each party, and in particular on the applicant for the order, to keep the need for it under review.

A party who wants the court to vary or discharge a witness anonymity order, or a witness who wants the judge to do so when the case is over, must apply in writing, as soon as reasonably practicable after becoming aware of the grounds for doing so, and serve the application on the Crown Court officer, and on each other party:

(1) explaining what material circumstances have changed since the order was made (or last varied, if applicable);
(2) explaining why the order should be varied or discharged, taking account of the conditions for making an order; and
(3) asking for a hearing, if the applicant wants one.

Where an application includes information that the applicant thinks might reveal the witness's identity, the applicant must:

(a) omit that information from the application that is served on an accused;
(b) mark the information to show that it is only for the court and the prosecutor (if the prosecutor is not the applicant); and
(c) with that information include an explanation of why it has been withheld.

Where a party applies to vary or discharge an order after the trial and any appeal are over, the party who introduced the witness's evidence must serve the application on the witness (CorJA 2009 s.91; CrimPR 29.21).

Discharge or variation after proceedings

62-057 If:

(1) a court has made a witness anonymity order in relation to a witness in criminal proceedings ("the old proceedings"); and
(2) the old proceedings have come to an end, the court that made the order may discharge or vary (or further vary) the order if it appears to the judge to be appropriate to do so in view of:
    (a) the provisions that apply to the making of a witness anonymity order; and
    (b) such other matters as he considers relevant.

A judge may do so on an application made by a party to the old proceedings if there has been a material change of circumstances since the relevant time, or on an application made by the witness if there has been a material change of circumstances since the relevant time.

A judge may not determine such an application unless, in the case of each of the parties to the old proceedings and the witness, he has given the person the opportunity to be heard, or he is satisfied that it is not reasonably practicable to communicate with the person.

These provisions do not prevent the court hearing one or more of the persons mentioned above in the absence of a person who was an accused in the old proceedings and that person's legal representatives, if it appears to be appropriate to do so in the circumstances of the case.

The "relevant time" means the time when the old proceedings came to an end, or, if a previous application has been made the time when the application (or the last application) was made (CorJA 2009 s.92).

15. WARNING TO THE JURY

62-058 Where, on a trial on indictment with a jury, any evidence has been given by a witness at a time when a witness anonymity order applied to the witness, the judge must give the jury such warning as the judge considers appropriate to ensure that the fact that the order was made in relation to the witness does not prejudice the accused (CorJA 2009 s.90).

F. WITNESS PREPARATION

General

There is a dramatic difference between: **62-059**

(1) witness training or coaching; and
(2) witness familiarisation.

The training or coaching of witnesses in criminal proceedings, whether for the prosecution or the defence, is not permitted.

Such a rule:

(a) minimises the risk inherent in witness training, that a witness may tailor his evidence in the light of what someone else said; and, equally
(b) avoids any unfounded perception that he may have done so.

That is so even where the training takes place one-to-one with someone completely remote from the facts of the case; the witness may come, even unconsciously, to appreciate which aspects of his evidence are perhaps not quite consistent with what others are saying, or indeed not quite what is required of him.

But this principle does not extend to preclude pre-trial arrangements to familiarise witnesses with:

(i) the layout of the court;
(ii) the likely sequence of events when the witness is giving evidence; and
(iii) a balanced appraisal of the different responsibilities of the various participants.

Such arrangements are to be welcomed. Nor does the principle prohibit the training of expert and similar witnesses in, for example, the technique of giving comprehensive evidence of a specialist kind to a jury, or the developing of the ability to resist the inevitable pressure of going further in evidence than matters covered by the witness's specific expertise (*R. v Momodou* [2005] EWCA Crim 177; [2005] 2 Cr. App. R. 6).

Guidance from the CACD

The CACD (in *R. v Momodou* [2005] EWCA Crim 177; [2005] 2 Cr. App. R. 6) **62-060**
stated that if arrangements are made for familiarisation with outside agencies rather than the witness service then the following guidance should be followed:

(1) in relation to prosecution witnesses, the CPS should be informed in advance of any proposal for familiarisation; if appropriate after obtaining police input, they should be invited to comment in advance on the proposals;
(2) if relevant information comes to the police, the police should inform the CPS; the proposals for the intended familiarisation programme should be reduced into writing, rather than left to informal conversations; if, having examined them, the CPS suggest that the programme may be breaching the permitted limits, it should be amended; if the defence engage in the process, it would be wise for counsel's advice to be sought, again in advance, and again with written information about the nature and extent of the training;
(3) in any event, it is a matter of professional duty on counsel and solicitors to ensure that the judge is informed of any familiarisation process organised

by the defence using outside agencies, and it will follow that the prosecution will be made aware of what has happened;

(4) the familiarisation process should normally be supervised or conducted by a criminal justice process, and preferably by an organisation accredited for the purpose by the Bar Council and Law Society;

(5) none of those involved should have any personal knowledge of the matters in issue;

(6) records should be maintained of all those present and the identity of those responsible for the familiarisation process, whenever it takes place; the programme should be retained, together with all the written material (or appropriate copies) used during the familiarisation sessions; none of the material should bear any similarity whatsoever to the issues in the proceedings to be attended by the witnesses, and nothing in it should play on or trigger the witness's recollection of events;

(7) if discussion of the instant criminal proceedings begins, as it almost inevitably will, it must be stopped, and advice given about precisely why it is impermissible, with a warning against the danger of evidence contamination and the risk that the course of justice may be perverted; a note should be made if and when any such warning is given; and

(8) all documents used in the process should be retained, and if relevant to prosecution witnesses, handed to the CPS as a matter of course, and in relation to defence witnesses, produced to the court; none should be destroyed; it should be a matter of professional obligation for lawyers involved in these processes, or indeed the trial itself, to see that the guidance is followed.

On 20 December 2004 the Attorney General issued a report in which he signalled his decision to permit prosecutors to speak to prosecution witnesses. In the light of the judgment in *Momodou* the Bar Standards Board issued a formal Guidance on Witness Preparation (see *http://www.barstandardsboard.org.uk* [Accessed September 2022]).

G. Restraint (handcuffing of accused)

62-061 Unless there is sufficient reason (which usually means a real risk of violence or escape) an accused ought not to be visibly restrained by handcuffs or otherwise in the dock or in the witness box. Even if there is some relevant risk, alternative forms of avoiding it ought to be investigated before resort is made to visible restraint; thus:

(1) a secure dock;

(2) the interposition of prison officers between accused or on either side of a particular accused;

(3) police officers inside or outside the courtroom; or

(4) in an extreme case, authorisation from the Senior Presiding Judge for armed officers to be in the court building,

are alternatives which may be employed.

The jury must be free to decide on the guilt or otherwise of an accused without the risk of being influenced against him by the sight of restraint which, in their minds, suggests that he is regarded, with good cause, as a dangerous criminal (*R. v Horden* [2009] EWCA Crim 388; [2009] 2 Cr. App. R. 24).

63. SPENT CONVICTIONS

Where a person has been convicted of an offence and certain conditions are satisfied, he is, after the applicable rehabilitation period has expired, treated for the purposes of the Rehabilitation of Offenders Act 1974 ("ROA 1974") as a "rehabilitated person" in respect of that conviction, and the conviction is treated as "spent". **63-001**

The ROA 1974 seeks to reconcile the competing demands of rehabilitation and public protection. In the attempt to do so fairly, the legislation has been frequently amended, resulting in legislative texts, some of which are complicated. These competing demands have also led to case law that is difficult to reconcile. In *Hussain v Waltham Forest LBC* [2020] EWCA Civ 1539; [2021] 1 W.L.R. 922: it was held that whilst the ROA 1974 sought to balance the policy intention to alleviate the legal and practical burden of past convictions against the requirement to ensure that the public were protected from the risk of repeat criminal conduct, the focus of that Act was rehabilitation, and criminal conduct not giving rise to a conviction could not be the subject of rehabilitation under the Act. However, the part governing the status of spent convictions in subsequent criminal proceedings is relatively straightforward.

Substantial amendments are to be made to s.5 of the ROA 1974 (on a date to be appointed) by the Police, Crime, Sentencing and Courts Act 2022 (PCSCA 2022) (see 63-006).

Effect of rehabilitation

The effect of ROA 1974 s.4(1), is that a person who has become a rehabilitated person for the purpose of the Act in respect of a conviction (known as a "spent" conviction) must be treated for all purposes in law as a person who has not committed, been charged with, prosecuted for, convicted of or sentenced for the offence or offences which were the subject of that conviction. **63-002**

Section 4(1) does not apply, however, to evidence given in criminal proceedings (see s.7(2)(a)), where convictions are often disclosed.

The approach to be adopted is set out in *CPD* 2015 V 21A as follows:

(1) During the trial of a criminal charge, reference to previous convictions (and therefore to spent convictions) can arise in a number of ways. The most common is when a bad character application is made under the Criminal Justice Act 2003. When considering bad character applications under the 2003 Act, regard should always be had to the general principles of the Rehabilitation of Offenders Act 1974.

(2) On conviction, the judge must be provided with a statement of the offender's record for the purposes of sentence. The record supplied should contain all previous convictions, but those which are spent should, so far as practicable, be marked as such.

(3) Nobody should refer in open court to a spent conviction without the authority of the judge, who should not give it unless the interests of justice require.

(4) When announcing sentence the judge should make no reference to a spent

conviction unless it is necessary to do so for the purpose of explaining the sentence to be passed.

Convictions excluded from rehabilitation

63-003 The following are excluded from rehabilitation:

(1) sentences of imprisonment for life;
(2) sentences of imprisonment, youth custody, detention in a young offender institution or corrective training for a period exceeding 48 months;
(3) sentences of preventive detention;
(4) a sentence of detention during HM Pleasure or for life under PCC(S)A 2000 ss.90 or 91 [SA 2020 ss.250 or 259], or under the Armed Forces Act 2006 ss.209 or 218, or under the Criminal Procedure (Scotland) Act 1975 s.205(2) or (3), or a sentence of detention for a term exceeding 48 months under PCC(S)A 2000 s.91 [SA 2020 s.250] or the Armed Forces Act 2006 s.209;
(5) a sentence of custody for life; and
(6) a sentence of imprisonment for public protection under CJA 2003 s.225, a sentence of detention for public protection under CJA 2003 ss.225 or 226, or an extended sentence under CJA 2003 ss.227 or 228 (SA 2020 ss.254, 266 or 279), or a sentence passed as a result of the provisions of the Armed Forces Act 2006 ss.219–222.

(ROA 1974 s.5(1))

Special provisions apply to spent cautions under ROA 1974 ss.8A, 8AA, 9A and Sch.2, and as to orders under s.1(2)(a) of the Street Offences Act 1959, see the Policing and Crime Act 2009 s.18.

Periods required for rehabilitation for those convictions not so excluded are set out in the TABLE at 63-005.

There is no rehabilitation period for an order of discharge or any other sentence in respect of a conviction the sentence for which is not dealt with in the Table or under LASPOA 2012 s.139.

Relevant orders

63-004 A "relevant order" in the Table below means:

- a conditional discharge;
- a bind over;
- an order under the Street Offences Act 1959 s.1(2A);
- a hospital order (with or without restriction);
- a referral order under SA 2020 Pt 6 Ch.1;
- an earlier statutory order (see below); or
- any order which imposes a disqualification, disability, prohibition or other penalty and is not otherwise dealt with in the Table or s.139(3), (4),

but does not include a reparation order under SA 2020 Pt 6 Ch.2.

Table

63-005

Sentence	End of rehabilitation period for adult offenders	End of rehabilitation period for offenders under 18 at time of conviction
Custodial sentence of more than 30 months and up to, or consisting of, 48 months	The end of the period of 7 years beginning with the day on which the sentence (including any licence period) is completed	The end of the period of 42 months beginning with the day on which the sentence (including any licence period) is completed
Custodial sentence of more than 6 months and up to, or consisting of, 30 months	The end of the period of 48 months beginning with the day on which the sentence (including any licence period) is completed	The end of the period of 24 months beginning with the day on which the sentence (including any licence period) is completed
Custodial sentence of 6 months or less	The end of the period of 24 months beginning with the day on which the sentence (including any licence period) is completed	The end of the period of 18 months beginning with the day on which the sentence (including any licence period) is completed
Removal from HM service	The end of the period of 12 months beginning with the date of the conviction in respect of which the sentence is imposed	The end of the period of 6 months beginning with the date of the conviction in respect of which the sentence is imposed
Sentence of service detention	The end of the period of 12 months beginning with the day on which the sentence is completed	The end of the period of 6 months beginning with the day on which the sentence is completed
A fine	The end of the period of 12 months beginning with the date of the conviction in respect of which the sentence is imposed	The end of the period of 6 months beginning with the date of the conviction in respect of which the sentence is imposed
A compensation order	The date on which the payment is made in full	The date on which the payment is made in full
A community or youth rehabilitation order	The end of the period of 12 months beginning with the day provided for by or under order as	The end of the period of 6 months beginning with the day provided for by or under order as the last day on

Sentence	End of rehabilitation period for adult offenders	End of rehabilitation period for offenders under 18 at time of conviction
	the last day on which the order is to have effect*	which the order is to have effect
A "relevant order" (see 63-004)	The day provided for by or under order as the last day on which the order is to have effect*	The day provided for by or under order as the last day on which the order is to have effect

Notes
*Where no provision is made in the order for the last day on which it is to have effect, the period is 24 months beginning with the date of conviction.
Where the table refers to a custodial sentence, suspended sentences are treated as if they had been sentences of immediate imprisonment.
The current version of the table was substituted by LASPOA 2012 s.139.
LASPOA 2012 s.141 provides that the changes introduced by s.139 apply retrospectively, save for road traffic endorsements which are still governed by the previous law, thus the rehabilitation period for road traffic endorsements remains 5 years.

Amendments to s.5 ROA 1974

63-006 With effect from 1 May 2022, s.5 of ROA 1974 is amended by the Armed Forces Act 2021 s.18 so that in the table following subs.2(b) (reproduced above) the following is inserted after the fifth entry:

A severe reprimand or reprimand under the Armed Forces Act 2006	The end of the period of 12 months beginning with the date of the conviction in respect of which the sentence is imposed	The end of the period of 6 months beginning with the date of the conviction in respect of which the sentence is imposed

On a date to be appointed, significant changes are to be made to ROA 1974 s.5 by PCSCA 2022 s.193.

64. SURCHARGES

Duty to order payment of surcharge

A court dealing with an offender for one or more offences committed on or after 1 April 2007 must also order the offender to pay a surcharge. **64-001**

The means of the offender are relevant only where a compensation order, an unlawful profit order or a slavery and trafficking reparation order are imposed. In such a case, where the offender has insufficient means to pay both the compensation order (or unlawful profit order or slavery and trafficking reparation order) *and* the surcharge, the surcharge should be reduced (if necessary to nil).

(SA 2020 s.42)

Where the judge orders the parent or guardian of a young offender to pay the surcharge a reference to the means of the offender is a reference to the means of the parent or guardian (SA 2020 s.42(4)).

In so far as appeals against the surcharge are concerned:

(i) MCA 1980 s.108(d) does not prevent an appeal to the Crown Court against a surcharge imposed under s.163A (MCA 1980 s.108(4)); and

(ii) CAA 1968 s.50(1), for the purposes of an appeal from the Crown Court to the CACD "sentence" includes any order made by a court when dealing with an offender, plainly wide enough to embrace the statutory surcharge order.

In *R. v Abbott* [2020] EWCA Crim 516 the CACD provided guidance on the calculation of surcharge orders:

- When fines are imposed for more than one offence, the surcharge is for 10 per cent of the total, rather than 10 per cent of the highest individual fine, subject to the overall cap of £181.
- In a case involving a fine and a period of imprisonment, the surcharge is the higher of the amount corresponding to the aggregate fine and the amount corresponding to the aggregate period of imprisonment. This applies to any other available combination of orders, and the position is the same whether there is a mixed disposal in relation to a single offence or different disposals in relation to different offences.
- A second surcharge should not be imposed upon resentencing for a breach (see also *R. v George* [2015] EWCA Crim 1096; [2015] 2 Cr. App. R. (S.) 58).

It is the duty of counsel to remind the judge to impose the surcharge; the CACD may not necessarily have the power to do so (*R. v Taylor* [2013] EWCA Crim 1704; [2013] 9 WLUK 500). The judge must refer to the imposition of the surcharge in his sentencing remarks—even though such an order is mandatory, if the judge does not impose the surcharge, the CACD is precluded from imposing it as to do so would be to deal with the offender more severely than he had been dealt with by the court below (*R. v Jones* [2018] EWCA Crim 2994; [2019] 1 Cr. App. R. (S.) 50).

The Council of His Majesty's Circuit Judges has proposed the use of a form of words which has been approved by the Senior Presiding Judge, as follows: "The surcharge provisions apply to this case and the order can be drawn up accordingly".

The rates of surcharge depend on whether the offender is under 18 or over, the offences straddle the age threshold, or whether the offender is a corporation.

Where an offender has been convicted by a magistrates' court of some offences, and has been committed to the Crown Court for sentence in respect of other offences, both courts are required to impose a surcharge order (*R. v Cuthbertson* [2020] EWCA Crim 1883; [2021] 2 Cr. App. R. (S.) 14). The statute does not permit an exception based upon general considerations of fairness.

Enforcement

64-002 Until guidance is issued, it may be helpful to note the following:

(1) where the surcharge is imposed in addition to a non-custodial sentence, enforcement is a matter for the magistrates' court and it will be collected in the same way as a fine; if the surcharge is imposed in addition to a custodial sentence it appears that the money will be recovered from the offender while he is serving his sentence;
(2) there is no power to fix a term in default of payment of the surcharge but there is power to afford time for payment (*R. v Holden* [2013] EWCA Crim 2017).

Tables

64-003 Sentencing Act 2020 (Surcharge) (Amendment) Regulations 2022: These regulations came into force on 16 June 2022 and amend the surcharge amounts payable as set out in the Criminal Justice Act 2003 (Surcharge) Order 2012.

The amendments do not apply where a court deals with a person for a single offence committed before 16 June 2022 or where it deals with a person for more than one offence and at least one of those offences was committed before that date.

Where there is more than one disposal, the surcharge must be whichever specified amount is highest.

Surcharges for offences committed by an individual aged under 18

Column 1	*Column 2*
An order for conditional discharge as defined in section 80 of the Sentencing Act 2020	£20
A fine	£26
A youth rehabilitation order as defined in section 173 of the Sentencing Act 2020	£26
A referral order as defined in section 83 of the Sentencing Act 2020	£26
A community order as defined in section 200 of the Sentencing Act 2020	£26
A custodial sentence as defined in section 222 of the Sentencing Act 2020	£41

Surcharges for offences committed by an individual aged 18 or over

Column 1	*Column 2*
An order for conditional discharge as defined in section 80 of the Sentencing Act 2020	£26
A fine	40 per cent of the value of the fine, rounded up or down to the nearest pound, subject to a maximum of £2,000
A community order as defined in section 200 of the Sentencing Act 2020	£114
A suspended sentence of imprisonment, as defined in section 286 of the Sentencing Act 2020, where the sentence of imprisonment or detention in a young offender institution is for a period of up to and including 6 months	£154
A suspended sentence of imprisonment, as defined in section 286 of the Sentencing Act 2020 where the sentence of imprisonment or detention in a young offender institution is for a determinate period of more than 6 months	£187
A sentence of imprisonment, or detention in a young offender institution, for a determinate period of up to and including 6 months	£154
A sentence of imprisonment, or detention in a young offender institution, for a determinate period of more than 6 months and up to and including 24 months	£187
A sentence of imprisonment, or detention in a young offender institution, for a determinate period exceeding 24 months	£228
A sentence of imprisonment or custody for life	£228

Surcharges for offences committed by a person who is not an individual

Column 1	*Column 2*
An order for conditional discharge, as defined in section 80 of the Sentencing Act 2020	£26
A fine	40 per cent of the value of the fine, rounded up or down to the nearest pound, subject to a maximum of £2,000

65. SUSPENDED SENTENCE ORDERS

Quick Guide

1. Making of order

General

65-001 Where, in relation to an offence committed after 4 April 2005, a judge passes a sentence of:

(1) imprisonment; or
(2) detention in a young offender institution in the case of a person aged at least 18 but under 21,

for a term *of at least 14 days but not more than two years*, he *may* make an order providing that the sentence is not to take effect unless:

(a) during a period specified in the order for the purposes of this paragraph ("the operational period") the offender commits another offence in the UK (whether or not punishable with imprisonment); and
(b) a judge having the power to do so subsequently orders (under SA 2020 Sch.16 para.13—see 65-014) that the original sentence is to take effect.

Where two or more sentences imposed on the same occasion are to be served consecutively, the power to suspend is not exercisable in relation to any of them unless the aggregate of the terms of the sentences does not exceed two years (SA 2020 s.264).

The "supervision period" (if any) and the "operational period" (which may not be the same (*R. v Lees-Wolfenden* [2006] EWCA Crim 3068; [2007] 1 Cr. App. R. (S.) 119)), must each be for a period of not less than 14 days (the SA 2020 still says six months) and not more than two years beginning with the date of the order, and where an order imposes one or more community requirements, the supervision period must not end later than the operational period (SA 2020 s.288(5)).

Subject to any provision to the contrary contained in the CJA 1967 or any other enactment passed or instrument made under any enactment after 31 December 1967, a suspended sentence which has not taken effect (under Sch.16 para.13) is to be treated as a sentence of imprisonment, or in the case of a person aged at least 18 but under 21, a sentence of detention in a young offender institution] for the purposes of all enactments and instruments made under enactments (SA 2020 s.289).

As to the position on commission of a further offence, see 65-014. As to the combination of other sentences with a suspended sentence order, see 65-004.

Addition of community requirement

65-002 An order *may* also provide that the offender must comply during a period specified in the order for the purposes of this subsection ("the supervision period") with one or more requirements falling within SA 2020 s.287 (see 65-006) and specified in the order. Where an order imposes one or more community requirements the supervision period must not end later than the operational period.

Where an order contains such a provision it must provide that the sentence of imprisonment suspended under 65-001 will also take effect if:

(1) during the supervision period the offender fails to comply with a requirement so imposed; and
(2) a judge having the power to do so subsequently orders (under Sch.12 para.8—65-014) that the original sentence is to take effect.

(SA 2020 ss.286, 287 and 288)

Periodic reviews of the offender's compliance with the community requirements may be ordered (65-008). As to breach of the requirements, see 65-014. As to amendment and revocation of the order, see 65-024.

As to transfer to Scotland and Northern Ireland, see SA 2020 s.204.

Additional Provisions

Several matters need to be borne in mind, namely: 65-003

(1) a sentence must not be suspended for longer than two years;
(2) the imposition of a community requirement is now discretionary rather than mandatory;
(3) the judge must specify not only the operational period of the sentence, but also the supervision period for the purpose of the community requirements; these may not be the same.

Where the judge feels able to take a merciful course and not impose an immediate and substantial custodial sentence, it may be more sensible for him to impose a community sentence rather than a suspended sentence of imprisonment kept artificially low, since on the breach of:

(a) a suspended sentence, the judge is restricted to activating the term of the suspended sentence, or a lesser term (see 65-014); while
(b) a community order, the offender may be dealt with in any manner originally available to the sentencing court had a community order not been made.

(*R. v Phipps* [2007] EWCA Crim 2923; [2008] 2 Cr. App. R. (S.) 20)

Pre- conditions to Suspension; Sentencing Council Guidance

The Sentencing Council Imposition of Community and Custodial Sentences Definitive Guideline set out four questions on the imposition of a custodial sentence. 65-004

(1) Has the custody threshold been passed?
    - A custodial sentence must not be imposed unless the offence or the combination of the offence and one or more offences associated with it was so serious that neither a fine alone nor a community sentence can be justified for the offence.
    - There is no general definition of where the custody threshold lies. The circumstances of the individual offence and the factors to be assessed by offence-specific guidelines will determine whether an offence is so serious that neither a fine alone nor a community sentence can be justified. Where no offence specific guideline is available to determine serious-

ness, the harm caused by the offence, the culpability of the offender and any previous convictions will be relevant to the assessment.
- The clear intention of the threshold test is to reserve prison as a punishment for the most serious offences.

(2) Is it avoidable that a sentence of imprisonment be imposed?
- Passing the custody threshold does not mean that a custodial sentence should be deemed inevitable. Custody should not be imposed where a community order could provide sufficient restriction on an offender's liberty (by way of punishment) while addressing the rehabilitation of the offender to prevent future crime.
- For offenders on the cusp of custody, imprisonment should not be imposed where there would be an impact on defendants which would make a custodial sentence disproportionate to achieving the aims of sentencing.

(3) What is the shortest term commensurate with the seriousness of the offence?
- In considering this the court must NOT consider any licence or post sentence supervision requirements which may subsequently be imposed upon the offender's release.

(4) Can the sentence be suspended?
- A suspended sentence MUST NOT be imposed as a more severe form of community order. A suspended sentence is a custodial sentence. Sentencers should be clear that they would impose an immediate custodial sentence if the power to suspend were not available. If not, a non-custodial sentence should be imposed.

The guidelines set out a number of factors that should be weighed in considering whether it is possible to suspend the sentence. Those factors indicating that it would not be appropriate to suspend include where the offender presents a risk or danger to the public, where appropriate punishment can only be achieved by immediate custody or where there is a history of poor compliance with court orders. The factors indicating that it may be appropriate to suspend include a realistic prospect of rehabilitation, strong personal mitigation and where immediate custody will result in significant harmful impact upon others.

It is not appropriate to impose a suspended sentence when a sentence of immediate custody would have resulted in the offender getting the benefit of a substantial period spent on remand. In such circumstances the sentence should not be suspended but should be constructed in such a way as to give the appellant the benefit of the time spent on remand (see *R. v Barrett* [2010] EWCA Crim 365; [2010] 2 Cr. App. R. (S.) 86).

Suspended Sentences: General Guidance

65-005 *A prison sentence which is suspended should be for the same term which would have applied if the offender were being sentenced to immediate custody.*

The Sentencing Council make clear that the guidance on pre-sentence reports applies if suspending custody. If the court imposes a term of imprisonment of between 14 days and 2 years (subject to magistrates' sentencing powers), it may suspend for between 6 months and 2 years. That is also the case where the court imposes two or more sentences to be served consecutively. The time for which a sentence is suspended should reflect the length of the sentence; up to 12 months might normally be appropriate for a suspended sentence of up to 6 months. Where a court suspends a sentence it may impose one or more requirements for an offender to undertake in the community.

Imposition of requirements

The requirements which may be imposed under SA 2020 s.287 are those set out in the TABLE in COMMUNITY SENTENCES, subject to the restrictions of ss.150 (sentences fixed by law, etc.) and 290 and 291 (availability of arrangements) and the provisions as to particular requirements stated in that paragraph, and include an electronic monitoring requirement (as defined by SA 2020 Sch.9 Pt 14 paras 29–35). **65-006**

Where the judge:

(1) imposes a curfew requirement or an exclusion requirement, he *must* also impose an electronic monitoring requirement (as defined by s.215) unless:
  (a) he is prevented from doing so by ss.215(2) or 218(4) (SA 2020 s.291); or
  (b) in the particular circumstances of the case, he considers it inappropriate to do so;

(2) imposes:
  - an unpaid work requirement;
  - rehabilitation activity requirement;
  - a programme requirement;
  - a prohibited activity requirement;
  - curfew requirement;
  - exclusion requirement;
  - a residence requirement;
  - a foreign travel prohibition requirement;
  - a mental health treatment requirement;
  - a drug rehabilitation requirement;
  - an alcohol treatment requirement;
  - alcohol abstinence and monitoring requirement (where available); or
  - an attendance centre requirement,

  he *may* also impose an electronic compliance monitoring and/or an electronic whereabouts monitoring requirement unless he is prevented from doing so by SA 2020 ss.290(2) or s.291.

(SA 2020 s.291(4))

LASPOA 2012 s.76 inserted into s.212A of CJA 2003, now SA 2020 s.291, provision providing for an alcohol abstinence and monitoring requirement to be imposed as part of a requirement of a community order or suspended sentence order. The requirement is at present the subject of a pilot scheme in the South London local justice area (SI 2014/1777). Monitoring is by means of a transdermal electronic tag fitted to an offender to measure the level of alcohol contained in their sweat.

Under ORA 14 a "rehabilitation activity requirement" replaced the familiar "rehabilitation requirement". The "activity requirement" has been abolished and replaced by the "rehabilitation activity requirement".

The particular requirement(s) will need to ensure that they properly address those factors that are most likely to reduce the risk of re-offending.

As the Sentencing Council guidance and decision flow chart point out it is important to see that the requirements are compatible with each other (SA 2020 s.292(3)).

Combinations of other custodial sentences

65-007 A judge who passes a suspended sentence order on any person for an offence may not impose a community sentence in his case in respect of that offence or any other offence of which he is convicted by or before the court, or for which he is dealt with by the court (SA 2020 s.203).

Since the whole purpose of suspending a sentence of imprisonment is to avoid sending an offender to prison, it is bad sentencing practice to:

(1) impose on the same occasion, an immediate term in respect of one offence and make a suspended sentence order in respect of another (*R. v Sapiano* (1968) 52 Cr. App. R. 674);
(2) make a suspended sentence order in respect of an offender already serving an immediate custodial term for another offence (*R. v Hammond* [1969] Crim. L.R. 500).

2. REVIEW OF REQUIREMENTS

(1) General review

Power to order

65-008 There is power to provide for a periodic review of an order, either;

(1) generally, under SA 2020 s.293; or
(2) in the case of an order imposing a drug rehabilitation requirement (under SA 2020 s.293(3) (65-011)).

A suspended sentence order that imposes one or more community requirements may:

(a) provide for the order to be reviewed periodically at specified intervals;
(b) provide for each review to be made (subject to SA 2020 s.294), at a review hearing held for the purpose by the judge;
(c) require the offender to attend each review hearing; and
(d) provide for the responsible officer to make to "the court responsible for the order" before each review, a report on the offender's progress in complying with the community requirements of the order.

(SA 2020 s.293(3); the provision does not apply in the case of an order imposing a drug rehabilitation requirement (provision for such a requirement to be subject to review being made by s.293—see 65-011).

"The court responsible for a suspended sentence order" is:

(i) where a court is specified in the order (in accordance with s.293(4)), that court; and
(ii) in any other case, it is the court by which the order is made.

A suspended sentence order made on an appeal brought from the Crown Court or from the CACD is deemed for this purpose to have been made by the Crown Court (SA 2020 s.293(6)).

Powers on periodic review

At a review hearing the judge may, after considering the responsible officer's report, amend the community requirements, or any provision of the order, which relates to those requirements, but *may not amend*: **65-009**

(1) the community requirements of the order so as to impose a requirement of *a different kind* unless the offender consents to that requirement;
(2) a *treatment* requirement (i.e. a mental health treatment, drug rehabilitation or alcohol treatment requirement) unless the offender expresses willingness to comply with the amended requirement;
(3) *the operational period* of the suspended sentence; or
(4) except with the offender's consent, the order while it is being *appealed*.

He *may* amend the *supervision period* only if the period, as amended, complies with s.288(4) (see 65-001).

For the purposes of (1) above a community requirement falling within any paragraph of s.287 is of the same kind as another community requirement if it falls within the same paragraph of s.287. An electronic compliance monitoring requirement is a requirement of the same kind as any requirement within that table to which it relates (SA 2020 s.294(4)).

Conduct of Hearing

If: **65-010**

(1) before a review hearing is held the judge, after considering the responsible officer's report, is of the opinion that the offender's progress in complying with the community requirements of the order is satisfactory, he may order that no review hearing be held at that review; and
(2) before a review hearing is held, or at a hearing, the judge, after considering that report, is of that opinion, may amend the suspended sentence order so as to provide for each subsequent review to be held without a hearing.

If:

(a) at a review held without a hearing, the judge, after considering the responsible officer's report, is of the opinion that the offender's progress under the order is no longer satisfactory, he may require the offender to attend a hearing at a specified time and place;
(b) at a review hearing, the judge is of the opinion that the offender has without reasonable excuse failed to comply with any of the community requirements of the order, he may adjourn the hearing for the purpose of dealing with the case under SA 2020 Sch.16 para.13 (65-012);
(c) at a review hearing the judge may amend the suspended sentence order so as to vary the intervals specified under s.293(2)(a) (periodic reviews).

(SA 2020 ss.294 and 295)

(2) Drug rehabilitation requirement

Where appropriate

A suspended sentence order imposing a drug rehabilitation requirement may, (and *must* if the treatment and testing period is more than 12 months): **65-011**

(1) provide for the requirement to be reviewed periodically at intervals of not less than one month;
(2) provide for each review of the requirement to be made, subject to the provisions of SA 2020 s.287 and Sch.9 para.22(6) (see 65-012) at a hearing held for the purpose by the court responsible for the order (a "review hearing");
(3) require the offender to attend each review hearing;
(4) provide for the responsible officer to make to the court responsible for the order, before each review, a report in writing on the offender's progress under the requirement; and
(5) provide for each such report to include the test results communicated to the responsible officer (under SA 2020 Sch.9 para.19(7)) otherwise and the views of the treatment provider as to the treatment and testing of the offender.

References to "the court responsible" for a suspended sentence order imposing a drug rehabilitation requirement are references:

(a) where a court is specified in the order, to that court;
(b) in any other case, to the court by which the order is made.

Where a suspended sentence order imposing a drug rehabilitation requirement has been made on an appeal brought from the Crown Court or from the CACD, for the purposes of (b), above, it is taken to have been made by the Crown Court (SA 2020 Sch.9 para.21(6)).

Powers at hearing

65-012 At a review hearing within the meaning of SA 2020 s.294 and Sch.9 para.22, the judge may, after considering the responsible officer's report, amend the suspended sentence order, so far as it relates to the drug rehabilitation requirement, but may not amend the drug rehabilitation requirement unless the offender expresses his willingness to comply with the requirement as amended, and, except with the consent of the offender, may not amend any requirement or provision of the order while an appeal against the order is pending.

If the offender fails to express his willingness to comply with the drug rehabilitation requirement as proposed to be amended, the judge may:

(1) revoke the suspended sentence order and the suspended sentence to which it relates; and
(2) deal with him, for the offence in respect of which the order was made, in any way in which he could have been dealt with for that offence by the court which made the order if the order had not been made.

In dealing with the offender under (2) the judge:

(a) must take into account the extent to which the offender has complied with the requirements of the order; and
(b) may impose a custodial sentence (where the order was made in respect of an offence punishable with such a sentence) notwithstanding anything in SA 2020 s.230(2) (restrictions on the imposition of custodial sentences) for which see DEALING WITH AN OFFENDER.

If at such a review hearing, the judge, after considering the responsible officer's report, is of the opinion that the offender's progress under the requirement:

(i) is satisfactory, he may so amend the order as to provide for each subsequent review to be made without a hearing;
(ii) is no longer satisfactory, he may require the offender to attend a hearing at a specified time and place.

At that hearing the judge, after considering that report, may exercise the powers conferred by this section as if the hearing were a review hearing, and so amend the order as to provide for each subsequent review to be made at a review hearing (SA 2020 Sch.9 para.22).

3. Breach of Community Requirement(s); Further Offence

Process; Summons or Warrant

If at any time while a suspended sentence order made by the Crown Court (*save one where a direction was included that failure to comply with the community requirements of it be dealt with by a magistrates' court*) is in force in respect of an offender it appears on information that the offender has failed to comply with any of the community requirements of the order, the Crown Court may: **65-013**

(1) issue a summons requiring the offender to appear at the place and time specified in it;
(2) if the information is in writing and on oath, issue a warrant for his arrest;
(3) where the summons requires the offender to appear before the Crown Court and the offender does not appear in answer to it, issue a warrant for his arrest.

(SA 2020 Sch.16 para.9)

Powers on the breach

Where it is proved: **65-014**

(1) to the judge's satisfaction, that the offender has failed, without reasonable excuse, to comply with any of the community requirements of the order; or
(2) the offender is convicted of an offence committed during the operational period of the order (other than one which has already taken effect);

the judge before whom he is brought must consider the case and deal with him, by:

(a) ordering that the suspended sentence take effect with the *original term unaltered*;
(b) ordering that the suspended sentence take effect with the substitution for the original term of a *lesser term*;
(c) ordering the offender to pay *a fine* of an amount not exceeding £2,500; or
(d) in the case of an order which imposes one or more community requirements, amending the order by imposing *more onerous requirements* or *extending* the supervision period (for not less than six months nor more than two years) or the operational period;
(e) in the case of an order which does not impose any community requirements, subject to s.288(2) (which limits the length of the operational and supervision periods (see 65-001), amending the order by extending the operational period).

(SA 2020 Sch.16 paras 12–14)

He may not, however, increase the length of the original sentence by converting it into an immediate term (*R. v Cassidy* [2010] EWCA Crim 3146; [2011] 2 Cr. App. R. (S.) 40); nor may he make "no order" (*R. v Anderson* [2014] EWCA Crim 797). One of the options listed in Sch.12 para.8 must be adopted.

Any question whether the offender has complied with any of the community requirements of the order, and any question whether the offender has been convicted of an offence during the operational period of the sentence, is to be decided by the judge and not by the verdict of a jury.

Obligation to activate sentence

65-015 The judge *must* activate the suspended term under (a) or (b) of 65-014 unless he considers that, in all the circumstances it would be unjust to do so, taking into account, in particular:

(1) the extent to which the offender has complied with any community requirements of the order (*R. v Zeca* [2009] EWCA Crim 133; [2009] 2 Cr. App. R. (S.) 65); and
(2) the facts of the subsequent offence in the case of (2) in 65-014.

A suspended sentence order must be complied with in full; non-compliance risks activation of the suspended sentence in full. An offender who does not comply with the terms of the order, has only himself to blame if non-compliance leads to activation of the suspended sentence in full (*R. v Finn* [2012] EWCA Crim 881; [2012] 2 Cr. App. R. (S.) 96).

Where the judge deals with an offender in respect of a suspended sentence order, the Crown Court officer will notify the appropriate officer of the court which passed of the method adopted.

(SA 2020 Sch.16 para.14)

Where the judge decides not to order, where he has the power, that the suspended term take effect, he must explain why he has not done so, in his sentencing remarks (CrimPR 28.1(c)).

A Two Stage Test

65-016 In *R. v Sheppard* [2008] EWCA Crim 799; [2008] 2 Cr. App. R. (S.) 93 the CACD interpreted the statutory provisions as envisaging a two-stage test:

(1) where there has been a breach, the judge *must* order that the suspended sentence take effect, either in whole or in part, *unless* it would be unjust to do so; the extent of compliance with the original order is relevant to that decision (thus, if for example, 95 per cent of the order had been complied with, the judge might conclude that it was unjust to order that any part of the custodial term should take effect); and
(2) if it is not unjust to activate the suspended sentence, the judge must decide whether or not to order the offender to serve *the whole* of the original term or *modify* the term.

In those cases where an unpaid work requirement is included in the order, and that requirement has been completed, or substantially completed:

(a) *if there have been no other breaches*, it will generally be appropriate to reduce the term to reflect this (*R. v Zeca* [2009] EWCA Crim 133; [2009] 2 Cr. App. R. (S.) 65; *R. v Kavanagh* [2010] EWCA Crim 1737; [2011] 1

Cr. App. R. (S.) 63; *R. v Swallow* [2013] EWCA Crim 719); on the other hand;

(b) if the offender has (as in *R. v Sheppard* [2008] EWCA Crim 799; [2008] 2 Cr. App. R. (S.) 93), also committed a large number of breaches of the order; or, (as in *R. v Finn* [2012] EWCA Crim 881; [2012] 2 Cr. App. R. (S.) 96), there has been otherwise a "wholesale failure to comply"; or completion of a requirement has done nothing to alter the offender's thinking or attitude (see *R. v Abdille* [2009] EWCA Crim 1195; [2010] 1 Cr. App. R. (S.) 18; *R. v Collins-Reed* [2012] EWCA Crim 2036; [2013] 1 Cr. App. R. (S.) 95) it may well not be appropriate to reduce the term at all.

The commission of a further offence during the operational period of the suspended sentence is not a factor justifying the increase of the second sentence, not, at least, in circumstances where the suspended sentence is activated in full (*R. v Levesconte* [2011] EWCA Crim 2754; [2012] Crim. L.R. 236).

For the purpose of any enactment conferring rights of appeal in criminal cases, an order made is to be treated as a "sentence" passed on the offender by that court for the offence for which the suspended sentence was passed (SA 2020 s.293(6)).

Concurrent or Consecutive

When making an order that a sentence is to take effect (with or without any variation of the original term), the judge may order that: **65-017**

(1) the sentence is to take effect immediately; or
(2) that the term of that is to commence on the expiry of another term of imprisonment passed on the offender by him or by another court,

subject to SA 2020 s.225 (restriction on consecutive sentences for released prisoners), for which see IMPRISONMENT. Any term activated under (2) in 65-014 should ordinarily be made consecutive to any sentence imposed for the further offence (SA 2020 Sch.16).

Care needs to be taken where there are breaches of two orders, as where there is a suspended sentence containing a community requirement, and a community order from another court, which may depend on whether the orders run concurrently or consecutively (*R. v Butt* [2012] EWCA Crim 462, distinguishing *R. v Meredith* [1994] 15 Cr. App. R. (S.) 5).

Sentencing Council Guidelines on breach

The Sentencing Council Breach Offences Definitive Guidelines (with effect from 1 October 2018) set out the approach to be taken where there is a conviction for a further offence committed during the operational period of the order or where there has been a failure to comply with a community requirement. In both situations the guidelines make clear that the court must activate the custodial sentence unless it would be unjust in all the circumstances to do so. The predominant factor in making such a determination relates to the level of compliance with the SSO. The guidelines also make clear that this factor is already provided for in the penalties suggested which are determined by the level of compliance, but permit a reduction to the custodial term for relevant completed or partially completed requirements where appropriate. **65-018**

(1) Further offence:

The facts or nature of the new offence is the primary consideration in assessing the action to be taken. Three categories are provided. Where the breach is in the second or third categories, the prior level of compliance is also relevant.

(2) Failure to comply with a community requirement during the supervision period:

The court must take into account the extent to which the offender has complied with the SSO when imposing a sentence.

In assessing the level of compliance (in either of the situation 1 or 2 above) with the order the court should consider:

- the overall attitude and engagement with the order as well as the proportion of elements completed;
- the impact of any completed or partially completed requirements on the offender's behaviour;
- the proximity of the breach to imposition of order; and
- evidence of circumstances or offender characteristics, such as disability, mental health issues or leaning difficulties which have impeded compliance.

For 1 (Further offence), the guidelines provide that where the breach involves:

(i) Multiple and/or more serious new offence(s) committed, the penalty is full activation of the original custodial term.

(ii) Where it involves a new offence similar in type and gravity to the offence for which the suspended sentence order was imposed and: (a) no/low level of compliance with SSO, the penalty is full activation of the original term; (b) where medium or high level of compliance with the SSO then the penalty is to activate the sentence but to apply an appropriate proportionate reduction to the custodial term taking into consideration any unpaid work or curfew requirements completed.

(iii) For a new offence less serious that the original offence but which requires a custodial sentence and: (a) no/low level of compliance with the SSO, the penalty is full activation of the custodial term; (b) where medium or high level of compliance with the SSO, then the penalty is to activate the sentence but to apply an appropriate proportionate reduction to the custodial term taking into consideration any unpaid work or curfew requirements completed.

(iv) For a new offence that does not require a custodial sentence, then the penalty is to activate the sentence but to apply an appropriate proportionate reduction to the custodial term taking into consideration any unpaid work or curfew requirements completed, or to impose more onerous requirement(s) and/or extend the supervision period and/or extend the operational period and/or impose a fine.

For 2 (Failure to comply), the guidelines provide that where the breach involves:

(i) No/low level of compliance, the full activation of the original custodial term.

(ii) Medium level of compliance, to activate the sentence but to apply an appropriate proportionate reduction to the original custodial term taking into consideration any unpaid work or curfew requirements completed.

(iii) High level of compliance, to activate the sentence but to apply an appropriate proportionate reduction to the original custodial term taking into consideration any unpaid work or curfew requirements completed, or to impose more onerous requirement(s) and/or extend the supervision period and/or extend the operational period and/or impose a fine.

The Sentencing Council guidelines also make clear that the court dealing with the breach should remember that the court imposing the original sentence determined that a custodial sentence was appropriate in the original case.

In considering whether if there are factors which would cause activation to be unjust, the court may consider all factors including any strong personal mitigation, whether there is a realistic prospect of rehabilitation, and whether immediate custody will result in significant impact on others.

The guidelines also say that only new and exceptional factors/circumstances not present at the time the SSO was imposed should be taken into account. Where a court considers that it would be unjust to order the custodial sentence to take effect, it must state its reasons and it must deal with the offender as set out at 65-014.

"Treatment cases"; Surgical, Electrical or Other Treatment

An offender who is required by: **65-019**

(1) a mental health treatment requirement;
(2) a drug rehabilitation requirement; or
(3) an alcohol treatment requirement,

to submit to treatment for his mental condition, or his dependency on, or propensity to misuse, drugs or alcohol, is not to be treated as having failed to comply with that requirement on the ground only that he has refused to undergo any surgical, electrical or other treatment if, in the judge's opinion, his refusal was reasonable having regard to all the circumstances.

A judge may not amend the requirements (1)–(3) above unless the offender consents to the amended requirement (SA 2020 Sch.9 paras 21, 22 and 23).

4. Commission of Further Offence

Appropriate Court

An offender may be dealt with in respect of a suspended sentence order by the Crown Court or, where the sentence was passed by a magistrates' court, by any magistrates' court before which he appears or is brought. **65-020**

Where an offender is convicted by a magistrates' court of any offence and the court is satisfied that the offence was committed during the operational period of a suspended sentence passed by the Crown Court:

(1) that court may, if it thinks fit, commit the offender to the Crown Court; and
(2) if it does not, will give written notice of the conviction to the Crown Court officer.

(SA 2020 Sch.16 paras 11 and 13)

For these purposes, a suspended sentence passed on an offender on appeal is to be treated as having been passed by the court by which he was originally sentenced.

Appropriate Court; Process

Where it appears to a judge, where the Crown Court has jurisdiction that: **65-021**

(1) an offender has been convicted in the UK of an offence committed during the operational period of a suspended sentence order; and

(2) he has not been dealt with in respect of the suspended sentence, the judge may, subject to the following provisions of this paragraph, issue a summons requiring the offender to appear at the place and time specified in it, or a warrant for his arrest.

Jurisdiction may be exercised by a judge of the Crown Court if the suspended sentence was passed by the Crown Court.

For these purposes, a suspended sentence passed on an offender on appeal is to be treated as having been passed by the court by which he was originally sentenced.

Where an offender is convicted by a magistrates' court of an offence and the court is satisfied that the offence was committed during the operational period of a suspended sentence passed by the Crown Court, the offender may, if the court thinks fit, be committed to the Crown Court, or if he is not committed, written notice of the conviction will be given to the Crown Court officer (SA 2020 Sch.16).

5. Cancellation or Amendment of Order

(1) Cancellation of Community Requirements

65-022 Where at any time while a suspended sentence order is in force, it appears to the Crown Court that:

(1) the order was made by the Crown Court; or

(2) in the case of an order which is subject to review, the Crown Court is "responsible for the order" (see 65-008),

then, on the application of the offender or the responsible officer that, having regard to the circumstances which have arisen since the order was made, it would be in the interests of justice to do so, a judge may cancel the community requirements of the suspended sentence order.

The circumstances in which he may exercise this power in these circumstances include the offender's making good progress or his responding satisfactorily to supervision.

No application may be made by the offender while an appeal against the suspended sentence is pending (SA 2020 Sch.11 paras 24 and 26).

(2) Amendment of Community Requirements

Change of residence

65-023 SA 2020 s.302 imposes a duty on an offender to obtain permission before changing residence, prohibiting him, where a relevant order is in force from changing residence without permission given in accordance with the section by either the responsible officer, or a court.

Where at any time while a suspended sentence order is in force in respect of an offender the offender is given permission under s.302 to change residence, and the local justice area in which the new residence is situated ("the new local justice area") is different from the local justice area specified in the order, then, if the permission is given by:

(1) a court, the court must amend the order to specify the new local justice area;

(2) the responsible officer:
   (a) the officer must apply to the appropriate court to amend the order to specify the new local justice area; and
   (b) the court will make that amendment.

"The appropriate court" has the same meaning as in para.13.

Where the order as amended includes a residence requirement requiring the offender to reside at a specified place, and the local justice area in which that place is situated ("the new local justice area") is different from the local justice area specified in the order, the court must amend the order to specify the new local justice area (SA 2020 Sch.16 Pt 3).

As to the transfer of an order to Scotland or Northern Ireland, see SA 2020 Sch.11.

Amendment of community requirements

At any time during the supervision period, a judge of the Crown Court, as the appropriate court (see 65-020) may, on the application of the offender or the responsible officer, by order amend any community requirement of a suspended sentence order, by: **65-024**

(1) cancelling it;
(2) or replacing it with a requirement of the same kind which he could include if he were then making the order.

Note that:

(a) a requirement is of the same kind as another if both fall within the same paragraph of SA 2020 s.287, (setting out the requirements which may be imposed);
(b) an electronic monitoring requirement is a requirement of the same kind as any requirement falling within s.287 to which it relates.

The judge may *not*, however, under this paragraph, amend a mental health treatment requirement, a drug rehabilitation requirement or an alcohol treatment requirement unless the offender consents to the amended requirement. In this latter case, if the offender fails to express his willingness to comply with any of the proposed amended requirements, the judge may:

(i) revoke the suspended order and the suspended sentence to which it relates; and
(ii) deal with him, for the offence in respect of which the suspended sentence order was made, in any way in which he could deal with him if he had just been convicted by or before the court of the offence.

In dealing with the offender under (ii), he must take into account the extent to which the offender has complied with the requirements of the order (SA 2020 Sch.16 para.25).

The provision that no order might be made under this provision while an appeal against the suspended sentence was pending is omitted by ORA 2013 s.18(9) (SA 2020 Sch.16 para.23 and 24).

Where the judge proposes to exercise his powers under this provision, apart from cancelling the requirement, the offender must be summoned before the court. If he does not answer to the summons, a warrant may be issued (SA 2020 Sch.16 para.25).

As to the amendment of "treatment" requirements on the report of the medical practitioner concerned, see 65-025.

Amendment of treatment requirements on practitioner's report

65-025 Where the medical practitioner or other person by whom, or under whose direction, an offender is, in pursuance of any requirement, being treated for his mental condition, or his dependency on, or propensity to misuse, drugs or alcohol:

(1) is of opinion that:
   (a) the treatment of the offender should be continued beyond the period specified in that behalf in the order;
   (b) the offender needs different treatment;
   (c) the offender is not susceptible to treatment; or
   (d) the offender does not require further treatment; or
(2) the offender is for any reason unwilling to continue to treat or direct the treatment of the offender,

he will make a report in writing to that effect to the responsible officer and that officer will apply under 65-024 to the appropriate court for the variation or cancellation of the requirement (SA 2020 Sch.16 para.26).

Review of drug rehabilitation requirement

65-026 Where the responsible officer is of opinion that a suspended sentence order imposing a drug rehabilitation requirement which is subject to review should be amended so as to provide for each periodic review (see 65-008 and following) to be made without a hearing instead of at a review hearing, or vice versa, he will apply under 65-024 to the court responsible for the order for a variation of the order (SA 2020 Sch.16 para.26).

Extension of unpaid work requirement

65-027 Where:

(1) a suspended sentence order imposing an unpaid work requirement is in force in respect of the offender; and
(2) on the application of the offender or the responsible officer, it appears to the judge, where the Crown Court is the appropriate court (see 65-020), that it would be in the interests of justice to do so having regard to circumstances which have arisen since the order was made,

the judge may extend the period of 12 months (SA 2020 Sch.16 para.27).

6. Administrative matters

Duties of Crown Court officer

65-028 Crown Court officer will provide:

(1) copies of the amending order to the offender and to the responsible officer; and
(2) in the case of an amending order which substitutes a new local justice area, a copy of the amending order to:

(a) the appropriate probation officer; and
(b) the magistrates' court acting for that area; and

in the case of an amending order which imposes or amends a requirement specified in the first column of Sch.14, a copy of so much of the amending order as relates to that requirement to the person specified in relation to that requirement in the second column of that Schedule.

Where under (2)(b) above, the proper officer provides a copy of an amending order to a magistrates' court acting for a different area, he will also provide to that court such documents and information relating to the case as he considers likely to be of assistance to a court acting for that area in the exercise of its functions in relation to the order (SA 2020 Sch.16 para.28).

66. TRAVEL RESTRICTION ORDERS

General

66-001 Where:

(1) an offender is convicted of a drug trafficking offence (as to the meaning of which see 66-004) committed on or after 1 April 2002;
(2) the judge determines that it is appropriate to impose a sentence of imprisonment for that offence; and
(3) the term of imprisonment which he considers appropriate is a term of four years or more,

the judge *must* in sentencing the offender consider whether it would be appropriate for the sentence to include a travel restriction order ("TRO") (CJPA 2001 s.33).

The term in (3) above refers to a single sentence of four years for a drug offence, and not a combination of consecutive sentences making a total of four years in all (*R. v Alexander* [2011] EWCA Crim 89; [2011] 2 Cr. App. R. 52).

If the judge:

(a) considers that it is appropriate to make such an order in all the circumstances (including any other convictions of the offender for drug trafficking offences in respect of which he is also passing sentence), he should make such an order in relation to him; or
(b) determines that it is not so appropriate, he must state his reasons for not making an order.

A TRO prohibits the offender from leaving the UK at any time in the period which:

(i) begins with release from custody; and
(ii) continues after that time for such period of not less than two years as may be specified in the order.

The order cannot be made retrospectively or, in the case of offences added by statutory order under s.34(1)(c), in respect of an offence committed before the date of the coming into force of the relevant order.

A TRO must be for at least two years (CJPA 2001 s.33(3)(b)). There is no statutory maximum. The general presumption is that the travel ban should escalate based on the level of the sentence. It is for the judge to weigh the respective lengths of the term of imprisonment and the TRO in any given case. The order begins on the day on which the offender is released from custody (s.33(3)(a)).

The provisions of the order do not prevent deportation, extradition or other statutory removal action (see 66-008).

Approach to order

66-002 When imposing a sentence of four years or more for a drug trafficking offence, the judge has a duty to consider making an order. It is wrong to interpret s.33 as requiring an order to be made unless it is inappropriate (*R. v Graham* [2011] EWCA Crim 1905; [2012] 1 Cr. App. R. (S) 57; *R. v Powell* [2014] EWCA Crim 1606).

The correct approach to considering making an order was set out in *R. v Mee* [2004] EWCA Crim 629; [2004] 2 Cr. App. R. (S.) 81. The court has a broad discretion which must be exercised proportionately and fairly for the purpose for which it was granted, namely to prevent or reduce the risk of offending after the defendant's release from prison (the TRO was not intended to be a substitute for the appropriate period of imprisonment). If the judge is considering imposing a TRO he should indicate that he intends to do so and invite specific submissions on the relevant factors. He should then make a realistic assessment of the risk.

Various factors will come into play:

(1) the quantity, quality and type of the drug imported;
(2) the degree of sophistication demonstrated in committing the offence;
(3) the offender's past travel pattern;
(4) the degree of the offender's contact with the drug trade;
(5) the offender's role, as demonstrated by the facts;
(6) the offender's character and antecedents; and
(7) the impact of an order upon the offender's dependents, his employment and any other connections, both here and abroad.

The fact that the offender has been convicted of an offence of importation does not necessarily give rise to a risk that he will do it again on release.

For examples of cases in which a TRO was *not* considered to be appropriate, see *R. v Fuller* [2005] EWCA Crim 1029; [2006] 1 Cr. App. R. (S.) 8; *R. v Blackman* [2008] EWCA Crim 2833; *R. v Gee* [2009] EWCA Crim 1843; *R. v Graham* [2011] EWCA Crim 1905; [2012] 1 Cr. App. R. (S.) 57; and *R. v Powell* [2014] EWCA Crim 1606.

Where the judge decides to make an order he should include, in his sentencing remarks, a brief indication of his reasons.

In assessing the period of the order, the more serious the case, the longer the likely order; in any event its length should be proportionate both to the offence and to the circumstances of the case (*R. v Mee* [2004] EWCA Crim 629; [2004] 2 Cr. App. R. (S.) 81). Freedom to travel is a significant aspect of modern life. In restricting a person's freedom in that respect there is a need for balance; the length of any order should be restricted to that which is necessary to protect the public. The drug trade being truly international, the Act does not contemplate an order being made in relation to certain parts of the world only.

Direction to deliver up passport

The order may contain a direction to the offender to deliver up, or cause to be delivered up to the court, any UK passport held by him. Where such a direction is given, the court will send any passport delivered to the Secretary of State (in practice to the nearest Passport Office), who (without prejudice to any other power or duty of his to retain the passport) may retain it for so long as the prohibition imposed by the order applies to the offender (and is not for the time being suspended) and will not return the passport after the prohibition has ceased to apply, or when it is suspended, except when the passport has not expired and an application for its return is made to him by the offender. **66-003**

(CJPA 2001 s.33(5))

Definitions

66-004 "Drug trafficking offence" has the same meaning as under the DTA 1994 s.1(3) except that it includes any such offence under the MDA 1971 as may be designated by an order made by the Secretary of State under s.34(1)(c). It does not include an offence of possession with intent to supply (*R. v Boland* [2012] EWCA Crim 1953) (CJPA 2001 s.34(1) and (2)).

"UK passport" means a UK passport within the meaning of IA 1971 (CJPA 2001 s.33(8)). This includes a current or expired UK passport. The passports of foreign nationals and the non-British passports of those with dual nationality, whatever their domicile, remain the property of the issuing government. The court should record details of non-British passports.

"Release from custody" refers to an offender's first release from custody after the imposition of the travel restriction order, which is neither:

(1) a release on bail; nor
(2) a temporary release for a fixed period.

(CJPA 2001 s.33(7))

Revocation and suspension

66-005 An offender who has had a TRO made against him may apply to the court which made the order for the order to be either revoked or suspended.

An application for revocation may be made by that person at any time which is:

(a) after the end of the minimum period (as to the meaning of which, see 66-006); and
(b) not within three months after the making of any previous application for the revocation of the prohibition.

The judge may revoke the prohibition imposed by the order with effect from such date as the court may determine.

An application for suspension may be made by that person at any time after the making of the order. The prohibition can be suspended for such period as the court may determine.

The judge must not revoke the prohibition unless he considers it appropriate to do so in all the circumstances of the case and having regard, in particular, to:

(i) that person's character;
(ii) his conduct since the making of the order; and
(iii) the offences of which he was convicted on the occasion on which the order was made.

The judge must not suspend a prohibition for any period unless he is satisfied that there are exceptional circumstances that justify the suspension of the prohibition on compassionate grounds for that period (CJPA 2001 s.35). The judge must have regard to the same three requirements for revocation mentioned above under (i), (ii) and (iii) and to any other circumstances of the case that he considers relevant (CJPA 2001 s.35(5)).

Any application to revoke or suspend must be made in accordance with CrimPR 28.6.

Effect of suspension

Where the prohibition is suspended, the person who is the subject of the suspension must: **66-006**

(1) be in the UK when the period of suspension ends; and
(2) if the order contains a direction under s.33(4) above, surrender, before the end of that period, any passport returned or issued to him in respect of that suspension by the Secretary of State.

A passport that is required to be surrendered (under (2) above) must be surrendered to the Secretary of State in such manner, or by being sent to such address, as he may direct at the time when he returns or issues it.

Where the prohibition imposed on any person by a TRO is suspended for any period under this section, the end of the period, of the prohibition imposed by the order is treated (except for the purposes of s.35(7); see below) as postponed or, if there has been one or more previous suspensions further postponed, by the length of the period of suspension (CJPA 2001 s.35(6)).

"The minimum period" means:

(a) in the case of a TRO imposing a prohibition for a period of four years or less, the period of two years beginning at the time when the period of prohibition began;
(b) in the case of a TRO imposing a prohibition of more than four but less than 10 years, the period of four years beginning at that time; and
(c) in any other case, the period of five years beginning at that time.

(CJPA 2001 s.35(7))

Contravention of order

A person commits an offence if he: **66-007**

(1) leaves the UK at a time when he is prohibited from doing so by a travel restriction order; or
(2) is not in the UK at the end of the period during which a prohibition imposed on him by such an order has been suspended.

For each of these offences, the offender is liable on summary conviction to up to six months' imprisonment or to a fine or both and on indictment to up to five years' imprisonment and an unlimited fine or both.

A person who fails to comply with a direction contained in a TRO to deliver up, or cause to be delivered up, a passport to a court, commits an offence and is liable on summary conviction to up to six months' imprisonment or to a fine or to both (CJPA 2001 s.36).

Removal powers

Special savings and provisions in relation to TROs are made in respect of the Secretary of State's prescribed removal powers (CJPA 2001 s.37). **66-008**

67. TRIAL WITHOUT A JURY

Quick Guide

1. Jury tampering (CJA 2003 Pt 7)

67-001 CJA 2003 s.44 makes provision for trial on indictment without a jury where there is a real and present danger of jury tampering.

CJA 2003 s.46 provides for the discharge of a jury where jury tampering has taken place, and the continuation of the trial by judge alone.

See the observations of the Lord Chief Justice on the justification for holding trials without a jury in *R. v Twomey* [2009] EWCA Crim 1035; [2009] 2 Cr. App. R. 25.

Danger of jury tampering

67-002 Where one or more accused are to be tried on indictment for one or more offences, the prosecution may apply to a judge of the Crown Court for the trial to be conducted without a jury where there is said to be a real and present danger of the jury being tampered with (CJA 2003 s.44(1)–(5)).

The judge must make an order that the trial is to be conducted without a jury where he is satisfied that:

(1) there is a real and present danger that jury tampering would take place; and
(2) notwithstanding any steps (including the provision of police protection) which might reasonably be taken to prevent jury tampering, the likelihood that it would take place would be so substantial as to make it necessary in the interests of justice for the trial to be conducted without a jury (CJA 2003 s.44(4) and (5)).

As to *continuing* a trial without a jury after the sitting jury has been discharged, see CJA 2003 s.46 below.

The Act gives examples of cases where there may be evidence of a "real and present danger" that jury tampering would take place, namely a case where:

(a) the trial is a retrial and the jury in the previous trial was discharged because jury tampering had taken place;
(b) jury tampering has taken place in previous criminal proceedings involving the accused or any of the accused;
(c) there has been intimidation, or attempted intimidation, of any person who is likely to be a witness at the trial.

(CJA 2003 s.44(6))

Procedure "of last resort"

67-003 Ordering a trial without a jury under s.44 remains a decision of last resort, only to be ordered when the judge is sure (and not when he entertains doubts, suspicions or reservations) that the statutory conditions are fulfilled. Save in extreme cases, where the necessary protective measures would constitute an unreasonable intrusion into the lives of the jurors (where, for example, there might be a constant police presence in or near their homes, day and night and at the weekends, or police protection, which meant that at all times when they are out of their homes, they are accompanied or overseen by police officers, with its consequent impact on the availability of police officers to carry out their ordinary duties), the confident expectation must be that the jury will perform their duties with their customary determination to do justice (*R. v J* [2010] EWCA Crim 1755; [2011] 1 Cr. App. R. 5).

However, the description of the procedure as "the decision of last resort" is not relevant or applicable to a decision made under s.46 (see 67-005). Where jury tampering had occurred, the ordinary course was an order discharging the jury and the continuation of the trial by judge alone.

There will be cases where it will be quite inappropriate for the particular judge to continue to try the case alone, as where his knowledge of the accused's antecedents and his personal involvement in a series of trials which were directly concerned with a fraud in which the accused was said to have been a central figure (*R. v Twomey* [2009] EWCA Crim 1035; [2009] 2 Cr. App. R. 25; see also *R. v S(K)* [2009] EWCA Crim 2377; [2010] 1 Cr. App. R. 20).

Applications under s.44

An application under s.44 must be determined at a preparatory hearing, the parties to such preparatory hearing being given an opportunity to make representations with respect to the application (CJA 2003 s.45). **67-004**

CJA 1987 s.7(1) (which sets out the purposes of preparatory hearings) is modified for this purpose by CJA 2003 s.45(4) in that for paras (a)–(c) there is substituted:

(1) identifying issues which are likely to be material to determinations and findings which are likely to be required during the trial;
(2) if there is to be a jury, assisting their comprehension of those issues and expediting the proceedings before them;
(3) determining an application to which CJA 2003 s.45 applies.

The evidence which may demonstrate the statutory danger is not confined to evidence which would be admissible at the trial of the accused. The second condition in s.44 requires that:

(a) after making due allowance for any reasonable steps which might address and minimise the danger of jury tampering;
(b) the judge should be sure that there would be a sufficiently high likelihood of jury tampering to make a judge-alone trial necessary.

(CJA 2003 s.45(1)–(3))

In *R. v Twomey* [2009] EWCA Crim 1035; [2009] 2 Cr. App. R. 25, the CACD approved the approach taken in *R. v Mackle* [2008] NI 183 where attention was drawn to

> "the feasibility of measures, the cost of providing them, the logistical difficulties that they may give rise to, and the anticipated duration of any necessary precautions"

as well as whether the level of protection appropriate to protect the integrity of the jury might

> "affect unfavourably the way in which the jury approached its task. If a misguided percep-

tion was created in the minds of the jury by the provision of high level protection this would plainly sound on the reasonableness of such a step."

In *R. v Twomey*, the CACD examined the likely impact of possible measures on the ordinary lives of the jurors and considered whether even the most intensive protective measures for individual jurors would be sufficient to prevent the improper exercise of pressure on them through members of their families who would not fall within the ambit of the protective measures.

See also *R. v J* [2010] EWCA Crim 1755; [2011] 1 Cr. App. R. 5, where the CACD held that, where a trial was expected to last two weeks, the necessary protective measures would not impose an unacceptable burden on the jurors or inhibit them from giving the case proper attention and returning true verdicts.

Section 45(3) requires the judge to permit representations to be made by the accused when an application is being made. There will be cases, however, where the evidence to demonstrate the risk of jury tampering will be so sensitive that it can only be addressed under public immunity interest principles. The evidence should be disclosed to the fullest extent possible, but it would be contrary to the legislative purpose to make an order for disclosure which would, in effect, bring the prosecution to an end, and enable those who had been involved in jury tampering to derail the trial and avoid the consequences prescribed by statute, trial by judge alone (*R. v Twomey* [2009] EWCA Crim 1035; [2009] 2 Cr. App. R. 25).

For the procedure governing applications and responses, see CrimPR 3.23–3.25 (summarised at 67-011).

Trials under way: discharge of jury because of tampering

67-005 Where a trial on indictment is under way, and the judge is minded to discharge the jury because jury tampering appears to have taken place, he must, before taking any steps to discharge the jury:

(1) notify the parties that he is minded to discharge the jury;
(2) inform the parties of the grounds on which he is so minded; and
(3) allow the parties an opportunity to make representations.

Where, after considering any such representations, the judge discharges the jury, he may make an order that the trial is to continue without a jury if, but only if, he is satisfied:

(a) that jury tampering has taken place; and
(b) that to continue the trial without a jury would be fair to the accused.

However, if he considers that it is necessary in the interests of justice for the trial to be terminated, he must terminate it. Where he does so, he may make an order that any new trial which is to take place be conducted without a jury if he is satisfied in respect of the new trial that both of the conditions set out in s.44 are likely to be fulfilled (CJA 2003 s.46(1)–(5)).

If, during the course of the trial, attempts are made to tamper with the jury to the extent that the judge feels it necessary to discharge the jury, it should be clearly understood that the judge may continue with the trial and deliver a judgment and verdict on his own; the principle of trial by jury is precious, but any accused who is responsible for abusing this principle by attempting to subvert the process has no justified complaint that he has been deprived of a right which, by his own actions, he himself has spurned (*R. v J* [2010] EWCA Crim 1755; [2011] 1 Cr. App. R. 5).

It is not necessary to prove that the defendant himself was involved in the jury tampering. In *R. v McManaman* [2016] EWCA Crim 3; [2016] 1 Cr. App. R. 4. The CACD stated that a situation where tampering occurred wholly without the involvement of the defendant was highly unlikely to arise, but even if it did arise

> "it is difficult to see why it should make any difference, as the terms of CJA 2003 are clear and there are sound reasons for the maintenance of the efficacy of trial by jury why that is so" ([25]).

The description of the procedure as "the decision of last resort" is not relevant or applicable to a decision made under s.46 (see 67-005). Where jury tampering had occurred, the ordinary course was an order discharging the jury and the continuation of the trial by judge alone.

This provision is without prejudice to any other power that the judge may have on terminating the trial, nor does anything in it affect the application of s.44, above, in relation to any new trial which takes place following the termination of the trial (CJA 2003 s.46(6)–(7)).

There is nothing in the legislation to suggest that a trial judge who has made findings about the pre-conditions to the discharge of the jury and the continuation of the trial must then recuse himself. The fact that the judge, in ruling on jury tampering and discharge, heard material about that conduct does not mean that he will be unable to exclude inadmissible material from his consideration of whether or not the accused is guilty (*R. v Guthrie* [2011] EWCA Crim 1338; [2011] 2 Cr. App. R. 20; *R. v Twomey* [2009] EWCA Crim 1035; [2009] 2 Cr. App. R. 25). However, there will be cases where it will be appropriate for him to recuse himself (for example, where the judge has become aware of a vast body of information concerning the defendant over the course of a series of trials, information to which the defence did not have access and so could not address; see *R. v S(K)* [2009] EWCA Crim 2377; [2010] 1 Cr. App. R. 20).

Appeal

Part 7 provides a right of appeal to the CACD by the accused or the prosecutor from an order under s.46(3) or (5) but only with the leave of the judge or the CACD. An order from which the appeal lies is not to take effect before the expiration of the period for bringing the appeal, or, if such an appeal is brought, before it is finally disposed of (CJA 2003 s.47). **67-006**

Effect of order

Where an order is made: **67-007**

(1) under ss.44 or 46(5), the trial to which the order relates is then conducted without a jury; and
(2) under s.46(3), the trial is continued without a jury.

In either case the trial will proceed in the usual way, the judge having all the powers, authority and jurisdiction which the court would have had if the trial had been with a jury (including power to determine any question and to make any finding which would be required to be determined or made by a jury) (CJA 2003 s.48(1)–(3)).

Except where the context otherwise requires, any reference in an enactment to a jury, the verdict of a jury or the finding of a jury, is to be read, in relation to a trial conducted or continued without a jury, as a reference to the court, the verdict of the court or the finding of the court (CJA 2003 s.48(4)).

Where a trial is conducted or continued without a jury and the judge convicts an accused, he must give a judgment which states the reasons for the conviction at, or as soon as reasonably practicable after, the time of the conviction (CJA 2003 s.48(4) and (6)).

The reference in CAA 1968 s.18(2) (notice of appeal or of application for leave to appeal to be given within 28 days from date of conviction, etc.) to the date of the conviction is to read as a reference to the date of that judgment (CJA 2003 s.48(5)(b)).

2. Multiple counts (DVA 2004)

Trial of part of indictment without a jury

67-008 The prosecution may apply to a judge of the Crown Court for a trial to take place on the basis that the trial of some, but not all, of the counts included in an indictment be conducted without a jury. Three conditions must be satisfied:

(1) the number of counts in the indictment is likely to mean that a trial by jury involving all of them would be impracticable;
(2) each count or group of counts which would be tried by jury, if such an order was made, can be regarded as a sample of counts which could accordingly be tried without a jury; and
(3) it is in the interests of justice to do so.

(DVA 2004 s.17(1)–(5))

In deciding whether to make an order, the judge must have regard to any steps which might reasonably be taken to facilitate trial by jury, but a step is not "reasonable" if it might result in the defendant receiving a lesser sentence (DVA 2004 s.17(6)–(7)).

A count can only be a sample of other counts if the defendant in each count is the same person (DVA 2004 s.17(9)).

Procedure under DVA 2004 ss.17–21

67-009 The use of the powers under these sections is likely to be appropriate where justice cannot be done without charging a large number of separate offences and the allegations against the defendant appear to fall into distinct groups by:

(1) reference to the identity of the victim;
(2) reference to the dates of the offences; or
(3) some other distinction in the nature of the offending conduct alleged.

In such a case it is essential to make clear from the outset the association asserted by the prosecutor between those counts to be tried by a jury and those counts which it is proposed should be tried by judge alone, if the jury convict on the former (*CPD* II 10A.16).

An order for such a trial may be made only at a preparatory hearing. It follows that where the prosecutor intends to invite the court to order such a trial it will normally be appropriate to proceed as follows:

(a) the draft indictment served under CrimPR 10.1 should be in the form appropriate to such a trial;

(b) the indictment should be accompanied by an application under CrimPR 3.23 for a preparatory hearing;
(c) on receipt of a draft two part indictment, a Crown Court officer should sign it at the end of Pt Two; at the start of the preparatory hearing, the accused should be arraigned on all counts in Pt One of the indictment. Arraignment on Pt Two need not take place until after there has been either a guilty plea to, or finding of guilt on, an associated count in Pt One of the indictment;
(d) if the prosecution application is successful, the prosecutor should prepare an abstract of the indictment, containing the counts from Pt One only, for use in the jury trial. Preparation of such an abstract does not involve "amendment" of the indictment; it is akin to where an accused pleads guilty to certain counts in an indictment and is put in the charge of the jury on the remaining counts only; and
(e) if the prosecution application for a two-stage trial is unsuccessful, the prosecutor may apply to amend the indictment to remove from it any counts in Pt Two which would make jury trial on the whole indictment impracticable and to revert to a standard form of indictment; it will be a matter for the judge whether arraignment on outstanding counts takes place at the preparatory hearing, or at a future date.

(*CPD* II 10A.17–20)

Effect of order

The effect of an order under DVA 2004 s.17 is that where an accused is found guilty by a jury of a count which is a "sample" of other counts to be tried in those proceedings, those other counts may be tried without a jury in those proceedings (DVA 2004 s.19). **67-010**

3. Procedure

CrimPR 3.23, which applies to applications for a preparatory hearing, applies also to applications for a trial without a jury under CJA 2003 s.44 and DVA 2004 s.17. **67-011**

The procedure is to be found at CASE MANAGEMENT.

A prosecutor who wants the judge to order a trial without a jury must explain, in his application:

(1) where the prosecutor alleges a danger of jury tampering:
   (a) what evidence there is of a real and present danger that jury tampering would take place;
   (b) what steps, if any, reasonably might be taken to prevent jury tampering; and
   (c) why, notwithstanding such steps, the likelihood of jury tampering is so substantial as to make it necessary in the interests of justice to order such a trial; or
(2) where the prosecutor proposes trial without a jury on some counts on the indictment:
   (a) why a trial by jury involving all the counts would be impracticable;
   (b) how the counts proposed for jury trial can be regarded as samples of the others; and

(c) why it would be in the interests of justice to order such a trial.

(CrimPR 3.23(3))

Where:

(i) the prosecutor applies for an order for a trial without a jury because of a danger of jury tampering; and
(ii) the application includes information that the prosecutor thinks ought not be revealed to an accused,

he must:

- omit that information from the part of the application that is served on that accused;
- mark the other part to show that, unless the judge otherwise directs, it is only for the court; and
- in that other part, explain why the prosecutor has withheld that information from that accused.

The hearing of an application must be in private, unless the judge otherwise directs. If the judge so directs, the hearing may be, wholly or in part, in the absence of an accused from whom information has been withheld.

(CrimPR 3.24)

68. UNFITNESS TO PLEAD/INSANITY

1. General

Where, on the trial of any person, the question arises, at the instance of the defence or otherwise, whether the defendant is under a disability such that, apart from CP(I)A 1964 (as amended by CP(IUP) A 1991 and the DVA 2004), would constitute a bar to his being tried, then, though ordinarily such a question falls to be determined as soon as it arises: **68-001**

(1) if, having regard to the nature of the supposed disability, the judge is of the opinion that it is inexpedient to do so, he may postpone consideration of the question of fitness to be tried, until any time up to the opening of the case for the defence; and

(2) if, before the question of fitness to be tried falls to be determined, the jury return a verdict of acquittal on all or each of the counts on which the defendant is being tried, that question shall not be determined.

Where one of several defendants becomes unfit after a jury has been empanelled, there is nothing to prevent the same jury from considering whether that defendant has committed the actus reus although the question of guilt would be removed. A fortiori, in a case of several defendants, where the principal is found unfit to stand trial by reason of mental illness, and a second as a result of a stroke, there is nothing to prevent a single jury once empanelled, proceeding to consider whether the principal defendant committed the actus reus while looking, in the case of the other fit defendant to both actus reus and mens rea (*R. v B* [2008] EWCA Crim 1997; [2009] 1 Cr. App. R. 19); it is not "inescapable" that separate trials should take place.

Proceedings under s.4 determine whether the defendant is fit to plead: it is not a criminal charge. In proceedings under s.4A:

(a) if a defendant is found to have committed the act, the verdict is not one of guilty, but a finding that he did the act or made the omission charged against him;

(b) the finding of the jury that a defendant has committed the act lacks a finding as to intent and is not, therefore, a finding of guilty of the offence;

(c) the criminal charge provisions of ECHR art.6 do not apply to proceedings which cannot result in a conviction; and

(d) proceedings under ss.4 and 4A comply with the requirements of art.6.

The submission that a person who is unfit to plead cannot have the fair trial required by art.6 because he cannot sufficiently understand the proceedings or give proper instructions and may therefore be unable to give evidence, is to confuse the rights assured by art.6 with the enjoyment of those rights. Persons under mental disabilities, whose condition does not prevent their being fit to plead to a criminal charge, may well be under a disadvantage in legal proceedings, whether civil or criminal. A judge should do his best to minimise that disadvantage, but might be unable to remove it totally (CP(I)A 1964 s.4(1)–(6)).

A trial in civil or criminal proceedings where the disadvantage has been minimised could be "fair" (*R. v Kerr* considering *T v United Kingdom* [2000] Crim. L.R. 187; *Brown v Stott* [2001] 2 All E.R. 97; *R. v Antoine* [1999] 2 Cr. App. R. 225).

2. THE TEST FOR UNFITNESS TO PLEAD

68-002 The classic test for fitness to plead was set out in *R. v Pritchard* (1836) 7 Car. & P. 303. There are three points to be enquired into:

(1) whether the defendant is mute of malice or not;
(2) whether he can plead to the indictment or not; and
(3) whether he is of sufficient intellect to comprehend the course of the proceedings in the trial so as to make a proper defence—to know that he might challenge any of the jury to whom he might object—and to comprehend the details of the evidence.

That test was reaffirmed in *R. v Podola* (1959) 43 Cr. App. R. 220. The word "comprehend" being considered to go no further in meaning than the word "understand". See also *R. v Robertson* (1968) 52 Cr. App. R. 690; *R. v Berry* (1978) 66 Cr. App. R. 156, where the court emphasised that although a person was highly abnormal, it did not mean that he was incapable of doing those things set out in *Pritchard* and *R. v Walls* [2011] EWCA Crim 443; [2011] 2 Cr. App. R. 6 where the court stated that the duty of the court is to consider whether the defendant is *unfit to plead according to those criteria in the light of all the evidence before it, including the expert psychiatric evidence*.

Assistance is also to be found in the decision of the Court of Appeal in *R. v M (John)* [2003] EWCA Crim 3452 where the directions of the trial judge on the six things he said that a defendant must be capable of doing were commended. A number of psychiatrists refer to this decision as a good example of the points they need to address.

Another relatively recent and helpful case on insanity and the availability of the defence is the decision of the Court of Appeal in *Loake v CPS* [2017] EWHC 2855 (Admin).

Most recently in *R. v Keal* [2022] EWCA Crim 341; [2022] 4 W.L.R. 41, this area of the law was considered. The CACD held that to establish the defence of insanity within the M'Naghten Rules on the ground of not knowing the act was "wrong", the defendant must establish both that: (a) he did not know that his act was unlawful; and (b) he did not know that his act was "morally" wrong. "Wrong" means both against the law and wrong by the standards of ordinary reasonable people.

> "Strictly a jury must be satisfied that the defendant did not know that what he was doing was against the law nor wrong by the standards of reasonable ordinary people. In practice how the jury is directed on this issue will depend on the facts and issues in the particular case."

The Court also determined that under the M'Naghten Rules, the defence of insanity is not available to a defendant who, although he knew what he was doing was wrong, he believed that he had no choice but to commit the act in question.

3. DETERMINATION OF FITNESS BY THE JUDGE; EVIDENCE

Legal representatives for the defendant are the persons best placed to decide whether to raise the issue of fitness to plead, and indeed to seek medical assistance to resolve the problem. There is, however, a separate and distinct responsibility in the judge to oversee the process so that if there is any question of the defendant's fitness to plead, he can raise it directly with his legal advisers (*R. v Erskine* [2009] EWCA Crim 1425; [2010] 2 Cr. App. R. 29). **68-003**

If the question of fitness to be tried is raised, it is determined by the judge. Although a judge can determine that someone is fit to be tried he must not make a determination that he is unfit except on the written evidence of two registered medical practitioners at least one of whom is duly approved—*R. v Ghalam* [2009] EWCA Crim 2285; [2010] 1 Cr. App. R. 12 (see also *R. v Borkan* [2004] EWCA Crim 1642; [2004] M.H.L.R. 216). There is no need for oral evidence (cf. MHA 1983 s.41(2)): *Narey v Customs and Excise Commissioners* [2005] EWHC 784 (Admin); [2005] M.H.L.R. 194.

The purpose of CP(I)A 1964 s.4A is to prevent a person from being detained unless he would have been found guilty at a criminal trial. It is imperative, therefore, that the same rules of evidence be applied to proceedings under s.4A as to those that would have applied if the trial were a criminal trial in the strict sense. The judge is entitled to admit a witness statement as hearsay evidence in accordance with the present practice (*R. v Chal* [2007] EWCA Crim 2647; [2008] 1 Cr. App. R. 18, followed in *R. v Creed* [2011] EWCA Crim 144; [2011] Crim. L.R. 644).

Save in clear cases, the judge must rigorously examine evidence of psychiatrists adduced before him and subject that evidence to careful analysis against the *Pritchard* criteria as interpreted in *Podola*. Unless the unfitness is clear, the fact that psychiatrists agree is not sufficient (*R. v Walls* [2011] EWCA Crim 443; [2011] 2 Cr. App. R. 6).

Finding that the defendant did the act, etc.

Where the judge determines that the defendant is under a disability, the trial will not proceed further, but a jury must then determine whether: **68-004**

(1) on the evidence, if any, already given at the trial; or
(2) on such evidence as may be adduced or further adduced by the prosecutor or by such person appointed by the court to put the case for the defendant,

it is satisfied, as respects each of the counts on which he was to be, or is being tried, that he did the act or made the omission charged against him as the offence (CP(I)A 1964 s.4A).

In such circumstances, the procedure on plea of not guilty (under CrimPR 25.9) applies, if the steps it lists have not already been taken, except that everything which that rule requires to be done by the defendant may be done instead by the person appointed to put the case for the defence. Under CrimPR 25.10(3)(c)(ii), the judge will explain to the jurors that their duty is to decide whether or not the defendant did the act or made the omission charged as an offence, not whether he is guilty of that offence. CrimPR 25.9(2)(e) (warning of consequences of defendant not giving evidence) does not apply (see CrimPR 25.10).

Care needs to be taken to ensure that the act to be proved is accurately particularised—see *R. v McKenzie* [2011] EWCA Crim 1550; [2011] 2 Cr. App. R. 27.

If, as respects that or any of the counts, the jury are:

(a) so satisfied, they must make a finding that he did the act or made the omission charged against him; or
(b) not so satisfied, they must return a verdict of acquittal, as if, on that count, the trial had proceeded to a conclusion.

Once it is clear that there is an issue, such cases need very careful case management to ensure that full information is provided to the court without delay. When full information is available, the judge will need to consider whether to postpone the issue of trial of fitness to plead under s.4(2), given the consequences that a finding of unfitness has for the defendant (see, e.g. *R. v M* [2001] EWCA Crim 2024).

In *R. v B* [2012] EWCA Crim 1799 the Court of Appeal reinforced the view that these cases require very careful case management and that they are quite different from the ordinary case before the Crown Court. In B the trial judge had refused to exclude evidence from an interview of the defendant despite finding that the defendant's condition was the same at the time of interview as it was at trial:

> "There is the extremely important public interest of ensuring that, where the court proceeds to see whether the defendant did the act, time is taken to ensure that the inquiry is handled justly and fairly."

If the judge determines that the defendant is unfit to plead, then it is his duty under s.4A(2) to consider who is the best person to be appointed by the court to put the case for the defence.

Note that:

- the duty is personal to the judge, who must consider afresh who is the best person to be appointed; and
- the person appointed should not necessarily be the same person who has represented the defendant to date, as it is the responsibility of the judge to be satisfied that the person appointed is the right person for this difficult task. The responsibility placed on the person so appointed is quite different to the responsibility placed on an advocate where he can take instructions from a client.

(*R. v Norman* [2008] EWCA Crim 1810; [2009] 1 Cr. App. R. 13)

CrimPR 25.10(3) provides that in exercising that power he must take account of all the circumstances, and in particular:

(i) the willingness and suitability (including the qualifications and experience) of that person;
(ii) the nature and complexity of the case;
(iii) any advantage of continuity of representation; and
(iv) the defendant's wishes and needs.

Under the present legislation the CACD, should it consider the resulting verdict unsafe or unsatisfactory, cannot order a retrial save in certain very limited circumstances (see *R. v Norman* [2008] EWCA Crim 1810; [2009] 1 Cr. App. R. 13):

- where the question of disability is determined after arraignment, the question of whether or not the defendant did the act or made the omission charged is to be determined by the jury by whom the defendant is being tried; and

- in the exceptional case, where despite the original finding of disability, at a later hearing the defendant is found to be fit to be tried, the procedure under ss.4A and 5 are inapplicable. The proper course is for the judge to hold a second s.4 hearing, and if the defendant is found fit to plead to order his arraignment (*R. (on the application of Hasani) v Blackfriars Crown Court* [2005] EWHC 3016 (Admin); [2006] 1 Cr. App. R. 27).

4. Disposal after special verdict of finding a disability

Where a special verdict is returned that the defendant is not guilty by reason of insanity, or findings have been made that the defendant is under a disability and that he did the act or made the omission charged against him the judge's powers of sentencing in relation to a case where the defendant was arraigned on or after 31 March 2005 are limited to making: **68-005**

(1) a hospital order (with or without a restriction order);
(2) a supervision order within the meaning of CP(I)A 1964 Sch.1A Pt 1 as added by DVA 2004 s.24 Sch.2; or
(3) an order for absolute discharge.

(CP(I)A 1964 s.5)

Where the offence to which the special verdict or findings relate is one where the sentence is fixed by law, and the court has the power to make a hospital order, then the hospital order must be one with a restriction order whether or not the court would otherwise have the power to make a restriction order (CP(I)A 1964 as substituted by DVA 2004 s.24).

DVA 2004 abolishes admission orders. Two important changes introduced by DVA 2004 are that the Secretary of State no longer has a role in deciding whether or not the defendant is admitted to hospital, and the judge is no longer able to order the defendant's admission to a psychiatric hospital without hearing any medical evidence (CP(I)A 1964 Sch.1A para.5).

Where a defendant is acquitted of all counts of the indictment, save a summary offence attached to it by virtue of CJA 1988 s.40, the judge is restricted to magistrates' powers; there is no finding of guilt, as such, and the defendant is not therefore an offender (*R. v Southwark Crown Court Ex p. Koncar* [1998] 1 Cr. App. R. 321).

In *The Secretary of State for the Home Department v MZ* [2020] UKUT 225 (IAC) it was held that an individual sentenced to a hospital order following a finding that he "is under a disability and that he did the act or made the omission charged against him" is neither subject to s.117C of the 2002 Act (as amended) nor to paras A398–399 of the Immigration Rules. He is excluded from the statutory provisions by s.117D(3)(a) and from the Immigration Rules concerning deportation.

Supervision order; CP(I)A 1964 Sch.1A

The supervision order introduced by DVA 2004 is an order which requires the person in respect of whom it is made ("the supervised person") to be under the supervision of a social worker or a probation officer ("the supervising officer") for a period specified in the order of not more than two years. It may require the **68-006** supervised person to submit, during the whole of that period, or such part of it as may be specified in the order, to treatment by or under the direction of a registered medical practitioner (CP(I)A 1964 para.1(1)).

The judge must not make a supervision order unless he is satisfied that:

(1) having regard to all the circumstances of the case, the making of such an order is the most suitable means of dealing with the defendant or appellant;
(2) the supervising officer intended to be specified in the order is willing to undertake the supervision; and
(3) arrangements have been made for the treatment intended to be specified in the order.

The order must either:

(a) specify the local social services authority area in which the supervised person resides or will reside, and require him to be under the supervision of a social worker of the local social services authority for that area; or
(b) specify the local justice area in which that person resides or will reside, and require him to be under the supervision of a probation officer appointed for or assigned to that area.

(CP(I)A 1964 s.5A and Sch.1A para.1(1))

Before making such an order, the judge must explain to the supervised person in ordinary language the effect of the order (including any requirements proposed to be included in it) and that a magistrates' court has power to review the order on the application either of the supervised person or of the supervising officer (CP(I)A 1964 Sch.1A paras 2 and 3(1)–(3)).

The offender has a duty to keep in touch with the supervising officer in accordance with instructions given to him and to notify him of any change of address (CP(I)A 1964 Sch.1A para.3(5)).

Administrative provisions

68-007 After making an order, the Crown Court officer will give CP(I)A 1964, copies of the order to a probation officer assigned to the court, and also to the supervised person, and to the supervising officer.

The officer will also send to the designated officer for the local justice area in which the supervised person resides or will reside a copy of the order; and such documents and information relating to the case as it considers likely to be of assistance to a court acting for that area in the exercise of its functions in relation to the order (CP(I)A 1964 Sch.1A para.3(4)).

Requirement as to medical treatment

68-008 An order may, if the judge is satisfied as set out in the next paragraph, include a requirement that the supervised person submit, during the whole of the period specified in the order or during such part of that period as may be so specified, to treatment by or under the direction of a registered medical practitioner with a view to the improvement of his mental condition.

The judge must however be satisfied on the written or oral evidence of two or more registered medical practitioners, at least one of whom is duly registered, that the mental condition of the supervised person:

(1) is such as requires and may be susceptible to treatment; but

(2) is not such as to warrant the making of a hospital order within the meaning of the MHA 1983.

The treatment required by the order must be one of the following kinds of treatment, specified in the order, that is to say:

(a) treatment as a non-resident patient at such institution or place as may be specified in the order; and
(b) treatment by or under the direction of such registered medical practitioner as may be so specified,

but the nature of the treatment must not be specified in the order except as mentioned in para.(a) or (b) (CP(I)A 1964 Sch.1A para.4(1)–(4)).

Treatment by a medical practitioner

Where the judge is satisfied on the written or oral evidence of two or more registered medical practitioners that, because of his medical condition, other than his mental condition, the supervised person is likely to pose a risk to himself or others, and the condition may be susceptible to treatment: **68-009**

(1) the order may (whether or not it includes a requirement under Sch.1A para.4) include a requirement that the supervised person submit, during the whole of the period specified in the order, or during such part of that period as may be so specified, to treatment by or under the direction of a registered medical practitioner with a view to the improvement of the condition;
(2) the treatment required by any such order must be such one of the following as may be specified in the order:
    (a) treatment as a non-resident patient at such institution or place as may be specified in the order; and
    (b) treatment by or under the direction of such registered medical practitioner, but

the treatment must not be specified in the order except as mentioned in (a) or (b) in 68-008.

Where the medical practitioner by whom, or under whose direction, the supervised person is being treated in pursuance of a requirement is of the opinion that part of the treatment can be better or more conveniently be given in, or at, an institution or place which is not specified in the order, and is one in, or at, which the treatment of the supervised person will be given by or under the direction of a registered medical practitioner, he may, with the consent of the supervised person, make arrangements for him to be treated accordingly. Such arrangements may provide for the supervised person to receive part of his treatment as a resident patient in an institution or place of any description (CP(I)A 1964 Sch.1A para.5).

Where any such arrangements are made for the treatment of a supervised person, the medical practitioner by whom the arrangements are made must give notice in writing to the supervising officer, specifying the institution or place, in or at, which the treatment is to be carried out; and the treatment provided for by the arrangements will be deemed to be treatment to which he is required to submit in pursuance of the supervision order.

While the supervised person is under treatment as a resident patient in pursuance of arrangements under para.6, the supervising officer will carry out the supervision to such extent only as may be necessary for the purpose of the revocation or amendment of the order (CP(I)A 1964 Sch.1A para.7).

Requirements as to residence

68-010 A supervision order may include requirements as to the residence of the supervised person, but before making such an order containing any such requirement, the judge must consider the home surroundings of the supervised person (CP(I)A 1964 Sch.1A para.8).

5. APPEAL AGAINST ORDER

68-011 A person in whose case a judge of the Crown Court makes:

(1) a hospital order or interim hospital order by virtue of CP(I)A 1964 ss.5 or 5A; or
(2) a supervision order under s.5,

may appeal to the CACD against the order, but only:

(a) with the leave of the CACD; or
(b) if the judge of the court of trial grants a certificate that the case is fit for appeal.

If, on such an appeal, the CACD considers that the appellant should be dealt with differently from the way in which the court below dealt with him, it may quash any order which is the subject of the appeal and may make such order, whether by substitution for the original order or by variation of or addition to it, as it thinks appropriate for the case and as the court below had power to make (CAA 1968 s.16A). The CACD may not order a retrial of the facts should it quash a finding that the defendant did the act *R. v McKenzie* ([2011] EWCA Crim 1550); [2011] 2 Cr. App. R. 27.

Note that:

(i) the fact that an appeal is pending against an interim hospital order under MHA 1983 does not affect the power of the Crown Court to renew or terminate the order or deal with the appellant on its termination;
(ii) where the CACD makes an interim hospital order by virtue of these provisions, the power of renewing or terminating it and of dealing with the appellant on its termination is exercisable by the Crown Court and not by the CACD, and the Crown Court is treated for the purposes of MHA 1983 s.38(7) (absconding offenders) as the court that made the order; and
(iii) the fact that an appeal is pending against a supervision order under CP(I)A 1964 s.5 does not affect the power of the Crown Court to revoke the order.

Where the CACD makes a supervision order the power of revoking or amending it is exercised as if the order had been made by the Crown Court (CAA 1968 s.16B inserted by the DVA 2004).

6. RESUMPTION OF A PROSECUTION WHEN A PATIENT BECOMES FIT TO PLEAD.

68-012 Where a defendant is subject to s.37/41 following a finding of unfitness, the Secretary of State requires from the responsible clinician a report every year updating the Secretary of State as to whether that defendant remains unfit or whether fitness has been regained.

There is nothing preventing the responsible clinician alerting the Secretary of State to any recovery of fitness at any point of the admission.

Where fitness has been regained, and the Secretary of State refers matters to the CPS who refer the case back to the court, then the s.37/41 order will remain in force until as such time as the defendant appears before the court or is returned to prison by the Hospital.

Hospitals minded to retain the patient for treatment would need to apply for a s.48 transfer following the ending of the s.37/41 and a remand into custody by the court. The potential difficulties if there is not a fresh transfer under s.48 or another section of the MHA would be a relapse in the defendant's mental state and their becoming unfit.

Should the prosecution decide to offer no evidence following a defendant who regains their fitness and was originally dealt with by way of a s.37/41 disposal under s.4A and the defendant has does not appear in court, then may be a consequential lack of clarity as to whether the s.37/41 remains in place or not.

There is guidance explaining the powers and responsibilities of the Secretary of State for Justice, the CPS and HMCTS when a restricted patient becomes fit to plead. The document sets out the procedure to be followed when a prosecution is resumed. The guidance can be found on the MoJ website (see *https://assets.publishing.service.gov.uk/government/uploads/system/uploads/attachment_data/file/612502/resuming-guidance-prosecution-fit-to-plead.pdf* [Accessed September 2022]).

69. VARIATION OF SENTENCE

Quick Guide

Introduction

69-001 Ordinarily, a sentence imposed or other order made by the Crown Court when dealing with an offender takes effect from the beginning of the day on which it is imposed unless the judge otherwise directs, but:

(1) as a court of record, the Crown Court has an inherent jurisdiction to rectify mistakes in its record (*R. v Saville* (1980) 70 Cr. App. R. 204); and, more importantly
(2) a sentence or order may be varied or rescinded under the provisions of SA 2020 s.385; and
(3) a "discounted" sentence, passed upon an offender in view of an undertaking to assist the authorities, may be subsequently reviewed (under SA 2020 ss.387–388) where it is shown that such assistance is not forthcoming.

1. Variation of sentence: SA 2020 s.385

General

69-002 A sentence may be varied or rescinded:

(1) within, and only within the period of 56 days beginning with the day on which the sentence was imposed or order made (SA 2020 s.385(2)) (*R. v Menocal* (1979) 69 Cr. App. R. 148; *R. v Hart* (1983) 5 Cr. App. R. (S.) 25; *R. v Stillwell* (1992) 94 Cr. App. R. 65; *R. v Bukhari* [2009] Crim. L.R. 300);
(2) in open court (*R. v Dowling* (1989) 88 Cr. App. R. 88) in the presence of the offender (*R. v Hussein* [2000] 1 Cr. App. R. (S.) 181) and after his representatives have had an opportunity to make submissions on the alteration. The hearing must be properly listed so that all interested parties may attend (*R. v Perkins* [2013] EWCA Crim 323; [2013] 2 Cr. App. R. (S.) 72).

A sentence cannot be varied or rescinded except by the court constituted as it was when the sentence was imposed or made, or, where the Crown Court comprised one or more justices, a court so constituted save for the omission of any one or more of those justices (SA 2020 s.385(4)). Where a sentence is rescinded and the matter considered afresh at a further sentencing hearing, there is no irregularity or impropriety in sentence being adjourned to a different judge; *R. v Catchpole* [2014] EWCA Crim 1037; [2014] 2 Cr. App. R. (S.) 66.

In *R. v Gordon* [2007] EWCA Crim 165; [2007] 2 Cr. App. R. (S.) 66 the CACD pointed out that the correction of an error, notwithstanding the expiry of the 56-day period, was permitted in *R. v Saville* [1980] 2 Cr. App. R. (S.) 26. In *R. v Nnaji* [2009] EWCA Crim 468; [2009] 2 Cr. App. R. (S.) 107 it was held that the 56-day limit does not prohibit the correction of a mere procedural irregularity in the way in which the order of the court was recorded, or a later procedural step to complete an inchoate order, but without affecting what has already been announced; (in that case, the calculation of days spent on remand would have no effect on the recorded sentence passed). However, any variation of substance made after the expiry of the 56-day period will be of no effect as it will have been made without jurisdiction (*R. v D* [2014] EWCA Crim 2340; [2015] 1 Cr. App. R. (S.) 23; *R. v Nguyen* [2016] EWCA Crim 448; [2016] 2 Cr. App. R. (S.) 18).

Section 385 provides a valuable safety net in the sentencing process, enabling the judge to reflect on the sentencing decision and if so minded, within the statutory period, to amend it. It is however no more and no less than a further hearing in the original case. As such it should be listed so that all the interested parties, not only the accused but also the victims, the public and the media, may be present if they wish.

Where the original sentence is rescinded within the 56-day period, there is nothing to prevent the judge from exercising his common law powers of adjournment to hear further argument and passing a fresh sentence after the expiry of the statutory period (*R. v Reynolds* [2007] EWCA Crim 538; [2007] 2 Cr. App. R. (S.), cf. *R. v Dunham* [1996] 1 Cr. App. R. (S.) 438).

The sentence or order as varied takes effect from the beginning of the day on which it was originally imposed or made, unless the court otherwise directs (SA 2020 s.385(5)).

"Sentence" defined

A "sentence" includes any order made by the court when dealing with the offender in respect of the offence (SA 2020 s.401), including recommendation for deportation (SA 2020 s.385(8)). **69-003**

"Variation" defined

The word "varied" is an ordinary English word and bears its dictionary meaning (*R. v Sodhi* (1978) 66 Cr. App. R. 260). The provisions empower the judge, in an appropriate case, to: **69-004**

(1) correct minor errors made in sentencing;
(2) change the nature of the sentence where necessary (e.g. *R. v Grice* (1978) 66 Cr. App. R. 167 (imprisonment varied to hospital order));
(3) reduce the sentence imposed if, after further reflection, it appears too severe; and
(4) increase the sentence originally passed, but only in exceptional cases (*R. v Newsome* (1970) 54 Cr. App. R. 485 under previous legislation); cf. *R. v Grice* (above) where, e.g.:
    (a) additional material is put before the judge (*R. v Reilly* (1982) 75 Cr. App. R. 266); or
    (b) it is clear that the original sentence was passed on an incorrect factual basis (*R. v Hart* (1983) 5 Cr. App. R. (S.) 25; *R. v McLean* (1988) 10 Cr. App. R. (S.) 18; *R. v Hadley* (1995) 16 Cr. App. R. (S.) 358, cf. *R. v Woop* [2002] EWCA Crim 58; [2002] 2 Cr. App. R. (S.) 65).

In *R. v White (Horace)* [2021] EWCA Crim 1511; [2022] 4 W.L.R. 10 it was held that the "slip rule" only applied to cases where there had been an error of law or where the court had proceeded on a basis of an obvious and material error of fact; and did not provide a means for the Crown simply to invite the court to impose a higher sentence.

As to the problems caused by "rescinding" rather than varying a sentence, see *R. v Smith* (1995) 16 Cr. App. R. (S.) 974, and *R. v Dunham* [1996] 1 Cr. App. R. (S.) 438. Where the judge, in imposing consecutive sentences for two offences, has properly had regard to the totality principle but in imposing one of the sentences has exceeded the maximum, he may vary the sentence so as to reduce the unlawful sentence and increase the other, provided the total is not increased (*R. v Lees* [1999] 1 Cr. App. R. (S.) 194, cf. *R. v Evans* (1992) 13 Cr. App. R. (S.) 377).

Procedure

69-005 CrimPR 28.4 applies where the Crown Court can vary or rescind a sentence or order, and authorises a judge, in addition to his other powers, to do so within the period of 56 days beginning with another accused's acquittal or sentencing where:

(1) accused persons are tried separately in the Crown Court on the same or related facts alleged in one or more indictments; and
(2) one is sentenced before another is acquitted or sentenced.

A judge may exercise his power:

(a) on application by a party; or
(b) on his own initiative; or
(c) at a hearing, in public or in private, or without a hearing.

The judge must announce at a public hearing:

(a) a decision to vary or rescind a sentence or order, or to refuse to do so; and
(b) the reasons for that decision.

However, the announcement need not be made by the same member or members as the court which has made the decision to be announced.

A party who wants a judge to exercise that power must:

(a) apply in writing as soon as reasonably practicable after:
 (i) the sentence or order that that party wants the court to vary or rescind; or
 (ii) where para.(2) above applies, the other accused's acquittal or sentencing;
(b) serve the application on the Crown Court officer, and each other party;
(c) in the application, explain why the sentence should be varied or rescinded; and
(d) specify the variation that the applicant proposes, and if the application is late, explain why.

The judge must not exercise his power in the accused's absence unless either: (a) he makes a variation proposed by the accused, or the effect of which is that the accused is no more severely dealt with under the sentence as varied than before; or (b) the accused has had an opportunity to make representations at a hearing (whether or not he in fact attends) (CrimPR 28.4).

In relation to proceeding in the absence of the offender, there may be cases where it is proper to proceed in the absence of the offender, including where he has clearly waived his right to be present (either expressly or by implication) or where he has absconded, but this ought to be an exceptional course (see *R. v May* (1981) 3 Cr. App. R. (S.) 165; *R. v Cleere* (1983) 5 Cr. App. R. (S.) 465; *R. v McLean* (1988) 10 Cr. App. R. (S.) 18; *R. v Hussein* [2000] 1 Cr. App. R. (S.) 181).

In *R. v Perkins* [2013] EWCA Crim 323; [2013] 2 Cr. App. R. (S.) 72 the variation hearing took place on a day when the judge ordered the case to be heard but without formal listing. Coincidentally, both counsel in the case happened to be appearing before him in a different case. Neither of them had their original papers. The judge obtained the court file and proceeded with his decision, notwithstanding submissions that the proposed variation should not take place in the absence of the accused, whether in court or by video link, unless he had waived his right to be present. The judge did not invite submissions from either counsel, observing that to require the accused to travel to court would be detrimental to his health and he proceeded to order the variation. In the opinion of the CACD, since no one with a direct interest in the case had any idea that it was to be listed, for those most closely concerned the hearing was effectively a private hearing. That should not happen.

Where a sentence has been passed or order made which is defective in form, it may be permissible to correct the error after the expiration of the time limit, so long as the correction can be treated as a matter of form rather than substance: *R. v Saville* [1981] Q.B. 12; [1980] 3 W.L.R. 151. The scope of the power to vary a sentence outside the statutory period appears to have been narrowed by *R. v D* [2014] EWCA Crim 2340; [2015] 1 Cr. App. R. (S.) 23, where the CACD held that a judge had not been entitled to vary an extended sentence to correct a defect in the way in which the sentence had been expressed, notwithstanding the fact that the offender would not have been adversely affected by the variation.

In *R. v Warren* [2017] EWCA Crim 226; [2017] 2 Cr. App. R. (S.) 5, the CACD summarised the current state of the law concerning the application of PCC(S)A 2000 s.155 (now SA 2020 s.385):

(a) where an error had occurred in the factual basis of sentence, this should be pointed out to the court as soon as possible and consideration should be given to correcting this at the earliest opportunity, preferably by revisiting sentence on the same day rather than on a subsequent day;
(b) a judge should not use the slip rule simply because there was a change of mind about the nature or length of sentence but the slip rule was available where the judge was persuaded that he had made a material error in the sentencing process whether of fact or of law. It was relevant in considering whether or not he had made a material error that the error might be corrected by the Court of Appeal on the Attorney General's application;
(c) the sooner the slip rule was invoked in such a case the better. The passage of time from the first decision to its revision was a material consideration as to how the power should be exercised (but there was a 56-day cut off in any event);
(d) a judge should not be unduly influenced by the prospect of a reference being made to change a sentence that he thought was right at the time by the mere threat of a review by the Attorney General. If the judge concluded that the sentence was not wrong in principle and was not unduly lenient, he should not change his mind simply because there was the possibility of a reference. The judge could then use the opportunity at the further sentencing hearing to give any further explanations for the original decision for the sentence;
(e) sentencing and re-sentencing should take place in the presence of the appellant and administrative convenience should not be allowed to degrade that principle. But, if for one reason or another, the appellant could not be brought to court within the 56-day period, there was a discretion to proceed

in his absence so long as there was an advocate who could fully represent the appellant in the sense of who was properly instructed as to the relevant facts and was able to assist the court to make pertinent submissions on the facts and the law; and

(f) although *Nodjoumi* no longer identified the basic rule in such cases, the appearance of justice and the impact of the change on a defendant where an error had not been induced by anything that he had said or done were relevant considerations and, in appropriate cases, could be reflected in a modest discount to the proposed revised sentence to reflect that fact.

The *CPD* has now been amended to provide further guidance on the application of SA 2020 s.385 (*CPD* VII s.1–s.4). The circumstances in which a variation of sentence may properly be made without a hearing will be confined to cases in which neither party objects to the proposed variation and in which the consequences for the defendant will be neutral or benign. Even where there is no objection to the making of a variation without a hearing, the court retains a discretion to convene a hearing, having regard to the overriding objective and the importance of dealing with criminal cases in public. See also *R. v Cox* [2019] EWCA Crim 71; [2019] 2 Cr. App. R. (S.) 6. In reaching a decision, the court should consider each of the relevant factors in CrimPR 1.1, and be astute to distinguish between variations involving the correction of errors of a quasi-administrative character, and variations of sentence in which the determination will be a matter of legitimate public interest. Not every error of law or fact would lead to a material increase in sentence. If the error would not lead to a material increase in sentence, then the power ought not be used. If, however, the error was relevant to an important component of the law or guidelines relating to sentencing, then this would militate in favour of using the slip rule procedure (*R. v George* [2019] EWCA Crim 2177; [2020] 4 W.L.R. 41).

Ancillary orders

69-006 Where the judge is contemplating making an ancillary order, such as a compensation order or a confiscation order, which requires consideration of further evidence as to the amount, etc., he ought to state that he is postponing that question at the time he passes the substantive sentence. He cannot otherwise make, for example, a compensation order after the expiration of the 56-day period (see *R. v Dorrian* [2001] 1 Cr. App. R. (S.) 135).

2. Review of discounted sentence under SA 2020 ss.387–388

General

69-007 Where a judge of the Crown Court has passed a sentence on a person in respect of an offence, and that person receives:

(1) a discounted sentence in consequence of his having offered in pursuance of a written agreement to give assistance to the prosecutor or investigator of an offence: but

  (a) knowingly fails to any extent to give assistance in accordance with the agreement; or

  (b) having given the assistance in accordance with the agreement, in pursuance of another written agreement gives or agrees to give further assistance;

OR

(2) a sentence which is not discounted, and in pursuance of a written agreement he subsequently gives or offers to give assistance to the prosecutor or investigator of an offence,

a specified prosecutor (i.e. the DPP, the DSFO, the DPP for Northern Ireland, or a prosecutor designated for the purposes of this section by one of those) may at any time refer the case back to the court by which the sentence was passed if that person is still serving his sentence and the specified prosecutor thinks it is in the interests of justice to do so.

A person does not fall within this provision if he was convicted of an offence for which the sentence is fixed by law and he did not plead guilty to the offence for which he was sentenced (see DISCOUNTS ON SENTENCE).

(SA 2020 ss.387–388).

A prosecutor who wants the court to exercise this power must:

(i) apply in writing as soon as practicable after becoming aware of the grounds for doing so;
(ii) serve the application on the court officer and the defendant; and
(iii) in the application:
  - explain why the sentence should be reduced, or increased, as appropriate; and
  - identify any other matter relevant to the court's decision, including any sentencing guideline or guideline case.

The general rule is that the application must be determined by the judge who passed the sentence, unless that judge is unavailable.

The judge must not determine the application in the accused's absence unless the accused has had an opportunity to make representations at a hearing (whether or not he in fact attends) (CrimPR 28.11).

The hearing

Where that judge is satisfied that the person concerned knowingly failed to give the assistance, he may substitute for the sentence to which the referral relates such greater sentence (not exceeding that which the original judge would have passed but for the agreement to give assistance) as he thinks appropriate. **69-008**

Note that:

(1) in a case of a person who falls within SA 2020 s.388, the judge may take into account the extent and nature of the assistance given or offered and substitute for the sentence to which the referral relates such lesser sentence as he thinks appropriate;
(2) any part of the sentence to which the referral relates which the person has already served must be taken into account in determining when the substitute sentence has been served (SA 2020 ss.387(9) and 388(11)); and
(3) the duty to give reasons applies to a sentence substituted under this provision above unless the judge thinks that it is not in the public interest to disclose that the original sentence was a discounted sentence or that the

substitute sentence is a discounted sentence (SA 2020 ss.387(7)–(8) and 388(9)–(10)).

Appeal

69-009 A person in respect of whom a reference is made under ss.387 or 388, and the specified prosecutor, are each given the right, subject to the leave of the CACD, to appeal against the decision of the judge of the Crown Court; CAA 1968 s.33(3) (limitation on appeal from the CACD) does not prevent a further appeal to the Supreme Court (SA 2020 s.389(2)).

Procedure on such an appeal is governed by CrimPR 39.

A defendant who denies guilt and withholds co-operation before conviction cannot hope to negotiate a reduced sentence in the CACD by co-operating after conviction. To do so might be to reward the offender for good behaviour during the course of his sentence. Furthermore, some offenders may be motivated to manufacture assistance after conviction; *R. v ZTR* [2015] EWCA Crim 1427; [2016] 1 Cr. App. R (S.) 15; see also *R. v ZAR, R. v AXN* [2016] EWCA Crim 590; [2016] 2 Cr. App. R. (S.) 33.

3. REDUCTION AND AMENDMENT OF SENTENCE ON SUBSEQUENT PROCEEDINGS UNDER POCA 2002

69-010 Where a judge varies a confiscation order under POCA 2002 ss.21, 22, 23, 29, 32 or 33, the effect of the variation is to vary the maximum period applicable in relation to the order under s.35(2A) and:

(1) if the result is that that maximum period is less than the term of imprisonment or detention fixed in respect of the order under SA 2020 s.129(3), the judge must fix a reduced term of imprisonment or detention in respect of the confiscation order under s.129(3) in place of the term previously fixed; or
(2) if (1) is not the case, the judge may amend the term of imprisonment or detention fixed in respect of the confiscation order under s.129(3).

(POCA 2002 s.39)

See generally CONFISCATION ORDERS.

70. VICTIM PERSONAL STATEMENTS

Views on sentence

The damaging and distressing effects of a crime on the victim clearly represent an important factor in the sentencing decision, and those effects may include the anguish and emotional suffering of the victim or, in a case of death, the surviving close family (*R. v Nunn* [1996] Crim. L.R. 210), but: **70-001**

(1) the sentence imposed by the court cannot *depend* upon the views of the victim of the offence; it is for the judge to assess the impact of the offence(s) on the particular victim, though where:
   (a) the sentence passed may actually aggravate the victim's distress, this may be a consideration; and
   (b) the victim's forgiveness may be treated as showing that the harm done by the offender is less than would otherwise be the case (see *R. v Roche* [1999] Crim. L.R. 339);

(2) the judge needs to balance the victim's views with the nature of the offence and the particular facts of the case (*R. v Nunn* [1996] Crim. L.R. 210; *R. v Hayes*, *The Times*, 5 April 1999; *R. v Roche* [1999] Crim. L.R. 339); and

(3) the judge is entitled to receive evidence of the psychological effects of the offence on the victim.

SCEW Guidelines on domestic abuse emphasise that point (1) above is particularly important in such cases; the victim's feelings of being responsible for the offender's incarceration being a familiar consequence of controlling and intimidating behaviour.

Victim personal statements

Victims of crime are invited to make a statement, known as a Victim Personal Statement ("VPS"). The statement gives victims a formal opportunity to say how a crime has affected them. It may help to identify whether they have a particular need for information, support and protection. The judge will take the statement into account when determining sentence. **70-002**

In some circumstances, it may be appropriate for relatives of a victim to make a VPS, for example where the victim has died as a result of the relevant criminal conduct. The Code of Practice for Victims of Crime, in force from 10 December 2013, gives further information about victims' entitlements within the criminal justice system, and the duties placed on criminal justice agencies when dealing with victims of crime (*CPD* VII: Sentencing Victim Personal statements F.1).

Such statements provide a practical way of ensuring that the sentencing judge considers (SA 2020 s.63) "any harm which the offence caused". They may, albeit incidentally to the purposes of the sentencing judge, identify a need for additional or specific support or protection for the victim of crime, to be considered at the end of the sentencing process (*R. v Perkins* [2013] EWCA Crim 323; [2013] 2 Cr. App. R. (S.) 72).

As to family impact statements by surviving members of the family of a deceased, see 70-005.

Procedure

70-003 When a police officer takes a statement from a victim, the victim should be told about the scheme and given the chance to make a VPS.

Note that:

(1) the decision about whether or not to make a VPS is entirely a matter for the victim; no pressure should be brought to bear on his decision, and no conclusion should be drawn if he chooses not to make such a statement;
(2) a VPS or an updated VPS may be made (in proper s.9 form, see 70-004) at any time prior to the disposal of the case. It will not normally be appropriate for a VPS to be made after the disposal of the case; there may be rare occasions between sentence and appeal when an update to the VPS may be necessary, for example, when the victim was injured and the final prognosis was not available at the date of sentence;
(3) however, VPS after disposal should be confined to presenting up-to-date factual material, such as medical information, and should be used sparingly.

(*CPD* VII Sentencing: VPS F.2)

Approach to statement

70-004 If the court is presented with a VPS the following approach, subject to the further guidance given by the CACD in *R. v Perkins* [2013] EWCA Crim 323; [2013] 2 Cr. App. R. (S.) 72 should be adopted:

(1) the VPS and any evidence in support should be considered and taken into account by the judge, prior to passing sentence;
(2) evidence of the effects of an offence on the victim contained in the VPS or other statement, must be in proper form, that is a witness statement made under CJA 1967 s.9 or an expert's report; and served in good time upon the accused's solicitor or the accused, if he is not represented;
(3) except where inferences can properly be drawn from the nature of or circumstances surrounding the offence, a sentencing judge must not make assumptions unsupported by evidence about the effects of an offence on the victim;
(4) in all cases it will be appropriate for a VPS to be referred to in the course of the sentencing hearing and/or in the sentencing remarks. Whilst there is a presumption that a VPS will be read aloud, if the victim wishes, this remain subject to judicial discretion as to whether and, if so, how much of, the statement may be read and by whom;
(5) the judge must pass what he considers to be the appropriate sentence having regard to the circumstances of the offence and of the offender, taking into account, so far as he considers it appropriate, the impact on the victim; and
(6) the opinions of the victim or the victim's close relatives as to what the sentence should be are therefore not relevant, unlike the consequences of the offence on them; victims should be advised of this. If, despite the advice, opinions as to sentence are included in the statement, the judge should pay no attention to them.

In *R. v Perkins* the CACD called attention to the "somewhat haphazard and slovenly approach" to the time when the statement was served that may have developed in some parts of the country. Unless there was some breakdown in communication, late service of the statements was wholly inappropriate and wrong in principle.

VC 1.12, 13 and 14 make it clear that:

(a) the CPS must ensure that the VPS and information about the victim's preference is served on the court in a timely manner to enable the judge to consider whether, and what sections of, the VPS should be read aloud or played, and who will read it;

(b) HMCTS court staff must ensure wherever possible that the police or relevant Witness Care Unit are notified within one working day of the judge's decision about whether, and what sections of, the VPS should be read aloud or played, and who will read it; and

(c) the Witness Care Unit (or police if they are acting as the main point of contact in the case) must wherever possible notify the victim of the judge's decision about whether, and what sections of, the VPS should be read aloud or played, and who will read it in a timely manner so that the victim can make arrangements to attend court if necessary.

The procedure under (a) is not necessary where the case is not proceeding on the charges to which the VPS relates, since in which that case the VPS remains unused material.

The process does not create or constitute an opportunity for the victim to suggest or discuss the type or level of sentence to be imposed. The distinction is important, and is sometimes misunderstood. It is, however, well exemplified in *Nunn* [1996] 2 Cr. App. R. (S.) 136 (*CPD* VII F.3).

Family impact statements

In cases in which the victim has died as a result of the relevant criminal conduct, the victim's family is not a party to the proceedings, but does have an interest in the case. Bereaved families have particular entitlements under the Code of Practice for Victims of Crime. All parties should have regard to the needs of the victim's family and ensure that the trial process does not expose bereaved families to avoidable intimidation, humiliation or distress. **70-005**

In so far as it is compatible with family members' roles as witnesses, the court should consider the following measures:

(1) practical arrangements being discussed with the family and made in good time before the trial, such as seating for family members in the courtroom; if appropriate, in an alternative area, away from the public gallery;

(2) warning being given to families if the evidence on a certain day is expected to be particularly distressing; and

(3) ensuring that appropriate use is made of the scheme for VPS, in accordance with the Procedure in this chapter.

The judge should consider providing a written copy of his sentencing remarks to the family after sentence has been passed. Judges should tend in favour of providing such a copy, unless there is good reason not to do so, and the copy should be provided as soon as is reasonably practicable after the sentencing hearing (*CPD* VII Sentencing: Families bereaved by homicide and other criminal conduct G.1–3).

Impact statements for businesses

70-006 If the victim, or one of the victims, is a business or enterprise (including charities or public body; for example, a school or hospital), of any size, a nominated representative may make an Impact Statement for Business ("ISB"). The ISB gives a formal opportunity for the judge to be informed how a crime has affected a business or other body. He will take the statement into account when determining sentence. This does not prevent individual employees from making a VPS about the impact of the same crime on them as individuals. Indeed the ISB should be about the impact on the business or other body exclusively, and the impact on any individual included within a VPS (*CPD* VII Sentencing I: Impact Statements for Businesses I.1 as amended by *Amendment No.8* [2019] EWCA Crim 495). An ISB or an updated ISB may be made (in proper s.9 form) at any time prior to the disposal of the case. It will not be appropriate for an ISB to be made after disposal of the case but before an appeal (*CPD* VII I.3).

A person making an ISB on behalf of a business or other body, the nominated representative, must be authorised to do so on behalf of the business or other body, either by nature of their position, such as a director or owner, or a senior official, or by having been suitably authorised, such as by the owner or Board of Directors or governing body. The nominated representative must also be in a position to give admissible evidence about the impact of the crime on the business. This will usually be through first hand personal knowledge, or using business documents (as defined in CJA 2003 s.117) (*CPD* VII I.4).

If the nominated representative leaves the business before the case comes to court, he will usually remain the representative, as the ISB made by him or her will still provide the best evidence of the impact of the crime, and he could still be asked to attend court. If necessary, a further ISB may be provided to the police if there is a change in circumstances. This could be made by an alternative nominated representative. However, the new ISB will usually supplement, not replace, the original ISB and again must contain admissible evidence. The prosecutor will decide which ISB to serve on the defence as evidence, and any ISB that is not served in evidence will be included in the unused material and considered for disclosure to the defence (*CPD* VII I.5).

The ISB must be made in proper form, that is as a witness statement made under s.9 of the CJA 1967 or an expert's report; and served in good time upon the defendant's solicitor or the defendant, if he or she is not represented. The maker of an ISB can be cross-examined on its content (*CPD* VII. I.7).

The ISB and any evidence in support should be considered and taken into account by the judge, prior to passing sentence. The statement should be referred to in the course of the sentencing hearing and/or in the sentencing remarks. Subject to the judge's discretion, the contents of the statement may be summarised or read out in open court; the views of the business or body should be taken into account in reaching a decision. The judge will pass what he judges to be the appropriate sentence having regard to the circumstances of the offence and of the offender, taking into account, so far as the court considers it appropriate, the impact on the victims and others affected, including any business or other corporate victim. Opinions as to what the sentence should be are therefore not relevant. If, despite the advice, opinions as to sentence are included in the statement, the judge will pay no attention to them (*CPD* VII I.8 and 9).

Except where inferences can properly be drawn from the nature of or circumstances surrounding the offence, the judge will not make assumptions unsupported by evidence about the effects of an offence on a business or other body (*CPD* VII I.10).

71. VIEW BY JURY

Introduction

71-001 The trial judge on application, or on the judge's own initiative, may permit the jury:

(1) where such procedure is relevant to an issue in the case;
(2) at any time up to the commencement of the summing up,

to view real evidence of a nature which makes it impracticable to produce in the court room; and this includes a view of the locus of the alleged offence.

It is for the judge to say what is relevant, not the jury. If the judge is of the opinion that it is relevant for the jury to view the scene of the crime, a formal view ought to be ordered, under the guidance of the judge with the assistance of the advocates. If it is not relevant, the jury should not be directed towards it (*R. v Albarus* [1989] Crim. L.R. 905).

It is always entirely in the judge's discretion whether to allow a view or not; though such precautions, as may seem necessary to the judge, ought to be taken to secure that the jury does not improperly receive evidence out of court (*R. v Martin* (1865–72) L.R. 1 C.C.R. 378).

In *R. v Gurney*, the then Lord Chief Justice (Lord Widgery) suggested that a view is a slightly dangerous thing for a judge to order because there are certain rules, and, if they are not observed, difficulties are bound to arise.

Unless the judge otherwise directs, the court officer will arrange a trial to take place in a courtroom provided by the Lord Chancellor. He will, however, arrange for the court and the jury (if there is one) to view any place required by the judge (CrimPR 3.33). A note to the rule indicates that there may be circumstances in which the court may conduct all or part of the hearing outside a courtroom.

Simple views and formal views

71-002 The authorities show that a distinction is to be drawn between:

(1) a simple view at which no witnesses attend; and
(2) a formal view at which witnesses attend, objects are pointed out and, positions and lines of sight identified and measurements made.

A view such as that in (1) is on a par with the common case where a thing is too large or cumbrous to bring into court but is left in the yard outside. It is everyday practice for the jury in such a case to be taken to see the thing. There are no witnesses and there is no demonstration.

It is very different when a witness demonstrates to the jury at the scene of a crime. By giving a demonstration he gives evidence just as much as when in the witness box he describes the place in words or refers to it on a plan. Such a demonstration on the spot is more effective than words can ever be, because it is more readily understood. It is more vivid as the witness points to the very place where he stood. It is more dramatic as he re-enacts the scene. He will not, as a rule, go stolidly to the spot without saying a word. To make it intelligible, he will say at least: "I stood here" or "I did this," and, unless held in check, he will start to give his evidence all over again as he remembers "with advantages what [things] he did that day." But however much, or however little, the witness repeats his evidence or improves on it, the fact remains that every demonstration by a witness is itself evidence in the case. A simple pointing out of a spot is a demonstration and part of the evidence. Whilst giving it the witness is still bound by the oath which he has taken to tell the truth. If he wilfully makes a demonstration which he knew to be false, he would be guilty of perjury.

Personal visits by jurors

In *Parry v Boyle* (1986) 83 Cr. App. R. 310, a case dealing with magistrates, Glidewell LJ said as follows (substituting the phrase "fact finding body" for "the justices"): **71-003**

> "I myself regard it as undesirable that [the fact finding body] should have a view unaccompanied by the parties or their representatives. There are two matters which may arise upon which the parties may wish to comment further. The first is that it may be that some feature of the locality has altered since the time of the incident itself. The second matter is that the [fact finding body] on a view may see something which impresses them, which the parties then have not seen and the parties of course have no opportunity to comment upon it because it is not very helpful for the[fact finding body] to come back and say: 'We noticed such and such a feature', when the parties themselves had not seen it and cannot, therefore, evaluate its significance.
>
> Of course, I appreciate that [the fact finding body] sitting in their own localities will very often have what will be a quite considerable knowledge of the places at which offences with which they are dealing, are alleged to have taken place. But if they think it right and helpful to them to view the scene of an alleged criminal offence before arriving at their decision, as a general rule they should not do so without being accompanied by the parties or the parties' representatives. Moreover, they should not do so after speeches have been concluded or at least, if they do, they should give the parties the opportunity of commenting on any feature that the parties may themselves have observed and may wish to comment on. Accordingly, since that which is to be derived from the view forms part of the evidence, it should, as I advise, take place at or before the conclusion of the evidence."

Formal view as part of the evidence in the case

A formal view is part of the evidence and must be treated as such; it is in substitution for, or supplemental to, plans, photographs and the like. It follows that it must be held in the presence of the judge: **71-004**

(1) it is the very essence of a criminal trial that it must be decided on the evidence before the court and not on any outside information; and
(2) the judge and jury must be present throughout the giving of the evidence and every part of it, so as to be able to appreciate it and assess its worth, and throughout the speeches of the advocates too;
(3) the summing-up of the evidence by an impartial judge with a trained mind is an essential part of every criminal trial: but it can only properly be done by a judge who has heard all the evidence and seen all the demonstrations by witnesses; and
(4) the judge, for instance, may notice something at a demonstration which may be of vital import, but passes unnoticed by everyone else until he draws at-

tention to it; his presence ensures not only that the proceedings are properly conducted but also that no relevant point on either side is overlooked.

Presence of parties; the jury

71-005 It is a cardinal principle that once a court is composed and a defendant is in the jury's charge nothing which thereafter ensues must occur unless all the persons taking part in the trial are present. The only time when it is permissible for the jury to be absent is when a point of law, or some other matter which necessarily has to be dealt with in their absence, is being discussed. All participating members of the court must be present at a viewing of the scene of the crime, and the judge should be present to control proceedings (see *R. v Hunter* (1985) 81 Cr. App. R. 40).

The jury must stay together and hear all the evidence together; it is not possible to divide them by allowing some to view something which the others do not (see *R. v Gurney* [1977] R.T.R. 211; [1976] Crim. L.R. 567).

It follows that it is quite wrong for the judge to suggest that members of the jury go along and have a look, or that one or two do and then report back. It is not possible under our system for the jury's work to be apportioned out, as it were, and for two jurors to be sent off to look at one thing and two others to look at another. That has no sort of place in our system (*R. v Gurney*; *R. v Smyth*, *The Times*, 16 September 1998).

In *R. v Davies* [2000] 1 Cr. App. R. 8, the CACD thought that whether or not in the particular case there might be a risk of a juror acting on his own initiative, the judge ought to give some further appropriate direction.

With the enactment of CJCA 2015 and the new offences of jurors researching details of a case and the use of the internet, it will be even more important for the judge to give specific warnings to jurors over conducting an informal view or their own investigations. In many homicide and other complex cases footage from a 360 degree camera forms part of the evidence placed before the jury and this material may, in many cases, take the place of need for a traditional view for the jury.

Presence of parties; the defendant

71-006 In the absence of exceptional circumstances the presence of the defendant is as necessary at a formal view as at any other part of the trial; he may be able to point out some matter of which his legal advisers are unaware or about which others on the view are mistaken (*R. v Ely Justices Ex p. Burgess* [1992] Crim. L.R. 888; *Gibbons v DPP* [2000] All E.R. (D.) 2250).

Where the judge is informed that the defendant does not desire to attend, the judge need not insist on his presence, this is equivalent to allowing him to be absent; if a defendant declines to attend a view which the judge thinks desirable in the interests of justice, he cannot afterwards raise the objection that his absence of itself made the view illegal and a ground for quashing the conviction, if one follows, though he could, of course, object if any evidence were given outside the scope of the view as ordered.

Preparation for a formal view

71-007 Before embarking on a formal view there must be absolute clarity about precisely what is to happen on it, about who is to stand in what position, about what, if any, objects should be placed in a specific position and about who will do what (*M v DPP* [2009] EWHC 752 (Admin); [2009] 2 Cr. App. R. 12).

The judge should produce ground rules for the view, after discussion with the advocates. The rules should contain details of what the jury will be shown and in what order and who, if anyone, will be permitted to speak and what will be said. The rules should also make provision for the jury to ask questions and receive a response from the judge, following submissions from the advocates, while the view is taking place (*CPD* VI Trial 26J: Juries: Views 26J.1).

Procedure at a formal view

Procedure on a formal view might follow this course (based on the speeches of the Privy Council in *Karamat v The Queen* (1956) 40 Cr. App. R. 13): **71-008**

(1) a court officer ought to be sworn to keep the jury;
(2) the jury may be transported to the locus where they may be joined by the judge, advocates and court officers;
(3) where jurors and witnesses travel in the same transport as advocates, there must be no conversation between them relating to the case;
(4) at their destination the jury may be checked by the court officer, and also checked at any other place where they stopped during the day;
(5) any juror who wishes to ask a question ought to put it through the judge, and the witness may give a demonstration as the answer, and counsel may be invited by the judge to put questions through him, but no cross-examination may be allowed;
(6) the judge ought to be present the whole time so that he can observe and control the proceedings; he may ask a witness to place himself at a particular spot which he has mentioned in his evidence or to show to the jury the place where someone else stood or the direction from which someone came;
(7) the judge must make every effort to see that the witnesses make no communication to the jury except to give a demonstration; and
(8) at the conclusion of the view, the court should return to the courtroom, where cross-examination of the witnesses, and speeches will be heard.

Evidence given after jury enclosed

Once they have retired to consider their verdict, the jury may not be given any additional evidence, additional matter or material to assist them. They may come back and ask the judge to repeat for their benefit evidence which has been given, but they may not come back and ask for anything new and the judge must now allow them to have anything else (*R. v Davies* (1976) 62 Cr. App. R. 194). As to views see *R. v Lawrence* (1968) 52 Cr. App. R. 163 (cf. *R. v Nixon* (1968) 52 Cr. App. R. 218 where the view was at the request of the defence). As to distances and measurements, see *R. v Corless* (1972) 56 Cr. App. R. 341. **71-009**

72. VULNERABLE ACCUSED AND WITNESSES

QUICK GUIDE

1. GENERAL

The background

72-001 In respect of eligibility for special measures, "vulnerable" and "intimidated" witnesses are defined (in YJCEA 1999 s.16); "vulnerable" includes those under 18 years of age and persons with a mental disorder or learning disability, a physical disorder or disability, or are likely to suffer fear or distress in giving evidence because of their own circumstances or those relating to the case.

However, many other people giving evidence in a criminal case, whether as a witness or defendant, may require assistance: the judge is required to take "every reasonable step" to encourage and facilitate the attendance of witnesses and to facilitate the participation of any person, including the defendant (CrimPR 3.8(3)(a) and (b)). This includes enabling a witness or accused person to give their best evidence, and enabling an accused to comprehend the proceedings and engage fully with his defence. The pre-trial and trial process should, so far as necessary, be adapted to meet those ends. Regard should be had to the welfare of a young accused as required by CYPA 1933 s.44, and generally to CrimPR 1 and 3 (the overriding objective and the court's powers of case management) (*CPD* I General Matters 3 Vulnerable people in the courts D.1 and 2). Section 28 of the YJCEA 1999 has now been rolled out across the courts in England and Wales for the pre-recording of cross-examination and re-examination in certain cases (see SPECIAL MEASURES DIRECTIONS).

The rules

72-002 Under Pt 3 of the CrimPR, the judge:

(1) must identify the needs of witnesses at an early stage (CrimPR 3.2(2)(b)); and
(2) may require the parties to identify arrangements to facilitate the giving of evidence and participation (CrimPR 3.13(c)(iv) and (v)).

There are various statutory special measures that the court may utilise to assist a witness in giving evidence (see also SPECIAL MEASURES DIRECTIONS) CrimPR 18 gives the procedures to be followed. A judge should note the "primary rule" which requires him to give a direction for a special measure to assist a child witness or qualifying witness and that in such cases an application to the court is not required (CrimPR 18.9) (see *R. v Cox* [2012] EWCA Crim 549; [2012] 2 Cr. App. R. 6; *R. v Wills* [2011] EWCA Crim 1938; [2012] 1 Cr. App. R. 2; and *R. v E* [2011] EWCA Crim 3028; [2012] Crim. L.R. 563).

Part 3 also provides for directions for the participation of a witness companion while a witness gives evidence.

In *R. v Wills* [2011] EWCA Crim 1938; [2012] 1 Cr. App. R. 2, the CACD endorsed the approach taken by the report of the Advocacy Training Council (ATC) "*Raising the Bar: the Handling of Vulnerable Witnesses, Victims and Defendants in Court*" (2011). The report includes and recommends the use of "toolkits" to assist advocates as they prepare to question vulnerable people at court. The Inns of Court College of Advocacy, which was formerly the ATC, was established by the Council of the Inns of Court which now covers this area: *https://icca.ac.uk* [Accessed September 2022].

Note that:

(a) further toolkits are available through the Advocate's Gateway which is managed by the ATC's Management Committee: *http://www.theadvocatesgateway.org/* [Accessed September 2022];
(b) these toolkits represent best practice. Advocates should consult and follow the relevant guidance whenever they prepare to question a young or otherwise vulnerable witness or accused; judges may find it helpful to refer advocates to this material and to use the toolkits in case management;
(c) "*Achieving Best Evidence in Criminal Proceedings*" (MoJ 2022) describes best practice in preparation for the investigative interview and trial: *https://www.gov.uk/government/publications/achieving-best-evidence-in-criminal-proceedings* [Accessed September 2002]. The 2022 revision promotes a "victim-centered" and "trauma-informed" approach.

(*CPD* I 3D: Vulnerable people in the courts 6–8)

2. QUESTIONING WITNESSES

Responsibility of judge

All witnesses, including the defendant and defence witnesses, should be enabled to give the best evidence they can. In relation to young and/or vulnerable people, this may mean departing radically from traditional cross-examination. The form and extent of appropriate cross examination will vary from case to case (*CPD* I General Matters 3E and 3G—Ground rules hearings to plan the questioning of a vulnerable witness or defendant and Vulnerable defendants) (see also CrimPR 3.9 in relation to ground rules hearings). **72-003**

The judge is responsible for controlling questioning. Over-rigorous or repetitive cross-examination of a child or a vulnerable witness should be stopped. Intervention by the judge or intermediary (if any) is minimised if questioning, taking account of the individual's communication needs, is discussed in advance and ground rules are agreed and adhered to (*CPD* I 3E.1).

The Court of Appeal recognised that in some cases there may be compelling reasons why a time limit upon cross-examination should be strictly enforced (*R. v Bhatt (Manoj)* [2022] EWCA Crim 926; [2022] 7 WLUK 44).

Planning the questioning; ground rules

Discussion of ground rules is: **72-004**

(1) *required* in all intermediary trials; they must be discussed between the judge or advocates and intermediary before the witness gives evidence; the intermediary must be present but is not required to take the oath (the intermediary's declaration is made just before the witness gives evidence);

(2) good practice, even if no intermediary is used, in all young witness cases and in other cases where a witness or an accused has communication needs; discussion before the day of trial is preferable to give advocates time to adapt their questions to the witness's needs.

It may be helpful for a trial practice note of boundaries to be created at the end of the discussion; the judge may use such a document in ensuring that the agreed ground rules are complied with (*CPD* I 3E.2 and 3).

Form of cross-examination

72-005 For adult non-vulnerable witnesses an advocate will usually put his case so that the witness will have the opportunity of commenting upon it and/or answering it. When the witness is young or otherwise vulnerable, the judge may dispense with the normal practice and impose restrictions on the advocate "putting his case" where there is a risk of a young or otherwise vulnerable witness failing to understand, becoming distressed or acquiescing to leading questions. If there is more than one accused, the judge should not permit each advocate to repeat the questioning of a vulnerable witness; in advance of the trial, the advocates should divide the topics between them, with the advocate for the first accused leading the questioning, and the advocate(s) for the other accused asking only ancillary questions relevant to their client's case, without repeating the questioning that has already taken place on behalf of the others (*CPD* I 3E.5).

Where limitations on questioning are necessary and appropriate, they must be clearly defined. The judge has a duty to ensure that they are complied with and should explain them to the jury and the reasons for them (*CPD* I 3E.4).

In relation to inconsistencies during cross-examination:

(1) instead of commenting on inconsistencies during cross-examination, following discussion between the judge and the advocates, the advocate or the judge may point out important inconsistencies after (instead of during) the witness's evidence; the judge should also remind the jury of these during his summing up; but
(2) the judge should be alert to alleged inconsistencies that are not in fact inconsistent, or are trivial.

(*CPD* I 3E.4)

As to the use of "body maps" in sexual offences, see *CPD* I 3E.6.

3. INTERMEDIARIES

72-006 Intermediaries are communication specialists (not supporters or expert witnesses) whose role is to facilitate communication between the witness and the court, including the advocates. Intermediaries are independent of the parties and owe their duty to the court (see *Registered Intermediaries Procedural Guidance Manual*, Ministry of Justice, 2020): *https://assets.publishing.service.gov.uk/government/uploads/system/uploads/attachment_data/file/955316/registered-intermediary-procedural-guidance-manual.pdf* [Accessed September 2022] (*CPD* I General Matters 3F: Intermediaries—*CPD 2015 (Amendment No.1)* March 23, 2016 [2016] EWCA Crim 97).

Intermediaries for witnesses, with the exception of the accused, are one of the special measures available under the YJCEA 1999 (see SPECIAL MEASURES

DIRECTIONS). There is currently no statutory provision in force for intermediaries for accused persons (CorJA 2009 s.104 (not yet implemented) creates a new section (YJCEA 1999 s.33BA) which will provide an intermediary to an eligible accused only while giving evidence) (*CPD* I 3F.11).

The judge may direct the appointment of an intermediary to assist a defendant at trial (either solely when giving evidence or throughout the trial) and, where necessary, in preparation for trial: *R. (on the application of AS) v Great Yarmouth Youth Court* [2011] EWHC 2059 (Admin); [2012] Crim. L.R. 478; *R. v H* [2003] EWCA Crim 1208; *The Times,* 15 April 2003; *R. (on the application of C) v Sevenoaks Youth Court* [2009] EWHC 3088 (Admin); [2010] 1 All E.R. 735; *R. (on the application of D) v Camberwell Green Youth Court* [2005] UKHL 4; [2005] 2 Cr. App. R. 1; *R. (on the application of TP) v West London Youth Court* [2005] EWHC 2583 (Admin); [2006] 1 Cr. App. R. 25. There is, however, no presumption that a defendant will be so assisted and, even where an intermediary would improve the trial process, appointment is not mandatory (*R. v Cox* [2012] EWCA Crim 549; [2012] 2 Cr. App. R. 6). The court should adapt the trial process to address a defendant's communication needs (*R. v Cox*). It will rarely exercise its inherent powers to direct appointment of an intermediary but where a defendant is vulnerable or for some other reason experiences communication or hearing difficulties, such that he or she needs more help to follow the proceedings than her or his legal representatives readily can give having regards to their other functions on the defendant's behalf, then the court should consider sympathetically any application for the defendant to be accompanied throughout the trial by a support worker or other appropriate companion who can provide that assistance. This is consistent with CrimPR 3.9(3)(b) (see *CPD* I 3D.2); consistent with the observations in *R. v Cox* (see *CPD* I D.4); *R. (OP) v Ministry of Justice* [2014] EWHC 1944 (Admin) and *R. v Rashid* [2017] EWCA Crim 2; and consistent with the arrangements contemplated at *CPD* I 3G.8.

(*CPD* I 3F.12 as amended by amendment 7 to the CPD)

Selection assessment

Ministry of Justice regulations only apply to Registered Intermediaries appointed for prosecution and defence witnesses through its Witness Intermediary Scheme. All defendant intermediaries—professionally qualified or otherwise—are "non-registered" in this context, even though they may be a Registered Intermediary in respect of witnesses. 72-007

Even where a judge concludes he has a common law power to direct the provision of an intermediary, the direction will be ineffective if no intermediary can be identified for whom funding would be available.

The process of appointment should begin with assessment by an intermediary and a report. The revised *CPD* refers to the scarcity of intermediaries. Whereas the position was that assessment should be considered if a child or young person under 18, as a result of the revised *CPD* there is now no presumption that witnesses and defendants under 18 (including those under 11) will be assessed by an intermediary. In the light of the scarcity of intermediaries, the appropriateness of assessment must be decided with care to ensure their availability for those witnesses and defendants who are most in need. The decision should be made on an individual basis, in the context of the circumstances of the particular case (*CPD* I 3F.4 and 5).

The court may exercise its inherent powers to direct appointment of an intermediary to assist a defendant giving evidence or for the whole trial. Terms of appointment are for the court and there is no illogicality in restricting the appointment to the defendant's evidence (*R. v R* [2015] EWCA Crim 1870), when the "most pressing need" arises (*OP v Secretary of State for Justice* [2014] EWHC 1944 (Admin); [2015] 1 Cr. App. R. 7, DC). Directions to appoint an intermediary for a defendant's evidence will thus be rare, but for the entire trial extremely rare (*CPD* I F.13).

An application for an intermediary to assist a defendant must be made in accordance with Pt 18 CrimPR. Where an intermediary report is available it should be with the application. Arrangements for funding of intermediaries for defendants depend on the stage of the appointment process (*CPD* I F.14–16).

Absence of intermediary; adapting the trial process

72-008 In the absence of an intermediary for the accused, trials should not be stayed where an asserted unfairness can be met by the trial judge adapting the trial process with appropriate and necessary caution (*R. v Cox* [2012] EWCA Crim 549; [2012] 2 Cr. App. R. 6).

This includes setting ground rules for all witness testimony to help the accused follow proceedings; for example, directing that all witness evidence be adduced by simple questions, with witnesses asked to answer in short sentences; and short periods of evidence, followed by breaks to enable the defendant to relax and for counsel to summarise the evidence for him and to take further instructions (*CPD* I 3F.21).

4. Familiarisation; photographs of court facilities

72-009 Resident Judges in the Crown Court should, in consultation with HMCTS managers responsible for court security matters, develop a policy to govern under what circumstances photographs or other visual recordings may be made of court facilities, such as a live link room, to assist vulnerable or child witnesses to familiarise themselves with the setting, so as to be enabled to give their best evidence. For example, a photograph may provide a helpful reminder to a witness whose court visit has taken place sometime earlier. Resident Judges should tend to permit photographs to be taken for this purpose by intermediaries or supporters, subject to whatever restrictions the Resident Judge or responsible person considers to be appropriate, having regard to the security requirements of the court (*CPD* I 3F.29).

5. Court procedure: vulnerable accused

Before the proceedings

72-010 If a vulnerable accused, especially one who is young, is to be tried jointly with one who is not, the judge should consider at the PCMH whether the vulnerable accused should be tried on his own, but should only so order if satisfied that a fair trial cannot be achieved by use of appropriate special measures or other support for the accused.

If a vulnerable accused is tried jointly with one who is not, the judge should consider whether any of the modifications set out in this direction should apply in the circumstances of the joint trial and, so far as practicable, make orders to give effect to any such modifications (*CPD* I General Matters 3G: Vulnerable defendants 3G.1).

Thus, it may be appropriate to arrange that a vulnerable accused should visit, out of court hours and before the trial, sentencing or appeal hearing, the courtroom in which that hearing is to take place so that he can familiarise himself with it.

Note that:

(1) where an intermediary is being used to help the accused to communicate at court, the intermediary should accompany the accused on his pre-trial visit;
(2) the visit will enable the accused to familiarise himself with the layout of the court, and may include matters such as: where he will sit, either in the dock or otherwise; court officials (what their roles are and where they sit); who else might be in the court, for example those in the public gallery and press box; the location of the witness box; basic court procedure; and the facilities available in the court;
(3) if the accused's use of the live link is being considered, he should have an opportunity to have a practice session.

(*CPD* I 3G.2, 3 and 4)

Public or media interest

If any case against a vulnerable accused has attracted or may attract widespread public or media interest, the assistance of the police should be enlisted to try and ensure that he is not, when attending the court, exposed to intimidation, vilification or abuse. **72-011**

Note that:

(1) CJA 1925 s.41 prohibits the taking of photographs (see CONTEMPT OF COURT) of accused and witnesses (among others) in the court building or in its precincts, or when entering or leaving those precincts; a direction reminding media representatives of the prohibition may be appropriate;
(2) the judge should also be ready at this stage, if he has not already done so, where relevant to make a reporting restriction under CYPA 1933 s.39 (see REPORTING AND ACCESS RESTRICTIONS) or, on an appeal to the Crown Court from a youth court, to remind media representatives of the application of CYPA 1933 s.49; and
(3) the provisions of *CPD* accompanying Pt 6 should be followed.

(*CPD* I 3G.5 and 6)

The trial, sentencing or appeal hearing: general

Subject to the need for appropriate security arrangements, the proceedings should, if practicable, be held in a courtroom in which all the participants are on the same or almost the same level. Subject again to the need for appropriate security arrangements, a vulnerable accused, especially if he is young, should normally, if he wishes, be free to sit with members of his family or others in a like relationship, and with some other suitable supporting adult such as a social worker, and in a place which permits easy, informal communication with his legal representatives. The court should ensure that a suitable supporting adult is available throughout the course of the proceedings (*CPD* I 3G.7 and 8). **72-012**

It is generally desirable that those responsible for the security of a vulnerable accused who is in custody, especially if he is young, should not be in uniform, and that there should be no recognisable *police presence* in the courtroom save for good reason (*CPD* I 3G.12).

The judge should consider whether *robes and wigs* should be worn, and should take account of the wishes of both a vulnerable accused and any vulnerable witness.

The trial, sentencing or appeal hearing: proceedings

72-013 It is essential that at the beginning of the proceedings, the judge should:

(1) ensure that what is to take place has been explained to a vulnerable accused in terms he can understand; and
(2) ensure in particular that the role of the jury has been explained;
(3) remind those representing the vulnerable accused and the supporting adult of their responsibility to explain each step as it takes place and, at trial, explain the possible consequences of a guilty verdict and credit for a guilty plea; and
(4) remind any intermediary of their responsibility to ensure that the vulnerable accused has understood the explanations given to him.

Throughout the trial he should continue to ensure, by any appropriate means, that the accused understands what is happening and what has been said by him, the advocates and witnesses.

The trial should be conducted according to a timetable which takes full account of a vulnerable defendant's ability to concentrate, thus:

(a) frequent and regular breaks will often be appropriate;
(b) the whole trial is conducted in clear language that the defendant can understand; and
(c) the judge should ensure that evidence-in-chief and cross-examination are conducted using questions that are short and clear; the conclusions of the "ground rules" should be followed, and advocates should use and follow the "toolkits" (see 72-002).

A vulnerable accused who wishes to give evidence by *live link*, in accordance with YJCEA 1999 s.33A may apply for a direction to that effect; the procedure in CrimPR 18.14–18.17 should be followed. Before making such a direction, the court must be satisfied that it is in the interests of justice to do so and that the use of a live link would enable the defendant to participate more effectively as a witness in the proceedings. The direction will need to deal with the practical arrangements to be made, including the identity of the person or persons who will accompany him (*CPD* I 3G.11).

The trial, sentencing or appeal hearing: public and press

72-014 The judge should be prepared to restrict attendance by members of the public in the court room to a small number, perhaps limited to those with an immediate and direct interest in the outcome. He should rule on any challenged claim to attend. However, facilities for reporting the proceedings (subject to any restrictions under CYPA 1933 ss.39 or 49) must be provided.

He may restrict the number of reporters attending in the courtroom to such number as is judged practicable and desirable. In ruling on any challenged claim to attend in the court room for the purpose of reporting, the court should be mindful of the public's general right to be informed about the administration of justice.

Where it has been decided to limit access to the courtroom, whether by reporters or generally, arrangements should be made for the proceedings to be relayed, audibly and if possible visually, to another room in the same court complex to which the media and the public have access if it appears that there will be a need for such additional facilities.

Those making use of such a facility should be reminded that it is to be treated as an extension of the court room and that they are required to conduct themselves accordingly (*CPD* I 3G.13 and 14).

73. WELSH LANGUAGE CASES

Introduction

73-001 Section 22(1) of the Welsh Language Act 1993 provides that in any legal proceedings in Wales the Welsh language may be spoken by any party, witness or other person who desires to use it, subject in the case of proceedings in a court other than a magistrates' court, to such prior notice as may be required by rules of court; and any necessary provision for interpretation shall be made accordingly.

A number of matters concerning Welsh language cases have been dealt with by means of practice directions and protocols, including:

(1) the Practice Direction issued by the Lord Chief Justice in 1998;
(2) a supplementary Practice Direction issued by the Presiding Judges on 28 February 2000;
(3) a Practice Direction issued by the Presiding Judges in May 2001 on appeals from magistrates' courts against conviction; and
(4) a Protocol for the Listing of Cases where the Welsh language is used, issued by the Presiding Judges in December 2005.

However, see now *CPD* I 3H, 3J and 3K; CrimPR 3.34 (Use of Welsh language at Crown Court trial); also the *Guide for Judges: Use of the Welsh Language in Wales*, published online to the judiciary on 15 November 2012.

The purpose of the Directions is that, in the administration of justice in Wales, the English and Welsh languages should be treated on a basis of equality (*CPD* I 3K.1).

As to forms, see 73-010.

General

73-002 *CPD* makes it the responsibility of the legal representatives in every case in which the Welsh language may be used by any witnesses or party, or in any document which may be placed before the court, to inform the Crown Court of that fact so that appropriate arrangements can be made for the listing of the case (*CPD* I 3K.2). [NB: the position is different in the magistrates' court, where any party or witness is entitled to use Welsh without giving prior notice; see the *Magistrates Court Protocol for Listing Cases where the Welsh Language is used*, January 2008.]

In particular:

(1) if the possible use of the Welsh language is known at the time of sending or appeal to the Crown Court, the court should be informed immediately after sending, or when the notice of appeal is lodged; otherwise the court should be informed as soon as the possible use of the Welsh language becomes known;
(2) if costs are incurred as a result of failure to comply with these Directions, a wasted costs order may be made against the defaulting party and/or his legal representatives.

(*CPD* I 3K.4–5)

An advocate in a case in which the Welsh language may be used must raise that matter at the PTPH and endorse details of it on the form, so that appropriate directions may be given for the progress of the case.

Where the trial will take place in Wales and a participant wishes to use the Welsh language, he must serve notice on the court officer, or arrange for such a notice to be served on his behalf:

(1) at or before the PTPH; or
(2) in accordance with any direction given by the court; and

if such a notice is served, the court officer must arrange for an interpreter to attend the hearing (CrimPR 3.34).

If a defendant in a court in England asks to give or call evidence in the Welsh language, the case should not be transferred to Wales. In ordinary circumstances, interpreters can be provided upon request (*CPD* I 3J.1).

Listing

The listing officer, in consultation with the Resident Judge, should ensure that a case in which the Welsh language may be used is listed, wherever practicable, before a Welsh-speaking Judge, and in a court in Wales with simultaneous translation facilities (*CPD* I 3K.8). **73-003**

Interpreters

Whenever an interpreter is needed to translate evidence from English into Welsh or from Welsh into English, the court listing officer will contact the Welsh Language Unit who will ensure that an accredited interpreter attends (*CPD* I 3K.9). **73-004**

Jurors

The law does not permit the selection of jurors in a manner which enables the court to discover whether a juror does or does not speak Welsh, or to secure a jury whose members are bilingual, to try a case in which the Welsh language may be used (*CPD* I 3K.6). **73-005**

The Jury Bailiff when addressing the jurors at the start of their period of jury service must inform them that each may take an oath or affirm in Welsh or English as he or she wishes. After the jury has been selected to try a case, and before it is sworn, the court officer swearing in the jury must inform the jurors in open court that each may take an oath or affirm in Welsh or English as he or she wishes. A juror who takes the oath or affirms in Welsh should not be asked to repeat it in English.

Where Welsh is used by any party or witness in a trial, an accredited interpreter will provide simultaneous translation from Welsh to English for the jurors who do not speak Welsh. There is no provision for the translation of evidence from English to Welsh for a Welsh-speaking juror.

The jury's deliberations must be conducted in private with no other person present and therefore no interpreter may be provided to translate the discussion for the benefit of one or more of the jurors (*CPD* I 3K.10–13).

Witnesses

When each witness is called the court officer administering the oath or affirmation must inform the witness that he or she may be sworn or affirm in Welsh or English as he or she wishes. **73-006**

A witness who takes the oath or affirms in Welsh should not be asked to repeat it in English (*CPD* I 3K.14).

Documents and evidence

73-007 A person who wishes to use the Welsh language is entitled to file all documents and evidence in Welsh. They are not required (and should not be directed) to file documents or evidence in English, or to provide translated copies. The HMCTS Welsh Language Unit will translate the documents.

Opening/closing of Crown Courts

73-008 Unless it is not reasonably practicable to do so, the opening and closing of the court should be performed in Welsh and English (*CPD* I 3K.15).

Role of Liaison Judge

73-009 If any question or problem arises concerning the implementation of these directions, contact should in the first place be made with the Liaison Judge for the Welsh language through the Wales Circuit Office: HMCTS WALES/GLITEM CYMRU, 3rd Floor, Churchill House/3ydd Llawr Tŷ Churchill, Churchill Way/Ffordd Churchill, Cardiff/Caerdydd, CF10 2HH, 029 2067 8300 (*CPD* 3K.16).

Forms

73-010 CrimPR 5.2 provides that:

(1) any Welsh language form set out in *CPD*, or in the *Criminal Costs Practice Direction*, is for use in connection with proceedings in courts in Wales;
(2) both a Welsh form and an English form may be contained in the same document; and
(3) where only a Welsh form, or only the corresponding English form, is served, rubric in Welsh and English must be added; the Crown Court officer, or the person who served the form, must, on request, supply the corresponding form in the other language to the person served.

74. WITNESS SUMMONSES AND WARRANTS

Witness summons on application

Where a judge of the Crown Court is satisfied that: 74-001

(1) a person is likely to be able to give evidence likely to be material evidence, or produce any document or thing likely to be material evidence, for the purpose of any criminal proceedings before the court; and
(2) it is in the interests of justice to issue a summons to secure the attendance of that person to give evidence or to produce the document or thing, he must, subject to the following provisions, issue a witness summons directed to the person concerned and requiring him to:
   (a) attend before the Crown Court at the time and place stated in the summons; and
   (b) give the evidence or produce the document or thing.

The judge may refuse to issue the summons if any requirement relating to the application is not fulfilled (CP(AW)A 1965 ss.2 and 2D).

An application must be made as soon as reasonably practicable, after service on that person, of the relevant documents under CDA 1998 Sch.3 para.1, the transfer of the proceedings to the Crown Court or preferment of any voluntary bill.

As to procedure, see 74-004. As to the issue of a summons of the judge's own motion, see 74-009. As to the issue of a warrant, see 74-010.

Penalty for disobedience

A person who, without just excuse, disobeys a witness summons requiring him to attend the court is guilty of contempt and may be punished summarily as if his contempt had been committed in the face of the court. 74-002

The same applies to a person who, without just excuse, disobeys a requirement made by the court under s.2A. The punishment must not exceed three months imprisonment (see CONTEMPT OF COURT) (CP(AW)A 1965 s.3).

Power to require advance production

A witness summons which is issued under s.2 (74-001) and which requires a person to produce a document or thing as mentioned in s.2(2) (74-001) may also require him to produce the document or thing: 74-003

(1) at a place stated in the summons; and
(2) at a time which is so stated and precedes that stated under s.2(2),

for inspection by the person applying for the summons (CP(AW)A 1965 s.2A).

Application for summons, etc.: general rule

A party wishing the judge to issue a summons, warrant or order must apply as soon as practicable after becoming aware of the grounds for doing so: 74-004

(1) identifying the proposed witness; and

(2) explaining:
 (a) what evidence the proposed witness can give or produce;
 (b) why it is likely to be material evidence; and
 (c) why it would be in the interests of justice to issue such process.

(CP(AW)A 1965 s.2A; CrimPR 17.3, 17.4 and 17.8)

Where the proceedings concerned relate to an offence that is the subject of a deferred prosecution agreement within the meaning of CCA 2013 Sch.17, an application must be made as soon as is reasonably practicable after the suspension of the proceedings is lifted under para.2(3) of that Schedule.

The application may be made orally unless CrimPR 17.5 (see 74-005) applies or the judge otherwise directs.

Where someone wishes the judge to allow an application to be made orally, he must give as much notice as the urgency of his application permits to those on whom he would otherwise have served the application in writing, and in doing so, explain the reasons for the application and for wishing the judge to consider it orally.

Where it is in writing it must be in the form set out in the *CPD* containing the same declaration of truth as a witness statement.

The party applying must serve the application in every case on the court officer, as directed by the judge, and as required by CrimPR 17.5.

The procedure is set out in CrimPR 17.3.

The judge may issue (or withdraw) a witness summons, warrant or order with or without a hearing. If there is a hearing it must be in private unless the court otherwise directs. The procedure (which applies also to applications under BBEA 1879 s.7, see INVESTIGATIVE ORDERS AND WARRANTS) is set out in CrimPR 17.

The judge may shorten or extend (even after it has expired) a time limit under the CrimPR; he may also allow an application required to be in writing under the CrimPR to be given orally (CP(AW)A 1965 s.2(6A)).

Where summons is to produce document, etc.

74-005 Where (apart from an application to produce in evidence a copy of an entry in bank records) the witness summons applied for requires a proposed witness:

(1) to produce in evidence a document or thing; or
(2) to give evidence about information apparently held in confidence, that relates to another person, the application must be in writing in the form required by CrimPR 17 and the party applying must serve it:
 (a) on the proposed witness, unless the judge otherwise directs; and
 (b) if the judge so directs, on a person to whom the proposed evidence relates, or another party.

Where this rule applies, a witness summons must not be issued unless:

(i) everyone served has had at least 14 days in which to make representations, including representations about whether there should be a hearing before the summons is issued; and
(ii) the judge is satisfied that he has been able to take account of the rights and duties, including rights of confidentiality, of the proposed witness and of any person to whom the evidence relates (see, e.g. *R. (on the application*

of B) v Stafford Combined Court [2006] EWHC 1645 (Admin); [2006] 2 Cr. App. R. 34 in relation to a patient's medical records).

(CrimPR 17.5)

Summons no longer needed

If: **74-006**

(1) a document or thing is produced in pursuance of a requirement imposed by a witness summons under s.2A (74-001);
(2) the person applying for the summons concludes that a requirement imposed by the summons under s.2(2) (74-001) is no longer needed; and
(3) accordingly he applies to the Crown Court for a direction that the summons shall be of no further effect, a judge may direct accordingly.

(CP(AW)A 1965 s.2B)

The procedure is governed by CrimPR 17.7 (74-008).

Application to make summons ineffective

If a witness summons issued under s.2 (74-001) is directed to a person who: **74-007**

(1) applies to the Crown Court;
(2) satisfies the court that he was not served with notice of the application to issue the summons and that he was neither present nor represented at the hearing of the application; and
(3) satisfies the court that he cannot give any evidence likely to be material evidence or, as the case may be, produce any document or thing likely to be material evidence,

the judge may direct that the summons be of no effect (CP(AW)A 1965 s.2C).

The general principles are that material required to be produced on a summons:

(a) must be prima facie admissible (*R. v Cheltenham Justices Ex p. Secretary of State for Trade* [1977] 1 All E.R. 460; see also *R. v Derby Magistrates Court Ex p. B* [1996] 1 Cr. App. R. 385; *R. v H(L)* [1997] 1 Cr. App. R. 176);
(b) must be material, i.e. relevant to an issue in the case (*R. v Reading Justices Ex p. Berkshire CC* [1996] 1 Cr. App. R. 239); and
(c) must *not* be subject to public interest immunity (*R. v Cheltenham Justices Ex p. Secretary of State for Trade* [1977] 1 All. E.R. 460; *R. v K* (1993) 97 Cr. App. R. 342).

It is immaterial whether or not the CrimPR require the person to be served with notice of the application to issue the summons, or whether they enable the person to be present or represented at the hearing of the application.

An application under this section must be made in accordance with CrimPR 17.7.

In (2) in this paragraph "served" means:

(i) served in accordance with the CrimPR in a case where such rules require the person to be served with notice of the application to issue the summons;
(ii) served in such way as appears reasonable to the court to which the application is made, in any other case.

The judge may refuse to make a direction under this section if any requirement relating to the application under this section is not fulfilled (CP(AW)A 1965 s.2C(4)).

Where a summons is issued on application by a party and the judge later makes a direction that it shall be of no effect, the person on whose application the summons was issued may be ordered to pay the whole or any part of the costs of the application under this section, to be assessed by the Crown Court officer (CP(AW)A 1965 s.2C(8) and (9)).

The issue of a purely speculative summons may well amount to an "improper, unreasonable or negligent act" capable of being the subject of a wasted costs order (*R. v Cheltenham Justices v Secretary of State for Trade* [1977] 1 All. E.R. 460; also *Re Ronald A Prior & Co (Solicitors)* [1996] 1 Cr. App. R. 248).

Application to withdraw; assessment of relevance and confidentiality

74-008 Where a person served with an application for a witness summons requiring him to produce in evidence a document or thing objects to its production on the ground either that:

(1) it is not likely to be material evidence; or
(2) even if it is likely to be material evidence, the duties or rights, including rights of confidentiality, of the proposed witness or of any person to whom the document or thing relates outweigh the reasons for issuing a summons,

the judge may:

(a) require the proposed witness to make the document or thing available for the objection to be assessed; and
(b) invite the proposed witness or any representative of his, or a person to whom the document or thing relates or any representative of his, to help him assess the objection.

(CrimPR 17.6)

Issue of witness summons of judge's own motion

74-009 For the purpose of any criminal proceedings before him a judge may of his own motion issue a witness summons directed to a person and requiring him to:

(1) attend before the court at the time and place stated in the summons; and
(2) give evidence, or produce any document or thing specified in the summons.

If such a witness summons is directed to a person who:

(a) applies to the Crown Court; and
(b) satisfies the judge that he cannot give any evidence likely to be material evidence or, as the case may be, produce any document or thing likely to be material evidence,

the judge may direct that the summons be of no effect (CP(AW)A 1965 ss.2D and 2E).

The procedure is governed by CrimPR 17.

The judge may refuse to make a direction under this section if any requirement relating to the application under this section is not fulfilled.

Issue of warrant

If a judge of the Crown Court is satisfied by evidence on oath that a witness in respect of whom a witness summons is in force is unlikely to comply with the summons, he may issue a warrant to arrest the witness and bring him before the court before which he is required to attend, provided that a warrant must not be issued unless the judge is satisfied by such evidence that the witness is likely to be able to give material evidence or produce any document or thing likely to be material evidence in the proceedings. **74-010**

Where a witness who is required to attend before the Crown Court by virtue of a witness summons fails to attend in compliance with the summons, a judge may:

(1) in any case, cause to be served on him a notice requiring him to attend the court forthwith or at such time as may be specified in the notice;
(2) if he is satisfied that there are reasonable grounds for believing that that person has failed to attend without just excuse, or if he has failed to comply with a notice under (1) issue a warrant to arrest him and bring him before the court,

provided the prosecutor proves that notice has been given (*R. v Abdulaziz* [1989] Crim. L.R. 717) (CP(AW)A 1965 s.4).

Culpable forgetfulness is not a "reasonable excuse" (*R. v Lennock* (1993) 97 Cr. App. R. 228).

Remand of witness

A witness brought before the court in pursuance of a warrant under s.4 may be remanded: **74-011**

(1) in custody; or
(2) on bail (with or without sureties),

until such time as the court may appoint for receiving his evidence or dealing with him under s.3 of the Act (see 74-002); and where a witness attends a court in pursuance of a notice under (1) of 74-009 the judge may direct that the notice shall have effect as if it required him to attend at any later time appointed by the court for receiving his evidence or dealing with him (CP(AW)A 1965 s.4(3)).

The power to remand in custody under s.4 is to remand until such time as the witness is released from further attendance at court (*R. (on the application of TH) v Wood Green Crown Court* [2006] EWHC 2683 (Admin); [2007] Crim. L.R. 727).

There is no appeal from a remand in custody; no separate appeal procedure is provided, and being a matter relating to trial on indictment judicial review is currently excluded by virtue of SCA 1981 s.29(3). It is distinct from the contempt of court punishable under CP(AW)A 1965 s.3 (see 74-002).

The Law Commission has recommended (Law Com. No.324 (2010)) that the statute be amended to permit judicial review in such cases.

In order to avoid a witness who fails to appear in response to a summons having to be remanded, it is better practice either:

(a) for the warrant to be backed for bail; or
(b) for the officers to be directed not to execute the warrant, except at the Crown

Court, if satisfied that the witness will attend voluntarily or will accompany them.

(*R. v Popat* [2008] EWCA Crim 1927; (2009) 172 J.P. 24)

Service outside the UK

74-012 A summons or order requiring a person to attend before the court for the purpose of giving evidence in criminal proceedings may be issued or made notwithstanding that the person in question is outside the UK, and may be served outside the UK in accordance with arrangements made by the Secretary of State.

Such service does not impose any obligation under the law of England and Wales to comply with it, so that failure to do so does not constitute contempt of court, nor is it a ground for issuing a warrant, unless that person is subsequently served in the UK.

Where a witness summons is issued or a witness order is made by the Crown Court in such circumstances, it is sent to the Secretary of State with a view to its being served in accordance with arrangements made by him (CJ(IC)A s.2).

75. YOUTH REHABILITATION ORDERS

Quick Guide

1. General

The youth rehabilitation order ("YRO") provides in relation to offenders under 18, like the community order for those aged 18 and over, a single generic community sentence, within which the judge may include one or more requirements variously designed to provide for punishment, protection of the public, reduction of re-offending and reparation. **75-001**

A YRO with intensive supervision and surveillance, or with fostering, may be imposed, but only where the court is dealing with an imprisonable offence (SA 2020 ss.178 and 180) (see 75-011). The YRO replaces curfew orders, exclusion orders, supervision orders and action plan orders, which will continue in force in relation to offences committed before 30 November 2009. The YRO will apply to offences committed on or after that date.

The commencement order expressly saves attendance centre orders, which may, it seems, be made in respect of offenders aged 16 or 17.

A YRO is not, save in the two instances mentioned above, dependent on the offence being punishable with imprisonment.

As to failure to comply with the requirements of such an order, and its revocation and amendment, see 75-020.

The Sentencing Council (Sentencing Children and Young People) (SC(SCYP)) came into effect for those sentenced from 1 June 2017 onwards. Paragraphs 6.23 to 6.41 set out general guidance on YROs.

SA 2020 s.196 makes provision for the transfer of such an order to Northern Ireland.

Power to make order

Where a person under 18 is convicted of an offence, the judge before whom he is convicted may make a YRO, imposing on him any one or more of the requirements set out in SA 2020 ss.184–186 and Sch.6. These requirements are set out in the table at 75-008. **75-002**

The judge's power to make a YRO is subject to ss.179 and 180 of the SA 2020. Before imposing a YRO the judge must be satisfied that the offence/s is/are serious enough to warrant such a sentence (s.179(2)). SA 2020 s.177 specifies a range of situations where the judge does not have the power to make a YRO, for example, where the sentence is fixed by law.

Before making a YRO the judge must obtain and consider information about the offender's family circumstances and the likely effect of such an order on those circumstances (SA 2020 s.179(6)).

Requirements of the order

75-003 Where the judge imposes a YRO, he must be satisfied that:

- the requirement/s is/are the most suitable for the offender (SA 2020 s.186(3)); and
- the restrictions on liberty are commensurate with the seriousness of the offence/s (SA 2020 s.186(6)). Both the content and length of the order are relevant to this consideration.

Before making:

- a YRO imposing two or more requirements; or
- two or more YROs in respect of associated offences,

the judge must consider whether, in the circumstances of the case, the requirements to be imposed by the order/s is/are compatible with each other (SA 2020 s.186(10)).

The judge must ensure, as far as practicable, that any requirement imposed by an order is such as to avoid:

- any conflict with the offender's religious beliefs;
- any interference with the times, if any, at which the offender normally works or attends school or any other educational establishment; and
- any conflict with the requirements of any other YRO to which the offender may be subject (SA 2020 s.186(11)(c)).

Effect of plea of guilty

75-004 The SC(SC&YP) guideline sets out that the maximum level of reduction for a guilty plea is one-third (para.5.4). The guideline also sets out that the reduction in sentence for a guilty plea can be taken into account by imposing one type of sentence rather than another, for example by reducing a custodial sentence to a community sentence, or by reducing a community sentence to a different means of disposal. Alternatively, the court could reduce the length or severity of any punitive requirements attached to a community sentence (para.5.10). It also provides that the court must always have regard to the principal aim of the youth justice system, which is to prevent offending by children and young people. It is, therefore, important that the court ensures that any sentence imposed is an effective disposal (para.5.11) and where a court has imposed one sentence rather than another to reflect the guilty plea, there should normally be no further reduction on account of the guilty plea. Where, however, the less severe type of sentence is justified by other factors, the appropriate reduction for the plea should be applied in the normal way (para.5.12).

Date of taking effect

75-005 A YRO ordinarily takes effect on the day on which it is made (SA 2020 s.189). However, the judge may order that it takes effect on a later date (SA 2020 s.189(2)).

If a detention and training order ("DTO") is in force in respect of an offender, the judge making a YRO in respect of the offender may order that it is to take effect instead, either:

- when the period of supervision begins in relation to the DTO; or

- on the expiry of the term of the DTO (SA 2020 s.181(1)(b)).

The references to a DTO include an order made under s.211 of the Armed Forces Act 2006 (DTOs made by service courts) (SA 2020 s.181(2)).

Other existing orders

The judge must not make a YRO in respect of an offender at a time when: **75-006**

- another YRO; or
- a reparation order,

is in force in respect of the offender, unless when he makes the order he revokes the earlier order (SA 2020 s.181(4)). Where the earlier order is revoked, SA 2020 Sch.7 para.12 (provision of copies of orders) applies to the revocation as it applies to the revocation of a YRO (SA 2020 Sch.7 para.27(5)).

Concurrent and consecutive orders

Where the judge is dealing with an offender who has been convicted of two or more associated offences, and in respect of *one of the offences*, he makes an order of *any* of the following kinds: **75-007**

- a YRO with intensive supervision and surveillance ("ISS");
- a YRO with fostering; or
- any other YRO,

he may not make an order of *any other* of those kinds in respect of the other offence/s (SA 2020 s.183) (emphasis added).

If the judge makes two or more YROs with ISS, or with fostering, both or all of the orders must take effect at the same time (SA 2020 s.183(3)).

Where requirements of the *same kind* are included in two or more YROs, the judge must direct, in relation to each requirement of that kind, whether:

- it is to be concurrent with the other requirement/s of that kind, or any of them; or
- it and the other requirement/s of that kind, or any of them, is/are to be consecutive (SA 2020 s.183(5)) (emphasis added).

However, the judge may not direct that two or more fostering requirements are to be consecutive (SA 2020 s.183(6)). Where the judge directs that two or more requirements of the same kind are to be consecutive:

- the number of hours, days or months specified in relation to one of them is additional to the number of hours, days, or months specified in relation to the other/s; but
- the aggregate number of hours, days or months specified in relation to both or all of them must not exceed the maximum number which may be specified in relation to any one of them (SA 2020 s.183(7)).

Requirements are "of the same kind" if they fall within the same part of Sch.6 to the SA 2020 (s.183(8)).

75-008

2. TABLE OF AVAILABLE REQUIREMENTS

The table sets out the requirements which may be included in a youth rehabilitation order: (As mentioned above, note that from 1 December 2020 the provisions in CJA 2003 and CJIA 2008 are repealed and replaced by SA 2020 ss.173–199 and Sch.6 and the table should be read accordingly).

No.	Name	Requirements	SA 2020 Sch.6	Restrictions	Notes
1	Activity	To: (1) participate, on such number of days as may be specified in the order, in activities at a specified place, or places; (2) participate in a specified activity, or activities, on a specified number of days; (3) participate in one or more residential exercises for a continuous period, or periods comprising such number or numbers of days as may be specified in the order; (4) engage in activities in accordance with instructions of the responsible officer on such number of days as may be specified in the order.	Pt 1	Unless imposed as part of an ISS requirement (see No.17), the number of days specified in an order must not, in the aggregate, be more than 90. A requirement such as is mentioned in (1) or (2) requires the offender, in accordance with instructions given by the responsible officer, on the number of days specified in the order in relation to the requirement, in the case of a requirement such as is mentioned in: (1), to present himself or herself at a place specified in the order to person of a description so specified; or (2) to participate in an activity specified in the order, and, on each such day, to com-	Not to be imposed unless: (a) a member of a youth offending team has been consulted; or (b) a probation officer; or (c) an officer of a provider of probation services; nor unless (d) arrangements for such activities exist in the local justice area in which the offender resides or will reside. An activity may consist of, or include an activity whose purpose is that of reparation, such as an activity involving contact between an offender and persons affected by the offence(s) in respect of which the

No.	Name	Requirements	SA 2020 Sch.6	Restrictions	Notes
		As to (3) residential exercises, see 75-019		ply with instructions given by, or under the authority of, the person in charge of the place or the activity (as the case may be).	order is made, but only where such other persons consent.
2	Supervision	To attend appointments with the responsible officer or another person determined by the responsible officer, at such times and places as may be determined by the responsible officer.	Pt 2	During the period for which the order remains in force.	Not to be imposed unless the judge: (a) is satisfied that the offender is a suitable person to perform work under such a requirement; and (b) he is satisfied that provision for such work under such a requirement can be made.
3	Unpaid work	To perform unpaid work for the number of hours specified in the order at such times as the responsible officer may specify in instructions.	Pt 3	In the aggregate, for: (1) not less than 40; and (2) not more than 240 Subject to Sch.7 paras 10(7) and 19 the work required to be performed under such a requirement must be performed during the period of 12 months beginning with the day on which the order takes effect. Unless revoked, an order imposing an unpaid work requirement remains in force until the offender has worked under it for the number of hours specified in it.	Not to be included unless arrangements for such work exist in the local justice area in which offender resides or will reside.

No.	Name	Requirements	SA 2020 Sch.6	Restrictions	Notes
4	Programme	To participate in accordance with instructions given by the responsible officer in the programme at the place or places specified in the order on the number of days so specified; and while at any of those places, to comply with instructions given by, or under the authority of, the person in charge of the programme. May require the offender to reside at any place specified in the order for a specified period if it is necessary for him to reside there for that period in order to participate in the programme.	Pt 4	No minimum or maximum period prescribed save for days specified in requirement.	Not to be specified unless: (1) the programme proposed has been recommended by: (a) a member of a youth offending team; (b) an officer of a local probation board; or (c) a probation officer, as being suitable for the offender; (2) the judge is satisfied that the programme is available at the place Not to be specified unless: or places proposed to be specified; and (3) if compliance with that requirement would involve the cooperation of a person other than the offender and the offender's responsible officer, only where that other person consents to its inclusion.
		To attend at an attendance centre specified in the order for such number of hours as may be specified. It requires the offender to attend at the centre at the beginning of the period and during that period, to engage in oc-		If: (1) the offender is aged 16 or over at the time of conviction, the hours specified must be not less than 12 and not more than	The commencement order (see 75-001) expressly saves attendance centre orders under PCC(S)A 2000 s.50 and now the SA 2020, which remain available in the case of offenders aged 16 and 17, in respect of offences committed before 9 No-

No.	Name	Requirements	SA 2020 Sch.6	Restrictions	Notes
5	Attendance centre	cupation, or receive instruction, under the supervision of and in accordance with instructions given by, or under the authority of, the officer in charge, whether at the centre or elsewhere. The first time at which the offender is required to attend at the centre will be a time notified to the offender by the responsible officer. The subsequent hours will be fixed by the officer in charge of the centre, in accordance with arrangements made by the responsible officer, having regard to the offender's circumstances.	Pt 5	36; (2) the offender is aged 14 or over but under 16 at the time of conviction, they must be not less than 12 and not more than 24; (3) the offender is aged under 14 at the time of conviction, must not be more than 12. An offender may not be required under this requirement to attend at an attendance centre on more than one occasion on any day, or for more than three hours on any occasion.	vember 2009 see AGE OF OFFENDER. A requirement may not be included in an order unless the court: (a) has been notified by the Secretary of State that: (i) an attendance centre is available for persons of the offender's description; and (ii) provision can be made at the centre for the offender; and (b) the judge is satisfied that the centre proposed to be specified is reasonably accessible to the offender, having regard to the means of access available to the offender and any other circumstances.
6	Prohibited activity	To refrain from participating in activities specified in the order, on a specified day or days or during a specified period. May include a requirement that the offender does not possess, use or carry a firearm within the meaning of the FA 1968.	Pt 6		Such a requirement may be included only after consultation with: (1) a member of a youth offending team; (2) an officer of a local probation board; or (3) an officer of a provider of probation services.

No.	Name	Requirements	SA 2020 Sch.6	Restrictions	Notes
7	Curfew	To remain, for periods specified in the order, at a specified place.	Pt 7	Order may specify different places or different periods for different days, but may not specify periods which amount to less than two hours or more than 20 hours in any day, nor may it specify periods which fall outside the period of 12 months beginning with the day on which the requirement first takes effect.	Only after the judge has obtained information about the place proposed to be specified in the order (including information as to the attitude of persons likely to be affected by the enforced presence there of the offender).
8	Exclusion	Prohibits the offender from entering a place specified in the order for a specified period. An exclusion requirement may: (1) provide for the prohibition to operate only during the periods specified in the order; and (2) may specify different places for different periods or days. "Place" includes an area.	Pt 8	The period specified must not be more than three months.	
				An order under (2) is referred to as "a place of residence requirement," and may not be included	Before making a youth rehabilitation order containing a place of residence requirement, the judge must consider the offender's home surroundings. A requirement under: (1) may not be

No.	Name	Requirements	SA 2020 Sch.6	Restrictions	Notes
9	Residence	A "residence requirement" is a requirement that, during the period specified in the order, the offender reside: (1) with an individual; or (2) at a place specified in the order.	Pt 9	unless the offender was aged 16 or over at the time of conviction. If the order so provides, a place of residence requirement does not prohibit the offender from residing, with the prior approval of the responsible officer, at a place other than that specified in the order.	included unless that individual has consented to the requirement. A hostel or other institution as the place where an offender must reside may not be specified except on the recommendation of: (a) a member of a youth offending team; (b) an officer of a local probation board; (c) an officer of a provider of probation services; or (d) a social worker of a local authority.
10	Local authority residence	To reside, during the period specified in the order, in specified accommodation provided by or on behalf of a local authority. An order which imposes such a requirement may also stipulate that the offender is *not* to reside with a person specified in the order.	Pt 10	Any period specified in the order as a period for which the offender must reside in accommodation provided by or on behalf of a local authority must not be longer than six months, and must not include any period after the offender has reached the age of 18.	Judge must be satisfied that: (1) the behaviour which constituted the offence was due to a significant extent to the circumstances in which the offender was living; and (2) the imposition of that requirement will assist in the offender's rehabilitation. Parent or guardian must be consulted (unless impracticable) also local authority which is to receive the offender. The order must specify, as the local authority which is to receive the offender, the local authority in

No.	Name	Requirements	SA 2020 Sch.6	Restrictions	Notes
					whose area the offender resides or is to reside.
					Only where the judge is satisfied: (a) that the mental condition of the offender: (i) is such as requires and may be susceptible to treatment; but (ii) is not such as to warrant the making of a hospital order or guardianship order within the meaning of MHA 1983; and (b) that arrangements have been or can be made for the treatment intended to be specified in the order (including, where the offender is to be required to submit to treatment as a resident patient, arrangements for the reception of the offender); and (c) the offender has expressed willingness to comply with the requirement. Note. Treatment does not include taking medication. This can often get confused with what treatment is. YJB guidance states: *"For a YRO with a*

No.	Name	Requirements	SA 2020 Sch.6	Restrictions	Notes
				Treatment must be: (1) as a resident patient in an independent hospital or care home within the	*Mental Health Treatment Requirement to be made, the young person must have expressed a willingness to comply with it. It is important to note that 'willingness to comply with the requirement' and 'consent to treatment' are two separate issues. Where a young person withdraws his/her willingness to comply with the requirement, the YOT case manager should return the case to court for revocation/amendment as the requirement is unworkable. The court may consider, depending on the circumstances, that the unwillingness by the young person constitutes a breach of the requirement."* It is important to note that the child or young person is not admitted under the Mental Health Act 1983 and therefore cannot be compulsorily treated in accordance with the provisions of that Act. Whether the

No.	Name	Requirements	SA 2020 Sch.6	Restrictions	Notes
11	Mental health treatment	To submit, during a specified period or periods to treatment by or under the direction of a registered medical practitioner or a chartered psychologist, (or both, for different periods) with a view to the improvement of the offender's mental condition.	Pt 12	meaning of the Care Standards Act 2000 or a hospital within the meaning of MHA 1983, but not in hospital premises where high security psychiatric services within the meaning of that Act are provided; (2) as a non-resident patient at such institution or place as may be specified in the order; (3) by or under the direction of such registered medical practitioner or chartered psychologist (or both) as may be so specified; but the order must	child or young person is resident in hospital or not, they can only be treated if they consent. Having made the YRO with the Mental Health Treatment Requirement, the child or young person must expressly consent to any treatment. The Code of Practice for the Mental Health Act 1983 at para.23.31 states: "*Consent is the voluntary and continuing permission of a patient to be given… treatment, based on a sufficient knowledge of the purpose, nature, likely effects and risks of that treatment, including the likelihood of its success and any alternatives to it. Permission given under any unfair or undue pressure is not consent.*" Not only must all this be clearly explained to the child or young person, but the child or young person must be able to

No.	Name	Requirements	SA 2020 Sch.6	Restrictions	Notes
				not otherwise specify the nature of the treatment.	understand all this when s/he expresses willingness. A lack of consent to a particular form of treatment being provided by the medical practitioner once the requirement is in place does not itself constitute an unwillingness to comply with the requirement and is not therefore a potential breach. The medical practitioner will approach the matter of consent to treatment with their patient in the legally accepted way.
12	Drug treatment	To submit, during a specified period or periods to treatment, by or under the direction of a specified person having the necessary qualifications or experience ("the treatment provider"), with a view to the reduction or elimination of the offender's dependency on, or propensity to misuse, drugs.	Pt 13	Treatment must be: (a) as a resident in such institution or place as may be specified in the order; or (b) as a non-resident at such institution or place, and at such intervals, as may be so specified, but the order must not otherwise specify the nature of the treatment.	
					Drug testing requirement arrangements should be outlined

No.	Name	Requirements	SA 2020 Sch.6	Restrictions	Notes
13	Drug testing		Pt 14		in local protocols between the YOT and young people's substance misuse services and should be managed by specialist substance misuse staff. The test results are used to inform the treatment agency and YOT of the progress the young person is making through drug treatment. The test may not always be used with the purpose of requiring abstinence as it is accepted that time is needed to effectively change the drug use of a young person supported by treatment. Therefore, judgments in relation to expectations of abstinence by the young person need to be made in this context. If a young person fails to take the test itself, this could result in breach action being taken but this will need to be considered by the YOT responsible officer together with the specialist substance misuse treatment provider and taking into account other is-

No.	Name	Requirements	SA 2020 Sch.6	Restrictions	Notes
					sues regarding compliance. This could include consideration of the young person's general behaviour and compliance with the rest of the order. Failing this test—that is the test showing positive for drugs—is not a breach.
14	Intoxicating substance treatment	To submit, during a specified period or periods to treatment by or under the direction of a specified person having the necessary qualifications or experience, with a view to the reduction or elimination of the offender's dependency on or propensity to misuse intoxicating substances.	Pt 15		
15	Education	To comply, during a specified period or periods, with approved education arrangements: (1) made for the time being by the offender's parent or guardian; and (2) approved by the local education authority specified in the order, being the local educa-	Pt 16		Good practice would be by a YOT to also gain written confirmation from the specified education provider that they will liaise with the YOT in regards to absences once a joint meeting has been held with YP, School, Parents and YOT to agree a % tar-

No.	Name	Requirements	SA 2020 Sch.6	Restrictions	Notes
		tion authority for the area in which the offender resides or is to reside.			get for attendance. This should be discussed in the PSR to inform Court.
16	Electronic monitoring	To secure the electronic monitoring of the offender's compliance with other requirements imposed by the order during a period specified in the order or determined by the responsible officer in accordance with the order. A standalone "electronic whereabouts monitoring requirement" is currently being piloted.	Pt 17	Must be imposed where: (1) a curfew requirement is imposed; or (2) an exclusion requirement is imposed, the order must also impose an electronic monitoring requirement unless the judge: (a) in the particular circumstances of the case, considers it inappropriate for the order to do so; or (b) is prevented from including such a requirement in the order. Location monitoring is mandatory for YROs with ISS.	The duty of notification by the Crown Court officer under CPR r.42.2(3) is the same as in the case of a community order (see 14-021).
17	Intensive supervision	An order that contains an extended activity requirement, i.e. an activity requirement of a maximum of 180 days. An order which imposes an extended activity requirement (and other requirements) is referred to as "a	SA 2020 s.178 and	Must be coupled with a supervision requirement and a curfew requirement (and accordingly, if so required by para.2, an electronic monitoring requirement). Where appropriate may include additional requirements provided that whole set is most suitable for the offender, and restric-	Only where: (a) an offence is punishable with imprisonment; (b) the judge is of the opinion that the offence, or the combination of the offence and one or more offences associated with it, is so serious that, but for paras 3 or 4, a custodial sentence would be appropriate (or, if the of-

No.	Name	Requirements	SA 2020 Sch.6	Restrictions	Notes
	with surveillance	youth rehabilitation order with intensive supervision and surveillance" (whether or not it also imposes any such other requirements as mentioned in column 5).	Sch.7 para.11(2)	tions on liberty are commensurate with the seriousness of the offence. Judge should ensure that requirements are not so onerous as to make likelihood of breach almost inevitable (SGC(Y) (10.27)), and see 75-013.	fender is aged under 12 at the time of conviction, would be appropriate if the offender had been aged 12); and (c) the offender is aged under 15 at the time of conviction and the judge is of opinion that the offender is a persistent offender (see 28-010).
18	Fostering	To reside for a period specified in the order, with a local authority foster parent. An order which imposes a fostering requirement is referred to as "a youth rehabilitation order with fostering" (whatever other requirements it imposes). An order with intensive supervision and surveillance may not impose a fostering requirement.	Pt 11	Period must: (1) end no later than the end of the period of 12 months beginning with the date on which the requirement first has effect (but subject to extension or new periods permitted by Sch.7 paras 10(9), (10) and 17(5) and (6); and (2) not include any period after the offender has reached the age of 18.	Requirements A–D of para.27 of Pt 11 of Sch.6 must be met and the judge satisfied: (1) that the behaviour which constituted the offence was due to a significant extent to the circumstances in which the offender was living; and (2) that the imposition of a fostering requirement would assist in the offender's rehabilitation, but only where: (a) he has consulted the offender's parents or guardians (unless it is impracticable to do so); and (b) has consulted the local authority which is to place the offender with a local authority foster parent.

LASPOA 2012 s.76 inserted s.212A into CJA 2003 providing for an alcohol abstinence and monitoring requirement to be imposed as part of a requirement of a community order. It is not yet in force, but is being piloted in the South London local justice (SI 2014/1777). Monitoring is by means of a transdermal electronic tag fitted to an offender to measure the level of alcohol contained in their sweat.

Approach to determining nature and extent of requirements

75-009 The SC(SC&YP) guideline states that the requirements included and the length must be proportionate to the seriousness of the offence and suitable for the child or young person. The requirements should not be too onerous so as to make a breach almost inevitable. The guideline also suggests that in determining the nature and extent of the requirements to be included within a YRO the court should primarily consider the likelihood of the child or young person re-offending and the risk of the child or young person causing serious harm. A higher risk of re-offending does not in itself justify a greater restriction on liberty than is warranted by the seriousness of the offence. Regard must be had to the welfare of the child or young person (paras 6.26 and 6.28).

Before making a YRO the judge will need to consider a pre-sentence report from the Youth Offending Team ("YOT"). The YOT will assess the requirements and recommend an intervention level to the court. The court can ask the YOT to consider particular requirements. The guidelines set out three levels of a YRO: standard, enhanced and intensive depending on the likelihood of re-offending and the risk of serious harm with the examples of requirements likely to be considered.

Duration of order and date for compliance

75-010 An order must specify an end date not more than three years after the date on which the order takes effect, by which time all the requirements in it must have been complied with (SA 2020 s.187).

If a YRO imposes two or more different requirements the order may also specify a date by which each of those requirements must have been complied with and the last of those dates must be the same as the end date (SA 2020 s.187(3)).

In the case of a YRO with intensive supervision and surveillance, the end date must not be earlier than six months after the date on which the order takes effect (s.187(2)(b)).

Subject to SA 2020 Sch.6 Pt 3 (duration of YRO imposing unpaid work requirement), a YRO ceases to be in force on the end date. Unless revoked, a YRO imposing an unpaid work requirement remains in force until the offender has completed the number of hours specified in it (SA 2020 Sch.6).

Order with intensive supervision and surveillance

75-011 A YRO with intensive supervision and surveillance ("ISS") is an order that contains an extended activity requirement, that is, an activity requirement of more than 90 but no more than 365 days (SA 2020 s.180).

An ISS requirement must also include:

- a supervision requirement;
- location monitoring; and
- a curfew requirement.

The curfew requirement must be electronically monitored unless:

- in the particular circumstances of the case it is inappropriate;
- the court does not have the consent of a person (other than the offender) without whose cooperation it will not be practicable to secure that the monitoring takes place.

The SC(SC&YP) states that where appropriate, a YRO with ISS may also include additional requirements, although the order as a whole must comply with the obligation that the requirements must be those most suitable for the offender and that any restrictions on liberty must be commensurate with the seriousness of the offence (para.6.35). The judge must ensure that the requirements are not so onerous as to make the likelihood of breach almost inevitable (para.6.36).

A YRO with an ISS requirement may not include an additional *fostering* requirement.

As to a fostering requirement, see 75-015.

3. Duties of officers

Meaning of "the responsible officer"

Each YRO is managed by a "responsible officer". This role is defined as: **75-012**

- in a case where the order imposes *only* a curfew or an exclusion requirement with electronic monitoring, the person who is responsible for the electronic monitoring (SA 2020 s.191). A YRO which imposes electronic monitoring must include provision for making a person responsible for the monitoring (Sch.6 Pt 17 para.42);
- in a case where the *only* requirement imposed by the order is an attendance centre requirement, the officer in charge of the attendance centre in question (s.191(3)); and
- in *any other case*, the qualifying officer who is for the time being responsible for discharging the functions conferred on the responsible officer (s.191(4)).

Meaning of "qualifying officer"

"Qualifying officer", in relation to a YRO means: **75-013**

- a member of a youth offending team established by a local authority for the time being specified in the order for the purposes of this section; or
- a probation officer appointed for, or assigned to, the local justice area for the time being so specified, or (as the case may be) an officer of a provider of probation services acting in the local justice area for the time being so specified (SA 2020 s.191(5)).

Duties of responsible officer and offender in relation to the order

Where a YRO has effect, it is the duty of the responsible officer: **75-014**

- to make any arrangements that are necessary in connection with the requirements of the order;
- to promote the offender's compliance with those requirements; and
- where appropriate, to take steps to enforce those requirements (SA 2020 s.192(2)(c)).

These duties do not apply to a person falling within s.191(2) (i.e. someone who is merely responsible for electronic monitoring where only a curfew or an exclusion requirement has been imposed) (s.192(3)).

When giving instructions in pursuance of a YRO, the responsible officer must ensure, as far as practicable, that they avoid:

- any conflict with the offender's religious beliefs;
- any interference with the times, if any, at which the offender normally works or attends school, or any other educational establishment; and
- any conflict with the requirements of any other youth rehabilitation order to which the offender may be subject (s.192(4)(c)).

An offender in respect of whom a YRO is in force:

- must keep in touch with the responsible officer in accordance with such instructions as he may from time to time be given by that officer; and
- must notify the responsible officer of any change of address (s.193(2)(b)).

These obligations are enforceable as if they were a requirement imposed by the order (s.193(3)).

4. INDIVIDUAL REQUIREMENTS—ADDITIONAL MATERIAL

Intensive supervision and fostering requirements

75-015 A YRO with an intensive supervision and surveillance ("ISS") or a fostering requirement may be made only where:

- the judge is dealing with the offender for an offence which is punishable with imprisonment;
- the judge is of the opinion that the offence/s is/are so serious that, but for the option of imposing an ISS or a fostering requirement, a custodial sentence would be appropriate (or, if the offender is aged under 12 at the time of conviction, would be appropriate if the offender had been aged 12); and
- the offender is aged under 15 at the time of conviction, the judge is of opinion that the offender is a persistent offender (SA 2020 s.178 and Sch.7 para.11(2)) (see 28-010).

Activity requirement with residential exercise

75-016 Where the YRO requires the offender to participate in a residential exercise as part of an activity requirement (see the Table at 75-008), it must specify in relation to the exercise:

- a place; or
- an activity (SA 2020 Sch.6 paras 4 and 5).

A requirement to participate in a residential exercise operates to require the offender, in accordance with instructions given by the responsible officer:

- if a *place* is specified, to present him/herself at the beginning of the period specified in the order in relation to the exercise, at the place so specified to a person of a description specified in the instructions, and to reside there for that period;

- if an *activity* is specified, to participate, for the period specified in the order in relation to the exercise, in the activity so specified,

and, during that period, to comply with instructions given by, or under the authority of, the person in charge of the place or the activity (as the case may be) (para.4(2)).

5. ADMINISTRATIVE

Local justice area to be specified in order

75-017 A YRO must specify the local justice area in which the offender resides or will reside (SA 2020 s.188).

Provision of copies of orders

75-018 The court by which any YRO is made must forthwith provide copies of the order:

- to the offender;
- if the offender is aged under 14, to his parent or guardian; and
- to a member of a youth offending team assigned to the court, to a probation officer assigned to the court or to an officer of a provider of probation services (SA 2020 s.190).

Where a YRO is made by the Crown Court, the court making the order must:

- provide to the magistrates' court acting in the local justice area specified in the order a copy of the order and such documents and information relating to the case as it considers likely to be of assistance to a court acting in that area in the exercise of its functions in relation to the order; and
- provide a copy of the order to the local probation board acting for that area or (as the case may be) a provider of probation services operating in that area (SA 2020 s.190(3)).

Where a YRO imposes any requirement specified in the first column of the Table at s.190, the court must also forthwith provide the person specified in the second column with a copy of so much of the order as relates to that requirement (s.190(3)).

Direction in relation to further proceedings

75-019 Where the Crown Court makes a YRO, it may include in the order a direction that further proceedings relating to the order be in a youth court or other magistrates' court (SA 2020 s.189).

"Further proceedings" in relation to such an order means proceedings:

- for any failure to comply with the order; or

- on any application for amendment or revocation of the order (SA 2020 Sch.7).

6. BREACH, REVOCATION AND AMENDMENT

(1) Breach of order

Powers of Crown Court

75-020 Where an offender appears or is brought before the Crown Court, either under the SA 2020 Sch.7 Pt 2 para.5 (i.e. on a summons or warrant) or by virtue of para.6 (i.e. on referral from the magistrates' court), and it is proved to the judge's satisfaction that the offender has failed without reasonable excuse to comply with the YRO, the judge may deal with the offender in any one of the following ways:

- by taking no action and allowing the order to continue in its original form. This can be contrasted with the judge's powers relating to an adult offender which entail an obligation to make the order more onerous;
- by ordering the offender to pay a fine of an amount not exceeding £2,500 (SA 2020 Sch.7 Pt 2 para.7(2)(c));
- by amending the terms of the order so as to impose any requirement which could have been included in the order when it was made, either in addition to, or in substitution for, any requirement/s already imposed by the order (para.7(2)(b)). However, the judge may not impose an extended activity requirement, or a fostering requirement, if the order does not already impose such a requirement (para.10(8)); and
- by dealing with the offender, for the offence in respect of which the order was made, in any way in which the Crown Court could have dealt with him for that offence (para.7(2)(c)). The judge must revoke the original order if it is still in force (para.7(6)).

In dealing with the offender in one of these three ways, the judge must take into account the extent to which the offender has complied with the YRO (para.7(5)).

Any question whether the offender has failed to comply with the YRO is to be determined by the judge and not by a jury (para.7(7)).

Subject to the rules outlined at 75-021, any requirement imposed in addition to, or in substitution for, any requirement/s already imposed by the YRO under para.7(2)(b) must be capable of being complied with before the original end date (para.10(3)) (see 75-010).

Imposing a new requirement

75-021 When imposing a requirement under para.7(2)(b) (see 75-022), the judge may amend the YRO to specify a later end date to that previously expressed in the order (see 75-010) (SA 2020 Sch.7 Pt 2 para.10(4) and (5)).

However, the new end date:

- may not fall outside the period of six months beginning with the end date previously specified; but
- subject to that, may fall more than three years after the date on which the order took effect (para.10(5)(b)).

This power may not be exercised in relation to a YRO if it (or the equivalent power available to the magistrates' court under para.6(6A)) has previously been exercised in relation to that order (para.10(6)).

The end date substituted under para.10(5) is to be treated as having been specified as the original end date (see 75-010).

SC(SC&YP) Guidance on non-compliance

The SC(SC&YP) suggests that where the failure arises primarily from non-compliance with reporting or other similar obligations and a sanction is necessary, the most appropriate response is likely to be: 75-022

- the inclusion of (or increase in) a primarily punitive requirement such as the curfew requirement, unpaid work, the exclusion requirement and the prohibited activity requirement; or
- in the imposition of a fine.

However, continuing failure to comply with the order is likely to lead to revocation of the order and re-sentencing for the original offence (para.7.16).

Where the judge proposes to deal with the offender by imposing a new requirement (see 75-021), the YRO does not include an unpaid work requirement, and the judge decides to impose such a requirement, the minimum period of unpaid work must be 20 hours (para.10.37). The SA 2020 Sch.7 explains that, in these circumstances, Sch.6 para.10(4) (which requires "not less than 40" hours to be imposed as part of an unpaid work requirement) applies as if, instead of "40", it reads "20".

Fostering requirement

Where: 75-023

- the *original requirement* of the YRO is a fostering requirement; and
- the judge proposes to *substitute* a new fostering requirement (under the SA 2020 Sch.7—see 75-021) for the original requirement,

Sch.7 Pt 2 para.10(10) (which limits the period for which the fostering may continue) applies in relation to the *substitute requirement* as if the reference to the period of *12 months* beginning with the date on which the *original requirement* first had effect were a reference to the period of *18 months* beginning with that date (emphasis added).

Persistent offenders

Where an offender has wilfully and persistently failed to comply with a YRO and the judge proposes to revoke the order and resentence him for the original offence (under SA 2020 Sch.7 para.11—see 75-020), the judge may impose a YRO with intensive supervision and surveillance ("ISS"). This option is available to the judge even though the original offence is not imprisonable and would not in itself warrant a custodial sentence (SA 2020 Sch.7 para.11(3)). 75-024

Where the existing order is a YRO imposed under SA 2020 Sch.7 para.7 or 6 (the equivalent power in the magistrates' court), the judge, in exercising his power under SA 2020 Sch.7 para 7(2)(c) (to resentence), may deal with the offender by making a DTO for a term not exceeding 4 months. As above, this option is available to the judge even though the original offence was not punishable with imprisonment (SA 2020 Sch.7 para.11(3)).

In considering whether the failure to comply is "persistent", account should be taken of the principles set out in DETENTION OF YOUNG OFFENDERS.

SC(SC&YP) Guidance on breach

75-025 The SC(SC&YP) suggests that the primary objective when sentencing for breach of a YRO is to ensure that the offender completes the requirements imposed by the court. Therefore:

- where the failure arises primarily from non-compliance with reporting or other similar obligations and a sanction is necessary, the most appropriate disposal is likely to be the inclusion of (or increase in) a primarily punitive requirement;
- the judge must ensure that he has sufficient information to enable him to understand why the order has been breached and that all steps have been taken by the youth offending team and other local authority services to give the young person appropriate opportunity and support. This will be particularly important if the judge is considering a custodial sentence as a result of the breach; and
- where the judge is determining whether the young person has "wilfully and persistently" breached an order, he should apply the same approach as when determining whether an offender is a "persistent offender" (see DETENTION OF YOUNG OFFENDERS). In particular, almost certainly an offender will have "persistently" breached a YRO where there have been three breaches (each resulting in an appearance before a court) demonstrating a lack of willingness to comply with the order (see para.7.19).

Treatment cases: surgical, electrical or other treatment

75-026 Where a YRO imposes in respect of an offender:

- a mental health treatment requirement;
- a drug treatment requirement; or
- an intoxicating substance treatment requirement,

the offender is not to be treated as having failed to comply with the order on the ground only that he has refused to undergo any surgical, electrical or other treatment if, in the opinion of the judge, the refusal was reasonable having regard to all the circumstances (CJIA 2008 Sch.2 para.9).

(2) Revocation of order

Crown Court's powers

75-027 The revocation of a YRO will generally be a matter for a magistrates' court acting under the SA 2020 Sch.7. However, in appropriate circumstances a judge may revoke a YRO, providing:

- such an order is in force in respect of an offender;
- the order was made by the Crown Court and does not contain a direction that further proceedings should take place in a youth or magistrates' court (under SA 2020 s.189 and Sch.7 Pt 1 para.2); and
- the offender or responsible officer makes an application to the Crown Court (Sch.7 Pt 3 para.13).

If it appears to be in the interests of justice to do so, having regard to circumstances which have arisen since the YRO was made, the judge may:

- revoke the order; or
- both revoke the order and deal with the offender, for the offence in respect of which the order was made, in any way in which he could have dealt with him for that offence (para.13(4)).

The circumstances in which a YRO may be revoked include the offender's making good progress or responding satisfactorily to supervision or treatment (as the case requires) (para.13(5)).

In dealing with an offender under para.13(4) (as above), the judge must take into account the extent to which the offender has complied with the YRO (para.13(6)).

No application may be made by the offender while an appeal against the YRO is pending (para.13(2)).

If an application for revocation of a YRO is dismissed then, during the period of three months beginning with the date on which it was dismissed, no further such application may be made in relation to the order by any person, except with the consent of the Crown Court (para.13(7)).

(3) Amendment of the order

General

In the majority of cases, amendments to a YRO will be made in the appropriate magistrates' court. However, in appropriate circumstances a judge may amend a YRO, providing: **75-028**

- such an order is in force in respect of an offender;
- the order was made by the Crown Court and does not contain a direction that further proceedings should take place in a youth or magistrates' court (under Sch.7 Pt 4 para.14); and
- an application for the amendment of the order is made to the Crown Court by the offender or responsible officer (SA 2020 Sch.7 Pt 4 para.15).

If the judge is satisfied that the offender proposes to reside, or is residing, in a local justice area other than the local justice area for the time being specified in the order, he *must*, if the application was made by the *responsible officer*, or *may* in *any other case*, amend the YRO by substituting the new local justice area for the area specified in the order (para.15(2)) (emphasis added). However, the judge's power to do so in either case is subject to para.16 (para.15(3)) (see 75-031).

Subject to para.17 (see 75-033 and 75-034), the judge may also amend the YRO by cancelling any of the requirements of the order, or by replacing any of those requirements with a requirement of the same kind which could have been included in the order when it was made (para.17(1)–(9)).

Subject to para.18 (see 75-035), any such requirement must be capable of being complied with before the end date specified in the order (see 75-010) (para.17(3)).

Specific area requirements and programme requirements

A "specific area requirement", in relation to a YRO, means a requirement contained in the order which, in the opinion of the judge, cannot be complied with unless the offender continues to reside in the local justice area specified in the order (SA 2020 Sch.6). **75-029**

A YRO with specific area requirements may not be amended to substitute a new local justice area (under para.16(3)—see 75-028) unless either:

- those requirements are cancelled; or
- those requirements are substituted for other requirements which can be complied with if the offender resides in the new local justice area (para.15(3)).

If the application to amend the YRO was made by the *responsible officer* and the order contains specific area requirements, the judge must, unless he considers it inappropriate to do so, exercise his powers to cancel/replace the requirements of the order (under para.16(4) (see 75-028)) that he is not prevented by sub-para.(2) from amending the order under para.16(2).

The judge may not amend a YRO by substituting a new local justice area (under para.15(2)—see 75-028) unless he is satisfied that a programme which:

- corresponds as nearly as practicable to the programme specified in the order for the purposes of that requirement; and
- is suitable for the offender,

is available in the new local justice area (para.16(6)).

Programme requirement

75-030 A "programme requirement", in relation to a relevant order, means a requirement that the offender must participate in an accredited programme on the number of days specified in the order (SA 2020 Sch.6 Pt 4 para.12).

A programme requirement operates to require the offender:

- in accordance with instructions given by the responsible officer, to participate in the accredited programme that is from time to time specified by the responsible officer at the place that is so specified on the number of days specified in the order; and
- while at that place, to comply with instructions given by, or under the authority of, the person in charge of the programme (para.12(2)).

A place specified by the responsible officer must be a place which has been approved by the probation authorities for the area in which the premises are situated as providing facilities suitable for persons subject to a programme requirement.

Fostering requirement

75-031 Where:

- a YRO imposes a fostering requirement; and
- the judge proposes to substitute a new fostering requirement for the original one,

para.26(2) of Sch.6 Pt 11 (limiting the period for which an offender may reside with a local authority foster parent) applies in relation to the substitute requirement as if the reference to the period of *12 months* beginning with the date on which the original requirement first had effect were a reference to a period of *18 months* beginning with that date (emphasis added).

Mental health and drug treatment

The judge may not under para.15(3) (power to cancel or replace requirements of a YRO) impose: **75-032**

- a mental health treatment requirement;
- a drug treatment requirement; or
- a drug testing requirement,

unless the offender has expressed willingness to comply with the requirement (SA 2020 Sch.7 Pt 4 para.17(7)).

If an offender fails to express willingness to comply with any of these requirements which the judge proposes to impose, the judge may:

- revoke the YRO; and
- deal with the offender, for the offence in respect of which the order was made, in any way in which that court could have dealt with the offender for that offence (para.17(8)).

When exercising this power, the judge must take into account the extent to which the offender has complied with the order (para.17(9)).

Extension of order

The appropriate court may, on the application of the offender or the responsible officer, amend a YRO by substituting a later end date for that originally specified (see 75-010) (SA 2020 Sch.7 Pt 4 para.18). **75-033**

The substituted date:

- may not fall outside the period of six months beginning with the end date originally specified; but
- subject to that, may fall more than three years after the date on which the order took effect (para.18(3)).

However, the power to substitute a later end date may not be exercised if it has previously been exercised in relation to that order (para.18(4)).

"The appropriate court" is the Crown Court if the YRO was made by a judge of the Crown Court and does not contain a direction for further proceedings to take place in the youth or magistrates' court (under Sch.7—see 75-021) (para.14).

Extension of unpaid work requirement

Where: **75-034**

- a YRO imposing an unpaid work requirement is in force in respect of an offender; and
- on the application of the offender or the responsible officer, it appears to the judge that it would be in the interests of justice to do so having regard to circumstances which have arisen since the order was made,

the court may, in relation to the order, extend the period of 12 months in which, by Sch.6 para.10(1)(b), an unpaid work requirement must usually be completed (SA 2020 Sch.7 Pt 4 para.19).

(4) Powers following subsequent conviction

General

75-035 Where:

- a YRO is in force in respect of an offender; and
- the offender is convicted by the Crown Court of an offence, is brought or appears before the Crown Court following committal by the magistrates' court (under para.22(2) or (4)), or has been committed by the magistrates' court to the Crown Court for sentence,

the judge may revoke the YRO (SA 2020 Sch.7 Pt 5 para.23(1) and (2)).

Where the judge revokes the order, he may deal with the offender in any way in which the court that made the order could have dealt with him for the original offence (para.23(2)), providing he considers that it would be in the interests of justice to do so, having regard to the circumstances which have arisen since the YRO was made (para.23(2)).

In exercising his power to re-sentence the offender under para.23(2)(b), the judge must take into account the extent to which he has complied with the YRO (para.23(5)).

Care needs to be taken in complying with the statutory restrictions. See, for example, *R. v RH* [2012] EWCA Crim 3039.

Appearance of offender

75-036 Where, otherwise than on the application of the offender, a judge of the Crown Court proposes to exercise his powers in relation to the breach, amendment or revocation of a YRO, the offender must be summoned to appear before the court. If the offender does not appear in answer to the summons, the judge may issue a warrant for his arrest (SA 2020 Sch.7 Pt 5 para.23(4)).

This does not apply, however, where the judge proposes to make an order:

- revoking a YRO;
- cancelling, or reducing the duration of, a requirement of a YRO; or
- substituting a new local justice area or place for one specified in a YRO (para.16).

(5) Administrative provisions

Duties of proper officer

75-037 Where an order is made, revoking or amending a YRO, the proper officer of the Crown Court must forthwith:

- provide copies of the revoking or amending order to the offender and, if the offender is aged under 14, to his parent or guardian;
- provide a copy of the revoking or amending order to the responsible officer;
- in the case of an amending order which substitutes a new local justice area, provide copies of the amending order to the local probation board acting for that area and the magistrates' court acting in that area;
- in the case of an amending order which imposes or cancels a requirement specified in the first column of the Table in SA 2020 s.190 (see below)

provide a copy of so much of the amending order as relates to that requirement to the person specified in relation to that requirement in the second column; and

- in the case of an order which revokes a requirement specified in the first column of that Table, provide a copy of the revoking order to the person specified in relation to that requirement in the second column (SA 2020 s.190 and Sch.7 Pt 6 para.27).

Where the Crown Court officer provides a copy of an amending order to a magistrates' court acting in a different area, the officer must also provide to that court such documents and information relating to the case as appear likely to be of assistance to a court acting in that area in the exercise of its functions in relation to the order (SA 2020 s.190(4)).

Requirement	Person to whom copy of requirement is to be given
Activity requirement specifying a place obligation	The person in charge of that place para.3(1)(b) of Sch.6
Activity requirement specifying an activity requirement	The person in charge of that activity para.4(1)(b) of Sch.6
Activity requirement specifying a residential exercise obligation	The person in charge of the place or activity specified under para.5(1)(b) of Sch.6 in relation to that residential exercise
Attendance centre requirement	The officer in charge of the attendance centre specified under para.14(2)(a) of Sch.6
Exclusion requirement imposed for the purpose (or partly for the purpose) of protecting a person from being approached by the offender	The person intended to be protected
Residence requirement requiring residence with an individual	The individual specified under para.22(2)(b) of Sch.6
Place of residence requirement (within the meaning of para.22 of Sch.6) relating to residence in an institution	The person in charge of the institution
Local authority residence requirement	The local authority specified in para.24(3)(b) of Sch.6
Mental health treatment requirement	The person in charge of the institution or place specified under para.(3)(b)(i) or (ii) of para.28 of Sch.6, or the person specified under subpara.(3)(b)(iii)
Drug treatment requirement	The treatment director specified under para.31(3)(b)(i) of Sch.6
Drug testing requirement	The treatment director specified under para.31(3)(b)(i) of Sch.6
Intoxicating substance treatment requirement	The treatment director specified under para.36(3)(b)(i) of Sch.6

Education requirement	The relevant authority specified under para.39(2)(a) of Sch.6
Electronic monitoring requirement	Anyone who, by virtue of para.42(1) of Sch.6 will be responsible for the electronic monitoring, and any person without whose consent the requirement could not have been included in the order

INDEX

Also available:

Sentencing Principles, Procedure and Practice, 3rd edn
Lyndon Harris and Sebastian Walker
ISBN: 9780414108851 Publication date: November 2022
Formats: Hardback/ProView eBook
The essential sentencing text, updated with all the latest changes from the Police, Crime, Sentencing and Courts Act 2022 and all important cases from the Court of Appeal (Criminal Division).

The work guides practitioners though the various stages of a sentencing hearing and clearly indicates the considerations applicable to a sentencing decision. The title includes extensive expert commentary from the authors and other expert practitioners and academics, and concise summaries of all the relevant case law. The book is intended for use in sentencing hearings and appeals, in court and for research.

New coverage in this edition includes revised sections and commentary on terrorism, burglary and sexual offences to reflect new Sentencing Council guidelines and various other changes to reflect new legislation and case law.

Rook and Ward on Sexual Offences Law and Practice, 6th edn
HH Peter Rook KC and Robert Ward CBE KC
ISBN: 9780414089297 Publication date: October 2021
Formats: Hardback/ProView eBook/Westlaw UK
The leading work on sexual offences, **Rook and Ward** provides coverage of the most up-to-date legislation including key decisions relating to the Sexual Offences Act 2003 and important developments in respect of evidence, practice and procedure. It is an essential tool for all those involved in prosecuting, defending and trying sexual offence cases, including lawyers, police and medical practitioners.

Archbold: Criminal Pleading, Evidence & Practice, 2023 edn
General Editor: HHJ Mark Lucraft KC
ISBN: 9780414110212 Publication date: October 2022
Formats: Hardback/ProView eBook/Westlaw UK
The 2023 edition of **Archbold**, the leading criminal court book for the Crown Court, published in October 2022.

2022 marked a special year for Archbold as it celebrated the 200th anniversary since the first edition published in 1822. The aim of the work remains as originally set out: to capture the essential materials for the criminal law practitioner, and, as Archbold himself intended, to be a "practically useful book".

Archbold 2023 continues the ethos of being an invaluable aid to practising criminal law in the Crown Court and being reliable, current and comprehensive. It's the same tried, tested and trusted content. The new edition is as up to date and authoritative as ever: amendments made, in particular, by the Police, Crime, Sentencing and Courts Act 2022 and the Judicial Review and Courts Act 2022 have been fully taken in, and the Criminal Procedure Rules are up to date to 3rd October 2022 with the coming into force of the Criminal Procedure (Amendment No.2) Rules 2022 (SI 2022/815), plus significant case law decisions.

Archbold 2023 - The essential criminal law text since 1822.